American Combat Planes of the 20th Century

A.S.23-1

American Combat Planes of the 20th Century

A Comprehensive Reference

By

Ray Wagner

Jack Bacon & Company
Reno, Nevada
2004

Designed by Jim Richards

Printed by R. R. Donnelley & Sons
in the United States of America

ISBN 0-930083-17-2

Jack Bacon & Company
516 South Virginia Street
Reno, Nevada 89501

Dedicated to the men and women who
designed, built, crewed, and flew these warplanes.

CONTENTS

INTRODUCTION

Fighter styles of four wars: the Spad biplane of World War I, is circled by a P-51 monoplane of World War II, an F-86 jet of the Korean War, and the supersonic F-100 used in Vietnam.

Purpose

The 20th century has seen thousands of airplanes built in the United States. Those designed for combat have made world history as the striking weapons of air power. Yet, despite their importance, a comprehensive and objective history of all these bombers, fighters and attack types and their characteristics was not available for many years.

Military secrecy often veiled reality and allowed myth and inaccuracy to confuse the story, but only in recent years have archives opened in America, Britain, and Russia to provide the more accurate picture presented in this book.

The purpose of *American Combat Planes of the 20th Century* is to tell the story of the marriage of aircraft and war and provide a quick reference. Every combat type built in the United States for the Air Force, Navy, or for foreign governments is included, together with foreign aircraft bought for American fighting outfits.

Data and photographs are chosen to present the most authentic and representative description of each type. An objective examination is offered, despite the different views of builders, each military service, and national bias.

Plan

This book describes all the planes designed to attack an enemy with guns, bombs, or rockets. This excludes the trainers, transports, and most unarmed liaison or reconnaissance aircraft, which also contribute to airpower, but can be better described in separate studies. Armed reconnaissance aircraft, and those derived from fighter designs are included.

This book arranges all those planes by their fighting purpose and their appearance in history. Even by simply viewing their photographs page by page, the reader sees the story of combat plane design over the years. Below each picture are the vital facts of each type: the engine's name and power, how big and how heavy that plane is, as well as how fast, how high, and how far it can go. These are what military documents call the characteristics of each warplane.

As the reader follows the text, he will learn who made these planes and when. Dates are to history what dimensions are to engineering; they tell us what happened first and why. The many numbers in each story are the mathematics of policy, each measuring the effort people made to produce such weapons. What could each plane do, how many were made, and where were they used?

Attention is given to both the famous mass-production types, like the Liberator, Mustang, and Hellcat, with their major modifications, and also to little-known experimental efforts. The description, armament, and history of each type is related to other designs, as well as to its intended military missions.

Each chapter describes the aircraft designed for each mission in the order of their appearance. This tells a better story of progress than any listing of aircraft only by alphabet, or by numerical designation, which is often a poor guide to chronology or even design antecedents. Photographs enable identification of each type, and are accompanied by dimensions, weights, and performance. Most of these characteristics are drawn from flight tests and specifications given in once classified official documents.

Why each combat plane was built is the most important question about each type, and is best answered by placing each design in the historical context in which it was developed. Beginning with America's entrance into World War I in 1917, most aircraft are biplanes with open cockpits, constructed of a fabric-covered wooden frame. Their missions are intended to fit into the kind of fighting seen in Europe over the trenches of the Western Front, or over the warships at Jutland.

Part One describes how observation, ground attack, bombing, and fighting missions emerged from World War I, along with parallel naval missions. The first chapter orients readers on the historical and technical factors influencing early aircraft design and gives a brief summary of the background needed to follow warplane history, such as their weapons and how aircraft and their engines are designated. Then the story of the warplanes emerges in the separate chapters for each class, as aircraft design styles developed that continued after the war.

Part Two shows how the technical revolution in design style from biplane to monoplane prepared the way for the aircraft fleets built for World War II. This period began around 1931, when the all-metal monoplane appears with refinements like enclosed cockpits, retractable wheels, and more powerful engines with variable-pitch propellers.

Such progress fulfilled the ambitious strategic role played by aircraft in World War II, which came to its climax in 1945. Again, an introductory chapter orients the reader, followed by separate chapters for each combat mission.

This organization is continued in Part Three, which covers the early Cold War's types from 1945 to 1962. Aviation, like politics, would be dominated by the confrontation of two superpowers armed with nuclear weapons. During this period, the piston engine was replaced by the gas turbine, and aircraft performance, along with aircraft costs, reached undreamed of heights.

In Part Four, a generation of long-lived aircraft, many of them serving to the next century, witnessed the Gulf War and the end of Cold War in 1991. An awesome expansion of military capability has resulted from this century of air power, with supersonic speeds, nuclear weapons, and electronics.

This book concludes with a bibliography designed to be a guide for readers seeking colorful details about any of the more famous combat planes, as well as the archival sources of the historical facts presented here.

Acknowledgments

The author gratefully thanks the people who contributed to American Combat Planes over the last forty years. Many of these people published valuable studies of aircraft development that are listed in the bibliography. All deserve the thanks of aviation history enthusiasts.

The origins of this material are discussed in full in the bibliography, which is also a reader's guide to further study. When the author made his first research trip to the National Archives and the Smithsonian Institution in 1956, he had the good fortune to meet Naval Air historian Lee M. Pearson and Major James F. Sunderman of the Air Force Book Program, who encouraged this project on its first steps. Peter M. Bowers was the first of many American Aviation Historical Society members to provide hundreds of photographs and information not otherwise available.

Doubleday published the progenitor in 1960, with 1968 and 1982 editions as more documentation was declassified. That book found wide acceptance, and the Cold War's end has finally allowed new information and insights for this larger volume.

The author would like to thank Jack Bacon, who is bold enough to publish this book, Jim Richards, who designed the layout, and Cindy Coan for the index and many corrections. For Mary and Roger Wagner, whose caring made it happen, my love and appreciation.

Correspondents and Informants

Not everyone's name may be given, but the following each shared in some personal way to make this book possible. We begin with the San Diego Aerospace Museum's archival staff now headed by John Bolthouse, aided by Ron Bulinski, Pam Gay, A.J. Lutz, & Casey Smith.

Harold Andrews	Gerald Balzer	Dana Bell
Roger F. Besecker	Warren M. Bodie	Peter M. Bowers
Walter J. Boyne	Ron Bulinski	Richard Bueschel
Santiago A. Flores	Harry S. Gann	Richard P. Hallion
Chuck Hansen	Edward Heineman	Meyers K. Jacobsen
Lloyd S. Jones	Gerald L. Landry	William T. Larkins
Robert L. Lawson	Edward A. Leiser	Corwin H. Meyer
David C. Montgomery	Merle C. Olmstead	Lee M. Pearson
Larry Peterson	Gennady Petrov	Dominick Pisano
Mauno A. Salo	Arthur L. Schoeni	William E. Scarborough
John Underwood	Mary K. Wagner	Roger R. Wagner

Photo credits are abbreviated in the right-hand bottom corner of each picture, and these sources are listed in the bibliography section.

PART ONE

THE BIPLANE PERIOD, 1917 TO 1932

CHAPTER 1

THE ROLE OF THE COMBAT PLANE: THE FIRST GENERATION

A Modest Beginning

When the first military airplane was purchased by the American government, no combat future was envisioned. The specification issued called for no weapons, just a two-place aircraft with a speed of 40 mph, a range of 125 miles, "and the ability to steer in all directions without difficulty." A contract was signed February 10, 1908, with the Wright brothers, who began testing the 30-hp biplane that September. The first fatal airplane crash of history delayed acceptance of the rebuilt aircraft until August 2, 1909.

That $25,000 "flying machine" had no blood-thirsty intentions. Its only use was to train the first Army aviators to fly its kite-like successors. Only gradually did the Army try such missions as message-carrying, scouting, and spotting for coast artillery. The Wright brothers themselves, "the bishop's boys", had no interest in weapons.

The Army gradually experimented with airborne weapons, firing a rifle from an aircraft on August 20, 1910, and dropping live bombs in January 1911. A prototype of the new Lewis machine gun was fired at a ground target from a Wright biplane by Capt. Charles D. Chandler on June 7, 1912, (a week after Wilbur Wright died) but the Army was not yet ready to purchase the Lewis gun. The inventor took his weapon to Europe, where it won rapid acceptance by Belgium, Great Britain, and France.

European countries faced an immediate threat of invasion by powerful nations on their immediate borders. Even the most conservative military leaders had to notice aviation's wartime potential. France began developing an aircraft industry with military funding, because the lack of practical commercial application discouraged private investment. Britain, Germany, and Russia were also rivals in producing aircraft useful to their armed forces.

The First War in the Air

When World War I began in 1914, Europe's airplanes were as bare of weapons as America's, but existed in much larger numbers. The initial mission of these aircraft was reconnaissance, and however violent the ground fighting, the soldiers of the skies found their flights across the lines relatively peaceful. For such purposes unarmed, single-engine, two-place aircraft were adequate.

But the temptation to use the advantage of flight for attack purposes was too strong. On August 14, 1914, a pair of French biplanes dropped artillery shells on hangars at Metz, and on November 21, three British Avros bombed Zeppelin sheds. A German plane dropped the first bomb on English soil on December 24, 1914. Zeppelins began raids in January 1915, and warfare had truly entered a new dimension.

Later chapters of this book will describe how the "military aeroplane" became the combat plane by developing a series of specialties. Single-engine, two-seat observation biplanes were fitted with bomb racks under the wings and became light bombers. Smaller single-seaters with a machine gun became *avions de chasse,* or pursuit ships, for attacking enemy aircraft, while larger multi-engine machines were built for long-range bombing.

Flying these early open-cockpit combat planes was very different than today's missions. Without radar location, fighter patrols cruised over the trench lines until encountering an enemy. Since there was no radio talk between aviators, hand signals were used to direct action. There were no parachutes to escape a burning plane.

The airplane as a scout had developed into the airplane as a bomber and as a destroyer of other aircraft, but this development was European, not American, and happened without comparable activity on this side of the Atlantic. New fighters often made sensational appearances over the front and disappeared from battle in only a few months. America missed the rapid technological advances that produced five generations of fighters in four years.

SDAM

The Eaton seaplane launched in September 1916 was the first American aircraft designed for coast defense, but never had weapons installed.

American Beginnings

Although the United States had produced the world's first successful powered plane, and purchased the first military plane, it had not participated in the air weapon's wartime development. Not even a prototype of up-to-date pattern was available when we entered the war.

Aircraft had been used by the U.S. Army in Mexico in 1916, when the 1st Aero Squadron's eight Curtiss JN-3 two-seaters had searched for Pancho Villa's cavalry. While much more serviceable aircraft than the Wright B, and later developed into the famous JN-4 primary trainer, these biplanes had no combat capability.

American weakness in military aviation was due not only to reluctance to arm, but to the military posture of the day. The specific missions of the armed forces were defense of the continental United States, its overseas possessions, and its maritime commerce. For these purposes a strong Navy was needed, but mass armies of the European type were unnecessary, since only Mexico's small army presented any possible threat on land.

The pride of American military technology was the giant cannon; the 14-inch rifles installed in coastal fortifications and battleship turrets that could fire a 1,560-pound projectile over 13 miles. Compared to such destructive power, little airplanes seemed properly limited to the Aviation Section of the Signal Corps.

When the United States Army prepared its first three specifications for military aircraft in 1916, the aircraft envisioned were first: Aeronautical Specification No. 1000 for a 90-hp primary trainer, and second, Specification No. 1001 for an advanced trainer. Third was Specification No. 1002 dated October 1, 1916, for a "Hydroplane" adapted to coast defense reconnaissance. This two-place, twin-engine "aeroplane" should carry up to 500 pounds for two men, accessories, and instruments, and enough fuel to sustain five hours of flight at full power, with a stalling speed of 45 mph. No mention was made of top speed or armament.

SDAM

EATON AI seaplane
Two Hall-Scott A7a, 100 hp
DIMENSIONS: Span 73', Lg. 37', Wing Area 820 sq. ft.
WEIGHT: Empty 2700 lb., Gross 4400 lb.
PERFORMANCE: No data available to confirm the 70 mph and five-hour endurance promised.

Such a seaplane "designed especially for coast defense" was first built by the New York Aero Construction Company at Newark, New Jersey. Designed by Warren S. Eaton (1891-1966), this biplane had two long floats under two 100-hp Hall-Scott water-cooled engines, and supported a biplane tail with three rudders on outrigger struts. The pilot sat in the back of a center nacelle with fuel tanks between him and a front cockpit for an observer, who could be provided with a Lewis gun.

After the Eaton AI seaplane was launched on September 4, 1916, it accidentally overturned, delaying flight tests until November. But the Army preferred to deal with more established aircraft builders and on December 9, 1916, ordered 96 "Twin Hydro" seaplanes spread among designs by Aeromarine, Burgess, Standard, and later, Thomas-Morse. None of these were ever built, because the whole program was canceled in 1917 to clear the way for aircraft more necessary for the war in Europe.

When the United States declared war on April 6, 1917, there were no specific plans to use airpower on a mass basis, but it was realized how far the United States had fallen behind Europe. There were no guns or bomb racks on any of the 130 Army aircraft in commission at that time. Most of these were the famous Curtiss JN-4 "Jenny" trainers.

The 1st Aero Squadron at Columbus, New Mexico, and the 3rd, at San Antonio, Texas, faced the Mexican border with eleven Curtiss R-2 and six Curtiss R-4s between them. These were heavier two-seaters than the "Jenny", using 160-hp (R-2) and 200-hp (R-4) engines, but there is no evidence that guns or bombs were ever carried, except perhaps for a test. The only other Aero Squadron was the 2nd, at Manila with only three Martin floatplanes to spot for coast artillery.

PMB

Most of the Army's fliers in 1918 flew French-built aircraft like the Nieuport 28, first AEF fighter to score air victories.

The AEF's Air Arm

When the French Prime Minister on May 24, 1917, requested an American force of 4,500 planes in 1918, a massive aviation program was launched, requiring a production and training effort far beyond previous American experience. One front-line squadron of 25 single-seat fighters in 1918 would need 31 officers and 181 enlisted men; the latter including 21 chauffeurs, 6 cooks, and two buglers. From the Major in command to his airplane pilots, technical sergeants, and the privates at their service, all these men would have to be taught their new jobs.

An estimated aircraft attrition rate of 50% per month from combat and ordinary accidents would require 100 planes per squadron each six months, and by 1918 it appeared that 200 squadrons might be needed for 1919. United States production had to begin with training planes to provide fliers for the war in France.

Raw materials needed would include vast quantities of spruce for air frame structures and cotton for covering them, along their varnish (then called dope) finish, as well as metal for their power plants and weapons. When these needs were added to the demands of a huge land army and naval expansion, America quickly changed from a market economy to a command economy.

Two LePere two-seat fighters were the only U.S.-designed combat planes to reach France.

On June 17, 1917, a joint Army-Navy Mission led by Major R.C. Bolling sailed for France to gain information on aircraft types. Samples of several Allied warplanes were selected and shipped to the United States for production here, but of the combat types selected, only the DH-4 would be produced in quantity. To fill the gap until American-built aircraft would be available, the French contracted on August 30, 1917, to supply 5,875 aircraft to the American Expeditionary Force (AEF).

As the following chapters will tell, the American squadrons at the front depended principally on French equipment. The 36 squadrons at the front on November 1, 1918, included 15 with the Spad and one with SE-5A single-seaters, and 10 with the Salmson, eight with the U.S.-built DH-4, and two with the Breguet two-seaters. None had twin-engine equipment.

When the U.S. Navy began World War I patrols from shore bases, only Curtiss HS-1L flying boats could be quickly produced.

During the war, the Army received 11,754 planes from United States contractors, of which 1,216 were delivered to the AEF before the Armistice. France provided 4,791 aircraft (incl. 2,186 service types) to the AEF, Britain 261 (incl. 189 service types) and Italy 19 trainers. This gave the AEF a total of 6,287 planes, including 2,696 trainers and 3,591 service types. On Armistice Day the AEF had 740 planes at the front. Table 1 shows how this number compared with the forces of other countries.

Table 1 • November 11, 1918

Comparison of airplane strengths of Allied and enemy air services.

Airplanes	Pursuit	Observation	Bombardment Day	Bombardment Night	Total
British	759	503	306	190	1,758
French	1,344	1,505	225	247	3,321
American	330	293	117	0	740
Italian	336	360	36	80	812
Belgian	45	100	0	8	153
Combined Allies	2,814	2,761	684	525	6,784
German	1,020	1,442	0	268	2,730
Austrian	220	391	0	11	622
Combined Enemy	1,240	1,833	0	279	3,352

Beginning Navy Air Power

Naval aviation developed its own specialties: flying boats to patrol the sea, and torpedo-carrying seaplanes to attack enemy shipping were joined by fighters carried by the British fleet on vessels with flight decks.

The United States Navy had some experience with shore-based aircraft, but when war was declared had only 45 training seaplanes, six flying boats, and three landplanes, none of them armed or designed for combat.

U-boats were the war's chief threat to Britain, so when a British flying boat claimed to have sunk one for the first time on May 20, 1917, Allied naval aviation's most important mission was clear. Hundreds of American flying boats were ordered for shore-based patrols.

Because of the difficulty encountered in getting enough aircraft, the government built its own Naval Aircraft Factory in Philadelphia. Unlike the Army's Engineering Division at Dayton, which built only prototypes, the NAF produced flying boats in quantity, and would be the only government-owned aircraft factory for thirty years.

Flying boats were valued for spotting enemy submarines, but a more direct attack could be made by bombing the sub bases on the English Channel. For that purpose, a Northern Bombing Group was organized with DH-4, DH-9, and Caproni landplanes obtained from the Army and the Allies.

Unlike the AEF, the Navy obtained most of its planes at home; only 142 of 2,705 Navy machines were procured abroad. United States production for the Navy was 1,444 service types, 1,084 training planes, and 36 experimentals, as well as 155 DH-4s and 144 trainers transferred from Army stocks.

American Air Power Between the Wars

The Armistice left the United States with an enormous stock of rifles, machine guns, and artillery for the ground forces. These could be expected to provide the Army with a secure arsenal for at least twenty years. But the aircraft stockpile was a different matter, for warplanes were rapidly made obsolete by technical advances.

The thousands of DH-4 two-seaters, several hundred pursuit ships of foreign origin, and a few night bombers, would need to be replaced by more modern types. Military leaders accustomed to buying hardware that would last 20 years were reluctant to spend much money on aircraft with less than a six-year service life. Funding for fiscal year 1921 allowed Army contracts in June 1920 for only 170 new combat planes: 100 fighter, 40 observation, 20 night bomber, and 10 attack planes, as well as beginning work on the large Barling bomber prototype.

Marine pilots used DH-4Bs from 1918 until 1927.

With only limited experience in air warfare and rudiments of a theory of air power, the Army Air Service had an uncertain future. The existing organization reflected the conservative view that aviation existed primarily to assist the ground army, and that bombing and pursuit aircraft in themselves were unlikely to affect the course of war. (An example of this thinking was a lengthy World War I history that mentioned only scouting as a wartime aviation activity.) The view once expressed that "the duty of the aviator is to see, not to fight" seemed to be reflected in the dispersal of air force strength into observation squadrons attached to various ground units.

Subordination of the Air Service to the Army had a bad effect on both morale and equipment. Of 517 Air Service crash deaths from January 1919 to June 1925, all but 12 were in aging aircraft built before the end of the war. The lack of improved and safer replacements was criticized, and a long debate on the control of air power ensued. Since this argument centered around the use of the bomber, it is discussed in the chapters devoted to that weapon.

The organizational impasse of the period was reflected in the relatively slow technical advance. Most of the aviation headlines were made by the skill of individual aviators, rather than by a startling advance in performance. Compare the service aircraft of 1930, a dozen years after the Armistice, with those of the war period. Still we see the same open cockpit, fabric-covered biplanes dragging struts and exposed undercarriages. Advances in top speed were modest. Fighters had gone from the 132 mph of a Spad to 166 mph for a P-12B, bombers from the 94 mph of a Handley-Page to 114 mph for a B-3A, two-seaters from the 124 mph of a DH-4 to 139 mph for an A-3B.

The Army Air Service, as it was constituted from 1920 to 1926, was viewed almost entirely as an organization to support the ground arms: infantry and cavalry, coast and field artillery. In case of war, plans called for the mobilization of six field armies, each of nine divisions in three corps. Each army would have an attack group, two pursuit groups, and an observation group, as well as observation squadrons for each division and corps, or a total force of four attack, eight pursuit and 16 observation squadrons per army. A General Headquarters element would have the only bomber group, along with attack, observation and pursuit groups.

The actual peacetime Army Air Service was planned as the cadre for a rapid wartime expansion and in 1922 consisted of 14 observation, four attack, seven bombing and seven pursuit squadrons. They were deployed in the United States as the 1st Pursuit, 2nd Bombardment, 3rd Attack, and 9th Observation Groups, as well as an observation squadron for each of the nine Army corps. Overseas possessions were protected by three composite groups with mixed squadrons; the 4th Composite Group in the Philippines, the 5th in Hawaii, and the 6th in the Panama Canal Zone.

In 1926, the Air Service became the Air Corps, and began a five-year expansion of pursuit and bomber squadrons. By 1932 there were 15 groups of combat planes, including ten in the United States and five overseas, and the Air Corps kept this organizational framework until 1940.

Navy Aviation Between the Wars

Naval aviation in the 1920s began with shore bases at Hampton Roads, Virginia, and San Diego, California, to support the fleets in the Atlantic and Pacific, as well as the training establishment at Pensacola and the testing station at Anacostia. Overseas operations were based on the air stations at Coco Solo at the Panama Canal and at Pearl Harbor.

Most operational Navy service planes in 1919 were shore-based flying boats, plus some Marine DH-4s. The Naval Aircraft Factory kept busy with the overhaul and repair of flying boats continuously damaged by waves and sea water soaking.

The first American aircraft carrier, the *Langley* (CV-1) taking aboard a Martin MO-l.

A small postwar force, including fighting, observation, and torpedo planes, was established to operate on wheels or floats from shore bases. The next step was to perfect means by which these aircraft could accompany the fleet to sea, and the Bureau of Aeronautics (BuAer), established

Before electric starters, propellers had be pulled by hand, as on this Standard-built Italian Caproni at Love Field, Texas, in June 1919.

In between flight operations, Vought VE-7s of VF-2 rest on the deck, while the Langley's smokestacks and radio masts are up.

September 1,1921, devoted itself to this problem. Early shipboard operations were by seaplanes catapulted from battleships and cruisers, and lifted back by cranes after landing on the sea. There were disadvantages to this method: only a few seaplanes could be carried without impairing the ship's fighting ability; it was difficult to recover the launched aircraft; and most important, the seaplanes were inferior in performance to landplanes.

As early as July 1917, the British Royal Navy had commissioned *HMS Furious,* which answered the problem by adding to the fleet a specialized aircraft carrier that could launch and recover landplanes from a large flight deck. Congress authorized, in July 1919, conversion of a collier to the first American aircraft carrier, the *USS Langley* (CV-l). The first takeoff from the Langley was made on October 17, 1922, by a Vought VE-7SF. Conventional landplanes were thus able to begin operations with the fleet, modified by strengthened landing gear and arresting hooks.

The *Langley* arrived in the Pacific in November 1924, and became the Flagship, Aircraft Squadrons, Battle Fleet. For a dozen years it operated out of San Diego, taking two squadrons to sea at a time to perfect carrier operations. However, the CV-l lacked the speed and defenses to be fit for combat, and would be converted to an aircraft tender in 1937.

PMB

Flotation bags could be inflated to save this Hanriot HD-2 fighter from sinking. All-metal aircraft with water-tight compartments no longer had to use that system.

USN

An F-5L flying boat, seen on August 1, 1924, would remain the principal Navy patrol type all through the 1920s.

USN

Shore-based floatplanes like the Martin T3M-2 combined scouting, bombing, and torpedo work during the 1920s

Launching an O2U-1 by catapult from the battleship *New Mexico.*

Two big battle-cruisers canceled by the Washington Naval Treaty in 1922, the *Lexington* and *Saratoga,* were ordered completed as aircraft carriers. In March 1925, the Navy called upon designers for models to fit the fine new ships and the industry responded with the Curtiss F6C fighter, the Vought O2U scout, and the Martin T3M torpedo plane.

The Saratoga (CV-3), which made surprise attacks on Hawaii during maneuvers, and her sister ship the Lexington (CV-2), were the Navy's first really combat-ready carriers.

In 1928 the two carriers began operations, each with two squadrons of fighters, one of scouts, and one of torpedo bombers. The largest Navy ships yet, they soon proved themselves powerful weapons in Pacific Fleet maneuvers. On January 26, 1929, the *Saratoga* achieved the theoretical destruction of the Panama Canal with 83 aircraft launched in a surprise attack.

Hawaii was defended by Army 23rd Bombardment Squadron's Keystone open-cockpit B-5A biplanes.

A surprise attack on Pearl Harbor one Sunday morning, February 7, 1932, was made by the two big carriers during maneuvers. Rear Admiral Harry Yarnell used the cover of night to bring his task force northeast of Oahu, launching 152 biplanes just before dawn. Boeing fighters and Martin dive-bombers and torpedo planes caught the defenders unready and had to be credited, in the theoretical sense of war games, of knocking out the defender's ships and aircraft. The concept of a carrier strike had been demonstrated, and instead of simply following the battleships, the carriers now operated as separate task forces.

Much of the Navy's success in developing the carrier-based strike force during the biplane period was due to the leadership of air-minded admirals such as the tall, white-bearded, Joseph Reeves, Commander of Aircraft Squadrons, Battle Fleet, William Moffett, the first Chief of the Bureau of Aeronautics, and William Sims, Naval War College

USN

Carrier operations required special gear, like the arresting hook on this Vought 02U-2.

USN

Amphibians like this Loening OL-8A filled Army and Navy observation roles in 1929.

PMB

Army and National Guard observation squadrons continued to fly Douglas biplanes until 1940, like this 116th OS O-38 seen on August 6, 1932.

ARC

Defense of the Panama Canal, shown below a Douglas P2D-l from Coco Solo, was a primary U.S. objective between the World Wars.

PMB

Twin ,303-caliber Vickers guns on Spad 13 were synchronized with propeller.

President, who foresaw the carrier becoming the capital ship of the future.

Building the Warplane: the designer's task

Military leaders demand of the plane builders not only a machine to do a certain job, but a machine that can do that job better than foreign types. Since the physical laws of aerodynamics are true all over the world, and the engineering textbooks everywhere have much the same formulas, the engineer can only hope to be a little earlier than his competitors.

French Salmsons provided American observers with a Scarff ring for twin Lewis guns with their drum magazines.

The first airplane designers had no computers and little relevant experience to guide them through their difficulties, and trial and error was the chief learning method. In this section of the chapter we give the reader a very simplified introduction to the characteristics of the early combat plane.

Essentially, the combat plane is an airborne weapons carrier whose value is its ability to get from point to point in the skies. The four physical forces that act on aircraft in flight are thrust and lift on the positive side, and drag and gravity on the negative side.

Thrust, the energy converted into forward motion by the engine, is counteracted by drag, or air resistance. This age of streamlining has made us conscious of the problem of reducing drag. Air movement around the wings creates lift to counteract gravity. The designer's task is to manipulate these forces to produce the best possible performance.

Armament and Equipment

Armament is the part of a combat plane's weight that is the reason for its existence. The weapons carried must be sufficient for their task, but yet not unduly hamper performance. In this respect, a lesson was taught by the first British effort to attack an enemy plane.

On August 22, 1914, a Farman pusher, with a Lewis gun attached to the bow, took off in pursuit of an Albatros patrolling at a 5,000-foot altitude. The added weight of the gun had depressed the Farman's climb, however, and the Allied plane found itself unable to pass the 3,500-foot level, while the Albatros went home undisturbed.

Such incidents suggest why armament is always limited by the power of the aircraft. With improvements in design, the weights carried have steadily increased. During World War I, the bombs dropped were seldom as large as the shells from the heaviest artillery, but by the end of World War Two, the bombs had grown as heavy as the 44,000-pound T-10.

The first American-built combat plane, the DH-4, had twin Lewis guns in the rear cockpit and twin Marlins for the pilot. The extra Lewis pointed forward and down was only a test installation.

To fight other aircraft, the rifle-caliber machine gun came into general use in 1915. The Lewis was the first Allied machine gun favored for aircraft work. Of light weight, it was used throughout the 1914-1918 war, but its

Browning .30-caliber M1922 flexible gun lifted out of recess on Curtiss XO-16, replaced Lewis guns on Scarff ring.

Lewis gun mounts tested on a Navy F-5L flying boat in August 1918. The standing position was discarded in favor of a simple hatch.

drum feeding required frequent reloading, and it could not be synchronized to fire through propellers. The belt feeding of the heavier Vickers gun was more suitable for a pilot-fired synchronized weapon.

Both of these weapons had been invented by Americans, but were first put into mass production by Britain using caliber .303-inch (7.7-mm) ammunition, and aircraft delivered by the Allies to American forces standardized on the Vickers for fixed and the Lewis gun for flexible mountings. By 1917, both were being produced in the United States for the Allies, so the American services were able to get over 39,000 Lewis guns, modified with 97-round drums of United States .30-caliber (7.62-mm) ammunition.

Vickers gun output here was already committed to the ground forces, so the Marlin M1917, an air-cooled gas-operated weapon, was provided as the forward synchronized weapon on aircraft built in the United States. The first American DH-4 squadron arrived at the front in August 1918. Two Marlins with 1,000 rounds weighed 122 pounds, plus 35 pounds for the synchronization gear, while the twin Lewis guns and ten bullet drums weighed 128 pounds, plus 23 pounds for the Scarff mount around the observer's cockpit. This became the usual gun weight allowance for American two-seaters.

Sometimes a water-cooling system, like these wing radiators on the Curtiss XO-13 and XPW-8A on September 9, 1927, just was not practical.

About 38,000 Marlins were made before production shifted in October 1918 to the new gun developed by John Browning. Although that air-cooled recoil-operated aircraft machine gun appeared too late for combat use in the war, its high rate of fire (1,000 rpm) and reliability made it the standard weapon between the wars; first as a fixed synchronized gun. The first 3,000 30-.caliber Browning aircraft guns, Model 1918, were deemed faulty in construction. Refined as the M1921, it replaced the Marlin as the fixed gun installed on all Army and Navy aircraft. Then the M1922 flexible gun was provided, but did not replace stocks of the Lewis gun in service until about 1931.

The need for larger caliber guns, especially against ground targets and armored aircraft, resulted in the Browning .50-caliber (12.7-mm) gun developed at the war's end, successfully adopted as the .50-caliber M1921 aircraft gun designed for use against light armor. That weapon's size seemed too heavy to be aimed from open cockpits, so .50-caliber guns were used as fixed forward-firing guns until the development of enclosed turrets.

A 37-mm Puteaux aircraft smooth-barrel gun firing explosive shells, or canister shot with 24 half-inch steel balls, was introduced by France, but its loading by hand was slow and inconvenient. An American development of the Puteaux was the 37-mm Baldwin automatic cannon.

Trials began September 4, 1919 at McCook Field, but suffered many malfunctions. Development of that cumbersome Baldwin was discontinued November 22, 1921. Not until 1937 did Army Ordinance produce the rapid-firing, high-velocity, 37-mm gun famous on the Bell fighters.

Performance Goals

Once an aircraft has been provided with the crew, weapons, and equipment appropriate for its mission the warplane's value is determined by its mobility, or performance. Speed, climb, ceiling, and range are the measurements of performance- how fast, high, and far the plane's weapons can be taken.

To the early designers, the chief enemy of performance was weight, against whom thrust and lift must be arrayed. The measurement of the burden of gravity against thrust is *power loading*- the gross weight divided by the power or thrust available. The measurement of the burden upon lift is *wing loading*- the gross weight divided by the area of the wing. These expressions must be kept in mind in describing the achievement of high performance.

Top speed is the measurement of the airplane's ability to catch or to escape the enemy. Primarily, it is determined by an aircraft's power loading and its drag. The lower the power loading, the faster the aircraft, thus the lighter the weight and the greater the power, the higher the speed. The drag of any airframe is steadily reduced as the aircraft gains in altitude, due to the thinning density of the air. Therefore, the higher the altitude of a given power loading, the faster the plane.

As a plane goes higher the air gets thinner and power also decreases; an unsupercharged piston engine will lose a third of its power at 10,000 feet and 60% by 20,000 feet. That condition may be corrected by supercharging that compresses the air so that sea-level pressures and engine power are maintained up to the unit's critical altitude, where power starts to fall off.

Since thinner air at higher altitudes means less drag, the aircraft can go nearly 1% faster with every 1,000 feet of height, and an airplane makes its highest speed at the altitude at which the advantage of the lower drag is greater than the disadvantage of the loss of power due to the thinning air. This is known as the critical altitude. In unsupercharged airplanes, the critical altitude is at sea level, for the loss of power as the plane goes higher is not compensated by the reduction in drag.

In the Curtiss P-6E, the last unsupercharged Army pursuit, top speed dropped from 198 mph at sea level to

1. Propulsive efficiency is also a factor, but since propellers tended to be standardized, they are not considered in comparing aircraft designs in this book.

194 at 5,000 feet, 189 at 10,000 feet, and 182 at 15,000 feet. On the other hand, the Boeing 281 had a single-stage supercharger that maintained power into higher altitudes. Top speed therefore went from 215 mph at sea level to 235 at 6,000 feet (its critical altitude), and to 232 at 11,000 feet.

This effect was gained by a built-in, or integral supercharger run by the crankshaft of the engine. Later types used turbosuperchargers, run by the engine exhaust, which are heavier, and can maintain power up to 35,000 feet. The disadvantage of superchargers is their increased weight, which handicaps the supercharged aircraft's performance at sea level.

As far as fighter aircraft are concerned, rate of climb and ceiling come second only to top speed as performance criteria. *Rate of climb* is simply the time taken to reach a given altitude, or the feet gained in one minute's climb. *Service ceiling* is the altitude at which rate of climb is 100 feet per minute for a fully loaded aircraft, while *absolute ceiling* is the highest altitude an aircraft may achieve. Service ceiling was the criteria for tactical purposes, and absolute ceiling is no longer cited in government tables after 1938.

The climbing ability of an aircraft is determined by both power loading and wing loading. The lower each is, the better the climb. Unfortunately a low power loading and high speed are not always compatible with a low wing loading and good climb. The larger the wing, the lower the wing loading, but the larger the wing, the more the drag.

Therefore it can be seen that a fast plane with a small wing may not match the climbing ability of a slower plane with a more generous wing area. An example of this was the Japanese Zero, whose low wing loading gave it a distinct advantage in climb and maneuverability over faster American types.

Maneuverability is the plane's ability to change direction. Wing loading and inertia are determining factors here. Maneuverability is adversely affected by aircraft inertia, or the natural resistance to any rotation about its center of gravity. Any heavy weight at a distance from the center of gravity will make maneuvers more difficult. The more compact and lighter the aircraft, the more maneuverable it will be, often forcing designers to choose between a fighter's ability to catch his enemy and his ability to maneuver into a good firing position.

Endurance was given in hours and minutes on older aircraft and usually quoted at full throttle. After World War I, *Range* was a vital characteristic and is determined by the number of hours an aircraft's fuel will allow it to stay in the air, times the cruising speed. *Cruising speed* depends on altitude, gross weight, and power used, and thus is very variable. The range of an aircraft also has numerous possibilities depending on the amount of fuel carried. Throughout this book, range is usually given at the normal cruising condition with the usual fuel load. Maximum ranges suggest the possibilities of the plane with its largest possible fuel load, and the most economical speed and altitude. *Radius of action* is about 40 per cent or less of range.

Running engines at too high a speed may waste fuel, as in this example: With 2,290 gallons of fuel and a gross weight of 55,000 pounds, the B-24D could achieve a range of about 2,950 miles at a cruising speed of 200 mph at 25,000 feet. Increasing the speed to 250 mph reduces the range to 2,400 miles. At an altitude of 5,000 feet, however, B-24D range is only 1,000 miles at 250 mph, and 2,400 miles at 200 mph. The inefficiency of the supercharged engines at lower altitudes is evident. Any increase in the bomb load carried will reduce this range, while a substitution of fuel for bombs can increase the range.

Landing speed, while not tactically significant, is included in the specifications because it is a measure of relative safety, and is one of the earliest limiting points selected in the design of an aircraft. The faster the necessary landing speed, the more difficult the landing. Landing speed depends on wing loading and the lifting efficiency of the wing. *Stalling speed,* at which the airplane stalls, is the minimum speed of flight, and is often cited in tables instead of landing speed.

A designer begins his task with a proposed specification that gives the armament and performance required. Traditional design procedure began with an estimate of weight, as this is the prime limiting factor of aircraft. A list of the essential parts of the *useful load* is totaled, including crew, armament, equipment, and probable fuel required. This is added to a rough estimate, from past experience, of the engine and airframe weight required to support such a load. Useful load and empty weight are added to make estimated gross weight.

An appropriate wing section and form is then selected; a high-lift *airfoil* profile for a bomber, or a low-drag airfoil for the fighter. *Aspect ratio* (the ratio of the wing span to the mean wing chord) is decided upon; a high aspect ratio for a long-range machine like the B-29, or a short, stubby wing for an interceptor.

Sliding pilot's enclosure ready for trials on this Curtiss XO-1E on March 10, 1931.

American World War I aircraft used the thin airfoil profiles developed in Britain and France by the Royal Aircraft Factory and Eiffel laboratories. But while such thin wings had less drag, they required bracing by outside struts and wires. Germany, however, often favored the thick airfoils developed at the Goettingen wind tunnel. On planes like the Fokker D VII, they provided higher lift without much more drag. Most important was that thicker wings allowed a stronger internal structure, even a *cantilever* beam supported at one end only, without external struts.

The Clark Y airfoil appeared in 1923, and used on most Curtiss and Douglas warplanes, combined the Goettingen profile with a flat undersurface for easier manufacturing. By 1933, the Variable-Density wind tunnel at Langley Field enabled the NACA (National Advisory Committee for Aeronautics) to develop a family of 78 airfoil profiles of different qualities. World War II aircraft especially used the 230 series.

Once the airfoil and aspect ratio have been chosen, designers must determine what wing loading would permit the desired landing speed and desired flight qualities. Then the necessary wing area is given by dividing the gross weight by the wing loading. Lift-increasing devices such as landing flaps and wing slots can be added to reduce the wing area without raising the landing speed. The introduction of tricycle landing gear on combat planes in 1939 made feasible higher landing speeds, since the nose wheel permits more sudden stops. However, wing loading should not be increased to a point too detrimental to climb and maneuverability.

When the weight has been estimated, the wing chosen, and the general layout planned, the performance of aircraft depends on its power loading. This leads to the next problem: the selection of a power plant.

Power Plants

To a designer the important features of an airplane engine are its power, weight, size, arrangement and number of cylinders, and the method of cooling. The reader should notice what the official designation tells about an engine. Allison's V-1710 has an inline Vee cylinder arrangement, and an approximate engine displacement of 1,710 cubic inches, while Wright's R-2600 is a radial of some 2,600 cubic inch engine displacement.

A piston engine's power is rated in horsepower available for takeoff, and at a rated altitude. Jet (gas turbine) engines are rated by pounds of static thrust.

Early aircraft engines had their cylinders lined up behind one another in two rows, and were liquid cooled. (Water until the 1930s; with chemical additives since then.) The most widely used inline engines were the Liberty 12 (V-1650) of 1918, the Curtiss D-12 (V-1150) of 1922, the Curtiss Conqueror (V-1570) of 1926, the Allison V-1710 of 1935, and the Packard Merlin (V-1650) of 1941. All had 12 cylinders. The reader is reminded that these military designations indicate the engine's size in cubic inches, so the higher the number, the larger the power plant

The radiator and cooling systems required by liquid-cooled engines added weight, drag, and maintenance problems. Air cooling offered the obvious advantage of low weight and simplified servicing, if only the engine could be kept from overheating. The rotary engines used on the World War I Nieuports, with their circle of whirling cylinders, represented an effort in this direction, but could develop only limited power.

The radial engine first used on American combat planes was the 200-hp 9-cylinder Lawrance J-l of 1922, used in the Navy's Curtiss TS fighter. Air cooling became so popular in the Navy, that after the more powerful 9-cylinder Pratt & Whitney Wasp (R-1340), Hornet (R-1690), and the early Wright Cyclone (R-1750) became available in 1927, radial engines were standard on Navy combat planes.

Although the period after World War I had not changed the basic shape of combat aircraft, and open-cockpit biplanes remained the common style, still engineers and aviators had built a solid foundation of experience to prepare the way for the next generation of aircraft.

A Guide to Designations of Combat Aircraft

During World War I, aircraft were known by the rather random names and numbers given by their own manufacturers. Most companies continued their own numbering series, but from 1919 to 1924 the Air Service used an adaptation of the French system. A more simplified classification was then used until 1948, with many modifications. Table 2 lists older designations used by Army combat planes, with the dates in use.

The basic mission symbol could also be preceded by status symbols such as "X" for experimental, or "Y" for service test aircraft procured in limited quantities.

Table 2
Army Air Corps/Force Combat Type Designations

A-	Attack and light bombardment, 1925-48
B-	Bombardment, 1926 to present
DB-	Day bombardment, 1920-23
F-	Photographic reconnaissance, 1938-48
F-	Fighter, 1948 to present
FM-	Fighter-multiplace, 1937-40
GA-	Ground attack, 1920-22
HB-	Heavy bombardment, 1926-27
LB-	Light bombardment, 1925-33
NBL-	Night bombardment, long distance, 1923
NBS-	Night bombardment, short distance, 1921-24
P-	Pursuit, 1925-48
PA-	Pursuit, air-cooled, 1922
PB-	Pursuit, biplace, 1935
PG-	Pursuit, ground attack, 1922
PN-	Pursuit, night, 1921
PW-	Pursuit, water cooled, 1921-28

In World War II, block designations were added to Army planes to denote minor modifications and factory of origin. Thus, the Douglas A-24A-DE was built at the El Segundo, California, plant; the A-20B-DL at the Long Beach, California, facility; the A-20C-DO at the main Santa Monica, California, shop, and the A-24B-DT at the firm's Tulsa, Oklahoma, shop. The Boeing-designed B-17G-VE was built by Lockheed's subsidiary, Vega. Block designations are used in this work only when needed to indicate which of several factories built the models described.

Air Corps flying at the end of the biplane era; a 17th Pursuit Squadron P-6E formation.

From 1923 to 1962, Navy combat aircraft were designated by a system that began with mission symbols alone or in combinations:

A = Attack (since 1946)
B = Bomber BF = Bomber-Fighter
F = Fighter
O = Observation OS = Observation-Scout
P = Patrol PB = Patrol-bomber
S = Scout SB = Scout-bomber SO = Scout-Observation
T = Torpedo TB = Torpedo-bomber

These letters were followed by a manufacturer's letter and model, as in PM-1 for Martin's first patrol plane, while P5M-2 is the fifth patrol design by Martin, the second modification, and the F6C-l is the sixth fighter by Curtiss, first model. Like the Army, the Navy used X as a prefix for experimental, as the XF12C-l.

Table 3

Letters assigned to builders of combat aircraft
(Dates indicate last deliveries of firms defunct by 1948)

Navy 1923-62	Army 1941-62	Company	Location
A	—	Atlantic-Fokker (1931)	Teterboro, New Jersey
A	—	Brewster (1944)	Long Island City, N.Y.
B	BH	Beech	Wichita, Kansas
B	BO	Boeing	Seattle, Washington
B	BN	Boeing	Renton, Washington
B	BW	Boeing	Wichita, Kansas
C	CU	Curtiss (1948)	Buffalo, N.Y.
D	DO	Douglas	Santa Monica, Cal.
D	DL	Douglas	Long Beach, Cal.
D	DT	Douglas	Tulsa, Oklahoma
E	—	Bellanca	New Castle, Del.
F	GR	Grumman	Bethpage, N.Y.
G	—	Great Lakes (1936)	Cleveland, Ohio
G	GO	Goodyear	Akron, Ohio
H	—	Hall (1940)	Bristol, Penna.
H	MC	McDonnell	St. Louis, Mo.
J	—	Berliner-Joyce (1934)	Dundalk, Md.
J	NA	North American	Inglewood, Cal.
J	NH	North American	Columbus, Ohio
K	—	Keystone (1932)	Bristol, Penna.
K	—	Kaiser (1946)	Bristol, Penna.
L	—	Loening (1932)	New York, N.Y.
L	BE	Bell	Buffalo, N.Y.
M	MA	Martin	Baltimore, Md.

Navy 1923-62	Army 1941-62	Company	Location
M	—	Eastern (General Motors)	Trenton, N. J.
N	—	Naval Aircraft Factory	Philadelphia, Pa.
O	LO	Lockheed	Burbank, Cal.
—	LM	Lockheed	Marietta, Ga.
—	RE	Republic	Farmingdale, N.Y.
R	RY	Ryan	San Diego, Cal.
S	SI	Sikorsky	Stratford, Conn.
T	NO	Northrop	Hawthorne, Cal.
U	—	Vought	Dallas, Texas
V	—	Lockheed (ex-Vega)	Burbank, Cal.
W	—	Canadian Car & Foundry	Fort William, Ont. Canada
Y	CO	Consolidated (Convair)	San Diego, Cal.
Y	CF	Consolidated (Convair)	Fort Worth, Texas

To the above list can be added suffixes sometimes added during and since World War II to denote special modifications such as the F4U-5N. On combat types they include:

A -Amphibious
B -Special Armament
C -Carrier
D -Special Drop Tank
E -Electronic Gear
G -Search-Rescue
K - Target Drone
L - Searchlight
M -Missile launcher
N - Night version
P - Photographic
Q - Radar Countermeasures
S - Anti-sub
W -Early Warning

CHAPTER 2

CLOSE SUPPORT FOR THE ARMY, 1917-1923

The only American-built plane used in combat by the Army in World War I was the De Havilland DH-4.

Two-seat Biplanes for the AEF, 1918

When America entered the war, the most common aircraft type at the front was the two-seat biplane used for observation and light bomber work. Germany confronted the Allies with 1,557 two-seaters at the front on April 30, 1917, compared to 686 single-seat fighters and 71 twin-engine bombers.

Missions of these two-seaters included observation of enemy activities behind the front-lines, the direction of artillery fire, photographic reconnaissance, and daytime light bombing. Such close support aircraft had the first priority for army leaders, and the Bolling Commission chose Britain's De Havilland 4 as the best type for production in America.

Since the first American two-seater squadrons arrived at the front before their DH-4s, French types were used. The 1st Aero Squadron made its first mission on April 11, 1918, with Spad llA2s, and on May 8, this squadron was joined to the 12th (A.R.l) and 88th (French-built Sopwith 1A2) Aero Squadrons to become the I Corps Observation Group.

SALMSON 2 A2
Salmson 9Z, 250 hp
DIMENSIONS: Span 38'6", Lg. 27'10", Ht. 9'6", Wing Area 401 sq. ft.
WEIGHT: Empty 1835 lb., Gross 3036 lb. Fuel 70 gal.
PERFORMANCE: Speed- Top 116 mph at s.l., 114 mph at 6500', Service Ceiling 20,500', Climb 6560'/11 min. Range 310 miles.

These aircraft were considered obsolete, and would be replaced in June by the Salmson 2A2. Fortunately, the Group sector was quiet, without enemy fighters, and there was no air combat in the first weeks. Corps observation missions were short-range, with each squadron assigned to support an infantry division on the ground. From dawn to dusk, single planes would fly along the trench lines, watching for enemy activity. Occasionally, the observer in the rear cockpit would take photos, or signal in Morse code to adjust the shots of divisional artillery batteries.

Observation squadrons directly attached to 1st Army headquarters were expected to make deep penetrations for photographs. The first such American squadron was the 91st, whose Salmsons made their first sorties on June 7, 1918. In September the 1st Army Observation Group was formed with the 91st and 24th Observation Squadrons, and 9th Night Observation Squadron.

A Salmson pilot sat ahead of the wings behind a radial engine water-cooled by a circular radiator; future American-made radials would all be air-cooled. Armament consisted of a Vickers gun for the pilot and a pair of Lewis flexible guns for the observer behind the wings.

The AEF in France received 705 Salmsons, which were used in combat by ten squadrons. These Salmsons had to do a lot of hard fighting to bring their information back home, usually flying in formations of three or four planes for protection against enemy fighters. During the Argonne drive, observation squadrons were credited with destroying 26 enemy planes, 17 of these being downed by the 91st Squadron's Salmsons. Unlike later concepts of reconnaissance by single unarmed fast aircraft, 1918 missions usually expected to fight their way.

The first American bombing mission was flown by the 96th Aero Squadron against a railroad yard on June 12, 1918. They used the standard French light bomber, the Breguet 14B2 powered by the 300-hp Renault 12F with a prominent exhaust stack pointing upwards. The lower wing had full-span trailing edge flaps for landing, and the racks for 32 16-pound bombs, or their 520-pound equivalent in larger bombs.

BREGUET 14 B2
Renault 12F, 300 hp
DIMENSIONS: Span 47'1", Lg. 29'6", Ht. 10'10", Wing Area 540 sq. ft.
WEIGHT: Empty 2283 lb., Gross 3892 lb. Fuel 70 gal.
PERFORMANCE: Speed- Top 110 mph at 6500'. Service Ceiling 19,000', Climb 10,000'/16.5 min. Endurance 2.75 hours. Range 300 miles.

Defensive armament comprised one fixed Vickers and two flexible Lewis guns. Forty-seven Breguet 14B2 bombers were sold to the AEF in 1918, along with 229 14A2 and 100 14E2 models mostly used for training. The Breguet 14A2 was equipped for observation work with a camera and wireless transmitter, but fewer bombs.

A second AEF Breguet squadron, the 9th with 14A2 models, was assigned to the front on August 26 for night observation work, while the 96th continued to be the only American bomber outfit until it joined with the new DH-4s of the 11th and 20th Squadrons on September 10, to form the First Day Bombardment Group. Their first mission would be bombing the German army transportation system during the St. Mihiel offensive.

The DH-4

The long-heralded DH-4 was the only American-built Army plane to be flown in combat in World War I, and became the most widely used American warplane of its decade. Typical of the period, it had two open cockpits, a big flat nose radiator for its water-cooled engine, wooden frame construction, and fabric-covered wings held together with four pairs of struts and numerous bracing wires. Cotton cloth replaced the scarce linen used in Britain and was made taut and waterproof by varnish called "dope" – so called because the mixtures gave off strong fumes that seemed to make workers dopey.

The DH-4 had first flown in Britain in August 1916, used a 250-hp Rolls-Royce engine when the first squadron began operations at the front in March 1917, and its performance was highly recommended to the Americans. A sample airframe, without engine or equipment, arrived in the United States on July 18, 1917, and was sent to the Aviation Section's Technical Staff at McCook Field, Dayton, Ohio by August 15.

The Dayton-Wright Airplane Company, a new Ohio firm formed three days after war was declared, was chosen on August 14 to produce an American version. Although Orville Wright's name as "Consulting Engineer" was invoked, company executives were automobile industry leaders who planned to achieve rapid mass production, bypass the small aircraft manufacturers, and thereby win the major share of government aviation spending. Much publicity was given to their promises, but production of wooden airplanes requiring thousands of engineering changes had little resemblance to automobile production.

A pre-production prototype, quickly hand-built using the new 12-cylinder Liberty engine, was first flown on October 29, 1917, by Howard M. Rinehardt. While the Dayton company had been awarded a production contract on October 8, 1917, the DH-4 structural details had to be redesigned to fit American manufacturing methods and the heavier engine. No less than 10,000 DH-4s would be ordered from three companies in 1917.

Nine Dayton-Wright DH-4s were delivered in February 1918, but tests also indicated that many mechanical problems or "bugs" had to be worked out; for example 11 different makes of radiators were tried. Not until the 31st aircraft was completed in April was the production configuration fixed. While the basic British shape remained, along with the RAF-15 airfoil section, the internal structure was very different than the original De Havilland airframe.

The "Liberty Plane" looked warlike enough, armed with two fixed .30-caliber Marlin guns with 1,000 rounds over the engine, two flexible .30-caliber Lewis guns with 970 rounds in ten drums, and bomb racks under the wings for four 112-pound, or ten 25-pound bombs. A Wimperis sight was used for bombing, or a De Ram automatic camera was provided with 48 plates to photograph enemy positions. When adjusting artillery fire, a 50-pound wireless with a Morse code key, generator, and a wind-out trailing antenna was used. This was a transmitter only, not a receiver, and voice radio was not yet available for that war.

DAYTON-WRIGHT DH-4
Liberty 12, 400 hp
DIMENSIONS: Span 42'5", Lg. 29'11", Ht. 9'8", Wing Area 440 sq. ft.
WEIGHT: Empty 2391 lb., Gross 3582 lb. Fuel 66 gal.
PERFORMANCE: Speed- Top 124 mph at s.1., 120 mph at 6500'. Absolute Ceiling 19,500', Climb 10,000'/14 min. Range 270 miles.

Flight tests in April 1918 demonstrated a top speed at full 400 hp of 124.7 mph, then as fast as many fighters. Endurance was one hour, 13 minutes at full power, and three hours at half-power. If the 19,500 foot ceiling was to be utilized, a 23-pound oxygen apparatus was provided.

Quantity deliveries from Dayton gathered force with 153 planes in May 1918, and increased to 556 by October.

Fisher Body (General Motors) at Cleveland, Ohio, had been added to the program on November 7, 1917, and Standard Aircraft of Patterson, New Jersey, who had been building trainers, got a DH order on January 24, 1918. Fisher's first DH-4 flew on June 26, and Standard delivered its first four in August. In the month of October 1918, total DH-4 deliveries reached 1,097 planes.

While four Dayton DH-4s reached France on May 6, 1918, they were from the first test batch, and judged unsuitable for front-line use. Not until August 9, 1918, did the first squadron to use the DH-4 at the front, the 135th Aero, make its first mission, with fifteen planes and General Benjamin Foulois as an observer. America had already been in the war sixteen months, with only three months left to go, yet that first sortie by American pilots in American aircraft did not even cross the front lines!

Heavy criticism would be leveled at the DH-4's combat record. The wooden construction was considered weak compared to the duralumin tube Breguet framework, the pilot's view upwards was blocked by the wing, and the fuel tanks lacked the leak-proof rubber covering of the Salmson and (after July) Breguet. Worst of all, the main gas tank was between the crewmen, which prevented easy communication, was a danger in crashes, and vulnerable to enemy fire. The phrase "flaming coffin" was used, although not statistically justified by actual losses.

DH-4 production in the United States reached 3,431 by Armistice Day, of which 1,213 had been received in France by the AEF. Of these, 499 had actually been delivered to squadrons on the front, 249 crashed at the front and 33 lost over the lines to enemy action. At the war's end on November 11, there were 196 with five day bombing, five corps observation, and two Army observation squadrons, along with 157 Salmsons and 43 Breguets in the thirteen other two-seater squadrons.

The AEF also had 332 DH-4s in depots and 270 in flying schools. The U.S. Navy received 155 Dayton-built DH-4s during the war, of which 51 went to the Marines of the Northern Bomber Group in September 1918 for operations on the Channel Coast.

Of 5,000 DH-4s ordered from Dayton-Wright, 3,106 were built when production ended in March 1919. Fisher Body built 1,600 of the 2,000 ordered, and Standard just 140 of 1,000 ordered, for a total of 4,846. The government paid about $5,500 for each plane, and the first one built at Dayton is exhibited in the National Air and Space Museum.

Improved De Havillands

In July 1917, the British had developed a new De Havilland version, the DH-9, with a larger gas tank moved ahead of, instead of behind, the pilot's cockpit. Two aircraft were purchased without engines by the AEF in July 1918, and 13,750 were ordered from American firms by the Army before full details were available. They were to be built in 1919 with Liberty engines, be known as USD-9s and be substituted for the DH-4 on production lines as soon as possible.

The British themselves, however, found the DH-9 unsuccessful and it was replaced by the DH-9A, which had wider wings, more fuel, and American Liberty engines, with deliveries to the RAF beginning in June 1918. The U.S. counterpart of this would be the USD-9A, a development pushed by the Army's Engineering Division at McCook Field. Army engineers built two USD-9 prototypes in July 1918, and Dayton-Wright also completed two shortly afterwards. The first of five Engineering Division USD-9A models built to American manufacturing standards began flight tests September 24, 1918. Dayton-Wright also received an order in September for four USD-9As completed in April 1919 after the last DH-4s. With an enlarged self-sealing fuel tank in front of the crew cockpits, now close together, the USD-9A overcame the DH-4's worst fault. Armament included a new .30-caliber Browning gun under the right-hand side of the cowl with 750 rounds, and two Lewis guns with 970 rounds in the rear cockpit. The 550-pound bomb load was carried in racks below the wings and fuselage, while wireless and camera equipment could be fitted to the reconnaissance version.

While the war's end closed the USD-9A program, its main improvements could be made on rebuilt DH-4s. Dayton-Wright had delivered two improved DH-4s in July 1918; the first was the DH-4A with a modified 110-gallon fuel system, and the other was reworked by October to the DH-4B with a 88-gallon main tank forward of the pilot, the second cockpit directly behind, and the landing gear enlarged and moved forward.

ENGINEERING DIVISION USD-9A
Liberty 12, 400 hp
DIMENSIONS: Span 45'11", Lg. 30'3", Ht. 11'2", Wing Area 490 sq. ft.
WEIGHT: Empty 2815 lb., Gross 4322 lb. as recon. (4872 lb. as bomber) Fuel 142 gal.
PERFORMANCE: Speed- Top 126 (121) mph at s.l., 117 (115) mph at 10,000'. Service Ceiling 18,700" (14,400'), Climb 6500'/7.5 (12) min. Range 400 miles as recon, 350 miles as bomber.

After the war, the Army's stockpile was so huge that it was cheaper to destroy most of those in Europe in the "Billion Dollar Bonfire" than to repack and ship them home. But several American aircraft factories were kept going between 1919-1923 with "maintenance" contracts modifying some 1,538 DH-4s to several DH-4B configurations. Along with the standard observation model armed with one fixed Browning and twin Lewis guns, numerous DH-4B variations were flown. These planes equipped most of the post-war Army Air Service squadrons, the Marines, the Air Mail Service, and the Border Patrol

MFR

DAYTON-WRIGHT DH-4B
Liberty 12A, 421 hp
DIMENSIONS: Span 42'5", Lg. 29'11", Ht. 9'8", Wing Area 439 sq. ft.
WEIGHT: Empty 2732 lb., Gross 4297 lb. Fuel 94 gal.
PERFORMANCE: Speed- Top 123.7 mph at s.1., 120 mph at 6,500',
Landing 61.5 mph. Service Ceiling 15,800', Absolute Ceiling 17,600', Climb 10,000'/14.8 min. Endurance 3.2 hours at 116 mph. Range 370 miles.

A further development was the DH-4M (for modernized) whose fuselage was of welded steel tubing covered by fabric, assembled with parts from old DH-4s. Boeing delivered 147 DH-4M-ls from January to September, 1924, and 30 similar Marine Corps O2B-ls in March 1925, while Atlantic Aircraft rebuilt 135 DH-4M-2s. These aircraft

AF

BOEING DH-4M-1
Liberty 12A, 416 hp
DIMENSIONS: Span 42'5", Lg. 29'11", Ht. 9'8", Wing Area 439 sq. ft.
WEIGHT: Empty 2939 lb., Gross 4595 lb. Fuel 76 gal.
PERFORMANCE: Speed- Top 118 mph at s.1., Landing 64 mph. Service Ceiling 12,800', Climb 5000'/8.2 min. Endurance 3.25 hours at 94 mph.

PMB

LWF G-2
Liberty 12, 435 hp
DIMENSIONS: Span 41'7", Lg. 29'1", Ht. 9'4", Wing Area 516 sq. ft.
WEIGHT: Empty 2675 lb., Gross 4023 lb., Max. 4880 lb. Fuel 90-120 gal.
PERFORMANCE: Speed- Top 138 mph at s.1., 130 mph at 10,000', Landing 50 mph. Service Ceiling 24,000', Climb 10,000'/9.3 min. Endurance 3 to 4 hours at 90 mph.

lingered on with the Army; in April 1926, 623 of 1,510 Air Service planes were De Havillands, and two DH-4B and 78 DH-4Ms remained in 1931, the last retired in April 1932.

ENGINEERING DIV. LUSAGH-11
Liberty 12, 408 hp
DIMENSIONS: Span 47'1", Lg. 24'4", Ht. 10'10", Wing Area 601 sq. ft.
WEIGHT: Empty 3913 lb., Gross 5109 lb., Max. 5600 lb. Fuel 67-80 gal.
PERFORMANCE: Speed- Top 114 mph at s.1., 110 mph at 6,500', Stalling 61 mph. Service Ceiling 15,300', Absolute Ceiling 17,000', Climb 875'/1 min., 6500'/9.4 min., Endurance 2.6 hours at 107 mph.

It is interesting to note that De Havilland's design played a similar role in Russia, where most Red Air Force planes in 1929 were still R-1s, the Soviet-built version of the Liberty-powered DH-9A. R-1 squadrons fought tribal rebellions in Central Asia, and production actually continued until 1931! Britain's Royal Air Force also used their own DH-9A squadrons to attack insurgent tribesmen in Iraq and Northwest India.

ENGINEERING DIVISION LUSAO-11
Two Liberty 12, 425 hp
DIMENSIONS: Span 54'6", Lg. 38'2", Ht. 13'6", Wing Area 870 sq. ft.
WEIGHT: Empty 5455 lb., Gross 8577 lb. Fuel 272 gal.
PERFORMANCE: Speed- Top 112 mph at s.1., 109 mph at 6,500', Stalling 61.5 mph. Service Ceiling 15,350', Climb 6500'/9.3 min. Endurance 4.5 hours at 106 mph, Range 475 miles .

Experimental Army tactical support designs

To back up the DH-4/-9 program with new designs for possible production in 1919, four new prototypes were begun for the Army in 1918. The LWF Company of College Point, New York, begun as a partnership of Edmond Lowe, Jr., Charles Willard, and Charles Fowler, was building a series of trainers with a unique laminated wood monocoque *(single shell)* fuselage. After the LWF Model F first tested the 235-hp 8-cylinder Liberty on August 20, 1917, they received a contract on September 14, 1917, for two advanced trainers to be test beds for the "U.S. Standard Aircraft Engine" as the Liberty was known. The Model G was flown with the early 350-hp Liberty 12, and had a fatal crash on January 16, 1918.

It had been unarmed like previous LWF aircraft, but the second prototype, LWF G-2, was heavily armed with seven guns and under wing bomb racks. Four fixed Marlin guns were grouped around the engine, two guns were on the gunner's ring, and another fired through a hole behind and below the gunner. According to company claims, flight tests in summer 1918 at a gross weight of 4,023 pounds, including 90 gallons of fuel, showed a remarkable 138 mph and four hours endurance. Equipped for bombing with full fuel, up to 592 pounds of bombs, and 66 pounds of cockpit armor, the G-2 weighed 4,880 pounds. Great hopes were held, but the war ended, and the two-seater crashed on November 18.

POMILIO BVL-12
Liberty 12, 400 hp
DIMENSIONS: Span 48'3", Lg. 31'7", Ht. 9'9", Wing Area 578 sq. ft.
WEIGHT: Empty 2824 lb., Gross 4552 lb. Fuel 115 gal.
PERFORMANCE: Speed- Top 111 mph at s.1., 106.5 mph at 6500', Stalling 61.5 mph. Service Ceiling 13,700', Absolute Ceiling 15,900', Climb 710'/1 min., 6500'/11.8 min. Range 485 miles/350-lb. bombs at 94 mph.

A French engineer, Captain Georges LePere, had been loaned to the Army to design aircraft around the Liberty engine, and a prototype LUSAGH-11 (LePere United States Army Ground Harassment) ordered May 6, 1918, from the Engineering Division at McCook Field began tests on September 22. With 408-hp, (flight test output of Liberty engines varied) the heavy, squared-off, LUSAGH-11 had the forward fuselage built with 1,390 pounds of armor to protect pilot and gunner seated side-by-side in one cockpit.

For low-level work supporting infantry, a new .50-caliber Browning heavy gun firing down and forward, a flexible .30-caliber Lewis gun protecting the upper rear, and 450 pounds of bombs were provided. A second prototype, LUSAGH-21, with a new 420-hp Bugatti, was completed in January 1919, but by then the need for any production was gone.

Unique among American aircraft designed for observation missions was LePere's USAO-1, a triplane with two

Liberty engines, a pilot and two observers with two pairs of Lewis guns, and a four-hour endurance at 106 mph for "long-range" penetrations. Two prototypes ordered from the Engineering Division on May 6, 1918, were delivered in February and May 1919.

An Italian engineer, Ottorino Pomilio, was also loaned to the United States, and he designed the BVL-12 day bomber ordered September 21, 1918. A plywood fuselage was suspended between the wings, three pairs of struts connected the wings, while one fixed Browning gun, two Lewis flexible guns, and 350 pounds of bombs comprised the armament. Six were delivered from January to May 1919 from Indianapolis.

Ground Attack

During the war's last year, German fliers gave outstanding close-support to their own troops by low-level attacks on Allied infantry. Special squadrons (*Schlachstaffeln*) of light two-seaters were formed in 1917 to strafe enemy trench and road systems with machine-gun fire. In 1918, they were joined by heavy two-seaters with added firepower and armor protection.

After the war, the Americans considered these methods and in 1921, the First Surveillance Group at Kelly Field, Texas, which had been patrolling the Mexican border, was redesignated the Third Attack Group. Their equipment remained the DH-4B for many years, while the Air Service made several unsuccessful attempts to develop a specialized attack plane.

Such a type should give armor protection and heavier firepower, including the 37-mm Baldwin semi-automatic cannon experimentally mounted in a Martin GMB bomber in September 1919. The Air Service issued a circular proposal for an armored ground-attack design on October 15, 1919, but not a single private company responded- despite post-war hunger for contracts. This left the task to the Army's own prototype producer, the Engineering Division at McCook Field, Dayton, Ohio.

AF

ORENCO IL-1
Liberty 12, 408 hp
DIMENSIONS: Span 46', Lg. 32', Ht. 11'9", Wing Area 602 sq. ft.
WEIGHT: Empty 4437 lb., Gross 5686 lb. Fuel 86 gal.
PERFORMANCE: Speed- Top 107 mph at s.l., 103 mph at 6500', Landing 60 mph. Service Ceiling 11,500', Absolute Ceiling 13,100', Climb 685'/1 min., 6500'/13 min. Endurance 3.5 hours at 98 mph, Range 343 miles.

The GAX (Ground Attack Experimental) was designed by Isaac M. Laddon (1897-1977), of the Engineering Division. Mr. Laddon had not yet reached the competence that his famous PBY and B-24 designs would show and he faced a task that private aircraft companies had rejected.

Powered by two Liberty engines turning four-bladed pusher propellers, the GAX was a triplane. All that lift seemed necessary for the ton of 3/16-inch armor protecting the engines and three crewmen. Slow and awkward, it had a 37-mm Baldwin cannon in front that swung 45 degrees right or left, 60 degrees down or 15 degrees up. Eight .30-caliber Lewis guns were mounted: four pointed front and downwards 45 degrees, another one faced aft over the wings, and all were fired by the busy front gunner. The rear gunner handled two belly guns and one upper gun. Ten small fragmentation bombs could be carried, if some guns were removed.

AMC

BOEING GA-2
Engineering Div. W-1A-18, 700 hp
DIMENSIONS: Span 54', Lg. 37', Ht. 12', Wing Area 851 sq. ft.
WEIGHT: Empty 6908 lb., Gross 9150 lb. Fuel 90 gal.
PERFORMANCE: Speed- Top 110 mph at s.l., Service Ceiling 11,500', Absolute Ceiling 13,100', Climb 6500'/16.5 min. Range 165 miles.

The GAX began tests on April 3, 1920, but was severely criticized by test pilot Lt. Harold R. Harris, who found it unmaneuverable and complained of the long take-off run, poor visibility, and especially of vibration and noise from the armored sides. Nevertheless, a contract for 20, to be designated GA-l, was given to Boeing on June 15, 1920, but the quantity was reduced to ten before the first example was tested May 2, 1921. Shipped to Kelly Field for the 3rd Attack Group, the GA-ls were seldom flown, and were scrapped in April 1926.

More conventional was the Orenco IL-l (Ordinance Engineering Infantry Liaison), an armored two-seat biplane for low-altitude infantry support work ordered on January 26, 1920. Two were delivered, closely resembling a DH-4B with the same RAF-15 airfoil, but with double-bay triple struts, a .50-caliber Browning in the nose, and twin Lewis guns. Flight tests begun March 21, 1921, indicated that the IL-l was far too heavy for the performance needed.

Two single-engine attack biplanes designed by Army engineers around an experimental 700-hp Engineering Division W-lA-18 engine were ordered December 20, 1920, from Boeing. Like the GA-l, this three-place GA-2 sacrificed performance for ferocity and was first flown December 18, 1921.

Mounted behind the engine, at the leading edge of the lower wing, was a 37-mm cannon and two .30-caliber guns

ENGINEERING DIVISION GAX
Two Liberty 12, 435 hp
DIMENSIONS: Span 65'6", Lg. 33'7", Ht. 14'3", Wing Area 1016 sq. ft.
WEIGHT: Empty 7532 lb., Gross 9740 lb. Fuel 102 gal.
PERFORMANCE: Speed- Top 105 mph at s.1., 102 mph at 4,000', Stalling 63.6 mph. Service Ceiling 9,600', Climb 6000'/ 14.1 min. Endurance 1.8 hours at 95 mph, Range 170 miles.

movable 60° in the vertical plane and 15° in the horizontal. The gunner sat beneath the pilot and also had a .50-caliber Browning to fire back and down, while the third crewman in a turret behind the pilot guarded the upper hemisphere with two Lewis guns. Ten 20-pound bombs could be attached to wing racks. Protection from ground fire was furnished by 1,600 pounds of 1/4-inch armor and the duplication of all struts, bracing and control wires, and spars.

BOEING GA-2 (close-up)

The GA-2 is the sole example of this weighty and expensive safety device.

The general failure of these armored ground-strafers was due to inadequacies of the time's engineering: not enough strength and power, and too much weight and drag. All through the decade following the war, therefore, attack-squadron equipment, like that of the observation outfits, had to be drawn from the wartime stock of DH-4s.

The most advanced aircraft style of that time was the all-metal, Junkers monoplane whose low wing was thick enough to allow a cantilever structure without outside supporting struts. A New York dealer, John Larsen, imported from Germany several Junkers F13 cabin planes built of corrugated dural.

Two designated JL-6 with a 243-hp 6-cylinder BMW engine were purchased by the Army in 1920. Larsen also modified another as the JL-12 attack by installing a 420-hp Liberty 12 engine, replacing the German metal skin with .025-inch Alcoa duralumin, twice the original thickness, and 400 pounds of 1/8-inch armor.

Thirty Thompson M1921 submachine guns with 3,000 rounds of .45-caliber ammunition were added. Two "Tommy guns" could be fired out of the cabin windows on each side, while the rest were fixed to fire downward. The 28 belly guns were mounted in the floor; twelve pointed slightly forward, six directly down, and ten inclined to the rear. Half the guns could be fired at once, or a single trig-

GALLAUDET DB-1B
Engineering Div. W-1A-18, 700 hp
DIMENSIONS: Span 66'7", Lg. 42' 6", Ht. 12'7", Wing Area 684 sq. ft.
WEIGHT: Empty 5060 lb., Gross 8600 lb. Fuel 248 gal.
PERFORMANCE: Speed- Top 127 mph at s.1., 118 mph at 5.000', Service Ceiling 13,400', Absolute Ceiling 15,500', Climb 706'/1 min.

JUNKERS-LARSEN JL-12
Liberty 12, 420 hp
DIMENSIONS: Span 49', Lg. 33', Ht. 10'4", Wing Area 417 sq. ft.
WEIGHT: Empty 2900 lb., Gross 5000 lb. Fuel 140 gal.
PERFORMANCE: Speed- Top 125 mph at s.1., Stalling 60 mph. Climb 10,000'/18 min. Range 400 miles.

ger could set off all 28, delivering a fire volume for once justifying the cliché about a rain of bullets. While the JL-12 was offered to the Army in December 1921, the test pilot opposed purchase of the plane, described as a bad flier, expensive, and with an pistol-caliber armament array of doubtful efficiency.

The last prototype actually ordered by the Army in 1920 was a light bomber of advanced layout. Stimulated by the success of the Junkers metal internally-braced low-wing monoplanes, the two Gallaudet DB-1 monoplanes contracted on December 24, 1920, were low-wing two-seaters without any struts outside of the thick wing. Powered by a 700-hp Engineering Division W-1A 18-cylinder water-cooled engine, the all-metal DB-1 (Day Bomber One) design promised to carry 600 pounds of bombs with eight hours of fuel and have a top speed of 141 mph.

But when the first DB-1 was delivered on December 5, 1921, it proved to be overweight; 9,207 pounds empty instead of the 7,050 pounds estimated. When the control system made the duralumin skin buckle, it was decided unsafe to fly the monoplane, but to use it only for static tests.

On March 11, 1922, the second example was reordered as the DB-1B with a lighter structure of welded steel tubing with fabric covering on the rear fuselage, wing sections, and control surfaces. Between the pilot and gunner's cockpit was a bay for the 600-pound bomb load and 1,367 rounds were carried for four .30-caliber guns; a Browning in the nose, two Lewis guns in the rear cockpit, and one in the belly.

Careful testing of structural components delayed delivery to McCook Field until May 26, 1923, and the first flight until August 1. New difficulties delayed any more flights until April 1924, and the design seemed too advanced for the structural technique of that time. Gallaudet General Manager Rueben Fleet advised against any more flight tests.

CHAPTER 3

THE FIRST FIGHTERS, 1915-1920

FOKKER E I
The first true fighter plane

SDAM

The Gun and the Airplane

In the beginning, aerial warfare was an unspectacular routine of trips across the lines for scouting and artillery spotting, only occasionally enlivened by picayune bombing raids. The first attack by one aircraft upon another has not been definitely recorded, but there were awkward engagements between reconnaissance pilots who fired pistols, rifles, and crudely-mounted machine guns.

But as the importance of aerial observation grew, so did the desirability of preventing enemy flights over your own forces. The French were the most aggressive, killing a German flier with pistol shots on August 26, 1914, and on October 5, an Aviatik was downed by a machine-gun mounted on a Voisin two-seater pusher.

MdA

NIEUPORT 11

The tractor plane, with its propeller facing forward, was more efficient, but how could a machine-gun be mounted to avoid hitting the propeller? Roland Garros fired his machine gun forward through his Morane single-seat monoplane's propeller. Metal deflector blades on the wooden propeller blades threw off those bullets that struck them.

When Garros and his Morane were captured by the Germans in April 1915, Anthony Fokker (1890–1939) was asked to produce a response. Fokker's answer was the E I, the single-seat monoplane armed with a 7.9-mm gun synchronized to fire through the propeller with a mechanical interrupter gear. These Fokkers were the first true fighter planes, making their first kill on July 1, 1915, and in a few months became the "Fokker Scourge" that destroyed many Allied planes that had dared to cross the German lines. A race to build a better fighter plane began that would last the rest of the century.

The French answer to the Fokker was the Nieuport 11 appearing at the front in January 1916. It was called a sesquiplane, since the narrow lower wing was about half the size of the upper one, with Vee struts between them. An air-cooled rotary engine, usually an 80-hp Le Rhone, gave a top speed of 97 mph. Since the Lewis gun could not be synchronized, it was mounted on the top wing and fired over the propeller. The gun's 47-round ammunition drum was replaced late in 1916 with the 97-round drum used for the rest of the war.

Nieuports became the principal Allied fighter and were issued to the first American fighter pilots in the war, the volunteers of the Lafayette Escadrille. That famous squadron, flying the Nieuport 11 "chasse," or pursuit, plane in the massive battle of Verdun, scored their first victory on May 18, 1916.

Nieuport fighters went through a rapid development by increasing in horsepower and size, and by replacing the Lewis gun with a synchronized, belt-fed Vickers. Model 27 with an 130-hp Le Rhone, in 1917, was the last of the sesquiplane series used until the French Army selected the stronger Spad as its standard fighter.

Spad fighters had the Hispano-Suiza water-cooled eight-cylinder inline engine behind a rounded radiator, and equal-span wings strengthened by a second pair of articulated struts between the fuselage and the outer struts. The first model used by the French was the Spad 7, introduced late in 1916 with a 150-hp direct-drive Hispano-Suiza 8A and a single Vickers gun. By 1917, an 180-hp "Hisso" was standard, and the Spad 7 was replacing Nieuports in the French, British, Italian, and even Russian squadrons.

Development continued in 1917 with the 220-hp Spad 11 two-seater and the Spad 12, which incorporated the first cannon on a single-seat fighter. Armament consisted of one Vickers .303-caliber machine gun and a 37-mm cannon mounted to fire through a hollow propeller shaft. Twelve rounds of buck-shot type ammunition were carried for the single-shot, hand-loaded cannon. The French ace Captain Rene Fonck downed seven Germans with the experimental weapon, but felt hand-loading an inconvenient distraction. A single example of the Spad 12 went to the Americans in July 1918.

When the Spad 13, with two Vickers guns and a geared 220-hp Hispano-Suiza 8B became available, it was chosen to equip every French single-seat fighter squadron at the front in 1918.

Native Single-seaters

When the United States declared war on April 6, 1917, the Army had no armed fighter planes in service. The only single-seater available was the Curtiss S-3 the Army tested in October 1916. Called the Curtiss "Scout" the S-3 was a triplane with a 100-hp OX-2 and big prop spinner. Four had been ordered November 20, 1916, and delivered, without spinner or guns, in June-July 1917. An example appearing in December as the S-6 did display a pair of forward-firing Lewis guns, but these were not actually tested.

CURTISS S-3

Such scouts were not by any means up to combat on the Western Front, and neither were two unarmed single-seat prototypes ordered with American-built 100-hp Gnome rotaries. They were the Victor Aircraft Corporation's "Pursuit," a neatly streamlined biplane design by Albert S. Heinrich, ordered April 11, 1917, and delivered in December, and the obscure Pigeon Fraser monoplane ordered April 30 and delivered in September 1917. Despite publicity as fighters, they were really only possible trainers.

On May 1, 1917, the Army issued its first specification, No.1003, for an airplane "adapted to combat and pursuit of hostile aircraft". A pilot and two guns would be carried along with two and 1/2 hours of fuel for an approved engine of between 100 and 150 horsepower. Only modest instrumentation was considered needed for 1917 fighter pilots: a compass, clock, altimeter, tachometer, and rolling map case.

VICTOR PURSUIT

French influence was so strong that wartime performance would be measured in metric equivalents, and endurance would be given at full power. Specified performance should include a climb in 13 minutes to 3,000 meters (9,840 feet), where top speed will be "not less than 165 kilometers per hour" (102 mph).

But neither such a fighter design nor adequate power plants then existed in America, and even if they had, that specification was quickly surpassed by the fighters reaching the front. In fact, no American-designed single-seat fighters would be delivered during the nineteen months of war.

SCHIEFER-ROBBINS "PURSUIT"

A Nieuport-like Schiefer-Robbins single-seater offered as a private venture by a San Diego furniture firm flew on December 9, 1917. Although purchased by the Army on January 17, 1918, its 100-hp Gnome meant it could only duplicate other trainers and had no potential. Although several low-powered single-seaters were produced, such as the Standard E-l, Thomas-Morse S-4, and Orenco C, all were unarmed trainers.

While none of the earlier light single-seaters passed the prototype stage, the Thomas-Morse S-4 tested in June 1917 was successful. The Air Service had realized that for cadet pilots to jump from the "Jenny" to a high-powered pursuit was too much, and so 100 Thomas-Morse S-4Bs were ordered on October 3, 1917, as pursuit-trainers. Designed by a British immigrant, B.D. Thomas (1890-1966), and using the 100-hp Gnome, they were delivered from November 1917 to May 1918 and followed by 50 S-4Cs with modified controls. The Gnome engine proved unsatisfactory, and the 80-hp Le Rhone was substituted in June 1918 for the remaining 447 S-4Cs completed when production ended in December 1918.

The "Tommy" became well-known to would-be fighter pilots. Although sometimes fitted with a Marlin gun for target practice, it was a trainer, not a fighter, but is included in this book because of its close association with pursuit aviation.

THOMAS-MORSE S-4C
Le Rhone, 80 hp
DIMENSIONS: Span 26'6", Lg. 19'10", Ht. 8'1", Wing Area 234 sq. ft.
WEIGHT: Empty 963 lb., Gross 1373 lb., Fuel 27 gal.
PERFORMANCE: Speed- Top 95 mph. Service Ceiling 15,000', Climb 7500'/10 min.

With the same mission, two Standard E-l double-bay biplane prototypes were ordered December 13, 1917, and delivered in January and April 1918 with 100-hp Gnomes. Of 126 production E-ls completed between August and December 1918, 30 had Gnomes and the rest had 80-hp Le Rhones.

STANDARD E-1
Le Rhone 80 hp
DIMENSIONS: Span 24', Lg. 18'11", Ht. 7'10", Wing Area 153 sq. ft.
WEIGHT: Empty 828 lb., Gross 1144 lb., Fuel 17 gal.
PERFORMANCE: Speed- Top 100 mph at s.l., 85 mph at 6,500', Absolute Ceiling 14,800', Climb 6000'/10 min. Endurance 2 hours.

Six rather similar single-seaters were also ordered on December 13, 1917, from the Ordinance Engineering Company (Orenco) at Baldwin, New York. The Orenco B was

ORENCO C
Le Rhone 80 hp
DIMENSIONS: Span 26', Lg. 19', Ht. 7'7", Wing Area 180 sq. ft.
WEIGHT: Empty 835 lb., Gross 1117 lb. Fuel 18 gal.
PERFORMANCE: Speed- Top 98 mph at s.l., 94 mph at 6,500', Stalling 33 mph. Service Ceiling 13,500', Climb 10,000'/10 min. Endurance 2.25 hours.

designed to use a 150-hp Gnome, but U.S. production of that engine was canceled and only the first had an imported Gnome in June 1918. Five were delivered from July to November as the Orenco C pursuit-trainers with the 80-hp Le Rhone and added wing stagger.

American design of real fighters was officially foregone in favor of tested foreign types. The Bolling Commission on July 30, 1917, had selected the Spad single-seater and

Bristol two-seater fighters for production in America, but a sample Spad did not arrive until September 18, and Curtiss received an order for 3,000 on October 8, 1917.

A December 14, 1917, cable from General Pershing had recommended leaving single-seat fighter production to Europe, and a suitable American power plant could not be produced in time for the Spad. Fighter design in Europe was moving too rapidly for American industry to catch up. April 1917 was called "Bloody April" for the heavy Allied losses to German fighters, but only three months later, the German fighters were being defeated by new Allied types.

Cancellation of the Curtiss Spad program on January 28, 1918, meant the AEF would depend entirely upon its Allies for fighters in 1918. The Hispano-Suiza had been licensed for production by the Wright-Martin company on behalf of the French, but production deliveries beginning in November 1917 were of the 150-hp Model A, suitable only for trainers. By the time the 180-hp model arrived from American factories in August 1918, the geared 220-hp version was being used in Europe, and an improved American 300-hp model was not available in quantity until 1919.

The United States Bristol

As for the Liberty 12, that big engine could not be fitted into any existing single-seater, but heavier two-seat fighters might be designed around the Liberty. These designs found their main inspiration in England's Bristol Fighter, a double-bay biplane with a 275-hp Rolls-Royce engine, pilot and gunner back to back, and fuselage suspended between the wings. It went to war in April 1917 with a fixed Vickers gun and two flexible Lewis guns, and had excellent maneuverability, which made the Bristol successful against enemy fighters. The combination of the front gun with the rear guns for tail protection helped Canadian ace Major Andrew E. McKeever win thirty victories and established the two-seater biplane as a standard fighter type.

PMB

CURTISS-BRISTOL FIGHTER (LIBERTY 12)

A sample Bristol arrived in New York on August 25, 1917, and immediately the Americans tried to redesign it to use the "United States Standard Aircraft Engine" as the Liberty 12 was called. Curtiss received a contract on November 3 to produce 1,000, later increased to 2,000, Liberty-powered Bristols designated USAO-1. Armament was to be two Marlin fixed and two Lewis flexible guns.

The first Curtiss Bristol with the Liberty began flight tests on March 5, 1918. While the British Bristol had done 119 mph weighing 2,779 pounds, the Curtiss version was supposed to do 138 mph at 2,937 pounds, but the actual weight came to 3,600 pounds and the engine was too much for the airframe.

It was also unsafe, for the second example crashed on May 5, another on June 10, and a third, on July 25. On July 20, 1918, the Curtiss-Bristol program was canceled after 27 aircraft had been completed, and the factory then concentrated on the S.E.5 program. Yet the Bristol's RAF-15 airfoil section would become the wing pattern for most 1918 American fighters.

Curtiss did attempt to meet the contract by designing its own two-seater fighter with the Liberty engine and biplane wings so close together that the top wing was level with the laminated wood veneer fuselage top. This gave the observer a good fire field, but the pilot's view down was poor. Known as the CB, for "Curtiss Battler," the machine crashed during testing in 1918 and no technical details have been located.

PMB

THOMAS-MORSE MB-1
Liberty 12, 400 hp
DIMENSIONS: Span 31', Lg. 22'.
WEIGHT: Gross 2375 lb.
PERFORMANCE: Never flown.

Thomas-Morse received an order on November 12, 1917, to build two two-seater fighters around the 400-hp Liberty 12. The MB-l was a light high-wing monoplane braced by a wide strut, to be armed with two Marlin and

AMC

THOMAS-MORSE MB-2
Liberty 12, 400 hp
DIMENSIONS: Span 31', Lg. 24', Ht. 8', Wing Area 323 sq. ft.
WEIGHT: Empty 2047 lb., Gross 2773 lb. Fuel 50 gal.
PERFORMANCE: Not available.

two Lewis guns. The Ithaca, New York, firm towed it out to frozen Lake Cayuga late in January 1918. But the 900-pound direct-drive engine's vibrations weakened the light airframe so much that the machine collapsed while being taxied out for flight trials.

The company replaced it with the MB-2 biplane, with a four-bladed propeller to absorb the power of a geared Liberty 12C cooled by radiators on the lower wings, and the same four guns. The difficult task of mating the big engine and light airframe delayed delivery until November 1918. The war's end canceled this project and its half-finished sister ship, but Thomas-Morse would be more successful with its MB-3 single-seater.

Fighters with the AEF

When the two 94th Aero Squadron pilots scored the first American Army fighter victories of World War I on April 14, 1918, the United States had been at war for more than a year. Yet the first Air Service pilots had to begin combat with the Nieuport 28, for there still were no American fighters available.

Since the AEF came to France without planes, its future fighter pilots were trained on some 872 old-model Nieuports. The idea was that pilot proficiency would increase with the power of the planes flown. Anxious to begin fighting, the AEF decided to buy the Nieuport 28, which had already been rejected by the French in favor of the Spad.

PMB

NIEUPORT 28
Gnome 9N, 155 hp
DIMENSIONS: Span 26'9", Lg. 21', Ht. 8'1", Wing Area 172 sq. ft.
WEIGHT: Empty 961 lb., Gross 1539 lb. Fuel 33 gal .
PERFORMANCE: Speed- Top 128 mph at s.1., 123 mph at 6500'. Service Ceiling 19,685', Climb 6500'/5.3 min. Endurance 2 hours.

Powered by a 150-hp Gnome with nine cylinders spinning around until the two-hour fuel supply ran out, this Nieuport had straight equal-span wings connected by an even pair of struts on each side, instead of the Vee struts of earlier Nieuports. Two Vickers guns were mounted on the left side ahead of the pilot.

The first 36 Nieuport 28s were turned over to the Americans in March 1918, but the lack of guns delayed their debut into combat until April. By the end of May, all four squadrons of the First Pursuit Group were at the front, and they continued to use Nieuports until Spads began

PMB

SPAD 13
Hispano-Suiza 8Be, 220 hp
DIMENSIONS: Span 26'4", Lg. 20'4", Ht. 7'6", Wing Area 227 sq. ft.
WEIGHT: Empty 1464 lb., Gross 2036 lb. Fuel 30 gal.
PERFORMANCE: Speed- Top 131.5 mph at s.1., 128 mph at 6500', Stalling 65 mph. Service Ceiling 18,400', Climb 6500'/6.5 min. Endurance 2 hours at 124.5 mph.

arriving in July. The AEF had 297 of some 310 Nieuport 28s built, but the Nieuport's reputation for wing failures led the Americans to quickly discard the type when the more robust Spads became available.

The first Spad 13 was ferried in to the First Pursuit Group on July 5 by Captain "Eddie" Rickenbacker (1890-1973). During the last four months of the war, he, Frank Luke, and other AEF pilots made the French fighter part of the American military tradition. Spad 13s were already being used by the Lafayette Escadrille that became the Army's 103rd Aero Squadron, but continued operating with the French Army until August 1918, when it became part of the AEF's new 3rd Pursuit Group.

Two .303-caliber (7.7-mm) Vickers synchronized guns provided with 800 rounds were mounted over the Spad 13's 220-hp geared Hispano-Suiza. Beginning in September 1918, four 25-pound bombs could be carried under the fuselage for attacking ground troops. By the time the American squadrons got their Spads, the double-bay wings had been modified with square tips.

By the war's end, 15 of the 16 AEF pursuit squadrons at the front used the Spad 13. As well as the 893 Spad 13s acquired by the Air Service, there were also 189 Spad 7s being used for training. After the Armistice, American forces in Europe until April 1919 included two Spad 7 and six Spad 13 squadrons.

SOPWITH CAMEL F-1
Clerget 9-Bc, 130 hp
DIMENSIONS: Span 28', Lg. 18'9", Ht. 8'6", Wing Area 231 sq. ft.
WEIGHT: Empty 929 lb., Gross 1453 lb. Fuel 31 gal.
PERFORMANCE: Speed- Top 115 mph at 6500', 113 mph at 10,000', Service Ceiling 19,000', Climb 6500'/6 min. Endurance 2.5 hours.

About 58 Spad 7 and 435 Spad 13 fighters were shipped to the United States for service in the schools and with the active squadrons of the First Pursuit Group in Texas. Marlin guns were substituted for the Vickers, while the 180-hp direct-drive engine available in the U.S. was preferred for postwar flying because it was less troublesome. The Spad 13 specifications given here are those using the Army's flight test methods at McCook Field in 1921.

American fighter pilots trained by the British went into action on the British sector of the front with British fighters. Of these, by far the most famous was the Sopwith Camel, which had appeared at the front in July 1917 as the first Allied fighter with two synchronized guns. Most often powered by an air-cooled 130-hp Clerget rotary and armed with two .303 Vickers guns under the hump, and racks for four 25-pound bombs, the Camel was very maneuverable, but considered dangerous and tricky to fly. It has been credited with more victories than any other Allied fighter plane of that war, despite a relatively low top speed.

The two AEF Camel Squadrons were the 17th and 148th. Both squadrons were involved in hard fighting, the 148th scoring the first kill on July 13, 1918, and George Vaughn became the leading American Camel ace by scoring 13 victories. During 1918, the AEF received 143 Camels. While the 17th and 148th turned theirs in for Spads on November 1, 1918, the 41st Aero Squadron used Camels on post-Armistice duties.

Another famous British fighter used by Americans was the Royal Aircraft Factory's S.E.5A which used the 200-hp geared Hispano-Suiza 8B, nose water radiator, one synchronized Vickers over the engine and one Lewis gun on the upper wing. Although the S.E.5A was used in large numbers by the British, only 38 were acquired by the AEF in October 1918.

They were issued to the 25th Aero Squadron, whose arrival at the front on November 1 was too late for combat, but its leader, Reed Landis, had scored 10 victories flying the S.E.5A with the RAF. Back in the United States, however, the S.E.5A played a small role in American efforts to make their own fighters.

Two-seat Fighters

Actually, the American aircraft industry had better luck during the First World War with two-seat fighter designs than with single-seaters. Several prototypes flown in 1918 were good enough to have been sent to France had the war lasted another year.

Captain Georges LePere had been loaned to the Engineering Division by the French government, and began his first project on January 4, 1918, as a two-seat fighter designed around the Liberty 12 and armed with two Marlin and two Lewis guns. Construction was ordered on

PACKARD-LEPERE LUSAC-11
Liberty 12, 425 hp
DIMENSIONS: Span 41'7", Lg. 25'3", Ht. 10'7", Wing Area 415 sq. ft.
WEIGHT: Empty 2561 lb., Gross 3746 lb. Fuel 65 gal.
PERFORMANCE: Speed-Top 133 mph at s. 1., 130 mph at 6500', Cruising 118 mph, Landing 50 mph. Service Ceiling 20,200', Absolute Ceiling 21,500', Climb 6500'/6 min. Range 320 miles.

PACKARD-LEPERE LUSAC-11
(with first U.S. turbosupercharger)

March 1, 1918, by the Packard Motor Company in Detroit, which rushed the first LUSAC-11 prototype to delivery on April 30, and flight tests at McCook Field began May 15.

With a plywood fuselage, double-bay box struts, and radiator on the upper wing, the business-like biplane looked promising enough to order 25 LUSAC-11s from Packard on June 15, 1918. Packard delivered two more prototypes by June, and seven production LePeres from July to October 1918. By October 23, 3,500 had been ordered from Fisher, Packard and Brewster, but these contracts ended with the war. Packard did finish 18 LePeres in January 1919, along with three test planes in February for a total of 31 LUSAC-11s. Three LUSAC-21 airframes for the experimental Bugatti engine were also built in 1918, but that project never flew.

Two of the Packard planes went to France in time for tests begun on November 4, 1918; the only U.S.-designed Army planes there for World War I. One hung in the *Musee de l'Air* until 1989, when it was transferred to the Air Force Museum, the oldest American fighter on exhibit. A prototype at McCook Field became the first U.S. plane to test an exhaust-driven turbosupercharger, beginning in September 1919. Several altitude records were set, including a flight to 34,508 feet on September 28, 1921.

An alternate program with lighter engines was begun with the USB-1 (United States Bristol), actually the first imported Bristol airframe powered with the first 300-hp Wright-Hispano and test flown July 4, 1918. A second imported Bristol with the Liberty 8, the USB-2, was readied, but crashed on September 6, 1918.

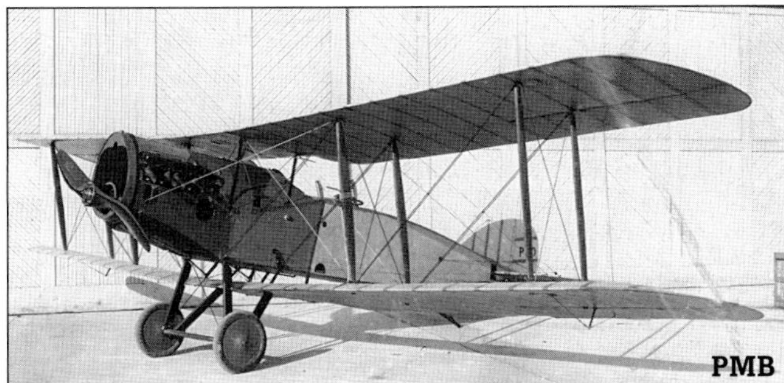

ENGINEERING DIVISION USB-1
Hispano H, 300 hp
DIMENSIONS: Span 39'4", Lg. 25'5", Ht. 8'3", Wing Area 403 sq. ft.
WEIGHT: Empty 1842 lb., Gross 2910 lb. Fuel 52 gal.
PERFORMANCE: Speed- Top 114.5 mph at s.1, Climb 6500'/3.5 min.

The Engineering Division developed a new stronger and lighter plywood monocoupe fuselage, and this was used on three US XB-1A prototypes powered by the 360-hp Wright-Hispano and armed with two Browning and two Lewis guns. While the first flight on July 3, 1919, had missed the war, the third model added another leak proof fuel tank on the upper wing and was equipped as a night observation type. Forty XB-1As ordered June 28, 1920, from Dayton-Wright were used in 1921-22 by the 12th Observation and 13th Attack Squadrons in Texas.

ENGINEERING DIVISION U.S. XB1A (P90 -1919)
Wright-Hispano H, 300 hp
DIMENSIONS: Span 39'4", Lg. 25'5", Ht. 9'8", Wing Area 406 sq. ft.
WEIGHT: Empty 2010 lb., Gross 2994 lb. Fuel 54 gal.
PERFORMANCE: Speed- Top 124 mph at s.l., 121 mph at 6500', Stalling 59 mph. Service Ceiling 20,900', Climb 6500'/7.8 min. Endurance 2.4 hours at 118 mph.

A 300-hp Wright-Hispano H powered the first American monoplane fighter, the remarkable M-8 of Grover Loening (1888-1976). The wings were joined to the top of a narrow fuselage and braced by struts underneath, leaving the upper field of fire clear for the observer's Lewis guns. Two Marlin guns were mounted at the engine's sides, above a neat tunnel radiator.

Careful design reduced the time required to produce the type. Ordered in March 1918, the M-8 was first flown in August at Mineola, New York. Two went to the Army by January 1919, before peace ended plans to put the

LOENING M-8
Wright-Hispano H, 300 hp
DIMENSIONS: Span 32'9", Lg. 24', Ht. 8'4", Wing Area 215 sq. ft.
WEIGHT: Empty 1663 lb., Gross 2639 lb. Fuel 55 gal.
PERFORMANCE: Speed- Top 143.5 mph at s.1., 138 mph at 6500', Stalling 58 mph. Service Ceiling 18,600' Absolute Ceiling 19,900', Climb 6500'/5.2 min., 10,000'/9.2 min. Endurance 2 hours at top speed.

DAYTON-WRIGHT XB-lA (P151)
Wright-Hispano H, 330 hp
DIMENSIONS: Span 39'4", Lg. 25'6", Ht. 9'9", Wing Area 406 sq. ft.
WEIGHT: Empty 2128 lb., Gross 3590 lb. Fuel 90 gal.
PERFORMANCE: Speed- Top 127 mph at s.l., 124 mph at 6500', Stalling 63 mph. Service Ceiling 18,500', Absolute Ceiling 20,400', Climb 6500'/7.3 min. Endurance 4 hours at 121 mph.

Loening into-production, but six were ordered as observation planes by the Navy in June 1919.

Charles Kirkham, chief engineer at the Curtiss Garden City plant, had produced a new K-12 engine with the same 400 hp as the Liberty, but lighter and smaller. A two-seater triplane fighter designed around that power plant for the Navy was first flown on July 5, 1918, and on July 10 the Army ordered four examples and borrowed the Navy's Model 18-T prototype for tests in August 1918.

With a nicely streamlined round wooden monocoupe fuselage and side radiators, the triplane was claimed to be the fastest fighter aloft, with a 163-mph top speed. Later tests suggested a more modest 151 mph, when carrying the full armament of two Marlin nose guns and two Lewis guns on the Scarff ring, plus a third aimed through an opening underneath the rear cockpit.

The first Army Model 18-T delivered in January 1919 and the second in February were triplanes, while two

PMB

CURTISS 18-T
Curtiss K-12, 400 hp
DIMENSIONS: Span 31'11", Lg. 23'3", Ht. 9'10", Wing Area 309 sq. ft.
WEIGHT: Empty 1825 lb., Gross 2901 lb. Fuel 67 gal.
PERFORMANCE: Speed- Top 163 mph at s.1., 145 mph at 10,000', Stalling 58 mph. Service Ceiling 22,000', Climb 10,000'/6.9 min. Endurance l:75 hours. Range 550 miles "at economic speed."

PMB

CURTISS 18-B
Curtiss K-12, 400 hp
DIMENSIONS: Span 37'6", Lg. 23'4", Height 8'10", Wing Area 306 sq. ft.
WEIGHT: Empty 1988 lb., Gross 3001 lb. Fuel 53 gal.
PERFORMANCE: Speed- Top 160 mph at s.1., 157 mph at 10,000', Stalling 59 mph. Service Ceiling 22,000', Climb 10,000'/6.3 min. Endurance l:75 hours at 160 mph, 6.7 hours at 80 mph. Range 536 miles.

Model 18-B biplane versions were delivered in June 1919. No more of these planes were purchased by the Army, although a single civil triplane was sold to Bolivia.

American Single-seat Fighters

After much rivalry between the Allied military missions on behalf of their own designs, Curtiss received a contract on June 8, 1918, for 1,000 S.E.5A single-seaters to use the 180-hp Wright-Hispano. Only one example was completed with the first of these engines, beginning flight tests on August 20, but the Armistice canceled the rest. To fill the gap until U.S. production got underway, 56 S.E.5A air-frames had been imported from Britain for assembly by Curtiss. Curtiss delivered one in September, three in October, 13 by the year's end, and the rest in 1919, all with the Wright-Hispano engines.

The specification in this book gives the test results of the first Curtiss S.E.5A. In 1922-23, 50 were rebuilt with plywood fuselages by Eberhardt as S.E.5E pursuit-trainers.

Strong German offensives in the Western Front stimulated an American decision to provide single-seat fighters for a 1919 campaign, but the Armistice would halt production programs. An Italian engineer at McCook Field, Ottorino Pomilio, designed the FVL-8 around the eight-cylinder version of the Liberty. A plywood fuselage hung above the lower wing and a four-bladed propeller were distinctive features. Six FVL-8s ordered September 21, 1918, were delivered at Indianapolis from January to June 1919.

AMC

CURTISS S.E.5A
Wright-Hispano E, 180 hp
DIMENSIONS: Span 26'9", Lg. 20'10", Ht. 10', Wing Area 247 sq. ft.
WEIGHT: Empty 1486 lb., Gross 2060 lb. Fuel 35 gal.
PERFORMANCE: Speed- Top 122 mph at s.1., 120 mph at 6500'. Service Ceiling 20,400', Climb 6500'/8 min. Range 280 miles at top speed.

Three private companies won contracts to build four prototypes each of conventional Spad layout, as double-bay biplanes of wood construction with RAF-15 airfoils, a Wright-Hispano and two .30 caliber Brownings with an Aldis telescopic sight. Power of the water-cooled, eight-cylinder Hispano had been boosted to 300 hp by the American licensee. The Thomas-Morse MB-3 was ordered on September 27, 1918, the Lewis & Vought VE-8 ordered October 11, and the Orenco D ordered October 16.

PMB

EBERHART S.E.5E

Not until after the Armistice did these fighters appear. Largest and least successful was the first VE-8 delivered in June 1919. A development of the VE-7 trainer with the upper wing joined to the fuselage, flight tests showed it too sluggish for a fighter, and the others were canceled.

AMC

POMILIO FVL-8
Liberty 8, 275 hp
DIMENSIONS: Span 26'8", Lg. 21'8", Ht. 8'2", Wing Area 264 sq. ft.
WEIGHT: Empty 1726 lb., Gross 2284 lb. Fuel 40 gal.
PERFORMANCE: Speed- Top 135 mph at s.1., 134 mph at 6,500', Stalling 60 mph. Service Ceiling 21,000', Climb 1245'/ 1 min., 6500'/6.7 min. Endurance 2 hours at 131 mph.

Four Orenco D fighters, delivered from January to October 1919, were built by the Ordnance Engineering Corporation from an Army Engineering Division design. Powered by a 300-hp Wright-Hispano H, this double-bay biplane had a plywood fuselage, flat nose radiator, one-piece elevator, and according to the test pilot, "had good flying qualities," handling better than the Spad and other rival fighters.

At that time, all military designs became Army property, and bidding on production contracts was open. Curtiss won with the lowest bid, building 50 heavier production models with balanced ailerons ordered June 16, 1920, the first being flown on November 10. Such cut-throat competition would put Orenco out of business, but workmanship on the Curtiss Ds was considered poor, and they were soon retired from the First Pursuit Group.

The most successful single-seater of this period, and the one finally selected to equip all the postwar Army pursuit squadrons was the Thomas-Morse MB-3 designed by B.D. Thomas. The first prototype from the Ithaca, New

PMB

CURTISS-ORENCO D
Wright H, 330 hp
DIMENSIONS: Span 33', Lg. 21'5", Ht. 8'4", Wing Area 273 sq. ft.
WEIGHT: Empty 1908 lb., Cross 2820 lb. Fuel 58 gal.
PERFORMANCE: Speed- Top 139.5 mph at s.1., 136 mph at 6500', Stalling 64.5 mph. Service Ceiling 18,450', Absolute Ceiling 20,250', Climb 1140'/1 min., 6500'/6.9 min. Endurance 2.5 hours at 125 mph.

York, company was shipped to Dayton for static tests, and the second first flew on February 21, 1919, with the best streamlined nose of that time. Moving the flat radiator from the nose to the upper wing allowed a metal prop spinner and metal cowl for the 300-hp Wright-Hispano. Performance of the four prototypes delivered by August 1919 was so superior to the S.E.5s and Spads then with the Air Service that 50 more MB-3s were ordered June 19, 1920. They were delivered in 1921, followed by 11 built for the Marine Corps squadron at Quantico in February 1922.

Nine companies offered bids on February 21, 1921, for MB-3 mass production, including Curtiss and Thomas-Morse, but Boeing's low bid won a contract for 200 MB-3As at $1,455,740 ($7,279 each) on April 8. It would be the largest pursuit contract until 1937 and placed Boeing firmly on the road to become the most successful American airplane builder.

Delivered between July and December 1922, the MB-3A differed from the original in many details. Its radiator was moved from the upper wing, split, and placed on each side of the fuselage, and the new metal engine cowling was high enough to cover the cylinders and guns. While

AMC

VOUGHT VE-8
Wright-Hispano H, 338 hp
DIMENSIONS: Span 31', Lg. 21'4", Ht. 8'8", Wing Area 307 sq. ft.
WEIGHT: Empty 1764 lb., Gross 2657 lb. Fuel 68 gal.
Performance: Speed- Top 127.5 mph at s.1., 121 mph at 10,000', Service Ceiling 18,400', Absolute Ceiling 20,250", Climb 6500'/7.2 min. Endurance 3.8 hours. Range 460 miles.

AMC

ORENCO D
Hispano-Suiza H, 300 hp
DIMENSIONS: Span 30', Lg. 21'6", Ht. 7'9", Wing Area 261 sq. ft.
WEIGHT: Empty 1776 lb., Gross 2432 lb. Fuel 55 gal.
PERFORMANCE: Speed- Top 147 mph at s.1., 142 mph at 6500', Stalling 56 mph. Service Ceiling 23,000', Absolute Ceiling 23,600', Climb 1460'/1, 6500'/5.2 min. Endurance 2.5 hours at 139 mph.

PMB

THOMAS-MORSE MB-3
Wright-Hispano H, 300 hp
DIMENSIONS: Span 26', Lg. 20', Ht. 8'6", Wing Area 250.5 sq. ft.
WEIGHT: Empty 1506 lb., Gross 2094 lb. Fuel 41 gal.
PERFORMANCE: Speed-Top 152 mph at s.1., 148 mph at 6500', Stalling 58 mph. Service Ceiling 23,700', Absolute Ceiling 24,900', Climb 1930'/1 min., 6500'/3.9 min. Endurance 2 hours at 144 mph.

BOEING MB-3A
Wright H-3, 300 hp
DIMENSIONS: Span 26', Lg. 20', Ht. 8'7", Wing Area 229 sq. ft.
WEIGHT: Empty 1716 lb., Gross 2539 lb. Fuel 44 gal.
PERFORMANCE: Speed- Top 141 mph at s.1., 138 mph at 6500',
Landing 55 mph. Service Ceiling 19,500', Absolute Ceiling 21,200', Climb 1235'/1 min., 6500'/6.7 min. Endurance 2.25 hours at 125 mph.

the MB-3's two .30-caliber guns had been exposed in 1918 fashion, the MB-3A's Brownings were under the cowl. One of the .30-caliber M1921s was replaced by a new .50-caliber M1921 gun when desired, an arrangement standard on Army fighters up to the Second World War.

A low vertical fin on most MB-3As was replaced by a more normal fin on the last 50. Although performance of the MB-3A was good, visibility was hampered by the upper wing. In March 1923, one was fitted with the first drop tank in the United States, adding 37 gallons of fuel under the fuselage to extend the range to 400 miles.

BOEING MB-3A with revised fin

All eight Army pursuit squadrons of this period used the MB-3A, their deployment reflecting the American defense posture of those times. Four squadrons made up the First Pursuit Group, which was to remain at Selfridge Field, Michigan, from July 1, 1922, to December 8, 1941. Two more squadrons were stationed in Hawaii, one in the Philippines, and one in the Canal Zone. After the Curtiss Hawk became a standard Army fighter in 1926, the MB-3As were gradually retired to Kelly Field, Texas, the tactical training school.

The First World War had provided American fighter pilots with a pattern for future development. The well-liked Spad was superseded in the postwar period by the MB-3A, which followed the same general arrangement. Two-seater fighters, however, were not incorporated into the postwar air service, in spite of the success of the wartime Bristol and the promising Loening monoplane. The dozen years following the war would produce a great variety of pursuit types, for fighters are cheaper and easier to build than bombers, but there was only a small advance from the wartime tradition.

CHAPTER 4

MULTI-ENGINE BOMBERS, 1917-1932

The **HANDLEY-PAGE** set the style for American bombers.

The First Big Bombers

When land warfare settled down to a long deadlock in World War I, the airplane's appeal as an offensive weapon grew. Attacks against people on the ground became more serious, and aircraft specialized for bomb-carrying over long distances were demanded by the warring powers.

Respectable bomb loads, increased fuel supply, and a crew sufficient to operate the airplane and its armament, required much larger machines than the frail scouting types then available. Builders began bomber designs by adding a second or more engines to their aircraft for the additional power needed.

STANDARD HANDLEY-PAGE
Two Liberty 12-N, 350 hp at sea level
DIMENSIONS: Span 100', Lg. 62'11", Ht. 22', Wing Area 1655 sq. ft.
WEIGHT: Empty 8721 lb., Gross 14,425 lb. Fuel 390 gal.
PERFORMANCE: Speed- Top 94 mph at s.1., 82 mph at 6500'. Service Ceiling 7400', Absolute Ceiling 9600', Climb 400'/1 min., 6500'/27 min. Range 550 miles/2000 lb. bombs.

Only Russia had such a plane at the war's beginning: Igor Sikorsky's Ilya Mourometz was an improvement on the world's first four-engine airplane, the Sikorsky Grand flown on April 27, 1913. The 113-foot span Mourometz had four 100-hp engines on the lower wing and an enclosed cabin for the crew. It was ordered into production in 1914, and after the war began, a "squadron of flying ships" was formed. On February 15, 1915, an Ilya Mourometz V carried 600 pounds of bombs over the German lines on its first combat mission.

Germany also formed bombing units in 1915 using the twin-engine G types by AEG and Gotha, and the larger multi-engine R types by Siemens and VGO. Italy began operations with the three-engine Caproni biplanes in 1915.

The general arrangement which became the classic pattern for the next dozen years of bombers was established by the first British Handley-Page O/100 bomber flown on December 18, 1915. While the Handley-Page first went into action in March 1917 with a Royal Navy unit, the improved O/400 version was also ordered for the RAF's strategic bombing "Independent Force" which began operations in 1918. These twin-engine planes were listed as night bombers, since deep penetrations of hostile areas by these slow biplanes were considered too dangerous unless covered by darkness.

The upper wing spanned 100 feet, overhanging a smaller lower wing; between them was suspended two 350-hp Rolls-Royce engines. A squared fuselage began with a gunner's cockpit in the bow, followed by side-by-side seats for the pilot and co-pilot. A rear gunner sitting behind the wings had his rearward view limited by a box-like tail of two horizontal and two vertical surfaces. A pair of .30-caliber Lewis guns were mounted at the front and rear cockpits, and a fifth gun aimed downward through a trap door. Eight 250 or 16 112-pound bombs could be carried on eight-hour missions, or a single 1,650-pound bomb could be used.

Although none of these big bombers made any real difference as far as the strategy or outcome of the war was concerned, they brought the war to civilians behind the lines who, in past history, had not feared for their lives. The most severe of these raids was on June 13, 1917, when twenty Gothas attacking London killed 162 and injured 432 persons. A modest piece of homicide, considering World War II, but it was the best the earlier war could offer, and caused many to imagine then that the likelihood of such horrors might cause nations to abstain from any more war.

Early Americans

After the United States entered the war, the Bolling Mission in July 1917 did recommend building Caproni bombers, but consideration of the Handley-Page caused a rivalry that delayed the placing of contracts. Finally both were ordered, to be powered with U.S.-designed Liberty engines.

STANDARD CAPRONI
Three Liberty 12-N, 350 hp at s.l.
DIMENSIONS: Span 76'3", Lg. 41'2", Ht. 12'1", Wing Area 1420 sq. ft.
WEIGHT: Empty 7700 lb., Gross 12,350 lb., Max. 12,904 lb. Fuel 400 gal.
PERFORMANCE: Speed- Top 103 mph at s.1., Landing 61.5 mph. Service Ceiling 11,500', Absolute Ceiling 13,500', Climb 670'/1 min., 6500'/14 min. Range 762 miles/1330 lb. bombs.

Bomber production in the United States, however, was delayed by the inability to decide how many should be made, and of what type. The role of fighters had been clear, to destroy enemy aircraft, and the Army also knew what it wanted from its short-range two-seater observation/day bomber types. But how much long-distance bombing would be done, and of what targets? No such doctrine of airpower employment had yet been formulated by American military leaders.

Therefore, the number of bombers programmed was based on an inaccurate guess of production capacity. Production goals fluctuated until the program of July 1918 finally projected a ratio of 3:5:2 for pursuit, observation, and bombardment plane production.

The first true multi-engine bomber seen in the United States was the three-engine Caproni Ca 33 sent from Italy with Italian pilots and flown at Langley Field September 11, 1917. As the largest plane yet seen in America, it attracted much attention flying over Liberty Bond parades to drop patriotic leaflets and advertise the Italian air force.

Although Curtiss had received a contract on September 19, 1917, to build 500 Capronis with Liberty engines, it was canceled November 17 because there were no plans on hand for that aircraft, nor any firm decision as to whether the Caproni or Handley-Page bombers would be used.

While the Caproni project was stalled, in December 1917 the British proposed that parts for Handley-Page bombers be manufactured in America for assembly in England, along with Liberty engines. An agreement was signed on January 26, 1918, by British and American officials, and several manufacturers were lined up to make the parts for 500 aircraft by contracts made from March 12 to April 13, 1918. Standard Aircraft, at Elizabeth, New Jersey, contracted on April 1 to assemble 50 of the bombers for tests and training in America, while the other components were to be packed and shipped to England.

The first Standard Handley-Page was flown on July 1, 1918, christened the *Langley*, and successfully passed its tests with the performance listed on our table. Parts for 100 were shipped to England from July to October, and a second example was flown by Standard just before the war ended and production curtailed. Standard completed five more by January 1919, assembled by the Air Service itself. The aircraft parts shipped abroad were not assembled, but were returned to America and soon forgotten.

In the meantime, work on the Caproni was revived by the arrival on January 17, 1918, of an Italian engineering mission to organize design, manufacture, and testing of a Liberty-powered bomber. Count Caproni had insisted that his engineer have absolute control, "even in the slightest detail", of the project. Standard Aircraft was chosen as the builder, although an order for the first prototype was not signed until April 9, and that was replaced by a contract for four on May 20.

The Standard-Caproni first flown on July 4, 1918, was powered by three Liberty engines; one at the rear of the center nacelle, and the others at the front of the twin booms leading back to the stabilizer and triple rudders. The engines used in both the Caproni and Handley-Page were the 350-hp, low-compression models thought more reliable for long distance work. One or two Lewis guns could be mounted in the bow cockpit, and another pair were operated by a gunner standing on a platform over the Caproni's rear engine. Performance was better than that of the Handley-Page, but armament accommodation was awkward.

As it turned out, that first Standard-Caproni was the only one flown before the war's end. The reasons for this have been analyzed by John Casari, but in the limited space here we can state the main facts of the program's breakdown. Five hundred Capronis had been ordered from Curtiss on June 7, 1918, and 500 more from Fisher the next day.

But development at Standard had gone so slowly that prototype work was shifted to Fisher in Cleveland, who undertook to build three with entirely new drawings. The first Fisher airframe was forwarded to McCook Field for static tests on November 21, 1918. The production program had been canceled on Armistice Day, but a second Fisher prototype was flown on January 16, 1919, and in June the Air Service accepted both the last Fisher-built prototype and the second Standard prototype, which had been completed by Fisher.

Besides the five American-built Capronis, Air Service pilots also flew Italian-built imports; the original Ca 33 named after Julius Caesar, and a Ca 5 of 1918 that was also tested by the Navy on a sea sled. The latter was a

MARTIN GMB
Two Liberty 12A, 400 hp at s.l.
Dimensions: Span 71'5", Lg. 46'10", Ht. 14'7", Wing Area 1070 sq. ft.
WEIGHT: Empty 6702 lb., Gross 10,225 lb. Fuel 214 gal.
PERFORMANCE: Speed- Top 105 mph at s.1., 100 mph at 6500', Landing 67.5 mph. Service Ceiling 10,300', Absolute Ceiling 12,250', Climb 630'/1 min., 6000'/14.6 min. Range 390 miles/1040 lb. bombs at 92 mph.

device to tow bombers across the North Sea until they were near enough to the target to launch.

American pilots in Italy attached to the Italian Air Force also flew Capronis on 65 bombing missions, beginning on June 20, 1918. Navy pilots also trained in Italy on Capronis, which were chosen for the Night Wing, Northern Bomber Group, and were flown from Milan to fields in northern France. Nine Ca 5s were delivered in July, and nine in August, but there were 16 crashes with nine pilot fatalities on the way to the Calais area from Italy. In those days, flight delivery of aircraft was as dangerous as combat. Nevertheless, the first Navy raid by a single Caproni was made August 15, 1918, and 13 did arrive by the war's end.

Martin Bombers

Concentrating on foreign-designed planes, the government was reluctant to purchase untried native designs, but on January 17, 1918, Glenn L. Martin (1886-1955) received a contract for six twin-engine four-place "corps-de-Armee" reconnaissance biplanes, that could also be used for bombing. Designed for Martin by Donald W. Douglas (1892-1981) and built in a new Cleveland factory, the first was flown on August 15, 1918. That the first American bomber was ordered as a scout for land armies is symbolic of the outlook that was to limit Army bomber development in its early history.

The Martin GMB (MB-l) was of similar layout to the Handley-Page, but smaller, with the popular RAF-15 airfoil. Two 400-hp Liberties were suspended between the wings, four wheels were aligned on a single axle, and the tail assembly of two rudders obstructed the rear gunner's view less than the older type's empennage. Five .30-caliber Lewis guns and 1,040 pounds of bombs comprised the armament. The original contract was enlarged to 50 on October 22, 1918, but then cut back in January 1919 to ten. The first 37-mm cannon on an Army plane was fitted in the ninth GMB's nose, swinging 60 degrees down and 45 degrees to either side, and was tested in September 1919. The last Martin was completed as a GMT transport in February 1920.

MARTIN MB-2 (to NBS-1)
Two Liberty 12A, 418 hp at s.l.
DIMENSIONS: Span 74'2", Lg. 42'8", Ht. 14'8", Wing Area 1121 sq. ft.
WEIGHT: Empty 7069 lb., Gross 12,027 lb. Fuel 292 gal.
PERFORMANCE: Speed- Top 97.5 mph at s.1., 91 mph at 6,500', Landing 59 mph. Service Ceiling 7700', Absolute Ceiling 9900', Climb 445'/1 min., 6500'/23.8 min. Range 400 miles/2000 lb. bombs.

An improved version of the Martin bomber, the MB-2, was ordered on June 9, 1920, and first flown December 12. This model had larger wings to carry a heavier load, with the Liberty engines lowered to the bottom wing and a simplified landing gear with two wheels. Five Lewis guns were mounted; paired in the front and rear cockpits, with one aimed downwards and to the rear through a trapdoor. Six 300 or 600-pound bombs could be carried inside the fuselage, or external racks could hold two 1,100 or one 2,000-pound bomb.

The larger bomb had been developed to give bombers a punch equal to that of the biggest guns of battleships and coastal forts. More extravagant was a 4,300-pound, 172-inch long bomb; too big for the Martins, it was first test dropped from a Standard Handley-Page on September 28, 1921.

MARTIN NBS-1 with turbosuperchargers in 1921.

Twenty Martin MB-2s were built in Cleveland and redesignated NBS-l (Night Bomber, Short distance), and the first was later fitted with General Electric turbosuperchargers which, on a December 8, 1921, test, enabled the NBS-l to climb past its normal 9,900-foot ceiling to 25,341 feet. The plan to use superchargers in service was premature, however, for reliable and serviceable applications would not be available on bombers until the B-17B of 1939.

Those 20 Martins were a modest force even for 1921, but with them the airmen were about to challenge the traditional champions of American defense, the battleship and the coastal fortification.

Bombers Against Battleships

After the war, a return to "normalcy" was expected, and the nation turned to domestic problems. However, any return to the conservative military habits of the past was resisted by those who saw in new weapons a need for a complete re-organization of America's defense establishment.

Foremost in the campaign for greater emphasis on aviation was Brigadier General William Mitchell (1879-1936), Assistant Chief of Air Service, and wartime commander of AEF combat planes. General Mitchell's life and arguments are studied in detail elsewhere (see Bibliography), but bomber history here requires a summary of his position.

Mitchell said that air bombardment would become the most important instrument of warfare. Instead of a tedious wearing down of hostile land forces, bombers would strike immediately at enemy industrial centers, destroying the enemy's ability and will to make war before his armies need be defeated.

For a nation surrounded by the sea, bombers could replace battleships, and with the aid of submarines, cause surface fleets to "disappear" as a major military force. If air power was to play this role, it must be freed from the dominance of ground commanders, and have its own leadership, doctrine, and equipment. The organization most suitable for this purpose was a unified department of defense, with a department of air co-equal with the Army and Navy.

Greatest resistance to these views came from those who held Mahan's theory of sea power as the basis of national strength, and so Mitchell aimed his attack at sixteen expensive 16-inch gun capital ships then being built as part of a naval race with Britain and Japan. His bombers could sink any battleship afloat, he insisted, and offered to prove it by actual test. Then he struck at the big ships, "1,000 bombardment airplanes can be built and operated for the price of one battleship." Irritated by Mitchell's appeal to an economy-minded public, Secretary of the Navy Josephus Daniels had offered to stand bareheaded on a battleship deck while bombers tried to hit it. That offer was not accepted, but target ships were provided.

The tests were carried out in July 1921, on captured German ships. Attacking with Martins from Langley Field, Virginia, the airmen first sank a destroyer with 300-pound bombs, then a cruiser with 600-pound bombs, and finally climaxed the demonstration by sinking the 22,800-ton battleship *Ostfriesland* with six new 2,000-pound bombs, then the largest available.

There was no agreement on the experiment's significance; a joint Army and Navy board report signed by General Pershing concluded that the "battleship was still the backbone of the fleet and the bulwark of the nation's

AF

MARTIN-CURTISS NBS-1
Two Liberty 12A, 418 hp at s.l.
DIMENSIONS: Span 74'2", Lg. 42'8", Ht. 14'8", Wing Area 1121 sq. ft.
WEIGHT: Empty 7269 lb., Gross 12,064 lb., Fuel 300 gal.
PERFORMANCE: Speed- Top 98.7 mph at s.1., 91 mph at 6500', Landing 62 mph. Service Ceiling 8500' Absolute Ceiling 10,000', Climb 391'/1 min., 6500'/22.5 min. Range 429 miles/1797 lb. bombs, 558 miles/1262 lb. at 91 mph.

sea defense," while Mitchell's own report flatly contradicted this position, asserting that bombers alone could accomplish the defense of our coasts. In Congress, Senator William E. Borah questioned the necessity of the expensive battleship building program, while a bill was introduced providing for conversion of two forthcoming battle-cruisers into aircraft carriers.

In the midst of this debate, the Washington Conference on the Limitation of Armaments was held. At the suggestion of the United States, an agreement was made to limit battleship construction; many ships on hand or on order were to be scrapped and the size of future ships limited. As a result, the United States halted work on eleven capital ships, converted two others to aircraft carriers, and scrapped some prewar battleships, including three sunk in more bombing tests in 1923. The Washington Treaty of 1922 began a 15-year holiday in battleship building, and Japanese Navy aircraft in December 1941 would demonstrate the ability of bombers to destroy these giant ships.

But those who thought the end of the battleship race would result in more funds for bombers were disappointed. With Europe and Asia apparently pacified by diplomacy, there was little interest in armaments – not even in substituting economy-sized wood-frame airplanes for costly steel dreadnoughts. Air Service appropriations dropped from 35.1 million in fiscal 1921 to 12.6 million in fiscal 1924.

Bomber Design from 1921 to 1924

Glenn L. Martin didn't profit from his bomber's exploits in 1921, however, because proprietary rights to military designs were then held by the government, which could assign production to the company offering the lowest bid. Trying to spread limited funds further, the Army purchased more bombers by inviting competitive bids from prospective contractors. Martin offered to build more NBS-ls for $23,925 each, but was underbid by his competitors.

Instead, on June 28, 1921, Curtiss received a contract for 50 NBS-ls at a price of $17,490 each, while another 35 were ordered from the LWF Engineering Company, and 25 more from Aeromarine. Tests on the first Curtiss ship began September 11, 1922, and showed characteristics similar to its predecessors. Curtiss officials admitted a loss of $300,000 on that NBS-l contract, which did keep their work force together during this period of cut-throat competition. But the money lost by LWF and Aeromarine to complete their contracts forced those firms out of business.

LWF H-1 OWL
Three Liberty 12, 400 hp at s.l.
DIMENSIONS: Span 106'8", Lg. 53'9", Ht. 17'6", Wing Area 2216 sq. ft.
WEIGHT: Empty 13,386 lb., Gross 21,186 lb.
PERFORMANCE: Speed- Top 110 mph at s.l., Landing 56 mph. Service Ceiling 15,000', Climb 6000'/10 Min. Range 1000 miles/2000 lb. bombs.

All eight Army bombing squadrons of this period used the NBS-l: the 11th, 20th, 49th, and 96th with the 2nd Bomb Group at Langley Field, Virginia (today the oldest USAF base in service), the 23rd and 72nd with the 5th Composite Group in Hawaii, the 25th with the 6th Composite Group in the Canal Zone, and the 28th with the 4th Composite Group in the Philippines. They remained in service until replaced by Keystone bombers in 1928-29.

Liberty engines from the wartime stockpile were used on these planes, as well as on the long-range bomber projects of the Air Service. The first project was the three-engine LWF H-l Owl, a private venture designed by Raoul Hoffman for mail or bombing work. A Caproni-like layout included a center plywood nacelle for a crew of three and the center Liberty, with booms running back from the outboard engines to triple rudders. The center nacelle was equipped only for carrying mail when the Army purchased the Owl on April 16, 1920, and began tests at Mitchel Field on May 22.

After a June 1921 crash, the aircraft went back to the factory and reappeared at Mitchel Field in September 1922 with a nacelle equipped for bombing, a new nose radiator, the pilot's cockpit ahead of the wings, and a rear gunner's cockpit with twin Lewis guns on the ring and a third firing downward. Fuel for ten hours was contained in the outer booms, and a 2,000-pound bomb might be carried between the wheels.

The flight data given here was evidently an estimate, not actually achieved in tests, for the Owl did not hold Army interest and was scrapped. LWF proposed a twin-engine metal bomber called the XNBS-2, but the company went out of business in April 1923 before it could be built.

The largest aircraft of that generation was designed for the Engineering Division by Walter H. Barling (1890-1965) in response to General Mitchell's desire for an Army equal of the six-engine German Giant bombers. Designated NBL-l (Night Bombardment Long-distance), the Barling plans were dated May 15, 1920, and a contract for two was made June 23, with Witteman-Lewis in Teterboro, New Jersey, the company that made the lowest bid for the work.

Since the aircraft had to be built in sections and shipped in crates for assembly at Dayton's Wilbur Wright Field, components had to be framed with the dimensions of railroad tunnels in mind. The parts arrived in Dayton on July 22, 1922, but final assembly had to await construction of a hangar big enough to shelter the giant. The second prototype had been canceled on January 31, 1922, but cost increased to $525,000 for one airplane, instead of the $375,000 estimated for two!

BARLING NBL-1
Six Liberty 12A, 420 hp at s.l.
DIMENSIONS: Span 120', Lg. 65', Ht. 27', Wing Area 4200 sq. ft.
WEIGHT: Empty 27,703 lb., Gross 32,203 lb., Max. 42,569 lb. Fuel 2000 gal.
PERFORMANCE: Speed- Top 96 mph at s.l., 93 mph at 5,000', Cruising 61 mph, Landing 55 mph. Service Ceiling 7,725', Absolute Ceiling 10,200', Climb 352'/1, min., 5000'/1 9.7 min. Range 170 miles/5000 lb. bombs, 335 miles max.

Lt. Harold R. Harris made the NBL-l's first flight on August 22, 1923. Three wings, four rudders, six engines, and ten landing wheels gave this behemoth a configuration more likely to antagonize the air than to pass through it. Four 420-hp Liberty 12A engines were arranged as tractors, two as pushers. Seven .30-caliber Lewis guns guarded a crew of ten in the spruce barrel fuselage, including two pilots, engineer, bombardier, navigator, radio operator, and four gunners. Up to 2,000 gallons of gasoline made a six-ton load, or half of that fuel could be replaced by 5,000 pounds of bombs. A record flight was made to 6,722 feet with a 4,400-pound load, but this modest altitude capability prevented flight over the mountains to either coast.

Although Mitchell said the Barling "was entirely successful from an experimental standpoint," it was elsewhere described as "Mitchell's Folly", and an Air Force history admits it had "disappointing speed, load, and endurance," with a range of 170 miles with load divided between fuel and bombs, and 335 miles with fuel only.

Mitchell also wanted to go ahead with the Martin NBL-2, a less-complicated biplane with two 700-hp, 18-

cylinder, W-1A Engineering Division engines on the 98-foot lower wing's leading edge, and a contract for two prototypes was signed on June 17, 1922. Glenn L. Martin had planned the NBL-2, after the *Ostfriesland* test, as a battleship buster. Essentially an enlarged NBS-1 with four main wheels and four rudders instead of two each, it had four times the bomb load, but only the same four crewmen were needed.

NASM

MARTIN NBL-2 (model)
Two Engineering Division W-1A, 700 hp at s.l.
DIMENSIONS: Span 98', Lg. 53', Wing Area 3000 sq. ft.
WEIGHT: Empty 14,704 lb., Gross 26,190 lb., Fuel 740 gal.
PERFORMANCE: Speed- Top 95 mph at s.l., Service Ceiling 9,000'. Contract estimates; NBL-2 never built.

Armament included five Lewis guns and a bomb bay for six 600 or four 1,100-pound bombs, or four 2,000 or even two 4,000-pound bombs could be carried underneath the fuselage. This project was canceled, probably because funds had been used up on the Barling triplane which itself was scrapped in June 1928. Nothing like its size was to be seen in the U.S. bombers until 1937.

After an April 1922 design competition, traditional bomber patterns reappeared in the Elias NBS-3 and Curtiss NBS-4 ordered June 17, 1922; four-place biplanes with box-like biplane tails, and five .30-caliber guns in the usual nose, rear, and tunnel positions. Powered by two Libertys, they had a welded steel tube, instead of wood, fuselage framework. Tested in August 1924, the XNBS-3 was built in Buffalo, did 101 mph with a 1,692-pound bomb load, and the wings could fold back for storage.

The Curtiss NBS-4, first flown on May 13, 1924, by Harold R. Harris, had 90-foot wings with a new Curtiss airfoil and offset windows on each side for the pilots behind the bow cockpit. The first of two examples tested could carry a 1,907-pound bomb load 608 miles.

Neither of these ships was ordered, for they incorporated no real advance over service types. With little performance progress made since the war, Air Service bomber squadrons hardly seemed likely to replace the battleship as the first line of defense. In July 1925, the bomber force was limited to 90 NBS-ls, the same type used five years earlier.

The Debate over National Air Power

Despite the modest size of his striking force Mitchell continued attacking "battleship admirals" and ground generals and predicted enormous capabilities for future aircraft. President Calvin Coolidge demoted him to the rank of

AMC

ELIAS NBS-3
Two Liberty 12A, 425 hp at s.l.
DIMENSIONS: Span 77'6", Lg. 48'5", Ht. 16'10", Wing Area 1542 sq. ft.
WEIGHT: Empty 8809 lb., Gross 14,343 lb. Fuel 340-356 gal.
PERFORMANCE: Speed- Top 101 mph at s.1., 96 mph at 6500', Landing 65 mph. Service Ceiling 8680', Absolute ceiling 11,500', Climb 405 ft/1 min., 5000'/16 min. Range 485 miles/1692 lb. bombs.

AMC

CURTISS NBS-4
Two Liberty 12A, 436 hp at s.l.
DIMENSIONS: Span 90'2", Lg. 46'5", Ht. 16'9", Wing Area 1524 sq. ft.
WEIGHT: Empty 7864 lb., Gross 13,795 lb. Fuel 334 gal.
PERFORMANCE: Speed- Top 100 mph at s.1., 95 mph at 5000', Landing 53 mph. Service Ceiling 10,750', Absolute Ceiling 13,000', Climb 529'/1 min., 5000'/11.5 min. Range 608 miles/1907 lb. bombs.

colonel, and he was sent to "exile" in Texas, but the disaster of the dirigible *Shenandoah* in September 1925 gave Mitchell an excuse to issue his most violent denunciation of "incompetency, criminal negligence, and almost treasonable administration."

This statement resulted in Mitchell's famous court martial in the fall of 1925, and the accompanying publicity led to Presidential appointment that same year of a board to investigate aviation, under chairmanship of banker-diplomat Dwight W. Morrow. Scores of witnesses presented data and opinions of air power to the board, most of them hostile to Mitchell.

It was against the limited range of the existing bombers that witnesses before the Morrow Board directed their main fire. The conservative position was put very strongly by the assistant director of the Navy's War plans Division, Captain Claude S. Pye. In the first place, argued the Navy spokesman, since bombers were then very limited in striking radius, to abandon battleships for bombers would be to assume an "essentially defensive" military posture. Without a fleet, our world trade would soon become a sacrifice to the air fetish." Do we wish to adopt a policy "like that of China and build a wall of air defense along our shores, outside of which the nations of the world can rob us of our commerce on which our national prosperity...depends?

Even if one were to suppose, Captain Pye continued, that offensive operations by aircraft alone were possible, could Americans use such weapons? No, he said, quoting liberally from Mitchell's book, *Winged Defense* to show that air bombardment meant "ruthlessly" bombing "civil population and economic resources." But under then existing international law this "means of coercing an enemy people is banned."

The Navy "does not subscribe to the theory of ruthlessness and believes that any organization based on... war according to such a theory is unsound. The Navy further believes that if the people of the United States will seriously consider this subject, they will reject this theory of ruthlessness and with such rejection the principal excuse for an independent air service will disappear."

Thus testified a Navy representative on October 14, 1925. Not all Navy men deprecated bomber striking power, and later chapters in this book detail progress made in carrier aviation. Yet aviation was seen by the majority as an arm of surface elements, whether fighting ships or infantry divisions. An independent air force built around bombers would be unsound because it could not protect our overseas commerce, and because it would commit the United States to a "theory of ruthlessness". The Morrow Board must have been impressed, for the final report firmly rejected Mitchell's theories, and two weeks later he was found "guilty as charged" of insubordination, and resigned from the Army effective February 1, 1926.

Bomber Designs from 1925 to 1927

Aside from changing the Air Service name to Air Corps, and promising enough funds to build a modern force of 1,800 planes, the Air Corps Act of 1926 embodied Morrow Board ideas and left the airmen still under the thumb of a General Staff of ground officers. Appropriations steadily increased from 13.5 million dollars in 1925 to 38.9 million in fiscal 1931, but much was siphoned off for observation planes. On June 30, 1925, the Army had 90 bombers compared with 249 observation planes and 28 fighters; on December 31, 1928, there were only 60 bombers to 506 observation planes, 190 fighters, and 69 attack planes.

Bomber strength was declining, and a replacement for the NBS-1 was required. More range was needed if bombers were to grow in importance, and this aim seemed advanced by the Huff Daland XLB-1 (Light Bomber), which appeared in August 1925. Substituting a single 750-hp Packard lA-2540 for the usual two Libertys, the XLB-1 was of fabric-covered steel-tube construction with two men side by side behind the engine, and a gunner near the single tail. Tapered wings used a USA-45 airfoil. Two Lewis guns were mounted at the gunner's pit, a third on the floor, and two .30-caliber Brownings were fixed on the lower wings' leading edge. About 1,500 pounds of bombs could be carried 8.25 hours over a range of 940 miles, the best yet for an American bomber.

AMC

HUFF DALAND XLB-l
Packard 2A-2540, rated 800 hp, actual 750 hp
DIMENSIONS: Span 66'6", Lg. 46'2", Ht. 14'11", Wing Area 1137 sq. ft.
WEIGHT: Empty 5740 lb., Gross 10,346 lb. Fuel 290 gal.
PERFORMANCE: Speed- Top 121 mph at s.1., 117 mph at 6500', Cruising 114 mph, Landing 55 mph. Service Ceiling 14,425', Absolute Ceiling 17,300', Climb 176'/1 min., 6500'/23.5 min. Range 940 miles.

SDAM

HUFF DALAND LB-1
Packard 2A-2540, 787 hp at s.l.
DIMENSIONS: Span 66'6", Lg. 46'2", Ht. 14'1", Wing Area 1137 sq. ft.
WEIGHT: Empty 6237 lb., Gross 12,415 lb. Fuel 295-350 gal.
PERFORMANCE: Speed- Top 120 mph at s.1., 114 mph at 5000', Cruising 105 mph, Landing 61 mph. Service Ceiling 11,150', Absolute Ceiling 13,700', Climb 530'/1 min., 6500'/14 min. Range 430 miles/2750 lb. bombs.

Ten LB-ls, called Pegasus by the company, were ordered in November 1925 for service trials. In July 1926, deliveries began on the LB-1, which had provision for a fourth crewman and larger useful loads than the prototype. An enlarged heavy bomber version of the LB-1 appeared in October 1926 as the XHB-1.

Since an expected 1,200-hp engine had failed to materialize, the same 787-hp Packard 2A-2540 had to be used. Christened Cyclops by the company, the only Army plane bearing "HB" letters carried four men; two in an open cockpit ahead of the wing, one near the tail with twin Lewis guns, and the other with a "retractable gun platform" which could be lowered below the fuselage. Two fixed Browning wing guns and up to 4,000 pounds of bombs were also carried.

The Cyclops was the Army's last single-engine bomber, for as early as April 1926 an Army board declared single-engine aircraft unsatisfactory for bombardment missions. A twin-engine layout was safer, and allowed a nose cockpit for gunnery and bomb-aiming. The Army began shopping for better twin-engine replacements for the aging NBS-1s.

HUFF DALAND XHB-1
Packard 2A-2540, 787 hp at s.l.
DIMENSIONS: Span 87', Lg. 59'7", Ht. 17'2", Wing Area 1648.5 sq. ft.
WEIGHT: Empty 8070 lb., Gross 16,838 lb. Fuel 412 gal.
PERFORMANCE: Speed- Top 109 mph.

Huff Daland, which in March 1927 became the Keystone Aircraft Corporation, received a contract on May 24, 1926, for an XLB-3, using two inverted air-cooled Liberty engines, the LB-l's tapered wings, and single rudder. The Bristol, Pennsylvania, factory preceded that model with an XLB-5 accepted November 12, 1926, with war-surplus water-cooled Libertys and a single rudder. This five-place biplane was designed by C. Talbot Porter and called the Pirate by the company.

KEYSTONE XLB-5
Two Liberty V-1650-3, 430 hp at s.l.
DIMENSIONS: Span 66'6", Lg. 45', Ht. 16'6", Wing Area 1137 sq. ft.
WEIGHT: Empty 6848 lb., Gross 11,992 lb. Fuel 200-340 gal.
PERFORMANCE: Speed- Top 108 mph at s.l., 99 mph at 6000', Cruising 87 mph, Landing 60 mph. Service Ceiling 7,875', Absolute Ceiling 10,300', Climb 420'/1 min., 4000'/12 min.

Nine LB-5 bombers delivered from August to December 1927 to Langley Field, added two small fins to the tail after delivery. Gunners in the bow and rear were armed with five .30-caliber Lewis guns and 2,000 pounds of bombs were carried. Their most famous mission was bombing the Pee Dee River bridge on December 23, 1927, a test that demonstrated that nothing less than 1,100-pound bombs could smash concrete bridges. Twenty-five LB-5As ordered May 6, 1927, at a cost of $28,000 each, appeared with new twin rudders from February to July 1928.

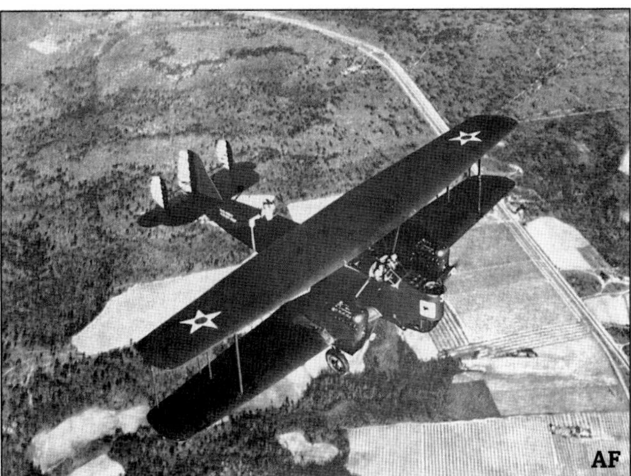

KEYSTONE LB-5
Two Liberty V-1650-3, 420 hp at s.l.
DIMENSIONS: Span 66'6", Lg. 44'8" Ht. 16'10", Wing Area 1139
WEIGHT: Empty 7024 1b., Gross 12,155 lb. Fuel 200 gal.
PERFORMANCE: Speed- Top 107 mph. Service Ceiling 8000', Absolute Ceiling 8800', Climb 5000'/20 min. Range 435 miles/2000 lb. bombs.

The XBL-3 had been delivered in December 1927 with experimental air-cooled Liberty engines, but they were replaced by 410-hp R-1340 Wasp radials and the designation became XLB-3A. These air-cooled radial engines were introduced along with the two 525-hp R-1750-1 Wrights on the XLB-6 converted from the 10th LB-5 and also delivered that December.

KEYSTONE XLB-3
as LB-5, with inverted air-cooled Liberty V-1410-1.

Keystone's newest bomber had twin rudders and larger wings, with engine nacelles between them, above the turbulent air flow over the lower wing. A stability problem persisted until dihedral and sweep-back were added to the wings and the tail modified.

At the same time those light bombers were being developed, Keystone had also received a contract on May 20, 1926, for a heavy bomber, the XB-l, a twin-engine development of the XHB-l, with 510-hp Packard 2A-1530s. Now that funds were available to reequip Army bomber squadrons, Keystone found itself in competition with a Curtiss design by George Page.

The Curtiss XB-2 Condor ordered June 2, 1926, with new 600-hp Curtiss Conquerors, was also a large five-

KEYSTONE LB-5A *As LB-5 with twin rudders*

KEYSTONE XLB-3A
Two Pratt & Whitney R-1340-1, 410 hp at s.l.
DIMENSIONS: Span 67', Lg. 45', Ht. 16'10", Wing Area 1139 sq. ft.
WEIGHT: Empty 6065 lb., Gross 11,682 lb. Fuel 245-350 gal.
PERFORMANCE: Speed- Top 116 mph at s.1., 113 mph at 5000', cruising 93 mph, Landing 59 mph. Service Ceiling 11,210', Absolute Ceiling 13,700', Climb 550'/1 min. Range 545 miles at top speed.

KEYSTONE XLB-6
Two Wright R-1750-1, 525 hp at s.l.
DIMENSIONS: Span 74'9", Lg. 43'6", Ht. 18'1", Wing Area 1148 sq. ft.
WEIGHT: Empty 6605 lb., Gross 13,018 lb. Fuel 350 gal.
PERFORMANCE: Speed- Top 116 mph at s.1., 114 mph at 5000', Cruising 93 mph, Landing 58 mph. Service Ceiling 14,770', Absolute Ceiling 17,000', Climb 746'/1 min., 5000'/7.9 min. Range 440 miles/2000 lb. bombs.

place biplane with twin rudders. A Clark Y airfoil was used on the Keystone, while the XB-2 used a new Curtiss-72 airfoil and a double tail.

Both the XB-1 and the XB-2 shared the first improvement in defensive armament since the war; instead of a single rear gunner with view blocked by the tail assembly, there were two gunners, one seated in each engine nacelle with a clear fire to the rear and below. Two Lewis guns were provided for each, with a third pair in the nose. A normal bomb load of 2,500 pounds, could be increased to 4,000 on short flights.

When the XB-1 was built by September 1927, it had Packard engines, and in 1928, they were replaced by 600-hp Curtiss V-1570-5 Conquerors and the Keystone became the XB-1B. But the Curtiss Condor, first tested in July 1927 at Mitchel Field, showed the best performance of any bomber of that decade. The $115,000 contract had the usual penalty clause of $1,000 for each 100 pounds overweight, but the Garden City, New York, factory had come below the design estimate.

The first twin-engine Air Corps bomber built as a monoplane, the Atlantic* XLB-2 was ordered May 28, 1926, and first flown August 5, 1927 at Teterboro, New

*Anthony Fokker formed Atlantic Aircraft as the American branch of his Dutch firm. It became Fokker Aircraft in 1928, and then was sold and renamed General Aviation in 1930.

AF

CURTISS B-2
Two Curtiss V-1570-7, 633 hp at s.l.
DIMENSIONS: Span 90', Lg. 47'6", Ht. 16'3", Wing Area 1499 sq. ft.
WEIGHT: Empty 9039 lb., Gross 16,516 lb. Fuel 444 gal.
PERFORMANCE: Speed- Top 132 mph at s.1., 128 mph at 5000', Cruising 114 mph, Landing 53 mph. Service Ceiling 17,100', Absolute Ceiling 19,400', Climb 850'/1 min., 5000'/6.8 min. Range 780 miles/2508 lb. bombs.

MFR

KEYSTONE XB-1 (data for XB-1B remodel)
Two Curtiss V-1570-5, 600 hp at s.l.
DIMENSIONS: Span 85', Lg. 62', Ht. 19'3", Wing Area 1604 sq. ft.
WEIGHT: Empty 9462 lb., Gross 16,500 lb., Max. 17,039 lb. Fuel 444 gal.
PERFORMANCE: Speed- Top 117 mph at s.1., Landing 56 mph. Service Ceiling 15,000'. Range 700 miles/2508 lb. bombs.

MFR

CURTISS XB-2
Two Curtiss GV-1570, 600 hp at s.l.
DIMENSIONS: Span 90', Lg. 47'6", Ht. 16'3", Wing Area 1499 sq. ft.
WEIGHT: Empty 8732 lb., Gross 16,344 lb. Fuel 444 gal.
PERFORMANCE: Speed- Top 130 mph at s.1., 122 mph at 10,000', Cruising 104 mph, Landing 53 mph. Service Ceiling 16,140', Absolute Ceiling 18,435', Climb 912'/1 min.

Jersey. Developed from the Fokker C-2 transport, the XLB-2 had 410-hp Pratt & Whitney R-1340 Wasps suspended below the high cantilever plywood wing. Top speed with these engines was 116 mph, but speed was later increased to 123 mph by using the 525-hp R-1690-1. The crew of five was armed with five .30-caliber guns and 2,052 pounds of bombs.

This firm also planned a larger high-wing monoplane in 1926; the five-place XHB-2 with two 800-hp Packard 2A-2540s, double tandem wheels, twin rudders, a tail gunner, and up to 5,981 pounds of bombs. It was never built, for, as in the case of Martin's NBL-2 and a projected Huff Daland XHB-3, authorities were unready to trust a big monoplane. Doubts about all-metal aircraft also halted the XLB-4 project, a biplane proposed by Martin with R-1690 Hornets.

Atlantic-Fokker built another bomber monoplane at the Teterboro plant in May 1929. Powered by two R-1690 Hornets, it was registered X9165, but was never tested by the Army before being rebuilt as an conventional F-10A trimotor transport.

Igor Sikorsky (1889-1972), now transplanted to America, had a contract with Consolidated Aircraft in April 1927 to finance his Sikorsky S-37B Guardian bomber completed on December 9, 1927, at College Point, New York,. Powered

ATLANTIC XLB-2
Two Pratt & Whitney R-1340, 410 hp (later R-1690-1, 525 hp)
DIMENSIONS: Span 72'10", Lg. 51'5", Ht. 13'3", Wing Area 748 sq. ft.
WEIGHT: Empty 5916 (6236) lb., Gross 12,039 (12,655) lb. Fuel 295 (340) gal.
PERFORMANCE: Speed- Top 116 (123) mph at s.1., 112 mph at 5000', Cruising 93 mph, Landing 67 mph. Service Ceiling 10,925' (13,700'), Absolute Ceiling 13,400', Climb 540'/ 1 min. (762'/1 min.), 5000'/11.5 min. Range 540 (650) miles/2057 lb. bombs.

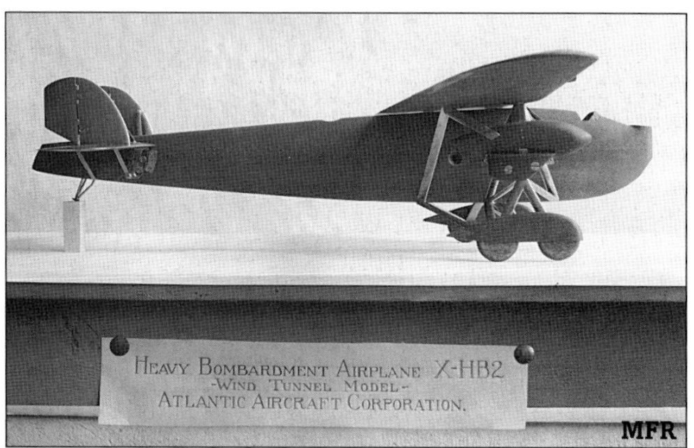

ATLANTIC XHB-2
Two Packard 2A-2540, 800-hp at s.l.
DIMENSIONS: Span 108'4", Lg. 71'3", Wing Area 1600 sq. ft.
WEIGHT: Empty 12,054 lb., Gross 24,473 lb. Fuel 590 gal.
Wind tunnel model and engineering data only.

by two air-cooled Pratt & Whitney 525-hp Hornets, the S-37B had a 100-foot span upper wing overhanging a 58-foot lower wing. Five men were arranged in the traditional manner in the fuselage; twin rudders made up the tail. Armed with five Lewis guns and 1,952 pounds of bombs, the Guardian used the Army bailment designation XB-936.

Consolidated would have done the production version, had the S-37B won a contract, but the duralumin, fabric-covered airframe weight was nearly 1,000 pounds over the design estimate. Consolidated refused to pay for the failed project, so Sikorsky remodeled it into a civil transport, which operated until 1934.

When an Army board of seven officers met in February 1928 to choose a bomber type for production, it dismissed the XB-1B, XLB-2, and S-37, but disagreed on the merits of the Curtiss XB-2 and Keystone XLB-6. Although the former had by far the best performance, critics complained that it cost too much and was "too big for existing hangars." A four-to-three decision put the Keystone ship

FOKKER X9165

SIKORSKY S-37B
Two Pratt & Whitney R-1690, 525 hp at s.l.
Dimensions: Span 100', Lg. 45', Ht. 16'2", Wing Area 1074 sq. ft.
Weight: Empty 8794 lb., Gross 15,109 lb. Fuel 350-550 gal.
Performance: Speed- Top 108 mph, Landing 57 mph. Service Ceiling 12,800', Climb 546'/1 min. Range 575 miles/1,952 lb. bombs.

into production, but on June 23, 1928, Curtiss did get a $1,050,473 contract for twelve B-2s, which were delivered at Buffalo from August 10, 1929, to January 16, 1930. The B-2 "Condors" remained in service with the 11th Bomb Squadron in California until 1934.

Keystone Bombers, 1928-1932

Although the Keystone bombers were conservative in design and performance, they were favored because of their low cost, economical operation, and stable flying qualities. Between 1927 and 1932, 210 Keystones were delivered to the Air Corps, representing 19 different models. All were twin-engine, five-place biplanes constructed of steel tubing covered by fabric. Below the bow gunner were windows for the bombardier, and behind and above him sat the pilots. The rear gunner behind the wings had two Lewis guns on a ring, like the front gunner, and another gun firing downward through the floor opening.

With their open cockpits, struts, wires, and exposed wheels, they looked and performed much the same as the NBS-ls they replaced- certainly not enough to make national policy makers feel they had advanced far beyond the planes that sank the old target ships. The first Keystone production series was the LB-5A Pirates mentioned earlier; they could be recognized by their water-cooled Libertys and 67-foot tapered wings.

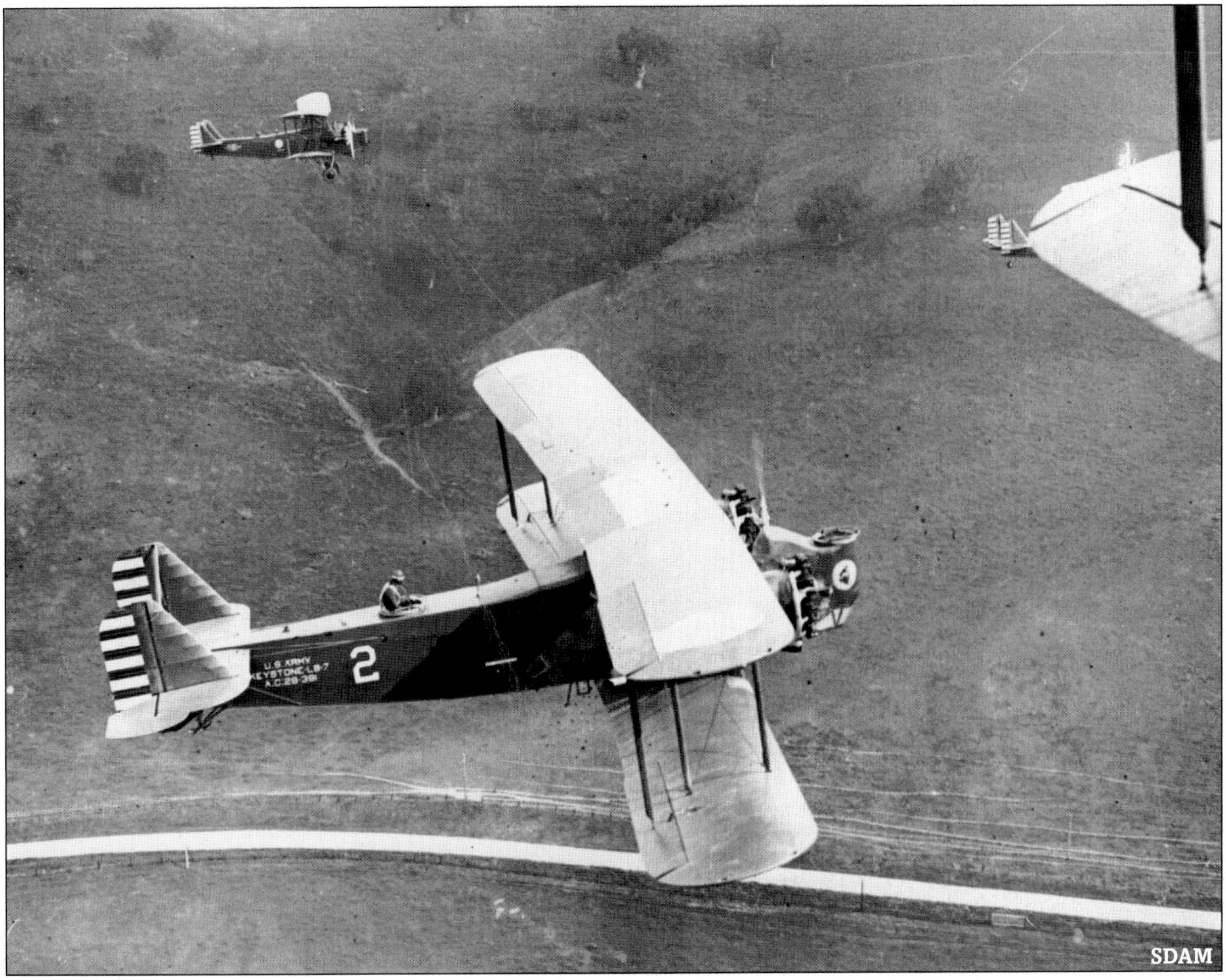

SDAM

KEYSTONE LB-7
Two Pratt & Whitney R-1690-3, 525 hp at s.l.
DIMENSIONS: As LB-6
WEIGHT: Empty 6556 lb., Gross 12,903 lb. Fuel 350 gal.
PERFORMANCE: Speed- Top 114 mph at s.1., 110 mph at 5,000', Cruising 95 mph, Landing 55 mph. Service Ceiling 13,325', Absolute Ceiling 15,700', Climb 660'/1 min., 5000'/9.1 min. Range 432 miles/2,000 lb. bombs.

PMB

KEYSTONE LB-6
Two Wright R-1750-1, rated 575 hp at s.1., actual 536 hp
DIMENSIONS: Span 75', Lg. 43'5", Ht. 18'1", Wing Area 1148 sq. ft.
WEIGHT: Empty 6836 lb., Gross 13,440 lb. Fuel 352 gal.
PERFORMANCE: Speed- Top 114 mph at s.1., 106 mph at 5000', Cruising 95 mph, Landing 58 mph. Service Ceiling 11,650' Absolute Ceiling 14,000', Climb 600'/1 min., 5000'/10.3 min. Range 632 miles/2000 lb. bombs.

On May 7, 1928, 35 Keystones were ordered at a cost of $24,750 each. Labeled Panther by the company, they had a longer fuselage, 75-foot wings, and twin rudders. Sixteen LB-6s with Wright R-1750-1 Cyclones had exhaust collector rings on the front of their cylinders, while 16 LB-7s had Pratt & Whitney R-1690-3 Hornets distinguished by their exhaust collectors behind the cylinders. The LB-7s were delivered first, from February to June 1929, and the LB-6s arrived in July to October of that year. Armament included five Lewis guns and a ton of bombs in internal racks. The five crewmen were provided with radio and oxygen gear.

The 17th aircraft on this contract became the LB-8, delivered in November 1929 with the geared GR-1860-3 Hornet, followed by an LB-9 with the GR-1750-1 Cyclone. A new single rudder was introduced on the LB-10, with the R-1750-1, as early as July 1929, while the LB-11 was the last LB-6 converted in 1930 to direct-drive R-1750-3 Cyclones. The first LB-7 became the XLB-12 when R-1860-1

PMB

KEYSTONE LB-8
Two Pratt & Whitney GR-1860-3, 550 hp at s.l.
DIMENSIONS: Span 75', Lg. 42'6", Ht. 18'1", Wing Area 1148 sq. ft.
WEIGHT: Empty 7357 lb., Gross 13,745 lb. Fuel 363 gal.
PERFORMANCE: Speed- Top 126 mph at s.1., 121 mph at 5000', Cruising 100 mph, Landing 59 mph. Service Ceiling 16,800', Absolute Ceiling 18,700', Climb 977'/1 min., 5000'/14.5 min.

PMB

KEYSTONE LB-10
Two Wright R-1750-1, 525 hp at s.l.
DIMENSIONS: Span 75', Lg. 49'3", Ht. 15'6", Wing Area 1148 sq. ft.
WEIGHT: Empty 6993 lb., Gross 13,285 lb. Fuel 340 gal.
PERFORMANCE: Speed- Top 116 mph at s.1., 113 mph at 5000', Cruising 93 mph, Landing 58 mph. Service Ceiling 13,440', Absolute Ceiling 15,800', Climb 660'/1 min., 5000'/ 9 min. Range 352 miles/2587 lb. bombs.

Hornets were installed. The purpose of these modifications was to choose the best engines for the next bomber series.

On March 15, 1930, the Bristol builder got an order for 73 ships originally labeled LB-l0A, LB-13, and LB-14. But by the time delivery began, the Army had dropped the LB designation and was listing all bombers in the B series beginning with XB-l and XB-2 and continuing to the XB-70. All ships in this new Keystone series had a 74-foot 9-inch span wing with a Goettingen-398 airfoil and were distinguished from their predecessors by a single balanced rudder. Three Browning M1922 flexible guns with 500 rounds per gun (rpg) replaced Lewis guns by 1932, and the bomb bay held up to 2,496 pounds (4 x 624) of bombs.

First was the B-3A that appeared in October 1930 with 525-hp R-1690-3 Hornets, two-bladed propellers and aft exhaust rings. Thirty-six B-3As delivered by March 1931, were followed by 27 B-5As with 525-hp R-1750-3 Cyclones and forward exhaust rings.

AF

KEYSTONE B-3A
Two Pratt & Whitney R-1690-3, 525 hp at s.1.
DIMENSIONS: Span 74'8", Lg. 48'10", Ht. 15'9", Wing Area 1145 sq. ft.
WEIGHT: Empty 7705 lb., Gross 12,952 lb. Fuel 235-535 gal.
PERFORMANCE: Speed- Top 114 mph at s.1., 109.5 mph at 5000', Cruising 98 mph, Landing 56 mph. Service Ceiling 12,700', Absolute Ceiling 15,000', Climb 650'/1 min., 5000'/ 9.4 min. Range 480 miles/2496 lb. bombs, 1050 miles max.

PMB

KEYSTONE B-5A
Two Wright R-1750-3, 525 hp at s.1.
DIMENSIONS: As B-3A
WEIGHT: Empty 7705 lb., Gross 12,952 lb. Fuel 235-535 gal.
PERFORMANCE: Speed- Top 111 mph at s.1., 106 mph at 5000', Cruising 98 mph, Landing 57 mph. Service Ceiling 10,600', Absolute Ceiling 13,000', Climb 540'/1 min., 5000'/11.7 min. Range 440-964 miles.

In June 1931, Keystone also completed five YlB-4s with 575-hp R-1860-7 Hornets and five YlB-6s with 575-hp R-1820-1 Cyclones. These Cyclones were the first to use three-bladed propellers and the first model of the engine series that would power World War II's B-17 bombers.

On April 28, 1931, the Army placed its last biplane bomber contract, for 25 B-4A and 39 B-6A Keystones. First came the B-6As delivered from August 1931 to January 1932 with Cyclones, while the Hornet-powered B-4As were accepted from January to April 1932. Both had three-blade propellers, but could be distinguished by the exhaust rings; which were positioned in front on the Cyclones, and aft on the Hornets.

SDAM

KEYSTONE B-4A
Two Pratt & Whitney R-1860-7, 575 hp at s.l.
DIMENSIONS: Span 74'8", Lg. 48'10", Ht. 15'9", Wing Area 1162 sq. ft.
WEIGHT: Empty 7951 lb., Gross 13,209 lb. Fuel 235-535 gal
PERFORMANCE: Speed- Top 121 mph at s.l., Cruising 103 mph, Landing 57 mph. Service Ceiling 14,000'. Range 885-1040 miles.

AF

KEYSTONE Y1B-4

AF

KEYSTONE B-6A
Two Wright R-1820-1, 575 hp at s.l.
DIMENSIONS: Span 74'8", Lg. 48'10", Ht. 15'9", Wing Area 1182 sq. ft.
WEIGHT: Empty 8057 lb., Gross 13,334 lb. Fuel 235-535 gal.
PERFORMANCE: Speed- Top 121 mph at s.l., 116 mph at 5000', Cruising 103 mph, Landing 57 mph. Service Ceiling 14,100', Absolute Ceiling 16,500', Climb 690'/1 min., 5000'/8.6 min. Range 463 miles/2496 lb. bombs, 944 miles max.

PMB

KEYSTONE B-4A

When biplane bomber production ended in 1932, the ten Air Corps bombardment squadrons included:

20th, 49th, and 96th Sqs., 2nd Bomb Group, Langley Field, with B-6A.

9th and 31st Sqs., 7th Bomb Group, March Field, with B-4A.

11th Sq., 7th Bomb Group, March Field, with B-2.

23rd Sq. 5th Composite Group, Luke Field (Hawaii), with LB-6.

72nd Sq. 5th Composite Group, Luke Field, with B-5A.

25th Sq., 6th Composite. Group, France Field (Canal Zone), with B-3A.

28th Sq., 4th Composite Group, Nichols Field (Philippines), with B-3A.

In addition, the 19th Bomb Group was activated in June 1932 at Rockwell Field with only nine B-3As, and the training squadron at Kelly Field had a few B-5A and LB-7s.

Keystone biplanes formed almost the entire U.S. Army bombardment strength during the international social crisis of 1931-1933, which finally led to World War II. But their striking power, range, and ability to defend themselves were little greater than that of their predecessors, and their top speed reflected only that improvement offered by more horsepower. These fabric-covered biplanes could not go as fast or as far as needed for strategic bombing, but a new monoplane bomber generation would change that situation.

CHAPTER 5

ARMY PURSUITS THE BIPLANE PERIOD, 1920-1932

VERVILLE VCP-1
(original version)

Postwar Experiments

Fighter development from 1920 to 1932 was usually based on traditional biplane designs, and began with a group of prototypes exploring the immediate technical possibilities available when the war ended.

The first single-seat fighter of the postwar generation was the VCP-l designed by Alfred Verville (1890-1970) of the Army's Engineering Division. Verville had been on a technical mission sent to France to evaluate the latest innovations in fighter design. Although the mission's report on November 1, 1918, was too late to affect wartime projects, the Engineering Division began the "Verville Chase Plane", and two examples were ordered, the first for static tests and the second for flight trials.

PMB

VERVILLE VCP-1
Wright-Hispano H, 300 hp at s.l.
DIMENSIONS: Span 32', Lg. 22'6", Ht. 8'4", Wing Area 269 sq. ft.
WEIGHT: Empty 2014 lb., Gross 2669 lb. Fuel 41 gal.
PERFORMANCE: Speed- Top 154 mph at s.1., 152 mph at 6500', Stalling 61.5 mph. Service Ceiling 25,400', Absolute Ceiling 27,000', Climb 1690'/1 min., 6500'/ 4.4 min. Endurance 2 hours at 149 mph.

Powered by a 300-hp Wright-Hispano and armed with two Browning guns, the VCP-l had a laminated wood-veneer fuselage and "I" struts between the tapered wings with balanced ailerons on the lower surfaces. The first was delivered for the sandbag ordeal in August 1919, and the second made flight trials on January 12 and 26, 1920, with an odd "annular" radiator arranged around the nose. When this proved unsatisfactory, it was replaced with a conventional nose radiator by April 12, 1920.

Since increased speed was becoming the chief objective of pursuit development, a practical way of promoting speed was for the services themselves to participate in the air racing becoming popular. The Air Service obtained a May 25, 1920, appropriation to convert the original VCP-1 to the VCP-R racer with a 636-hp 12-cylinder Packard 1A-2025.

AF

VERVILLE VCP-R

First flown with the new engine and the same wings on July 15, the racer was provided with smaller wings by August 1920. An attempt at the Gordon Bennett Race failed, but the VCP-R won the first Pulitzer Race on November 25, beating standard MB-3 and Orenco D entrants. The Verville would be rebuilt as the R-l for the 1922 Pulitzer, but then it was eclipsed by the speeds made by the Curtiss R-6. That Curtiss was the best of a series of Army racers built in 1921-22.

The Army adopted a system of aircraft designation to replace the previous confusion of builders' letters and numbers. The new system provided for PW, PA, and PN types (Pursuit, Water-cooled, Pursuit, Air-cooled, and Pursuit, Night). The first of these fighters was the Engineering Division's PW-1 ordered April 23, 1920. Based on Verville's VCP design, it would retain the VCP-l's tapered I strut wings with an RAF-15 airfoil section, but had a Packard lA-1237 with a tunnel radiator and introduced a fuselage of fabric-covered welded steel tubing.

ENGINEERING DIV. PW-1
Packard lA-1237, 350 hp at s.l.
DIMENSIONS: Span 32', Lg. 22'6", Ht. 8'4", Wing Area 269 sq. ft.
WEIGHT: Empty 2069 lb., Gross 3005 lb. Fuel 61 gal.
PERFORMANCE: Speed- Top 146 mph at s.1., 144 mph at 6500', Stalling 69 mph. Service Ceiling 19,300', Absolute Ceiling 21,000', Climb 10,000'/11 min. Endurance 2.5 hours at 131.5 mph.

When the PW-1 began flight tests in June 1921, it had the standard one .30-caliber M1921 over the engine, but the new .50-caliber M1921 was added, along with provisions for a rack of four 25-pound bombs under the fuselage and emergency jettisoning of the main fuel tank. The PW-1 was rebuilt in December 1921 as the PW-lA with Fokker-style straight cantilever wings and metal N struts. Test flights begun December 13 showed the thick wing section that had worked on the famous Fokker D VII only slowed the Verville design down, so the original wings were restored.

ENGINEERING DIV. PW-1A
Packard lA-1237, 350 hp at s.l.
DIMENSIONS: Span 31'2", Lg. 22'6", Ht. 8'10", Wing Area 288 sq. ft.
WEIGHT: Empty 2139 lb., Gross 3075 lb. Fuel 61 gal.
PERFORMANCE: Speed- Top 134 mph at s.1., 133 mph at 6500', Service Ceiling 17,200', Absolute Ceiling 18,800', Climb 10,000'/1 2.3 min. Endurance 2.5 hours at 115.5 mph.

The only example of the specialized night fighter was the Curtiss PN-l biplane ordered February 23, 1920, with a six-cylinder 220-hp Liberty L-825 engine, long exhaust pipes to hide the flames, and an overhanging upper wing with balanced ailerons. The theory behind this design seems to have been to get a low wing loading for easy operation out of small blacked-out wartime fields.

Since the top speed was barely above that of the bombers it was supposed to stop, only two such planes were built. The first had cantilever wings, but failed static tests in December 1920, so N struts were added to the second PN-l that began flight tests on August 18, 1921. The PN-1 project was terminated on December 2.

CURTISS PN-1
Liberty 6, L-825, 220 hp at s.l.
DIMENSIONS: Span 30'10", Lg. 23'6", Ht. 10'3", Wing Area 300 sq. ft.
WEIGHT: Empty 1631 lb., Gross 2311 lb. Fuel 50 gal.
PERFORMANCE: Speed- Top 108 mph at s.l. Service Ceiling 23,900', Absolute Ceiling 25,600', Climb 6500'/5.5 min. Range 255 miles.

Grover Loening, the leading American advocate of monoplanes, received a contract for three PW-2 high-wing fighters on April 10, 1920. As was the procedure then, the first prototype was used for static tests and was delivered in February 1921, and the second began flight tests in May. Powered by a 320-hp Wright H, the PW-2 was armed with the usual .30 and .50-caliber guns.

LOENING PW-2
Wright H, 320 hp at s.l.
DIMENSIONS: Span 39'8", Lg. 24'2", Ht. 9', Wing Area 287 sq. ft.
WEIGHT: Empty 1876 lb., Gross 2788 lb. Fuel 59 gal.
PERFORMANCE: Speed- Top 132 mph at s.1., 131 mph at 6500', Stalling 61 mph. Service Ceiling 20,000', Absolute Ceiling 21,800', Climb 6500'/6.2 min., 10,000'/10.6 min. Endurance 2.5 hours at 132 mph.

LOENING PW-2 (2nd version)

A third PW-2 was delivered on November 22 with twin rudders and a four-bladed propeller. Although two PW-2As had been ordered June 21, 1921, and ten more Loening monoplanes added later, dangerous weaknesses appeared. While wing flutter was little known when Loening built his first monoplanes, but as the designer wryly remarked that after the first flights, "We knew all we wanted to know about it."

LOENING PW-2A
Wright H, 322 hp at s.l.
DIMENSIONS: Span 39'9", Lg. 26', Ht. 8'4", Wing Area 299 sq. ft.
WEIGHT: Empty 1858 lb., Gross 2770 lb. Fuel 60 gal.
PERFORMANCE: Speed- Top 136 mph at s.1., 133 mph at 6500', Stalling 63 mph. Service Ceiling 21,200', Absolute Ceiling 23,000', Climb 6500'/5.7 min., 10,000'/9.8 min. Endurance 2.5 hours at 131 mph.

A PW-2A with a new rudder first flew on January 31, 1922, and the second delivered as the PW-2B with a Packard lA-1237 and side radiators on March 24. After the PW-2A lost its wing and gave Lieutenant Harold R. Harris the unwanted distinction of being the first American pilot to save himself by parachute on October 20, the contract was cut back to four.

The PW-3 biplane began as the Orenco D-2 with wood construction and a 320-hp Wright H with side radiators. Three were ordered April 23, 1920, and the first delivered on April 26, 1921, but all were condemned as unsafe because of unsatisfactory workmanship, and never flown.

The contract to build the Army's first fighter with an air-cooled radial attracted bids from nine companies on November 15, 1920. Loening won the right to build the PA-l with a Wright R-1454 on January 20, 1921. A static test example was delivered in September, 1921, and the flight article delivered in April 1922 had a steel-tube fuselage, short for quick turns, and placed the gas tank up in the thick upper wing. Lacking an engine, flight tests were delayed until 1923, and the 3rd example was canceled on February 6, 1923.

LOENING PW-2B
Packard lA-1237, 352 hp at s.l.
DIMENSIONS: Span 34'1", Lg. 23'4", Ht. 8'1", Wing Area 225 sq. ft.
WEIGHT: Empty 2040 lb., Gross 2976 lb. Fuel 61 gal.
PERFORMANCE: Speed- Top 140 mph at s.1., 137 mph at 6500', Stalling 71 mph. Service Ceiling 17,150', Absolute Ceiling 18,600', Climb 6500'/6.1 min., 10,000'/11 min. Endurance 2.75 hours at 134 mph.

ORENCO PW-3
Wright H, 300 hp at s.l.
DIMENSIONS: Span 27'9", Lg. 23'10", Ht. 8'1", Wing Area 240 sq. ft.
WEIGHT: Empty 1870 lb., Gross 2669 lb. Fuel 50 gal.
PERFORMANCE: Unsafe for flight.

Previously, the Army had tested, in July 1921, an imported air-cooled fighter, the British Aerial Transport F.K. 23 "Bantam," a very light design by Koolhoven with a monocoque fuselage and 184-hp A.B.C. Wasp A radial.

A single-seat ground-attack sesquiplane was designed by I. M. Laddon around the Wright K, a Hispano H with a 37-mm Baldwin cannon firing through the hollow engine crankshaft. Armor weighing 165 pounds protected the engine and cockpit, and a .50-caliber gun was added so the PG-l (Pursuit, Ground) could be used both for ground strafing and attacking hostile armored aircraft. Vee struts connected the narrow lower wing to the upper wing atop the fuselage, with the pilot's head poking through the center section. A radiator in front of his face further ruined his visibility.

After a test cannon-engine was produced in July 1920, bids for the PG-l were requested from private firms. Four submitted bids, and Aeromarine, at Keyport, New Jersey, received the order on March 15, 1921, for three prototypes. The first was delivered as a static test airframe on November 28, 1921, for static tests and the second was flown on July 14, 1922, with a Wright H, which failed on takeoff, destroying the aircraft. A 346-hp Packard 1237 was used on the third prototype, tested in 1923. Its top speed of

GALLAUDET PW-4
Packard lA-1237, 350 hp at s.l.
DIMENSIONS: Span 29'10", Lg. 22'8", Ht. 8', Wing Area 245 sq. ft.
WEIGHT: Empty 2203 lb., Gross 3040 lb. Fuel 60 gal.
PERFORMANCE: Speed- Estimated 145 mph, but never flown.

116 mph at 3,342 pounds gross weight was below that expected of the original configuration, as shown in the accompanying data.

Gallaudet's single PW-4 ordered June 21, 1921, was the Army's first all-metal fighter. With very modern bullet lines, "I" struts, and a 350-hp Packard lA-1237, the PW-4 began taxi tests on February 17, 1922, but after static tests was considered unsafe to fly. Two other examples on the contract were canceled November 17, 1922.

LOENING PA-1
Wright R-1 (R-1454), 350 hp at s.l.
DIMENSIONS: Span 28', Lg. 19'9", Ht. 8'8", Wing Area 282 sq. ft.
WEIGHT: Empty 1536 lb., Gross 2463 lb. Fuel 69 gal.
PERFORMANCE: Speed- Top 124 mph at s.1., Service Ceiling 19,200' Absolute Ceiling 21,000', Climb 10,000'/12 min.

More extreme was the Dayton-Wright PS-l (Pursuit Special), a high-wing parasol monoplane ordered on June 29, 1921, and first delivered for static tests on November 13, 1922. Powered by a 200-hp Lawrance J-l radial within a streamlined cowling, it introduced one of the first retractable wheel arrangements. The wheels folded up into

AEROMARINE PG-1
Wright K-2, 330 hp at s.l.
DIMENSIONS: Span 40', Lg. 24'6", Ht. 8', Wing Area 389 sq. ft.
WEIGHT: Empty 3030 lb., Cross 3918 lb. Fuel 45 gal.
PERFORMANCE: Speed-Top 130 mph at s.l., Landing 58 mph. Service Ceiling 17,000', Absolute Ceiling 19,000', Climb 6500'/9.5 min. Range 195 miles at top speed.

the fuselage, as on the Grummans a decade later. Two more were completed in June/July 1923, but they flew badly, their tactical use was unclear, and they became another unsatisfactory project.

Anthony Fokker had built many successful fighters for the Kaiser's Air Force during World War I, the most famous being the D VII. After the Armistice, he moved his factory to the Netherlands and began selling planes to his erstwhile adversaries. The Air Service had brought back 142 D VIIs captured from Germany, actually used them in service, and respected Fokker's sturdy cantilever wing structures.

AF

DAYTON-WRIGHT PS-1
Lawrance J-1, 200 hp at s.l.
DIMENSIONS: Span 30', Lg. 19'2", Wing Area 143 sq. ft.
WEIGHT: Empty 1143 lb.,Gross 1715 lb. Fuel 28 gal.
PERFORMANCE: Speed- Estimated 145 mph.

On December 4, 1920, the Army ordered two examples of the Fokker V-40, a high-wing monoplane development of the wartime D VIII. While the welded steel tube fuselage was long enough to make a vertical fin unnecessary for the balanced rudder, the cantilever wing was all wood. They arrived at McCook Field on January 22, 1922, and the first was flown with a 334-hp Wright H.

AMC

FOKKER V-40
Wright H, 334 hp at s.l.
DIMENSIONS: Span 39'5", Lg. 26'1", Ht. 9', Wing Area 247 sq. ft.
WEIGHT: Empty 1935 lb., Gross 2686 lb. Fuel 51 gal.
PERFORMANCE: Speed- Top 144 mph at s.1., 141 at 10,000', Stalling 62 mph. Service Ceiling 23,750', Absolute Ceiling 25,400', Climb 10,000'/8 min. Endurance 2 hours at top speed.

During a mock dogfight with a Loening PW-2 on March 13, 1922, the V-40's wing failed, and the pilot was killed. The second V-40, which had thin 4-mm armor on the forward fuselage, was then gradually loaded with sand bags until the wing broke.

Nevertheless, ten heavier models were purchased on May 27, 1922, for service tests. Designated PW-5, they were armed with the .30/.50-caliber gun combination then standard on Army fighters, and deliveries began October 26, 1922. Nine PW-5s and two PW-2As served with the First Pursuit Group in 1923, but pilots never really trusted the high-wing monoplanes' strength.

Fokker also sent a D IX biplane purchased June 30, 1922, and tested at McCook Field in September as the PW-6. Like the PW-5 monoplane, the PW-6 had a nose radiator for the Wright H-2, and had no fin in front of the balanced rudder. "N" struts between the wings would become common on later American biplanes.

AMC

FOKKER PW-5
Wright H-2, 300 hp at s.l.
DIMENSIONS: Span 39'5", Lg. 27'2", Ht. 9', Wing Area 246 sq. ft.
WEIGHT: Empty 2170 lb., Gross 3015 lb. Fuel 61 gal.
PERFORMANCE: Speed- Top 138 mph at s.1.

On August 10, 1922, the Army ordered three Fokker D XI sesquiplanes from the Dutch builder. Known here as the PW-7, the first began tests at McCook in February 1924 with a 440-hp Curtiss D-12 engine, side radiators, and tapered plywood upper wing connected by V struts with the much smaller lower wings. The heavier second and third example had N struts between fabric-covered wings. It is noteworthy that the Fokker D XI with an Hispano engine became the standard Soviet Air Force fighter in 1924-29.

All-metal construction and cantilever monoplanes were audacious experiments in those days, but some German designers combined both in fighter design. One was the all-metal single-seat Dornier "Falke" with a high-wing built in Switzerland. Inspected at McCook Field in April 1923, its clean lines were defeated by high costs and the fear the wing might come off.

The last pursuit type built by the Army's own Engineering Division was the TP-l two-seater ordered in 1922. A biplane whose lower wing was larger than the upper, it added two flexible Lewis guns on the rear cockpit ring, and another at a floor trapdoor, to the usual two fixed guns.

FOKKER PW-6 (D IX)
Wright H-2, 315 hp at s.l.
DIMENSIONS: Span 29'6", Lg. 23'3", Ht. 9', Wing Area 238 sq. ft.
WEIGHT: Empty 1926 lb., Gross 2763 1b. Fuel 58 gal.
PERFORMANCE: Speed- Top 138.5 mph at s.1., 129 mph at 10,000', Stalling 62 mph. Service Ceiling 16,750', Absolute Ceiling 18,200', Climb 6500'/6.3 min., 10,000'/11.4 min. Endurance 2.5 hours at 117 mph.

FOKKER PW-7 (D XI)
Curtiss D-12, 440 hp at s.l.
DIMENSIONS: Span 38'4", Lg. 23'11", Ht. 9'4", Wing Area 250 sq. ft.
WEIGHT: Empty 2271 lb., Gross 3176 lb. Fuel 65 gal.
PERFORMANCE: Speed- Top 151 mph at s.1., Stalling 63 mph. Service Ceiling 20,700', Absolute Ceiling 22,000', Climb 1690'/1 min. Endurance 2.4 hours at 145 mph.

FOKKER PW-7 (3rd prototype)

DORNIER Falke at McCook Field

Tests with two versions of the Liberty engine were made in 1924. When fitted with an experimental Type F turbosupercharger and a radiator in the top wing, the top speed increased from 125 mph at sea level to 150 mph at 20,300 ft., and a ceiling of 29,462 feet was reached on March 27, 1924. When tested with a conventional Liberty and nose radiator in November 1924, only 129 mph at sea level and 123 mph at 6,500 feet was achieved, too slow for success. A second prototype was finished as the XCO-5.

ENGINEERING DIV. TP-l (with turbosupercharger)
Liberty 12, 415 hp
DIMENSIONS: Span 36', Lg. 25'1", Ht. 10' Wing Area 375 sq. ft.
WEIGHT: Empty 2787 lb., Gross 4416 lb. Fuel 93 gal.
PERFORMANCE: Speed- Top 125 mph at s.1., 132 mph at 6500', 150 mph at 20,000'. Service Ceiling 20,300', Absolute Ceiling 29,462', Climb 6500'/6.5 min. Range 380 miles.

None of these 16 pursuit types planes tested by the Army were good enough to win production contract, and the need to replace the old MB-3As was growing.

Curtiss Army Hawks versus Boeing biplanes

For several years, the Curtiss Hawk became the dominant Army fighter type, until vigorous competition from Boeing elbowed these single-seaters aside. The Curtiss company's engineers at Garden City, New York, began a fighter design in May 1922 using the 440-hp Curtiss D-12 and streamlined "eversharp pencil" nose developed in the Curtiss racer series.

ENGINEERING DIV. TP-1
Liberty 12, 423 hp
DIMENSIONS: Span 36', Lg. 25'1", Ht. 10', Wing Area 375 sq. ft.
WEIGHT: Empty 2748 lb., Gross 4363 lb. Fuel 93 gal.
PERFORMANCE: Speed- Top 129 mph at s.l., 123 mph at 6500', Stalling 63 mph. Service Ceiling 13,450', Absolute Ceiling 15,200', Climb 6500'/9.2 min. Endurance 3.6 hours at 117 mph.

Other features were wood-covered wings with a thin Curtiss airfoil, connected by two pairs of steel "N" struts. The welded steel tube fuselage was covered by dural back to the cockpit and fabric in the rear and tail. Engine cooling was by brass water radiators on the upper wing. Two .30-caliber guns with 600 rounds each were mounted under the cowl, unless the right-hand one was replaced by a .50-caliber gun with 200 rounds.

The first Curtiss PW-8 was built with company funds, flown in January 1923, and was sold to the Army on April 27, 1923, with two more prototypes to be built later. It became the XPW-8 when the Air Service adopted the X prefix on May 14, 1924, as the symbol for experimental planes. Twenty-five PW-8 production models were ordered September 14, 1923.

The second prototype was tested at McCook in March 1924 with landing gear and wing refinements also used on production PW-8s delivered from June to August 1924. Made famous by Lieutenant Russell L. Maughan's "dawn to dusk" 22-hour transcontinental flight on June 24, 1924, the PW-8 demonstrated an Air Service capability of moving squadrons from one coast to the other. The wing radiators were the least desirable feature of the Army's last double-bay biplane fighter, for maintenance was poor and a puncture in their wide area might subject the pilot to a stream of hot water.

CURTISS XPW-8 (First prototype)
Curtiss D-12, 440 hp
DIMENSIONS: Span 32', Lg. 22'6", Ht. 8'8", Wing Area 265 sq. ft.
WEIGHT: Empty 1879 lb., Gross 2784 lb. Fuel 75 gal.
PERFORMANCE: Speed- Top 169 mph at s.l., 160 mph at 10,000', Landing 70 mph. Service Ceiling 27,150', Absolute Ceiling 28,600', Climb 2500'/1 min. Endurance 2.8 hours.

Boeing was also eager to provide the replacement for the MB-3A fighters built by the Seattle firm in 1922. Model 15, first flown June 2, 1923, had single-bay tapered wooden wings with a thick Goettingen 436 airfoil, Curtiss D-12 engine, a tunnel radiator, cross-axle landing gear and an arc-welded steel tube fuselage structure that owed much to through study of the Fokker D VII. Delivered to McCook Field in June, it soon showed an advantage in maneuverability over the Curtiss and Fokker designs, so the Army purchased the Boeing as the PW-9 on September 29, 1923, along with ordering two more prototypes. Armament was the same two guns in the nose as on the Curtiss fighters.

CURTISS XPW-8 (2nd prototype)
Curtiss D-12 (Low-Compression), 438 hp
DIMENSIONS: Span 32' Lg. 22'6", Ht. 8'10", Wing Area 267 sq. ft.
WEIGHT: Empty 2191 lb., Gross 3151 lb. Fuel 75 gal.
PERFORMANCE: Speed- Top 168 mph at s.l., 163 mph at 6500', Landing 63 mph. Service Ceiling 20,350', Absolute Ceiling 21,500', Climb 1830'/1 min., 10,000'/7.4 min. Endurance 2.75 hours at 159 mph.

These two modified XPW-9s were delivered May 6, 1924, and while performance varied on different tests with changes in propeller and weight, comparative testing against the Curtiss design won Boeing a contract for 12 PW-9s on September 19, increased to 30 on December 16, 1924.*

Deliveries of the PW-9, which had split-axle landing gear, were made from October to December 1925, and were followed by 25 similar PW-9As delivered from June 1926 to February 1927 with the D-12C engine. The last of these became the PW-9B when temporarily fitted with a D-12D, which also powered 40 strengthened PW-9Cs delivered from July to August 1927. Last came 16 PW-9Ds ordered August 12, 1927 and delivered in April/May 1928.

Additional weight such as wheel brakes, reduced performance below that of earlier models and required a balanced rudder, but still the Boeing fighters were usually

*Eight different PW-9 and five different PW-8 Official Performance Tests were seen in Army files; those cited here seem most representative.

SDAM

CURTISS PW-8 (First production article)
Curtiss D-12, 440 hp
DIMENSIONS: Span 32', Lg. 22'6", Ht. 8'10", Wing Area 279 sq. ft.
WEIGHT: Empty 2191 lb., Gross 3151 lb. Fuel 75 gal.
PERFORMANCE: Speed- Top 165 mph at s.l., 162 mph at 6,500', Landing 61 mph. Service Ceiling 21,700', Absolute Ceiling 23,300', Climb 10,000'/9 min. Endurance 2.75 hours at 160 mph. Range 440 miles.

considered a bit more maneuverable than the Curtiss types. Total PW-9 production, after the three prototypes, was 111, most of them serving with the overseas squadrons, and Boeing sold the similar FB series to the Navy.

Curtiss responded to Boeing's challenge by rebuilding the third XPW-8 prototype by August 1924 as the XPW-8A with shorter single-bay wings like those of the PW-9. At first the radiator was put in the XPW-8A wing's center section, but then a tunnel radiator under the engine, again like the Boeing's, was fitted for competitive flight tests in October. Top speed was greatly improved, but the Boeing's maneuverability advantage remained.

AMC

BOEING XPW-9
Curtiss D-12, 440 hp
DIMENSIONS: Span 32'1", Lg. 22'10", Ht. 8'9", Wing Area 253 sq. ft.
WEIGHT: Empty 2011 lb., Gross 2971 lb. Fuel 69 gal.
PERFORMANCE: Speed- Top 161 mph at s.1., 154 mph at 6500', Landing 64 mph. Service Ceiling 22,000', Absolute Ceiling 22,850', Climb 2055'/1 min., 10,000'/6.7 min. Endurance 2.83 hours at 150 mph.

In December 1924, the same prototype was ordered converted to the XPW-8B with new tapered wings. Designed by George Page, Jr., the new Clark Y airfoil wings and tail became standard on future Curtiss Hawks from the P-l to P-23. The P-ls ordered into production parallel with the Boeing PW-9 in March 1925 were nearly identical to the XPW-8B prototype.

While Boeing and Curtiss had profitable results from their fighter initiatives, the Thomas-Morse company at Ithaca, New York, would lose money on its efforts. All-metal construction was boldly tried on the TM-23 single-seat

PMB

BOEING XPW-9 (3rd prototype)
Curtiss D-12, 448 hp
DIMENSIONS: Same as PW-9.
WEIGHT: Empty 2052 lb., Gross 3015 lb. Fuel 75 gal.
PERFORMANCE: Speed- Top 163 mph at s.l., 159 mph at 6,500', Landing 64 mph. Service Ceiling 21,000', Absolute Ceiling 22,600', Climb 10,000'/9.1 min. Endurance 2.6 hours at 156 mph.

PMB

BOEING PW-9 (First production model)
Curtiss D-12, 430 hp
DIMENSIONS: Span 32'1", Lg. 22'10", Ht. 8'8", Wing Area 242 sq. ft.
WEIGHT: Empty 2166 lb., Gross 3020 lb. Fuel 62 gal.
PERFORMANCE: Speed- Top 165 mph at s.l., 160 mph at 10,000', Landing 65 mph. Service Ceiling 20,175', Absolute Ceiling 21,400', Climb 1710'/1 min., 10,000'/7.8' min. Endurance 2.6 hours at top speed. Range 437 miles

biplane with the same Curtiss D-12, a short corrugated aluminum fuselage, and small wings joined by "I" struts. But many difficulties interrupted company tests in 1924.

The same construction was used by the Thomas-Morse TM-24 two-seat fighter tested at McCook Field in February 1925 with a 440-hp Curtiss D-12 cooled by radiators in the wing roots. This biplane's upper wing was smaller than the lower wing, and was supported by an ugly arrangement of "V" and "N" struts.

BOEING PW-9C

BOEING PW-9D
Curtiss D-12, 430 hp
DIMENSIONS: Span 32', Lg. 24'2", Ht. 8'8", Wing Area 241 sq. ft.
WEIGHT: Empty 2328 lb., Gross 3234 1b. Fuel 62 gal.
PERFORMANCE: Speed- Top 155 mph at s.1., 152 mph at 5000', Cruising 124 mph, Landing 63 mph. Service Ceiling 18,230', Absolute Ceiling 19,600', Climb 1456'/1, 10,000'/9.5 min. Endurance 2.87 hours. Range 396 miles

PMB

CURTISS PW-8A
Curtiss D-12, 440 hp
DIMENSIONS: Span 30', Lg. 22'6", Ht. 8', Wing Area 255 sq. ft.
WEIGHT: Empty 2007 lb., Gross 2830 lb. Fuel 53 gal.
PERFORMANCE: Speed- Top 178 mph at s.1., 171 mph at 6500', Landing 68 mph. Service Ceiling 22,250', Absolute Ceiling 23,400', Climb 10,000'/6.91 min. Endurance 2 hours at 169 mph.

Since the first version of the single-seat TM-23 was unsuccessful, it was rebuilt with a new strut system and the radiator under the fuselage, but official performance tests in March 1926, brought complaints that the TM-23 flew badly and had too high a landing speed. No Army contract or designation was given either effort, so the company lost over $77,000 on the TM-23 and $46,000 on the TM-24, showing how risky expensive technical innovation was for a small company competing against large ones. The day of the all-metal fighter waited for better aluminum technology.

AMC

CURTISS XPW-8B
Curtiss D-12, 435 hp
DIMENSIONS: Span 31'6", Lg. 22'2", Ht. 8'6", Wing Area 250 sq. ft.
WEIGHT: Empty 2032 lb., Gross 2802 lb., Max. 2926 lb. Fuel 50+50 gal.
PERFORMANCE: Speed- Top 167 mph at s.1. (162 mph with drop tank), 163 mph at 5000', Landing 61 mph. Service Ceiling 21,400', Absolute Ceiling 22,600', Climb 10,000'/7.3 min. Endurance 1.6 to 3.2 hours.

As Boeing's PW-9 series made progress, and Thomas-Morse tried unsuccessfully to get some fighter business, production on the popular Curtiss Hawks began with ten P-ls ordered March 7, 1925, starting the fighter designation

AMC

THOMAS-MORSE TM-23
Curtiss D-12, 440 hp
DIMENSIONS: Span 23', Lg. 16'8", Wing Area 200 sq. ft.
WEIGHT: Empty 1918 lb., Gross 2706 lb. Fuel 61 gal.
PERFORMANCE: Speed- Top 167 mph at s.1., 150 mph at 15,000', Landing 80 mph. Service Ceiling 20,150', Absolute Ceiling 21,275', Climb 10,000'/7.3 min. Endurance 2.25 hours at 125 mph.

series that continued until 1962. Essentially a refined PW-8B with a 435-hp V-1150-1 (the new Curtiss D-12 engine designation), the P-l, delivered from August to October 1925, had fabric covering over wooden wing spars and a steel-tube rear fuselage and tail. A 50-gallon main tank could be supplemented by a 50-gallon auxiliary tank attached behind the tunnel radiator, increasing endurance from two to four hours. Armament remained one .30 and one .50-caliber fixed gun.

ARC

THOMAS-MORSE TM-24
Curtiss D-12, 440 hp
DIMENSIONS: Span 30', Lg. 20'5", Wing Area 237 sq. ft.
WEIGHT: Empty 1969 lb., Cross 3470 lb. Fuel 84 gal.
PERFORMANCE: Speed- Top 143 mph at s.1., 138 mph at 15,000', Landing 63 mph. Service Ceiling 15,600', Absolute Ceiling 17,000', Climb 1178'/1 min., 5000'/5.1 min. Endurance 2.75 hours at 114 mph.

Twenty-five similar P-lAs ordered September 9, 1925, were delivered beginning in April 1926, and 25 P-lBs were purchased August 17, 1926. Deliveries from Garden City began in November on the P-lB with a V-1150-3, larger wheels and improved radiator. A V-1150-5 and wheel brakes distinguished 33 P-lCs ordered October 3, 1928, and delivered from January to April 1929.

AF

CURTISS P-1B
Curtiss V-1150-3, 435 hp
DIMENSIONS: Span 31'0", Lg. 22'8", Ht. 8'11", Wing Area 250 sq. ft.
WEIGHT: Empty 2105 lb., Gross 2932 lb., Max. 3562 lb. Fuel 50+50 gal.
PERFORMANCE: Speed- Top 159.6 mph at s.l., 153 mph at 10,000', Cruising 127 mph, Landing 57 mph.Service Ceiling 21,400', Absolute Ceiling 22,900', Climb 1,540'/1 min., 10.000'/8.6 min. Range 414 miles

CURTISS P-1
Curtiss V-1150-1, 435 hp
DIMENSIONS: Span 31'7", Lg. 22'10", Ht. 8'7", Wing Area 250 sq. ft.
WEIGHT: Empty 2058 lb., Gross 2846 lb., Max. 3238 lb. Fuel 50+50 gal.
PERFORMANCE: Speed- Top 163 mph at s.1., 159 mph at 5000', 153 mph at 10,000', Cruising 136 mph, Landing 59 mph. Service Ceiling 22,500', Absolute Ceiling 23,800', Climb 1810'/1 min., 5000'/3.1 min., 10,000'/7.2 min. Endurance 2.46 hours at top speed. Range 400 miles.

CURTISS P-1A
Curtiss V-1150-1, 435 hp
DIMENSIONS: As P-l
WEIGHT: Empty 2041 lb., Gross 2866 lb. Fuel 50+50 gal.
PERFORMANCE: Speed- Top 160 mph at s.l., 155 mph at 10,000', Cruising 128 mph, Service Ceiling 20,200', Absolute Ceiling 21,350', Climb 2170'/1 min., 5000'/2.6 min.

Tests indicated that continuous increments of weight had depressed the Hawk's performance. Cost of the P-1C, $9,862 each, was very low compared to today's fighters. Navy Hawks of this type were F6C-3s built at Buffalo, while one P-1A was sold to Japan, and Chile bought eight P-1As and eight P-1Bs in 1927.

PMB

CURTISS P-1C
Curtiss V-1150-5, 435 hp
DIMENSIONS: Span 31'6", Lg. 23'3", Ht. 8'6", Wing Area 252 sq. ft.
WEIGHT: Empty 2136 lb., Gross 2973 lb. Fuel 50 gal.
PERFORMANCE: Speed- Top 154 mph at s.1., 148 mph at 10,000', Cruising 124 mph, Landing 58 mph. Service Ceiling 20,800', Absolute Ceiling 22,300', Climb 1460'/1 min., 5000'/3.9 min. 10,000'/9.1 min.
Endurance 1.32 hours at top speed. Range 203 miles.

In addition, 52 of 71 Hawks built as low-powered AT-4 and AT-5 advanced trainers were converted with D-12 engines in 1929 to P-1D, P-1E, and P-1F fighter trainers used at Kelly Field for advanced students. Standard P-1 pursuits equipped the four squadrons (17, 27, 94 and 95) of the First Pursuit Group.

While these Hawks went into service, the same basic airframe tested other engine arrangements. Five Curtiss P-2s bought on the first P-1 contract and flown in December 1925, had the 505-hp Curtiss V-1400. Like most previous types, this was a water-cooled inline engine, but the Curtiss XP-3 was the last P-1A set aside in October 1926 for a 400-hp air-cooled Curtiss R-1454 radial.

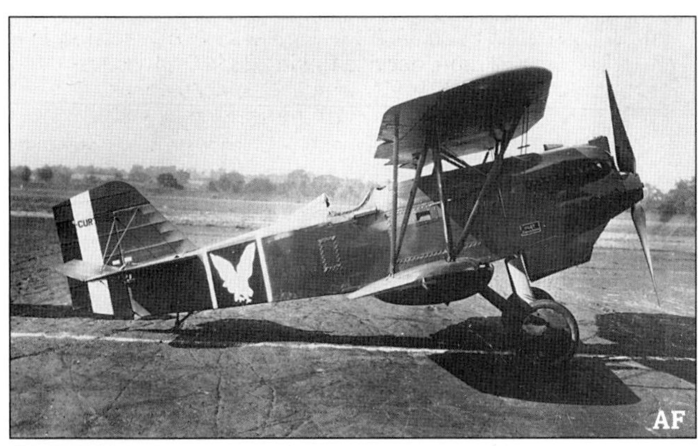

AF

CURTISS P-2
Curtiss V-1400, 505 hp
DIMENSIONS: Span 31'7", Lg. 22'10", Ht. 8'6", Wing Area 250 sq. ft.
WEIGHT: Empty 2081 lb., Gross 2869 lb., Max. 3255 lb. Fuel 50+50 gal.
PERFORMANCE: Speed- Top 172 mph at s.l., 162 mph at 10,000', Cruising 138 mph, Landing 65 mph. Service Ceiling 22,950', Absolute Ceiling 24,000', Climb 2170'/1 min., 5,000'/2.6 min. Endurance 2.33 hours at full speed. Range 401 miles.

But that power plant failed, so a 410-hp Pratt & Whitney R-1340-9 radial was substituted for the XP-3A (project XP-451) delivered in October 1927. Five P-3As with the R-1340-3 had been ordered December 27, 1927, and delivery began on October 5, 1928. Early flights showed that the naked ring of cylinders handicapped performance, but in May 1929, Air Corps engineers at Wright Field* added a cowl with front shutters and prop spinner to the first P-3A, while Curtiss in Buffalo modified the XP-3A the same month with a deeper cowl of their own design.

MFR

CURTISS P-3A
Pratt & Whitney R-1340-3, 410 hp (432 hp effective)
DIMENSIONS: Span 31'7", Lg. 22'5", Ht. 8'9", Wing Area 252 sq. ft.
WEIGHT: Empty 1956 lb., Gross 2788 lb. Fuel 50+50 gal.
PERFORMANCE: Speed- Top 153 mph at s.1., 151 mph at 5000', 148 mph at 10,000', Cruising 122 mph, Landing 58 mph. Service Ceiling 23,000', Absolute Ceiling 24,400', Climb 1742'/1 min., 5000'/3.2 min.
Data applies to standard version without cowl.

AF

CURTISS XP-3A (XP-524)
Pratt & Whitney R-1340-3, 410 hp (440 hp effective)
DIMENSIONS: Span 31'6", Lg. 22'5", Ht. 8'9", Wing Area 252 sq. ft.
WEIGHT: Empty 2107 lb., Gross 2788 lb. Fuel 37 gal.
PERFORMANCE: Speed- Top 171 mph at s.l., 168 mph at 5000', 164 mph at 10,000', Cruising 136 mph, Landing 58 mph. Service Ceiling 23,525', Absolute Ceiling 24,900', Climb 1800'/1 min., 5000'/3.1 min.

*Air Corps testing moved from McCook Field to nearby Wright Field in Dayton Ohio, on October 12, 1927.

MFR

CURTISS XP-3A (XP-451)

Both were known as XP-3A, but the Army version carried the XP-524 project number, and the Curtiss conversion retained the XP-451 number. The former demonstrated a speed increase of from 153 mph to 171 mph on its May 22, 1929, trials and by June 1930, 190 mph had been achieved. Other P-3As were given simple Townsend ring cowls and the two XP-3As that became temporary test beds for the 300-hp R-985-1 Wasp Jr. in December 1930 were labeled XP-21.

AF

CURTISS P-3A (with ring cowl)

AMC

BOEING XP-4
Packard 1A-1500, 510 hp
DIMENSIONS: Span 32', Lg. 23'11", Ht. 8'10", Wing Area 308 sq. ft.
WEIGHT: Empty 2783 lb. Gross 3650 lb. Fuel 100 gal.
PERFORMANCE: Speed- Top 161 mph. Cruising 137 mph, Service Ceiling 22,000', Absolute Ceiling 22,850', Climb 2055'/1 min. Range 375 miles.

Another path of engine development was the turbosupercharger developed by Dr. Sanford A. Moss (1872-1949) of General Electric. After static tests at Pikes Peak in September 1918, flight trials had been made on a LePere fighter in February 1920, and further tests had been made on an MB-2 bomber, the TP-l, a PW-8, and the first P-2.

Boeing also delivered a turbosupercharged high-altitude fighter, the XP-4, in July 1926. Actually the last PW-9 reworked with a 510-hp Packard, four-bladed propeller, a new airfoil section and an enlarged lower wing, the overweight XP-4 was grounded after only 4.5 flying hours. An unusual feature was provision for two .30-caliber guns in the lower wings.

A contract placed April 30, 1927, purchased five Curtiss P-5 Hawks with turbosuperchargers on V-1150-3 engines. Delivery began in January 1928. Except for cockpit heater, oxygen supply, and longer wheel struts for the enlarged propeller, the P-5 was similar to the P-l. The supercharger's weight reduced sea level speed to 146 mph, but 173 mph was attained at 25,000 feet.

PMB

CURTISS P-5
Curtiss V-1150-3, 435 hp to 25,000'
DIMENSIONS: Span 31'6", Lg. 23'8", Ht. 9'3", Wing Area 252 sq. ft.
WEIGHT: Empty 2520 lb., Gross 3349 lb. Fuel 50+50 gal.
PERFORMANCE: Speed- Top 146 mph at s.l., 159 mph at 10,000', 170 mph at 20,000', 173 mph at 25,000', Cruising 117 mph, Landing 62 mph. Service Ceiling 31,900', Absolute Ceiling 32,500', Climb 1150'/1 min., 10,000'/8.4 min., 15,000'/12.4 min., Endurance 1.3 hours at top speed.

Since these superchargers were driven by hot exhaust gases, and compressed frigid high-altitude air, they required metals able to withstand great extremes of temperature. It was to take another decade of work before turbosuperchargers would be reliable enough for production and service.

When the 600-hp Curtiss V-1570-1 Conqueror became available, two Hawks were rebuilt to try it out at the September 1927 air races. The XP-6 was a P-2 with a Conqueror installed, while the XP-6A had a high-compression Conqueror and a P-lA body with XPW-8A wings and wing radiators. At the races, the XP-6A came first with a speed of 201 mph, leaving the XP-6 second place, but it should be remembered that the XP-6A was strictly a racer whose wing radiators had already been found unsuitable

PMB

CURTISS P-6A
Curtiss V-1570-23, 600 hp
DIMENSIONS: Span 31'6", Lg. 23'7", Ht. 8'7", Wing Area 252 sq. ft.
WEIGHT: Empty 2389 lb., Gross 3172 lb. Fuel 50 gal.
PERFORMANCE: Speed- Top 178 mph at s.1., 177 mph at 5000', 173.5 mph at 10,000', 160 mph at 20,000', Cruising 154 mph, Landing 60 mph. Service Ceiling 27,200', Absolute Ceiling 28,400', Climb 10,000'/5.8 min.

for service. Another conversion was the XP-6B, a P-1C built with a Conqueror and a 250-gallon fuel capacity for a July 1929 flight to Alaska.

Eighteen P-6s were ordered with the P-lC on October 19, 1928, and like previous Hawks, were to have water-cooling for their V-1570-17, but in October 1929 the first had a V-1570-23 cooled by ethylene glycol (commercially sold as Prestone). Chemical cooling permitted smaller radiators, and had been tried on modified P-lB and P-lCs. Eight with Prestone coolers were redesignated P-6A, while ten P-6s delivered with the original engines were modified to P-6A standards and used by the 27th Pursuit Squadron.

Cuba ordered three P-6S Hawks in October 1929, but they were delivered in January 1930 with a 450-hp Pratt & Whitney air-cooled radial. An export P-6 with the usual Conqueror engine was called the Hawk I and flown around

PMB

XP-6
Curtiss V-1570-1, 600 hp
DIMENSIONS: Span 31'7", Lg. 22'8", Ht. 8'11", Wing Area 252 sq. ft.
WEIGHT: Empty 2204 lb., Gross 3037 lb. Fuel 50 gal
PERFORMANCE: Speed- Top 176 mph at s.1., 168 mph at 10,000', 143 mph at 20,000', Cruising 141 mph, Landing 61 mph. Service Ceiling 23,110', Absolute Ceiling 24,200', Climb 2271'/1 min., 10,000'/5.7 min.

PMB

CURTISS P-6
Curtiss V-1570-17, 600 hp
DIMENSIONS: Span 31'6", Lg. 23'7" Ht. 8'11", Wing Area 252 sq. ft.
WEIGHT: Empty 2430 lb., Gross 3150 lb., Max. 3310 lb. Fuel 50+50 gal
PERFORMANCE: Speed- Top 176 mph at s.1., 171 mph at 10,000', 144 mph at 20,000', Service Ceiling 22,700', Absolute Ceiling 24,000', Climb 2140'/1 min., 10,000'/6.6 min. Range 260 miles normal, 520 miles max.

CURTISS XP-6A racer

CURTISS P-6 HAWK for Japan

CURTISS XP-6B
Curtiss V-1570-1, 600 hp
DIMENSIONS: Span 31'6", Lg. 23'7", Ht. 8'9", Wing Area 252 sq. ft.
WEIGHT: Empty 2545 lb., Gross 3269 lb. Fuel 250 gal.
PERFORMANCE: Speed- Top 178 mph at s.1., 175 mph at 5000', Cruising 142 mph, Landing 62 mph. Service Ceiling 22,600', Absolute Ceiling 23,800', Climb 5000'/2.7 min. Endurance 1.9 to 3.8 hours max.

Europe in 1930 by Jimmy Doolittle. Eight P-6s bought for the Dutch East Indies in February 1930 were delivered from April to September, and together with six more built in Holland by Aviolande, served the first fighter squadron there until 1937. Mitsubishi purchased another P-6 in March 1930. Incidentally, the Japanese firm's inspector at Curtiss then was Jiro Horikoshi, who later became chief designer of the Zero and earlier Japanese fighters.

No P-6C appeared, but the XP-6D was a P-6A modified by an F-2 turbosupercharger on a V-1570-23. This ship had a two-bladed propeller like most biplanes, but a dozen P-6Ds, converted from February to August 1932 from P-6 and P-6As, had three-bladed propellers whose bite would take better advantage of the turbosupercharger's high-altitude capabilities. They served with the 37th Pursuit Squadron at Langley Field until 1935.

CURTISS HAWK P-6S (Cuba)
Pratt & Whitney R- 1340, 450 hp
DIMENSIONS: Span 31'6", Lg. 22'10", Ht. 8'6", Wing Area 252 sq. ft.
WEIGHT: Gross 2910 lb., Fuel 50+50 gal.
PERFORMANCE: Speed- Top 157 mph at s.1. Service Ceiling 21,800', Climb 1820'/1 min., 12,500'/10 min. Endurance 2.54 hr.

CURTISS HAWK I (export)
Curtiss V-1570, 630 hp
DIMENSIONS: Span 31'6", Lg. 22', Ht. 9'1", Wing Area 252 sq. ft.
WEIGHT: Empty 2542 lb., Gross 3376 lb. Fuel 50+48 gal.
PERFORMANCE: Speed- Top 187 mph at s.1., Cruising 144 mph, Stalling 61 mph. Service Ceiling 22,000' Climb 10,000'/5.7 min. Endurance 1 hour, 40 min. at s.1., 2.5 hours at 15,000'.

CURTISS P-6D
Curtiss V-1570-23, 600 hp
DIMENSIONS: Span 31'6", Lg. 23'7", Ht. 8'7", Wing Area 252 sq. ft.
WEIGHT: Empty 2698 lb., Gross 3483 lb. Fuel 50+50 gal.
PERFORMANCE: Speed- Top 172 mph at s.1., 190 mph at 10,000', 197 mph at 15,000', Landing 63 mph. Service Ceiling 32,000', Climb 1720'/1 min., 15,000;/8.7 min. Range 515 miles.

CURTISS XP-10
Curtiss V-1710-15, 600 hp
DIMENSIONS: Span 33', Lg. 23'3", Ht. 8'8", Wing Area 270 sq. ft.
WEIGHT: Empty 3043 lb., Gross 3975 lb.
PERFORMANCE: No test data located.

Boeing continued to give Curtiss stiff competition for fighter contracts during this period. Like other firms, they had failures as well as successes. The Army ordered that the last PW-9D be fitted with a V-1570-1 Conqueror and that aircraft was delivered as the XP-7 on September 4, 1928.

However, Boeing had also completed a new design, Model 66, in July 1927. With an inverted 600-hp Packard 2A-1530 cooled by a radiator built into the juncture of lower wing and fuselage, this prototype was purchased by the Air Corps on January 27, 1928. Designated XP-8, that design was similar to the Navy's F2B, but was handicapped by an unsatisfactory engine.

Although biplanes dominated the aviation picture, the Army and Boeing signed a $60,000 contract on June 13, 1928, for an XP-9 monoplane with a V-1570-15 engine, and strut-braced gull wings attached to the top of an all-metal stressed skin fuselage, the first since 1922. When the XP-9 was, at last, flown on November 18, 1930, the pilot called it "a menace" due to exceedingly poor vision and dangerous flying qualities.

BOEING XP-7
Curtiss V-1570-1, 600 hp
DIMENSIONS: Span 32', Lg. 24', Ht. 9' Wing Area 241 sq. ft.
WEIGHT: Empty 2323 lb., Gross 3157 lb. Fuel 50 gal.
PERFORMANCE: Speed- Top 167.5 mph at s.1., 163 mph at 5000', Cruising 134 mph, Landing 62 mph. Service Ceiling 21,120', Absolute Ceiling 22,300', Climb 1867'/1 min., 10,000'/7.1 min. Endurance .92 hour at top speed.

BOEING XP-8
Packard 2A-1530, 600 hp at s.l.
DIMENSIONS: Span 30'1", Lg. 23'4", Ht. 8'4", Wing Area 237 sq. ft.
WEIGHT: Empty 2320 lb., Gross 3116 lb., Max. 3422 lb. Fuel 90 gal.
PERFORMANCE: Speed- Top 173 mph at s.1., 172 mph at 5000', Cruising 138 mph, Landing 64 mph. Service Ceiling 23,000', Absolute Ceiling 24,175', Climb 2138'/1 min., 5000'/2.6 min.

BOEING XP-9
Curtiss V-1570-15, 600 hp (583 hp actual)
DIMENSIONS: Span 36'7", Lg. 25'8", Ht. 7'9", Wing Area 214 sq. ft.
WEIGHT: Empty 2694 lb., Gross 3604 lb. Fuel 81-135 gal.
PERFORMANCE: Speed- Top 181 mph at s.1., 179.5 mph at 5000', Cruising 144 mph, Landing 70 mph. Service Ceiling 25,300', Absolute Ceiling 26,400', Climb 2430'/1 min., 5000'/2.3 min. Endurance 1.5 hours at top speed.

BOEING P-12
Pratt & Whitney R-1340-7 (SR-1340C), 450 hp at 5000'
DIMENSIONS: Span 30', Lg. 20'1", Ht. 9'7", Wing Area 227.5 sq. ft.
WEIGHT: Empty 1758 lb., Gross 2536 lb. Fuel 52+47 gal.
PERFORMANCE: Speed- Top 158 mph at s.1., 171 mph at 5000', Cruising 135 mph, Landing 60 mph. Service Ceiling 28,200', Absolute Ceiling 29,600', Climb 2080'/1 min., 10,000'/5.7 min. Range 520 miles.

When the Army ordered the Curtiss XP-10 biplane on June 18, 1928, the specification included an integral geared supercharger. This design's top speed was expected to increase from 191 mph at sea level to 215 mph at 12,000 feet, with a 26,500-foot service ceiling, and have good maneuverability and pilot visibility as well. But when the XP-10 was completed in May 1930 at Garden City, only an unsupercharged sea-level V-1570-15 was installed. The XP-10 also featured plywood wings gulled into the fuselage, and wing surface radiators, but that cooling system was too vulnerable to bullet damage and tests were stopped in October 1930 due to trouble with these coolers, which were not used again.

The next Curtiss design developed the familiar Hawk layout. The XP-11 was to be a P-6 with the experimental 600-hp Curtiss H-1640-1. That engine, flight-tested on the Thomas-Morse XP-13, was a failure, so the XP-11 project, together with a more advanced Curtiss XP-14 designed around that engine, was abandoned. Two of three P-11 airframes ordered in January 1929 were completed as P-6s, while the third became the YP-20.

BOEING XP-12A

Boeing P-12 series

The most successful Boeing fighter family began in June 1928 as the Model 83 biplane, a private venture powered by a 400-hp Pratt & Whitney R-1340C Wasp. Together with the later Model 89, it was submitted to the Navy and became the XF4B-l. Impressed by Navy reports, the Army on November 7, 1928, ordered nine P-12s and one XP-12A for service trials.

First flown on April 11, 1929, the P-12 had a 450-hp R-1310-7 with cylinder fairings and the usual two guns in front of the pilot. Fabric covered the fuselage metal tube framework, but the tail surfaces and ailerons were of corrugated aluminum. Boeing designed its own airfoil section for the wooden wings, as it would for most future projects. The lone XP-12A displayed a deep NACA cowl, new Frise ailerons, and shorter landing gear, but was destroyed in a collision with a P-12 in May 1929 after only four flying hours.

The first air-cooled pursuits widely used by the Army were 90 P-12Bs ordered June 10, 1929, and delivered from February to May 1930 by rail, since Boeing then had no airfield for flyaway delivery. First flown May 30, the P-12B had the XP-12A's ailerons and elevators, but omitted the cylinder fairings.

Meanwhile, Boeing turned out four Model 100 unarmed demonstrators in 1929, civilian P-12s powered by 525-hp SR-1340Ds. One tested at Wright Field in March 1930 showed a top speed of 177.5 mph, or 192 mph when a 10-pound ring cowl was added. The last Model 100 was sold to Japan.

A monoplane development of the P-12 series was Boeing's 202, built with a 525-hp SR-1340D, metal fuselage, and high, strut-braced, metal-covered wing. The model 202 was completed in January 1930, and loaned to the Army for tests on March 10. Designated XP-15, it did 185 mph with a ring cowl on May 3, 1930, and 178 mph when flown with bare cylinders. A curved rudder on an XF5B-l Navy version was later installed on the XP-15, but that aircraft was returned to Boeing without purchase.

BOEING P-12B
Pratt & Whitney R-1340-7, 450 hp at 5000'
DIMENSIONS: Span 30', Lg. 20'3", Ht. 8'10", Wing Area 227.5 sq. ft.
WEIGHT: Empty 1945 lb., Gross 2638 lb. Fuel 50+49 gal.
PERFORMANCE: Speed- Top 157 mph at s.l., 166.5 mph at 5000', Cruising 135 mph, Landing 59 mph. Service Ceiling 27,450', Absolute Ceiling 28,800', Climb 2040'/1 min., 10,000'/5.9 min. Range 540 miles.

Although the XP-15's performance was good, the Army preferred to order 96 P-12C and 35 P-12D biplanes on June 20, 1930. Delivered from August 1930 to February 1931, the P-12C had a 450-hp R-1340-9 under a ring cowl and a crossed-axle landing gear, instead of the older split-axle style. The P-12Ds delivered from February to March 1931 were similar, but for a 500-hp R-1340-17 and different auxiliary tank.

BOEING MODEL 100
Pratt & Whitney SR-1310D, 525 hp
DIMENSIONS: Span 30', Lg. 20'1", Ht. 9'3", Wing Area 227.5 sq. ft.
WEIGHT: Empty 1815 lb., Gross 2597 lb. Fuel 50 gal.
PERFORMANCE: Speed- Top 168 mph at s.1., 192 mph at 8000', Cruising 155 mph, Landing 60 mph. Service Ceiling 29,900', Absolute Ceiling 31,000', Climb 2010'/1 min., 10,000'/15.9 min.

BOEING MODEL 202

The fabric-covered metal tube structure of early P-12 fuselages was replaced by the XP-15's all-metal semi-monocoque body on the Boeing Model 218 first flown September 29, 1930, and tested by the Army in December as the XP-925. Sometimes seen with wheel pants, it became the XP-925A in August 1931 when the 450-hp SR-1340C was replaced by a 500-hp R-1340F, and was also tested by the Navy.

Sent to China for demonstration, it became the first American fighter to combat Japanese planes, but was destroyed near Soochow on February 22, 1932, in the Japanese Navy's first air victory. Pilot Robert Short had attacked three Type 13 three-place bombers from the *Kaga,* killing the commander and wounding the gunner of one,

PMB

BOEING XP-15
Pratt & Whitney SR-1.340D, 525 hp at 8000'
DIMENSIONS: Span 30'6", Lg. 21', Ht. 9', Wing Area 157 sq. ft.
WEIGHT: Empty 2050 lb., Gross 2790 lb. Fuel 50+60 gal.
PERFORMANCE: Speed- Top 163.5 mph at s.1., 180 mph at 8000', Cruising 150 mph, Landing 71 mph. Service Ceiling 26,550', Absolute Ceiling 27,650', Climb 1860'/1 min.

PMB

BOEING 218 (later XP-925)
Pratt & Whitney SR-1340C, 450 hp
DIMENSIONS: Span 30', Lg. 20'5", Ht. 9'1", Wing Area 227.5 sq. ft.
WEIGHT: Empty 1976 lb., Gross 2667 lb. Fuel 50 gal
PERFORMANCE: Speed Top 190 mph at 5000', Cruising 157 mph, Landing 58 mph. Service Ceiling 29,000', Absolute Ceiling 30,000', Climb 10,000'/2.3 min.

SDAM

BOEING P-12C
Pratt & Whitney R-1340-9, 450 hp at 8,000'
DIMENSIONS: Span 30', Lg. 20'1", Ht. 8'8", Wing Area 227.5 sq. ft.
WEIGHT: Empty 1938 lb., Gross 2630 lb. Fuel 50+50 gal.
PERFORMANCE: Speed- Top 178 mph at 8000', Cruising 141 mph, Landing 58 mph. Service Ceiling 26,200', Absolute Ceiling 27,600', Climb 1410'/1 min., 10,000'/6.1 min. Range 580 miles max.

PMB

BOEING XP-925A (Modified 218)
Pratt & Whitney SR-1340F, 500 hp at 10,000'
DIMENSIONS: Span 30', Lg. 23', Ht. 8'10", Wing Area 227.5 sq. ft.
WEIGHT: Empty 1981 lb., Gross 2673 lb. Fuel 50 gal.
PERFORMANCE: Speed- Top 176 mph at s.1., 205 mph at 10,000', Landing 58 mph. Service Ceiling 31,925', Absolute Ceiling 33,000', Climb 2310'/1 min., 10,000'/4.8 min.

PMB

BOEING P-12D
Pratt & Whitney R-1340-17, 500 hp at 7000'
DIMENSIONS: As P-12C
WEIGHT: Empty 1956 lb., Gross 2648 lb. Fuel 50+60 gal.
PERFORMANCE: Speed-Top 188 mph at 7000', Cruising 163 mph, Landing 58 mph. Service Ceiling 25,400', Climb 10,000'/5.8 min. Range 622 miles.

AF

BOEING P-12E
Pratt & Whitney R-1340-17 (SR-1340E), 500 hp at 7000'
DIMENSIONS: Span 30', Lg. 20'3", Ht. 9', Wing Area 227.5 sq. ft.
WEIGHT: Empty 1999 lb., Gross 2690 lb. Fuel 55+55 gal.
PERFORMANCE: Speed- Top 189 mph at 7000', Cruising 160 mph, Landing 58 mph. Service Ceiling 26,300', Absolute Ceiling 27,400', Climb 10,000'/5.8. Range 570 miles.

BOEING P-12F
Pratt & Whitney R-1340-19, 600 hp takeoff, 500 hp at 10,000'
DIMENSIONS: As P-12E
WEIGHT: Empty 2035 lb., Gross 2726 lb. Fuel 55+55 gal
PERFORMANCE: Speed- Top 194.5 mph at 10,000', Cruising 186 mph, Landing 59 mph. Service Ceiling 31,100', Absolute Ceiling 32,400', Climb 2595'/1 min., 10,000'/4.2 min. Range 600 miles.

but when a Type 3 fighter escort joined the fight, Short became the first American pilot killed defending China.

Best-known of the Boeing biplanes became the P-12E, which had the Model 281's metal fuselage. Powered by an R-1340-17, it had a 55-gallon fuel tank behind the engine and a 55-gallon auxiliary belly tank could be added. Like the others in the series, it was armed with two .30-caliber guns, the right one replaceable by a .50-caliber weapon when required. Bomb racks handled five 30 or two 122-pound bombs.

Ordered on March 20, 1931, the P-12E cost $10,197 each. Delivered by train between September 15 and October 15, 1931, the 110 P-12Es were popular with Air Corps pilots for their maneuverability and flying qualities.

BOEING P-12F (with canopy)

Twenty-five P-12F pursuits delivered on the same contract from March 6 to May 17, 1932, had the R-1340-19 Wasp and the last one tested a cockpit canopy. Boeing delivered in total 336 Army P-12 series aircraft, in addition to two 100E (P-12E) fighters shipped to Siam in November 1931, the civilian and export models mentioned and the Navy's F4B series described in Chapter 10.

A number of P-12 models were converted by engine changes. They include the XP-12G, the first P-12B fitted with a turbosupercharger and three-bladed propeller. The XP-12H was a D with a geared Wasp, and the P-12J was an E testing the H Wasp. In 1934, seven P-12Es service testing the first Marvel fuel injection systems became the YP-12Ks, and one trying an F-7 supercharger was briefly designated XP-12L.

Ebb Tide for Biplanes

Thomas-Morse, luckless since the MB-3, again ventured a fighter called the XP-13 after the Army purchased it during flight tests in June 1929. An all-metal biplane with a Clark Y airfoil, "I" struts, and a corrugated metal fuselage, the Viper had an experimental air-cooled 600-hp Curtiss H-1640-1. A twin-row radial with the second row of six cylinders directly behind the first row of six, the engine had cooling difficulties that were not solved until later twin-row radials were introduced with a staggered cylinder arrangement.

THOMAS-MORSE XP-13
Curtiss H-1640-1, 600 hp
DIMENSIONS: Span 28', Lg. 23'6", Ht. 8'5", Wing Area 189 sq. ft.
WEIGHT: Empty 2262 lb., Gross 3256 lb. Fuel 80 gal.
PERFORMANCE: Speed- Top 173 mph at s.1., 170 mph at 5000', Cruising 138 mph, Landing 67 mph. Service Ceiling 20,775', Absolute Ceiling 22,000', Climb 5000'/3 min.

THOMAS-MORSE XP-13A
Pratt & Whitney SR-1340C, 450 hp
DIMENSIONS: As XP-13
WEIGHT: Empty 2224 lb., Gross 3194 lb. Fuel 74 gal.
PERFORMANCE: Speed- Top 188 mph at 5000', Cruising 150 mph, Landing 67 mph. Service Ceiling 24,150', Absolute Ceiling 25,600', Climb 5000'/3.5.

CURTISS XP-17
Wright V-l460-3, 480 hp
DIMENSIONS: Span 31'7",Lg. 22'10", Ht. 8'7", Wing Area 250 sq. ft.
WEIGHT: Empty 2204 lb., Gross 2994 lb. Fuel 43 gal.
PERFORMANCE: Speed- Top 165 mph at s.l., 161 mph at 5000', Cruising 130 mph, Landing 62 mph. Service Ceiling 21,400', Absolute Ceiling 22,800', Climb 10,000'/8 min.

When the XP-13 failed to win a contract, the Thomas-Morse firm was absorbed by Consolidated in August 1929. A Pratt & Whitney Wasp and a new tail were installed on the aircraft by the Army by September 1930, and the fighter redesignated XP-13A.

CURTISS YP-20
Wright R-1820-9, 575 hp
DIMENSIONS: Span 31'6", Lg. 23'9", Ht. 9'2", Wing Area 252 sq. ft.
WEIGHT: Empty 2477 lb., Gross 3233 lb. Fuel 50+49 gal.
PERFORMANCE: Speed- Top 187 mph at s.l., 184 mph at 5000', Cruising 149 mph, Landing 61 mph. Service Ceiling 26,700', Absolute Ceiling 27,800', Climb 2400'/1 min., 5000'/2.3 min. Endurance 1.1 hour at top speed.

Boeing had been doing well in the fight for pursuit contracts, but Curtiss did not let their West Coast competitor capture the field entirely. New versions of the Hawk appeared sporting the latest wrinkles in design. The Curtiss XP-17 was actually the first P-l airframe modified by Army engineers in June 1930 to test the 480-hp air-cooled inverted inline Wright V-1460-3 Tornado. A pair of Curtiss designs, the XP-18 biplane and the XP-19 low-wing monoplane, were planned for the 600-hp Wright V-1560-1, but both were discarded on the drawing board.

CURTISS XP-22
Curtiss V-1570-23, 600 hp at s.l.
DIMENSIONS: Span 3l'6", Lg. 23'7", Ht. 8'9", Wing Area 252 sq. ft.
WEIGHT: Empty 2597 lb., Gross 3354 lb. Fuel 50+50 gal.
PERFORMANCE: Speed- Top 202 mph at s.l., 200 mph at 5000', 195.5 mph at 10,000', Cruising 172 mph, Landing 61 mph. Service Ceiling 26,500', Absolute Ceiling 27,700', Climb 2400'/1 min., 5000'/2.3 min., 10,000'/5.2 min.

The next Curtiss Hawk also had an air-cooled power plant, in this case the Wright R-1820-9 Cyclone. The YP-20 was actually a P-11 completed in October 1930 with this new radial, a ring cowl, and wheel pants. This was a very busy year in pursuit aviation at Wright Field, what with testing the P-6A, XP-9, XP-10, Model 100, P-12B, P-12C, XP-13A, XP-15, XP-16, XP-17, and the YP-20.

The Curtiss XP-22 appeared in May 1931 as a rebuilt P-6A with a V-1570-23 in a neatly streamlined nose, three-bladed propeller, and Prestone cooler between the legs of a single-strut panted landing gear. Flight tests in June demonstrated a 202-mph speed, the highest yet for an Army fighter.

In June 1931, an Army board met to consider the respective merits of the best fighters then on hand: the turbosupercharged XP-6D, the air-cooled P-12D and YP-20, and the liquid-cooled XP-22. The supercharger still seemed unready for squadron service, and the YP-20, while slightly superior in speed and climb to 5000 feet, was inferior to the P-12D in maneuverability and visibility. The XP-22 was the fastest up to 15,000 feet, but was less maneuverable than the Boeing fighters.

While the P-12 was the more acceptable pursuit, the board recommended purchase of 46 P-22s to further development of the liquid-cooled engine in pursuit airplanes, and for "the desirability of giving the Curtiss Company business." Lt. Colonel Henry H. Arnold recommended a contract on July 10, 1931, for 46 Curtiss fighters at $12,211 each, but these aircraft were designated P-6E.

The contract was approved July 24, and by November 4, 1931, Curtiss had assembled a prototype XP-6E by installing the XP-22's engine, nose, and landing gear on the YP-20's airframe. A shallower fuselage, larger headrest, and tail wheel distinguished it from the XP-22. During January 1932 tests, this ship did 198 mph at sea level, but the 45 regular P-6E production ships delivered at Buffalo from December 1931 to March 1932 were less quick. Fifty gallons of fuel were contained behind the V-1570-23 engine with a three-blade Hamilton propeller, and a 50-gallon belly drop tank or two 116-pound bombs on wing racks could be added.

PMB

CURTISS XP-6E
Curtiss V-1570-23, 600 hp
DIMENSIONS: Span 31'6", Lg. 23'2", Ht. 8'10", Wing Area 252 sq. ft.
WEIGHT: Empty 2699 lb., Gross 3392 lb. Fuel 50+50 gal.
PERFORMANCE: Speed- Top 198 mph at s.l., 194.5 mph at 5000', 189.5 mph at 10,000', Cruising 175 mph, Landing 61 mph. Service Ceiling 24,700', Absolute Ceiling 25,800', Climb 2400'/1 min., 5000'/2.3 min., 10,000'/5.3 min. Range 285 miles normal, 572 miles max.

The first P-6E went to Wright Field, as was customary, and 44 went to Selfridge Field for the 17th and 94th Pursuit Squadrons. Famous at the time for their good-looking markings, the Curtiss Hawk was easy to fly, but was usually outturned in mock dog-fights with the lighter P-12Es of the other 1st Pursuit Group squadron, the 27th. Seven P-6Es were lost from February 10 to June 2, 1932, by the 94th Squadron, but these accidents were due to collisions and weather, not the aircraft.

PMB

CURTISS P-6E
Curtiss V-1570-23, 600 hp
DIMENSIONS: Span 31'6", Lg. 23'2", Ht. 8'11", Wing Area 252 sq. ft.
WEIGHT: Empty 2743 lb., Gross 3436 lb., Max. 3797 lb. Fuel 50+50 gal.
PERFORMANCE: Speed- Top 193 mph at s.l., 188 mph at 10,000', Cruising 167 mph, Landing 61 mph. Service Ceiling 23,900', Absolute Ceiling 24,900', Climb 2460'/1 min., 10,000'/5.2 min. Range 572 miles max.

PMB

CURTISS XP-6F
Curtiss V-1570-55, 600 hp at 15,000'
DIMENSIONS: As P-6E
WEIGHT: Empty 3149 lb., Gross 3842 lb. Fuel 50+50 gal.
PERFORMANCE: Speed- Top 183 mph at s.l., 212 mph at 10,000', 225 mph at 18,000'. Service Ceiling not determined. Climb 1400'/1 min., 10,000'/6.1 min. Range 200 miles at top speed.

In March 1933 the XP-6E became the XP-6F when modified with a turbosupercharged V-1570-55, a cockpit canopy and open-sided wheel pants. Top speed of the XP-6F increased with altitude from 183 mph at sea level to 225 mph at 18,000 feet; but engine overheating prevented higher flights, and tests were discontinued on August 1, 1933.

A temporary installation of a V-1570-51 on a P-6E in August 1932 was represented by the XP-6G designation, but more significant was the XP-6H, the first Army multi-

PMB

CURTISS XP-6H
Curtiss V-1570-51, 600 hp
DIMENSIONS: As P-6E
WEIGHT: Gross 3854 lb. Fuel 50+50 gal.
PERFORMANCE: Speed- Top 190 mph at s.1. Service Ceiling 22,800', Climb 2000'/1 min., 13,400'/10 min. Range 256 miles.

gun single-seater. Two .30-caliber synchronized guns, with 600 rpg, had been standard on pursuit ships since 1918, the only difference on the P-6E being that the guns were lowered from their usual position on the cowl, to fire through troughs below the exhaust stacks. But the need for more firepower was felt, and a P-1B with another pair of .30-caliber guns in the upper wing had been tested in December 1931.

Conversion of the first P-6E into a six-gun XP-6H, with an additional pair of .30-caliber guns in the upper wing with 600 rounds each, and one with 450 rounds in each lower wing, was approved on September 11, 1932, and completed at Wright Field in April 1933. Wing guns added too much weight for airframe safety and the project was discontinued.

AMC

CURTISS XP-23
Curtiss V-1570-23, 600 hp
DIMENSIONS: Span 31'6", Lg. 23'10", Ht. 9'6",'Wing Area 252 sq. ft.
WEIGHT: Empty 3274 lb., Gross 4124 lb. Fuel 78+50 gal.
PERFORMANCE: Speed- Top 180 mph at s.l., 223 mph at 15,000', Cruising 190 mph, Stalling 70 mph. Service Ceiling 33,000', Climb 1370'/1 min. Range 435 miles normal, 703 miles max.

The last and finest of the Army's 247 Curtiss Hawks was the final aircraft on the P-6E contract. An all-metal monocoque fuselage and tail, with a 600-hp V-1570-23 Conqueror and F-2G turbosupercharger on the left side, and a finely streamlined nose pointed by a three-bladed prop, characterized the XP-23. Delivered April 16, 1932, the XP-23 kept the P-6 wing structure, but raised the upper wing four inches higher. For easier maintenance, open-sided wheel pants were fitted, and later also used on the P-6Es, and the guns were moved back into the cockpit sides.

This good-looking Curtiss resembled Britain's Hawker Fury, and it is too bad that new monoplanes elbowed it out of the way. A company report credited the XP-23 with 223 mph at 15,000 feet. A June 22, 1932, order had the prototype refitted with a geared 600-hp V-1570-27 minus the turbo and a two-bladed prop. Redesignated YP-23, this version had a more prosaic performance.

AMC

CURTISS YP-23

The last biplane fighter to enter service with an Army squadron was also the only two-seat biplane pursuit in production for the Army since 1918. A design competition for

BERLINER-JOYCE XP-16
Curtiss V-1570A, 600 hp
DIMENSIONS: Span 34', Lg. 28'5", Ht. 8'11", Wing Area 279 sq. ft.
WEIGHT: Empty 2756 lb., Gross 3927 lb. Fuel 78 gal.
PERFORMANCE: Speed- Top 176 mph at s.l., 186 mph at 5000', Cruising 148 mph, Landing 68 mph. Service Ceiling 26,200', Absolute Ceiling 28,000', Climb 2260'/1 min., 5000'/2.6 min.

two-seat fighters was held in April 1929, and Berliner-Joyce was chosen over Boeing and Curtiss proposals for a prototype contract on June 19. The first two-seat fighter since the TM-24, the Berliner-Joyce XP-16 arrived at Wright Field by September 1, 1930. A 600-hp Curtiss V-1570A Conqueror turned a two-bladed prop above the tunnel radiator, and biplane Clark Y airfoil wings were gulled into the fuselage. Armament included two .30-caliber nose guns, a flexible .30-caliber rear gun, and two 122-pound bombs.

A three-bladed propeller distinguished 25 YP-16s first ordered March 31, 1931. The first arrived at Wright Field by March 1, 1932, and the others went to the 94th Pursuit Squadron, which passed its P-6Es on to the 33rd Squadron. Redesignated PB-l (pursuit-biplace) in 1935, P-16s had better endurance than contemporary single-seaters, but were handicapped by low speed and bad visibility for landing.

As the biplane period drew to an end, Army pursuit strength had increased from 12 squadrons in 1931 to 20

BERLINER-JOYCE YIP-16
Curtiss V-1570-25, 600 hp
DIMENSIONS: Span 34', Lg. 28'2", Ht. 9', Wing Area 279 sq. ft.
WEIGHT: Empty 2803 lb., Gross 6996 lb. Fuel 85+75 gal.
PERFORMANCE: Speed- Top 175 mph at s.1., 172 mph at 5000', 167 mph at 10,000', Cruising 151 mph, Landing 66 mph. Service Ceiling 21,600', Absolute Ceiling 22,800', Climb 1970'/1 min., 5000'/2.9 min., 10,000'/6.7 min. Range 423 miles normal, 720 miles max.

squadrons in 1933. These included one squadron each of P-6E, P-12E and P-16s (the 17th, 27th and 94th Squadrons) with the 1st Pursuit Group at Selfridge, while the 8th Pursuit Group at Langley had the 33rd Squadron with the P-6E, the 37th with the P-6D, and the 35th and 36th with P-12s.

Boeings were also used by the 17th Pursuit Group (34th, 73rd, and 95th Squadrons) at March Field, and the 20th Pursuit Group (55th, 77th, and 79 Squadrons) at Barksdale Field. Older P-12s equipped the overseas units: the 3rd Squadron in the Philippines, the 16th Pursuit Group (24th, 29th, 74th and 78th Squadrons) in the Canal Zone, and the 18th Pursuit Group (6th and 19th Squadrons) in Hawaii. Finally, there were the elderly pursuit-trainers at Kelly Field.

CHAPTER 6
OBSERVATION AND ATTACK AIRCRAFT, 1922-1933

PMB

GALLAUDET CO-l
Liberty 12A, 420 hp
DIMENSIONS: Span 56'2", Lg. 33'8", Ht. 10'2", Wing Area 492 sq. ft.
WEIGHT: Empty 3042 lb., Gross 4751 lb. Fuel 117 gal.
PERFORMANCE: Speed- Top 121 mph at s.l.

Experiments in Corps Observation, 1922-1924

For the top Army leadership, the most important role of aviation was still that of the observation squadrons. Improvements in speed or firepower were secondary to the ability to respond to needs of the ground units. A prototype development program of two-seat Corps Observation (CO) aircraft, aimed at missions up to 12 miles behind the enemy lines, explored the technical means of serving artillery and infantry forces.

All of these prototypes were Liberty-powered biplanes, except the first, the CO-l. Designed by I. M. Laddon, of the Engineering Division, the CO-l was the Army's first all-metal, high-wing monoplane. Two prototypes were built at McCook Field, one for static test, and the other first flown on July 26, 1922. Two crewmen were carried along with 287 pounds of observation equipment and 300 pounds of defensive armament; two fixed Browning and two flexible Lewis guns.

AF

ENGINEERING DIVISION CO-l
Liberty 12, 390 hp
DIMENSIONS: Span 55'9", Lg. 33'7", Ht. 10'4", Wing Area 480 sq. ft.
WEIGHT: Empty 2977 lb., Gross 4751 lb. Fuel 119 gal.
PERFORMANCE: Speed - Top 118 mph at s.l., 114 mph at 6500', 111 mph at 10,000', Stalling 58 mph. Service Ceiling 16,000', Absolute Ceiling 18,400', Climb 775'/1 min., 10,000'/18.6 min. Endurance 4.6 hours. Range 510 miles at 111 mph.

On June 22, 1922, Gallaudet received a contract to develop a production version, because of Gallaudet's work on the low-wing, all-metal DB-l bomber. Their CO-l version, improved with balanced ailerons and strengthened landing gear, first flew June 20, 1923, but only one example was built. The wing arrangement was considered bad for the observer's vision, so a projected CO-3 replacing the corrugated dural skin with fabric-covering was dropped.

The Engineering Division also built a conventional biplane in 1922, the CO-2, designed by Jean A. Roche with the usual Liberty, four guns, and fabric covering, but that prototype crashed during tests.

AF

ENGINEERING DIVISION CO-2
Liberty 12, 390 hp
DIMENSIONS: Span 41'1", Lg. 30'9", Ht. 10'9", Wing Area 402 sq. ft.
WEIGHT: Empty 2669 lb., Gross 4084 lb. Fuel 89 gal.
PERFORMANCE: Speed- Top 115.5 mph at s.l., 124.5 mph at 10,000'. Service Ceiling 21,250', Absolute Ceiling 23,300', Climb 550'/1 min., 10,000''/17.1 min. Endurance 4 hours, Range 500 miles.

General Mitchell had visited the Fokker factory in the Netherlands and saw the C IV, a two-seat biplane based on the D VII fighter, but powered by a Liberty engine. One was imported and, after tests, purchased May 29, 1922, along with two more. Designated CO-4 by the Air Service, it had the typical Fokker style steel-tube, fabric-covered fuselage, wooden cantilever wing structure with N struts, and square nose radiator. The main gas tank was between the wheels, a feature intended to protect the crew in case of fire.

However, that would be a hazard in a crash landing, and was not used on the two CO-4s delivered in 1923 with

FOKKER CO-4A
Liberty 12A, 423 hp
DIMENSIONS: Span 39'6", Lg. 30'4", Ht. 10'7", Wing Area 407 sq. ft.
WEIGHT: Empty 3140 lb., Gross 4694 lb. Fuel 92 gal.
PERFORMANCE: Speed - Top 134 mph at s.l., 121 mph at 10,000', Landing 58 mph. Service Ceiling 14,950', Absolute Ceiling 17,060', Climb 820'/1 min., 10,000'/18.4 min. Endurance 3.7 hours.

a rounded radiator, larger tail, and other changes to meet Air Service standards. Five CO-4A two-seaters were delivered in 1924 with a streamlined nose and side radiators that could be extended as the temperature required. Three of these planes were service tested at Langley Field, armed with one fixed .30-caliber Browning and the usual two Lewis guns.

The last Fokker observation biplane tested by the Army was the Atlantic AO-l built by the New Jersey factory affiliated with Fokker. Essentially it was a CO-4 refinement with the circular radiator and was tested October 7, 1924.

Another foreign design tried in 1924 was the Cox-Klemin CO, a modified Heinkel HD 17 powered by a British 450-hp Napier Lion with internal supercharger. It was labeled the CK CO-2 and had no provisions for military equipment during Army tests.

FOKKER CO-4 (1922 version)
Liberty 12A, 420 hp
DIMENSIONS: Span 39'4", Lg. 29'2", Ht. 10'10", Wing Area 417 sq. ft.
WEIGHT: Empty 2911 lb., Gross 4494 lb. Fuel 90 gal.
PERFORMANCE: Speed- Top 131 mph at s.l., 122.6 mph at 10,000', Stalling 67 mph. Service Ceiling 16,100', Absolute Ceiling 17,900', Climb 990'1 min., 10,000'/ 14,8 min. Endurance 3 hours, Range 367 miles.

FOKKER CO-4 (1923 version)
Liberty 12A, 417 hp
DIMENSIONS: Span 39'6", Lg. 29'8", Ht. 10'10", Wing Area 417 sq. ft.
WEIGHT: Empty 3018 lb., Gross 4493 lb. Fuel 90 gal.
PERFORMANCE: Speed- Top 132 mph at s.l., 119.6 mph at 10,000', Landing 58 mph. Service Ceiling 16,550', Absolute Ceiling 18,700', Climb 875'/1 min., 10,000'/16.1 min. Endurance 3.3 hours, Range 398 miles.

The Engineering Division next offered the CO-5, which used the wings of the second TP-l fighter, but reversed them, putting the larger one above the fuselage to improve visibility downward. The first version was tested in October 1923 with 375-square-foot, single-bay wings and frontal radiator, but in November 1924 reappeared with wider 438-square-foot wings and a "chin" radiator. The data given here is for this version, but the picture shows the aircraft after a turbosupercharger and wider, two-bay wings were installed to enable it, as the XCO-5A, to set an American altitude record of 38,704 feet on January 29, 1926.

AF

ATLANTIC AO-l
Liberty 12, 435 hp
DIMENSIONS: Span 39'6", Lg. 30'4", Ht. 10'7", Wing Area 397 sq. ft.
WEIGHT: Empty 2967 lb., Gross 4525 lb. Fuel 92 gal.
PERFORMANCE: Speed- Top 135 mph at s.l., 122 mph at 10,000', Landing 58 mph. Service Ceiling 15,300', Absolute Ceiling 16,850', Climb 1050'/1 min., 10,000'/14.25 min. Range 439 miles.

The last Engineering Division prototype was the XCO-6 (by now experimental aircraft had the X prefix). Designed by Jean Roche, it was first fitted with an inverted Liberty, but was tested on November 30, 1924, with a standard engine and chin radiator (later called the XCO-6B),

AMC

COX-KLEMIN CK-CO2
Napier-Lion 450 hp
DIMENSIONS: Span 42'4", Lg. 30'6", Ht. 10'8", Wing Area 420 sq. ft.
WEIGHT: Empty 3021 lb., Gross 4741 lb. Fuel 89 gal.
PERFORMANCE: Speed- Top 144 mph at s.1., 133 mph at 10,000', Landing 55 mph. Service Ceiling 19,150', Absolute Ceiling 20,850', Climb 1230'/1 min., 10,000'/11 min. Range 498 miles.

and finally, became the XCO-6C test bed for an inverted air-cooled Liberty. Performance and flying qualities were said to be excellent, but the double-bay, wire-braced wing was bad for maintenance work. Three guns were provided.

The officer's board which met in December 1924 to evaluate observation planes considered the XCO-6 the best of the observation types discussed here so far, followed in order of merit by the AO-l, CO-5, CO-8 and the Cox-Klemin, but the Board stated that the new Curtiss and Douglas types were "so far superior to all of the others that no consideration should be given to the rest." After this, the Army left all aircraft construction to private firms, and the McCook Field facility limited itself to testing. Since 1918, the Engineering Division had designed and built 27 prototypes, some of which had made important advances in the "state of the art."

AF

ENGINEERING DIVISION CO-5 (original)
Liberty 12A, 416 hp
DIMENSIONS: Span 36', Lg. 26'5", Ht. 9'7", Wing Area 375 sq. ft.
WEIGHT: Empty 2718 lb., Gross 4193 lb. Fuel 75 gal.
PERFORMANCE: Speed- Top 137 mph at s.1., 120 mph at 10,000', Stalling 60 mph. Service Ceiling 16,200', Absolute Ceiling 18,000', Climb 1010'/1 min., 10,000'/14.3 min. Range 360 miles.

AF

ENGINEERING DIVISION XCO-5A
Liberty 12A, 428 hp (turbosupercharger added in photo)
DIMENSIONS: Span 43', Lg. 27'2", Ht. 10'2", Wing Area 438 sq. ft.
WEIGHT: Empty 2869 lb., Gross 4427 lb. Fuel 93 gal.
PERFORMANCE: Speed- Top 133 mph at s.1., 123 mph at 10,000', Stalling 58 mph. Service Ceiling 17,750', Absolute Ceiling 19,500', Climb 1090'/1 min., 10,000'/12.8 min. Range 450 miles.

The observation board also agreed that the worst of the observation types tested was the "very poor" CO-7 that Boeing made by combining a standard DH-4M-l fuse-

MFR

BOEING XCO-7B
Liberty 12 (V-1410) inverted, 420 hp
DIMENSIONS: Span 45', Lg. 30'1", Ht. 10'8", Wing Area 440 sq. ft.
WEIGHT: Empty 3107 lb., Gross 4665 lb. Fuel 93 gal.
PERFORMANCE: Speed- Top 122 mph at s.l., 110.5 mph at 10,000', Stalling 55 mph. Service Ceiling 13,050', Absolute Ceiling 14,850', Climb 810'/1 min., 10,000'/20.5 min. Range 330 miles.

AF

ENGINEERING DIVISION XCO-6
Liberty 12, 428 hp
DIMENSIONS: Span 48', Lg. 29'8", Ht. 9'8", Wing Area 481 sq. ft.
WEIGHT: Empty 3049 lb., Gross 4607 lb. Fuel 91 gal.
PERFORMANCE: Speed- Top 134 mph at s.l., 122 mph at 10,000', Stalling 64.5 mph. Service Ceiling 15,900', Absolute Ceiling 17,450', Climb 1125'/1 min., 10,000'/13 min. Range 440 miles.

AF

ATLANTIC XCO-8
Liberty 12A, 400 hp
DIMENSIONS: Span 45', Lg. 30', Wing Area 495 sq. ft.
WEIGHT: Empty 3065 lb., Gross 4680 lb. Fuel 93 gal.
PERFORMANCE: Speed- Top 130 mph at s.l., 117 mph at 10,000', Stalling 62 mph. Service Ceiling 16,350', Absolute Ceiling 18,000', Climb 1080'/1 min., 10,000'/13.5 min. Range 450 miles.

lage with a tapered wing and new landing gear. Three airframes were made: one without engine for static tests, the XCO-7A with a standard Liberty on November 29, 1924, and the XCO-7B flown with an inverted Liberty.

The last corps observation series aircraft was the Atlantic XCO-8. After that, all observation planes were numbered in a series from O-l to O-63. The XCO-8 was simply a DH-4M-2 with the Loening wings used in the COA-l. Performance was better than on the standard DH-4, but inferior to the other types being considered. Twenty sets of Loening wings were ordered for use on DH-4s in airmail service.

Amphibians

Grover Loening had proposed to the Air Service on September 23, 1923, an amphibian aircraft that would use the same engine and layout as the DH-4B and have superior performance. Realizing the usefulness of such a type, especially to the three overseas observation squadrons in the "islands" and the Canal Zone, the Army ordered a prototype as the XCOA-l.

LOENING COA-l
Liberty V-1650-1, 428 hp
DIMENSIONS: Span 45', Lg. 34'7", Ht. 12'1", Wing Area 495 sq. ft.
WEIGHT: Empty 3440 lb., Gross 5010 lb. Fuel 91 gal.
PERFORMANCE: Speed- Top 119 mph at s.l., 107 mph at 10,000', Cruising 90 mph, Landing 63 mph. Service Ceiling 11,900', Absolute Ceiling 14,160', Climb 630'/1 min., 5000'/9.8 min. Range 308 miles.

The prototype was ready on June 9, 1924, and although the first day's trials ended with a wreck, ten COA-l amphibians were ordered in July. The first was flight delivered January 17, 1925, and immediately lived up to its promise. The wheels folded up by hand crank into the fuselage above the metal-covered hull, an inverted Liberty turned a four-bladed propeller, and while the wing had the DH-4 plan form, the Loening had an improved airfoil section, metal ribs and steel N struts. A Scarff ring around the observer's cockpit could accommodate a Lewis gun for defense, and a fixed M1921 Browning was on the engine cowl.

LOENING OA-lA
Liberty V-1650-1, 428 hp
DIMENSIONS: Span 45', Lg. 35'3", Ht. 12'11", Wing Area 502 sq. ft.
WEIGHT: Empty 3665 lb., Gross 5250 lb. Fuel 90-140 gal.
PERFORMANCE: Speed- Top 124 mph at s.l., Cruising 90 mph, Landing 57 mph. Range 405-630 miles.

Four COA-1s were transferred to the Navy and redesignated OL-2s for the 1925 McMillian Arctic Expedition. Army contracts for 15 OA-lA, 9 OA-lB, and 10 OA-lC amphibians followed. Similar to the OA-l, but for a three-bladed metal propeller, and new vertical tail, they were delivered from October 1926 to February 1928 from the Manhattan factory, and rapidly became famous for their usefulness in exploration, mapping and patrol of the overseas departments. The Army's Pan-American Goodwill Flight begun from Texas on December 21, 1926, by five OA-1As, attracted international attention.

LOENING OA-lC
Liberty V-1650-1, 428 hp
DIMENSIONS: Span 44'11", Lg. 35'6", Ht. 11'11", Wing Area 504 sq. ft.
WEIGHT: Empty 3745 lb., Gross 5316 lb. Fuel 90-110 gal.
PERFORMANCE: Speed- Top 120 mph at s.l., 110 mph at 10,000', Cruising 96 mph, Landing 58 mph. Service Ceiling 13,225', Absolute Ceiling 15,450', Climb 5000'/8.8 min. Range 363 miles at top speed.

The XO-10 was a new Loening version, which was also known as the XOA-2. Powered by an experimental Wright Tornado inverted, air-cooled engine with a two-bladed propeller, it had a single main wheel retracting into the hull's centerline. The XO-10 was flight delivered July 3, 1929, after eight more had been ordered as the OA-2. Performance tests were not completed until November and showed marked degradation of climb at high altitude.

LOENING XO-10
Wright V-l460-1, 480 hp
DIMENSIONS: Span 46'1", Lg. 35', Wing Area 488 sq. ft .
WEIGHT: Empty 3565 lb., Gross 5395 lb. Fuel 145 gal.
PERFORMANCE: Speed- Top 116.5 mph at s.l., 104 mph at 10,000', Cruising 95 mph, Landing 58 mph. Service Ceiling 11,090', Absolute Ceiling 13,650', Climb 533'/1 min., 10,000'/33.7 min.

The eight OA-2s were built at Bristol, Pennsylvania, by Keystone, who had bought Loening's amphibian company, and delivered with the regular retractable twin-wheel gear from June to September 1930. The Tornado engine's output was so poor that it took more than 59 minutes to climb to 10,000 feet, and this engine was never again used in an Army plane. While Keystone then offered an O-37 design as a counterpart of the Navy's Wasp-powered OL-9, none were actually built.

KEYSTONE OA-2
Wright V-1460-1, 480 hp
DIMENSIONS: Span 44'11", Lg. 34'11", Ht. 12', Wing Area 504 sq. ft.
WEIGHT: Empty 3841 lb., Gross 5414 lb. Fuel 90 gal.
PERFORMANCE: Speed- Top 112 mph at s.1., 106.5 mph at 5000', 86 mph at 10,000', Cruising 89 mph, Landing 56 mph. Service Ceiling 8475', Absolute Ceiling 10,725', Climb 5000'/14.1 min.

Although the Army continued buying amphibians with OA designations, they were no longer combat planes with gun mounts, but were ordinary commercial types used for transport and utility service until World War II.

Douglas O-2 Series

The most important event in observation aviation was the work of the officer's board convened to select a standard replacement for the DH-4B. By December 1, 1925, seven officers led by Captain Gerald Brower had begun flight trials on eleven two-seat biplane types.

DOUGLAS XO-2
Liberty V-1650-1, 425 hp
DIMENSIONS: Span 39'8", Lg. 29'6", Wing Area 411 sq. ft.
WEIGHT: Empty 2812 lb., Gross 4427 lb. Fuel 92.5 gal.
PERFORMANCE: Speed- Top 137 mph at s.l., 127 mph at 10,000', Cruising 116 mph, Landing 60 mph. Service Ceiling 16,900', Absolute Ceiling 18,600', Climb 1075'/1 min., 10,000'/13.4 min. Range 408 miles.

What was wanted was a "good general utility ship" for the observation squadrons, and speed was not a major objective. The Liberty engine would be the power plant, although the airframe should be adaptable to more recent units like the Packard. As stated in the board's report, the new type should have these characteristics:

a. Ability to get in and out of small, poor fields easily and safely with comparatively inexperienced pilots.
b. Best possible safety features (flying characteristics, structure, tank location, etc.).
c. Tank capacity sufficient for long cruising range.
d. Good vision for cross-country work in bad weather.
e. Provision for carrying quantities of freight, baggage, etc., on airways, transport and similar work, including the ability to carry varying loads without changing the balance of the airplane.
f. Best possible accommodations, arrangements, vision, gun fire, comfort, etc., in the rear cockpit for observation work, attack work, gunnery training, transformation flying, and passengers on cross-country.
g. Rugged construction, ability to withstand rough handling by inexperienced mechanics, accessibility of parts, ability to stand weathering in all climates.
h. Adaptability to being fitted with skis and pontoons.

DOUGLAS O-2
Liberty V-1650-1, 439 hp
DIMENSIONS: Span 39'8", Lg. 29'7", Ht. 10'10", Wing Area 411 sq. ft.
WEIGHT: Empty 3032 lb., Gross 4785 lb. Fuel 13 0 gal.
PERFORMANCE: Speed- Top 128 mph at s.l., 114 mph at 10,000', Cruising 103 mph, Landing 65 mph. Service Ceiling 12,275', Absolute Ceiling 14,025', Climb 807'/1 min., 6500'/10.9 min. Range 400 miles.

The board was unanimous in recommending that the Douglas O-2 be adopted as the standard observation type, adding:

"This airplane with Liberty engine proved to be without doubt the logical successor to the DH-4B. Its flying qualities appeared to be perfect, it was very maneuverable and controlled beautifully, it could not be made to spin from a stall and when attempts were made to force it in, it brought itself out immediately. It appeared to have no tricks, landed very easily and handled well on the ground. An outstanding characteristic was that each one who flew it felt perfectly at home in it from the first moment. For observation work, the plane was exceptionally good. The angles of vision and of flexible gun fire were excellent, the cockpit location nearly ideal and the arrangement very well worked out. The flexible guns were operated at high speed in dives and zooms with very pleasing results, the slipstream not affecting the accuracy of fire. The pilot's angles of vision were very good for cross-country. In construction, the plane is a very simple and straightforward chrome molybdenum steel tube, wire-braced, fuselage, with single-bay wire-braced wings and wide tread axle less landing gear...."

Douglas had already won Army favor with their successful "World Cruiser" planes of 1924, and the new XO-2's simple and neat proportions seemed to fit its role. Ordered in July 1924, the XO-2 was built by the Santa Monica firm in time for McCook Field tests to be completed December 11. A second airframe for static tests was supplied in May 1925. Fabric covered the usual steel tube fuselage and wood wing structure, and the new Clark Y airfoil was used.

DOUGLAS XO-2 (Short wings)
Packard 1A-1500, 502 hp
DIMENSIONS: Span 36'3", Lg. 29'6", Wing Area 370 sq. ft.
WEIGHT: Empty 2650 lb. Gross 4235 lb. Fuel 106 gal.
PERFORMANCE: Speed- Top 150 mph at s.l., 138 mph at 10,000', Cruising 129 mph, Stalling 60 mph. Service Ceiling 21,200', Absolute Ceiling 23,100', Climb 1075'/1 min., 10,000'/13.4 min. Range 387 miles.

The prototype had a Liberty with a smoothly shuttered chin radiator, but was also tested on January 12, 1925, with the 500-hp Packard lA-1500 and shorter wings. Top speed rose from 137 mph to 150 mph due to the reduced weight and size. That engine seemed unready for service adoption, however, so Liberty engines were specified for 75 production aircraft ordered February 16, 1925. It was the largest contract Douglas had received to date, and the largest Army two-seater contract since 1918.

Production deliveries on the first 45 Douglas O-2s began in January 1926. Normal armament was one .30-caliber M1921 Browning fixed gun over the engine and one or two Lewis guns on the observer's Scarff ring, but when the Third Attack Group became the first to receive the O-2s to replace its DH-4Bs, a pair of .30-caliber Brownings and bomb racks were added to the lower wings.

Aircraft specialized for ground attack were required, and in March 1926, the 46th O-2 was ordered converted to the XA-2 attack (the XA-l designation had been used for a Cox-Klemin ambulance plane). Powered by an inverted Liberty, air-cooled to dispense with the vulnerable water radiator, the XA-2 was armed with six .30-caliber Brownings firing forward, and two flexible Lewis guns for the gunner. Two of the fixed guns were in the nose, two were in the upper wing, two were in the lower wing, and bombs were in internal racks.

AF

DOUGLAS XA-2
Liberty V-1410, 433 hp
DIMENSIONS: Span 39'8", Lg. 29'7", Ht. 11', Wing Area 411 sq. ft.
WEIGHT: Empty 3,179 lb., Gross 4985 1b. Fuel 130 gal.
PERFORMANCE: Speed- Top 130 mph. Climb 800'/1 min.

Eighteen Douglas biplanes were delivered in 1926 as O-2As with night flying equipment and six unarmed O-2Bs had dual controls for use as senior officers' personal transports, while the last five aircraft on the contract were used for power plant development. Douglas also delivered five O-5 seaplanes, an armed twin-float version of the famed Liberty-powered World Cruiser that was used in the Philippines, and Thomas-Morse contracted April 21, 1926, to build an all-metal version of the O-2 called the O-6. The first of five O-6 biplanes was tested at McCook Field May 18, 1926.

Three O-2s with Packard engines were known as the O-7 and first tested April 26, 1926. The O-8 was another O-2 tested in October with a 400-hp Wright R-1454 radial, while the last O-2 became the O-9 with a geared Packard and four-bladed propeller. All five of these aircraft reverted to the normal Liberty engine O-2 configuration after their tests.

Douglas next received a contract for the O-2C, which introduced a new nose flat radiator, and built 46 O-2Cs, two unarmed O-2D transports and an O-2E with modified tail fin. Two more O-2Cs went to a San Diego Marine unit

AF

THOMAS-MORSE O-6
Liberty V-1650-1, 435 hp
DIMENSIONS: Span 39'9", Lg. 28'8", Ht. 11', Wing Area 418 sq. ft.
WEIGHT: Empty 2947 lb., Gross 4734 lb. Fuel 118 gal.
PERFORMANCE: Speed- Top 129 mph at s.1., 116 mph at 10,000', Cruising 101 mph, Stalling 66 mph. Service Ceiling 13,175', Absolute Ceiling 14,825', Climb 892'/1 min., 10,000'/18.6 min. Range 424 miles.

MFR

DOUGLAS O-7
Packard lA-1500, 504 hp
DIMENSIONS: Span 39'8", Lg. 29'6", Wing Area 411 sq. ft.
WEIGHT: Empty 2914 lb., Gross 4708 lb. Fuel 120 gal .
PERFORMANCE: Speed- Top 137 mph at s.1., 131 mph at 10,000', Cruising 110 mph, Stalling 67 mph. Service Ceiling 17,350', Absolute Ceiling 19,125', Climb 1065'/1 min., 10,000'/13.3 min.

MFR

DOUGLAS O-8

as the OD-l, and eight were sold to the Mexican army. There was no O-2F or G model.

The most widely used model was the O-2H, whose new wings had a Goettingen 398 airfoil of German origin and a pronounced forward stagger, along with landing gear and tail refinements. Armament still included the standard fixed M1921 Browning gun, but an M1922 flexible Browning replaced the traditional drum-fed Lewis guns in the rear cockpit.

SDAM

DOUGLAS O-2C (as OD-1)
Liberty V-1650, 439 hp
DIMENSIONS: Span 39'8", Lg. 29'6", Ht. 10'10", Wing Area 411 sq. ft.
WEIGHT: Empty 2941 lb., Gross 4630 lb. Fuel 110 gal.
PERFORMANCE: Speed- Top 126 mph at s.1. Service Ceiling 12,275', Absolute Ceiling 14,025', Climb 10,000'/21.7 min. Range 606 miles.

There were 140 O-2Hs delivered in 1927-29, to both Air Corps and National Guard squadrons, along with three O-2J officer transports and 57 O-2K dual-control basic trainers. The latter were redesignated BT-l for school use and were the last Liberty-powered Army planes to remain in service, not retiring until 1935.

AF

DOUGLAS O-2H
Liberty V-1650, 433 hp
DIMENSIONS: Span 40', Lg. 30', Ht. 10'6", Wing Area 368 sq. ft.
WEIGHT: Empty 2818 lb., Gross 4485 lb. Fuel 113 gal.
PERFORMANCE: Speed- Top 133 mph at s.1., 128 mph at 10,000', Cruising 107 mph, Landing 58 mph. Service Ceiling 17,100', Absolute Ceiling 18,900', Climb 1050'/1 min., 10,000'/13.6 min. Range 512 miles.

Army observation aviation in this period consisted of a twelve-plane squadron for each of the nine continental corps areas and three overseas departments. By January 1930, 19 National Guard squadrons were active, and two School squadrons at Kelly and Maxwell fields got the second-hand aircraft. Douglas O-2 biplanes were used by nearly all of these squadrons by the end of the Twenties.

Curtiss Falcons

While the Curtiss Falcon came second in the observation competition, it seemed to hold first place in the public imagination, possibly both because of its sharp-looking engine cowl and swept-back upper wing and the appropriate name given it by company publicity.

AF

CURTISS XO-1
Liberty V-1650-1, 431 hp
DIMENSIONS: Span 38', Lg. 28'7", Wing Area 350 sq. ft.
WEIGHT: Empty 2460 lb., Gross 4075 lb. Fuel 92-119 gal.
PERFORMANCE: Speed- Top 152 mph at s.l., 136 mph at 10,000", Cruising 126 mph, Landing 63 mph. Service Ceiling 18,700', Absolute Ceiling 20,300', Climb 1235'/1 min., 10,000'/11.1 min. Range 440 miles.

With Packard lA-1500, 510 hp:
WEIGHT: Empty 2277 lb., Gross 3857 lb. Fuel 93 gal.
PERFORMANCE: Speed- Top 154 mph at s.1., 147 mph at 10,000', Service Ceiling 23,400', Absolute Ceiling 24,800', Climb 1725'/1 min., 10,000'/7.4 min. Range 424 miles.

AF

WRIGHT XO-3
Wright V-1950 (T-3) 645 hp
DIMENSIONS: Span 45', Lg. 31', Ht. 10'7".
WEIGHT: Empty 4193 lb., Gross 5997 lb.
PERFORMANCE: Speed- Top 146 mph., Cruising 132 mph. Service Ceiling 18,450', Absolute Ceiling 20,200', Climb 6500'/6.9 min. Range 395 miles.

Designed by Rex Beisel, the XO-l prototype was tested with a Liberty engine by Lt. Harold Harris on November 30, 1924, and showed "remarkably high performance," excellent flying qualities, and "handled exactly like a pursuit plane." Doubts were raised by the observation board about its suitability for "average pilots," and the maintenance of its riveted duralumin tube fuselage structure. The board suggested a service test purchase of the Curtiss type.

On December 1, 1924, the XO-l, like the XO-2, was also tested with the Packard lA-1500, and although the Curtiss competitor's performance was best, no order for that version was placed. The Wright XO-3 tested on January 23, 1925, was a double-bay biplane with an experimen-

CURTISS O-1
This March 1926 construction photo shows the Curtiss Falcon's duralumin tube structure, engine, radiator, oil and fuel tanks, and the blast tube for the M1921 forward gun, before the fabric covering and metal cowl are added.

tal Wright V-1950 engine. It was not purchased by the Army, and the Wright company abandoned efforts at aircraft construction to concentrate quite successfully on engines. Another observation project of the period, a Liberty-powered Martin XO-4, was canceled before completion.

Ten Curtiss Falcons were ordered for service test, the first appearing in February 1926 with the small and neatly cowled Curtiss D-12 (V-1150), while the ninth was tested in October 1926 as the O-lA with a 430-hp Liberty, and another became the XO-11. That Liberty version was first ordered in 1926 for observation squadrons as the O-11. Sixty-six O-11s went into service in 1927-28, armed with the one .30-caliber fixed and twin .30-caliber flexible guns usual on observation planes. They served with the 5th, 12th and 99th Squadrons, as well as with the National Guard.

As for the Army's attack units, a board convened on August 2, 1926 had agreed that the Curtiss was the most suitable model until a more satisfactory type could be developed. On February 2, 1927, 65 Falcons were ordered, and a September contract added 36 more. They were delivered as 76 A-3, 21 O-lB, and four O-lC Falcons, the latter being unarmed official transports.

CURTISS O-1
Curtiss V-1150, 448 hp
DIMENSIONS: Span 38', Lg. 28'4", Ht. 10'1", Wing Area 350 sq. ft.
WEIGHT: Empty 2417 lb., Gross 4165 lb. Fuel 113+56 gal.
PERFORMANCE: Speed- Top 143 mph at s.1., 135.5 at 10,000', Landing 64 mph. Service Ceiling 17,375', Absolute Ceiling 19,100', Climb 1070'/1 min., 10,000'/13.1 min. Range 560 miles at 112 mph.

CURTISS O-11
Liberty V-1650-1, 433 hp
DIMENSIONS: Span 38', Lg. 28'4", Ht. 10'1", Wing Area 353 sq. ft.
WEIGHT: Empty 2887 lb., Gross 4561 lb. Fuel 113+56 gal.
PERFORMANCE: Speed- Top 146 mph at s.1., 134 mph at 10,000', Cruising 115 mph, Landing 64 mph. Service Ceiling 16,630', Absolute Ceiling 18,350', Climb 1066'/1 min., 10,000'/13.6 min. Range 689 miles.

The first A-3 was ready by October 31, 1927. A 435-hp Curtiss D-12D engine was under the smooth cowling, the radiator was underneath, and a neat prop spinner gave the nose the characteristic "Eversharp pencil" appearance. The wood-frame wings used the Clark Y airfoil, with the upper wing swept back from a straight center section, while the lower wings were straight. There were two M1921 Browning guns in the nose, two wing guns firing forward, and two flexible Lewis rear guns. All were .30-caliber, with 400 rounds provided for the wing guns and 600 rounds for the others. Wing racks for 200 pounds of fragmentation bombs were attached, or a 56-gallon auxiliary tank could be carried behind the tunnel radiator.

AF

CURTISS A-3
Curtiss V-1150-3, 435 hp
DIMENSIONS: Span 38', Lg. 28'4", Ht. 10'1", Wing Area 353 sq. ft.
WEIGHT: Empty 2612 lb., Gross 4378 lb. Fuel 113+56 gal.
PERFORMANCE: Speed- Top 141 mph, Cruising 116 mph, Landing 61 mph. Service Ceiling 15,600', Absolute Ceiling 17,300', Climb 1046'/1 min., 5000'/5.8 min. Range 630 miles at top speed.

Weapons were removed and dual controls installed on six A-3s, which became the A-3A trainers. The second A-3 was completed with the new air-cooled Pratt & Whitney Wasp radial and tested in May 1928 as the XA-4. Twenty-one O-lB observation versions were similar to the A-3, but had only one Browning gun firing forward.

MFR

CURTISS XA-4
Pratt & Whitney R-1340-1, 410 hp (421 hp actual)
DIMENSIONS: Span 38', Lg. 28'4", Ht. 10'1", Wing Area 353 sq. ft.
WEIGHT: Empty 2348 lb., Gross 4114 lb. Fuel 113 gal.
PERFORMANCE: Speed- Top 139 mph at s.l., 136 mph at 5000', Cruising 112 mph, Landing 58 mph. Service Ceiling 15,975', Absolute Ceiling 17,700', Climb 1040'/1 min.

The next Falcon contract on June 19, 1929, ordered the A-3B and O-1E versions using the V-1150-5, balanced (Frise) ailerons and elevators, and a .30-caliber M1922 Browning flexible gun in the rear, instead of the drum-fed Lewis guns. Seventy-eight A-3Bs were built on two contracts, the first tested in April 1930 and armed with five Browning guns, 2,700 rounds, and two 116-pound bombs on wing racks. Attack Falcons equipped all four of the Air Corps ground-attack squadrons; the 8th, 13th, and 90th of the 3rd Attack Group at Fort Crockett, Texas, and the 26th Attack Squadron in Hawaii.

MFR

CURTISS O-lB
Curtiss V-1150-3, 435 hp
DIMENSIONS: same as A-3 and O-11
WEIGHT: Empty 2577 lb., Gross 4240 lb. Fuel 113+56 gal.
PERFORMANCE: Speed- Top 140 mph at s.l., 132 mph at 10,000', Cruising 111 mph, Landing 60 mph. Service Ceiling 16,325', Absolute Ceiling 18,350', Climb 1060'/1 min., 10,000'/13.7 min. Range 612 miles.

PMB

CURTISS A-3B
Curtiss V-1150-5, 435 hp
DIMENSIONS: Span 38', Lg. 27'2", Ht. 10'6", Wing Area 353 sq. ft.
WEIGHT: Empty 2875 lb., Gross 4458 lb., Max. 4476 lb. Fuel 113+56 gal.
PERFORMANCE: Speed- Top 139 mph at s.l., 136 mph at 5000', Cruising 122 mph, Landing 60 mph. Service Ceiling 14,100', Absolute Ceiling 16,100', Climb 948'/1 min., 5000'/6.5 min. Range 550 miles.

Similar to the A-3B, but armed with just one fixed and one flexible Browning with 500 rounds per gun, was the O-lE appearing in December 1929. Curtiss built 35 O-lE, one unarmed O-lF transport, and in October 1930, one XO-lG (later Y1O-lG) introducing such refinements as a new rear gun post mount allowing more cockpit room and a recess

CURTISS O-IE
Curtiss V-1150-5, 435 hp
DIMENSIONS: same as A-3B
WEIGHT: Empty 2922 lb., Gross 4347 lb. Fuel 113+56 gal.
PERFORMANCE: Speed- Top 141 mph at s.1., 128 mph at 10,000', Cruising 122 mph, Landing 59 mph. Service Ceiling 15,300', Climb 980'/1 min., 10,000'/14.4 min. Range 550 miles.

to fold the gun away, wheel pants, and tail wheel. The latter was adopted and retrofitted to earlier Falcons, but the pants proved unsuitable for service use.

Thirty O-lG Falcons were ordered January 17, 1931 and delivery began in May 1931. Their equipment included the usual two Brownings, camera, and a 109-pound radio (SCR-134) with a 30-mile range with voice and 150 miles with Morse code.

Since each Army observation squadron was assigned to work on its own with particular infantry corps and divisions, group organization had been limited to the 9th Observation Group formed with the three squadrons (1st, 5th and 99th) based at Mitchel Field, New York. That group was equipped with Curtiss Falcons, which also went to the 12th and 16th Observation squadrons. In October 1930, the 12th Observation Group was activated at Brooks Field, Texas, to control O-l, O-2 and O-l9 squadrons in the western states.

CURTISS XO-lG (Y1O-lG)
Curtiss V-1150-5, 435 hp
DIMENSIONS: same as A-3B, O-lE
WEIGHT: Empty 3143 lb., Gross 4488 lb. Fuel 103+56 gal.
PERFORMANCE: Speed- Top 145 mph at s.1., 136 mph at 10,000', Cruising 116 mph, Landing 61 mph. Service Ceiling 16,750', Climb 1060'/1 min., 10,000'/13.6 min. Range 510 miles.

The Falcon series also included several examples testing new engines. First was the air-cooled-Pratt & Whitney R-1340-1 flown May 21, 1928, on the XO-12, which looked like the XA-4 and had originally been an O-l1 airframe. The Curtiss V-1570-1 Conqueror was introduced in September 1927 on the XO-13 and XO-13A conversions of O-1 airframes, with the XO-13A having wing radiators good for racing, but not service use. There was also an O-13B transport converted from an O-1C, and three YO-13C Falcons with the usual tunnel radiators followed the O-1E off the Curtiss line in August 1930.

The Conqueror engine was adapted for Prestone cooling and used on the XO-16 ordered December 28, 1927, and completed in May 1930. The usual two Brownings were carried, but the rear M1922 gun was on the new fold-away post mount.

An experimental air-cooled Curtiss H-1640-1 engine was tried on the XO-18. The XO-16 and XO-18 were to have attack counterparts as the XA-5 and XA-6, but these projects were canceled. The XO-18 had been converted

AF

CURTISS O-1G
Curtiss V-1150-5, 435 hp
DIMENSIONS: Span 38', Lg. 27'4", Ht. 9'11", Wing Area 360 sq. ft.
WEIGHT: Empty 3090 lb., Gross 4425 lb. Fuel 104 gal.
PERFORMANCE: Speed- Top 143.5 at s.l., 131 mph at 10,000', Cruising 123 mph, Landing 60 mph. Service Ceiling 14,275', Absolute Ceiling 16,075', Climb 910'/1 min., 10,000'/17.5 min.

PMB

CURTISS XO-13
Curtiss V-1570-1, 600 hp
DIMENSIONS: Span 38', Lg. 28'4", Ht. 10'1", Wing Area 353 sq. ft.
WEIGHT: Empty 2637 lb., Gross 4318 lb. Fuel 112 gal.
PERFORMANCE: Speed- Top 164 mph at s.l., 157 mph at 10,000', Cruising 130 mph, Landing 60 mph. Service Ceiling 21,775' Absolute Ceiling 23,300', Climb 1540'/1 min., 10,000'/8.5 min. Range 346 miles.

PMB

CURTISS XO-13A as racer

from the first O-1B, but tests were stopped on July 24, 1930, because the cooling failed. A second O-18 converted from an O-11 was tested in January 1931, but the engine never did work out. The last aircraft on the O-1E contract was completed with a geared, Prestone-cooled Conqueror as the Y1O-26.

The last Air Corps Falcons were ten O-39s with V-1570-25 engines ordered May 12, 1931, and the first ap-

AF

CURTISS YO-13C
Curtiss V-1570-1, 600 hp
DIMENSIONS: Span 38', Lg. 27'6", Wing Area 353 sq. ft.
WEIGHT: Empty 3144 lb., Gross 4542 lb. Fuel 108+56 gal.
PERFORMANCE: Speed- Top 156 mph at s.l., 146 mph at 10,000', Cruising 125 mph, Landing 60 mph. Service Ceiling 19,750', Absolute Ceiling 21,400', Climb 1290'/1 min., 10,000'/10.46 min.

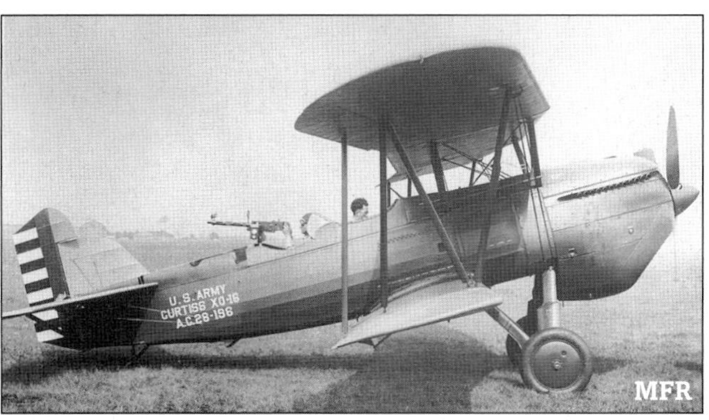

MFR

CURTISS XO-16
Curtiss V-1750-1, 600 hp
DIMENSIONS: same as YO-13C
WEIGHT: Empty 3025 lb., Gross 4305 lb. Fuel 100 gal.
PERFORMANCE: Speed- Top 162 mph at s.l., 156 mph at 10,000', Cruising 130 mph, Landing 59 mph. Service Ceiling, 21,750', Absolute Ceiling 23,300', Climb 10,000'/8.6 min.

AF

CURTISS XO-18
Curtiss H-1640-1, 600 hp
DIMENSIONS: Span 38', Lg. 27'4", Ht. 10'3", Wing Area 353 sq. ft.
WEIGHT: Empty 2814 lb., Gross 4296 lb. Fuel 113 gal.
PERFORMANCE: Speed- Top 148.5 mph at s.1., 142.5 mph at 10,000', Cruising 127 mph, Landing 59 mph. Service Ceiling 17,650', Absolute Ceiling 19,200', Climb 1255'/1 min., 10,000'/11.6 min.

peared in July 1931. They had a smooth engine cowl with small Prestone radiator underneath and a smaller rudder, but the wheel pants and cockpit canopy on the first example were usually removed from the aircraft serving at Mitchel Field. Two Browning guns were fitted, and the

CURTISS FALCON seaplane for Colombia
Wright SR-1820F-2, 712 hp at 3300'
DIMENSIONS: Span 38', Lg. 29'3", Ht. 12'8", Wing Area 348 sq. ft.
WEIGHT: Empty 3660 lb., Gross 4983 lb., Max. 5777 lb. Fuel 103+55 gal.
PERFORMANCE: Speed- Top 178 mph at 3300', Stalling 61 mph. Service Ceiling 22,900', Climb 1530'/1 min. Range 384-680 miles.

CURTISS YIO-26
Curtiss V-1570-11, 600 hp
DIMENSIONS: Span 38', Lg. 27'6", Ht. 10'6", Wing Area 353 sq. ft.
WEIGHT: Empty 3179 lb., Gross 4587 lb. Fuel 109 gal.
PERFORMANCE: Speed- Top 167.5 mph at s.l., 159.5 mph, at 10,000', Cruising 143 mph, Landing 60 mph. Service Ceiling 20,400', Absolute Ceiling 21,800', Climb 10,000'/9.4 min.

CURTISS O-39
Curtiss V-1570-25, 600 hp
DIMENSIONS: Span 38', Lg. 27'7", Ht. 10'11", Wing Area 349.6 sq. ft.
WEIGHT: Empty 3301 lb., Gross 4647 lb. Fuel 103+36 gal.
PERFORMANCE: Speed- Top 174 mph at s.l., 167 at 10,000', Cruising 153 mph, Landing 57 mph. Service Ceiling 22,400', Climb 1550'/1 min., 10,000'/8.3 min. Range 540-730 miles.

drop tank under the fuselage could be replaced by two 116-pound bombs.

Export Falcons

Curtiss also built Falcons for export, beginning with an O-1B type mounted on a single float and flown to Colombia in March 1928. D-12 engines also powered 18 O-1E types delivered to Chile by April 1929, and followed later by another batch (20?)assembled in Chile. Nine of those were sold to Brazil in August 1932, with one lost on the delivery flight, and another taken over by Paraguay.

CURTISS FALCON for Colombia
Wright SR-1820F-2, 712 hp at 3300'
DIMENSIONS: Span 38', Lg. 26'6", Ht. 10'3", Wing Area 348 sq. ft.
WEIGHT: Empty 3261 lb., Gross 4584 lb., Max. 5378 lb. Fuel 103+55 gal.
PERFORMANCE: Speed- Top 182 mph at 3300', Stalling 59 mph. Service Ceiling 24,000', Climb 1650'/1 min. Range 394-700 miles.

Wright R-1820 Cyclone radials powered 23 Falcons completed for Colombia, beginning in May 1933, and used

CURTISS FALCON II
Wright SR-1820F-3, 750 hp at 8000'
DIMENSIONS: Span 38', Lg. 26'6", Ht. 10', Wing Area 348 sq. ft.
WEIGHT: Empty 3447 lb., Gross 4770 lb., Max. 5100 lb. Fuel 103+55 gal.
PERFORMANCE: Speed- Top 205 mph at 8000', Cruising 183 mph, Stalling 60 mph. Service Ceiling 26,000', Climb 1600'/1 min., Range 367-560 miles.

in the Leticia war with Peru. These Falcons had interchangeable landing gear of wheels or twin floats, and had a sliding cockpit canopy. Armament included a .30-caliber gun in the nose, two in the lower wings, another in the rear cockpit, and four 110-pound bombs on racks under the wings.

Bolivia also received nine Cyclone-powered Falcons, beginning in September 1934. Similar, but omitting the two wing guns, they entered the Chaco war against Paraguay, replacing the light Curtiss-Wright Osprey armed trainers previously used. Peru acquired about ten Cyclone Falcons about that time.

The last Falcon built was a prototype with a 750-hp R-1820, streamlined landing gear, full-length cockpit enclosure, and known only as F-1-37, or Falcon II. First flown on November 6, 1934, it was soon destroyed during company tests, and none were sold.

Observation Biplanes, 1928-1931

The next trio of prototypes was designed as light-weight, unarmed two-seaters for training National Guard pilots. Ordered December 12, 1927, and completed around November 23, 1928, the Douglas XO-14 had a Wright Whirlwind, as did the Keystone XO-15 ordered the same week.

In April 1928, a Consolidated PT-3 trainer using the same engine was tested with observation equipment as the XO-17, and it was decided the most economical way of meeting the requirement was by use of standard primary trainers. Twenty-nine O-17s were purchased for the National Guard in 1928, along with one O-17A (R-790-3 engine), ending any need for the XO-14/15 types.

Thomas-Morse received a contract for four all-metal, air-cooled observation biplanes on June 16, 1928, with two more added on December 20. They were constructed of riveted dural tubing with corrugated dural covering the fuselage and control surfaces. The fabric-covered wings had the Clark Y airfoil.

DOUGLAS XO-14
Wright R-790-5, 240 hp
DIMENSIONS: Span 30'1", Lg. 23'10", Ht. 8'8", Wing Area 237 sq. ft.
WEIGHT: Empty 1758 lb., Gross 2500 lb. Fuel 40 gal.
PERFORMANCE: Speed- Top 121 mph at s.l., 113 mph at 10,000', Cruising 100 mph, Landing 53 mph. Service Ceiling 15,250', Absolute Ceiling 17,100', Climb 925'/1 min., 10,000'/16.3 min. Range 250 miles.

KEYSTONE XO-15
Wright R-790-5, 236 hp
DIMENSIONS: Span 37'3", Lg. 27'1", Ht. 9'9", Wing Area 256 sq. ft.
WEIGHT: Empty 1784 lb., Gross 2518 lb. Fuel 40 gal.
PERFORMANCE: Speed- Top 119 mph at s.l., 112 mph at 10,000', Cruising 95 mph, Landing 52 mph. Service Ceiling 16,600', Absolute Ceiling 18,625', Climb 925'/1 min., 10,000'/15.5 min. Range 240 miles.

CONSOLIDATED XO-17
Wright R-790-1, 237 hp
DIMENSIONS: Span 34'6", Lg. 28'1", Ht. 10'3", Wing Area 295 sq. ft.
WEIGHT: Empty 1881 lb., Gross 2770 lb. Fuel 60 gal.
PERFORMANCE: Speed- Top 103 mph at s.1., 91 mph at 10,000', Cruising 83 mph, Landing 52 mph. Service Ceiling 11,880', Absolute Ceiling 14,100'. Climb 636'/1 min., 10,000'/27.4 min.

THOMAS-MORSE XO-19
Pratt & Whitney R-1340-3, 450 hp
DIMENSIONS: Span 39'9", Lg. 28'6", Ht. 9'10", Wing Area 348 sq. ft .
WEIGHT: Empty 2342 lb., Gross 3994 lb. Fuel 112 gal.
PERFORMANCE: Speed- Top 146 mph at s.1., 141 mph at 10,000', Landing 58 mph. Service Ceiling 21,425', Absolute Ceiling 23,000', Climb 1250'/1 min., 10,000'/9.7 min.

THOMAS-MORSE YO-20
Pratt & Whitney R-1690-1, 525 hp
DIMENSIONS: same as XO-19
WEIGHT: Empty 2559 lb., Gross 3907 lb. Fuel 103 gal.
PERFORMANCE: Speed- Top 147 mph at s.1., 140 mph at 10,000', Service Ceiling 22,600', Absolute Ceiling 24,400', Climb 1350'/1 min., 10,000'/9.5 min.

THOMAS-MORSE XO-21
Curtiss H-1640-1, 600 hp
DIMENSIONS: Span 39'9", Lg. 29'2", Ht. 10'4", Wing Area 348 sq. ft.
WEIGHT: Empty 2659 lb., Gross 4280 lb. Fuel 106 gal.
PERFORMANCE: Test data unavailable.

The first prototype was the XO-19 of April 1929, with an R-1340-3 Wasp, fixed Browning gun, and a Lewis gun on the observer's ring, while the R-1340-9 was used on the O-19. Next was the YO-20 in September 1929 with an R-1690-1 Hornet, and the fourth prototype became the XO-21 with a Curtiss H-1690-1, which later changed to the XO-21A with a Wright R-1750. A second prototype contract produced another Wasp-powered O-19 and an O-19A with a smaller, 88-gallon, fuel tank.

Thomas-Morse also produced a prototype with a water-cooled V-1570-1 Conqueror engine. The YO-23 ordered November 3, 1928, was tested September 18, 1929, but lost out to the Douglas O-25 as the Army's Conqueror-powered two-seater.

Another company tried to compete with the O-19 as the Wasp-powered observation type. Chance Vought's O-28 was an Army version of the Navy's O2U-3. Purchased May 5, 1928, off the Vought production line, the O-28 had an R-1340 Wasp C rated at 450 hp, but actually yielding 625 hp. The Air Corps choice, however, was the Thomas-Morse design.

Seventy O-19B aircraft were ordered August 16, 1929, a few days after the Thomas-Morse Company had been

THOMAS-MORSE O-19B
Pratt & Whitney R-1340-7, 450 hp
DIMENSIONS: Span 39'9", Lg. 28'9", Ht. 10', Wing Area 348 sq. ft.
WEIGHT: Empty 2732 lb., Gross 3910 lb., Max. 4233 lb. Fuel 80+40 gal.
PERFORMANCE: Speed- Top 139 mph at s.l., 135 mph at 10,000', Cruising 121 mph, Landing 57 mph. Service Ceiling 20,500', Climb 1780'/1 min., 10,000'/11 min. Range 397 miles normal, 462 miles max.

THOMAS-MORSE YO-23
Curtiss V-1570, 600 hp
DIMENSIONS: Span 39'9", Lg. 28'10", Wing Area 348 sq. ft.
WEIGHT: Empty 2842 lb., Gross 4190 lb. Fuel 105 gal.
PERFORMANCE: Speed- Top 156 mph at s.l., 151 mph at 10,000', Cruising 125 mph, Landing 59 mph. Service Ceiling 22,275', Absolute Ceiling 23,750', Climb 1596'/1 min., 10,000'/8.2 min.

VOUGHT O-28
Pratt & Whitney R-1340-C, 625 hp
DIMENSIONS: Span 36', Lg. 24'8", Ht. 10'1", Wing Area 327 sq. ft.
WEIGHT: Empty 2404 lb., Gross 3865 lb. Fuel 110 gal.
PERFORMANCE: Speed- Top 156.5 mph at s.1., 152 mph at 10,000', Cruising 125 mph, Landing 58 mph. Service Ceiling 22,100', Absolute Ceiling 23,600', Climb 1570'/1 min., 10,000'/8.3 min.

sold to Consolidated Aircraft. A new assembly line in Buffalo delivered the O-19Bs from March to June 1930. Armed with one Browning fixed and one Browning flexible gun with 900 .30-caliber rounds, the O-19B could carry a 40-gallon drop tank or two 116-pound bombs under the fuselage. The useful load could include a 102-pound radio, 96-pound camera, or add 63 pounds for a pair of night landing lights under the wings.

Seventy-one O-19Cs ordered June 12, 1930, began appearing in November 1930 with ring cowls and tail wheels. The O-19D was a C converted to transport service while a new R-1340-15, supercharged to 5,000 feet, powered 30 O-19Es ordered February 21, 1931, and delivered beginning in September. They became the last aircraft built by Thomas-Morse, whose few assets merged with Consolidated.

THOMAS-MORSE O-19C
Pratt & Whitney R-1340-7, 450 hp
DIMENSIONS: Span 39'9", Lg. 29', Ht. 10', Wing Area 348 sq. ft.
WEIGHT: Empty 2769 lb., Gross 3921 lb., Max. 4269 lb. Fuel 76+39 gal.
PERFORMANCE: Speed- Top 143 mph at s.l., 137 mph at 10,000', Cruising 124 mph, Landing 57 mph. Service Ceiling 20,000', Absolute Ceiling 21,800', Climb 1810'/1 min., 10,000'/11 min. Range 377 miles normal, 436 miles max.

The O-19 series totaled 177 aircraft and served with eight of the 13 Army observation squadrons in 1931. These included all four overseas units (the 2nd in the Philippines, 4th and 50th in Hawaii, and the 7th in the Canal Zone) as well as the 12th, 15th, 22nd and 88th in the United States. They also served to demonstrate the suitability of all-metal construction for Army aircraft.

THOMAS-MORSE O-19E
Pratt & Whitney R-1340-15, 575 hp at 5000'
DIMENSIONS: Span 40', Lg. 28'10", Ht. 10'4", Wing Area 359 sq. ft.
WEIGHT: Empty 2774 lb., Gross 3938 lb., Max. 4275 lb. Fuel 80+40 gal.
PERFORMANCE: Speed- Top 156 mph at 5000', 153 mph at 10,000', Cruising 136 mph, Landing 57 mph. Service Ceiling 23,500', Climb 10,000'/10.7 min. Range 473 miles.

Thomas-Morse had been less successful in adapting their aircraft to the more powerful Curtiss Conqueror engine with Prestone cooling. A geared V-1570-11 was installed in the first O-19B, rebuilt and flown on April 23, 1930, as the YlO-33, but the Douglas O-25C and Curtiss O-39 got the Air Corps contracts for observation types with this engine.

The last prototype designed by B.D. Thomas with the Thomas-Morse name was a sesquiplane (small lower wing) known as the XO-932 when first flown on May 4, 1931, and tested at Wright Field in June. A geared, Prestone-cooled Conqueror in a neat cowl, N struts, and wheel pants were featured.

That model was rejected by an Army board because the basic structure seemed weak and the board now believed that "a monoplane is the most desirable type for observation purposes because of its superior qualities of vision." While not sold to the Army, the aircraft received the YlO-41 designation, and was used as a Consolidated Company hack until sold to a Mexican officer in December 1936. The end of the biplane was in sight, as the Army in July 1931 rejected a proposed Consolidated Y1O-42 with an even smaller lower wing.

THOMAS-MORSE Y1O-33
Curtiss V-1570-11, 600 hp
DIMENSIONS: Span 39'9", Lg. 29'2", Ht. 10'2", Wing Area 348 sq. ft.
WEIGHT: Empty 3130 lb., Gross 4291 lb. Fuel 77.5 gal.
PERFORMANCE: Speed- Top 165 mph at s.l., 158 mph at 10,000', Cruising 143 mph, Landing 58 mph. Service Ceiling 22,600', Absolute Ceiling 24,000', Climb 1840'/1 min., 10,000'/6 min. Range 443 miles.

THOMAS-MORSE YlO-41 (XO-932)
Curtiss V-1570-29, 600 hp
DIMENSIONS: Span 40'8", Lg. 29'3", Ht. 10', Wing Area 299 sq. ft.
WEIGHT: Empty 3254 lb., Gross 4394 lb. Fuel 79 gal.
PERFORMANCE: Speed- Top 188 mph at s.l., 181 mph at 10,000', Cruising 164 mph, Landing 63 mph. Service Ceiling 24,250', Absolute Ceiling 25,500', Climb 1840'/1 min., 10,000'/6.9 min.

The last Douglas biplanes

Despite vigorous competition from Curtiss and Thomas-Morse, Douglas kept winning most of the Air Corps observation business during the biplane period, and Douglas two-seaters were the last combat biplanes bought by the

DOUGLAS O-22
Pratt & Whitney R-1340-1, 450 hp
DIMENSIONS: Span 38'1", Lg. 28'4", Ht. 9'8", Wing Area 316 sq. ft.
WEIGHT: Empty 2389 lb., Gross 3841 lb. Fuel 88 gal.
PERFORMANCE: Speed- Top 146 mph at s.l., 137 mph at 10,000', Cruising 115 mph, Landing 59 mph. Service Ceiling 20,750', Absolute Ceiling 22,600', Climb 1207'/1 min., 10,000'/10.9 min. Range 403 miles.

Army. Part of its success was due to variety in developing the basic airframe, and when the Air Corps seemed uncertain in choosing between air-cooled or liquid-cooled power plants, Douglas could sell aircraft of both styles.

DOUGLAS O-25
Curtiss V-1570-5, 600 hp
DIMENSIONS: Span 40', Lg. 30'8", Ht. 10'7", Wing Area 364 sq. ft.
WEIGHT: Empty 2951 lb., Gross 4573 lb. Fuel 110 gal.
PERFORMANCE: Speed- Top 158 mph at s.l., 153 mph at 10,000', Cruising 126 mph, Landing 60 mph. Service Ceiling 22,375', Climb 1480'/1 min., 10,000'/8.7 min.

Five two-seat configurations of Douglas biplanes appeared in 1929. First was the three light YO-22s ordered January 17, 1929, and first delivered to Wright Field in September 1929 with a Pratt & Whitney R-1340-1 Wasp radial and swept back upper wing, N struts, ring cowl, tail wheel, and auxiliary tank under the fuselage.

The other prototypes were standard O-2K airframes with the Liberty engines replaced by new power plants. A 600-hp Curtiss V-1570-5 Conqueror turned an O-2K into an O-25, tested in September 1929 with water-cooling and in November with a Prestone cooler. The O-29 was flown in September with an air-cooled 525-hp Wright R-1750-1 Cyclone, and later as the O-29A with a 575-hp R-1820-1 Cyclone.

DOUGLAS O-25A
Curtiss V-1570-7, 600 hp
DIMENSIONS: Span 40', Lg. 30'8", Ht. 10'7", Wing Area 364 sq. ft.
WEIGHT: Empty 3260 lb., Gross 4657 lb. Fuel 110-146 gal.
PERFORMANCE: Speed- Top 153 mph at s.l., 151 mph at 10,000', Cruising 136 mph, Landing 61 mph. Service Ceiling 21,100', Climb 1560'/1 min., 10,000'/8.1 min. Range 553 miles normal, 612 miles max.

A smaller 450-hp R-1340-3 Wasp was used in September 1929 to make the O-32, which later became the BT-2 basic trainer series, while another O-2K tested with the 525-hp Pratt & Whitney Hornet was the predecessor of the O-38 series.

An Air Corps production contract on October 18, 1929, first called for 36 O-25A and 30 O-32A aircraft, but the latter were transformed to BT-2A trainers after delivery in 1930. Future observation aircraft built with single-row Wasps would be trainers, while the standard observation type would have larger engines. The first O-25A appeared at Wright in June 1930 with a water-cooled 600 hp V-1570-7 and, with a contract addition, Douglas built 50 O-25As armed with two .30-caliber Brownings and 1,000 rounds, and three O-25B unarmed transports.

DOUGLAS O-29
Wright Cyclone R-1750-1, 525 hp
DIMENSIONS: Span 40', Wing Area 364 sq. ft.
WEIGHT: Empty 2781 lb., Gross 4095 lb.
PERFORMANCE: Speed- Top 137 mph at s.l., 131 mph at 10,000'. Service Ceiling 20,600', Absolute Ceiling 22,300'.

The Curtiss Conqueror was also used on the YO-34, converted from the third YO-22 in March 1930, but the Army preferred to develop the O2M series airframe with the air-cooled Pratt & Whitney Hornet radial. Deliveries of this type actually began in April 1929 with nine O2M

Ortiz

DOUGLAS O-2M for Mexico
Pratt & Whitney R-1690 "Hornet A," 525 hp
DIMENSIONS: Span 40', Lg. 30', Ht. 10'10", Wing Area 361 sq. ft.
WEIGHT: Empty 2580 lb., Gross 4550 1b. Fuel 206 gal.
PERFORMANCE: Speed- Top 145 mph at s.1., Cruising 120 mph, Landing 56 mph. Service Ceiling 17,500', Absolute Ceiling 18,900', Climb 1350'/1 min., Range 800 miles.

biplanes built for Mexico with Hornet engines, enlarged fuel tanks, bomb racks, and twin Lewis guns on a rear cockpit ring. They were followed in 1930 by three Mexican O2M2s.

MFR

DOUGLAS YO-34
Curtiss V-1570-11, 600 hp
DIMENSIONS: Span 38', Lg. 28', Ht. 10'5", Wing Area 316 sq. ft.
WEIGHT: Empty 2871 lb., Gross 4656 lb. Fuel 80 gal.
PERFORMANCE: Speed- Top 156 mph at s.1., 149 mph at 10,000', Cruising 125 mph, Landing 63 mph. Service Ceiling 21,500', Absolute Ceiling 23,075', Climb 10,000'/8.68 min.

On June 13, 1930, the Army ordered the Hornet-powered Douglas as the O-38, and the first four aircraft were delivered to the National Guard on October 30, 1930. While the first was an unarmed O-38A transport, 45 O-38s had the usual M1921 fixed and M1922 flexible gun, with 800 rounds, and their bumped ring cowls were familiar sights on National Guard fields (none went to Air Corps units) for many years. Except for an increased forward stagger, their wings were the same shape and Goettingen airfoil as the O-2 series.

Under wing bomb racks for four 116 or ten 30-pound bombs were added to the O-38B, first ordered December 22, 1930, with deliveries beginning in April 1931. Forty-five were built to Air Corps contracts while eighteen more for the National Guard began appearing in December 1931 with a new smooth cowl and exhaust system that was later retrofitted to earlier O-38s. A single O-38C delivered to the Coast Guard in December 1931 had an R-1690-7 engine, but no guns.

The Air Corps was not yet finished with inline engines, however, and on May 12, 1931, ordered 30 O-25Cs with Prestone-

AF

DOUGLAS O-38
Pratt & Whitney R-1690-3, 525 hp
DIMENSIONS: Span 40', Lg. 31'3", Ht. 10'10", Wing Area 364 sq. ft.
WEIGHT: Empty 3046 lb., Gross 4421 lb. Fuel 110-146 gal.
PERFORMANCE: Speed- Top 143 mph at s.1., 139 mph at 10,000', Cruising 121 mph, Landing 59 mph. Service Ceiling 19,750', Absolute Ceiling 21,600', Climb 1140'/1 min., 10,000'/11.7 min. Range 325 miles at top speed.

MFR

DOUGLAS O2MC for China
Pratt & Whitney R-1690-5, 525 hp
DIMENSIONS: Span 40', Lg. 30'4", Ht. 10'10", Wing Area 362 sq. ft.
WEIGHT: Empty 3032 lb., Gross 5006 1b. Fue1 146-206 gal.
PERFORMANCE: Speed- Top 150 mph at s.1., Cruising 130 mph, Service Ceiling 19,000', Climb 1240'/1 min. Range 840 miles.

AF

DOUGLAS O-38B
Pratt & Whitney R-1690-5, 525 hp
DIMENSIONS: Span 40', Lg. 32', Ht. 10'8", Wing Area 371 sq. ft.
WEIGHT: Empty 3072 lb., Gross 4458 lb., Fuel 110-146 gal.
PERFORMANCE: Speed- Top 149 mph at s.1., 143 mph at 10,000', Cruising 128 mph, Landing 59 mph. Service Ceiling 20,700', Absolute Ceiling 22,500', Climb 1240'/1 min., 10,000'/10.6 min. Range 600 miles normal, 706 miles max.

MFR

DOUGLAS O-38P
Pratt & Whitney R-1820F-21, 640 hp
DIMENSIONS: Span 40', Lg. 30', Ht. 10'10", Wing Area 371 sq. ft.
WEIGHT: Empty 3389 lb., Gross 4887 lb. Fuel 146-206 gal.
PERFORMANCE: Speed- Top 172 mph at s.l., Cruising 140 mph, Landing 61 mph. Service Ceiling 21,500', Climb 1500'/1 min.

PMB

DOUGLAS O-38E
Pratt & Whitney R-1690-13, 625 hp
DIMENSIONS: Span 40', Lg. 32', Ht. 10'5", Wing Area 371 sq. ft.
WEIGHT: Empty 3481 lb., Gross 4870 lb. Fuel 110-146 gal.
PERFORMANCE: Speed- Top 154 mph at s.l., 147 mph at 10,000', Cruising 133 mph, Landing 60 mph. Service Ceiling 19,200', Climb 1230'/1 min., 10,000'/11.1 min. Range 468 miles.

PMB

DOUGLAS O-38F in Russia.

DOUGLAS O-25C
Curtiss V-1570-7, 600 hp
DIMENSIONS: Span 40', Lg. 31'4", Ht. 10'10", Wing Area 376 sq. ft.
WEIGHT: Empty 3438 lb., Gross 4816 lb. Fuel 110-146 gal.
PERFORMANCE: Speed- Top 161 mph at s.l., 153 mph at l0,000', Cruising 139 mph, Landing 61 mph. Service Ceiling 21,000', Absolute Ceiling 22,600', Climb 1510'/1 min., 10,000'/8.8 min. Range 542 miles.

cooled V-1570-27 Conquerors. Tested at Wright October 23, 1931, the O-25C was the fastest of the O-2 developments, with a neatly streamlined nose and the same armament, two-guns and 464 pounds of bombs, of its O-38B contemporary. They served with the 16th and 91st Observation Squadrons at Fort Riley, Kansas, and Crissy Field, San Francisco.

Even before the Air Corps bought its O-38, Douglas sold export versions to China, beginning with ten O2MC two-seaters with 525-hp Hornets delivered in May 1930. These did not have the smooth ring cowls used on 20 O2MC-2 models arriving in August 1931. These were similar to the O-38B, and were followed by five O2MC-3s with 575 hp Hornet B engines, while 24 O2MC-4/5s were basic trainers with 420-hp R-1340 Wasps, 22 O2MC-6s used 575-hp Wright R-1820E Cyclones in 1935 and a single O2MC-10 had a 670-hp R-1820F in 1936.

These Douglas biplanes played an active role in civil warfare with Kuomintang attacks on warlord rebels at Fukien, and on the Long March. They were delivered without guns, which were fitted in China, and some added two .30-caliber guns on the lower wings. But these two-seaters were too slow to evade Japanese fighters, so they were replaced by I-15b fighters as soon as Soviet planes arrived in 1938.

Air Corps observation contracts had reached a peak during the six months of 1931, with seven different types ordered: 115 O-lG, O-19E, O-25C, O-38B and O-39 biplanes, and 18 YO-27 and YO-31 monoplanes for service test. The day of the open-cockpit biplane was ending, and after 1932, monoplanes with enclosed cockpits would be the prevailing combat plane style.

Enclosed cockpits were used on the last batch of Army service biplanes. Such an enclosure had been introduced on the single O-38D, a dual-control, unarmed transport with a 575-hp R-1820-1 Cyclone built in June 1932 and bought for a National Guard general on October 4. Peru's Navy received six armed 640-hp Cyclone-powered O-38P convertible land or seaplanes with enclosed cockpits, beginning November 1932.

The O-38E, first ordered December 7, 1932, also had a canopy over the pilot and his observer, and a rounded fuselage obtained by adding wooden stringers built over the steel tube framework. Powered by a 625-hp Hornet with a three-bladed propeller, the O-38E had the usual two guns and bomb racks. Thirty were delivered, beginning in May 1933, and scattered among the 19 National Guard Squadrons. Five O-38B, the O-38D, and five O-38E biplanes still remained in Guard service in November 1941, the last biplanes in squadron use.

Among the last biplanes were eight O-38F dual-control, enclosed cockpit, unarmed transports. They were used for high-ranking officers at locations like Bolling Field, and one was flown in Russia by the Army's military attaché in Moscow. Since the O-lC, some 30 officers' transports had been delivered under the "O" designation, which tended to cover the use of Army funds for this purpose.

CHAPTER 7

FLYING BOATS FOR NAVY PATROLS, 1917-1934

CURTISS H-12
prototype

Patrol planes were the first American aircraft in wartime service, and were the first to sink an enemy vessel, so they are an appropriate beginning for the story of Navy combat types. Certainly their heavy armament and long battle record qualify patrol planes as combat types, despite the monotonous nature of the average wartime patrol.

Flying Boats versus U-boats

Throughout its history, the naval patrol plane has been linked to the submarine. Originally envisioned as passive observers of fleet movements, patrol planes were called into combat action when German U-boats were inflicting heavy losses on Allied shipping in World War I. With land warfare stalemated, the only possible German answer to the British blockade had been a counter-blockade by submarine.

Unrestricted submarine warfare by the Germans shocked American public opinion (which never dreamed the U.S. would later use the same methods against Japan) into accepting war, but was calculated to starve England out before a single U.S. division arrived. In April 1917, sinkings rose so high that it seemed the Germans calculated rightly.

CURTISS H-12
Two Liberty 12, 360 hp
DIMENSIONS: Span 92'8", Lg. 46'6", Ht. 16'6". Wing Area 1216 sq. ft.
WEIGHT: Empty 7293 lb., Gross 10,650 lb.
PERFORMANCE: Speed- Top 85 mph at 2000', Stalling 55 mph. Service Ceiling 10,800', Climb 2000'/3.3 min. Endurance 6 hours.

In this emergency, British flying boats patrolled the most dangerous areas, and in 1917, a Curtiss H-12 hit the first German U-boat sunk by aircraft. Others were not usually so successful, but flying boats handicapped the subs by reporting their location and driving them below the surface, where their speed was reduced. Other devices played a larger part in beating the subs and saving England- the convoy system, mine barrage, and hydrophones- so aircraft shared the credit for only five of 140 U-boats sunk, but the flying boat had demonstrated its future possibilities.

The flying boats used then were developments of the first twin-engine Curtiss *America,* a 5,000-pound, 72-foot span biplane. Built in 1914 at Hammondsport, New York, it had a single-step boat-like hull, Curtiss engines, and 300 gallons of fuel for a proposed attempt to fly the Atlantic. The war prevented that flight, but a British officer, John C. Porte, saw its possibilities, and the two experimental Curtiss *America* boats were shipped to Britain on September 30, 1914. Like eight similar H-4s delivered in 1915, they had two 90-hp Curtiss OX-5 water-cooled engines, but when this power plant proved inadequate, 100-hp Anzanis were used on 50 H-4s ordered March 1915 and used for training and limited patrols by the Royal Naval Air Service.

These flying boats were called *Small Americas* by the British and were followed by bigger Curtiss H-8 *Large Americas.* Two 160-hp Curtiss engines powered the first one delivered July 1916, but again the biplane was underpowered, and 275-hp Rolls-Royce Eagles were substituted. These aircraft became the Curtiss H-12, the first American plane used in combat.

Open cockpits were provided for a pilot, co-pilot, engineer, and "wireless operator", two 230-pound bombs were carried under the wings, a pair of .30-caliber Lewis guns were in the bow cockpit, and another Lewis gun was in the rear cockpit. These guns destroyed the first enemy aircraft downed by an American airplane. On May 14, 1917, a Curtiss H-12 swept down below and alongside a German Zeppelin. A short burst from the bow guns, and the L-22 caught fire and fell into the North Sea.

On May 20, another H-12 attacked a submarine, the UC-36, and an H-12 sank UB-32 with two 230-pound bombs with two-second delay fuses on September 22, 1917. Official RAF history counts UC-36 as sunk by the H-12, but a German historian blames that loss on mines,

CURTISS HS-1

while UB-32's sinking is accepted by historians. It should be noted that the first submarines destroyed by aircraft were two Allied submarines sunk in the Adriatic by Austrians in 1916.

Eighty-one Curtiss H-12s built to British orders were shipped without engines, but another 20 were turned over to the United States Navy. The first Navy H-12 in March 1917 had the original Curtiss engines, while the rest were delivered early in 1918 with Liberty 12 engines.

When the United States entered the war, the Navy looked for a single-engine flying boat which could be put into production more quickly, take up less shipping space, and use shallow water. Curtiss offered the HS-1 (for Hydroplane, single-engine) in July 1917 with an America-style single-step wooden hull and a 200-hp Curtiss VXX eight-cylinder engine between the wings.

Copied from the R-type seaplane, the wings had an RAF-6 airfoil and three pairs of interplane struts on each side. When the 360-hp Liberty 12 first became available for tests, the Curtiss prototype was flown as the HS-1L (for Liberty) on October 21, 1917, and all production aircraft received this engine.

CURTISS HS-1L
Liberty 12, 360 hp
DIMENSIONS: Span 62'1", Lg. 38'6", Ht. 14'7", Wing Area 653 sq. ft.
WEIGHT: Empty 4070 lb., Gross 5910 lb. Fuel 110-153 gal.
PERFORMANCE: Speed- Top 87 mph at s.l., Stalling 57 mph. Service Ceiling 2500', Climb 1725'/10 min. Endurance 3.7 hours at top speed, 5.7 hours cruising.

The first HS-1s were delivered to NAS Hampton Roads in January 1918, began service at Miami in March, and eight became the first American aircraft shipped to France, arriving on May 24. American Navy pilots in France had been flying their first patrols in French Tellier and Donnet-Denhaut flying boats until the HS boats were ready to begin patrols on June 13, 1918.

The three-seat HS-1L was armed with a Lewis gun in the front cockpit and two 180-pound depth bombs under the wings. To increase the lift so that heavier loads like 230-pound bombs could be carried, the wings were increased twelve feet in span, a fourth pair of struts were added on each side, and the rudder enlarged. This version became the HS-2L and most of the HS boats in production were completed or converted to this standard.

CURTISS HS-2L
Liberty 12, 360 hp
DIMENSIONS: Span 74'1", Lg. 39', Ht. 14'7", Wing Area 803 sq. ft.
WEIGHT: Empty 4359 lb., Gross 6432 lb. Fuel 153 gal.
PERFORMANCE: Speed- Top 82.5 mph at s.l., Cruising 78 mph, Stalling 50 mph. Service Ceiling 5200', Climb 2300'/10 min. Endurance 4.6 hours at top speed, 7.6 hours cruising.

The first recorded attack by an HS boat on a submarine was that of July 21, 1918, on the U-156 off Cape Cod, but the bomb was a dud, and there is no evidence that other incidents were much more successful. Ten Navy Air Stations (NAS) in France got 182 HS boats during the war, but most served on the American east coast or at San Diego, then the only west coast NAS. A 110-pound wireless transmitter was sometimes carried, but carrier pigeons were more often used for emergency dispatches.

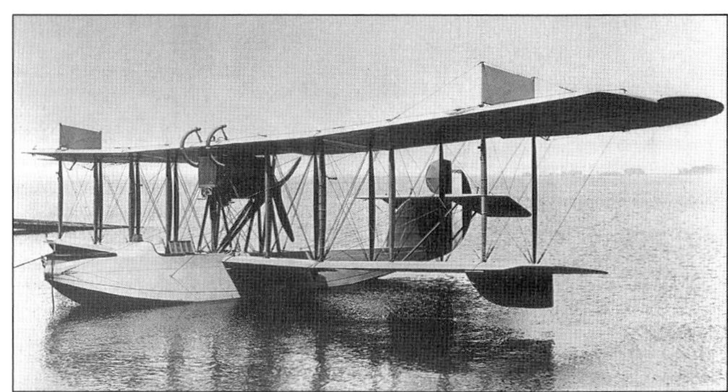

CURTISS HS-3

NAVAL AIRCRAFT FACTORY H-16 (modified)
Data as below, but with two Liberty 12A, 400 hp
WEIGHT: Empty 7400 lb., Gross 10,900 lb. Fuel 410 gal. max.

Navy demands for the HS boats were too great for Curtiss to build in its Buffalo and Garden City, New York, factories, and other firms became involved in that work. Between January 4 and December 27, 1918, Curtiss built 674 HS boats. LWF added 253 from June 1918 to February 1919, while Standard built 138, and Gallaudet 60. After the war, Loughead was allowed to assemble two in January 1919, Boeing added 25 by June, and 24 were erected from spare parts at naval air stations.

Many HS boats were sold to private operators in America and abroad after the war. Modified hulls and wings were tried on four HS-3s built by Curtiss in 1919, and two more HS-3s reworked at the Naval Aircraft Factory in 1922 had wing frames of steel tubing designed by Charles Ward Hall. These reduced empty weight about 10%, improving performance.

Liberty engines on Navy flying boats were low-compression versions whose shorter piston stroke sacrificed power to gain less-troubled engine reliability and endurance. High-compression models were sometimes used after the war.

Curtiss also delivered the first twin-engine H-16 on February 1, 1918; a larger H-12 development with a two-step hull and heavier armament. Britain ordered 125, and fitted the 75 that were actually shipped with 345-hp Rolls-Royce Eagles, but 124 Curtiss H-16s for the U.S. Navy had 400-hp Liberty engines. On November 20, 1917, an order

CURTISS H-16
Two Liberty 12, 330 hp
DIMENSIONS: Span 95'1", Lg. 46'2", Ht. 17'9", Wing area 1164 sq. ft.
WEIGHT: Empty 7148 lb., Gross 10,476 lb. Fuel 235-324 gal.
PERFORMANCE: Speed- Top 95 mph at 2,000', Stalling 56 mph. Service Ceiling 9950', Climb 5000'/10 min. Range 342 miles normal, 465 miles max.

for H-16s had been given to the new Naval Aircraft Factory (NAF) in Philadelphia and 150 were completed between March and October 1918. The first NAF H-16 flown March 27, 1918, was forwarded to a Navy station in England, and differed from the Curtiss model in detail, since plans had been redrawn to expedite production.

Armament of the H-16 included four 230-pound bombs, and four or five Lewis guns- one or two in the bow, one in the rear cockpit, and one at an opening on each side of the hull. The H-16 cost $37,850, compared to $16,900 for each HS-2.

The British improved on the Curtiss hull design at their Felixstowe station with a series of twin-engine flying boats, called the F-1 to F-5. While retaining the biplane configuration and RAF-6 airfoil, the larger F-5 had a stronger and more streamlined hull. Plans of the F-5 were brought to the NAF in March 1918, and this design was modified for quantity production with American manufacturing details and Liberty engines as the F-5L, to distinguish it from British types powered by Rolls-Royce engines.

The first NAF F-5L was flown at Philadelphia by John C. Porte on July 15, 1918, with straight balanced ailerons and a rounded rudder balanced below the horizontal surface. They arrived at Hampton Roads on September 3, 1918, too late for action, and 33 were built by the NAF by December 31. Although 543 F-5Ls were canceled, production continued until 137 were completed by September 1919. Sixty more were built by Curtiss, and 30 were produced in Canada.

USN

NAVAL AIRCRAFT FACTORY F-5L (July 1918)

The $34,800 F-5L carried four 230-pound bombs under the wings and four Lewis guns at the bow and rear cockpits and waist openings. A crew of four or five were provided with a 260-pound radio, Very signal pistol, and two pigeons. A taller rudder, horn-balanced at the top, and tested on two F-6 prototypes delivered in January 1919, was fitted to all the F-5L boats in service, as well as to the H-16s, which also adopted the balanced ailerons and open pilots' cockpits.

Curtiss also built for Britain a single triplane flying boat in 1916, which had four 250-hp engines and a 134-foot wing span. Known as the Curtiss T, it was shipped to Britain for its first flight, but was wrecked on its first test. A more practical approach was begun by an August 27, 1917, Navy proposal to design Liberty-powered aircraft capable of flying directly to Britain.

USN

NAF F-5L (post-war modified)
Two Liberty 12, 330 hp, or 12A, 420 hp
DIMENSIONS: Span 103'9", Lg. 49'4", Ht. 18'9", Wing Area 1397 sq. ft.
WEIGHT: Empty 8720 lb., Gross 13,256 lb., Max. 13,659 lb. Fuel 495 gal.
PERFORMANCE: Speed - Top 90 mph at s.1., Landing 52 mph. Service Ceiling 5500', Climb 2625'/10 min. Range- 608 miles at top speed, 830 miles cruising.

Four NC (Navy Curtiss) boats ordered in December 1917 were the largest American planes of 1918, designed to fly across the Atlantic to join in anti-submarine patrols. When first flown on October 4, 1918, at Rockaway NAS, the NC-l had three 350-hp Libertys, but NC-2 had four paired in two nacelles.

A fourth was added behind NC-1's center engine to turn a pusher propeller, and that arrangement was chosen for the next two built at the Curtiss Garden City factory. A gunner's position installed on the NC-1's upper wing was not on the others. The last, NC-4, first flew April 30, 1919.

Biplane tail surfaces were mounted high on spruce outriggers from the hull and huge RAF-6 wings, an arrangement calculated to clear waves and "permit a machine gun to be fired straight aft... without interference," although the field of fire in almost every other direction was cluttered. A 45-foot hull contained a bow cockpit, side-by-side pilot's cockpits, rear compartment, radio, and fuel tanks. Top speed was 90 mph light, and 81 mph loaded, not much of a margin over the landing speed.

USN

NAVY-CURTISS NC-4
Four Liberty 12, 420 hp
DIMENSIONS: Span 126', Lg. 68'3", Ht. 24'6", Wing Area 2380 sq. ft.
WEIGHT: Empty 15,874 lb., Gross 21,500 lb., Max. 28,000 lb. Fuel 1800 gal.
PERFORMANCE: Speed - Top 90 mph light, 81 mph fully loaded, Landing 62 mph. Service Ceiling 4500', Climb 1050'/5 min. Range 1470 miles.

In May 1919, the NC-4 became the first plane to fly across the Atlantic, and became an exhibit in the Naval Air Museum at Pensacola. Two sister ships, NC-1 & NC-3, which also attempted the Newfoundland-Azores-Lisbon-Plymouth flight, landed at sea and were unable to take-off again.

The NAF received an order for four NC boats in 1919, and after NC-5 and 6 were delivered in May 1920, two more were added. While the first two had three engines, the third a pusher in the center nacelle, the others, NC-7/-10, had four when delivered in 1921. They had a high accident rate and seemed unreliable for steady patrol work.

NAF NC-6

NAF TF
Two Wright-Hispano H, 300 hp
DIMENSIONS: Span 60', Lg. 44'5", Ht. 17', Wing Area 930 sq. ft.
WEIGHT: Gross 8846 lb.
PERFORMANCE: Speed- Top 107 mph at s.l. Service Ceiling 8000'.

A smaller flying boat was designed by the Navy to provide a twin-engine, three-place escort fighter to support the larger patrol planes. Called the NAF TF for "Tandem Fighter", it resembled a small-sized NC, with two Wright-Hispano engines back-to-back in a center nacelle, and twin rudders. Four were ordered April 9, 1919, and the first was flown at Philadelphia on October 13, 1920. Unsatisfactory tests halted further development.

The largest flying boat project designed at Philadelphia was a "Giant Boat" for use over the vast distances of the Pacific. It was to be a 70,000-pound, 150-foot span triplane with nine Liberty engines in three Gallaudet-built nacelles, tandem geared to turn tractor propellers.

Construction was authorized June 7, 1920, and promised range was 1,877 miles at 78 mph, with up to 4,000 gallons of gas and 6,000 pounds of bombs, and cockpits for five .50-caliber guns. Work on the NC-style Giant halted in 1922 as high costs and technical problems discouraged the Navy. At that stage of engineering, it would probably have been even less successful than the Army's Barling bomber.

Navy Patrol Flying Boats, 1920-1932

When the Navy entered World War I it had only six flying boats; by Armistice Day 1,172 were on hand, most of them single-engine HS types. After the German U-boats were gone, so was the reason, it seemed, to build any more patrol planes, although millions were invested in new battleships, with their tall basket masts and armored turrets. It was a decade before new flying boats were built in quantity.

The twin-engine biplane pattern of the H-12, H-16 and F-5 established a tradition for Navy flying boats. There were 347 HS, 106 H-16 and 172 F-5L boats on hand July 1, 1921, and by June 30, 1925, the Navy's aging patrol force consisted of 44 F-5L and 33 H-16 twin-engine boats, 40 single-engine HS-2s, and 80 assorted unserviceable air-frames of these types. Fortunately, the Naval Aircraft Factory was developing a new series of flying boats to relieve the spruce framework of these antiques. The first improvement needed was metal hulls instead of the wooden surfaces so threatened by salt water and waves.

Since private industry was not expected to risk the capital investment required to develop advanced patrol planes, the Naval Aircraft Factory built 13 trial flying boats. The first two were authorized in January 1923 and designated PN-7, for Patrol, Navy, the 7 following redesignation of the wartime F-5 and F-6 as PN-5/6.

Traditional wood and fabric biplanes, the PN-7s had a modified F-5 hull and new 72-foot 10-inch span wings with the USA-27 airfoil and only one pair of interplane struts on each side. Two 525-hp Wright T-2 Tornado inline engines and two-bladed propellers were mounted in streamlined nacelles, with the water radiators hanging from the upper wing. A crew of five, four 230-pound bombs, and four Lewis guns were carried.

The first PN-7 was tested at Philadelphia in November 1923, and delivered in January 1924, but the second was not accepted until August. The next pair of Navy boats were built with lighter metal hulls and a new tail. The first, A-6799, flew on March 19, 1925, as the PN-8 with Wright T-3 engines, while the second, A-6878, was tested in April as the PN-9 with 525-hp Packard lA-1500 engines behind large water radiators and increased fuel capacity for a proposed flight to Hawaii.

The PN-8 was soon converted to PN-9 configuration, and on August 31, 1925, both PN-9s took off for the first attempt to fly from San Francisco to Hawaii. While A-6799 was soon forced down, the A-6878's fuel lasted over 25 hours; long enough to cover 1,841 miles against head winds and set a world's distance record, but after it ran out of fuel, the PN-9 came down at sea some 360 miles short of Pearl Harbor. Then the metal hull demonstrated good flotation qualities, keeping the five-man crew safe for ten days, until they reached the islands using sails improvised from the wing's fabric covering.

USN

NAF PN-7
Two Wright T-2, 525 hp
DIMENSIONS: Span 72'10", Lg. 49'1", Ht. 15'4", Wing Area 1217 sq. ft.
WEIGHT: Empty 9637 lb., Gross 14,203 lb. Fuel 489 gal.
PERFORMANCE: Speed- Top 104.5 mph at s.1., Landing 54 5 mph. Service Ceiling 9200', Climb 5000'/10.2 min. Range 655 miles.

The first flying boat built since 1919 by a private company to a Navy design was the Boeing PB-l ordered September 23, 1924, for the same trans-Pacific flight as the PN-9. Two big 800-hp Packard 2A-2540s back-to-back between the hull and upper wing, turned one tractor and one pusher propeller. First flown at Seattle July 29, 1925, the

USN

NAF PN-9
Two Packard 1A-1500, 525 hp
DIMENSIONS: Span 72'10", Lg. 49'2", Ht. 16'6", Wing Area 1217 sq. ft.
WEIGHT: Empty 9125 lb., Gross 19,610 lb. Fuel 1270 gal.
PERFORMANCE: Speed- Top 114.5 mph at s.1., Stalling 68 mph. Service Ceiling 3080', Climb 1750'/10 min. Range 2550 miles.

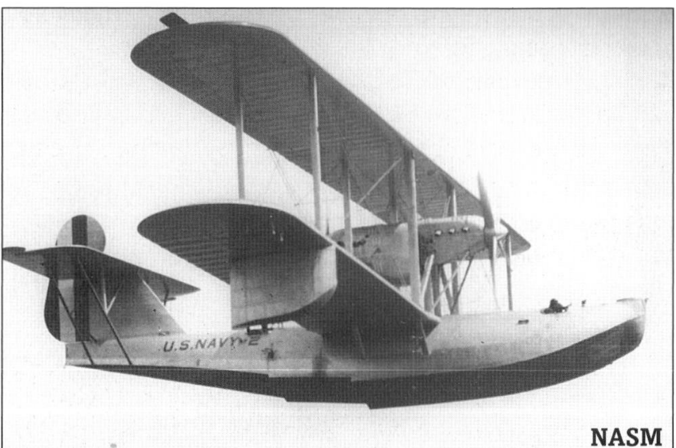

NASM

BOEING PB-1
Two Packard 2A-2540, 800 hp
DIMENSIONS: Span 87'6", Lg. 59'5", Ht. 22'2", Wing Area 1823 sq. ft.
WEIGHT: Empty 12,742 lb., Gross 24,000 lb., Max. 26,822 lb. Fuel 1881 gal.
PERFORMANCE: Speed- Top 125 mph at s.1., Cruising 80 mph, Stalling 69 mph. Service Ceiling 3300', Climb 5000'/46 min. Range 2230 miles.

BOEING XPB-2
Pratt & Whitney GR-1690, 475 hp
DIMENSIONS: Span 87'6", Lg. 59'5", Ht. 20'10" Wing Area 1823 sq. ft..
WEIGHT: Gross 24,374 lb. Fuel 1881 gal.
PERFORMANCE: Speed- Top 112 mph at s.1., Stalling 64.4 mph. Service Ceiling 4470', Climb 2500'/10 min.

PB-l had five cockpits, the Clark Y airfoil, and a new composite hull design with metal bottom and plywood deck. Three Lewis guns and up to 4,000 pounds of bombs could be carried, but engine difficulties prevented participation in the Hawaii flight.

The next pair of boats were the PN-l0s with geared 525-hp Packard 2A-1500s, and three-bladed propellers. They were expected to introduce a metal wing structure covered by fabric, but delay of the duralumin parts caused the first flight on June 21, 1926, to be made with wooden wings. Distance records set in August 1927 by a PN-10 at San Diego included one of 1,569 miles in 20 hours, 15 minutes, with an 1,100-pound load. Two more PN-l0s were ordered with the metal wings and the first flew November 30, 1927, the first Navy flying boat with an all-metal structure, although cotton fabric still covered wings and control surfaces.

NAF PN-10
Two Packard 2A-1500, 525 hp
DIMENSIONS: Span 72'10", Lg. 49'2", Ht. 16'9", Wing Area 1217 sq. ft.
WEIGHT: Empty 10,060 lb., Gross 18,994 lb., Max. 19,029 lb. Fuel 858 gal.
PERFORMANCE: Speed- Top 114 mph at s.1., Stalling 66 mph. Service Ceiling 4500', Climb 5000'/29 min. Range 1508 miles.

Up to this point, water-cooled engines had been used on Navy patrol planes, but in 1928 the Navy changed to air-cooled radials on flying boats. The second PN-10 became the XPN-12 when fitted with 525-hp Wright R-1750 Cyclones in December 1927, and the same engines powered the boat ordered as the fourth PN-10, but delivered in June 1928 as a PN-12.

Pratt & Whitney R-1690 Hornets were mounted on the other two PN-10s, which were also redesignated PN-12, and set an altitude record in June 1928 of 15,426 feet with 4,400 pounds. Boeing's ship was also rebuilt at the NAF as the XPB-2 with two Pratt & Whitney R-1690 Hornets, instead of the unsatisfactory Packards, and was test flown in April 1928.

SDAM

NAF PN-12
Two Wright R-1750D, 525 hp
DIMENSIONS: Span 72'10", Lg. 49'2", Ht. 16'9", Wing Area 1217 sq. ft.
WEIGHT: Empty 7669 lb., Gross 14,122 lb. Fuel 858 gal.
PERFORMANCE: Speed- Top 114 mph at s.l., Stalling 58 mph. Service Ceiling 10,900', Climb 5500'/16 min. Range 1309 miles.

The first PN-12 version with Wright engines was the prototype for the first production flying boats ordered since the war. Twenty-five Douglas PD-ls ordered December 29, 1927, entered service in June 1929 with VP-7 at San Diego, and were then all concentrated at Pearl Harbor with VP-4 and VP-6. Armament comprised two flexible guns and four 500-pound bombs, with automatic pilot and radio equipment.

On May 31, 1929, the Navy ordered 25 Martin PM-l and three NAF XP2N boats. Martin's contract was increased to 30 PM-ls delivered at Baltimore from July to October 1930 with 525-hp Wright R-1750D Cyclones, but the last three boats were diverted to Brazil, and replaced by PM-2s. Six each went to Scouting Force squadrons VP-2 at Coco Solo and VP-8, VP-9, and VP-10 based on tenders *Argonne* and *Wright*.

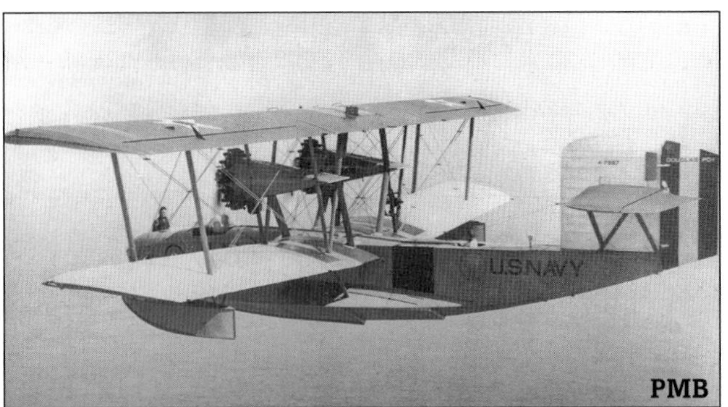

PMB

DOUGLAS PD-l
Two Wright R-1750A, 525 hp
DIMENSIONS: Span 72'10", Lg. 49'2", Ht. 16', Wing Area 1162 sq. ft.
WEIGHT: Empty 8319 lb., Gross 14,988 lb. Fuel 759 gal.
PERFORMANCE: Speed- Top 121 mph at s.1., Cruising 100 mph, Stalling 59 mph. Service Ceiling 11,600', Climb 5000'/9.8 min. Range 1465 miles.

The PM-ls were almost identical to the Douglas PD-ls except for rounded engine nacelles, and had four .30-caliber guns in the forward cockpit, rear cockpit, and side openings. Four 500 or two 1,000-pound bombs could be carried under the wings, and a 239-pound radio and a five-man life raft were standard equipment.

Meanwhile, the Naval Aircraft Factory built two PN-11 boats with a wider metal hull minus the sponsons seen on Navy boats since the H-12, a new airfoil section for the wings, and twin rudders. The first with 525-hp Hornet engines began tests in October 1928, and the second with 575-hp Cyclones began flying in April 1929.

The Navy XP2Ns were redesignated, and the first was delivered December 23, 1930, as the XP4N-l with the PN-11 hull, twin rudders, and 575-hp Wright Cyclones. Two X4PN-2s, similar but for increased fuel capacity, were not delivered until March 1932, the last prototype flying boats from Philadelphia.

USN

MARTIN PM-1 (1930)
Two Wright R-1750D, 525 hp
DIMENSIONS: Span 72'10", Lg. 49'2", Ht. 16'4", Wing Area 1236 sq.ft.
WEIGHT: Empty 8679 lb., Gross 15,826 lb., Max. 17,908 lb. Fuel 600-750 gal.
PERFORMANCE: Speed- Top 118 mph at s.1., Cruising 79 mph. Stalling 61 mph. Service Ceiling 9260', Climb 4000'/10 min. Range 945 miles/2,000-lb. bombs, 1274 miles as patrol.

The twin rudder tail was chosen for 18 Keystone PK-ls ordered November 30, 1929, and 25 Martin PM-2s bought June 10, 1930, but ring cowls on their 575-hp Cyclones gave them a little more speed. Keystone deliveries from Bristol, Pennsylvania, went to VP-l at Pearl Harbor from April to December 1931, while 28 Martin boats were delivered from June to September 1931, filling out squadrons VP-2, VP-5, and VP-10. Pilot cockpit enclosures were fitted in 1934 to both the PM-l and PM-2, as well as Norden Mk. XI bombsights, and the PM-1s were modified with R-1820-64 Cyclones in ring cowls.

Charles Ward Hall was a specialist in aluminum aircraft structures who was given a contract on December 29, 1927, to build a refined all-metal version of the PN series. The prototype XPH-l was built in a Buffalo factory shared with Consolidated and appeared in December 1929 with an improved all-metal hull, cowled 537-hp GR-1750D Cyclones, Clark Y airfoil, a tall, balanced single rudder, four open cockpits with twin Lewis guns on the bow and stern cockpit rings, and 2,000-pounds of bombs.

Nine production PH-ls ordered June 10, 1930, were first tested on October 19, 1931, and served with VP-8 at Pearl Harbor from 1932 to 1937. They had enclosed pilot's cockpits, R-1820-86 Cyclones, and four separate Browning guns at the fore, aft, and side positions.

These were the last twin-engine biplanes built for the Navy, since the big Consolidated monoplanes were coming in. But the biplane was not quite through; since the

USN

MARTIN PM-1 (modified)
Two Wright R-1820-64, 575 hp
DIMENSIONS: Span 72'10", Lg. 49'2", Ht. 16'4", Wing Area 1236 sq. ft.
WEIGHT: Empty 8970 lb., Gross 16,117 lb. Fuel 750 gal.
PERFORMANCE: Speed- Top 118.7 mph at s.1., Stalling 60.5 mph. Service Ceiling 8500', Climb 5000'/13.3 min. Range 1305 miles.

USN

NAF XP4N-1
Two Wright R-1820-64, 575 hp
DIMENSIONS: Span 72'10", Lg. 54', Ht. 17'7", Wing Area 1154 sq. ft.
WEIGHT: Empty 9770 lb., Gross 17,900 lb., Max. 20,340 lb. Fuel 1270 gal.
PERFORMANCE: Speed- Top 115 mph at s.l., Stalling 65 mph. Service Ceiling 9000', Climb 5000'/11.3 min. Range 1510 miles normal, 1930 miles max.

SDAM

NAF XPN-11
Two Pratt & Whitney R-1690, 525 hp
DIMENSIONS: Span 72'10", Lg. 53'6", Ht. 17'6", Wing Area 1154 sq. ft.
WEIGHT: Empty 7923 lb., Gross 16,870 lb.
PERFORMANCE: Speed- Top 120 mph at s.l., Stalling 63 mph. Service Ceiling 7700', Climb 5000'/16.1 min. Range 1948 miles.

USN

NAF XP4N-2
Two Wright R-1820-64, 575 hp
DIMENSIONS: As XP4N-1
WEIGHT: Empty 9843 lb., Gross 17,595 lb., Max. 21,585 lb. Fuel 1420 gal.
PERFORMANCE: Speed- Top 114 mph at s.l., Stalling 64 mph. Service Ceiling 9300', Climb 5000'/11.7 min. Range 1350 normal, 2050 miles max.

Coast Guard had need of a patrol and rescue boat smaller than the PBYs, Hall got an order for a new version of the old design in June 1936. Deliveries began in April 1938 on seven Hall PH-2s with 750-hp Wright R-1820-F51 Cyclones, followed in 1940 by seven PH-3s with improved engine cowls and pilots' enclosure. Built in the old Keystone-Fleetwings factory alongside the Delaware River at Bristol, the Hall boats were armed during the war for anti-submarine work.

By 1932, the Navy had eight patrol squadrons with twin-engine biplanes developed from the PN series. Three squadrons served at Pearl Harbor (VP-1,-4,-6,), three with the aircraft tenders *USS Argonne* and *Wright* at San Diego (VP-7,-8 -9), and two at Coco Solo in the Canal Zone (VP-2,-5), along with the twin-float torpedo planes of VP-3. The end of the biplane was in sight, however, when VP-10 was activated to handle the big new P3M monoplanes. Until monoplanes like the PBY came into large-scale production in 1937, the biplanes continued to serve, often embellished with refinements like cockpit enclosures, and late-model Cyclone engines.

USN

KEYSTONE PK-1
Two Wright R-1820-64, 575 hp
DIMENSIONS: Span 72'10", Lg. 48'11", Ht. 16'9", Wing Area 1226 sq. ft.
WEIGHT: Empty 9387 lb., Gross 16,534 lb., Max. 17,074 lb. Fuel 750-840 gal.
PERFORMANCE: Speed- Top 120 mph at s.1., Stalling 67 mph. Service Ceiling 9700', Climb 5000'/11 min. Range 1250 miles normal, 1355 miles max.

MARTIN PM-2
Two Wright R 1820-64, 575 hp
DIMENSIONS: Span 72'10", Lg. 49', Ht. 16'9" Wing Area 1236 sq. ft.
WEIGHT: Empty 9826 lb., Gross 17,083 lb., Max. 19,062 lb. Fuel 750-858 gal.
PERFORMANCE: Speed- Top 118.5 mph at s.l., Service Ceiling 9500', Climb 5000'/13.8 min. Range 937 miles as bomber, 1347 miles max.

The patrol designation was briefly carried by Navy versions of the twin-engine Sikorsky commercial amphibians, which were not really combat types. One XPS-l with 220-hp Wright R-790s and a gunner's cockpit in the bow of the short fuselage ordered January 28, 1928, and completed at College Point, NY, on March 16, was too underpowered for service. Two XPS-2 (S-38A) amphibians with 450-hp Pratt & Whitney R-1340Bs and the usual ten-place cabins ordered October 13, 1928, were delivered to Utility Squadron VJ-1 at San Diego in January 1929.

USN

HALL XPH-l
Two Wright GR-1750; 537 hp
DIMENSIONS: Span 72'10", Lg. 51'1", Ht 17'5", Wing Area 1170 sq. ft.
WEIGHT: Empty 6576 lb., Gross 13,228 lb., Max. 18,000 lb. Fuel 750 gal.
PERFORMANCE: Speed- Top 124 mph at s. l., Stalling 56 mph. Service Ceiling 12,050'. Climb 5,000'/9.5 min. Range 1790 miles.

ARC

HALL PH-1
Two Wright R 1820-86, 620 hp
DIMENSIONS: Span 72'10", Lg. 51'10", Ht. 17'6", Wing Area 1223 sq.ft.
WEIGHT: Empty 8251 lb., Gross 15,479 lb., Max. 16,379 lb. Fuel 900 gal.
PERFORMANCE: Speed- Top 134.5 mph at s.l. Stalling 60 mph. Service Ceiling 11,200', Climb 5000'/ 8 4 min. Range 1580 miles normal, 1868 miles max.

HALL PH-2
Two Wright GR-1820F-51, 750 hp
DIMENSIONS: Span 72'10", Lg. 51', Ht. 17'10", Wing Area 1170 sq. ft.
WEIGHT: Empty 9150 lb., Gross 15,411 lb., Max. 16,370 lb. Fuel 750-892 gal.
PERFORMANCE: Speed- Top 145 mph at s. l., 151 mph at 2800', Cruising 126 mph, Stalling 60 mph. Service Ceiling 21,000', Climb 1550'/1 min. Range 1830 miles normal, 2170 miles max.

Four PS-3s ordered on April 30, 1929, were completed with gun positions in the bow and stern of the hulls. The first was destroyed at Anacostia during its tests in June 1929, while one did serve VP-2 and the others VJ-1. The gun cockpits were soon covered over when the aircraft reverted to normal S-38B configuration. Redesignated RS-3, these amphibians served with utility squadrons along with six more assorted RS types added later.

HALL PH-3
Two Wright GR-1820F-51, 750 hp at 3200'
DIMENSIONS: Span 72'10", Lg. 51', Ht. 19'10", Wing Area 1170 sq. ft.
WEIGHT: Empty 9614 lb., Gross 16,152 lb., Max. 17,679 lb. Fuel 750-892 gal.
PERFORMANCE: Speed- Top 153 mph at s.1., 159 mph at 3200', Cruising 136 mph, Stalling 60 mph. Service Ceiling 21,350'. Range 1937 miles normal, 2300 miles max.

Sikorsky did build a true patrol biplane, the three-place XP2S-1 with 450-hp Wasps mounted in tandem over the hull, two .30-caliber flexible Brownings, and two 500-pound bombs. Ordered June 3, 1930, the XP2S-1 was tested in June 1932, but won no production contracts.

SIKORSKY XPS-1

SIKORSKY XP2S-1
Two Pratt & Whitney R-1340-88, 450 hp
DIMENSIONS: Span 56', Lg. 44'2", Ht. 16'4", Wing Area 762 sq. ft.
WEIGHT: Empty 6040 lb., Gross 9745 lb. Fuel 180-350 gal.
PERFORMANCE: Speed- Top 124 mph at s.1., Stalling 59.5 mph. Service Ceiling 10,500', Climb 660'/1 min.

The Big Boats

Perfection of patrol types capable of safely flying to overseas bases in Alaska, Hawaii, the Philippines, or the Canal Zone was seen as the major problem facing American flying boat designers. Bureau of Aeronautics engineers planned a 100-foot span monoplane that was a big step toward this capability, and on February 28, 1928, ordered Consolidated Aircraft, then in Buffalo, New York, to build a prototype.

SIKORSKY XPS-2

SIKORSKY PS-3
Two Pratt & Whitney R-1340C, 450 hp at s.1.
DIMENSIONS: Span 71'8", Lg. 40'3", Ht. 13'10", Wing Area 720 sq. ft.
WEIGHT: Empty 6740 lb., Gross 10,323 lb. Fuel 330 gal.
PERFORMANCE: Speed- Top 123.5 mph at s.1., Cruising 110 mph, Stalling 64 mph. Service Ceiling 15,300', Climb 5000'/8 min. Range 594 miles.

CONSOLDATED XPY-1
Two Pratt & Whitney R-1340-38, 450 hp
DIMENSIONS: Span 100', Lg. 61'9", Ht. 17'4" Wing Area 1110 sq. ft.
WEIGHT. Empty 8369 lb. Gross 13,734 1b., Max. 16,492 lb. Fuel 600-1021 gal.
PERFORMANCE: Speed- Top 118 mph at s.l., Cruising 70 mph. Stalling 56 mph. Service Ceiling 15,300', Climb 730'/1 min., 5,000'/8.3 min. Range 1716 miles normal, 2620 miles max.

First flown January 10, 1929, the XPY-l had two 450-hp Pratt & Whitney R-1340-38 Wasps suspended on struts between a fabric-covered, metal-frame wing and an all-metal single-step hull with five open cockpits. Isaac M. Laddon designed the first Navy monoplane patrol type with outboard pontoons to keep the wing tips out of the water and a twin rudder tail assembly. At the Navy's request, a third Wasp was installed above the wing in August, an effort to increase speed that Laddon regarded with distaste.

CONSOLIDATED XPY-1 (3 engines)
As above, but gross weight 14,900 1b.
Speed- Top 118 mph at s.l., Stalling 58 mph, Service Ceiling 18,100', Climb 880'/1 min., 7,050'/10 min.

Glenn L. Martin, however, underbid Consolidated for production of the type, starting a patrol plane rivalry that continued for over two decades. Consolidated did build a successful commercial XPY-l development known as the Commodore.

Nine examples of Martin's version ordered June 29, 1929, were designated P3M-l. The first, tested January 26, 1931, was similar to the twin-engine XPY-1 with R-1340-38 Wasps and had five crewmen, four .30-caliber guns, and four 500-pound bombs. All nine were delivered by May 1931, the P3M-ls being modified to P3M-2 standard by September with 525-hp R-1690-32 Hornets, ring cowls, and enclosed pilots' seats. They served VP-10 in 1932 and VP-15 in 1936, but most of the time were at training stations.

Martin P3M-1
Two Pratt & Whitney R-1340-38, 450 hp
DIMENSIONS: Span 100', Lg. 61'9", Ht. 16'8", Wing Area 1119 sq. ft.
WEIGHT: Empty 9988 lb. Gross 14,797 lb., Max. 17,122 lb. Fuel 500-850 gal.
PERFORMANCE: Speed- Top 114 mph at s.1., Cruising 70 mph, Stalling 60 mph. Service Ceiling 12,600', Climb 4600'/10 min. Range 427 miles/2000 lb. bombs, 911 miles normal (500 gal.) patrol, 1540 miles max.

Martin P3M-2
Two Pratt & Whitney R-1690-32, 525 hp
DIMENSIONS: Span 100', Lg. 61'9", Ht. 16'8", Wing Area 1119 sq. ft.
WEIGHT: Empty 10,032 1b. Gross 15,688 lb., Max. 17,977 lb. Fuel 844 gal.
PERFORMANCE: Speed- Top 115 mph at s.1. Stalling 61 mph. Service Ceiling 11,900' Climb 5000'/10.9 min. Range 1010 miles normal, 1770 miles max.

Martin also received a contract June 28, 1929, for a developmental prototype with the same Clark Y wing section, but lowered, and with two cowled 575-hp Wright R-1820-64 Cyclones installed on the leading edge. It was first tested June 22, 1931, as the XP2M-l with a third Cyclone mounted above the wing, but this engine was deleted when the aircraft was modified to the XP2M-2 in 1932. This reduction in power lowered performance, except for an increase in range obtained from reduced fuel consumption.

Enclosures covered the original open pilots' cockpits on this Martin and a Mk 11 sight in the bow aimed bombs hung above the struts connecting the fuselage and the floats that contained the fuel tanks. Flexible .30-caliber guns in the bow and rear cockpits could be supported by weapons in the waist doors, if needed.

USN

Martin XP2M-2
Two Wright R-1820-64, 575 hp
DIMENSIONS: Span 100', Lg. 61'2", Ht. 15'10", Wing Area 1204 sq. ft.
WEIGHT: Empty 11,138 lb., Gross 18,935 lb., Max. 20,146 lb. Fuel 750-1191 gal.
PERFORMANCE: Speed- Top 128 at s.1. Stalling 66 mph. Service Ceiling 7,600', Climb 4200'/10 min. Range 1900 miles normal.

USN

Martin XP2M-1
Three Wright R-1820-64, 575 hp
DIMENSIONS: Span 100', Lg. 61'2", Ht. 20'9", Wing Area 1204 sq. ft.
WEIGHT: Empty 12,467 lb., Gross 19,937 lb., Max. 22,916 lb. Fuel 750-1194 gal.
PERFORMANCE: Speed- Top 143 at s.1. Stalling 68 mph. Service Ceiling 13,400', Climb 5000'/5.9 min. Range 1257 miles normal, 1855 miles max.

USN

HALL XP2H-1
Four Curtiss V-1570-54, 600 hp
DIMENSIONS: Span 112', Lg. 70'10", Ht. 25'6", Wing Area 2742 sq. ft.
WEIGHT: Empty 20,417 lb., Gross 35,393 lb., Max. 43,193 lb. Fuel 3368 gal.
PERFORMANCE: Speed- Top 139 at s.1., Cruising 120 mph, Stalling 59 mph. Service Ceiling 10,900', Climb 5000'/8.7 min. Range 2150 miles normal, 3350 miles max.

The last patrol biplane built for the Navy, and the last with inline engines, was the Hall XP2H-1 ordered June 30, 1930, and first flown November 15, 1932. Largest American flying boat since NC-4, it had a crew of six and four 600-hp Curtiss V-1570-54 Conquerors mounted in tandem pairs and cooled by radiators below the front engines. Armament included a 2,000-pound bomb load and five .30-caliber Browning guns at positions in the nose, rear deck, waist and tail. The last weapon was aimed by a prone gunner between clamshell doors, the first tail gun on a Navy plane.

SDAM

CONSOLIDATED XP2Y-1 (original 3-engine form)

Consolidated offered an improved XPY-l design with 575-hp Wright R-1820 Cyclones and a small lower wing, making a sesquiplane (1+l/2 wing) layout with room for more fuel tanks and bomb racks. This design won the next Navy design competition, with contracts for an XP2Y-1 prototype on May 26, 1931, and 23 similar P2Y-ls July 7.

SDAM

CONSOLIDATED XP2Y-1
Two Wright R-1820-E, 575 hp
DIMENSIONS: Span 100', Lg. 61'9", Ht. 16'8", Wing Area 1430 sq. ft.
WEIGHT: Empty 10,950 lb., Gross 20,852 lb., Max. 21,547 lb. Fuel 1200 gal.
PERFORMANCE: Speed- Top 126 at s.1., Stalling 61 mph. Service Ceiling 11,000', Climb 5000'/10.7 min. Range 1768 miles normal, 1940 miles max.

The XP2Y-1 was first flown March 26, 1932, with three engines, but on May 18, tests began with the two-engine layout chosen for production ships. Three-bladed propellers, ring cowls, and enclosed pilot cockpits were featured on the five-place patrol plane. Armament included up to 2,000 pounds of bombs under the wings, a .30-caliber Browning in the bow cockpit, and two others beneath the sliding hatches of the twin waist openings.

ARC

CONSOLIDATED P2Y-1
Two Wright R-1820-E, 575 hp
DIMENSIONS: Span 100', Lg. 61'9", Ht. 17'3", Wing Area 1430 sq. ft.
WEIGHT: Empty 10,950 lb., Gross 19,852 lb., Max. 21,052 lb. Fuel 1200 gal.
PERFORMANCE: Speed- Top 126 at s.1., Stalling 60.4 mph. Service Ceiling 11,200', Climb 5000'/10.2 min. Range 1750 miles normal, 2050 miles max.

On February 1, 1933, the first P2Y-1s went to Norfolk for Patrol Squadron Ten (VP-10), who found them far superior in endurance to the old biplane boats. Two then spectacular demonstrations of their capabilities are remembered; the nonstop flight from Norfolk to Coco Solo, the Canal Zone base, by VP-5 in September 1933, and by six VP-10 boats from San Francisco to Pearl Harbor in January 1934. The latter 2,400-mile formation flight took 24 hours, 35 minutes, and satisfied a Navy ambition

SDAM

CONSOLIDATED XP2Y-2
Two Wright R-1820-88, 750 hp at takeoff
DIMENSIONS: Span 100', Lg. 61'9", Ht. 17'3", Wing Area 1430 sq. ft.
WEIGHT: Empty 11,349 lb., Gross 20,251 lb., Max. 24,043 lb. Fuel 1632 gal.
PERFORMANCE: Speed- Top 138 at 4,000', Stalling 61 mph. Service Ceiling 10,800', Climb 5000'/12.6 min. Range 1890 miles normal, 2900 miles max.

ARC

CONSOLIDATED P2Y-3
Two Wright R-1820-90, 750 hp at takeoff, 700 hp at 4,000'
DIMENSIONS: Span 100', Lg. 61'9", Ht. 19'1", Wing Area 1514 sq. ft.
WEIGHT: Empty 12,769 lb., Gross 25,266 lb., Max. 27,291 lb. Fuel 1620 gal.
PERFORMANCE: Speed- Top 131 mph at s. l., 139 at 4,000', Cruising 117 mph, Stalling 63 mph. Service Ceiling 16,100', Climb 650'/ 1 min. Range 1800 miles patrol, 1180 miles/2,000-lb. bombs.

frustrated in 1925, when the PN-9 biplane ran out of fuel and had to go the rest of the way by sail!

The last P2Y-1 became the XP2Y-2 in August 1933, with the R-1820-88 Cyclones inserted into the upper wing's leading edge. This layout was adopted for 23 P2Y-3 models ordered December 27, 1933 and delivered from January to May 1935, with 700-hp R-1820-90 Cyclones.

This new engine position was so successful that the P2Y-ls in service were modernized to P2Y-2 configuration with conversion kits made up by Consolidated and shipped to Pearl Harbor and Coco Solo. Consolidated's P2Y-2 and P2Y-3 boats were to continue in squadron service until sent to Pensacola as trainers in 1941.

Foreign sales included a P2Y-lC for Colombia flown on December 23, 1932, and a P2Y-lJ, the latter assembled and flown in Japan by the Kawanishi Company on April 12, 1935, for evaluation by the Japanese Navy. Six P2Y-3A boats were ordered by Argentina in May 1936, and first flown June 3, 1937. Delivered from San Diego by August 1937, they served Argentina's patrol squadron for ten years.

SDAM

CONSOLIDATED P2Y-3A for Argentina

CHAPTER 8

NEW WEAPONS FOR THE NAVY, 1918-1933

Shore-based seaplanes like the Curtiss R-6L were the first Navy torpedo planes.

Aircraft bearing the Navy's "Attack" designation have replaced the battleship's heavy guns as the hammer of the fleet's fighting power. During World War II, carrier-based attack planes were attacking enemy vessels with torpedoes or dive-bombing, strafing with cannon and rockets, or striking hundreds of miles inland at surface targets, with a radius of action and striking speed never equaled by a naval weapon.

Radar and the potential of nuclear weapons since 1945 would add to the destructive capability of carrier aircraft. Attack planes have made more of a change in naval tactics and strategy than did the armored steamship when it replaced wooden sailing ships.

NAF N-1
Liberty 12, 360 hp
DIMENSIONS: Span 51', Lg. 31'7", Ht. 15'4", Wing Area 694 sq. ft.
WEIGHT: Empty 4330 lb., Gross 5900 lb.
PERFORMANCE: Speed- Top 94 mph. Climb 3250'/10 min.

The weapon was not easily developed, however. It began with frail, short-range seaplanes designed to make torpedo attacks from shore bases. Then the torpedo plane was adapted to the aircraft carrier, making it a part of the fleet. Specialized scouting and dive-bombing types were also developed for the carriers, and shore-based types abandoned. After World War II substituted the carrier for the battleship as the principle arm of the fleet, scouting, bombing, and torpedo functions were successfully combined into a single attack type.

When World War I began, the Navy had no aircraft suitable for attacking either shipping or land targets, and practical weapons for aircraft use were slow in coming. As early as October 3, 1912, however, the first ground test had been made of a recoilless gun to be fired from aircraft at surface targets. Commander Cleland Davis had designed a two-inch rifle firing a six-pound shell out one end of the barrel and ejecting a counter-weight out the other. This weapon was mounted, with an attached Lewis gun for aiming, on the bow of a Curtiss flying boat and test fired August 4, 1917.

An aircraft to carry a Davis gun was designed by Jerome Hunsaker at the Naval Aircraft Factory by January 24, 1918, and two prototypes were begun. The first aircraft designed and built for the attack role, the NAF N-l was a two-seat biplane with a Liberty 12 and pusher propeller, giving the gunner a clear field of fire.

The first example was finished on May 22, 1918, but an accidental fire destroyed it before tests began. A second N-l was rolled into the Delaware River and made its first flight July 25, testing the Davis gun two days later. British Handley Pages, however, had already tried that weapon, against submarines, and they had withdrawn the Davis gun from service in February 1918. Clearly, more formidable ordinance would be needed, and the N-1 program was canceled after four examples.

Shore-based Torpedo Planes

Rear Admiral Bradley A. Fiske had received a patent in July 1912 for a method of carrying and delivering a torpedo by air, but the first nation to actually use torpedo planes in warfare was Great Britain. In 1915, the British made attacks on Turkish vessels with two-place Short seaplanes handling a small torpedo between the floats. Germany began torpedo attacks on Russian ships in September 1916.

CURTISS R-6L
Liberty 12, 360 hp
DIMENSIONS: Span 57'1", Lg. 33'5", Ht. 14'2", Wing Area 613 sq. ft.
WEIGHT: Empty 3513 lb., Gross 5662 lb. Fuel 112 gal.
PERFORMANCE: Speed- Top 104 mph at s.1., Stalling 55.5 mph. Service Ceiling 9900', Climb 5000'/12.3 min. Range 368 miles/1036 lb. torpedo.

United States Navy developments had been hampered by the lack of a lightweight torpedo. Available aircraft could carry no more than 600 pounds of ordinance, not enough for a torpedo with enough explosive to damage a large warship, said a Chief of Naval Operations report on November 24, 1917. Not until November 22, 1918, is there a successful air launching, when an F-5L flying boat dropped a 400-pound dummy torpedo.

While still without a real torpedo plane at the war's end, the Navy did have the Curtiss R-6, an unarmed twin-float biplane with a 200-hp Curtiss V-X-X engine that arrived at NAS Pensacola in June 1917. With the pilot sitting in the rear seat, the R-6 was of very limited usefulness. Nevertheless, one squadron became the first American Navy planes overseas when, in January 1918, they were sent to the Azores to patrol with two 50-pound bombs against submarines.

The last 40 of 158 built were fitted with Liberty engines and designated R-6L. The increased power enabled them to handle a light (1,036-pound) torpedo and tests began on May 3, 1919. Torpedo detachments were then organized at Hampton Roads and San Diego, but the R-6L was not nearly rugged enough for service conditions.

A more practical system was the torpedo-carrying version of Martin's Army MB-l bomber. The first of ten ordered September 30, 1919, was flown February 4, 1920, called the MBT by the Navy, and had two Liberty engines between the wings. Beginning with the third example, which was first flown on April 26 and tested by the Army at McCook Field in August, they had their engines on the lower wing and were designated MT-l (would become TM-l under the system adopted in March 1923 for new aircraft).

The pilot sat ahead of the biplane wings and cockpits for the front and rear gunner were fitted with Scarff rings for Lewis guns, and the outer wings folded back for stowage. A 1,628-pound Mk 7 torpedo or a 1,000 or 1,650-pound bomb, or six 250-pound bombs were carried between the four-wheeled landing gear. Martin delivered the last from Cleveland in August 1920. Six went to NAS Hampton Roads until replaced by PT-1 seaplanes in September 1921, and then went to the Marines at Quantico, while four served NAS San Diego until also transferred to Quantico in April 1923.

MARTIN MT-1
Liberty 12, 400 hp
DIMENSIONS: Span 71'5", Lg. 45'8", Ht. 15'8", Wing Area 1080 sq. ft.
WEIGHT: Empty 7150 lb., Gross 12,098 lb., Fuel 273 gal.
PERFORMANCE: Speed- Top 105 mph at s.l., 101 mph at 6500'. Stalling 61 mph. Service Ceiling 8500', Absolute Ceiling 10,600', Climb 6500'/19.6 min. Endurance 5.5 hours, range 480 miles.

NAF PT-l
Liberty 12, 360 hp
DIMENSIONS: Span 62'1", Lg. 34'5", Ht. 16'8", Wing Area 652 sq. ft.
WEIGHT: Empty 4231 lb., Gross 6798 lb. Fuel 110 gal.
PERFORMANCE: Speed- Top 96 mph at s.1., Stalling 49 mph. Service Ceiling 4500', Climb 5000'/15.7 min. Endurance 2 hours at top speed, 3.5 hours cruising.

Philadelphia's Naval Aircraft Factory combined surplus R-6L fuselages, HS-1L wings, and Liberty engines, to produce 15 PT-l two-place twin-float seaplanes ordered January 1921 and delivered beginning in August. Larger HS-2 wings were used on 18 PT-2s completed by June 1922. Torpedo and Bombing Plane Squadron One conducted the first mass torpedo practice on a live target on September 27, 1922. Eighteen PTs attacked the *USS Arkansas*, running at full speed, and scored eight hits with their Mk 7 torpedoes. But the PTs could lift a Mk 7 torpedo only if a single pilot and no guns were carried.

During the summer of 1922, the Navy tested five prototypes competing for a torpedo-plane contract. Two were

SDAM

CURTISS CT-1
Two Curtiss CD-12, 350 hp
DIMENSIONS: Span 65', Lg. 52', Ht. 15'11", Wing Area 830 sq. ft.
WEIGHT: Empty 7684 lb., Gross 11,208 lb. Fuel 111 gal.
PERFORMANCE: Speed- Top 107 mph at s.1., Landing 58 mph. Service Ceiling 5200', Climb 2600'/10 min. Range 350 miles.

twin-engine two-place types venturing a low-wing monoplane layout new for that period. Ordered June 30, 1920, and first flown on May 2, 1921, at NAS Rockaway Beach, N.Y., the Curtiss CT-l had two 300-hp Wright-Hispano engines above twin floats, but used 350-hp Curtiss D-12s when flown to Anacostia on January 13, 1922. A short fuselage of wooden construction had the pilot ahead of a rear gunner, while tail booms extended behind to a biplane tail. A Mk 7 torpedo could be carried, but only one of nine CT-ls ordered was completed.

NAF PT-2
Liberty 12, 360 hp
DIMENSIONS: Span 73'11", Lg. 36'4", Ht. 16'7", Wing Area 803 sq. ft.
WEIGHT: Empty 4478 lb., Gross 7075 lb., Fuel 112 gal.
PERFORMANCE: Speed- Top 92 mph at s.l. Service Ceiling 6100', Climb 5000'/16.4 min. Range 286 miles at top speed, 334 miles at cruising speed.

The Navy's first all-metal low-wing monoplane was the Stout ST torpedo plane, a clean design with two 300-hp Packard Liberty engines, twin rudders, and wheeled landing gear. Five had been ordered from designer William B. Stout's (1880-1956) Metal Plane company in Detroit, with the first flown April 25, 1922, but the rest were canceled when the prototype crashed after the 13th flight.

Two foreign-built single-engine designs were also studied. Three twin-float, low, cantilever-wing Fokker FT three-seaters were imported from the Netherlands, and the first was flown there on January 22, 1922, with a 400-hp Liberty engine. The first reached Anacostia June 29, along with a pair of Blackburn Swifts from Britain, biplanes with a 450-hp Napier Lion, wheels "releasable" in emergencies, flotation gear, and folding wings. These single-seat torpedo planes had the pilot sitting in a humped cockpit.

SDAM

STOUT ST-1
Two Packard Liberty V-1237, 330 hp
DIMENSIONS: Span 60', Lg. 37', Ht. 14', Wing Area 790 sq. ft.
WEIGHT: Empty 6557 lb., Gross 9817 lb. Fuel 195 gal.
PERFORMANCE: Speed- Top 110 mph, Landing 58 mph. Service Ceiling 10,000'. Range 385 miles at top speed.

USN

FOKKER FT

USN

BLACKBURN SWIFT

Donald W. Douglas (1892-1981) had developed a solid-looking two-place biplane from the Cloudster, his first airplane since he left Glenn L. Martin to become an independent producer. Three were ordered on April 14, 1921, and the first delivered as the single-seat DT-l on November 10 to NAS San Diego. The next two were DT-2 two-seaters, and the third was flown April 18, 1922, with the radiator in front of the Liberty engine, instead of at the sides. The landing gear could be either twin floats or wheels for land-based operations, and the wings could fold back.

MFR

DOUGLAS DT-1
Liberty, 400 hp
DIMENSIONS: Span 50', Lg. 37'8", Ht. 15'1", Wing Area 707 sq. ft.
WEIGHT: Empty 4367 lb., Gross 6895 lb. Fuel 115 gal.
PERFORMANCE: Speed- Top 101 mph, Landing 45 mph. Service Ceiling 8700', Climb 5000'/15.6 min. Range 232 miles at top speed.

USN

DOUGLAS-LWF DT-2 landplane
Liberty 12A, 420 hp
DIMENSIONS: Span 50', Lg. 34'2", Ht. 13'7", Wing Area 707 sq. ft.
WEIGHT: Empty 3737 lb., Gross 6502 lb. Fuel 115 gal.
PERFORMANCE: Speed- Top 101 mph at s.l., Landing 49 mph. Service Ceiling 7800', Climb 4050'/10 min. Range 293 miles/torpedo.

A 1,835-pound Mk 6 torpedo, or the 1,628-pound Mk 7, was carried beneath the fuselage between the fuselage, and a Lewis gun provided for rear defense. Launching torpedoes was a delicate matter, for they were prone to fail or misdirect if the plane wasn't flying absolutely straight or more than 32 feet high, or more than 100 mph. Actually, less than 25 feet high and 90 mph worked best.

The Navy ordered 38 more DT-2s delivered from the Douglas Santa Monica factory from October 1922 to October 1923. Another 11 were built by Dayton-Wright, 20 by LWF, and six by the NAF. DT-2s first entered service at San Diego with VT-2 in December 1922, and served with squadrons VT-1 at Hampton Roads, VT-5 at Pearl Harbor, and VT-20 at Cavite in the Philippines. Norway got one DT-2B from Douglas in 1924 and built eight more in Oslo, and four DTB models with 650-hp Wright Typhoon engines were later sold to Peru.

USN

DOUGLAS DT-2 seaplane
Liberty 12A, 420 hp
DIMENSIONS: Span 50', Lg. 37'8", Ht. 15'1", Wing Area 707 sq. ft.
WEIGHT: Empty 4528 lb., Gross 7293 lb. Fuel 115 gal.
PERFORMANCE: Speed- Top 99.5 mph at s.l., Landing 51 mph. Service Ceiling 7400', Climb 3850'/10 min. Range 274 miles/torpedo.

USN

DOUGLAS DT-4 landplane
Wright T-2, 525 hp
DIMENSIONS: Span 50', Lg. 34'5", Ht. 13'5", Wing Area 707 sq. ft.
WEIGHT: Empty 4224 lb., Gross 6989 lb. Fuel 115 gal.
PERFORMANCE: Speed-Top 108 mph, Landing 51 mph. Service Ceiling 11,075', Climb 5000'/10 min. Range 240 miles.

USN

DOUGLAS DT-6

MFR

CURTISS CS-1
Wright T-2 Typhoon, 525 hp
DIMENSIONS: Span 56'6", Lg. 38'5", Ht. 15'2", Wing Area 856 sq. ft.
WEIGHT: Empty 4690 lb., Gross 7908 lb. Fuel 214-370 gal.
PERFORMANCE: Speed- Top 101.5 mph at s.1., Landing 51 mph. Service Ceiling 9100', Climb 5000'/12.2 min. Range 452 miles.

Post-delivery modifications of DT-2s included four NAF DT-4s of 1924 with 525-hp Wright T-2s, one becoming a DT-5 with a geared T-2, and the DT-6 flown April 27, 1925, as a test bed for the first 400-hp Wright P-l air-cooled radial. Dayton-Wright modified three LWF ships as SDW-l long-range scouts.

Curtiss won a contract to build six examples of a BuAer design for a three-place biplane capable of scouting, torpedo, or bombing missions. The first CS-l was completed in November 1923 with a 525-hp inline Wright T-2 Tornado, two cockpits behind the folding wings, and twin floats interchangeable with wheels. The upper wing was smaller in span than the lower, a reverse of usual biplane practice, and a 1,628-pound torpedo was carried under the fuselage along with a flexible Lewis for the gunner, and a radio for an operator within the fuselage.

USN

DAYTON-WRIGHT SDW-1

One CS-1 became a CS-2 with a 585-hp Wright T-3 and radiators on the upper wing in January 1924, and Curtiss delivered two more CS-2s with increased fuel capacity. The last CS-1 tested the Packard engine with a three-blade propeller proposed for the future T3M-1.

CURTISS CS-l seaplane
Wright T-2, 525 hp
DIMENSIONS: Span 56'6", Lg. 40'3", Ht. 16', Wing Area 856 sq. ft.
WEIGHT: Empty 5390 lb., Gross 8670 lb. Fuel 214-370 gal.
PERFORMANCE: Speed- Top 100 mph at s.1., Landing 53 mph. Service Ceiling 6900', Climb 5000'/17.5 min. Range 430 miles.

The CS design was chosen to replace the DT-2s in service and contracts were let in June 1924 after open bidding in which Curtiss, asking $32,000, was underbid by Martin, asking $20,000. Thirty-five three-place Martin SC-1s with T-2 engines, similar to the CS-1, were delivered between February and August 1925. Forty SC-2s with T-3s were ordered in January and delivered by December 1925. They equipped VS-1, VS-3, VT-1, and VT-2, and carried their Lewis gun on a ring in the center cockpit, the third crewman located behind him inside the fuselage.

CURTISS CS-2
Wright T-3, 585 hp
DIMENSIONS: Span 56'6" Lg. 40'3", Ht. 16', Wing Area 856 sq. ft.
WEIGHT: Empty 6235 lb., Gross 11,233 lb.
PERFORMANCE: 102.5 mph at s.l., Landing 61 mph. Service Ceiling 4020', Climb 1450'/10 min.

Boeing received the next contract to build prototypes to a Navy design built around the 710-hp Packard 1A-2500. The pilot and torpedo-man sat side-by-side ahead of the folding wings, with a gunner in the rear, and the landing gear was convertible from twin floats to four wheels. Although three Boeing TB-1 torpedo planes were purchased in May 1925, the first was not flown until May 4, 1927.

BOEING TB-1
Packard lA-2500, 770 hp at s. 1.
DIMENSIONS: Span 55, Lg. 42'7", Ht. 15'1", Wing Area 868 sq. ft. (Landplane Lg. 40'10", Ht. 14'4")
WEIGHT: Empty 6298 lb., Gross as scout 10,537 lb./torpedo 10,703 lb. Fuel 450 gal. (landplane Gross 10,015 lb.)
PERFORMANCE: Speed- Top 106 mph at s.1., Landing, scout 58.5 mph, /torpedo 59 mph. Service Ceiling 2600', Climb 1900'/10 min. Range 850 miles.

MARTIN SC-1 seaplane (Also landplane data)
Wright T-2, 525 hp
DIMENSIONS: Span 56'6", Lg. 40'3", Ht. 16', Wing Area 856 sq. ft. (Landplane Lg. 38'6", Ht. 15'3")
WEIGHT: Empty 5610 lb., Gross 9025 lb. Fuel 389 gal. (Landplane: Empty 4895 lb., Gross 8310 lb.)
PERFORMANCE: Speed- Top 101 mph at s.1., Landing 55 mph. Service Ceiling 5850', Climb 5000'/20.6 min. Range 381 miles/torpedo, 562 miles max. (Landplane: Speed- Top 100 mph at s.1., Landing 52.5 mph, Service Ceiling 7950', Climb 5000'/14.7 min. Range 403 miles/torpedo, 595 miles max.)

A twin-engine biplane was ordered from the Naval Aircraft Factory in May 1925 and three more designed to the same BuAer specification were assigned to Douglas in July. The first Douglas XT2D-1 was flown January 27, 1927, at Santa Monica with wheels, and the NAF XTN-l was completed in May. Both had two air-cooled 500-hp Wright P-2 radials, folding wings and a narrow fuselage with three cockpits.

MARTIN SC-2 seaplane
Wright T-3, 540 hp
DIMENSIONS: Span 56'6", Lg. 41'9", Ht. 16', Wing Area 856 sq. ft.
WEIGHT: Empty 5908 lb., Gross 9323 lb. Fuel 389 gal.
PERFORMANCE: Speed- Top 101 mph at s.1. Landing 56 mph. Service Ceiling 5430', Climb 5000'/24.2 min. Range 335 miles/torpedo, 570 miles max.

MARTIN SC-2 landplane
Wright T-3, 540 hp
DIMENSIONS: Span 56'6", Lg. 37'9", Ht. 14'8", Wing Area 856 sq. ft.
WEIGHT: Empty 5007 lb., Gross 8422 lb. Fuel 389 gal.
PERFORMANCE: Speed- Top 102 mph at s.1., Landing 53 mph. Service Ceiling 7470', Range 336 miles/torpedo, 540 miles max.

USN

DOUGLAS T2D-1 seaplane
Two Wright R-1750, 525 hp
DIMENSIONS: Span 57', Lg. 44'4", Ht. 16'11", Wing Area 886 sq. ft.
WEIGHT: Empty 6528 lb., Gross 10,503 lb., Max. 11,357 lb. Fuel 250 gal.
PERFORMANCE: Speed- Top 124 mph at s.1./ Mk. 7 torpedo (125 mph as bomber), Landing 58 mph. Service Ceiling 11,400' (12,520' as bomber), Climb 5000'/6.4 min. Range 384 miles/torpedo, 454 miles max.

USN

NAF XTN-1 seaplane
Two Wright R-1750, 525 hp
DIMENSIONS: Span 57', Lg. 44'10", Ht. 15'7", Wing Area 886 sq. ft.
WEIGHT: Empty 6003 lb., Gross 10,413 lb., Max. 11,926 lb. Fuel 450 gal.
PERFORMANCE: Speed- Top 121 mph at s.1. with torpedo (123 mph as bomber), Landing 58 mph. Service Ceiling 11,300' (12,600' as bomber), Climb 5000'/8.1(7.1) min. min. Range 375 miles /torpedo, 764 miles max.

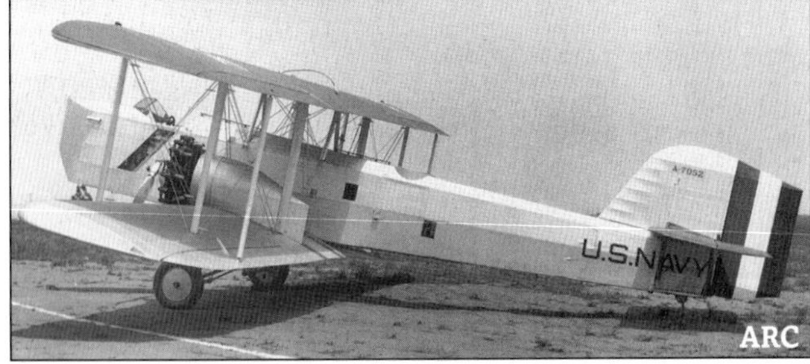

ARC

DOUGLAS T2D-1 landplane
Two Wright R-1750, 525 hp
DIMENSIONS: Span 57', Lg. 42', Ht. 15'11", Wing Area 886 sq. ft.
WEIGHT: Empty 6011 lb., Gross 9986 lb., Max. 10,840 lb. Fuel 250 gal.
PERFORMANCE: Speed- Top 124 mph at s.1. Service Ceiling 13,830' Climb 5000'/5.9 min. Range 457 miles.

ARC

DOUGLAS P2D-1
Two Wright R-1820E, 575 hp
DIMENSIONS: Span 57', Lg. 43'11", Ht. 17'6", Wing Area 909 sq. ft.
WEIGHT: Empty 7624 lb., Gross 12,791 lb. Fuel 356-572 gal.
PERFORMANCE: Speed- Top 135 mph, Cruising 108 mph, Landing 62.5 mph. Service Ceiling 11,700', Climb 5000'/7.6. min. Range 1,010 miles.

A 1,628-pound Mk 7 torpedo or bombs was carried between twin floats, which could be exchanged for wheels. The Douglas XT2D-l joined VT-2 at San Diego in May 1927, and was the only twin-engine aircraft actually intended for tests on the *Langley*. These trials were canceled when the P-2 proved unreliable, and had to be replaced by 525-hp Wright R-1750 Cyclones with three-blade propellers.

Nine more T2D-ls ordered from Douglas had a balanced rudder and four cockpits. Delivered in 1928, they did most of their service on floats at Pearl Harbor, since the Navy decided that carrier deck space was better used by larger numbers of single-engine types.

Eighteen more Douglas twin-engine aircraft were ordered on June 12, 1930, with R-1820E Cyclones, more fuel and twin rudders. By the time they were delivered, shore-based torpedo units had been redesignated as Patrol squadrons, for land-based attack was held an Army mission. Designated P2D-l, the Douglas ships were completed by June 1932 and served with VP-3 in the Canal Zone until replaced by PBYs in February 1937. Armament comprised two flexible Brownings, a torpedo, or bombs.

Three Men, Two Wings, and a Torpedo

All the torpedo planes described so far did most of the operations chained to shore bases, with only occasional practice from the *Langley*. As the new carriers *Saratoga* and *Lexington* neared completion, it was necessary to provide planes designed primarily for flight deck operation.

MFR

MARTIN T3M-l
Wright T-3B, 575 hp
DIMENSIONS: Span 56'7", Lg., 41'9", Ht 15'1", Wing Area 848 sq. ft.
WEIGHT: Empty 5462 lb., Gross 8839 lb. bomber, 8979 lb./torpedo. Fuel 132-180 gal.
PERFORMANCE: Speed- Top 109 mph at s.1., Cruising 78 mph, Stalling 54 mph. Service Ceiling 5700'. Range 520 miles/torpedo, 1045 miles as scout.

Such a type was available in the Martin T3M-1, 24 of which were ordered October 12, 1925, and entered service with VT-l in September 1926. A development of the SC-2 (T2M), it had the same short upper wing, a 575-hp Wright T-3B, and an all-welded steel tube fuselage framework, with the pilot and torpedo-man seated side-by-side ahead of the wing. A gunner in the rear cockpit had a Scarff ring and a floor opening for his Lewis guns. Twin floats or wheels were interchangeable as landing gear.

SDAM

MARTIN T3M-l seaplane
Wright T-3B Typhoon, 575 hp
DIMENSIONS: Span 56'7", Lg. 42'9", Ht 16', Wing Area 848 sq. ft.
WEIGHT: Empty 6323 lb., Gross 9855 lb. Fuel 132-180 gal
PERFORMANCE: Speed- Top 107 mph at s.1., Stalling 59 mph Service Ceiling 3500'. Range 972 miles.

One hundred T3M-2s with a 710-hp inline Packard 3A-2500, equal-span wings, and three seats in tandem, began appearing by February 1927 and equipped the first squadron (VT-l) to go aboard the *Lexington* after its commissioning in December. This meant the Navy carried its aerial punch to sea, but few realized that an actual substitute for battleships was appearing. VT-2 also flew from the *Saratoga* 's deck, while VP-2D, VT-3D, and VT-4D at Coco Solo, VT-5A with the Asiatic Fleet in the Philippines, VT-6 and VT-7 at Pearl Harbor, and VT-9 on the *Wright,* usually operated the T3M-2 on floats. NAS Pearl Harbor also flew the twin-engine T2D-ls of VP-1D.*

SDAM

MARTIN T3M-2 landplane
Packard 3A-2500, 710 hp
DIMENSIONS: Span 56'7", Lg. 41'4", Ht. 15'1", Wing Area 883 sq. ft.
WEIGHT: Empty 5814 lb., Gross 9503 lb./torpedo. Fuel 300 gal.
PERFORMANCE: Speed- Top 109 mph at s.1., Stalling 55 mph. Service Ceiling 7900', Climb 5000'/16.8 min. Range 634 miles/torpedo.

USN

MARTIN T3M-2 seaplane
Packard 3A-2500, 710 hp
DIMENSIONS: Span 56'7", Lg. 42'6", Ht. 15'11", Wing Area 883 sq. ft.
WEIGHT: Empty 6500 lb., Gross 10,209 lb./torpedo. Fuel 300 gal.
PERFORMANCE: Speed- Top 107 mph at s.1., Service Ceiling 5950', Range 755 miles/torpedo

These biplanes used water-cooled inline engines, but development of the air-cooled Pratt & Whitney Hornet radial provided a lighter power plant and reduced empty

*The D indicated a Naval District shore-based unit.

weight by a third. This engine was tested on the XT3M-3, converted from the first T3M-2, and also used on the XT4M-1 (Martin Model 74), a prototype first flown in Cleveland on April 27, 1927, with the previous wooden structure replaced by a new folding-wing metal framework covered by fabric.

USN

MARTIN XT3M-3
Pratt & Whitney R-1690, 525 hp
DIMENSIONS: Span 56'7", Lg. 41'4", Ht. 15'1", Wing Area 883 sq. ft.
WEIGHT: Empty 4600 lb., Gross 8304 lb. Fuel 300 gal.
PERFORMANCE: Speed- Top 102 mph, Landing 52 mph. Service Ceiling 3750', Climb 5000'/15.3 min. Range 423 miles at top speed.

Production T4M-ls first ordered June 30, 1927, appeared in April 1928 with a larger, balanced rudder, and were armed with two Lewis guns, a Mk 7 torpedo, or three 500 or 12 100-pound bombs. Three tandem cockpits were provided for the observer, pilot, and gunner, with room inside for a fourth man to operate the radio, or fire a gun at the floor opening. By then the Navy had the 1,740-pound 2A version of the Mk 7 torpedo, but the long, slow, launching run still put the torpedo plane at great risk to enemy guns.

ARC

MARTIN T4M-l
Pratt & Whitney R-1690-24, 525 hp.
DIMENSIONS: Span 53', Lg. 35'7", Ht 14'9", Wing Area 656 sq. ft.
WEIGHT: Empty 3931 lb., Gross 7387 lb., Max. 8071 lb. Fuel 104-200 gal.
PERFORMANCE: Speed- Top 114 mph at s.1. with torpedo, 113 mph with bombs, Cruising 98 mph, Landing 57 mph. Service Ceiling 10,150', Climb 5000'/14 min. Range 363 miles/torpedo, 694 miles max.

The Navy put 102 T4M-ls into service, beginning in August 1928 with VT-2B on the *Saratoga*. The *Lexington's* VT-lB also got the T4M-l, while twin-float versions were used by VT-9S, usually working in the Atlantic with the tender *Wright*.

USN

MARTIN T4M-l seaplane
Pratt & Whitney R-1690-24, 525 hp
DIMENSIONS: Span 53', Lg. 37'8", Ht. 16', Wing Area 656 sq. ft.
WEIGHT: Empty 4441 lb., Gross 7897 lb., Fuel 78-132 gal.
PERFORMANCE: Speed- Top 111 mph at s.l., Landing 59 mph. Service Ceiling 8400', Climb 3020'/10 min.

Glenn L. Martin decided to move his firm to Baltimore, Maryland in 1929, and sold his old Cleveland, Ohio plant to the Great Lakes Corporation, which received a Navy contract June 25, 1929, to continue torpedo-plane production. Eighteen TG-l biplanes were similar to the T4M-l, but for an R-1690-28 Hornet, modified landing gear and folding wings. The first TG-l was tested at Anacostia in April 1930 with twin floats and armed with a torpedo or 1,000 pounds of bombs, two Lewis flexible guns on the rear cockpit ring, and a fixed .30-caliber Browning in the upper wing, the first forward gun on a single-engine torpedo type. Most TG-ls went to VT-2, beginning in June 1930, with tail hook, main wheels with brakes, and new tail wheels.

USN

GREAT LAKES TG-l as seaplane

A Wright R-1820-86 Cyclone powered the Great Lakes TG-2 that had two .30-caliber flexible Brownings, one in the rear cockpit, and the other in the front cockpit with a guard rail to protect the propeller when the gun moved. The fixed gun was deleted. Thirty-two TG-2s were ordered July 2, 1930, and delivered from June to December 1931, serving on the *Saratoga* with VT-2 until replaced by TBD-l monoplanes late in 1937.

USN

GREAT LAKES TG-1
Pratt & Whitney R-1690-28, 525 hp
DIMENSIONS. Span 53', Lg. 34'8", Ht. 14'10", Wing Area 656 sq. ft.
WEIGHT: Empty 4179 lb., Gross 7652 lb., Max. 7922 lb. Fuel 200 gal.
PERFORMANCE: Speed- Top 108 mph at s.l., Stalling 58 mph. Service Ceiling 8000', Climb 5000'/10 min. Range 447 miles/torpedo, 547 miles max.

USN

GREAT LAKES TG-2
Wright R-1820E, 620 hp
DIMENSIONS: As TG-1
WEIGHT: Empty 4670 lb., Gross 8463 lb. Max. 9236 lb. Fuel 220 gal
PERFORMANCE: Speed- Top 127 mph at s.l., Stalling 61 mph. Service Ceiling 11,500', Climb 5000'/10 min. Range 330 miles/ torpedo, 547 miles max.

ARC

MARTIN XT6M-1
Pratt & Whitney R-1860, 600 hp
DIMENSIONS: Span 47'3", Lg. 33'8", Ht. 13'10", Wing Area 502 sq. ft.
WEIGHT: Empty: 3569 lb., Gross 6841 lb. Fuel 104 gal
PERFORMANCE: Speed- Top 124 mph, Landing 61.5 mph. Service Ceiling 11,600', Climb 5000'/8.8 min. Range 323 miles/torpedo.

DOUGLAS XT3D-2
Pratt & Whitney R-1830-54, 800 hp at s.l.
DIMENSIONS: Span 50', Lg. 35'6", Ht. 14', Wing Area 649 sq. ft.
WEIGHT: Empty 1876 lb., Gross 8543 1b. Fuel 225 gal.
PERFORMANCE: Speed- Top 142 mph at s.l., Landing 62 mph. Service Ceiling 13,800', Climb 5000'/8.7 min. Range 748 miles.

DOUGLAS XT3D-1
Pratt & Whitney R-1860B, 575 hp at 8000'
DIMENSIONS: Span 50', Lg. 35'1", Ht. 14'8", Wing Area 636 sq. ft.
WEIGHT: Empty: 4319 lb., Gross 7744 lb. Max. 7941 lb. Fuel 180 gal
PERFORMANCE: Speed- Top 120 mph at s.l., 134 mph at 8000', Landing 59 mph. Service Ceiling 17,300', Climb 5000'/7.7 min. Endurance 6.1 hours. at 75% power.

During most of this time VT-2 was the only torpedo plane squadron in service, for the shore-based units had become patrol squadrons and VT-1 replaced its T4M-1s with BM-1 dive-bombers. Until development of a new weapon, the Mk 13, which could be dropped from faster and higher attacks, the torpedo was less effective than dive-bombing.

There were two efforts to design a TG-2 replacement, the first being Martin's XT6M-1 ordered June 28, 1929, and completed in December 1930 as an all-metal, long-nosed biplane with a Wright Cyclone, a fixed upper wing gun and two Lewis guns. This was a two-seater specialized for torpedo work, but the Navy was losing faith in that weapon. It had no more success than the three-place Douglas XT3D-1, ordered on June 30, 1930, and tested in October 1931 with a 575-hp Hornet B single-row radial and a flexible Browning in the rear cockpit. The front cockpit also had a flexible gun, and the bomber window facing forward indicated the greater emphasis on level bombing, instead of torpedoes. In May 1932 this aircraft was returned to Douglas for installation of an 800-hp twin-row XR-1830-54.

Redesignated XT3D-2, it reappeared in January 1933 with a NACA cowl, wheel pants, and low enclosures for the three crewmen. Badly streamlined, was the official verdict, and no production orders were placed. On March 28, 1935, a Norden Mk XV bombsight and automatic pilot was installed to demonstrate the new Stabilized Bombing Approach Equipment (SBAE) system planned for the new PBY and TBD types. Weighing 178 pounds for that trial, this bomb aiming system would become most famous when used by the Army Air Force heavy bombers in World War II.

The First Dive Bombers

During expeditions to Haiti (1919) and Nicaragua (1927) the Marines had developed dive-bombing as a technique for hitting guerrilla-groups with 50-pound bombs dropped by DH-4Bs. The Curtiss F8C Helldiver, 1928's two-seat fighter, was the first type built especially for dive-bombing, which, as war would amply show, was far more accurate against small or moving targets than horizontal bombing.

If dive-bombing by fighters was effective against enemy personnel, it was apparent that large warships would be threatened by a dive-bomber sturdy enough to attack with an 1,000-pound bomb. Because of their weight, such designs were begun first under the old "T" for torpedo designation, and later received a "B" label for bombing.

MFR

MARTIN XT5M-1
Pratt & Whitney R-1690-22, 525 hp
DIMENSIONS: Span 41', Lg. 28'4", Ht. 12'4", Wing Area 417 sq. ft.
WEIGHT: Empty 3084 lb., Gross 5693 lb. Fuel 100 gal. .
PERFORMANCE: Speed- Top 134 mph at s.1. Service Ceiling 13,250', Climb 5000'/7.8 min. Range 442 miles.

Two very similar two-seat biplanes designed by BuAer for this requirement and ordered June 18, 1928, were the Martin XT5M-1 with a Pratt & Whitney R-1690-22, and the Naval Aircraft Factory's XT2N-1 with a Wright R-1750D. The first planes designed to pull out of a dive while carrying a 1,000-pound bomb, they had a metal monocoque fuselage and fabric-covered metal wing structure. Twin Lewis guns were provided for the observer, and the XT2N-1 had two fixed guns in the upper wing, while the Martin had a fixed synchronized gun on the cowl.

Martin's dive-bomber began tests at Anacostia on May 17, 1929, but on October 14, the right wing was damaged in a dive. The plane was rebuilt and pilot William McAvoy resumed tests on March 20, 1930, and the XT5M-1 became the first successful dive-bomber with the 1,000-pound bomb. The NAF XT2N-1 was also tested in March 1930, but many mechanical difficulties discouraged production.

USN

NAF XT2N-1
Wright R-1750, 525 hp
DIMENSIONS: Span 41', Lg. 27'9", Ht. 12'2", Wing Area 416 sq. ft.
WEIGHT: Empty 2735 lb., Gross 5333 lb. Fuel 100 gal.
PERFORMANCE: Speed- Top 134.5 mph at s.1., Landing 60 mph. Service Ceiling 14,100', Climb 5000'/7 min. Range 408 miles.

Another innovation was development of a bomb displacing gear to prevent the bomb striking the propeller when released in a near-vertical dive. Two arms swung the released bomb away from the fuselage, and this system passed final tests on January 7, 1931. Standard on all Navy dive-bombers, it was considered an official secret, not for export, until 1940.

Martin received contracts for 12 BM-1s on April 9, 1931, and 16 BM-2s on October 17. These were to be similar to the XT5M-1, but had R-1690-44s, ring cowls, and wheel pants, although the latter streamlining details were omitted after the type went into service. The first example was received on September 28, 1931, but the pilot was killed when it failed to recover from a dive in November. Better luck was had with the stronger second example in January 1932, and a replacement aircraft was built.

USN

MARTIN BM-1
Pratt & Whitney R-1690-44, 625 hp at 6000'
DIMENSIONS: Span 41', Lg. 28'9", Ht. 12'4", Wing Area 417 sq. ft.
WEIGHT: Empty 3700 lb., Gross 5749 lb., Max. 6259 lb. Fuel 100+60 gal.
PERFORMANCE: Speed- Top 145 mph at 6000', Landing 59 mph. Service Ceiling 16,400', Climb 5000'/5.9 min. Range 409 miles/1000 lb. bomb, 689 miles max.

The two-seat BM-1 had an M1921 .30-caliber Browning fixed gun in front of the pilot, and an M1922 .30-caliber

USN

MARTIN BM-2
Pratt & Whitney R-1690-44, 625 hp at 6000'
DIMENSIONS: Span 41', Lg. 28'9", Ht. 12'4", Wing Area 417 sq. ft.
WEIGHT: Empty 3662 lb. Gross 5657 lb. Max. 6218 lb. Fuel 104+60 gal.
PERFORMANCE: Speed- Top 146 mph at 6000', Landing 59 mph. Service Ceiling 16,800', Climb 5000'/5.7 min. Range 413 miles/ 1000 lb. bomb, 695 miles max.

Browning flexible gun for the observer, who also operated the 95-pound radio. The Mk V bomb actually weighed 989 pounds, and could be replaced by a 60-gallon drop tank. Arresting gear and emergency flotation bags were standard.

Four more BM-ls were added to the contract, which added an unarmed XBM-l delivered for special NACA tests on August 1, 1932. Sixteen BM-2s were completed from August 1932 to January 1933, for a total of 35 BMs. Squadron service began on the *Lexington* in July 1932 with VT-lB, which became VB-l in 1934.

Along with the TG-2s of VT-2, the BM squadron constituted the Navy's carrier-based attack strength from 1932-1934, until another BM squadron, VB-3, was formed on the new *Ranger* in July 1934. Dive-bombers and torpedo planes, unused by the Navy in World War I, had taken their place as first-line naval weapons.

CHAPTER 9

NAVY OBSERVATION AIRCRAFT, 1917-1932

GALLAUDET D-4
Liberty 12, 400 hp
DIMENSIONS: Span 46'6", Lg. 33'6", Ht. 11'8", Wing Area 612 sq. ft.
WEIGHT: Empty 4228 lb., Gross 5440 lb. Fuel 89 gal.
PERFORMANCE: Speed- Top 119 mph at s.1., Landing 58 mph Service Ceiling 14,000'. Endurance 3.5 hours.

ARC

Every Navy combat flight of World War I was made from shore bases and not from ships. But even before the war, the Navy had investigated the possibilities of operating seaplanes from its warships, and had begun developing catapults to launch them while the ship was underway.

In those days, sea warfare was centered on the battleships, which would win or lose the war in great collisions of sea power. Fast cruisers could locate enemy vessels, but the capital ship's big guns would sink them. Aircraft offered over-the-horizon eyesight, warning of the enemy's appearance, and more importantly, correct the big gun's aim by spotting the fall of shells aimed at ships too distant to be seen by a surface observer.

The armored cruiser *North Carolina* was the first U.S. Navy ship equipped to operate aircraft, using a catapult on the stern to launch a small AB-3 flying boat trainer on July 12, 1916. By the time war came, the cruiser *Huntington* also had a stern catapult, which launched a Curtiss R-6 floatplane in July 1917.

These fixed catapults blocked the after gun turrets and both launching and recovery of the aircraft by crane required that the ship be stopped, an unattractive prospect. The *Huntington* and its two R-6 floatplanes accompanied just one convoy to Britain and returned without using its aircraft. In October 1917, the catapults and all aviation gear were removed from both the *Huntington and North Carolina so* these ships' normal cruiser operations would be unimpeded.

The clumsy R-6 two-seater had shown little promise for shipboard work, because the observer sat in the front cockpit, where the wings blocked his view. Much better visibility was available in the unusual Gallaudet D-4 biplane, whose observer sat in the nose, followed by the pilot and a 360-hp Liberty within the fuselage, which turned four propeller blades on a ring around the fuselage. A large pontoon under the fuselage and small outboard floats near the tip of the sweptback wings became the float system most common on later Navy seaplanes.

The first Gallaudet floatplane prototype was the D-l with Duesenberg engines flown on July 17, 1916. Despite numerous mechanical difficulties, the Army bought four D-2 versions, and the Navy ordered two D-4 models in February 1918. Powered by a Liberty engine, the first D-4 crashed on a July 19, 1918, test, but the second was successfully flown in October 1918. The Navy accepted it, but no more of these interesting seaplanes were ordered, and wartime Gallaudet production centered on HS-2 flying boats.

USN

LOENING LS-1
Wright-Hispano H, 300 hp
DIMENSIONS: Span 34'10", Lg. 28'8", Ht. 10'5" Wing Area 229 sq. ft.
WEIGHT: Gross 2530 lb.
PERFORMANCE: Speed- Top 122 mph at s.l. Service Ceiling 15,500'.

Post-war shore-based observation aircraft displayed some advanced design styles. The first production monoplane for the Navy was the Loening two-seater first developed as an Army fighter. Grover C. Loening won a Navy order in June 1919, but his first Navy M-8 with a 300-hp Wright-Hispano was demolished on its delivery flight, September 17, 1919.

Nevertheless, work went ahead on a similar LS-l built with twin floats also flown in September 1919 and ten M-8-O observation landplanes armed with two fixed and two flexible guns. Larger wings were used in 1920 on the M-8-l (M-81) monoplanes, including six landplanes built by Loening and 36 with twin floats made by the Naval Aircraft Factory from September 1920 to March 1921.

LOENING M-81
Wright-Hispano H, 300 hp
DIMENSIONS: Span 37'10", Lg. 24'2", Ht. 6'10", Wing Area 260 sq. ft.
WEIGHT: Empty 1790 lb., Gross 2742 lb. Fuel 55 gal.
PERFORMANCE: Speed- Top 125 mph at s.l. Service Ceiling 13,750', Climb 5000'/5.4 min.

Aeromarine built three AS-l biplanes in 1920. Two were redesignated AS-2 in 1921 when the radiator was moved to the front of the 300-hp Hispano. Charles Willard designed this two-seater with two pairs of N struts, twin floats, and tail fin lowered to give the rear gunner a clear fire field.

AEROMARINE AS-2
Wright-Hispano H, 300 hp
DIMENSIONS: Span 37'6", Lg. 30'5", Ht. 10'8", Wing Area 380.5 sq. ft.
WEIGHT: Empty 2377 lb, Gross 3597 lb. Fuel 98 gal.
PERFORMANCE: Speed- Top 116.5 mph at s.1., Stalling 51 mph. Service Ceiling 16,000', Climb 5000'/6.4 min. Endurance 8 hours.

The largest Navy contracts went to Chance Vought, who had developed the VE-7 advanced trainer for the Army in 1918, and after the war the Navy had purchased its first twenty VE-7 two-seaters with the 180-hp Wright-Hispano E-2 cooled by a nose radiator. The structure was a conventional fabric-covered wood frame, with thin RAF-15 airfoils braced by double-bay struts.

Vought at Long Island City, New York, built sixty Navy VE-7 series and the Naval Aircraft Factory also received an order on September 17, 1919. Beginning in September 1920, that Philadelphia factory built 69. The first Navy VE-7 was delivered May 27, 1920, as a landplane trainer, but the Navy modified other versions.

VOUGHT VE-7H
Wright-Hispano E-2, 180 hp
DIMENSIONS: Span 34'1", Lg. 31'1", Ht. 10'2", Wing Area 248.5 sq. ft.
WEIGHT: Gross 2300 lb. Fuel 32 gal.
PERFORMANCE: Speed- Top 110 mph at s.l. Service Ceiling 14,800'. Endurance 2.33 hours.

The VE-7G was armed with a flexible Lewis gun in the rear cockpit and a fixed Vickers gun on the cowl, and became the VE-7GF when emergency flotation gear was added. A large central pontoon and wingtip floats were fitted to the VE-7H hydroplane, while the VE-7S, VE-7SF and VE-7SH were single-seat fighter versions with the forward cockpit sealed and two synchronized guns installed. One VE-7 fitted with the Wright-Hispano E-3 became the VE-9 in 1922, and Vought also built 21 Navy VE-9s by July 1923.

Catapult Seaplanes

After the war, the Navy operated observation aircraft from shore bases, but its principal concern was still development of shipboard aircraft, and here Vought biplanes dominated the postwar decade. Light and simple in construction, they easily fitted the compressed-air turntable Mark I catapult developed in 1921, which could launch a 3,500-pound aircraft at 48 mph.

First to get the catapult was the new battleship *Maryland*, whose 16-inch guns really needed aircraft to spot their shell splashes, so a Vought VE-7H trainer was launched on May 24, 1922. Next, the battleship *Oklahoma* catapulted a VE-7H on December 1. Meanwhile, a VE-7SF made the first takeoff from the *Langley*, the Navy's first carrier, on October 17, 1922.

The Navy appreciated the advantages of the air-cooled engine for shipboard aircraft, and quickly adopted the 200-hp nine-cylinder Lawrance radial that became the Wright J-3 when Wright bought out the Lawrance Company. Essentially, the Vought UO-l was a VE-7 with that radial engine, a new tail fin, and rounded fuselage with twin fuel tanks on each side of the front cockpit. Either UO-l float or wheel landing gear could be used. The first began Navy tests on June 13, 1923.

The Chance Vought company built 140 UO-ls between 1923 and 1927, including one converted in 1922 to the UO-2 racer with a water-cooled Aeromarine engine. One or two UO-ls served on every U.S. light cruiser, beginning with the *Detroit*, on August 23, 1923, and on the

VOUGHT UO-1
Wright R-790, 200 hp
DIMENSIONS: Span 34'3", Lg. 28'4", Ht. 10', Wing Area 290 sq. ft.
WEIGHT: Empty 1860 lb., Gross 2785 lb. Fuel 46 gal.
PERFORMANCE: Speed- Top 122 mph at s.l., Stalling 55.5 mph. Service Ceiling 14,900'. Climb 5000'/6.3 min. Range 418 miles.

VOUGHT UO-1 as landplane
Wright R-790, 200 hp
DIMENSIONS: Span 34'3", Lg. 24'5", Ht. 8'9", Wing Area 290 sq. ft.
WEIGHT: Empty 1544 lb., Gross 2469 lb. Fuel 46 gal.
PERFORMANCE: Speed- Top 124 mph at s.l., Stalling 52.5 mph. Climb 5000'/4.9 min. Range 448 miles.

MARTIN MO-1 as landplane
Curtiss D-12, 350 hp
DIMENSIONS: Span 53'1", Lg. 38'1", Ht. 12'2", Wing Area 488 sq. ft.
WEIGHT: Empty 3137 lb., Gross 4642 lb. Fuel 112 gal.
PERFORMANCE: Speed- Top 104.5 mph at s. 1., Stalling 49 mph. Service Ceiling 10,600', Climb 5000'/11 min. Range 483 miles.

battleships, beginning with the *Mississippi* in November. Two production Mark II catapults, with a launch capacity of 6,000-pounds at 60-mph, were mounted behind the four smoke stacks on each of the ten Omaha-class light cruisers, and a single catapult was placed on the fantail of each battleship.

Since UO-1s had no armament, FU-1 fighters begun as 20 UO-3s and described in the next chapter might accompany them. Two Voughts were built for the Coast Guard as the UO-4, and four sent to Cuba in October 1924 were the first Voughts sold abroad.

The Navy also prepared a requirement for a three-place observation type to use the new Curtiss D-12 water-cooled engine. Glenn Martin responded with an advanced mid-wing monoplane with a fabric-covered metal structure designed by a former Junkers engineer. Two open cockpits were provided, seating the pilot behind the engine, the gunner behind the wing, and the observer between them inside the fuselage had narrow windows under the wing.

The landing wheels were exchanged for twin floats when the MO-1 went aboard battleships. Radio was carried to direct the ships' big guns, along with a .30-caliber Lewis for the gunner. Six MO-1s were ordered in April 1922 from the Cleveland factory, and the first flew on November 11, 1922. Thirty more ordered in February 1923 were delivered from October 1923 to January 1924.

ARC

MARTIN MO-l as seaplane
DIMENSIONS: Span 53'1", Lg. 38'1", Ht. 12'11", Wing Area 488 sq. ft.
WEIGHT: Empty 3440 lb., Gross 4945 lb. Fuel 112 gal.
PERFORMANCE: Speed- Top 102 mph at s. 1., Stalling 50 mph. Service Ceiling 10,000', Climb 5000'/12 min. Range 467 miles.

ARC

MARTIN M2O-1
Curtiss D-12, 350 hp
DIMENSIONS: Span 43'6", Lg. 33', Ht. 12'8"", Wing Area 462 sq. ft.
WEIGHT: Empty 3063 lb., Gross 4643 lb. Fuel 112 gal.
PERFORMANCE: Speed- Top 102 mph at s.l., Stalling 50 mph. Service Ceiling 11,750'. Climb 5000'/11 min. Range 497 miles.

The first 18 went to San Diego for VO-1 and VO-2, and others went to Hampton Roads for VO-6. The battleship *Mississippi* got the first of the more powerful Mark IV gunpowder catapults that were being mounted on the upper rear turrets, but the first MO-1 launching was delayed until December 14, 1924. The big monoplanes proved too heavy and large for shipboard operation, and were soon retired.

ARC

NAVAL AIRCRAFT FACTORY NO-l
Curtiss D-12, 350 hp
DIMENSIONS: Span 43'6", Lg. 32'9", Ht. 12'6", Wing Area 462 sq. ft.
WEIGHT: Empty 3337 lb., Gross 4842 lb. Fuel 112 gal.
PERFORMANCE: Speed- Top 102.8 mph at s.l., Stalling 50 mph. Service Ceiling 11,200', Climb 5000'/8.75 min. Range 490 miles.

A more traditional approach to the three-place spotter requirement was the Navy-designed M2O-1 wood-framed biplane also built by Martin. Three were made and appeared in April 1923, followed by three made at the Naval Aircraft Factory as the NO-l, which appeared in December 1923. They had heavily braced wings, twin floats, a gun ring on the third cockpit, and differed in details. Curtiss D-12 engines powered all but the third NAF aircraft, which became the NO-2 with a Packard lA-1500. The decision to limit catapult operations to lighter air-cooled UO-1s ended the heavier programs.

Marine Observation Types

Elias delivered seven two-seat biplanes designed as "Marine Expeditionary" types intended to replace the DH-4B then used by Marine observation squadrons. The Buffalo company's EM-1 design was convertible from wheels to a single-float configuration and had a 300-hp Wright-Hispano, but the second appeared in January 1922 with a 400-hp Liberty, the power plant used on the remaining five aircraft. For economy's sake, however, the Marine squadrons were filled up with ex-Army DH-4Bs.

Despite efforts to produce advanced types, De Havilland's venerable DH-4 received another lease on life when the last 30 DH-4M-ls from Boeing in March 1925 were designated O2B-l and given to the Marines to supplement the aging DH-4Bs. At that time the Marines had observation planes with their First Aviation Group at Quantico, the Second Aviation Group at San Diego, and Observation Squadron Two in Haiti.

In 1927, the O2B-1 went to Nicaragua and China with VO-7M and VO-l0M. The China tour was quiet, but on July 17, 1927, VO-7M pilots made diving attacks on insurgent forces at Ocotal, Nicaragua, that are now remembered as the first use of organized dive bombing in combat.

Loening Navy Amphibians

The success of Grover Loening's amphibian concept led the Navy to order two examples designated OL-l. They dif-

SDAM

ELIAS EM-1

ELIAS EM-2 (Data as seaplane)
Liberty 12, 400 hp
DIMENSIONS: Span 39'8", Lg. 32'11", Ht. 13'4", Wing Area 482 sq. ft.
WEIGHT: Empty 2933 lb., Gross 4093 lb. Fuel 100 gal.
PERFORMANCE: Speed- Top 111 mph at s.l., Stalling 47 mph.
Service Ceiling 17,600', Climb 5000'/5 min. Endurance 5.4 hours.

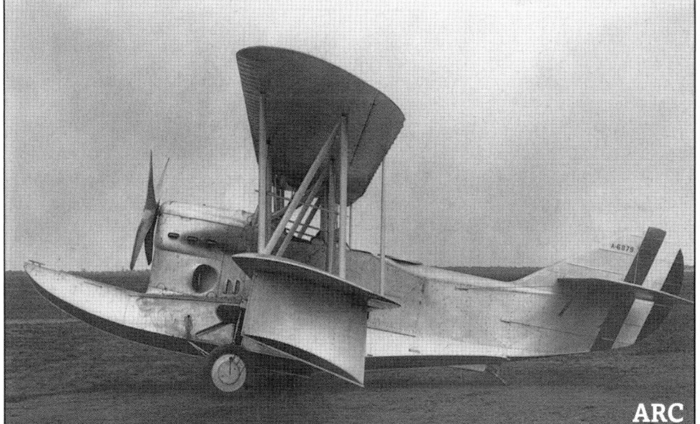

LOENING OL-1
Packard lA-1500, 440 hp
DIMENSIONS: Span 45', Lg. 35'4", Ht. 12'8", Wing Area 504.5 sq. ft.
WEIGHT: Empty 3576 lb., Gross 5208 lb. Fuel 148 gal.
PERFORMANCE: Speed- Top 125 mph at s.l., Stalling 59 mph.
Service Ceiling 12,750', Climb 5000'/7 min. Range 415 miles.

fered from the Army COA-1 models in having a Packard lA-1500, three crew cockpits, and a hull strengthened for catapult launching. First flight for the OL-1 was May 1, 1925.

Shortly afterward, the Navy got five OL-2 amphibians, two-seaters built as the Army's Liberty-powered COA-1. They had been requisitioned for Admiral Richard Byrd's naval air unit in the Arctic expedition of 1925, and were afterwards all used by the Marines.

The Packard engine was again chosen for six OL-3 three-seaters, which were, however, preceded by four

BOEING O2B-1
Liberty 12, 400 hp
DIMENSIONS: Span 42'5", Lg. 30'1", Ht. 10'6", Wing Area 440 sq. ft.
WEIGHT: Empty 2647 lb., Gross 4214 lb. Fuel 132 gal.
PERFORMANCE: Speed- Top 122.5 mph at s.l., Stalling 57.6 mph. Service Ceiling 14,000', Climb 5000'/6.8 min. Range 550 miles.

LOENING OL-2
Liberty 12, 400 hp
DIMENSIONS: Span 45', Lg. 33'10", Ht. 12'6", Wing Area 500 sq. ft.
WEIGHT: Empty 3540 lb., Gross 5010 lb., Fuel 140 gal.
PERFORMANCE: Speed- Top 121 mph at s.l., Stalling 57 mph. Service Ceiling 12,100', Climb 5000'/8 min. Range 405 miles.

LOENING OL-4
Liberty 12, 400 hp
DIMENSIONS: Span 45', Lg. 35'1", Ht. 12'9", Wing Area 504 sq. ft.
WEIGHT: Empty 3805 lb., Gross 5448 lb. Fuel 140 gal.
PERFORMANCE: Speed- Top 117 mph at s.l., Stalling 61 mph. Service Ceiling 11,000', Climb 4500'/10 min. Range 378 miles.

OL-4s fitted with Liberty engines; still considered more reliable for the planned Alaskan aerial survey. The first OL-4s, with three-bladed propellers and a new balanced rudder, were delivered in April 1926, and the last OL-3 went to San Diego in August 1926. The first aircraft built new for the Coast Guard were three Liberty-powered, unarmed, OL-5s delivered in October 1926.

By August 1926 the Navy thought well enough of amphibians to order 27 three-seat OL-6s with 475-hp 2A-1500 Packards. They were delivered from December 1926 to July 1927 and scattered among various battleships, shore stations, and a Marine squadron in China. A single Lewis gun was mounted at the rear cockpit. Grover Loening wrote that these aircraft had been made by a 190-man labor force in his Manhattan factory at a price of $32,500 per plane, of which nearly $15,000 was profit.

The greatest obstacle to using Loenings on aircraft carriers was that they had too large a wingspan for the elevators. The Navy redesigned one OL-6 contract aircraft to be the XOL-7, whose single-bay wings had a thicker Goettingen 398 airfoil and folded backwards. Delivered July 6, 1927, it proved too heavy and was slower than the OL-6.

The new air-cooled Pratt & Whitney Wasp radial engine gave the same horsepower as the water-cooled power

SDAM

LOENING OL-6
Packard 2A-1500, 475 hp
DIMENSIONS: Span 45', Lg. 34'11", Ht. 12'9", Wing Area 504 sq. ft.
WEIGHT: Empty 3671 lb., Gross 5350 lb. Fuel 147 gal.
PERFORMANCE: Speed- Top 122 mph at s.l., Stalling 60 mph. Service Ceiling 13,000', Climb 5000'/9.1 min. Range 423 miles.

USN

LOENING XOL-7
Packard 2A-1500, 475 hp
DIMENSIONS: Span 44'4", Lg. 35'3", Ht. 12'9"
WEIGHT: Empty 3944 lb., Gross 5623 lb.
PERFORMANCE: Speed- Top 117.5 mph at s.l. Service Ceiling 9750', Climb 5000'/11.5 min. Range 476 miles.

ARC

LOENING OL-8
Pratt & Whitney R-1340B, 450 hp
DIMENSIONS: Span 45', Lg. 34'9", Ht. 13', Wing Area 502 sq. ft.
WEIGHT: Empty 3429 lb., Gross 4802 lb. Fuel 96 gal.
PERFORMANCE: Speed- Top 121.5 mph at s.l., 112 mph at 10,000', Cruising 110 mph, Stalling 56.5 mph. Service Ceiling 14,300', Climb 5000'/7.1 min. Endurance 3.1 hours. Range 341 mph

ARC

KEYSTONE OL-9
Pratt & Whitney R-1340-4, 450 hp
DIMENSIONS: Same as OL-8
WEIGHT: Empty 3565 lb., Gross 5044 lb.
PERFORMANCE: Speed- Top 121 mph at s.l., 110 mph at 10,000', Cruising 110 mph, Stalling 58 mph. Service Ceiling 13,400', Climb 5000;/7 min. Endurance 3.1 hours.

USN

KEYSTONE-LOENING XO2L-1
Pratt & Whitney R-1340-4, 450 hp
DIMENSIONS: Span 37', Lg. 29'10", Ht. 11'7", Wing Area 348 sq. ft.
WEIGHT: Empty 2742 lb., Gross 4053 lb. Fuel 112 gal.
PERFORMANCE: Speed- Top 132 mph at s.l., Stalling 59 mph. Service Ceiling 16,200'. Endurance 3.1 hours at 110 mph.

ARC

KEYSTONE-LOENING XO2L-2
Pratt & Whitney R-1340-12, 550 hp
DIMENSIONS: Span 37', Lg. 33'3", Ht. 13'5", Wing Area 348 sq. ft.
WEIGHT: Gross 4829 lb.
PERFORMANCE: Speed- Top 142 mph at s.l. Service Ceiling 15,600'.

SDAM

LOENING OL-8A

plants, but at a lighter weight. One was installed on the last OL-6 contract aircraft, which was first flown August 19, 1927 as the XOL-8.

Twenty Loening OL-8s with two cockpits ordered in October 1927 were delivered from April to August 1928, and followed by 20 similar OL-8As from February to June 1929. Although wing racks for four 116 or ten 30-pound bombs had been added, most OL-8s served with utility, rather than with observation, squadrons.

Loening sold his company to Keystone Aircraft, which moved amphibian production to Bristol, Pennsylvania, where 26 OL-9s were delivered from May 1931 to March 1932. They were similar to the OL-8, but armament now included a .30-caliber fixed Browning with 500 rounds in the upper wing, the flexible Lewis gun with six 97-round drums, and four 116-pound bombs.

The Navy received 110 OL amphibians, but in April 1931 Keystone offered a new XO2L-1 with a more streamlined all-metal fuselage and a 450-hp Wasp. A second prototype, the XO2L-2, had a larger rudder and 550 hp. Both were tested aboard battleships, cruisers, and the *Saratoga* in 1932, but no production order was given.

Grover Loening Aircraft, a small new firm begun by that designer at Garden City, built the XSL-1, a small flying boat intended to operate from a submarine. Ordered June 7, 1930, the XSL-1 was first flown on February 5, 1931, by B. A. Gillies. With only an 110-hp Warner pusher engine, this single-seat monoplane could be folded into an eight-foot tube on the deck of the submarine S-1. Like the little Cox-Klemin XS-1 and similar Martin MS-1 single-seat biplanes of 1923, the unarmed XSL-1 was by no means a combat type, but is included here to complete the "S" category.

On March 27, 1933, the Loening was flown rebuilt as the XSL-2 with an inline Menasco B-6, but no more submarine-based aircraft were attempted by the United States, especially after the disastrous loss of Britain's M-2 submarine with its own aircraft hangar. The Japanese Navy, however, would develop submarine-based aircraft for World War II.

ARC

LOENING XSL-1
Warner Scarab, 110 hp at s.1.
DIMENSIONS: Span 31', Lg. 27'2", Ht. 8'11", Wing Area 148 sq. ft.
WEIGHT: Empty 1114 lb., Gross 1512 lb. Fuel 20 gal.
PERFORMANCE: Speed- Top 101 mph at s.l., Stalling 55 mph. Service Ceiling 13,000'.

ARC

LOENING XSL-2

The First Corsairs

Corsair is the name given to famous Vought planes of three generations. In Viet Nam, the Corsair was the A-7 attack, in World War II, it was the F4U fighter and for the

ARC

VOUGHT O2U-l seaplane
Pratt & Whitney R-1340-4, 450 hp
DIMENSIONS: Span 34'6", Lg. 28'7", Ht. 11'7", Wing Area 320 sq. ft.
WEIGHT: Empty 2600 lb., Gross 3893 lb. Fuel 88 gal.
PERFORMANCE: Speed- Top 147 mph at s.l. 140 mph at 10,000', Cruising 110 mph, Stalling 59 mph. Service Ceiling 18,700', Climb 10,000'/11.5 min. Range 571 miles.

previous generation, it was applied to the most successful Navy observation biplane.

Chance Vought, the vigorous chief of the Long Island City company, realized his basic VE-7/UO-l line had exhausted its potential and planned the O2U-l two-seater around the new Pratt & Whitney Wasp radial. The fuselage and tail were constructed of steel tubing with fabric covering and aluminum fuel tanks on each side of the front cockpit. The wings were fabric-covered spruce structures with the Clark Y airfoil, single-bay steel N struts and a 4.75-degree sweep back on the upper wing.

MFR

VOUGHT XO2U-l
Pratt & Whitney R-1340-4, 450 hp
DIMENSIONS: Span 34'6", Lg. 24'6", Ht. 10'1", Wing Area 320 sq. ft.
WEIGHT: Empty 2342 lb., Gross 3635 lb. Fuel 88 gal.
PERFORMANCE: Speed- Top 149.6 mph at s.l., 142 mph at 10,000', Cruising 110 mph, Stalling 57 mph. Service Ceiling 18,700', Climb 5000'/3.6 min. Range 608 miles.

Armament comprised a .30-caliber Browning gun in the right upper wing with 400 rounds, and a Lewis gun and five 97-round drums for the Scarff gun ring on the rear cockpit. A headrest replaced the gun ring when desired. Underwing bomb racks could hold four 116 or ten 30-pound bombs.

Two prototypes had been ordered by the Navy, the first flying on November 2, 1926, with a propeller spinner and straight axle landing gear. Later, it was fitted with central pontoon gear and in April 1927 set new world's seaplane records for speed and altitude. The second O2U-1 (the X prefix was added to the first aircraft later) deleted the spinner and had the split-axle wheeled gear used on the remaining Corsairs when they were not on pontoons.

On April 14, 1927, the Chance Vought Corporation received an order for the first 33 production planes, and while pairs of those fitted with floats replaced the UO-1s on light cruisers, six O2U-1s went as landplanes to the Marines' VO-7M in December 1927. They replaced the

O2B-ls (modernized DH-4) being used by this squadron in Nicaragua, and became involved in the fighting against Sandino's insurgents. Marine aviators flew observation, bombing and rescue missions, the latter winning a pilot the Medal of Honor. They were introduced to the kind of guerrilla warfare that later would make Viet Nam a bad memory.

Hasse

VOUGHT O2U-2
Pratt & Whitney R-1340-4, 450 hp
DIMENSIONS: Span 36', Lg. 25'4", Ht. 11', Wing Area 318.5 sq. ft.
WEIGHT: Empty 2371 lb., Gross 3830 lb. Fuel 80 gal.
PERFORMANCE: Speed- Top 147 mph at s.l., 141 mph at 10,000', Cruising 110 mph, Stalling 59.5 mph. Service Ceiling 20,100', Climb 10,000'/11 min. Range 725 miles.

New Navy contracts added 97 more O2U-1s for the battleships and cruisers. Another Marine squadron, VO-9M, used the O2U-l landplane in Haiti in 1928.

The next version of the Corsair was the O2U-2. Thirty-seven were delivered and used with wheels and arresting gear by VS-lB, VS-2B, and VS-3B aboard the three carriers in 1929 (the B meant the squadrons were assigned to the Battle Fleet) and by the Marine's VS-14M in 1931. The O2U-2's upper wingspan had increased to the 36-feet standard for later shipboard types, with a larger center section cutout, and provided the lift for potential heavier loads. A few were later fitted with ring cowls to reduce drag.

USN

VOUGHT O2U-3 seaplane
Pratt & Whitney R-1340C, 450 hp
DIMENSIONS: Span 36', Lg. 28'10", Ht. 13'2", Wing Area 318.5 sq. ft.
WEIGHT: Empty 2705 lb., Gross 3991 lb. Fuel 80 gal.
PERFORMANCE: Speed- Top 136 mph at s.l., 128 mph at 10,000', Cruising 110 mph, Stalling 61 mph. Service Ceiling 16,100', Climb 10,000'/12 min. Range 440 miles.

Vought also built 80 O2U-3 Corsairs with refined tail surfaces, and 42 O2U-4s by February 1930. Both were also convertible land or seaplanes used on both catapults and flight decks. Amphibian floats were also developed, the first being Brewster-built with the wheels outside the pontoon, and then Grumman made eight floats in 1930 with the wheels retracting into the pontoon itself.

USN

VOUGHT O2U-3 landplane
Pratt & Whitney R-1340C, 450 hp
DIMENSIONS: Span 36', Lg. 25'3/4", Ht. 11'6", Wing Area 318.5 sq. ft.
WEIGHT: Empty 2490 lb., Gross 3967 lb. Fuel 80 gal.
PERFORMANCE: Speed- Top 138 mph at s.l., 130 mph at 10,000', Cruising 110 mph, Stalling 61 mph. Service Ceiling 17,100', Climb 10,000'/12 min. Range 632 miles.

Corsairs were also sold abroad, beginning in March 1929 with 12 O2U-2Ms rushed to put down the last military rebellion in Mexico. Another 31 were built under license with 425-hp Wasps in Mexico City from May 1931 to March 1932. Some served until 1942. One tested a Watters engine cowl in October 1934. Japan bought an O2U-l, which Nakajima developed into the Type 90-II (E4N) seaplane.

USN

VOUGHT O2U-4 landplane
Pratt & Whitney R-1340C, 450 hp
DIMENSIONS: Span 36', Lg. 25'1", Ht. 11'6", Wing Area 318.5 sq. ft.
WEIGHT: Empty 2518 lb., Gross 3995 lb. Fuel 110 gal.
PERFORMANCE: Speed- Top 138 mph at s.l., 130 mph at 10,000', Cruising 110 mph, Stalling 61 mph. Service Ceiling 17,900', Climb 10,000'/11.2 min. Range 495 miles.

Warplane sales to China had been stalled by a State Department embargo until the Central Government was allowed to buy 12 O2U-1D Corsair landplanes with R-1340 engines in October 1929. Although first shipped in

December without weapons, relaxed regulations allowed fitting a Colt fixed and a Lewis flexible gun when serving with the 4th Squadron in Changsha. One downed a Junkers W-33 of a rival warlord to win the first aerial victory for Chiang Kai-Shek's forces, and one landed in Communist territory in February 1930. Named after Lenin, it became the first plane flown for the Chinese Red Army. Another 20 Corsairs with guns and bomb racks arrived in China by September 1930.

VOUGHT O2U-4 seaplane
Pratt & Whitney R-1340C, 450 hp
DIMENSIONS: Span 36', Lg. 28'10", Ht. 13'2", Wing Area 318.5 sq. ft.
WEIGHT: Empty 2526 lb., Gross 4004 lb. Fuel 110 gal.
PERFORMANCE: Speed- Top 136 mph at s.l. Service Ceiling 16,900'.

Cuba ordered six O2U-1As in May 1929, and added at least eight later. Other Voughts were exported in 1929/30: two O2U-ls to Canada, four O2U-1As to Argentina, and six O2U-2As to Brazil's Navy, beginning in December 1930. Peru bought six O2U-lE and two O2U-3B models. The Dominican Republic one O2U-1 in May and two O2U-3SDs in September 1933. These also had R-1340 engines and usually operated as wheeled aircraft. Seven O2Us were sold to civilian agencies and one became the Army's O-28.

Curtiss Helldivers

With the appearance of the Curtiss Helldiver in 1928 the Marines were finally able to replace the reconditioned DH-4s of their observation squadrons. This type began with an air-cooled version of the Army's Falcon biplanes, called the XF8C-l two-seat fighter. Prototypes had been ordered on June 30, 1927, but on November 21, a rush order for 25 more was added to supply the Marine forces in Nicaragua and China.

While the first F8C-1 arrived at Anacostia in January 1928, the aircraft were redesignated to match their assignment to observation squadrons. Four F8C-1s and 21 F8C-3s delivered by April 1928 were called the OC-1 and OC-2 when they reached VO-8M and VO-10M in San Diego, and later both were also used in Nicaragua by VO-7M.

Powered by the 410-hp Pratt & Whitney Wasp, these biplanes were armed with two .30-caliber Browning guns with 800 rounds in the lower wings, two Lewis guns with ten drums in the rear cockpit, and wing racks for ten 30-pound bombs. A single XOC-3 was the second XF8C-l modified to test the 600-hp Curtiss H-1640-1 engine in 1930.

VOUGHT O2U-4 with Grumman amphibian float

CURTISS OC-2
Pratt & Whitney R-1340, 410 hp
DIMENSIONS: Span 38', Lg. 27'11", Ht. 11'8", Wing Area 351 sq. ft.
WEIGHT: Empty 2508 lb., Gross 4021 lb., Fuel 110 gal.
PERFORMANCE: Speed- Top 137 mph at s.l., 131 mph at 10,000', Cruising 110 mph, Stalling 59 mph. Service Ceiling 16,850', Climb 10,000'/12.9 min. Range 550 miles.

CURTISS XOC-3

A more advanced version was the Curtiss O2C-1 "Helldiver", which was stressed for dive-bombing with four 116-pound bombs under the wings. The two fixed guns were now in the upper wing, whose span was reduced to match that of the lower wing. A tail wheel replaced the

NASM

CURTISS O2C-2
Wright R-1820-58, 575 hp
DIMENSIONS: Span 32', Lg. 25'8", Ht. 10'11", Wing Area 308 sq. ft. WEIGHT: Empty 2997 lb., Gross 4627 lb. Fuel 120 gal.
PERFORMANCE: Speed- Top 174 mph at s.l., 172 mph at 5000', Stalling 65.5 mph. Service Ceiling 20,000', Climb 5000'/3 min. Range 696 miles.

skid, and later ring cowls were added to streamline the 450-hp Wasp. Ring cowls were also added to some of the OCs and Corsairs in service.

USN

CURTISS O2C-1 (F8C-5)
Pratt & Whitney R-1340C
DIMENSIONS: Span 32', Lg. 26', Ht. 10'3" . Wing Area 308 sq. ft.
WEIGHT: Empty 2520 lb., Gross 4020 lb. Fuel 120 gal.
PERFORMANCE: Speed- Top 140 mph, Cruising 110 mph. Landing 63 mph. Service Ceiling 16,050'. Range 560 miles.

Ninety-three O2C-1 Helldivers, originally F8C-5s, were issued to VO-6M, VO-7M, VO-9M, and to Naval Reserve stations from September 1930 to November 1931. A Wright R-1820 Cyclone was installed in the unarmed XF8C-7 purchased in November 1930 as a transport for the Assistant Secretary of the Navy, and this aircraft was briefly redesignated XO2C-2 before reverting to the XF8F-7 label.

NASM

CURTISS O2C-2 (With R-1510, June 1933)

Three more Cyclone-powered O2C-2 Helldivers were purchased December 30, 1930, and two appeared in January 1931 with ring cowls, wheel pants, and sliding cockpit canopies. Armed with two Brownings in the upper wing and a third in the rear cockpit, they served as command planes on the two big carriers in 1931. The second

O2C-2 became a test bed for the twin-row Wright XR-1510 in June 1933.

CURTISS O2C-2 Modified (O3C-l)

The third aircraft was completed in September 1931 with a new fuselage structure and metal tail. While still marked O2C-2 on its rudder, this aircraft was designated O3C-l in Navy documents. It crashed during a test dive, killing the company pilot, so Curtiss had to build another two-seater using the same serial number, 8847, to fulfill the contract.

CURTISS XS3C-l
Wright R-1820-E, 620 hp
DIMENSIONS: Same as 02C-2
WEIGHT: Empty 3387 lb., Gross 4959 lb. Fuel 120 gal.
PERFORMANCE: Speed- Top 178 mph at s.l., Stalling 64 mph. Service Ceiling 19,800', Climb 1680'/1 min., 10,900'/10 min.

This aircraft became the XS3C-l, reflecting a new designation for carrier or land-based scout planes. The riveted duralumin tube structure of previous Helldivers was replaced with a welded steel frame fuselage, and the XS3C-1 had a new, panted single-strut, landing gear, balanced elevators and open cockpits. Armed with the usual three guns, the XS3C-1 may have been known as the XFl0C-l on paper. But it was as the XS3C-1 that this two-seater was first tested at Buffalo January 29, 1932, flown to Anacostia on February 14, and destroyed on February 25, when it lost its elevators in a dive.

Vought O3U-1

Vought retained leadership of the naval observation class with the O3U-1, developed from the O2U series except that the lower wing now had the same span and sweep as the upper. Powered by the 450-hp Wasp and convertible from wheels to floats, it had a .30-caliber Browning with 500 rounds in the upper wing, a Lewis gun and six drums in the rear cockpit, and bomb racks for the same 300 to 464-pound load as the Helldivers.

VOUGHT O3U-l
Pratt & Whitney R-1340-96, 450 hp
DIMENSIONS: Span 36', Lg. 26'1", Ht. 10'8", Wing Area 325.6 sq. ft.
WEIGHT: Empty 2546 lb., Gross 4005 lb. Fuel 80-110 gal.
PERFORMANCE: Speed- Top 138 mph at s.l., 129 mph at 10,000', Cruising 110 mph, Stalling 59 mph. Service Ceiling 16,300', Climb 10,000'/13.7 min. Range 506 miles.

The O3U-1 had been ordered January 18, 1930, and entered service with VO-3B in July 1930, with 87 built by September 1931 to three contracts in the new Vought plant at East Hartford, Connecticut. Generally, the O3U-1s operated as float planes from battleships and heavy cruisers until 1936. In May 1931, the O3U-l was tested with an improved Grumman amphibian float and 15 such floats were purchased for occasional service use.

VOUGHT XO4U-l
Pratt & Whitney R-1340D, 500 hp
DIMENSIONS: Span 37', Lg. 27'9", Ht. 9'7", Wing Area 335 sq. ft.
WEIGHT: Empty 2178 lb., Gross 3696 lb. Fuel 110 lb.
PERFORMANCE: Speed- Top 143 mph at s.l., 137 mph at 10,000', Stalling 56 mph. Service Ceiling 21,200', Climb 10,000'/10.6 min. Endurance 4.9 hours at 110 mph.

Vought attempted a more advanced structural design in the XO4U-l. with all-metal monocoque fuselage and fabric-covered metal wings, the swept-back upper one attached to the fuselage. Ordered May 13, 1930, the XO4U-l landplane crashed shortly after its first flight on February 28, 1931. Vought designers then preferred to stay with the proven structure of the O3U Corsair series.

VOUGHT O3U-1 seaplane
Pratt & Whitney R-1340-96, 450 hp
DIMENSIONS: Span 36', Lg. 29'11", Ht. 12', Wing Area 325.6 sq. ft.
WEIGHT: Empty 2747 lb., Gross 4057 lb. Fuel 80 gal.
PERFORMANCE: Speed- Top 135 mph at s.l., 126 mph at 10,000', Cruising 110 mph, Stalling 59 mph. Service Ceiling 15,200', Climb 10,000'/16.5 min. Range 352 miles.

Berliner-Joyce OJ-2

Another Navy effort was made to develop a lightweight observation type for the *Omaha*-class cruisers, whose catapults had a 6,000-pound limit. BuAer Design No. 86 was prepared, and on June 28,1929, prototypes were ordered from Keystone (XOK-l) and Berliner-Joyce (XOJ-l).

Using a 400-hp Wright Whirlwind and a ring cowl, the XOK-l was flown on January 5, 1931. By April, it had a new cowl, vertical tail, and guns on the upper wing and in the rear cockpit, but was destroyed in a crash April 15th.

NASM

KEYSTONE XOK-1 (Seaplane data added)
Wright R-975C, 400 hp
DIMENSIONS: Span 34'8", Lg. 24'10" (28'9"), Ht. 9'9" (11'4"), Wing Area 293 sq. ft.
WEIGHT: Empty 2000 (2219) lb., Gross 3176 (3395) lb. Fuel 60 gal.
PERFORMANCE: Speed- Top 143 (139) mph at s.l., 137 (133) mph at 10,000', Stalling 55 (57) mph. Service Ceiling 22,500' (19,900'). Endurance 3 (2.9) hours at 110 mph.

MFR

BERLINER-JOYCE XOJ-l seaplane
Pratt & Whitney R-985A, 400 hp
DIMENSIONS: Span 33', Lg. 29'1", Wing Area 284 sq. ft.
WEIGHT: Empty 2214 lb., Gross 3378 lb. Fuel 60 gal.
PERFORMANCE: Speed- Top 149 mph at s.l., 136 mph at 10,000', Stalling 60 mph. Service Ceiling 17,400', Climb 10,000'/9.2 min. Endurance 3 hours at 110 mph.

Instead of the XOK-1's monocoque fuselage, the XOJ-1 was completed with conventional fabric-covered welded steel tubing in June 1931, by the company now named simply the B/J Corp., instead of Berliner-Joyce. Powered by a 400-hp Pratt & Whitney R-985A, it passed acceptance tests in September and won the first Navy order for 18 OJ-2s on October 26, 1931.

In October 1932, full-span Zap flaps on both wings, allowing more lift with smaller wing area, were tried on the XOJ-1, but test results were unsatisfactory, and the flaps would not be used on production aircraft.

Beginning in March 1933, the lightweight B/J OJ-2s served in pairs aboard the light cruisers with VS-5B and VS-6B, and 39 were delivered from Dundalk, Maryland, by December 1934. Landing gear was interchangeable between wheels and floats, and the usual .30-caliber Browning gun was mounted on the upper wing, with another in the rear cockpit, and a 136-pound radio was provided. The OJs were replaced by the SOC-1 in 1936 and retired to Naval Reserve stations.

The company's last Navy contract, in June 1934, sent one OJ-2 back to the Dundalk factory to be rebuilt by October as an XOJ-3 with a new cowl, cockpit canopy, more fuel, and wing flaps, but it crashed in March 1935, no longer a contender for Navy orders.

Although the Navy's observation planes were roughly handled by catapulting and by the hoist back

MFR

BERLINER-JOYCE XOJ-l landplane
Pratt & Whitney R-985A, 400 hp
DIMENSIONS: Span 33', Lg. 25'8", Wing Area 284 sq. ft.
WEIGHT: Empty 1961 lb., Gross 3125 lb. Fuel 60 gal.
PERFORMANCE: Speed- Top 154 mph at s.l., 140 mph at 10,000', Stalling 58 mph. Service Ceiling 20,900', Climb 10,000'/8.9 min. Endurance 3.1 hours at 110 mph.

BERLINER-JOYCE XOJ-l with Zap flaps

BERLINER-JOYCE OJ-2 seaplane
Pratt & Whitney R-985-38, 400 hp at s.l.
DIMENSIONS: Span 33'8", Lg. 29'1", Ht. 12'7", Wing Area 284 sq. ft.
WEIGHT: Empty 2520 lb., Gross 3851 lb. Max. 3911 lb. Fuel 90 gal.
PERFORMANCE: Speed- Top 149 mph at s.l., 147 mph at 5000', Stalling 61 mph. Service Ceiling 13,500', Climb 5000'/6 min. Endurance 5.09 hours at 149 mph.

Vought O2U-1s on the *New Mexico* about 1930 show typical battleship scene between the wars.

BERLINER-JOYCE OJ-2 as landplane
Pratt & Whitney R-985-38, 400 hp at s.l.
DIMENSIONS: Span 33'8", Lg. 25'8", Ht. 10'9", Wing Area 284 sq. ft.
WEIGHT: Empty 2367 lb., Gross 3726 lb. Fuel 90 gal.
PERFORMANCE: Speed- Top 150 mph at s.l., 149 mph at 5000', Stalling 60 mph. Service Ceiling 15,300', Climb 5000'/4.7 min. Endurance 5.09 hours at 150 mph.

aboard, they provided warships with valuable over-the-horizon vision. The 16-inch guns reached up to 35,000 yards, so only aircraft could correct their aim by spotting their shell splashes. Each battleship carried a O3U-1

BERLINER-JOYCE XOJ-3
Pratt & Whitney R-985-38, 400 hp
DIMENSIONS: Span 33'8", Lg. 29'5", Ht. 12'6", Wing Area 284 sq. ft.
WEIGHT: Empty 2932 lb., Gross 4531 lb. Fuel 130 gal.
PERFORMANCE: Speed- Top 149 mph at s.l., 144 mph at 5000', Cruising 110 mph, Stalling 61 mph. Service Ceiling 14,100', Climb 5000'/6.3 min. Endurance 7.32 hours.

floatplane on the quarterdeck catapult, another waited on a cradle nearby to be hoisted up by the stern crane, and a third could be launched from a catapult on the third gun turret.

CHAPTER 10
ADAPTING FIGHTERS TO FLIGHT DECKS

CURTISS HA-1
Liberty 12, 380 hp
DIMENSIONS: Span 38'6", Lg. 30'9", Ht. 10'7", Wing Area 387 sq. ft.
WEIGHT: Empty 2648 lb., Gross 3687 lb. Fuel 100 gal.
PERFORMANCE: Speed- Top 123 mph at s.1., Landing 70 mph. Climb 7100'/10 min. Endurance 2.5 hours.

A Humble Beginning

The Navy's fighters have had the same basic mission as those of the Air Force: destruction of enemy aircraft. Since they are based on aircraft carriers, however, they present a more difficult designing problem. The carrier fighter must have a short takeoff and landing run for operations from a limited flight deck. To conserve space, carrier types should have either small wings, or some way of folding large ones. An arresting hook is necessary for deck landing, and safety gear should be available for overwater flying.

In World War I, the United States had no aircraft carriers, so the first Navy fighter was shore-based. The Curtiss HA single-float seaplane was a short-nosed two-place biplane with a Liberty engine and four-bladed wooden propeller, two .30-caliber Marlin synchronized nose guns, and twin .30-caliber Lewis guns in the rear cockpit.

CURTISS HA-2
Liberty 12, 360 hp
DIMENSIONS: Span 42', Lg. 30'9", Ht. 12'8", Wing Area 490 sq. ft.
WEIGHT: Empty 2946 lb., Gross 3907 lb.
PERFORMANCE: Speed- Top 118 mph at s.1., Climb 7900'/10 min. Endurance 2.5 hours.

Called the "Dunkirk fighter" since it was intended for operations in that area, the HA was ordered December 7, 1917, and first flown March 21, 1918, at Port Washington, Long Island by Roland Rohlfs. Crashed during tests, it was followed by a modified second prototype, HA-2, flown on December 23. A third, even more modified example with wingspan increased from 36 to 42 feet, was not completed until May 1919, when it was no longer needed.

The second fighter for the Navy was also a four-gun two-seater, but the Curtiss 18-T was a triplane with a new Curtiss engine designed by Charles B. Kirkham. Two examples ordered March 30, 1918, were first flown July 5 with wheeled landing gear; it didn't take long to build a prototype in those days. Yet the streamlined wooden monocoque fuselage contributed to good performance and flying qualities, compared to the dreadful experiences with the unstable HA type, and the Army bought two more examples.

CURTISS 18-T
Curtiss Kirkham K-12, 400 hp
DIMENSIONS: Span 31'11", Lg. 23'3", Ht. 9'10", Wing Area 309 sq. ft.
WEIGHT: Gross 1825 lb., Max. 2902 lb. Fuel 67 gal.
PERFORMANCE: Speed- Top 163 mph. Stalling 58 mph. Service Ceiling 23,000', Climb 15,000'/10 min. Range 550 miles.

The first Navy prototype was returned to the company and fitted with wider wings to set a world's altitude record of 34,910 feet on September 18, 1919. Both Navy prototypes competed in the 1922 and 1923 National Air Races. An unarmed fifth example delivered in September 1919 became the first plane to fly over Bolivia's capital city.

No Navy fighters were actually used in World War I, but David Ingalls became the first Navy ace, flying a Sopwith Camel with the RAF. Eight Camels, 12 Nieuport 28s, and two S.E.5s were transferred from the U.S. Army to the Navy in 1919, along with a Loening M-8 two-seater used as a prototype for the M-80 observation series.

In an effort to take these fighters to sea with the fleet, wooden flying platforms were built on two turrets of eight battleships, and the single-seaters mentioned above had a takeoff run short enough, with luck, to fly off these ships

MFR

CURTISS TS-1 seaplane
Wright J-4, 200 hp
DIMENSIONS: Span 25', Lg. 24'9", Ht. 9'7", Wing Area 228 sq. ft.
WEIGHT: Empty 1443 lb., Gross 2123 lb. Fuel 50 gal.
PERFORMANCE: Speed- Top 122 mph, Landing 50 mph. Service Ceiling 14,450'. Range 339 miles.

PMB

CURTISS 18-T-2

PMB

HANRIOT HD-2
Clerget 9B, 130 hp
DIMENSIONS: Span 28'6", Lg. 19'6", Ht. 8'6", Wing Area 203 sq. ft.
WEIGHT: Empty 904 lb., Gross 1521 lb.
PERFORMANCE: Speed- Top 112 mph.

and land at the nearest shore base. The first such flight was made by a Camel from the *USS Texas* on March 9, 1919, followed in August by a French Hanriot from the *Mississippi.* These Hanriots were developed from the HD-1 fighter popular in Belgium and Italy. The U.S. Navy had purchased 26 of a naval version, the HD-2 with twin floats, in 1918 to protect its flying boats at Dunkirk. Ten of these were imported and assembled with wheels at the Naval Aircraft Factory, and also served on the battleships *New York* and *Pennsylvania.*

Nieuport 28s also served on seven battleships, but the platform technique had apparent limitations, and was abandoned after 1920. The Marines, however, established a shore-based fighter unit with 11 Thomas-Morse MB-3s acquired in January 1922.

When the first U.S. carrier, the *Langley,* was commissioned, the Navy had two fighter squadrons, but they were equipped only with Vought VE-7SF double-bay biplanes designed as trainers. Powered by a 180-hp Wright E-2 and converted to a single-seater with one Vickers gun, a VE-7SF made the Navy's first carrier takeoff on October 17, 1922. The SF stood for single-seat, with flotation gear equipment. At least 50 Voughts were so modified in 1921, two Marlin fixed guns replacing the Vickers of the first ships. Both VF-l and VF-2 were based at San Diego at that time.

The first single-seater specially designed for operation from Navy ships was the TS-1, with the 200-hp Lawrance J-1 air-cooled radial (later became the Wright J-4). It was a single-bay biplane with the lower wing hung below the fuselage and containing the fuel in a droppable center-

Hasse

VOUGHT VE-7SF
Wright E-2, 180 hp
DIMENSIONS: Span 34'1", Lg. 24'5", Ht. 8'7", Wing Area 284 sq. ft.
WEIGHT: Empty 1505 lb. Gross 2100 lb. Fuel 30 gal.
PERFORMANCE: Speed- Top 117 mph at s.l., Landing 51 mph. Service Ceiling 15,000', Climb 5000'/5.5 min. Range 291 miles.

section fuel tank. Either wheels or twin floats could be used, and twin .30-caliber fixed guns were mounted on the cowl. The structure of the fuselage was welded steel tubing, and the wings were of wood; both fabric covered.

Rex Beisel, at BuAer's design department, was put in charge of the TS (for tractor single-seater) project in March 1921, and a contract for production of his small lightweight design was made with Curtiss on June 30, 1921. The Naval Aircraft Factory also built five TS-1s as a cost-yardstick project, and the first of these was delivered on May 9, 1922.

Curtiss built 34 TS-1 fighters, the first completed in June 1922, and the rest from March to June 1923, differing in some details from the NAF planes. Squadron VF-1 at San Diego operated the TS-1 until 1927, both from the *Langley* and with floats from battleship catapults.

CURTISS TS-1 landplane
Wright J-4, 200 hp
DIMENSIONS: Span 25', Lg. 22'1", Ht. 9', Wing Area 228 sq. ft.
WEIGHT: Empty 1240 lb., Gross 1920 lb. Fuel 50 gal.
PERFORMANCE: Speed- Top 125 mph, Landing 48 mph. Service Ceiling 16,200', Climb 5000'/5.5 min. Range 482 miles.

Four race versions with water-cooled engines and racing wings were also built by the NAF. These were two TS-2s with 240-hp Aeromarine U-8D engines and two TS-3s with Wright E-2 (later called TR-2 and TR-3). The last versions of the TS to be built were two aircraft with an all-metal fabric-covered structure designed by Charles W. Hall with lower wings raised to the fuselage bottom and braced by metal struts instead of wires. This version carried the same load, including two Marlin guns, as the TS-1. Flight tests begun September 4, 1924, as the Curtiss F4C-1, demonstrated that a metal airframe need weigh no more than the traditional wood and wire structure.

MFR

CURTISS F4C-1
Lawrance-Wright J-4, 200 hp
DIMENSIONS: Span 25', Lg. 18'4", Ht. 8'9", Wing Area 185 sq. ft.
WEIGHT: Empty 1027 lb., Gross 1707 1b. Fuel 50 gal.
PERFORMANCE: Speed- Top 126 mph, Landing 49 mph. Service Ceiling 17,400', Climb 5000'/3.9 min. Range 525 miles cruising.

That designation reflected the system of designating aircraft by their manufacturer, irrespective of design origin, and was affected by the Navy's efforts to explore high-speed flight by building unarmed racers. Curtiss had built the CR, R2C, and R3C racers, and they were considered to have covered the FC, F2C, and F3C designations. There was no F5C fighter, to avoid confusion with the F-5 flying boats.

Boeing's first naval fighter was the FB-l biplane, based on the Army's PW-9 with tapered single-bay wooden wings with the Goettingen 436 airfoil. The welded steel tube fuselage was fabric-covered, except for duralumin over a Curtiss D-12 inline engine with a tunnel water radiator under the nose. Armament was the arrangement standard on Navy fighters before World War II; two .30-caliber synchronized guns on the cowl, with one replaceable by a .50-caliber weapon.

Fourteen Boeings were ordered in December 1924, and delivery was made in December 1925 on ten FB-1s used by a Marine fighter squadron that served in China. Two FB-2s with arresting gear for carrier trials were

MFR

BOEING FB-3 on floats

BOEING FB-1
Curtiss D-12, 400 hp
DIMENSIONS: Span 32', Lg. 23'6", Ht. 8'9", Wing Area 241 sq. ft.
WEIGHT: Empty 2132 lb., Gross 2949 lb. Fuel 62+50 gal.
PERFORMANCE: Speed- Top 167 mph at s.1., Landing 57.5 mph. Service Ceiling 21,200', Climb 5000'/2.8 min. Range 509 miles.

BOEING FB-3
Packard lA-1500, 510 hp
DIMENSIONS: Span 32', Lg. 22'11", Ht. 8'9", Wing Area 241 sq. ft.
WEIGHT: Empty 2387 lb., Gross 3204 lb. Fuel 62+50 gal.
PERFORMANCE: Speed- Top 170 mph, Landing 59 mph.
Service Ceiling 23,100', Climb 5000'/3 min. Range 460 miles.

BOEING FB-4
Wright P-2, 410 hp
DIMENSIONS: Span 32', Lg. 22'10", Ht. 8'9", Wing Area 241 sq. ft.
WEIGHT: Empty 2000 lb., Gross 2817 lb. Fuel 62+50 gal.
PERFORMANCE: Speed- Top 160 mph, Landing 58 mph.
Service Ceiling 22,500', Climb 5000'/:3.18 min. Range 428 miles.

delivered December 8. An FB-3 with a Packard 1A-1500 and twin wooden floats crashed on December 31, 1925, and an FB-4 was delivered with a Wright radial and twin floats in January 1926. In April 1926, two more FB-3s were built with Packards and wheels, and the FB-4 became the FB-6 with a Pratt & Whitney R-1340 Wasp in August 1926.

The production version of that Boeing was the FB-5 with a Packard 2A-1500, convertible wheels or float gear, auxiliary fuel drop tank, and a balanced rudder. The first example was tested on October 7, 1926, and all 27 were delivered to the *Langley* by barge in Seattle on January 21, 1927.

Curtiss gave Boeing strong competition in this period with a seagoing version of the Army's P-1 Hawk series. Tapered wings, N struts, and a tunnel radiator for their D-12 engines were features shared by both the Boeing and Curtiss fighters, but the Hawks used Clark Y airfoils. Nine Hawks were ordered in January 1925, and the first F6C-1 was completed in August with four being delivered in September. Powered by the Curtiss D-12, they had inter-

USN

BOEING FB-5
Packard 2A-1500, 525 hp
DIMENSIONS: Span 32', Lg. 23'8", Ht. 9'1", Wing Area 241 sq. ft.
WEIGHT: Empty 2416 lb., Gross 3196 lb. Fuel 50+50 gal
PERFORMANCE: Speed- Top 169 mph at s.1., 163 mph at 5000', Cruising 110 mph, Landing 60 mph. Service Ceiling 20,200', Climb 5000'/3.2 min. Range 323 miles.

USN

BOEING FB-6
Pratt & Whitney R-1340, 400 hp
DIMENSIONS: Same as FB-4
WEIGHT: Empty 1904 lb., Gross 2737 lb.
PERFORMANCE: Speed- Top 159 mph at s.l. Service Ceiling 22,800', Climb 5000'/2.5 min. Range 414 miles.

MFR

CURTISS F6C-1 seaplane
Curtiss D-12, 412 hp
DIMENSIONS: Span 31'6", Lg. 25'5", Ht 10'8", Wing Area 252 sq. ft.
WEIGHT: Empty 2510 lb., Gross 3253 lb. Fuel 50+50 gal.
PERFORMANCE: Speed- Top 155 mph at s.l., Landing 65 mph. Service Ceiling 19,100', Climb 5000'/3.7 min.

changable wheels or twin-float landing gear, but four F6C-2s delivered in November 1925 had straight axle wheels and arresting gear for the *Langley*.

USN

CURTISS F6C-2
Curtiss D-12, 400 hp
DIMENSIONS: As F6C-1
WEIGHT: Empty 2090 lb., Gross 3838 lb. Fuel 50+50 gal.
PERFORMANCE: Speed- Top 159 mph at s.1., Landing 59 mph. Service Ceiling 22,700', Range 330 miles.

Thirty-five Curtiss F6C-3 Hawks, delivered beginning in October 1926, were the last Navy service fighters with water-cooled engines. At that time, the Navy's fighter force comprised VF-1, VF-6, and later VF-3 with FB-5s, VF-5 with F6C-3s, and VF-2 testing the first FB-2s, F6C-1, and F6C-2 types. The Marines had VF-1M, VF-2M, and VF-3M, with F6C-3, F6C-1 and FB-1 fighters.

USN

CURTISS F6C-3
Curtiss D-12, 400 hp
DIMENSIONS: Span 31'6", Lg. 22'10", Ht. 10'8", Wing Area 252 sq. ft.
WEIGHT: Empty 2161 lb., Gross 2963 lb., Max. 3349 lb. Fuel 50+50 gal.
PERFORMANCE: Speed- Top 154 mph at s.1., Landing 59 mph. Service Ceiling 20,300', Climb 5000'/3.5 min. Range 351 miles normal, 655 miles max.

In addition to their two guns, these fighters could carry five 25-pound bombs under the fuselage and on October 22, 1926, VF-2 made the first fleet demonstration of near-vertical dive-bombing with F6Cs from San Diego's North Island. Further success with this method led to the redesignation of VF-5 and VF-6 as VB-lB and VB-2B on July 1, 1928. This meant that the second single-seat squadron on the *Saratoga* and *Lexington* would be trained as bomber-fighter units.

USN

CURTISS F6C-1
Curtiss D-12, 412 hp
DIMENSIONS: Span 31'6", Lg. 22'8", Ht 10', Wing Area 252 sq. ft.
WEIGHT: Empty 2055 lb., Gross 2803 lb. Fuel 50+50 gal.
PERFORMANCE: Speed- Top 163.5 mph at s.l., Cruising 110 mph, Landing 59 mph. Service Ceiling 21,700', Climb 5000'/2.9 min. Range 350 miles.

Battleship Fighters

In 1927, VF-2 was deployed among the twelve battleships of the Pacific Battle Fleet, operating as individual floatplanes from their catapults along with the UO-1 and OL-6 observation aircraft. These fighters were supposed to protect the spotter planes from enemy aircraft.

The type selected for this role was the Vought FU-1, a single-seat fighter version of the UO-1 with new double-bay wings and steel struts. Armed with two .30-caliber M1919 Brownings, the FU-1 had a 220-hp Wright J-5 with a Rootes integral supercharger, making them the first Navy fighters faster at altitude than sea level. They operated with a central main float from ships and with wheels ashore.

Twenty FU-1s ordered June 30, 1926, were delivered from January to April 1927 and served on the battleships until September 1928. After that time, Navy fighter squadrons would be carrier-based, and the Voughts were converted to FU-2s with a second cockpit for utility service. Float fighters would always be inferior to land-planes, and only squadrons of fighters from flight decks could assure air superiority.

VOUGHT FU-1 landplane
Wright R-790, 220 hp
DIMENSIONS: Span 34'4", Lg. 24'5", Ht. 8'10", Wing Area 290 sq. ft.
WEIGHT: Empty 1715 1b., Gross 2409 lb. Fuel 46 gal.
PERFORMANCE: Speed- Top 130 mph at s.1., 151 mph at 15,000', Service Ceiling 29,600', Range 430 miles.

PMB

CURTISS XF6C-4

Hasse

VOUGHT FU-l seaplane
Wright R-790, 220 hp
DIMENSIONS: Span 34'4", Lg. 28'4", Ht. 10'6", Wing Area 290 sq. ft.
WEIGHT: Empty 2074 1b., Gross 2774 lb. Fuel 46 gal.
PERFORMANCE: Speed- Top 125 mph at s.1., 147 mph at 13,000', Landing 53 mph. Service Ceiling 27,300', Climb 5000'/5.1 min. Range 410 miles.

Air-cooled Single-seaters

The adoption of the Pratt & Whitney R-1340 Wasp as the standard engine for fighters came as the Navy squadrons prepared to go aboard the new *Lexington* and *Saratoga*. This engine was first airborne on May 5, 1926, with the Wright F3W-l biplane.

That single-seater was the last of several prototypes (NW and F2W) designed to explore new engine and design arrangements and had been intended for a Wright P-1 radial until that engine failed to work out. Using either wheels or floats, it was actually built in Vought's factory, but called the F3W-1 Apache. Never intended as a production prototype, the F3W-l was used for research from 1927 to 1930, setting many altitude records.

PMB

Wright F3W-1
Pratt & Whitney R-1340B, 450 hp
DIMENSIONS: Span 27'4", Lg. 22'1", Ht. 8'6", Wing Area 215 sq. ft.
WEIGHT: Empty 1414 lb., Gross 2128 lb. Fuel 47 gal
PERFORMANCE: Speed- Top 162 mph at s.l., Landing 54 mph. Service Ceiling 33,000'.

The first Curtiss Navy fighter with the Wasp was the XF6C-4,* converted in July 1926 from the first F6C-l. Thirty-one production F6C-4s were delivered from February to June 1927, most of them going to the Marines, and some were fitted with ring cowls in 1930. A further

*The X was not actually applied to Navy prototype aircraft until 1927, but we use it here for convenience.

development was the XF6C-5, which was the XF6C-4 airframe fitted with the Pratt & Whitney R-1690 Hornet in September 1927.

PMB

CURTISS F6C-4
Pratt & Whitney R-1340, 410 hp
DIMENSIONS: Span 31'6", Lg., 22'6", Ht. 10'11", Wing Area 252 sq. ft.
WEIGHT: Empty 1980 lb., Gross 2785 lb., Max. 3171 lb. Fuel 50+50 gal.
PERFORMANCE: Speed- Top 155 mph at s.1., Landing 57 mph. Service Ceiling 22,900', Climb 5000'/2.5 min. Range 361 miles normal, 676 max.

PMB

CURTISS XF6C-5
Pratt & Whitney R-1690, 525 hp
DIMENSIONS: Span 31'6", Lg. 22'6", Ht. 9'8", Wing Area 252 sq. ft.
WEIGHT: Empty 2109 lb., Gross 2960 lb. Fuel 50+50 gal.
PERFORMANCE: Speed- Top 159 mph, Landing 60 mph. Service Ceiling 21,900', Climb 5000'/2.5 min. Range 329 miles.

The unarmed XF6C-6 was specially built for the 1930 air races with lower wing removed, wheel pants, and a Curtiss Conqueror inline engine. The latter machine's fatal crash killed the pilot and ended Navy competition in the air races. Wind tunnel experiments and careful engineering were proving a more efficient method of advancing performance than trial-and-error racers unsuitable for actual service work. The last of the F6C series was an F6C-4 converted at the NAF in 1932 to a test bed for the 350-hp air-cooled inverted inline Ranger SGV-770 and designated XF6C-7.

USN

CURTISS XF7C-1

Designed from the very beginning as a carrier type by Rex Beisel, the Curtiss XF7C-1 had a R-1340B neatly mounted behind a large prop spinner, an upper wing swept back seven degrees over a straight lower wing, and a life raft in a tube behind the pilot. The XF7C-1 was ordered December 8, 1926, and first flew on February 28, 1927. Seventeen production F7C-ls ordered August 28, 1927, and completed from November 1928 to January 1929 had strengthened landing gear, omitted the spinner, and served with the Marines of VF-5M at Quantico.

MFR

CURTISS F7C-l
Pratt & Whitney R-1340B, 450 hp
DIMENSIONS: Span 32'8", Lg. 22'2", Ht. 9'8", Wing Area 275 sq. ft.
WEIGHT: Empty 2075 lb., Gross 2838 lb., Max. 3275 lb. Fuel 83+30 gal.
PERFORMANCE: Speed- Top 151 mph at s.1. Stalling 53 mph. Service Ceiling 23,350', Climb 5000'/2.6 min. Range 330 miles normal, 671 miles max.

More Boeing Fighters

Designed especially for carrier use with the R-1340B Wasp, the Boeing XF2B-1 was first flown November 3, 1926, and was developed from the FB-6 and XP-8 designs. Boeing had designed a new airfoil for the wing's spruce frame-

SDAM

BOEING XF2B-1
Pratt & Whitney R-1340, 425 hp
DIMENSIONS: Span 30'1", Lg. 23', Ht. 9'1", Wing Area 243 sq. ft.
WEIGHT: Empty 1875 lb., Gross 2660 lb. Fuel 50 gal.
PERFORMANCE: Speed- Top 154.5 mph at s.1., Landing 56 mph. Service Ceiling 21,300', Climb 1890'/1 min.

BOEING F3B-1
Pratt & Whitney R-1340-80, 450 hp
DIMENSIONS: Span 33', Lg. 24'10", Ht. 10'1", Wing Area 275 sq. ft.
WEIGHT: Empty 2183 lb., Gross 2950 lb., Max. 3340 lb. Fuel 60+50 gal.
PERFORMANCE: Speed- Top 156 mph at s.1., Landing 55 mph. Service Ceiling 20,900', Climb 5000'/3.1 min. Range 382 miles.

work, and used a welded steel tubing fuselage structure covered with cotton fabric behind an aluminum cowling. Tests at Anacostia began December 17, but before production, much refinement was needed.

BOEING F2B-1
Pratt & Whitney R-1340B, 450 hp
DIMENSIONS: Span 30'1", Lg. 22'11", Ht. 9'3", Wing Area 243 sq. ft.
WEIGHT: Empty 1991 lb., Gross 2808 lb. Fuel 50+50 gal.
PERFORMANCE: Speed- Top 158 mph at s.1., Landing 57 mph. Service Ceiling 21,500', Climb 2090'/1 min., 12,700'/10 min. Range 317 miles at 118 mph, 630 miles max.

The large nose spinner was omitted from production ships, which added the balanced rudder of the FB-5, and had one .30-caliber and one .50-caliber Browning gun under the cowl, wing racks for 25-pound bombs, an auxiliary drop tank, tail hook, and twin flotation bags under the top wing. Thirty-two F2B-1s ordered in March 1927 were delivered from October 1927 to March 1928 and were the first fighters on the new *Saratoga* with VF-1B and VB-2B. They also were used by the Navy's first precision aerobatics

BOEING XF3B-1
Pratt & Whitney R-1340B, 450 hp
DIMENSIONS: Span 30'1", Lg. 22'9", Ht. 9'3", Wing Area 235 sq. ft.
WEIGHT: Empty 1919 lb., Gross 2715 lb.
PERFORMANCE: Speed- Top 157 mph at s.1., Cruising 131 mph. Service Ceiling 21,800', Climb 2020'/1 min. Range 336 miles.

team, the "Three Sea Hawks" to perform at air shows. One example each was also sold to Brazil and Japan.

The Boeing XF3B-1 first flew March 2, 1927, as a company venture called Model 74 with a 425-hp Wasp, landing gear interchangable with wheels or a central float, and wings and tail surfaces like those of the F2B-l. Rejected by the Navy, it returned to the factory to be rebuilt. When flown again on February 3, 1928, it had larger wings with constant chord and sweptback on the upper wing. The tail surfaces and ailerons were made of corrugated aluminum.

Hasse

BOEING F3B-l for VB-1

This aircraft was accepted and followed by 73 F3B-1 fighters delivered from August to December 1928. Production articles differed from the original by a new vertical fin and deletion of the float provisions, no longer required for Navy fighters. Armament comprised two .30-caliber guns and five 25-pound bombs, and flotation bags were provided in the fuselage. The F3B-1 served on all three carriers with VF-2 and VF-3, and in 1929 was reworked as fighter-bombers for VB-1 and VB-2.

USN

CURTISS F8C-1 (to OC-1)
Pratt & Whitney R-1340, 432 hp
DIMENSIONS: Span 32', Lg. 25'11", Ht. 10'6", Wing Area 353 sq. ft.
WEIGHT: Empty 2440 1b., Gross 3918 lb. Max. 4367 lb. Fuel 120 gal.
PERFORMANCE: Speed- Top 137.5 mph at s.1., 129 mph at 10,000', Landing 58 mph. Service Ceiling 17,300'. Climb 8500'/10 min. Range 378 miles.

Two-seat Fighters

On June 30, 1927, the Navy ordered the Curtiss factory at Garden City to build three two-seaters capable of fighting and light bombing missions. The first two, designated F8C-1, were to be air-cooled Wasp-powered versions of the Army's O-1B Falcon, while the last was a more powerful dive-bomber prototype, the XF8C-2.

PMB

CURTISS XF8C-2
Pratt & Whitney R-1340-80, 450 hp
DIMENSIONS: Span 32', Lg. 25'5", Ht. 10'6", Wing Area 308 sq. ft.
WEIGHT: Empty 2229 lb., Cross 3332 lb. Max. 3620 lb. Fuel 90 gal.
PERFORMANCE: Speed- Top 145 mph at s.1., Landing 56 mph. Service Ceiling 20,800', Climb 5000'/4 min. Range 333 miles normal, 512 miles max.

But the Marine Corps had become involved in Nicaragua's civil war with the Sandanistas and had developed a dive-bombing technique with small fragmentation bombs using the old DH-4Bs (O2B-1) of World War I design. Better replacements were needed quickly and the Curtiss contract was revised on November 21 to add 25 production aircraft.

The first Curtiss F8C-l (Model 37) appeared in January 1928 with the upper wing swept back from the center section and a balanced rudder. Six F8C-ls and 21 F8C-3s delivered by April 1928 soon joined Marine observation squadrons and so were redesignated OC-l and OC-2, as mentioned before in Chapter 9 on naval observation planes.

They were used by VO-7M in Nicaragua, VO-8M at San Diego and VO-l0M in China, and later some received ring cowls. Armament included ten 17 or two 116-pound bombs under the wings, and two Lewis guns on the observer's Scarff ring, and while the F8C-1 had one nose gun, the OC-2 had two .30-caliber Brownings with 800 rounds, mounted in the lower wing and firing outside of the propeller arc.

A more advanced version was the XF8C-2, reordered March 15, 1928, and flown in November 1928. The upper wing was reduced to the same span as the lower and stressed for dive-bombing, with two 116-pound bombs under each wing, or a 500-pound bomb below the fuselage, and the pilot had a telescopic sight alongside the ring sight for the two .30-caliber guns in the upper wing. Although the first prototype lost its tail in a dive on December 2, another was delivered April 22, 1929, originally with a cowl around the engine cylinders.

ARC

CURTISS XF8C-7 (983V, to XF8C-8)

Hasse

CURTISS F8C-4
Pratt & Whitney R-1340-88, 450 hp at s.1.
DIMENSIONS: Span 32', Lg. 26' Ht 10'10" Wing Area 308 sq. ft.
WEIGHT. Empty 2513 lb., Gross 3783 lb., Max. 4238 lb. Fuel 86+50 gal.
PERFORMANCE: Speed- Top 137 mph at s.1. Landing 59 mph. Service Ceiling 15,000', Climb 5000'/6 min. Range 455 miles normal, 722 miles max.

In June 1929 orders were placed for an XF8C-4 and 36 production aircraft from the Buffalo factory. The XF8C-4 appeared in April 1930, like the XF8C-2 except for replacing the centerline bomb rack with a drop tank and wing racks for eight 30 or four 116-pound bombs. Two .30-caliber Browning guns were in the upper wing, and the gunner had two Lewis guns.

Twenty-five F8C-4s entered service with VF-1B aboard the *Saratoga* in August 1930 as the only two-seater Navy fighter squadron. The Curtiss company named this plane the Helldiver, a name made famous by a 1931 movie, and revived in World War II dive-bombers. More agile F4B-3 single-seaters replaced the F8C-4s in January 1932.

Hasse

CURTISS XF8C-7 (Data for unarmed model)
Wright R-1820-64, 575 hp
DIMENSIONS: Span 32', Lg. 26', Ht. 11', Wing Area 308 sq. ft.
WEIGHT: Empty 2958 lb., Gross 4274 lb. Fuel 120 gal.
PERFORMANCE: Speed- Top 179 mph at s.1., Landing 63 mph. Service Ceiling 20,800', Climb 5000'/3.2 min. Range 736 miles.

Ninety-three aircraft originally designated F8C-5 had no arresting gear and were allotted to Marine observation squadrons. Redesignated O2C-1, they served with VO-6M, VO-7M, and various reserve air stations. A new wing with leading edge slots and trailing edge flaps was tested on the first two F8C-5s, which were designated XF8C-6 until restored to standard O2C-1 configuration.

Four more Helldivers were built with Wright R-1820 Cyclones. The first was the XF8C-7 purchased in November 1930 as an unarmed command transport for David Ingalls, Assistant Secretary of the Navy. It had a 575-hp R-1820-65, wheel pants and cockpit enclosure. Another, built in December 1930 as a private venture registered N983V, had a flexible .30-caliber Browning gun in the rear cockpit, as well as two fixed in the top wing. This aircraft was labeled F8C-7 by Curtiss, but was also designated XF8C-8 before becoming one of the three O2C-2s purchased by the Navy on December 30, 1930, (described in the previous chapter).

Vought also tried to enter the two-seat fighter field with the XF2U-1 delivered June 25, 1929. It introduced the wing shape later used on the O2U-2, but had a cowled R-1340C Wasp, two fixed Brownings in the upper wing, and a Lewis gun on a pivot in the rear cockpit. Vought's biplane did not, however, dislodge the Helldiver from its place.

VOUGHT XF2U-1
Pratt & Whitney R-1340C, 450 mph
DIMENSIONS: Span 36', Lg. 27', Ht. 10', Wing Area 318 sq. ft.
WEIGHT: Empty 2539 lb., Gross 3907 lb. Max. 4208 lb. Fuel 110 gal.
PERFORMANCE: Speed- Top 146 mph, Cruising 110 mph, Landing 57.5 mph. Service Ceiling 18,700', Climb 9100'/10 min. Range 495 miles.

Single-seat Experiments, 1926-1932

Several other companies made unsuccessful attempts to capture Navy single-seat fighter contracts from the successful Boeing ships. Earliest of these was the Eberhart FG-l with a Wasp engine and fabric-covered welded steel tube fuselage. The wings had a fabric-covered dural structure with a seven-degree sweepback on the upper wing and a six-degree sweep forward on the upper wing. Tested as a landplane in November 1926, the FG-1 reappeared in January 1928 as a single-float seaplane with modified wings and an XF2G-1 designation.

Another biplane with sweepback on the upper wing and forward sweep on the lower was the Hall XFH-1, whose main feature was an all-metal watertight monocoque fuselage. The structure was of duralumin except for fabric covering on the Clark Y section wings, and the landing gear could be dropped for emergencies. Armament was one .30-caliber and one .50-caliber Browning gun under the cowl, and wing racks for two 116-pound bombs. Built in Buffalo, the XFH-l was delivered June 18, 1929, but crashed February 3, 1930, after generally unsatisfactory performance.

EBERHART FG-1
Pratt & Whitney R-1340C, 425 hp
DIMENSIONS: Span 32', Lg., 27'3", Ht. 9'10", Wing Area 241 sq. ft.
WEIGHT: Empty 2145 lb., Gross 2938 lb. Max. 3208 lb.
PERFORMANCE: Speed- Top 154 mph at s.1., Service Ceiling 18,700' Climb 5000'/3.5 min.

HALL XFH-l
Pratt & Whitney R-1340B, 450 hp
DIMENSIONS: Span 32', Lg. 22'6", Ht. 11', Wing Area 255 sq. ft.
WEIGHT: Empty 1773 lb., Gross 2514 lb. Fuel 80 gal.
PERFORMANCE: Speed- Top 153 mph at s.1., Cruising 110 mph, Landing 55 mph. Service Ceiling 25,300', Climb 5000'/2.8 min. Range 275 miles.

To compare American technique with developments abroad, the Navy imported the British Bristol Bulldog fighter for tests. The first example crashed in November 1929, but a second was purchased in March 1930. Powered by a 515-hp Bristol Jupiter VII, the Bulldog had good performance, but was not considered as rugged as American types.

Among this period's most interesting types was the Berliner-Joyce XFJ-l, which was distinguished by a gap between the metal monocoque fuselage and the lower wing, while the upper wing was gulled into the fuselage behind a 450-hp R-1340C Wasp. Ordered May 16, 1929, the XFJ-l was tested in May 1930, armed with two .30-caliber guns, but was damaged in a crash and was returned to the Dundalk, Maryland factory for modification in November.

On May 22, 1931, the prototype, later designated XFJ-2, resumed tests at Anacostia using a supercharged 500-hp

BERLINER-JOYCE XFJ-1
Pratt & Whitney R-1340C, 450 hp at s.1.
DIMENSIONS: Span 28', Lg. 19'11" , Ht. 7'11", Wing Area 179 sq. ft.
WEIGHT: Empty 2046 lb., Gross 2797 lb. Fuel 50 gal.
PERFORMANCE: Speed- Top 172 mph at s.1., Cruising 138 mph, Stalling 65 mph. Service Ceiling 23,800', Climb 5000'/3.9 min. Range 404 miles.

BRISTOL BULLDOG (Navy test)
Bristol Jupiter VII, 515 hp at 9000'
DIMENSIONS: Span 33'10", Lg. 27'6", Ht. 9'4", Wing Area 306 sq. ft.
WEIGHT: Empty 2174 lb., Gross 3264 lb. Fuel 70 gal.
PERFORMANCE: Speed- Top 141 mph at s.1., 173 mph at 9000', Landing 59 mph. Service Ceiling 27,300', Climb 5000'/2. min.

BERLINER-JOYCE XFJ-2
Pratt & Whitney R-1340-92, 500 hp at 6000'
DIMENSIONS: Span 28', Lg. 20'10", Ht. 9'10", Wing Area 179 sq. ft.
WEIGHT: Empty 2102 lb., Gross 2847 lb., Max. 3116 lb. Fuel 91 gal.
PERFORMANCE: Speed- Top 193 mph at 6000', Stalling Landing 65 mph. Service Ceiling 24,700', Climb 14,300'/ 10 min. Range 520 miles.

R-1340D, wheel pants, ring cowl, prop spinner, wings raised six inches, and a larger vertical tail. While performance improved, the aircraft was now unstable, and no longer satisfactory.

Another biplane with the upper wings gulled into an all-metal fuselage was the XFA-1 built by General Aviation, formerly Atlantic-Fokker. A 450-hp R-1340C Wasp was fitted with a two-bladed propeller and a ring cowl. Ordered June 24, 1930, the XFA-1 could be distinguished by a fairing over the landing-gear struts, and was also seen with a three-bladed propeller. Not delivered to the Navy until March 5, 1932, it was built to BuAer Design 96, the same small-size fighter specification that produced the Curtiss Sparrowhawk. More aircraft might be stored on a carrier, if smaller sized planes would be adequate.

The Curtiss XF9C-1 Sparrowhawk was a little biplane who's fabric-covered, Clark YH airfoil, upper wings were joined to the metal fuselage behind a ring-cowled Wright R-975C Whirlwind. Ordered June 30, 1930, the XF9C-1 made its first flight on February 12, 1931, the last plane built at the

USN

CURTISS F9C-2
Wright R-975-22, 420 hp
DIMENSIONS: Span 25'6", Lg. 20'1", Ht. 7'1", Wing Area 173 sq. ft.
WEIGHT: Empty 2114 lb., Gross 2776 lb. Max. 2888 lb. Fuel 60+30 gal.
PERFORMANCE: Speed- Top 176.5 mph at 4000', Stalling 65 mph. Service Ceiling 19,200', Climb 5000'/3.5 min., 11,300'/10 min. Range 366 miles normal, 507 miles max.

Curtiss Garden City facility. Another prototype, the XF9C-2, was built at Buffalo by September 1931 with a higher upper wing, modified landing gear and larger vertical fin.

PMB

FOKKER XFA-1
Pratt & Whitney R-1340C, 450 hp at s.1.
DIMENSIONS: Span 25'6", Lg. 20'2", Ht. 9'3", Wing Area 175 sq. ft.
WEIGHT: Empty 1837 lb., Gross 2508 lb. Fuel 60 gal.
PERFORMANCE: Speed- Top 170 mph at s.1., Stalling 64 mph, Service Ceiling 20,200', Climb 5000'/3.4 min. Range 375 miles normal, 518 miles max.

ARC

CURTISS XF9C-1
Wright R-975C, 421 hp
DIMENSIONS: Span 25'6", Lg. 19'5", Ht. 7'1", Wing Area 173 sq. ft.
WEIGHT: Empty 1836 lb., Gross 2502 lb. Fuel 59 gal.
PERFORMANCE: Speed- Top 176.5 mph at s.1., 160 mph at 10,000', Stalling 63 mph. Service Ceiling 22,600', Climb 5000'/2.6 min., 13,800'/10 min. Range 396 miles normal, 536 miles max.

At that time the Navy's giant airship, the 785-foot long *Akron*, was entering service, and its sister ship, the *Macon*, was under construction. Their hangar held four small aircraft on a monorail, and a trapeze was provided to launch and recover them. Compared to a cruiser and its floatplanes, these rigid airships could move twice as fast and their more agile planes allowed a far more extensive search area.

The Sparrowhawk's small size recommended it for this mission, so the XF9C-l had a hook-on device erected in front of the cockpit in September and six production F9C-2s were ordered on October 14, 1931. The XF9C-l successfully hooked on to the training dirigible *Los Angeles* on October 23, and the first F9C-2 flew on Apri1 14, 1932.

After the disaster to the *Akron* that killed BuAer Chief Rear Admiral Moffett on April 4, 1933, operations shifted to the *Macon* commissioned June 23, and the classic photo made July 7 of a hook-on illustrates the F9F-2 in this book.

Provided with two .30-caliber guns and a radio, the Sparrowhawks sometimes operated from the *Macon* with wheeled gear removed and 30-gallon auxiliary tanks to extend range. During maneuvers, however, the airships seemed unable to avoid destruction by hostile aircraft. After the *Macon* was also lost in a storm on February 12, 1935, with four F9C-2s aboard, no other large rigid airships were built by the Navy.

Boeing's F4B

To many, the height of traditional biplane design in the Navy was the F4B series. Compact and maneuverable, they captured public interest in their time, and remain a favorite of model builders today.

PMB

BOEING XF4B-1 (Model 83)
Pratt & Whitney R-1340B, 500 hp at s.1.
DIMENSIONS: Span 30', Lg. 20'7", Ht. 9'3", Wing Area 227.5 sq. ft.
WEIGHT: Empty 1811 lb., Gross 2557 lb. Max. 3087 lb.
PERFORMANCE: Speed- Top 169 mph at s.1., Cruising 142 mph, Stalling 56 mph. Service Ceiling 26,900', Climb 2920'/1 min. Range 520 miles.

The first prototype was the Boeing Model 83 powered by a 500-hp Pratt & Whitney Wasp and constructed with fabric-covered bolted and welded dural and steel tube fuselage and wooden wings, with corrugated metal control surfaces. First flown June 25, 1928, and shipped to San Diego for Navy tests, Model 83 had cross-axle landing gear.

A second prototype, Model 89, made its first flight at Anacostia on August 7 with a split-axle landing gear that allowed room for a 500-pound bomb or 49-gallon belly tank. Both were armed with the usual two fixed guns, had cylinder fairings, and were known as XF4B-ls in Navy documents. The ineffective fairings later were removed when both aircraft were reworked to production form, and accepted as part of F4B-1 order.

MFR

BOEING XF4B-1 (Model 89)

Twenty-seven F4B-l (Model 99) were ordered with supercharged Wasps and split-axle gear on November 28, 1928, and the Army purchased a parallel P-12 version. First flown May 6, 1929, and delivered in June, the F4B-1 was used by VF-5B on the *Lexington*. All Boeings in this series had one .30-caliber and one .50-caliber Browning gun under the cowl and wing racks for ten 30 or two 116-pound bombs.

Hasse

BOEING F4B-l
Pratt & Whitney R-1340-8, 500 hp at 6000'
DIMENSIONS: Span 30', Lg. 20'7", Ht. 9'7", Wing Area 227.5 sq. ft.
WEIGHT: Empty 1925 lb., Gross 2725 lb., Max. 3268 lb. Fuel 57+50 gal.
PERFORMANCE: Speed- Top 166 mph at 6000', Stalling 59 mph. Service Ceiling 27,700', Climb 5000'/2.9 min. Range 371 miles normal, 771 miles max.

Another Boeing private venture was the Model 205, which reached Anacostia on February 14, 1930, for tests and was purchased May 10 as the XF5B-l. Resembling the F4B-l, it was a high-wing monoplane and, like the XP-15 offered to the Army at the same time, used a 450-hp R-1340D and metal-covered fuselage and wings. Trials were made with the bare cylinders under a ring cowl, adding 15 mph to the top speed.

MFR

BOEING XF5B-1
Pratt & Whitney R-1340D, 500 hp at 6000'
DIMENSIONS: Span 30'6", Lg. 21', Ht. 9'4", Wing Area 157 sq. ft.
WEIGHT Empty 2091 lb., Gross 2848 lb. Fuel 52+50 gal.
PERFORMANCE: Speed-Top 183 mph at 6000', Stalling 71 mph. Service Ceiling 27,100', Climb 5000'/2.7 min.

Hasse

BOEING F4B-2
Pratt & Whitney R-1340-8, 500 hp at 6000'
DIMENSIONS: Span 30', Lg. 20'1", Ht. 9'1", Wing Area 227.5 sq. ft.
WEIGHT: Empty 2067 lb., Gross 2799 lb., Max. 3260 lb. Fuel 55+55 gal.
PERFORMANCE: Speed-Top 170 mph at s.1., 186 mph at 6000', Stalling 59 mph. Service Ceiling 26,900', Climb 5000'/2.5 min. Range 403 miles normal, 812 miles max.

The Navy, however, was not yet ready for monoplanes aboard carriers, and instead contracted for 46 F4B-2s in June 1930. Delivered from January 2 to May 2, 1931, they were similar to the F4B-1 except for ring cowl, Frise ailerons, and a spreader-bar axle landing gear with a tail wheel. Similar to the P-12C, they served VF-6, VF-2, and later, VF-5.

In December 1930, Boeing offered Model 218 with a new all-metal fuselage to both the Army and Navy, leading to orders for the P-12E and F4B-3. Contracts let on April 23, and August 15, 1931, called for 75 F4B-3s, but 54 of these aircraft were delivered as F4B-4s. The 21 F4B-3s were powered by R-1340-10s and were delivered from December 24, 1931, to the following January 20. They replaced the Helldivers of VF-1, on the *Saratoga,* where they served until transferred to the Marine's VB-4M in 1933.

The most famous of the series was the F4B-4, similar to the F4B-3 but for an R-1340-16, wider fin, and on the

MFR

BOEING F4B-3
Pratt & Whitney R-1340-10, 500 hp at 6000'
DIMENSIONS: Span 30', Lg. 20'5", Ht. 9'9", Wing Area 227.5 sq. ft.
WEIGHT: Empty 2242 lb., Gross 2958 lb., Max. 3419 lb. Fuel 55+55 gal.
PERFORMANCE: Speed- Top 167 mph at s.l., 187 mph at 6000', Cruising 160 mph, Stalling 61 mph. Service Ceiling 27,500'. Climb 5000'/2.9 min. Range 370 miles normal, 734 miles max.

PMB

BOEING Model 218, Navy test

ARC

BOEING F4B-4
Pratt & Whitney R-1340-16, 550 hp at 6000"
DIMENSIONS: As F4B-3
WEIGHT: Empty 2354 lb., Gross 3128 lb. Max. 3611 lb. Fuel 55+55 gal.
PERFORMANCE: Speed- Top 188 mph at 6000', Stalling 62.5 mph. Service Ceiling 26,900'. Range 370 miles normal, 734 miles max.

last 45, an headrest enlarged to hold a life raft. Armed with the usual two guns under the cowl, the F4B-4 had wing bomb racks for two 116-pound bombs and a 55-gallon drop tank under the fuselage could double the internal fuel load. A telescopic sight for dive-bombing, alongside the gun sight ring, helps distinguish the F4B from its Army P-12 sister ships. Radios were ordered for all Navy fighters in November 1932.

Another contract brought Boeing's F4B-4 order to 92, delivered from July 21, 1932, to February 28, 1933. Brazil also got 14 F4B-4s, minus Navy gear, in September 1932, and nine more in February 1933. Altogether, Boeing built 586 of this series, including 188 for the Navy, 32 for export, and 366 for the Army. F4B-4As were 23 various Army P-12s turned over to the Navy in 1940 for radio-controlled targets.

Although the F4B series was used by both the Army and the Navy, it was two decades before another fighter type could be successful in both roles (North American F-86 and FJ series). The Army's shift to high-speed monoplanes could not be followed for many years, and when it was, monoplanes designed for carrier work were quite different from their land-based counterparts.

Early in 1933, the Navy's fighter force consisted of five carrier-based and two Marine squadrons, all using Boeings and all with F4B-4s but VF-l (F4B-3) and VF-2 (F4B-2). These F4B-4s were not replaced in Marine service by Grumman F3F-2s until June 1938.

PART TWO

MONOPLANES FOR WORLD WAR II, 1931 TO 1945

CHAPTER 11

BACKGROUND OF WORLD WAR II DEVELOPMENT

The first Boeing bomber, the Y1B-9A, wore camouflage paint for May 1933 maneuvers, carried one ton of bombs 540 miles, with a 186-mph top speed. Boeing B-29s in 1944 carried up to ten tons of bombs 3,150 miles, with a 358-mph top speed. A tremendous advance over the B-9 in only a few years!

To even the most casual observer, World War II aircraft are very different from those of World War I and the biplane period. Streamlined monoplanes with enclosed cockpits, retractable wheels, and all-metal structure replaced the open cockpits, struts, and fabric covering of the first generation of combat planes.

Lockheed introduced the sliding cockpit canopy on the YP-24 in 1931, but the .30 caliber M1922 Browning in rear seat was nearly impossible to aim in a 200-mph air stream.

How this change in appearance came about is the subject of this section. A decade before Pearl Harbor, biplanes filled the squadrons of both the Army and Navy, but rather suddenly they were replaced by the new generation of aircraft. A technical revolution in aircraft design was under way. It had appeared on drawing boards in the 1920s and, with little encouragement by the military, took the form of commercial aircraft built by Boeing, Consolidated, and Northrop. Meanwhile, Army squadrons continued to operate their old biplanes. The technical revolution had two elements: the use of new discoveries in metallurgy for lightweight all-metal structures of new strength and reliability; and the shaping of these structures into which dragging struts, undercarriages, and open cockpits were submerged into the streamlined forms of cantilever wings, retractable landing gear, and Plexiglas enclosures.

The availability of monoplanes – due to increased knowledge of internally braced metal cantilever wing construction and of the cause and cure of wing flutter and other aberrations – was about to make a radical improvement in the appearance and performance of combat planes.

An old-fashioned strut-braced thin high wing is joined with flaps, enclosed cockpit, and retractable wheels on the XF13C-1.

The relatively slow-paced aviation progress of the 1920s contrasts sharply with the changes that took place in the air forces during the 1930s. The depression knocked the bottom from the private plane market, although U.S. expenditures on military aircraft rose from $25 million in fiscal 1925 to $69 million in fiscal 1931. This same depression caused an international social crisis that changed governmental leadership around the world.

An enclosed bomb bay is featured in 1935's XB2G-1 biplane.

Wheels retracting back partway into the XF7B-1's low-wing allowed a safety margin for forced landings.

The most fateful of the changes was the rise of aggressive rulers in Japan and Germany. Japan's invasion of Manchuria in September 1931 directly indicated the direction of the next threat to America, created a market for 600 aircraft in 1932-38 when China became the largest customer of American aircraft exports, and stimulated a Soviet industrial drive that included the purchase of 4,990 American aircraft engines in 1932-34.

In Washington, a new presidential administration was friendly to social and technical progress, while Nazi rule and rearmament in Germany put Europe on the road to war. The social climate promoted an arms race, with air power the largest concern, and American airplanes took a leading place.

The smooth lines of the first XPBY-1 in March 1937 contrast with the Martin PM-1 biplanes it will replace.

Export sales like these Curtiss Hawk seaplanes for Colombia, in 1933 helped the aircraft industry survive the depression.

During 1935, Hitler officially announced the formation of his air force, the Luftwaffe, Mussolini invaded Ethiopia, Congress passed a legislative program of social reforms, and the Army's combat aviation made a big step forward. An Air Corps of 2,320 planes and a General Headquarters (GHQ) Air Force command for operations free of dependence on particular ground armies, was implemented as recommended the previous year by the Baker Board.

China was the leading U.S. warplane customer in 1933-38, and the Northrop 2E made the first bombing attacks on Japanese forces at Shanghai on August 14, 1937.

Officially begun March 1, 1935, the GHQ Air Force could be concentrated against a threat from any direction. Consisting of all of the two attack, four bomber and three pursuit groups in the United States, the GHQ-AF was deployed in the 1st Wing facing the Pacific from its chief base at March Field, California; while the 2nd Wing, headquarters at Langley Field, Virginia, faced the Atlantic; and the 3rd Wing faced the Gulf of Mexico from Barksdale Field, Louisiana.

March Field was the headquarters of GHQ's First Wing, including A-17s of the 17th Attack Group on October 20, 1936.

Only the five groups in overseas departments and the observation squadrons of the nine corps areas were outside GHQ-AF control. Total Air Corps unit strength remained at 15 active groups from June 1932 to January 1940. The Army General Staff saw no need for more and seldom spent the full amount of money allotted to the Air Corps each fiscal year by Congress.

Army maneuvers in May 1938, demonstrated how the defense system was supposed to work. That war game presumed the Navy entirely occupied fighting Japan in the Pacific, leaving the GHQAF to oppose an attack on the East Coast by another enemy fleet. The games included an unsuccessful pursuit defense against a simulated night bombing of Farmingdale, New York, and Northrop attack planes smashing a simulated landing in Virginia, but the most memorable mission was by three B-17s that located the Italian liner *Rex* 725 miles east of New York. That demonstrated the heavy bomber's reach to the whole aviation world.

Army Air Corps flying in 1938 is remembered for formations like these 1st Pursuit Group P-35s at the National Air Races.

Fortunately, technical progress in those years was rapid and when the time for expansion came, a new generation of advanced aircraft was ready. The results of the Munich crisis made a general war inevitable, and President Roosevelt called a meeting of government leaders on September 28, 1938, in which he gave air power the first priority in American rearmament.

Not only were the Army and Navy air arms to be enlarged, but also the aircraft industry should reach a production of 10,000 planes a year, with the manufacturers encouraged by cost-plus-fee contracts whose profits would be a strong incentive for expansion. Roosevelt asserted that aircraft would impress Hitler, not minor improvements in facilities for ground forces. This view reflected the widespread opinion that fear of the Luftwaffe had promoted the disastrous appeasement policy of Britain.

General Henry H. Arnold, who had become Air Corps Chief that same month, left that meeting "with the feeling that the Air Corps had finally achieved its Magna Carta." Expansion of the Air Corps and of the aircraft industry was launched.

Britain and France also began contracting for large numbers of aircraft in 1938. While their early delivery requirements often conflicted with the immediate supply of Air Corps and Navy aircraft, these orders expanded plant capacity for future wartime needs. On March 25, 1940, permission was granted for the sale of Army and Navy service types as soon as a newer model was available.

Grumman F2F-l fighters with colorful markings, like the *Lexington*'s VF-2, represent Navy carrier-based planes in 1938.

France ordered 3,526 aircraft, of which 1,300 were delivered by June 17, 1940, when the British Air Commission took over the rest. Britain purchased 10,507 American aircraft before the Lend-Lease Act in March 1941 took over the cost of government contracts for more thousands of planes to be built for foreign Allies.

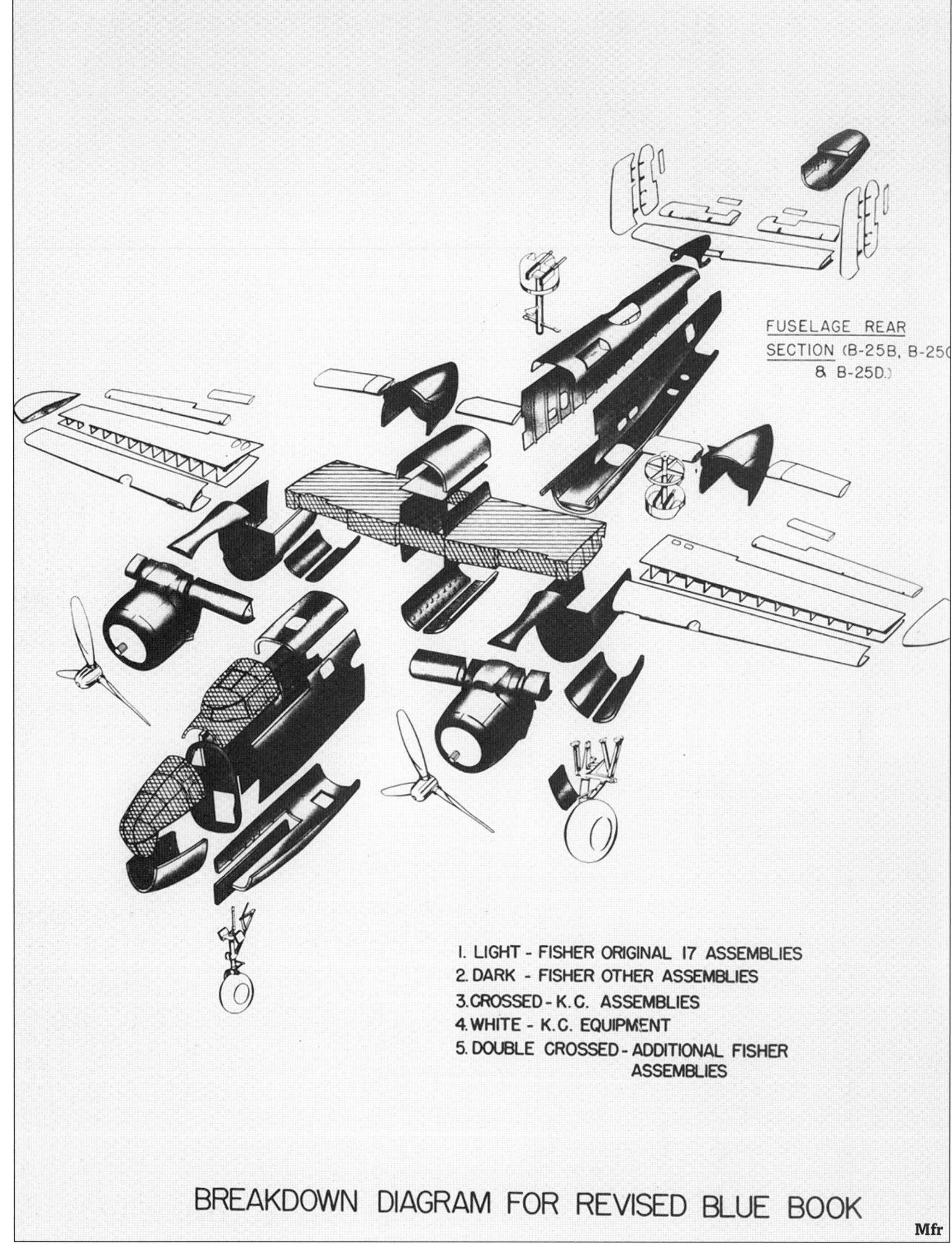

North American B-25s were an example of mass final assembly from numerous sub-assemblies.

AF

Heavy bombers like this Fifteenth Air Force B-24L-10 from Ford's Willow Run factory, were the main thrust of the AAF's wartime power.

The rugged Northrop BT-1 of 1938 is the Navy's first monoplane dive-bomber.

The largest American bomber, the XB-19, never reached production.

Building planes for the Allies and for America itself required such an enormous factory expansion that the American aircraft manufacturing industry became the largest single industry in the world during the war. Not only did squadrons have to be filled out, but also replenished. General Arnold had feared that combat squadrons in action would suffer attrition at a rate of 25% of aircraft and personnel per month.

Mass production included Consolidated PBY-5 flying boats in San Diego.

From 50,000 employees prewar, the prime contractor labor force increased to 425,027 at the end of 1941 and to its highest total of 1,247,182 on April 30, 1944. Annual production of military aircraft in the United States rose from 1,800 in 1938 to 6,086 in 1940, 19,290 in 1941, and reached a high of 96,369 in 1944.

Of 295,959 aircraft delivered from July 1940 to August 1945, the AAF received 158,880, the U.S. Navy 73,711, British Commonwealth forces 38,811, the Soviet Union 14,717, and the rest to others.

History's Largest Air Force:

The Army and Navy had some 2,400 and 1,700 planes respectively when the 1939 expansion program proposed an Army Air Corps of 5,500 planes with 24 groups, and a Navy air service with 3,000. This expansion had hardly gotten under way when German successes in Europe led President Roosevelt to call for 50,000 service planes in May 1940. That figure then seemed preposterous to some, but was authorized by Congress: 13,500 for the Navy, and 36,500 for a 54-group Army Air Corps.

AF

Attacks on enemy airfields and ships were the main work of medium bombers like these B-25D-20s and B-26s combined in the 22nd Bomb Group.

In 1941, still another plan calling for 84 groups by mid-1942, hardly seemed realistic in view of lend-lease commitments. Although by December 7, 1941, 70 groups had been activated in the now virtually autonomous "Army Air Forces" (that name replacing Air Corps on June 20, 1941), the 24 fighter, 13 heavy bomber, ten medium bomber, five light bomber, nine observation, two composite, one photographic mapping and six transport groups had only 3,305 combat planes plus 7,024 other types. Navy aviation also expanded in 1941 from 2,553 planes in January to 5,260 in December.

For the cross-Channel invasion of Europe in June 1944, the AAF alone assembled 10,637 planes (8,351 combat) in 98 groups: 40 heavy bomber, eight medium bomber, three light bomber, 33 fighter, and 14 troop carrier. By 1945, the United States had the largest air force ever built in history, with 243 groups* and 65 separate squadrons with 72,726 aircraft (41,961 combat) in the Army Air Force on January 1, and 41,180 naval aircraft (28,032 combat) on June 30.

USN

The Navy's heaviest punch was the dive-bomber, like the Curtiss SB2C-1 Helldiver.

Petrov

Lend-lease light bombers included this A-20G-35 modified for the Soviet Baltic Fleet's 51st Mine-torpedo Air Regiment.

The Navy assaulted Okinawa in April 1945 with the support of 919 planes on fast carriers and 564 planes on escort carriers. Navy combat planes on hand in mid-1945 included 13,940 fighters, 5,101 scout bombers, 4,937 torpedo bombers, and 4,054 patrol bombers, operating from 28 large carriers, 72 escort carriers, and numerous land bases.

Mfr

Fowler flaps on the Lockheed P-38L enabled a modest wing area to lift off with twin engines and heavy armament.

*Seventy-one fighter, 72 heavy, 25 very heavy, 20 medium, and eight light bombardment groups, with 29 troop carrier, 13 reconnaissance and five composite groups.

The 50-caliber M1921 was too big for a open cockpit mount, so this enclosed, but still manual, nose turret was designed for Boeing's XB-15 in 1937.

The .30 caliber M2, recognizable by the perforated barrel jacket, points down from a PBY-1 tunnel opening in September 1936.

What these planes did in the war has been described in detail in both official and academic histories. Air power, both carrier and land-based, was the largest single factor in Japan's defeat. More controversial is the role of air power against Germany, although it is significant that no Allied victories were won until after Germany's early control of the air was smashed.

Aircraft Design for World War II

From 1931-1939, the chief concern of designers had been the rapid improvement of performance through better streamlining and more powerful engines. Flaps were added to supplement the monoplane's limited wing area during takeoff and landing, while controllable-pitch propellers, supercharging, and high-octane fuels added to power plant efficiency.

Both the added useful load of the new plane and the threat of combat compelled designers to improve armament. Two fixed guns had been sufficient firepower for an Army fighter from 1918 to 1938, three flexible guns provided for most bombers, and five guns provided for attack types. Caliber .30 (7.6-mm) armament was customary, except for the occasional use of .50-caliber (12.7-mm) on pursuits; less than five percent of the ammunition practice-fired by a typical pursuit group was of .50-caliber.

In Europe, firepower increased quickly. Four-gun fighters were becoming common in 1935, when Britain introduced the eight-gun Hurricane and Spitfire. Most multi-gun fighters mounted their weapons in the wings, where there was more room than in the nose, and where synchronization was unnecessary.

The standardized Browning machine gun, Caliber .30, M2, was the fully developed model of the gun used in World War II. It can be distinguished by the barrel jacket's round perforations, instead of the slots seen on earlier models.

A waist blister on early B-17 of 1937 shelters a .30 caliber M2 from the air stream.

The improved .50-caliber Browning M2 model authorized in 1933 became the principal American aircraft weapon of World War II, and again can be recognized by the barrel jacket's round perforations, instead of slots. That weapon's size seemed too heavy to be aimed from open cockpits, so .50-caliber guns were used as fixed forward-firing guns until the development of enclosed turrets.

Hand-held 50-caliber M2s at a B-24 waist position.

In the following chapters, the reader will see how American aircraft gradually adopted these armament systems. After a transition period in 1939-40, six .50-caliber guns were mounted in the wings of most fighters. Bomber armament increased from the single, hand-held .30-caliber Browning to .50-caliber Browning M-2s paired in power-operated turrets. Power-operated turrets had appeared on British bombers by 1936, but RAF practice favored two or four .30-caliber weapons. Computing sights were introduced on American bombers in 1942, and appeared on fighters in 1944.

Larger caliber guns have a slower rate of fire, but are especially effective against bombers and ground targets. The 37-mm Baldwin aircraft gun with exploding shells in 1921 had been unsatisfactory, but the Army's Ordinance Department developed the rapid-firing, high-velocity 37-mm guns that began production in 1939 for the Bell fighters.

This Martin power turret with twin 50-caliber M2s was favorite Air Force wartime turret.

In Europe, the 20-mm (.78-inch) Oerlikon gun, produced by a Swiss company originally established by Germans, offered a faster rate of fire for a relatively light weight. The United States Army bought two Type FF wing guns, as well as one flexible type L model that was loaned to the Glenn Martin Company for tests in a B-10's rear cockpit. The Army also requested a 25-mm Hotchkiss cannon in 1937, but the French were unwilling to sell one, and that weapon never reached production.

Retractable Sperry ball turret with twin 50-caliber guns on B-24.

A 23-mm Madsen gun from Denmark appeared on the Fokker G-1 at December 1936 Paris Air Show. The U.S. Army ordered four on May 18, 1937, and the first reached New York in November. Reliability and rate of fire (rpm) were poor, but two were used on the P-36G, and the Navy tested the others. While the Navy did request 20 Madsen guns for F2A-1 fighters in July 1938, on October 15 the Navy decided against buying guns of foreign manufacture.

The most important aircraft cannon was the 20-mm Hispano-Suiza. That company had been founded in Barcelona by Marc Birkigt and also established its headquarters in Paris. Birkigt improved the 20-mm Oerlikon gun as Type 404 with a higher rate of fire and also produced Hispano engines with the gun mounted between cylinder banks to fire through an offset hollow propeller shaft.

Remote-controlled bottom rear turret of B-29.

A bomber escort conversion of a YB-29 in 1943 added five pairs of .50-caliber guns in new mounts.

The French Air Ministry adopted that system for Dewoitine fighters. While RAF trials began in January 1937, British engines did not fit the centerline arrangement. Instead, British-made guns first delivered in December 1938 were intended for installation in the nose of twin-engine fighters like the Westland Whirlwind, or in the wings of Hurricanes.

Automatic 37-mm cannon were introduced on the Bell XFM-1, but the Airacuda was too big to be a good fighter.

The United States Army ordered a sample HS 404 gun on July 27, 1937, which arrived in New York on March 26, 1938, and tests began June 21, 1938, at the Aberdeen Proving Ground. Successful trials led to an order placed with the French firm on December 14, 1939, for 33 guns; 13 for the Army, and 20 for the Navy. The first ten reached Aberdeen on February 20, 1940.

General Arnold urged Air Force adoption of the 20-mm gun on April 12, 1940, and on September 23, Bendix got

A 20-mm Oerlikon cannon tried in a Martin bomber was too large for manual use.

contract approval for 1,202 20-mm M-1 guns, mostly for P-38 and P-39 fighters. Only 14 M-1s went to the Navy. They were intended for Brewster fighters, but the 18-inch height with the 60-round drum discouraged mounting in the wings.

The first 20-mm gun on a production bomber was in the B-29's tail turret.

Later guns would all be heavier M-2 models, and in 1942 the Navy provided a belt-feed system for 20-mm gun M-2 guns on SB2C dive-bombers and some F4U fighters. Bendix made 22,642 guns from 1941 to the end of deliveries in December 1943. Oldsmobile made 77,010 from November 1941 to February 1944, and International Harvester and IBM joined the work. A total of 134,663 20-mm guns were produced by February 1944: 21,228 for the Navy, 13,272 for the AAF, and the rest to Lend-lease or storage.

The most heavily armed combat plane in action, the B-25H with a 75-mm cannon and 14 .50-caliber guns.

Table 4 • American Aircraft Guns, 1940-1945

Type	Length (inches	Weight Gun (lb.)	Weight of Bullet (ounces)	Muzzle Velocity (ft./sec)	Rate of fire (rds/min)	Range (yards)
.30-cal. M-2	40	21	.34	2,600	1,350	1,800
.50-cal. M-2	57	64	1.71	2,810	800	7,200
20-mm M-2	94	102	4.82	2,850	650	5,500
20-mm M-3	78	112	4.82	2,750	800	—
37-mm M-4	89	248	21.44	2,000	135	4,000
37-mm M-9	104	365	21.44	2,900	125	8,875
75-mm M-4	141	1,297	208.00	2,090	-	12,000

Armor protection in the pilot's cockpit became standard on Soviet fighters in 1937, and by 1940 all of the warring countries had adopted pilot armor and revived the 1918 fuel tank protection system of an inner self-sealing lining of rubber to make the tank leak proof. Another Soviet development, air-launched rockets, were first used in 1939 against Japan, and appeared in American combat units in 1944.

CHAPTER 12

ARMY OBSERVATION AIRCRAFT, 1930-1942

While the XO-47 was the most advanced observation type of 1935, it was completely unsuitable for combat.

The First Observation Monoplanes: 1930-1932

Most of the fighting planes in World War I were two-seat biplanes on observation sorties, perhaps with some light bombs along, and always depending on the observer's guns to drive off the enemy. But despite the change to faster monoplanes, armed observation types would disappear from World War II's center stage.

When monoplanes replaced biplanes in Air Corps and National Guard observation squadrons, the monoplanes were not the low-wing type standard in attack and pursuit aviation. Since visibility was the first consideration, observation monoplanes had their wing in a high position, either the gull or "parasol" style.

FOKKER XO-27
Two Curtiss V-1570-9, 600 hp
DIMENSIONS: Span 64', Lg. 47'4", Ht. 11'9", Wing Area 615 sq. ft.
WEIGHT: Empty 6522 lb., Gross 8918 lb. Fuel 202-412 gal.
PERFORMANCE: Speed- Top 160 mph at s.1., 152 mph at 10,000', Cruising 128 mph, Landing 65 mph. Service Ceiling 22,600', Absolute Ceiling 24,400', Climb 1350'/1 min., 10,000'/9.5 min.

The higher performance offered by the monoplanes was especially attractive to the long-neglected requirement for a twin-engine, three-place army observation type capable of deep penetrations into enemy territory to get information for GHQ and Air Force commands. Such-aircraft could also be configured as light bombers.

Two such prototypes, the XO-27 and XB-8, were ordered from Fokker Aircraft on June 19, 1929. The XO-27 was completed in August 1930, and tested at Wright Field on October 20, with two V-1570-9 Conquerors in the leading edge of the thick cantilever wing and the first retractable landing gear on an Air Corps observation type. Wing construction was all wood and the fuselage was of fabric-covered steel-tubing. Three open cockpits were provided, with a .30-caliber Lewis gun in the bow and another in the rear.

FOKKER XO-27A

Later, the prototype was modified with the pilot's cabin and geared V-1570-29 engines chosen for the YO-27 version. Fokker, which had become the General Aviation Company in May 1930, received a service test contract April 11, 1931, for six aircraft, increased to 12 the following month. The first YO-27 was completed in May 1932, at Dundalk, Maryland, tested at Wright in September, and service trials were made by the 12th Observation Group at Brooks Field, Texas. Longer nacelles with three-bladed Hamilton propellers, bow windows, and rudder tabs distinguished the YO-27 from the XO-27.

Douglas also prepared twin-engine three-place designs as the XO-35/36 project and two prototypes were ordered from the Santa Monica factory on April 14, 1930. The XO-35 was delivered October 24, 1931, but the XO-36 variant was replaced by an XB-7. An all-metal, strut braced gull-wing monoplane with V-1570-29 engines, the XO-35 had two .30-caliber flexible guns, a 100-pound camera, and a 75-pound radio.

Twelve service test examples ordered August 27, 1931, were delivered, beginning in August 1932, as five

AF

DOUGLAS Y1O-35
Two Curtiss V-1570-53, 600 hp
DIMENSIONS: Span 65'8", Lg. 45'11", Ht. 12'6", Wing Area 621 sq. ft.
WEIGHT: Empty 7896 lb., Gross 10,376 lb. Fuel 297 gal.
PERFORMANCE: Speed- Top 179 mph at s.1., Cruising 157 mph, Service Ceiling 21,750', Range 700 miles.

AAHS

GENERAL AVIATION YO-27
Two Curtiss V-1570-29, 600 hp
DIMENSIONS: Span 64', Lg. 47'6", Ht. 14'6", Wing Area 628 sq. ft.
WEIGHT: Empty 8092 lb., Gross 10,639 lb. Fuel 207-409 gal.
PERFORMANCE: Speed- Top 177 mph at s.1., 174 mph at 10,000', Cruising 152 mph, Landing 68 mph. Service Ceiling 20,750', Absolute Ceiling 22,400', Climb 1370'/1 min., 10,000'/9.7 min. Range 425-840 miles.

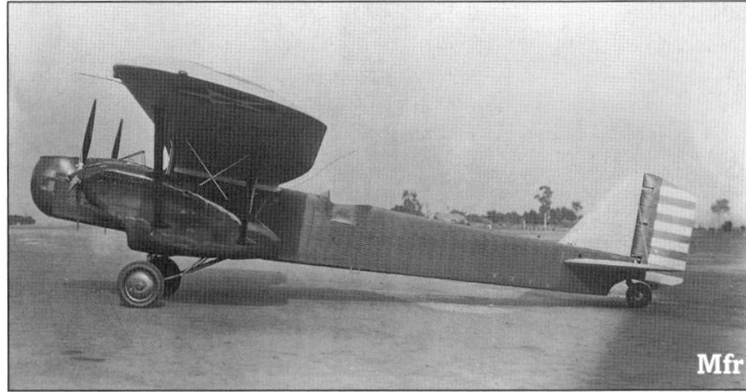

Mfr

DOUGLAS XO-35
Two Curtiss V-1570-29, 600 hp
DIMENSIONS: Span 65', Lg. 45'6", Ht. 12'6", Wing Area 609 sq. ft.
WEIGHT: Empty 7296 lb., Gross 10,376 lb. Fuel 297 gal.
PERFORMANCE: Speed- Top 178 mph at s.1., 172 mph at 10,000', Cruising 156 mph, Landing 65 mph. Service Ceiling 21,750', Absolute Ceiling 23,300', Climb 1560'/1 min., 10,000'/8.4 min. Range 765 miles.

Y1O-35s and seven Y1B-7s. They differed from the prototypes by the smooth, instead of corrugated, skins on their monocoque fuselages, and by their fabric-covered control surfaces. Our 12th Observation Squadron Y1O-35 photo shows the bulge under floor for the camera, behind the rear cockpit, that is the only visible difference from the B-7 bomber version.

Despite promising performance, the twin-engine observation types never went into production, because it was decided that missions beyond a 50-mile penetration of enemy territory could be done best by using the same type aircraft as in bomber units, with more fuel substituted for bombs. Long-range, multi-engine observation aircraft would be designated "reconnaissance" aircraft, and several observation squadrons were redesignated reconnaissance squadrons in 1937-38 and equipped with twin-engine B-10 and B-18 bombers.

Mfr

DOUGLAS XO-31
Curtiss V-1570-25, 600 hp
DIMENSIONS: Span 45'8", Lg. 33'2", Ht. 12', Wing Area 335 sq. ft.
WEIGHT: Empty 3277 lb., Gross 4428 lb. Fuel 82-136 gal.
PERFORMANCE: Speed- Top 176 mph at s.1., 168 mph at 10,000', Cruising 152 mph, Landing 62 mph. Service Ceiling 23,000', Absolute Ceiling 24,600', Climb 1620'/1 min., 10,000'/7.9 min. Range 498 miles.

This left the army observation squadrons with the conventional single-engine two-seater, which had to be adapted to the all-metal monoplane style coming in. The first was the Douglas XO-31, an all-metal monoplane with corrugated dural fuselage, straight, fabric-covered gull-wings braced by wires to a cabane, wheel pants, and the inline Curtiss Conqueror engine.

Mfr

DOUGLAS YO-31
Curtiss V-1570-7, 600 hp
DIMENSIONS: Span 45'8", Lg. 33'5", Ht.12', Wing Area 335 sq. ft.
WEIGHT: Empty 3496 lb., Gross 4654 lb. Fuel 82-136 gal.
PERFORMANCE: Speed- Top 182 mph at s.1., 177 mph at 10,000', Cruising 157 mph, Landing 65 mph. Service Ceiling 24,300', Absolute Ceiling 25,800', Climb 1700'/1 min., 10,000'/7.4 min.

Two prototypes were ordered January 7, 1930, and the XO-31 was first completed in December 1930 with a blunt nose and chin Prestone cooler, but was revised in February 1931 by moving that radiator back and adding a nose spinner. The second prototype, the YO-31, was completed in April 1931 with a geared Conqueror and numerous refinements. One fixed and one flexible .30-caliber M1922 Browning were mounted, standard armament for all of these Douglas observation monoplanes. The fixed gun was placed in the right wing and had 300 rounds of ammunition, and 500 rounds were provided in the rear cockpit.

Six service test examples were ordered June 23, 1931, and the first four were built as the YO-31A. Delivered in December 1931, the YO-31A had a new smooth-surfaced

Mfr

DOUGLAS YO-31A
Curtiss V-1570-53, 600 hp
DIMENSIONS: Span 45'11", Lg. 33'10", Ht. 11'9", Wing Area 340 sq. ft.
WEIGHT: Empty 3751 lb., Gross 4865 lb. Fuel 78-130 gal.
PERFORMANCE: Speed- Top 191 mph at s.1., 187 mph at 10,000', Cruising 168 mph, Landing 65 mph. Service Ceiling 22,700', Climb 1870'/1 min., 10,000'/6.9 min. Range 635 miles.

PMB

DOUGLAS YO-31A modified

monocoque fuselage, cockpit canopy, elliptical wing plan form and a V-1570-53 with three-bladed propeller. The YO-31B was a General's unarmed transport finished in April 1932 with dual-control cockpits completely enclosed and faired back to a high fin. It was delivered to the Militia Bureau, the National Guard command post in Washington D.C.

SDAM

DOUGLAS YO-31B

Last on the order was the YO-31C of July 1932, which had a high peaked tail, new gull wing joint, and single-strut landing gear. Under the cockpit was a bulge in the floor to give the observer's legs more room. The Douglas O-31s, like the twin-engine O-35s, were transferred back and forth around Brooks, Langley, and Mitchel fields to give the biplane-equipped squadrons experience with the high-wing monoplane concept.

DOUGLAS YO-31C
Curtiss V-1570-53, 600 hp
DIMENSIONS: Span 45'11", Lg. 33'10", Ht. 11'9", Wing Area 340 sq. ft.
WEIGHT: Empty 3852 lb., Gross 4982 lb. Fuel 78-130 gal.
PERFORMANCE: Speed- Top 190 mph at s.1., Cruising 171 mph, Landing 73 mph. Service Ceiling 22,700', 10,000'/7.1 min.

Curtiss O-40 Raven

Curtiss tried to follow its Falcon series with the Raven, featuring the Wright Cyclone radial, metal monocoque fuselage, cockpit canopy, and swept-back upper wing. The landing gear in the roots of the narrow lower wing retracted inwards into the fuselage.

A YO-40 prototype ordered October 10, 1931, was completed in January 1932, and forwarded to Wright Field in February. Tests soon demonstrated a useful turn of speed, but that Curtiss crashed on May 20.

CURTISS YO-40
Wright YR-1820-F, 630 hp
DIMENSIONS: Span 44'1", Lg. 28'6", Ht. 10'7", Wing Area 325 sq. ft.
WEIGHT: Empty 3429 lb., Gross 4565 lb. Fuel 78-136 gal.
PERFORMANCE: Speed- Top 193 mph at s.1., 185 mph at 10,000', Cruising 165 mph, Landing 64 mph. Service Ceiling 24,000',Absolute Ceiling 25'600', Climb 1685'/1 min., 10,000'/7.5 min. Range 324 miles.

The Air Corps had Curtiss rebuild the sesquiplane as the YO-40A, while giving the company a contract on June 30, 1932, for four YO-40Bs, a development in monoplane form. In that version, the stubs for landing gear remained, but to make up for the lift lost by removing the lower wings, a system of slots and flaps was used.

The first YO-40B monoplane was finished in June 1933, and retained the cockpit canopy of the YO-40, but the rebuilt YO-40A differed from the original in having separate open cockpits. Instead of the original two-bladed propeller, both the YO-40A and YO-40B were tested together at Wright Field with three-bladed propellers in August 1933. Later YO-40Bs were used at Mitchel Field.

CURTISS YO-40A
Wright R-1820-37, 670 hp
DIMENSIONS: Span 44'1", Lg. 28'10", Ht.10'7", Wing Area 312 sq. ft.
WEIGHT: Empty 3590 lb., Gross 4744 lb. Fuel 78-136 gal.
PERFORMANCE: Speed- Top 181 mph at s.1., 177 mph at 10,000', Cruising 156 mph, Landing 66 mph. Service Ceiling 23,900', Absolute Ceiling 25,400', Climb 1740'/1 min., 10,000'/7.3 min. Range 315 miles.

An Officers Board met September 15, 1933, to compare the sesquiplane and monoplane configurations. Both models were credited with very satisfactory flying characteristics, with the YO-40B monoplane rated the fastest, with the best vision and with a lower landing speed due to the slots. The YO-40A exceeded in climb and slightly in maneuverability, but the cockpit arrangement was undesirable. Both types were criticized for inadequate fuel capacity, and neither were considered entirely satisfactory.

The Parasols

Douglas won the contracts to equip Air Corps observation squadrons with monoplanes by changing from the O-31's gull-wing to the parasol wing of the O-43, which gave the crew the best downward visibility. The elliptical wings retained their fabric-covered aluminum structure.

CURTISS Y1O-40B
Wright P-l820-37, 670 hp
DIMENSIONS: Span 41'8", Lg. 28'10", Ht. 10'8", Wing Area 266 sq. ft.
WEIGHT: Empty 3754 lb., Gross 4908 lb., Fuel 78-136 gal.
PERFORMANCE: Speed- Top 188 mph at s.1., 182 mph at 10,000', Cruising 160 mph, Landing 62 mph. Service Ceiling 23,100', Absolute Ceiling 24,600', Climb 1645'/1 min., 10,000'/7.7 min. Range 324-650 miles.

AF

DOUGLAS Y1O-43 with V-1570-59

Five Y1O-43 monoplanes ordered August 26, 1931, and delivered from February to April 1933 may be the best-looking observation planes built, with smooth lines from the 9.5-foot propeller's nose spinner, through the geared V-1570-53, the small oil and Prestone radiators, and cockpit canopy, to the rounded tail cone and fin. Equipment included camera, radio, flares, a fixed .30-caliber gun in the right wing with 200 rounds, and the flexible .30-caliber M1922 with 500 rounds.

One Y1O-43 was modified at Wright with the 675-hp, hi-compression V-1510-59 selected for 24 O-43As ordered March 2, 1933. The first O-43A was seen in May 1934 with the rounded tail of the Y1O-43, but the tall fin of the O-31C was standardized for the other O-43As and retrofitted to YO-31As. No nose spinner was used, and exhaust collector pipes were added. Another change was the roomier cockpit that made the belly bulge unnecessary.

The O-43s went into service from July to November 1934 at Brooks Field with the 12th and 22nd Observation Squadrons, the first to entirely use monoplanes, while the

DOUGLAS Y1O-43
Curtiss V-1570-53, 600 hp
DIMENSIONS: Span 45'8", Lg. 33'11", Ht. 12'3", Wing Area 335 sq. ft.
WEIGHT: Empty 3834 lb., Gross 4982 lb. Fuel 78-130 gal.
PERFORMANCE: Speed- Top 188 mph at s.1., 181 mph at 10,000', Cruising 163 mph, Landing 69 mph. Service Ceiling 23,200', Absolute Ceiling 24,600', Climb 1800'/1 min., 10,000'/7.1 min. Range 327-630 miles.

DOUGLAS O-43A
Curtiss V-1570-59, 675 hp
DIMENSIONS: Span 45'8", Lg. 34'4", Ht. 12'1", Wing Area 335 sq. ft.
WEIGHT: Empty 4151 lb., Gross 5331 lb. Fuel 78-129 gal.
PERFORMANCE: Speed- Top 191 mph at s.1., 183 mph at 10,000', Cruising 166 mph, Landing 67 mph. Service Ceiling 22,400', Absolute Ceiling 23,800', Climb 1690'/1 min., 10,000'/7.7 min. Range 383 miles.

12 remaining observation squadrons still flew O-19, O-25, and O-38 biplanes. Later, the O-43As passed to the Texas National Guard, who's 111th Squadron still had five in November 1941.

The last O-43A was completed in October 1934 as the XO-46 with an air-cooled Pratt & Whitney Twin Wasp and trailing edge flaps on the wing braced by metal struts, instead of wires. That was the fastest version; 204 mph when weighing 5,325 pounds. Later, it was proposed to rework that prototype to be an XO-48 with a Wright R-1670-3, but that project was canceled.

AF

DOUGLAS XO-46

An O-46A production contract was made April 29, 1935, and the first rolled out of Douglas about January 29, 1936. Ninety O-46As delivered from May 1936 to April 1937 went into Air Corps and National Guard squadrons. The cockpit enclosure was now faired into the fuselage, and was folded back to expose the gun. Ammunition supply was increased to 250 and 1,000 rounds for the fixed and flexible guns. Although no bombs were carried by other observation monoplanes, a rack for two 116-pound bombs was fitted on some O-46As in 1940.

AF

DOUGLAS O-46A
Pratt & Whitney R-1535-7, 725 hp at 4000'
DIMENSIONS: Span 45'9", Lg. 34'9", Ht. 10'4", Wing Area 335 sq. ft.
WEIGHT: Empty 4700 lb., Gross 6135 lb. Fuel 88-130 gal.
PERFORMANCE: Speed- Top 200 mph at s.1., Cruising 171 mph, Landing 58 mph. Service Ceiling 24,150', Absolute Ceiling 25,400', Climb 1765'/1 min., 10,000'/6.4 min. Range 383 miles/88 gal.

Bombers had replaced observation aircraft in several units by 1936, when these squadrons were redesignated reconnaissance squadrons, and the 9th Observation became the 9th Bombing Group. Aside from the school squadrons, only six corps observation squadrons remained in the United States: the 12th and 22nd at Brooks Field, the 15th at Scott, 16th at Fort Riley, 91st at Crissy Field, and the new 97th at Mitchel Field, along with the 19 National Guard units. Nearly all of these squadrons used O-46As at one time or another, usually along with older types and the new O-47s.

The O-47

In December 1934, the Air Corps formulated a requirement for an observation aircraft that could exceed 200 mph and yet not require more than 1500 feet to takeoff over a 50-foot obstacle. By November 1935, accommodation for three crewmen was also desired.

The only aircraft offered to fill this requirement was the General Aviation GA-15, built by the Dundalk, Maryland firm led by J. K. Kindelberger, who had been chief engineer at Douglas during the firm's domination of observation contracts. An all-metal mid-wing monoplane powered by a Wright Cyclone, the GA-15 had a long enclosure over its crew, with the observer sitting between the pilot and gunner while working as co-pilot, or moving down to his observation post in the deep belly. Windows under the wing gave him visibility, and for the first time the observer could concentrate on his camera and map work, leaving to the gunner the task of watching for other aircraft. The wheels and their long struts swung outwards into the wing.

Mfr

NORTH AMERICAN XO-47
Wright R-1820-41, 850 hp at 4000'
DIMENSIONS: Span 46'4", Lg. 33'6", Ht. 9'11", Wing Area 331 sq. ft.
WEIGHT: Empty 5552 lb., Gross 7319 lb. Fuel 156 gal.
PERFORMANCE: Speed- Top 225 mph at 4,000', Cruising 197 mph, Service Ceiling 23,800', Absolute Ceiling 25,000', Climb 10,000'/6.8 min.

Completed in May 1935, the GA-15 went to Wright late that year and was purchased by the Air Corps as the XO-47 on January 22, 1936. By that time, its builders had a new name, North American Aviation, and a new California factory.

The Air Corps hesitated with a production contract, because while the new plane's performance and crew accommodation was very superior to the older two-seaters, it did require twice as much room to takeoff and land; a serious consideration for a plane supposed to work closely with ground troops.

But no valid alternative seemed to be available, and 109 O-47s were ordered on February 19, 1937. It was the largest contract for observation planes since the war, but in

NORTH AMERICAN O-47A
Wright R-1820-49, 975 hp takeoff, 835 hp at 3900'
DIMENSIONS: Span 46'4", Lg. 33'7", Ht. 12'2", Wing Area 350 sq. ft.
WEIGHT: Empty 6028 lb., Gross 7650 lb. Fuel 150 gal.
PERFORMANCE: Speed- Top 223 mph at 4,000', Cruising 200 mph, Landing 76 mph. Service Ceiling 23,200', Climb 10,000'/6.8 min. Range 900 miles at 150 mph.

October was increased to 164 aircraft. The first O-47A was flown at Inglewood, California, March 7, 1938, armed with a .30-caliber M-2 gun in the right wing with 200 rounds and a flexible M-2 with 600 rounds, but no bombs. Modified to an April 1939 NA-60 specification, the last O-47A was completed in August with more windows in the belly, but this feature was not adopted for the O-47B.

Since the O-47A worked well in service, 74 O-47B versions with a 1,060-hp Cyclone were ordered March 18, 1939, and delivery began in August. Unlike fiscal year 1931, when the Air Corps had seven types to chose from, there was now only one Army observation aircraft in production. When the last O-47B was delivered in March 1940, enough deep-bellied North Americans were around to be used by nearly all of some 33 Army and National Guard observation squadrons.

They joined, rather than replaced, the O-46A, for both types served together. For example, Philadelphia's 103rd Observation Squadron (NG) had six O-46As, three O-47As, one O 47B, one O-38B, and a BC-lA trainer at the end of 1940,

NORTH AMERICAN NA-60 (Last O-47A)

NORTH AMERICAN O-47B
Wright R-1820-57, 1060 hp takeoff, 900 hp at 3800'
DIMENSIONS: Same as O-47A
WEIGHT: Empty 6218 lb., Gross 8045 lb. Fuel 134-200 gal.
PERFORMANCE: Speed- Top 227 mph at 4,000', Cruising 200 mph, Service Ceiling 24,100", Climb 15,000'/11.8 min. Range 840 miles.

when all 21 Guard squadrons together had 76 O-47A, 44 O-47B, 39 O-46A, six O-43A, 11 O-38B and 13 O-38E aircraft.

Tracing observation plane development from the DH-4 to the O-47, shows a remarkable improvement in capability, just as is seen with bombers and fighters. But the results of this development are quite different. While the end products of the 1918 to 1940 story of bombers went into battle in the Second World War, no O-47, or any other American armed, two or three-place observation type, played a significant role in the new war.

In short, the development had led to a technological dead end; the most widely used aircraft type of 1918 became the least important aircraft of 1940. In Europe, the Mureaux, Lysander, and Henschel observation aircraft proven unable to defend themselves against fighter attack. A single .30-caliber gun was almost useless against fighters with up to eight guns or cannon, and there was no way the heavy observation types could have enough speed to escape 350-mph fighters.

On December 7, 1941, seven sorties were flown by O-47Bs of the 86th Observation Squadron on Oahu in a vain effort to find attacking Japanese. They were fortunate not to encounter fighters that would have made short work of them. The O-47 flew no other real combat mission in World War Two.

From the O-49 to the O-53

Since the O-47 was too heavy for the short-field operation and low-altitude maneuverability needed to work directly with Army ground divisions, the Air Corps was looking for a "flying motorcycle" that could takeoff from and land on short unprepared fields, providing commanders with communication and artillery spotting services.

The trend towards high performance aircraft demanded heavier, more expensive planes requiring long runways; the opposite of what Army ground forces needed. An AMC (Approved Military Characteristics) dated March 30, 1938, for short-range liaison observation aircraft, was developed into Type Specification C-413 dated May 7, and in turn led to CP 39-2 (Circular Proposal) dated August 2.

Private builders were invited to offer bids for a two-place, high-wing monoplane capable of taking off over 50-foot obstacles in only 500 feet (the O-46 required 644 feet and the O-47A required 1,300 ft.), flying as slow as 40 mph, and, of course, too light for armament. In 1939, the Army planned to issue three such liaison planes to each observation squadron to supplement the armed types.

Germany's World War II liaison type, the Fieseler Storch, was demonstrated in America in September 1938 at the National Air Races and at Wright Field. It appeared that such light aircraft could have STOL short-field characteristics nearly matching the autogiros that had been unsuccessfully tested as a replacement for the captive balloons of World War One trenches.

Ten bids were received in February 1939 for the CP 39-2 design competition, and the winners were announced June 15. Fiscal 1940 funds provided contracts dated August 12, 1939, and approved September 20, for 100

Mfr

RYAN YO-51
Pratt & Whitney R-985-21, 440 hp takeoff, 420 hp at s.1.
DIMENSIONS: Span 52', Lg. 34'5", Ht. 11'1", Wing Area 400 sq. ft.
WEIGHT: Empty 3432 lb., Gross 4200 lb. Fuel 52 gal.
PERFORMANCE: Speed- Top 130 mph at s.1., Cruising 119 mph, Landing 30 mph. Service Ceiling 19,700', Climb 10,000'/13 min. Range 261 miles.

Stinson O-49s, and three each of the somewhat heavier Bellanca YO-50 and Ryan YO-51 types for back-up tests. All would be light two-seaters with fixed landing gear, wing flaps and slots, and no guns.

The Ryan company in San Diego wished to finish the YO-51 first, expecting better performance than the Stinson, whose lower price won the first contract. After the "Dragonfly" first flew on January 31, 1940, the press was invited to witness "almost unbelievably quick takeoffs, steep climbs over obstacles, nearly vertical approach, and extremely short landing roll."

Army charts record a 475-foot takeoff distance over the standard 50-foot obstacle height, and a 350-foot landing space. While the plywood-covered wing used the same

AF

STINSON O-49 (L-l)
Lycoming R-680-9, 295 hp takeoff, 280 hp at s.1.
DIMENSIONS: Span 51', Lg. 33'2", Ht. 9'4", Wing Area 330 sq. ft.
WEIGHT: Empty 2583 lb., Gross 3315 lb. Fuel 52 gal.
PERFORMANCE: Speed- Top 122 mph at s.1., Cruising 109 mph, Landing 31 mph. Service Ceiling 20,000', Climb 15,000'/27.2 min. Range 278 miles, Endurance 2.5 .hours.

Clark Y airfoil as Ryan's famous "Spirit of Saint Louis", its wing area increased nearly 40% when the full-span Fowler flaps were extended, and full-span slots on the wing's leading edge also added lift.

Mfr

CURTISS O-52
Pratt & Whitney R-1340-51, 600 hp takeoff, 550 hp at 4000'
DIMENSIONS: Span 40'9", Lg. 26'5", Ht. 10', Wing Area 210 sq. ft.
WEIGHT: Empty 4230 lb., Gross 5307 lb., Max. 5585 lb. Fuel 75-108 gal.
PERFORMANCE: Speed- Top 208 mph at 4,000', Cruising 153 mph, Landing 70 mph. Service Ceiling 23,200', Climb 10,000'/8.2 min. Range 450-770 miles.

Equipment in the aluminum-covered fuselage with two open cockpits included a 55-pound radio, but no guns or heavy cameras. Powered by a 420-hp R-985-21, the YO-51 speed range was from 32 mph for a careful look at ground activity to 130 mph for evasion. All three Ryans were accepted in July 1940.

The first O-49 flew July 15, 1940, at Nashville, with a 295-hp Lycoming radial, light-weight fabric-covered steel structure, and cockpit enclosure. Slots and flaps enabled a takeoff of 396 feet, and a landing at 31 mph in 415 feet. Production deliveries began in January 1941, and by the year's end, 172, then officially named the Vigilant, were parceled out to Army and Guard squadrons.

Bellanca's YO-50 was late, the first not accepted until April 1941. It introduced an inverted inline air-cooled Ranger V-770-1, and had an enclosed cabin, full-span slots and Fowler flaps. But it won little attention as the Army bought more Vigilants, building 324 (including 148 for the RAF) by March 1942.

Low speed and no guns were evidence that these were no combat planes, but depended for protection on friendly fighter cover or a quick landing sheltered by friendly ground troops. A new designation was appropriate and so the O-49 began the new Liaison series as the L-l and L-lA on April 8, 1942.

The Air Corps still expected to use traditional two-seat observation planes armed for shallow penetrations of enemy airspace, and ordered 203 Curtiss O-52 all-metal high-wing monoplanes on October 12, 1939. Powered by a 600 hp Wasp, the O-52 Owl owed its retractable wheels and cockpit enclosure to the Navy SBC series and was armed with a fixed .30-caliber M-2 gun in the nose and a flexible one in the rear cockpit with 500 rounds. Despite the use of leading edge slots and split flaps, takeoff required over 1,000 feet.

SDAM

BELLANCA YO-50
Ranger V-770-1, 420 hp at s.l.
DIMENSIONS: Span 55'6", Lg. 35'2", Ht. 9'10", Wing Area 490 sq. ft.
WEIGHT: Empty 3086 lb., Gross 3887 lb. Fuel 54 gal.
PERFORMANCE: Speed- Top 126 mph at s.1. Cruising 114 mph, Landing 27 mph. Service Ceiling 19,420', Climb 10,000'/8.2 min. Range 230 miles.

Delivered at Buffalo from June 1941 to January 1942, the O-52s were scattered among the Army and National Guard squadrons. Like other traditional observation types, the O-52 fell between two requirements; too slow and light to defend itself, but still too heavy for the small field operations needed for close service to ground forces. It was the last Army plane completed as an armed observation type.

All the O-52s were offered to the Soviet Union in September 1941, and 30 were shipped from the factory in October. Eleven were lost en route, and 19 arrived in Murmansk, but without assembly instructions or spare parts. The Russians refused to take any more, although a few were used by the 50th OKE squadron. Ten O-52s were sent to the Philippines for the Army's 2nd Observation Squadron.

In the fall of 1940, a committee representing various interested Army elements including the Air Corps, Artillery, and Infantry decided that two separate types of observation aircraft were needed: a short-range, unarmed, single-engine liaison type and a high-altitude twin-engine type armed for penetration of enemy airspace beyond the 50-mile pre-war limit.

Since the Air Corps had already ordered three Douglas A-20 light bombers converted for photographic reconnaissance duties, that type was selected as the three-place, twin-engine reconnaissance aircraft. On October 11, 1940, 775 Douglas O-53s were ordered with 1,700-hp turbosupercharged R-2600-7 Cyclones that were expected to confer 395 mph at 25,000 feet, with a 604-mile range and six machine guns. This program was canceled in June 1942 as Lockheed F-4 Lightnings succeeded in the mission, and other needs for A- 20 type aircraft had priority.

The End of the Observation Plane

At the other extreme of cost and size were the standard off-the-shelf sports planes that were quickly available. Stinson's Model 105 Voyager was a popular commercial type that had attracted French attention during the German invasion. Thirty-eight had been rounded up from various dealers, and 25 were shipped on the *Bearn* on June 16, 1940. The U.S. Army bought six from Stinson on August 24, 1940; and designated them YO-54. Cost of this 80-hp three-place cabin plane was $3,989 compared to $17,560 for an O-49, $24,578 for an O-52, or $31,780 for an O-47A.

At this point, the story of the "O" type separates itself from the combat types, for none of the remaining aircraft completed as "O" ships were armed. That twenty years development of the specialized armed observation types should have been abandoned in wartime in favor of light aircraft designed solely to provide sport pilots with safe fun at the lowest possible price seems remarkable. What actually happened is that procurement of light liaison aircraft, intended to give the ground forces the kind of close support they wanted, relieved the Air Force of the need to compromise combat plane performance with short field and special vision needs. This in turn allowed wartime Air Force reconnaissance to be done by standard fighter and bomber aircraft modified with cameras.

During the Louisiana maneuvers in August 1941, the Army had tested borrowed civilian light planes as observers for division and corps artillery. Success was immediate, and the first dozen Taylorcraft, Aeronca and Piper

CURTISS O-52 of 119th Sq., New Jersey National Guard

(four each) 65-hp light planes were purchased September 17, 1941, with the YO-57, YO-58 and YO-59 designations. They were able to work more intimately with artillery than the O-49s, and more were bought in November. These aircraft became the L-2, L-3 and L-4 liaison series in April 1942, the Army's own "grasshoppers" that were an organic part of the ground organizations, with each division getting its own aircraft. The most popular Piper L-4 cost only $2,432 each in 1942.

Details of that story, of course, are separate from combat plane history, and here we simply record the demise of observation aviation as such. For several months the situation in squadron equipment and organization was chaotic, as the Air Forces tried to assimilate the new developments.

In December 1941 the 29 now federalized Guard squadrons had 251 Observation aircraft of seven armed and four light types, and the regular army units included 11 squadrons in the United States, and four in the overseas possessions. These Army squadrons had 168 observation aircraft, including 15 O-46, 53 O-47A, 18 O-47B, 32 O-49, 31 O-52, and 19 light aircraft scattered through the units. The most important Guard types were 32 O-46, 61 O-47A, 37 O-47B, 51 O-49 and 19 O-52, and 42 light aircraft.

As the uselessness of the conventional armed types in combat was apparent, and the light aircraft-were redesignated as liaison aircraft on April 8, 1942, the Air Force tried to fit modified fighter and bomber aircraft into observation units. As late as July 1, 1942, a "standard observation squadron" was to comprise nine liaison, six fighter, and six twin-engine bomber type aircraft. This unlikely mixture was not practical, especially since combat units had first priority in getting the new fighter and bomber types. Instead, ten liaison planes became part of each division, while tactical and strategic reconnaissance groups served the Air Force.

CHAPTER 13

ARMY ATTACK MONOPLANES FROM A-7 TO A-41

D-Day stripes adorn the most widely used World War II attack-bombers, A-20Gs of the Ninth Air Force.

The first branch of American military aviation to completely replace biplanes with monoplanes was the Army attack force. Four Curtiss Falcon squadrons that comprised this branch in 1931 were replaced by monoplanes by 1936 and had expanded to eight squadrons of Curtiss and Northrop types by 1938.

First came the all-metal Fokker XA-7 and the Curtiss XA-8: two-place, low-wing monoplanes powered with the 600-hp inline liquid-cooled Curtiss Conqueror. Each was armed with four .30-caliber guns firing forward outside of the propeller arc, and a fifth Browning for the rear gunner. The XA-7 had a thick cantilever wing, wheel pants, open cockpits, and tunnel radiator. This prototype had been built to a contract approved January 8, 1930, and was completed in April, 1931. After tests at Wright Field the XA-7 was sent back to Fokker on June 6, had its radiator enlarged and landing gear configuration modified, and returned to Wright September 27.

FOKKER XA-7 on April 13, 1931

FOKKER XA-7 modified in August 1931
Curtiss V-1570-27, 600 hp at sea level
DIMENSIONS: Span 46'9", Lg. 31', Ht. 9'5", Wing Area 333 Sq. ft.
WEIGHT: Empty 3866 lb., Gross 5650 lb. Fuel 102 gal.
PERFORMANCE: Speed- Top 184 mph, Landing 61 mph.

Its competitor, the Curtiss XA-8 Shrike, had thin wings externally braced by wires, and landing gear entirely enclosed in spats. Construction was all-metal, the structure used in all Army attack and light-bomber aircraft following this machine. Cooling was accomplished by a radiator below and behind the engine, which was neatly streamlined behind the prop spinner. Modern features of the XA-8 were the first enclosed cockpits, several feet apart, for both crewmen, and the first appearance on a U.S. combat plane of wing slots and flaps to minimize landing speed. This system was licensed by the Handley Page company.

The XA-8 was ordered on June 6, 1930, and flown in June 1931, judged better than the Fokker, and Curtiss was awarded a contract on September 29, 1931, for 13 service

Mfr

CURTISS YA-8
Curtiss V-1570-31, 600 hp at sea level
DIMENSIONS: Span 44'3", Lg. 32'10", Ht. 9', Wing Area 285 sq. ft.
WEIGHT: Empty 3938 lb., Gross 5706 lb. Fuel 101+52 gal.
PERFORMANCE: Speed- Top 183 mph at s.1., 179.5 mph at 5000', Cruising 157.5 mph, Landing 69 mph. Service Ceiling 18,100', Absolute Ceiling 19,700', Climb 1375'/1 min., 5000'/4.4 min. Range 425 miles/464-lb. bombs, 734 miles max.

Mfr

CURTISS XA-8
Curtiss V-1570-23, 600 hp at sea level
DIMENSIONS: Span 44', Lg. 32'6", Ht. 9', Wing Area 285 sq. ft.
WEIGHT: Empty 3673 lb., Gross 5113 lb. Fuel 96-123 gal.
PERFORMANCE: Speed- Top 197 mph at s.1., 191 mph at 5000', Cruising 162.5 mph, Landing 70 mph (65 mph/flaps). Service Ceiling 19,800', Absolute Ceiling 21,450', Climb 1265'/1 min. Range 682 miles.

test examples. These went into service July 1932, as the YA-8 (later A-8). Like the original, they had a pair of .30-caliber Browning M1921 guns in each wheel spat, with 600 rounds for each of these, and a .30-caliber Browning M1922 rear gun. A 52-gallon tear-shaped drop tank or four 116-pound bombs could be carried below the fuselage.

Mfr

CURTISS YIA-8A (A-8A)
Curtiss V-1570-57, 675 hp at sea level
DIMENSIONS: Span 44'3", Lg. 33'7", Ht. 9'2", Wing Area 285 sq. ft.
WEIGHT: Empty 4330 lb., Gross 6287 lb. Fuel 105+52 gal.
PERFORMANCE: Speed- Top 181 mph at s.1., 176 mph at 5000', Cruising 156 mph, Landing 75.5 mph. Service Ceiling 17,000', Absolute Ceiling 18,600', Climb 1225'/1 min. Range 624 miles.

The last of these ships, the YlA-8A, was tested in October 1932 with a geared Conqueror "F" engine; which was less noisy, but heavier than the standard model. Field trials of the Shrike were successful enough to merit a 46-plane production order on February 27, 1933.

The first YA-8 was returned to Curtiss for installation of an air-cooled 625-hp Pratt & Whitney Hornet, renamed YA-10, and came back to Wright Field on September 8, 1932. Air-cooled radials were less streamlined than inline engines, but offered other advantages for attack planes. The Army found them less expensive to operate, and free of the radiator area exposed to hostile gunfire. Air-cooled engines were therefore favored for future production attack planes, despite a loss in speed, as a comparison of the A-12 with the A-8 and A-11 will show.

SDAM

CURTISS YA-10
Pratt & Whitney R-1690-9, 625 hp at sea level
DIMENSIONS: Span 44'3", Lg. 32'6", Ht. 9', Wing Area 285 sq. ft.
WEIGHT: Gross 6135 lb. Fuel 101+52 gal.
PERFORMANCE: Speed- Top 175 mph at s.1.

Curtiss offered a Navy version of the YA-10 as the XS2C-l (see page 400), and completed the 46 production Shrikes not as A-8Bs, but as the A-12 with the air-cooled 670-hp Wright Cyclone. Similar to the A-8s except for the radial engine and two open cockpits joined together, the A-12 had the usual five guns and bombs. Ten 30-pound bombs were carried inside the fuselage, or four 116-pound bombs beneath the fuselage. A 52-gallon drop tank could replace the latter. The forward .30-caliber guns in the wheel pants could be adjusted 2° down, 1° up, or 1° to either side.

AF

CURTISS A-12
Wright R-1820-21, 670 hp at sea level
DIMENSIONS: Span 44', Lg. 32'3", Ht. 9'4" Wing Area 285 sq. ft.
WEIGHT: Empty 3898 lb., Gross 5756 lb., Max. 5900 lb. Fuel 114+52 gal.
PERFORMANCE: Speed- Top 177 mph at s.1., 173.5 mph at 5000', Cruising 150.5 mph, Landing 69.5 mph. Service Ceiling 15,150', Absolute Ceiling 16,600', Climb 5000'/5.1 min. Range 510 miles/464-lb. bombs.

The A-12s were delivered from November 1933 to February 1934 and used by the 3rd Attack Group at Fort Crockett, Texas. In 1935, the A-8s and an A-12 were passed to the new 37th Attack Squadron at Langley Field. When the 3rd Attack Group received A-17s in 1936, 15 A-12s went to Kelly Field as trainers, and 20 to the 26th Attack Squadron in Hawaii, where they served until 1941.

China purchased 20 Curtiss Shrikes (labeled Model 60 by the company) powered by Wright SR-1820-F52 Cyclones rated at 775-hp at 6,800 feet, improving performance over the Army version. Delivery began in July 1936, and the Shrikes were used by the two squadrons of China's 9th Group against the Japanese invasion in August 1937.

Mfr

CURTISS SHRIKE Model 60 for China
Wright SR-1820-F52, 775 hp at 6800'
DIMENSIONS: Span 44', Lg. 31'6", Ht. 9'4", Wing Area 285 sq. ft.
WEIGHT: Empty 4024 lb., Gross 5925 lb. Fuel 114+52 gal.
PERFORMANCE: Speed- Top 182 mph at s.l., 202 mph at 6800', Cruising 171 mph. Service Ceiling 20,700', Range 481 miles/300-lb. bombs.

While attack squadrons were receiving the Curtiss products, work proceeded on some more advanced projects. The first of these was the Lockheed YA-9, projected as an attack version of the experimental YP-24. This design incorporated the most modern features then available, including fully retractable landing gear, flaps and enclosed cockpits. Its misfortunes are described in Chapter 16.

When Lockheed proved unable to fulfill the five-plane YA-9 service test order placed in September 1931, Consolidated produced a development of that basic design in January 1933 called the YlA-11. With increased power and improved nose lines, it was similar to the YlP-25, but minus its turbo-supercharger. Despite a crash on January 20, four more A-11s were ordered on February 27, 1933, the same day as the A-12s.

Using the 675-hp V-1710-59 Curtiss Conqueror engine, and armed with four .30-caliber fixed wing guns, one flexible gun, and ten 30-pound bombs on wing racks, the A-11 had a performance far advanced over its contemporaries when delivered from August 30 to September 28, 1934. Apparently the Army's policy opposing liquid-cooled engines in attack ships blocked its wider acceptance. However, the pursuit versions of the ship (P-30 and PB-2A) won larger orders. The first A-11 was modified by Bell Aircraft to the A-llA engine test ship, becoming the first to take the 1,000-hp Allison XV-1710-7 into the air on December 14, 1936.

CONSOLIDATED A-11
Curtiss V-1570-59, 675 hp at sea level
DIMENSIONS: Span 43'11", Lg. 29'3", Ht. 9'10", Wing Area 297 sq. ft.
WEIGHT: Empty 3805 lb., Gross 5490 lb. Fuel 90+90 gal.
PERFORMANCE: Speed- Top 227.5 mph at s.l., Cruising 193 mph, Landing 84 mph. Service Ceiling 23,300', Absolute Ceiling 24,900', Climb 5000'/3.4 min. Range 470 miles/327-lb. bombs, 950 miles max.

Northrop Attack Planes

The most famous attack plane of the 30s and the first American monoplane bomber to enter combat was the low-wing two-seater designed by John K. Northrop. His company had been formed in 1932 at El Segundo as a Douglas subsidiary to manufacture the Gamma, a civilian all-metal monoplane with multi-cellular wing, stressed-skin fuselage construction, large wheel pants, a deep engine cowl, and split trailing edge flaps.

NORTHROP A-13
Wright R-1820-37, 712 hp at 3300'
DIMENSIONS: Span 48', Lg. 29'2", Ht. 9'2", Wing Area 362 sq. ft.
WEIGHT: Empty 3600 lb., Gross 6575 lb. Fuel 245 gal.
PERFORMANCE: Speed- Top 198 mph at s.1., 207 mph at 3300', 202 mph at 10,000', Cruising 172 mph, Landing 70 mph. Service Ceiling 21,700', Absolute Ceiling 23,600', Climb 1300'/min., 5000'/4.3 min. Range 1100 miles.

These features were seen in the first military Northrop, the Gamma 2C completed in May 1933, and delivered to Wright Field on July 18 with an enclosure over the two cockpits, a 712-hp Wright Cyclone, and two-bladed propeller. The Army purchased this aircraft June 28, 1934, as the YA-13, armed with four fixed guns in the wings, a flexible Browning in the rear cockpit, 3,000 .30-caliber rounds, and twenty 30-pound fragmentation bombs in an internal bomb rack between the cockpits.

These were appropriate weapons for the tree-top flying expected by the U.S. Army, but an export version was planned as a bomber. Larger bombs required that the plane to fly high enough to escape the blasts from its own bombs, and needed a bombsight and engine supercharging. Model 2E had external bomb racks for one 1,100, two 600, or ten 100-pound bombs, two .30-caliber guns in the wings, a third in the rear, and a retractable tub under the rear cockpit for a bombsight and window.

NORTHROP 2E
Wright SR-1820-F3, 710 hp at 7000'
DIMENSIONS: Span 48', Lg. 28'10", Ht. 9'1", Wing Area 363 sq. ft.
WEIGHT: Empty 3850 lb., Gross 6400 lb., Max. 7500 lb. Fuel 362 gal.
PERFORMANCE: Speed- Top 198 mph at s.l., 219 mph at 7000', Landing 64 mph. Service Ceiling 23,300', Climb 972'/1 min., 10,000'/12.5 min.

China purchased the first Model 2E light bombers on August 30, 1933, and the first 24, each powered by an R-1820-F3 rated at 710-hp at 7,000 feet, were delivered from February 20 to September 21, 1934. Another 25 were ordered August 30, 1934, as unassembled parts which were shipped in May 1935 for assembly at Shien Chiao by CAMCO.

NORTHROP 2E in China

Northrop-equipped Groups 1 and 2 of the Chinese Air Force became the first planes sent against the Japanese invaders, on August 14, 1937. That morning, 21 Chinese Northrop bombers of the 2nd Group attacked ships and enemy positions at Shanghai, supported by eight Curtiss Hawk III dive-bombers, and an afternoon raid by 22 Northrops followed. This attack had tragic results when bombs hit among Shanghai civilians. Most of these Northrops were expended in the next three months of air fighting.

NORTHROP 2E for the USSR

NORTHROP 5A for Japan

An example of the 2E (K5093) was purchased by Britain on July 31, 1934, and delivered in November. Another (X13760) was used for a demonstrator in Latin America and then, fitted with a 750-hp SR-1820-F53 and three-bladed propeller, became the first American combat plane sold to the Soviet Union, on November 20, 1935. Top speed of this model ranged from 210 mph at 11,000 feet, fully loaded to 7,600 pounds, to 228 mph in light 6,400-pound condition. These Northrops demonstrated the advantages of modern design over the open-cockpit biplane light bombers then used by the RAF and VVS.

NORTHROP 5B

Various canopy and tail refinements were used to produce the 750-hp R-1820-F52 Cyclone-powered Northrop 5A completed October 21, 1935, and quickly sold to the Japanese Navy, which designated it BXN1 for tests. A Northrop 5B was completed in December with a Pratt & Whitney engine, but was fitted with a R-1820F-52 for demonstrations in Argentina in September 1936, and was later sold to a broker in Mexico, who finally shipped it to Spain in December, 1937.

NORTHROP 2F

In the meantime, Northrop had built another prototype for the Army, which appeared October 6, 1934, as Model 2F with a Pratt & Whitney twin-row R-1535-11, three-bladed propeller, new tail, and wheels folding back into bulky fairings. Northrop then won the largest prewar Army attack contract, for 110 aircraft purchased December 19, 1934, for $2,047,774.

It was hoped to install the bigger Twin Wasp in the production version, so the YA-13 was returned to Northrop in January 1935 for rework. It flew in March, redesignated XA-16 with the R-1830-7, but on April 25, the Army was told that either a larger tail or a smaller engine would be necessary. To prevent disruption of production, the Army chose to retain the R-1535, whose smaller diameter improved pilot visibility, for production ships.

NORTHROP XA-16
Pratt & Whitney R-1830-9, 950 hp takeoff, 850 hp at 8000'
DIMENSIONS: Span 48', Lg. 29'8", Wing Area 362 sq. ft.
WEIGHT: Gross 6750 lb. Fuel 362 gals.
PERFORMANCE: Speed- Top 199 mph at s.l., 220 mph at 5800', Landing 60 mph. Service Ceiling 26,800', Climb 1120'/1 min., Range 1430 miles.

The 2F prototype was rebuilt with the 750-hp R-1535-11 Wasp Jr., new open-sided wheel fairings for easier service, and further canopy and tail changes. The armament, specialized for low-level attack, was five .30-caliber guns with 600 rpg and twenty 30-pound fragmentation bombs carried in chutes inside the fuselage. Or, four 116-pound bombs might be carried externally, the maximum bomb load being 654 pounds. Thus redone, the 2F became the first A-17 (35-51) when delivered to Wright Field July 27, 1935, and accepted in November.

Northrop did persevere with the Twin Wasp installation on the XA-16, which was redelivered to the Army in

NORTHROP A-17
Pratt & Whitney R-1535-11, 750 hp at s.l.
DIMENSIONS: Span 47'9", Lg. 32', Ht. 12', Wing Area 362 sq. ft.
WEIGHT: Empty 4913 lb., Gross 7337 lb. Fuel 150-287 gal.
PERFORMANCE: Speed- Top 206 mph at s.1., Cruising 170 mph, Landing 67.5 mph. Service Ceiling 20,700', Absolute Ceiling 22,150', Climb 5000'/3.8 min, Range 600 miles/654-lb. bombs, 1242 miles max.

August 1936 with an 850-hp XR-1830-9, armed with five guns and 24 30-pound bombs.

A-17 deliveries went on with the first true production aircraft (35-52), adding perforated flaps, sent to Wright Field on December 23, 1935. In February 1936, A-17s began arriving at the 3rd Attack Group's new base at Barksdale Field. When the last was completed in December 1936, Army attack units also included the 17th Attack Group, which had begun conversion from P-26A Pursuits at March Field in June 1936, and 15 A-17s with Langley Field's 37th Attack Squadron.

Retractable wheels distinguished 100 A-17As ordered January 29, 1936, but they were preceded by delivery in July 1936 of two A-17AS three-place unarmed command planes, powered by 600-hp R-1340 Wasps, for the Air Corps Chief and his Deputy. General Oscar Westover was killed in his on September 21, 1938, and his Deputy, General Henry H. Arnold, became Air Corps Chief for a term that was to include all of World War II.

Delayed by various problems, the first true A-17A was completed on February 4, 1937, and 100 were delivered by December 21, 1937, with 29 more added from June 10 to August 31, 1938. They replaced the A-17s in the 3rd and 17th Groups* and the 37th Squadron, so 15 A-17s were shipped to the new 74th Attack Squadron in the Canal Zone, and the rest to Kelly Field or to depots as trainers, although Hawaii's 26th Squadron continued to make do with their A-12s.

Ninety-three of these A-17As were transferred back to Douglas on June 20, 1940, leaving about 20 in the Army. In exchange, Douglas added twenty planes to the current A-20A order. Of the 93 A-17As, 32 went to Canada in August 1940, 43 were shipped to South Africa for training and target-towing, 14 were lost at sea, and four retained by the RAF were named the Nomad I.

Attack-bombers for Export

After serious labor and production problems at the factory, Douglas took complete control, dissolved the Northrop

*3rd Attack Group: 8th, 13th and 90th Squadrons.
17th Attack Group: 34th, 73rd and 95th Squadrons.

NORTHROP A-17A
Pratt & Whitney R-1535-13, 825 hp takeoff, 750 hp at 2500'
DIMENSIONS: Span 47'9", Lg. 31'8", Ht. 12', Wing Area 362 sq. ft.
WEIGHT: Empty 5106 lb., Gross 7550 lb. Fuel 151-247 gal.
PERFORMANCE: Speed- Top 220 mph at 2500', Cruising 170 mph, Landing 64 mph. Service Ceiling 19,400', Absolute Ceiling 20,800', Climb 1350'/1 min., 5000'/3.9 min. Range 732 miles/654 lb. bombs, 1195 miles max.

Corporation on September 8, 1937, and the factory became the Douglas El Segundo Division. Jack Northrop left, and his design was exported as the Douglas 8A attack bomber.

DOUGLAS 8A-l for Sweden
Bristol Pegasus XII, 875 hp at 6250'
DIMENSIONS: Span 47'9", Lg. 31'9", Ht. 12'4", Wing Area 363 sq. ft.
WEIGHT: Empty 5369 lb., Gross 7497 lb., Max. 9371 lb. Fuel 290 gal.
PERFORMANCE: Speed- Top 208 mph at 6250'/bombs, (219 mph clean), Cruising 185 mph, Landing 66 mph. Service Ceiling 22,600', Climb 9840'/7.5 min. Range 500 miles/1000 lb. bombs, 930 miles max.

Sweden had ordered the 8A-1 on March 30, 1937, and Argentina the 8A-2 on April 15. These were the last fixed gear types, for the remaining models had retractable wheels. Powered by a 875-hp Bristol Pegasus, the 8A-1 embarked for Sweden (six months late) on April 22, 1938. Along with a second example shipped in parts in August, it was the prototype for 101 B-5 dive bombers built under license with Swedish-made engines from March 1940 to November 1941. These were the first planes made by Saab at Linkoping.

SAAB B-5B dive-bomber in Sweden

While the Army Air Corps had not yet accepted dive-bombing, Sweden had, and so the retractable bomber's window tub under the rear cockpit was omitted on the 8A-1, but was standard on the 8A-2 and later models. Instead, the Swedes would provide a crutch under the fuselage to release a 550-pound bomb clear of the propeller. Four 110-pound bombs could be added, or up to eleven of the smaller or two of the larger bombs could be carried with reduced fuel, along with five 8-mm Colt guns. Wheels could be replaced by skis in wintertime.

Argentina received 30 8A-2s with 840-hp Wright Cyclones from February 22 to May 17, 1938. Armament included two 12.7-mm and two 7.6-mm Madsen guns in the wings, a 7.6-mm gun in the rear cockpit, and racks under the fuselage for one 1,105-pound bomb, or two 624, four 288, or seven 116-pound bombs.

DOUGLAS 8A-2 for Argentina
Wright R-1820-G3, 875 hp takeoff, 840 hp at 8700'
DIMENSIONS: Span 47'9", Lg. 31'6", Ht. 12'4", Wing Area 363 sq. ft.
WEIGHT: Empty 4930 lb., Gross 7884 lb. Max. 9435 lb. Fuel 225 gal.
PERFORMANCE: Speed- Top 223 mph at 8700', Cruising 200 mph, Landing 65 mph. Service Ceiling 25,400', Climb 1300'/ 1 min. Range 1190 miles max.

Ten Cyclone-powered 8A-3Ps with retractable wheels were ordered by Peru on August 4, 1938, and were delivered from January to June 1939, but twin-row Wasps powered 18 8A-3Ns that the Netherlands ordered March 14, 1939. First flown July 31, 1939, they were completed on November 14, and shipped to Rotterdam, but were destroyed in the German invasion on May 10, 1940. Armament included four 7.9-mm guns in the wings, a flexible gun in the rear cockpit, and both internal and external racks for up to 1,200 pounds of bombs.

DOUGLAS 8A-3P for Peru
Wright R-1820-G3, 875 hp takeoff, 840 hp at 8700'
DIMENSIONS: Span 47'9", Lg. 32'1", Ht. 9'9", Wing Area 363 sq. ft.
WEIGHT: Empty 4820 lb., Gross 7500 lb. Fuel 235 gal.
PERFORMANCE: Speed- Top 208 mph at s.l., 238 mph at 8700', Cruising 208 mph, Landing 66 mph. Service Ceiling 24,000', Climb 1200'/1 min. Range 1180 miles.

Fifteen similar 8A-4s with Cyclone engines were the first combat planes ordered by Iraq, on October 23, 1939. Completed from April to June 1940, they had four .50-caliber wing guns along with the usual .30-caliber flexible gun and bomb racks.

Mfr

CURTISS XA-14
Two Wright R-1670-5, 775 hp at 10,000'
DIMENSIONS: Span 59'5", Lg. 40'3", Ht. 10'9", Wing Area 526 sq. ft.
WEIGHT: Empty 8456 lb., Gross 11,738 lb. Fuel 287-617 gal.
PERFORMANCE: Speed- Top 249 mph at 4550', 254 mph at 9750', Cruising 211 mph, Landing 75 mph. Service Ceiling 27,125', Climb 1685'/1 min. Range 816 miles/600 lb. bombs.

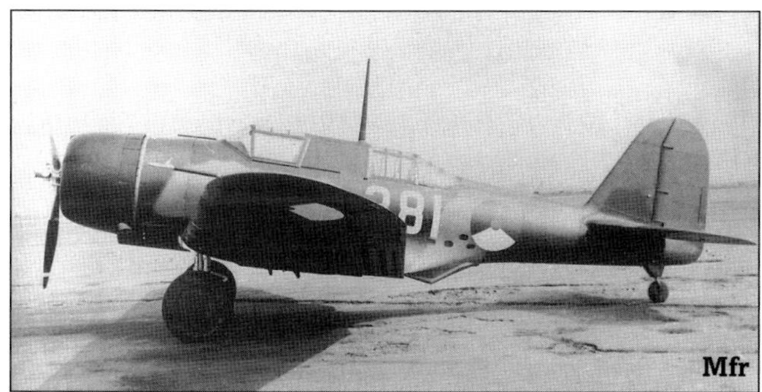

Mfr

DOUGLAS 8A-3N for the Netherlands
Pratt & Whitney R-1830-SC3G, 1050 hp takeoff, 900 hp at 12,000'
DIMENSIONS: Span 47'9", Lg. 32'5", Ht. 9'9", Wing Area 363 sq. ft.
WEIGHT: Empty 5508 lb., Gross 7848 lb., Max. 8775 lb. Fuel 250 gal.
PERFORMANCE: Speed- Top 214 mph at s.l., 232 mph at 13,000', Cruising 205 mph, Landing 66 mph. Service Ceiling 24,900', Climb 1460'/1 min. Range 910 miles.

Mfr

DOUGLAS 8A-5 (to A-33)
Wright R-1820-G205A (-87) 1200 hp takeoff, 900 hp at 15,200'
DIMENSIONS: Span 47'9", Lg. 32'6", Ht. 12', Wing Area 363 sq. ft.
WEIGHT: Empty 5510 lb., Gross 7800 lb., Max. 9200 lb. Fuel 173-252 gal.
PERFORMANCE: Speed- Top 207 mph at s.l., 248 mph at 15,200', Landing 67. Service Ceiling 26,200', Climb 1470'/1 min.,10,000'/5.8 min.

Thirty-six Douglas 8A-5 attack planes ordered by Norway on March 1, 1940, were completed from October 24, 1940 to January 31, 1941, and sent to the Norwegians training in Toronto, Canada. Distinguished from Army A-17As by a 1,200-hp Wright R-1820-G205A Cyclone and a hinged bomber's tub, the 8A-5 had four .50-caliber wing guns, a 30-caliber flexible gun, and could carry twenty 30-pound bombs in the internal chutes and up to 1,200 pounds of bombs under the fuselage.

Peru purchased 18 from Norway in August 1941, but the U.S. State Department objected because the aircraft might be used against Ecuador. Therefore, the Army requisitioned these 18 8A-5s on December 9, 1941, designated them A-33s and used them for general utility service. Peru finally did get the other 13 surviving A-33s from July to November 1943.

Curtiss Twin-engine Types

Although the use of two engines would improve performance and safety, the Army was cautious about adding to the cost and complexity of its attack planes. In May 1934, an attack version of the Martin YB-10 bomber was projected. Designated XA-15, it was to have two Wright R-1820-25s, weigh 12,356 pounds gross, and do 214 mph at 4,500 feet. This design was dropped in the paper stage in favor of the faster Curtiss XA-14.

The XA-14 was a carefully streamlined all-metal monoplane with retractable wheels, pencil-pointed nose and crew of two under a long enclosure. Two Wright 775-hp twin-row R-1670-5 Whirlwinds turned two-bladed propellers. Standard armament was the same as the A-17s (five .30-caliber guns with twenty 30 or four 116-pound bombs) but the four fixed guns were grouped in the nose.

SDAM

CURTISS XA-14 with 37-mm gun, April 1937

First flown as Curtiss Model 76 on July 17, 1935, the prototype was purchased by the Army on November 29. Although top speed was much higher than other attack or bomber types, the Army hesitated to begin large-scale production, for the plane cost more than three times that of the A-17A. Curtiss wanted to try to break some records with the

AF

CURTISS A-18

Two Wright R-1820 47, 930 hp takeoff, 850 hp at 2500'

DIMENSIONS: Span 59'5", Lg. 42'4", Ht. 15'9", Wing Area 526 sq. ft.

WEIGHT: Empty 9410 lb., Gross 12,679 lb., Max. 15,016 lb. Fuel 287-639 gal.

PERFORMANCE: Speed- Top 238.5 mph at 3500', Cruising 211 mph, Landing 73 mph. Service Ceiling 28,650', Absolute Ceiling 30,000', Climb 5000'/2.2 min. Range 1445 miles/ 654-lb. bombs, 1700 miles max.

prototype, but instead it was decided in June 1936 to use the XA-14 to test the new 37-mm gun planned for the XFM-1.

Thirteen examples were ordered July 23, 1936, for service tests with single-row Cyclones and three-bladed propellers. Designated YlA-18, the first was flown July 3, 1937, and the contract completed in October. Twelve YlA-18s served the 8th Attack Squadron at Barksdale until transferred to the 15th Attack Squadron at Lawson Field in 1941.

Four 30-caliber nose guns with 500 rpg were aimed with a reflector sight, replacing the bar sights on previous attack types. The rear gunner's weapon had 1,000 rounds, and internal chutes carried twenty 30-pound bombs, or four 116-pound bombs were carried below the wings. But the Air Corps now wanted twin-engine types to have a worthy bomb load and sight. Neither were buyers found for an export version, the Curtiss 76-D with the Cyclone G3 of 840 hp at 10,200 feet.

Vultee's Bombers

Vultee offered Douglas competition with the V-11, a development of that firm's 1934 V-lA transport. When single-engine transports were banned from commercial airlines, Vultee turned to the military market. The V-11 attack was a low-wing monoplane with retractable wheels and a long cockpit enclosure over two crewmen.

Mfr

VULTEE V-11 prototype

The V-11G could be operated as a low-level attack plane with 20 30-pound bombs in internal racks, four .30-caliber wing guns and the flexible gun used on Army attack planes, with a 1,125-mile range. Alternatively, it was a bomber carrying an 1,100, or four 300-pound bombs, and two 30-caliber wing guns, with a range of 2,380 miles. That V-11GB model accommodated a third crew member in the fuselage behind the gunner, adding a bombsight, and another gun in a retractable belly mounting.

The first V-11 two-seater began its flight tests at Glendale on September 18, 1935, but the next day the 750-hp SR-1820-F53 failed on takeoff, and both the pilot and the project engineer were killed in the crash. A second prototype (NR 14980) was completed October 9, and its successful tests won contracts for 100 aircraft built at a new Downey, California, factory for four foreign countries. This second prototype was rebuilt in 1940 and sold to Pratt & Whitney as an engine test ship.

Although no V-11s reached the Spanish civil war, several V-1A transports were acquired by both sides, and were sometimes armed for use as light bombers.

VULTEE V-11GB
Wright R-1820-G2, 850 hp at 5800'
DIMENSIONS: Span 50', Lg. 37'6", Ht 10', Wing Area 384 sq. ft.
WEIGHT: Empty 6176 lb., Gross 9441 lb., Max. 11,437 lb. Fuel 250-504 gal.
PERFORMANCE: Speed- Top 214 mph at s.l., 229 mph at 5800' as attack (203 mph at s.l.,220 mph at 11,000' as bomber), Cruising 207 (188) mph, Landing 68 mph. Service Ceiling 23,000' (18,500'), Climb 1285'/1 min. (885') Range 1225 miles/600-lb. bombs, 2380 miles max.

China bought 30 V-11 bombers. The first was completed in December 1936 with an F53 Cyclone, and the rest were V-11GBs completed, beginning July 1937, with the 850-hp R-1820-G2. They were used on raids beginning on February 7, 1938, by the 14th Squadron, an international unit with American and French pilots with Chinese gunners.

VULTEE V-11
Wright SR-1820-F53, 750 hp at 11,000'
DIMENSIONS: Span 50', Lg. 37'10", Ht 10', Wing Area 384 sq. ft.
WEIGHT: Empty 5662 lb., Gross 8500 lb., Max. 10,950 lb. Fuel 186-500 gal.
PERFORMANCE: Speed- Top 200 mph at s.l., 230 mph at 11,000' as attack (181 mph at s.l., 209 mph at 11,000' as bomber), Cruising 217 (193) mph, Landing 65 (70) mph. Service Ceiling 24,000' (19,000'), Climb 1100'/1 min. Range 900 miles/600-lb. bombs, 2200 miles max.

On September 7, 1936, the Soviet Union bought two three-place V-11GB attack bombers with the G-2 Cyclones, plus two sets of parts, along with the license and tools to manufacture them as replacements for their R-5 ground-attack biplanes. The first V-11GB (NX17328) was completed January 31, 1937, at Downey and arrived in Russia on April 30 with American specialists to help production. The V-11's all-metal structure was very different than the I-15 biplanes then produced by Moscow's Aircraft Factory #1.

But the Americans found their Soviet counterparts so secretive that they weren't even told the Vultee's new name. While the Soviet examples looked alike, except for the enclosed cowling on the M-62 engine, the BSh-l designation meant armored assault. Crew armor had become standard for VVS combat planes, but U.S. Army service types didn't add armor until 1941. The added weight reduced the Vultee's speed, and Soviet production stopped in December 1938 after only 36 aircraft, including those with American parts.

During 1938, Chinese Vultees and I-15bis biplanes had operated from the same fields, observed by Russian pilots. Their Air Force decided that to continue production of the maneuverable fighters would provide better interim attack aircraft while awaiting delivery of the BB-1 (Su-2) light bomber and development of the BSh-2, the prototype

VULTEE lower gun mount

for the most famous World War II attack plane, the Il-2 *Shturmovik*. The Russian-built Vultees were stripped and turned over to Aeroflot as PS-43 mail planes.

VULTEE YA-19
Pratt & Whitney R-1830-17, 1200 hp takeoff, 1050 hp at 6500'
DIMENSIONS: Span 50', Lg. 37'10", Ht. 10', Wing Area 384 sq. ft.
WEIGHT: Empty 6452 lb., Gross 10,421 lb. Fuel 311-330 gal.
PERFORMANCE: Speed- Top 230 mph at 6500', Cruising 207 mph, Landing 80 mph. Service Ceiling 20,400', Absolute Ceiling 22,000', Climb 1320'/1 min. Range 1110 miles/1080-lb. bombs, 1385 miles max.

Turkey received 40 V-11GBs completed between September 1937 and April 1938 for its 2nd Air Regiment. The Turkish president's daughter, Sabiha Gokcen, flew a Vultee on a tour of nearby capitals, as the first Muslim female military pilot. Brazil ordered 26 Vultees, delivery beginning in June 1938. Twin floats and a modified tail fin were seen on the last Brazilian Vultee, flown March 7, 1939.

Not until after the V-11 became popular abroad was it tested by the U.S. Army, which was committed to the smaller, more economical Northrops. Seven service test examples were ordered June 24, 1938, as the YA-19. Unlike the export versions, they were powered by Pratt & Whitney Wasps, the twin-row R-1830-17 giving 1,200-hp for takeoff. Six .30-caliber guns and 36 30-pound bombs were the usual armament.

The first YA-19 was flown January 27, 1939, and five more were delivered in June/July, but the last became an engine test bed; the XA-19A with a 1,200-hp Lycoming 0-1230-1 inline engine balanced by a lengthened tail, and first flown May 22, 1940. Pratt & Whitney's big new R-2800-1, programmed for the B-26, was also first flown on July 12, 1939, in the XA-19B, which had been the second YA-19. The remaining YA-19s served at March Field until moved to the Canal Zone, where they were utilized by military attaches to nearby countries.

Canary

VULTEE YA-19A

Mfr

VULTEE V-12 (AB-2)
Wright GR-1820-G105A, 1100 hp takeoff, 900 hp to 6,500', 750 hp at 18,000'.
DIMENSIONS: Span 50', Lg. 37'6", Ht. 12'11", Wing Area 384 sq. ft.
WEIGHT: Empty 6602 lb., Gross 9,941 lb., Max. 12,043 lb. Fuel 250-494 gal.
PERFORMANCE: Speed- Top 217 mph at s.l., 243 mph at 19,000' as attack, (204 mph at s.l., 222 mph at 19,000' as bomber), Cruising 218 mph (190 mph), Landing 69 mph (72 mph). Service Ceiling 25,500' (22,000'), Climb 6560'/ 5.1 min.(7.6 min.). Range 1200 miles/600-lb. bombs, (2,070 miles/1125- lb. bomb)

Mfr

VULTEE V-12D
Wright GR-2600-A5B, 1600 hp takeoff, 1275 hp at 11,500'
DIMENSIONS: Span 50', Lg. 38'3", Ht. 14'6", Wing Area 384 sq. ft.
WEIGHT: Empty 7427 lb., Gross 10,584 lb., Max. 12,025 lb. Fuel 200-350 gal.
PERFORMANCE: Speed- Top 256 mph at s.l.. 281 mph at 11,000' as attack, (248 mph at s.l., 270 mph at 11,000' as bomber), Cruising 248 mph (230 mph). Service Ceiling 28,800' (25,400'), Climb 6560'/3.3 min. (4.3 min.) Range 1050 miles/200 gal./600-lb. bombs, (1700 miles/350 gal./1125-lb. bomb)

In an effort to improve the type, Vultee produced a prototype V-12 (NX18935), which was flown September 13, 1938, with a more streamlined canopy, flush riveting, a GR-1830-SlC3-G Twin Wasp with two-stage supercharger, and .50-caliber guns on the inboard wing mounts, along with two .30-caliber wing guns and two .30-caliber flexible guns. This prototype was sold to Pratt & Whitney in May 1940 as another engine test ship.

On November 22, 1939, China ordered 26 V-12Cs completed with a Wright R-1820-G105B and 52 V-12Ds with the big R-2600-A5B, deeper fuselage, and new vertical fin. The first V-12C (NX28367) appeared with a modified canopy, but was wrecked January 25, 1941, in a taxiing accident, and not flown. Others were to be assembled in China, but that project failed.

The V-12D was armed with one .50-caliber and one .30-caliber gun in the nose, two flexible .30-caliber guns, 20 30-lb. bombs in the internal bay, or an 1,100-lb. bomb underneath the fuselage. One was tested by Vultee in May 1941, but the others were shipped in parts for assembly in Asia. After their intended assembly plant at Loiwing, China, was bombed out in 1940, the assemblies were sent to Bangalore, India, where only three were completed by Hindustani Aircraft before that factory became otherwise occupied.

Other Light Bombers

The potential market for light bombers lured commercial aircraft companies to adapt their designs for combat. Bellanca's "Flash", for example, was a two-place monoplane whose fabric-covered construction included a wooden wing structure braced by external wires running to two steel cabane struts below the fuselage. The prototype had first flown September 1, 1934, as a long-range racer with retractable wheels.

When the Spanish Civil War began in 1936, this prototype was purchased by the Republicans. By June 1937, 20 more were built with a 900-hp Pratt & Whitney Wasp as model 28-90, alleged to be high-speed mail planes for Air France. After the State Department blocked their delivery when it learned they were intended for Spain, 19 were sold to China, and they appeared at Hankow in January 1938 without guns, until armament as light bombers was improvised.

SDAM

BELLANCA 28-90
Pratt & Whitney R-1830-SBG, 900 hp at 6500'
DIMENSIONS: Span 46'2", Lg. 25'11" Ht. 8'8", Wing Area 279 sq. ft.
WEIGHT: Empty 4450 lb., Gross 6755 lb., Max. 7849 lb. Fuel 150 gal.
PERFORMANCE: Speed- Top 280 mph at 6,500', Cruising 250 mph, Landing 68 mph. Service Ceiling 30,500', Climb 2800'/1 min., 15,000'/7.5 min. Range 800 miles.

One example had been retained by the company as a "fighter-bomber" demonstrator armed with four .30-caliber fixed guns, one flexible gun, and racks under the wings for eight 120-pound bombs. Another batch was ordered in December 1937 by a fictitious Greek firm, but again Spain was the intended destination for the 28-90B (which added flaps), and export permits were refused. In 1939, 22

NORTH AMERICAN NA-40
Two Pratt & Whitney R-1830-S6C3-6, 1100 hp at 5000'
DIMENSIONS: Span 66', Lg. 47'10", Ht. 15', Wing Area 598.5 sq. ft.
WEIGHT: Empty 13,700 lb., Gross 19,500 lb. Fuel 476 gal.
PERFORMANCE: Speed- Top 268 mph at 5000', Cruising 243 mph, Landing 67 mph. Service Ceiling 26,000'. Range 1245 miles/ 1200-lb. bombs.

Bellancas were moved to Vera Cruz, where they were purchased by the Mexican Air Force in September 1939 after the Spanish Republic lost the war. After two fatal crashes, they were withdrawn from Mexican service.

SPARTAN ZEUS
Pratt & Whitney R-1340-S3H-l, 550 hp at 5000'
DIMENSIONS: Span 39', Lg. 27'3", Ht. 8'6", Wing Area 256 sq. ft.
WEIGHT: Empty 3440 lb., Gross 4953 lb. Fuel 112 gal.
PERFORMANCE: Speed- Top 234 mph at 5000', Cruising 218 mph, Landing 65 mph. Service Ceiling 29,400', Climb 2100'/ 1 min. Range 760 miles.

The story of the single-engine Army attack plane may be concluded with light-weight two-seaters built to offer a low-cost aircraft to the Latin American market. The Spartan Executive was a popular cabin low-wing monoplane, and the company built a military version, called the Zeus, with two crewmen, two .30-caliber wing guns, a flexible gun in the rear, wing racks for ten 25-pound bombs, and powered by a 550-hp Wasp. It was offered to Mexico in September 1937 and to Cuba in 1938, but was not purchased, and remained in Tulsa as an instructional airframe for the Spartan School.

NORTH AMERICAN NA-44

North American Aviation had some success with a souped-up attack version of the famous AT-6 trainer. A demonstration model, the NA-44 begun in December 1937, flew in 1938 with five guns and a 775-hp R-1820-F52, and was eventually sold to Canada in July 1940. Ten ordered on November 29, 1939, by Thailand were completed as NA-69s in July 1940, and shipped abroad via Manila, but were intercepted on October 10, 1940, because of fear that they might be used against French Indo-China.

On March 5, 1941, they were turned over to the U.S. Army in the Philippines and designated the A-27. Powered by the Wright R-1820-75, the A-27 carried five 110-pound (or one 550-pound) bombs, and three .30-caliber guns; two in the nose, and the flexible rear gun, but the A-27s were of little use when the war began.

NORTH AMERICAN A-27 (NA-69)
Wright R-1820-75, 785 hp takeoff, 745 hp at 9600'
DIMENSIONS: Span 42', Lg. 29', Ht. 12'2", Wing Area 258 sq. ft.
WEIGHT: Empty 4520 lb., Gross 6006 lb., Max. 6700 lb. Fuel 120-170 gal.
PERFORMANCE: Speed- Top 250 mph at 11,500', Cruising 220 mph, Landing 70 mph. Service Ceiling 28,000'. Range 575 miles/400-lb. bombs, 800 miles max.

Brazil also ordered 30 similar attack planes on January 13, 1940, designated NA-72, which were flight delivered to Brazil beginning on September 11, 1940. Twelve more ordered by Chile on August 7 as the NA-74 were completed by February 1941.

Twin-engine Attack Bombers

Shortly after WW II began, all Air Corps Attack Squadrons were renamed Bombardment (Light) Squadrons on September 15, 1939. Instead of single-engine two-seaters, they were to fight the war with twin-engine three-seaters, even if such types were too large for good close support work.

Twin-engine attack types meant more than improved performance and safety. Additional power also allowed larger bomb loads, so that America could match the capabilities of the swift twin-engine light bombers then being acquired by European powers. The first such type was the Tupolev SB that entered production in 1936, followed by the Dornier Do 17. Both types joined the air war in Spain.

Prodded by threatening war, the Army announced a design competition for "attack bombers," A new specification (98-102 dated December 16, 1937), had been foreshadowed by the A-18's two engines and the A-19's three crewmen. The minimum requirements included a 1,200-pound bomb load to be carried 1,200 miles at an operating speed of at least 200 mph. This would permit a "tactical operating radius" (25% of total economical range) of 300 miles. Crew accommodations would include stations for a bomb sight and lower rear defense gun, but four forward guns and fragmentation bombs for low-level attacks would be retained.

The preliminary designs submitted in July 1938 included one with inline engines, Bell's Model 9. Two Allison V-1710s were expected to yield a top speed of 255 mph at 3,000 feet with a 19,500-lb. gross weight, including two 37-mm guns. Faster speeds, however, were promised by lighter radial-engine proposals including the 17,470-pound Stearman X-100 at 269 mph, the 15,800-pound Martin 167F at 275 mph, and the 14,700-pound Douglas Model 7B offering 280 mph.

Encouraged by these designs, the Army invited the companies to build sample planes and submit bids to be opened March 17, 1939. Bell dropped out, but the other three firms, plus North American, did build prototypes for the competition that determined the World War II attack-bomber pattern.

All four prototypes built for Circular Proposal 38-385 were all-metal monoplanes with two radial engines, three-bladed propellers, and retractable wheels, reflecting European light bombers like the Bristol Blenheim. All had four .30-caliber fixed guns for ground attack and an internal bay for the bomb load.

The North American NA-40 was a five-place high-wing design with twin rudders, and tricycle landing gear. Armament included seven .30-caliber guns; four in the wings, one in the ball and socket nose mount, and the rear gunner's upper and lower flexible guns. Engineering began in December 1937, and NA-40 construction was ordered May 20, 1938. Two 1,100-hp Pratt & Whitney R-1830-S6C3-G Wasps powered the aircraft on tests begun January 29, 1939, but Wright GR-2600-A71 Double Cyclones were fitted when tests resumed as the NA-40B on March 1.

NORTH AMERICAN NA-40B
Two Wright GR-2600-A71, 1500 hp takeoff, 1350 hp at 5,000', 1275 hp at 12,000'
DIMENSIONS: Span 66', Lg. 47'10", Ht. 15', Wing Area 598.5 sq. ft.
WEIGHT: Empty 14,002 lb., Gross 19,741 lb. Fuel 476 gal.
Performance: Speed- Top 287 mph at 5000', 309 mph at 14,000', Cruising 282 mph, Landing 70 mph. Service Ceiling 25,000'. Range 1176 miles/1200- lb. bombs.

Top speed was 287 mph at 5,000 feet, which increased to a company guaranteed 309 mph at 14,000 feet after the second stage of the superchargers kicked in. When flown to the Air Corps tests at Wright Field on March 12, the NA-40B was briefly the fastest bomber in America, but crashed April 11 during a single-engine test. While the North American design failed the attack-bomber competition, its layout was the forerunner of the B-25 medium bomber.

Two Pratt & Whitney R-2180-7 Twin Hornets powered the four-place Stearman X-100, which had its wing mounted high on a squared-off fuselage. A socket in the nose allowed a flexible gun, while two rear gunners had a .30-caliber gun in a turret behind the wing, side guns, and another in a belly fixture. Four wing guns and 90 30-pound bombs could be used from low levels, or one 2,000, two 600, six 300 or twelve 100-pound bombs could be dropped from higher altitudes.

Mfr

DOUGLAS 7B (prototype A-20)
Two Pratt & Whitney R-1830-S6C3-6, 1100 hp at 5000'
DIMENSIONS: Span 61', Lg. 45'5", Wing Area 464 sq. ft.
WEIGHT: Gross 15,200 lb. Fuel 370 gal.
PERFORMANCE: Speed- Top 304 mph at 5000', Cruising 200 mph, Landing 72 mph. Service Ceiling 27,600'. Range 1350 miles

STEARMAN X-100

STEARMAN XA-21
Two Pratt & Whitney R-2180-7, 1400 hp takeoff, 1150 hp at 7000'
DIMENSIONS: Span 65', Lg. 53'1', Ht. 14'2", Wing Area 607 sq. ft.
WEIGHT: Empty 12,760 lb., Gross 18,257 lb. Max. 20, 200 lb. Fuel 450-520 gal.
PERFORMANCE: Speed- Top 257 mph at 5000', Cruising 200 mph, Landing 72 mph. Service Ceiling 20,000'. Range 725 miles/1200-lb. bombs, 1500 miles max.

First flown March 3, 1939, at Wichita with its bombardier and pilot under an unbroken Plexiglas nose, it was purchased by the Army with orders to rework the front. The Stearman returned to the factory April 30 and tests resumed on August 28 as the XA-21 with a separate pilot's windshield; the broken nose sacrificing streamlining for visibility, causing top speed to drop. The Army used the XA-21 at Eglin Field to develop low-level high-speed bombing methods.

Douglas A-20 Havoc

The most important and famous Army attack-bomber of World War II was the Douglas A-20, winner of the 1939 competition. Its design was actually begun in 1936 at El Segundo as the Northrop 7A, before that organization became part of the Douglas company. That design was revised as the Douglas Model 7B for submission in the July 1938 attack-bomber design contest, and a prototype was constructed to compete for the 1939 production contract.

As first flown October 26, 1938, the 7B had two 1,100-hp Pratt & Whitney Twin Wasps, a shoulder-high wing, and the first tricycle landing gear on an American combat plane. This nose-wheel gear permitted faster landing speeds and thus a smaller wing, leading in turn to the highest speed of any contemporary American bomber.

For the low-level attack mission, the 7B had a metal-covered nose and could be armed with two .50-caliber and six .30-caliber fixed guns, 80 30-pound or 14 100-pound

DOUGLAS 7B with bomber nose

bombs. A different nose with Plexiglas windows for a bombardier allowed the use of one 2,000 or four 300-pound bombs, while retaining four .30-caliber fixed guns in blisters. Both versions were defended by a rear gunner with a retractable "birdcage" turret, and another .30-caliber gun to fire downwards from a retractable floor mount.

The first flights were not announced to the public, but a crash on January 23, 1939, brought the plane widespread controversial attention. It was discovered that a French officer had been aboard, in violation of the Air Corps policy of not releasing information on new aircraft types until they were approaching obsolescence. An investigation revealed that President Roosevelt himself had made the decision to allow France and Britain to buy up-to-date American warplanes, thus rejecting traditional isolationism.

DOUGLAS DB-7 in France (later BOSTON I)
Two Pratt & Whitney R-1830-SC3G, 1050 hp takeoff, 900 hp at 12,000'
DIMENSIONS: Span 61'4", Lg. 46'11", Ht. 15'10", Wing Area 464 sq. ft.
WEIGHT: Empty 11,400 lb., Gross 16,427 lb., Max. 17,031 lb. Fuel 325 gal.
PERFORMANCE: Speed- Top 278 mph at s.l., 307 mph at 11,650', Cruising 261 mph, Landing 81 mph. Service Ceiling 30,840', Climb 2440'/1 min. Range 869 miles/1760-lb. bombs.

France did order 100 Douglas DB-7s on February 15, 1939, and the first flew at El Segundo in only six months, on August 17, 1939, with 900-hp R-1830-SC3G Twin Wasps with 87-octane fuel and Hamilton propellers. Designer Edward Heinemann (1908-1991) provided the French with a transparent bombardier's nose, engine nacelles lowered below the wings, intakes on the cowl tops, cockpit armor, and replaced the rear turret with a simple sliding canopy. Armament, to be fitted in France, included four 7.5-mm nose guns, a 7.5-mm upper rear gun, another for the ventral opening, and a choice of 64 22-pound, 16 110-pound, eight 220-pound, or four 440-pound bombs.

An additional 170 DB-7s were ordered October 14, 1939, and, beginning with DB-7 number 131, 1,000-hp R-1830-S3C4-G Twin Wasps using 100-octane fuel were installed on the remainder of the 270 DB-7s completed by September 3, 1940. The 131st DB-7 had also been tested July 26, 1940, with a twin rudder arrangement requested by the French, whose Leo 45 bomber was thought to have a better rear gunner's fire field due to twin tails. This system was not adopted for production, however, for firepower, not field of fire, was the common weakness of bomber defense in those days.

Not until December 25, 1939, did ships carrying the first eight DB-7s arrive in Casablanca, where they were slowly assembled and delivered to the French air force in March 1940. By June 25, 121 arrived in crates, and 64 had reached five squadrons when the DB-7 entered combat on May 22. Fastest bombers at the front, they flew about 134 sorties, losing 16 DB-7s before France surrendered and the Douglas squadrons were withdrawn to North Africa. Britain took over all French contracts and 138 undelivered DB-7s on June 17.

DOUGLAS HAVOC I
Two Pratt & Whitney Wasp SC4-G, 1100 hp at 6200'; 1000 hp at 14,500'
DIMENSIONS: As DB-7
WEIGHT: Empty 11,520 lb., Max. 17,151 lb. Fuel 325 gal.
PERFORMANCE: Speed- Top 293 mph at s.l., 322 mph at 15,300', Landing 86 mph. Service Ceiling 33,800', Range 462 miles/2,080-lb. bombs, 875 miles max.

The British named the earlier DB-7 Boston I, using four as trainers introducing nose-wheel gear to RAF pilots, and briefly called the 134 S3C4-G models the Boston II. Night operations had become a major RAF concern, so the Bostons went to six Fighter Command Squadrons renamed the Havoc I (Intruder) with black paint, flame-damper exhausts, and four .303-caliber fixed guns to supplement the bomb load. As aircraft intercept (AI) radar became available, the Havoc I (Night Fighter) appeared with the bomber's compartment replaced by four more guns in a solid nose fairing. Instead of guns, 21 Havocs fitted with a searchlight in the nose became the "Turbinlite' version. (See Chapter 18 for details)

Britain also inherited a French contract made October 20, 1939, for 100 DB-7As with 1,275-hp R-2600-A5B Cyclones. With longer nacelles, armor, and broader vertical

DOUGLAS DB-7A
Two Wright R-2600-A5B, 1500 hp takeoff, 1275 hp at 11,500'
DIMENSIONS: Span 61'4", Lg. 48', Ht. 15'10", Wing Area 464 sq. ft.
WEIGHT: Empty 13,584 lb., Design Gross 16,700 lb., Max. 19,322 lb. Fuel 325 gal.
PERFORMANCE: Speed- Top 308 mph at s.l., 344 mph at 12,500', Landing 97 mph. Service Ceiling 32,000', Range 490 miles/2,129-lb. bombs.

tail, the first DB-7A was flown on July 30, 1940, but crashed before acceptance. The remainder were accepted from November 20, 1940, to February 13, 1941, and, less eight lost at sea, were converted in Britain to Havoc II night fighters with twelve .303-caliber nose guns, added fuel tanks, and AI Mk. IV radar, while 39 became Havoc II (Turbinlite).

DOUGLAS HAVOC II

DOUGLAS HAVOC II (Turbinlite)

Meanwhile, work on the Army version proceeded more slowly. The crashes of the 7B and NA-40 left the Stearman and Martin ships the only survivors of the March 38-385 competition. To these firms' disappointment, no contract was awarded then; the Army instead waiting for new bids on April 17 for Circular Proposal 39-460, a modified specification not requiring prototypes.

Among the eight firms submitting new bids, Douglas offered a new version of their plane with Wright R-2600 engines instead of the R-1830 Wasps used on the 7B prototype. This won the order announced May 20, 1939, for 186 attack bombers, while only the prototypes of Stearman and Martin were purchased.

DOUGLAS A-20A
Two Wright R-2600-11, 1600 hp takeoff, 1275 hp at 12,000'
DIMENSIONS: Span 61'4", Lg. 47'7", Ht. 17'7"" Wing Area 464 sq. ft.
WEIGHT: Empty 15,165 lb., Design Gross 19,750 lb., Max. 20,711 lb. Fuel 388 gal.
PERFORMANCE: Speed- Top 347 mph at 12,400', Cruising 295 mph, Landing 85 mph. Service Ceiling 28,175', Climb 10,000'/5.1 min. Range 525 miles/2400-lb. bombs, 675 miles/1200-lb. bombs, 1000 miles max.

The first Army version was the A-20A, powered by Wright R-2600-11 Cyclones with a larger nose enclosure, stronger structure, and more fuel. For low-level attack, 80 30-pound, or 16 100-pound bombs could be carried, while alternately, one 1,100, two 600, or four 300-pound bombs could be dropped from greater heights. Four .30-caliber guns were set low in the nose, one (later two) in the rear cockpit, and one on the floor.

A contract approved on June 30 called for 123 A-20As, and 20 more were added a year later in exchange for the A-17As Douglas resold to Britain. The first A-20A flight was September 6, 1940, and that aircraft was delivered November 30. The fifth A-20A went to the Navy on December 2 as the BD-l, replaced by another A-20A added to the contract. Armor and leak-proof fuel tanks were not provided on the first 17, delivered by January 31, 1941, but were added to 127 remaining A-20As delivered from February 7 to August 29, 1941, and priced at $94,080 each. Fuel capacity was reduced from 500 to 388 gallons by the tank protection.

The 3rd Bombardment Group (Light) {formerly the 3rd Attack}, and the 27th Group was equipped with A-20As at their new Savannah base by April 1941. Hawaii and the Canal Zone got 12 each, while others were parceled out to the new Light Bombardment squadrons, the 15th at Lawson Field, the 46th at Bowman Field and the 48th at Will Rogers Field.

DOUGLAS A-20
Two Wright R-2600-7, 1700 hp at 20,000' (turbosuperchargers)
DIMENSIONS: As A-20A
WEIGHT: Empty 15,845 lb., Design Gross 20,329 lb. Fuel 414 gal.
PERFORMANCE: Speed- Top 388 mph at 20,000', Cruising 218 mph, Landing 93 mph. Service Ceiling 31,500', Climb 10,000' /5 min. Range 767 miles/1200-lb. bombs, 1100 miles max.

Sixty-three A-20 light bombers ordered the same day as the A-20As were to get R-2600-7 Cyclones turbosupercharged to give 1,700 hp at 20,000 feet. Those engines, however, delayed delivery and it was realized that high altitude performance (390 mph at 20,000 feet was promised) was of no value when the Norden bombsight supply was still limited to heavy bombers.

Turbosuperchargers were fitted to the 15th aircraft of the Douglas contract, which became the only actual pure A-20 tested. Since these components proved almost impossible to cool, the superchargers were deleted from the program and that A-20 became the XP-70 night fighter prototype.

Sixty-two A-20 airframes rested empty in the Douglas yard awaiting the equipment to convert three into YF-3 photographic planes as ordered May 11, 1940. The rest were considered for target towing, until assigned to the P-70 program by an October 15, 1941, order.

Previously, the Photographic designation had denoted stock civilian cabin planes modified as the Fairchild F-l and Beechcraft F-2 types used by the photographic mapping unit. In 1941, F became the code for camera-equipped combat planes intended to penetrate hostile airspace. Three YF-3s delivered in April 1942 were modified with R-2600-11 Cyclones, fuel tanks enlarged to carry 480 to 600 gallons, and tandem T-3A cameras.

DOUGLAS DB-7B (BOSTON III)
Two Wright R-2600-A5B 1500 hp takeoff, 1275 hp at 11,500'
DIMENSIONS: Span 61'4", Lg. 47'3", Ht. 18'1", Wing Area 464 sq. ft.
WEIGHT: Empty 15,051 lb., Gross 21,580 lb. Fuel 390 gal.
PERFORMANCE: Speed- Top 311 mph at sea level, 338 mph at 12,500', Landing 95 mph. Service Ceiling 27,600', Range 525 miles/2,000-lb. bombs.

Proposed armament consisted of seven .30-caliber guns: two fixed in the nose, two flexible top and one flexible tunnel weapons, with another fixed gun pointing from the rear of each engine nacelle. Fire from the nacelle guns converged about 100 yards behind the tail, and this rather uncertain defense was also planned for the A-20B series, but was not used on most production aircraft.

DOUGLAS A-20B
Two Wright R-2600-11, 1600 hp takeoff, 1275 hp at 11,500'
DIMENSIONS: Span 61'4", Lg. 48', Ht. 18'1", Wing Area 464 sq. ft.
WEIGHT: Empty 14,830 lb., Gross 21,000 lb., Max. 23,800 lb. Fuel 394-490 (+604 ferry) gal.
PERFORMANCE: Speed- Top 350 mph at 12,000', Cruising 278 mph, Landing 95 mph. Service Ceiling 28,600', Climb 10,000'/ 5 min. Range 825 miles/1000-lb. bombs, 2300 miles ferry.

On February 20, 1940, Britain had ordered the DB-7B version, similar in appearance to the A-20A but with R-2600-A5B Cyclones, armor and leak-proof fuel tanks, seven British .303-caliber guns, and four 500-pound bombs. The first was flown January 10, 1941, and 541 were delivered from April 4 to November 19, 1941. Boeing also received a French order for 240 bombers on May 18, 1940, which were accepted as DB-7Bs from August 1941 to January 1942.

DOUGLAS A-20B
Gun nose, 47th BG in North Africa

The United Kingdom received 325 of these DB-7Bs including 35 built by Boeing, another 116 were shipped to the Middle East, and 16 were lost in transit. Known as the Boston III, they replaced Blenheims in five RAF bomber squadrons and first sortied against the enemy in occupied France on February 12, 1942. Three night intruder squadrons received Bostons with four 20-mm guns in a tray under the fuselage, and several Boston IIIs were modified for the Turbinlite units.

One DB-7B for Brazil left on November 2, 1941, and the first four DB-7Bs for the Soviet Union were shipped on November 28, but others were diverted after the United States entered the war in December, when the USAF requisitioned 81 Douglas-built and 132 Boeing-built DB-7Bs.

Another 33 DB-7Bs had been allocated to the Chinese Air Force, but these were diverted to the Dutch East Indies, where six arrived on February 27, 1942. Java fell before they could be used, but one was captured and flown in Japan, and 22 others joined the Royal Australian Air Force (RAAF).

DOUGLAS A-20B
In Soviet Air Force with a 12.7-mm UBT in UBK-1 turret

The Dutch had ordered 48 DB-7Cs, similar but for adding torpedo gear, on October 16, 1941, although they were not ready until July 1942. Except for one sent to Newport, Rhode Island, for torpedo tests by the U.S. Navy, they went to Soviet naval air units.

On October 11, 1940, the AAF ordered 999 A-20Bs and 775 O-53 reconnaissance versions. The O-53s were canceled in June 1942, but the A-20Bs were delivered at the new Douglas Long Beach plant between December 1941 and January 1943. Eight went to the U.S. Navy as the BD-2 in May 1942, while Russia got 665 on lend-lease.

DOUGLAS A-20C
Two Wright R-2600-23, 1600 hp takeoff. 1275 hp at 11,500'
DIMENSIONS: Span 61'4", Lg. 47'3", Ht. 17'7", Wing Area 464 sq. ft.
WEIGHT: Empty 15,625 lb., Gross 21,000 lb., Max. 24,500 lb. Fuel 400-540 (+540 ferry) gal.
PERFORMANCE: Speed- Top 314 mph at s.1., 342 mph at 13,000', Cruising 280 mph, Landing 100 mph. Service Ceiling 25,320', Climb 10,000'/6.3 min. Range 800 miles/1000-lb. bombs, 2300 miles ferry.

The A-20B had R-2600-11 engines with ejection stacks, armor, leak proof tanks, two .50-caliber fixed nose guns, one .50-caliber flexible upper gun, a .30-caliber tunnel gun, and the stepped nose enclosure used on the French DB-7s. Provision was made to increase fuel capacity for transoceanic ferry to 1,094 gallons internal overload, or 1,479 gallons with a belly tank.

The A-20C has the distinction of being the first plane ordered by a "Lend-Lease" contract, dated April 28, 1941. Similar to the DB-7B, but for ejection exhaust stacks and more fuel, it was named Boston IIIA, and had R-2600-23 Cyclones, seven .30-caliber guns, 415 pounds of armor, and 2,076 pounds of bombs. Beginning with the A-20C-5 model, a torpedo could be attached below the fuselage.

Concurrently with the A-20B, Douglas built 808 A-20C-DOs at Santa Monica until January 1943, and Boeing made 140, the last A-20C-BO delivered on March 31, 1942. Most A-20Cs were taken by the AAF or shipped to Russia. RAF deliveries resumed with an effort to fly 200 of the lend-lease Boston IIIA (A-20C) models across the Atlantic, and 182 made it to the United Kingdom. Another 11 A-20C-10s from AAF stocks replenished RAF units in Africa.

The A-20D and A-20E models were A-20A variants that never actually materialized.* The XA-20F was an A-20A with a 37-mm fixed nose gun and two General Electric remote-control twin .50-caliber turrets installed to develop a new gunnery system. Successful flight tests in September 1941 encouraged the system's adoption for the projected A-26.

After America came into the war, the A-20 found itself in action all over the world, and the name "Havoc" was given to all Army Air Force A-20s. An A-20A squadron was hit in the Pearl Harbor attack. Except for those sent overseas, most A-20As were replaced by later models and converted into target-towing RA-20As.

The A-20A had not enough range to fly to the distant theaters of action, so the first Army crews trained on Havocs were shipped overseas without their aircraft; the 3rd Bomb Group (L) leaving for Australia in February 1942, and the 15th Bomb Squadron for England in May. Six crews from the 15th used borrowed DB-7Bs to join six RAF crews in a July 4th attack on German airfields in the Netherlands that was publicized (incorrectly) as the first American attack on German forces.

Three Havocs were lost and three damaged in what was essentially a propaganda operation to make up for previous American inactivity in Europe. After this squadron moved to North Africa, Air Force Havocs did not strike from England again until March 1944, but British and Soviet pilots used them in great numbers.

When the 3rd Group's 40 A-20As arrived in Australia, nine were given to an RAAF squadron in June 1942. The others were modified for ground strafing by adding four .50-caliber nose guns. The 89th squadron did not take them into combat in New Guinea until August 31, 1942,

*It appears that the first 17 A-20As with unprotected fuel tanks were to be redesignated A-20E, but no such change is noted on the individual Aircraft Record Cards.

the three other 3rd Group squadrons having previously substituted A-24 and B-25C bombers for attacks on Japanese forces.

American invasion of North Africa brought the A-20Bs of the 47th Bomb Group into combat on December 14, after using ferry tanks to cross the Atlantic. They were joined by the A-20Bs that equipped half of the 68th Observation Group, and by the Bostons of the 15th Squadron.

Some of these A-20Bs working in Africa had also been modified with solid "gun noses," and this fixed gun arrangement was chosen for the A-20G attack-bomber ordered June 1, 1942, and first delivered in February 1943 from Santa Monica with more firepower, armor and fuel. Powered by the R-2600-23, it carried four 500-pound bombs in the bay, or a 2,000-pound torpedo under the fuselage.

SDAM

DOUGLAS A-20G-1
Two Wright R-2600-23, 1600 hp takeoff, 1275 hp at 11,500'
DIMENSIONS: Span 61'4", Lg. 48', Ht. 17'7", Wing Area 464 sq. ft.
WEIGHT: Empty 15,958 lb., Gross 21,914 lb., Max. 24,000 lb. Fuel 540+536 gal.
PERFORMANCE: Speed- Top 339 mph at 12,400', Cruising 272 mph, Landing 95 mph. Service Ceiling 25,800', Climb 10,000'/7.1 min. Range 700 miles 2000-lb. bombs, 2200 miles ferry.

The first 250 (A-20G-1) had four 20-mm and two .50-caliber nose guns, while the remaining 2,600 Gs used six .50-caliber bow guns, with 350 rounds per gun. A hand-operated .50-caliber gun in the rear seat of the first 750 (to A-20G-15) was replaced by two .50s in a power-operated Martin turret in the A-20G-20 of August 1943. Beginning with this model, the .30-caliber belly gun was replaced by a .50-caliber weapon operated by a third crew member, four more 500-lb. bombs could be added under the wings for short ranges, or an additional belly tank added for ferry flights.

Wright R-2600-29 Cyclones of 1,700-hp were fitted to the three-place A-20H whose solid noses with six .50-caliber guns distinguished 412 delivered in 1944. The first four-place A-20J was an A-20G-25 with a transparent bombardier's nose enclosure and two .50-caliber nose guns, and 450 were produced in parallel with later A-20G models. Last of the series was the 413 A-20Ks with the bombardier nose; similar to the Js except for R-2600-29 engines.

When Havoc production ended September 20, 1944, 7,098 had been built by Douglas, and 380 under license by Boeing, while AAF inventories were at a peak of over 1,700 A-20s. Havocs then equipped seven USAF groups in action: the 3rd, 312th, and 417th with the Fifth Air Force in the Pacific, and the 47th with the Twelfth Air Force in Italy, while the 409th, 410th and 416th with the Ninth Air Force in Britain bombed ahead of the D-Day invasion of Normandy.

SDAM

DOUGLAS A-20G-5

AF

DOUGLAS A-20G-20
Two Wright R-2600-23, 1600 hp takeoff, 1275 hp at 11,500'
DIMENSIONS: As A-20G-1
WEIGHT: Empty 16,993 lb., Gross 24,127 lb., Max. 26,200 lb. Fuel 725+374 gal.
PERFORMANCE: Speed- Top 333 mph at 12,300', Cruising 272 mph, Landing 95 mph. Service Ceiling 23,700', Climb 10,000'/8.8 min. Range 1150 miles/2000-lb. bombs, 2100 miles ferry.

Mfr

DOUGLAS A-20G-40
Two Wright R-2600-23, 1600 hp takeoff, 1275 hp at 11,500'
DIMENSIONS: As A-20G-1
WEIGHT: Empty 16,910 lb., Gross 23,967 lb., Max. 26,200 lb. Fuel 725+374 gal.
PERFORMANCE: (at 26,000 lb.) Speed- Top 302 mph at s.l., 312 mph at 10,000', Cruising 240 mph, Landing 95 mph. Service Ceiling 22,400', Climb 10,000'/8.8 min. Range 1150 miles/2000-lb. bombs, 2100 miles ferry.

Petrov

DOUGLAS A-20G-45 of 51st MTAP, VMF-Baltic Fleet

AF

DOUGLAS A-20H-1
Two Wright R-2600-29, 1700 hp takeoff, 1450 hp at 13,000'
DIMENSIONS: Span 61'4", Lg. 48', Ht. 18'1", Wing Area 464 sq. ft.
WEIGHT: Empty 16,842 lb., Gross 23,987 lb., Max. 26,400 lb. Fuel 725+374 gal.
PERFORMANCE: (at 24,000 lb.) Speed- Top 333 mph at 15,600', Cruising 269 mph, Landing 100 mph. Service Ceiling 25,300', Climb 10,000'/8.8 min. Range 880 miles/2000-lb. bombs, 2200 miles ferry.

While treetop attacks were favored in the Pacific, European missions were at medium altitudes. Those groups usually operated a glass-nosed A-20J or K for every three gun-nose G or H models, the formation releasing their bombs at the leader's signal. Forty-six A-20J and Ks became F-3A night reconnaissance planes with K-19B camera, four flash bombs, and with the lower rear gun deleted. The last A-20 mission by American pilots in the Pacific was flown on August 12, 1945, by the 3rd Group, but Soviet pilots were still flying sorties against the Japanese.

With Foreign Pilots

As early as September 29, 1939, Douglas received a Soviet offer to purchase ten DB-7s and a license to produce them in Russia, along with a license to build Wright R-2600 engines. Those negotiations were ended by war in Finland and the resulting weapons embargo. In September 1941 the situation changed as the Nazi invasion added the Soviet Union to lend-lease programs.

MdA

DOUGLAS A-20J-10 (Boston IV of 342 Sq.)
Two Wright R-2600-23, 1600 hp takeoff, 1275 hp at 11,500'
DIMENSIONS: Span 61'4", Lg. 48'4", Ht. 17'7", Wing Area 464 sq. ft.
WEIGHT: Empty 17,117 lb., Gross 23,748 lb., Max. 26,200 lb. Fuel 725+374 gal.
PERFORMANCE: Speed- Top 317 mph at 10,700', Cruising 257 mph, Landing 95 mph. Service Ceiling 23,100', Climb 10,000'/8.8 min. Range 1090 miles/2000-lb. bombs, 2100 miles ferry.

Since the Havoc was produced to give close support to ground troops, and since the largest Allied army was Soviet, the USSR was allocated 3,125 Douglas Havocs at a promised rate of 100 a month. Of these, 2,908 actually arrived, including 869 flown over the South Atlantic and 550 shipped over to the Persian Gulf, plus 126 shipped to North Russia.

Another 1,363 were flown over the Alaska-Siberian (Alsib) route, the first 12 A-20Bs leaving Ladd Field with Soviet pilots on October 6, 1942. Regular deliveries were completed in July 1944, but the last 97 A-20H/Ks were added in May/August 1945, to replenish units to be used against Japan.

DOUGLAS A-20K-15 (BOSTON V)
Two Wright R-2600-29, 1700 hp takeoff, 1450 hp at 13,000'
DIMENSIONS: As A-20J
WEIGHT: Empty 17,266 lb., Gross 23,953 lb., Max. 26,400 lb. Fuel 725+374 gal.
PERFORMANCE: (at 24,000 lb.) Speed- Top 333 mph at 15,600', Cruising 269 mph, Landing 100 mph. Service Ceiling 25,100', Climb 10,000'/6.6 min. Range 830 miles/2000-lb. bombs, 2200 miles ferry.
(at 26,000 lb.) Top 320 mph at 10,000', Service Ceiling 23,600').

The first DB-7Bs for the Soviet Union shipped via the South Atlantic and Persian Gulf, began arriving at Basra in February 1942. Since the first to arrive were 77 Boston III (DB-7B) and 103 IIIA (A-20C) aircraft originally scheduled for Britain; they were designated B-3 in Soviet service, and entered combat on the Southwestern front in May 1942 with the 794th Bomber Air Regiment (BAP).

When joined by the 57th and 745th BAPs, they formed the 221st Bomber Air Division. Beginning in September 1942, a Soviet UTK-1 turret with a 12.7-mm UBT gun replaced the .30-caliber guns in the open rear cockpit. A-20s replaced the standard Pe-2 light bombers in 12 Red Army (VVS-RK) air regiments, including the 45th, 449th, 860th and 861st BAPs of the 244th Bomber Air Division; the 63rd, 277th, 367th, and 542nd BAPs of the 132nd Bomber Air Division, and the separate 201st BAP.

Cameras were introduced in July 1942 for reconnaissance by A-20Bs of the Baltic Fleet's 15th RAP and by the Black Sea's Fleet's 30th RAP in November. Two torpedoes test launched from a DB-7C in March 1943 showed that a Boston could handle those weapons better than the Il-4s then used by Soviet crews, so 36 A-20Bs were modified for torpedo attacks.

While American crews did not use the torpedo provisions added under the A-20G's fuselage, torpedoes became standard for the five Soviet Navy (VVS-VMF) Mine-Torpedo Air Regiments (MTAP). The 9th Guards MTAP and the 36th MTAP, operating against German convoys near Norway, the 1st Guards and 51st MTAP in the Baltic Sea, and the 5th Guards MTAP in the Black Sea, used A-20Gs modified for four crewmen with windows added in the nose and behind the turret.

A Soviet airborne intercept radar, *Gneys-2,* was tested on a few Pe-3 night fighters and a Boston III, and production ordered on June 16, 1943. The lend-lease A-20G-1 was considered the best type then available for night fighting because of its forward firepower and the space available for a navigator and an operator of the *Gneys-2* sets added to the planes at the Monino modification center. Extra 274-gallon bomb-bay fuel cells were added, but the flexible guns were usually removed.

The 45th and 173rd long-range night-fighter escort regiments (APON), of the 56th Fighter Air Division, each had 32 A-20G-1s. Like the AAF P-70s, they were seldom able to line up their guns on enemy bombers, flying 650 sorties in 1944 without definite result. The German night attack upon the U.S. bombers landed at Poltava showed the limitations of VVS night defense measures.

When the war with Germany neared its end on May 1, 1945, 127 A-20B, 105 Boston III/A, 147 A-20G-1, 115 A-20G-10, 376 A-20G-20, and 65 A-20J/K remained with the Red Army. Navy units also had 43 A-20Gs with the North Sea Fleet, another 43 with the Baltic Fleet, and 70 with the Black Sea Fleet. War against Japan in August 1945 involved A-20s of the Red Navy's 36th MTAP, 49th MTAP, and 50th MRAP regiments. The 36th MTAP was still flying A-20s from Port Arthur on September 4, 1950, when one was shot down by F4U-4Bs from the *Valley Forge.*

Australia acquired 69 Havocs from 1942 to 1944, including nine A-20A, 22 DB-7B, nine A-20C, 28 A-20G, and an A-20J. A Free French squadron, No. 342 "Lorraine", began operations from England on June 12, 1943, with Boston IIIA and IVs received via the RAF. Joined by 13 AAF and RAF squadrons in support of the 1944 Normandy invasion, these pilots had come a long way since the first twelve French DB-7s had sortied in 1940.

Britain, whose RAF medium-altitude operations had no need for the A-20G gun-nose versions, received 169 A-20Js and named them Boston IV. Of these, 129 were flown to the United Kingdom to replenish RAF squadrons on operations across the English Channel, 35 were flown to North Africa, and the rest crashed *en route.* Ninety A-20K-15s became the Boston V, and 86 of these were flown to replenish four RAF and two South African squadrons in the Mediterranean theatre.

Altogether, the RAF acquired 1,166 Boston series aircraft. Brazil also got 30 A-20Ks from July to September 1944, but did not use them in combat.

Martin Maryland

Martin's attack-bomber was a low-wing, tail-down, rival of the A-20, but had less performance than the Douglas. The prototype had two R-1830-37 Twin Wasps and three crewmen in a narrow fuselage, with a retractable manual rear-gun turret covered by a panel that slid back when the turret was raised. Armament included four .30-caliber guns in the wings, another in the turret, and another in a deeply-cut lower position behind the bay for 60 30-pound or four 300-pound bombs.

Martin's Model 167F design was begun in April 1938 by James S. McDonnell. First tested on March 13, 1939, the 167 flew from Baltimore to Wright Field the following day, and was purchased by the Air Corps as the XA-22 on September 26. Glenn L. Martin protested the production contract awarded Douglas on the grounds that the 7B prototype had crashed and was not present for the competition, but he could be consoled by his own French contract for 115 aircraft placed February 6, 1939.

AF

MARTIN XA-22
Two Pratt & Whitney R-1830-37, 1200 hp takeoff, 1100 hp at 5000'
DIMENSIONS: Span 61'4", Lg. 46'8", Ht. 16'6", Wing Area 538.5 sq.ft.
WEIGHT: Empty 11,170 lb., Gross 16,803 lb., Max. 17,000 lb. Fuel 433-528 gals.
PERFORMANCE: Speed- Top 279 mph at 5000', Cruising 261 mph. Service Ceiling 20,000'. Range 750 miles/1800lb. bombs, 820 miles/1200-1b. bombs, 1900 miles max.

French aircraft could carry eight 220-pound bombs and six 7.5-mm guns like the DB-7, but they had no cover over the turret and used 900-hp R-1830-SC3G Twin Wasps supercharged to 12,000 feet with 87-octane fuel and Curtiss propellers. The first 167F flew August 8, 1939, and by November the contract was increased to 345 aircraft completed by July 1940.

The first ship convoy carrying Martins did not reach Casablanca in French Morocco until December 25. There the Glenns, as the French called them, were uncrated and assembled, but late supply of their French radios and bomb racks delayed their combat readiness. After the German invasion, four groups flew 418 combat sorties from May 22 to June 24, 1940, losing 18 Martins in action. In the meantime, 234 had arrived in Casablanca by June 25, but only 189 had been assembled and turned over to the French Air Force.

More Martins from America arrived in Africa in July and replenished the squadrons that had fled Europe. They were used to retaliate against British pressure on French forces commanded by the Vichy government collaborating with Hitler. Fighting broke out in June 1941 in Syria, where 21 Martins were lost fighting British forces. Attacks on American forces near Casablanca in November 1942, led to four Glenns being shot down by Wildcats.

MdA

MARTIN 167F (France)
Two Pratt & Whitney R-1830-SC3G, 1050 hp takeoff, 900 hp at 12,000'
DIMENSIONS: As XA-22
WEIGHT: Empty 10,783 lb., Gross 15,707 lb., Max. 16,621 lb. Fuel 370-512+158 gal.
PERFORMANCE: Speed- Top 270 mph at s.1., 298 mph at 13,000', Cruising 254 mph, Landing 71 mph. Service Ceiling 29,000', Climb 13,130'/7.4 min. Range 762 miles/1,760-lb. bombs, 1015 miles max. with 670 gals.

After the French defeat, the RAF took over the last 62 167Fs in America, adding about 19 in transit or from escaping French pilots. Known as the Maryland I, they first served with a long-range reconnaissance unit at Malta in 1940, scouting the Italian Navy in preparation for the successful Swordfish attack on Taranto. One was credited with downing several Italian planes and another Maryland from Scotland was the first to discover the *Bismarck's* sortie from Norway.

A pause in production was followed by 150 heavier Maryland II bombers ordered June 7, and accepted by the RAF from December 1940 to April 1941, with R-1830-S3C4-G Wasps of 1,000-hp at 14,500 feet with 100-octane fuel. These RAF Marylands had self-sealing fuel tanks, armor plate behind the pilot and gunner, and carried 2,000 pounds of bombs with four crewmen. The turret now had two Vickers guns and two fixed "scare" guns firing backwards were added behind the bomb bay; these weapons being installed after the planes arrived in Egypt.

The Maryland IIs were used by four British and three South African light bomber squadrons in northeast Africa. Many bombing missions against Axis forces were flown until the Marylands were replaced by the heavier Baltimores in 1942.

Martin Baltimore

Martin had planned to use Wright R-3350-11 engines in an XA-23 designed for the Army. That project was dropped, but on May 18, 1940, an order had been placed for 400 Martin 187s better fitted to meet British requirements for increased power and armament.

First flown by E.D. Shannon on June 12, 1941, the Martin 187B was dubbed the Baltimore, and differed from the Maryland by having Wright 1,600-hp R-2600-A5B engines, self-sealing fuel tanks, 211 pounds of armor, and a deeper fuselage for a four-man crew and four 500-pound bombs.

Fifty Baltimore I and 100 Baltimore II types had eleven .30-caliber guns; four fixed in the wings, two flexible guns for the upper rear cockpit, another for the ventral

IWM

MARTIN MARYLAND II (167B)

spot, and an unusual mounting of four belly guns pointing aft and fixed at an angle 9° down and 1.5° out. Hand-held upper guns were replaced on the 250 Baltimore IIIs by a Boulton Paul power turret with four .303-caliber guns.

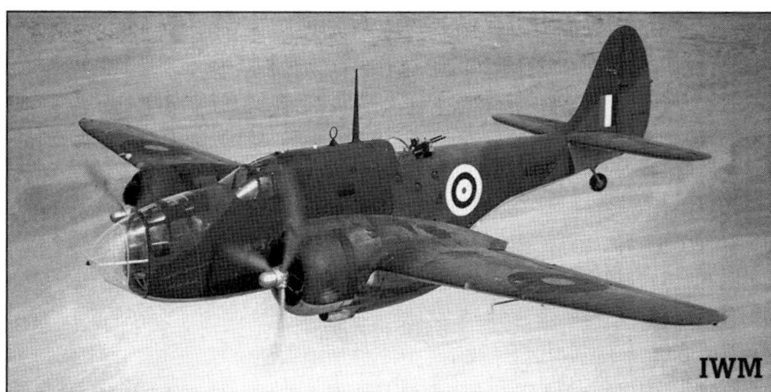

IWM

MARTIN BALTIMORE I (187B)
Two Wright R-2600-19 (A5B), 1600 hp takeoff, 1400 hp at 10,000'
DIMENSIONS: Span 61'4", Lg. 48'6", Ht. 11'3", Wing Area 538.5 sq. ft.
WEIGHT: Empty 15,149 lb., Gross 21,750 lb., Max. 22,958 lb. Fuel 490-980 gal.
PERFORMANCE: Speed- Top 284 mph at s.1., 308 mph at 13,000', Cruising 230 mph. Service Ceiling 22,300', Climb 13,130'/ 7.9 min. Range 1082 miles/1000-lb. bombs, 2800 miles max.

By 1941's end, 146 Baltimores had been accepted, and of the original 400 Baltimores accepted by June 1942, 356 went to RAF units in the Middle East, 35 were sunk on torpedoed ships, six went to the United Kingdom and one was retained by Martin. The first RAF mission was on May 23, 1942, in Libya, but Messerschmitts downed all four Baltimores, proving that light bombers still needed fighter escort.

After the Lend-Lease Act made available more funds for Britain, 575 more were ordered June 17, 1941. Since lend-lease aircraft were purchased by the United States government, they had AAF designations, including the Douglas A-20C Boston, the Lockheed A-28 and A-29 Hudsons, Martin A-30 Baltimore, and Vultee A-31 Vengence. (As the Hudsons were actually maritime patrol types, not attack planes, they are discussed in Chapter 20.)

IWM

MARTIN BALTIMORE III

The A-30 began appearing in August 1942, with two .50-caliber guns in a Martin power turret replacing the hand-held dorsal guns, and bomb bay ferry tanks so they could be ferried across the South Atlantic to Accra. The

281 Baltimore IIIA models were followed, beginning January 1943, by 294 Baltimore IV (A-30A-1/5). Six hundred Baltimore Vs (A-30A-10/30) with 1,700-hp Wright R-2600-29 Cyclones were ordered September 23, 1942, and delivery began by July 1943. Wing guns were now also of .50-caliber.

MARTIN BALTIMORE IV (A-30-1)
Two Wright R-2600-19, 1600 hp takeoff, 1275 hp at 11,500'
DIMENSIONS: Span 61'4", Lg. 48'6", Ht. 14'2", Wing Area 538.5 sq. ft.
WEIGHT: Empty 15,460 lb., Gross 22,600 lb., Max. 27,100 lb. Fuel 490-1440 gal.
PERFORMANCE: Speed- Top 305 mph at 11,500', Cruising 225 mph, Landing 87 mph. Service Ceiling 23,300', Climb 10,000'/7 min. Range 800 miles/2000-lb. bombs, 1100 miles/1000-lb. bombs, 2800 miles ferry.

When production ended in May 1944, 1,575 Baltimores had been built, 78 had been lost before or during flight deliveries to Africa, and the last one was retained by the U.S. Navy for tests. All combat missions were flown in the Mediterranean area.

MARTIN BALTIMORE V (A-30A-10)
Two Wright R-2600-29, 1700 hp takeoff, 1450 hp at 12,000'
DIMENSIONS: As A-30
WEIGHT: Empty 15,875 lb., Gross 22,622 lb., Max. 27,800 lb. Fuel 490-1440 gal.
PERFORMANCE: Speed- Top 320 mph at 15,000', Cruising 224 mph, Landing 87 mph. Service Ceiling 25,000', Climb 10,000'/4.8 min. Range 720 miles/2000-lb. bombs, 980 miles/1000-lb. bombs, 2600 miles ferry

Besides ten RAF and three South African squadrons, Baltimores also served a Greek squadron in 1944, and became the last bomber used by the Italian Air Force when 34 were supplied to a unit of the Co-Belligerent Air Force from November 1944 to May 1945. Although neutral, Turkey also received 72 Baltimore Vs, beginning in August 1944, while 12 were given in 1945 to a French squadron in Syria.

The Army's Dive Bombers

"Stuka" became a fearful word in 1940, as Junkers dive bombers, teamed with armored divisions, smashed the ground forces resisting the Nazi conquest of Europe. American authorities were startled into the realization that dive attacks were more accurate than conventional bombing techniques.

"Can the A-20 bomb from a dive?" asked General Henry Arnold on June 1, 1940. No, not from angles over 30°, but the Army might get Navy two-place dive bombers like the Douglas SBD. The Air Corps had to furnish two dive bomber groups to support the Army's new armored divisions, and a July 2, 1940, directive ordered procurement of 78 from a Navy contract.

The first was delivered from El Segundo to Wright Field on June 18, 1941, and 78 designated A-24 (SBD-3A on Navy lists) were completed by October. With a 1,000-hp Wright R-1820-52 Cyclone, they were like the Navy models except for Army colors, a new tail wheel, and no deck-landing gear. Armament included a 500 or 1,000-pound bomb on the center yoke, or a pair of 100-pound bombs on under-wing racks, as well as two .50-caliber nose guns and a .30-caliber flexible gun. Armor protection and leak-proof tanks were standard, along with perforated flap dive brakes.

The A-24 two-seaters went to the principal Army light bomber station at Savannah, Georgia, where they equipped three of the four squadrons of the new 27th Bombardment Group (Light) and one squadron of the veteran 3rd Bombardment Group (Light). These groups' other four squadrons had twin-engined A-20A level bombers.

The 27th Group's dive-bomber squadrons were shipped to the Philippines Islands, but unfortunately the airmen arrived without their aircraft, the 52 A-24s sailing in convoy from Honolulu November 29, 1941, and then being diverted by the war to Australia, which they reached December 22.

Some pilots were evacuated to rejoin their aircraft whose operations were delayed by missing parts. Eleven A-24s flew up to Java to join a losing fight and the first two Army dive-bomber sorties were made February 19, 1942, but the remainder didn't begin missions from Port Morseby with the 8th Bombardment Squadron until April 1. After five of seven were lost on the last mission on July 29, these dive-bombers were withdrawn from action as too slow, short-ranged, and ill-armed. This same type, of course, did excellent Navy work, but the Air Force was comparing it to land-based twin-engine types.

A new allocation of the Dauntless dive-bomber to the Army was made by an April 16, 1942, contract on which deliveries resumed July 2, 1942, with 90 more A-24s and 170 A-24A (SBD-4A) built by March 1943 at the Douglas El Segundo plant. Twin flexible guns and larger bomb sizes were provided on these aircraft along with a new 24-volt electrical system on the A-24A.

The new Douglas factory at Tulsa received a contract approved December 1, 1942, for 1,200 A-24B (SBD-5) powered by a 1,200-hp Wright R-1820-60. Deliveries began

AF

DOUGLAS A-24

Wright R-1820-52, 1000 hp takeoff, 800 hp at 16,000'

DIMENSIONS: Span 41'6", Lg. 32'8", Ht. 12'11", Wing Area 325 sq. ft.

WEIGHT: Empty 6265 lb., Gross 9200 lb., Max. 10,200 lb. Fuel 260 gal.

PERFORMANCE: Speed- Top 250 mph at 17,200', Cruising 173 mph, Landing 75 mph. Service Ceiling 26,000', Climb 10,000'/7 min. Range 950 miles/1000-lb. bomb, 1300 miles max.

DOUGLAS A-24B
Wright R-1820-60, 1200 hp takeoff, 900 hp at 14,000'
DIMENSIONS: Span 41'6", Lg. 33', Ht. 12'11", Wing Area 325 sq. ft.
WEIGHT: Empty 6330 lb., Gross 9250 lb.(with 1000 lb. bomb), Max. 10,250 lb. Fuel 260 gal.
PERFORMANCE: Speed- Top 254 mph at 15,000', Cruising 180 mph, Landing 75 mph. Service Ceiling 27,000', Climb 10,000'/ 6.1 min. Range 950 miles/1000-lb. bomb, 1250 miles as scout.

CURTISS A-25A (SB2C-1A)
Wright R-2600-8, 1700 hp takeoff, 1450 hp at 12,000'
DIMENSIONS: Span 49'9", Length 36'8", Ht. 14'9", Area 422 sq. ft.
WEIGHT: Empty 10,363 lb., Gross 15,076 lb., Max. 17,162 lb., Fuel 320+246 gal.
PERFORMANCE: Speed- Top 269 mph at s.l., 285 mph at 12,400', Cruising 155 mph, Stalling 74 mph. Service Ceiling, 24,500', Climb 1580'/1 min., 10,000'/7.4 min., Range 1130 miles/1000-lb. bomb, 1090 miles/2000-lb., 2020 miles ferry range.

in March 1943, but cancellations on October 30 reduced the total to 615 A-24Bs completed by December 1943.

Thirteen new Army groups were designated as dive-bomber units from July 1942 to August 1943, and ten used A-24s during this period, but the only unit to take them into combat was the 58th Bomb Squadron (Dive) at Wheeler Field, Hawaii. This squadron went to the Gilbert Islands and, redesignated the 531st Fighter-Bomber Squadron, used its A-24s to pound Japanese installations in December 1943.

Earlier, the 407th Bomb Group flew an August 4, 1943, mission against Kiska, but the enemy had already fled that island. Most A-24Bs were relegated to non-combat utility and training work, or offered to other nations. Mexico received 28 from June to November 1943 to train pilots who later turned to P-47Ds, and Chile got 12. In September 1944, Free French A-24Bs of GC1/18 attacked German positions in France.

The A-25 Failure

The Air Force intended to follow the A-24 with a more powerful Navy dive-bomber, the Curtiss SB2C-1 with an R-2600-8 Double Cyclone (whose design is described more fully in chapter 21). Even before the prototype was flown, the Army was authorized on November 6, 1940, to buy 100 as the A-25, or SB2C-1A, from a Navy contract. By April 3, 1941, the A-25 specification promised a top speed of 313 mph and a service ceiling of 29,000 feet at a weight of 7,868 pounds empty and 10,982 pounds gross. After Pearl Harbor, the Navy would need the Curtiss Columbus factory's full output, so a separate production line for the Army was set up in St. Louis to build the 3,100 A-25As ordered by February 18, 1942.

The A-25A was armed with four .50-caliber wing guns, a single .50-caliber flexible gun on a power-boosted rear cockpit mount, and an internal bomb bay for one 1,000-pound or a 1,600-pound armor-piercing bomb. Under wing racks could add two 58-gallon drop tanks or 500-pound bombs. Additional protection added under the nose and around the cockpits increased armor weight from the Navy's 195 pounds to 669 pounds on the Army version, which had no carrier gear and different wheels than its Navy sisters, and only the first ten had folding wings.

All these changes increased the weight to 10,363 pounds empty, and 15,076 pounds gross. Performance was reduced to a top speed of 285 mph and a 24,500 foot service ceiling. This data shows what wartime increases in armament, armor, and fuel often cost in performance.

The first A-25A was flown September 29, 1942, but not accepted until December, and only ten more were accepted by March 22, 1943, when an Air Force Board rejected the dive-bomber concept. Two-seat dive-bombers like the A-24, A-25, and A-35 were too slow to evade enemy fighters and should be replaced by single-seat fighter-bombers like the A-36 and P-39.

CURTISS A-25A for Australia

By June 12, 1943, the A-25A contract was reduced and production ended in March 1944 with 900 built, none of them ever deployed in combat units. Australia was to get 150, but only ten were actually delivered in November 1943. The last 410 went to the Marines and Navy as SB2C-1A operational trainers, the remainder considered "in excess of all military requirements."

Vultee Vengeance

The most widely-used American land-based dive-bomber originated as the Vultee V-72 two-seater, designed for France. Two hundred were ordered off the drawing board for the Royal Air Force on July 3, 1940. The reorganized Northrop corporation was enlisted on September 16 to build another 200 at Hawthorne, California.

Mfr

VULTEE V-72 prototype
Wright GR-2600-A5B-5, 1600 hp takeoff
DIMENSIONS: Span 48', Lg. 39'9", Ht. 15'4", Wing Area 332 sq. ft.
WEIGHT: Empty 9592 lb., Gross 11,338 lb. Max. 12,939 lb., Fuel 200-360 gal.
PERFORMANCE: Speed- Top 277 mph at 3,000', 285 mph at 12,000', Cruising 237 mph, Landing 82 mph. Service Ceiling 25,700'. Climb 8800'/5 min. Range 810 miles/1000-lb. bombs, 1420 miles max.

Since Vultee's Downey, California, factory was occupied by previous contracts, the Stinson plant at Nashville, Tennessee, was purchased for V-72 production and only the first two pre-production prototypes were built at Downey in 1941. By December 2, 1940, Britain had named the dive bomber the Vengeance and increased the Vultee order to 500. The RAF had now ordered 1,200 dive bombers, including 450 Brewster Bermudas and 50 Vought Chesapeakes, from America. No dive bombers were ordered from British factories, committed to fighters and heavy bombers.

The robust Vengeance used the 1,600-hp Wright Double Cyclone and had odd sweptback wings with lattice dive-brakes, armor and leak proof tanks. The main wheels rotated and retracted back into the wings. Armament included six .30-caliber guns and two 500-pound bombs in an internal bay, with room for two more 250-pound bombs as overload. The four wing guns had 750 rounds each, while 500 rounds were provided each of the two flexible guns.

Twin rudders on the original design were replaced with a single rudder by February 20, 1941, and the first example flew at Downey on March 30, 1941. Although the original 1940 specification promised 298 mph at 11,338 pounds gross weight, early tests indicated a 285-mph top speed in light condition, without camouflage. The first two aircraft were retained in America for test work, as was Northrop's first V-72 flown on November 30, 1941. Two hundred were accepted from Hawthorne from January 24 to August 15, 1942, as the Vengeance I. Nashville delivered 500 Vengeance IIs from March 1942 to January 1943.

Only two examples from each factory were shipped to the United Kingdom, for Japan's entrance into the war had opened new fronts. In January 1942, the AAF wanted to requisition 300 Vengeances to train its projected dive bomber groups. February tests of the V-72 at Wright Field were unsatisfactory, and when it was learned that parts of the Northrop and Vultee production ships were not interchangeable, all Northrops were allocated for export, while the AAF laid first claim to the Vultees.

Most V-72s were shipped to India, the first five arriving August 17, 1942. Although 172 Northrop and 227 Vultee V-72s arrived for four RAF and two Indian Air Force squadrons, adjusting the planes for tropic conditions, and training crews, delayed combat until March 19, 1943. Nine Northrop and two Vultee-built V-72s were lost at sea on the way to India.

Mfr

VULTEE Vengeance I (V-72-NO) for RAF

The Royal Australian Air Force (RAAF) had been promised 367 Vengeances, received 15 Northrop V-72s beginning May 30, 1942, but had to wait until February 1943 for more. Although 269 V-72s (Vengeance II) were flight delivered to the AAF from Nashville, 122 of these were boxed and shipped to Australia in 1943. Brazil got 26 of 28 V-72s dispatched from December 1942 to February 1943.

The Army designation A-31 was given to replenishments scheduled by Lend-lease contracts, approved June 28, 1941, that added 400 Vultees and 200 more from Northrop. They had better fuel tank protection and the same engine, now labeled R-2600-19. Northrop delivered these 200 Vengeance IA (A-31-NO) dive-bombers from October 20, 1942 to April 30, 1943, before that company shifted to P-61 production. The RAF in India received 116 of these Vengeance IAs, and the RAAF got 84. Vultee delivered 100 Vengeance IIIs (A-31C-VN) from Nashville for the RAF in India from February to May 1943.

The first V-72 had been designated XA-31A when accepted at Downey without engine or armament for use as an engine test ship. It became the XA-31B after the big Pratt & Whitney XR-4360-1 planned for the XA-41 was installed by April 25, 1942. Six Vultee V-72s modified to test Wright R-3350s with four-bladed propellers for the B-29 program were known as the XA-31C and five YA-31Cs.

Army pilots had recommended that the Vengeance be equipped according to AAF armament standards, with .50-caliber guns and a 1,000-pound size bomb, as well as a four-degree angle of wing incidence. These changes were incorporated on Vultee Model 88, the first A-35A in

Mfr

VULTEE A-31-NO (Vengeance IA)
Wright R-2600-19, 1600 hp takeoff, 1000 hp at 11,500'
DIMENSIONS: Span 48', Lg. 39'9", Ht.15'4", Wing Area 332 sq. ft.
WEIGHT: Empty 9725 lb., Gross 12,940 lb., Max. 14,300 lb. Fuel 320 gal.
PERFORMANCE: Speed- Top 275 mph at 11,000', Cruising 235 mph, Landing 80 mph. Service Ceiling 22,500', Climb 19,700'/ 20.4 min. Range 700 miles/1000-lb. bombs, 1400 miles ferry.

September 1942, whose satisfactory flying traits encouraged the purchase of 400 A-35s on September 22, 1942. An order for 2,330 more Vengeances was approved on December 17, 1942.

Mfr

VULTEE Vengeance II (V-72-VN)

The next 99 ships accepted by May 1943 on the lend-lease order were designated A-35A-1, and had five .50-caliber guns. The four fixed wing guns had 425 rounds each, and the flexible gun had 400 rounds. A 1,000-pound bomb was carried in the bay and two 500-pound bombs or ferry tanks could be added on wing racks. Last model to appear was the A-35B (Vengeance IV) of May 1943, which had a 1,700-hp R-2600-13 or Navy R-2600-8 and six .50-caliber wing guns.

About 140 Vultee V-72s were available in the U.S. in 1942 for three of the newly organized dive-bomber groups while two more groups got A-31s, and two had A-35 Vengeances to replace their A-24s. But in March 1943 the AAF decided against using two-seat dive-bombers in combat, and on May 20, 1943, A-35 contracts were canceled except for those necessary to keep the Nashville factory operating. All of the dive-bomber groups trained in the U.S. got single-seaters before the end of 1943. When Vengeance production ended on June 6, 1944, 1,931 had been built, including 831 A-35Bs. Some 320 of the latter were modified for target towing.

Mfr

VULTEE A-35A-1
Wright R-2600-19, 1600 hp takeoff, 1275 hp at 11,500'
DIMENSIONS: As A-31
WEIGHT: Empty 10,060 lb., Gross 13,500 lb., Max. 15,600 lb. Fuel 300 gal.
PERFORMANCE: Speed- Top 273 mph at 11,000', Cruising 235 mph, Landing 83 mph. Service Ceiling 21,500', Climb 15,000'/ 12.8 min. Range 600 miles/2000-lb. bombs, 1300 miles ferry.

Australia received 15 Vengeance I, 84 Vengeance IA (A-31), 122 Vengeance II (V-72), 23 A-35A and 98 A-35B models (342 total), and flew dive-bombing missions against Japanese-held island bases from June 13, 1943 to March 8, 1944.

The Free French in North Africa received 28 A-35As in July 1943 and 37 A-35Bs in December 1943, but none were used in combat. Brazil got only seven A-35Bs in September 1944, of 50 promised from the last batch produced.

AF

VULTEE A-35B (Vengeance IV)
Wright R-2600-13, 1700 hp takeoff, 1350 hp at 13,000'
DIMENSIONS: As A-31
WEIGHT: Empty 10,300 lb., Gross 16,400 lb., Max. 17,100 lb. Fuel 300+325 gal.
PERFORMANCE: Speed- Top 279 mph at 13,500', Cruising 230 mph, Landing 84 mph. Service Ceiling 22,300', Climb 15,000'/ 11.3 min. Range 530 miles/2000 lb. bombs, 1900 miles max.

Lend-lease provided the RAF with 538 Vengeance IVs, but limited their combat use to 114 on the Burma front, where operations continued until July 16, 1944. Later, 35 went to the Middle East, and most of the 389 Mark IVs in the United Kingdom served as target-tow aircraft.

Officials in the U.S. did not anticipate the lack of demand for the Vengeance planes, and their continued production was criticized as a "shining example of the waste... caused by pressure for sheer numbers of planes not actu-

IWM

NORTH AMERICAN A-36A as Mustang IA

ally needed at the front." Much the same could be said of the A-24B and A-25A contracts, yet in Burma the sturdy Vengeance was a successful RAF close-support weapon.

The disappearance of two-seat dive-bombers from AAF combat groups can be attributed to the greater success of single-seat fighter-bombers in the same mission. Bombed-up fighters like the A-36 and P-47 had much better performance, proved excellent for close support, and could take care of their own defense after their bombs were gone.

The A-36A Mustang

North American Aviation was building P-51 Mustangs for the RAF Army Cooperation Command in 1942, but these contracts would run out in the fall, and the AAF had yet to select the Mustang for its own fighter squadrons. Learning that the AAF was unsatisfied with the two-seaters then available, the company began to rework its single-seater as a dive-bomber on April 16, 1942.

Racks for two 500-pound bombs, or 75-gallon drop tanks, were added under the wings of a Mustang I along with four dive-brakes adapted from the A-31. The Air Force was impressed enough to order 500 as the A-36A, powered by an Allison V-1710-87 boosted to 1,325-hp for low-altitude operations. Six .50-caliber guns, two in the nose and the others in the wings, were provided with 1,200 rounds.

Bob Chilton flew the first on September 27, 1942, and 500 were accepted between October 1942 and March 1943, before production shifted to the P-51A fighter version. Three groups formerly using the Vengeance two-seaters trained on the A-36A, and the 27th Fighter-Bomber Group went into combat from Tunisia on June 6, 1943, joined by the 86th Fighter-Bomber Group in July. They flew 23,373 sorties and dropped over 16,000 bombs before replacement by P-47Ds in 1944. In India, the A-36A was operated by the 311th Fighter-Bomber Group.

AF

NORTH AMERICAN A-36A
Allison V-1710-87, 1325 hp at 3000',
(1500 hp at 5400' War Emergency)
DIMENSIONS: Span 37', Lg. 32'3", Ht. 12'2", Wing Area 233 sq. ft.
WEIGHT: Empty 6610 lb., Gross 8370-10,000 lb., Max. 11,000 lb., Fuel 180+300 gal.
PERFORMANCE: Speed- Top 310 mph at 5000'/two 500 lb. bombs, 366 mph clean, Cruising 250 mph, Landing 85 mph. Service Ceiling 25,100' (bombs), 27,000' clean. Climb Range 550 miles/two 500-lb. bombs, 2300 miles ferry.

They were the only liquid-cooled attack aircraft and the last dive-bombers used in the war by the Army Air Force. Their success demonstrated the value of single-seat fighter-bombers, and led to widespread use of later P-51 and P-47 models on close-support missions.

The Douglas Invader

Even as the first A-20A was tested, the Air Force on November 5, 1940, instigated a Douglas study of a better and larger light bomber with twice the A-20's bomb load and defensive firepower. The resulting design submitted on January 28, 1941, by E. H. Heinemann became the last propeller-driven twin-engine bomber in production for the Air Force, the A-26 Invader.

A wider body permitted side-by-side pilot seating and 4,000 pounds of bombs. Instead of hand-held guns, two 50-caliber guns in a top turret and two in a lower rear turret were aimed through periscopic sights and remote controls in the rear cockpit. Two 2,000-hp R-2800-27 Wasps and wings with a low-drag laminar-flow airfoil and double-slotted flaps, along with tricycle landing gear, were provided.

Contracts were placed June 2, 1941, for prototypes and on October 31 for the first 500 production aircraft. But it would be three years before the A-26 entered combat, unlike the rapid flow of Havocs from the Douglas plants in 1941-1944. The first XA-26 flew July 10, 1942, at El Segundo with three crewmen, a transparent bombardier nose, and six guns. Two guns were fixed on right side of the nose, and four in the turrets.

SDAM

DOUGLAS XA-26
Two Pratt & Whitney R-2800-27, 2000 hp takeoff, 1600 hp at 13,500'
DIMENSIONS: Span 70', Lg. 51'2", Ht. 18'6", Wing Area 540 sq. ft.
WEIGHT: Empty 21,150 lb., Gross 31,000 lb. Fuel 830+220 gal.
PERFORMANCE: Speed- Top 370 mph at 17,000', Cruising 212 mph, Landing 100 mph. Service Ceiling 31,300', Climb 20,000'/ 10.2 min. Range 1800 miles/3000-lb. bombs, 2500 miles ferry.

Night fighter equipment was installed on the second prototype, the two-seat XA-26A with AGL-1 radar in the nose, four 20-mm fixed guns in a belly tray, and a top turret with four .50-caliber guns. It was not flown until January 27, 1943, but this version was made redundant by the success of Northrop's P-61.

The third prototype was the XA-26B, completed by May 1943, which had a 75-mm T-7 cannon on the right side and two .50-caliber guns on the left side of a short solid nose and four .50-caliber guns paired in turrets. This gun nose had been chosen for the production model, but considerable gun variations were possible. A tank destroyer version with four 37-mm guns was proposed in January 1943, but was discarded by February 22.

SDAM

DOUGLAS XA-26A
Two Pratt & Whitney R-2800-27, 2000 hp takeoff, 1600 hp at 13,500'
DIMENSIONS: Span 70', Lg. 52'5", Wing Area 540 sq. ft.
WEIGHT: Empty 20,794 lb., Gross 25,300 lb., Max. 28,893 lb., Fuel 440-800 gal.
PERFORMANCE: Speed- Top 365 mph at 17,000', Cruising 264 mph. Service Ceiling 25,900', Climb 20,000'/10.5 min., Range 700 miles normal, 1420 miles max.

Mfr

DOUGLAS XA-26B
Two Pratt & Whitney R-2800-27, 2000 hp takeoff, 1600 hp at 13,500'
DIMENSIONS: Span 70', Lg. 50', Wing Area 540 sq. ft.
WEIGHT: Empty 20,225 lb., Gross 28,855 lb. Fuel 440-800 gal.
PERFORMANCE: Speed- Top 359 mph at 16,000'. Service Ceiling 25,700'. Range 695 miles normal, 1260 miles max.

The large propeller spinners on the prototypes were deleted from the production A-26Bs built at Long Beach. The first of five A-26B-l-DL Invaders appeared on September 10, 1943, and 15 A-26B-5-DLs completed by March 1944 had minor changes and eliminated the camouflage formerly customary on bombers. These models had the 75-mm gun in the nose with two .50-caliber guns on the left side, but a new all-purpose nose was installed on later aircraft, beginning with the A-26B-10. Extensive cockpit armor and self-sealing fuel tanks were provided.

Mfr

DOUGLAS A-26B-5-DL

Alternate gun arrangements could be chosen: two 37-mm and four .50-caliber, one 37-mm and one 75-mm, or one 75-mm and two .50-caliber guns. The usual arrange-

DOUGLAS A-26B-10-DL
Two Pratt & Whitney R-2800-27 or -71, 2000 hp takeoff, 1600 hp at 13,500'
DIMENSIONS: Span 70', Lg. 50', Ht. 18'6", Wing Area 540 sq. ft.
WEIGHT: Empty 22,370 lb., Gross 35,000 lb. Fuel 925+675 gal.
PERFORMANCE: Speed- Top 340 mph at s.l., 355 mph at 15,000', Cruising 284 mph. Landing 100 mph. Service Ceiling 22,200', Climb 10,000'/8.1 min. Range 1400 miles/4000-lb. bombs, 3200 miles ferry.

ment actually installed was six .50-caliber nose guns, with 400 rounds per gun, along with the usual guns paired in the two turrets with 500 rounds each. The bomb bay could accommodate six 500 or four 1,000-pound bombs. Beginning with the A-26B-15, fixtures under the wings could accommodate eight more .50-caliber guns or four more 500-pound bombs. Five aircraft from the A-26B-15-DL line were finished as A-26C-DL bombers with transparent nose enclosures and two nose guns.

Delays in achieving mass production brought much criticism from the Air Force, including General Arnold's complaint on March 13, 1944, that he wanted "A-26s for use in this war and not the next war." He hoped to replace not only the A-20, but the B-25 and B-26 medium bombers with the A-26.

While the first 500 Invaders (to A-26B-40-DL) rolled out of Long Beach, a parallel production line was established at Tulsa, Oklahoma, for 500 aircraft ordered March 17, 1943, the first appearing in January 1944. Of these, 205 were delivered as A-26B-5 to A-26B-25-DT models and the rest as A-26C-15 to A-26C-25-DT with glazed noses. On most of these the engine model was the R-2800-71, with a new ignition system.

New production contracts for 6,700 more Invaders were approved March 29, 1944, and later. The first appeared in January 1945 as the A-26B-45-DL, introducing the R-2800-79 water injection engine yielding 2,350-hp WE (war-emergency) power. Beginning with B-26B-50-DL, fourteen 5-in. rockets could be carried under the wings, and six .50-caliber guns were mounted within the wings. Eight .50-caliber nose guns brought the total to 14 fixed guns. Additional range could be attained from two 155-gallon external wing tanks, or a 125-gallon tank could replace the lower gun turret.

Parallel changes were made on the A-26C line at Tulsa. Invader deliveries ended at Long Beach on August 31, 1945, after 655 B-26B-45/-66-DLs had been built to that contract, and at Tulsa after 791 more B-26C-30/-55-DT. Altogether, 2,451 Invaders had been accepted, with wartime cancellations eliminating the proposed A-26D and E models.

Several experimental versions were tested, including an XA-26D-DL completed with R-2800-83 Wasps in 1945.

DOUGLAS A-26C-50-DT
Two Pratt & Whitney R-2800-79, 2000 hp takeoff, 2350 hp WE
DIMENSIONS: Span 70', Lg. 51'3", Ht. 18'6", Wing Area 540 sq. ft.
WEIGHT: Empty 22,690 lb., Combat 35,000 lb., Gross 37,740 lb. Fuel 925+985 gal.
PERFORMANCE: Speed- Top 361 mph at s.l., 372 mph at 10,000', Cruising 226 mph, Stalling 109 mph. Service Ceiling 20,450', Combat 23,100', Climb 2745/1 min. Range 892 miles/4000-lb. bombs, 3367 miles ferry.

One A-26B fitted with a 105-mm T7 gun and 30-round automatic feed was ground tested in 1945.

Perhaps the first tests of jet propulsion on an American bomber was made on the XA-26F, an A-26B delivered after the war with a I-16 jet engine and 125 gallons of jet fuel replacing the rear gunner and turrets. The jet intake was atop the fuselage and the exhaust was in the tail. Two 2,100-hp R-2800-83 Wasps turned four-bladed props, and although no rear guns were carried, eight nose and six wing .50-caliber guns were retained. In June 1946, the XA-26F averaged 413 mph over a 621-mile course.

Combat began for the Invaders used by the Ninth Air Force in Britain. The 416th Bomb Group flew the first full group mission November 17, 1944, its A-26Bs led on a medium altitude bombing strike by glass-nosed A-20Ks, since A-26Cs had not yet arrived. By January 23, 1945, the 409th Bomb Group joined the effort, making the first low-level attacks by Ninth Air Force bombers in Europe since

DOUGLAS A-26B-66-DL
Two Pratt & Whitney R-2800-79, 2000 hp takeoff, 2350 hp WE
DIMENSIONS: Span 70', Lg. 50', Ht. 18'6", Wing Area 540 sq. ft.
WEIGHT: Empty 22,850 lb., Gross 34,400 lb. Max. 37,200 lb. Fuel 925+1010 gal.
PERFORMANCE: Speed- Top 360 mph at s.l., 373 mph at 10,000', Cruising 284 mph. Landing 105 mph. Service Ceiling 22,200', Climb 10,000'/8.1 min. Range 1050 miles/4000-lb. bombs, 1250 miles/3000-lb. bombs, 3450 miles ferry.

1943. The third Ninth Air Force A-20 group, the 410th, used its first A-26s for night attacks.

Two groups with Martin B-26 Marauders, the 386th and 391st, changed to A-26s by April, with the final mission by 124 A-26s and eight B-26 pathfinders on May 3, 1945. Air Force A-26s flew 11,567 sorties in the European war.

The 47th Bomb Group in Italy also received some A-26s in 1945, but returned to the United States in July for specialized training in night attacks. While it did not go into combat again, its black-painted B-26Cs with radar served the group until replaced by B-45s in 1948.

The RAF received an A-26B-15 in July 1944, and was loaned two A-26C-25s for evaluation in February 1945. A plan to supply Britain with 140 A-26C Invaders canceled even before Germany's collapse, and those A-26Cs were assigned to the U.S. Navy's JD-1 program.

DOUGLAS XA-26F

In the Pacific, the veteran 3rd Bomb Group had tried five A-26B-5s in July 1944, but was not converted from A-20s to A-26s until a year later. They bombed for the Fifth Air Force from July 9 to August 12, 1945, while the 319th Bomb Group used them with the Seventh Air Force. After the war, the 3rd Bomb Group was stationed in Japan with the occupation forces. After 1948, it was the only light bomber group left in the Air Force.

Attack Prototypes, 1943-44

Several ground attack prototypes were built during 1943-44, but none of them won production contracts. The Brewster XA-32 was the only plane built by that company for the Air Force, and was the first designed as a single-seat dive-bomber.

A mid-wing, barrel-shaped monoplane with wide-tracked main wheels retracting into the wings and a fixed tail wheel, the XA-32 had a 2,100 hp Pratt & Whitney R-2800-37 Wasp and a four-bladed propeller. Heavy armor and increased speed was expected to compensate for the lack of a gunner. This design was proposed on April 15, 1941, and two prototypes ordered on October 31, 1941.

When the mockup was inspected in May 1942, Materiel Command officers considered the A-32 the "most desirable" dive-bomber design available, and a possible replacement for the A-25. But in June it was realized that the prototype would be delayed long past the scheduled September 1942 date, and Brewster was, in any case, too tied up by Navy orders to undertake new production. Immediate requirements for dive-bombers were then met

BREWSTER XA-32
Pratt & Whitney R-2800-37, 2100 hp takeoff, 1600 hp at 13,500'
DIMENSIONS: Span 45'1", Lg. 40'7", Ht. 12'8", Wing Area 425 sq. ft.
WEIGHT: Empty 11,820 lb., Gross 15,512 lb., Max. 19,9601b. Fuel 200+330 gal.
PERFORMANCE: Speed- Top 279 mph at s.1., 311 mph at 13,200', Cruising 236 mph, Landing 75 mph. Service Ceiling 26,000', Climb 10,000'/5.7 min. Range 500 miles/3000-lb. bombs, max. 1600 miles.

by ordering the P-51 Mustang's attack version, the A-36A, and the Vultee A-35B.

The Brewster did not begin flight tests until May 22, 1943, and then went to Eglin Field, Florida, for operational suitability trials. Armament on the XA-32 consisted of four 20-mm guns with 120 rpg in the wings, along with six .50-caliber guns with 400 rpg. Four 37-mm guns were provided on the second prototype, XA-32A. An internal bomb bay accommodated 1,000 pounds, with another 1,000-pound bomb under each wing. Split trailing-edge flaps were used as dive-brakes.

Tests showed the Brewster's speed and range below expectations, and below the standard A-20's capabilities. While flying qualities were satisfactory and armor protection (650 pounds) good, performance was not suitable for operations, and development ended. Brewster was also assigned the A-34 designation in May 1942 for the Bermuda dive-bombers for the RAF when 98 of those aircraft were requisitioned by the Army. (They are described with the Navy's SB2A series in Chapter 12.)

Two engines were used on the mysterious Hughes XA-37, which was kept so secret that no photograph of the completed aircraft was published. This project began with a company proposal on December 5, 1939, for a twin-boom fighter. But when the Air Corps signed an engineering contract on May 22, 1940, it was for design of a bomber to be built of Duramold, a process of heat-bonded wood and plastic. By March 1941, the design became a two-place long-range fighter powered by two projected liquid-cooled R-2160-3 Wright Tornado engines and provided with tricycle landing gear and seven .50-caliber guns.

The prototype built in Culver City, California, at company expense was called the D-2, for Hughes Design Two, Design One being the 1935 racer. Pratt & Whitney R-2800-49 Wasps replaced the Tornado when that engine failed to materialize. Hughes insistence on complete secrecy, even from the military, aroused Air Force suspicions, and doubts about the construction left the Materiel Command unwilling to commit government support. By May 1942, the two-seat, twin tail-boom, design had a 60-foot span, 23,900 to 36,000-pound gross weight, and was expected to have a 446 mph top speed at 25,000 feet and a 1,000-mile range with 2,200 pounds of bombs.

At first, the Hughes D-2A had no guns, like the all-wood de Haviland Mosquito bomber whose performance it was expected to exceed, but then six .50-caliber nose guns and a remote-controlled rear turret with four guns was added. The Air Force considered an XP-73 designation on June 30, 1942, but officially decided on XA-37 by July 3.

After a year with no contacts, Howard Hughes himself flew the aircraft on June 20, 1943, at an isolated California location, but the aircraft was never tested by the Air Force itself before it was destroyed in a hangar fire. So successful was the shroud of secrecy imposed by Mr. Hughes that no photographs or descriptions were released to the public.*

The project was revived when Colonel Elliott Roosevelt visited Hughes in July, and saw his design as the potential long-range photographic reconnaissance plane needed for the Pacific war. A new, much larger all-metal version called the D-5 resulted in an Air Force decision on October 6, 1943, to order 100 as the F-11. The first aircraft designed entirely for unarmed long-range reconnaissance, it would be delayed until after the war, like the giant Hughes flying boat built at the same time.

The next attack type actually began as a twin-engine, two-place fighter designed to destroy bombers with an automatic 75-mm gun. Since another aircraft for that purpose was already underway (the still-born Curtiss XP-71), an attack version of the Beech Model 28 was offered as a company proposal on September 23, 1942, and two prototypes ordered as the XA-38 on December 2, 1942.

First flown at Wichita May 7, 1944, the XA-38 was a two-place low-wing monoplane with two Wright R-3350-43 Cyclones, twin rudders, tail-down landing gear, and studs under the wings for four 500-pound bombs. The rear gun arrangement was like the A-26's; two pairs of .50-caliber guns in upper and lower General Electric remote-controlled turrets. The nose, however, was as individual as a swordfish's, with the long barrel of a 75-mm T15E1 cannon protruding far beyond the pair of .50s in the bow. Twenty rounds of ammunition were fed to the big gun by automatic loading, and 3,000 rounds were carried for the six machine guns.

Delayed by the lack of availability of engines, also needed for the B-29 program, the A-38 never reached production, although it had good flying qualities.

Meanwhile, development proceeded on a trio of heavily-armed single-seat, single-engine monoplanes, with large internal bomb bays. They were halfway between the single-seat fighter and the two-seat dive bomber. First were the Kaiser-Fleetwings XA-39 and Curtiss XA-40, neither of which got past the mockup stage. The former was to have used a 2,000 hp R-2800-27, and had two 37-mm

*Documentation can be found in the Summary of Hughes D-2, D-5, F-11 project, AMC Wright Field, August 1946, filed as 202.1-32 at the Air Force Historical Research Center, Air University, Maxwell AFB. See also Charles Barton, Howard Hughes and his Flying Boat, Fallbrook 1982: 103, 130, 259.

BEECH XA-38
Two Wright R-3350-43, 2530 hp takeoff, 2210 hp at 5800'
DIMENSIONS: Span 67'4", Lg. 51'9", Ht. 13'6", Wing Area 626 sq. ft.
WEIGHT: Empty 22,480 1b., Gross 32,000 1b., Max. 35,265 lb. Fuel 825+600 gal.
PERFORMANCE: Speed- Top 361 mph at s.l., 376 mph at 5800', Cruising 344 mph, Landing 103 mph. Service Ceiling 27,800', Climb 10,000'/5 min. Range 1070 miles/2000-lb. bombs, 1960 miles ferry.

and four .50-caliber wing guns. Six 500 or two 1,600-pound bombs could be carried in the bomb bay.

A 2,300 hp Wright R-3350-8 was planned for the XA-40 dive bomber, which was armed with four 20-mm and six .50-caliber guns in the wings. The internal bay could handle a 1,000-pound bomb or a 2,000-pound torpedo, and external wing racks for two 500-pound bombs.

By October, 1943, about a year after these projects were ordered, the AAF decided that it only wanted twin-engine attack-bombers, and single-engine type development was discontinued. Both companies then shifted their attention to bomber-torpedo single-seaters developed for the Navy, which became the XBTK-1, XSB3C-l, and XBTC-1 projects.

The Consolidated-Vultee XA-41 survived the cuts because it was the first type scheduled to fly with the big new

CONSOLIDATED-VULTEE XA-41
Pratt & Whitney XR-4360-9, 3000 hp takeoff, 2400 hp at 13,500'
DIMENSIONS: Span 54', Lg. 48'8", Ht. 14'6", Wing Area 540 sq. ft.
WEIGHT: Empty 13,400 1b., Gross 18,800 1b., Max. 23,260 lb. Fuel 350-445 gal. (1140 gal. ferry)
PERFORMANCE: Speed- Top 333 mph at s.l., 353 mph at 15,500', Cruising 270 mph, Landing 74 mph. Service Ceiling 27,000', Climb 10,000'/4.3 min. Range 800 miles/3000-lb. bombs, 3000 miles max

3,000-hp Pratt & Whitney XR-4360-9, and the Air Force wanted to see its performance. The XA-41 was begun at AAF request in September 1942 as the Vultee Model 90, ordered on a November 10, 1942, letter contract and first flown February 11, 1944, at Lomita, California.

The wing had a straight leading edge, tapered trailing edge, and eight-degree dihedral. Armament included four 37-mm and four .50-caliber guns in the wings, with 50 and 600 rounds per gun, respectively. The internal bomb bay normally carried four 500-pound bombs, but could accommodate two 1,600-pound bombs, a torpedo, or extra fuel tanks.

CURTISS XA-43 (mockup only)
Four General Electric J-35, 3835 lb. thrust at sea level
DIMENSIONS: Span 77'7", Lg. 71'10", Ht. 22'2", Wing Area 750 sq. ft.
WEIGHT: Empty 39,080 lb., Gross 62,000 lb. Fuel 2380-3950 gal.
PERFORMANCE: Speed- Top 585 mph at s.l., Cruising 400 mph, Landing 125 mph. Service Ceiling 40,000', Climb 20,000'/ 5 min. Range 1000 miles/4000-lb. bombs, 2400 miles max.

Flight tests showed much promise, but in 1944 close support bombing for the Army seemed well-provided for by the P-47 Thunderbolt's fighter-bomber operations, with the A-26 serving for heavier attacks. Only one XA-41 was built, and was the last new Army Air Force type flown with an attack designation. It was used after August 1944 by Pratt & Whitney for engine tests

Although four other designs were allotted attack designations during the war, none were completed in that class. The twin-engine Douglas XA-42 was quickly redesignated XB-42 in 1943, while the first jet-propelled attack-bomber was the Curtiss XA-43 whose mockup was seen in February 1945.

Planned armament included eight .50-caliber guns in the nose and four more in a remotely-controlled rear turret. Up to 16 500-pound bombs or 32 rockets might be carried, but instead this project was transformed into the XP-87 night fighter. Likewise, Convair's strange XA-44 jet with swept-forward wings became the XB-53, while Martin's XA-45 jet was completed as the XB-51. Both will be described in the chapter on jet bombers.

From 1932 to 1945 over 16,000 attack or light bombers were built in America, mostly by Douglas, to provide close support to American and allied ground forces. But after World War Two ended, interest in that tactical genre declined in favor of long-range strategic bombing. Yet the Douglas had more wars to fight, as chapter 25 will tell. Surplus Invaders left over after World War II were to turn up in many countries around the world.

CHAPTER 14

BOMBER MONOPLANES, 1931-1939

Most Army Air Corps bombers when war began in Europe in 1939 were like this Douglas B-18 of the 19th Bomb Group

American bombers were completely transformed between 1931 and 1939 from the old Keystone biplanes to the high-performance monoplane style that fought World War II. This transformation began when the new twin-engine monoplanes designed for long-range army observation missions were adapted for short-range bombing. In 1929, the Fokker XO-27 and Douglas XO-35 were the projected monoplanes chosen to have the second prototype of each completed as a light bomber.

Both aircraft were three-place high-wing monoplanes whose main landing wheels retracted back into the nacelles behind 600-hp Curtiss Conqueror engines, and both were armed with 1,200 pounds of bombs and a flexible .30-caliber Browning in the front and in the rear cockpits. The first bomber to appear with retractable wheels was the Fokker ordered June 19, 1929, and completed in December 1930 as the XB-8 and delivered to Wright Field in February 1931 with a straight, all-wood, cantilever wing and fabric-covered steel tube fuselage. All of the dozen service test aircraft, however, were completed as YO-27 observation types in 1932.

FOKKER XB-8
Two Curtiss V-1570-23, 600 hp
DIMENSIONS: Span 64', Lg. 47', Ht. 11'6", Wing Area 619 sq. ft.
WEIGHT: Empty 6861 lb., Gross 10,545 lb. Fuel 209 gal.
PERFORMANCE: Similar to XO-27, but with 1248 lb. bomb load added.

The Douglas XB-7, however, had the engines below fabric-covered gulled wings braced by metal struts, and had a corrugated aluminum fuselage. Ordered April 14, 1930, the XB-7 was completed in Santa Monica in June 1931. Seven YIB-7 bombers and five YIO-35 observation types were ordered for service tests on August 22, 1931. The first YIB-7 was completed in September 1932 with three-bladed propellers on its 675-hp engines, a smooth-skinned monocoque fuselage and an armament of two .30-caliber flexible guns with two 624-pound bombs beneath the fuselage. The Douglas monoplanes served the 31st Bomb Squadron at March Field, and flew the air mail during the 1934 crisis.

DOUGLAS XB-7
Two Curtiss V-1570-25, 600 hp
DIMENSIONS: Span 65', Lg. 45'6", Ht. 12'6", Wing Area 609 sq. ft.
WEIGHT: Empty 6865 lb., Gross 10,537 lb., Max. 11,287 lb. Fuel 200-300 gal.
PERFORMANCE: Speed— Top 169 mph at s.1., 165 mph at 5000', Cruising 147 mph, Landing 66 mph. Service Ceiling 18,950', Climb 1220'/1 min., 5000'/4.7 min. Range 632 miles.

Monoplanes built entirely of metal, including the skin, were operating successfully on airlines, and suggested themselves as bombers. A bomber version of Ford's famous trimotor was tested by the Army in June 1931. A high-wing monoplane with anti-drag rings on three 500-hp R-1340E radials, the Ford XB-906 was like the "Tin Goose" transport, but added bombardier's windows behind the front engine, a bay for 2,000 pounds of bombs, a front gun ring above and behind the pilot, and top and tunnel rear guns.

Wheel pants did not compensate enough for the landing gear's drag, and performance was far below that of new types with retractable gear. An Army board inspecting the XB-906 reported that the front gun could not be handled

AF

FORD XB-906
Three Pratt & Whitney R-1340E, 500 hp at 7000'
DIMENSIONS: Span 77'11", Lg. 51'6", Ht. 13'8", Wing Area 835 sq. ft.
WEIGHT: Empty 8345 lb., Gross 14,137 lb. Fuel 325 gal.
PERFORMANCE: Speed— Top 156 mph at 10,000', 145 mph at s.1., Cruising 135 mph, Landing 66 mph. Service Ceiling 18,400', Absolute Ceiling 20,000', Climb 775'/1 min., 7000'/11.9 min.

SDAM

DOUGLAS Y1B-7
Two Curtiss V-1570-27, 675 hp at s.1.
DIMENSIONS: Span 65'3", Lg. 46'7", Ht. 12'1", Wing Area 621 sq. ft.
WEIGHT: Empty 7519 lb., Gross 9953 lb., Max. 11,177 lb. Fuel 200-300 gal.
PERFORMANCE: Speed— Top 182 mph at s.1., 177 mph at 5000', Cruising 158 mph, Landing 78 mph. Service Ceiling 20,400', Absolute Ceiling 21,800', Climb 5000'/3 7 min. Range 411 miles/1248 lb. bombs, 632 miles max.

Mfr

BOEING XB-901 (YB-9)
Two Pratt & Whitney R-1860-13, 575 hp at s.1. (R-1860-11, 600 hp at 6000')
DIMENSIONS: Span 76'9", Lg. 51'6", Ht. 12'8", Wing Area 954 sq. ft.
WEIGHT: Empty 7650 (8362) lb., Gross 12,663 (13,351) lb. Fuel 250-308 gal.
PERFORMANCE: Speed— Top 163 mph at s.1., 158 mph at 5000', (188 mph at 6000'), Cruising 137 (165) mph, Landing 62 (63) mph. Service Ceiling 19,400' (22,600'), Absolute Ceiling 21,700' (24,400'), Climb 950'/1 min., 5000'/6 min. (1060'/1, 10,000'/4.5) Range (495 miles/1997 lb. bombs).

in the propeller slipstream and coverage of the rear guns was inadequate. On September 19, 1931, the XB-906 failed to recover from a dive, killing two company pilots.

Even less progress was made by the Keystone XB-908, designed as an all-metal low-wing monoplane with retractable wheels and two Curtiss V-1570 Conquerors. A mockup was inspected in April 1931, but neither the Army nor the company chose to finance the project further. When production of older Keystone biplanes ended in 1932, the Bristol, Pennsylvania, factory closed, and unemployment hurt the Bucks County community. A senator was asked to

Mfr

BOEING YlB-9A (YlP-26 in background)
Two Pratt & Whitney R-1860-11, 600 hp at 6000'
DIMENSIONS: Span 76'10", Lg. 52', Ht. 12', Wing Area 954 sq. ft.
WEIGHT: Empty 8941 lb., Gross 13,932 lb., Max. 14,320 lb. Fuel 306-528 gal.
PERFORMANCE: Speed- Top 186 mph at 6000', Cruising 165 mph, Landing 67 mph. Service Ceiling 20,150', Absolute Ceiling 21,900', Climb 900'/1 min., 10,000'/5.1 min. Range 540 miles/2260 lb. bombs, 990 miles max.

intercede for Army contracts, but new Boeing and Martin designs eclipsed their competition, and the company suffered the penalty of inadequate technical advance.

Boeing's aggressive design staff had developed in 1930 an all-metal low-wing transport with retractable wheels called the Monomail. The same principles were applied next to a twin-engine bomber built as a private venture and labeled XB-901. First flown April 13, 1931, the XB-901 had 575-hp Pratt & Whitney commercial engines and a top speed of 163 mph at sea level. The crew sat in four separate open cockpits along the narrow fuselage, with a radio operator inside, behind the front cockpit.

Excellent flying qualities won an Army contract for the prototype and six service test models approved August 21, 1931. Refitted with Hornets supercharged to yield 600 hp at 6,000 feet and with three-bladed propellers, the prototype was designated YB-9 and did 188 mph at that altitude during January 1932 tests. Armament included a .30-caliber M1922 Browning gun in the front and rear cockpits and an external 2,496-pound bomb load.

The second example was flown November 5, 1931, with Curtiss V-1570-29 Conquerors, the last inline engines to be used on an Army bomber for over eleven years. The top speed of the YB-9 was only 173 mph, so the engines were replaced by the R-1860-11 Hornets used on the remaining five ships. Designated YlB-9A and first flown July 4, 1932, they did 188 mph clean, and 186 mph with two 1,130-pound bombs underneath the fuselage. Five YlB-9As accepted by March 21, 1933, served at Langley Field with the 2nd Bomb Group, changing to a fabric-covered rudder with tabs in 1933.

Mfr

BOEING YlB-9
Two Curtiss V-1570-29, 600 hp at s.1.
DIMENSIONS: As YB-9
WEIGHT: Empty 8618 lb., Gross 13,591 lb. Fuel 263-308 gal.
PERFORMANCE: Speed- Top 173 mph at s.1., 171 mph at 5000', Cruising 151 mph, Landing 62 mph. Service Ceiling 19,200', Absolute Ceiling 21,000', Climb 1160'/1 min.

MARTIN YB-10
Two Wright R-1820-17, 675 hp at 4500'
DIMENSIONS: Span 70'6", Lg. 45'3", Ht. 11', Wing Area 678 sq. ft.
WEIGHT: Empty 7688 lb., Gross 12,829 lb, Max. 13,357 lb. Fuel 230-456 gal.
PERFORMANCE: Speed- Top 196 mph at s.1., 207 mph at 4500', Cruising 178 mph, Landing 80 mph. Service Ceiling 21,800', Absolute Ceiling 23,600'. Climb 1075'/1 min., 10,000'/10.2 min. Range 573 miles/2260 lb. bombs, 1360 miles max.

Boeing's bomber was a tremendous achievement, offering speeds more than 50 percent higher than that of the Keystones built at the same time. With bomber speed now comparable to that of the pursuit ships, defense problems became much greater than in biplane days. Boeing's metal monoplane became the parent of the bombers that fought the next war. But the B-9 itself was not built in quantity, for a new machine even more advanced in design eclipsed it and became the first American-built bomber to take part in actual warfare.

The Martin Bombers

Between the biplanes of the 20s and the heavily armed monoplanes of World War II, the most important American bomber was the Martin B-10 series. While retaining the modest armament and range of its elders, it suddenly displayed speeds faster than the biplane fighters that were supposed to catch it.

The bomber's role at that time was seen by the Army as that of coast defense. This had been formalized by the MacArthur-Pratt agreement on January 9, 1931, between the Army's Chief of Staff and the Chief of Naval Operations, which assigned Army air forces to defending the coasts of the continental United States and its overseas holdings, while Navy air forces would be free to move with the fleet on offensive missions. This arrangement continued the old tradition of concentrating Army efforts on coastal fortifications while the Navy would be the first offensive force. Seen in this perspective, the Army bombers were essentially long-range coastal guns.

The Martin Aircraft Company's Model 123 was developed in response to Air Corps pressure for a mid-wing all-metal monoplane. The stressed-skin monocoque fuselage had corrugated top and bottom surfaces with a deep belly and doors for the internal bomb bay. The wheels retracted into nacelles behind two 600-hp Wright SR-1820E Cyclones covered by anti-drag rings, and three open cockpits were provided, with room for a fourth crew member within the fuselage behind the bomb bay.

Known as the XB-907, the first version was flown February 26, 1932, at Baltimore, Maryland. Numerous difficulties delayed testing by the Army, but a July 1932 Wright Field report announced a 197-mph top speed and too-fast landing speeds. The aircraft was returned to the factory for rebuilding with a larger wing, flaps, and 675-hp R-1820F series Cyclones in full cowlings moved forward ahead of the wings.

MARTIN XB-907
Two Wright SR-1820E, 600 hp at 6000'
DIMENSIONS: Span 62'2", Lg. 46'2", Ht. 12'8", Wing Area 551 sq. ft.
WEIGHT: Empty 6978 lb., Gross 10,580 lb. Fuel 200-300 gal.
PERFORMANCE: Speed- Top 190 mph at s.l., 197 mph at 6000', Cruising 171 mph, Landing 91.5 mph. Service Ceiling 20,000', Absolute Ceiling 21,600', Climb 1600'/1 min. Range 513 miles, 980 miles max.

The new XB-907A, later designated XB-10, first flew October 4, 1932. The first rotating transparent turret on a U.S. bomber protected the front gunner from the slipstream of a 207-mph speed. Not only were the Keystones now totally obsolete, but the Martin was faster than any pursuit plane then in Army service. The technical revolution accomplished in bomber design by all-metal monoplanes would now be forced on fighter design. Little wonder that the Collier Trophy was awarded in 1933 to Glenn L. Martin for this ship. Army engineers, however, complained that the prestigious award ignored the role the Air Corps played with its insistence on incorporating the newest ideas in the prototype.

MARTIN XB-10 (XB-907A)
Two Wright R-1820-19, 675 hp at 6000'
DIMENSIONS: Span 70'7", Lg. 45', Ht. 10'4", Wing Area 640 sq. ft.
WEIGHT: Empty 7294 lb., Gross 12,230 lb., Max. 12,560 lb. Fuel 250 gal.
PERFORMANCE: Speed- Top 196 mph at s.1., 207 mph at 6000', Cruising 169.5 mph, Landing 71 mph. Service Ceiling 21,000', Absolute Ceiling 22,750', Climb 1380'/1 min. Range 600 miles/2260 lb. bombs.

The XB-10 prototype was purchased by the Army at the same time a contract approved January 24, 1933, ordered 48 production Martins at a unit cost of $50,840 each. (Costs had more than doubled in the decade since Martin's last bomber, the NBS-l.) These ships differed from the prototype in having a sliding canopy over the pilot's and rear gunner's cockpits and a simplified landing gear. Three .30-caliber Brownings with 500 rpg were located in the front turret, rear cockpit, and lower tunnel position. The bomb bay could accommodate two 1,130, three 624, or five 300-pound bombs, and accuracy was improved by provisions for the very secret Norden Mk XV bombsights that the Army began receiving via the Navy in April 1933. An external shackle could be fitted under the right wing for a 2,000-pound bomb.

The first Martin off the production line, a YB-10, was delivered to Wright Field in November 1933 with 675-hp R-1820-17 Cyclones; 14 YB-10s had been delivered by April 1934. They can be distinguished from their successors by an air intake atop the engine cowling. A single YB-l0A delivered in June 1934 had experimental turbo-supercharged R-1820-31 Cyclones, and top speed increased from 202 mph at 10,000 feet to 236 mph at 25,000 feet. This Cyclone-supercharger combination, after much development, would become standard for all the B-17s built after 1938.

MARTIN YB-l0A
Two Wright R-1820-31, 675 hp
DIMENSIONS: As YB-10
WEIGHT: Empty 8139 1b., Gross 13,212 lb. Fuel 230-456 gal.
PERFORMANCE: Speed- Top 178 mph at s.l., 202 mph at 10,000', 236 mph at 25,000', Climb 10,000'/7.1 min.

Pratt & Whitney Hornets of 700 hp were used on seven YB-12 and 25 YB-12A models, the first appearing in February 1934, with the air intakes on the nacelle's port side. These intakes were on top, behind the cowl, on the B-12As, first seen in June 1934 and introducing provisions for increasing fuel tankage to 580 gallons and sealed flotation compartments in the wings. A plan for a dozen YB-13s with R-1860-17 Hornet Bs was canceled, but one XB-14 in May 1934 introduced the Twin Wasp, YR-1830-1, which would become the power plant for World War II's B-24 bombers.

MARTIN YB-12 AF
Two Pratt & Whitney R-1690-11, 700 hp at 6500'
DIMENSIONS: Span 70'6", Lg. 45'3", Ht. 11', Wing Area 678 sq. ft.
WEIGHT: Empty 7745 lb., Gross 12,829 lb. Fuel 230-456 gal.
PERFORMANCE: Speed- Top 190 mph at s.1., 212 mph at 6500', Cruising 182 mph, Landing 71 mph. Service Ceiling 24,600', Absolute Ceiling 26,600'. Climb 1740'/1 min., 10,000'/10.1 min. Range 524 miles/2260 lb. bombs, 1360 miles max.

MARTIN B-12A

Adapting the Martin to a multi-seat fighter, of the style then favored in France, was discussed in March 1933. Gun turrets fore and aft, along with a retractable belly turret, were considered. Later, XA-15 attack and XO-45 observation versions of the YB-10 were proposed, but these were also dropped from plans. One B-12A was fitted with twin floats to set a seaplane speed record on August 24, 1935.

MARTIN XB-14
Two Pratt & Whitney YR-1830-1, 800 hp at 7500'; (later R-1830-9, 950 hp takeoff, 850 hp at 8000')
DIMENSIONS: As YB-12
WEIGHT: Empty 8467 lb., Gross 13,560 lb. Fuel 230-456 gal.
PERFORMANCE: Speed- Top 190 mph at s.1., 222.5 mph at 7900', Cruising 191 mph. Climb 1640'/1 min. Range 575 miles/2260 lb. bombs, 1210 miles/456 gal.

Most of the Martins were based at March Field, California. Ten YB-l0s demonstrated their serviceability with a survey flight to Alaska in July 1934, and then the YB-10s remained at March for the 19th Bomb Group. In December 1934 the Hornet-powered B-12/12A versions went with the 7th Bomb Group to the new Hamilton Field near San Francisco.

The main production version was the B-l0B, with 750-hp R-1820-23 Cyclones, intakes atop the nacelle, and behind them the exhaust pipes that were moved from the lower nacelle. A June 28, 1934, contract for 81 B-l0Bs was later increased to 103, with two more assembled by the Army from spare parts. The first B-l0B arrived at Wright Field in July 1935, where it remained for type tests, and quantity deliveries to Langley Field began in December 1935, at a cost of $55,299 each. The last B-10B from Martin was completed on August 8, 1936.

Martins reached all Army bomber groups, which in 1936 included the 2nd Bomb Group at Langley and the 9th at Mitchel Field with B-l0Bs on the East coast, and the 7th (B-l0B and B-12) and l9th (YB-10 and B-l0B) in California.

MARTIN B-10B
Two Wright R-1820-33, 775 hp takeoff, 750 hp at 5400'
DIMENSIONS: Span 70'6", Lg. 45'3", Ht. 11'6", Wing Area 678 sq. ft.
WEIGHT: Empty 9450 lb., Gross 14,621 lb., Max. 16,400 lb. Fuel 226-452 gal. (702 gal. ferry).
PERFORMANCE: Speed- Top 196 mph at s.1., 213 mph at 10,000', Cruising 188 mph, Landing 65 mph. Service Ceiling 24,400', Climb 10,000'/7 min. Range 590 miles normal, 1240 miles (overload)/2260 lb. bombs, 1830 miles ferry.

Most of the B-12As went to Hawaii's 5th Composite Group in 1936. When Douglas B-18s began arriving in 1937, B-l0Bs became available to fill out the 6th Composite Group in the Canal Zone, and the last squadron to get B-l0Bs was the 28th in the Philippines, where they were used until 1940. By that time most stateside Martins were relegated to target-towing and utility work, and designated B-10M.

With such a performance record, winning export orders would be easy, but the Army forbade release of the Martin bomber until its own deliveries were complete. In the meantime, attempts at export sales were made by less advanced designs.

The Curtiss-Wright BT-32 was a bomber version of the Condor transport armed with five .30-caliber guns and up to 3,940 pounds of bombs. The last large biplane built in the U.S., the BT-32 had two R-1820-F2 Cyclones, retractable wheels, and a fabric-covered steel tube structure. The pilots sat in the nose of the cabin with a dome for a top gunner before the wings and behind them were guns in another top dome, at side windows, and a bottom hatch for the rear gunner. The bomb bay could hold two 1,130, three 600, or six 300-pound bombs, and up to fourteen 120-pound bombs could be added on racks under the wings

Completed on February 9, 1934, the demonstration aircraft went to China and was sold to Chiang Kai-shek. Three Condors delivered in June 1934 with twin floats became the first bombers sold to Colombia. Four more, built for Bolivia before a trade embargo, became transports in Peru. Most of the 45 Condors built in St. Louis were passenger or cargo planes that were soon displaced by faster Douglas monoplanes.

Colombia was the only buyer of the Bellanca 77-140, a bulky fabric-covered, high-wing monoplane with R-1820-F3 Cyclones, externally-braced, squared-off wings, and fixed landing gear at the intersection of stub wings and struts. Armament included 2,500 pounds of bombs and five .30-caliber guns located in the nose pit, and at top, bottom, and side openings in the cabin. Unlike the Martin, there was room inside the cabin for cargo or a dozen people along with the four-man crew. The first example had wheels and a nose gunner's turret in September 1934. Three with twin floats and open gunner's pit flew to Colombia by March 1935, fire destroyed another.

Glenn L. Martin was finally allowed to offer an export version of the B-10 and the first was a single Model 139WR (X16706) sold to Russia in November 1935 for

NASM

CURTISS-WRIGHT CONDOR BT-32 for China
Two Wright R-1820F-2, 720 hp at 4000'
DIMENSIONS: Span 82', Lg. 49'6", Ht. 16'4" Wing Area l276 sq. ft.
WEIGHT: Empty 11,233 lb., Gross 17,500 lb. Fuel 447-728 gal.
PERFORMANCE: Speed- Top 176 mph at 4100', Cruising 161 mph, Landing 58 mph. Service Ceiling 22,000', Absolute Ceiling 24,200', Climb 1290'/1 min. Range 840 miles/2260 lb. bombs, 1400 miles max.

SDAM

CURTISS-WRIGHT CONDOR BT-32 seaplane for Colombia

Mfr

BELLANCA 77-140
Two Wright R-1820F-3, 715 hp at 7000'
DIMENSIONS: Span 76', Lg. 40', Ht. 14', Wing Area 770 sq ft.
WEIGHT: Empty 8216 lb., Gross 14,136 lb., Max. 16,333 lb. Fuel 300-635 gal.
PERFORMANCE: Speed- Top 190 mph at 7000', Cruising 172 mph, Landing 58 mph. Service Ceiling 23,500', Absolute Ceiling 25,000', Climb 1200'/1 min., 6500'/5.5 min. Range 710 miles normal, 1500 miles max.

$116,718. Finished in August 1936 and shipped in September, it had GR-1820-F53 Cyclones of 730 hp at 9,600 feet and Hamilton propellers.

NASM

BELLANCA 77-140 seaplane for Colombia
Two Wright R-1820F-3, 715 hp at 7000'
DIMENSIONS: Span 76', Lg. 45'2", Ht. 16'5", Wing Area 770 sq ft.
WEIGHT: Empty 9362 lb., Gross 15,282 lb., Max. 17,749 lb. Fuel 300-680 gal.
PERFORMANCE: Speed- Top 175 mph at 7000', Cruising 165 mph, Landing 58 mph. Service Ceiling 19,000', Absolute Ceiling 21,500', Climb 950'/1 min., Range 1500 miles max.

SDAM

MARTIN 139-WR for Russia

Ramon Franco, a famous Spanish pilot, had favorably recommended the Martin after visiting America, and in January 1936 his government was negotiating a contract for 50 bombers, the first eight to be completed by Martin and the rest in Spain. Approval of this deal in Spain was delayed by the Popular Front's election victory, and the revolt led by Franco's brother, Francisco, began in July. On August 11, 1936, the U.S. State Department blocked the sale, so the Spanish Republicans had to match the rebel's German and Italian aircraft with those from the Soviet Union. Tupolev SB bombers used in the Spanish Civil War were often incorrectly described as Martins, although they are quite different aircraft.

NASM

MARTIN 139-WA demonstrator

Martin was willing to forget the Spanish order because others were arriving, beginning with 13 ordered by the Netherlands on February 27, 1936. Orders from China and Siam followed that summer.

A demonstrator (NR 15563) with R-1820-G2 Cyclones (850 hp at 5,800 feet) was first flown August 28, 1936, by E.D. Shannon, who flew this aircraft to Argentina in September to compete against the Junkers Ju 86 and Savoia SM-79B. The Martin won, Argentina buying 13 bombers for the Navy on December 24, 1936.

The first Dutch Martins, Model 139WH-1, were completed from September 5, 1936, to February 2, 1937, with GR-1820-F53 Cyclones They were shipped across the Pacific to the Netherlands East Indies, now called Indonesia.

Six Martin 139WCs with the R-1820-G3 of 840 hp at 8,700 feet and Curtiss propellers, went to China in February 1937. Used by China's 30th Squadron, they became the first American-designed twin-engine bombers to enter combat, with an attack on Japanese vessels on August 25, 1937. Five were lost while on the ground to bombing raids, while the last was shot down on October 22 by an enemy fighter.

Three more Martins arrived after the war began and were used in February 1938 by American pilots of China's 14th Squadron. Two Martins were defiantly flown over Japan by Chinese crews on the night of May 19-20, 1938. At that range, only propaganda leaflets could be dropped on Nagasaki.

NASM

MARTIN 139WC for China
Two Wright R-1820-G3, 875 hp at takeoff, 840 hp at 8700'
DIMENSIONS: Span 70'6", Lg. 44'9", Ht. 11'5", Wing Area 678 sq. ft.
WEIGHT: Empty 9727 lb., Gross 14,995 lb. Max. 16,455 lb. Fuel 226-452 gal.
PERFORMANCE: Speed- Top 198 mph at s.l., 230 mph at 8700', Cruising 200 mph, Landing 65 mph. Service Ceiling 24,300', Climb 10,000'/6.6 min. Range 1350 miles.

Less eventful was the service of some other Martins sold aboard. These included six completed for Siam between March 5 and April 26, 1937, with R-1820-G3 Cyclones and 20 finished for Turkey from July to September 1937.

The Argentine Navy's 13 Model 139WANs with the R-1820-G2 were delivered by November 13, 1937, and an additional 26 for the Army with the R-1820-G3 were delivered by April 1938. One of the former was returned to the U.S. in 1976 to be refurbished for the Air Force Museum, and is on exhibit.

But the largest, first and last customer for the Martin export bomber was the Netherlands East Indies, whose rich oil fields were threatened by Japanese expansion. The first of the 121 Dutch Martins were the 13 139WH-1 bombers, followed by 26 Model 139WH-2s, powered by R-1820-G3s, added from November 1937 to March 1938.

The last version of the Martin bomber appeared in May 1938 as the 139WH-3, or Model 166, as it was described in advertising. Refined streamlining included a rounded nose, and a long unbroken canopy from the pilot's cockpit to the rear pit, while two external racks increased the bomb load to 4,400 pounds. The first 40 built with 900-hp R-1820-G5 Cyclones were followed by 40 139WH-3As with 1,000-hp R-1820-G105As. These were completed by May 5, 1939. Two replacements were added in February 1940, bringing the total to 192 Martin bombers built for export and 154 for the Army Air Corps.

NASM

MARTIN 166 (139WH-3) for the Dutch East Indies
Two Wright R-1820G-105A, 1,200 hp at takeoff, 1000 hp at 6890'
DIMENSIONS: Span 70'10", Lg. 44'9", Ht. 11'6", Wing Area 682 sq. ft.
WEIGHT: Empty 10,322 lb., Gross 15,624 lb. Max. 18,825 lb. Fuel 296-512+250 gal.
PERFORMANCE: Speed- Top 241 mph at 9850', Cruising 186 mph, Landing 68 mph. Service Ceiling 28,215', Climb 9850'/4.9 min. Range 1590 miles max.

Company specifications for the export models cited here may be viewed as optimistic, compared to the rigorous measurement of the Air Corps test results given here for the Army bombers.

Six Martin squadrons served in the Indies when Japan attacked and on December 17, 1941, they began strikes on advancing Japanese ships and landing forces. Severe losses were suffered from the fast and heavily-armed Zero fighters, whose development made the Martin's speed and protection inadequate. A surviving Martin 166 fled to Australia on March 7, 1942, and was taken over by the Americans as a utility aircraft. Nine Dutch Martins captured by Japan were given to Thailand.

Four-engine Bombers, 1935-1939

As early as July 1933, Wright Field engineers had studied the problem of maximum range with a one-ton bomb load. When a 5000-mile range seemed possible, the Air Corps prepared "Project A", a proposal to build such a plane. A request for design proposals was issued April 14, 1934, and the responses were Boeing's Model 294 and Martin's

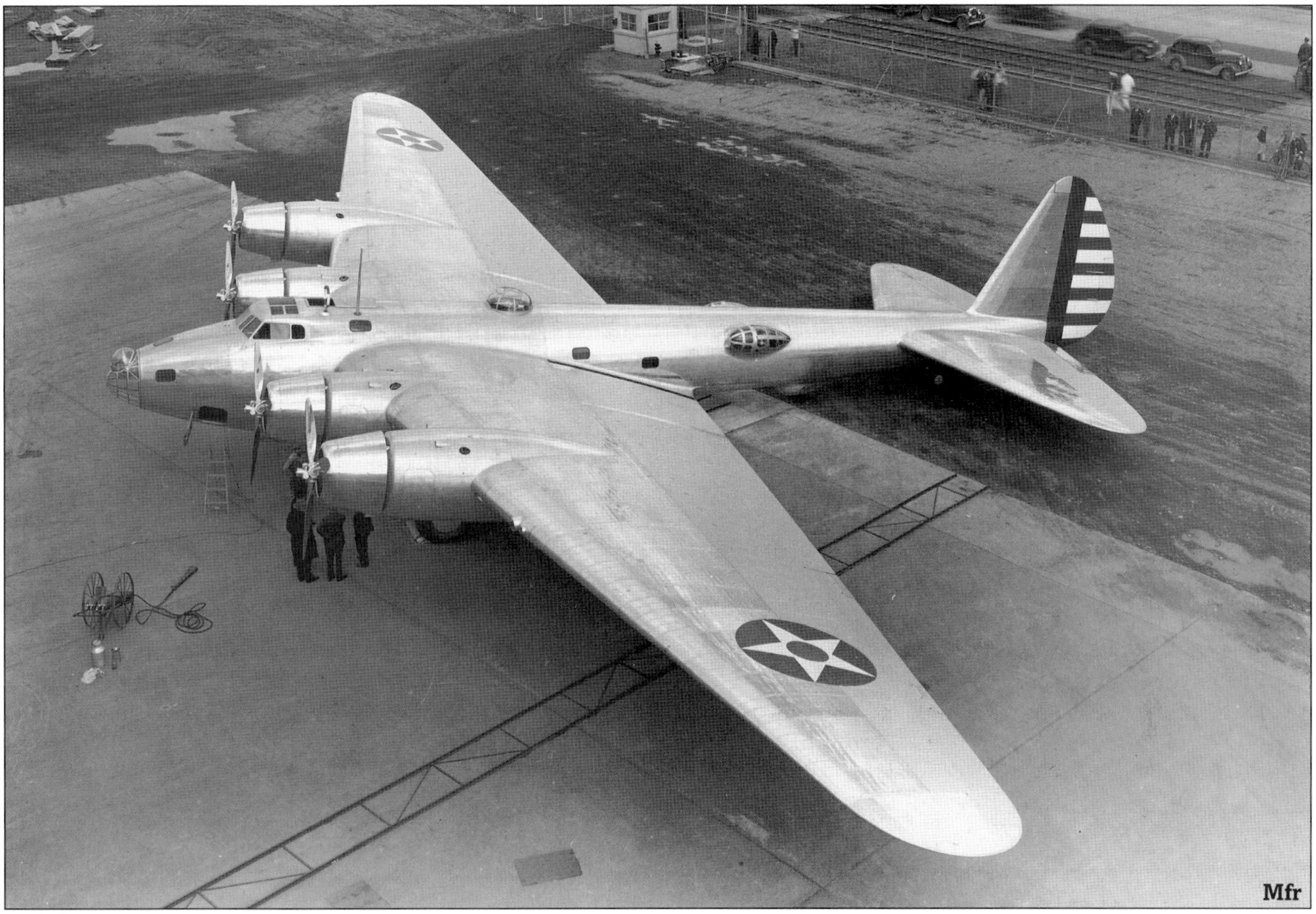

BOEING XB-15
Four Pratt & Whitney R-1830-11, 1000 hp takeoff, 850 hp at 6000'
DIMENSIONS: Span 149', Lg. 87'11" Ht. 18'5", Wing Area 2781 sq. ft.
WEIGHT: Empty 37,709 lb., Gross 65,068 lb., Max. 70,700 lb. Fuel 3350-4260 gal.
PERFORMANCE: Speed- Top 200 mph at 6000', Cruising 170 mph, Landing 70 mph. Service Ceiling 18,850', Absolute Ceiling 20,900', Climb 5000'/7.1 min., 10,000'/14.9 min. Range 3300 miles/2496 lb. bombs, 4000 miles max.

Mfr

The BOEING XB-15
It was the world's largest bomber from 1937 to 1941.

Model 145. Negotiations with Boeing and Martin for preliminary designs began at Wright Field on May 14, 1934.

Both projects originally planned to use four new Allison V-1710 inline engines expected to provide 1,000 hp, and became the Boeing XB-15 and Martin XB-16. Martin's first proposal had the engines buried within the 140-foot span wing with extension drive shafts turning the four propellers. The 32-ton low-wing monoplane offered twin rudders and a tail gunner, a new idea for American bombers.

By 1935, the Martin XB-16 became enlarged to a 173-foot span, 52-ton high-wing monoplane with six Allison V-1710-3 engines: four as tractors, and two as pushers. The twin rudders were out on twin tail booms, and tricycle landing gear was proposed, but this giant was far too expensive for the Air Corps budget.

However, Boeing's design won a contract on June 28, 1934, for design data, wind tunnel tests, and a mockup. Boeing proposed four 1,000-hp Pratt & Whitney R-1830-11 Twin Wasps, an air-cooled power plant much nearer to practical service than the Allison. On June 29, 1935, a contract was approved for Boeing to build the XB-15 as a 149-foot span, 35-ton monoplane. It was known for a while as the XBLR-l (Experimental Bomber, Long Range).

The designs prepared by these firms were heroic in size compared with the existing American bombers, but developments abroad already included such four-engine monoplanes as the Tupolev TB-3 in Soviet mass production and the Mitsubishi Ki-20 bomber tested in Japan. The Tupolev six-engine 177-foot span TB-4 bomber had been flown July 3, 1933, and the eight-engine 210-foot span ANT-20 transport was flown June 17, 1934, at Moscow.

By the time XB-15 construction began, Boeing had nearly finished the prototype of Model 299, which as the

B-17, would become the first Air Corps strategic bomber in production. The XB-15 itself would take much longer to build and made its first flight on October 15, 1937, as the largest aircraft then built in America.

The XB-15's wing was thick enough to have passageways in the leading edge out to the engines. Double wheels and two ailerons on each wing testified to the weight. The ten crewmen included a flight engineer and had "soundproofed, heated, and ventilated" quarters with four rest bunks, kitchen and lavatory, and, for the first time in an airplane, small auxiliary engines operated a 110-volt electrical system. All-metal construction was used, except for fabric covering aft of the rear wing spar and on all movable control surfaces.

Armament was the strongest then found on a bomber: three .30-caliber and three heavy .50-caliber guns. A nose turret with a 180-degree field of fire, a top turret rotating 360 degrees, and a rearward-facing ventral blister had the .50-caliber guns, with the lighter guns in a forward-facing blister below the pilot's cabin, and two waist blisters behind the wings. Every approach to the ship was covered except directly behind the huge tail – a weakness common to all U.S. bombers of that decade.

Strategically, the most important facts about the XB-15 was its 3,300 mile range with four 624-pound bombs, not only much greater than any other bomber, but enough to fly from Guam to Japan and back, dropping something heavier and noisier than the leaflets sprinkled by Chiang's Martins. Maximum capacity, including bays in the wing roots, allowed thirty 300, fourteen 624, or eight 1,130-pound bombs.

The XB-15 joined the 2nd Bomb Group's 49th Bomb Squadron in August 1938, and in 1939 set world records for payload distance and altitude. In 1941, the giant was converted to a cargo carrier, redesignated XC-105 on May 6, 1943, and served the Sixth (Caribbean) Air Force until it was dismantled in 1945. The large wing design was used on the Boeing 314 flying boats, and much of its experience would contribute to the B-19 and B-29 designs. It was underpowered for its size, but this was expected to be corrected in Boeing's YB-20, planned as an improved B-15 with 1,400-hp engines.

The most important four-engine bomber of the period, however, was Boeing's Flying Fortress, which led the strategic bombing offensive against Germany. For the Air Corps, the B-17 story started with a specification for a "multi-engine four to six place" bomber to replace the B-10.

Dated July 18, 1934, this specification stated the desired performance should include a top speed of 250 mph at 10,000 feet, a ten-hour endurance at cruising speed, a 25,000-foot service ceiling, and double the B-10's bomb capacity; minimum requirements were 200 mph and a 1,020-mile range. Interested aircraft builders were to produce prototypes at their own expense to compete for a production contract in August 1935.

When Boeing received this proposal on August 8, 1934, company president Clairmont Egtvedt made certain that "multi-engine" also permitted four, as well as two, power plants. A design study for a four-engine bomber, Model 299, was already underway, based on experience with the 247 transport and the Project A long-range bomber. Half-way in size between the B-10 and the B-15, Model 299 promised performance far beyond that which any twin-engine design could achieve. On September 26, the company's directors agreed to take the risk, which eventually required over $641,000. The Project Engineer was E. Gifford Emery until 1935, when his assistant, Edward C. Wells, became Project Engineer. He was then 24 years old, and in charge of the most important airplane of its time. It has been a long time since young men have been given such responsibility in the aviation industry.

First flown on July 28, 1935, four months after Hitler renounced the Versailles Pact and officially announced German rearmament, the Boeing 299 had four 750-hp Pratt & Whitney R-1690 Hornets on its low wing and could carry 2,500 pounds of bombs 2,040 miles. Immediately recognized as the most advanced bomber yet built, its nonstop delivery flight on August 20 from Seattle to Wright Field, covering 2,100 miles at 233 mph, attracted national attention. The eight-place 299 had five enclosed positions for .30-caliber guns. A nose turret could cover the whole forward hemisphere, while teardrop blisters studded the top, bottom and sides of the rear fuselage.

MARTIN 146
Two Wright R-1870G-5, 800 hp at 10,000'
DIMENSIONS: Span 75', Lg. 48'2", Wing Area 734 sq. ft.
WEIGHT: Empty 10,943 lb., Gross 16,000 lb., Max. 17,100 lb. Fuel 404 gal.
PERFORMANCE: Speed- Top 204 mph at s.1., 234 mph at 13,500', Cruising 170 mph. Service Ceiling 28,500'. Range 1237 miles normal, 1589 miles max.

Martin and Douglas also sent prototypes to Wright Field for the opening of bids and trials in August 1935. The Martin 146 was an enlarged B-10, with two Wright R-1820-G5 Cyclones and a wider fuselage to accommodate a larger bomb load and crew compartment with side-by-side pilot and co-pilot seats. To handle the increased landing weight, the usual trailing edge split flaps were replaced by introducing Fowler flaps that were extended behind the wing.

What was done with the Martin after the competition is not known, but Glenn L. Martin wrote the Secretary of War, complaining that despite the lowest bids and his $350,000 investment in the prototype, he had won no contract. The Fowler flaps, however, appeared on most wartime American bombers like the B-24 and B-29.

The Douglas DB-1 bore a family resemblance to that firm's DC-3 transports, even to a cabin with bunks on which the six-man crew might rest. Two Wright R-1820-G12

DOUGLAS DB-l (B-18 prototype)
Two Wright SR-1820G-12, 850 hp at 9000'
DIMENSIONS: Span 89'7", Lg. 57'3", Ht. 15'4", Wing Area 959 sq. ft.
WEIGHT. Empty 14,806 lb., Gross 20,159 lb. Fuel 204-802 gal.
PERFORMANCE: Speed— Top 220 mph at 10,000', Cruising 173 mph, Landing 62 mph. Service Ceiling 25,000', Climb 10,000'/8.8 min. Range 1034 miles/2260 lb. bombs.

Cyclones powered this mid-wing monoplane, which was armed with three .30-caliber guns. One was in a "birdcage" nose-turret like the Martin, a second fired through a trap-door in the floor at the rear, while the third was in a retractable, fully-rotating turret just ahead of the tail. A 2,260-pound bomb load could be carried only about half the distance of the Boeing competitor, and with less speed.

Quantity or Quality?

In spite of the prototype's destruction on October 30, in a crash due to pilot error, the Air Corps recommended adoption of the Boeing 299. Although airmen enthusiastically greeted the advanced performance, the Army's General Staff was concerned with economy. Prices quoted per ship (exclusive of engines), in lots of 25 and 220 were as follows: Martin, $85,910 and $48,880; Douglas $99,150 and $58,500; and Boeing $196,730 and $99,620. Operating under budgetary limitations, the Air Corps recommended purchase of 65 B-17s instead of 185 other aircraft authorized. The General Staff preferred quantity to quality, and contracts made in 1936 called for only 13 four-engine Boeing YB-17s and 133 twin-engine Douglas B-18s.

BOEING 299
Four Pratt & Whitney R-1690 S1EG, 750 hp at 7000'
DIMENSIONS: Span 103'9", Lg. 68'9', Ht. 15', Wing Area 1420 sq. ft.
WEIGHT: Empty 22,125 lb., Gross 34,432 lb., Max. 38,053 lb. Fuel 1700 gal.
PERFORMANCE: Speed- Top 236 mph at 10,000', Cruising 204 mph. Service Ceiling 24,620'. Range 2040 miles/2573 lb. bombs, 3010 miles max.

The first production versions of Boeing's Flying Fortress were the 13 YB-17s ordered, with a static test airframe, on January 17, 1936. Wright R-1820-39 Cyclones, rated at 775 hp at 14,000 feet, replaced the prototype's Hornets, and Cyclones remained standard on all future production B-17s. The landing gear and turret structure were simplified, and a long carburetor intake on top of the engine nacelles distinguished these aircraft from later models. Designated YB-17 at first, they became the YlB-17, and later just plain B-17.

Armament included five .30-caliber guns with 1,000 rpg, and room in the bomb bay for eight 600, four 1,100, or two 2,000-pound bombs, or two 396-gallon ferry tanks.* Top speed was 256 mph and range was 2,260 miles, with a normal load of 2,500 pounds of bombs and 850 gallons of fuel. Range in overload condition (4,000 pounds of bombs and 1,700 gallons) was 2,400 miles, or with 2,492 gallons and no bombs, 3,320 miles.

BOEING YB-17
Four Wright R-1820-39, 930 hp takeoff, 775 hp at 14,000'
DIMENSIONS: Span 103'9", Lg. 68'4", Ht. 19'3", Wing Area 1420 sq. ft.
WEIGHT: Empty 24,458 lb., Gross 34,873 lb., Max. 42,600 lb. Fuel 1700+792 gal.
PERFORMANCE: Speed- Top 256 mph at 14,000', Cruising 217 mph, Landing 72 mph. Service Ceiling 30,600', Climb 10,000'/6.5 min. Range 2260 miles/2500 lb. bombs and 850 gal., 1377 miles/10,400 lb. bombs, 3320 miles max.

This performance was the best of any heavy bomber in the world, and the Air Corps lost no opportunities to display its new weapon. The first YlB-17 was flown on December 2, 1936, and by January 11 was at Wright Field where it remained as the test example, as was the customary use of the first production aircraft. Langley Field received the other twelve from March 1 to August 4, 1937, and they served alongside the B-10Bs and B-18s of the 2nd Bomb Group. Over three years of vigorous flying without a serious accident, proved the B-17s practical weapons and they were transferred to the 19th Bomb Group at March Field by October 1940.

*The actual bomb weights were 624, 1,130, and 2,030 pounds respectively, but contemporary documentation used the approximations. New standard, Army-Navy (AN) sizes, including 500 & 1,000 pounds, were adopted in 1942.

DOUGLAS B-18
Two Wright R-1820-45, 930 hp takeoff, 810 hp at 10,300'
DIMENSIONS: Span 8'6", Lg. 56'8", Ht. 15'2", Wing Area 959 sq. ft.
WEIGHT: Empty 15,719 lb., Gross 21,130 1b. Max. 27,087 lb.
Fuel 802+368 gal.
PERFORMANCE: Speed- Top 217 mph at 10,000', Cruising 170 mph, Landing 64 mph. Service Ceiling 24,200', Absolute Ceiling 25,850', Climb 1355'/l min., 10,000'/9.1 min. Range 1082 miles/418 gal. with 2260 lb. bombs, 1200 miles/4000 lb. (Max. load), 2225 miles ferry.

Douglas Bombers, 1936-1942

The most widely used Air Corps bomber when World War II began was the Douglas B-18. Its acceptance was due to its low cost and reliable airline-type flying qualities, rather than its performance. Essentially, army leadership represented by the Chief of Staff and the Secretary of War, had rejected the strategic bombing idea. The B-18's role was seen as coast defense, for which a greater number of twin-engine aircraft seemed more helpful than a smaller number of expensive four-engine B-17s.

While the defensive armament was completely inadequate for wartime conditions, three .30-caliber guns were also what was carried by foreign bombers like the Heinkel He 111, Mitsubishi G3M, or Ilyushin DB-3. A normal load of 2,260 pounds of bombs and 418 gallons of fuel could take the B-18 1,082 miles with a modest 217-mph top speed. When in overload condition, the bomb bay could contain six 600, four 1,100, or two 2,000-pound bombs with 802 gallons for a 1,200-mile range, or two 184-gallon ferry tanks could be substituted.

A contract made January 28, 1936, for 82 B-18s, was increased to 132 by June, and the prototype DB-l was brought up to production standard and also purchased by the Air Corps in September 1936. The first true production B-18 arrived at Wright on February 23, 1937.

The Douglas DB-2 was actually a B-18 airframe fitted with the power-driven nose turret and large bombardier's enclosure designed for the XB-l9. After lengthy factory tests, it arrived at Wright Field November 8, 1937, and was eventually accepted as the last aircraft on the B-18 contract and rebuilt to standard configuration. Another armament experiment was the installation of a 75-mm M1897 cannon in the bomb bay of the B-18 prototype in August 1939, which led to the use of cannon on the A-26B and B-25G in 1943.

DOUGLAS DB-2 (Last B-18, with power turret)

A competing bomber design was begun January 13, 1936, by North American Aviation as the NA-21 "Dragon" and first flown December 22, 1936. Powered by two 1,200 hp Pratt & Whitney R-2180-1 Twin Hornets with F-10 turbosuperchargers first atop the nacelles, and then at the sides, this six-place mid-wing monoplane had a .50-caliber gun mounted in a hydraulic-powered ball-turret in the nose, another turret on top near the rear, and three .30-caliber guns at transparent panels in waist and ventral positions. Two 1,100-pound bombs could be carried 1,960 miles, or eight 1,100-pound bombs for a 660-mile range.

The NA-21 arrived at Wright Field in March 1937, but once again price was a competition factor, for North American had bid $122,600 each in quantities of 50, while cost savings due to previous production enabled Douglas to cut B-18A unit bids to $63,977. Beset by power plant problems, including superchargers that didn't work, limiting high altitude performance, the NA-21 was reworked in October 1937 and returned to the Air Corps as the XB-21 in May 1938. A plan to build five more for service tests was dropped.

AF

NORTH AMERICAN XB-21 (NA-21)
Two Pratt & Whitney R-2180-1, 1200 hp takeoff, 1000 hp at 9700'
DIMENSIONS: Span 95', Lg. 61', Ht. 14'9", Wing Area 1120 sq. ft.
WEIGHT: Empty 19,082 lb., Gross 27,253 lb., Max. 40,000 lb. Fuel 600-2400 gal.
PERFORMANCE: Speed— Top 220 mph at 10,000', Cruising 196 mph. Service Ceiling 25,000', Climb 10,000'/10 min. Range 1960 miles/2200 lb. bombs, 660 miles/10,000 lb. bombs, 3100 miles max.

Although Air Corps leaders wanted to buy B-17s instead of twin-engine bombers, the War Department insisted on the smaller and cheaper type. Douglas received the largest contract yet for 177 B-18As on June 10, 1937, and on June 30, 1938, 78 additional bombers (completed as 40 B-18A and 38 B-23) were added. Changes in the neat Douglas nose had been ordered on October 11, 1937, to give more visibility and comfort to the bombardier, whose position was hardly usable if the front turret was manned. This resulted in the B-18A's unusual nasal arrangement in which the bombardier sat above and ahead of the bow gunner. First flown April 15, 1938, 217 B-18As had R-1820-53 Cyclones and a dome top on the rear turret.

The Army's last B-18A was delivered February 22, 1940. Air Corps B-18 and B-18A bombers mingled in all four bomber groups in the U.S., each of which had four squadrons by 1940, one designated as reconnaissance. Hawaii's 5th Group got 40 B-18s in 1938, the Canal Zone's 6th got 34 in 1939, and finally the 28th Squadron in the Philippines was given 18 B-18s in 1941.

Canada ordered 20 B-18As for the RCAF, which named them the Digby. The Army opposed naming its aircraft until October 1941, when the B-18 was christened the Bolo. Actually, Americans continued to prefer the old type number designation. The first two Digbys were flown on December 18, 1939, from Santa Monica to the Canadian border, where the current neutrality law required that they be towed across the border (by farm horses!). The last Digbys were accepted on March 26,1940, and served with No. 10 Squadron based in Newfoundland to defend Canada's coast.. One made the first attack on a U-boat in

Mitchell

DOUGLAS B-18A
Two Wright R-1820-53, 1000 hp takeoff, 850 hp at 9,600'
DIMENSIONS: Span 89'6", Lg. 57'10", Ht. 15'2", Wing Area 959 sq. ft.
WEIGHT: Empty 16,321 lb., Gross 22,123 1b. Max. 27,673 lb. Fuel 802+368 gal.
PERFORMANCE: Speed— Top 215 mph at 10,000', Cruising 167 mph, Landing 68 mph. Service Ceiling 23,900', 10,000'/ 9.9 min. Range 1100 miles/4000 lb., 2100 miles ferry.

American waters on October 26, 1941. It was unsuccessful, but on October 30, 1942, a Digby sank the *U-520.*

As expansion multiplied the Army's bomber groups in 1941, the Douglas bombers were scattered about for training purposes. When war came, they were far too obsolete for combat, except in one manner. The first American experiment with airborne radar was on a B-18 first flown with an SCR-268 on November 4, 1940, and with an AI-10 on a B-18A flown March 10, 1941.

An anti-submarine version, the B-18B, with SCR-517 radar in the nose and magnetic airborne detection gear in the tail, was converted from 122 B-18As. Their monotonous patrols were occasionally interrupted, in the Caribbean, with several engagements with surfaced submarines. On one of these, the B-18B was shot down, but on August 22, 1942, another B-18B sank *U-654* near the Panama Canal, and a B-18B also sank *U-512* on October 2, 1942.

AF

DOUGLAS B-18B

Douglas had plans to improve their twin-engine design at first as the B-22, a B-18A with new R-2600-1 Cyclone engines. This project was superseded in November 1938 by the B-23, which had 1,600-hp Wright R-2600-3 Cyclones and a new streamlined fuselage incorporating the latest ideas in armament. It was thought that the 282-mph top speed reduced the threat of frontal attacks, so the bow turret of earlier years was replaced by a simple plastic nose with a flat bombardier's panel, and a ball-and-socket mount for a .30-caliber gun. Another .30 was placed on a floor ring while a waist gun could be fired by opening side and top windows. The first Air Corps tail gunner had a .50-caliber gun and telescopic sight with a narrow 40-degree cone of fire. Up to four 1,100-pound bombs were carried.

BOEING YB-17A
Four Wright R-1820-51, 1000 hp takeoff, 800 hp. at 25,000'
DIMENSIONS: Span 103'9", Lg. 68'4", Ht. 19'3", Wing Area 1420 sq. ft.
WEIGHT: Empty 26,520 lb., Gross 37,000 lb., Max. 45,650 lb. Fuel 1700+792 gal.
PERFORMANCE: Speed- Top 295 mph at 25,000', Cruising 230 mph, Landing 78 mph. Service Ceiling 38,000', Climb 10,000'/7.8 min. Range 2400 miles/4000 lb. bombs, 3600 miles max.

There was no B-23 prototype, as they had been ordered as part of the B-18A contract, so the first B-23 was flown by Douglas July 27, 1939, and arrived at Wright on October 14th. The remaining 37 were delivered from February 11 to September 20, 1940. Aside from test ships, 13 went to Maxwell Field, and 18 to McChord Field for the 17th Bomb Group, until that group got new B-25s and the B-23s were passed on to the 12th Bomb Group. In no case did they see combat, but about 15 were converted to UC-67 transports, 11 others were fitted with C-5 tow target gear, and after the war, most B-23s were modified to civilian executive transports.

DOUGLAS B-23
Two Wright R-2600-3, 1600 hp takeoff, 1275 hp at 12,000'
DIMENSIONS: Span 92', Lg. 58'4", Ht. 18'6", Wing Area 993 sq. ft.
WEIGHT: Empty 19,089 lb., Gross 26,500 lb., Max. 31,199 lb. Fuel 870-1290 gal.
PERFORMANCE: Speed- Top 282 mph at 12,000', Cruising 225 mph, Landing 80 mph. Service Ceiling 31,600', Climb 10,000'/6.7 min. Range 1400 miles/4000 lb. bombs, 2750 miles ferry.

Strategic Bombers Advance in Performance

Four-engine bombers were what Air Corps leaders really wanted, and the GHQ Air Force Commander, General Frank Andrews, had urged the War Department on June 1, 1937, that all future bombers bought should be four-engine, since enough B-18s were on order already. He favored only two bomber types; the heavy bomber for long-range missions, and the attack-bomber for close support. Bombers were seen as the basic element of air power and as vital to the nation as land or sea power.

Constant improvement of performance was needed if strategic bombing was to become a reality and the exhaust-driven turbosupercharger, developed over the years, offered the main chance of improving the B-17. The static test airframe of the first contract was chosen for completion with turbosuperchargers on May 12, 1937.

Designated YIB-17A, it made its first flight on April 29, 1938, with the turbos installed on top of the nacelles. When this system proved unworkable, they were moved to the bottom and the reworked aircraft flown again on November 20. This time the system worked so well and improved performance so much that turbos became standard on the B-17B and all future B-17 models.

The B-17B also had R-1820-51 Cyclones giving 800 hp up to 25,000 feet, and a new, cleaner, nose better accommodating the bombardier. The nose turret was replaced by a short transparency with the flat bomb-aiming panel, formerly in a fuselage cutout, and a simple socket for a .30-caliber flexible gun. The flaps were enlarged, a plastic dome for the navigator added to the cabin roof, and external bomb racks could be added to increase the capacity another 4,000 pounds if needed.

While the first B-17B contract on August 3, 1937, called for ten aircraft, by June 30, 1938, the total was increased to 38, each costing $251,178. Boeing flew the first June 27, 1939, and delivered the last March 30, 1940. They served with the 2nd, 7th, and 19th Groups except for

BOEING B-17B
Four Wright R-1820-51, 1000 hp takeoff, 800 hp. at 25,000'
DIMENSIONS: Span 103'9", Lg. 67'11", Ht. 15'5", Wing Area 1420 sq. ft.
WEIGHT: Empty 27,650 lb., Gross 38,000 lb., Max. 45,650 lb. Fuel 1700+792 gal.
PERFORMANCE: Speed- Top 292 mph at 25,000', Cruising 230 mph, Landing 80 mph. Service Ceiling 36,000', Climb 10,000'/ 7 min. Range 2400 miles/4000 lb. bombs, 3600 miles max.

the first B-17B, which was retained at Wright. This aircraft was reworked to test the new armament installations planned for the future B-17C version. Many of the service B-17Bs were modernized in 1941 to use such features as the flush-type side openings for .50-caliber guns.

When replaced at their original stations by newer models in 1941, the B-17Bs were scattered among several bomb groups to train new crews. Ten went to the Canal Zone, two to Alaska for cold weather tests, and six to Newfoundland with the 41st Reconnaissance Squadron, 2nd Bomb Group. One of the latter dropped the first bomb in anger by the Air Force when the B-17B attacked a U-boat on October 27, 1941, without producing visible results. Since we were not officially at war, the incident was not reported in the press.

The XB-19

Largest airplane ever built until after World War Two, the Douglas XB-19 of 1941 was among the most famous planes of its day. Although only one was built, and it never flew a combat mission, the XB-19 became a symbol of prewar American air power. A 212-foot wing span and the 162,000-pound gross weight made the big Douglas the largest in the air until the B-36 of 1946.

This design's main purpose was to find out just how far a bomber could be made to fly in the prewar state of the art. This led inevitably to a giant airplane, whose development made possible future air monsters.

In February 1935, the U.S. Army Air Corps began Project D, a long-range bomber idea "investigating the maximum feasible distance into the future," and classified the whole project Secret. Contracts with Douglas Aircraft and Sikorsky Aviation were prepared to cover preliminary design and wooden mockups, with an option to purchase a completed aircraft, if prospects looked good.

DOUGLAS XB-19
Four Wright R-3350-5, 2000 hp takeoff, 1500 hp at 15,000'
DIMENSIONS: Span 212', Lg. 132'2", Ht. 42'9", Wing Area 4285 sq. ft.
WEIGHT: Empty 84,431 lb., Gross 140,000 lb., Max. 162,000 lb. Fuel 10,350+824 gal.
PERFORMANCE: Speed- Top 224 mph at 15,700', Cruising 135 mph, Landing 73 mph. Service Ceiling 23,000', Absolute Ceiling 24,500', Climb 545'/1 min. Range 7300 miles/6000 lb. bombs, 7900 miles max.

Douglas was assigned the designation XBLR-2 (Experimental Bomber Long Range) on July 9, 1935, the same month the first B-17 flew. Originally, they had estimated that the plane could be completed by March 31, 1938, so a design contract was approved on October 31, 1935, and a model tested in the Galcit wind tunnel in December. The wooden mockups of both Douglas and Sikorsky were inspected in March 1936, and the former was considered superior as a military weapon. Sikorsky's XBLR-3 contract was canceled with a $103,000 payment.

Among the then-new features of the Douglas design were retractable tricycle gear, power turrets and a tail gun position. None of these features had yet been seen on an American combat type. A Douglas OA-4 Dolphin amphibian was loaned back by the Army in May 1936 to test the tricycle gear idea, and experiments were so successful that the nose-wheel plan was also adopted for the company's forthcoming DC-4 transport and A-20 attack bomber series.

The power-operated nose turret was tested on the DB-2, but the tail turret was then considered of "questionable value." Originally 1,600-hp Allison XV-3420-1 liquid-cooled inline engines (actually two V-1710s joined together) were to be used on both the Douglas and Sikorsky designs, but on November 2, 1936, 2,000-hp Wright R-3350-5 air-cooled radials were substituted. This was the first use on a military plane of these power plants, which would eventually power the vast B-29 program. Passages in the low wing gave direct access to the engines, with their three-bladed Hamilton propellers.

After a staff study examining a Navy contention that long-range flying was a function of only that service, the Air Corps was granted authority to proceed with Project D detailed design and tests on September 29, 1936. A contract change calling for a prototype to be completed and designated XB-19, instead of XBLR-2, was dated November 19, 1937, but not approved until the following March 8.

On December 22, 1937, the Air Corps also invited plans to follow-up the B-15 with a more advanced bomber of the same size. In response, the Boeing Model 316 and

Douglas DB-4 were offered as four-engine long-range bomber projects with tricycle landing gear and 1,400-hp R-2180 Twin Hornets. The low-wing Douglas offered March 12, 1938, based on the DC-4 transport with a 138-foot wing span, was to weigh 71,000 pounds gross, have a crew of nine, and six .50-caliber guns in four power turrets and two waist openings. Estimated performance included 260 mph at 15,000 feet and a 4,000-mile range with 4,500 pounds of bombs, and 1,000 miles with 20,000 pounds.

Boeing's high-wing project was offered in several forms, and the 80,000 lb. gross, seven-gun, ten-place, 152-foot span, pressurized cabin 316D version was designated YlB-20 in June 1938. But prototypes of these designs were considered too expensive, because an Army and Navy Joint Board insisted on June 29, 1938, that the Air Corps would not require bombers of greater range and carrying capacity than those of the B-17. The YlB-20 was dropped, and the Douglas DC-4 transport prototype was sold to Japan, where it was rebuilt in 1941 as a bomber, the G5N-1, for the Japanese Navy.

The XB-19 was endangered when the Douglas Company itself recommended cancellation of the contract on August 30, 1938, arguing that the expensive ship was becoming obsolete, that weight was increasing excessively, and that the personnel was needed on designs more likely to be produced in quantity. The Army insisted that the company proceed with the $1,400,000 contract, (which was eventually to cost the company nearly $4,000,000) because only actual flight tests could establish the data needed for future development of such large aircraft.

Since the B-19 would operate far beyond the reach of fighter escort, armament was quite formidable for those days. As specified on January 1, 1939, the armament included two 37-mm guns, five .50-caliber guns, and six .30-caliber guns with 50, 200, and 600 rpg, respectively. The big bomb bay could accommodate eight 2,000, sixteen 1,100, or thirty 600-pound bombs, while ten external wing racks accommodating bombs up to 2,000 pounds could be added for short-range missions, for a maximum capacity of 37,100 pounds. No armor plate or leak-proof fuel tanks were included, as these features were not specified for Army planes before 1940.

The crew included up to sixteen men. The front gunner sat in the power-operated turret with a 37-mm gun, and a .30-caliber weapon attached above it, so its tracers might help the gunner's aim. But this would not help at long ranges, due to the differing ballistics of these guns. Another power-operated turret with a 37-mm and attached .30-caliber gun was provided on top for the main upper gunner.

Behind and below the front turret were the bombardier and another gunner with .30-caliber machine guns in sockets on each side of their compartment. Above them the main cabin accommodated the pilot, co-pilot, plane commander, navigator, engineer, and radio operator. Behind the bomb bay, two waist gunners, an upper rear turret gunner, and a belly gunner each had a single .50-caliber gun. The tail compartment had a .30-caliber gun on each side for a gunner below the stabilizer and the last crewman operated the .50-caliber tail gun. Above the bomb bay was a crew compartment with six bunks and eight seats for a relief crew or extra flight mechanics.

After many delays, the XB-19 was flown on June 27, 1941, from Santa Monica to March Field, where contractor's tests were made. Despite all the guns, the XB-19 was less of a weapon than a flying laboratory to test technical problems, such as how control forces, stability, vibration, stress and weight increases affected large aircraft. As such, it encouraged work on the B-29 and B-36 projects. After America entered the war, it was painted olive-drab, armed, and flown to Wright Field on January 23, 1942.

DOUGLAS XB-19A
Four Allison V-3420-11, 2600 hp at 25,000'
DIMENSIONS: As XB-19.
WEIGHT: Empty 92,397 lb., Gross 140,230 lb., Fuel 6400 gal.
PERFORMANCE: Speed- Top 265 mph at 25,000', Cruising 185 mph. Service Ceiling 39,000'. Range 4240 miles/2500 lb. bombs.

Flight tests began in January 1943 with 2,600-hp Allison V-3420-11 turbosupercharged engines installed at Detroit, Michigan. Designated XB-19A, this version tested the power plants and four-bladed Curtiss propellers that would be used on the Boeing XB-39.

In March 1944, the XB-19A was to be fitted as a cargo carrier with a 45,000 pound payload, but actual modifications were not completed. Its last flight on August 17, 1946, was a few days after the first XB-36 had taken its place as the world's largest airplane. The XB-19A was scrapped in June 1949.

When we compare the B-9 of a decade earlier with the XB-l9, the improvement in range, bomb load, and firepower is obvious. When the speed and ceiling developed by the concurrent B-17 is added to the comparison, the performance improvement of the pre-war bomber decade is striking. In ten years the technology for a new kind of war had been prepared.

But the outbreak of World War Two in Europe quickly demonstrated that mass production of bombers with armor, leak-proof fuel tanks, and powered gun turrets would be needed before American airmen could force their way to enemy targets.

CHAPTER 15

BOMBERS FOR WORLD WAR II, 1939-1945

BOEING B-17C
Four Wright R-1820-65, 1200 hp at 25,000'
DIMENSIONS: Span 103'9", Lg. 67'11", Ht. 15'5", Wing Area 1420 sq. ft. / WEIGHT: Empty 30,900 lb., Design Gross 39,320 lb., Max. 49,650 lb. Fuel 1700+792 gal. / PERFORMANCE: Speed- Top 323 mph at 25,000', Cruising 250 mph, Landing 84 mph. Service Ceiling 37,000', Climb 10,000'/7.5 min. Range 2000 miles/4000 lb. bombs, 3400 miles max.

American bombers began their attacks on Germany when three B-17Cs flown by RAF pilots hit Wilhelmshaven on July 8, 1941. This small raid introduced a bombardment that by 1945 involved thousands of planes, and this chapter tells the story of how those bombers were developed.

The small American bomber force available at the end of 1938 was far from combat ready. While the six Army bomber groups were then equipped with 180 B-18s and only a dozen B-17s, the Army's General Staff saw them as a coast defense, rather than as a strategic force.

Turning point after Munich

But warfare in China and Spain had made the public, and younger military leaders in particular, more concerned about air power. A European crisis in September 1938 led to the Munich pact with Hitler and dramatized the importance of bombers in power politics, alerting Americans to the need for air power.

Some advocates of appeasement had been motivated by Hitler's professed intention to expand only eastward, but much acceptance of Czech dismemberment was due to fear of Germany's well-advertised bombers. Wrote General Henry H. Arnold, who had just been appointed Chief of the Army Air Corps: "the nation with the greatest navy in the world in alliance with the nation having the most powerful army in the world [Britain and France] capitulated without a struggle to Germany's newly created air power."

When President Roosevelt decided to enlarge the Army and Navy air forces, General Arnold prepared expansion plans, and appropriations were requested in the Presidential message to Congress in January 1939.

In April, the Air Corps was authorized to expand from 2,300 planes to 5,500 in 24 groups by June 1941. Bombers, in five heavy, six medium, and two attack (light) bombardment groups, were the big stick of the new force. In the words of its chief, "The No. 1 job of an air force is bombardment. We must have the long-range bombers which can hit the enemy before he hits us; the best defense is attack." No longer was the bomber seen merely as a long-range coast-defense gun.

On August 10, 1939, the Army ordered 461 new bombers of four different models. One contract was for improved Boeing B-17Cs, but others were for B-24, B-25, and B-26 types not yet even flown in prototype form. So urgent was the need for improved bombers that the Army took the unprecedented risk of ordering production of designs that had yet to be tested.

When war was declared in Europe in September 1939, Roosevelt appealed to every belligerent government that "under no circumstances" there be any bombing of civilians in unfortified cities, upon the understanding that the same rules be observed by all belligerents. Except for the quick conquest of Poland, the "phony war" phase gave some hopes that the air weapon would remain sheathed; no one then realized that the United States itself would demonstrate bombing of cities in its most violent form.

German invasion of Western Europe in May 1940 was accompanied by unrestrained air attacks on civilians, and Britain began her struggle for survival. President Roosevelt called for expansion of Army and Navy aviation to 50,000 planes. On June 26, 1940, the Army approved the First Aviation Objective of 54 groups and 12,835 planes by April 1942. Basic equipment of the bomber component was to be a pair each of four-engine and twin-engine types; the B-17 and B-24, and the B-25 and B-26.

Before any of the 461 bombers ordered in 1939 had reached Army groups in 1941, 2,753 more of these four types had been added to Army contracts. With this expansion, specific strategic plans for their use was made.

Rainbow Five

Since autumn of 1939, the Army had been preparing basic war plans against the potential enemies; hostilities with Japan had already been studied as War Plan Orange for many years. The new threat from the German-Japanese alliance had inspired Rainbow No. 5, code name for the plan finally adopted, which contemplated an offensive in Europe while maintaining a strategic defense against Japan. After talks with British officials in February 1941, this strategy was approved on May 14, 1941, by the Army and Navy Joint Board.

At the President's request, the now virtually autonomous Army Air Forces prepared, by August 12, 1941, AWPD/1 (Air War Plans Division), which defined the Air Force plan to fulfill Rainbow Five. AWPD/1 was approved and included in the joint Army-Navy report to Roosevelt on September 11, 1941. This remarkably precise program projected German defeat by the destruction of 154 selected targets in the electric power, petroleum, aluminum, magnesium, aircraft, and transportation industries.

Required for this bombardment would be 6,834 bombers in 98 groups: 20 heavy (B-17 and 24), 24 very heavy (B-29 and 32), and 10 medium groups (B-25 and 26), the latter "included because of availability only." Larger planes would be "far more economical" and it was hoped that by 1944, 44 groups of bombers with a 4,000-mile radius would be available. Sixteen pursuit groups were to protect the bombers' bases in England and Egypt.

Now that a war plan and the bomber designs to meet its requirements had been prepared, the problem remaining was one of improving the weapons to meet battle conditions and building them in numbers sufficient to execute the plan, and still have enough to allot some to allies.

B-17s at War

Boeing's B-17 led the strategic bombing offensive against Germany, but at first, the company's "Flying Fortress" name represented journalistic and advertising hyperbole. Before sustained daylight operations could be made, protection against enemy fighters had to be improved. Describing how the airmen fought their battles in the B-17 and other wartime bombers would fill whole books by itself; in our bibliography we list the best. For this chapter, we must be limited to identification of the major steps in weapons development.

The first Flying Fortress used in air combat was the nine-place B-17C with four Wright Cyclones, up to 800 pounds of armor, leak proof tanks, and the four gun blisters replaced by new openings for each .50-caliber gun. Flush panels were provided on the sides, another over the radio compartment, and a tub for the kneeling bottom gunner. A single .30-caliber gun could be fired from any of six sockets in the nose. Bomb bay capacity remained the same (4,992 pounds with eight 624-pound bombs) as on the YB-17.

Thirty-eight B-17Cs were ordered August 10, 1939, and Poland had been overrun by the Germans before this contract was approved on September 20 by the Secretary of War. The first B-17C flew July 21, 1940, and was retained by the company for tests, while the last was delivered by November 29.

Boeing had guaranteed a top speed of 274 mph at 15,000 feet and 300 mph at 25,000 feet at design weight with a normal 1,000 hp from the R-1820-65 engines, but the Army credited the B-17C with 323 mph when the B-2 turbosuperchargers boosted 1,200 hp at 25,000 feet. Twenty B-17Cs were sold to Britain as the Fortress I, and all were returned to Boeing in January 1941 to be modified to B-17D standards with seven guns and Goodrich self-sealing fuel tanks.

Mfr

BOEING B-17D

Forty-two more had been ordered April 17, 1940, but were redesignated B-17D on September 6. Delivered from February 3 to April 29, 1941, they could be distinguished from the Cs by their cowl flaps. Improved protection included a new self-sealing fuel tank system and paired guns in the belly and top positions to bring the total up to one .30-caliber and six .50-caliber guns with 500 rpg.

Britain's own four-engine bomber in 1940, the Short Stirling, contrasted sharply with the B-17, for it carried 14,000 pounds of bombs and power-operated turrets, with a top speed of 260 mph and a ceiling of only 18,000 feet instead of the 37,000 feet of the American aircraft.

All British heavy bombers were then attacking at night, but a new squadron, No. 90, was selected to try day bombing from high-altitude to avoid AAA fire and fighter interception. The RAF Fortresses began arriving in Britain on April 14, 1941, fitted with Sperry bombsights, as the Norden sight was considered too secret for export. A Lend-lease contract made June 2, 1941, promised 300 B-17F-1s (Fortress II) to the RAF, if the first efforts succeeded.

"The desire to use an American bomber at the earliest opportunity is to be expected and has propaganda value". But a secret memo on May 22 went on to warn "...that this aircraft has been given world-wide publicity, and if it fails...no hiding of the news will be possible and the whole world will know, with the expected effect on British and American prestige and morale."

Results were disappointing, due to problems with freezing equipment and operation of the first turbosuperchargers in RAF service. Four 1,100-pound bombs were to be dropped from 30,000 feet from each Fortress on the first Wilhelmshaven raid on July 8, 1941, but mechanical difficulties hampered the mission. Three sent July 23 on a prestige raid to Berlin were turned back by the weather. Brest and Emden were attacked next, and on August 2, gunners downed a Bf 109F, the first such victory by an American heavy bomber. But two of the three Boeings near Oslo were destroyed by Bf 109T fighters on August 9th.

Raids from England ended by September 26 after 51 sorties, of which 27 had aborted. Seven B-17Cs had been lost during that time to accidents and enemy fighters, and few direct hits were confirmed.

Americans blamed this poor record on excessively high attack altitudes, and on not flying in formation to promote defensive firepower and a good bombing pattern; but it was evident that something had to be done to counter the speed and firepower added by fighter planes since the original B-17 had been designed. RAF Bomber Command decided against more heavy bomber daylight raids and pushed production of Stirlings with improved Halifax and Lancaster types, while in the future, RAF B-17s would be used by the Coastal Command.

America's APWD/1 war plan would be useless unless the bombers could be protected well-enough to penetrate to their targets, an ability not yet demonstrated by U.S. planes. Part of the answer was to replace most of the hand-held gun mounts with power-operated turrets and provide a tail gunner with a clear field of fire to the rear.

The Sperry company designed a 650-pound electric-powered dome with twin .50-caliber guns, 400 rpg, and a computer sight. Located behind the pilots' seats, it swung 360 degrees around and 85 degrees up. Another pair of guns in a Sperry belly turret was remote-controlled from a periscope sight by a prone gunner. These turrets armed the B-17E, ordered August 30, 1940, and first flown September 5, 1941, about four months behind schedule.

BOEING B-17E
Four Wright R-1820-65, 1200 hp at 25,000'
DIMENSIONS: Span 103'9", Lg. 73'10", Ht. 19'2", Wing Area 1420 sq. ft.
WEIGHT: Empty 32,250 lb., Gross 40,250 lb., Max. 53,000 lb. Fuel 1700+792 gal.
PERFORMANCE: Speed- Top 317 mph at 25,000', Cruising 224 mph, Landing 88 mph. Service Ceiling 36,600', Climb 10,000'/ 7.5 min. Range 2000 miles/4000 lb. bombs, 3200 miles max.

Another pair of .50-caliber guns, aimed with a simple bar sight, was provided in a tail emplacement, with a narrow 60-degree cone of fire. A .50-caliber gun at each squared waist opening was hand-operated, as was the .30-caliber gun fired from sockets in the nose enclosure. Since power plants were the same as on the previous Fortress models, the increased weight and drag of protruding turrets reduced the speed, although its ability to defend itself was greatly improved. Distinguishing feature of this and all succeeding Fortress models was a large dorsal fin and wider stabilizer.

As early as December 1940, the original belly turret was seen as unsatisfactory and, after the first 112 B-17Es, was replaced in January 1942 by an 850-pound Sperry ball turret with the gunner curled up inside. But the weakness of the protection from frontal attacks was not recognized until after heavy combat losses.

BOEING B-17E with ball turret

The B-17E arrived just as America entered the war. Forty-two were delivered by November 30, 1941, mostly to the 7th Bomb Group, with 60 more B-17Es in December, and the last of 512 by May 28, 1942.

In 1941, there were 13 heavy bomber groups, but they were far below the plane strength planned. Only some 150 B-17s were on hand December 1, 1941, including older models, together with some B-18s for training. First priority was given to the groups deployed overseas. Twenty-one B-17Ds had been flown to Hawaii in May 1941, and the rest joined older models in the 7th and 19th Bomb Groups.

Six B-17Cs and 29 B-17Ds of the 19th Bomb Group were flown to the Philippines via Hawaii, Midway and Wake islands, and Australia. They had expected to be joined by the 38th Reconnaissance Squadron that arrived in Hawaii with four B-17C and two B-17Es in the middle of the Japanese attack on December 7, along with six B-17Es of the 88th Reconnaissance Squadron. Parked at Hickam Field were 12 B-17Ds of the 5th Bomb Group. Of 24 present that morning, seven B-17s were destroyed and four damaged.

Defending the Canal Zone was the 6th Bomb Group with nine B-17Bs and 19 B-18s, plus nine new B-17Es that arrived early in December. Newfoundland had six B-17Bs and a B-18A with the 41st Reconnaissance Squadron, and one B-17B was stationed in Alaska.

The only combat-ready group in the United States was the 7th, whose 35 B-17Es left Salt Lake City, Utah, on December 5 for deployment to the Far East. Six had arrived in Hawaii, as mentioned above, but the rest were diverted to Muroc to parry any threat to California. Most were then transferred to Hawaii, but in January their new replacements would begin to fly almost around the world via Africa to Java. To help the 39th Bomb Group at Geiger Field, Spokane, cover the Northwest, only 19 B-17Bs, five B-17Cs, and a B-17D were left to be gathered from scattered training sites. This group would remain a replacement training unit, sending off crews in factory-fresh aircraft to the war zones.

BOEING B-17F-30-VE
Four Wright R-1820-97, 1200 hp at 25,000', (1380 hp War Emer. [WE])
DIMENSIONS: Span 103'9", Lg. 74'9", Ht. 19'1", Wing Area 1420 sq. ft.
WEIGHT: Empty 34,000 lb.,(35,728 lb. on late models) Gross 55,000 lb., Max. 65,500 lb. Fuel 1730+820 gal. (3630 gal. max.).
PERFORMANCE: Speed- Top 252 mph at 5000', 299 mph at 25,000' (265-314 mph WE), Cruising 200 mph, Landing 90 mph. Service Ceiling 37,500', Climb 20,000'/25.7 min. Range 2200 miles/6000 lb. bombs, 2880 miles with 2810 gals, 3800 miles max.

After heavy losses in the Philippines, 14 surviving Boeings of the 19th Bomb Group retreated to Australia. Then came the battle for Java, with the arrival of 39 B-17E and 12 LB-30s from January 13 to February 20 with 7th Bomb Group crews; 22 of the Es and eight LB-30s would be lost in that fight. Remnants of that Group fled to India. The 19th continued to fight from Australia and the 5th and 11th groups were in Hawaii for the Battle of Midway, while the 36th Bombardment Squadron was in Alaska at that same time.

Replenishments for the Southwest Pacific included 90 more B-17Es arriving with the 5th and 11th groups from July to December. When the 19th BG retired to America in October, the last Flying Fortress outfit deployed against Japan was the 43rd Bomb Group, who's 49 B-17Fs had began operations in August 1942.

Yet by September 1943, B-17s had been withdrawn from the Pacific in favor of the longer-ranged B-24. The B-17 had not been very successful in its originally intended role of attacking moving surface ships, a job better done by low-altitude twin-engine bombers.

Instead, the B-17 flew over 98% of its combat sorties in Europe. On July 1, 1942, the first 97th Bomb Group B-17E reached the United Kingdom (the first Air Force combat aircraft to do so), the group losing four of its 49 aircraft over the North Atlantic ferry route. This group flew the first B-17E mission against Nazi-occupied Europe on August 17, 1942. (A heavy bomber group's authorized strength was 48 bombers in four squadrons, during most of the war.)

Forty-five B-17Es also went to the RAF Coastal Command from March to July 1942 as the Fortress IIA. Fitted with ASW radar, they would sink seven enemy U-boats.

BOEING-LOCKHEED XB-38
Four Allison V-1710-89, 1425 hp at 25,000'
DIMENSIONS: Span 103'9", Lg. 74', Ht. 19'2", Wing Area 1420 sq. ft.
WEIGHT: Empty 34,748 lb., Gross 56,000 lb., Max. 64,000 lb. Fuel 1730+790 gal.
PERFORMANCE: Speed- Top 327 mph at 25,000', Cruising 226 mph. Service Ceiling 29,000'. Range 2400 miles/3000 lb. bombs, 1900 miles/6000 lb. bombs, 3600 miles max.

The ninth B-17E was fitted with 1425 hp Allison V-1710-89 inline engines by Lockheed Vega and called XB-38. The first liquid-cooled bomber design in a decade was begun in March 1942, ordered the following July 10, and flown on May 19, 1943. This attempt to compare performance was frustrated by a crash on June 15.

B17F and G Models

The B-17F followed the B-17E into production with a new molded Plexiglas nose, more armor, new propellers, and R-1820-97 Cyclones. While normal bomb load remained 4,000 pounds, the bomb bay could accommodate up to twelve 500, six 1,000 or 1,600, or two 2,000-pound bombs of the new AN (Army/Navy) standard sizes.

Production history of the B-17F series began with a Lend-lease contract made in June 1941 for 300 Fortress II bombers for the RAF. When the British decided to use the Boeings not as bombers, but only for ocean patrols, most of them became available for the Army. The first B-17F-1-BO was delivered May 30, 1942, and as they rolled out of the Seattle factory, the first two were used for testing, the next 12 allocated to the Eighth AF in England, the next six flown to the Fifth AF in the Pacific, and then more were allocated to each destination as the war developed. Beginning in October, 19 B-17Fs did go to RAF Coastal Command as the Fortress II, eventually sinking two more U-boats.

Later contracts for B-17F-30-BO to B-17F-130-BO brought the total to 2,300 built at Boeing by September 2, 1943. Douglas had received an order for 600 B-17F-DL on August 28, 1941, and Lockheed-Vega for 500 B-17F-VE on September 13, and delivery from their Long Beach and Burbank factories began in June 1942.

Many mechanical modifications made on the production lines were reflected by block numbers for each batch, often of 50 to 100 planes. For example, from B-17F-30 to B-17F-90-BO, two external racks under the wings could each hold a 4,000-pound bomb, but this option was seldom used. Modification centers made changes, especially in armament, when these could not be easily done at the factory.

Armament operated by the ten crewmen was originally the same as that of the E, but protection for the nose increased when the .30-caliber gun was deleted in August 1942, after 264 planes, and .50-caliber weapons were installed in the nose. Positions varied with model and modification center, but two were usually mounted on the nose side windows, and one in the nose itself. Another gun was added at the opening on top of the radio compartment, beginning with the B-17F-30-BO in September 1942. Some Eighth Air Force B-17Fs had two .50-caliber guns with armor in the bow; this left no room for a bomb sight, for usually bombs were released when the lead plane directed.

Extra tankage was added, beginning with B-17F-55-BO, to allow up to 2,810 gallons in the wings and 820 gallons in the bomb bay. In 1944, a water injection system could be added to raise the standard 1,200-hp to 1,380 "War Emergency" power for up to five minutes. Top speed, in 55,000-pound condition, was then increased from 299 mph to 314 mph.

These were the bombers that launched the American share of Operation POINTBLANK, the Combined Bomber Offensive against Germany. So-called "precision" bombing in daylight was more effective than the night "area" bombing practiced by the RAF, and it was supposed that bomber firepower in mass formation would frustrate fighter defense.

The first Eighth Air Force attack on Germany, on January 27, 1943, was on the navy base at Wilhelmshaven, the same target as the first RAF B-17 raid. Of 84 B-17Fs dispatched, 53 found and bombed the primary target. Bomber strength would grow until the massive December 24, 1944, attack that sent into Germany 1,400 B-17G and 634 B-24 heavy bombers, supported by 792 P-51 fighters.

At first, Eighth Air Force commander General Ira Eaker had insisted that "we can make penetration without fighter support."

But in 1943, resistance by German fighters grew more bitter and effective as bomb tonnage delivered increased, and raids like those on Ploesti and Schweinfurt in August through October 1943 cost such losses that ability of the bombers to execute their part of the war plan was in doubt.

As early as September 17, 1941, an air force board had suggested that bombers be accompanied by "destroyer escort" planes. Existing fighters being too short-ranged to protect the bombers, the logical answer by April 1, 1942, was specially armed B-17 and B-24s. A proposal by Vega was accepted, and on August 2, 1942, Vega received the second B-17F-1-BO for conversion to the XB-40.

BOEING XB-40
Four Wright R-1820-97, 1200 hp at 25,000'
DIMENSIONS: Span 103'9", Lg. 74'9", Ht. 19'1", Wing Area 1420 sq. ft.
WEIGHT: Empty 36,898 1b, Gross 58,000 lb., Max. 63,295 lb. Fuel 1730+790 gal.
PERFORMANCE: Speed- Top 248 mph at s.l., 292 mph at 25,000', Cruising 196 mph, Landing 94 mph. Service Ceiling 29,200', Climb 780'/1 min., 10,000'/13.3 min. Range 2460 miles.

That escort plane was first delivered on September 9, 1942, and finally revised by November 17, with the bomb capacity replaced by 2,150 pounds of armor for the crew, up to 11,200 rounds of ammunition, and fourteen .50-caliber guns. These were placed in pairs in the usual top and belly turrets, as well as in a new Bendix chin turret, a Martin power turret amidships, and on power-operated mounts at each side window and the tail.

Thirteen B-17F-10-VEs went to the Tulsa modification center in November 1942 for conversion to YB-40 escorts delivered from February 28 to March 14, 1943. Another 12 modifications were ordered, but only one of these followed the first 13 to the Eighth Air Force, the rest being stripped down as TB-40 trainers, after the escort function failed in combat.

Between May 29 and July 4, 1943, nine YB-40 combat missions were flown from England, claiming five kills and two probable for one YB-40 lost to AAA, but the experiment failed as a protection system. According to the official history, "Being heavily armored and loaded, they could not climb or keep speed with the standard B-17, a fact which...

BOEING B-17G-80-BO
Four Wright R-1820-97, 1200 hp at 25,000', (1380 hp War Emer.)
DIMENSIONS: Span 103'9", Lg. 74'4", Ht. 19'1", Wing Area 1420 sq. ft.
WEIGHT: Empty 36,135 lb., Gross 55,000 lb., Max. 65,500 lb., Fuel 2810+820 gal. (3630 gal. max.).
PERFORMANCE: Speed- Top 246 mph at 5000', 287 mph at 25,000' (258-302 mph WE), Cruising 182 mph, Landing 90 mph. Service Ceiling 35,600', Climb 20,000'/37 min. Range 2000 miles/6000 lb. bombs and 2810 gals, 3400 miles max.

resulted in the disorganization of the formation they were supposed to protect."

An effort to strengthen the standard bomber armament was made by fitting one B-17E in September 1943 with front and rear Consolidated power turrets, but the lighter 412-pound Bendix chin turret developed for the B-40 was adopted for the last Fortress production model, the B-17G (British Fortress III).

The first G was a rebuilt B-17F-115-BO flown on May 21, 1943. Production deliveries began September 4, 1943, with two guns in the chin turret below the nose, which swung 180 degrees left and right, and 85 degrees up and down. Above them a pair of hand-operated "cheek" guns were added, beginning with the B-17G-55-BO.

Armament of the B-17G now included thirteen .50-caliber guns with 6,380 rounds, and from 6,000 to 9,600 (6 x 1,600) pounds of bombs in the bay. The waist positions were enclosed and the right side moved forward to ease the gunners' movement. Later models deleted the seldom-used radio operator's gun and introduced an improved "Cheyenne" tail turret with a reflector sight on the B-17G-80-BO, B-17G-50-DL, and B-17G-55-VE.

Of 8,680 Gs built, 2,395 were by Douglas, 2,250 by Vega, and the rest by Boeing, who completed Fortress production April 13, 1945. With Germany defeated, production closed at the other plants in July. About 878 had been delivered as TB-17G trainers for replacement training units (RTU). B-17 costs dropped from $301,000 each in

BOEING YB-40 with RP-63 target planes.

BOEING B-17G prototype, from B-17F-115-BO

BOEING B-17G-30-DL

1941 to $204,000 in 1944.

B-17Gs went to Britain as the Fortress III, beginning in March 1944, and 85 were used by two RAF radar countermeasures squadrons and by a Coastal Command squadron. Another 14 2nd-hand AAF B-17F bombers were acquired in 1944.

The AAF also benefited from RAF radar progress when the H2X (APS-15 *Mickey*) radar navigation and bombing set became available to find targets at night or in bad weather. Over 260 AAF B-17Gs, fitted with H2X scanners in radomes that replaced the belly turrets, became squadron leaders bombing through overcast (BTO).

Total B-17 production was 12,276 and the peak AAF inventory was 4,574 in August 1944, with 27 combat groups in the Eighth Air Force in England and six groups with the Fifteenth Air Force in Italy. Their combat record is summarized in Table 5, which compares the work of AAF bombers in the air offensive against Germany and her European Allies.

Table 5
AAF Bombers in the European War, 1942–45

Type	Number of Sorties	Bomb Tonnage	U. S. Aircraft Lost in Combat	Enemy Aircraft Claimed Destroyed in Air
B-17	291,508	640,036	4,688	6,659
B-24	226,775	452,508	3,626	2,617
B-26	129,943	169,382	911	402
B-25	63,177	84,980	380	193
A-20	39,492	31,856	265	11
A-26	11,567	18,054	67	7
Total	762,462	1,396,816	9,937	9,889

How the bomber crews found the courage to meet the violence, pain and death to complete their missions has been dramatized in story and film, like *"Twelve O'clock High."* Until friendly long-range fighters dominated the sky, failure always threatened the bomber offensive. One group's history illustrates the experience; flying 340 missions, averaging 28 group planes on each, from November 7, 1942, to April 25, 1945, the 91st Bomb Group lost 197 B-17s missing in action and claimed 420 enemy fighters downed.

Besides the bombing missions, B-17s filled other roles. None were more dramatic than the BQ-7, which was a radio-controlled drone loaded with 20,000 pounds of explosives (Torpex). The secret project gave the code name Aphrodite to the bombers, often named simply Weary Willie to the participants. The first ten were converted from worn B-17Fs at Burtonwood, England, in July 1944. Visual control from a guide plane equipped with a 50-pound control box was used, and later a TV camera in the nose was tried. Wooden guns disguised the aircraft's role, and smoke bombs could be used to simulate an aircraft in distress.

The first drones were launched against V-l flying bomb sites on August 4. Their effect was less than expected, for essentially this was a light-case weapon with no penetrating power, and was limited to a 30-degree slant descent. The program was soon canceled.

Non-combat conversions of the B-17 were many, but are outside of this book's scope. The most numerous were 41 F-9, F-9A and F-9B trimetragon camera ships converted from B-17Fs, while in 1945, modified B-17Gs became the F-9C. Renamed RB-17G in 1948, about 28 served the 5th Reconnaissance Group's photographic mapping missions until 1950.

Some 130 late-model B-17Gs, no longer needed as bombing in Europe ended, were modified in 1945 to B-17H (later SB-17G) rescue planes carrying a lifeboat and SCR-717 radar, including 16 that became PB-lG Coast Guard aircraft. Gun provisions were retained, although not usually installed in peacetime until the Korean War.

On July 31, 1945, the Navy redesignated 20 late-model B-17Gs from Douglas as PB-lW aircraft with APS-20 radar under the bomb bay. They joined the Navy's first land-based early warning squadron, VPB-101, which evolved by 1952 into two units, VW-1 and VW-2, on the East and West Coasts. Replenished by several more conversions from storage dumps, they retained gun provisions and were not completely replaced by Lockheed WV-2 Warning Stars until 1956.

Although no B-17s were supplied to the Soviet Union by Lend-lease, enough damaged aircraft found in Red Army occupied-areas were salvaged to provide 17 B-17Gs to the 890th Bomber Air Regiment at the end of the war in Europe. These planes, along with that regiment's Pe-8 bombers, provided the VVS with valuable training in four-engine flying.

Petrov

BOEING B-17G with Soviet 890th BAP

The last B-17s to bomb were three civilian B-17Gs purchased by Israel, and armed in Czechoslovakia, where they took off and raided the Cairo area July 14, 1948, on their way to Israel. They flew about 200 sorties in Israel's Liberation War, and served that country's bomber force for ten years.

In 1952, two B-17s were flown to Taiwan for special spy missions by Chinese crews with CIA equipment. These missions ended on May 29, 1959, when a B-17 with 14 men and ELINT equipment was shot down by MiG jets. More peaceful operations were made in Brazil by a B-17G search-rescue squadron for over twenty years, and by American civilian fire-fighters who used some B-17 chemical bombers into the 1970s to preserve, not destroy.

B-24 Liberator

More B-24 Liberators were built than any other American warplane, and more than any bomber type in any other country in the world. Although less famous than the B-17, the B-24 was much more widely used.

The Liberator began in January 1939, when the Chief of the Army Air Corps decided that a second heavy bomber type should join the B-17 in production. Consolidated Aircraft's chief designer, Isaac M. Laddon, could respond with Model 32, which used a new Davis airfoil on a high aspect ratio wing with Fowler flaps to add lift for take-off and landings.

Since this wing was already being built on the Model 31 flying boat, and Consolidated had also flown the four-engine XPB2Y-1 bomber for the Navy, Laddon was able to present a proposal to Wright Field on January 30, and begin wind tunnel tests on a model by February 16. The XB-24 prototype was ordered March 30, 1939, and additional orders were placed for seven YB-24s on April 27, and 38 B-24As on September 20.

Mfr

CONSOLIDATED XB-24

Four Pratt & Whitney R-1830-33, 1200 hp takeoff, 1000 hp at 14,500'

DIMENSIONS: Span 110', Lg. 63'9", Ht. 18'8", Wing Area 1048 sq. ft.

WEIGHT: Empty 27,470 lb., Gross 38,351 lb., Max. 47,174 lb. Fuel 924-2400 gal.

PERFORMANCE: Speed- Top 258 mph at s.l., 292 mph at 15,000', Cruising 186 mph, Landing 90 mph. Service Ceiling 31,500', Climb 10,000'/6 min. Range 3000 miles/2496 lb. bombs.

What became the most important flight from San Diego's Lindbergh Field was made on Friday, December 29, 1939, by William Wheatley, only nine months after the original contract was approved. The XB-24 had the first tricycle landing gear flown on a large bomber. The nose wheel permitted faster landings and take-offs, and thus allowed a heavier wing loading on the narrow wing. Power plants were four Pratt & Whitney R-1830-33 Wasps of 1,000 hp at 14,500 feet.

A bombardier's Plexiglas enclosure began the nose of the deep fuselage, which terminated behind twin rudders with a tail gunner's position. Armament included three .50-caliber hand-operated guns fired after opening panels in the rear fuselage top, bottom, and tail, while four .30-caliber guns were provided for two sockets in the nose and two mounts at the waist panels. Eight 1,130-pound bombs could be accommodated, twice the capacity of the B-17's bay, and the wing tanks could hold 40 percent more fuel.

Problems discovered on early tests led to exchanges of the twin fins with the Model 31, and were solved by extending the horizontal tail from 22 to 26 feet, beginning with the 23rd test on April 12, 1940. Slots in the outer wings were found an unnecessary drag. The prototype's speed was measured at from 291 to 298 mph during the first 30 flights, instead of the 311-mph promised by the specification.

On July 26, 1940, the Air Corps ordered that leak proof fuel tanks and B-2 turbosuperchargers be installed. Redesignated XB-24B with 1,200-hp R-1830-41 Wasps and with wing slots deleted, the reworked prototype would be flown February 1, 1941. Each turbosupercharger added 135 pounds of weight, but they raised critical altitude to 25,000 feet, where top speed could be over the 320-mph level.

Until these improvements could be incorporated into production B-24s for the Air Corps, Consolidated could export earlier models. In April 1940, the French became interested in the LB-30 version with commercial R-1830-S3C4G engines. By the time a contract was made in June 4, 1940, France was near defeat. Britain took over the contract on June 17, specifying 165 LB-30s with self-sealing fuel tanks, armor, and power-operated turrets.

CONSOLIDATED LIBERATOR IA (LB-30A)

These features, plus turbosuperchargers, were also specified for the future Air Corps B-24C/D versions, by a contract change dated June 24, 1940. Delivery on the B-24s ordered in 1939 was deferred by the Air Corps announcement on November 9, 1940, that 26 would go to Britain, and be replaced later by modernized B-24C/D models. The RAF aircraft would be delivered with commercial R-1830-S3C4G engines and without armament.

The first YB-24 was painted in RAF colors when first flown on November 19, 1940, and was similar to the original XB-24 except for R-1830-S3C4G engines, omitting wingtip slots, and adding deicers. Six were accepted in December and redesignated LB-30A. They provided Britain with fast transatlantic mail and ferry service, and in 1943 flew a risky route to Moscow.

CONSOLIDATED YB-24

Using R-1830-33 Wasps, the seventh YB-24 added self-sealing fuel tanks and 637 pounds of armor. First flown on March 4, 1941, it was delivered in Army olive-drab paint to Wright Field on April 7, seven months behind schedule, and assigned to the Ferry Command school on July 5. As the prototype for the B-24A, it was armed with six .50-caliber hand-operated guns in the rear fuselage's top, waist, bottom, and tail openings, with two .30-caliber guns for the nose enclosure's upper and lower sockets.

Design gross weight of all early B-24s was "assumed" to be 41,000 pounds, although this would allow only six crewmen, 854 gallons, and 2,500 pounds of bombs. There was room to add 6,000 pounds of bombs or another 1,000 gallons, as the mission demanded. Actual combat would require at least a third more gross weight.

The first 20 B-24As were delivered with R-1830-S3C4G Wasps from March 29 to May 26, 1941, as the RAF's Liberator I (LB-30B), serials AM910/929. A hard landing in Britain wrecked one, and three became transports.

CONSOLIDATED B-24A

Four Pratt & Whitney R-1830-33, 1200 hp takeoff, 1000 hp at 14,500'
DIMENSIONS: Span 110', Lg. 63'9", Ht. 18'8", Wing Area 1048 sq. ft.
WEIGHT: Empty 29,863 lb., Design Gross 41,000 lb., Max. 53,600 lb. Fuel 778- 2400+600 gal.
PERFORMANCE: Speed- Top 293 mph at 15,000', Cruising 228, Landing 92 mph. Service Ceiling 30,500', Climb 10,000'/5.6 min. Range 2200 miles/4000 lb. bombs, 4000 miles max. at 190 mph.

CONSOLIDATED XB-24B

The other 15 joined No. 120 Coastal Command Squadron, based at Nutts Corner in Northern Ireland, the first RAF unit able to cover the mid-Atlantic submarine gap. After gradually learning to find their difficult targets, they began, in October 1942, attacks that sank eight U-boats, five by Liberator AM929's crew alone.

Equipment installed at Prestwick, Scotland, included a complicated radar installation, the ASV Mark II, with both forward and sideways-looking aerial arrays. Six to eight 250-pound depth charges could be carried on 16-hour patrols, along with four 20-mm fixed guns in a tray under the fuselage and six .303-caliber guns (British Brownings), paired on the waist and tail mounts.

Another LB-30B, AM927, remained in the U.S. after an accident, became a Consolidated company transport and prototype for the C-87, and lasted many years after the war with the Confederate Air Force as the oldest Liberator still flying.

Nine B-24As accepted by the Army from June 16 to July 10, 1941, had R-1830-33 Wasps like the YB-24. Mounts for six .50 and two .30-caliber guns and 519 pounds of armor

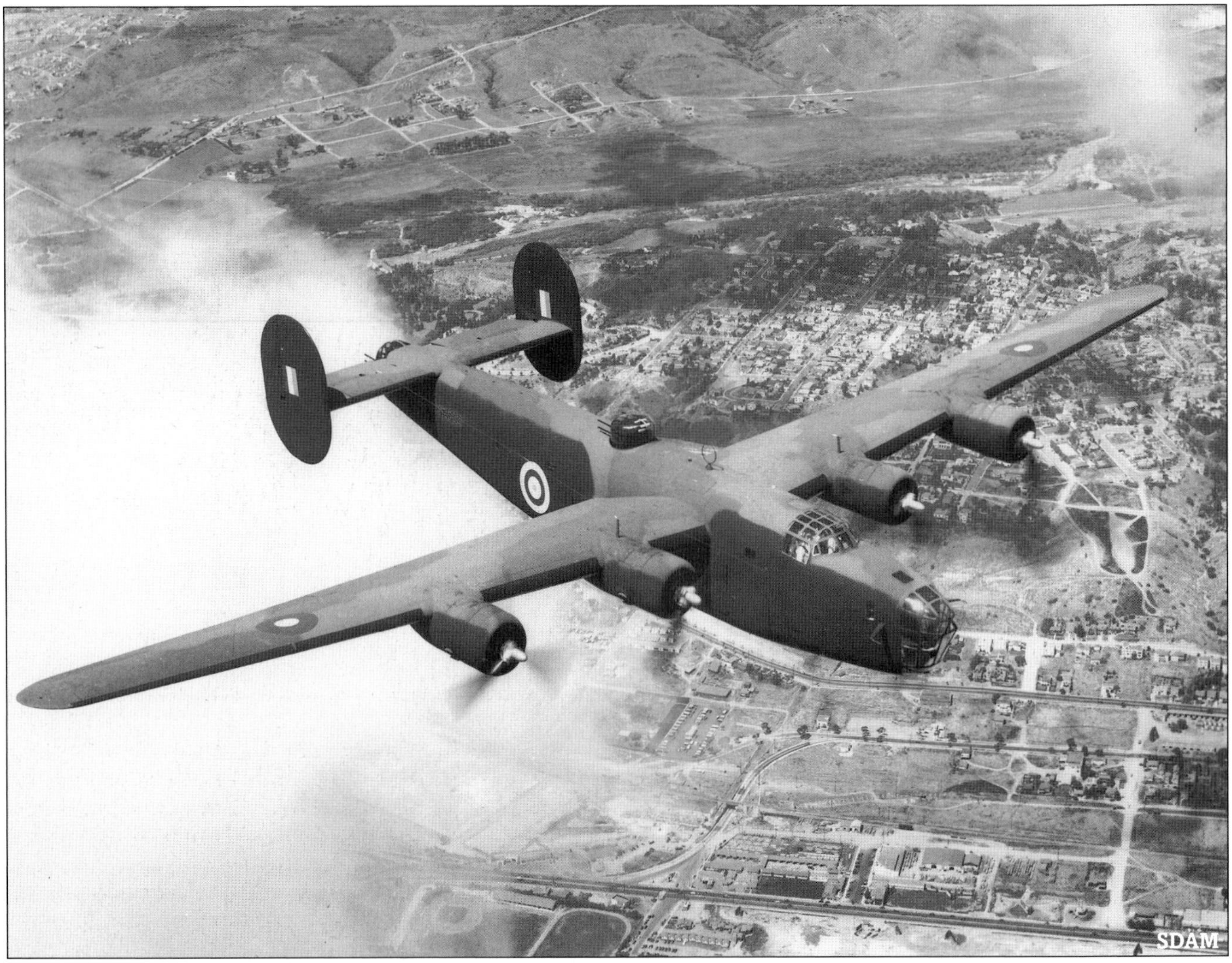

CONSOLIDATED LIBERATOR II (LB-30)
Four Pratt & Whitney R-1830-S3C4-G 1200 hp takeoff, 1050 hp at 13,100'
DIMENSIONS: Span 110', Lg. 66', Ht. 17'11", Wing Area 1048 sq. ft.
WEIGHT: Empty 32,314 lb., Design Gross 41,000 lb., Max. 56,000 lb. Fuel 915-2308 gal.
PERFORMANCE: Speed- Top 278 mph at 15,100'. Service Ceiling 24,300'. Range 1420 miles/6000 lb. bombs, 3020 miles max.

were provided, but these planes went to the newly organized Army Air Force Ferry Command, which retained only a tail gun and used them to pioneer intercontinental routes vital to Allied cooperation. They were the only Army planes with enough range for flights like the mission carrying Americans from Scotland to Moscow in September 1941. Passengers sat for 15 hours on bare benches in the unheated bomb bay.

CONSOLIDATED LIBERATOR I (LB-30B)

The first B-24A to be lost to enemy action was at Hickam Field on December 7, 1941; it had been fitted with cameras and three guns for a secret mission to photograph Japanese mandated islands in the Pacific. Four more were lost in Australia by March 19, 1942.

The Liberator II, built on the LB-30 contract with R-1830-S3C4G engines and Curtiss (instead of the usual Hamilton) propellers, was the first model with a longer nose and provision for two 850-pound power-operated gun turrets, along with 14 .303-caliber guns. Four were in the Boulton Paul top turret, four in the tail turret, two in each waist window, one at the tunnel hatch, and another in the nose. Except for test examples, the armament was to be installed in Britain.

Seven crewmen with a Sperry bombsight and twelve 500-pound bombs were the standard load, which could be carried 3,020 miles. The first LB-30 (AL503) was flown May 26, 1941, but was destroyed by a fatal crash on June 2. Another 139 were delivered from August 8 to December 31, 1941.

Most Liberators had been flown by American pilots to Montreal, where British pilots took them across the Atlantic. The AAF's own Ferry Command next undertook to fly them across the South Atlantic and Africa to an RAF bomber squadron in Egypt, and the first five began that pioneering flight on November 21, 1941. The first raid by one of these RAF Liberator IIs was on Tripoli on the night of January 10, 1942.

When the United States entered the war, there still were no Liberators with AAF bomber squadrons, so the remaining 74 LB-30s were taken over by the Air Force. Two days after the Pearl Harbor attack, provisions for British armament were ordered to be replaced by eight .50-caliber guns, including two hand-operated guns on posts at the tail and waist openings, with single guns in the nose and tunnel positions. Instead of the Boulton Paul turret on top behind the rear wing spar, a two-gun Martin power turret, like that of a B-26, was installed at the Tucson modification center.

Twelve of these LB-30s were flown by 7th Bomb Group crews to Java, six via the South Atlantic and Africa, and the others across the Pacific via Hawaii, various islands, and Australia. The first three to arrive flew the first Air Force Liberator combat sorties on January 17, 1942.

Seventeen others were rushed to the Canal Zone in March/April 1942 to fill out the 6th Bomb Group, and that summer were fitted with ASV Mark II radar. The 30th Bomb Group had LB-30s at March Field and sent six to Hawaii and three to Alaska in time to fly a few sorties in June 1942. Others served the AAF as transports, but 23 Army LB-30s were returned to British control in 1942, to bring the RAF LB-30 total to 88, less four lost en route. Most went to RAF squadrons in India.

Turbosupercharged 1,200-hp R-1830-41 Wasps in elliptical cowls, like those of the XB-24B, were used on nine B-24Cs, the first flown October 14, 1941. Seven .50-caliber guns and 2,900 rounds of ammunition were carried, two guns in a 954-pound Consolidated armored hydraulic-powered tail turret. A swing of 122-degrees sideways and 111-degrees up and down gave the B-24 a much better arc of fire than the B-17E's tail guns. Another pair was in a Martin power turret behind the pilots' cabin, two more were in a retractable Bendix belly turret behind the bomb bay, and one hand-held gun remained in the nose.

Rearranged crew stations moved the navigator's table into the nose, as it was assumed he would operate the bombsight, while the radio operator now sat behind the co-pilot, instead of behind the bomb bay. Eight B-24Cs were accepted from December 20 to 31, 1941, but the last was delayed to February 10, 1942, as it was a test bed for the General Electric remote-control turrets planned for the B-29.

The first mass-production Liberator version was the B-24D, first flown on January 12, 1942, which was similar at first to the B-24C, except for R-1830-43 engines. While the first 26 replaced the early Liberators given to the RAF, Consolidated had received orders for 56 more on August 16, and for 352 on September 20, 1940.

CONSOLIDATED B-24C
Four Pratt & Whitney R-1830-41, 1200 hp at 25,000'
DIMENSIONS: Span 110', Lg. 66'4", Ht. 17'11", Wing Area 1048 sq. ft.
WEIGHT: Empty 33,473 lb., Design Gross 41,000 lb., Max. 54,000 lb. Fuel 836-2364+780 gal.
PERFORMANCE: Speed- Top 313 mph at 25,000', Cruising 233 mph, Landing 93 mph. Service Ceiling 34,000', Climb 10,000'/ 6.1 min. Range 2100 miles/5000 lb. bombs, 3600 miles ferry.

The Lend-lease program contracted on May 12, 1941, for 700 more Liberators for Britain, and as later contracts were added for the AAF, a production pool of five factories was established. These included a new Consolidated factory at Fort Worth, a Douglas factory at Tulsa, and an enormous Ford plant at Willow Run, Michigan, that produced both complete B-24E aircraft and KD (knock-down) subassemblies for the Fort Worth and Tulsa factories. North American joined the pool when it received a letter contract in January 1942 to build 750 at a new Dallas factory.

The first 26 B-24Ds accepted at Consolidated's San Diego factory from January 22 to February 12, 1942, had seven guns and lacked the astrodome in the nose common to all later models. Their specified weight was 33,822

CONSOLIDATED B-24D-CO
Four Pratt & Whitney R-1830-43, 1200 hp at 25,000'
DIMENSIONS: Span 110', Lg. 66'4", Ht. 17'11", Wing Area 1048 sq. ft.
WEIGHT: Empty 33,822 lb., Design Gross 41,000 lb., Max. 56.000 lb., Fuel 2364+780 gal.
PERFORMANCE of first 26 similar to B-24C. Photo of 40-2358, the 17th B-24D, dated March 6, 1942, at San Diego.

pounds empty and only 41,000 pounds design gross. This unrealistic low loading would permit a 316-mph top speed, claimed the Model Specification dated February 1, 1942.

Liberator weight would rise due to operational requirements. The top Martin power turret and a Consolidated power turret in the tail remained with two .50-caliber guns each, but the Bendix belly turret with its awkward periscope sight was removed from the first 287 B-24Ds.

Most remained in the United States, beginning with the 44th BG which first trained crews for new units. Aircraft sent overseas, beginning with the HALPRO unit, added three hand-held .50-caliber guns. These were mounted at each waist window and at the bottom camera door behind them, as planned for early models.

A system of block numbers and letters was adopted to identify the numerous changes and factory of origin, starting with the B-24D-1-CO accepted at San Diego on June 30, 1942. Beginning with the B-24D-20-CO and Fort Worth's B-24D-1-CF model, outboard 450-gallon wing tanks could augment the normal 2,364 gallon fuel capacity. Another 780 gallons could be provided in bomb-bay ferry tanks when bombs were not needed.

Mfr

CONSOLIDATED B-24D-13-CO
Four Pratt & Whitney R-1830-43, 1200 hp at 25,000'
DIMENSIONS: Span 110', Lg. 66'4", Ht. 17'11", Wing Area 1048 sq. ft.
WEIGHT: Empty 34,985 lb., Gross 56,000 lb., Max. 64,000 lb., Fuel 2814+780 gal.
PERFORMANCE: Speed- Top 252 mph at 5000', 303 mph at 25,000', Cruising 215 mph, Landing 95 mph. Service Ceiling 32,000', Climb 20.000'/22 min. Range 2300 miles/5000 lb. bombs, 3500 miles ferry.

In December 1942, a hand-operated gun was added behind each side of the nose enclosure, with another at the bottom. The B-24D-25-CO now had ten .50-caliber guns with 4,800 rounds and 901 pounds of armor and bulletproof glass to protect crewmen. Bomb capacity was up to eight 1,130-pound bombs, but the B-24D-25-CO, B-24D-10-CF, and later models could accommodate eight 1,600-pound bombs. Under wing racks for two 4,000-pound bombs were tested, but proved unsuitable.

The B-24D-25-CO's weight had reached 34,985 pounds empty and 56,000 pounds gross before the end of 1942, and top speed was given as 303 mph. In 1943, the R-1830-65, with a new carburetor, was installed, beginning with the B-24D-135-CO, but the -43 engine continued to be used in some later aircraft for production reasons. Beginning with a B-24D-140-CO, the last 293 B-24Ds had a Sperry ball turret like that of the B-17, but made retractable by Briggs to clear the ground. Deliveries were completed July 22, 1943, with the B-24D-170 version, weighing 35,345 pounds empty.

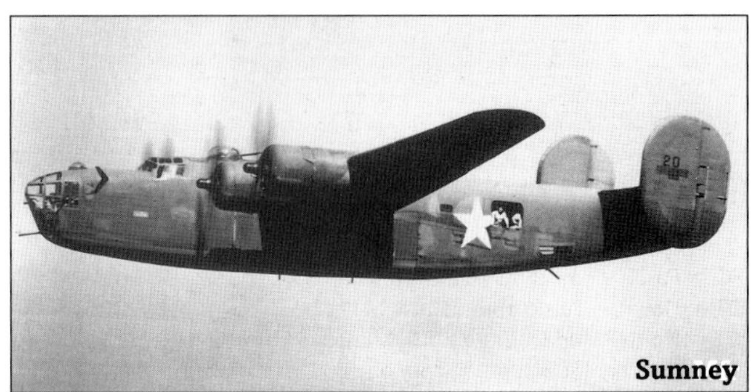
Sumney

CONSOLIDATED B-24D-25-CO of 9th BS over India

Consolidated built 2,415 B-24D-CO bombers at San Diego, and shipped eight KD sets to Fort Worth, which completed them from April 30 to July 10, 1942, followed by kits for the first 44 C-87 transports, whose delivery began September 14, 1942. Fort Worth added 295 B-24D-1-CF to D-20-CF models from December 17, 1942, to September 10, 1943. Ten more B-24D KD sets were sent to Tulsa in 1942, to give Douglas Liberator experience while waiting for B-24E sets from Ford.

AF

CONSOLIDATED B-24D-145-CO with Convair nose turret

Ford's B-24E was produced to the same specification as the B-24D, but reflected the auto builder's own practices. Willow Run did fly a B-24E assembled from San Diego parts on May 19, 1942, but acceptances on the remaining 490 B-24E-1-FO to B-24E-25-FO Liberators began on September 30, about four months late. B-24E KD kits were shipped to Tulsa and Fort Worth for completion in 1943. North American's first 25 B-24G-NTs (March/October 1943) were like late B-24Ds, but for the A-5 autopilot and Sperry S-1 bombsight used by the B-24E.

Table 6
B-24 Liberator Production from 1940 to 1945

Builder =	CO	CF	FO	DT	NT	Total
B-24A/C	20	——	——	——	——	20
LB-30/B	166	——	——	——	——	166
B-24D	2415	303	——	10	——	2728
B-24E	——	144	490	167	——	801
B-24G	——	——	——	——	430	430
B-24H	——	738	1780	582	——	3100
B-24J	2792	1558	1587	205	536	6678
B-24L	417	——	1250	——	——	1667
B-24M	916	——	1677	——	——	2593
B-24N	——	——	8	——	——	8
AT-22	——	5	——	——	——	5
C-87,A	——	286	——	——	——	286
Total	6726	3034	6792	964	966	18,482

CO = San Diego; from December 1940 to May 1945.
CF = Convair, Fort Worth; from April 1942 to August 1944.
(Fort Worth is the only factory still building aircraft in 2002)
FO = Ford, Willow Run; from September 1942 to June 1945.
DT = Douglas, Tulsa; from August 1942 to July 1944.
NT = North American Av., Dallas; March 1943 to November 1944.
Data selected from "History of the B-24 Airplane," AAF Wright Field.

Table 6 indicates how many Liberators of each model were completed from 1942 to 1945 by each of the five Liberator builders. So many changes in equipment were requested by the various Air Forces that new aircraft accepted at the factory were then flown to modification centers and depots for final preparations. Unmodified B-24Ds and nearly all B-24E aircraft were used for replacement training in the U.S., the crews getting the most recent models when they went overseas. Certain aircraft were retained for development, such as a B-24D that became the XB-24F when modified to test treated-surface anti-icing equipment in May 1942.

IWM

CONSOLIDATED LIBERATOR III

The first B-24Ds to go abroad were 23 of Col. Henry Halvorsen's detachment, called HALPRO, originally organized to bomb Japan from China, but rerouted to Egypt. From there, 12 struck at the Ploesti oil center on June 12, 1942, the first AAF strategic mission into Europe. Four of those B-24Ds were interned in Turkey, after running out of fuel. HALPRO planes remained in Egypt to fly raids with the Ninth Air Force, and later became part of the 376th Bomb Group.

Britain-based B-24Ds of the 93rd Bomb Group began operations October 9, 1942, and were joined by the 44th BG on November 7. The 33rd would fly 8,169 sorties on 396 missions, losing 140 planes and claiming 93 fighters by the war's end, while the 44th flew 8,039 sorties on 343 missions, losing 192 planes but claiming 93 fighters.

The first B-24D squadron in the Pacific attacked Kiska June 11, 1942, and the 90th Group came to the Southwest Pacific in November 1942. Because of their superior range, Liberators eventually replaced all B-17s in the heavy bomb groups opposing Japan, like the 7th in India, the 28th in Alaska, and the 5th and 43rd in the South Pacific.

Like the Boeings, the Liberator also suffered from enemy fighters and on September 29, 1942, construction of an escort fighter counterpart to Boeing's B-40 was approved. Converted from a B-24D, the Consolidated XB-41 had 1,980 pounds of crew and engine armor and 11,135 rounds for fourteen .50-caliber guns. These were placed in pairs in a new Bendix chin turret, two Martin top turrets, a Motor Products tail turret, a Sperry ball turret, and on power-operated mounts at each waist opening. One was delivered January 29, 1943, but 13 YB-41s were canceled March 16, 1943. Experience with the B-40 had convinced the Air Force that the converted bomber type of escort "would never be satisfactory".

Mfr

CONSOLIDATED XB-41
Four Pratt & Whitney R-1830-43, 1200 hp at 25,000'
DIMENSIONS: Span 110', Lg. 66'4", Ht. 17'11", Wing Area 1048 sq. ft.
WEIGHT: Empty 39,900 lb., Gross 63,000 lb. Fuel 2814 gal.
PERFORMANCE: Speed- Top 289 mph at 25,000', Cruising 200 mph, Service Ceiling 28,500', Climb 1050'/1 min. Range 3100 miles.

The "most urgent" change recommended by combat commanders was to improve frontal protection. Colonel Arthur H. Rogers, of the 90th Bomb Group, had suggested placing a Consolidated tail turret in the B-24s nose. Such a mockup was begun at Ford in August 1942, and the Hawaiian Air Depot installed this turret in the nose of a B-24D.

After successful tests in November, this aircraft participated in the Wake Island raid by 26 307th Bomb Group B-24s on December 22, 1942. By March 1, 1943, 35 turrets had been shipped to Australia for nose installations, and 20 more turrets went to Hawaii. The first B-24D-5 modified in Australia was tested on March 3, and flew a combat mission April 10, 1943. Nose turrets for Pacific-based B-24Ds were also added at the Oklahoma City modification center.

CONSOLIDATED B-24G-15-NA

On February 25, 1943, it was decided that Emerson electric nose turrets, weighing 1,006 pounds each, would be incorporated into B-24 production, while the 412-pound Bendix chin turret was chosen for the B-17G. Ford first delivered the B-24H-1-FO with an Emerson nose turret and a retractable belly Sperry ball turret on June 30, 1943. Ten .50-caliber guns with 4,700 rounds of ammunition were carried, paired in the nose, top, belly and tail turrets, and at hand-operated waist mounts where panel coverings were provided on later blocks. The A-5 autopilot and S-1 bombsight were standard on all B-24H models built at Fort Worth and Tulsa, as well as at Willow Run.

CONSOLIDATED B-24H-5-FO
Four Pratt & Whitney R-1830-43 1200 hp at 25.000'
DIMENSIONS: Span 110', Lg. 67'3", Ht. 17'11", Wing Area 1048 sq. ft.
WEIGHT: Empty 36,500 lb., Gross 56,000 lb., Max. 65,000 lb., Fuel 2364-2814+780 gal.
PERFORMANCE: Speed- Top 244 mph at 5000', 290 mph at 25,000', Cruising 215 mph, Landing 95 mph. Service Ceiling 30,000', Climb 20,000'/25 min. Range 2100 miles/5000 lb. bombs, 3300 miles max.

All but the first 25 of 430 B-24Gs built at Dallas were similar to the B-24H. Consolidated put its own nose turret on the B-24J-1-CO, which first appeared August 13, 1943, with a C-1 autopilot and Norden M-9 bombsight. This version was built by all five factories.

Motor Products hydraulic nose turrets installed, beginning January 1944, on the B-24J-75-CO, were replaced by the heavier Emerson electric turrets on the B-24J-200-CO in September 1944. These turrets altered aircraft length by a few inches. The R-1830-65 Wasps were fitted with new B-22 turbosuperchargers, increasing critical altitude, starting with the B-24J-90-CO. New Liberators, beginning with a B-24J-145, stopped getting camouflage when an order dated March 1, 1944, had them finished in bare metal; saving about 140 pounds.

CONSOLIDATED B-24J-25-CO

Production accelerated until 985 Liberators were delivered in one month, May 1944, from the five factories. Peak AAF B-24 inventory was in September, 1944, when 6,043 were on hand, including 2,257 in U.S. depots or training units, 1,471 with the Eighth and 1,190 with the 15th Air Force, and 874 confronting Japan. Tulsa had delivered its last B-24J in July and changed to the A-26, Dallas stopped B-24Js in November in favor of P-51s, and Fort Worth completed its last B-24J-105-CF on December 17, 1944, and turned to the B-32.

CONSOLIDATED B-24J-175-CO
Four Pratt & Whitney R-1830-65, 1200 hp at 28,000'
DIMENSIONS: Span 110', Lg. 67'7", Ht. 17'11", Wing Area 1048 sq. ft.
WEIGHT: Empty 36,510 lb., Gross 56,000 lb., Max. 65,000 lb., Fuel 2364-2814+780 gal.
PERFORMANCE: Speed- Top 244 mph at 5000', 290 mph at 25,000', 300 mph at 30,000', Cruising 215 mph, Landing 95 mph. Service Ceiling 30,000', Climb 20,000'/25 min. Range 2100 miles/5000 lb. bombs, 3300 miles max.

The development of airborne radar soon introduced a variety of aerial protrusions on Liberators modified for special missions. These included electronics designed for air to surface vessel search (ASV), electronic intelligence (ELINT), and electronic counter-measures (ECM). No American planes on the Pacific coast had ASV radar when the war began. British ASV sets used by Coastal Command were imported until American SCR-517s could be produced for anti-submarine patrols.

Dreadful Aleutian weather inspired the use of SCR-621 sets whose Yagi antennae cluttered the wings of the B-24D-7 model. The most widely used surface search radar was the

CONSOLIDATED B-24J-1-FO

APS-15 (H2X), first used with chin "Dumbo" radome in the nose of B-24Ds and then in a retractable radome in place of the belly turret. Most of them went to the 8th and 15th Air Force to lead "blind" bombing missions over heavy overcast. "Carpetbagger" B-24s of the 492nd BG were modified to drop agents and supplies into occupied Europe at night.

The first ELINT mission in the Pacific was flown to Kiska on March 6, 1943, by a B-24D-13 "Ferret" with an SCR-729. Liberators modified for ECM had APQ-9 jammers and chaff in the bomb bay, and added two operators to support the operations of conventional bombers. The 20th Air Force also used 35 B-24 and F-7 Ferrets to map radar sites protecting the Japanese homeland. Low-level night attacks on Japanese shipping were begun in September 1943 by the 394th Bomb Squadron, whose B-24Js had SCR-717 radar.

Several attempts to develop lighter nose and tail turrets were tried with limited success. A new hand-held tail gun mount had been specified for the B-24L, but only 186 B-24L-CO Liberators actually received them, the rest getting standard turrets. Armor steel and glass weight was reduced to 240 pounds, and side guns were enclosed, as on later J models. San Diego delivered 417 from July 1944 to January 1945 while Willow Run delivered 1,250 B-24L-FOs at the same time.

New light-weight power tail turrets appeared on 916 B-24M-COs, beginning in October 1944, and on 1,677 B-24M-FOs built by Ford from December 1944 to June 1945. Performance of models B-24G through M was essentially the same, depending on each aircraft's load. In this book, data from the model specifications is offered as representative of typical loadings.

A single vertical tail was first tested on an early B-24D first flown with a Douglas B-23 fin on March 6, 1943. Then the XB-24K, a modified B-24D-40-CO was first flown September 9, 1943, with a high single tail fin, R-1830-65 engines, and Convair nose turret. Improvements in flight handling and field of fire for the rear guns was so great that the Eglin Field proving ground recommended on April 26, 1944, that all future B-24s be ordered with single tails.

CONSOLIDATED XB-24K
Four Pratt & Whitney R-1830-65, 1350 hp at 30,000'
DIMENSIONS: Span 110', Lg. 67'1", Ht. 26'3", Wing Area 1048 sq. ft.
WEIGHT: Empty 36,723 lb., Gross 56,000 lb., Max. 65,000 lb. Fuel 2061-2814+780 gal.
PERFORMANCE: Speed- Top 297 mph at 25,000', Cruising 213 mph, Landing 95 mph. Service Ceiling 28,000'. Range 2530 miles/2000 lb. bombs.

An XB-24N-FO with the single tail, R-1830-75 Wasps and new Emerson nose and tail ball turrets ordered January 28, 1944, was first flown on November 5, but the end of the war in Europe curtailed production. Of 5,176 single-tailed Liberators ordered from Ford, only seven YB-24Ns were delivered in May-June 1945.

AF

CONSOLIDATED B-24L-5-CO
Four Pratt & Whitney R-1830-65A, 1200 hp at 28,000'
DIMENSIONS: Span 110', Lg. 66', Ht. 17'11", Wing Area 1048 sq. ft.
WEIGHT: Empty 36,075 lb., Gross 56,000 lb., Max. 65,000 lb., Fuel 2364-2814+780 gal.
PERFORMANCE: Speed- Top 294 mph at 25,000', 300 mph at 30,000', Cruising 230 mph, Landing 95 mph. Service Ceiling 32,000', Climb 20,000'/25 min. Range 2250 miles/2000 lb. bombs, 3300 miles max.

San Diego delivered the last B-24M-45-CO on May 31, and the last B-24M-30-FO came off the Ford line on June 29, 1945. Total Liberator production was 18,482, the largest of any American military airplane. Costs had dropped from $304,391 in 1942 to $215,516 per plane in 1945. They flew 312,743 sorties during the war, including 226,775 in the ETO.

As with any aircraft built in large numbers, there were many variations, and only the most important can be given here. The C-87 was the 20-passenger transport version first accepted in September 1942. Since each C-87 meant one less bomber, the needs of the bomber and transport commands had to be balanced, and only 286 transports were delivered from Fort Worth. Five AT-22s were built from June to September 1943 to train flight engineers

To support B-29s by flying fuel into their China-bases, 204 B-24s were converted to C-109 aerial tankers in 1944.

Mfr

CONSOLIDATED B-24M-40-CO
Four Pratt & Whitney R-1830-65A, 1200 hp at 31,750'
DIMENSIONS: Span 110', Lg. 66', Ht. 17'11", Wing Area 1048 sq. ft.
WEIGHT: Empty 36,099 lb., Gross 56,000 lb., Max. 65,000 lb., Fuel 2056-2814+780 gal.
PERFORMANCE: Speed- Top 234 mph at s.l., 294 mph at 25,000', 308 mph at 31,750', Cruising 216 mph, Landing 95 mph. Service Ceiling 32,000', Climb 8,500'/10 min. Range 2480 miles/2000 lb. bombs, 3300 miles max.

CONSOLIDATED XB-24N
Four Pratt & Whitney R-1830-75, 1350 hp at 30,000'
DIMENSIONS: Span 110', Lg. 67'2", Ht. 26'9", Wing Area 1048 sq. ft.
WEIGHT: Empty 38,300 lb., Gross 56,000 lb., Max. 65,000 lb. Fuel 2814-3614 gal.
PERFORMANCE: Speed- Top 291 mph at 30,000', Cruising 213 mph, Landing 95 mph. Service Ceiling 28,000', Climb 20,000' /29 min. Range 2000 miles/5000 lb. bombs, 3000 miles max.

A B-24D was converted to an XF-7 photographic aircraft with 11 cameras in January 1943, and was followed by 213 conversions of later aircraft to F-7, F-7A, and F-7B aircraft for use by Pacific reconnaissance units. Other rarely seen Liberators were the XB-24P, a B-24D modified in July 1945 to test Sperry fire control systems, and the XB-24Q, a B-24L testing the General Electric radar-controlled tail gun system in July 1946.

Nineteen Eighth Air Force groups used Liberators, but five of these were re-equipped with B-17Gs by September 1944. The Eighth Air Force in Britain favored the B-17 because it was easier to fly, had a higher ceiling, and seemed more resistant to enemy gunfire (see Table 5, page 243 for comparisons). Both heavy bombers had added much weight, but the smaller area of the B-24's narrow wing handicapped it at high altitudes.

In most areas, because of their superior range, B-24s were preferred over the B-17. Fifteen Liberator groups worked with the Fifteenth Air Force in the Mediterranean and eleven groups operated against Japan, plus the single Aleutian-based 404th Squadron that made its first attack against the Kurils on July 18, 1943.

The longest daylight bombing raid by B-24 formations were the Thirteenth Air Force's strikes against the Balikpapan oil center. The full fuel load of 3,590 gallons was needed to carry 2,500 pounds of bombs the 1,280-mile distance to the target. The 68,000-pound takeoff weight was far beyond that ever planned by the plane's designers.

The story of the Navy's use of the Liberator, and its development, the Privateer, will be told in a later chapter, but eight U-boats were sunk in the Atlantic by USAF anti-submarine squadrons in 1943. When the 13 U-boats sunk by the Navy and 68 by the RAF/RCAF are added, the Liberator became the most successful anti-submarine aircraft of the war.

The Lend-lease program in 1942 allocated Britain 164 B-24Ds designated Liberator III, and 204 Liberator GR. V with Coastal Command radar and equipment. Deliveries began with early B-24Ds rushed in March 1942, followed by a flow thru modification centers and other transfer, losing about six in transit by 1943. The anti-submarine patrols of 120 Squadron was soon joined by seven more squadrons scoring kills in the Atlantic.

A nine-place B-24D-60-CO, GR. V, was loaded with 3,393 U.S. gallons of fuel and eight 270-pound depth charges to a gross weight of 62,169 pounds. A 16.45-hour patrol was flown at an average speed of 160 mph and an altitude of 2,500 feet. Equipment included an APS-15 radar in the nose, a Boulton Paul tail turret with four .303-caliber guns, and three .50-caliber guns in the nose and waist, but no upper or belly turret, armor, or oxygen were carried.

Another B-24D-21-CF version had the radome in place of the belly turret, a Leigh light outboard of the right engines, and carried the same weapons with 3,193 gallons. Gross weight for a 15.5-hour patrol was 60,981 pounds.

Nose turrets were provided on the Liberator B.VI (1,049 B-24J and 164 B-24L), Liberator GR.VI (287 B-24J), and Liberator B.VIII (38 B-24J and 72 B-24L), and Liberator GR.VIII (182 B-24J and 130 B-24L) bombers, while 24 Liberator C-VII (C-87) and 48 Liberator C-IX (RY-3) were provided as cargo versions. When the LB-30 versions are included, the RAF gained 2,015 Liberators, less those lost in transit.

In addition to the anti-submarine, transport, and special units in Britain, about 900 were flown to heavy bomber units in the Middle East and India. A special RAF unit for ECM work, Nr. 223 Squadron, had 18 B-24H and 10 B-24J-30s transferred from the Eighth Air Force, and their modifications were also incorporated into some AAF aircraft

Australia received 13 B-24D, 144 B-24J, 83 B-24L, and 47 B-24M Liberators, for a total of 287. Canada's Nr. 10 Squadron at Gander replaced its B-18As with 15 GR VIs in May 1943, equipped with APS-15 radar, usually in the chin radome, and six .50-caliber guns, mounted in the nose, waist, tunnel, and Convair tail turret. Another four B-24D, 38 B-24J, 16 B-24L, and four B-24M bombers were added by 1945. An operational training squadron at Boundary Bay also borrowed 40 RAF Mk. VIs in 1944.

An AAF Ferry Command B-24D was stranded at Yakutsk in November 1942, and the USSR also got a 404th Bomb Squadron B-24D-10-CO that made an emergency landing in Kamchatka in September 1943. That Liberator was placed in the 45th Long-Range Bomber Air Division, the only VVS group with Pe-8 four-engine bombers, on October 23, 1943. In April 1944, the VVS requested 540 B-24 or B-17 bombers, but the AAF preferred that American units operate any strategic bombers from Soviet bases. Neither side was granted its wish.

As more American crews landed damaged bombers in Soviet-held territory, the 45th BAD-DD added aircraft to replace Pe-8s. By July 1, 1945, that division included 19 B-24s with the 25th Guards ADD Regiment and 17 B-17s with the 890th BAP, as well as 44 B-25s and 26 surviving Pe-8s. Then the 203rd Guards Bomber Air Regiment was assigned all the B-24s for long-range training, with 21 of the 29 salvaged still in flying condition in October 1945, after the war ended.

China received 37 B-24Ms in 1945, too late to fight Japan, but they were used in the civil war. On June 26, 1946, a B-24M flown to Yenan became the first of 26 aircraft with 69 Nationalist pilots to defect to the Communists. A Taiwan-based B-24M raid on Communist-held Shanghai on February 6, 1950, killed over 1,400 civilians, and caused the first request to Stalin for a VVS MiG-15 regiment to block more attacks from Taiwan. Soviet MiGs and pilots arrived, and a Liberator shot down on May 11 ended the last combat missions.

Most Liberators, of course, were processed for scrap metal after the war. Some survived many transfers, but the last Liberators in service were among 42 ex-RAF B-24Js flown by two Indian Air Force reconnaissance squadrons from 1948 to 1968.

Flying alone on anti-sub patrols, or in mass formations deep into enemy territory, Liberators were seen from Alaska to the Indian Ocean, and often their missions were as dangerous and violent as the famous low-level attack on Ploesti on August 1, 1943. Their service has been recorded in many wartime histories, and a Liberator enthusiasts' club still publicized its career a generation after the war.

Medium Bombers in Wartime

Although four-engine heavy bombers flew most of the Air Force's bombing missions, there were many targets for which twin-engine medium bombers were more appropriate. The North American B-25 and Martin B-26 were the types used by the Air Force for attacks over shorter ranges and at lower altitudes than those usual for their larger companions.

Development of the medium bombers proceeded in parallel, both being designed to a five-place bomber specification issued by the Air Corps on January 25, 1939. Bids were opened July 5, and contracts for 184 B-25 and 201 B-26 aircraft were announced August 10, and finally approved September 20. These production contracts were made without testing a prototype, so that deliveries could be made more quickly. Both types did begin arriving at Army bases in February 1941, and both entered combat in April 1942.

North American's B-25 design (NA-62) by Leland Atwood (1904-1999) and Raymond Rice was developed from the earlier NA-40 attack-bomber, but with a larger fuselage and fuel capacity. Two 1,700-hp Wright R-2600-9 Cyclones had Bendix carburetors and three-bladed Hamilton propellers, and the airframe was designed for easy production by component sub-assemblies.

Mfr

NORTH AMERICAN B-25
The first B-25 and the first B-26, factory-fresh and ready for their first flights in 1940, display each type's similarities and differences.

The wing originally had unbroken dihedral from root to tip, but to improve directional stability, the outer panels were made horizontal and the tail fins enlarged. This shape remained on all production B-25s, along with the twin rudders and tricycle gear.

The bomb bay could accommodate one 2,000, or two 1,130, or four 624-pound, or more smaller bombs, or an extra 420-gallon tank. Four hand-held flexible guns reflected 1939's modest armament levels. A .30-caliber gun was provided in the bombardier's nose enclosure. Two more hand-held .30-caliber guns were mounted to fire through waist windows and panels in the fuselage top and bottom. A .50-caliber gun in the tail was fired by a seated gunner.

The first B-25 was flown August 19, 1940, at Inglewood, California, by Vance Breese. It was never delivered to the Army, but was retained by the company as a test aircraft. This policy had replaced the previous custom of delivering the first aircraft of each type to Wright Field. Eventually, this aircraft became a company executive transport.

Martin's B-26, designed by Peyton Magruder, was a more expensive and heavily-armed medium bomber. Although also a mid-wing monoplane with tricycle gear, the B-26 was highly streamlined with a circular fuselage, single rudder, and a smaller wing, despite the heavier weight. Two Pratt & Whitney 1,850-hp R-1830-5 Wasps with four-bladed Curtiss propellers, the most powerful power plants then available, were used. A double bomb bay could hold up to two 2,000, four 1,130, six 624, or 16 300-pound bombs, up to a 4,800-pound maximum.

Mfr

MARTIN B-26

Four .30-caliber guns had been specified for the original armament, but the war in Europe made the need for more protection obvious. Drawing on its experience with turrets for the Navy's PBM, Martin developed an electric-power gun turret, the first such to go into American production. With built-in 3/8th-inch armor and a full 360-degree sweep, it weighed 522 pounds and was also adopted for the B-24 and other warplanes.

Two .50-caliber guns were placed in the top turret, and another was for the gunner seated in the tail. A .30-caliber gun was provided in the conical nose enclosure, and a second could be fired from an opening in the fuselage bottom behind the turret. Self-sealing fuel tanks and 553 pounds of armor were specified for the B-26A version added on option to the original contract, and by Septem-

NASM

NORTH AMERICAN B-25
Two Wright R-2600-9, 1700 hp takeoff, 1300 hp at 13,000'
DIMENSIONS: Span 67'6", Lg. 54'1", Ht. 14'10", Wing Area 610 sq. ft.
WEIGHT: Empty 16,767 lb., Gross 23,714 lb., Max. 27,310 lb.
Fuel 434-916 gal. (+420 gal. bomb bay).
PERFORMANCE: Speed- Top 322 mph at 15,000', Landing 90 mph. Service Ceiling 30,000', Climb 2090'/1 min. Range 2000 miles/916 gal. /3000 lb. bombs.

ber 30, 1940, the Army decided to include these features on all B-26s under construction.

On November 25, 1940, the first B-26 was flown at Baltimore by William K. Ebel. By that time, the estimated gross weight had increased from 26,625 to over 28,700 pounds, and top speed had dropped from an estimated 323 mph to 315 mph; still 100 mph faster than the B-18As it would replace.

B-25 Development

North American's bomber soon added the improved protection features introduced on the B-26. The first 24 B-25s accepted from February to May 1941 had no internal protection, but were followed by 40 B-25As with 3/8-inch armor back of the crew's seats, and self-sealing fuel tanks. This additional weight naturally began the gradual performance degradation of wartime models.

The bombardier's hand-held .30-caliber gun, with 600 rounds, was retained in the nose, but Bendix power-operated turrets were provided for the remaining ships on the contract, labeled B-25B. The tail and waist guns and windows were deleted, and two .50-caliber guns with 400 rounds each were in the top turret, which added 525 pounds to the weight. Two more guns with 350 rounds each were in a retractable belly turret lowered behind the bomb bay and aimed through a periscope sight by a kneeling crewman. A 3/8-inch armor bulkhead was provided behind the gunners.

PMB

NORTH AMERICAN B-25A
Two Wright R-2600-9, 1700 hp takeoff, 1300 hp at 13,000'
DIMENSIONS: Span 67'7", Lg. 54'1", Ht. 15'9", Wing Area 610 sq. ft.
WEIGHT: Empty 17,870 lb., Gross 27,100 lb., Max. 27,100 lb.
Fuel 434-670 gal. (+420 gal. bomb bay).
PERFORMANCE: Speed- Top 315 mph at 15,000', Cruising 262 mph Landing 90 mph. Service Ceiling 27,000', Climb 15,000'/8.4 min. Range 1350 miles with 3000 lb. bombs.

While the Bendix top turret remained throughout the war, the lower turret's gunner found it difficult to pick up targets. Condemned as "completely hopeless" as early as October 1941, the lower turret was often deleted by operational units to save the 497-pound full weight.

The first 14 B-25Bs were accepted in August 1941, but the 15th was destroyed before delivery and deleted from the order. This was before their turrets were available, but after August all were finished with them. North American had delivered 130 bombers on this contract at the time of the Pearl Harbor attack, and 171 by the end of 1941. During January 1942, with 119 B-25Bs accepted, deliveries shifted to the new B-25C contract. By that time, the bomber had been named the Mitchell, after the most famous advocate of American air power.

NORTH AMERICAN B-25B (RAF Mitchell I)
Two Wright R-2600-9, 1700 hp takeoff, 1300 hp at 13,000'
DIMENSIONS: Span 67'7", Lg. 52'11", Ht. 15'9", Wing Area 610 sq. ft.
WEIGHT: Empty 18,840 lb., Gross 26,208 lb., Max. 28,460 lb. Fuel 434-670 gal. (+420 gal. ferry tank).
PERFORMANCE: Speed- Top 300 mph at 15,000', Cruising 262 mph Landing 93 mph. Service Ceiling 23,500', Climb 15,000'/8.8 min. Range 1300 miles with 3000 lb. bombs, 2900 miles ferry.

The first Air Force group to use the Mitchell was the 17th Bomb Group at Pendleton, Oregon, which reached 52-plane strength (four 13-plane squadrons) in September 1941. At that time, the Air Force had ten medium bomber groups, but except for one with B-26s, the other groups had Douglas B-18 and B-23 aircraft, too obsolete for combat. When war came, these groups were assigned to offshore anti-submarine patrols.

Crewmen from the 17th Bomb Group, however, were given a unique mission; flying the only Army bombers ever to attack from an aircraft carrier. Led by LtCol. James H. Doolittle, 16 B-25Bs were launched from the *USS Hornet* on April 18, 1941, each loaded with 2,000 pounds of bombs and 1,141 gallons of fuel, and made a low-level attack on Tokyo and other targets in Japan.

The first mass-production Mitchell was the B-25C (NA-82) with 863 ordered from the Inglewood factory September 28, 1940, and 162 for the Netherlands East Indies on June 24, 1941. A new bomber factory was also begun in Kansas City in December 1940, and an initial order for 1,200 B-25D Mitchells was approved June 28, 1941. This model (NA-87) was to be identical to the B-25C, and the first 100 were assembled from parts made in Inglewood until the Fisher Body Division of General Motors took over parts supply.

The first B-25C, flown on November 9, 1941, was identical to the B-25B except for the R-2600-13 engines with new Holley carburetors, an anti-icing system, and new 24-volt electrical system. Changes introduced on later production aircraft were increased fuel capacity and a navigator's scanning blister atop the fuselage on plane #385, and these were included on parallel B-25D aircraft.

NORTH AMERICAN B-25C

Most of the first 100 B-25Cs finished by March 1942 were rushed out of the country to help Dutch and Soviet pilots. The first to see combat were 42 B-25Cs flown across the Pacific to Australia. Although intended for the Netherlands East Indies, they were taken over by the 3rd Bomb Group's 13th and 90th squadrons, which had arrived in Australia without their own aircraft.

On April 6, 1942, the 13th Squadron attacked a Japanese air base on New Guinea with 12 Mitchells, and the 90th flew ten to the Philippines on April 11, where they raided Japanese shipping and returned without loss. These two squadrons were joined in September by a Dutch squadron (No. 18) that had obtained another 18 B-25Cs, and the 38th Bomb Group added two more B-25C squadrons to the Fifth Air Force defending Australia.

NORTH AMERICAN B-25C-5

China had been told to prepare for a B-25 squadron's arrival in April, but Doolittle's force was unable to locate the landing fields at night. In June 1942, two 7th Bombardment Group squadrons got B-25Cs, with the 11th Squadron flying into China, and the 22nd remaining in India to become the nucleus of the 341st Group activated in September by the Tenth Air Force.

The next Mitchell unit in combat was the 12th Bomb Group, which flew 57 B-25Cs across the South Atlantic and Africa to Egypt without a loss. They made their first raid in support of British forces on August 14, 1942.

After the Americans landed in North Africa, three more B-25 groups (310th, 321st, and 340th) had by April

1943 joined the struggle for the Mediterranean under the direction of the Twelfth Air Force. The AAF, however, never used the Mitchell on raids from United Kingdom bases, reserving that role for the B-26.

After 605 B-25Cs were completed at Inglewood by July 1942, and 200 B-25Ds accepted at Kansas City from February to October, production continued with 258 B-25C-l and 100 B-25D-l bombers. They added external wing bomb racks that could hold eight 250-pound bombs in addition to the bomb bay's racks for two 1,600, three 1,000, or six 500-pound bombs, up to a maximum of 5,200 pounds. A 2,000-pound torpedo could be carried externally, although that was not used in combat by the Army.

NORTH AMERICAN B-25C-10
Two Wright R-2600-13, 1700 hp takeoff, 1450 hp at 12,000'
DIMENSIONS: Span 67'7", Lg. 52'11", Ht. 15'9", Wing Area 610 sq. ft.
WEIGHT: Empty 20,300 lb., Gross 33,500 lb., Max. 34,900 lb. Fuel 974 gal. (+585 gal. ferry tank).
PERFORMANCE: Speed- Top 264 mph at s.l., 284 mph at 15,000', Cruising 237 mph Landing 105 mph. Service Ceiling 21,500', Climb 15,000'/16.5 min. Range 1500 miles/3000 lb. bombs, 2750 miles ferry.

Beginning in October 1942, a .50-caliber flexible gun and a .50-caliber fixed gun were mounted in the nose of 162 B-25C-5 (NA-90) and 225 B-25D-5 bombers and most subsequent aircraft, for a total of six .50-caliber guns with 1,350 rounds. Winterization changes were made by December on 150 B-25C-10s and 180 B-25D-10s, while in January 1943, the B-25C-15, and later the B-25D-15, had multiple flame dampening exhaust stacks.

NORTH AMERICAN B-25C of Fifth Air Force

That corrected the bright flame spurts from the older exhaust pipes that could betray the bomber on night raids. Only minor changes were made on the C-20/-25 and parallel D-20/-25 models. Modification centers were set up at Kansas City to prepare newly-delivered aircraft with the different paint and climate gear desired by each user.

Production of the B-25C series was completed in May 1943 with 1,619 built. Deliveries of 1,540 B-25Ds to block D-25 accelerated at Kansas City until they surpassed the output of the California factory. From September 1943 to March 1944, the last blocks of 500 B-25D-30s and 250 B-25D-35s were completed with a single .50-caliber gun in a tail position and the belly turret replaced by a pair of waist guns like those of the B-25H/J models.

NORTH AMERICAN B-25D-5

A B-25C-10 modified to test a heated surface anti-icing system was designated XB-25E and first flown February 4, 1943, but an XB-25F planned for an alternate system was not completed. Forty-five B-25Ds stripped of armament and fitted with trimetrogon cameras for photo mapping were redesignated as the F-10 on August 18, 1943.

The Fifth Air Force in the Southwest Pacific added its third medium bomber group when the 345th left California with 62 B-25D-5s in May 1943, and began operations in June. The 38th Bomb Group increased from two to four B-25 squadrons by October 1943, and the 22nd Group completely converted to B-25s after the departure of the Martin B-26 Marauder from the Pacific war scene in February 1944. Since the B-26 needed larger airfields and had less range, the B-25's rival was considered more suitable for Europe.

NORTH AMERICAN B-25D-15 with BTO radar, 77th Bomb Sq.

More pressure on Japan was added with the arrival of the 42nd Group in the South Pacific's Thirteenth Air Force by April 1943 and the 41st Group in the Central Pacific's Seventh Air Force in October.

The 11th Bomb Squadron remained the only Fourteenth Air Force B-25 unit until the Chinese-American

Composite Wing's B-25 group arrived in November 1943. The 341st Group continued operations from India, joined by the 12th in March 1944. In the Aleutians, both medium bomber squadrons, (73rd and 77th), replaced B-26s with B-25s that usually added radar search gear to penetrate the northern fogs.

Improving the B-25's Firepower

The Fifth Air Force added a new modification to the Mitchell type when they modified B-25s for strafing. The bombardier's position and the lower turret were removed, and two pairs of guns were added to the nose, and another pair attached in blisters on each side. These eight forward-firing .50s were supplemented by the two in the upper turret. A crew of three operated this strafer, and sixty small fragmentation bombs, plus six 100-pound demolition bombs, could be carried. The four fixed guns in side packages were also added back in the U.S. to new B-25D-30 models.

The first B-25C strafer was tested in December 1942, and 175 B-25C and Ds were so converted for low-level strafing at the Townsville, Australia, depot by September 1943. Deadly work was done by these Mitchells against shipping in the Battle of the Bismarck Sea, and against Japanese airfields in the Rabaul area.

A remarkable Mitchell modification was to fit a standard 75-mm M-4 cannon to the last B-25C-l, which became the XB-25G tested on October 22, 1942. Five B-25C-15s were completed as B-25G-ls, the first flown March 16, 1943, and the last 400 B-25C-25s were completed as B-25G-1/-10s by August 1943.

The 75-mm gun was mounted in the lower left nose and hand-loaded with 21 rounds from the loading tray behind the pilot. The shortened solid nose had two fixed .50-caliber nose guns with 400 rounds each, and armor 3/8-inch thick covered the front and left side of the pilot's cockpit. The usual two-gun top turret and its armor bulkhead was retained, but the two-gun lower turret on the first 221 Gs was omitted on later ships.

AF

NORTH AMERICAN B-25G-10
Two Wright R-2600-13, 1700 hp takeoff, 1450 hp at 12,000'
DIMENSIONS: Span 67'7", Lg. 51', Ht. 15'9", Wing Area 610 sq. ft.
WEIGHT: Empty 19,975 lb., Gross 33,500 lb., Max. 35,000 lb. Fuel 974 gal. (+675 gal. ferry tank).
PERFORMANCE: Speed- Top 268 mph at s.l., 281 mph at 15,000', Cruising 248 mph Landing 105 mph. Service Ceiling 24,300', Climb 15,000'/16.5 min. Range 1500 miles/3000 lb. bombs, 2450 miles ferry.

The cannon was accurate if the aircraft was held steady, but only about four shells could be fired in a single run. Although the Fifth Air Force often used them against shipping and ground targets, the cannons were taken out of 82 B-25Gs and replaced by two .50-caliber guns in the cannon tunnel, two more in the nose, and a pair of .30s in the tail. Beginning in November 1943, these modifications were made in the Townsville depot.

Heavier armament was introduced on the B-25H-1, which had a 75-mm T13E-1 in the nose along with four fixed .50-caliber guns, and two more in blisters on the right side of the fuselage. The two-gun power turret was moved forward to just behind the pilot, improving its field of fire. The unpopular retractable belly turret was replaced in the waist by a flexible gun firing out of a window on each side, and a tail gunner was seated in a power-operated Bell two-gun turret with an 84-degree vertical and 76-degree horizontal swing. The load included 3,200 pounds of bombs, with provisions on late models for eight 5-inch rockets under the wings.

A thousand B-25Hs (NA-98) had been ordered on August 21, 1942, and the first B-25H-1 flew July 31, 1943. Twelve .50-caliber guns were carried on the 300 B-25H-ls, but the remaining blocks, beginning in December with the B-25H-5, carried 14, with twin package guns on both sides of the nose. Armor weight was 869 pounds.

One B-25H-5, 34408, was flown as the NA-98X with 2,000-hp Pratt & Whitney R-2800-51 engines on March 31, 1944, but crashed on April 24. Production of the five-place B-25H ended in July 1944, when North American's Inglewood factory changed entirely to P-51 fighter production.

Mfr

NORTH AMERICAN B-25H-5
Two Wright R-2600-13, 1700 hp takeoff, 1450 hp at 12,000'
DIMENSIONS: Span 67'7", Lg. 51'4", Ht. 16'5", Wing Area 610 sq. ft.
WEIGHT: Empty 19,924 lb., Gross 28,330 lb. with 434 gal., 2000 lb. bombs; 33,500 lb., with 974 gal., 3000 lb. bombs, Max. 36,600 lb. Fuel 974 gal. (+650 gal. ferry tank).
PERFORMANCE: Speed- Top: at 27,000 lb.: 293 mph at 13,000'; at 33,500 lb.: 266 mph at s.l., 275 mph at 15,000', Cruising 230 mph Landing 105 mph. Service Ceiling 23,800-25,500', Climb 15,000'/16.5 min. Range 940 miles/2000 lb. bombs and 434 gal., 1350 miles/3000 lb. bombs and 974 gal., 2700 miles ferry.

Mfr

NORTH AMERICAN B-25J-22

The most widely used Mitchell was the B-25J (NA-108) that followed the B-25D at the Kansas City factory. A six-place model with the B-25D's transparent bombardier's nose enclosure, the B-25J had no cannon, but instead had a flexible gun in the nose, with a fixed gun on the right side of the nose. The rest of the 12 .50-caliber guns were the same as those on the B-25H-5, with four fixed in packages and six for the three gunners.

The first B-25J-1 flew December 14, 1943, and 4,318 B-25Js were accepted from the Kansas factory. Later production blocks to varied in detail and gradually increased in normal weight from 26,783 pounds on the B-25J-1 to 27,738 pounds on the B-25J-30 in 1945. Power plants were the R-2600-13 or the similar R-2600-29 Cyclone. Another .50-caliber fixed gun was added below the fixed gun in the right-hand side of the nose of the B-25J-20. When in a radar training configuration, these aircraft were designated AT-24D, and later TB-25J.

An attack modification replaced the bombardier's compartment with eight .50-caliber fixed guns and 400 rpg in a solid nose. Appearing in August 1944, the B-25J-22 had twelve .50-caliber fixed guns, as well as the six flexible guns, with a total of 7,300 rounds of ammunition. This was the most heavily armed aircraft of its size in service. There were 510 Mitchells completed in this configuration, designated B-25J-22, -27, -32, and -37, according to their production block.

All B-25Js had up to 944 pounds of 3/8-inch armor for crew members, and the bomb bay normally accommodated two 1,600, three 1,000, or six 500-pound bombs. Other racks could be fitted to hold a 2,000-pound bomb or eight 500-pound bombs inside, or a Mark 13 torpedo externally. Eight 5-inch rockets could be added under the wings.

By the end of 1944, the Air Force had 11 B-25 groups overseas, (plus the 77th Bomb Squadron on Shemya) with each medium bomber group normally having 64 aircraft

Mfr

NORTH AMERICAN B-25J-5

Two Wright R-2600-13, 1700 hp takeoff, 1450 hp at 12,000'

DIMENSIONS: Span 67'7", Lg. 53'6", Ht. 16'5", Wing Area 610 sq. ft.

WEIGHT: Empty 19,480 lb., Gross 27,000 lb. with 434 gal., 2000 lb. bombs; 33,500 lb., with 974 gal., 3000 lb. bombs. Max. 35,831 lb. Fuel 434-974 gal. (+650 gal. ferry tank)

PERFORMANCE: Speed- Top at 27,000 lb.: 292 mph at 14,200', at 33,500 lb.: 266 mph at s.l. & 275 mph at 15,000', Cruising 204 mph Landing 105 mph. Service Ceiling 24,200-25,500', Climb 15,000'/16.5 min. Range 990 miles/2000 lb. bombs and 434 gal., 1350 miles/3000 lb. bombs and 974 gal., 2700 miles ferry.

among four squadrons. Total inventory, including those in reserve and at training stations, reached a peak of 2,656 in July 1944. Production ended in August 1945 with 9,816 Mitchells accepted, not including 72 B-25J-35s in flyable condition at the war's end, but not accepted contractually. Costs had dropped from $180,031 in 1941 to $116,752 per plane in 1945.

Marine Corps medium bomber squadrons were also activated to use the Mitchell, beginning with VMB-413, whose first combat mission was against Rabaul on March 15, 1944. Six more squadrons, each with 15 aircraft and 30 crews, served in the Pacific war, and five more squadrons were commissioned too late for combat.

USN

NORTH AMERICAN PBJ-1D (B-25D-30)

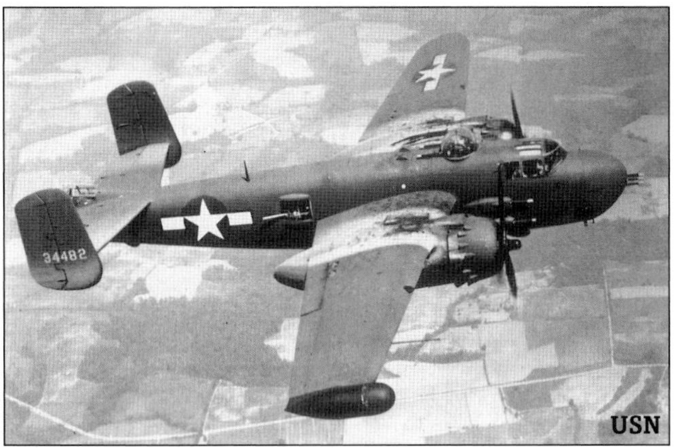
USN

NORTH AMERICAN PBJ-1H (B-25H-5 for Marines)
Two Wright R-2600-13, 1700 hp takeoff, 1450 hp at 12,000'
DIMENSIONS: Span 67'7", Lg. 51'7", Ht. 16'5", Wing Area 610 sq. ft.
WEIGHT: Empty 20,216 lb., Gross 33,728 lb., Max. 35,106 lb. Fuel 974 gal. (+585 gal. ferry tank).
PERFORMANCE: Speed- Top 265 mph at s.l., 275 mph at 12,700', Cruising 159 mph, Landing 91 mph., Service Ceiling 20,600' ,Range 1560 miles/3000 lb. bombs, 2850 miles ferry.

For these Marines, 25 B-25C-20 and 25 B-25C-25 bombers were redesignated PBJ-lC when delivered in February/April 1943, while 49 B-25D-20, 25 B-25D-25, and 78 B-25D-30s delivered from June 1943 to February 1944 became the PBJ-1D in the Marines. Instead of the belly turret, a retractable APS-3 radar scanner was added, although another modification mounted the radar in the nose. They were followed by one B-25G-5, 248 B-25Hs (which had the radar on the right wingtip), and 255 B-25Js with PBJ-1G,-1H, and -1J designations by June 1945. One PBJ-1H made experimental deck landings and takeoffs from the carrier, *Shangri-La,* on November 15, 1944.

Mfr

NORTH AMERICAN PBJ-1J (B-25J-25 for Marines)
Two Wright R-2600-13, 1700 hp takeoff, 1450 hp at 12,000'
DIMENSIONS: Span 67'7", Lg. 53'7", Ht. 16'4", Wing Area 610 sq. ft.
WEIGHT: Empty 20,273 lb., Gross 32,516 lb., Max. 34,846 lb. Fuel 974 gal. (+550 gal. ferry tank).
PERFORMANCE: Speed- Top 264 mph at s.l., 278 mph at 12,700', Cruising 159 mph, Landing 112 mph. Service Ceiling 24,300', Range 1940 miles/1,200 lb. bombs, 1520 miles/4000 lb. bombs.

The Mitchell in Allied Forces

The Mitchell was the only medium bomber supplied to the Soviet Union under Lend-Lease. Soviet fliers who came to the U.S. in September 1941 were given five B-25As to test, but considered them inadequate, and also found the B-26 unsuitable. Five B-25Bs were substituted in November, and shipped to North Russia by sea.

Beginning in March 1942, 128 B-25Cs started from Florida to be delivered by air through Africa and Iran. Four were lost on the way, but 103 arrived by the end of 1942, and Russian pilots flew 124 from Tehran in 1942- 43. They first served the 37th Bomber Air Regiment (BAP) in summer 1942, which, joined by the 16th and 125th BAP, became the 222nd DBAD (Long-range Bomber Division) on September 29, 1942. This division's combat success with B-25Cs earned it the title of 4th Guards BAD-DD in March 1943.

Another 733 Mitchells arrived in Russia via the Alaska-Siberia route, including B-25C-5/25, B-25D-20/25, B-25DP (Soviet term for B-25D-30/35), and B-25J models. Two more Guards divisions, the 14th and 15th, were added to the long-range bomber force (ADD) in 1944, and the Baltic Fleet's reconnaissance regiment, the 15th OMRAP, also used Mitchells. A single B-25G arrived in September 1943, but after testing, its cannon was removed and it became a transport for the Northern Fleet's reconnaissance regiment. The VVS also acquired a dozen B-25s landed by the 77th Bomb Squadron in Kamchatka from September 1943 to July 1945.

Mfr

NORTH AMERICAN B-25J-25 for VVS

The Royal Air Force mainly used the B-25 to attack German-occupied Europe from the United Kingdom in

Mfr

NORTH AMERICAN B-25J interior cutaway

1943-44. Deliveries began in May 1942 with 23 B-25Bs, named the Mitchell I. Three were flown to Britain for tests, one stayed in Canada, one crashed before delivery, and the rest served the operational training unit at Nassau, in the Bahamas.

Five B-25Cs flown from Florida to India for Dutch airmen in April 1942 eventually became, with their crews, part of an RAF recon squadron there, but the first RAF Mitchells in combat were 68 B-25Cs flown across the North Atlantic in July-August 1942. Named the Mitchell II, they were issued to No. 98 and No. 180 squadrons in September, and flew their first combat mission on January 22, 1943.

As deliveries increased in 1943, the RAF converted three more squadrons, No. 226, 305, and 320 (Dutch Navy pilots), to the Mitchell II, including both the B-25C and B-25D. Replenishments after August 1944 were of the Mitchell III (B-25J) model. By the time Lend-lease deliveries were completed in April 1945, the RAF had been allocated 23 B-25B, 162 B-25C, 285 B-25D, two B-25G, and 266 B-25J models; 738 aircraft, less those lost in transit.

The Netherlands East Indies squadron (No. 18) operating with the Australian Air Force (RAAF) replenished its original 18 B-25Cs with eight B-25C-15s in April 1943, followed by 34 B-25D and 39 B-24J Mitchells by June 1945.

AF

MARTIN B-26

Two Pratt & Whitney R-2800-5, 1850 hp takeoff, 1500 hp at 14,000'

DIMENSIONS: SPAN 65', Lg. 56', Ht. 19'10", Wing Area 602 sq. ft.

WEIGHT: Empty 21,375 lb., Gross 27,200 lb., Max. 32,000 lb. Fuel 465-962+250 gal.

PERFORMANCE: Speed- Top 315 mph at 15,000', Cruising 265 mph, Landing 102 mph. Service Ceiling 25,000', Climb 15,000'/ 12.5 min. Range 1000 miles/3000 lb. bombs, 2200 miles max.

The RAAF received 30 B-25D and 20 B-25J bombers for No. 2 Squadron from January 1944 to August 1945.

An operational training unit with 15 B-25Ds was set up in 1943 for Chinese airmen in India, but about 120 B-25H and Js were not delivered to China itself until 1945. Canada received 13 B-25D-20/25, 55 B-25D-30/35, and 83 B-25J models during the war, and Brazil got six B-25Bs in 1942 and 21 B-25Js in 1944.

The war's end also finished AAF B-25's combat career, and their place in this book, but for many years they were flown around the U.S. in both civil and military work. Dutch bombers opposed Indonesian independence and Chinese Mitchells fought in the civil war until 1949. Canada and eight Latin American countries were supplied with many war-surplus B-25Js in 1947-52.

In 1950/53, the USAF converted B-25Js to new training configurations: the TB-25K to TB-25N models prolonging the Mitchell's service life until 1960. Thousands of memories were left behind by the B-25, from the Tokyo raid to a spectacular crash into the world's tallest skyscraper, the Empire State Building, on July 28, 1945. Building damage was limited.

B-26 Development

The Martin Marauder was not built in as large numbers as the Mitchell, because it proved more expensive to produce and maintain, and had a higher accident rate. On paper, the Martin seemed the more advanced design, and even before the first flight, the original B-26 contract had been increased by orders for 139 B-26As on September 16, and 791 B-26Bs on September 28, 1940. This brought the total to 1,131 aircraft, a big risk on an untested aircraft.

Since Martin had designed its own power turret and self-sealing tanks, the B-26 could be the first to be ready for combat. While the B-25 entered service on the West Coast, the B-26 first arrived at Langley Field, Virginia, for the 22nd Bomb Group on February 18, 1941. After delays caused by numerous mechanical difficulties and the accidental loss of five aircraft, the group had 52 B-26s by September 30. The remaining aircraft waited undelivered because of the lack of power turrets and propellers. As they were made ready, the 38th and 42nd Bomb Groups began the difficult training demanded by the B-26.

The day after the Pearl Harbor attack, the 22nd Group, still the only operational B-26 unit, was ordered from Langley Field to Muroc, California, losing one plane on the way. It remained there until February 6, 1942, when its 56 B-26s were moved by ship to Hawaii, where ferry tanks were fitted on the 48 bombers their seven-man crews would fly to Australia by April.

On April 5, 1942, this group flew the war's first Air Force medium bomber mission, attacking Rabaul with six B-26s. In a series of unescorted attacks against Japanese-held bases against strong opposition by Zero fighters, the B-26's speed and ruggedness won praise from its crews.

Two 42nd Bomb Group squadrons were moved to Alaska to join the 28th Group. The 77th Squadron lost five of the first 14 Marauders flown up in January 1942 from California, but there were 24 B-26s of the 73rd and 77th squadrons in Alaska by May. There, weather proved a greater problem than the Japanese when they attacked on June 3, 1942, and the B-26s had to hunt through fog for the enemy.

Two British battleships had been sunk on December 10, 1941, by torpedoes carried on 50 twin-engine Japanese Navy bombers. This disaster inspired improvisation of an external rack underneath the B-26 fuselage for a 1,927-pound Navy Mark 13-1 torpedo. This rack had been tested before the war, so kits could be forwarded to combat units. There was no time for the Army pilots to practice the very different attack technique required before attempts were made against enemy ships near Midway and Dutch Harbor on June 4, 1942.

While the first five B-26As were accepted on October 31, 1941, this model did not enter service until 1942 and that contract was completed in April. Thirty still had R-2800-5 Wasps, while the rest had R-2800-39s with different carburetors, beginning on December 31, 1941, and were known as B-26A-ls.

IWM

MARTIN B-26A (Marauder IA for RAF)

The B-26A differed mainly by provision for two 250-gallon ferry tanks in the bomb bay; a feature later added to some of the early B-26s. Armament remained three .50-caliber guns with 1,200 rounds and two .30-caliber guns with 1,200 rounds. Top speed was listed as 313 mph by the specification, but that was with a design gross weight of only 27,200 pounds. Since empty weight was 21,959 pounds, these Marauders usually weighed some 32,200 pounds with the full fuel, bomb, and crew carried into combat.

AF

MARTIN B-26A-1 with torpedo

The first Marauders in action against Germany were those of the RAF, which had first been promised 500 B-26B-1s by a lend-lease contract placed on June 26, 1941, but these were rescheduled for the AAF after Pearl

Harbor. However, in May 1942, General Rommel's offensive threatened British forces in Egypt, and immediate help was required. To fill a gap in Martin Baltimore deliveries, 52 B-26A-1s at AAF stations were allocated to the RAF as the Marauder I. An additional 19 B-26As were named the Marauder IA.

After accidents in the U.S. and in transit, the RAF received 14 B-26A and 43 B-26A-1 bombers. They had been prepared for British use at Omaha, and four were ferried across the North Atlantic in June 1942 for tests in Britain. The rest were intended for North Africa and had enlarged air intakes so that filters could be fitted to protect carburetor intakes during desert operations.

By August 1942, the first had been flown down to Brazil and across the South Atlantic and Africa to No. 14 Squadron in Egypt. Their first operational sortie was made on October 28, 1942, and two months later, this squadron began torpedo reconnaissance flights over the Mediterranean.

The B-26B

A new tail defense distinguished the B-26B, the model used in the greatest quantity. In place of the single hand-held gun with 400 rounds of ammunition, two .50-caliber guns, each supplied with 1,500 rounds, were in a stepped down tail position. Ammunition was fed on a pair of roller tracks from containers behind the bomb bay. Slightly longer than earlier models and with a new 24-volt electric system, the B-26B could accommodate 4,000 pounds in the bomb bay, or a torpedo on an external rack. An Estoppey D-8 bombsight was provided, instead of the more complex Norden favored on the high-altitude heavy bombers.

Mfr

MARTIN B-26B

The first B-26B was accepted on April 5, 1942, and 26 re-equipped the 69th and 70th squadrons, 38th Group, which made the first B-26 overwater flight to Hawaii. The first two B-26Bs arrived in time for the Battle of Midway, when they and two 22nd Bomb Group B-26s made a gallant, but unsuccessful, torpedo attack on June 4, 1942. The Marauder was the only Army bomber to use torpedoes in combat, aside from the A-20 Havocs provided the Soviet Navy.

Those two squadrons later moved to the South Pacific, and then began combat sorties on November 15, 1942, while other B-26Bs replenished some 22nd and 38th Group losses. In 1943, however, the B-26s in the Pacific were replaced by B-25s, whose longer range and shorter

NASM

MARTIN B-26B with two 20-mm and six .50-caliber fixed guns

takeoffs were more suitable for island-hopping than the fast, "hot" Martins. One 22nd Group squadron, the 19th, used the B-26 until January 6, 1944, bringing the group's total to 1,376 Marauder sorties and a loss of 77 aircraft, 38 to enemy action.

The first 307 B-26Bs had the R-2800-5, but the 2,000-hp R-2800-41 was introduced on June 17, 1942, on the first of 96 B-26B-2 aircraft. One .50-caliber flexible gun and one fixed gun were provided in the nose cone. Armor weighed 1,094 pounds. The similar R-2800-43, license-built by Ford, was used on the remaining Marauder models, along with the enlarged air intakes for desert conditions introduced on 28 B-26B-3s.

AF

MARTIN B-26B-2
Two Pratt & Whitney R-2800-41, 2000 hp takeoff, 1600 hp at 13,500'
DIMENSIONS: Span 65', Lg. 58'3", Ht. 19'10", Wing Area 602 sq. ft.
WEIGHT: Empty 22,380 lb., Gross 29,725 lb., Max. 34,000 lb. Fuel 962+500 gal.
PERFORMANCE: Speed- Top 317 mph at 14,500', Cruising 260 mph, Landing 103 mph, Service Ceiling 23,500', Climb 15,000'/ 12 min. Range 1150 miles/3000 lb. bombs, 2800 miles max.

The B-26B-4 appeared in September 1942 with a lengthened nose wheel strut, equipment changes and 1,041 pounds of armor. Of 211 built, the last 141 added a pair of .50-caliber waist guns firing through side hatches at

MARTIN B-26B-3

the fuselage bottom; an arrangement previously seen on some aircraft modified by combat units. Four .50-caliber fixed guns could be arranged in outside packages below the pilots' cabin. Most of the early B-26B models were reworked at Omaha to incorporate the armament changes of the B-4 version and became known as B-26B-1s.

MARTIN B-26B-4

The first AAF Marauder group to cross the Atlantic was the 319th, which trained at Barksdale Field on B-26A-1s, and began to fly 57 B-26Bs to England in September 1942, but accidents and bad weather left the group with only 34 B-26Bs. In November, 25 reached Algeria to begin combat on November 28. Withdrawn in February after 17 losses on 165 sorties, it was rebuilt to full 64-plane strength and returned to combat in June 1943.

While the 17th and 320th groups had also been assigned to support North African operations, their route was changed to the South Atlantic. The 17th Group, the pioneer B-25 Mitchell outfit that had converted to B-26B and B-26B-2s at Barksdale Field in summer 1942, flew 57 over the South Atlantic to North Africa (losing three), and made its first combat mission over Tunis on December 30, 1942. The third B-26 group in the Mediterranean area with the 12th Air Force was the 320th, which trained at MacDill Field and entered combat on April 22, 1943, with B-26B-4s.

Nine new AAF medium bomber groups had been activated in 1942 as Marauder units, but it was in this period that criticism of the type reached its heights. A series of bad accidents in training the new pilots had brought upon the B-26 such names as "Widow Maker" and "Flying Prostitute". In the United States, the B-26 accident rate was much higher than that of the B-25, and despite improved training methods after 1942, accident rate was 55 per 100,00 flying hours from 1942 to 1945, compared to 33 for the B-25.

The Marauder's bad reputation at home contrasted sharply with its success in combat, and is to be explained primarily by the pilots involved. Increases in weight were steadily making the B-26's wing loading, and therefore its stalling and landing speeds, higher and higher. The veteran pilots of the overseas units had the experience to deal with such an aircraft, the new pilots at home did not. Many of the new pilots had not flown any twin-engine aircraft at all, and when inexperienced ground crews and overloading of the type was added, the accident rate was understandable.

Air Force inspection boards, therefore, decided to solve the problems by a new training program and accepting Martin's offer to enlarge the aircraft's wing. The new wing increased span from 65 to 71 feet and area from 602 to 658 square feet and was introduced on the 642nd B-26B and the new B-26C models. In the meantime, in July and again in October 1942, the AAF considered canceling the B-26, but commendations from the 5th Air Force, kept it in production.

To increase forward firepower, several B-26s were fitted with two 20-mm and two .50-caliber guns in the nose, and tried by the 28th Group in the Aleutians. The system adopted for production was four .50-caliber fixed guns in outside packages. In September 1942, the 28th B-26B had been tested with the fixed package guns and a new Bell tail turret, and these features were to be included on the wide-winged production aircraft as soon as possible.

The first Marauder with the new wing and larger tail was the B-26C-5-MO ordered on June 28, 1941, from a new Martin factory in Omaha. The first three were accepted in August 1942, and 86 were accepted by the year's end. The wide wing was also introduced on Baltimore's production line after 641 short-winged B-26Bs had been built by the end of 1942. The first was the B-26B-10-MA in January 1943, with 150 built on the original B-26B contract.

Except for place of manufacture, the B-26B-10 and the 175 B-26C-5s were alike. Twelve .50-caliber guns with 4,250 rounds were carried: one flexible and one fixed gun in the nose, four fixed package guns on the sides, two in the top turret, two in the lower waist, and two in the tail.

A power-operated Bell M-6 tail turret with a 90-degree cone of fire was introduced in March 1943 on the B-26B-20-MA and B-26C-10-MO. The double bomb bay could accommodate two 2,000, four 1,000, eight 500, or thirty 100-pound bombs, or 1,000 gallons of extra fuel. However, on the B-26B-25 and B-26C-30 and later models, the external torpedo rack and the rear bays were deleted. While four 1,000-pound bombs could still be carried, there was room now for just six 500 or twenty 100-pound bombs, or 500 gallons of added fuel. The nose fixed gun was also deleted from the B-26B-45 and later models.

Production of 1,883 B-26Bs ended at Baltimore in February 1944, with the last B-26B-55-MA. In addition, Martin built 208 AT-23As for the Air Force. First appearing in August 1943, the AT-23A had no armor, guns, or turret, but had a tow target windlass installed for its gunnery training mission.

Marauder production ended at Omaha on April 4, 1944, after 1,210 B-25C-5 to B-25C-45-MO and 375 AT-23B tow target trainers. Of the tow target ships, the U.S. Navy got 200 in September-October 1943 and the last 25 in 1944. Known as the JM-l, their bright orange yellow finish was familiar at Navy stations around the country. Air Force AT-23Bs, however, retained a natural metal finish and were redesignated TB-26 in 1944.

Wide-wing B-26B-10 and B-26C-5s replenished the 17th and 319th groups by June 1943. Lend-lease schedules originally designated the Marauder II as a B-26B-1, but no B-26B actually reached the RAF. Instead, the Marauder IIs were 20 B-26C-25, 45 B-26C-30 and 30 B-26C-45 bombers supplied to South African squadrons in the Mediterranean in 1943, and three Free French squadrons had another 50 B-26C-45s in 1944.

MARTIN B-26C-5
Two Pratt & Whitney R-2800-43, 1920 hp takeoff, 1490 hp at 14,300'
DIMENSIONS: Span 71', Lg. 58'3", Ht. 21'6", Wing Area 658 sq. ft.
WEIGHT: Empty 24,000 lb., Gross 37,000 lb., Max. 38,200 lb. Fuel 962+1000 gal.
PERFORMANCE: Speed- Top 270 mph at s.l., 282 mph at 15,000', Cruising 214 mph, Landing 135 mph. Service Ceiling 21,700', Climb 15,000'/23 min. Range 1150 miles/3000 lb. bombs, 2850 miles max.

The first Marauder group to fly a combat mission from England was the 322nd, which made its first sorties May 14, 1943. On the second mission three days later, all ten B-26B-4s crossing the Channel were downed by the enemy. This defeat showed that the low-level attack for which the B-26 crews had trained with D-8 bombsights was impractical against strong German anti-aircraft forces with quadruple heavy 20-mm guns.

New medium-height (10-14,000 feet) tactics with Norden M-7 bombsights were chosen for missions resumed on July 17 by the 323rd Group with wide-winged B-26C-6s, and much reduced losses. The Marauders in Britain were assigned to the Ninth Air Force, which by April 1944 had eight B-26 groups and a pathfinder squadron.

AF

MARTIN B-26B-25 "Flack Bait"

AF

MARTIN B-26B-55

In March 1944, the AAF B-26 inventory peaked at 1,931 aircraft, with 11 groups of 64 planes each, deployed against Germany, and two replacement training (RTU) units in the United States. On June 6, 1944, 742 B-26 sorties were flown in support of the cross-channel invasion.

The Last B-26 Models

The lone XB-26D was an early B-26 modified to test heated surface type de-icing equipment. The B-26E designation in September 1943 was used for three Marauders with modified armament, including a stripped B-26C-5 with less weight, and the upper turret moved forward to the navigator's compartment, as well as a B-26B-40 with six fixed guns paired in the nose and in each wing.

Three hundred B-26F-MAs, ordered September 1942, began appearing in February 1944 with the wing's angle of attack increased 3.5 degrees to reduce the takeoff run and landing speed. All had four fixed and seven flexible .50-caliber guns. The first 100 went to the AAF and the rest to the RAF.

AF

MARTIN B-26F-1
Two Pratt & Whitney R-2800-43, 1920 hp takeoff, 1490 hp at 14,300'
DIMENSIONS: Span 71', Lg. 56'1;, Ht. 20'4", Wing Area 658 sq. ft.
WEIGHT: Empty 23,700 lb., Gross 37,200 lb., Max. 38,200 lb. Fuel 1002+500 gal.
PERFORMANCE: Speed- Top 281 mph at s.l., 277 mph at 10,000', Cruising 225 mph, Landing 122 mph. Service Ceiling 20,000', Climb 10,000'/17.2 min. Range 1300 miles/3000 lb., 2100 miles max.

The B-26G was the last variant, and differed only in mechanical details. Production amounted to 893 B-26G-MA as well as 57 TB-26Gs that went to the U.S. Navy as the JM-2 target tow types in March 1945. Production ceased on March 26, 1945, with the 5,266th Marauder, the last of 56 B-26G-25s diverted in May 1945 to replenish the B-26C-45 and B-26G-10s in six French squadrons. Lend-lease had provided 200 B-26F-2, 75 B-26G-10, and 75 B-26G-21 bombers in 1944-45 as the Marauder III to replenish two RAF and five South African squadrons in Italy.

B-26 costs had dropped from about $261,000 each in 1941 to $192,000 in 1944. A single B-26G-25 modified in May 1945 to try out the bicycle landing gear planned for the B-47 and B-48 jets became the XB-26H.

The AAF record against the European Axis powers included 129,943 Marauder sorties, and a bomb tonnage of 169,382 pounds, with a loss of 911 B-26s lost in combat as shown in Table 5. Enemy air bases, transportation, V-1 missile sites, and other targets had been pounded by the medium bomber groups.

MARTIN B-26G-15

A 322nd Group B-26B-25, "Flak Bait", from August 16, 1943 to April 17, 1945, became the first American bomber to complete 200 combat missions. The last group-sized B-26 attacks in April 1945, were opposed by Me 262 jets, but time was running out for Hitler. The final B-26 mission, on May 3, 1945, was by eight pathfinder squadron planes leading 124 A-26 light bombers against an ammunition plant.

Experimental Types

The next twin-engine bomber to appear had been designed originally in August 1939 to a specification for high-altitude versions of the B-25 and B-26. Both the Martin XB-27 (Model 182) and North American XB-28 (NA-63) were to have turbosupercharged Pratt & Whitney Wasps and pressurized cabins. The Martin project was to have a wingspan increased to 84 feet, but was never built.

Two XB-28s, however, were ordered on February 13, 1940, and the first was flown on April 26, 1942. Powered by the R-2800-11, the XB-28 had tricycle landing gear, single rudder, five men in a pressure cabin, and carried 4,000 pounds of bombs and six .50-caliber guns with 1,200 rounds. The guns were paired in upper, lower, and tail turrets remote-controlled by pairs of periscope sights above and below the forward cabin. The second prototype was completed as the XB-28A photo version with R-2800-27s.

NORTH AMERICAN XB-28
Two Pratt & Whitney R-2800-11, 2000 hp takeoff, 1840 hp at 25,000'
DIMENSIONS: Span 72'7", Lg. 56'5", Ht. 14', Wing Area 676 sq. ft.
WEIGHT: Empty 25,575 lb., Gross 35,740 lb., Max. 37,200 lb. Fuel 1170-1508 gal.
PERFORMANCE: Speed— Top 372 mph at 25,000', Cruising 255 mph, Landing 86 mph. Service Ceiling 34,600', Climb 10,000'/9 min. Range 2040 miles/600 lb. bombs.

Although the high-altitude performance of the XB-28 far exceeded that of service types, wartime medium bombing was done at relatively low altitudes and authorities were unwilling to interrupt Mitchell production for an untried type. Instead, the main emphasis of bomber design in 1940-1942, from the B-29 to the B-39, would be on large long-range types.

A fitting end to the story of bomber designs with two propellers was the Douglas Model 459 begun in May 1943 and proposed to the AAF on June 15, 1943. The original design was designated XA-42 with two Allison V-1710-93 liquid-cooled engines in the fuselage. When the experimental contract was awarded on June 25, however, it was seen as a way of "increasing the heavy long-range bombing attack with minimum industrial effort."

Redesignated XB-42 on November 25, 1943, it became a high-speed bomber that could match the B-29s striking range at much less cost in economic strain, fuel, and crew requirements. First flown on May 6, 1944, the XB-42 minimized drag by burying both inline engines in the fuselage behind the pilots and extending drive shafts (each of five P-39 shafts) to co-axial Curtiss pusher propellers behind the tail. Radiators in the wings cooled 1,800-hp Allison V-1710-103s.

The usual bombardier sat in the transparent nose, with the pilot and co-pilot seated under individual canopies, the latter facing backward when operating the remote-controlled guns. Two .50-caliber guns in the trailing edge of each wing were limited to a 50 degree horizontal and 45 degree vertical swing, but were thought enough to meet attacks that, because of the bomber's speed, could come only from the rear. Two fixed forward guns were located in the nose, and a total of 2,400 rounds were provided for all six guns. An alternate attack solid nose with eight guns was anticipated. A range of over 5,000 miles with a one-ton bomb load was expected, but the bomb bay had an 8,000-pound capacity, and normal range was 1,840 miles.

DOUGLAS XB-42A
Two Allison V-1710-137, 1790 hp takeoff, 1900 hp WE at s.1., and two Westinghouse 19B-2, 1600 lb. static thrust.
DIMENSIONS: Span 70'7", Lg. 53'10", Ht. 18'10", Wing Area 555 sq. ft.
WEIGHT: Empty 24,775 lb., Gross 39,000 lb., Max. 44,900 lb. Fuel 650-2402 gal. (2570 gal. max.)
PERFORMANCE: Speed— Top 488 mph at 14,000', Cruising 251 mph. Range 4750 miles max.

DOUGLAS XB-42
Two Allison V-1710-103, 1325 hp takeoff, 1820 hp WE.
DIMENSIONS: Span 70'6", Lg. 53'7", Ht. 20'9", Wing Area 555 sq. ft.
WEIGHT: Empty 20,888 lb., Gross 33,208 lb., Max. 35,702 lb. Fuel 650-1750 gal.
PERFORMANCE: Speed- Top 344 mph at s.1., 410 mph at 23,440', Service Ceiling 29,400', Range 1840 miles normal, 5400 miles max.

A second XB-42 flown on August 1, 1944, was later given a more conventional canopy, and was lost on December 16, 1945, shortly after setting a 433-mph transcontinental flight record, with the help of tail winds. When jet engines became available, the design evolved into the XB-43 described in a later chapter. Douglas did propose the addition of a 1,600-pound static thrust Westinghouse jet under each wing on February 23, 1945, so the first prototype was reworked in this manner and flown again as the XB-42A on May 27, 1947. All guns were removed, but fuel capacity was increased.

Although none of the experimental medium bombers designed after 1939 went into production, more than enough of earlier models to win the war were available. From 1940-1945, over 30,000 four-engine heavy and over 15,000 twin-engine medium bombers had been built. Germany was defeated and the Japanese Empire had been pushed back, but the vast distances across the Pacific protected Japan from deadly attacks by those types. Closing these distances required a naval offensive and the massing of very long-range giant bombers, so these aircraft developments are described in later chapters.

CHAPTER 16

FIGHTER MONOPLANES, FROM THE P-24 TO THE P-37

An all-metal low-wing monoplane with enclosed cockpits and retractable landing gear, the Y1P-25 tested in January 1933 already has the shape of World War Two fighters.

TWO-SEAT FIGHTERS

The Lockheed YP-24 began a turn in American fighter history, the shift from the open-cockpit biplanes of World War I to the enclosed-cockpit, low-wing monoplanes of World War II. The first monoplane to show this new trend in Army Air Corps fighters was built by the Detroit Aircraft Development Co., which in 1931 also owned the Lockheed Aircraft Company in Burbank.

Robert J. Woods, then 26-years old, was hired in Detroit to design a fighter based on the low-wing Lockheed Sirius, built for Colonel Charles Lindbergh in 1929, with two cockpits enclosed by a new sliding canopy installed at Ann Lindbergh's suggestion. This design had become the Altair when fitted with landing gear retracting inward into the wings, and the Army purchased one example as the Y1C-23.

During the Depression years, the Air Corps offered bailment contracts, in which a company-owned aircraft was loaned to the Air Corps for tests. The Air Corps would provide the engine and equipment, and if the tests were successful, purchase the aircraft.

LOCKHEED YP-24 (XP-900)
Curtiss V-1570-23, 600 hp at s.1.
DIMENSIONS: Span 42'9", Lg. 28'9", Ht. 8'6", Wing Area 292 sq. ft. Weight: Empty 3193 lb., Gross 4360 lb. Fuel 80 gal.
PERFORMANCE: Speed— Top 214.5 mph at s.1., 210.5 mph at 5000', Cruising 186 mph, Landing 73 mph. Service Ceiling 26,400', Absolute Ceiling 28,000', Climb 1800'/1 min., 5000'/3.1 min., 10,000'/6.9 min. Range 556 miles.

After a mockup inspection at Detroit in March 1931, a bailment contract was issued to Detroit Aircraft for a two-place fighter. The Army's exploration of the performance advantages of low wings and retractable wheels on a fighter was designated the XP-900 project and matched by a contract with Boeing to design the XB-901 (later B-9) bomber with the same features .

Twelve engineers worked overtime at half-pay to complete the design in five months. A metal fuselage was built in Detroit and a spruce plywood wing was shipped from Burbank. On September 23, 1931, the XP-900 prototype was purchased and assigned the designation YP-24, along with four additional examples designated Y1P-24. Five Y1A-9 attack versions were also planned.

Vance Breese was the test pilot and on September 29, 1931, the YP-24 flew to Wright Field with designer Woods in the rear cockpit "to save train fare". Powered by a 600-hp Curtiss Conqueror V-1570C (-23) engine, the YP-24 soon proved itself the fastest fighter yet offered to the Air Corps, with a top speed of 214 mph at sea level. This compared to 193 mph at sea level for the Curtiss P-6E single-seat biplane with the same engine, or 175 mph for the Berliner-Joyce P-16 two-seater it might replace.

One .50-caliber and one .30-caliber synchronized M1921 Browning gun was mounted atop the engine, and a .30-caliber M1922 gun was provided for the gunner sitting back to back behind the pilot. A rack could be added under the fuselage for five 30 or two 116-pound bombs.

Encouraged by this contract, the project work was moved to Burbank. But Detroit Aircraft had been raiding Lockheed division profits for other less-successful company branches, and company debts were too large to go ahead with the Air Corps contract. On October 24, Detroit Aircraft went out of business and the contract for more aircraft was rescinded. The prototype itself was lost on October 19 when the retractable landing gear failed to extend and the pilot bailed out.

Fortunately, the YP-24's young designer had been hired by Consolidated Aircraft, then located in Buffalo, and was able to plan a new two-seater of similar layout, but of all-metal construction. The Army canceled the Lockheed contract and ordered all drawings, tools, and work in progress shipped to Buffalo. On April 4, 1932, Air Corps funds for the service test of four fighters were allocated to Consolidated for Wood's new design.

Two were to be Y1P-25s with liquid-cooled Curtiss Conqueror engines while air-cooled Pratt & Whitney Wasps were planned for other models proposed in May 1932. The Y1P-27 was to use a 550-hp R-1340-21 and the Y1P-28 a 600-hp R-1340-19, but both aircraft were later canceled.

Mfr

CONSOLIDATED YIP-25
Curtiss V-1570-27, 600 hp at 15,000'
DIMENSION5: Span 43'10", Lg. 29'4", Ht. 8'7", Wing Area 296 sq. ft.
WEIGHT: Empty 3887 lb., Gross 5110 lb. Fuel 90—173 gal.
PERFORMANCE: Speed- Top 205 mph at s.1., 247 mph at 15,000', Climb 10,000'/6.7 min.

First flown by William Wheatley on November 17, 1932, and delivered to Wright Field December 11, the Y1P-25 had a 600-hp turbosupercharged V-1570-27 and did 247 mph at 15,000 feet. The second prototype was completed without the turbosupercharger and labeled Y1A-11 for low-altitude attack work. Although the Y1P-25 crashed January 13, 1933, followed by another fatal accident to the Y1A-11 a week later, an Army board recommended purchase of a new version, the P-30.

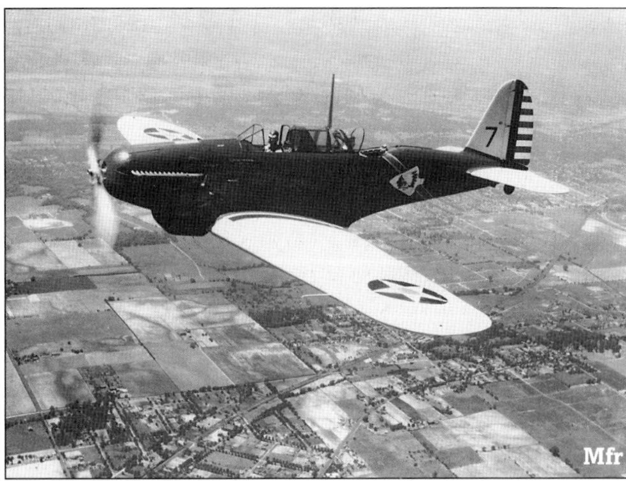

Mfr

CONSOLIDATED P-30
Curtiss V-1570-57, 675 hp at 15,000'
DIMENSIONS: Span 43'11", Lg. 29'4", Ht. 8'4", Wing Area 297 sq. ft.
WEIGHT: Empty 3832 lb., Gross 5092 lb. Fuel 92-141 gal.
PERFORMANCE: Speed- Top 194 mph at s.1., 239 mph at 15,000', Cruising 201.5 mph, Landing 77 mph. Climb 10,000'/7.6 min.,15,000'/10.9 min. Range 484 miles.

There was good reason to demand fast fighters. New all-metal monoplane bombers like the Martin XB-10 sharply reduced interception capabilities of biplane pursuits. The XB-10's 207-mph speed was faster than any 1932 Army biplane like the P-12E, and the Army abruptly turned to the monoplane pattern for its fighters. The switch was made sooner than that of the Navy, which persisted with the Grumman biplanes, and was far ahead of most foreign powers that, as late as 1941, were still fighting with biplanes like the British Gladiator, Italian Fiat, and Soviet I-153.

The Consolidated P-30 two-seater was like the Y1P-25 except for a 675-hp turbosupercharged V-1570-57 and changes in the landing gear and nose. Four were purchased with a contract approved March 1, 1933. Delivery was made from January 12 to May 17, 1934, followed by four A-11 attack versions. Useful load included three .30-caliber guns, 90 gallons of fuel, a 50-pound radio, and could add 45 more gallons if needed, or ten 30-pound bombs in racks under the wings.

Consolidated offered an air-cooled design called the P-33 in November, 1933, with the proposed new 800-hp R-1830-1 Twin Wasp. But the Army thought it to be too heavy, and instead waited until December 6, 1934, to order 50 P-30A two-seaters.

Consolidated moved its plant from Buffalo to San Diego and these aircraft were the first built in the new factory. First flown on December 17, 1935, the P-30A was redesignated PB-2A (pursuit biplace), while the P-16 and P-30 models became the PB-1 and PB-2. Armament included the usual two fixed and one flexible .30-caliber gun, and ten 17-pound fragmentation bombs.

Shipp

CONSOLIDATED PB-2A
Curtiss V-1570-61, 700 hp at 15,000'
DIMENSIONS: Span 43'11", Lg. 30', Ht. 8'3", Wing Area 297 sq. ft.
WEIGHT: Empty 4306 lb., Gross 5643 lb. Fuel 90-135 gal.
PERFORMANCE: Speed- Top 214 mph at s.1., 255.5 mph at 15,000', 274.5 mph at 25,000', Cruising 215 mph, Landing 62 mph. Service Ceiling 28,000', Climb 15,000'/7.78 min. Range 495 miles.

These Consolidated two-seaters were innovations for American production fighters: the first low-wing monoplanes with completely retractable landing gear, first with enclosed cockpits, and first with a constant-speed controllable-pitch propeller for the 700-hp V-1570-61 engine. They were also the last pursuits to use the old bar gun sight, and to be delivered in bright blue and yellow colors. Hand cranks were used by the pilot to wind up the wheels (37 turns) and by a mechanic to start the engine; the last Air Corps combat planes without electrical power for these jobs.

The effect of the General Electric F-2H turbosupercharger on speed was revealed in April 1936 trials when a

BOEING P-26A
Pratt & Whitney R-1340-27, 570 hp at 7,500'
DIMENSIONS: Span 27'11", Lg. 23'7", Ht. 10'5", Wing Area 149.5 sq. ft.
WEIGHT: Empty 2271 Lb., Gross 3012 lb. Fuel 52-107 gal.
PERFORMANCE: Speed- Top 211 mph at s.1., 234 mph at 7500', Cruising 199 mph, Landing 82.5 mph (74 mph with flaps). Service Ceiling 27,800', Absolute Ceiling 28,300', Climb 2360'/1 min., 6000'/3 min. Range 378 miles normal, 570 miles max.

PB-2A did 214 mph at sea level, 255 mph at 15,000 feet, and 274 mph at 25,000 feet. At that altitude, however, overheating interfered and the actual ceiling was not obtained. For comparison, the British Hawker Demon two-seat fighters, biplanes built the same year, had a top speed of only 182 mph at 16,400 feet.

The seventh PB-2A had been flown on March 28, 1936, as a single-seater, with the rear gunner replaced by 130 gallons of fuel, for the pursuit competition won by the P-35. The first PB-2A was lost at Wright on May 25 during tests the remainder were delivered by July 23, 1936, and divided between the 1st and 8th Pursuit groups, until all were concentrated in the latter group at Langley Field in 1937. There they served until replaced by P-36As in 1939.

The PB-2A was the last of the two-seat, back-to-back, fighter tradition begun by the Bristol Fighter in 1917. Pilots of the P-30 had complained that the gunner became valueless if even the simplest maneuvers were performed. Experience soon indicated that the flexible .30-caliber gun could not be aimed well at high speeds, and by 1938, pursuit commanders said they had no use for the two-seaters.

The PB-2A's value was in the service experience with the new design style and the turbosupercharger. Consolidated engineers again offered the Air Corps an air-cooled version in July 1938, and as late as 1940 were considering a version with a Rolls-Royce Merlin and a Boulton Paul four-gun turret for the RAF.

Boeing's P-26

The Army's approach to single-seat fighter monoplanes was somewhat more cautious, for the P-26 was the first all-metal monoplane in pursuit squadron service, but was also the last Army fighter with an open cockpit, fixed landing gear, and external wires to brace the wings.

Boeing began this design in September 1931 as Model 248 and got a bailment contract for three aircraft as project XP-936 on December 5, 1931. Built at company expense with a 525-hp Pratt & Whitney R-1340-21, the first was flown March 20, 1932, the second shipped to Wright Field for static structure tests, and the third was delivered April 25 to Selfridge Field. All three were purchased June 15, 1932, and became the Y1P-26.

A production contract for 111 P-26A pursuits at $9,999 each* was approved January 28, 1933, and the first was flown December 7, 1933, at Seattle. Although deliveries were completed on June 30, 1934, all of these planes had

* Minus such government-furnished equipment (GFE) as engines and instruments, of course.

Mfr

BOEING YIP-26 (XP-936)
Pratt & Whitney R-1340-21 (SR-1340G), 525 hp at 6000'
DIMENSIONS: Span 27'5", Lg. 23'9", Ht. 7'6", Wing Area 150 sq. ft.
WEIGHT: Empty 2120 lb., Gross 2789 lb. Fuel 50-106 gal.
PERFORMANCE: Speed- Top 227 mph at 6000', Cruising 193 mph, Landing 73.5 mph. Service Ceiling 27,800', Absolute Ceiling 28,900', Climb 2230'/1 min.

Mfr

BOEING XP-936 #3

to be reworked for safety's sake with a higher headrest and wing flaps to reduce landing speed.

Powered by an R-1340-27 giving 570 hp at 7,500 feet, the P-26A had two .30-caliber guns, with 500 rpg, at the pilot's floor-level (with the right gun replaceable by a .50-caliber one if needed). A rack could be attached under the fuselage to carry two 116 or five 30-pound bombs, and a radio was standard equipment for this and all future fighters.

The Boeing Model 281 was the export version first flown August 2, 1934, and shipped to China. Although it crashed during a demonstration flight near Shanghai on November 27, the Çantonese Air Force would purchase ten with funds raised in America. The second Model 281 arrived in Spain March 10, 1935, but the less-expensive Hawker Fury was chosen instead for production in Spain. No radio was provided on export models.

Twenty-five P-26Bs had been ordered by the U.S. Army, to be powered with 600-hp R-1340-33 Wasps using fuel injection. The first P-26B was delivered June 20, 1935, and the second June 21. Delivery of the rest was delayed while waiting for more fuel-injection engines. The price of a P-26B had increased to $14,009, due to minor model changes, the New Deal's minimum hourly wage of 40 cents, and a reduction of the aircraft worker's week from 52 to 40 hours.

Boeing then turned out the Chinese order placed in July 1935 with the last of ten delivered at Seattle on

Mfr

BOEING 281
Pratt & Whitney R-1340 S1H1G, 550 hp at 5,000'
DIMENSIONS: Same as P-26A
WEIGHT: Empty 2354 1b., Gross 3039 lb., Max. 3390 Lb. Fuel 55-107 gal.
PERFORMANCE: Speed- Top 215 mph at s.1., 235 mph at 6000', Cruising 210 mph, Landing 68 mph. Service Ceiling 28,200', Climb 2210'/1 min., 10,000'/4.6 min. Range 386 miles normal, 745 miles max.

January 5, 1936. When the rest of the Army order was completed March 7, 1936, they went to Selfridge Field with standard R-1340-27 Wasps. They carried a temporary P-26C designation for several months until more fuel injection Wasps arrived and 17 regained their P-26B identity. While the Marvel fuel injection system improved critical altitude, other limitations caused the Air Corps to stick to conventional carburetors for its standard engines.

Air Corps Boeings were issued to the 20th, 17th, and 1st Pursuit Groups, in that order. The 17th, at March Field, was soon re-equipped as an A-17 attack outfit. After four years service with the other two pursuit groups, they were replaced by P-35s and P-36s and most surviving Boeings went to the three overseas fighter units. In December 1938, these were Hawaii's 18th Group, with 21 P-26A, 12 P-26B, and 24 P-12E pursuits; the Canal Zone's 16th Group, with 25 P-26A, 17 P-12E, and 10 P-12F models; and the 3rd Pursuit Squadron in the Philippines, with 20 P-26A, three P-12E and three P-12C aircraft.

The first of these Boeings to see combat was the one in Spain when the civil war erupted in July 1936. It was one of the last three fighters at Getafe defending Madrid when it was shot down by Fiats on October 21.

Eight Boeings were left in China when the "War of Resistance" against Japan began in 1937. They were flown by the 17th Squadron of the 3rd Pursuit Group, commanded by John Wong (Huang Pan-Yang), a Seattle-born pilot trained in Portland who, with other expatriate classmates, had joined the Chinese Air Force, and became the first American ace of the war.

From August 15 to October 12, 1937, they defended Nanking against Japanese raids. At first, they were successful in downing unescorted G3M bombers, but the arrival of Japanese A5M fighters defeated the Chinese pilots. That Boeing squadron is credited with six confirmed victories for a loss of four. The remaining Boeings were grounded by damage and the lack of spare parts.

Of 34 P-26As shipped to the Philippines in 1937-1940, 14 were transferred to Filipino pilots in 1941 and several led by Capt. Jesus Villamor attacked Japanese bombers in

December. Six old Boeings went to Guatemala in May 1943, and two of these eventually returned to the United States for museum display.

Curtiss XP-31

Boeing's success had eclipsed the Curtiss effort, the XP-934 "Swift" which resembled the A-8 attack type. An all-metal monoplane with wheel pants and V-struts under the wings, the XP-934 had a .30-caliber gun in a fairing on each side of the enclosed cockpit. The wings had leading edge slots as well as flaps to reduce landing speed. A streamlined 50-gallon drop tank was attached underneath, but Air Corps fighters would not adopt this feature until 1941.

Mfr

CURTISS XP-934 (with R-1340 engine)

This private venture had a Curtiss Conqueror when the mockup was inspected in May 1932, but the Air Corps insisted on provisions for either air-cooled or liquid-cooled motors. When the prototype was completed in July 1932, a Pratt & Whitney SR-1340G radial was provided. By August 23, the 600-hp Curtiss V-1570-53 replaced it.

AF

CURTISS XP-31 (XP-934)
Curtiss V-1570-53, 600 hp at s.1.
DIMENSIONS: Span 36', Lg. 26'3", Ht. 7'9", Wing Area 203 sq. ft.
WEIGHT: Empty 3334 lb., Gross 4143 lb. Fuel 75-125 gal.
PERFORMANCE: Speed- Top 208 mph at s.1., 202.5 mph at 5000', Cruising 184 mph, Landing 80.5 mph. Service Ceiling 24,400', Absolute Ceiling 25,600', Climb 2130'/1 min., 5000'/2.6 min. Range 370 miles.

Tests at Wright Field in December revealed the top speed to be only 208 mph instead of the promised 215 mph at sea level, for the Curtiss weighed more than 1,300 pounds more than the Y1P-26. Yet it was purchased as the XP-31 on March 1, 1933.

Boeing P-29

Even before the P-26 entered service, the Army pressed for a single-seat cantilever (no external struts) monoplane with retractable landing gear. In response to an Air Corps specification dated May 19, 1933, Boeing offered its Model 264 design, which would become the P-29. Similar to the Navy's XF7B-1 fighter, it was built as the XP-940 on a bailment contract and had a full NACA cowl for the same 570-hp R-1340-27 used by the P-26A.

Mfr

BOEING XP-940

The pilot's cockpit was enclosed and armament included two .30-caliber guns and an A-3 rack for five 30-pound bombs. The wheels retracted back about halfway into the low wing, providing for safer wheels-up emergency landings.

Boeing also prepared a Model 278 design offered to the Army in November 1933 as the XP-32. Using a 700-hp R-1535-1 Twin Wasp, it was a mid-wing monoplane with wheels retracting into the fuselage, like the Navy's Grumman fighters. With two .30-caliber guns and wing racks for ten 30-pound bombs, it was expected to weigh 3,895 pounds.

The Army rejected that proposal, although the XP-940 was completed and flown on January 20, 1934. Tests at Wright Field won a contract for three Boeings designated YP-29, YP-29A, and YP-29B, but the cramped cockpit enclosure was rejected.

The YP-29 was delivered by September 4, 1934, with a simple ring cowl around an R-1340-31, a roomy pilot's canopy, 6° dihedral, and oleo tail wheel. Two .30-caliber guns and ten 30-pound bombs were provided.

The YP-29A was actually the reworked XP-940 prototype delivered September 7 with an R-1340-27, open cockpit, 7° dihedral, and P-26A tail-wheel. On October 11, the YP-29B arrived with an R-1340-27* and open cockpit, but added a one-piece flap.

This flap was later added to the other two aircraft, which became the P-29 and P-29A, respectively, when tests were completed. But the Air Corps chose to place production orders with the cheaper P-26B and faster P-30A. Boeing went out of the Army fighter business in 1936 to concentrate on bombers and transports.

*Although the P-29s were supposed to get a 600-hp R-1340-35 with fuel injection, this engine was not produced, and the conventional carburetor model was substituted.

BOEING YP-29 (P-29)
Pratt & Whitney R-1340-31 (or -39), 550 hp at 10,000'
DIMENSIONS: Span 29'5", Lg. 25'2", Ht. 7'8", Wing Area 177 sq. ft.
WEIGHT: Empty 2573 lb., Gross 3572 lb. Fuel 75-110 gal.
PERFORMANCE: Speed- Top 244 mph at 10,000', Cruising 208 mph, Landing 81 mph. Service Ceiling 24,200', Climb 1570'/1 min., 10,000'/6.8 min. Range 520 miles normal, 707 miles max.

BOEING YP-29A (P-29A)
Pratt & Whitney R-1340-27, 570 hp at 7500'
DIMENSIONS: Span 29'5", Lg. 25'1", Ht. 7'8", Wing Area 177 sq. ft.
WEIGHT: Empty 2502 lb., Gross 3270 lb. Fuel 75-110 gal.
PERFORMANCE: Speed- Top 242 mph at 7500', Cruising 206 mph, Landing 82 mph. Climb 1840'/1 min.

BOEING P-29B

Reaching for 300 mph

The fastest plane in America in 1934 was the Wedell-Williams No. 44, which had set a landplane speed record of 305 mph at sea level with a special R-1340 Wasp boosted to 745 hp. On November 10, 1933, the Air Corps Engineering Section at Wright Field requested data on this racer, built in a Louisiana hangar without blueprints by a pair of brothers who were amateur engineers. After studying their data, however, the Army rejected that type as needing too many changes in strength, visibility, equipment, and a reduced landing speed, to be useable.

But Claire Chennault, then an instructor at the Air Corps Tactical School at Maxwell Field, had seen a new version of the racer with retractable wheels and on February 14, 1935, recommended that it be developed as an interceptor of hostile bombers. Chennault saw that new bomber monoplanes like the B-10 were too fast to be intercepted by the biplanes then in service. He argued that faster pursuits (as fighters were called then) could defeat bombers, given enough warning by ground spotters. Pursuit advocates realized that speed, rather than maneuverability, had become the main criteria for success.

It was now evident that a new generation of monoplane fighters was necessary. While rejecting the 1933 Wedell-Williams design, Wright Field planned a new family of pursuit plane specifications, beginning in July 1934, which set 300 mph as the desired top speed. These specifications were used in a series of competitions intended to produce a new fighter generation.

Choosing the best designs for the Army Air Corps meant the open bidding required by a law intended to foster free enterprise and avoid possible political influence. According to the Air Corps Act of 1926, aircraft should be chosen by circulating requests for bids among private manufacturing companies, comparing their proposals, and purchasing the best offer. The task of selecting the best design was up to the Air Corps' Materiel Division, at Wright Field, near Dayton, Ohio.

Unlike today's agencies, this was not an especially large bureaucracy, and had many other duties. The Technical Executive was Major Oliver P. Echols, and coordination of engineering and procurement was the task of special project offices. The Air Corps Pursuit Project Branch itself consisted of one First Lieutenant, one civilian engineer, and a secretary. Lt. Benjamin S. Kelsey, an M.I.T. graduate, became chief of this office in 1934, and held that post nine years. He personally examined, and usually flew, each prototype offered.

The actual selections, however, were made by a "Board of Officers" set up for each competition to evaluate these proposals by awarding points for a "Figure of Merit". The project officer acted as the board's recorder, and could talk directly to company officials about their proposals. Company officials were not allowed meetings with board members themselves.

In 1935, the different boards set up to choose new bomber and pursuit types met in critical times. Many of the warplanes that became famous in World War Two made their first appearance that year, including the Boeing B-17, Hawker Hurricane, Messerschmitt 109, and the Consolidated PBY flying boat. While other famous warplanes, like the North American P-51 of 1940, came later, their design shapes usually followed the general patterns established in 1935.

Looking forward to the funding for fiscal 1936 (the budget year from July 1, 1935 to June 30, 1936) the Army Air Corps planned to buy new fighter types. On January 15, 1935, the Air Corps announced two Design and two Production

Competitions for pursuit planes with an all-metal monocoque fuselage and cantilever monoplane wings.

In a Design Competition, the Air Corps invited private companies to offer preliminary drawings of proposed aircraft to fulfil an Army specification. This envisioned a long-term development program intended to produce superior fighters three years down the line. Bids were to be opened May 6 on proposals to fit two specifications: X-602 for Pursuit, Two-place, and X-603 for Pursuit, One-place. The winning designs would be given an Army designation and a contract for engineering data, an experimental prototype, or perhaps even a service test contract for three to fifteen planes.

Production contract competitions required private builders to submit a sample aircraft, built at their own expense, for testing at Wright Field. For more immediate use, the Army needed to buy about 80 pursuits in fiscal 1936 to replace aircraft in service, so bids were also requested for two-place and for one-place pursuits, to be opened May 27 and May 29, 1935, respectively.

Since only paper designs had to be offered for the first design competition in May, no less than 16 bids were opened. After five months of evaluation, an unexpected choice was made. Although they had no real factory, the Wedell-Williams company was awarded a development contract on October 1, 1935, for an XP-34 design based on their racers. At first, the XP-34 was expected to use a 700-hp Pratt & Whitney R-1535-1, weigh 4,250 pounds, and do 286 mph at 15,000 feet.

Another bid based on a racer design by Howard Hughes had been rejected, but his new company went on to build a beautifully streamlined monoplane that set a new world's speed record of 352 mph on September 13,1935. Perhaps such speeds might be possible for fighters of similar layout, but the little racer couldn't carry the weight of a combat type, of course, and had used special 100-octane fuel. Major Echols asked that the Hughes plane visit Dayton for inspection, but Hughes did not accept the suggestion. The wealthy pilot's future relationship with officials would usually be rather erratic.

Since both Curtiss and Seversky had produced fighters for the production competitions with more powerful engines than the one on the XP-34, that paper design had to be upgraded. On June 26, 1936, a new design contract called for a 900-hp R-1830 and a speed of 308 mph. But no XP-34 ever appeared due to the death of the Wedell brothers and their backer Williams in flying accidents, and the inability of their survivors to complete the contract requirements. The lesson learned was that a company with mass production capacity was needed.

But the production contract competitions in 1935 failed to produce an eligible winner. Only Curtiss had a sample plane ready, and that had an unsatisfactory engine. Fortunately, rescheduling the single-seat pursuit competition to August 9, 1935, produced prototypes whose performance would exceed the unfulfilled XP-34's promise. These were built to specification X-600A, which required sample aircraft with these minimum and desired performance levels: a 250 to 300-mph top speed at 10,000 feet, a service ceiling of 25,000 to 30,000 feet, a 3 to 4.5 hour endurance, and a landing speed of only 65 to 70-mph to permit using a small fields. Other desired features were two guns, racks for ten 17-pound time-fused bombs, two-way radio, life raft, oxygen, controllable-pitch propellers, and a choice among nine power plants with provisions for a future turbosupercharger.

Mfr

NORTHROP 3A
Pratt & Whitney SR-1535-G, 830 hp at takeoff
DIMENSIONS: Span 33'6", Lg. 21'10", Wing Area 187 sq. ft.
WEIGHT: Gross 4185 lb.
PERFORMANCE: Speed- Top 278 mph at s.l., 266 mph at 10,000', Stalling 67 mph. Service Ceiling 31,600', Climb 10,000'/3.3 min.

Northrop responded to the challenge by beginning a rapid redesign of its XFT-1 Navy fighter on February 12, 1935. Model 3A had an R-1535-G Twin Wasp Jr. and wheels retracting into the wing roots as on the A-17A. On July 30, 1935, this prototype disappeared on a test flight over the Pacific coast.

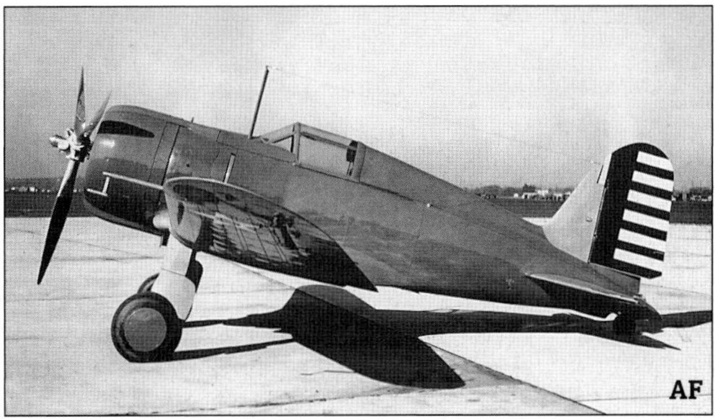

AF

VOUGHT V-141
Pratt & Whitney R-1535-A5G, 750 hp at 8000'
DIMENSIONS: Span 33'6", Lg. 22'10", Ht. 9'8", Wing Area 187 sq. ft.
WEIGHT: Empty 3515 lb., Gross 4430 lb. Fuel 75-112 gal.
PERFORMANCE: Speed- Top 274 mph at 10,000', Cruising 249 mph, Landing 73 mph. Service Ceiling 28,300', Climb 10,000'/3.86 min. Range 704 miles.

Chance Vought then purchased Northrop's fighter design and it first flew March 29, 1936, as the V-141 with a 750-hp R-1535. Smallest contender in the April 1936 trials, it suffered from tail vibrations, and the Army preferred the larger Seversky. With a modified tail and called the V-143, it arrived in Argentina by September 7, 1936, but did not win

Mfr

CONSOLIDATED PB-2A #7 as single-seat fighter
Curtiss V-1570-61, 700 hp at 15,000'
DIMENSIONS : Span 43'11", Lg. 30', Ht. 8'3", Wing Area 297 sq. ft.
WEIGHT: Empty 4315 lb., Gross 5602 lb. Fuel 90-180 gal.
PERFORMANCE: Speed- Top 250 mph at 15,000', 275 mph at 25,000', Cruising 220 mph, Service Ceiling 30,000', Climb 10,000'/5 min. Range 1012 miles max.

a contract because of its poor spin recovery. Instead, the Argentine Army waited to buy the Curtiss Hawk 75 in 1938.

Mfr

VOUGHT 143 (July 1937)
Pratt & Whitney R-1535-SB4G, 825 hp takeoff, 750 hp at 9,000'
DIMENSIONS: Span 33'6" Lg. 26', Ht. 9'4", Wing Area 187 sq. ft.
WEIGHT: Empty 3490 lb., Gross 4400 lb. Fuel 112 gal.
PERFORMANCE: Speed- Top 256 mph at s.l., 292 mph at 11,485', Cruising 243 mph. Landing 65 mph. Service Ceiling 30,600', Climb.10,000'/3.1 min. Range 808 miles.

Vought then rebuilt the V-143 with a longer fuselage and new tail. This export version was armed with the same two 30-caliber guns with 500-rpg and bomb racks as the other U.S. Army contract competitors. First flown June 18, 1937, it was sold to the Japanese Army in July 1937. A similarity in layout to the later Mitsubishi Zero caused some wartime comment, but the A6M Zero was a carrier-based fighter with a very different mission concept.

Seversky P-35

The successful bidder for the production contract was a colorful Russian immigrant, Alexander de Seversky (1894-1974). He was the president, designer, and test pilot of his own airplane company, with a fellow immigrant, Alexander Kartveli (1896-1974), as the chief engineer. In 1933, Seversky built an advanced all-metal low-wing monoplane on twin floats. Piloting it himself, Seversky set a new world's speed record for amphibians, and then reworked his craft as a landplane.

His demonstrations won his company its first contracts: for three SEV-3M military amphibians for Colombia, and 30 BT-8s, the first Air Corps monoplane basic trainers. The first SEV-3M appeared in August 1935 with a 440-hp Wright Whirlwind R-975, sliding canopy over the two cockpits, and two guns.

Using the same one-piece semi-elliptical wing, Seversky had completed a second prototype as a two-seat fighter with deep wheel pants. The SEV-2XP used a 775-hp Wright GR-1670-5, and was the only sample plane built for

SEVERSKY SEV-3M-WW for Colombia
Wright R-975E3, 440 hp for takeoff, 420 hp at 1600'
DIMENSIONS: Span 36', Lg. 28', Ht. 10'2", Wing Area 220 sq. ft.
WEIGHT: Empty 3205 lb., Gross 4600 lb. Fuel 130 gal.
PERFORMANCE: Speed-Top175 mph, Cruising 152 mph, Landing 65 mph. Service Ceiling 16,200'. Range 900 miles.

the two-place competition. But it was damaged on the way to Wright Field and didn't arrive until June 18, 1935, too late for the specified May date.

SEVERSKY SEV-2XP

When he realized the Army was more interested in single-seat fighters, Seversky replaced the rear seat with a baggage compartment, and retracted the wheels backwards into fairings under the wings. Next, an 850-hp XR-1820-G5 Wright Cyclone, the single-row radial used by Army bombers, replaced the twin-row radial. The fuel tank was integral with the center section of the Seversky wing, whose shape remained the same for the whole fighter series.

The resulting Sev-1XP returned to Wright Field on August 15, demonstrated a 289-mph top speed, and won the favor of the evaluation board. But Curtiss protested that the competition was unfair since, among other things, the Seversky had arrived late after changing to the larger engine. Army officials were not entirely happy with the result, either.

For one thing, only two of the companies interested in fighter design had actually provided prototypes. General Frank M. Andrews, GHQ Air Force commander, complained that the selection board did very little test flying, and recommended more thorough suitability trials.

Assistant Secretary of War Harry H. Woodring set a new date, April 15, 1936, for pursuit proposals, giving the builders a chance to improve their craft. Four builders responded with sample aircraft painted blue and yellow. Consolidated sent the seventh PB-2A (P-30A) modified as a single-seater with a 700-hp Curtiss V-1570-61, the only inline engine in the competition. But that was old technology, with an airframe too big for the power, and the price, $44,000 each for 25, too high for the Air Corps. The Vought V-141 was too small to have the growth potential of the Seversky and Curtiss ships.

Although the Hawk 75 reappeared in April powered by a single-row Wright XR-1820-39 Cyclone, Seversky again stepped up to an 850-hp Pratt & Whitney Twin Wasp R-1830-9 twin-row radial. While the power was the same, the smaller diameter of the Twin Wasp reduced drag and improved visibility.

As it turned out, the Air Corps decided to standardize on the Twin Wasp for production pursuits, and use the Cyclone, because of its lower fuel consumption, on bombers. Seversky won a contract, approved June 30, 1936, for 77 P-35 pursuits, while Curtiss had to be content, for the time being, with three Y1P-36s on a service test contract. To raise capital and get factory space in Farmingdale, Long Island, Seversky sold stock in his company. These investors would take control away from him in less than three years.

SEVERSKY SEV-1
Wright R-1820-G5, 850 hp at 5,000', 775 hp at 14,000'
DIMENSIONS: Span 36', Lg. 25', Wing Area 220 sq. ft.
WEIGHT: Empty 3706 lb., Gross 5014 lb.
PERFORMANCE: Speed- Top 300 mph at 10,000' (actually 289 mph on test), Cruising 265 mph. Service Ceiling 30,000', Climb 10,000'/3 min. Range 1192 miles.

SEVERSKY SEV-1
(Pratt & Whitney R-1830-9, April 1936)

Mfr

SEVERSKY P-35 (1st production aircraft, flown by Major Seversky)
Pratt & Whitney R-1830-9, 950 hp take-off, 850 hp at 8000'
DIMENSIONS: Span 36', Lg. 25'2", Ht. 9'1", Wing Area 220 sq. ft.
WEIGHT: Empty 4279 lb., Gross 5563 lb. Fuel 134-200 gal.
PERFORMANCE (As guaranteed by company, Feb. 1937): Speed- Top 300 mph at 10,000', Cruising 270 mph, Landing 70 mph. Service Ceiling 29,685', Climb 10,000'/3.15 min. Range 1134 miles/200 gal.

Major Seversky and Frank Sinclair used the original SEV-1 prototype as a personal plane and racer in 1937. A larger contract was to be awarded from bids opened April 2, 1937, so another prototype was built and Seversky challenged Curtiss again when he flew his AP-1 to Wright in March, 1937. Actually a preproduction P-35, the AP-1 had a bulged windshield, and the retracting wheels fully enclosed in fairings. But this time Curtiss got the contract.

The AP-1 was having various problems, including landing gear failures, Seversky's Farmingdale factory was behind schedule, and General H.H. Arnold was, by April 15, complaining that the company "misrepresented the performance" of its planes in advertising.

Seversky had trouble producing his P-35s. The first true P-35 arrived late at Wright Field on May 7, 1937, (contract date had been January 30) with what became the standard windshield. In July, the second P-35 appeared with practical open-sided wheel fairings and added more dihedral to the wing. Making these changes delayed deliveries so that only four Army P-35s had been accepted by the end of 1937, along with six variants built for others.

Powered by an 850-hp R-1830-9, the P-35 had a guaranteed top speed at 10,000 feet of 300 mph and a stalling speed of 65 mph, but actual test results were 281.5-mph top and 79-mph stalling. Since performance guarantees were not met, payments were reduced to $22,610 each and Seversky lost money on the contract.

The P-35s went to the First Pursuit Group at Selfridge Field. They were 20% faster and had over double the range of the P-26s they replaced. The usual two guns were fitted, but the P-35s were the first Air Corps fighters to replace bar sights with the N-2 optical reflector gun sights that would be common to WW II fighters. They were also the first Army production fighters delivered in unpainted natural metal and powered by the Pratt & Whitney Twin Wasp.

AF

SEVERSKY AP-1

SEVERSKY P-35 (Standard Army service)
Pratt & Whitney R-1830-9, 950 hp takeoff, 850 hp at 8000'
DIMENSIONS: Span 36', Lg. 25'2", Ht. 9'1", Wing Area 220 sq. ft.
WEIGHT: Empty 4315 lb., Gross 5599 lb., Max. 6295 lb. Fuel 110-200 gal.
PERFORMANCE: Speed- Top 281.5 mph at 10,000', Cruising 259.5 mph, Landing 79 mph. Service Ceiling 30,600', Absolute Ceiling 31,750', Climb 2440'/1 min., 5000'/2.05 min., 15,000', 6.9 min. Range 800 miles/134 gal. at 200 mph, 1150 miles/ 200 gal. at 259.5 mph.

The new power plants presented their own problems and the Severskys had to be grounded on April 28, 1938, due to engine bearing failures, until Pratt & Whitney solved the problem. The last of 76 P-35 fighters was delivered to Selfridge Field on August 8, 1938. When they were replaced by more advanced types in 1940-41, they were passed on to the 31st, 49th, and 53rd groups for training.

Seversky wrote the Air Corps on June 7, 1938, to propose using a new engine and wheels retracting flat into the center section. Such an aircraft, his AP-2 racer in June 1937, did 307 mph at 10,000 feet, he claimed. On June 27, 1938, the Army ordered that the last plane on the P-35 contract be completed as the XP-41 with a 1,200-hp R-1830-19 and wheels retracting inwardly.

Private versions of the P-35 for Frank Fuller and Jacqueline Cochran won the Bendix air race three years in a row (1937-39). Two Cyclone-powered examples were also built; one similar to the AP-1 for Navy fighter tests (see NF-1 in Chapter 22) and the other for James Doolittle.*

SEVERSKY AP-l with spinner

A two-seat export version known as the 2PA "Convoy Fighter," with an 875-hp R-1820-G3, was developed in July 1937 by reworking the Sev-XBT advanced trainer demonstrator. This aircraft arrived by ship in Argentina by September 29, 1937, but that country chose the Curtiss Hawk 75 as its standard fighter.

The Soviet Union bought one 2PA-L two-seater, first flown November 2, 1937, with a GR-1820-G7, and one 2PA-A delivered in March 1938 with amphibian floats and extended wings. Armament on both included a .30-caliber flexible gun, two fixed guns with bar sight, and up to 600 pounds of bombs. Manufacturing rights were also acquired by the Soviet Union, although its air force subsequently decided against replacing their DI-6 biplanes with more two-seat fighters.

SEVERSKY 2PA-L for USSR
Wright GR-1820-G3, 1000 hp takeoff, 840 hp at 8700'
DIMENSIONS: Span 36', Lg. 25'4", Ht. 9'6", Wing Area 220 sq. ft.
WEIGHT: Empty 4190 lb, Gross 6437 lb, Max. 8035 lb. Fuel 166-373 gal.
PERFORMANCE: Speed- Top 245 mph at s.l., 285 mph at 10,000', Cruising 242 mph, Stalling 74 mph. Service Ceiling 24,000', Climb 1666'/1 min., 10,000'/6 min. Range 1200 miles.

Twenty more Convoy Fighters, 2PA-B3, were built from April to August 1938, for the Japanese Navy (which called them the A8V1), although the company had claimed that Siam was their destination. They were the only American-built combat planes used operationally by a Japanese squadron, the 12th Kokutai. Their landing gear was similar to the P-35, and they had extended 41-foot wings to add fuel capacity.

---

*Civilian registrations for Seversky aircraft, listed to aid photo identification:

NR2106 Original Sev-3 as racer, was X2106 in 1933, sold to Spain in 1937.
NR 18Y Sev-1XP, c/n 2, was X18Y in 1935; wrecked December 1937.
NR189M 2PA, c/n 6, was X189 as XBT trainer with R-1340 in 1936.
R1250 AP-2, c/n 39, was X1250 in June 1937, wrecked September 1, 1937.
X1254 NF-1 naval fighter, R-1820-22, c/n 41, June 1937.
NR1291 Sev-DS, c/n 42, Doolittle Special with R-1820-G5, September 1937.
R70Y Sev S2, c/n 43, to F. Fuller in August1937, R-1830SC-G, won Bendix Trophy.
R1390 AP-1, c/n 44, March 1937, was X1390, burned April 1938.
NX1307 2PA-A, R-1820-G5, amphibian for USSR.
NX1391 2PA-B3, first for Japan, April 1938.
NX1384 AP-7, c/n 145, for J. Cochran, September 1938; flush wheels in 1939.
NX2586 2PA-200 demonstrator, c/n 146, October 1938.
NX2587 EP-1 demonstrator, c/n 147, October 1938.
NX2597 AP-4, c/n 144, December 1938, prototype for P-43.
NX2598 AP-9, c/n 148 January 1939.

SDAM

SEVERSKY 2PA-L for Japan

A 950-hp R-1830-S3C3-G with 92-octane fuel, the intake for the downdraft carburetor moved to the top, and a longer, flush-riveted fuselage was used on the two-seat 2PA-202 first flown October 23, 1938. It was joined by a similar single-seat version called the EP-1 (Export Pursuit).

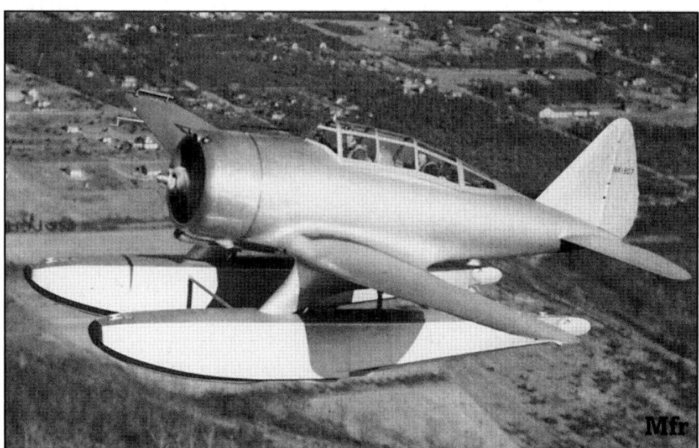

Mfr

SEVERSKY 2PA-A for USSR
Wright GR-1820-G2, 1000 hp takeoff, 850 HP at 5800'
DIMENSIONS: Span 41', Lg. 30'5", Ht. 10'9", Wing Area 250 sq. ft.
WEIGHT: Empty 4200 lb, Gross 5900 lb. Fuel 166 gal.
PERFORMANCE: Speed- Top 220 mph at s.l., 250 mph at 5800', Cruising 220 mph, Landing 68 mph. Service Ceiling 23,000', Climb 2100'/1 min. Range 850 miles.

Company publicity credited the EP-1 with 320 mph and the 2PA-202 with 315 mph, and Seversky took both prototypes to Europe on a sales tour in November. While he was abroad, the company tried for an Army contract with the single-seat AP-9, with an 825-hp R-1830-S3C5, flush riveting, the top intake for the downdraft carburetor, a sharper leading edge, and wheels retracting flat into the center section. Reaching Wright Field on January 17, 1939, it only placed last in the pursuit competition won by the P-40.

They might have had better luck with the XP-41, which was the last aircraft of the P-35 contract, but also had the wheels retracting inwardly, and introduced a 1,050-hp R-1830-19 with a two-stage supercharger. However, it was delivered too late for that competition and will be seen in the next chapter.

Seversky's bad luck continued when the 2PA-202 was wrecked after a demonstration in England on April 1, 1939, and he returned from Europe to learn that he had lost con-

Mfr

SEVERSKY 2PA-BX-202
Pratt & Whitney R-1830 S3C3-G, 1100 hp takeoff, 950 hp at 14,300'
DIMENSIONS: Span 36', Lg. 26'10", Ht. 9'10", Wing Area 225 sq. ft.
WEIGHT: Empty 4581 lb., Gross 6140 lb., Max. 7658 lb. Fuel 130-378 gal.
PERFORMANCE: Speed- Top 316 mph at 15,000', Cruising 279 mph, Service Ceiling 33,100', Climb 2600'/1 min. Range 675 miles/130 gal., 1,950 miles max.

AF

SEVERSKY AP-9

trol of the company he founded. An expected Chinese contract for 54 fighters fell through in June 1939, although the EP-1 prototype, the AP-7, Sev-DS, and the Sev-S2 were eventually sold to Ecuador in October 1941 to counter a Peruvian threat.

Sweden's Royal Air Force (RSwAF), however, did order the EP-1 on June 29, 1939, to replace its Gladiator biplanes, and while the first was damaged October 14, 1939 on its first test, sixty completed by May 1940 entered Swedish service as the J9 fighter. Sixty more ordered January 6, 1940, along with 52 two-seat dive-bombers, were completed from July 1940 to January 1941.

But these EP-1 fighters became the U.S. Army's Republic P-35A.* On October 16, 1940, General H. H. Arnold ordered that these planes were needed to replace the 28 P-26s that were then the only fighters in the Philippines, and the EP-1s were taken over two days later. The Swedes replaced the P-35A in their plans with a remarkably similar Italian fighter, the Reggiane 2000.

The RSwAF had also ordered the two-seat 2PA-204A Guardsman with extended wings, fitted as a dive-bomber with two nose guns, a flexible gun, a yoke under the fuse-

* After Seversky left the firm, the name was changed to Republic on October 18, 1939.

Mfr

REPUBLIC 2PA-204 Guardsman (to AT-12)
Pratt & Whitney R-1830-45, 1050 hp takeoff, 1000 hp at 11,500'
DIMENSIONS: Span 41', Lg. 27'8", Ht. 9'10", Wing Area 250 sq. ft.
WEIGHT: Empty 5135 lb., Gross 7462 lb., Max. 7700 lb. Fuel 130-340 gal.
PERFORMANCE: Speed- Top 293 mph at 11,500', Cruising 250 mph, Landing 86 mph. Service Ceiling 27,900', Climb 9840'/4.8 min. Range 584 miles as bomber.

SDAM

SEVERSKY EP-1 (J9)

lage for a 550-pound bomb, and wing racks for six 110-pound bombs. Only two were received in Sweden on August 1, 1940, and designated B6, before 50 others were taken over by the United States Army in October 1940 as AT-12 advanced trainers.

The P-35A added a .50-caliber gun in each wing to the two .30-caliber guns on the cowl and wing racks for ten 35-pound bombs. It could be distinguished from older P-35s by the top intake for the R-1830-45 Wasp, the longer oil cooler intake under the cowl, and gun blast tubes. Fifty-seven P-35As were shipped to the 24th Pursuit Group in the Philippines. When the Japanese invasion began in December 1941, the enemy's Zero fighters outclassed them, but they fought through the war's early weeks.

AF

REPUBLIC P-35A
Pratt & Whitney R-1830-45, 1050 hp takeoff, 1000 hp at 11,500'
DIMENSIONS: Span 36', Lg. 26'10", Ht. 9'10", Wing Area 220 sq. ft.
WEIGHT: Empty 4575 lb., Gross 6118 lb., Max. 6723 lb. Fuel 130-200 gal.
PERFORMANCE: Speed- Top 290 mph at 12,000', Cruising 260 mph, Landing 85 mph. Service Ceiling 31,400', Climb 1920'/1 min., 15,000'/6.9 min. Range 600 miles/130 gal. at 260 mph, 950 miles/200 gal. at 220 mph with 350 lb. bombs.

Curtiss P-36

The most successful pursuit effort of 1935 was the Curtiss design by Donovan R. Berlin (1898-1982) that became the P-36. Berlin had been hired as Chief Engineer by the Buffalo, New York firm, because of his experience at Northrop with all-metal construction. His P-36 would be the first American-built fighter to shoot down German

PMB

REPUBLIC 2PA-204 Guardsman as AT-12

planes, the first to pass a 1,000-plane production total, and was developed into the P-40, the principle U.S. production fighter of the war's early years

Work began on the prototype, known as Curtiss Model 75, on November 1, 1934. Seeing that engines are the pacing element in aircraft design and development, he planned from the beginning an aircraft large enough in size and wing area for growth in power plants. Berlin wanted to "provide the ultimate in performance, stability, maneuverability, controllability and maintenance, and ... a structure which would lend itself to quantity production."*

Salo

CURTISS Design 75 (Prototype P-36)
Wright SGR-1510-C5, 750 hp at takeoff, 700 hp 10,000'
DIMENSIONS: Span 37'4", Lg. 28'3", Ht. 9', Wing Area 236 sq. ft.
WEIGHT: Empty 3698 lb., Gross 4781 lb. Fuel 100-150 gal.
PERFORMANCE: Speed- Top 221 mph at s.l., 253 mph at 10,000', Cruising 229 mph. Absolute Ceiling 33,600', Climb 10,000'/4.06 min. Range 687-973 miles.

When the design was first offered to the Army on May 24, 1935, three different power plants were proposed, and the prototype actually experienced four engine changes within a year's testing. For the generous 236-square-foot area wing, a new NACA 2300-series airfoil was chosen, with less drag than the Clark CHY profile used by Seversky. Using a unique retractable landing gear whose wheels rotated as they folded back flat within the wings, the Model 75 had a 700-hp Wright XR-1510-C5 when test pilot H. Lloyd Child made the first flight on May 13, 1935.

Top speed was estimated as a modest 253-mph at 10,000 feet, but this experimental radial engine was replaced in July by a 775-hp Wright XR-1670-5, which promised 263 mph. Neither of these power plants was accepted for Air Corps production, so another air-cooled

NASM

CURTISS 75 (2nd version)
Wright SGR-1670-5, 825 hp at takeoff, 775 hp 10,000'
DIMENSIONS: As first Design 75.
WEIGHT: Empty 3760 lb., Gross 4843 lb. Overload 5177 lb. Fuel 100-150 gal.
PERFORMANCE: Speed- Top 233 mph at s.l., 263 mph at 10,000', Cruising 228 mph. Absolute Ceiling 33,200', Climb 10,000'/4 min. Range 687-973 miles.

AF

CURTISS 75 (With R-1535)

AF

CURTISS 75B (4th version)
Wright XR-1820-39, 1000 hp takeoff, 850 hp at 10,000'
DIMENSIONS: Span 37'4", Lg. 28'1", Ht. 9', Wing Area 236 sq. ft.
WEIGHT: Empty 4017 lb., Gross 5075 lb., Max. 5409 lb. Fuel 133-151 gal.
PERFORMANCE: Speed- Top 285 mph at 10,000', Cruising 260 mph, Landing 66 mph. Service Ceiling 32,500', Climb 10,000'/3.87 min. Range 730 miles.

radial, the 750-hp Pratt & Whitney R-1535 adopted by the Army for attack and observation planes, powered the Curtiss Model 75 when it appeared on August 7 for the Army competition.

The larger Wright R-1820 on Seversky's entry gave it an advantage in speed. When Curtiss complained, the Secretary of War set back the contract competition to

* Don R. Berlin, "Development of the Curtiss P-36A." Aero Digest.. Dec. 1937: 54-58.

AF

CURTISS Y1P-36 (Model 75E)
Pratt & Whitney R-1830-13, 1050 hp takeoff, 900 hp at 12,000'
DIMENSIONS: Span 37'4", Lg. 28'2", Ht. 9', Wing Area 236 sq. ft.
WEIGHT: Empty 4389 lb., Gross 5437 lb., Max. 5960 lb. Fuel 100-154 gal.
PERFORMANCE: Speed- Top 294.5 mph at 10,000', Cruising 256 mph, Landing 65 mph. Service Ceiling 35,100', Absolute Ceiling 36,150', Climb 3145'/1 min., 10,000'/3.44 min. Range 752 miles/150 gal.

April 15, 1936. Don Berlin's Hawk was flown again as Model 75B on April 4, 1936, powered by an 850-hp single-row Wright XR-1820-G5 Cyclone, and with indentations behind the cockpit to help visibility. Curtiss estimated the top speed of their Hawk as 294 mph with the Cyclone, or 297 mph if provided with a Twin Wasp, but only 285 mph was actually obtained during the tests.

Although Seversky won the Fiscal 1936 contract, Curtiss did get an order on August 7, 1936, for three Y1P-36s. The first Y1P-36, was delivered to Wright Field with a twin-row Pratt & Whitney R-1830-13 and Hamilton propeller on March 4, 1937, and was soon followed by its two service test companions. The gear-driven supercharger built into the back of the R-1830-13 yielded 1,050-hp for takeoff and 900-hp at 12,000 feet with 92-octane fuel, giving the Y1P-36 a top speed of 295 mph.

Fiscal 1938 funds would allow purchase of about 220 new pursuits, so both companies tried again with bids opened April 2, 1937. Specification 98-605 called for 300-mph and deleted the old bomb rack requirement; the Air Corps then didn't want its fighters diverted to ground-attack work.

CURTISS P-36A
Pratt & Whitney R-1830-17, 1200 hp takeoff, 1050 hp to 8,500'
DIMENSIONS: Span 37'4", Lg. 28'6", Ht. 8'5", Wing Area 236 sq. ft.
WEIGHT: Empty 4493 lb., Gross 5556 lb., Max. 5840 lb. Fuel 105-162 gal.
PERFORMANCE: Speed- Top 313 mph at 8,500', 307 mph at 12,500'. Cruising 270 mph, Stalling 69 mph. Service Ceiling 32,700', Absolute Ceiling 33,700', Climb 3900'/1 min., 10,000'/2.8 min. 15,000'/4.8 min. Range 830 miles at 270 mph.

Seversky offered its AP-1 at $15,900 each, while Curtiss wanted $18,720 for its P-36. This time the lowest bidder lost. Curtiss won the largest fighter contract since 1918: for 210 P-36s on July 30, 1937.

The first production P-36A was flown April 20, 1938, using the same Twin Wasp as the Y1P-36, but with a Curtiss propeller, and a new cowl with cooling flaps and blast tubes for the usual two nose guns. When the fourth P-36A, 38-4, was delivered on September 12, it had a new R-1830-17 with a carburetor for 100-octane fuel. These engines were standardized, beginning with the 15th P-36A. They delivered 1,050 hp at altitude, improving performance, so the P-36A did 313 mph at 8,500 feet. (P-36A 38-4 was flown back on October 26 to Buffalo, where it would be converted to the XP-42.)

The 20th Hawk was accepted on November 4 and designated P-36B with an R-1830-25 giving 1,100-hp at takeoff and 950-hp at 14,300 feet. Top speed was 327-mph at 17,000 feet. After a decision not to produce more of this engine model, the plane reverted to the standard P-36A power plant.

PMB

CURTISS P-36B
Pratt & Whitney R-1830-23, 1,100 hp at takeoff and 950 hp at 14,300'
DIMENSIONS: As P-36A.
WEIGHT: Empty 4533 lb., Gross 5634 lb. Fuel 105-162 gal.
PERFORMANCE: Speed- Top 327 mph at 17,000'. Service Ceiling 35,500', Climb 10,000'/2.75 min.

Two guns in the nose had armed American single-seat fighters in 1918, and still did twenty years later. Curtiss P-36A Hawks of 1938 had a .30-caliber Browning on the left side of the engine cowl with 500 rpg and another on the right side that could be replaced by a .50-caliber gun with 200 rpg. No bomb racks were used on any Army P-36s.

Not until September 12, 1938, was the Curtiss proposal to add two .30-caliber guns in the wings accepted, and the 85th aircraft was delivered as a P-36C on December 2. These wing guns were also authorized on December 9 for the last 30 contract aircraft. Retainer boxes were added under the P-36C wing guns to prevent used cartridges from damaging other aircraft. These P-36Cs were delivered to the 27th Pursuit Squadron at Selfridge from April 4 to May 5, 1939.

The Curtiss fighter was a "much better flying plane than the P-35" wrote Colonel Charles Lindbergh in 1939, and other pilots usually agreed. Air Corps pursuit strength then consisted of the 1st Group (with one squadron each

AF

CURTISS P-36C
Pratt & Whitney R-1830-17, 1200 hp at takeoff, 1050 hp at 8,500'
DIMENSIONS: As P-36A.
WEIGHT: Empty 4620 lb., Gross 5754 lb., Max. 6150 lb. Fuel 105-162 gal.
PERFORMANCE: Speed- Top 311 mph at 10,000', Cruising 270 mph, Stalling 69 mph. Service Ceiling 32,000', Climb 15,000'/4.9 min., Range 820 miles at 270 mph.

AF

CURTISS XP-36F
Pratt & Whitney R-1830-17, 1200 hp at takeoff, 1050 hp at 6,500'
DIMENSIONS: As P-36A.
WEIGHT: Empty 4493 lb., Gross 5840 lb., Max. 6850 lb. Fuel 105-162 gal.
PERFORMANCE: Speed- Top 265 mph at 9,000', Cruising 211 mph, Range 790 miles at 211 mph.

of P-35, P-36A, and P-36C fighters and a large reserve of the former), and the 8th and 20th Groups with P-36As.

At last Air Corps pilots had a plus 300-mph fighter, but this speed was surpassed abroad. In June 1936, the same month the Army ordered 77 P-35s, the Royal Air Force had ordered 600 Hurricane and 310 Spitfire fighters with *eight* guns. Hurricanes entered service in December 1937 with a 320-mph speed and the 362-mph Spitfire joined a squadron in August 1938. Their streamlined nose enclosing Rolls-Royce inline engines contrasted with the built-in drag of the Wasp radials.*

Curtiss P-37

The first fighter with the new Allison inline engine was the XP-37, actually the original Hawk 75 airframe rebuilt with

*American cross-country tests in 1941 would reveal Spitfire limitations: short range, requiring frequent landings, and the marginal stability that added to the superb maneuverability but became tiring and uncomfortable on long flights. "The plane that was superior in all respects in its own country would not have met our standards or been accepted...by our evaluating boards" asserted Ben Kelsey.

the liquid-cooled YV-1710-7 in its streamlined nose, side scoops for the radiator and intercooler inside the fuselage, and the pilot's cockpit moved back behind the fuel tank. With an external exhaust-driven F-10 turbosupercharger by General Electric under the engine, 1,000 hp was developed at 20,000 feet, enabling the XP-37 to reach 340-mph at that altitude.

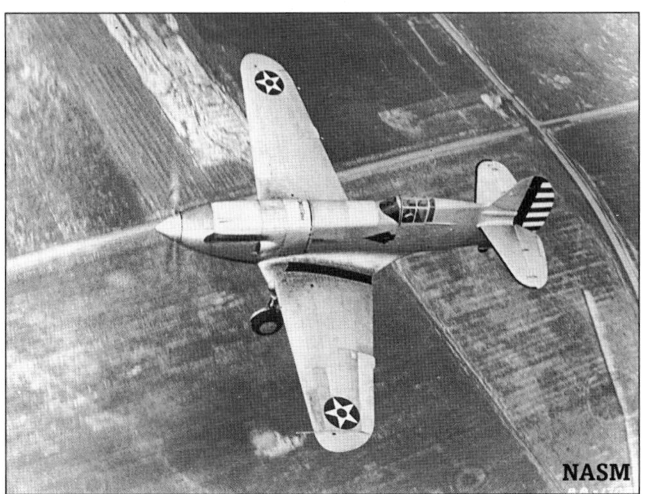
NASM

CURTISS XP-37
Allison V-1710-11, 1150 hp takeoff, 1000 hp at 20,000'
DIMENSIONS: Wing Span 37'4", Lg. 31', Ht. 9'6", Wing Area 236 sq. ft.
WEIGHT: Empty 5272 lb., Gross 6350 lb., Max. 6643 lb. Fuel 104-148 gals.
PERFORMANCE: Speed- Top 340 mph at 20,000', Cruising 304 mph. Landing 75 mph. Service Ceiling 35,000', Climb 20,000'/7 min. Range 485 miles normal, 625 miles max.

Purchased from Curtiss on February 16, 1937, the XP-37 was damaged when flown to Wright Field on April 20 and had to be repaired and redelivered for its official first flight on July 23. After another accident in 1938, the aircraft was reworked with an 1,150-hp V-1710-11 and B-1 (F-13) supercharger, and again in January 1939 to test the engine arrangement of the YP-37.

Thirteen Curtiss YP-37s were ordered on December 11, 1937, and the first two were delivered on April 29, 1939, to service test their Allison V-1710-21 engine and B-2 supercharger. Ten more were accepted in November and the last was received on December 5, 1939. They could be distinguished by the lengthened fuselage behind the cockpit, a small air scoop on the left side for the intercooler, and a larger scoop on the right side for the engine radiator.

Ten served the 8th Pursuit Group at Langley, which had experience with the supercharged PB-2A, and the 36th Group in 1940. Pilot visibility was poor during landings and the superchargers constantly gave trouble. Since these turbosuperchargers were an American development unequaled in Europe, it was tempting to see them as a kind of magic for high-altitude speed, and the devices were not allowed to be exported before 1941.

But they did have important disadvantages. Turbosuperchargers were heavy, had to be placed outside of the engine cowling to obtain enough cooling, and generated so much heat and pressure that explosions of their rotor blades and in-flight fires were frequent. Prewar models

AF

CURTISS YP-37
Allison V-1710-21, 1150 hp takeoff, 1000 hp at 20,000'
DIMENSIONS: Span 37'4", Lg. 32'10", Ht. 9'6", Wing Area 236 sq. ft.
WEIGHT: Empty 5723 lb., Gross 6889 lb., Max. 7178 lb. Fuel 108-164 gal.
PERFORMANCE: Speed- Top 331 mph at 20,000', Cruising 305 mph, Landing 85 mph. Service Ceiling 34,000', Climb 2920'/1 min., 20,000'/8.1 min. Range 570 miles normal, 870 miles max.

lacked an automatic regulator, so their control was a distraction for already preoccupied fighter pilots. With such problems, designers preferred the simpler gear-driven internal supercharger unless high-altitude speed was absolutely demanded.

Curtiss also tried to improve the air-cooled versions with the Hawk 75R, a private-venture P-36 modification, whose R-1830-19 Wasp had a two-stage internal supercharger and added an auxiliary gear-driven supercharger with external coolers behind the radial. First flown on December 13, 1938, and delivered to Wright Field on January 20, 1939, the complicated power plant proved unsatisfactory and the 75R was returned to the company for further work.

AF

CURTISS 75R
Pratt & Whitney R-1830-19, 1200 hp takeoff, 1050 hp at 17,500'
DIMENSIONS: As P-36A
WEIGHT: Empty 5074 lb., Gross 6163 lb.
PERFORMANCE: Speed- Top 330 mph at 15,000', Cruising 302 mph, Climb 15,000'/4.75 min. Range 600 miles.

The fourth P-36A returned to Wright Field on March 5, 1939, modified as the XP-42. Reflecting an attempt to give the radial engine the streamlining associated with inline power plants, the XP-42's R-1830-31 Wasp had an extended propeller shaft enclosed behind a large spinner with an intake for air cooling underneath and paired carburetor air intakes on top. Maximum speed was only 315 mph at first, but a large variety of cowl forms were tested at Langley Field, and by August 1941, 343 mph had been achieved with a short-cowled configuration.

CURTISS XP-42
Pratt & Whitney R-1830-31, 1050 hp take-off, 1000 hp at 14,500'
DIMENSIONS: Span 37'4", Lg. 30'7", Ht. 12', Wing Area 236 sq. ft.
WEIGHT: Empty 4818 lb., Cross 5919 lb., Max. 6260 lb. Fuel 105-161 gal.
PERFORMANCE: Speed- Top 315 mph at 15,000', Cruising 286 mph. Range 730 miles normal, 1200 miles max.

CURTISS XP-42 (Short-nose version)

Air Corps concern with its inadequate fighter armament was reflected in an August 23, 1939, contract that produced two P-36A conversions: an XP-36D with two .50-caliber guns in the nose and four .30-caliber wing guns, along with the XP-36E, which had eight .30-caliber guns in the wings, like British fighters. Both were at Wright Field by October, and after tests at the Eglin proving ground, the XP-36D's armament was chosen for the future XP-46 and P-40B types.

Four Danish 23-mm Madsen guns had been ordered by the Army on May 18, 1937, but tests in 1938 displayed poor reliability and a slow rate of fire. Nevertheless, a September 6, 1939, order converted a P-36A to the XP-36F, which appeared in December with an imported Madsen with 50 rpg attached below each wing, as well as the usual .50-caliber and .30-caliber guns on the cowl.

A sample of the 20-mm Hispano Type 404 gun had been ordered from France on July 27, 1937, and Army tests begun June 21, 1938, demonstrated twice the Madsen's rate of fire. Another 33 were ordered December 14, 1939, and after the first arrived from France in February 1940, a pair replaced the Madsens on the XP-36F. Since their height with the 60-round ammunition drum prevented installation within the wings, large fairings were required. After successful firing tests in July, these 20-mm weapons were chosen for Air Corps production by Bendix in September 1940, but in 1941, this gun was limited to the roomy noses of the P-38 and export models of the P-39.

The 27th Squadron's P-36Cs at Selfridge were transferred to the 1st Pursuit Squadron at the Eglin Field Proving Ground in September 1939. By 1940, the P-36A was being replaced by the P-40. The 8th Pursuit Group passed its P-36As and YP-37s to the 36th Group in 1940 and to the 56th Group in 1941, while the 20th Group's P-36As went to the 35th at Hamilton Field and then to the 51st at March Field.

Overseas squadrons still used old Boeings until September 1939, when 30 P-36As were flown to the 16th Group in the Panama Canal. Three were lost on that ferry flight. Overseas deployment sent 20 P-36As to Hawaii in October 1939, followed by 31 more flown off the carrier *Enterprise* on February 21, 1941, a preview of wartime fighter deliveries. There were 39 left at Wheeler Field, with 20 in commission, on December 7, 1941.

Twenty P-36As went to Anchorage, Alaska, with the 18th Pursuit Squadron on February 20, 1941. By November 30, 1941, 15 P-36As remained in the Canal Zone with the 16th Group and Puerto Rico's 36th Group had 16.

Only once did the P-36A fight while carrying U.S. markings. On the morning of December 7, 1941, 14 P-36A and 11 P-40B sorties were flown during the surprise attack on Pearl Harbor. The older Hawks were credited with at least two victories, for one loss to enemy fighters and one to American anti-aircraft fire.

Hawks for export

Unlike Seversky, the Curtiss fighter did not seek publicity from civilian exploits. Instead, the strong Curtiss sales office promoted more heavily-armed export models. The first Curtiss monoplane fighter built for export first flew on May 18, 1937, following the Y1P-36s. Called the Hawk 75H, it differed from the P-36 in having fixed, panted wheels and a Wright R-1820-G3 Cyclone giving 840-hp at 8,700 feet. Armament included two cowl guns (one .30-caliber with 600 rounds and one .50-caliber with 200 rounds), two .30-caliber wing guns, and wing racks for ten 30-pound bombs.

Shipped to China and demonstrated there in August, it was purchased for use as a command and reconnaissance plane by Colonel Claire Chennault, who was the senior "advisor" to China during the Japanese invasion. Once, on October 12, 1937, while flown by John Wong, the 75H shot down a Japanese E7K1 seaplane. This is the first confirmed Hawk 75 victory.

SDAM

CURTISS 75H in China

NASM

CURTISS 75H
Wright GR-1820-G3; 875 hp at takeoff, 840 hp at 8700'
DIMENSIONS: Span 37'4", Lg. 28'10", Ht. 9'3", Wing Area 236 sq. ft.
WEIGHT: Empty 3975 lb., Gross 5305 lb., Max. 6465 lb. Fuel 120-220 gal.
PERFORMANCE: Speed- Top 239 mph at s.l., 280 mph at 10,700', Cruising 240 mph, Landing 68 mph. Service Ceiling 31,800', Climb 2340'/1 min. Range 537 miles normal, 1210 miles max.

Thirty Hawk H75M fighters were ordered by China in September 1937, first flown June 8, 1938, and completed by August. Serving with the 5th Group, they were not very successful in combating the lighter Japanese fighters, due to frequent accidents by inexperienced pilots. Only five were left in December 1940. A second Hawk 75H arrived in Argentina on June 19, 1937, and, after lengthy but successful demonstrations, crashed March 10, 1938, on the way to Chile. The Argentine Army did purchase 30 H75O models delivered with the R-1820-G3, one 11.35-mm, and three 7.65-mm Madsen guns from November 29 to December 30, 1938. With 20 more built under license at Cordoba in 1940, with the R-1820-G5, Argentina had the best fighter force in South America.

Mfr

CURTISS HAWK 75M

Twelve H75Ns were ordered by Thailand in April 1938 and the first flight was on November 1, 1938. They had an R-1820-G3 and an armament of two 8-mm nose guns and under wing mounts for two 23-mm Madsen guns to be fitted by the customer. The Thai fighters flew attacks against French air bases in Cambodia during a border dispute that climaxed in January 1941.

Powered by a GR-1820-G105A whose two-speed supercharger offered 900 hp at 8,000 feet and 750 hp at 19,000 feet, the Hawk H75Q was the first export model with retractable wheels like the P-36. First flown by Robert W. Fausel on October 7, 1938, the 75Q was shipped to

NASM

CURTISS H-75Q
Wright GR-1820-Gl05A, 1100 hp at takeoff, 900 hp at 8000', 750 hp at 19,000'
DIMENSIONS: Same as Hawk 75H.
WEIGHT: Empty 4483 lb., Gross 5692 lb., Max. 6940 lb., Fuel 105-163 gal.
PERFORMANCE: Speed- Top 259 mph at s.l., 303 mph at 19,000', Cruising 260 mph, Landing 68 mph. Service Ceiling 32,800', Climb 2800'/1 min., 10,000'/3.4 min., 20,000'/9 min. Range 677 miles/105 gal., 1040 miles/163 gal.

China, where Fausel flew competitive tests with Soviet fighters in February, 1939.

Equipment included a 67-pound armor plate behind the pilot, racks for ten 30-pound bombs, one .30-caliber and one .50-caliber nose gun, and two 23-mm Madsen guns under the wings. These cannons were sent from Denmark and tested March 8 in China with such success that Curtiss urged the Air Corps to try them. Madsens were installed on the XP-36F nine months later.

The H75Q was destroyed in a crash on May 5, but the Chinese did decide to order 50 H75A-5 fighters and 100 Madsen guns in June 1939, with one pattern fighter to be completed at Buffalo in 1940 and the rest at a new Chinese factory at Loiwing, near the Burma border.

NASM

CURTISS H-75R with GR-1820-GR205A in November 1939

Hawks for France

No major country seemed more in need of fighters than France, for that country's industry had failed to produce, in quantity or quality, aircraft equal to the threat presented by Germany's bombers and Bf 109 fighters. Curtiss Hawks were attractive, but obstacles arose; among them the refusal of the Air Corps to allow the French to examine retractable-wheeled versions and the fact that the price was nearly twice that of contemporary French equipment.

President Roosevelt, however, forced the Air Corps to allow French pilot Michel Detroyat to secretly test a Y1P-36 on March 20, 1938, and on May 13, 1938, France did buy 100 H75A-1s, along with an option for 100 H75A-2s taken when initial deliveries met expectations. The French version, styled H75-C1 (chasse, one-place, according to their system) had a 900-hp R-1830-SC3G with 87-octane fuel, French instrumentation, four 7.5-mm FN guns and pilot's seat-back 9-mm armor. This was the first armor on American production aircraft, although Soviet fighters had used pilot armor since 1935.

Lloyd Child flew the first French Hawk on November 21, 1938, and the first two reached France by sea on December 24, 1938. Beginning with plane #131, six 7.5-mm guns were carried, with four located in the wings. Production of the full order was completed on July 29, 1939, with 200 H75As sent to France. When the war began, they equipped two *escadres** of 54 planes each, plus reserves. On September 8, 1939, the first French victory of

Mfr

CURTISS HAWK 75A-1
Pratt & Whitney R-1830-SC3G, 1050 hp at takeoff, 900 hp at 13,200'
DIMENSIONS: As P-36A
WEIGHT: Empty 4715 lb., Gross 5932 1b., Fuel 105-162 gal.
PERFORMANCE: Speed- Top 258 mph at s.l., 302 mph at 13,120', Cruising 217 mph, Landing 75 mph. Service Ceiling 31,826', Climb 9,840'/3 min. Range 524 miles normal.

MdA

CURTISS H75A-2 (France)

Salo

CURTISS H75A-3 (In Finland)
Pratt & Whitney R-1830-S1C3G, 1200 hp at takeoff, 1050 hp at 7,500'
DIMENSIONS: As P-36A
WEIGHT: Empty 4619 lb., Gross 5998 1b. Fuel 105-162 gal.
PERFORMANCE: Speed- Top 311 mph at 13,120', Cruising 270 mph, Landing 75 mph. Service Ceiling 33,790', Climb 13,120'/6 min. Range 820 miles.

the war was scored when Curtiss Hawks downed two Bf 109Ds without loss to themselves.

French pilots found the H75A more maneuverable than its adversaries, and this superiority even showed up in a comparison with the Spitfire. Of course, the latter had a big edge in firepower and speed, and when the Germans replaced the Messerschmitt Bf 109Ds with improved Bf 109Es, the Hawk was at a disadvantage.

* Two groupes each, viz. I/4, II/4, I/5 and II/5

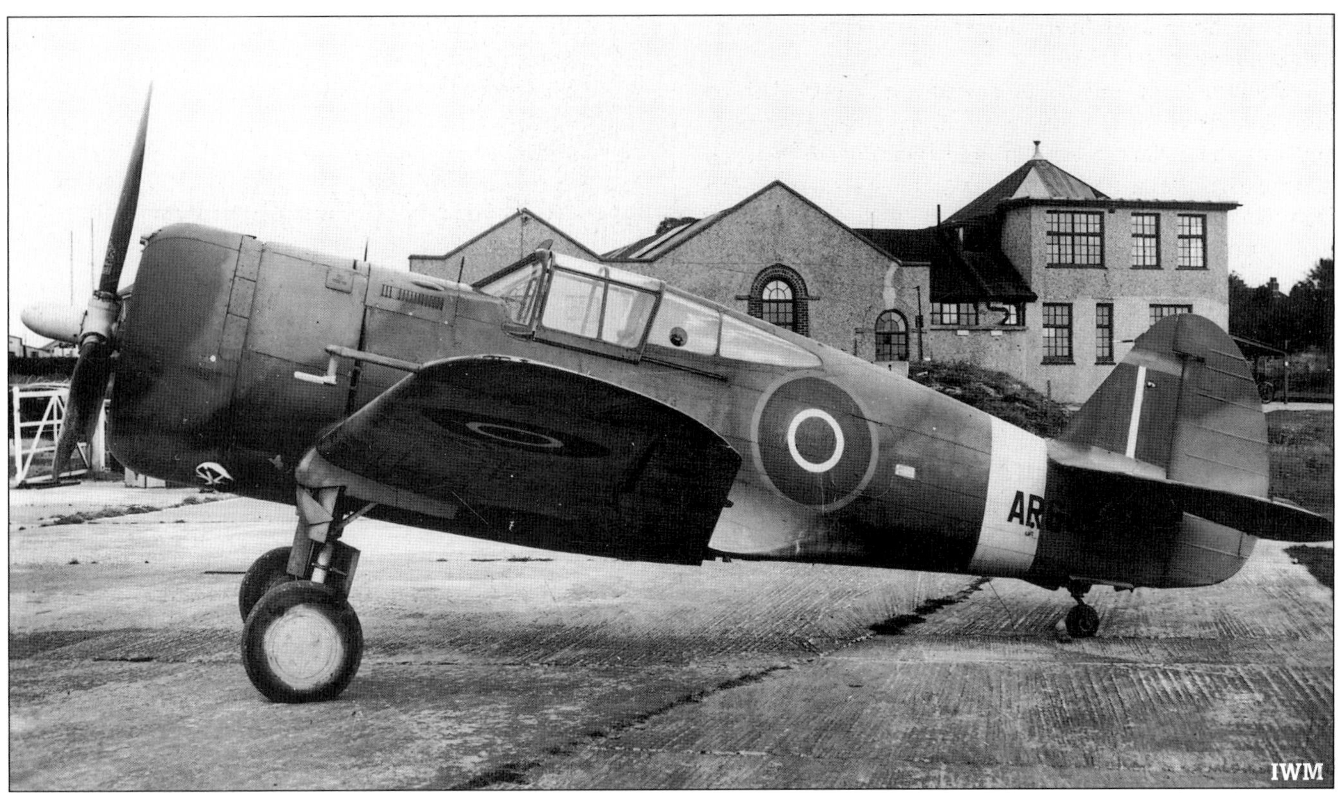

CURTISS H75A-4 MOHAWK
Wright GR-1820-G205A, 1200 hp takeoff, 900 hp at 15,100'
DIMENSIONS: Span 37'4", Lg. 28'10", Ht. 9'6", Wing Area 236 sq. ft.
WEIGHT: Empty 4669 lb., Gross 5800 lb. Max. 6163. Fuel 105-163 gal.
PERFORMANCE: Speed- Top 287 mph at s.l., 323 mph at 15,100', Cruising 262 mph, Landing 69 mph. Service Ceiling 32,700', Range 647 miles normal, 1005 miles max.

Hoping for more contracts, Curtiss offered new power-plant installations: one with a fully-rated high-octane twin-row Wasp and another with the single-row Cyclone. These would become the H75A-3 and H75A-4, although the French did not feel pressed enough to order them until after war actually began.

Norway also ordered 12 Hawks on August 12, 1939, and added 12 more in September. These 24 H75A-6s came off the reopened Hawk assembly line from February 5 to March 19, 1940, with SC3G engines like the H75A-1 and mounts for four 7.9-mm guns. Beginning February 15, deliveries also proceeded on a new French contract placed October 9, 1939, for 135 H75A-3s with six 7.5-mm guns and an R-1830-S1C3G Wasp of 1,050-hp at 7,500 feet, increasing speed from 302 to 311 mph.

In the meantime, the affiliated engine maker of the Curtiss-Wright combine had been developing the single-row Wright R-1820-G205 Cyclone with 1,200-hp for takeoff and 900-hp at 14,000 feet with 90 octane fuel. This power plant was flight tested on the Hawk H75R, beginning on November 2, 1939.

The remaining Hawks were powered by Wright GR-1820-G205A Cyclones of 900 hp at 15,200 feet, later designated R-1820-95 by the Army. A single H75A-5 pattern aircraft built in March 1940 for China was shipped to Rangoon, but its final delivery was not completed. The H75A-4 for France was first flown on March 31, 1940. Provision was made for six 7.5-mm guns, wing racks for ten 30-pound bombs, pilot back-armor, a 74-pound radio, and Superflexite-covered fuel tanks; the first leak-proof, or self-sealing, tanks on an American fighter. By August 10, 1940, 285 H75A-4s were completed on that contract.

Hawk H75A-7s ordered for the Dutch East Indies in October 1939 also had the G205A engines using 90-octane fuel, Curtiss propellers, and four 12.7-mm Browning guns. The first flew April 16, 1940, and 20 were completed by May 31. They reached Java in July, but the 15 remaining to fight the Japanese invasion were wiped out in February 1942.

Norway bought 36 H75A-8 Hawks, first flown on December 9, 1940, with two 12.7-mm nose guns, four 7.9-mm wing guns and a radio direction-finder. The last were delivered February 4, 1941, to the Norwegian training base in Toronto, Canada, yet most remained in their crates until 1942.

The last of the Curtiss Hawks were ten H75A-9s purchased by Iran on May 20, 1940; the first American fighters built for that country. The first was flown March 19, 1941, and shipped to Iran, and the rest completed by April 8. All these export models had bomb racks under the wing and pilot armor.

Most of these Hawks never flew for their original buyers and some fought against the Allies. Norwegian H75A-6s were being assembled there as Germany attacked on April 9, 1940, when four planes were destroyed by bombs and 15 were captured by Germany. Five others on a ship diverted to Scotland became the first Hawks to join the RAF.

CURTISS H75A-8 (to P-36G)
Wright R-1820-87, 1200 hp takeoff, 900 hp at 15,200'
DIMENSIONS: Same as H75A-4
WEIGHT: Empty 4929 lb., Gross 5753 1b. Fuel 105-163 gal.
PERFORMANCE: Speed- Top 313 mph at 15,100', Service Ceiling 32,200', (Test report shows 308 mph and Ceiling 33,300').

With capitulation near, France turned over to Britain the 204 H75A-4 Hawks that were undelivered on June 17, 1940. France had been shipped 416 Hawks, including the first 81 H75A-4s, but only 316 were actually received by the French air force. Missing were 15 more Hawk H75A-4s, along with eight in crates, on the carrier *Bearn* and its escort, 30 on a sunken freighter, and ten H-75A-4s that fell into German hands. The *Bearn* was diverted to Martinique where the Hawks remained until demolished in 1942, except for the crated eight that eventually reached the Free French in 1944/45.

The Hawks were the most successful of the French fighters, five *groupes* being credited with 233 confirmed victories by June 1940, after which most were transferred to North Africa. On November 8-9, 1942, two *groupes* used by Vichy French forces fought against American Navy Wildcats over Morocco.

Britain designated the Wasp-powered and Cyclone-powered H75s the Mohawk III and IV, respectively, and armed them with six .303-caliber Brownings. Although they arrived during the Battle of Britain in September 1940, there was little use for the Curtiss fighters there, where they were not considered equal to the RAF fighters. Instead, South Africa was sent 76, beginning in March 1941, and a squadron operated against Italian East Africa from October 5 to November 27, 1941. Portugal also received 16 from August to October 1941.

Altogether, some 230 Mohawks, including a few French defectors, received RAF serial numbers, along with nine Iranian H75-9s captured, while still in crates, by the British occupation begun August 25, 1941. About 100 Mohawks went to the RAF in India between October 1941 and August 1942. Mohawks of No. 5 Squadron began combat patrols as northern India's only air defense against Japan, until they were joined by No. 155 Squadron in November 1942. They claimed 12 kills from April 5, 1942, to November 9, 1943.

The RAF also inherited China's H75A-5 program, including the pattern aircraft. Bombed out of Loiwing October 26, 1940, and with Madsen guns never delivered, the remaining Hawk parts had been turned over to India's first airplane factory, Hindustani Aircraft. Only five H75A-5s were completed at Bangalore, the first not until July 31, 1942. By that time the Mohawk was quite obsolete, so the factory was better used as a repair facility.

Finland arranged to buy captured Hawks from Germany on October 1, 1940. Seven H75A-4 and 13 H75A-6 types arrived, beginning June 23, 1941, just before Finland joined the war against the Soviet Union. Nine ex-French Hawks were received from the German War Booty Depot by November, and 15 replacement aircraft began arriving in June 1943, including six H75A-1, nine A-2, and nine A-3 types. These 44 Curtiss fighters, flown in combat by Finns from July 14, 1941, to September 4, 1944, were credited with 190 victories for only 24 losses.

Latin America saw Curtiss Hawks when Brazil received ten P-36As in March 1942 and 29 P-36G Hawks began arriving in Peru in October. The latter were from the Norwegian H75A-8s stored in Canada until purchased by the United States in May 1942 for resale to Peru with a lend-lease designation.

Bell Airacuda

He named his first fighter the Airacuda, suggesting the fierce attack of the barracuda fish. Larry Bell, president of the newly-formed Bell Aircraft, wanted his first product, the XFM-l, to be noticed. It was. The radical big fighter appeared on the front cover of every aviation magazine in America at the time. By the time World War II began, however, it had been rejected by the Air Corps as a serious combat type.

Certainly the twin-engine Airacuda looked fierce enough from the front, with a 37-mm cannon in the nacelle out on each wing in front of the Allison engines turning the first pusher propellers on an American fighter. Five men comprised the crew: a gunner in each nacelle, the pilot in front of the fuselage, a navigator behind him, and a radioman-gunner behind the wing. Blisters were provided for a .50-caliber gun aimed from each side of the rear fuselage. No notice was made of the gunner's blind spot in the rear, for this was then a fault of all multi-engine Army Air Corps types.

The idea for this plane came from the Air Corps, which had considered a "multi-place fighter" version of the Martin B-10 bomber as early as February 1933, and the Plans Division on December 17, 1934, had recommended "development of a multi-engine, multi-place fighter armed with heavy machine guns and cannon". Army Ordnance was developing an automatic 37-mm cannon for anti-aircraft use, whose rapid rate of fire with explosive shells also offered stronger firepower for an airplane big enough to use it.

Robert J. Woods, Bell's chief engineer, had prepared a basic design in September 1934 and the Bell Aircraft Corporation opened its doors on July 1, 1935. Bell and Lockheed each received engineering contracts for XFM (Experimental Fighter, Multi-place) types in September 1935. Lockheed's XFM-2 designed by February 1936, also used two V-1710 engines, but in a conventional layout with twin rudders, tricycle landing gear, and just one 37-mm gun in the nose. Larry Bell delivered Wood's proposal on March

PMB

BELL XFM-1
Two Allison V-1710-13, 1150 hp takeoff, 1150 hp at 20,000'
DIMENSIONS: Span 69'10", Lg. 44'10", Ht. 13'7", Wing Area 684 sq. ft.
WEIGHT: Empty 13,376 lb., Gross 17,333 lb. Max. 18,462 lb. Fuel 400-800 gal.
PERFORMANCE: Speed- Top 271 mph at 20,000', Cruising 244 mph, Landing 77 mph. Service Ceiling 30,500', Climb 15,000'/10 min. Range 800 miles normal, 1600 miles max.

4, 1936, and won the competition by a very narrow margin of 72 to 71.6 points. Lockheed went on to work on another twin-engine design that later became the famous P-38.

On May 12, 1936, Bell received a $403,057 Air Corps contract for one XFM-1, which was approved by the War Department on June 4. This prototype was built and taken to the Buffalo Municipal Airport for final assembly on July 25, 1937. First Lt. Benjamin S. Kelsey, then in charge of Air Corps fighter projects, made the first flight September 1, 1937. After 25 minutes, he returned, discovering that backfire had damaged the intercooler for the F-10 turbosupercharger on the port YV-1710-9. After repairs and tests with V-1710-13s, the XFM-l went to Wright Field on October 21 for acceptance trials.

Performance data was a closely-held secret at the time. A request for simple plans by Strombecker, a company making little wood models, was refused. But when Model Airplane News published Airacuda plans, Air Corps Chief General Westover wrote an alarmed letter to Larry Bell on Feb 29, 1938, about the breach in security. Bell replied that an error on the plans showed they hadn't come from within the company. Apparently the artist had simply visited the municipal airport.

One reason for secrecy was the embarrassing difference between the manufacturer's Performance Guarantee and actual test results. The promised high speed of 317 mph at 20,000 feet with 2,500 hp, with 300 mph guaranteed, actually turned out to be 271 mph, with only 2,000 hp available from the two engines. A climb to 15,000 feet in 7.5 minutes and a service ceiling of 35,000 feet had been promised, but the XFM-1 took ten minutes to get to 15,000 feet, and had a 30,500 foot service ceiling. However, a normal 400-gallon fuel load in inboard wing tanks could be doubled to get ten hours of endurance, or twenty 30-pound fragmentation bombs could be carried in the fuselage. Each cannon was supplied with 110 rounds, and each .50-caliber gun had 600 rounds.

Wooden dummy cannon had been carried until Colt had readied a working example. On March 25, 1938, the XFM-1 first tested a 37-mm T-9 gun and fired 16 rounds with satisfactory results. The weapon fired five-round clips and could be aimed through a 25-degree cone of fire. A .30-caliber gun was attached alongside each cannon so that its tracers could be used to adjust the gunner's aim. This was unsatisfactory, since the cannon had different ballistic characteristics than the machine gun, and fired twice as far.

A solution to the problem was offered by the first use on aircraft of a remote fire-control system. The Sperry Gyroscope company proposed a telescopic sight, computing unit, and joystick to enable the navigator to aim both cannons, which would be reloaded by the nacelle gunners. Other improvements planned for the service test version included relocating the turbosuperchargers underneath the nacelle, eliminating the side blisters and the nacelle .30s, adding a new 24-volt auxiliary power system, flush rivets, and changing the shape of the nose and nacelles. A top speed of 305 mph at 20,000 feet was guaranteed by the company.

Larry Bell told the Army he could build ten YFM-1 and three YMF-1As, starting deliveries 11 months after a contract, with three a month afterwards. The YMF-lA would have tricycle landing gear. On May 20, 1938, these 13 planes were ordered at $3,168,265. Thirteen Sperry fire-control systems were ordered for $27,400 on December 9.

BELL YFM-l
Two Allison V-1710-23, 1150 hp takeoff, 1150 hp at 20,000'
DIMENSIONS: Span 70', Lg. 45'11", Ht. 12'5", Wing Area 688 sq. ft.
WEIGHT: Empty 13,630 lb., Gross 18,000 lb., Max. 19,000 lb. Fuel 400-800 gal.
PERFORMANCE: Speed- Top 270 mph at 12,600', Landing 77 mph. Service Ceiling 30,500', Climb 15,000'/10.3 min. Range 940 miles normal, 1800 miles max.

The Air Corps planned to buy enough Airacudas with fiscal 1940 funds to equip two "Fighter Pursuit" groups. Before the first YFM-1 was ready, however, the Air Corps had second thoughts. Lockheed's P-38 was becoming available, with over 100-mph more speed and much less production and operation cost. The Airacuda was very specialized in its fighting role; making long-distance patrols to attack unescorted enemy long-range bombers. It wasn't quick enough to cope with faster, more maneuverable, enemy fighters.

At the same time as war began with the invasion of Poland, a September 2, 1939, headquarters memo reported that the Air Corps had dropped the multi-place fighter concept in favor of single-seat pursuits. Contracts were increased, however, for Bell's P-39, which carried one 37-mm gun at more than one-third faster speed and less than one-third the price.

Although the first production 37-mm guns had been delivered on time in April, the first YFM-1 wasn't flown until September 28, and that flight was interrupted by another supercharger explosion. Not until February 23, 1940, was the YMF-1 delivered and later sent to Hamilton Field, California, for service tests by the 20th Pursuit Group.

Eight YFM-1s with V-1710-23 engines and B-1 superchargers were completed by June, but one crashed before it could be accepted by the Army. Armament included two .50 caliber guns in the waist, a .30-caliber gun in a small retractable top turret, and another .30-caliber gun mounted to fire back under the tail. The Sperry sight for the two cannon firing forward protruded beneath the pilots' cabin.

BELL YFM-lA
Two Allison V-1710-23, 1150 hp takeoff, 1150 hp at 20,000'
DIMENSIONS: Span 70', Lg. 45'11", Ht. 19'6", Wing Area 688 sq. ft.
WEIGHT: Empty 13,962 lb., Gross 18,431 lb., Max. 19,301 lb., Fuel 400-800 gal.
PERFORMANCE: As YFM-1.

BELL YFM-lB
Two Allison V-1710-41, 1090 hp at 13,200'
DIMENSIONS: Span 70', Lg. 45'11", Ht. 12'5", Wing Area 688 sq. ft.
WEIGHT: Empty 13,023 lb., Gross 18,373 lb., Max. 21,150 lb. Fuel 400-800 gal.
PERFORMANCE: Speed- Top 268 mph at 12,600', Cruising 200 mph, Landing 77 mph. Service Ceiling 29,900', Climb 1520'/1 min., 15,000'/10.6 min. Range 650 miles normal, 1670 miles max.

Two more examples were completed without turbosuperchargers, using V-1710-41 engines. The YFM-lB first appeared in March and both were delivered July 30, 1940. The first YFM-lA with tricycle gear and V-1710-23 engines was seen by August 13 and two more rolled out in October. While the Army had lost all interest in the Airacuda as a combat type, experience gained by Sperry with fire control and Bell with heavy gun mountings proved very useful in building armament systems for bombers like the B-17.

Export Fighters

Two single-seaters that appeared just before the war were developed from trainer designs to provide relatively low-cost fighters for the export market. They were the Curtiss-Wright CW-21 and the North American NA-50.

The St. Louis branch of the Curtiss-Wright corporation produced the CW-21 as a fast-climbing interceptor developed from the CW-l9 trainer. Powered by a Wright Cyclone, it had a sweptback leading edge and wheels retracting backwards into fairings below the wings. The CW-21 prototype was first flown November 2, 1938, and due to

CURTISS-WRIGHT CW-21
A company pilot used this demonstrator to attack a Japanese bomber in May 1939, before World War II began.

very light-weight construction, was able to climb nearly twice as fast as the Hawk 75s.

It was shipped to China by March 2, 1939, where Robert Fausel demonstrated in competitive tests that the interceptor was better in climb and maneuverability than other available fighters. Fausel also shot down one of the Japanese Army Fiat bombers raiding Chungking on May 3.*

When China bought the Hawk H75A-5 in June 1939, CW-21 Interceptors were also ordered, with three made in St. Louis and 29 to be assembled at Loiwing. While the prototype had the usual one .30-caliber and one .50-caliber nose gun, the Chinese specified two .50-caliber and two .30-caliber synchronized guns, with 1/4-inch armor installed behind the pilot, and an 85-gallon drop tank. The first production CW-21 first flew on March 20, 1940, and was loaned to the US. Navy for tests begun March 28. All three pattern aircraft were completed by June 1940, and shipped to Rangoon, Burma.

CURTISS-WRIGHT CW-21 for China
Wright R-1820-G5, 1000 hp takeoff, 850 hp at 6000', 750 hp at 15,200'
DIMENSIONS: Span 35', Lg. 26'6", Ht. 8'8", Wing Area 174 sq. ft.
WEIGHT: Empty 3050 lb., Gross 4092 lb. normal, Max. 4250 lb., Fuel 96 gal.
PERFORMANCE: Speed- Top 296 mph at 7500', 315 mph at 17,000', Cruising 274 mph, Landing 68 mph. Service Ceiling 35,600'. Climb 4800'/1 min., Range 530 miles.

Not until December 23, 1941, was a ferry flight to China attempted, in which all three were destroyed. Just before the first examples were to be finished at Loiwing, the factory was burned and abandoned on May 1, 1942, before advancing Japanese troops. After three years of waiting, not a single CW-21 had reached Chinese squadrons. The ill-fated attempt to build them in China instead of America had left the Chinese without anything to match the Japanese Zero.

On April 17, 1940, the Netherlands ordered 24 CW-21B interceptors, whose wheels folded inward completely into the wing. Armament provisions were made for four 7.9-mm guns under the cowl. Completed between October and December 1940, they went to a squadron in Java.

CURTISS-WRIGHT CW-21B
Wright R-1820-G5, 1000 hp takeoff, 850 hp at 6000', 750 hp at 15,200'
DIMENSIONS: Span 35', Lg. 27'2", Ht. 8'2", Wing Area 174 sq. ft.
WEIGHT: Empty 3382 lb., Gross 4500 lb. Fuel 100 gal.
PERFORMANCE: Speed- Top 314 mph at 5,600', 333 mph at 18,000', Cruising 282 mph, Landing 68 mph. Service Ceiling 34,300', Climb 4500'/1 min., 13,120'/4 min. Range 630 miles.

On February 3, 1942, these fighters, along with H75A-7s, rose against the Japanese invaders, but the Dutch lost nine of the 12 interceptors aloft in that first day's attack; the Zeros were too much for them. All were lost by March 5.

NORTH AMERICAN NA-50
Wright R-1820-G3, 840 hp at 8700'
DIMENSIONS: Span 37'5", Lg. 27'8", Ht. 8'11", Wing Area 227.5 sq.ft.
WEIGHT: Empty 4120 lb., Gross 5350 lb., Max. 5680 lb. Fuel 120-170 gal.
PERFORMANCE: Speed- Top 270 mph at 10,700', Cruising 235 mph, Landing 70 mph. Service Ceiling 31,500'. Range 675 miles normal, 945 miles max.

*Fausel's single firing pass, unpublicized at the time, was exaggerated by post-war gossip into a epic fight, but with the wrong plane and pilot!

NORTH AMERICAN NA-68
(P-64 with original 20-mm armament and Thai markings)

The NA-50 built by North American Aviation was a single-seat fighter version of their famous trainer series. Peru ordered seven on August 4, 1938, and they were completed between February and April 1939. Powered by an 840-hp Wright R-1820-G3 Cyclone, the NA-50 had two .30-caliber cowl guns with a bar sight and bomb racks under the wings. This project gave the company's small design office experience that would promote the P-51 Mustang concept a year later, and the NA-50s would serve Peru in a 1941 border war with Ecuador.

A redesigned version was ordered by Thailand November 30, 1939, as the NA-68 with a revised cowl and rudder. Armament could include four 8-mm Colt guns (two in the nose and two in the wings) and two 20-mm Madsen guns under the wings, with racks for two 110-pound bombs. The first was flown on September 1, 1940, but export permission was revoked by the State Department on October 19, 1940.

All six were taken over by the Air Corps on March 5, 1941, and instead of being shipped overseas, served at western training bases without armament. The Air Corps designated the NA-68 as the P-64, since it was a single-seat design. This number was so late in the Army's fighter catalog because intervening numbers had been issued to the many projects already in progress.

NORTH AMERICAN P-64 (NA-68)
Wright R-1820-77, 875 hp at takeoff, 840 hp at 8700'
DIMENSIONS: Span 37'3", Lg. 27', Ht. 9', Wing Area 227.5 sq. ft.
WEIGHT: Empty 4660 lb., Gross 5990 lb., Max. 6800 lb. Fuel 120-170 gal.
PERFORMANCE: Speed- Top 270 mph at 8700', Cruising 235 mph, Landing 70 mph. Service Ceiling 27,500'. Range 630 miles normal, 965 miles max.

CHAPTER 17
WARHAWKS TO MUSTANGS

The three best Army fighters in 1940: the P-40, YP-38, and the P-39.

The Army Air Force won air supremacy with fighters designed and first flown before the United States entered the war.

The Long P-40 Line

Although seven different fighter types were in mass production for the Air Force during World War II, the Curtiss P-40 was the first available in large numbers. From 1940 to 1942, more P-40s were built than all of the other major types together, and so the Warhawk was seen on nearly every front.

The P-40 offered little new in design over the P-36 except a streamlined nose with an inline engine; in fact, the prototype was a P-36A with an Allison V-1710-19. Since the P-37's high-altitude turbosupercharger was still unreliable, designer Don Berlin advocated a less complex medium-altitude, single-stage blower built into the engine. He later complained that the P-37's "supercharger wasn't working, and we didn't have time to develop that, too."

CURTISS XP-40 (Original version)

Instead, on March 3, 1938, Berlin proposed to fit a P-36 with a 1,000-hp Allison using a single-stage geared supercharger, raising medium altitude speed without the turbo's disadvantages. The Air Corps quickly responded on April 26 with a contract to modify the tenth P-36A to the XP-40. First flown October 14, 1938, by Ed Elliot, the XP-40 was further modified in February 1939 by moving the radiator from behind the wing to under the nose and installing the usual two guns in blast tubes over the engine.

The Army's pursuit competition had called for bids on January 25, 1939, for designs whose top speeds of 310 to 370 mph were to be reached at 15,000 feet, with a two-hour endurance at cruising speed. Besides the XP-40, Curtiss also offered the P-36B, the P-37, and the Hawk 75R, while Seversky had the AP-4 and AP-9A with radial engines. The Seversky XP-41 arrived too late to compete.

Higher critical altitudes and speeds were offered by the turbo-superchargers on the Lockheed XP-38 and Bell XP-39 "interceptor-pursuits" designed for "cannon" armament, but neither had been tested. At that time, the Air Corps still preferred to mass-produce a medium-altitude pursuit first, and compared to the air-cooled types, the XP-40 was faster, less expensive, and available for rapid delivery.

According to the evaluation, of 1,000 possible points, Figure of Merit scores were: XP-40, 744 points; AP-4A, 713 points; H75R, 660 points; P-37, 622 points; P-36B, 604 points; and AP-9, 502 points.

CURTISS XP-40 (Modified)
Allison V-1710-19, 1060 hp takeoff, 1000 hp at 10,000'
DIMENSIONS: Span 37'4", Lg. 31'1", Ht. 12'4", Wing Area 236 sq. ft.
WEIGHT: Empty 5417 lb., Gross 6260 lb., Max. 6870 lb. Fuel 100-158 gal.
PERFORMANCE: Speed- Top 342 mph at 12,200', Cruising 299 mph, Landing 72 mph. Range 460 miles normal, 1180 miles at 200 mph with full load.

Although Curtiss was the low bidder, and had guaranteed a 360-mph top speed at 15,000 feet, only 342 mph at 12,200 feet had been attained in tests.

AF

CURTISS P-40s of 8th PG on the Wasp, October 12, 1940

On March 28, the Army ordered the XP-40 sent to the National Advisory Committee for Aeronautics (NACA) for tests in that government agency's full-scale wind tunnel, where several ways of cleaning up the design's streamlining were tried. Then the XP-40 was returned to the company on April 11 for refinements such as a new radiator arrangement under the nose, individual exhaust stacks replacing the one-piece manifold, a carburetor intake between and ahead of the gun muzzles, and improved landing gear. These features, plus flush riveting, were adopted on production P-40s.

The P-40 had arrived at the right time, for President Roosevelt was asking Congress to expand the Air Corps from 2,300 to 5,500 planes. He understood the influence of German air power on the Munich crisis, and that American air power needed to be rapidly increased. Only the P-40 was nearly ready for production, while the best of the others would need service tests.

The President signed the Air Corps Expansion Act on April 26, 1939, and on the same day, 524 Curtiss P-40 low-altitude pursuits were ordered for $12,872,398; the largest Air Corps contract to that date. Thirteen each of the YP-38 and YP-39 interceptor-pursuits were approved the next day. All would have Allison engines, which became the only American-designed liquid-cooled engine available in World War II, as none of the liquid-cooled projects begun by four other companies would ever reach mass production.

AF

CURTISS P-40
Allison V-1710-33, 1040 hp at 14,300'
DIMENSIONS: Span 37'4", Lg. 31'9", Ht. 12'4", Wing Area 236 sq. ft.
WEIGHT: Empty 5367 lb., Gross 6807 lb., Max. 7173 lb. Fuel 120-180 gal.
PERFORMANCE: Speed- Top 357 mph at 15,000', Cruising 277 mph, Landing 80 mph. Service Ceiling 32,750', Climb 3080'/1 min., 15,000'/5.3 min. Range 650 miles normal, 950 miles at 250 mph, 1400 miles max. at 188 mph.

The first production P-40 was flown April 4, 1940, with an Allison C-15 (V-1710-33) originally rated at 1,090 hp at 15,000 feet. Although 366-mph was achieved in early tests, bearing problems caused the Army to restrict this engine to 1,040 hp and limited top speed to 357-mph.

Armament included two .50-caliber guns with 200 rpg on the cowl and provision for a .30-caliber gun with 500 rpg in each wing, but no armor or bomb racks were carried. The first three aircraft were delivered in natural metal, but the remainder introduced the olive drab paint with gray under bottom of wartime Army planes, while these P-40s were the last model delivered with the traditional tail stripes.

Two hundred of the P-40 model reached the Army by October 15, 1940. Three went to Wright Field for tests, and technical schools at Chanute and Lowry Fields each got one. Eighty reached the 8th Pursuit Group, which moved from Langley to Mitchel Field in November; 80 went to California's 20th Pursuit Group, which went from Moffet to Hamilton Field in September; and 35 to Selfridge Field for the new 31st Pursuit Group. Now the Army squadrons had a type comparable with the Bf 109E, although weaker in speed and firepower to the Spitfire.

On October 12, 1940, near Norfolk, the *USS Wasp* flew off 24 P-40s from the 8th Pursuit Group and nine O-47As of the 2nd Observation Squadron. This was the first time U.S. Army fighters flew off a Navy carrier, and would become a common wartime delivery method. *HMS Argus* had flown off 12 Hurricanes for Malta the previous August 2.

The remaining 324 P-40s had been deferred in April 1940 to enable earlier delivery on the Curtiss H81A-1s ordered by France and taken over by Britain. The deferred Army aircraft were to be replaced later by ships incorporating armor, fuel tank protection, and more firepower. Some may have been expected to get the P-40A designation not used on actual production aircraft.

Mfr

CURTISS H-81A-1 (#1 in French markings)
Allison V-1710-C15, 1040 hp at 14,300'
DIMENSIONS: As P-40
WEIGHT: Empty 5365 lb., Gross 6748 lb., Max. 7070 lb. Fuel 120-159 gal.
PERFORMANCE: (At 6835 lb.) Speed- Top 321 mph at 5000', 358 mph at 15,000', Landing 74 mph. Service Ceiling 33,200'. Range 893 miles.

France had ordered 100 Curtiss H81A-1 fighters, along with H75As on October 5, 1939, with a guaranteed top speed of 360-mph. The first example was flown June 6, 1940, with French equipment, provisions for four 7.5-mm wing guns and two 13-mm nose guns, and wavy camouflage paint. After the RAF took over Curtiss fighter contracts on June 17, 1940, when France surrendered, H81A contracts were increased to 1,180 aircraft.

Delivery of 100 H81A-ls, named the Tomahawk I by the RAF, began September 18, 1940. They differed from the P-40 in having 83 pounds of pilot seat armor, Superflexite fuel tank covers, four .30-cal. wing guns with 1,960 rounds and two .50-cal. nose guns with 380 rounds each. They were followed in October by 40 Tomahawk IA models with .303-cal. British wing guns. The Tomahawk Mk. IIA, or H81A-2, whose deliveries began October 30, had standard British equipment with 89 pounds of armor. Top speed had been reduced to 345 mph by the increased weight. By the end of 1940, 558 Tomahawks had been accepted at the factory by the RAF.

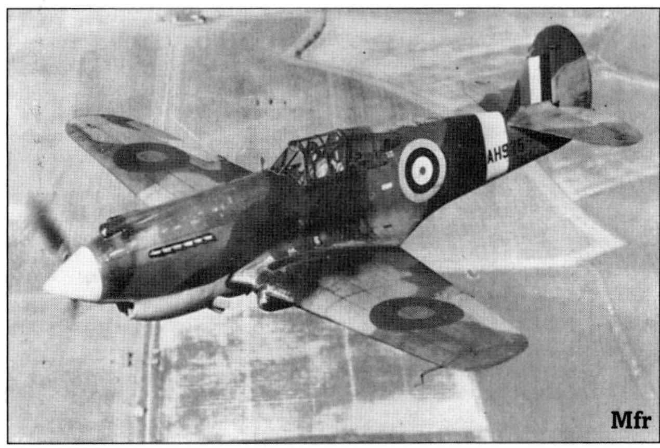

Mfr

CURTISS Tomahawk IIA (RAF)

The Army's equivalent of the H81A-2 was the P-40B ordered September 12, 1940, which was the first Air Corps fighter with Superflexite self-sealing tanks. There were 93 pounds of armor, two .50-caliber nose guns with 760 rounds, and four .30-caliber wing guns with 1,960 rounds. Delivery of 131 began January 3, 1941, followed, beginning March 31, by 193 P-40C fighters. That model had a new radio, 24-volt electrical system, a new fuel system with Hewitt internal self-sealing, and a drop tank.

The first P-40Bs and P-40Cs delivered were deployed to Hawaii, beginning April 1941, by Navy carrier, flying off the deck to Army airfields. To modernize some older Army P-40s, sets of H81A-2 wings with four guns and protected tanks were installed on 46 aircraft redesignated P-40G from August 1 to September 25, 1941.

AF

CURTISS P-40B
Allison V-1710-33, 1040 hp at 14,300'
DIMENSIONS: As P-40
WEIGHT: Empty 5615 lb., Gross 7352 lb., Max. 7624 lb. Fuel 120-158 gal.
PERFORMANCE: Speed- Top 352 mph at 15,000', Cruising 280 mph, Landing 80 mph. Service Ceiling 32,400', Climb 15,000'/5.1 min. Range 730 miles normal, 1230 miles max.

The Tomahawk IIB was the concurrent British P-40C version, first flown April 23, 1941, with deliveries until

Arnold

CURTISS P-40C
Allison V-1710-33, 1040 hp at 14,300'
DIMENSIONS: As P-40
WEIGHT: Empty 5767 lb., Gross 7504 lb., Max. 8050 lb. Fuel 120+68 gal.
PERFORMANCE: (At 7327 lb.) Speed- Top 345 mph at 15,000', Cruising 280 mph, Landing 82 mph. Service Ceiling 29,500', Climb 15,000'/5.1 min. Range 730 miles normal, 1350 miles at 195 mph.

August 21, 1941, when Curtiss had finished 1,180 Tomahawks. About 516 Tomahawks were sent to the Middle East to replace RAF Hurricanes, and the first P-40 victory was scored June 8, 1941, when an Italian bomber was destroyed near Alexandria by a No. 250 Squadron pilot. No. 3 Squadron (Australians) used Tomahawks in Syria, downing three Ju 88s on June 18, and six Vichy French Martin Marylands on June 28. Then this squadron joined Number 112 and 250 Squadron Tomahawks in Egypt, along with two South African squadrons.

During the brisk desert fighting, the Tomahawk was reputed to be a heavy, but robust aircraft, inferior to the new Bf 109F in speed and climb, while better in maneuverability. Superior German pilot experience added to the difficulties, but Australian Clive Caldwell did score 20 victories flying P-40s, probably the most successful ace on the type.

While 54 Tomahawks were lost at sea, many remained in reserve, so on January 6, 1941, 100 H81A-2s were sold to China and shipped from New York to Burma for the American Volunteer Group (AVG). Turkey also received 30 from Middle East stocks, beginning in November 1941.

R. T. Smith

CURTISS H-81A-2 (AVG)
Allison V-1710-C15, 1040 hp at 14,300'
DIMENSIONS: As P-40
WEIGHT: Empty 5600 lb., Gross 7444 lb., Max. 7778 lb. Fuel 120-161 gal.
PERFORMANCE: (At 7778 lb.) Speed- Top 301 mph at 5000', 345 mph at 15,000', Cruising 289 mph, Stalling 81 mph. Service Ceiling 30,500', Climb 15,000'/7.6 min. Range 600 miles normal, 805 miles max.

The 316 that remained in Britain took some 1,000 hours apiece to assemble and deliver to units. Unwanted by Fighter Command, Tomahawks were first used in 1941 to replace the two-place Lysanders of 11 Army Cooperation squadrons, whose Tomahawks were fitted with an oblique camera for tactical reconnaissance. Four more squadrons later got them for training. These squadrons served only in the United Kingdom and fought no air battles before the Tomahawks were replaced in 1942/43 by Mustang Is.

After the Soviet Union was invaded, Churchill promised 200 surplus Tomahawks to Stalin on July 25, 1941. The last 49 Tomahawk IIBs built were shipped directly from the United States with 10 P-40Cs and 16 P-40Gs, while 24 IIA and 147 IIB types came from British depots. Convoys carrying these aircraft began arriving at Archangel on September 1, where two Army pilots, Lts. John Alison and Hubert Zemke, between September 10 and 29, qualified the first 120 Soviet pilots on the P-40 with only one loss.

The first Soviet P-40 units were the 126th Fighter Air Regiment (IAP), which first introduced the Tomahawk into combat defending Moscow on October 12, 1941; the 147th IAP, replacing its I-153 biplanes at Murmansk, and the 154th IAP, replacing I-16s and entering combat on the Leningrad Front on November 26.

Improving the P-40

Even before the P-40 entered service, Curtiss engineers planned a replacement. The first possibility was a response to an Army circular proposal dated June 15, 1939, for pursuit designs intended for 1941 production. An improved 1,150-hp Allison with new reduction gears (V-1710-39) was specified for the Curtiss offer dated July 27. Although it took third place to the Republic P-44 and Bell P-45 proposals, prototype development of the Curtiss XP-46 was authorized September 29, 1939.

PMB

CURTISS XP-46
Allison V-1710-39, 1150 hp at 11,800'
DIMENSIONS: Span 34'4", Lg. 30'2", Ht. 13', Wing Area 208 sq. ft.
WEIGHT: Empty 5625 lb., Gross 7322 lb., Max. 7665 lb. Fuel 103-156 gal.
PERFORMANCE: Speed- Top 355 mph at 12,200', Landing 79 mph. Service Ceiling 29,500', Climb 12,300'/5 min. Range 325 miles at 332 mph, 717 miles at 305 mph.

The original light-weight concept was replaced by October 19 with provisions for two .50-caliber nose guns, four .30-caliber wing guns, 65 pounds of pilot armor, and self-sealing fuel tanks, apparently the first to be required by an Air Corps specification. The armament was that later specified for the P-40B, although the XP-46 was a smaller aircraft, with the wheels retracting inward instead of backward, and the radiator moved back below the wings.

The Air Corps contract signed October 31 and approved January 17, 1940, was the first to call for two prototypes, one (XP-46A) to be delivered without armament to expedite tests and insure against accidents like the one that interrupted XP-38 development. Mockup inspection began March 4, 1940.

WT

CURTISS XP-46A

British and French officials meeting with the President's Liaison Committee on March 14, 1940, insisted that they had to have the P-38 and P-39, as well as the P-46, in 1941. Air Corps leaders had resisted these requests before, but now they realized that the 789 pursuits the Army had ordered in 1939 had no armor, self-sealing tanks, or enough firepower. Letting the Allies buy into the fighter program was a way of funding these crucial modernizations.

On March 25, the government's new "Release of Aircraft Policy" was completed. The Allies would be allowed to buy certain modern types, providing that their manufacturers would offer a more advanced design to the Army and the Allies would provide information about their own combat experience. By April 10 (the day after the invasion of Norway), the Anglo-French Purchasing Commission was told they could complete contracts for 2,440 American fighters.

Curtiss could offer early delivery of its P-40s, since the first production model for the Army was already in the air. A Foreign Release Agreement made with the Army on April 18, 1940, would halt P-40 deliveries at 200 planes and released the advanced P-46 for export.

This allowed Curtiss to concentrate on the export P-40, the H81A Tomahawk, for the rest of 1940, and promise P-46s to the Allies in 1941. In return, Curtiss could replace the Army's deferred 324 P-40s with 324 P-46s, beginning in March 1941, and would develop a new design for the Army, designated the XP-53.

An export version of the P-46, called the H86A, was proposed on May 1, 1940, using the same engine, but armed RAF-style with eight .30-cal. wing guns. A top speed of 410-mph at 15,000 feet was promised, providing gross weight was limited to 6,750 pounds and fuel to 105 gallons, with armor and self-sealing tanks not included. On May 10, France ordered 140 H86As to follow the 260 H81A fighters scheduled in 1940, and 300 more were planned for the RAF.

But changing to the very different P-46 would interrupt production in 1941, just when fighters might be most needed. On May 24, 1940, the Curtiss company proposed discarding P-46 production and substituting a redesigned P-40 with the same 1,150-hp Allison F3R engine, heavier armament, armor, and fuel-tank protection. That version was the H87A, named the Kittyhawk by the British and produced concurrently for the Air Corps as the P-40D. Originally planned armament was four .50-caliber guns in the wings with two 20-mm guns mounted externally below them.

Expecting to get a better airplane at an earlier date, the Army's Materiel Division accepted the substitution of the modified P-40 for the P-46 on June 10, 1940, and the RAF also bought 471 more H81A-2 Tomahawks and 560 H87A Kittyhawks. These were intended for use in the Middle East, rather than for Fighter Command in Britain.

Mfr

CURTISS H87A-1 (Kittyhawk I)
Allison V-1710-F3R, 1150 hp at 11,800'
DIMENSIONS: Span 37'4", Lg. 31'9", Ht. 12'4", Wing Area 236 sq. ft.
WEIGHT: Empty 5898 1b., Gross 8170 lb., Max. 8535 lb. Fuel 120-148 gal.
PERFORMANCE: Speed- Top 326 mph at 5000', 361 mph at 15,000', Cruising 296 mph, Stalling 84 mph. Service Ceiling 29,500', Climb 15,000'/7.1 min. Range 730 miles with 148 gal.

Thus, long before the XP-46A flew on February 15, 1941, production plans had been rejected. Both prototypes were delivered in September and the company suffered a financial penalty when performance failed to meet contract guarantees. Fortunately, the P-40D development, which also used the 1150-hp V-1710-39, was more successful.

The first P-40D from the deferred 324-plane contract began tests on April 12, 1941. The modified fuselage had the radiator and top intakes moved forward on a nose given a new shape by the V-1710-39. Four .50-cal. guns with 2,000 rounds were carried in the wings and 111 pounds of pilot armor was provided. Self-sealing internal fuel tanks contained 148 gallons, and there were fittings for a 52-gallon

Mfr

CURTISS H87A-2 (Kittyhawk IA)

drop tank or 500-pound bomb under the fuselage, or six 20-pound fragmentation bombs under the wings.

Curtiss kept the first P-40D at Buffalo until it was modified and delivered as a P-40E on August 20. The second P-40D, delivered May 7, was loaned to Allison for engine studies. The next article was completed as the XP-40F and the fourth was delivered on May 20 to Patterson Field for accelerated service tests. The remaining 20 were accepted on June 30, and 18 went to the 20th Pursuit Group at Hamilton Field on August 8, 1941.

Mfr

CURTISS P-40D
Allison V-1710-39, 1150 hp at 11,800'
DIMENSIONS: Span 37'4", Lg. 31'9", Ht. 12'4", Wing Area 236 sq. ft.
WEIGHT: Empty 5993 lb., Gross 8063 lb., Max. 8499 lb. Fuel 148+52 gal.
PERFORMANCE: Speed- Top 362 mph at 15,000', Cruising 258 mph Landing 82 mph. Service Ceiling 30,600', Climb 15,000'/6.4 min. Range 800 miles normal, 1150 miles at 195 mph.

Since the 20-mm guns planned for the P-40D could not be made available in time, a February 18, 1941, order fixed six .50-caliber M2 guns with 1,686 rounds for the P-40E version. These six wing guns became standard for most American wartime fighters. The first P-40E, with six guns and a new radio, began test flights on August 17, 1941, and 300 P-40Es were delivered by October 15. They went first to the 20th Group and then to the Philippines and the Panama Canal Zone. Another 519 P-40Es that had been ordered on September 13, 1940, were coming off the

PMB

CURTISS P-40E
Allison V-1710-39, 1150 hp at 11,800'
DIMENSIONS: Span 37'4", Lg. 31'9", Ht. 12'4", Wing Area 236 sq. ft.
WEIGHT: Empty 6079 lb., Gross 8122 lb., Max. 8679 lb. Fuel 148+52 gal.
PERFORMANCE: Speed- Top 362 mph at 15,000', Cruising 258 mph., Landing 84 mph. Service Ceiling 29,000', Climb 15,000'/7.6 min. Range 700 miles normal, 950 miles ferry.

production line and were rushed to Pacific combat zones when America entered the war.

The 560 H87A Kittyhawks ordered by Britain in 1940 were in concurrent production with the Army planes as the first Kittyhawk I began flight tests on May 22, 1941. The first 20 Kittyhawk Is were delivered, beginning August 27, with four guns and 119 pounds of armor and armor glass, but the remaining 540 had six guns and were completed by December 16.

About 476 Kittyhawks were moved to Egypt where they replaced the Tomahawk in nine squadrons, beginning December 1941, but 72 went to Canada, beginning in October 1941, and only ten reached the United Kingdom (UK) itself. At least 14 were passed from RAF bases to Turkey in 1943.

CURTISS P-40E-1

The third contract (DA-3) of the Lend-lease program approved May 12, 1941, provided 1,500 P-40E-l (Kittyhawk IA) models, which replaced the Kittyhawk I on production lines in December 1941 and were produced alongside the Army P-40Es until both contracts were completed in May 1942. Most Kittyhawk IAs (the A indicated Lend-lease funding, instead of direct purchase), went under that name to the Soviet Union, the RAF Middle East, and Commonwealth Air Forces, but all Army P-40s were renamed Warhawks in January 1942.

Army Pursuit Strength in December 1941

Army pursuit strength had increased from five groups plus one separate squadron, with 464 fighters in January 1940, to 24 groups plus two squadrons, with 1,618 aircraft at the beginning of December 1941. Curtiss fighters were in the majority, with older models being passed on to the less experienced units being trained.

Hawaii had been sent 87 P-40B and 13 P-40C fighters for the 15th and 18th Pursuit Groups. Eleven P-40B sorties were flown during the December 7th attack when Lt. George S. Welch downed four attacking planes, but 42 P-40s were destroyed and 30 damaged that morning.

In the Philippines, the 24th Pursuit Group's five squadrons had received 31 P-40Bs on May 17, 50 P-40Es on September 29, and 24 more November 10. The war began with 51 P-35A, 28 P-40B and about 64 operational P-40E pursuits available. Despite losses during the surprise attack, they fought on until all were lost by April, although Lt. Boyd D. Wagner downed five enemies with his P-40E to become the war's first AAF ace.

Defense forces in the Canal Zone on November 30, 1941, included the 16th, 32nd, and 37th Pursuit Groups with 10 P-26A, 15 P-36A, 5 P-40B, 59 P-40C, and 15 P-40E fighters. Puerto Rico's 36th Pursuit Group began December with 16 P-36As, 34 P-39Ds, 19 P-40Cs and 30 P-40Es scattered on several eastern Caribbean fields.

In the northeast United States, the First Air Force had six pursuit groups. The 8th had turned over its old model P-40s to the 33rd at Mitchel and sent one squadron with 30 P-40Cs to Iceland via the *USS Wasp* on August 6, 1941. Most remaining P-40Cs served at Windsor Locks with the 57th, which had lost nine planes in a cross-country flight begun October 24. Bell P-39Ds had been issued to the rest of the 8th Group, as well as to the 31st and 52nd at Selfridge with the lst Pursuit's P-38s and P-43s.

The Second Air Force in the Northwest had older model P-40s with the 54th, and P-43s with the 55th Group. The Third Air Force had five pursuit groups in the Southeast: the 49th, 50th and 58th had P-40s, while the 53rd and 56th had P-39 and P-36 types. In the Southwest, the Fourth Air Force had P-40E and P-40G fighters at Hamilton Field for the 20th and 35th Groups (the latter's personnel in transit to the Philippines), while the 14th and 51st Groups at March Field were getting P-38s and P-40Es, respectively.

At War in the Pacific

As the Pacific war got under way, the P-40 became the most important fighter against the enemy advance. The most famous were the Tomahawks of the "Flying Tigers", the AVG pilots commanded by Claire Chennault, fighting Japanese Army squadrons over Burma and southern China. Beginning on December 20, 1941, by defeating a Kawasaki Ki-48 bomber squadron near Kunming, the AVG pilots became by far the most successful fighters against the enemy.

Their air victories did not change the rapidly deteriorating ground situation, and not until March 22, 1942, did the first of 25 P-40E replacements begin arriving from their flight from Accra across Africa and Asia. In July, the remaining AVG aircraft and a few of its pilots became part of the AAF's 23rd Pursuit Group in China. During its 30 weeks in combat, the AVG was credited with 297 victories for the loss of 80 aircraft: 12 in air combat, 10 to anti-aircraft fire, 13 on the ground, 23 in accidents, and 22 destroyed in evacuations.

Much of the P-40's success was due to the tactics developed by Chennault. Fighting in pairs, his men avoided turning dogfights with the more maneuverable Japanese fighters and utilized superior P-40 speed and firepower to "bounce" the enemy with quick passes and breakaways.

As the Japanese advanced southward in the Pacific, 337 P-40Es arrived in Australia between December 23, 1941, and March 18, 1942. Of these, 120 in provisional squadrons tried to reach Java, but only 36 actually arrived able to join the fight lost there by March 1st. Thirty-two had gone down with the *USS Langley*.

The 49th Group used the P-40E to defend Darwin and Port Moresby against frequent Japanese raids, beginning on March 14. Australian pilots also received P-40Es and went into combat with No. 75 squadron on March 21. P-40 pilots in Pacific areas were seldom as successful as the Flying Tigers, for Japanese Navy Zero fighters were tougher opponents, and the American pilots less experienced.

The *USS Ranger* took 68 P-40E-1s across the Atlantic and launched them off the deck on May 10, 1942, 150 miles from Accra, where they began difficult ferry flights across Africa through the Middle East to fill up the 51st Fighter Group* in India and the 23rd FG in China.

Entirely different weather conditions faced the 50 P-40Es of the 11th and 18th Fighter Squadrons in the Aleutians when Japan attacked Dutch Harbor June 3, 1942. They operated against Japanese forces on Attu and Kiska, and were joined to a P-38 squadron to form the 343rd Fighter Group on September 11, 1942.

By that time, Japan was surrounded by a ring of Warhawk units: the 343rd Group in Alaska, the 15th and 18th Groups in Hawaii (with 134 P-40B, C and Es in June) the 68th Fighter Squadron with 25 P-40Es on Tongatabu in the South Pacific, the 49th Fighter Group and the Australian squadrons in the southwest Pacific, and the 23rd and 51st Groups in China and India. In addition, there were Warhawks serving defense and training units from California to Panama, and in the Zone of the Interior.

Rolls-Royce Warhawks

The Allison engine's poor high-altitude output limited P-40 performance severely below that of the Bf 109F used by the Germans. Better possibilities were offered with the production in America by Packard of the Rolls-Royce Merlin with a two-speed integral supercharger. Packard Merlins were scheduled for 1,000 aircraft in a September 1940 contract, as well as 312 added by a contract approved on May 3, 1941.

A prototype was made by installing an imported Merlin 28 on the third P-40D airframe. The new XP-40F first flew June 30, 1941, and eliminated the carburetor intake above the nose that had been the Allison-engine P-40's trademark. Beginning on January 3, 1942, Curtiss delivered 1,311 P-40F's powered by the Packard V-1650-1 Merlin yielding 1,300 hp at 12,000 feet and 1,120 hp at 18,500 feet. They went down assembly lines side by side with the P-40E-l, for the supply of Merlin engines was insufficient to fill half of the Curtiss fighter's production.

CURTISS P-40F
Packard V-1650-1, 1300 takeoff, 1120 hp at 18,500'
DIMENSIONS: Span 37'4", Lg. 31'9", Ht. 12'4", Wing Area 236 sq. ft.
WEIGHT: Empty 65761b., Gross 8509 lb., Max. 9350 lb. Fuel 148+75 or 109 gal.
PERFORMANCE: Speed- Top 364 mph at 20,000', Landing 82 mph. Service Ceiling 34,400', Climb 12,300'/5 min. Range 375 miles/ 500 lb. bomb, 1500 miles ferry.

The first 699 P-40Fs had the same fuselage as the P-40E, but the P-40F-5 of August 1942, had 20 inches added to the length to improve directional stability. Minor mechanical changes were made on the P-40F-10, F-15, and F-20 series. Armed with six .50-caliber guns with 1,410 rounds in the wings, a 500-pound bomb, the P-40F's armor weighed 149 pounds, the armor glass windshield weighed 36 pounds, and a 170-gallon drop tank could be attached on ferry flights.

Seven hundred P-40Ls with V-1650-1 Merlins ordered June 15, 1942, replaced the P-40F-20 on the production line in January 1943 and were similar in appearance. In fact, the first 50 P-40L-ls were identical to the last Fs, but the P-40L-5 was lightened by the deletion of the two .50-caliber outboard guns and a 37-gallon wing tank. Production of Merlin-powered Warhawks ended with the last P-40L-20 on April 28, 1943, as the new P-51B and P-51C Mustangs took the full Packard engine output.

Most of these Merlin-powered Hawks were allocated to the five groups sent to the Mediterranean theater. Because of the shortage of Packard engines, 300 P-40F and P-40L aircraft used in the U.S. for training had to be re-engined with Allison V-1710-81s, and were redesignated P-40R.

The 57th Fighter Group first took the P-40F-1 across the Atlantic on the *USS Ranger*, flying 72 Warhawks off the deck on July 19, 1942, to Accra and then in stages across Africa to Palestine. Their first mission supporting the British in Egypt was on August 9, 1942, and they fought in the Battle of El Alamein in October.

The *Ranger's* next trip brought the 79th Group the same way, arriving in Egypt by November 12. A third P-40F group, the 324th, was added December 23 to what had become the Ninth Air Force.

The Twelfth Air Force, formed to support the American occupation of North Africa, had two Warhawk groups, the 33rd and 325th. The former flew 76 P-40Fs from the *USS Chenango* on November 8, 1942, but only 58 landed without damage near Casablanca. Twenty-four of those P-40Fs went to a French squadron in December 1942, which was later supplied with 49 P-40L-10s in March 1943.

The 33rd FG began combat with the Germans in December 1942 and was joined by the 325th, whose 72 P-40F-10s came from the *Ranger* on January 19, 1943, and entered combat on April 17. After the Axis surrender in North Africa on May 13, the Warhawks were strengthened for the invasion of Italy by the arrival on June 2 of P-40L-ls of the 99th Squadron. That was the first squadron entirely flown by African-American pilots, then barred from regular units by segregation.

Warhawks in Italy were replaced in AAF groups by the P-47, and their last P-40 mission was flown July 18, 1944, by the 324th Group. In 67,054 sorties, the P-40s lost 553, downed 481 enemies, and destroyed 40 on the ground.** Their best day was the "Palm Sunday Massacre" (April 18, 1943) of 59 Axis transports and 16 fighters, and the top P-40

*Pursuit Groups were renamed Fighter Groups in May 1942.
**See Table 7, page 337 for data comparing fighter scores.

ace in that area was Major Levi Chase with ten victories. But the main Warhawk role was as a fighter-bomber.

In the South Pacific, the only P-40Fs were those used by the 44th Fighter Squadron at Guadalcanal in 1943.

Later P-40 Models

Development of the P-40 continued with efforts to catch up with the performance of more advanced types. The third P-40F was remodeled with a deep radiator back under the wing and called the YP-40F. A P-40H, apparently with a more advanced Merlin engine, and a P-40J with a turbo-supercharged Allison were projected, but when the company lacked interest, designer Don Berlin left Curtiss in December 1941, and both projects were dropped. The creative impulse at Curtiss seems to have left with him, for no more new fighter projects there met success.

PMB

CURTISS YP-40F

Had the P-40 been replaced by the P-60A as planned, the last Warhawks would have been 600 P-40K-ls ordered October 28, 1941, for lend-lease to China. Fearing to interrupt production for an unproven type, authorities canceled the P-60A program in January 1942 in favor of the P-47G and more P-40s. A new contract approved June 15, 1942, added 1,400 more P-40K and M types to the schedule.

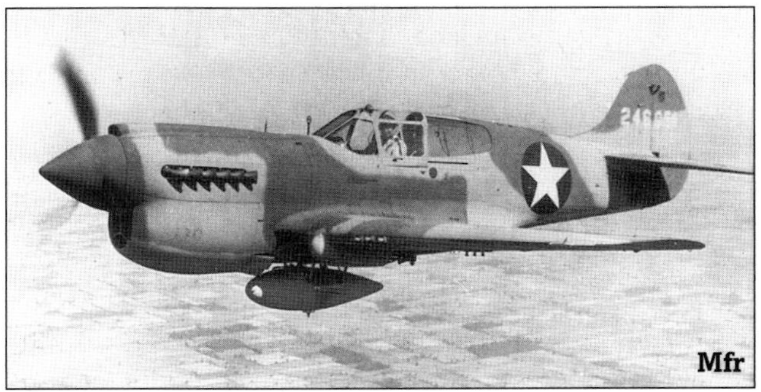

Mfr

CURTISS P-40K-1
Allison V-1710-73, 1325 hp takeoff, 1150 hp at 11,800'
DIMENSIONS: Span 37'4", Lg. 33'4", Ht. 12'4", Wing Area 236 sq. ft.
WEIGHT: Empty 6367 1b., Gross 8335 lb., Max. 10,000 lb. Fuel 157+75/170 gal.
PERFORMANCE: Speed- Top 362 mph at 15,000', Landing 82 mph. Service Ceiling 28,000', Climb 15,000'/7.5 min. Range 350 miles/500 lb. bomb, 1500 miles ferry.

The first P-40K-l delivered May 5, 1942, was similar to the P-40E-l except for an improved V-1710-73 engine. A small dorsal fin was fitted to late P-40E-ls, the P-40K-l, and 200 P-40K-5s, to correct a swinging tendency during take-off, but the lengthened fuselage of parallel late F models was introduced in October 1942 on 500 P-40K-10 and K-15 aircraft. Armament was six .50-caliber guns with 1,410 rounds in the wings, armor weighed 136 pounds, the armor glass windshield weighed 36 pounds, while some were delivered with only four guns and winterization. The Ks replaced the Es in AAF groups facing Japan, while some went to the 57th FG, and 765 were shipped as the lend-lease Kittyhawk III.

Mfr

CURTISS P-40L-20
Packard V-1650-1, 1300 takeoff, 1120 hp at 18,500'
DIMENSIONS: Span 37'4", Lg. 33'4", Ht. 12'4", Wing Area 236 sq. ft.
WEIGHT: Empty 6485 1b., Gross 8120 lb., Max. 9750 lb. Fuel 120+75/170 gal.
PERFORMANCE: Speed- Top 364 mph at 20,000', Landing 83 mph. Service Ceiling 34,400', Climb 15,000'/7.6 min. Range 275 miles/500 lb. bomb, 1375 miles ferry.

In November 1942, the P-40M replaced the K on the production lines. Ordered for lend-lease contracts, the 600 P-40Ms had six guns and a V-1710-81 with war-emergency power boost (WE) and a cooling grill behind the propeller spinner.

Mfr

CURTISS P-40M-1
Allison V-1710-81, 1200 hp takeoff, 1125 hp at 14,600', 1360 hp WE
DIMENSIONS: As P-40L
WEIGHT: Empty 6464 1b., Gross 8400 lb., Max. 10,000 lb. Fuel 120-157 gal.,(327 gal. ferry).
PERFORMANCE: Speed- Top 350 mph at 20,000', Cruising 272 mph, Landing 82 mph. Service Ceiling 30,000', Climb 15,000'/ 7.2 min. Range 350 miles/500 lb. bomb, 1600 miles ferry.

Four thousand P-40N fighters were ordered by a contract approved January 25, 1943, and this type began to replace the P-40M and L models at Curtiss in March 1943. By then, the much-superior P-38, P-47 and P-51 fighters were scheduled to equip all AAF groups in Europe and most of the Pacific, but increasing P-40 output provided a quick and less expensive way to meet commitments to lend-lease schedules and secondary Pacific sectors.

AF

CURTISS P-40N-1
Allison V-1710-81, 1200 hp takeoff, 1125 hp at 14,600', 1360 hp WE
DIMENSIONS: As P-40L
WEIGHT: Empty 60001b., Gross 7400 lb., Max. 8850 lb. Fuel 122+170 gal.
PERFORMANCE: Speed- Top 378 mph at 10,000', Cruising 288 mph, Landing 82 mph. Service Ceiling 38,000', Climb 15,000'/6.7 min. Range 260 miles/500 lb. bomb, 1400 miles ferry.

Four hundred P-40N-ls had a lighter structure with only four guns and the V-1710-81, and were the fastest production Warhawks, at 378 mph. Six guns, and wing racks for drop tanks or 500-pound bombs, greatly increased the ground attack or ferry capability of the P-40N-5, which also introduced an improved canopy. Allison V-1710-81 engines were also used on 1,100 P-40N-5s, 100 P-40N-10s winterized for Alaska's 343rd Group, and 377 P-40N-15s with more internal fuel.

CURTISS P-40N-5

Warhawk production reached a height of 463 P-40Ns in August 1943, and the following month the 80th Group in India became the seventh P-40 group in continuous combat against Japan. The other groups (15, 18, 23, 49, 51, and 343rd) also used P-40Ns, along with the 8th Group's 35th Squadron.

Allison V-1710-99s with an automatic engine control unit were used on 3,022 P-40N-20 to N-35 blocks, which differed in minor details. Twenty-five of these were completed as TP-40N two-place trainers. As late as June 30, 1944, another thousand were ordered, but that contract was cut back to 220 P-40N-40s with V-1710-115 engines and metal-covered ailerons. This last service model was delivered without camouflage paint and included five finished as two-seaters.

Mfr

CURTISS P-40N-30

AF

CURTISS P-40N-20
Allison V-1710-99, 1200 hp takeoff, 1125 hp at 14,600'
DIMENSIONS: As P-40L
WEIGHT: Empty 62001b., Gross 8350 lb., Max.11,400 lb. Fuel 159+450 gal.
PERFORMANCE: Speed- Top 350 mph at 16,400', Cruising 290 mph, Landing 82 mph. Service Ceiling 31,000', Climb 14,000'/7.3 min. Range 360 miles/500 lb. bomb, 3100 miles ferry at 198 mph.

There was a development effort to advance P-40 performance with the P-40P and P-40Q programs, but the Packard-powered P-40P was canceled with none built. The P-40Q project included two reworked P-40K-l0s and another begun as a P-40N-25, and the first flown on June 15, 1943. The best example was the XP-40Q example shown on the next page; actually the first P-40K-1 rebuilt in 1944 with a bubble canopy, V-1710-121 with two-stage supercharger, four-bladed propeller, clipped wingtips, new radiators, and four wing guns.

When the last P-40N-40 was accepted November 30, 1944, the Curtiss Buffalo factory had delivered 13,738 P-40 fighters since 1940. Peak AAF inventory had been 2,499 in April 1944 and eight foreign Air Forces used them under lend-lease. Production had continued on long past the P-40's prime and the end of the P-40 also meant the end of quantity fighter production by Curtiss.

PMB

CURTISS P-40N-40

The Kittyhawk I became the RAF's most important fighter in North Africa after it entered combat January 1, 1942, but never operated from the United Kingdom itself. Precise enumeration of RAF Kittyhawks is complicated by accidents and local transfers, but lend-lease shipments included 200 Kittyhawk IA (P-40E-1) that arrived for the Mediterranean Allied Air Forces (MAAF), but 34 were sunk at sea, and two more were tested in the UK.

CURTISS XP-40Q
Allison V-1710-121, 1425 hp takeoff, 1100 hp at 25,000'
DIMENSIONS: Span 35'3", Lg. 35'1;
WEIGHT: Gross 9000 lb.
PERFORMANCE: Speed- Top 422 mph at 20,500', Service Ceiling 39,000', Climb 20,000'/4.8 min.

The RAF allotted 130 serial numbers to the P-40F and 100 to the P-40L-10 as the Kittyhawk II, but only 103 P-40Fs and 45 P-40L-10s reached the RAF in North Africa, while 21 were lost at sea. Some served with No. 260 Squadron, and others were retained by the AAF.

Beginning in September 1942, the area's MAAF command received the Kittyhawk III, including 338 P-40K and 94 P-40Ms shipped from the U.S., plus a few P-40Ks transferred from local AAF units. The 456 Kittyhawk IVs shipped in 1943-44, less 15 sunk, were P-40Ns. While they won their last air battle in Italy on April 7, 1944, one squadron continued in the ground support role until the war's end.

Australia formed eight Kittyhawk squadrons, receiving 811: 37 P-40E and 126 P-40E-l, 42 P-40K-10 and K-15, 90 P-40M-5 and M-10, and 516 P-40N-1 to N-40 models. New Zealand equipped its seven fighter squadrons with 62 P-40E-1, 23 P-40K, one P-40L, 35 P-40M and 172 P-40N Kittyhawks. Besides the 72 Kittyhawk Is obtained from the RAF, Canada got replenishments through lend-lease: 12 P-40E-1, 15 P-40M-5 to M-10, and 35 P-40N-1 to N-20 models, while nine P-40K-ls were borrowed, but returned in 1943.

The Soviet Union was lend-leased 2,430 P-40s from the U.S., (in addition to the 171 Tomahawks shipped from Britain) of which 304 were lost in transit. Models sent included 75 more Tomahawks, about 840 P-40E-1s, 313 P-40Ks, 220 P-40Ms, and 980 P-40Ns.

At first they were sent on the Northern route, but in 1942. that route was the most dangerous, with 248 Kittyhawks sunk and 959 reaching Archangel or Murmansk. Forty-eight P-40Ks came via Alaska, starting in October 1942, but 1,091 Warhawks arrived on ships reaching the Persian Gulf, beginning on November 15, 1942, with 54 lost at sea.

A total of 320 of these Warhawks (or Kittyhawks in RAF/VVS usage) went to the Soviet North and Black Sea Fleets. The first to get the P-40E in May 1942 was the 72nd Fighter Air Regiment near Murmansk, joined in 1943 by the 27th and 78th IAPs, who promoted the fighter-bomber role, while a 118th MRAP squadron did naval reconnaissance. Black Sea Fleet regiments like the 7th and 62nd IAP and the 30th RAP, received 109 of the Navy's P-40s.

Red Army regiments with Kittyhawks included the 126th, 147th, 154th, 159th, 191st, 196th and 436th IAPs. To avoid a problem with the Allison engine's bearings, Soviet M-105 power plants were used by some P-40Es of the 196th IAP.

Apart from AVG aircraft, 14 P-40K, 15 P-40M and 299 P-40N fighters were shipped to China, but diversions to the 10th and 14th Air Forces reduced actual deliveries to 65 for the operational training unit in India and 139 for the Chinese air force itself. Two Chinese squadrons training in India received their first P-40N-5s on October 15, 1943. Eight fighter squadrons in the Chinese-American Composite Wing used P-40Ns by 1945.

Brazil acquired six P-40E-1, 29 P-40K, 9 P-40M-5 and 41 P-40N Warhawks to train a fighter group. Apparently, the last P-40 in combat was among the 59 P-40N-20s received by the Dutch No. 120 Squadron in Australia from December 1943 to July 1945 and used after the war against Indonesian nationalists.

Lockheed Lightning

The fastest American fighter available when World War II began, the Lockheed Lightning was the first twin-engine single-seat fighter ever in mass production and nothing like it had been seen before in the Air Corps.

Europe already had twin-engine fighters in 1937 with the Messerschmitt Bf 110 and Fokker G-l, the latter even anticipating the Lightning's tail booms, but these ships were long-range two-seaters. Lockheed's XP-38 was a single-seat fighter far outdoing the comparable Westland Whirlwind built in Britain in 1938.

On January 8, 1937, the Air Corps secretly invited five companies to participate in a competition to design a experimental fighter, whose mission was to intercept enemy long-range bombers. Since such bombers would be unlikely

LOCKHEED XP-38
Two Allison V-1710-11/-15, 1150 hp takeoff, 1000 hp at 20,000'
DIMENSIONS: Span 52', Lg. 37'10", Ht. 12'10", Wing Area 327.5 sq. ft.
WEIGHT: Empty 11,507 lb., Gross 13,964 lb., Max. 15,416 lb. Fuel 230-400 gal.
PERFORMANCE: Speed- Top 413 mph at 20,000', Landing 80 mph. Service Ceiling 38,000', Climb 20,000'/6.5 min. Range 890 miles normal, 1390 miles max.

LOCKHEED P-38
Two Allison V-1710-27/-29, 1150 hp takeoff and at 25,000'
DIMENSIONS: Span 52', Lg. 37'10", Ht. 12'10", Wing Area 327.5 sq. ft.
WEIGHT: Empty 11,672 lb., Gross 14,178 lb., Max. 15,340 lb. Fuel 230-410 gal.
PERFORMANCE: Speed- Top 390 mph at 20,000', Cruising 290 mph, Landing 80 mph. Service Ceiling 38,000', Climb 20,000'/6.8 min. Range 825 miles normal, 1490 miles max.

to be escorted by fighters, the defender's speed, climb, and firepower would be more important than aerobatic and endurance potential.

The specification, X-608 Interceptor Pursuit (Twin-engine), called for a top speed of 360 to 400 mph at 20,000 feet and a climb to that altitude in six minutes. This performance required turbosupercharged Allison engines, and armament should include a cannon and four machine guns.

Lockheed's experience with twin-engine designs, including the Electra transport and the proposed XFM-2, prepared the way for C.L. "Kelly" Johnson's bold Model 22 design, which became the XP-38.

The engines were the same Allisons, rated at 1,150 hp for takeoff, used on the XP-37, but they had their propellers turning inward to counteract each other's torque. Designated V-1710-11 and V-1710-15, they had General Electric B-1 turbosuperchargers in the twin booms that extended back to twin rudders. A short central nacelle held the pilot and proposed armament of one 23-mm Madsen and four .50-caliber Browning guns, which shot a concentrated stream of bullets from the nose uninterrupted by synchronization.

The first tricycle gear on a fighter permitted faster landings than were safe for older types, although Fowler extended flaps were needed to keep stalling speed within reason. Designer Johnson also provided a control wheel, instead of the usual stick, for the metal-covered control surfaces.

A wind-tunnel model was tested at the California Institute of Technology on April 1, 1937, a week after they had tested a model of the rival Vultee XP-1015. Using the same power plants and armament as the Model 22, the even larger Vultee had a long fuselage and conventional tail-down landing gear. Lockheed's proposal was submitted to the Air Corps on April 13, along with the lowest price bid, compared to bids by Hughes, Vought, and Vultee. The XP-38 was ordered June 23, 1937, but it would take over five years before service versions could enter combat.

The original XP-38 specification called for a 417-mph top speed at 20,000 feet (which was to be reached in 4.5 minutes), a service ceiling of 39,100 feet, and an endurance of 1.75 hours at 393 mph. This was promised at weights of 7802 pounds empty and 10,500 pounds gross.

By the time of the XP-38's first flight by Lt. Ben Kelsey on January 27, 1939, 3,700 pounds had been added to that weight, and Lockheed had spent $761,000 on a $163,000 contract. It was a good investment, for despite flap trouble on its first flight, the XP-38 was clearly the most advanced anti-bomber weapon available in the world. Lockheed had reduced its top speed guarantee to a conservative 385 mph with a 14,200 pounds gross weight, but this was soon surpassed in tests at March Field.

The secrecy that had surrounded the project was lifted for a transcontinental speed dash on February 11, 1939. Although the flight ended in a crash landing that destroyed the prototype, thirteen YP-38s (Model 122) were ordered on April 27.

LOCKHEED YP-38
Two Allison V-1710-27/-29, 1150 hp takeoff and at 25,000'
DIMENSIONS: Span 52', Lg. 37'10", Ht. 12'10", Wing Area 327.5 sq. ft.
WEIGHT: Empty 11,171 lb., Gross 13,500 lb., Max. 14,348 lb. Fuel 230-400 gal.
PERFORMANCE: Speed- Top 405 mph at 20,000', 353 mph at 5000', Cruising 330 mph, Landing 80 mph. Service Ceiling 38,000', Climb 20,000'/6 min. Range 650 miles normal, 1150 miles max.

Sixty-six Model 222 production aircraft were added by a contract announced August 10 and approved September 16, 1939. These aircraft used Allison F-2s (V-1710-27/29) with outward turning propellers and whose short gearbox and higher thrust line gave a new shape to the engine nacelles. They were supposed to be delivered in 15 months, so the First Pursuit Group at Selfridge Field could replace its P-35 and P-36s by December 30, 1940.

When the Anglo-French Purchasing commission was allowed to buy the most advanced American fighters, Secretary of War Harry Woodring objected to the export of turbosuperchargers. An isolationist at heart, he felt them too secret and too scarce to share. While the mechanical principles were no secret, it had taken 20 years to develop the metallurgical technology for the Air Corps. On March 21, 1940, Lockheed offered an export version, Model 322-61 with two 1,090-hp V-1710-C15s, without a turbosupercharger, turning both propellers in the same direction. Since these were the same engines used by the P-40 Tomahawks, they presented an attractive alternative for the Allies.

On paper, the threat to the type's performance was not fully realized. Guaranteed YP-38 performance at the design weight of 13,500 pounds promised 353 mph at 5,000 feet, 405 mph at 20,000 feet, and a climb to 20,000 feet in six minutes, while the 322-61 without turbos was expected to do 361 mph at 5,000 feet, 404 mph at 16,000 feet, and climb to 16,000 feet in 5.6 minutes.

A Foreign Release Agreement was made between Lockheed and the Air Corps on April 12, releasing this model for export, providing that the Army's P-38s would add the pilot and gas tank protection incorporated in export planes, and that Lockheed would deliver, in 16 months, a new prototype to be designated XP-58. All this, stated the Agreement, "without any additional expense or cost to the government"; presumably the company expected to pass these costs on to the foreign customers.

The Joint Purchasing Commission ordered 667 export models on June 5, 1940. This very expensive commitment would later be regretted by the RAF, which named the Lockheed "Lightning I" and inherited the entire amount after France capitulated to Germany. Addition of armor and leak-proof tanks would increase the gross weight to 14,467 pounds, and performance with the C-15 engines was very disappointing.

The armament originally considered in 1937 involved a Hotchkiss 25-mm weapon, but when this did not materialize, the prototype was to get one of four Danish 23-mm Madsens the Army imported, although guns were never actually fitted to the XP-38. On the YP-38, two .50-caliber with 200 rpg and two .30-caliber guns with 500 rpg, were specified just as on the early P-40, but below them was a 37-mm M-4 with only a 15-round magazine. An August 5, 1940, order changed all four machine guns to .50-caliber on all later P-38 models, and provided pilot armor.

Since tests on Hispano 20-mm guns, which began arriving from France by February 10, 1940, were favorable, and this gun had been selected by the British for their fighters, the 20-mm M1 was ordered into U.S. production for 607 Army Lightnings contracted for on August 30, 1940. Army and British Lightning models were to be produced concurrently, with similar armament and numerous details simplified for mass production.

Shortly after Spitfires and Hurricanes broke the back of the German bomber offensive in the Battle of Britain, the first YP-38 was flown on September 18, 1940. It is fortunate that this victory could be won without recourse to U.S. fighter production, which that month was limited to 114 P-40s, with one each of the YP-38, YP-39, and YP-43. Only the Lockheed outperformed the British types.

The first YP-38 was retained by the company for developmental testing, the second went to Wright Field on January 28, 1941, while the third and fourth were delivered to Patterson Field in March. Examples then went to Chanute and Lowry, but the seven remaining YP-38s went to Selfridge Field by May 29 for service tests by the 1st Pursuit Group.

LOCKHEED XP-38A

From June 20 to August 15, 29 P-38s followed, also with V-1710-27/29 engines and B-2 turbosuperchargers, but with four .50-caliber guns, the 37-mm M4, 3/8-inch armor, and camouflage paint. Another P-38 was held back for completion with the pressurized cockpit planned for the XP-49. That unarmed aircraft began tests as the XP-38A in May 1942, but no B or C model ever appeared.

Self-sealing fuel tanks, reducing capacity from 410 to 300 gallons, were introduced on the P-38D. The first of 36 was accepted on July 1, while the rest were delivered from August 9 to October 1, 1941, completing that contract eight months late. These aircraft cost $80,311 each, compared to $30,800 for the less-capable P-40s delivered the same time.

LOCKHEED P-38D
Two Allison V-1710-27/-29, 1150 hp takeoff and at 25,000'
DIMENSIONS: As P-38
WEIGHT: Empty 11,780 lb., Gross 14,456 lb., Max. 15,500 lb. Fuel 230-300 gal.
PERFORMANCE: Speed- Top 390 mph at 25,000', Cruising 300 mph, Landing 83 mph. Service Ceiling 39,000', Climb 20,000'/8 min. Range 500 miles normal, 975 miles max. at 200 mph.

Tests had begun in August on the first British 322-61 Lightning I with the C-15 medium altitude engines and both propellers rotating in the same direction, which were scheduled to be replaced, beginning with the 144th ship in April 1942, with turbo-supercharged power plants on the Lightning II version. The second Model 322 was accepted October 8, but later 322s coming out of the factory were refused acceptance by the British because of their poor high-altitude performance.

Standard Lightning armament on the RAF's Model 322, the AAF's P-38E, and on all later models, was one 20-mm gun with 150 rpg and four .50-caliber guns with 500 rpg. There were 188 pounds of cockpit armor and a 20-pound armor-glass windshield. Another 1,000 Lockheeds were ordered by the Air Force on October 31, 1941, and the first P-38E was delivered November 16.

When the United States entered the war, the only pursuit group with Lightnings was the 1st, which left its twenty-year home at Selfridge on December 8, 1941, to fly to San Diego. With six YP-38, 23 P-38, and 19 P-38Ds, they became southern California's air defense force, joined by the 14th Group as P-38Es replaced that unit's P-66s early in 1942.

The British allocation of Lightnings was eliminated and 143 Lightning Is were taken as "P-322" by the Army. Three P-322s were shipped to Britain for evaluation in March 1942. Air Force pilots found P-322s nose-heavy,

LOCKHEED P-38E
Data as P-38D

unable to keep formation with regular P-38s over 12,000 feet, and therefore suitable only for training. The 524 Lightning IIs scheduled were absorbed into AAF P-38F and P-38G contracts, and 120 P-322s had their engines replaced later with Allison F series power plants.

LOCKHEED 322-61 (LIGHTNING I)
Two Allison V-1710-C15 (-33), 1040 hp at 14,300'
DIMENSIONS: As P-38
WEIGHT: Empty 11,945 lb., Gross 14,467 lb.
PERFORMANCE: Speed- Top 357 mph. Service Ceiling 40,000', Climb 2850'/1 min.

Delivery went ahead with 210 P-38Es and 100 F-4 photo models, which replaced the guns with four K-17 cameras. The first two F-4s were delivered in December 1941, giving the Air Force its first high-speed reconnaissance capability. The first Lightnings deployed to a war theater were F-4s shipped to Australia, where they flew their first missions for the Fifth Air Force April 16, 1942.

To increase the Lightning's range, Lockheed attached a pair of 75-gallon drop tanks to a P-38E on January 15, 1942, and these were standardized on all F-4s going overseas and on the P-38E's issued to the squadron dispatched to Alaska. This was much more practical than a still-born project to carry gas for transoceanic deliveries in twin floats, which would require the upswept tail tested on one P-38E in March 1942.

As the first fighter fast enough to encounter compressibility, the P-38 suffered buffeting when diving too steeply, and the first YP-38 lost its tail pulling out of a dive. With a

LOCKHEED P-38G
Two Allison V-1710-51,-55, 1325 hp takeoff, 1150 hp at 25,000'
DIMENSIONS: As P-38
WEIGHT: Empty 12,200 lb., Gross 15,800 lb., Max. 19,300 lb. Fuel 300+300 gal. (900 gal max.)
PERFORMANCE: Speed- Top 345 mph at 5000', 400 mph at 25,000', Cruising 310 mph, Landing 89 mph. Service Ceiling 39,000', Climb 20,000'/8.5 min. Range 350 miles with 2000 lb. bombs, 2400 miles ferry at 203 mph.

basic airframe speed limit of Mach .73, various fixes had small effect. Deployment into combat was delayed until this problem was alleviated with wing fillets, and until the range could be extended for offensive missions.

The P-38F introduced new Allison F-5s (V-1710-49/53) with B-13 turbos and 1,325 hp for 15 minutes at takeoff, although military power available for 15 minutes at altitude was limited to 1,150 hp by the Lightning's inadequate engine cooling system. A pair of 165-gallon drop tanks,* or 1,000-pound bombs could be carried. Delivery of 527 P-38F and 20 F-4A models began in March 1942, and maneuvering flaps were introduced with the P-38F-15 block.

They were followed after June 1942 by 1,082 P-38G-l to G-15 series aircraft with the Allison F-10 (-51/55) engines and under-wing racks for 300-gallon ferry tanks or 1,600-pound bombs.

More power became available with the Allison F-15 (-89/91) yielding 1,425 hp for takeoff, with military power limited to 1,240 hp by the inadequate engine cooling. This power plant was tested on a pre-production P-38H-1 in September 1942, beginning a series known as Model 422, with also introduced a flat 35-pound armor-glass windshield and 182 pounds of cockpit armor.

The cooling limit was overcome by the P-38J, which was distinguished from older models by a new chin intake below the engine, with core-type intercoolers. These allowed the V-1710-89/-91 engines full 1,425-hp military power or a five-minute war-emergency power boost (WE) of 1,600 hp. Ten P-38J-ls were completed, but until more of the new intercoolers were made, Lockheed built 225 P-38H-ls beginning in April 1943, followed by 375 P-38H-5 models whose B-33 turbos with higher manifold pressures raised critical altitude.

LOCKHEED P-38F
Two Allison V-1710-49,-53, 1325 hp takeoff, 1150 hp at 25,000'
DIMENSIONS: As P-38
WEIGHT: Empty 12,264 lb., Gross 14,850 lb., Max. 18,000 lb. Fuel 230-300 gal. (600 gal max.)
PERFORMANCE: Speed- Top 395 mph at 25,000', Cruising 305 mph, Landing 85 mph. Service Ceiling 39,000', Climb 20,000'/8.8 min. Range 350 miles normal at 305 mph, 1925 miles ferry at 195 mph.

*Often listed as 150 gallons, but the actual capacity is given here.

LOCKHEED P-38H-5
Two Allison V-1710-89,-91, 1425 hp takeoff, 1240 hp at 27,000'
DIMENSIONS: As P-38
WEIGHT: Empty 12,350 lb., Gross 16,300 lb., Max. 20,300 lb. Fuel 300+600 gal.
PERFORMANCE: Speed- Top 345 mph at 5000', 402 mph at 25,000', Cruising 300 mph, Landing 88 mph. Service Ceiling 34,000', Climb 20,000'/6.5 min. Range 960 miles normal, 1640 miles with 630 gal., 2400 miles ferry at 215 mph.

Then the assembly line turned, in August 1943, to build 2,960 P-38J-5 to J-25s with the last model adding dive flaps to allow recovery from faster dives. A 55-gallon leading edge fuel tank added in each wing, with two 300-gallon external tanks, increased Lightning ferry range to 2,600 miles at 198 mph. On combat missions, two 165-gallon drop tanks gave the P-38J a radius of 795 miles for fighter sweeps or medium bomber escort. Two 1,000-pound bombs instead of tanks could be carried out to a radius of 375 miles. Two 1,600-pound armor-piercing bombs could also be carried.

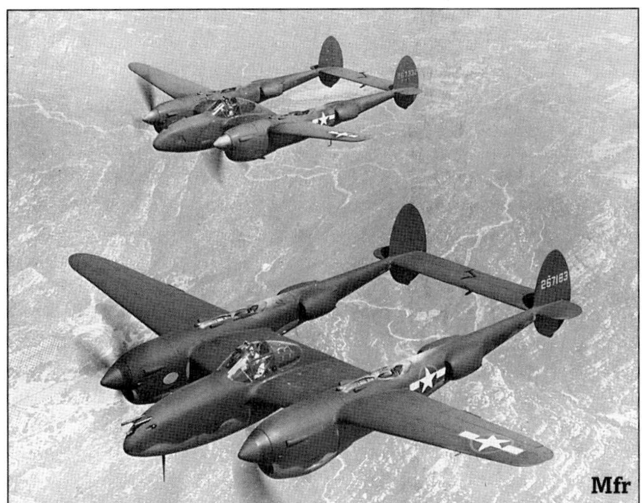

LOCKHEED P-38J with F-5B
Two Allison V-1710-89,-91, 1425 hp takeoff, 1600 hp at 27,000'(WE)
DIMENSIONS: As P-38
WEIGHT: Empty 12,780 lb., Gross 17,500 lb., Max. 21,600 lb. Fuel 410+600 gal.
PERFORMANCE: Speed- Top 360 mph at 5000', 414 mph at 25,000', Cruising 330 mph, Landing 105 mph. Service Ceiling 44,000', Climb 20,000'/7 min. Range 450 miles/3200 lb. bombs, 1220 miles with 410 gal., 1780 miles with 740 gal., 2600 miles ferry at 198 mph.

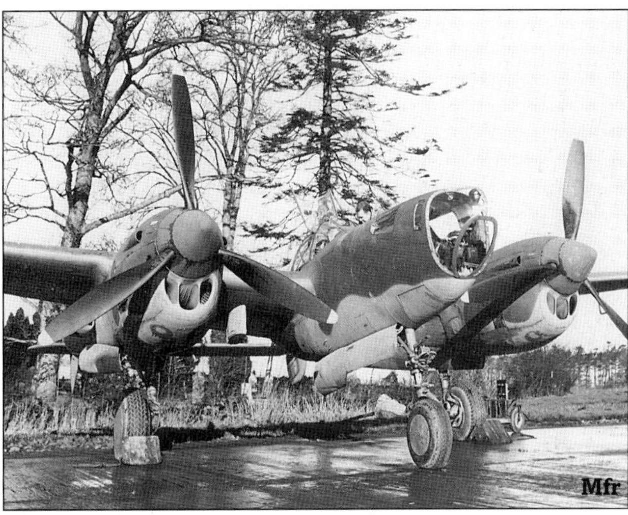

LOCKHEED P-38J (with "Droop snoot")

One Lightning was completed as the XP-38K, with 1,425 hp V-1710-75/77 Allisons and larger, 12-foot 6-inch, propellers. In June 1944, the P-38L appeared with 1,475-hp Allison F-30 engines, and could add fittings under the wing for ten 5-inch rockets. Before the war's end halted Lightning production in August 1945, 3,810 P-38L-LOs had been built at the Burbank factory. Two thousand P-38L-VNs had been ordered June 26, 1944, from Consolidated-Vultee's Nashville plant, but this contract was canceled after 113 were accepted between January and June 1945.

Mfr

LOCKHEED P-38L-5
Two Allison V-1710-111/-113, 1475 hp takeoff, 1600 hp WE at 28,700'
DIMENSIONS: As P-38
WEIGHT: Empty 12,800 lb., Gross 17,500 lb., Max. 21,600 lb. Fuel 410+600 gal.
PERFORMANCE: Speed- Top 414 mph at 25,000', Cruising 330 mph, Landing 105 mph. Service Ceiling 44,000', Climb 20,000'/7 min. Range 450 miles/3200 lb. bombs, 1210 miles with 410 gal., 1770 miles with 740 gal., 2600 miles ferry at 198 mph.

As the fastest strategic reconnaissance type available, unarmed Lightnings also operated on every front. Five K-17 cameras replaced guns in the F-5 series, the first being a single F-5A-2 converted from an F-4 in April 1942, and fitted with two 165-gallon drop tanks. Twenty F-5A-ls preceded the P-38G-1 off the line in June 1942, using the same engine, followed in August by 20 F-5A-3s with B-13 superchargers and by 140 F-5A-l0s beginning in November. Two hundred blue-painted F-5B-ls were essentially P-38J camera versions with an automatic pilot that were delivered from September to December 1943.

AF

LOCKHEED F-5A
Two Allison V-1710-51/-55, 1325 hp takeoff, 1150 hp at 25,000'
DIMENSIONS: As P-38
WEIGHT: Empty 12,185 lb., Gross 14,965 lb., Max. 18,580 lb. Fuel 300-600 gal. (900 gal max.)
PERFORMANCE: Speed- Top 400 mph at 27,000', Cruising 340 mph, Landing 90 mph. Service Ceiling 39,000', Climb 20,000'/10.6 min. Range 375 miles, 2400 miles ferry at 203 mph.

All later camera versions were converted at Lockheed's Modification Center in Dallas, and included 128 F-5Cs with special cameras, a single two-place XF-5D with a Plexiglas nose and three cameras, 205 F-5Es from P-38Js, and some 500 F-5F or F-5Gs from P-38Ls.

Modified Lightnings also tried special attack styles. Two torpedoes were test-dropped from a P-38F-13 in December 1942. The first glazed-nose P-38J "Droop-Snoot", with a bombardier and Norden bomb sight replacing nose armament, reached the Eighth Air Force on February 28, 1944. They guided formations of conventional P-38Js, each carrying two bombs, on horizontal bombing missions begun April 10, 1944. In 1945, the "Pathfinder" P-38L modification used an APS-15 radar in the nose to guide bomber missions.

AF

LOCKHEED F-5G
Two Allison V-1710-111/-113, 1475 hp takeoff, 1600 hp WE at 28,700'
DIMENSIONS: As P-38
WEIGHT: Empty 12,800 lb., Gross 15,800 lb., Max. 21,600 lb. Fuel 230-1010 gal.
PERFORMANCE: Speed- Top 418 mph at 25,000', Cruising 330 mph, Landing 100 mph. Service Ceiling 44,500', Climb 20,000'/6.5 min. Range 300 miles/230 gal., 500 miles with 300 gals., 2600 miles ferry at 198 mph.

The final Lightning model was the P-38M, a black-painted night fighter with an APS-4 radar under the nose and a radar operator seated behind and above the pilot. This model had been preceded by the modification of two P-38J-20 single-seaters in April 1944 with the radar behind the nose wheel, and a third fitted as a two-seater in September 1944 with the radar on the right wing. A P-38L-5 converted to a night fighter at the Dallas Modification Center was flown February 5, 1945, and 75 similar conversions were ordered as P-38Ms. Weighing 17,646 pounds with combat load, the two-seater's top speed was reduced from the P-38L's 414 mph to 391 mph at 27,700 feet for the P-38M. The war ended before the P-38M went overseas, and only four were sent to the 418th FIS on occupation duty in Japan.

By the war's end, 9,535 fighter and 500 reconnaissance Lightnings had been completed. The average 1944 cost of a P-38 was $97,147 compared to $44,892 for a P-40.

LOCKHEED P-38M

The P-38 in Combat

The P-38 was the fastest army fighter in the earliest part of the war and the first fighter useful for long-range escort. Its main limitation was the relatively awkward maneuverability inherent in the machine's size, but when proper tactics were devised to take advantage of the P-38's speed and ceiling, that fighter became successful in combat, and the safety factor of the second engine brought many damaged Lightnings home.

A threat to Alaska brought the first P-38 combat deployment when the 54th Squadron was detached from the 55th Group and sent to Elmendorf Field on May 29, 1942. The squadron's P-38Es had been winterized and fitted with drop tanks, and scored the first Lightning combat victories on August 4, 1942, when two Type 97 four-engine flying boats were shot down near Umnak. The 54th joined the 343rd Fighter Group in action until July 1943 in the Aleutians, and remained until the war's end.

Operation Bolero was the transatlantic movement of aircraft to build up the Eighth Air Force in the United Kingdom. The 1st and 14th Fighter Groups were the first to fly single-seat fighters across the Atlantic. Re-equipped with P-38Fs after their service as California's air defense, they moved to Maine, and crossed via Greenland and Iceland, led by B-17E guides.

During July and August, 164 Lockheeds made the flight safely. Although six others were forced down in Greenland; all the pilots were rescued. On the way over, a squadron stayed in Iceland long enough for the first P-38 victory against Germany, when an Fw 200 Condor was destroyed on August 15, 1942.

Although over 340 Lightning sorties were flown from Britain, none encountered the enemy, and both P-38 groups were transferred to Operation Torch, the Northwest Africa occupation, beginning their movement November 14, 1942. The first P-38 victory in Africa, over a Bf 109, was scored on November 21. On Christmas Day, the 82nd Group's P-38s joined the fighting over Tunisia. These three Lightning groups served in the Mediterranean Theater (MTO) through the war, flying first for the Twelfth, and then the Fifteenth Air Force. Top P-38 ace in the MTO was the 82nd Group's Lt. William J. Sloan, with twelve victories.

While the Eighth Air Force had lost all its P-38s to the Twelfth in 1942, it still needed them, since neither the P-39 nor P-40 was considered suitable for the cross-channel offensive. The 20th and 55th Groups left their Seattle area defense stations, and flew P-38Hs to Britain by August and September 1943. The 55th Group's first combat mission was on October 15th, just after the Schweinfurt attacks had proven that the daylight bombing offensive against Germany could not succeed without fighter escort. At that point, "Nothing [was] more critical....than the early arrival of P-38s and P-51s", urged General Ira C. Eaker, then Eighth Air Force commander.

The Eighth soon added the 364th and 479th Groups while the Ninth Tactical Air Force got the 367th, 370th, and 374th Groups. All seven P-38 groups in Britain were used to cover the D-Day landings in Normandy, for their distinctive shape made them less likely to be shot at by Allied gunners. In the following months, five of these groups re-equipped with P-51s, one with P-47s, and only the 374th still used the P-38 until VE Day.

In the Pacific, the Lightnings usually appeared one squadron at a time, to upgrade the scattered P-39 and P-40 groups. The first such squadron was the 39th, of the 35th Group, whose P-39s were replaced by P-38Fs. These Lightnings scored their first kills for the Fifth Air Force on December 27, 1942. Likewise, the 9th and 80th Squadrons of the 49th and 8th Groups, respectively, got P-38s early in 1943. Not until September 1944 were the remaining squadrons of these three groups provided with P-38s. One full P-38 group, the 475th, had already joined the Fifth in combat on August 13, 1943.

It was here in the Southwest Pacific that Lockheed's fighter had its greatest success, as the top AAF aces ran up their scores on P-38s: Majors Richard Bong with 40 victories from December 27, 1942, to December 17, 1944, and Thomas McGuire, Jr., with 38 from August 18, 1943 to December 26, 1944. These scores, and the 475th Group's wartime score of 545 victories in two years, were the product of very carefully worked out tactics. Another victory in P-38s, on July 28, 1944, was that of a famous civilian pilot, Charles Lindbergh, who flew 25 missions with that group. The 49th Group, which had the Air Force's highest score, of 678 planes, downed most of them on P-38s.

In addition, the P-38 was used by both Thirteenth Air Force fighter groups (8th and 347th) and by one squadron in each of these groups in other Air Forces: the 531st Squadron, 21st Group, Seventh Air Force; the 459th Squadron, 80th Group, Tenth Air Force; the 54th Squadron, 343rd Group, Eleventh Air Force; and the 449th Squadron, 51st Group, Fourteenth Air Force. We have omitted those P-38 units not using the Lightning in combat, nor will we list the F-5 equipped photo-recon groups or squadrons that served in every wartime theater.

Lend-lease programs seldom involved Lockheed fighters. However, Australia got three used F-4s in August

1942, and two Free French units (GR I and II/33) operated F-5 series aircraft in 1943-45. China received 12 P-38Ls and nine F-5Es in 1945, and after the war, 50 P-38L and F-5Es were passed to Italy. Some P-38Ls drifted to Latin America, including six to Cuba and 11 to the Dominican Republic in 1947, five to Honduras and two to Nicaragua in 1948.

Bell P-39 Airacobra

Placing the engine behind the pilot has become common since jet propulsion, but this arrangement was first introduced to American fighters by Bell's Airacobra. Previously, it had been seen abroad in Westland and Koolhoven designs, but the P-39 was the first such design in mass production.

Several advantages became apparent when the engine was moved back to the center of gravity. A slimmer nose allowed better streamlining and visibility, and made room for heavier armament and the retracted nose wheel of a tricycle landing gear. This undercarriage offered better ground handling and permitted higher landing speeds, which in turn led to smaller wings -not an unmixed blessing since the higher wing loading handicapped climb and maneuverability at high altitudes.

Another disadvantage was that the crowded interior limited the space available for fuel, but that did not seem serious since the Air Corps specification X-609, dated March 19, 1937, called for an single-engine interceptor pursuit with cannon and turbosupercharger, designed to meet attacking enemy bombers. Designer Robert Wood had experience with the new Allison engine in Bell Model 2, the XA-11A modification that first tested that power plant. The Buffalo company offered designs planned with a 25-mm cannon in the propeller shaft. Bell Model 3 had the cockpit behind the engine as usual, but Model 4, dated June 3, 1937, placed the cockpit ahead of the Allison.

AF

BELL XP-39
Allison V-1710-17, 1150 hp takeoff, 1000 hp at 20,000'
DIMENSIONS: Span 34', Lg. 29'8", Ht. 9'10", Wing Area 214 sq. ft.
WEIGHT: Empty 4545 lb., Gross 6104 lb., Max. 6659 lb. Fuel 115-200 gal.
PERFORMANCE: Speed- Top 365 mph at 20,000', Landing 70 mph. Service Ceiling 36,000', Climb 20,000'/6 min. Endurance 1 hr. at top speed.

Rival Curtiss Model 80 and Seversky AP-3 high-altitude interceptor proposals were also submitted. Model 80 was based on the XP-37 and offered to put a pair of 23-mm Madsen cannon under the wings, while Model 80A proposed a single 23-mm Madsen in the nose. Seversky's AP-3 offering had two .50-caliber guns in the nose and two in the wings, but AP-3A had just the nose guns, but added a 25-mm cannon two feet below the centerline.

The Army chose Model 4 over the more conventional layouts, and a prototype, designated XP-39, was ordered October 7, 1937. An Allison V-1710-17 with a ten-foot extension drive shaft to the reduction gear box behind the propeller and a B-5 turbosupercharger under the engine delivered 1,150 hp.

Mfr

BELL XP-39B
Allison V-1710-37, 1090 hp at 13,200'
DIMENSIONS: Span 34', Lg. 29'9", Ht. 11'10", Wing Area 213 sq. ft.
WEIGHT: Empty 4530 lb., Gross 5834 lb., Max. 6450 lb. Fuel 115-200 gal.
PERFORMANCE: Speed- Top 375 mph at 15,000', Cruising 310 mph, Landing 73 mph. Service Ceiling 36,000', Climb 20,000'/7.5 min. Range 600 miles normal, 1400 miles/200 gal. at 190 mph.

Provision was made for two synchronized .50-caliber guns above a 25-mm Hotchkiss gun with its barrel pointed through the propeller hub. Since that weapon never appeared, by December 31, 1937, it was decided to use the new 37-mm Colt T-9 cannon. (Actually, no weapons were ever installed on the prototype during flight tests.)

The original X-609 specification called for a minimum top speed of 290 mph at sea level and 360 mph at 20,000 feet, but 400 mph was the desired goal. Bell guaranteed a top speed of 330 mph at sea level and 400 mph at 20,000 feet, climbing to that altitude in five minutes, but this was for a weight of 3,995 pounds empty and 5,550 pounds gross.

After the XP-39 was moved to Wright Field in December 1938, Army inspectors listed the actual prototype weight as 4,545 pounds empty and 6,104 pounds gross. Air intakes protruded behind the engine, the left side to cool the oil radiator, the right side for the carburetor and for the turbosupercharger intercooler, The first test flight was made at Wright Field by James Taylor on April 6, 1939. Drive shaft vibration curtailed tests and excessive airframe drag limited speed to nearer the minimum than the desired level. While detailed reports are not available, one Army chart stated top speed was 365 mph at 20,000 feet.

On April 27, 1939, without waiting for complete XP-39 tests, a service test contract was approved for 12 YP-39s and one YP-39A, the first to be delivered in ten months. Originally, the YP-39 (Bell Model 12) was to have the same turbosupercharged engine as the prototype, do 375 mph at 20,000 feet, climb to that altitude in six minutes, and have a 41,300-foot service ceiling. The proposed YP-39A's V-1710-31 would utilize internal geared supercharging instead of a turbosupercharger. While top speed at 20,000 feet would be reduced to 360 mph, the lighter weight and reduced drag was expected to improve low-altitude performance.

After unsatisfactory trials, the XP-39 prototype went to NACA's full-scale wind tunnel on June 6, 1939. That study suggested several modifications: the front wheel should no longer protrude below the nose, smaller main wheels could be enclosed in the wings, the cockpit hood lowered, oil cooling duct moved to the wings, and the turbosupercharger replaced by an internal geared system. If these changes were made, Larry Bell wrote the Material Division on August 30, the P-39 could attain 400 mph at 15,000 feet with 1,150 hp.

By this time the Air Corps no longer saw the Bell as a high-altitude partner of the P-38, so this proposal was accepted and the XP-39 was shipped back to the factory for modifications. A carburetor air scoop was placed behind the cockpit, the turbosupercharger and side intakes removed, and the original engine replaced by an interim V-1710-37 rated at 1,090 hp at 13,200 feet with a single-stage geared supercharger.

First flown November 25, 1939, the revised prototype was designated XP-39B and proved satisfactory enough for its features to be incorporated into all 13 service-test aircraft. A guaranteed top speed of 375 mph was promised at 13,200 feet.

"We have eliminated a million and one problems by the removal of the supercharger..." rejoiced Larry Bell on January 17, 1940. This crucial decision to omit the turbosupercharger improved low-altitude performance, but seriously crippled high-altitude performance, a fault shared by earlier P-40s.

Air Corps production plans had begun with Circular Proposals issued March 11, 1939, for single-engine Interceptor Pursuits, twin-engine Interceptor Pursuits, and Multiplace Fighters, with specifications calling for clones of the P-39, P-38, and YFM-1A designs. The last category was dropped from Air Corps plans, while the P-38 naturally won the twin-engine contract, but by May 10, the Materiel Division was considering less restrictive requirements for the single-engine pursuits to be delivered in 1941.

Tricycle gear, cannon, and the type of supercharging became optional on a new specification dated June 24, which enabled Curtiss, Republic and Vultee to enter the contract competition. Republic won first place with an order for 80 P-44s with *Wasp* engines, while 80 Bell Model 4-F fighters, designated P-45, would have the new 1,150-hp V-1710-35 Allisons promised for delivery in 1941. Contracts for the XP-46 and XP-47 designs were also awarded by this competition.

Bell's contract was approved October 12, 1939, but this model was redesignated P-39C. The P-39C specification dated February 14, 1940, estimated top speed as 343 mph at sea level and 400 mph at 15,000 feet, with a 39,000 feet service ceiling, based on 1,150 hp expected at 15,000 feet.

A French request to buy Airacobras was turned down by the Air Corps on February 8, 1940, but that decision was reversed on March 25. A Bell Model 14 export version was offered then called the P-400, apparently because it promised a 400-mph top speed at 15,000 feet, and a 35,000-foot service ceiling, if gross weight was limited to 6,150 pounds.

Bell Aircraft obtained a Foreign Sales Agreement from the Army on April 4 that allowed them to sell Airacobras to the Allies in exchange for designing a new fighter, the Model 16, which began the XP-52 project. Always an aggressive salesman, Larry Bell hurried to convince the joint Anglo-French Purchasing Commission to buy his "P-400". Unlike the Army, which then paid only after its planes were delivered, the Allies paid two million of the nine million dollar contract in advance; money his company badly needed.

This contract, made for France on April 13, 1940, and approved May 8, specified a 20-mm Hispano gun as the cannon armament and added wing guns, armor, and leak proof tanks. Despite the increase in weight, Bell guaranteed a top speed of 383 mph at 15,000 feet. This contract was taken over in June by the RAF, which by June 20, 1941, increased the number from 170 to 675 aircraft and planned to make the P-400 the first single-seat American to enter Fighter Command itself, rather than serving overseas like the Buffalo and Kittyhawk.

P-39 Production

On September 13, 1940, 17 months after the contract, the first YP-39 was first flown by Max Stanley. Powered by the 1,090-hp V-1710-37, it had 5/8-inch armor steel and armor glass in front and back of the pilot. Stanley had to bail out of this YP-39 on October 12, using the unique auto-style side door that replaced the usual sliding canopy. Tests resumed when the next two were delivered on October 31, and top speed at 7,000 pounds gross was 368 mph.

Mfr

BELL YP-39
Allison V-1710-37, 1090 hp at 13,200'
DIMENSIONS: Span 34', Lg. 30'2", Ht. 11'10", Wing Area 213 sq. ft.
WEIGHT: Empty 5042 lb., Gross 7000 lb., Max. 7235 lb. Fuel 104-170 gal.
PERFORMANCE: Speed- Top 368 mph at 13,600', Cruising 257 mph, Landing 80 mph. Service Ceiling 33,300', Climb 20,000'/7.3 min. Range 600 miles normal, 1000 miles max.

The full set of weapons mounted in the nose included two .30-caliber guns with 1,000 rounds, two .50-caliber guns with 400 rounds and a 37-mm cannon with 15 rounds. This YP-39 gun's first air test firing of 500 rounds was from November 7 to 24 over Lake Ontario, and established that cannon as Bell's trademark weapon.

Mfr

BELL P-39C
Allison V-1710-35, 1150 hp at 12,000'
DIMENSIONS: As YP-39
WEIGHT: Empty 5070 lb., Gross 7075 lb., Max. 7480 lb. Fuel 104-170 gal.
PERFORMANCE: Speed- Top 379 mph at 13,000', Cruising 274 mph , Landing 80 mph. Service Ceiling 33,200', Climb 13,000'/3.6 min. Range 500 miles normal, 900 miles max.

All Army P-39s were ordered with that cannon, which, Capt. Kelsey explained in an October 25, 1940, memo, was preferable at lower altitudes against heavily armored aircraft and tanks. Since the Lockheed P-38E was expected to operate "at high altitudes against lightly armored planes", the 20-mm gun was chosen for the Lightning.

The fourth YP-39 was delivered to Wright Field on December 2, 1940, and the next YP-39s went to Chanute, Patterson, and Lowry Fields and to NACA for tests. The last five, delivered December 16, 1940, went to Selfridge Field.

By September 13, 1940, the Army had added contracts for 623 P-39D Airacobras, which was the Bell Model 15 with wing guns and Hewitt Rubber Co. self-sealing fuel bags, and ordered that these additions be made to the last 60 aircraft on the previous contract. To expedite production, it was soon agreed to standardize most P-39D and P-400 features except for the latter's 20-mm gun and British-installed systems like oxygen and radio.

The first 20 P-39C production aircraft were completed from January 16 to April 7, 1941, with 1,150-hp V-1710-35 engines, camouflage finish, and the same five guns as the YP-39. Selfridge Field got them for the 31st Pursuit Group, although three were shipped to Britain on June 26. Thirty more sets of leak proof tanks were ordered on March 8, 1941, for later installation on YP-39 and P-39C models.

The P-39D and export P-400 came off the assembly lines at the same time, both with the V-1710-35 engine, self-sealing tanks, four .30-caliber wing guns with 4,000 rounds, and two synchronized .50s with 400 rounds in the nose. The P-39D had a 37-mm M-9 gun with 30 rounds, 191 pounds of armor, and 66 pounds of armor-glass. Since tank protection reduced internal fuel capacity from 170 to 120 gallons, a February 1941 order added provisions for a 75-gallon belly drop tank, or a 600-pound bomb, on the P-39D.

The P-400 used the more rapid-firing 20-mm HS gun with a 60-round drum, 231 pounds of armor and 60 pounds of armor-glass, the heaviest protection of any American fighter, as well as the 240-pound leak proof fuel bags and a 110-pound radio.

The first P-39D, priced at $41,479, was delivered February 3, 1941, but remained at the factory until December, while regular deliveries to Selfridge Field began May 5. Bell completed 429 P-39D models in 1941, too quickly for the available guns or Curtiss Electric propellers; only 390 37-mm aircraft guns in total were completed that year. The aircraft were sometimes flown to an Army base where the propeller was removed, shipped back to Bell, and reused to fly away another plane.

Aeroproducts hydromatic propellers were substituted on 229 P-39Fs, delivered beginning in December 1941,

BELL P-39D
Allison V-1710-35, 1150 hp at 12,000'
DIMENSIONS: As YP-39
WEIGHT: Empty 5658 lb., Gross 7500 lb., Max. 8400 lb. Fuel 120+75 gal.
PERFORMANCE: Speed- Top 368 mph at 13,800', Cruising 213 mph , Landing 82 mph. Service Ceiling 32,100', Climb 15,000'/5.7 min. Range 800 miles/500 lb. bomb, 1545 miles ferry at 195 mph.

and 25 other ships on this contract were designated P-39J with Allison V-1710-59 engines rated at 1,100 hp at 15,200 feet with automatic boost control. All these aircraft were known as Model 15 on company records and had similar characteristics.

BELL P-39F of 54th PG

BELL P-39J of 57th PS, 54th PG

The British Model 14 planes were called Airacobra I by RAF and P-400 in U.S. records. When the second was tested in April 1941 in light and highly polished condition, Larry Bell wrote the Army that it had achieved a 392-mph top speed at 14,400 feet and a 35,000-foot service ceiling. He did not mention the limited gross weight, which omitted guns and armor. In August, a standard P-400 was claimed to have a 371-mph top speed at 14,090 feet and a 34,800-foot service ceiling.

But after the P-400 reached Britain on July 30, 1941, it was tested at a full weight of 7,830 pounds, and strict RAF standards listed the top speed as a disappointing 355 mph at 13,000 feet with a 29,000-foot service ceiling. This loss of speed could not be explained by the American support group, and it became apparent that the company had greatly exaggerated its product's virtues. Compared to the Spitfire VB, the Airacobra I was faster at low levels, but decidedly slower in climb, and increasingly slower at altitudes over 14,000 feet.

BELL P-400 (Airacobra I)
Allison V-1710-35 (E4), 1150 hp at 11,800'
DIMENSIONS: As YP-39
WEIGHT: Empty 5550 lb., Gross 7637 lb., Max. 7845 lb. Fuel 120 gal.
PERFORMANCE: Speed- Top 326 mph at 6000', 355 mph at 13,000', Cruising 217 mph, Landing 82 mph. Service Ceiling 29,000', Climb 10,000'/5.1 min. Range 760 miles.

The only Fighter Command squadron to use the Bell flew just nine strafing sorties across the Channel, from October 9th to 11th, before compass troubles ended operations. As Fighter Command no longer wanted the type, No. 601 Squadron re-equipped with Spitfires in March 1942. While the Airacobra could have given good service to Army Cooperation squadrons, these had a goodly number of Mustang Is on the way.

Of 675 Airacobra Is built, 477 were shipped to Britain, two lost in tests, and 196 requisitioned by the Army Air Force at the factory after the United States entered the war. The USSR received 195 from Britain via convoys to North Russia, and 71 others were sunk *en route.** Heavy convoy losses delayed shipment to Russia of another 179 P-400s which were instead transferred to two AAF groups in the United Kingdom, leaving only 32 retained or expended by the RAF.

Lend-lease funds were used for the Model 14A, first ordered June 11, 1941, to follow the Model 14 in 1942. The first 336 were designated P-39D-1 and had a 20-mm gun with 60 rounds, two synchronized .50s with 430 rounds in the nose, four .30-caliber wing guns with 4,000 rounds, 177 pounds of armor, and 65 pounds of armorglass, and a 129-pound radio. Most were requisitioned by the AAF, and 158 similar P-39D-2s were delivered to the AAF and the Soviet Union with V-1710-63 engines.

*British records give 266 sent to the USSR, with 53 sunk in British ships. Russian records state one received in December 1941, 192 in 1942, and 2 in January 1943. Losses on other ships sunk may account for the difference.

BELL P-39D-1

The P-39D-3s were 26 Ds with two cameras added aft of the engine for taking vertical and oblique pictures, and 11 D-1s with these cameras became the P-39D-4. Cameras were also fitted to 27 P-39F-2 models.

BELL P-39D-2 of 45th IAP, VVS
Allison V-1710-63, 1325 hp takeoff, 1150 hp at 11,800'
DIMENSIONS: As YP-39
WEIGHT: Empty 5607 lb., Gross 7837 lb., Max. 8376 lb. Fuel 120+75 gal.
PERFORMANCE: Speed- Top 368 mph at 12,000', 309 mph at s.l., Cruising 250 mph, Stalling 82 mph. Service Ceiling 30,850', Climb 15,000'/6.25 min. Range 780 miles normal, 1063 miles max.

A larger square-cut wing was designed for the XP-39E (Bell Model 23) and two prototypes were ordered April 11, 1941, with a replacement added in 1942. Armed with a 37-mm nose gun with 30 rounds, two .50-caliber guns in the nose, and four in the wings with 300 rpg, the XP-39E planned to use an Allison V-1710-47. This power plant was not ready in time and were replaced by an Allison V-1710-35 when the first prototype was flown February 21, 1942. It spun to a crash March 26, but the second prototype, flown April 4, and the last, flown September 19, had the new V-1710-47 with a two-stage supercharger.

Each of the three examples tested a different vertical tail surface, and engineering studies made on this project contributed to the development of the Bell P-63 Kingcobra. Four thousand production models, designated P-76, were ordered on February 24, 1942, from the new Bell plant then building at Marietta, Georgia, but this contract was canceled on May 20, so that this plant would be free for B-29 production, and Bell engineers could concentrate on the P-63.

The next Airacobra production batch was externally like the P-39D, and began with a contract approved August 25, 1941, for 1,800 P-39Gs, Bell Model 26. Changes in engine model led to different designations when their delivery began in July 1942 from the Niagara Falls factory, but all had the 37-mm gun.*

BELL XP-39E
Allison V-1710-47, 1325 hp takeoff, 1150 hp at 22,400'
DIMENSIONS: Span 35'10", Lg. 31'11", Ht. 9'10", Wing Area 236 sq. ft.
WEIGHT: Empty 7631 lb., Gross 8918 lb. Max. 9240 lb. Fuel 100-150 gal.
PERFORMANCE: Speed- Top 386 mph at 21,680', Cruising 205 mph, Landing 88 mph. Service Ceiling 35,200', Climb 20,000'/9.3 min. Range 800 miles.

Using a V-1710-63 of 1,325 hp for takeoff, the first 210 were P-39K-1s with an Aeroproducts propeller, while 250 P-39L-1s built at the same time had Curtiss propellers. Both appeared with the same 37-mm and two .50-caliber nose guns as the P-39D, but only 1,200 .30-caliber rounds were carried for the four wing guns, with 165 pounds of armor and 66 pounds of armor-glass. About 17 fitted with two cameras in the left rear fuselage were redesignated P-39K-2 and P-39L-2 as were eight P-39M-2 models.

BELL P-39K-1
Allison V-1710-63, 1325 hp takeoff, 1150 hp at 11,800'
DIMENSIONS: Span 34', Lg. 30'2", Ht. 11'10", Wing Area 213 sq. ft.
WEIGHT: Empty 5658 lb., Gross 7637 lb., Max. 8200 lb. Fuel 120+75 gal.
PERFORMANCE: Speed- Top 368 mph at 13,800', Cruising 213 mph, Landing 82 mph. Service Ceiling 32,000', Climb 15,000'/5.7 min. Range 800 miles/500 lb. bomb, 1500 miles ferry at 195 mph.

In November 1942, water injection appeared on the V-1710-83, of 1,200 hp for takeoff, boosting war emergency (WE) power to 1,420 hp at 9,500 feet on the P-39M-1.

*All the aircraft in these lots are known as Model 26 on company records, and are so alike in appearance that they can be told apart only by serial numbers. (Note that no P-39G, H or P was ever finished, and that I and O are not used for designation letters since they might be confused with numbers.)

BELL P-39M-1
Allison V-1710-83, 1200 hp takeoff, 1420 hp at 9000' (WE).
DIMENSIONS: As P-39K
WEIGHT: Empty 5729 lb., Gross 7700 lb., Max. 9100 lb. Fuel 120+175 gal.
PERFORMANCE: Speed- Top 386 mph at 9500', Cruising 200 mph, Landing 84 mph. Service Ceiling 36,000', Climb 15,000'/4.4 min. Range 650 miles/500 lb. bomb, 1500 miles ferry.

For long-range ferry flights like the ALSIB route, a flush belly tank could replace the usual 75-gallon drop tank and increase fuel capacity to 295 gallons. After 240 P-39M-1s had been accepted, Bell rolled out the fastest of the Airacobras, the P-39N.

The P-39N had the V-1710-85 of 1,420 hp at 9,700 feet for war emergency power with an Aeroproducts propeller, and was credited with 399-mph. To reduce weight, the normal fuel load was limited to 87 gallons and on the P-39N-5, rearranged armor weighed 171 pounds with a 22-pound armor glass windshield. Of 2,095 N models built, 1,113 were shipped to Russia. Of those kept by the AAF, 128 P-39N-2, 35 P-39N-3, and 84 P-39N-6 models were modified with cameras.

BELL P-39N of 16th Gv.IAP
Allison V-1710-85, 1200 hp takeoff, 1420 hp at 9000' (WE)
DIMENSIONS: Span 34', Lg. 30'2", Ht. 12'5", Wing Area 213 sq. ft.
WEIGHT: Empty 5698 lb., Gross 7400 lb., Max. 8000 lb. Fuel 87+75 gal.
PERFORMANCE: Speed- Top 399 mph at 9700', Landing 85 mph. Service Ceiling 36,500', Climb 15,000'/3.8 min. Range 750 miles/500 lb. bomb, 1250 miles ferry.

BELL P-39N-5
Allison V-1710-85, 1200 hp takeoff, 1420 hp at 9000' (WE)
DIMENSIONS: As P-39N
WEIGHT: Empty 5663 lb., Gross 7396 lb., Max. 7629 lb. Fuel 87+75 gal.
PERFORMANCE: Speed- Top 396 mph at 11,500', Landing 85 mph. Service Ceiling 34,300', Climb 15,000'/6.4 min. Range 750 miles/500 lb. bomb.

Larry Bell felt that the wing guns were unnecessary weight, but on September 17, 1942, the Airacobra's wing gun installation was ordered changed from four .30-caliber to two .50-caliber guns with 300 rpg. Too large to fit inside the wings, these under slung weapons distinguished the P-39Qs that began appearing in May 1943 with the V-1710-85. All had belly fittings for a 500-pound bomb, a 75-gallon drop tank, or a 175-gallon ferry tank. Of 4,905 P-39Qs built, 3,291 left the U.S. for the long trip to the Soviet Union.

Internal arrangements varied. The first 150 (P-39Q-l) were used by the AAF, and had 87 gallons of fuel and 193 pounds of armor and glass. The next 950 (Q-5) had 110 gallons, and the remainder (Q-10 to Q-30) had 120 gallons and

227 pounds of armor weight. Army tactical recon squadrons got five P-39Q-2, 148 P-39Q-6, and eight P-39Q-11s modified by adding two cameras. A dozen P-39Q-22 trainers were unarmed two-place versions of the P-39Q-20.

BELL P-39Q-1
Allison V-1710-85, 1200 hp takeoff, 1420 hp at 9000' (WE)
DIMENSIONS: As P-39N
WEIGHT: Empty 5684 lb., Gross 7570 lb., Max. 8106 lb. Fuel 120+75 gal. (Ferry weight 9000 lb. with 295 gal.)
PERFORMANCE: Speed- Top 385 mph at 11,000', Landing 88 mph. Service Ceiling 35,000', Climb 15,000'/4.5 min. Range 690 miles at 170 mph, 1250 miles ferry.

BELL P-39Q-20
Allison V-1710-85, 1200 hp takeoff, 1420 hp at 9000' (WE)
DIMENSIONS: As P-39N
WEIGHT: Empty 5910 lb., Gross 7994 lb. Fuel 120+75 gal. (Ferry weight 9200 lb. with 295 gal.)
PERFORMANCE: Speed- Top 385 mph at 11,000', Landing 88 mph. Service Ceiling 35,000', Climb 15,000'/4.5 min. Range 675 miles at 240 mph, 1475 miles ferry at 160 mph.

Blocks Q-21 to Q-25 could be recognized by a four-bladed propeller, and those ferried to Russia deleted the wing guns, saving 331 pounds. The last block, Q-30, reverted to three-blade props.

In 1943, Bell produced more fighters than any other manufacturer, April deliveries reaching 511 P-39Ns. Peak AAF inventory was 2,150 in February 1944, but then all P-39 groups were converted to more advanced types by August. When the last P-39Q-30 was accepted on August 5, 1944, 9,589 Airacobras had been completed, most of them for lend-lease. Average unit cost in 1944 was $50,666.

P-39s in Combat

When the U.S. entered the war, P-39Ds equipped five pursuit groups: the 8th at Mitchel Field, the 31st and 52nd at Selfridge, the 53rd at MacDill Field, and part of the 36th in Puerto Rico. On December 8, 1941, the 31st Group was rushed to Seattle and the 53rd to the Canal Zone for defense purposes.

Neither place suffered attack, and the 31st transferred its pilots to the reorganized 35th Group, while the 53rd returned to the mainland in November, leaving its Airacobras among the three groups remaining in Panama through the war. The Japanese offensive in the Southwest Pacific presented the greatest threat, so ships rushed across the ocean over 200 P-39D, P-39D-1, P-39F and P-400 models requisitioned from the British contracts.

Combat began for the P-39Ds based at Port Moresby on April 30, 1942, with sorties by the 8th Group's 35th and 36th Squadrons, which would be followed in July by the 80th Squadron. Ex-British P-400s equipped the 35th Group, which entered combat on June 2, although some P-39D-2s arrived later. The battle for Guadacanal added the 67th Squadron's P-400s to front-line combat in August 1942 and they were incorporated into the new 347th Fighter Group along with the 68th Squadron's P-39s from Tongatabu and the 70th on Fiji.

The threat to Alaska brought the 54th Group up from West Coast defense in June 1942, with P-39F and J models, and they escorted bombers on raids to Kiska until December 1942, after which the group returned to the United States as a replacement training unit. In the Central Pacific, two P-39Q-l squadrons, the 46th and 72nd, sortied from Makin Island from December 18, 1943 to February 12, 1944, but the last Airacobra missions in the Pacific were flown by the 347th Group in New Guinea in August 1944.

The first Airacobra groups scheduled for European operations had been the 31st and 52nd. But their most experienced pilots had been transferred to Pacific-based units, and their P-39Fs were inferior to German fighters like the Fw 190A-3. On May 6, 1942, the British agreed to provide Spitfires to the American groups, so the 31st's pilots sailed for England in June, leaving their own planes behind.*

BELL P-39Q-20 for France

Armed with two 20-mm. and four .303-caliber guns in the wings, the Spitfire Vs were superior in speed, climb,

*Reports that the 31st flew P-39s from England are incorrect.

and ceiling to the Airacobra, but quite short on range. Their characteristics are included here for comparison. The 31st Group flew their first six sorties July 26, 1942, losing one plane. On August 19, 123 sorties were flown to support the Dieppe raid. An Fw 190 was downed for the first USAAF victory in Europe, although eight American Spitfires were lost. Clearly, the American pilots' inexperience would be costly.

SUPERMARINE SPITFIRE VB
Rolls-Royce Merlin 45, 1100 hp at takeoff, 1415 hp at 14,000'
Dimensions: Span 36'10", Lg. 29'11", Ht. 11'5". Wing Area 242 sq. ft.
Weight: Empty 5065 1b., Gross 6662 lb., Max. 6700 lb. Fuel 102+108 gals.
Performance: Speed- Top 331 mph at 10,000', 351 mph at 15,000', 370 mph at 19,500', Stalling 68 mph. Service Ceiling 36,500', Climb 20,000'/7.5 min., Range 395 miles, ferry 1135 miles.

Two more Spitfire groups had joined the Eighth Air Force; the 52nd which had also come without its P-39s, and the 4th, made up from the RAF's "Eagle" squadrons of American volunteer pilots. Only the 4th remained with the Eighth, because Torch, the North African invasion, was to be supported by the Lightnings of the 1st and 14th Groups, Spitfires of the 31st and 52nd, and the P-39s of the 81st and 350th Groups. Airacobras had re-entered the scene in October when the latter two groups were equipped with P-400 and P-39D-1s that had been waiting in Britain for shipment to the USSR.

Both the 81st and 350th Groups flew from Britain to North Africa by January 1943, losing on the way 18 P-39D-1s that were interned in, and later purchased by, Portugal. The Airacobras served the Twelfth Air Force, along with P-39s of the 111th and 154th Tactical Reconnaissance Squadrons. In February 1944, the Twelfth added the 332nd Group, whose African-American pilots flew P-39Q-20s until June.

This survey does not include the P-39 groups who never reached combat, or the detached squadrons serving uneventful guard duties on islands like Ascension in the South Atlantic, or Canton, Christmas and the Galapagos in the Pacific. More active were the 33rd Squadron's P-39Ds on Iceland, downing two German bombers in October 1942.

The first Airacobras used by the Soviet Air Force (VVS) were 195 P-400s transferred by the British from their stock in the United Kingdom and shipped in crates over the northern route to Murmansk and Archangel. Assembly began in January 1942, but training Soviet pilots in the fighter, the first in VVS service with tricycle landing gear, was complicated by a lack of instructors and interpreters for the English language manuals.

Soviet tests in April 1942 credited the Airacobra I with top speeds of 363 mph at 13,780 feet and 306 mph at sea level. Six VVS fighter regiments (IAPs) took the Airacobra I into combat. The first was the 19th Guards Fighter Air Regiment (19th GvIAP), beginning operations near Murmansk on May 15, 1942, with 16 Airacobras and ten P-40Es. They were joined in June by the 2nd Guards and 78th Fighter Regiments of the Northern Fleet. All four of the IAPs near Murmansk, including the 147th IAP's P-40s, were using American fighters.

By June 30, 1942, the 153rd Fighter Regiment entered combat near Voronezh with 20 Airacobras. Flying 1,070 sorties by September 25, it was credited with 64 victories for eight combat losses, and was honored by becoming the 28th Guards IAP. The other VVS regiments with Airacobra Is in 1942 were the 180th and 185th IAPs.

While the P-400s had been paid for by the British, later P-39s were lend-leased to the USSR, for whom 4,924 were delivered at the factory, and 4,756 actually reached the VVS, beginning November 28, 1942. Shipments actually leaving the U.S. in 1942 included 108 P-39D-2, 40 P-39K-1, 137 P-39L-1, and 157 P-39M-1 models, followed by 1,113 P-39Ns, and 3,291 P-39Qs in 1943/44.

While the Northern route had been used to ship 120 P-39s, of which 108 arrived, the largest supply was flown over the Alaska-Siberia route, beginning with 13 P-39M-1s in November 1942. By September 1944, 2,618 Airacobras were turned over to Soviet pilots in Fairbanks, Alaska, after 71 were lost *en route* from the factory with American pilots.

Lend-lease shipments via the Persian Gulf totaled 2,115 P-39s, with 2,020 turned over at Abadan, in Iran, beginning on December 13, 1942. The first were a P-39D-1 and 60 P-39D-2s with 20-mm guns, but the rest all had the 37-mm cannon. They entered combat at Krasnodar on March 9, 1943, when the 45th IAP arrived with ten P-39D-2, eleven P-39K-1, and nine P-40E-1s. They were joined March 17 by the 298th IAP, with 20 P-39D-2 and 10 P-39K-1s.

The best known Soviet Airacobra unit was the 16th Guards Fighter Air Regiment, which arrived at the front on April 8, 1943, with 11 P-39D-2, seven P-39K-1, and 14 P-39L-1s, and used Airacobras in combat until October 1944, when La-7s replaced the American type. Alexander Pokryshkin used P-39s for the last 47 of his 59 victories in 600 sorties, which made him the second-highest Soviet ace, and the most successful ace on any American fighter. Another ace of this regiment, Gregori A. Rechkalov, scored 44 victories on P-39s of some 56 victories on 450 sorties. Dimitri B. Glinka flew a P-39K while winning about 40 of his 50 credits.

These successes with the P-39 were due to its use with the most experienced VVS pilots on short-range, low-altitude missions – the best for the P-39 – covering ground troops. On July 19, 1943, the VVS asked that P-39s replace the P-40 entirely on their lend-lease allocations. One Russian historian described the P-39's as "almost ideally suited" to the Soviet German front, and that they were preferred "to any other allied aircraft received" by the VVS.

Wing guns were often removed to save weight, and the heavier models had a dangerous spin tendency that killed three Russian test pilots. During 1944, most Airacobra units shifted to the PVO, the Air Defence command protecting Soviet industrial areas. Altogether, 25 fighter regiments, most in eight divisions, operated Airacobras. While most Airacobras were in Red Army units, Navy fighter regiments were given 626. At the end of the war in Europe, the VVS still had 1,178 P-39s, including 536 with the PVO, 164 with front-line units, and 478 with the Navy.

BELL P-39Q-25 for VVS

Australia used 22 P-39D and P-39F aircraft from the Fifth Air Force for a squadron at Sidney in May 1942, returning them in November 1943. French squadrons got 107 P-39Ns in North Africa, beginning April 1943, and 140 P-39Q-20/25s were shipped from the U.S. in 1944. Italian Co-belligerent forces also received second-hand 74 P-39Ns and 75 P-39Qs, began using them from September 1944 for ground support in the Balkans until the war's end, and retained these planes until 1951.

The Airacobra was a disappointment to the U.S. Army, for it was out-climbed by the Zero and seemed "practically useless over 17,000 ft." The P-40 was thought "much better" because a lower wing loading allowed a faster climb. In North Africa the P-39's internal armor and high sea-level speed made it useful for ground strafing. "Unusually resistant" to enemy flak, it had the lowest rate of losses per sortie of any AAF fighter in the ETO, but downed only 14 enemy aircraft.

Flying qualities, including a fast dive and roll, were good, but turns were slow and a flat spin was a dangerous possibility. It is likely that the wing was too small; 213 square feet of area may have been adequate for the prototype's weight, but production models were over a third heavier.

Fighter Designs with Radial Engines

Contrasting sharply with the pointed noses of inline engine types was the barrel-shaped P-47 Thunderbolt, largest single-engine fighter used in the war. The last successful air-cooled, radial-engine Air Force single-seater, it was the only survivor of a series of round-engine designs that resisted the Army's 1939 selection of liquid-cooled Allisons as the primary power plant for pursuits.

To compete with the Curtiss P-40, Seversky offered the private-venture AP-4, first flown December 22, 1938, the AP-9 of January 1939, and the XP-41 delivered to Wright Field on March 4, 1939, each with wheels retract-

SEVERSKY XP-41
Pratt & Whitney R-1830-19 1200 hp takeoff, 1050 hp at 17,500'
DIMENSIONS: Span 36', Lg. 27', Ht. 12'6", Wing Area 220 sq. ft.
WEIGHT: Empty 5390 lb., Gross 6600 lb. Max. 7200 lb. Fuel 150-230 gal.
PERFORMANCE: Speed- Top 323 mph at 15,000', Cruising 292 mph. Range 730 miles normal, 1860 miles max.

ing inwards flush into the center section and the usual .30 and .50-caliber guns paired over the engine. All had *Wasp* radials of 1,050 hp at critical altitudes, but the AP-9 and the XP-41 used a built-in two-stage mechanical supercharger, while the AP-4's R-1830-SC2-G went higher with a turbosupercharger added in the belly behind the pilot.

SEVERSKY AP-4
Pratt & Whitney R-1830-S5C3-G 1050 hp takeoff
DIMENSIONS: As XP-41
WEIGHT: Empty 5257 lb., Gross 6673 lb.
PERFORMANCE: Speed- Top 345 mph at 15,000', 365 mph at 25,000', Cruising 312 mph. Climb 15,000'/5 min. Range 624 miles normal.

While Seversky reduced drag with flush riveting and a cleanly-retracting landing gear, the radial engine's built-in drag remained a problem. In an attempt to improve stream-

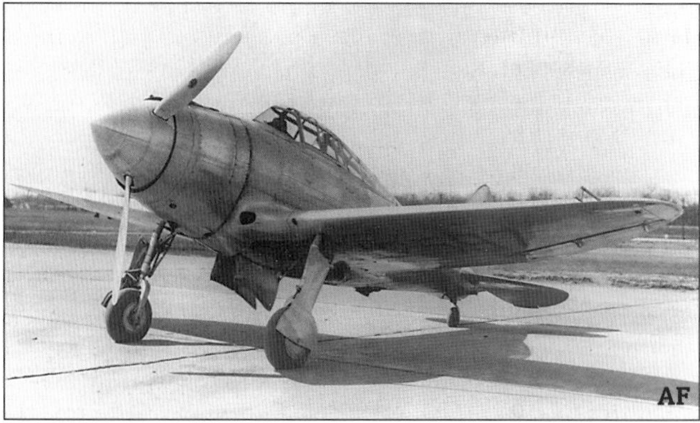

SEVERSKY AP-4A with nose spinner

Mfr

VULTEE VANGUARD 48C

lining, the AP-4 was also tested with its engine completely enclosed behind a huge spinner. An in-flight turbosupercharger fire destroyed this Seversky on March 22, 1939, but the AP-4A bid had secured second-place behind the P-40, provided wheel size would be increased from 27 to 30 inches.

General Arnold recommended a service test contract to determine the combat efficiency of high-altitude pursuits. These became the Republic YP-43, for the company's new owners had changed the firm's name and had not allowed Major Seversky inside the plant since November 1938. Thirteen YP-43s ordered May 12, 1939, were powered by a 1,200-hp turbosupercharged R-1830-35. Tests of the XP-41 prototype in NACA's full-scale wind tunnel in June determined the best streamlining for radial-engine fighters and the company's new specification guaranteed the YP-43 351-mph at 20,000 feet.

The last peacetime competition for pursuit production contracts began with CP-770, which was originally written to buy the P-39, but was changed on June 29, 1939, to be open to any single-engine interceptor pursuit design with a top speed of 360 to 420 mph at any critical altitude from 15,000 to 20,000 feet. Bids were opened on August 7.

Republic's Russian-born Chief Engineer Alexander Kartveli tried to surpass the speeds of liquid-cooled competitors by using larger Pratt & Whitney radials. His AP-4J proposal used a 1,400-hp R-2180-1, and was estimated to do 386 mph, while the AP-4L with the new turbosupercharged 2,000-hp R-2800-7 Double *Wasp* guaranteed speeds of 422 mph at 20,000 feet and 370 mph at 15,000 feet. This big power plant was to be installed in an airframe no larger than the P-43.

The AP-4L won first place in the competition and 80 designated P-44 were ordered October 12, 1939, with delivery guaranteed in 20 months. Proposed armament was two .50-caliber and four .30-caliber guns. A second-place contract went to Bell for the P-45 (P-39C), while prototype contracts went to Curtiss and Republic for the XP-46 and XP-47.

In contrast to the chunky P-44, Republic had also offered the AP-10 design at the same time, with a liquid-cooled 1,150-hp Allison V-1710-39, two synchronized guns, and a small (115 square foot) wing. Weighing only 4,900 pounds, it was supposed to do 415 mph and climb to 15,000 feet in only 3.5 minutes. A prototype contract was made in November, but Air Corps engineers requested an enlarged 6,150-pound design, increasing armament to two .50-caliber and four .30-caliber guns and reducing estimated speed to 400 mph. Two prototypes, an XP-47 and a stripped-down XP-47A, were approved on January 17, 1940, the same day as the Curtiss XP-46 contract.

Vultee Vanguard

Another air-cooled fighter, the Vultee Vanguard, had failed to win a place in the 39-770 competition. Designed by Richard W. Palmer, who had engineered the Hughes racer, Vultee Model 61 may be the most streamlined air-cooled fighter ever built. Designed for mass production, it was preceded by three trainer prototypes of the same basic design, one becoming the standard wartime BT-13 basic trainer.

VULTEE VANGUARD 61
Pratt & Whitney R-1830-S4C4-G, 1200 hp takeoff, 900 hp at 15,400'.
DIMENSIONS: Span 36', Lg. 29'2", Ht. 9'5", Wing Area 197 sq. ft.
WEIGHT: Empty 4657 lb., Gross 6029 lb. Fuel 124-240 gal.
PERFORMANCE: Speed- Top 322 mph at s.l., 358 mph at 15,600', Cruising 316 mph, Landing 73 mph. Service Ceiling 34,300', Climb 3300'/1 min. Range 738 miles normal.

When first seen as a wind-tunnel model in December 1938, the Vanguard had an R-1830 in a conventional cowl, but the design changed when the extended crankshaft Pratt & Whitney *Wasp* tested in the XP-42 became available. This engine was completely enclosed in a streamlined nose, with an air intake underneath to provide cooling. The first flight was made September 8, 1939, but the Air Corps rejected Vultee's offer to reduce the price for service test articles to $36,000, (compared to $64,035 given for the YP-43).

The new power plant arrangement's extra weight and persistent cooling difficulties caused the replacement of the 1,050-hp R-1830-S5C3-G with a conventional-cowled R-1830-S1C3-G by February 11, 1940. This version was known as the 48X and was wrecked on May 9 in a landing accident.

The only production order was placed by Sweden on February 6, 1940, for 144 model 48C Vanguards. A preproduction prototype in Swedish markings flown September 6, 1940, had added dihedral and a normal cowl for the S3C4-G, called the R-1830-33 by the Air Corps. Twin blast tubes were provided on the cowl for two .50-caliber guns, and on the wings for two 20-mm guns to be installed in Sweden.

When aircraft for Sweden were embargoed by the State Department in October, the Vanguards were considered by Britain, and the first three at the factory were painted in RAF colors. But the lack of self-sealing fuel tanks, and weaker performance than the Kittyhawk and Mustang blocked this sale. Instead, the Chinese Defense Supplies agency requested the Vultees on May 29, 1941, to replace the Soviet fighters then used. They were granted as Lend-Lease on June 19, priced at $53,133 each, and designated P-66.

Production ships were armed with two .50-caliber guns with 225 rpg on the cowl and four .30-caliber guns with 500 rpg in the wings, and pilot back armor was provided. Official acceptances began October 24, 1941, but the P-66s were drafted by the Air Force in December to fill out the 14th Fighter Group at March Field. After these were replaced by P-38s and production was completed on April 20, 1942, the Vultees were shipped to Asia, minus 15 planes lost in Air Force hands.

VULTEE P-66
Pratt & Whitney R-1830-33 (S3C4-G), 1200 hp takeoff, 1000 hp at 14,500'
DIMENSIONS: Span 35'10", Lg. 28'5", Ht.10', Wing Area 197 sq. ft.
WEIGHT: Empty 5237 lb, Gross 6985 lb., Max. 7385 lb. Fuel 124-185 gal.
PERFORMANCE: Speed- Top 332 mph at 6,900', 340 mph at 15,100', Cruising 290 mph, Landing 82 mph. Service Ceiling 28,200', Climb 2520'/1 min., 19,700'/9.2 min. Range 850 miles normal, 950 miles at 240 mph.

They were assembled at a depot at Karachi, then in India, but due to accidents during tests and delivery flights, only 104 P-66s actually reached the Chinese Air Force. They were used by two of the three Chinese fighter groups, the third getting the P-43A-1. Seldom seen in combat before a June 1943 battle in Hupeh, many were stored in dugouts and caves for possible future use, and the P-40N replaced them in Chinese squadrons.

Republic Lancer

Only the Chinese Air Force used the *Wasp*-powered Republic P-43 Lancer and Vultee P-66 Vanguard in combat. The Lancer had begun with a modest service test order for 13 YP-43s, and was to have been succeeded in 1941 by the P-44, while the XP-47 prototype would be tested.

Neither the P-44 or the XP-47 were ever flown, for war in Europe demonstrated the need for armor, self-sealing fuel tanks, and more firepower on future fighters. All this internal protection and eight guns were added to a new specification, dated June 12, 1940, offered by Alexander Kartveli. Built around a turbosupercharged 2,000-hp R-2800 Double *Wasp*, the gross weight would be 11,500 pounds, compared to 8,365 pounds expected for the P-44.

Evaluation by Wright Field engineers led to abandonment of the earlier projects, in spite of nearly a million dollars' worth of engineering study and a P-44 mockup. This meant replacing mass production plans for over 900 P-44s with the new design. On September 6, 1940, the XP-47 prototype contract was changed to call for an XP-47B with the Double *Wasp*, and on September 13, 1940, P-44 contracts negotiated during the previous two months were replaced by a $56,000,000 contract for 171 P-47Bs and 602 P-47Cs. Since such planes couldn't be made until 1942, the production gap would filled by 54 P-43s and 80 P-43As to replace the first 80 P-44s ordered in 1939.

The first of 13 YP-43s was completed September 13, 1940, but crashed November 19. Tests resumed when the second was delivered December 7, and the rest were completed from January 30 to March 31, 1941, nine going to Selfridge Field. Armament was the same as the early P-40s; two synchronized .50-caliber guns with 200 rpg on the cowl and two .30-caliber guns with 500 rpg in the wings. However, the YP-43 was the first pursuit since 1936 to have bomb racks; they held six 20-pound bombs. The third YP-43 was loaned to the U.S. Navy on May 25, 1941, so that service could try the B-1 turbosupercharger used with the R-1830-35.

Mfr

REPUBLIC YP-43

Fifty-four P-43 Lancers delivered from May 16 to August 28 were similar to the YP-43, with R-1830-47 engines rated at 1,200 hp at 25,000 feet. Eighty P-43As with new carburetors on R-1830-49 *Wasps* were received from September 3 to December 18, 1941. Guaranteed speed rose to 330 mph at 15,000 feet and 360 mph at 20,000 feet.

A lend-lease contract for China, approved June 30, 1941, assured production continuity at Republic with 125 P-43A-l fighters with an R-1830-57, 500 rpg for the .50-caliber guns, 3/8-inch pilot armor, Bendix radio, and wing racks for two 100-pound bombs or 25-gallon drop tanks. Delivered from December 1941 to March 1942, 17 were diverted in the U.S., 12 diverted to U.S. forces in India, two lost en route and 94 reached the Chinese, whose 4th Fighter Group first used them in combat on October 24, 1942.

Army Air Force Lancer service began with the 1st Pursuit Group at Selfridge, while the 55th at Portland got most of the P-43As. In each case they were interim equipment until replaced by P-38s, and a plan to modify 150 to P-43B photo-recon configurations in 1942 was tested on two P-43As with two K-14 cameras in the baggage compartment and designated P-43C. However, the program was curtailed after a few P-43D conversions as Lockheed F-4s became available. Only a few went to the Southwest Pacific, and of these, Australia obtained four P-43A-ls and four P-43D-1s.

PMB

REPUBLIC P-43 Lancer
Pratt & Whitney R-l830-47, 1200 hp at 20,000'
DIMENSIONS: Span 36', Lg. 28'6", Ht. 14', Wing Area 223 sq. ft.
WEIGHT: Empty 5671 lb., Gross 7111 lb., Max. 7933 lb. Fuel 145-218 gal.
PERFORMANCE: Speed- Top 349 mph at 20,000', Cruising 280 mph Landing 78 mph. Service Ceiling 38,000', Climb 15,000'/5.5 min. Range 600 miles normal, 1300 miles max.

AF

REPUBLIC P-43A

As the first turbosupercharged air-cooled fighter, the P-43 is remembered as the P-47's predecessor. Since the turbosupercharger lacked an automatic regulator, takeoff accidents were frequent due to improper use. This factor was responsible for an especially high crash rate in China.

Republic Thunderbolt

On May 6, 1941, Lowry Brabham piloted the first XP-47B flight. Largest single-engine fighter then built, it was the first with a four-bladed Curtiss propeller, and had pilot armor, leakproof tanks, and a low cockpit entered from the port side by a door. The XP-47B did achieve 412 mph at 25,800 feet, where 1,960 hp was available from the XR-2800-17. Eight .50-caliber guns in the wings were the strongest armament of any single-seater ordered into production. Combining the greatest horsepower with the heaviest firepower, more Thunderbolts would be built than any other American fighter.

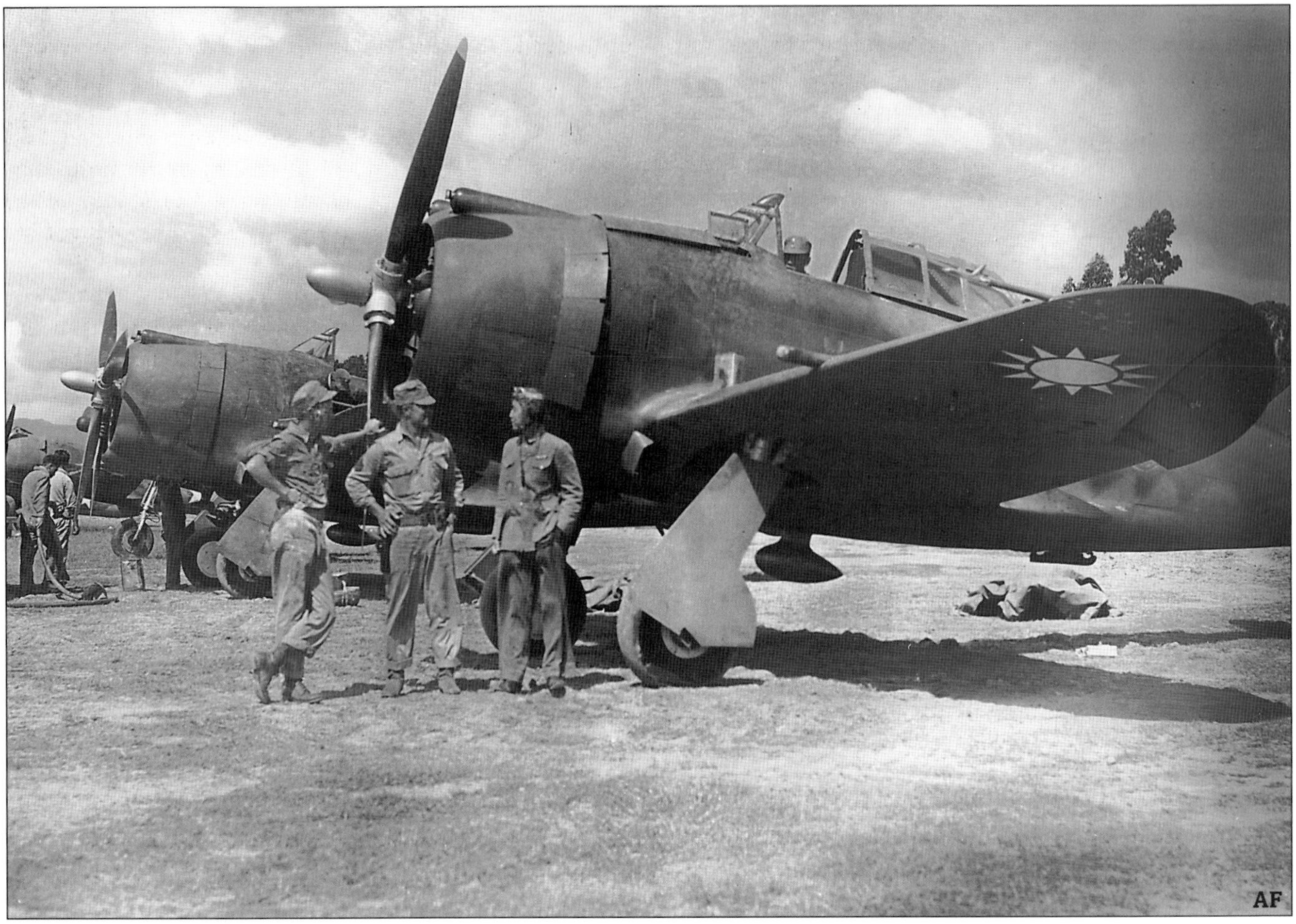

AF

REPUBLIC P-43A-1 Lancer
Pratt & Whitney R-1830-57, 1200 hp at 20,000'
DIMENSIONS: Span 36', Lg. 28'6", Ht. 14', Wing Area 223 sq. ft.
WEIGHT: Empty 5996 lb., Gross 7300 lb., Max. 8480 lb. Fuel 145-268 gal.
PERFORMANCE: Speed- Top 300 mph at 5,000', 356 mph at 20,000', Cruising 280 mph, Landing 76 mph. Service Ceiling 36,000', Climb 15,000'/6 min. Range 550 miles normal, 1450 miles max.

REPUBLIC XP-47B
Pratt & Whitney XR-2800-17, 2000 hp at 25,000'
DIMENSIONS: Span 40'9", Lg. 35'4", Ht. 12'8", Wing Area 300 sq. ft.
WEIGHT: Empty 9189 lb., Gross 12,085 lb., Max. 12,700 lb. Fuel 205-305 gal.
PERFORMANCE: Speed- Top 412 mph at 25,800' on test. Cruising 335 mph. Service Ceiling 38,000', Climb 15,000'/5 min. Range 575 miles normal.

REPUBLIC P-47B
Pratt & Whitney R-2800-21, 2000 hp at 25,000'
DIMENSIONS: As XP-47B
WEIGHT: Empty 9346 lb., Gross 12,343 lb., Max. 13,413 lb. Fuel 205-305 gal.
PERFORMANCE: Speed- Top 340 mph at 5000', 429 mph at 27,800', Cruising 335 mph, Landing 100 mph. Service Ceiling 42,000', Climb 15,000'/6.7 min. Range 540 miles normal, 750 miles max.

When the first of 169 P-47Bs was accepted on December 21, 1941, it had the cockpit door, as did the second, but a sliding canopy was used on the remaining production aircraft. Four more were accepted in March 1942, but failure of the tail section during a fatal dive of the 5th P-47B on March 26, and also on the 6th example on May 1, delayed further acceptances. Deliveries resumed May 26 after the fabric-covered elevators were replaced with metal-covered control surfaces.

These Republic Thunderbolts were broken in by the 56th Fighter Group, that unit being nearest to the Farmingdale, New York, factory. Tests and operational training went slowly, accompanied by the loss of 13 pilots and 41 aircraft. Completion of P-47B production in September enabled the formation of the 348th and 355th Groups shortly thereafter.

The first P-47C was delivered September 14, 1942, with a new radio and vertical mast. After 57 P-47Cs, the P-47C-1 introduced an extended engine mount that added ten inches to the length. Later block numbers were used to denote mechanical changes in the C and parallel D models. By February 1943, 602 P-47C, C-1, -2, and -5 models had been delivered from Farmingdale.

REPUBLIC P-47C-2
Pratt & Whitney R-2800-21, 2000 hp at 27,800'
DIMENSIONS: Span 40'9", Lg. 36'2", Ht. 14'2", Wing Area 300 sq. ft.
WEIGHT: Empty 9900 lb., Gross 13,300 lb., Max.14,925 lb. Fuel 305+200 gal.
PERFORMANCE: Speed- Top 420 mph at 30,000', Cruising 350 mph, Landing 104 mph. Service Ceiling 42,000', Climb 15,000'/7.2 min. Range 400 miles/305 gal., 835 miles max.

The Air Force chose the P-47 as its main fighter and expanded production with new contracts adding 850 P-47Ds to Farmingdale's schedule on October 14, 1941, 1,050 P-47Ds ordered January 31, 1942, from a new Republic facility in Evansville, Indiana, as well as 354 P-47Gs to be built by Curtiss in Buffalo along with the P-40. Evansville and Buffalo flew the first P-47D and P-47G in September 1942. The first four P-47Ds and first 20 P-47Gs at Curtiss were similar to the concurrent P-47C, while 110 more P-47D-RA followed the P-47C-5 pattern.

REPUBLIC P-47D-2-RA
Pratt & Whitney R-2800-21, 2000 hp at 27,800'
DIMENSIONS: Span 40'9", Lg. 36'2", Ht. 13'10", Wing Area 300 sq. ft.
WEIGHT: Empty 9960 lb., Gross 12,468 lb., Max.14,800 lb. Fuel 305+200 gal.
PERFORMANCE: Speed- Top 339 mph at 5,000', 372 mph at 15,000', 411 mph at 20,000', Climb 15,000'/6 min. Other data as C-2.

Additional cowl flaps and mechanical refinements distinguished the P-47D-l-RE of February 1943, as well as the P-47D-2-RA and P-47G-1-CU models, whose suffixes denoted the Republic Farmingdale, Evansville, and the Curtiss plants, respectively. The eight wing guns had 267 to 425 rounds each and 135 pounds of armor protected the pilot. Curtiss completed its contract in March 1944, with the P-47Gs used only for training, but production that month from Republic reached 641 Thunderbolts.

Early Thunderbolts used the R-2800-21 and C-1 turbosupercharger with an automatic regulator (lacking in P-43s), but water injection kits for emergency power boost were added, beginning with P-47D-3-RA and P-47D-5-RE. This increased output from 2,000 to 2,300 hp and top speed from 411 to 428 mph at 25,500 feet at design weight.

The 200-gallon flush ferry tank provisions on the P-47C series were replaced by shackles for a 75 or 110-gallon belly drop tank, or a 1,000-pound bomb on the P-47D-4-RA and P-47D-5-RE. The P-47D-10-RE series had R-2800-63 engines that raised the critical altitude to 29,000 feet, where top speed was 440 mph in light condition. By that time, however, Thunderbolts had to operate with all the fuel they could carry, so they could protect American bombers deep into enemy airspace. Drop tanks under the wings were added to the P-47D-15-RA and P-47D-16-RE.

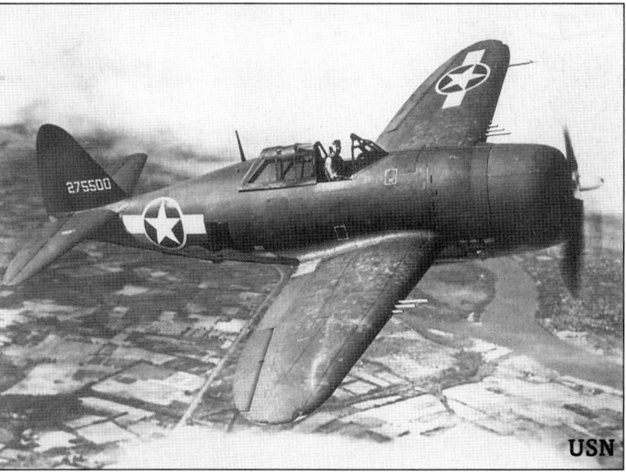

REPUBLIC P-47D-11-RE
Pratt & Whitney R-2800-63, 2000 hp at takeoff (WE 2300 hp at 25,000'
DIMENSIONS: As P-47D-2
WEIGHT: Empty 9978 lb., Gross 12,610 lb. Max. 18,300 lb., Fuel 305+110 gal.
PERFORMANCE: (at 12,610 lb.) Speed- Top 354 mph at 5,000', 390 mph at 15,000', 440 mph at 29,000', Climb 15,000'/5.1 min. (At 13,500 lb.) Speed- Top 353 mph at 5000', 433 mph at 30,000' (WE), Cruising 340 mph, Landing 100 mph. Service Ceiling 42,000', Climb 20,000'/11 min. Range 325 miles/ 305 gal., 835 miles max.

Pratt & Whitney R-2800-59 power plants were standardized on the P-47D-21 and all later D models. Larger, 13'2" Hamilton propellers were introduced on the P-47D-22-RE while the P-47D-23-RA got 13-foot Curtiss propellers. These were the first Thunderbolts delivered in natural metal finish, without camouflage. Armament included eight .50-caliber guns with 2,136 rounds, and under wing racks for two 1,000-pound bombs or 165-gallon tanks.

CURTISS P-47G-15-CU

Thunderbolts enter Combat

First priority for Thunderbolts was given the Eighth Air Force, whose bombers had the most important role in the air offensive against Germany and badly needed strong fighter support. When P-47C-2 and C-5s began arriving in Britain late in 1942 they were issued to three fighter groups: the veteran 4th, who reluctantly gave up their Spitfires; the 56th, fresh from flying P-47Bs in America; and the 78th, whose previous experience had been with P-38s.

REPUBLIC P-47D-21-RE leaving escort carrier for Saipan

Engine and radio problems caused delays, but on April 15, 1943, the first Thunderbolt kill was made by a 4th Group leader. As compared to the enemy Fw 190, the Thunderbolts were faster over 15,000 feet, had a higher ceiling and massive firepower, but their weaknesses were slow climb at low levels, and too wide a turn radius. Combat experience soon taught the American pilots the tactics to maximize their plane's advantages. Another Thunderbolt virtue was its sturdy construction.

The greatest problem was that of increasing the radius of action needed to support the bombers. The 200-gallon flush ferry tank provided for early C and D models was unsuitable for combat, and sufficient 75-gallon drop tanks were not available. The British were able to produce a 108-gallon tank of paper composition: one under the belly extended the P-47D's combat radius to 350 miles, and was first used on a July 28, 1943, mission. Two under the wings allowed a 445-mile radius, or two 165-gallon tanks could be attached for ferry flights.

There were ten Thunderbolt groups with the Eighth Air Force by the end of 1943, but since the P-51 promised better range, the P-47 was then directed into the Ninth Air Force, where its firepower could be used for ground attack. By June 1944, 17 P-47D groups were stationed in the United Kingdom.

In the Pacific, the Fifth Air Force got three P-47D groups, beginning with the arrival of the 348th at Port Moresby in June 1943. More Thunderbolts replaced the 35th Group's P-39s and the 58th Group arrived in November. The 49th Group operated one squadron each of P-38, P-40, and P-47 fighters in 1944. The 318th Group in Hawaii got 71 P-47D-21s that entered combat at Saipan after being flown off two escort carriers in June 1944.

Thunderbolts also re-equipped the 33rd and 81st Groups when they were sent to China in 1944, and in India they served the 1st Air Commando Group. In the Mediterranean, the P-47 replaced the 57th and 325th Groups' P-40s in December 1943, and P-47Ds were flown by five more Twelfth Air Force combat groups in Italy during 1944.

REPUBLIC P-47D-22-RE
Pratt & Whitney R-2800-59, 2000 hp at takeoff (WE 2300 hp at 25,000')
DIMENSIONS: As P-47D-2
WEIGHT: Empty 10,143 lb., Gross 12,777 lb., Max. 18,500 lb., Fuel 305+330 gal.
PERFORMANCE: (at 12,610 lb.) Speed- Top 358 mph at 5,000', 395 mph at 15,000', 443 mph at 29,000', Landing 104 mph. Service Ceiling 42,000', Climb 15,000'/4.8 min. Range 835 miles

Wartime Developments

New technology proposed for future fighters, like the XP-69, was tested on experimental aircraft begun as P-47Bs. The XP-47E ordered October 16, 1941, and completed in September 1942, was the 171st P-47B airframe with a pressurized pilot's cabin and side door installed.

A laminar-flow wing with straight trailing edges, 42-foot span, and 322-square foot area replaced the elliptical Republic S-3 airfoil on the 44th airframe by June 25, 1942. This XP-47F was flown in July and delivered to Wright Field September 17, 1942. Its 421-mph top speed did not justify more development.

The only pencil-nosed Thunderbolt was the XP-47H, a flying test bed for an experimental Chrysler 16-cylinder XIV-2220 inverted inline engine. Although the project was begun in August 1943, the two P-47D-15-RA airframes were not converted until 1945. Test flights began July 26, 1945, but speed fell below the 490 mph expected and jet propulsion killed official interest in the Chrysler power plant.

REPUBLIC P-47H
Chrysler XI-2220-11, 2500 hp takeoff to 25,000'
DIMENSIONS: Span 40'9", Lg. 38'4", Ht. 13'8", Wing Area 300 sq. ft.
WEIGHT: Empty11,442 lb., Gross 14,010 lb., Max.15,135 lb. Fuel 205-295 gal.
PERFORMANCE: Speed- Top 414 mph at 30,000'. Service Ceiling 36,000', Climb 2740'/1 min. Range 770 miles normal, 1000 miles max.

By November 1942, an XP-47J project was planned to reduce Thunderbolt weight and explore the speed limits of propeller-driven aircraft. Powered by an R-2800-57 giving 2,800-hp war emergency power, this type had a fan behind the prop spinner to suck cooling air over the cylinders, exhaust ejection to boost speed, and lightweight wing construction with ordnance reduced to six .50-caliber guns and 1,602 rounds. The contract was approved July 18, 1943, and the XP-47J first flew November 26.

A proposal to use counter-rotating propellers with an R-2800-61 on production P-47Js had been dropped in August 1943 in favor of P-72 development. On an August 5, 1944, test, the XP-47J did 505 mph, fastest speed for a propeller-driven aircraft officially announced during the war.

REPUBLIC XP-47J
Pratt & Whitney R-2800-57, 2100 hp at takeoff, 2800 hp at 30,000'
DIMENSIONS: Span 40'9", Lg. 36'3", Ht. 15', Wing Area 300 sq. ft.
WEIGHT: Empty 9,662 lb., Gross 12,400 lb., Fuel 287 gal.
PERFORMANCE: Speed- Top 505 mph at 34,450', Landing 92 mph. Service Ceiling 45,000', Climb 15,000'/4.5 min. Range 765 miles normal, 1070 miles max.

The next Thunderbolt models tested features more readily put on production aircraft. A bubble canopy was introduced on the XP-47K, completed July 3, 1943, from the last D-5, and on the XP-47L, which was the last D-20 with internal fuel capacity increased from 305 to 370 gallons.

REPUBLIC XP-47K

Visibility with this cockpit cover, copied from the Hawker Tempest, was so improved that production lines in both factories changed over from the old "razor-back" shape to the bubble canopy and larger tanks with the P-47-25-RE first delivered on February 3, 1944. The first 2,963 P-47D to P-47D-22-RE produced by April at Farmingdale had the old style cockpit while the last 2,546, with block numbers from P-47D-25 on, had the bubble canopy. At Evansville, the first 2,350 P-47D to P-47D-23-RA were old style; the last 3,743 (Blocks D-26 to 40) were new.

Characteristics of the P-47D-25 are typical of the line. Fuel load could include up to 370 gallons internally plus 330 in drop tanks, which could extend the radius of action to 690 miles for fighter sweeps. Radius with one 165-gallon drop tank and one 1,000-pound. bomb was 518 miles; with two 1,000-pound bombs, 320 miles. In this latter role, as a low-altitude fighter bomber, the heavily-armed Thunderbolt was outstanding through the last year of the European war. Dive recovery flaps appeared on the D-30 block along with rails for ten five-inch rockets. A dorsal fin extension was added in service, and on the P-47D-40-RA at the factory.

The new Thunderbolts went to the Ninth Air Force, which had 13 P-47D groups for the D-Day landing in France and 14 groups at VE Day. These Thunderbolts' attacks ahead of the Allied armies advancing into Germany helped cripple enemy resistance in the war's last stage.

Only one Eighth Air Force unit, the 56th Fighter Group, still used P-47s in 1945. That famous "Zemke's Wolf Pack" won the highest score of any Eighth Air Force group: 674 enemy aircraft destroyed in the air and 311 on the ground. Francis Gabreski and Robert Johnson won 28 air victories each on 153 and 91 combat missions, respectively. In both cases, all victories were over enemy fighters.

When the new R-2800-57 "C" series *Wasp* offering 2,800-hp war emergency power became available, four P-47D-27-RE aircraft fitted with the new *Wasps* and 13-foot Curtiss propellers were designated YP-47M. This installation was ordered in September for the last 130 P-47D-30-RE aircraft, which were delivered as P-47M-ls in December 1944. They were rushed to England for the 56th Fighter Group, but engine problems delayed their use until April 1945.

One YP-47M was actually completed as the XP-47N, using a new larger wing designed to accommodate addi-

Mfr

REPUBLIC P-47D-25-RE
Pratt & Whitney R-2800-59, 2000 hp at takeoff (WE 2300 hp at 25,000')
DIMENSIONS: Span 40'9", Lg. 36'2", Ht. 14'7" Wing Area 300 sq. ft.
WEIGHT: Empty 10,199 lb., Gross 14,500 lb., Max. 19,400 lb., Fuel 370+330 gal.
PERFORMANCE:(at 13,038 lb.) Speed- Top 358 mph at 5,000', 395 mph at 15,000', 443 mph at 29,000', Landing 104 mph. Service Ceiling 42,000', Climb 15,000'/4.8 min.; (at 14,500 lb.) Speed-Top 428 mph at 25,000', 363 mph at 5,000', Cruising 300 mph, Landing 106 mph. Service Ceiling 42,000', Climb 20,000'/9 min. Range 475 miles/500-lb. bomb, 590 miles normal, 1030 miles max.

Flores

REPUBLIC P-47D-30-RE in Mexico

tional fuel. This conversion had been ordered May 19, 1944, as it was realized that P-47D range limits, less than those of the P-38L or P-51D, made it less suitable for Pacific warfare.

Confidence in the Republic design, whose new wing had also been tried on the XP-47K, was such that 1,900 P-47Ns were ordered June 30, 1944, before the XP-47N flew July 22. The first P-47N-l-RE appeared in September, and 24 were delivered by the year's end. Farmingdale completed 1,667 P-47Ns before the Thunderbolt line closed in December 1945. Production in Evansville on the P-47D-30/-40-RA continued until July 1945, followed by 149 P-47N-20-RAs before VJ Day canceled the rest of the contract.

Heaviest single-engine fighter used in action, the P47N had an automatic pilot and could carry up to 1,156 gallons in internal and drop tanks. A radius of action of 1,000 miles was possible, provided the pilot's physical condition permitted a solo flight of nine or more hours. Alternately, ten 5-inch rockets or three 1,000-pound bombs could augment the eight .50-caliber guns with 2,136 rounds, in attacks on surface targets. Pilot protection included 112 pounds of metal armor and 28 pounds of armor glass.

The P-47N was first used in the Pacific by the 318th Group, which flew them from Hawaii to Le Shima, off Okinawa. On May 25, this group destroyed 34 Japanese aircraft without loss to themselves. They were joined on Le Shima by the 413th and 507th Groups by July 1, while

AF

REPUBLIC P-47D-30-RE
Pratt & Whitney R-2800-59, 2000 hp at takeoff (WE 2300 hp at 25,000')
DIMENSIONS: Span 40'9", Lg. 36'2", Ht. 14'7", Wing Area 300 sq. ft.
WEIGHT: Empty 10,180 lb., Gross 13,020 lb., Max. 19,400 lb., Fuel 370+330 gal.
PERFORMANCE: (at 13,020 lb.) Speed- Top 370 mph at 5,000', 437 mph at 24,500', Cruising 300 mph, Landing 100 mph. Service Ceiling 42,000', Climb 15,000'/4.4 min. Range 475 miles/500-lb. bomb, 1700 miles max.

REPUBLIC P-47M-1-RE
Pratt & Whitney R-2800-57, 2100 hp at takeoff (WE 2800 hp at 32,500')
DIMENSIONS: Span 40'9", Lg. 36'4", Ht. 14'9" Wing Area 300 sq. ft.
WEIGHT: Empty 10,423 lb., Gross 13,275 lb., Max. 15,500 lb., Fuel 370+330 gal.
PERFORMANCE: (at 13,275 lb.) Speed- Top 473 mph at 32,500', Cruising 360 mph, Landing 99 mph. Service Ceiling 41,000', Climb 32,000'/13.4 min. Range 530 miles/205 gal.

REPUBLIC XP-47N

REPUBLIC P-47N-1
Pratt & Whitney R-2800-57, or-73; 2100 hp at takeoff (WE 2800 hp at 32,500')
DIMENSIONS: Span 42'7", Lg. 36'2", Ht. 12'8" Wing Area 322 sq. ft.
WEIGHT: Empty 11,132 lb, Gross 16,300 lb., Max. 20,700 lb Fuel 556+600 gal.
PERFORMANCE: Speed- Top 384 mph at 5,000', 417 mph at 15,000', 467 mph at 32,500, Cruising 350 mph, Landing 98 mph. Service Ceiling 43,000', Climb 25,000'/14.2 min. Range 800 miles/2000 lb. bombs, 2200 miles at 281 mph.

another P-47N group, the 444th, was established on Iwo Jima in July. The last missions were flown in August.

The Thunderbolt production total of 15,683 is the largest in American fighter plane history, but is not as large as those for the Bf 109, Spitfire, or Yak series fighters abroad. There were 31 AAF P-47 groups in combat areas by the end of 1944, and a peak AAF inventory of 5,595 planes in May 1945. Average unit cost in 1945 was $83,000.

Lend-lease provided Britain with 240 P-47D-22-RE razorbacks as the Thunderbolt I, while the Thunderbolt II with the bubble canopy included 120 P-47D-25-RE, 420 P-47D-30-RE, 45 P-47D-30-RA and one P-47D-40-RA allocations. Two RAF Thunderbolt Is and four IIs were tested in the UK, 22 Thunderbolt Is and 48 IIs went to the MAAF, while 215 Thunderbolt Is and 534 IIs were shipped directly to India and began operations on the Burma front in September 1944 with 12 squadrons equipped by the war's end.

France was sent 446 P-47Ds to serve seven fighter squadrons, and they began operations over France on June 15, 1944. Three P-47D-10-REs flown to the Soviet Union via Alaska in October 1943 were to be followed by 100 P-47D-22-RE, shipped beginning in February 1944, and 100 P-47D-27-RE. Of these, 188 reached Russia via the Persian Gulf route, to serve Army regiments, and 72 were given to Soviet Navy regiments, replacing the P-39s of the 255th IAP, which escorted the Northern Fleet's 5th MTAD Division bombers.

Brazil received 66 P-47D-25/30-REs that served the Brazilian fighter squadron that began operations in Italy on October 14, 1944, the only Latin American air unit in Europe. Mexico's 201st Fighter Squadron flew ground support missions in the Philippines, beginning June 5, 1945, using 30 P-47Ds seconded from the Fifth Air Force, and got 25 new P-47D-35-RA after the war, in November 1945.

After the war's end, Thunderbolts continued to serve Air Force and National Guard units. One group, the 86th, remained in Germany with P-47Ds until it became the only USAF fighter group in Europe when the Berlin blockade began in 1948. Turkey received 180 P-47Ds beginning in March 1948, and Portugal got 50 in January 1952.

With the system of post-war alliances, the P-47D also became the standard fighter of Iran, with 60 delivered in 1949, and Yugoslavia (126). China had one P-47D group, and 116 second-hand aircraft were also allocated to Italy, beginning in December 1950.

The P-47D was chosen to supply Latin American countries and beginning in June 1947, Brazil got 30 P-47D-40-RA, Peru 25 P-47D-30-RA, and Ecuador 12 P-47D-30-RA. Columbia received eight Thunderbolts in 1947 and 12 more in 1949, while Venezuela got six in 1947 and 22 in 1949.

Another allocation in 1952-1953 gave Brazil another 25 P-47D-40-RA, Peru 19, Ecuador 12, and Columbia 14. Cuba received 27 and the Dominican Republic also received 25 P-47Ds. The Chinese on Taiwan received 190 of the P-47N model.

The last time the big Republic fighter fired its guns was during the overthrow of the Guatemalan government in June 1954. American pilots employed by the CIA flew at-

NORTH AMERICAN XP-51
Allison V-1710-39, 1150 hp at 11,800'
DIMENSIONS: span 37', Lg. 32'3", Ht. 12'2", Wing Area 233 sq. ft.
WEIGHT: Empty 6278 lb., Gross 7967 lb., Max. 8400 lb. Fuel 105-170 gal.
PERFORMANCE: Speed- Top 382 mph at 13,000', Cruising 325 mph, Landing 83 mph. Service Ceiling 30,800', Climb 15,000'/7 min. Range 780 miles.

tacks using several of seven P-47Ns secretly transferred to the Somoza dictatorship in Nicaragua.

North American Mustang

The most successful American fighter of World War II was designed for a foreign government and had a conventional appearance. It resembled the Messerschmitt, Spitfire, Yak, and other single-seat low-wing monoplanes powered by inline engines, but its superiority represented the highest refinement of the fighter layout introduced in 1931 by the YP-24.

North American Aviation, at Inglewood, California, had so favorably impressed Britain with its efficiency building Harvard trainers for the Royal Air Force that company president J. H. Kindelberger was asked to produce Curtiss P-40s in his factory. Instead, Kindelberger offered to build fighters designed by his own company.

German-born Chief Designer Edgar Schmued, who had done the NA-50, was by March 15, 1940, ordered to prepare a fighter proposal built around the Allison engine ordered for the Curtiss planes. The Anglo-French Purchasing Commission provided a letter of intent on April 11 for production in 1941 and told North American Vice-president Lee Atwood to obtain current fighter data from Curtiss.*

On April 24 the specification for Model NA-73 was ready and the company ordered construction of a prototype. An offer was made on May 1, 1940, to the Purchasing Commission to build 320 by September 30, 1941. The Army Air Corps granted permission on May 4 for the NA-73 sale, provided it was furnished two airframes, "without charge". The British ordered 320 on May 29, added 300 more on September 24, and named the fighter Mustang I.

NORTH AMERICAN NA-73X

The carefully-streamlined NA-73 was designed for mass production with a low square-cut wing that introduced the modified laminar-flow airfoil developed by

*Atwood met, in Buffalo on April 17, 1940, with Burdette Wright, who told him that Curtiss had invested $205,182 on engineering the P-37, P-40 and XP-46 (the latter about 21% of the total). Since British plans called for buying about 500 P-40, 300 P-46, and 300 North American fighters, Atwood paid 3/11 of this cost, or $56,000, for the Curtiss data. When these papers arrived in California, they appeared to add little to North American's design and Schmued himself never saw them.

Mfr

NORTH AMERICAN P-51
Allison V-1710-39, 1150 hp at 11,800'
DIMENSIONS: Span 37', Lg. 32'3", Ht. 12'2", Wing Area 233 sq. ft.
WEIGHT: Empty 6500 lb., Gross 8933 lb., Fuel 180 gal.
PERFORMANCE: Speed- Top 372 mph at 12,800', Cruising 303 mph, Landing 90 mph. Service Ceiling 30,600', Climb 20,000'/10 min. Range 1050 miles.

NACA to reduce drag. The radiator scoop was streamlined into the fuselage's underside behind the pilot.

An NA-73X prototype was completed by September 9, but had to wait for the engine, the first 1,150-hp V-1710-39 originally ordered for the P-46/P-40D program. Flight tests were begun by Vance Breese on October 26, 1940, but were interrupted by an accident November 20, 1940.

The first Mustang I production NA-73 was flown April 23, 1941, and was retained by the company for the necessary testing. Next to fly, on May 20, was the first XP-51 for the Air Corps. It was flown to Wright Field on August 24, while the second XP-51, actually the tenth NA-73, arrived December 16. Similar to the RAF Mustangs, they were equipped with armor, leakproof tanks, two .50-caliber guns with 200 rpg low in the nose, and two more in the wings between four .30-caliber guns with 500 rpg.

The second RAF Mustang first flew July 3, was accepted in August and began a long journey by ship through the Panama Canal to Liverpool, arriving October 24. By the end of 1941, 138 Mustangs had been accepted.

Tests soon showed the Mustang "certainly the best American fighter that has so far reached this country;" superior to the Kittyhawk, Airacobra, and Spitfire in both speed and maneuverability at low altitudes. RAF Mustangs were issued to Army Cooperation Squadrons, to replace Tomahawks, and were fitted with a camera facing left behind the pilot. Twenty Mustangs were lost on ships on the way to Britain, and four were sent to the Soviet Union in May 1942.

AF

NORTH AMERICAN MUSTANG I

Tactical reconnaissance calls for avoidance of enemy fighters, and so the Mustang's combat virtues were not yet often demonstrated. No. 26 Squadron flew its first sortie across the Channel on May 10, 1942, and the Mustang's first air battles were fought on August 19. On October 16, the Allison-powered Mustang was the first single-seat fighter from England to penetrate German air space, and 15 squadrons served the RAF in January 1943, with five remaining in June 1944.

A Lend-lease contract approved September 25. 1941, added 150 designated P-51s to the schedule, and these aircraft were armed with four 20 mm guns in the wings belt-fed with 125 rpg. The first P-51 was flown May 20, 1942, by Bob Chilton, and the first 20 P-51s to follow the last Mustang Is off the line in July 1942 were taken by the AAF and fitted with two cameras for tactical recon work.

This worked so well that they were sent to the 68th Observation Group, whose 154th squadron flew the first AAF P-51-2-NA mission on April 9, 1943. When this contract was completed in September, the RAF had gotten 93 as the Mustang IA, while the AAF got 55 P-51 photographic types (later redesignated F-6A) and two airframes were diverted to the XP-78 project.

Mustang production might have ended in 1942, but Air Force interest in the type was aroused when design began on the NA-97 dive-bomber version on April 16, 1942. Prospects of an improved engine and under wing racks for drop tanks or bombs convinced the AAF to contract for 500 A-36As on August 21, and 1,200 P-51As on August 24, 1942.

NORTH AMERICAN P-51A
Allison V-1710-81, 1200 hp takeoff, 1470 hp at 11,800'
DIMENSIONS: Span 37', Lg. 32'3", Ht. 12'2", Wing Area 233 sq. ft.
WEIGHT: Empty 6433 lb., Gross 8633 lb., Max. 10,300 lb. Fuel 180+300 gal.
PERFORMANCE: Speed- Top 340 mph at 5000', 390 mph at 20,000', Cruising 293 mph, Landing 90 mph. Service Ceiling 35,100', Climb 25,000'/12.7 min. Range 700 miles normal, 2400 miles ferry.

From October 1942 to March 1943, North American delivered the dive-bomber Mustangs designated A-36A, whose service was described in Chapter 13 on attack planes. They differed from the P-51 in their V-1710-87 boosted for low altitude operations, dive-brakes, bomb racks, and six-gun armament.

The P-51A used the V-1710-81 with 1,360-hp war emergency boost, and first flew February 3, 1943. By May 1943, 310 were delivered before production shifted to the P-51B. Armed with four .50-caliber wing guns with 1,260 rounds, and wing racks for two 500-pound bombs or two 75-gallon drop tanks, or fitted with two 150-gallon ferry tanks, the P-51A was judged to have "the best all-around fighting qualities of any present American fighter" below 22,000'.

The first group to get the P-51A was the 54th, which remained in Florida for replacement training, while later P-51As went to Asia for the 23rd and 311th Fighter groups, and flew their first missions October 16, 1943. Fifty went to replenish two RAF squadrons as the Mustang II, serving until the war's end in the low-altitude role. Another 35 became F-6Bs with two cameras added for the 107th Tactical Reconnaissance Squadron, which first sortied across the English Channel on December 20, 1943.

While serving the 1st Air Commando group in Burma, the P-51A became the first AAF fighter to fire rockets in combat. Three "bazooka" tubes installed under each wing launched 4.5-inch rockets at a Japanese air base on April 4, 1944.

Mustangs with Merlins

The major weakness of the early Mustang was that performance at high altitudes was limited by the Allison engine, and in the summer of 1942, "cross-breeding" of the airframe with the new Merlin 65 engine was proposed. Rolls-Royce decided on June 3 to install Merlins on five Mustang Is, with the first in the air by October 13, 1942, as the Mustang X.

In the United States, the Air Force authorized a parallel Merlin project on June 12, 1942, and North American submitted the NA-101 specification July 24. A contract was issued July 31 for two XP-78 aircraft to be converted from lend-lease P-51s by using the Packard Merlin V-1650-3 engine and two-stage supercharger rated by the Air Force at 1,295 hp at 28,750 feet with 1,595 war emergency hp available to 17,000 feet.

NORTH AMERICAN XP-51B
Packard V-1650-3, 1380 hp takeoff, 1595 hp WE at 17,000', 1295 hp at 28,800'
DIMENSIONS: Span 37', Lg. 32'3", Ht. 13'8", Wing Area 233 sq. ft.
WEIGHT: Empty 7038 lb., Gross 8350 lb. Max. 8880 lb. Fuel 180 gal.
PERFORMANCE: Speed- Top 441 mph at 29,800', Cruising 325 mph. Service Ceiling 42,000', Climb 20,000'/5.9 min. Range 750 miles normal.

Redesignated XP-51B in September, the first U.S. Merlin Mustang flew November 30, 1942, with a four-bladed Hamilton propeller and the carburetor intake below, instead of above, the engine. Even before tests, 2,290

Mustangs of this configuration were ordered, replacing 890 P-5lAs and adding 1,000 P-51Cs from a new assembly line at Dallas, Texas.

After severe cooling problems were overcome by an improved radiator, the first P-51B-l-NA was flown May 5, 1943. Armament still consisted of four .50-caliber guns, half that of a P-47, but the 440-mph top speed was the fastest of fighters then in combat. Even more important, the Mustang, with drop tanks, now had the range needed to accompany bombers to any target in Germany.

On July 6, 1943, the Air Force ordered that an 85-gallon fuel tank be added behind the cockpit, so a rebuilt P-51B was in the air by July 21, and these tanks were added by the AAF to 550 P-51B-5s, then redesignated P-51B-7. Such fuselage tanks became standard on all production models, beginning with the P-51B-10.

NORTH AMERICAN P-51B-1
Packard V-1650-3, 1380 hp takeoff, 1595 hp WE at 17,000', 1295 hp at 28,800'
DIMENSIONS: Span 37', Lg. 32'3", Ht. 13'8", Wing Area 233 sq. ft.
WEIGHT: Empty 6985 1b., Gross 9800 lb., Max. 11,800 lb. Fuel 269 +300 gal.
PERFORMANCE: Speed- Top 388 mph at 5000', 427 mph at 20,000', 440 mph at 30,000', Cruising 345 mph, Landing 100 mph. Service Ceiling 41,800', Climb 20,000'/7 min., 30,000'/12.5. Range 900 miles normal, 2900 miles ferry.

Mass production of the new Mustang at North American's California and Texas factories increased rapidly.

NORTH AMERICAN P-51C-1
Packard V-1650-7, 1490 hp takeoff, 1720 hp WE at 6,200', 1505 hp at 19,300'
DIMENSIONS: Span 37', Lg. 32'3", Ht. 13'8", Wing Area 233 sq. ft.
WEIGHT: Empty 6985 1b., Gross 9800 lb., Max. 11,800 lb. Fuel 269 +300 gal. (569 gal. max.)
PERFORMANCE: Speed- Top 395 mph at 5000', 426 mph at 20,000', 439 mph at 25,000', Cruising 362 mph, Landing 100 mph. Service Ceiling 41,900', Climb 30,000'/12.1 min. Range 950 miles/1000 lb. bombs, 2700 miles ferry.

Inglewood built 1,988 P-51Bs which had the V-1650-3 Merlin, except for the improved V-1650-7s on the last 390 P-51B-15-NAs. In August, 1943, Dallas began delivery on 350 similar P-51C-l-NT Mustangs with the V-1650-3, but the remaining 1,400 P-51Cs made there in 1944 had the V-1650-7.

A plastic canopy with all-around vision was installed on two P-51D-1s converted from P-51B-10s and first flown November 17, 1943. This canopy, along with a modified wing holding six .50-caliber guns and 1,880 rounds, the V-1650-7, and a Hamilton propeller, appeared on the P-51D-5-NA, which replaced the B model at Inglewood in March 1944. A small dorsal fillet was added to the P-51D-10 model and fittings for ten 5-inch rockets were added to the P-51D-20. Two 1,000-pound bombs or 110-gallon drop tanks could be carried below their wings.

Mustang production increased to a high of 857 in the month of January 1945. By July 1945, 6,502 P-51D-NAs were built in California. The Texas factory built 1,454 P-51D-DTs interspersed with 1,337 P-51Ks (similar except for an Aeroproducts electric propeller), and ten TP-51D two-place trainers. Seventy-one P-51B-1s and 20 P-51C-1s were modified to F-6Cs in 1943, while 136 F-6Ds and 163 F-6Ks were built at Dallas beginning in November 1944.

NORTH AMERICAN MUSTANG III

Mustangs in Battle

In 1943, American bombers had been suffering such severe losses when operating beyond the range of fighter escort that the whole strategic bombing offensive faced failure. Royal Air Force leaders had expected this defeat, believing that only night bombers could escape fighter defenses and that day bombers could not penetrate deep into Germany. An escort fighter with the range of a heavy bomber and the performance of an interceptor fighter was a technical impossibility, it seemed to RAF chief Sir Charles Portal.

American offensive operations from the United Kingdom were the new Mustangs' first priority, and the first P-51B group there, the 354th, flew its first cross-channel sweep December 1, 1943. Soon the Mustangs could go anywhere the bombers could, and on March 4, 1944, they went all the way to Berlin. This made the P-51 the most important factor in winning the air war against Germany.

The Eighth Air Force got a new commander in January 1944, General Jimmy Doolittle, who extended the fighter mission from bomber escort to seeking out and destroying enemy fighters wherever they could be found in the air or on their bases. Mustangs steadily replaced other

AF

NORTH AMERICAN P-51D-5
Packard V-1650-7, 1490 hp takeoff, 1720 hp WE at 6,200', 1505 hp at 19,300'
DIMENSIONS: As P-51B/C
WEIGHT: Empty 7125 lb., Gross 10,100 lb., Max. 11,600 lb. Fuel 269 +220 gal.
PERFORMANCE: Speed- Top 395 mph at 7000', 413 mph at 15,000', 437 mph at 25,000', Cruising 362 mph, Landing 100 mph. Service Ceiling 41,900', Climb 3475'/1 min., 30,000'/13 min. Range 950 miles/269 gal., 2300 miles/489 gal.

types after the invasion of France until 1945, when 14 P-51 groups and one P-47 group served the Eighth Air Force, responsible for strategic bombing, while 14 P-47 groups, three P-51 groups, and one P-38 fighter group served the Ninth Air Force, which operated in direct support of the ground armies.

The top Mustang group was the 357th, with 609 air and 106 ground kills from February 11, 1944, to April 25, 1945, while the 4th Group, which used Spitfires first, then P-47s, and finally P-51s in February 1944, had 583 air and 469 ground kills. Top Mustang aces were George Preddy with 25 victories, John C. Meyer, with 24, and Don Gentile, with 23.

In Italy, four fighter groups replaced older types with P-51s, (the 31st, 52nd, 325th, and 332nd) joining the Fifteenth Air Force's three P-38 groups and three Twelfth Air Force P-47 groups for the war's last year in Europe. Altogether, 43 AAF fighter groups, with about 75 planes each, confronted Germany in the war's last months. When Soviet, British, and French fighter units are considered, it is apparent that German defeat was inevitable.

Merlin-powered Mustangs were used against Japan in 1944 by the 23rd, 51st, and 311th Groups in China, while the Fifth Air Force received P-51Ds in 1945 for the 3rd Commando, 35th and 348th Groups. Perhaps the most significant Mustang missions in the Pacific were those flown from Iwo Jima by the 15th, 21st, and 506th Groups to support B-29 attacks on Japan.

NORTH AMERICAN F-6D

When fitted with two cameras behind the cockpit the Mustang made an excellent tactical reconnaissance supplement to Lockheed's F-5s, as the 68th Observation Group's F-6As had shown in 1942 for the Twelfth Air Force, and the 67th Tactical Reconnaissance Group of the

Ninth Air Force demonstrated during the battles for France in 1944. Merlin-powered F-6Cs, F-6Ds, and F-6Ks added high-altitude performance. These aircraft all still carried their wing guns, and often used them; in fact, the last German fighter destroyed in the war was an Fw 190 downed by an F-6C on May 8, 1945.

An Evaluation

Now that the major fighter types with which the Army Air Forces fought the war have been described, it may be helpful to summarize their role. Table 7 shows what fighters were used by the AAF in the European Theater of Operations from 1942 to 1945. The planes are given in order of number of sorties, as an indication of each type's relative importance, including Spitfires and Beaufighters obtained on reverse lend-lease, and P-6l night fighters. Unfortunately, we do not have this data for the Pacific theaters.

Table 7
AAF Fighters in the European War, 1942–1945

Type	No. of Sorties	Bomb Tonnage	U. S. a/c Lost in Combat	Enemy a/c Claimed Destroyed in Air	Enemy A/C Claimed Destroyed on Ground	Combat Missions Loss Rate Per Sortie
P-47	423,435	113,963	3,077	3,082	3,202	0.7%
P-51	213,873	5,668	2,520	4,950	4,131	1.2%
P-38	129,849	20,139	1,758	1,771	749	1.4%
P-40	67,059	11,014	553	481	40	0.8%
P-39	30,547	121	107	14	18	0.4%
Spitfire	28,981	212	191	256	3	0.7%
A-36	23,373	8,014	177	84	17	0.8%
Beauf/er	6,706	———	63	24	——	0.9%
P-61	3,637	141	25	58	——	0.7%
Total	927,460	159,272	8,471	10,720	8,160	0.9%

The first two columns give the number of sorties and show the decisive role in Europe of the Thunderbolt, Mustang, and Lightning. The next column indicates the extent that fighters were used for tactical bombing, and shows that the P-47 delivered over two-thirds of the bombs dropped by fighters.

Columns four and seven list total losses of each type on combat missions and the percentage of aircraft loss per sortie. The reader should remember this loss-rate reflects not only the type's vulnerability to enemy aircraft, but also the relative risk of anti-aircraft fire on its particular missions. With this in mind, Lightnings seem to have suffered the heaviest losses, 1.4 percent, and Airacobras the lowest, with only 0.4 per cent per sortie. The low losses of the night fighters and fighter bombers probably indicate that attacking enemy bombers or ground targets is less risky than tackling enemy fighters.

Column five indicates how many enemy aircraft were believed destroyed in the air by each type, while the sixth column tells the number of enemy aircraft destroyed when caught on the ground. This data gives only a rough index of each fighter design's relative efficiency in the job of destroying enemy aircraft, which is its *raison d'etre*. The effect of ground-fire and the uneven risks of interception and offensive missions, of course, limits this index's value.

Nevertheless, the Mustang accounted for almost half the enemy aircraft destroyed in Europe by U.S. fighters and emerges clearly as the most effective type, especially when we remember that Mustangs did relatively little bombing, and almost no interception, but were used for long-distance penetration of enemy fighter territory. Column six indicates Mustang success at strafing planes on their home fields, this largely in the war's last weeks.

The reader may draw his own conclusions from these figures. Why did Lightnings suffer losses greater than Airacobras when the former had a much better record in destroying the enemy? Possibly because the P-39's low-level maneuverability and extensive armor reduced the effects of hostile fire, while the P-38's speed and ceiling enabled it to close with an enemy that wished to avoid combat more often than to join it; but no doubt the where and when of each type's mission was more important here.

It would be highly interesting to have comparable data for the fighter types of other countries, but until then what we do have is a record of Air Force success in building fighters. The relative quality of fighter pilots is not constant, so it may not really be possible to make precise comparison of each type's efficiency, but quality of aircraft remains a significant factor, if not always the decisive one.

Lend-Lease Mustangs

British Mustang I and IAs continued through the war to serve Army Cooperation Command squadrons, replenished in June 1943 by 50 Mustang IIs (P-51A) plus a single A-36A for evaluation. Fighter Command did want the new Merlin-powered models, but had to wait for the AAF to get them before beginning operations in February 1944.

The Royal Air Force received 273 P-51B models shipped to the UK from California in 1944. These were named Mustang III, along with 630 P-51C fighters from Texas, including 353 shipped to the UK and 257 sent via Casablanca to RAF squadrons in Italy. A British-made sliding "Malcolm Hood" improved cockpit visibility on some used by RAF units.

The Mustang IVs were 280 P-51D and 588 P-51Ks shipped from Dallas in 1945, including 619 to the UK, 72 via Casablanca, and 277 to RAF squadrons in India. Actual totals of lend-lease aircraft often vary due to transfers made overseas, but the RAF operated 16 Merlin-powered Mustang squadrons in the United Kingdom and six in Italy at the war's end.

Australia replaced its P-40s in 1945 with 84 P-51K and 214 P-51D Mustangs from Texas, along with parts for the first 80 Mustang XXs assembled in Australia; the first flown April 29, 1945. Like 40 P-51D and 10 P-51Ks lend-leased to two Dutch East Indies squadrons, they were too late to enter combat against Japan.

China got 21 P-51C-10 Mustangs in 1944 to replace P-40s of the Chinese-American Composite Wing and, when 200 P-51D/Ks arrived after the war ended in 1945, there were three Chinese Mustang groups.

NORTH AMERICAN XP-51F
Packard V-1650-3, 1380 hp takeoff, 1505 hp at 17,000', 1295 hp at 28,800'.
DIMENSIONS: As P-51B/C
WEIGHT: Empty 5634 lb., Gross 7340 1b., Max. 9060 lb. Fuel 105-180 gal. (330 gal. max.)
PERFORMANCE: Speed- Top 491 mph at 21,500', Cruising 379 mph, Landing 82 mph. Service Ceiling 42,100', Climb 6530'/ 1 min.,19,500'/4.9 min. Range 1112 miles/180 gal.

Improved Mustangs

A new lightweight NA-105 design using load factors reduced to British standards and only four guns with 1,000 rounds was begun January 2, 1943, and five prototypes were ordered July 20. The first of three XP-51Fs with the Packard V-1650-3 was flown by Bob Chilton February 14, 1944, while the fourth, an XP-51G, flew on August 9 with an imported Rolls-Royce Merlin 145M and later added a wooden Rotol five-bladed prop. The third XP-51F and second XP-51G went to Britain.

NORTH AMERICAN P-51G
Rolls-Royce Merlin 145, 1675 hp takeoff, 1910 hp at 15,400', 2080 hp at 20,000'
DIMENSIONS: As P-51B/C
WEIGHT: Empty 5750 lb., Gross 7265 lb., Max. 8885 lb. Fuel 105-180 gal. (330 gal. max.).
PERFORMANCE: Speed- Top 472 mph at 20,750', Cruising 315 mph, Landing 100 mph. Service Ceiling 45,700', Climb 20,000'/ 3.4 min. Range 485 miles/1000 lb. bombs, 1865 miles max.

Lessons learned from these projects were incorporated into the last production Mustang, the P-51H with a V-1650-9, refined structure, and new wing and tail design. A thousand were ordered June 30, 1944, from Inglewood, the first P-51H-l-NA flying February 3, 1945. The war ended before any went overseas and the last of 555 H models was completed on November 9, 1945. One P-51H-5 went to the RAF in March 1945, and another to the U.S. Navy, which had tested a P-51D on a carrier in November 1944.

The P-51H was probably the fastest prop-driven plane in wartime production. Top speed was 487 mph at 25,000 feet when used as an interceptor, 450 mph when carrying two 500-pound bombs and added fuel. Range with two 110-gallon drop tanks could be extended to 2400 miles at 241 mph, or 850 miles when carrying two 1,000-pound bombs.

Armament was six .50-caliber guns, plus optional external loads of bombs or ten 5-inch rockets. Ammunition supply included 400 rounds for each inner wing gun, and 270 rounds for each of the others. Armor weighed 142 pounds, including 7/16-inch behind the pilot's head, 5/16-inch behind his back, and 1/4-inch at the front fire wall, and 93 pounds of bullet-proof glass were added.

NORTH AMERICAN P-51H-1
Packard V-1650-9, 1380 hp takeoff, 2220 hp at 10,200', 1800 hp WE at 25,000'
DIMENSIONS: Span 37', Lg. 33'4", Ht. 13'8", Wing Area 233 sq. ft.
WEIGHT: Empty 6585 lb., Gross 9500 lb., Max. 11,054 lb. Fuel 255+220 gal.
PERFORMANCE: Speed- Top 487 mph at 25,000', Cruising 380 mph, Landing 96 mph. Service Ceiling 41,600', Climb 30,000'/12.5 min. Range 850 miles/1000 lb. bombs, 940 miles normal, 2400 miles at 241 mph.

Two more prototypes were ordered June 30, 1944, to test an Allison V-1710-119 with a two-stage internal supercharger. These became the XP-51J, first flown April 23, 1945, but the engine presented too many mechanical problems to merit production.

P-51D production ended at Dallas in August 1945, with the last P-51D-30-NT actually completed as the only P-51M with a V-1650-9A engine. None of the 1,700 P-51Ls (V-1650-11) on order were completed. Total Mustangs completed -including attack, photographic, and experimental aircraft- amount to 15,486, with 5,541 on hand in the AAF when the war ended. Average unit cost in 1945 was $50,985.

Mustangs After 1946

The post-war Air Force used the Mustang, known as the F-51H since 1947, in its regular Wings (formerly called groups) until they were replaced by jet fighters. Air National Guard part-time fliers had F-51D and RF-51D models in 15 wings.

When the Korean War began in June 1950, 1,804 Mustangs remained with the Air Guard and in storage, and many were rapidly recalled to active service. Within a year, the Air Force had ten F-51 Wings, of which three with

NORTH AMERICAN P-51H-5 with P-51D-30

F-51Ds served in Korea, along with squadrons of South Korean, South African, and Australian pilots, the latter using some of the 200 Mustangs made in Australia. By the end of its Korean combat on January 23, 1953, the F-51 flew 62,607 sorties, and lost 194 to enemy action, usually by anti-aircraft guns, on missions that were primarily for ground support.

After the war, the last two F-51 Wings gave up their planes for jets, but the Air Guard didn't yield their last F-51D to the Air Force Museum until March 1957.

Sweden had become interested in the Mustang after examining a P-51B-5 that had run out of gas and landed in that neutral state on May 13,1944. Requests were made to the U.S. government for a supply to replace their obsolete Italian-made fighters. When confident of victory, the Americans sold 46 new and four interned Mustangs to Sweden on April 9, 1945. The first P-51D-20s were flown to Stockholm by AAF pilots on April 10th, and AAF veterans helped transition of the F16 group to the Mustangs, known there as the J26. More purchases in 1946/47 brought the total of Swedish P-51s to 161, serving with F16 and F4 until replaced by jets in1952.

Mustangs were the Nationalist fighters in the Chinese civil war that ended with a Communist victory in 1949, and 19 surviving Mustangs formed the first fighter squadron of the People's Republic. Chinese Nationalists took most of the remaining P-51D/Ks to Taiwan, and 18 more F-51Ds and 19 RF-51Ds arrived in 1953 to replenish the force until jet fighters came.

NORTH AMERICAN P-51J
Allison V-1710-119, 1500 hp takeoff, 1720 hp WE at 20,700'
Dimensions: Span 37', Lg. 32'11", Ht. 13'8"', Wing Area 233 sq. ft.
Weight: Empty 6030 lb., Gross 7550 lb. Max. 9185 lb. Fuel 180+150 gal.
Performance: Speed- Top 491 mph at 27,400', Landing 84 mph. Service Ceiling 43,700', Climb 20,000'/5 min.

Many second-hand Mustangs were sold or given to over a dozen different countries. Canada purchased 30 P-51D-30-NAs in March 1947 and 100 more Mustangs in 1950. Other deliveries included 100 for Switzerland and 100 to Italy in 1948. The Philippine Air Force used F-51Ds to attack guerrillas in 1948, and added 50 F-51Ds in 1950 and 40 more in 1953.

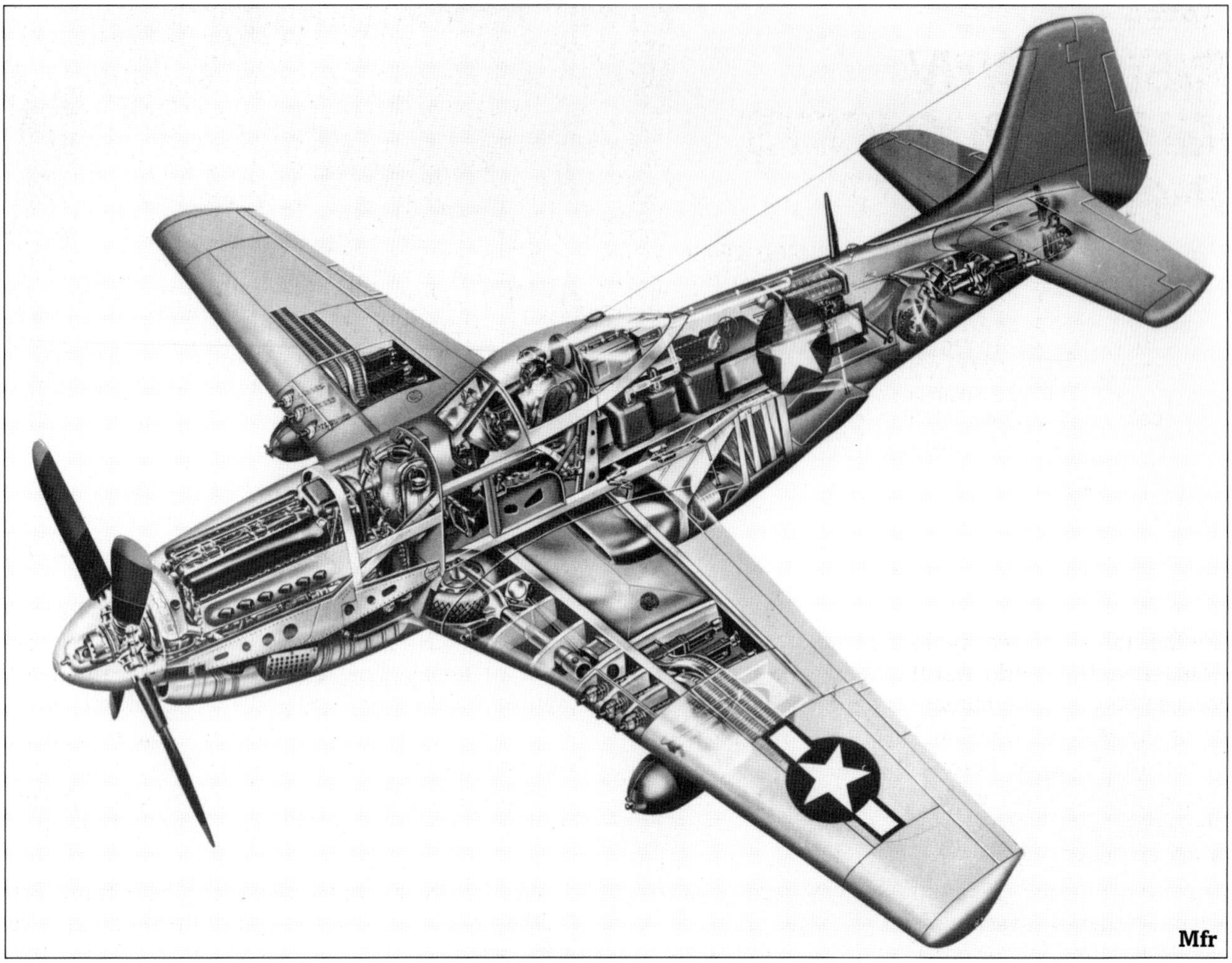

Mfr

NORTH AMERICAN P-51D
A cutaway drawing of the war's most successful fighter.

Israel acquired its first four Mustangs secretly in September1948, added more ex-AAF machines in 1950, and bought 25 P-51D-20s from Sweden on September 3, 1952. These were flown to Israel, which had 59 Mustangs by March 1954. More were found in Italy in 1955, and Mustangs once more went to war in October 1956 with Israel's successful Sinai campaign

Uruguay purchased 25 ex-AAF P-51D-20s in November 1950, but since Republic's P-47D had been chosen by the United States Defense Department to supply Latin American countries at U.S. expense during the post-war period, Mustangs dribbled into that area later from private dealers in a surreptitious manner. Instead of national defense, these air forces were usually involved in local power struggles between the haves and have-nots. Haiti found four ex-AAF P-51Ds in 1951, while Guatemala saw its first two during the CIA-sponsored June 1954 coup, and acquired 30 Mustangs by 1962.

Sweden was a reliable source for those with the foreign exchange, and on September 19, 1952, the RSwAF sold 32 P-51D-20s to the Dominican Republic. That air force, headed by the son of the dictator, Trujillo, added 10 more shipped in May 1953. These Mustangs actually lasted through a fierce civil war in 1965 until they were finally retired in 1984. Nicaragua also purchased 26 of the retired RSwAF Mustangs on September 16, 1954.

Dan Hagedorn estimates that some 185 Mustangs arrived in Latin America. Bolivia got about 23 from 1954 to 1958, even Costa Rica had four in January1955, while Cuban rebels had three in November 1958, and El Salvador's "Soccer War" involved at least 17 in 1968/69.

In 1958, several Philippine Air Force F-51 pilots were involved in CIA-sponsored operations against the Indonesian Republic, which itself had a small ex-Dutch P-51K squadron. When the last dozen Dominican survivors were sold to an American dealer in 1984, they brought almost six times their price brand-new 40 years earlier.

This survey must exclude details of the Mustang's long postwar career as a racer and air show performer. Fifty years after they were built, many fascinated show audiences and still held speed records. The most successful wartime fighter became the most popular post-war show plane. A Florida rally in 1999 turned out at least 65 privately owned Mustangs.

CHAPTER 18

CRISIS-BORN FIGHTER PROJECTS, XP-48 TO XP-77

Mfr

LOCKHEED XP-49
Two Continental XI-1430-13,-15, 1350 hp takeoff, 1600 hp at 25,000' / DIMENSIONS: Span 52', Lg. 40'1", Ht. 9'7", Wing Area 327 sq. ft. / WEIGHT: Empty 15,410 lb., Gross 18,750 lb., Max. 22,000 lb. Fuel 300-725 gal. / PERFORMANCE: Speed-Top 347 mph at s.l., 361 mph at 5,000', 406 mph at 25,000' Service Ceiling 37,500', Climb 3075'/1 min., 20,000'/ 8.7 min. Range 679 miles normal, 1800 miles ferry.

Now that the single-seat types that did most Air Force fighter work in World War II have been described, attention can be given the numerous experimental projects begun by the Materiel Division. In the two years between the outbreak of war in Europe and the attack on Pearl Harbor, an extraordinary variety of designs received pursuit designations from XP-46 to XP-71. Nevertheless, only three of over two dozen projects reached production in time to join the P-38, P-39, and P-40 types already on order when Germany's invasion of Poland began the war.

The first flurry of designs were the XP-46 to XP-50 fighters offered in the August 1939 design competitions. None passed the prototype stage, since the Curtiss XP-46, Republic XP-47, and Lockheed XP-49 were submerged by P-40, P-47B, and P-38 developments. Douglas made its only attempt at a land-based fighter with the XP-48 (Model 312), but it was never built.

Mfr

GRUMMAN XP-50
Two Wright R-1820-67, -69, 1200 hp takeoff, 1200 hp at 25,000'
DIMENSIONS: Span 42', Lg. 31'11", Ht. 12', Wing Area 304 sq. ft.
WEIGHT: Empty 8307 lb., Gross 10,558 lb., Max. 13,060 lb. Fuel 217-450 gal.
PERFORMANCE: Speed-Top 424 mph at 25,000', Cruising 317 mph. Service Ceiling 40,000', Climb 20,000'/5 min. Range 585 miles normal, 1250 miles ferry.

That Douglas specification, dated August 5, 1939, was for a lightweight 350-mph single-seater with a 525-hp Ranger SGV-770, tricycle gear, and two guns. Weight was expected to be only 3,400 pounds, with a wide, narrow wing requiring only 92 square feet of area. By February 1940, the Air Corps had rejected this approach.

Instead, prototypes were ordered of the top two competitors, the XP-49 and XP-50, in the August 1939 competition for twin-engine fighters. Lockheed attempted to improve the P-38 by using more advanced engines. This project, known as the XP-49 (Lockheed Model 522), began with a company proposal to the Air Corps in August 1939. A prototype contract was ready by November 30, but was not finally approved until January 22, 1940. Delivery in 14 months was promised.

The first specification called for the proposed Pratt & Whitney X-1800 (H-2600) 24-cylinder engine, and a speed of 473 mph at 20,000 feet was anticipated. When this engine was canceled, the Continental XI-1430, an inverted inline engine with 27% less frontal area than the Allison, was substituted by September 9, 1940. The new specification guaranteed top speed would be 372 mph at 5,000 feet, and 458 mph at 25,000 feet, where 1,600-hp per engine was expected.

Flight tests began on November 14, 1942, 33 months after the original contract, and continued until the following June with discouraging results. Top speed was only 361 mph at 5,000 feet and 406 mph at 15,000 feet. Armament was to include two 20-mm guns with 60 rpg and four .50-caliber guns with 300 rpg, but neither weapons or a proposed pressurized cabin were ever installed. The XP-49's only value was as a test bed for the Continental engine.

Grumman's only Army fighter, the XP-50, was a twin-engine counterpart of the Navy's XF5F-l, with a short squared-off wing, stubby fuselage, twin rudders, and tricycle landing gear. Equipment included front and back pilot armor, two 20-mm and two .50-caliber guns in the nose, and a rack for two 100-pound bombs. The XP-50 was ordered November 29, 1939, and since the power plant choice, turbosupercharged Wright Cyclones, was less speculative than that of the rival XP-49, the Grumman was first in the air. A maiden flight was made February 18, 1941, but a turbosupercharger explosion on May 14 caused the loss of the $353,828 prototype.

Undaunted, Grumman then proposed its Model 51 with two 1,700 hp Wright R-2600-10 Double Cyclones, and two prototypes designated XP-65 were recommended May 19, 1941, and authorized June 16. Essentially this design was like the Navy's XF7F-l prepared at the same time, but the Army wanted turbo supercharging, a pressurized cabin, and two 37-mm guns. The Army came to feel that "commonalties" with Navy design were a handicap, and since Grumman's concentration was on Navy projects, cancellation was recommended December 15, and completed by January 16, 1942.

Fighter Projects begun in 1940-1941

General Arnold urged a new emphasis on pursuit tactics and plane development on November 14, 1939, admitting that previous views that bombers could not be defeated by fighters had "now been proven wholly untenable." New pursuit requirements had to be established for World War Two.

Interceptor pursuit specification XC-622, dated November 27, 1939, called for a single-engine single-seater with a top speed at 15 to 20,000 feet of at least 425 mph. The "desired attainment" was 525 mph, which then seemed like a theoretical limit for propeller-driven planes. No more than seven minutes should be needed to climb to 20,000 feet, but endurance was limited to one and a half hours. At least four guns and six 20-pound bombs would be carried.

To find such fighter designs, Request for Data R40-C was circulated among potential fighter manufacturers on February 20, 1940. Replies from seven companies were opened April 15, 1940. The two designs considered most ready for construction were the Bell Model 13 and the Curtiss CP-40-2, both planned for the Continental XI-1430 inline engine. Designations XP-52 and XP-53 were assigned to these Bell and Curtiss projects. The Foreign Release Agreements made in April, releasing the P-39 and P-40 for export, obligated these companies to build new prototypes without cost to the Air Corps.

Republic's offering for the R40-C competition was the AP-12 with the proposed 2,350-hp Wright R-2160 Tornado engine enclosed behind the pilot, P-39 style, with an extension shaft and gear box driving contra-rotating propellers in the nose. Armament included a cannon and four machine-guns in the nose and two guns in the wings. While this very streamlined design was judged "the maximum that can be expected" from a conventional tractor arrangement, engine development would take over three years. Instead, Republic would develop the barrel-shaped AP-16, which became the XP-47B.

Pusher Prototypes

The highest marks of the R40-C evaluation made on May 15, 1940, were given to single-seaters with rearward-facing propellers and engines behind the pilot Fighters with pusher propellers offered advantages in drag reduction and a nose enhancing pilot visibility and heavy armament installations. Numerous structural complications presented themselves, however, and tricycle landing gear was a necessity.

Bell Aircraft's Model 13B, the proposed P-39 replacement, had won only 532 of 1,000 merit points from R40-C, so this company switched its XP-52 program to the Model 16, a pusher arrangement. The XP-52 had tricycle landing gear, laminar flow airfoil wings, twin booms to support the tail assembly, and a 1,600-hp Continental XI-1430-5 inline engine, cooled by a nose radiator and turning contra-rotating propellers. This specification, dated July 30, 1940, promised a 425-mph speed at 19,500 feet and an armament of two 20-mm and six .50-caliber guns.

As contract negotiations proceeded, Bell also offered a pusher interceptor on September 28 that had a 2000-hp Pratt & Whitney R-2800-23 cooled by air from a nose intake. This became the XP-59 on October 2, 1940, and by October 28 the Air Corps decided to abandon the XP-52. Two XP-59 prototypes ordered February 26, 1941, were to weigh 10,463 pounds each, do 450 mph at 22,000 feet, and have the XP-52's armament.

The XP-59 project was canceled on November 25, 1941, to relieve the load on Bell's engineering staff and clear the way for the XP-59A jet and the XP-63. Both would go into production in 1943 as the Airacomet and the Kingcobra.

The three R40-C winners were designated the Vultee XP-54, with a Figure of Merit of 817 points; the Curtiss-Wright XP-55 with 770 points, and the Northrop XP-56, with 725 points. Preliminary engineering contracts were issued June 22, 1940.

The XP-54 and XP-56 single-seat pushers were to be powered by the Pratt & Whitney 2,200-hp liquid-cooled 24-cylinder X-l800-A3G (H-2600-1), but this engine was canceled on October 4, 1940, and other power plants had to be chosen for the actual prototypes.

VULTEE XP-54
Lycoming XH-2470-1, 2300 hp at 25,000'
DIMENSIONS: Span 53'10", Lg. 54'9", Ht. 14'6", Wing Area 456 sq. ft.
WEIGHT: Empty 15,262 lb., Gross 18,233 lb., Max. 19,337 lb. Fuel 223-378 gal.
PERFORMANCE: Speed-Top 290 mph at s.l., 381 mph at 28,500'; Cruising 328 mph, Stalling 110 mph. Service Ceiling 37,000', Climb 26,000'/17 min. Range 500 miles normal, 870 miles ferry.

Vultee's XP-54 weight grew from 11,500 pounds in 1941 to 18,233 pounds when completed. When the first prototype order was approved on January 8, 1941, to be powered by a Lycoming XH-2470-1, a top speed of 510 mph at 20,000 feet was promised. But numerous changes resulted in a larger and heavier aircraft. By September 1941, turbosuperchargers and a pressurized pilot cabin had been added, and top speed was guaranteed at 476 mph at 30,000 feet with a 16,145 pound gross weight.

VULTEE XP-54 (2nd prototype)

The original nose armament of six .50-caliber guns was replaced by two 37-mm guns with 120 rounds mounted in the nose below a pair of .50-caliber guns with 1,000 rounds. A compensating gun sight could elevate the entire nose to give more reach to the cannon. Full armor and fuel tank protection was included.

Largest single-seater offered the Air Force, the XP-54 had twin rudders suspended on tail booms extending from the gulled wing. The bullet-shaped fuselage stood so high on tricycle gear that the pilot was raised up through the bottom into the cockpit by an elevating seat. In emergencies, the seat dropped downward on a swinging arm to throw the pilot clear of the four-bladed propeller. The XP-54 had excellent pilot's visibility, but its weapon system was never actually tested in flight.

More delay of the contract's July 1, 1942, delivery date came from a change of the Downey company's ownership that resulted in the XP-54's designer, Chief Engineer Richard Palmer, leaving Vultee. Flight tests begun January 15, 1943, by Frank Davis, produced only a disappointing 381 mph at 28,500 feet. Although the contractor polished and waxed the XP-54 so it did reach the 403 mph of the revised specification, the Air Force notified Vultee on May 25 that no production could be considered, and that the 24-cylinder Lycoming engine was being abandoned. A second prototype made the first of its ten flights on May 24, 1944. Total cost of the XP-54 project was $1,497,000.

The Curtiss-Wright XP-55 was the first Air Force fighter with swept wings, which angled back 45 degrees with twin vertical tail surfaces placed near the tips Since the pusher propeller eliminated the usual tail assembly, the elevators were placed at the nose in a "canard" layout.

Such a radical configuration required much new engineering and wind tunnel testing, and construction of a full-scale wood and fabric flying model powered by a 275-hp Menasco. Flight tests of this CW-24 begun in secret at Muroc Dry Lake on December 2, 1941, justified a contract, approved July 10, 1942, with the St. Louis firm for three prototypes.

The 1,600-hp Continental XI-1430-3, which was supposed to give the XP-55 a 507-mph top speed, was replaced by the available 1,125-hp Allison V-1710-95. A dorsal fin above and ventral fin below the engine contained air intakes for the engine and radiator while the three-bladed prop could be jettisoned to make a pilot's bailout safer. Armament consisted of four .50-caliber guns in the nose with 250 rpg and wing racks were provided for two 50-gallon drop tanks.

CURTISS XP-55
Allison V-1710-95, 1275 hp takeoff, 1125 hp at 15,560'
DIMENSIONS: Span 41', Lg. 29'7", Ht. 10'1", Wing Area 217 sq. ft.
WEIGHT: Empty 6,354 lb., Gross 7,931 lb. Max. 8,805 lb. Fuel 110+100 gal.
PERFORMANCE: Speed-Top 277.5 mph at 16,900' Landing 80 mph. Service Ceiling 36,200', Climb 2460'/1 min.

The first example flew on July 13, 1943, but was lost in an inverted spin November 15. The second XP-55 first flew on January 9, and the third on April 25, 1944, but an excessive takeoff run and dangerous stall behavior continued as problems. Over 1,000 pounds overweight, and costing $3,524,622, the XP-55 project did introduce the Air Force to the development of swept wing flight.

CURTISS XP-55 (2nd prototype)

The third and most radical of these pushers was the XP-56, a tailless interceptor with a very short elliptical fuselage. The newly reorganized Northrop company had designed a flying wing, the N-1M, with a control system of "elevon" control surfaces on the wings and rudders replaced by air-operated split flaps on the drooped wingtips. An NS-2 fighter design was ordered as the XP-56 prototype on September 26, 1940, and by March 12, 1941, the original X-1800 engine was replaced by an R-2800-29 Wasp cooled by air from wing-root intakes and turning contra rotating propellers behind dorsal and ventral fins. Delivery was planned for March 1942, and guaranteed top speed was 467 mph at 25,000 feet.

NORTHROP XP-56 (First Prototype)

The mockup was inspected on July 15, 1941, and a second prototype ordered on December 5, 1941, but progress was extremely slow at the Hawthorne plant because of difficulties with the welded magnesium construction introduced by Northrop. While the plane was completed in March 1943, gear box problems delayed the first cautious test hops by John Myers at Muroc to September 6, 1943. Poor directional stability prevented the next tests until a larger vertical fin was added to the prototype.

On October 8, the plane was wrecked when a tire blew out during a high speed taxi run. Empty weight was increased from 8,699 pounds on the first prototype to 9,879 pounds on the second XP-56. First flown March 23, 1944, by Harry Crosby, tests of that XP-56 ended with the 10th flight on August 11. Serious concerns about dangerous instability continued, and the calculated performance given by the specification was never validated by testing.

Armament was to include two 20-mm guns with 200 rounds and four .50-caliber guns with 1,600 rounds in the nose, but was never tested. Expenditures on the XP-56 "came to $12,265,555 with no visible benefit to the war effort " concluded an official report.

None of the radical designs offered for the Material Division's R40-C study had achieved tactical use. Ironically, the most successful designs of 1940 were Republic's big XP-47B and the conventional XP-51, which was not adopted by the Air Force until after it had been operated by Britain.

In sharp contrast to the design of heavy aircraft was the XP-57, which had been proposed in May 1940 by the newly-established Tucker Aviation of Detroit as a lightweight fighter of low construction cost. General Arnold ordered, by July 5, a contract negotiated for one plane, "at a cost not to exceed $40,000". With a design weight of only 3,000 pounds and armed with three .50-caliber, or one .50-caliber and one 20-mm gun, the wooden-winged Tucker was to attain 308 mph from a 720-hp Miller L-510 engine driving its propeller by an extended shaft like that on the P-39s. By February 1941, however, the little company was in financial difficulties, and since current fighter trends were to heavier and faster aircraft, the contract was allowed to lapse.

NORTHROP XP-56
Pratt & Whitney R-2800-29, 2000 hp takeoff, 1800 hp at 19,500'
DIMENSIONS: Span 42'6", Lg. 27'6", Ht. 11', Wing Area 306 sq. ft.
WEIGHT: Empty 9,879 lb., Gross 11,350 lb., Max. 12,145 lb. Fuel 215-314 gal.
PERFORMANCE: Speed-Top 417 mph at s.l., 465 mph at 19,500', Cruising 396 mph. Service Ceiling 33,000', Climb 20,000'/7.8 min. Range 445 miles normal, 660 miles max.

Lockheed XP-58 "Chain Lightning"

The last of 1940's fighter projects to be flown was the Lockheed XP-58, only two-seater begun that year, and the heaviest fighter built during the war. This type began with Lockheed's April 12, 1940, agreement to build an XP-58 prototype in exchange for the release of the P-38. This plane was to have twin Continental engines, a top speed of 450 mph and a range of not less than 1,600 miles, and be delivered in 16 months. By May 6, it was agreed that it would be a two-place convoy fighter whose tactical role was comparable to the Messerschmitt Bf 110 then active in Europe.

An XP-58 prototype ordered on October 14 was then scheduled to use the Pratt & Whitney X-1800 (H-2600) liquid-cooled engines also planned for several other 1940

Mfr

LOCKHEED XP-58
Two Allison V-3420-11/-13, 2600 hp takeoff, 3000 hp at 28,000'
DIMENSIONS: Span 70', Lg. 49'5", Ht. 13'8", Wing Area 600 sq. ft.
WEIGHT: Empty 31,624 lb., Gross 39,192 lb., Max. 43,000 lb. Fuel 656-760+930 gal.
PERFORMANCE: Speed-Top 417 mph at s.l., 436 mph at 25,000', Cruising 274 mph. Service Ceiling 38,400', Climb 25,000'/12.1 min. Range 1150 miles normal, 2650 miles ferry.

TUCKER XP-57
Miller L-510-1, 720 hp at takeoff, 615 hp at 20,000'
DIMENSIONS: Span 28'5", Lg. 26'7", Ht. 8'1", Wing Area 120 sq. ft.
WEIGHT: Empty 1920 lb., Gross 3000 lb., Max. 3400 lb. Fuel 75-125 gal.
PERFORMANCE: Speed-Top 308 mph at s.l., Cruising 257 mph. Service Ceiling 26,000', Climb 18,000'/11 min. Range 540 miles, 900 miles max. A sketch by Richard Dann of 1940s lightweight idea.

designs. After this program was dropped, Lockheed suggested Pratt & Whitney air-cooled R-2800s. In September 1941, these were replaced by 2,350-hp Wright R-2160s, and two remote-controlled turrets were added.

During 1942, the Air Force considered changing the design to a low-altitude attack type armed with a 75-mm cannon and a second prototype was begun. This role, however, was more effectively addressed by the Beech XA-38. By June 1943, the never-completed Wright engines were replaced by turbosupercharged Allison V-3420s originally developed as bomber power plants.

Looking much like an enlarged P-38 except for four-bladed propellers, double wheels on the tricycle gear, and the gunner at the rear of the center nacelle, the XP-58 had upper and lower remote-controlled turrets like the A-26. Two 50-caliber guns in each turret had 300 rpg, while the nose accommodated four 37-mm fixed guns with 250 rpg. Four 1,000 pound bombs or drop tanks could be carried, or the nose armament replaced by one 75-mm and two 50-caliber guns.

No armament was ever actually fitted to the XP-58, and the second prototype was canceled. After over four years of protracted development, the XP-58 made its first flight on June 6, 1944, from Burbank to Muroc. No production was ever scheduled.

Curtiss Developments

Curtiss planned to replace the P-40 with the XP-53, (Model 88) which was offered with the proposed Continental XI-1430-3 inverted inline engine for the R40-C design competition in April 1940. A revised specification dated July 10 had a laminar-flow wing with four .50-caliber guns, and promised 465 mph at 18,000 feet if 1,600 hp were available. A prototype contract was approved October 28, 1940, and an enlarged wing with eight guns was chosen in January 1941, reducing top speed to 430 mph.

When it was realized that the Continental engine would not be available in time to be useful, Curtiss offered an alternative Model 90 design by January 16; structurally identical, but substituting a Packard-built Merlin V-1650-1 engine. This aircraft was designated XP-60 and the contract change was approved May 16, 1941.

On September 18, 1941, the XP-60 was first flown, while the XP-53 airframe was used for static tests. A three-bladed propeller headed a neat nose, with the radiator ahead of the tapered wing and the wheels retracted inward of eight .50-caliber wing guns with 2,000 rounds.

CURTISS XP-60
Packard V-1650-1, 1300 hp takeoff, 1120 hp at 19,000'
DIMENSIONS: Span 41'5", Lg. 33'4", Ht. 10'9", Wing Area 275 sq. ft.
WEIGHT: Empty 7008 lb., Gross 9351 Lb., Max. 9961 Lb. Fuel 135-228 gal.
PERFORMANCE: Speed-Top 330 mph at 5150', 380 mph at 20,000', Landing 85 mph. Service Ceiling 29,000', Climb 15,000'/7.3 min. Range 995 miles/228 gal.

Production aircraft were planned with turbosupercharged Allison F10 engines and an order for 1,950 P-60As (Curtiss Model 95) was approved October 31, 1941. Had this plan been completed, the P-60A would have replaced the P-40 in production by 1943, but after the United States entered the war, there were second thoughts about the desirability of interrupting production at that crucial point. In January 1942, the P-60A program was replaced by more P-40s and some P-47Gs from Curtiss.

For developmental purposes, three aircraft labeled XP-60A, XP-60B, and XP-60C were allowed to survive the cut. The XP-60A was built with an Allison V-1710-75, General Electric B-14 turbosupercharger, a four-bladed propeller, and six .50-caliber wing guns with 1,200 rounds. While the XP-60 wing shape remained, with added dihedral, a new fuselage with a larger radiator was used.

CURTISS XP-60A
Allison V-1710-75, I425 hp at 25,000'
DIMENSIONS: Span 41'4", Lg. 33'7", Ht. 12'4", Wing Area 275 sq. ft.
WEIGHT: Empty 7806 lb., Gross 9616 lb. Max. 10,158 lb. Fuel 116-200 gal.
PERFORMANCE: Speed-Top 340 mph at 5000', 420 mph at 29,000'. Service Ceiling 32,500', Climb 15,000'/6.5 min.

CURTISS XP-60C
Pratt & Whitney R-2800-53, 2000 hp at 19,000'
DIMENSIONS: Span 41'4", Lg. 33'11", Ht. 10'9", Wing Area 275 sq. ft.
WEIGHT: Empty 8601 Lb., Gross 10,525 Lb., Max. 11,836 Lb. Fuel 178-360 gal.
PERFORMANCE: Speed- Top 340 mph at s.l., 414 mph at 20,350', Landing 89 mph. Service Ceiling 35,000', Climb 3890'/1 min., 20,000'/5.5 min.

A 420-mph top speed was promised, but after fires during ground runs, the turbosupercharger was removed before the XP-60A was flown on November 1, 1942. At first, the P-60B was to be similar with a new supercharger, and the P-60C was to try the Chrysler XIV-2220 eventually tested by the XP-47H. But on October 5, 1942, the AMC ordered the P-60C changed to a 2,000-hp R-2800-53 radial with contra rotating propellers and four .50-caliber wing guns with 1,000 rounds. This version began flight tests on January 27, 1943.

The original XP-60 was returned to Curtiss to be rebuilt as the XP-60D with the XP-60A tail and a two-stage V-1650-3 and four-bladed propeller like the P-51B. But before the new Merlin was installed, this aircraft's tail came off during dive demonstrations on May 6, 1943.

While XP-60A development had been canceled November 6, 1942, Curtiss had been given a letter contract November 27, 1942, for 500 fighters to be powered by two-

CURTISS XP-60D

stage Twin Wasps with an ordinary four-bladed propeller. An R-2800-10 was installed on the XP-60B airframe, so this aircraft was completed as the XP-60E, first flown on May 26, 1943, with four wing guns.

CURTISS XP-60E
Pratt & Whitney R-2800-10, 2000 hp at 20,000'
DIMENSIONS: As XP-60C
WEIGHT: Empty 8574 lb., Gross 10,320 lb., Max. 10,667 lb. Fuel 178-225 gal.
PERFORMANCE: Speed- Top 410 mph at 20,200', Landing 88 mph. Service Ceiling 38,000', Climb 4200'/1 min. 10,000'/2.5 min., 25,000'/6.5 min.

Since P-60 development had fallen behind the P-47, P-51, and P-63 fighters, the production order was canceled in June 1943. Only the first aircraft on that contract was completed as the YP-60E. First flown July 13, 1944, the YP-60E had an R-2800-l8, six .50-caliber wing guns with 1,602 rounds, an unbalanced rudder, and a bubble canopy that made it look much like a P-47D-25. By that time, the Air Force had lost interest in the type, so no tests were made to confirm the estimated performance.

Another single-seater, the largest single-engine Air Force fighter ever built, was developed by Curtiss during this same period. It began with a meeting in General Arnold's office on January 7, 1941, when Curtiss engineers proposed using the largest available radial engine, the Wright R-3350, with a supercharger, a pressure cabin, and twelve .50-caliber or eight 20-mm guns.

Designated XP-62 on January 16, this big low-wing monoplane had contra-rotating three-bladed propellers and laminar airfoil wings holding four to eight 20-mm guns with 150 rpg. The pressure cabin, designed to maintain a 10,000-foot interior altitude up to 35,000 feet, was entered

CURTISS YP-60E
Pratt & Whitney R-2800-18, 2100 hp at 23,000'
DIMENSIONS: As XP-60C
WEIGHT: Empty 8082 lb., Gross 10,213 lb., Max. 11,868 lb. Fuel 178-368 gal.
PERFORMANCE: Speed- Top 367 mph at s.l., 446 mph at 25,000', Landing 95 mph. Service Ceiling 40,800', Climb 4600'/1 min., 20,000'/5 min.

by a hatch that opened upward to the right, instead of sliding back.

Authority for purchase of the XP-62 was dated May 16, 1941, and a contract for two prototypes approved June 27 called for first delivery by September 28, 1942. The mockup was inspected on December 15, 1941.

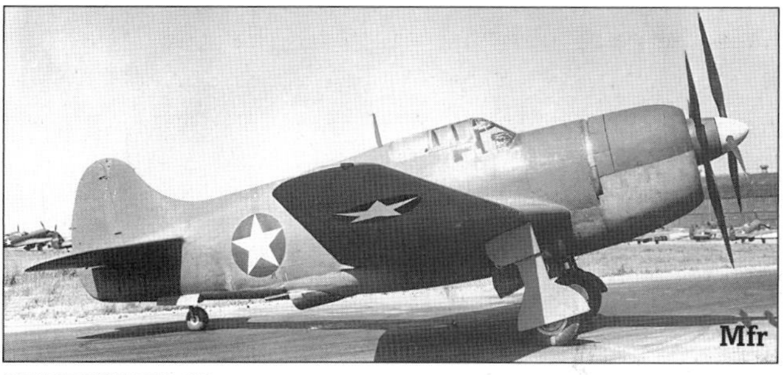

CURTISS XP-62
Wright R-3350-17, 2300 hp takeoff, 2250 hp at 25,000'
DIMENSIONS: Span 53'8", Lg. 39'6", Ht. 16'3", Wing Area 420 sq. ft.
WEIGHT: Empty 11,773 lb., Gross 14,660 lb., Max. 16,651 lb. Fuel 245-384 gal.
PERFORMANCE: Speed- Top 358 mph at 5000', 448 mph at 27,000', Cruising 340 mph, Landing 85 mph. Service Ceiling 35,700', Climb 15,000'/6.6 min. Range 900 miles normal, 1500 miles ferry.

A letter contract dated May 25, 1942, scheduled 100 P-62As, but R-3350 engine production was so taken up supplying B-29 bombers that the P-62 could not supplant the P-40 in production. Company hopes for production ended when the Air Force decided to stick with the P-47 and the P-62A project was canceled July 27, 1942. Only one XP-62 was completed, making its first flight July 21, 1943.

The Night-fighter Problem

In spite of the common division of European offensive aircraft into day- and night-bomber categories, few night attacks were made in the early months of World War II. Far less accurate than daylight bombing, night bombing was unnecessary for the Germans when they had air supremacy, and considered impolitic for the Allies. As more vigorous air operations developed in 1940, heavy

DOUGLAS P-70
Two Wright R-2600-11, 1600 hp takeoff, 1275 hp at 12,000'
DIMENSIONS: Span 61'4", Lg. 47'7", Ht. 17'7", Wing Area 464 sq. ft.
WEIGHT: Empty 16,031 lb, Gross 21,264 lb. Fuel 600 gal.
PERFORMANCE: Speed- Top 329 mph at 14,000', Cruising 270 mph, Landing 97 mph. Service Ceiling 28,250, Climb 12,000'/8 min. Range 1060 miles normal, 1460 miles ferry.

losses on daytime sorties led Britain's Bomber Command to concentrate on nocturnal raids. Their enemies began the Battle of Britain in the daytime, but when losses rose past a tolerable level despite fighter escort, the *Luftwaffe* turned more and more to night work.

Precision was still lacking, but as unhappy Coventry was to learn, increasing tonnage volume could severely hurt industrial targets. And difficult for bombers to find at night as a factory might be, it was much more difficult for fighters to find a moving airplane. The speedy interceptors that served London so well in sunshine groped about in darkness as Goering's bombers unloaded, and only occasional searchlight illumination gave opportunity for attack.

Perfection of radio-location equipment light enough to be airborne gave the fighter a better chance, and Britain developed a specialized night fighter large enough to carry the radar and its operator, plus armament sufficient to destroy any bomber. While speed and climb could not match that of a single-seater, enough margin over bomber performance was required to insure successful interception. Other requirements included a moderate landing speed for safe operation from small, blacked-out fields, and endurance enough to permit persistence in ambush or pursuit.

Such weight and relatively low wing loading requirements would severely limit a single-engine aircraft's performance, and therefore the first successful plane for this work was a development of the Blenheim twin-engine bomber. First flown in July 1939 powered by two Bristol Hercules radial engines, the Bristol Beaufighter first scored against the Germans in November 1940, and became the most important British night fighter. The pilot had good visibility forward, while the radar operator sat within the rear fuselage. Armament included four 20-mm guns firing forward from beneath the nose and six .30-caliber guns in the wings.

An example of the Beaufighter's AI (airborne interception) Mark IV radar was sent to the U.S., and on October 21 the Army Air Corps told the Northrop company to design a twin-engine night fighter. Jack Northrop submitted Specification NS-8A on December 22, 1940, and two XP-61 prototypes were ordered January 11, 1941, followed by 13 YP-61s on March 10. An American copy of the AI Mk 4 was to be produced as the SCR-540, while the Radiation Laboratory established at the Massachusetts Institute of Technology undertook the development of advanced radar.

Douglas Havoc

During the time required for the Northrop design to enter service, Douglas light bombers were pressed into night-fighter duty. In 1940, the British received Boston DB-7 bombers whose admirable agility suggested that type could function as a night fighter. The Boston's endurance and tricycle gear immediately made it a safer night operator than most, and when the nose enclosure was blocked in and replaced by twelve .30-caliber guns, and exhaust dampers and black paint added, it became the Havoc night fighter.

Other Havocs operated as night "intruders", which attempted to ambush enemy bombers over their home fields. Yet another modification was the "Turbinlight" of 1942; over 70 Havocs fitted with a 1,400-amp searchlight to be used after the Havoc closed within minimum range of its AI-IV radar. A beam of 30° divergence illuminated an area 150 yards wide at one-mile range, enabling accompanying conventional fighters to fire at the target. The powerful lamp was fitted behind an armored glass disk

Mfr

BRISTOL BEAUFIGHTER (RAF)

three feet in diameter and fed by a ton of batteries in the bomb bay. This system was a waste of good aircraft, for not one German bomber was destroyed.

In the United States, an imported AI-IV radar was installed in the first Douglas A-20, which became the XP-70 when delivered October 1, 1941. Sixty of the A-20s had been planned as high-altitude attack bombers, but the supercharged engines had failed. On October 15, the remaining A-20s were ordered to be converted to P-70 night fighters with SCR-540 radar, whose antennae included the arrow-like transmitter in the nose, azimuth receivers on each side, and elevation receivers on the port wing. The radar operator sat with his scope in the rear cockpit, while four 20-mm guns in a tub below the bomb bay had 60 rpg.

Powered by R-2600-11 Cyclones and fitted with self-sealing fuel tanks in the former bomb bay and the wings, the first P-70 was delivered April 4, 1942. The remaining 58 were accepted at Santa Monica from June to September. The four cannon were supplemented by two .50-caliber nose guns on some active duty planes.

Since the Air Force had no night fighter units when it entered the war, a training organization was established at Orlando, Florida. Then, 25 P-70s were deployed to Hawaii for the 6th Night Fighter Squadron in September 1942, and the last seven went to the Panama Canal Zone.

AF

DOUGLAS XP-70A-2

Additional Havocs included 13 P-70A-1 and 26 P-70A-2s converted from A-20C and A-20Gs with R-2600-23 Cyclones, SCR-540 radar, and six .50-caliber nose guns with 350 rpg instead of the 20-mm weapons. Since they retained the two flexible .50-caliber guns in the rear and 2,000 pounds of bombs, their performance remained that of their low-altitude bomber originals. Another 65 P-70A-2s were converted at modification centers.

SCR-720 radar was fitted in the nose of 105 P-70B trainers converted from A-20G aircraft in 1944. Six .50-caliber guns were in blisters on each side on the first P-70B-l, but were omitted from the remaining TP-70B-2 aircraft.

The first P-70s in action were a 6th NFS detachment on Guadalcanal from February to September 1943, which downed a bomber on April 19. Another six planes flew to New Guinea in March 1943, and scored their only confirmed victory on May 15. Three P-70A squadrons were also sent to the Pacific by February 1944, but were used mostly for attack missions. USAF Havocs were rather unsuccessful in combat; only two kills, due to their poor performance at altitude. In the Soviet Union, lend-lease A-20G-1s fitted with radar were no more successful.

Most P-70s remained in the U.S. to train the 12 night fighter squadrons formed in 1943 and six more squadrons formed in 1944. When four night fighter squadrons were sent to North Africa in 1943 for the Twelfth Air Force, they used Bristol Beaufort VI fighters obtained on reverse lend-lease.

The Black Widow

The first American night fighter designed just for that purpose, the P-61 was as big as a medium bomber, with two 2,000-hp Pratt & Whitney R-2800-10 Wasps, twin rudders supported by tail booms, and tricycle gear. The central nacelle had radar, the pilot's cabin with a gunner above and behind him, and finally a radar operator's enclosure. Retractable ailerons permitted flaps the full length of the wing's trailing edge. An ACR-720A radar transmitter designed for the P-61 had a rotating reflector dish in the Plexiglas (later fiberglass) nose, permitting location of targets ten miles away; depending on altitude and conditions.

Armament consisted of four 20-mm fixed guns with 800 rounds in a bulge below the fuselage, and four .50-caliber with 1,600 rounds in a top remote-controlled turret. The latter guns were usually fired forward like the cannon by the pilot, but could be unlocked and aimed by either gunner as flexible defense for the upper hemisphere.

NORTHROP XP-61
Two Pratt & Whitney R-2800-10, 2000 hp takeoff, 2000 hp at 19,000'
DIMENSIONS: Span 66', Lg. 48'11", Ht. 14'3", Wing Area 663 sq. ft.
WEIGHT: Empty 21,695 lb., Gross 27,575 lb., Max. 28,870 lb. Fuel 540-640 gal.
PERFORMANCE: Speed- Top 370 mph at 20,900', Cruising 200 mph, Landing 95 mph. Service Ceiling 33,100', Climb 2900'/1 min., 20,000'/9 min. Range 1200 miles normal, 1465 miles max.

Without waiting for the test aircraft's completion, the USAF ordered P-61A production begun with a 150-plane contract approved September 17, 1941, and increased to 560 by a new order approved February 26, 1942. On May 26, 1942, Vance Breese flew the first XP-61 at Hawthorne, and the second, with full-span flaps, flew November 18.

Production aircraft were slow to appear, for the first YP-61 was not finished until February 1943, or accepted until August 6, and the first P-61A-1 was accepted in October. Replacement of magnesium with aluminum in the structure added weight, and the P-61A added armor glass windshields to the crew's front armor.

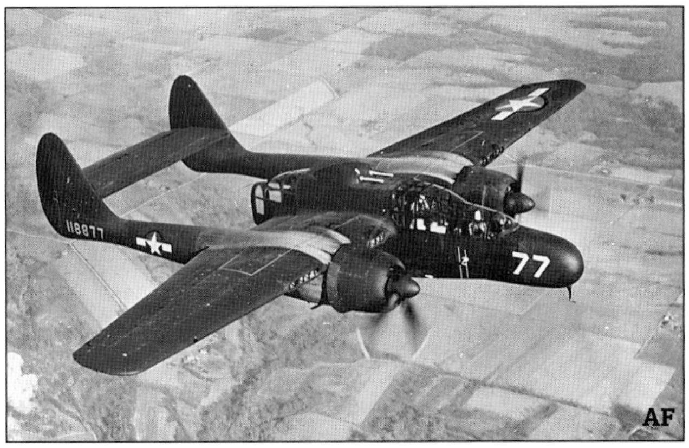

NORTHROP YP-61
Two Pratt & Whitney R-2800-10, 2000 hp takeoff, 2000 hp at 19,000'
DIMENSIONS: Span 66', Lg. 48'11", Ht. 14'3", Wing Area 663 sq. ft.
WEIGHT: Empty 21,910 lb., Gross 27,950 lb., max. 28,830 lb. Fuel 540-640 gal.
PERFORMANCE: As XP-61

Only the first 50 YP-61 and P-61A-1s had top turrets, because tail buffeting troubles and B-29 priority caused turret omission on 327 later ships. Forty-five P-61A-1s were followed by 35 P-61A-5s with provision for water injection, 100 P-61A-10s with the R-2800-65, and 20 P-61A-11s added fixtures for two 165-gallon drop tanks or bombs. Most of these entered service with two crewmen and the glossy paint that went with the Black Widow's official name.

NORTHROP P-65A
Two Pratt & Whitney R-2800-65, 2000 hp takeoff, 1930 hp at 17,000'
DIMENSIONS: Span 66', Lg. 48'11", Ht. 14'8", Wing Area 663 sq. ft.
WEIGHT: Empty 22,300 lb., Gross 29,240 lb. (with turret) . Fuel 640 gal.
PERFORMANCE: Speed-Top 330 mph at s.l., 369 mph at 17,600', Cruising 314 mph. Landing 95 mph. Service Ceiling 32,100', Climb 2610'/1 min., 20,000'/9.6 min. Range 1210 miles at 200 mph.
P-61A-10 without turret:
WEIGHT: Empty 20,965 lb., Gross 27,600 lb. Fuel 640 gal.
PERFORMANCE: Speed- Top 333 mph at s.l., 372 mph at 17,600', Stalling 85 mph. Service Ceiling 33,700', Climb 2920'/1 min., 20,000'/8 min.

Delivery of 163 P-61B-1 to P-61B-10s began in July 1944 with mechanical improvements including SCR-720C radar in a longer nose. The P-61B-10 had underwing fittings for four 1,600-pound bombs, or drop tanks of 165- or 300-gallon size. Four-gun turrets were restored on 286 P-61B-15 to P-61B-20, since the buffeting condition had been improved and turret deliveries had met B-29 needs.

Despite its size, the Black Widow was remarkably maneuverable. Its first success was won by the 6th Night Fighter Squadron, which landed on Saipan with P-61As on June 21, 1944, scored its first victory June 30, and the second July 6. Ten P-61 squadrons were deployed against the Japanese Empire by March 1945, two squadrons entered combat from England in July 1944, and four night fighter squadrons served the 12th Air Force. After the war, a dozen P-61Bs were used by the Marines as F2T-l trainers.

A program to improve performance by using turbosupercharged engines was begun in November 1943 with plans for a P-61C production model, preceded by two XP-61C prototypes prepared by Goodyear, an important Northrop sub-contractor. A P-61A-5 and an A-10 were flown to Akron in May 1944 for modification and, after a engine model change from the planned R-2800-77 altered their designation to XP-61D, flight tests began with 2,800 hp R-2800-57 Wasps and CH-5 turbos in November 1944.

The first P-61C-1 with R-2800-73s was accepted on July 14, 1945, just before V-J Day curtailed production, and only 41 were delivered, the last on January 28, 1946. Top speed had increased from 366 to 430 mph and speed brakes on the wings could prevent the P-61C from overshooting targets, but this model was too late for combat.

The XP-61E was a long-range day fighter with radar and turret removed to provide a smaller, more streamlined

NORTHROP P-61B-15
Two Pratt & Whitney R-2800-65, 2000 hp takeoff, 1930 hp at 17,000'
DIMENSIONS: Span 66', Lg. 49'7", Ht. 14'8", Wing Area 663 sq. ft.
WEIGHT: Empty 22,000 lb., Gross 29,700 lb., max. 38,000 lb. Fuel 640+1240 gal.
PERFORMANCE: Speed- Top 366 mph at 20,000', Cruising 318 mph.,Landing 93 mph. Service Ceiling 33,100', Climb 20,000'/12 min. Range 400 miles/2000 lb. bombs, 3000 miles ferry.

NORTHROP P-61C
Two Pratt & Whitney R-2800-73, 2000 hp takeoff, 2800 hp WE
DIMENSIONS: as P-61B
WEIGHT: Empty 24,000 lb., Gross 30,600 lb., max. 40,300 lb. Fuel 640+1240 gal.
PERFORMANCE: Speed- Top 430 mph at 30,000', Cruising 314 mph, Landing 87 mph. Service Ceiling 41,000', Climb 30,000'/14.6 min. Range 415 miles/4000 lb. bombs, 1725 miles ferry.

NORTHROP XP-61D
Two Pratt & Whitney R-2800-57, 2100 hp takeoff, 2800 hp at 30,000' WE
DIMENSIONS: Span 66', Lg. 48'11", Ht. 14'8", Wing Area 663 sq. ft.
WEIGHT: Empty 23,207 lb., Gross 29,208 lb., max. 39,715 lb. Fuel 606+1240 gal.
PERFORMANCE: Speed- Top 430 mph at 33,000', Landing 90 mph. Service Ceiling 43,000', Climb 30,000'/13.5 min. Range 3000 miles/205 mph ferry.

fuselage. Two crewmen sat under a bubble canopy ahead of a fuselage fuel tank, while four .50-caliber nose guns supplemented the usual four 20-mm belly guns. Converted from a P-61B-10 with R-2800-65 Wasps, the first prototype flew on January 3, 1945. A second prototype was wrecked in April, but the AAF had already decided on the P-82B Twin Mustang as its long-range fighter, and developed the Northrop as a photo-reconnaissance type.

With cameras replacing guns, the XP-61E was modified to the XF-15 and flew on July 3, 1945, while a turbo-supercharged XF-15A, a modified P-61C, flew October 17. Production as the F-15A Reporter was ordered in June

NORTHROP XP-61E
Two Pratt & Whitney R-2800-65, 2000 hp takeoff, 1930 hp at 17,000'
DIMENSIONS: Span 66', Lg. 49'7", Ht. 13'5", Wing Area 662 sq. ft.
WEIGHT: Empty 21,350 lb., Gross 31,425 lb., max. 40,180 lb. Fuel 1158+1240 gal.
PERFORMANCE: Speed- Top 376 mph at 17,000'. Service Ceiling 30,000', Climb 20,000'/13 min. Range 2250 miles normal, 3750 miles ferry.

1945, but post-war deliveries were limited to 36, delivered from September 1946 to April 1947.

The 706 Black Widows served adequately during the war's last year as the standard AAF night fighter. By then the Axis was on the defensive and no saturation raids were met. Generally, P-61s fought alone on their sorties, ambushing individual enemy raiders, and were credited with 127 victories up to the last night of the war. Postwar service continued until 1948, when they were replaced by the Twin Mustang.

America's First Jets

While visiting England in April 1941, Air Force General Henry H. Arnold saw the first jet-propelled British aircraft, the Gloster E28/39. He returned to the U.S. with information about its Whittle engine and on September 4 told General Electric, which had learned much from turbosupercharger experience about the heat-resistant alloys necessary for the whirling turbine blades, to build copies of the jet engine.

The next day, Bell Aircraft, because of its proximity to GE's Schenectady plant and Bell's talent for innovation, was assigned construction of three twin-jet prototypes. For security reasons the first Bell Model 27 airframes were designated XP-59A and the engines the "Type I" series, in hopes of disguising them as the canceled XP-59 pusher and General Electric superchargers.

The XP-59A contract was approved October 3, 1941, and 13 YP-59A interceptors were added on March 26, 1942, for service trials. Work went ahead with great secrecy in a Buffalo factory and Muroc Dry Lake in California was selected to conceal the initial flights. This site later became Edwards Air Force Base, which replaced Wright Field as the center of Air Force flight testing. The prototype was secretly shipped across the country by train, and on October 1, 1941, company test pilot Robert M. Stanley made the first 30-minute wheels-down flight. The next day, Stanley and Colonel Lawrence C. Craigie made the first official shakedown flights.

America's first jet fighter was a single-seat, mid-wing monoplane sitting low on tricycle landing gear. General

BELL XP-59A
Two General Electric I-A 1420 lb. s.t.
DIMENSIONS: Span 49', Lg. 38'10", Ht. 12'4", Wing Area 400 sq. ft.
WEIGHT: Empty 7,320 lb., Gross 10,186 lb. Fuel 290 gal.
PERFORMANCE: Speed- Top 397 mph at s. l., 418 mph at 25,000', Cruising 350 mph, Service Ceiling 41,000', Climb 3200'/min., 20,000'/8.2 min. Range 392 miles.

Electric I-A units under each wing root yielded only 1,250-pounds thrust each, instead of the expected 1,640 pounds. When more engines arrived, the second XP-59A could be flown on February 15, 1943. The top speed of 389 mph at 25,000 feet was below expectations, and newer 1420-lb thrust I-14B engines were installed. Although measured speed flights were not completed, the concluding Air Force report credited the XP-59A with 418 mph.

A sliding canopy, cockpit armor, and various modifications were seen on the YP-59A, the first two delivered to Muroc in June 1943 and first flown on August 13 with I-A engines. An improved engine model called the I-16 (later J31) became available by November and the wingtips were clipped. An unofficial altitude record for fighters of 47,600 feet was set December 15 by the first YP-59A with I-16 engines.

BELL YP-59A
Two General Electric I-16 (J31) 1650 lb. s.t.
DIMENSIONS: Span 45'6", Lg. 38'10", Ht. 12', Wing Area 385 sq. ft.
WEIGHT: Empty 7,626 lb., Gross 10,532 lb., max. 12,562 lb. Fuel 290+300 gal.
PERFORMANCE: Speed- Top 350 mph at s. l., 409 mph at 35,000', Cruising 314 mph, Landing 80 mph. Service Ceiling 43,200', Climb 2970'/min., 36,000'/20.5 min. Range 415 miles.

The third YP-59A went to Britain in September 1943 in trade for a Gloster Meteor, while the U.S. Navy got the 8th and 9th in December. These aircraft had the same two 37-mm guns with 88 rounds mounted in the nose as the prototypes, but the last four YP-59As were completed by August 1944 with the installation standard on later models; one 37-mm M-10 with 45 rounds, three .50-caliber M-2 guns with 600 rounds, and ferry drop tanks under the wings.

Mfr

BELL P-59B-1
Two General Electric J31-GE-5, 2000 lb. s.t.
DIMENSIONS: As P-59A
WEIGHT: Empty 8,165 lb., Gross 11,040 lb., max. 13,700 lb. Fuel 356+300 gal.
PERFORMANCE: As P-59A, but range 525 miles normal, 950 miles ferry.

While performance was inferior to prop fighters like the P-51, and a snaking tendency made them bad gun platforms, it is notable that there were no XP or YP-59A aircraft losses in 242 hours of testing, in spite of the very new technology. These pioneers had demonstrated the practicality of jet propulsion. Three single-engine XP-59Bs were ordered on the same day as the YP-59As, but this program was halted on June 15, 1943, when it became apparent that the I-16 engine was too weak to power an effective single-engine fighter.

A letter contract for 100 production Airacomets was sent to Bell on October 9, 1943, and secrecy was lifted January 7, 1944, with public announcements of the new fighters that flew without propellers. Photographs were not released until after the first P-59A-1 was delivered August 31,1944.

Successful development of Lockheed's P-80 jet fighter caused Bell's order to be cut in half. Twenty P-59A-1s were followed in December 1944 by the first of 30 P-59B-1s accepted by May 1945. The latter model had the J31-GE-5 and 66 gallons more of internal fuel. Most production P-59s went to the 412th Fighter Group at Bakersfield, California, where they gave useful training to future P-80 pilots.

Meanwhile, Germany not only developed jet fighters, but became the first to send them into combat. The world's first jet flight had been made on August 27, 1939, by the Heinkel He 178, and the He 280 twin-jet fighter flew on April 5, 1941. Messerschmitt's Me 262 flew with jets on July 27, 1942, and production deliveries of that 540-mph interceptor began in March 1944.

Mfr

BELL P-59A-1
Two General Electric J31-GE-5, 2000 lb. s.t.
DIMENSIONS: Span 45'6", Lg. 38'10", Ht. 12'4", Wing Area 385 sq. ft.
WEIGHT: Empty 7,950 lb., Gross 10,822 lb., max. 13,000 lb. Fuel 290+300 gal.
PERFORMANCE: Speed- Top 380 mph at 5,000', 413 mph at 30,000', Cruising 375 mph, Landing 80 mph. Service Ceiling 46,200', Climb 10,000'/3.2 min., 30,000'/15.5 min. Range 400 miles normal, 850 miles ferry.

Bell Kingcobra

Although nine new single-seat fighter types were flown in the two years following America's entry into the war, only the P-63, successor to the Bell Airacobra, reached mass production. Built mainly for lend-lease to the Soviet Union, the P-63 Kingcobra did not match the Mustang and Thunderbolt in high-altitude performance, and lacked the range for AAF needs.

The Kingcobra's design evolution began in February 1941, when Bell proposed Models 23 and 24 as improved P-39s with larger wings and alternative Allison and Continental engines. Model 23 became the XP-39E ordered in April and flown early in 1942 with a conventional airfoil section and an Allison V-1710-47 engine with a two-stage supercharger.

Two XP-63 prototypes were ordered on June 27, 1941, with a laminar-flow airfoil and a Continental engine. When progress with the Continental fell behind, in February 1942 the Allison V-1710-47 and square-cut tail of the XP-39E was chosen for the XP-63. Robert M. Stanley flew the first XP-63 on December 7, 1942, one year after the attack on Pearl Harbor.

BELL XP-63
Allison V-1710-47, 1325 hp takeoff, 1150 hp at 22,400'
DIMENSIONS: Span 38'4", Lg. 32'8", Ht. 11'5", Wing Area 248 sq. ft.
WEIGHT: Empty 6054 lb., Gross 7525 lb. Fuel 136+75 gal.
PERFORMANCE: Speed- Top 407 mph at 22,400', Climb 22,400'/7 min.

The Kingcobra's general arrangement was similar to the P-39s, with the Allison behind the pilot and tricycle gear, but the larger P-63 could be distinguished by its square-cut tail, wider wings, and four-bladed propeller. Bell's favorite armament of the 37-mm M-4 cannon with 30 rpg and twin .50-caliber guns with 250 rpg was mounted in the nose.

A production prototype, the XP-63A, had been ordered on September 24, 1942, and a contract for 3,200 production aircraft, Bell Model 33, was approved October 12, 1942. While both XP-63 prototypes were wrecked during tests, the XP-63A was flown on April 26, 1943. This prototype, powered by a V-1710-93 with a two-stage supercharger, added two .50-caliber guns attached under the wings and provided with 200 rpg, 123 pounds of armor, and provisions for a 75-gallon drop tank or 500-pound bomb beneath the fuselage.

Production began with 50 similar P-63A-1s, and when the first seven were accepted in October 1943, the AAF was planning to equip five fighter groups of the Ninth Air Force, based in England, with Kingcobras. But on November 10, 1943, it was decided to use only P-47D and P-51B fighters in all Ninth Air Force groups. Those fighters

BELL P-63A-1
Allison V-1710-93, 1325 hp takeoff, 1150 hp at 22,400' (1390 hp WE)
DIMENSIONS: Span 38'4", Lg. 32'8", Ht. 12'7", Wing Area 248 sq. ft.
WEIGHT: Empty 6030 lb., Gross 8330 lb. Max. 8860 lb. Fuel 136+75 gal.
PERFORMANCE: Speed- Top 372 mph at 10,000', 421 mph at 24,100', Cruising 341 mph, Landing 100 mph. Service Ceiling 44,400', Climb 20,000'/6.5 min. Range 587 miles, 1109 miles ferry.

had superior speed and room in their fuselages for much more fuel. Although P-63As replaced P-39s in AAF fighter groups training in the United States, they never went overseas with AAF units. Instead, the P-63 would fill lend-lease commitments to the USSR.

Weight gradually increased with successive additions to armor and external loads. In January 1944, armor weight increased to 179 pounds for the P-63A-5 block, then to 189 pounds on the A-8, and 199 pounds on the A-9. Beginning with block P-63A-6, two 75-gallon drop tanks or 500-pound bombs could be attached under the wings, and a 64-gallon flush ferry tank could be attached to the belly. In July 1944, ammunition for the new 37-mm M-10 gun was increased to 58 rounds on the P-63A-9. The P-63A-10 had 236 pounds of armor, provision for six rockets in tubes under the wings, and slightly larger stabilizers.

BELL P-63A-9 *en route* to USSR
Allison V-1710-93, 1325 hp takeoff, 1150 hp at 22,400' 1390 hp WE)
DIMENSIONS: As P-63A-1
WEIGHT: Empty 6375 lb., Gross 8815 lb. Max. 10,416 lb. Fuel 126+225 gal.
PERFORMANCE: Speed-Top 361 mph at 5000', 408 mph at 24,450', Cruising 378 mph, Landing 100 mph. Service Ceiling 43,000', Climb 25,000'/7.3 min. Range 450 miles/500 lb. bomb, 2575 miles ferry.

Except for three P-63A-6s shipped to North Russia in February 1944, most Kingcobras were flown to Alaska and turned over at Ladd Field to Soviet pilots, who then flew them to Siberia. On June 14, the first P-63A-7s began arriving at Ladd, but turnover to the Russians was delayed by mechanical problems. Another interruption to deliveries

Mfr

BELL P-63D
Allison V-1710-109, 1425 hp takeoff, 1100 hp at 29,000' (1300 hp WE)
DIMENSIONS: Span 39'2", Lg. 32'8", Ht. 11'2", Wing Area 255 sq. ft.
WEIGHT: Empty 7076 lb., Gross 9054 lb. Max. 11,044 lb. Fuel 168+225 gal.
PERFORMANCE: Speed- Top 437 mph at 30,000', Cruising 188 mph, Landing 91 mph. Service Ceiling 39,000', Climb 28,000'/11.2 min. Range 700 miles normal, 2000 miles ferry.

happened on October 7, when a serious rear fuselage weakness grounded the P-63A-10 until 223 aircraft in transit were modified, and deliveries resumed.

Of 1,725 P-63A models completed by December 1944, 1,324 had been turned over to the USSR, and a P-63A-6 reached the RAF in May 1944, followed later by a P-63A-9. From January to June 1945 Bell delivered 1,227 P-63Cs, which had the V-1710-117, 201 pounds of armor, an extended fin under the tail, and 1,076 went to the USSR.

The last two P-63C-5s reached Siberia in August 1945, just before Japan surrendered. Although 21 Kingcobras were lost in transit in North America, they were replaced, so that the Red Army Air Force received 2,400 of the 3,303 built by Bell, including experimental and target types. Most VVS fighter missions were less than two hours, so the limited fuel capacity was not a problem, and the wing guns were often omitted in Soviet service.

Mfr

BELL P-63C-5 for France
Allison V-1710-117, 1325 hp takeoff, 1100 hp at 27,000'
DIMENSIONS: As P-63A-1
WEIGHT: Empty 6856 lb., Gross 8640 lb., Max. 10,813 lb. Fuel 126+225 gal.
PERFORMANCE: Speed- Top 418 mph at 28,500', Cruising 356 mph, Landing 115 mph. Service Ceiling 38,600', Climb 25,000'/8.6 min. Range 320 miles/500 lb. bomb, 2100 miles ferry.

All this production and delivery effort resulted in the destruction of only one Axis plane, a Japanese fighter shot down during the invasion of Manchuria. The first P-63A regiment, the 28th IAP, was part of the Moscow area PVO, but there had been no raids on Moscow for three years. Most Kingcobras were still in Siberia when Germany had been defeated in May 1945. For the war against Japan in August, they equipped the 190th and 245th fighter air divisions (IAD) on the Transbaikal Front, while the 410th and 88th IAPs on Kamchata supported the attack on the Kuriles, and P-63s served the Soviet Pacific Fleet's 7th IAD. That division's 17th IAP scored the Kingcobras sole recorded victory over a Japanese fighter on August 15, 1945.

After the war, P-63s were flown by several VVS divisions and naval fighter regiments, until replaced by MiG-15 jets. As late as 1952, the P-63C was involved in Cold War episodes, when eight were destroyed by P-80s strafing a VVS base near Vladivostok, and those with a Soviet fighter regiment in Siberia unsuccessfully attempted to intercept RB-47 spy planes.

France also had the P-63C-5, receiving 114 from April to July 1945 as the war ended in Europe. From August 1949 to April 1951, four French groups flew ground support missions in Viet Nam.

Other P-63 Models

But the most unique versions were those built as manned aerial targets. Beginning with the first RP-63A-11 flown on September 1, 1944, combat equipment was removed, and a 1,488-pound extra-thick skin applied to shatter frangible dummy bullets fired by student gunners. A red nose light blinked like a pinball machine when hits were felt. One hundred RP-63A and 200 RP-63C target planes were built during the war to train bomber gunners, followed by 32 RP-63Gs after the war.

Efforts to improve the Kingcobra began with an XP-63B proposal to use the Packard V-1650-5 offering 1,300 hp at 24,000 feet, but when efforts to perfect the extension shaft and gears faltered, an Allison V-1710-109 was chosen for the single P-63D, or Bell Model 37. Featuring a bubble canopy and modified wing tips, the P-63D was followed in May 1945 by 13 P-63Es (Model 41) with the standard cockpit doors. Contracts for 2,930 more were canceled by the war's end. A tall tail and the 1,500-hp V-1710-133 distinguished the two P-63Fs, whose specification promised a 449-mph speed, but actual test results have not been located.

BELL P-63E
Allison V-1710-109, 1425 hp takeoff, 1100 hp at 29,000' (1300 hp WE)
DIMENSIONS: Span 39'2", Lg. 32'8", Ht. 12'9", Wing Area 255 sq. ft.
WEIGHT: Empty 7300 lb., Gross 9397 lb. Max. 11,033 lb. Fuel 126+225 gal.
PERFORMANCE: Speed- Top 410 mph at 25,000', Cruising 188 mph, Landing 117 mph. Climb 25,000'/7.6 min. Range 725 miles/500 lb. bomb, 2150 miles ferry.

BELL P-63F

After the war, P-63As were reworked for numerous tests, including those of a V-shaped "butterfly" tail, swept-back wings, and a second cockpit for instrument training. A P-63E became an XP-63H when testing a V-1710-127 engine. Five P-39Es found their way to Honduras in 1948.

Later Wartime Prototypes

Experimental fighters described so far have been those ordered by the end of fiscal 1941 (June 30, 1941), the federal fiscal year in which Air Force expansion gathered impetus toward wartime goals. Although the 1942 fiscal year added more fighter projects, production programs received higher priorities, and experimental ships lagged. After the Pearl Harbor attack only unusually high priority prototypes like the XP-59A jet and XP-61 night fighter were finished in less than 18 months. Other projects drifted for two or three years, with the longest gestation being the XP-58's four years.

An example of this delay is the twin-engine single-seat monoplane that began the career of the now well-known McDonnell Aircraft Corporation of St. Louis. The company begun by James S. McDonnell (1899-1980) had offered a fighter design for the R40-C competition in April 1940. Twin pusher propellers behind the wings were to be driven by an Allison V-3420 engine in the fuselage.

That proposal was rejected, but a new long-range fighter design was assigned the XP-67 designation on July 29,1941, and a contract was approved October 29, 1941, for two prototypes, the first to be delivered in 18 months. A fuselage, center section, and engine nacelles shaped to blend with the wing's laminar flow airfoil gave the XP-67 a unique appearance, and contained large fuel tanks, pressurized cockpit, tricycle landing gear, and six 37-mm fixed guns with 45 rpg. Two turbosupercharged Continental XIV-1430s drove four-bladed propellers and used their exhausts for extra thrust.

The XP-67 was first flown on January 6 , 1944, by Ed Elliot, but engine performance was unsatisfactory. In 1941,

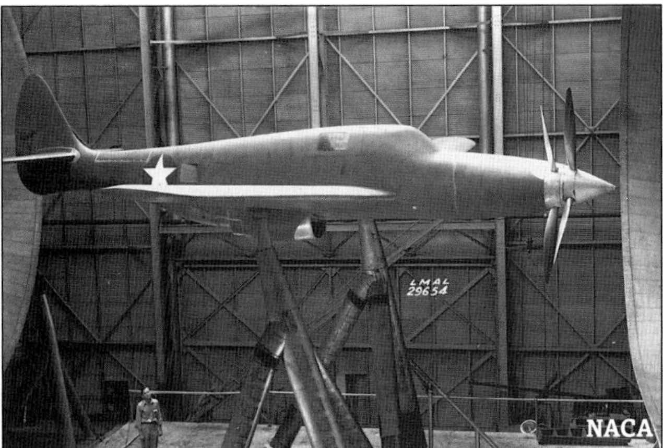

REPUBLIC XP-69 (Mockup)
Wright R-2160-3, 2350 hp at 25,000'
DIMENSIONS: Span 51'8", Lg. 51'6", Ht. 17'3", Wing Area 505 sq. ft.
WEIGHT: Empty 15,595 Lb., Gross 18,655 lb., Max. 26,165 lb. Fuel 240-700 gal. (1300 gal. ferry).
PERFORMANCE: Speed- Top 450 mph at 35,000', Cruising 260 mph. Service Ceiling 48,900', Climb 35,000'/20 min. Range 780 miles normal, 3000 miles ferry.

AF

McDONNELL XP-67
Two Continental XI-1430-17,-19, 1350 hp takeoff, 1600 hp at 25,000'
DIMENSIONS: Span 55', Lg. 44'9", Ht. 15'9", Wing Area 414 sq. ft.
WEIGHT: Empty 17,745 lb., Gross 22,114 lb., Max. 25,400 lb. Fuel 280-735 gal.
PERFORMANCE: Speed— Top 405 mph at 25,000', Cruising 270 mph, Landing 93 mph. Service Ceiling 37,400', Climb 2600'/1 min., 25,000'/17 min. Range 700 miles normal, 2385 miles ferry.

a 472-mph top speed with an 18,600-pound gross weight had been guaranteed. By 1944, the weight was 22,000 pounds and the speed estimated at 448 mph at 25,000 feet and 367 mph at sea level. But tests limited actual top speed to only 405 mph. After an engine fire on September 6 ended 43 hours of flight tests, the second example was canceled and the XP-67 abandoned.

The next two single-seat fighter designs were begun in September 1941 around the proposed 2,350-hp Wright R-2160 Tornado, a 42-cylinder, liquid-cooled six-row radial with contra rotating propellers. Vultee's XP-68 was similar to their XP-54 pusher, but the XP-69, begun as Republic's Model AP-18, had the engine behind the pilot with an extension shaft to the nose.

An air intake for cooling was placed under the XP-69's fuselage, and a pressurized cockpit and laminar wing were planned. Proposed armament was two 37-mm and four 50-caliber wing guns. Neither type was completed, as the XP-68 was canceled November 22, 1941, and while the XP-69 reached mockup inspection in June 1942, it was canceled May 11, 1943, when the engine program died.

The Curtiss-Wright XP-71 would have been the largest fighter plane built in America, if it had ever been finished. The idea of firing a 75-mm cannon from a plane had been proven on a B-18 bomber in 1940 and the Curtiss-Wright Corporation of St. Louis submitted fighter design studies in April 1941. By October a detailed prototype proposal was ready and designated XP-71 on October 28, 1941.

Mfr

CURTISS XP-71 (model)
Two Pratt & Whitney R-4360-13, 3000 hp takeoff, 2800 hp at 25,000'
DIMENSIONS: Span 82'3", Lg. 61'10", Ht. 19', Wing Area 602 sq. ft.
WEIGHT: Empty 31,060 lb., Gross 39,950 lb., Max. 46,950 lb. Fuel 900-1940 gal.
PERFORMANCE: Speed- Top 428 mph at 25,000', Cruising 270 mph, Landing 97 mph. Service Ceiling 40,000', Climb 25,000'/12.5 min. Range 3000 miles ferry.

Uncertainty about delivery of the fire-control system delayed approval of the contract for two prototypes until

March 6, 1942. When the mockup was inspected at St. Louis on November 16, 1942, the XP-71 was to have two 3,450-hp turbosupercharged R-4360-13 Wasp Majors turning contra rotating pusher propellers, a pressurized cockpit for two, a 75-mm gun in the nose with 20 rounds for automatic feed, and two 37-mm weapons with 60 rpg.

The 1942 specification proposed a 35,670-pound gross weight, a wing span of 77 feet and a top speed of 428 mph at 25,000 feet, but the size grew to 39,950 pounds and 82 feet. By August 26, 1943, Air Force leaders realized that long-range enemy bombers were no longer a threat, but our own bombers needed protection. Enemy fighters would never stand still long enough to be hit by slow-firing guns on a plane as big as the XP-71. The cannon could best be used against enemy shipping, a mission more suitable for low-altitude attack planes rather than a high-altitude fighters.

Only 21% complete, the XP-71 was finally canceled October 23, 1943, but a photo of the wind tunnel model is included to show what the largest American fighter would have looked like.

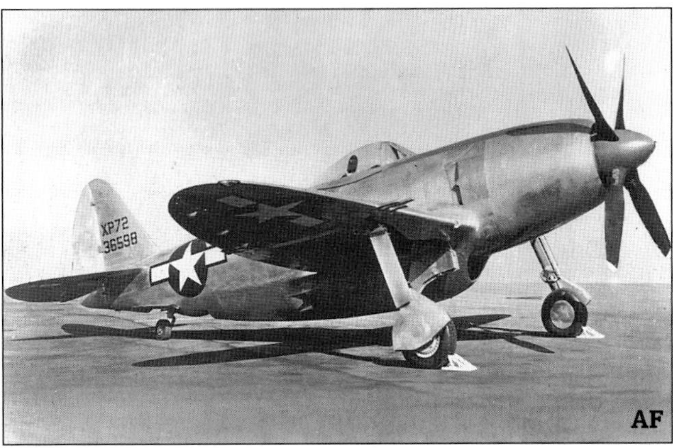

REPUBLIC XP-72
Pratt & Whitney R-4360-13, 3450 hp takeoff, 3000 hp at 25,000' (WE ratings)
DIMENSIONS: Span 40"1", Lg. 36'7", Ht. 12'4", Wing Area 300 sq. ft.
WEIGHT: Empty 11,476 lb., Gross 15,313 lb., Max. 17,492 lb. Fuel 370+300 gal.
PERFORMANCE: Speed- Top 405 mph at s.l., 490 mph at 25,000', Cruising 300 mph, Stalling 104 mph. Service Ceiling 42,000', Climb 15,000'/3.5 min. Range 1300 miles normal, 1530 miles ferry.

Republic XP-72

When Republic began work in September 1941 on the XP-69 with a Wright R-2160, it also studied a Model AP-19 designed at the same time around the Pratt & Whitney Wasp Major radial engine. No urgency was attached to the project until the Air Force realized that the Wright power plant was not going to be ready on time and that the air-cooled Wasp Major had better prospects. After the XP-69 was canceled, two XP-72 interceptor prototypes were ordered June 18, 1943.

Powered by an 3,450-hp R-4360-13 with a four-bladed propeller and a gear-driven supercharger, the XP-72 was similar in appearance to the P-47 except for the enlarged landing gear and air scoop under the fuselage. Six 50-caliber wing guns with 267 rpg and 3/8-inch cockpit armor was provided, as well as wing racks for two 1,000-pound bombs or 150-gallon drop tanks to increase the radius of action to 735 miles.

The first XP-72 flew on February 2, 1944, while the second one was flown June 26 with an R-4360-19 and six-bladed contra props. A plan to build 100 production P-72s was dropped when it was learned that jet propulsion would provide even faster fighters.

General Motors P-75

General Motors, the largest American auto manufacturer, had established a New Jersey branch to build Grumman aircraft, but the name recognition of producing its own design was attractive. In January 1942 Don R. Berlin, who designed the P-40, was hired to plan a fighter using the V-3420-19 of that company's Allison engine division.

A proposal presented at Wright Field on September 10 resulted in a letter contract dated October 10, 1942, for two XP-75 prototypes to be built in Detroit. How the P-75 designation was chosen isn't clear, for no P-73 or P-74 was assigned, although P-73 had been suggested for the Hughes D-2 in June 1942. Perhaps symbolism was a motive; the French 75-mm cannon in World War I, P-75 in World War II.

The largest liquid-cooled engine available mounted behind the pilot, Airacobra-style, drove two co-axial, three-bladed props in the nose with twin power shafts. To speed development, parts from aircraft already in production were used, including Curtiss P-40 outer wings, the Douglas A-24 tail section, and the Vought F4U landing gear. Armament included four .50-caliber synchronized nose guns with 300 rpg, six .50-caliber wing guns with 235 rpg, two 1,000-pound bombs, and 177-pounds of cockpit armor. The October 13, 1942, specification promised a top speed of 426 mph at 20,000 feet.

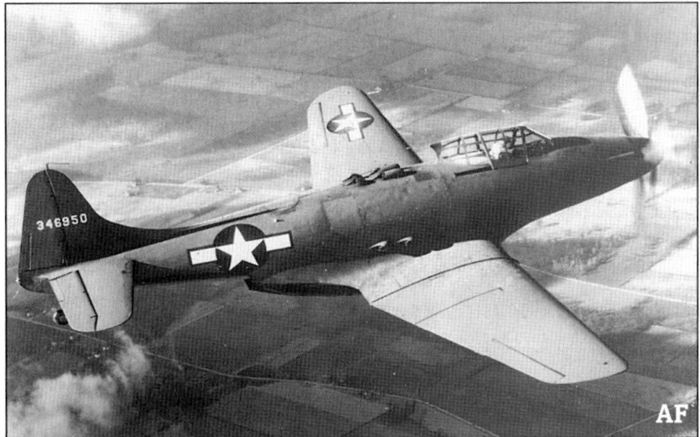

GENERAL MOTORS XP-75-GM
Allison V-3420-19, 2600 hp takeoff, 2300 hp at 20,000' (WE ratings)
DIMENSIONS: Span 49'1", Lg. 39'10", Ht. 15'6", Wing Area 342 sq. ft.
WEIGHT: Empty 9,883 lb., Gross 12,250 lb., Max. 16,007 lb. Fuel 210-511+150 gal.
PERFORMANCE: Speed- Top 429 mph at 25,000', Landing 88 mph. Service Ceiling 40,500', Climb 20,000'/4.1 min. Range 1227 miles normal, 2437 miles ferry.

Even before the XP-75-GM began flight tests, General Oliver P. Echols, Chief of Materiel Command, met with Don Berlin on July 6, 1943, to decide how the P-75 might meet the pressing need for an escort fighter to protect long-range bombers. It was decided to order six XP-75-GC preproduction prototypes with increased fuel capacity and production V-3420-23 engines. A letter of intent was written July 8, 1943, to produce 2,500 P-75A-GCs at the General Motors Fisher Body plant in Cleveland, originally built to make B-29 parts. The Air Force was told it would get the first P-75A-1 in May 1944, and have 586 by the end of October, with 250 delivered each month.

GENERAL MOTORS XP-75-GC
Allison V-3420-23, 2600 hp takeoff, 2300 hp at 20,000'(WE ratings)
DIMENSIONS: Span 49'4", Lg. 40'5", Ht. 15'6", Wing Area 342 sq. ft.
WEIGHT: Empty 11,495 lb., Gross 13,807 lb., Max. 18,210 lb. Fuel 535+220 gal.
PERFORMANCE: Speed- Top 389 mph at s.l. 433 mph at 20,000', Cruising 314 mph, Landing 88 mph. Service Ceiling 36,400', Climb 20,000'/5 min. Range 2050 miles normal, 3500 miles ferry.

GENERAL MOTORS P-75A-GC
Allison V-3420-23, 2600 hp takeoff, 2300 hp at 20,000' (WE ratings)
DIMENSIONS: Span 49'4", Lg. 41'4", Ht. 15'6", Wing Area 342 sq. ft.
WEIGHT: Empty 11,255 lb., Gross 17,875 lb., Max. 19,420 lb. Fuel 210-638+220 gal.
PERFORMANCE: Speed- Top 404 mph at 22,000', Cruising 250 mph, Landing 87 mph. Service Ceiling 38,000', Climb 20,000'/8.8 min. Range 1100 miles normal, 3150 miles/638 gal., 3850 miles ferry.

Flight tests started November 17, 1943, showed the XP-75 suffering from instability, low rate of roll, poor spinning characteristics, and trouble with the engine, (actually two V-1710s joined side by side). Redesign of the six Cleveland prototypes replaced the A-24 tail and improved things somewhat, but spoiled the quick-production advantage of the original components. Tests began at Cleveland in February, and the fifth XP-75 crashed on April 8.

The first production P-75A-1 "Fisher Eagle" was not flown until September 15, 1944, proved 30 mph below the guaranteed speed, and had a fatal crash on October 10. The P-75A program was terminated October 27, reducing production to only six aircraft. Fortunately the P-51 had solved the long-range fighter problem, but the XP-75 contract had cost $9,373,629, and the P-75 production fiasco millions more.

Bell XP-77

The last propeller-driven single-seat fighter prototype built for the Air Force, apart from P-47 and P-51 developments, was also the smallest and lightest type flown since the P-29. Emerging from the impression made by the maneuverability of Japan's Zero fighter, and a shortage of strategic metals, the XP-77 was a lightweight single-seater of wooden construction.

BELL XP-77
Ranger V-770-7, 520 hp at takeoff, 670 hp WE
DIMENSIONS: Span 27'6", Lg. 22'10", Ht. 8'2". Wing Area 100 sq. ft.
WEIGHT: Empty 2855 lb., Gross 3671 lb., Max. 3989 lb. Fuel 52-90 gal.
PERFORMANCE: Speed- Top 330 mph at 4,000', 328 mph at 12,600', Cruising 274 mph, Landing 92 mph. Service Ceiling 30,100', Climb 3600'/1 min., 9,000'/3.7 min. Range 305 miles at 330 mph, 990 miles ferry.

Designed to beat both the metal shortage and the Zero, the Bell Model 32 specification dated April 1, 1942, planned to use a 520-hp air-cooled, inline Ranger, modified to a supercharged XV-770-17 version with 670 hp. Procurement was authorized May 16, 1942, and after inspection of the mockup in September, a contract for six prototypes were approved October 10, 1942. A top speed of 350 mph at 8,500 feet was estimated, gross weight at only 3,700 pounds, and delivery was to begin in six months.

Ranger V-770-6 engines diverted from Navy stocks, until a more advanced model became available, were redesignated V-770-7. The only all-wood American fighter,

BELL XP-77 (2nd prototype)

the XP-77 had a sharply-tapered low wing, tricycle landing gear, two-bladed propeller, and a plastic canopy. Two .50-caliber synchronized guns with 200 rpg, a 77-pound armored seat and a 300-pound bomb were included. A planned 20-mm gun firing through the propeller shaft was omitted after 1943.

Long delayed by troubles with the sub-contracted wood construction, the contract was cut back in August 26, 1943, to two aircraft, the first flown on April 1, 1944. The basic concept that a small maneuverable fighter could be produced of non-strategic materials at less than average cost and time was not borne out. Performance fell below the estimates and a low-speed fighter that cannot force an enemy to do battle does not fit offensive combat tactics.

CHAPTER 19

NAVY PATROL BOMBERS, 1935-1945

DOUGLAS YOA-5
Two Wright YR-1820-45, 930 hp at takeoff, 860 hp at 3200' / DIMENSIONS: Span 89'9", Lg. 69'9", Ht. 21', Wing Area 1101 sq. ft. / WEIGHT: Empty 14,038 lb., Gross 20,813 lb. Fuel 700-1150 gal. / PERFORMANCE: Speed- Top 170 mph at 2800', Cruising 152 mph, Landing 75 mph. Service Ceiling 18,500', Climb 10,000'/13 min.

The wartime mission of the Navy is control of the sea. Shore-based patrol planes serve to discover the movements of enemy forces and attack those targets vulnerable to individual aircraft. From ten patrol squadrons in 1935, the Navy expanded to 112 patrol squadrons on January 1, 1945. The world-wide commitments of the Navy's war also demanded improvement of the performance and fighting ability of the patrol bomber.

A generous quantity of struts had been necessary to support the wings of Navy patrol planes before the perfection of cantilever, internally-braced wings made more streamlined design possible. Douglas Aircraft, of Santa Monica, California, built parallel prototypes for the Army and Navy developed as enlargements of the Dolphin amphibian.

An Army contract on December 7, 1932, called for an amphibian designated YB-11 with two Wright Cyclones. Since it was intended for long-range reconnaissance and carried no bombs, it became the YO-44 when the mockup was inspected in April 1933, and was designated YOA-5 when first flown in January 1935. The main wheels retracted into the hull, whose cabin enclosed five crewmen. Three .30-caliber guns were provided; one in a manual turret set back behind an open mooring hatch in the bow, and two for open gunners' hatches behind the wings.

Tests began at Wright Field in February and after October 1935 the Douglas YOA-5 was stationed at Langley Field. With 930-hp YR-1820-45s mounted in conical nacelles above the cantilever wings, it set world distance records for amphibians. As the first plane to land at Alaska's new Elmendorf Field, on November 8, 1940, the Army's YOA-5 remained to survey the Aleutian islands for future wartime landing sites.

Engineering studies for a larger Navy version had been ordered on May 20, 1933, and on February 16, 1934, the Navy exercised its option for construction of an XP3D-1 flying boat. First flown on February 6, 1935, it was similar to the YOA-5, but was powered by two Pratt & Whitney R-1830-58 Wasps, and had no landing wheels.

DOUGLAS XP3D-1
Two Pratt & Whitney R-1830-58, 825 hp at s. l.
DIMENSIONS: Span 95', Lg. 69'10", Ht. 22'5", Wing Area 1295 sq. ft.
WEIGHT: Empty 13,799 lb., Gross 21,346 lb., Max. 26,662 lb. Fuel 500-1667 gal.
PERFORMANCE: Speed- Top 161 mph at s. l., Landing 57 mph, Service Ceiling 18,500'. Climb 5,000'/7.1 min. Range 1900 miles normal, 3530 miles max.

Metal covered the hull and forward part of the wings, while fabric covered the rear wings and moveable control surfaces. Four .30-caliber guns, one in the first enclosed bow turret on an American patrol plane, two for the rear hatches, and one tunnel gun, were carried along with a 2,000-pound bomb load and five crewmen.

That model was not ordered by the Navy, since the Consolidated PBY offered better performance at a lower price. The Douglas prototype was rebuilt as XP3D-2 and flown to San Diego on May 15, 1936. Raised to the fuselage's top, the wing had R-1830-64 Wasps on the leading

DOUGLAS XP3D-2
Two Pratt & Whitney R-1830-64, 900 hp at takeoff, 850 hp at 8000'
DIMENSIONS: Span 95', Lg. 69'7", Ht. 22'5", Wing Area 1295 sq. ft.
WEIGHT: Empty 15,120 lb., Gross 22,909 lb., Max. 27,946 lb. Fuel 500-1620 gal.
PERFORMANCE: Speed- Top 161 mph at s. l., 183 mph at 8000', Landing 63 mph, Service Ceiling 18,900'. Climb 5,000'/6.1 min. Range 2050 miles normal, 3580 miles max.

Waist Gun
The open .30-caliber gun mount on the XP3Y-1 in 1935.

edge, increased incidence from five to seven degrees, and had the outboard floats retracting inwardly.

A new nose turret and both rear hatches could use either .30 or .50-caliber guns, and a Mark XV bombsight for two to four 1,000-pound bombs was provided. The cabin accommodated six crewmen, radio and navigation gear, and four rest bunks. Again, Consolidated won the year's patrol contract, but the XP3D-2 served VP-11 until a February 1937 crash. Russia and Japan each bought two of a 1937 transport version called the DF, before Douglas gave up on flying boats.

The Catalina

Consolidated's success with the P2Y series led to the design that was the principal Allied flying boat of World War II, and the PBY Catalina also became the most widely used flying boat in history.

Isaac M. Laddon designed the Consolidated Model 28 as a all-metal monoplane with two Pratt & Whitney Twin Wasps, the new 14-cylinder twin-row R-1830-58 giving 800 hp at sea level. Careful attention was paid to streamlining, even to having the outboard floats fold upward to become wing tips. The wings, mounted high on a pylon to clear the water, were metal except for fabric covering behind the rear spar and contained integral fuel tanks.

This design was submitted to the Navy on December 29, 1932, and an XP3Y-1 prototype was ordered June 16, 1933, for a $225,000 price. Two weeks later, the National Industrial Recovery Act precipitated a reduction of the work week in the Buffalo factory from 52 to 40 hours with the same pay. Total costs rose to $474,000 by the time the flying boat was shipped by train to Anacostia, and first flown March 21, 1935, by William B. Wheatley.

Mfr

CONSOLIDATED XP3Y-1
Two Pratt & Whitney R-1830-58, 825 hp at s. l.
DIMENSIONS: Span 104', Lg. 63'6", Ht. 18'6", Wing Area 1400 sq. ft.
WEIGHT: Empty 12,512 lb., Gross 19,793 lb., Max. 24,803 lb. Fuel 1750 gal.
PERFORMANCE: Speed- Top 169 mph at s. l., Landing 58 mph. Service ceiling 18,600', Climb 5000'/4.1 min. Range 2070 miles normal, 4270 miles max.

Consolidated's offer of a lower production price than that of Douglas won the largest Navy contract since World War I, $6,540,000 for 60 aircraft plus 20% spare parts, on June 29, 1935. Company president Reuben Fleet moved

Mfr

Waist Gun
The .50-caliber gun and armor of the PBY-5 blister in 1942.

his firm to San Diego to escape the Buffalo winter climate that had often blocked flight testing. In the new factory at Lindbergh Field, the prototype, which had set a new world's distance record for seaplanes on its way to California, was modified and flown again by April 4, 1936.

A new designation, XPBY-l, assigned on May 21, 1936, reflected the Mark XV Norden bomb sight and 4,000-pound load that added bomber to the patrol mission. Its configuration now included a rotating nose turret, modified rudder, a tunnel gun, and new Pratt & Whitney R-1830-64 Wasps giving 850 hp at 8,000 feet and 900 hp for takeoff. The improvements were needed because Douglas had also modified its prototype into the XP3D-2, with the same engines and retractable floats. But the XPBY-l was favored, and the Navy ordered 50 PBY-2s July 25, 1936.

CONSOLIDATED XPBY-1

On October 9, 1936, the first production PBY-l was flown from San Diego Bay by Wheatley, who would test all the new PBY models until 1940. The first full squadron, VP-6, flew 12 PBY-1s from San Diego to Hawaii on January 28, 1937; 2,553 miles in 21 hours, 43 minutes. Newly-organized VP-11 made the second delivery to Pearl Harbor in April, and turned over 12 PBY-1s to VP-8. These unprecedented direct non-stop deliveries were becoming routine when VP-3 flew its dozen PBY-1s 3,087 miles to Coco Solo in the Canal Zone.

Sixty PBY-ls completed by June 1937 were followed by 50 PBY-2s, similar except for modified elevators and exhausts. The first PBY-2 was flown on May 10, and went to VP-11, with the rest delivered to VP-2, -10, and -17 by February 1938. Crew space included the nose section for a gunner-bomb aimer, the flight deck for the pilot and copilot with instruments and automatic pilot, the cabin behind them for the navigator and the radio operator, a flight engineer up in the pylon, three rest bunks and galley, and the deck gunners' section.

A .30-caliber M-2 gun with 1,000 rpg was provided for the front turret, two more were mounted at the sliding waist hatches, and another with 500 rpg was aimed through a tunnel opening in the hull's bottom rear. Alternately, .50-caliber

CONSOLIDATED PBY-2
Two Pratt & Whitney R-1830-64, 900 hp takeoff, 850 hp at 8000'
DIMENSIONS: As PBY-1
WEIGHT: Empty 14,186 lb., Gross 21,747 lb., Max. 26,832 lb. Fuel 1570-1750 gal.
PERFORMANCE: Speed- Top 165 mph at s. l., 178 mph at 8000', Cruising 105 mph, Landing, 68 mph. Service Ceiling 21,100', Climb 860'/1 min. Range 2131 miles normal, 1242 miles/2000 lb. bombs, 4170 miles max.

Mfr

CONSOLIDATED PBY-1
Two Pratt & Whitney R-1830-64, 900 hp takeoff, 850 hp at 8000'
DIMENSIONS: Span 104', Lg. 65'2", Ht. 18'6", Wing Area 1400 sq. ft.
WEIGHT: Empty 14,576 lb., Gross 22,336 lb., Max. 28,447 lb. Fuel 1570-1750 gal.
PERFORMANCE: Speed- Top 164 mph at s. l., 177 mph at 8000', Cruising 105 mph, Landing 67 mph. Service ceiling 20,900', Climb 840'/1 min. Range 2115 miles normal, 1210 miles/2000 pound bombs, 4042 miles max.

guns and 800 rounds could be mounted in the waist if adapters were used. Under wing racks could accept four 325-pound Mark 17 depth charges, 500 or 1,000-pound bombs, or two 1,935-pound Mark 13 torpedoes.

An explorer, Richard Archbold, was allowed to order a civilian PBY-1 (Model 28-l) on January 27, 1937, and on February 28, the Soviet Union purchased three Model 28-2 cargo-mail boats, along with a license to build them in Russia. Archbold's PBY, called the Guba, was first flown on June 4,1937, but was sold on August 18 to the Soviet Union for an attempt to find a Russian crew lost in the Arctic. A second Guba (28-3), ready for Archbold by December 3, was used to explore New Guinea in 1938, was flown around the world, and sold to British Overseas Airways in October 1940.

The first Soviet Model 28-2 was flown on October 26, 1937, and delivered in December with the parts for the others for assembly in Taganrog, Russia. These were the only PBYs using Wright engines, R-1820-G3 Cyclones rated at 840 hp at 8,700 feet; Wright engines were chosen because they were already in Soviet production.

Mfr

CONSOLIDATED 28-2 for USSR

The PBYs were known as GSTs in Soviet aviation, and 27 Taganrog boats were built by 1940 with the front cargo hatch replaced by a Soviet-designed front turret, and cold-weather cowls often enclosed the M-62 engines. In June 1941, seven GSTs were attached to the Northern Fleet's 118th MRAP (Marine Reconnaissance Air Regiment), 11 to the Black Sea Fleet's 80th RAE squadron, and the others to Aeroflot bases in Siberia. Two flew the 37 members of General Gromov's lend-lease delegation to Seattle on September 4, 1941.

Petrov

GST of Soviet Navy (VVS-VMF)

Sixty-six PBY-3s with 1,000-hp R-1830-66 Wasps were ordered by the U.S. Navy on November 27, 1936, and the first was flown on October 11, 1937, with the rest delivered from March to August 1938. Their engine air intakes had been moved from the bottom to the tops of the cowlings for the down-draft carburetors.

Mfr

CONSOLIDATED PBY-3
Two Pratt & Whitney R-1830-66, 1050 hp takeoff, 900 hp at 10,000'
DIMENSIONS: As PBY-l
WEIGHT: Empty 14,657 lb., Gross 22,713 lb., Max. 28,863 lb. Fuel 1570-l750 gal.
PERFORMANCE: Speed- Top 171 mph at s. l., 191 mph at 12,000', Cruising 114 mph, Landing, 67 mph. Service Ceiling 24,400', Climb 930'/1 min. Range 2175 miles normal, 1258 miles/2000 lb. bombs, 4170 miles max.

Only 33 PBY-4s were ordered December 18, 1937, because the Navy began shifting funds to the new Martin

Mfr

CONSOLIDATED XPBY-5A
Two Pratt & Whitney R-1830-72, 1050 hp takeoff, 900 hp at 12,000'
DIMENSIONS: As PBY-l
WEIGHT: Empty 17,367 lb., Gross 24,817 lb., Max. 29,902 lb. Fuel 1570 gal.
PERFORMANCE: Speed- Top 171 mph at s. l., 192 mph at 12,000', Stalling 77 mph. Service Ceiling 20,200', Climb 850'/1 min.

USN

CONSOLIDATED PBY-4
Two Pratt & Whitney R-1830-72, 1050 hp takeoff, 900 hp at 12,000'
DIMENSIONS: As PBY-l
WEIGHT: Empty 14,819 lb., Gross 22,572 lb., Max. 32,011 lb. Fuel 1570-1750 gal.
PERFORMANCE: Speed- Top 176 mph at s. l., 197 mph at 12,000', Cruising 115 mph, Stalling, 71 mph. Service Ceiling 24,100, Climb 870'/1 min. Range 2070 miles normal, 1285 miles/2000 lb. bombs, 4430 miles max.

PBM type. The first PBY-4 was flown April 21, 1938, with R-1830-72 Wasps yielding 1,050 hp for takeoff, and prop spinners not seen on other PBYs. From October 1938 to March 1939, the next 28 PBY-4s were accepted, leaving delivery of the last four deferred for special modification.

A single Model 28-5 ordered on January 30, 1939, by the Royal Air Force with R-1830-SlC3C engines and standard PBY configuration first flew on June 14 and began the first trans-Atlantic flight delivery of a military aircraft on July 10. At that time, its long range impressed the

Mfr

CONSOLIDATED 28-5 for RAF (1939)
Two Pratt & Whitney S1C3G, 1200 hp takeoff, 1050 hp at 7,500'
DIMENSIONS: As PBY-l
WEIGHT: Empty 14,539 lb., Gross 27,000 lb. Fuel 1570-1750 gal.
PERFORMANCE: Speed- Top 199 mph at 7,500', Cruising 114 mph, Stalling, 68 mph. Service Ceiling 23,700', Climb 5000'/5.5 min. Range 3920 miles/1570 gal., 4290 miles max.

British, but their own Sunderland boats were faster and better protected. Only after the war began were more PBYs ordered for long-distance patrols.

A commercial version, the 28-4, was obtained by American Export Airlines in March 1939, and taken into the U.S. Navy in 1942. Another transport version was a PBY-3 rebuilt as the 30-passenger "Sea Horse" at Coco Solo in July 1943, and several PBY-5s also became converted transports in 1943.

Large transparent blisters at the waist would provide much better scanning and .50-caliber gun movement than the previous open hatches. After trials of wooden mock-ups on the first PBY-4 in October 1938, three of the last boats were fitted with the new enclosures and a straight rudder trailing edge and flight tests began May 8, 1939. The top speed was only slightly reduced from 197 to 195 mph.

Another big step towards wartime roles was the conversion of the last PBY-4 to the XPBY-5A amphibian by a Navy order of April 7, 1939. Provided with retractable tricycle wheels, it flew November 22, 1939. After hard service, it was rebuilt without wheels as the "Sea Mare" transport in 1943.

Wartime Expansion

When the war began in September 1939, the Navy had 190 Consolidated PBY and 35 P2Y boats with 19 squadrons deployed in five Patrol Wings. Patrol Wings One to Five, respectively, were based at Naval Air Stations (NAS) at San Diego, Pearl Harbor, Coco Solo, Seattle, and Norfolk. Seaplane tenders were provided to allow squadron movements to advanced bases. On September 21, VP-21 left Pearl Harbor with 14 PBY-4s to deploy to the Philippines via Midway, Wake and Guam.

There was a lull of over a year in PBY deliveries to service squadrons and its days in the front-line seemed numbered. New prototypes such as the XPBM-l, XPB2Y-l, and Consolidated's own Model 31, far surpassed it in performance. But now aircraft were needed by the Navy for its Neutrality Patrol and by the RAF for control of the Atlantic. Early delivery of a reliable patrol plane was now the main consideration.

WES

CONSOLIDATED PBY-5 (1940)
Two Pratt & Whitney R-1830-82, 1200 hp takeoff, 1050 hp at 5700'
DIMENSIONS: Span 104', Lg. 63'10", Ht. 18'10", Wing Area 1400 sq. ft.
WEIGHT: Empty 15,453 lb., Gross 26,487 lb., Max. 29,265 lb. Fuel 1570-1750 gal.
PERFORMANCE: Speed- Top 189 mph at s. l., 200 mph at 5700', Cruising 110 mph, Stalling 72 mph. Service Ceiling 21,600', Climb 990'/1 min. Range 1945 miles patrol, 1245 miles/2000 lb. bombs, 2895 miles max.

On December 20, 1939, the Navy ordered 200 Consolidated PBY-5s for 20 million dollars, again the largest single Navy aircraft order since World War I. Contracts were made with France on December 12, 1939, Britain on January 27, 1940, and Australia on August 5, for 108 similar 28-5Ms. The 40-plane French order would be absorbed by Britain, and a new assembly line was begun in San Diego.

The first PBY-5 was flown on August 23, 1940, with 1,200-hp (takeoff) R-1830-82 engines, the first to use 100-octane fuel, and with the oil coolers moved from the wings to beneath the nacelles. Armament included two .50-caliber guns in the waist blisters with 840 rounds and a .30-caliber gun in the bow, and another in the tunnel, with 1,500 rounds. The second PBY-5 was delivered to the Coast Guard in October 1940, and did extensive survey work in the Pacific during the war.

The first Model 28-5ME boat for Britain, tested by Russell Rogers on October 28, 1940, was named the Catalina I with R-1830-SlC3G Wasps of 1,050 hp with 90-octane fuel. British Catalina Is had eight crewmen and six .303-caliber Vickers guns, including two in each blister with 1,200 rounds, 225 pounds of 1/4-inch armor for the rear gunners, and 1,176 pounds of self-sealing fuel tank protection. RAF boats did not have the torpedo and oxygen provisions of the Navy's PBYs.

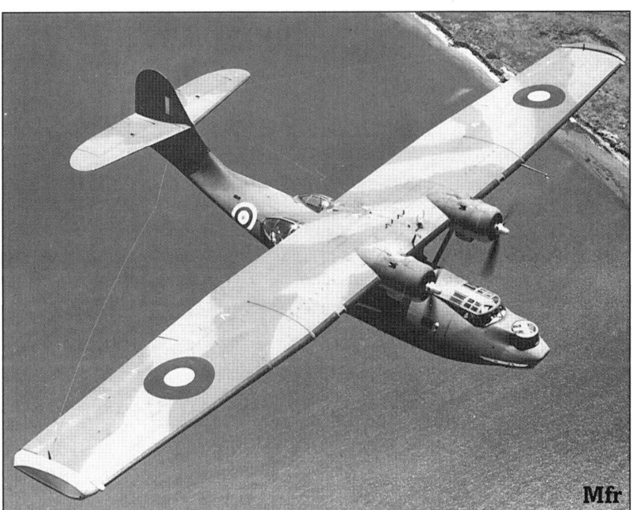
Mfr

CONSOLIDATED 28-5ME Catalina I
Two Pratt & Whitney S1C3G, 1200 hp takeoff, 1050 hp at 7,500'
DIMENSIONS: Span 104', Lg. 63'10", Ht. 18'10", Wing Area 1400 sq. ft.
WEIGHT: Empty 16,407 lb., Gross 29,547 lb., Max. 32,540 lb. Fuel 1285-1750 gal.
PERFORMANCE: Speed- Top 197 mph at 7,800', Cruising 110 mph, Stalling 72 mph. Service Ceiling 19,500', Climb 5000'/7 min. Range 2640 miles patrol, 3500 miles max.

Seven new PBY-5s were transferred from the Navy to become the Catalina II, tested on November 23 with R-1830-82 Wasps and .50-caliber waist guns, and used by the RAF's No. 240 Squadron stationed in Iceland from March 1941. By the end of 1940, nine PBY-5s, the first five Catalina Is, and all seven Catalina II boats had been accepted.

Most Catalinas were flown to Elizabeth City, North Carolina, and then to Bermuda and flown 3,400 miles

Catalina II of 240 Squadron

across the Atlantic to Britain. By July 21, 1941, Consolidated had delivered the 90 Catalina Is as well as the seven Catalina IIs on RAF orders, completed 18 similar model 28-5MAs for Australia (RAAF) from February 6 to October 7, and would add nine more Catalina Is from October 20 to November 7, 1941. Nine Catalina Is had been transferred to Canada's No. 116 Squadron in Nova Scotia in June 1941.

The first RAF Catalinas went to No. 240 Squadron and to No. 205 Squadron at Singapore. Catalina Is replaced the failed Lerwick boats with 209 Squadron based in Northern Ireland, and joined 202 Squadron at Gibraltar. No. 210 Squadron at Oban, Scotland, also received Catalina Is, as did 413 Squadron RCAF at Stranraer.

Thirty-six 28-5MNs ordered by the Dutch East Indies on November 10, 1940, were finished from August 8 to October 31, 1941. They were similar in engines and armament to the RAF boats.

By September 30, 1941, 167 PBY-5 boats had been accepted by the U.S. Navy, which in October also adopted Catalina as the official PBY name. To protect the original 1,750-gallon fuel system, self-sealing tankage could be provided, but reduced total capacity; 603-gallon Goodyear leak-proof cells could replace one or both 875-gallon spaces in the wings. As these tanks and armor were added, specified empty weight grew from 15,534 pounds on the first PBY-5 to 17,751 pounds in two years

Deployment first strengthened the Neutrality Patrol in the Atlantic, which was being extended to new bases in Bermuda, Newfoundland, and Iceland. First to operate from Bermuda on November 15, 1940, were the PBY-2s of VP-54. On May 18, 1941, PBY-5s of VP-52 arrived at Argentina, Newfoundland, operating from the seaplane tender, *USS Albemarle.*

Severe climate made patrol work hazardous, and on May 24, 1941, the squadron was ordered to look for the *Bismarck,* moving somewhere in the Atlantic after sinking *HMS Hood.* Catalinas of the RAF from Northern Ireland were also searching, flying 19 to 22 hours on each trip. On May 26, a No. 209 Squadron Catalina, with an American officer as copilot, found the *Bismarck.* Another Catalina took up contact, and the battleship was soon caught and destroyed by the British Navy.

The Catalina I's range allowed Harry Hopkins, President Roosevelt's personal representative, to be flown on July 28 by No. 210 Squadron from Scotland to Russia for the first top-level American conference with Stalin. The first U-boat victim of the Catalina was U-452, sunk by 209 Squadron from Ulster on August 23, 1941, and 202 Squadron at Gibraltar sank an Italian submarine on October 25.

CONSOLIDATED 28-5MC Catalina IIA
Two Pratt & Whitney S1C3G, 1200 hp takeoff, 1050 hp at 7500'
DIMENSIONS: Span 104', Lg. 63'10", Ht. 18'10", Wing Area 1400 sq. ft.
WEIGHT: Empty 16,179 lb., Gross 30,000 lb., Max. 32,540 lb. Fuel 1487-1750 gal.
PERFORMANCE: Speed- Top 196 mph at 7800', Cruising 110 mph, Stalling 72 mph. Service Ceiling 19,000', Climb 5000'/ 7 min. Range 3070 miles normal patrol, 3500 miles max.

The first Navy plane with airborne search radar early in 1941 was a PBY-2. By July 18, 1941, British ASV radar had been installed in one PBY-5 each of VP-71, 72 and 73, the first Navy squadrons with radar in service. Atlantic patrol units were reorganized, most of the squadrons becoming part of Patrol Wing Seven in July. On August 6, 1941, six PBY-5s of VP-73 and five Martin PBM-ls of VP-74 began operations from Iceland.

The success of the wheeled landing gear on the XPBY-5A led the Navy to have the last 33 aircraft on the 1939 PBY-5 contract completed as PBY-5A amphibians, and an November 25, 1940, order added 134 more. The first PBY-5A amphibian was delivered October 23, 1941, with R-1830-82 engines, self-sealing tanks, and armor. Patrol Wing Seven's VP-83 and 91 at Norfolk NAS received the first of 45 delivered by the end of 1941.

Canada ordered 50 Model 28-MCs with SlC3G Wasps on November 23, 1940, and 36 became Catalina IIA flying boats delivered from August 22 to November 4, 1941, and flown to Ottawa. Aircraft were sometimes reassigned among Commonwealth forces, so while seven were retained by Canada, nine Catalina IIAs joined the RAAF by April, and 20 (less two lost) went to the RAF by May 1942.

Fourteen Model 28-5AMC amphibians delivered from November 11 to December 31, 1941, were named the Canso A after a town in Nova Scotia, where they were stationed at Dartmouth with No. 116 Squadron for anti-submarine patrols. With 194 pounds of armor, they were similar to the Catalina I in armament, and are designated Catalina IA on some records.

Mfr

CONSOLIDATED PBY-5A (1942)
Two Pratt & Whitney R-1830-92, 1200 hp takeoff, 1050 hp at 7500'
DIMENSIONS: Span 104', Lg. 63'10" Ht. 20'2", Wing Area 1400 sq. ft.
WEIGHT: Empty 20,709 lb., Gross 30,043 lb., Max. 34,426 lb.
Fuel 785-1463 gal.
PERFORMANCE: Speed- Top 180 mph at s. l., 189 mph at 7000', Cruising 135 mph, Stalling 74 mph. Service Ceiling 19,200', Climb 660'/1 min. Range 2450 miles patrol, 2350 miles/4-325 lb. depth charges.

CONSOLIDATED 28-5AMC Canso A
Two Pratt & Whitney S1C3G, 1200 hp takeoff, 1050 hp at 7,500'
DIMENSIONS: Span 104', Lg. 63'10", Ht. 19'8", Wing Area 1400 sq. ft.
WEIGHT: Empty 18,950 lb., Gross 32,000 lb., Max. 34,500 lb.
Fuel 1368-1750 gal.
PERFORMANCE: Speed- Top 186 mph at 7500', Stalling 76 mph. Service Ceiling 16,100', Climb 5000'/7 min. Range 2430 miles max.

After Pearl Harbor

When America entered the war, the Navy had 16 patrol squadrons equipped with the PBY-5, three with the PBY-3, two each with the PBY-4 and PBY-5A, and one each with the PBM-l, PB2Y-2, and PBO-l types. A hundred older PBYs were located mostly at Gulf naval training stations.

Hawaii had seven squadrons with 54 PBY-5s and 27 PBY-3s, while two squadrons with 28 PBY-4s were in the Philippines, Seattle had 24 PBY-5s in four squadrons, and San Diego had a transition training squadron (VP-13) with four PB2Y-2s and a few PBYs. Two Canal Zone squadrons had 13 PBY-3s and 11 PBY-5s, while the Atlantic Fleet's eleven squadrons had 81 PBY-5s, 16 PBY-5As, 13 PBY-3s, 13 PBM-ls and the only landplanes; 14 PBO-l Hudsons.

A PBY-5 on patrol attacked a midget submarine just before most of Hawaii's PBYs were put out of action by the surprise attack on December 7th. Patrol Wing Ten in the Philippines carried out several PBY-4 bombing attacks before 15 survivors fled to the East Indies by December 26. Replacement PBY-5s were received from VP-22 and from the Dutch, but of 45 Catalinas used by PatWing l0, 14 were shot down and 24 destroyed on the water by March 3, 1942. The PBY's vulnerability to enemy fighter attack became obvious.

Deliveries of PBY-5 boats resumed from April 4 to May 26, 1942, with 90 aircraft using Pratt & Whitney R-1830-92 Wasps now rated at 1,050 hp from sea level to 7,500 feet and the elaborate antennae of British-designed ASV radar. A Lend-Lease contract dated June 30, 1941, provided 225 PBY-5B boats from May 28 to November 2, 1942. Powered by the R-1830-92, and armed with two .50-caliber and two 30-caliber guns, the PBY-5B had 361 pounds of armor with British equipment and deicers. Designated Catalina IB in RAF service, 162 reached the UK, 45 were kept by the U.S. Navy, eight went to Canada in December 1942, and the rest lost in transit.

CONSOLIDATED PBY-5B Catalina IB
Two Pratt & Whitney R-1830-92, 1200 hp takeoff, 1050 hp at 7500'
DIMENSIONS: Span 104', Lg. 63'10", Ht. 18'11", Wing Area 1400 sq. ft.
WEIGHT: Empty 16,429 1b., Gross 28,314 1b., Max. 34,500 1b. Fuel 515-1570 gal.
PERFORMANCE: similar to PBY-5

The last PBY-5 contract provided 496 boats from November 6, 1942, until boat deliveries at San Diego ended on July 31, 1943. They included 74 delivered to the RAF as the Catalina IVA, 12 to the RCAF, and eight to the RNZAF.

Production of the PBY-5A amphibian proceeded with 219 built by April 17, 1942. Although the RAF preferred the lighter boats to the amphibian, 12 PBY-5As were delivered as the Catalina III in June 1942 for No. 330 Squadron's Norwegian pilots in Iceland.

Catalina III of 330 Squadron

After a pause, PBY-5A deliveries resumed in August with 12 for a Dutch squadron; No. 321 in Ceylon, followed by 94 on a Navy contract by September 29, 1942. Another 430 PBY-5As were completed from July 20, 1943, to the end of Catalina production at San Diego on March 31, 1944. Their place was then taken by the PB4Y-2 Privateer.

Pressures of war lead to many changes in the Catalina. While most PBY-5As had one .30-caliber gun in the bow, two-gun turrets with 2,100 rounds had been retrofitted to many older examples by 1944. Steel 3/8-inches thick had been added behind the pilots' seats, increasing armor weight to 462 pounds. Primitive ASV radar had been added at the factory since April 1942, requiring addition of a ninth crewman, and APS-3 radar became available in 1944. There was much variation in weight among PBY-5 models, and the photos and data given here indicate representative characteristics of common examples.

By September 30, 1942, the Navy's 31 patrol squadrons included 16 with PBY-5 boats, 12 with PBY-5A amphibians and three still with the PBM-1, PBO, and PB2Y types. Gradually the boats were replaced until there were three PBY-5 boat and 20 PBY-5A amphibian squadrons on January 1, 1945.

CONSOLIDATED PBY-5 (1943)
Two Pratt & Whitney R-1830-92, 1200 hp takeoff, 1050 hp at 7500'
DIMENSIONS: Span 104', Lg. 63'10", Ht. 18'11", Wing Area 1400 sq. ft.
WEIGHT: Empty 17,859 1b., Gross 27,1731b., Max. 31,556-35,651 1b. Fuel 785-1463 gal.
PERFORMANCE: Speed-Top 185 mph at s. l., 195 mph at 7500', Cruising 110 mph, Stalling 71 mph. Service Ceiling 21,200', Climb 660'/1 min. Range 2980 miles patrol, 2370 miles/4-325 lb. depth charges, 2645 miles/2000 lb. bombs.

Catalinas were involved in every Navy campaign of the Pacific War. Everywhere there were endless patrol and search duties, with the threat of an encounter with a better-armed enemy combat plane. A PBY-5A was the first to sight the enemy 730 miles from Midway Island, where four with radar were sent on the Navy's first night torpedo attack. Patrol Wing Four Catalinas suffered heavy losses in the Aleutians in June 1942. At Guadalcanal, low-level night bombing against enemy shipping began the successful "Black Cat" squadrons' campaign in December 1942.

In the Atlantic, the hunt for U-boats was the primary task and sixteen submarines were sunk by Navy PBYs from August 1942 to July 1943. While depth charges were the usual weapon, VP-84 at Iceland sank U-657 on May 14 with the first use of the Mk. 24 acoustic homing torpedo.

One PBY-5A squadron, VP-63, became the first fitted with Magnetic Airborne Detector (MAD) gear, as well as the first Navy squadron in World War II to operate from Great Britain, when it arrived on July 23, 1943. Anti-submarine operations over the Bay of Biscay were pressed even against German long-range fighter attacks.

In January 1944, VP-63 went to Morocco, now equipped to fire 65-pound rocket bombs back and down at submerged U-boats. VP-63 set up barrier patrols across the Straits of Gibraltar, where three U-boats were sunk in early

WL

VICKERS OA-10A

1944 with help from surface ships. This squadron also sank U-1055, the last by Navy forces, on April 30, 1945.

USN

CONSOLIDATED PBY-5A of VP-63 in 1944

The most popular Catalina role, as far as fliers of other types was concerned, was the rescue of airmen down at sea. At first, this was done by the regular patrol squadrons, then special rescue squadrons of Catalinas were organized: Army Emergency Rescue Squadrons with OA-10 amphibians, and Navy Air-Sea Rescue Squadrons (VH) were first formed in the Pacific on April 15, 1944.

After San Diego finished Catalina deliveries, work continued in four satellite plants. On July 16, 1941, 156 PBN-1 Nomads had been ordered from Philadelphia's Naval Aircraft Factory (NAF). This enabled the adoption of a new hull design without disrupting established production. Engineering the longer clipper bow, extended after body, and enlarged fuel capacity delayed tests of the first PBN-1 until October 1942.

The added weight caused serious stability problems and although the first four were accepted in February 1943, the Navy decided on March 19 to add a higher fin and rudder to these and future PBNs. Armament included a .50-caliber gun in a powered nose turret and in each side blister as well as the usual small-caliber tunnel gun, and armor weighed 426 pounds.

USN

NAF PBN-1 Nomad

Two Pratt & Whitney R-1830-92, 1200 hp takeoff, 1050 hp at 7500'

DIMENSIONS: Span 104', Lg. 64'8", Ht. 21'3", Wing Area 1400 sq. ft.

WEIGHT: Empty 19,288 lb., Gross 36,350 lb., Max. 38,000 lb. Fuel 622-2070 gal.

PERFORMANCE: Speed- Top 174 mph at s. l., 186 mph at 6700', Cruising 111 mph, Stalling 78 mph. Service Ceiling 15,100'. Range 2590 miles/4-325 lb. depth charges, 3700 miles patrol.

Seventeen PBNs were completed for the Navy by September 1943, when the Navy canceled a 124-plane follow-on contract. The remainder of the 1941 contract, minus one accidentally burned, were allotted to the Soviet Navy Air Force (VVS-VMF) in Project ZEBRA. Soviet crews were trained at Elizabeth City, North Carolina.

Beginning on May 24, 1944, 48 were flown via Newfoundland and Iceland to the 118th MRAP (Marine Recon-

IWM

BOEING PB2B-1 Catalina IVB

naissance Air Regiment) and the 20th MRAE squadron near Murmansk, less one lost en route. Attacks on U-boats included the confirmed sinking of U-362 on September 5, 1944. Thirty were flown via Kodiak, Alaska, to Siberia and the 117th MRAP in September 1944. Sixty, less one crashed on takeoff, flew to Natal and over the South Atlantic and Africa to Lake Habbiniyah, Iraq, and then to the VMF station at Baku on the Caspian Sea. From there, they joined Black Sea units like the 82nd RAE, attacked small U-boats and on September 8, 1944, flew Bulgarian Communists to begin an anti-German uprising.

The last PBN left the NAF on March 19, 1945, and 107 PBN's were with Baltic, Black and Northern Fleets after war with Germany ended 9 May 1945. On August 9, the Pacific Fleet VMF went to war against Japan with 49 PBNs and 21 PBY-6As in the 16th, 48th, and 117th MRAPs. On August 24, 1945, ten Cats landed 135 Soviet marines at Port Arthur after the Japanese surrender.

Two Canadian facilities were involved in PBY production by an August 4, 1941, agreement. Boeing's factory at Vancouver began with 55 duplicates of Consolidated's 28-AMC amphibian, called the Canso A. Deliveries to the Royal Canadian Air Force began after the first flight on July 27, 1942, and were followed in July 1943 by 240 PB2B-1 (PBY-5 duplicates) flying boats built with lend-lease funds for the RAF. Called the Catalina IVB, they included 192 that reached the UK, 34 for New Zealand and seven for Australia.

The PB2B-2 (Catalina VI) flying boat appeared in September 1944 with the tall PBN tail. Of 67 built by March 1945, 47 went to Australia, six operated in U.S. Army markings, but 14 for the RAF never left Canada.. Canadian Vickers (Canadair since December 1944) at Montreal delivered 369 PBY-5A amphibians from April 1943 to May 1945, of which 139 were Canso As for the RCAF and the rest were OA-10As for the AAF.

PMB

BOEING PB2B-2 Catalina VI

Army Air Force procurement of the PBY-5A for rescue operations had begun with the promise of 74 from the contract made on November 25, 1940, but only 54, designated OA-10, were actually delivered, beginning in May 1942. They were so successful that the AAF was allotted 230 Vickers amphibians. Designated OA-l0A, they were accepted from December 1943 to February 1945, and similar to the PBY-5A with APS-3 radar and armament of two .50-caliber and two .30-caliber guns.

Mfr

CONSOLIDATED PBY-6A

Two Pratt & Whitney R-1830-92, 1200 hp takeoff, 1050 hp at 7500'

DIMENSIONS: Span 104', Lg. 62'11", Ht. 22'5, Wing Area 1400 sq. ft.

WEIGHT: Empty 21,480 1b., Gross 34,550 1b., Max. 36,400 1b. Fuel 1478+300 gal.

PERFORMANCE: Speed- Top 167 mph at s. l., 178 mph at 7000', Cruising 107 mph, Stalling 79 mph. Service Ceiling 14,900', Climb 530'/1 min. Range 2535 miles patrol, 2250 miles/4-325 lb. depth charges, 2195 miles/2000 lb. bombs, 3130 miles ferry.

The last factory to produce PBYs was the Consolidated-Vultee New Orleans facility, originally established to build the advanced P4Y-1, the Navy version of the Model 31. When this type's engine supply was absorbed by the B-29 program, the P4Y-1 program was replaced by a PBY contract on September 11, 1943.

The first aircraft completed in the New Orleans plant was a single PBY-5 delivered March 1, 1944, but on December 21, 1943, the Navy had decided to shift PBY-5A production from San Diego to New Orleans. From April 30, 1944, to January 27, 1945, 59 PBY-5As were delivered. All had the new bow turret with two .30-caliber guns that had been retrofitted to many older examples.

The last Catalina model was the PBY-6A amphibian, with PBN tail, two .50-caliber guns in the bow turret with 1,000 rounds, two more in the blisters with 1,156 rounds, the usual tunnel gun, 455 pounds of armor, and APS-3 radar over the cockpit. Of 175 built from January 31 to September 27, 1945, 75 went to the Army as the OA-10B and 48 to the USSR. Fifteen were flown through Alaska to the 48th MDRAP on Kamchatka, and the last aircraft group flew via Elizabeth City and Scotland to the Soviet Baltic Fleet in the war's closing days.

Nine PBY-5A squadrons and one of PBY-6As were operating for the U.S. Navy on July 1, 1945. The war's end closed the New Orleans plant and Catalina production. Production included: San Diego, 2,160; New Orleans, 235; Canada, 731; and Philadelphia, 156; a total of 3,282, including 1,418 amphibians.

As the largest foreign customer, the RAF purchased 90 Mk. I, seven Mk. II, and 20 Mk. IIA Catalinas by 1941, and Lend-Lease funds in 1942 provided 162 Mk. IB (PBY-5B) boats and only 12 Mk. III amphibians. In 1943, the RAF got

74 Mk. IVA flying boats from San Diego, followed by 192 Mk. IVB from Vancouver, and two Cansos in 1945. No Mk. V, the PBN, ever reached the RAF.

Some 556 Catalinas were actually delivered to serve 21 RAF squadrons and are credited with the confirmed sinking of 14 enemy submarines, the last on May 7, 1945.

Australia had its original 18 Catalina Is when Japan attacked, adding nine Mk. IIA boats in March/April 1942, one Model 28-MNE and two PBY-4 refugees, 38 PBY-5s from January 1943, 46 PBY-5As, seven PB2B-1s and 36 PB2B-2s from USN contracts. New Zealand's RNZAF got 14 PBY-5 and eight Catalina IVA boats from April to October 1943, and 34 PB2B-1s in 1944.

Canada chose Canso amphibians for Atlantic operations, with No. 5 squadron from Gander scoring first on May 4, 1943, and No. 162 Squadron at Wick, Scotland, sinking six U-boats in 1944. Canada's 15 squadrons received nine Mk. 1, eight Mk. IIA, 14 Mk. IA, eight Mk. IB, 12 Mk. IVA, 55 Canso A, and 139 Canadair PBY-5A.

Brazil received seven PBY-5 boats in January 1943, and on July 31, one sank the U-199, after it had been damaged by a PBM-3C. Starting in December 1944, 23 PBY-5As also went to Brazil. Chile got three PBY-5s and an OA-10A in June 1943.

France was given 30 PBY-5As, commissioned its first Catalina squadron in September 1943 at Norfolk, and French Navy aircrews were trained at Elizabeth City, NC. from Oct. 28, 1943, to March 5, 1944, to begin operations from Morocco.

With so many left over at the war's end, the Catalina was to have a long postwar history in at least 15 different air forces. Although, the last PBY-6A retired from the U.S. Navy on January 3, 1957, many still served in a variety of civilian functions from cargo to fire-fighting work twenty years after the war. The Catalina was a combat type that had lasted longer in peaceful tasks than in war.

Floatplanes for Patrol

During the PBY's long service life, many efforts were made to develop more advanced types for the shore-based patrol mission. While twin-float monoplanes like the Heinkel He 115 or Aichi E13A1 were common abroad, the only Navy prototype with twin floats instead of a boat hull, was the twin-engine Hall XPTBH-2, capable of patrol, torpedo, or bombing missions.

Ordered June 30, 1934, as an XPTBH-l with Wright R-1820 Cyclones, the high-wing monoplane was built in the Fleetwings plant at Bristol, Pennsylvania, with XR-1830-60 Wasps, redesignated XPTBH-2, and received by the Navy on January 30, 1937. A pair of large floats were installed under the engines, while the long fuselage contained the crew of four and a bay for a torpedo or bombs.

In the nose was a rotating turret with a .30-caliber M-2 gun. Behind the wings a hatch slid forward and up to reveal a rear gunner and .50-caliber M1921 Browning, while a floor panel opened for a .30-caliber M-2 tunnel gun. Since Navy procurement plans no longer included shore-based torpedo planes, no further contracts for this type

HALL XPTBH-2
Two Pratt & Whitney XR-1830-60, 800 hp at 8000'
DIMENSIONS: Span 79'4", Lg. 55'4", Ht. 24'1", Wing Area 828 sq. ft.
WEIGHT: Empty 11,922 lb., Gross 17,983 lb., Max. 21,467 lb. Fuel 830-1180 gal.
PERFORMANCE: Speed- Top 169 mph at s. l., 187 mph at 8000', Stalling 69 mph. Service Ceiling 20,900', Climb 5000'/5,3 min. Range 753 miles/torpedo, 2,360 miles max.

were made. The XPTBH-2 was at the Naval Torpedo Station at Newport, Rhode Island, when it was demolished by a hurricane in 1938.

The only American single-engine patrol monoplane was the Northrop N-3PB. Norway wanted a seaplane version of the 8A-5 light bomber just purchased from Douglas and on March 12, 1940, Jack Northrop's new independent company at Hawthorne, California, contracted to build 24 in less than a year.

NORTHROP N-3PB
Wright Cyclone R-1820-G205A, 1200 hp takeoff, 900 hp at 15,200'
DIMENSIONS: Span 48'11", Lg. 38', Ht. 12', Wing Area 377 sq. ft.
WEIGHT: Empty 6560 lb., Gross 9022 lb., Max. 11,213 lb. Fuel 320 gal.
PERFORMANCE: Speed- Top 220 mph at s. l., 257 mph at 16,400', Cruising 215 mph, Stalling 65 mph. Service Ceiling 28,400', Climb 2540'/1 min. Range 1400 miles max.

Powered by the Wright R-1820-G205A Cyclone, they carried three men, four .50-caliber fixed wing guns with 267 rpg, a .30-caliber flexible gun, another .30-caliber gun aimed through a trap door in the belly, and up to a ton of bombs, depth charges, or a torpedo. The first was flown from Lake Elsinore on December 22, 1940, and the last was delivered March 27, 1941.

Exiled Norwegian pilots in Canada trained on the Northrops and on April 24 formed No. 330 Squadron, RAF, in Iceland and began anti-submarine patrols on June 23, 1941. Usually, three 350-pound depth charges were carried on most of the 1,011 sorties by March 30, 1943, and several U-boats and Fw 200 bombers were attacked without confirmed success. Catalina III amphibians more suited for the Icelandic area had gradually replaced the Northrops.

Four-engine Flying Boats

As the PBY's prototype began flight tests, the Navy prepared a new Design Specification, February 14, 1935, using four engines to achieve a more advanced performance. Sikorsky contracted to build such a patrol-bomber, its Model S-44, on June 25, 1935, and another design by Consolidated, the XPB2Y-l, was ordered July 23, 1936.

First flown on August 13, 1937, from Stratford, Connecticut, by Edmund Allen, the Sikorsky XPBS-1 had XR-1830-68 Twin Wasps, fixed outboard floats, and a high single tail fin. The spacious hull accommodated living quarters for the crew, and a 110-volt electrical system powered the flaps, elaborate radio, and other electric appliances. Eight 1,000-pound bombs were carried within the wings, and the XPBS-1 was publicized as a "Flying Dreadnought".

Mfr

SIKORSKY XPBS-1 on first flight

SDAM

SIKORSKY XPBS-1

Four Pratt & Whitney XR-1830-68, 1050 hp takeoff, 900 hp at 12,000'

DIMENSIONS: Span 124', Lg. 76'2", Ht. 27'7", Wing Area 1670 sq. ft.

WEIGHT: Empty 26,407 lb., Gross 46,617 lb., Max. 48,451 lb. Fuel 1970-3600 gal.

PERFORMANCE: Speed- Top 203 mph at s. l., 227 mph at 12,000', Stalling 63 mph. Service ceiling 23,100', Climb 640'/ 1 min. Range 3170 miles/4000 lb. bombs, 4545 miles max.

Armament included a .50-caliber gun in a manual front turret that turned 200 degrees in horizon and 117 degrees in the vertical. Another .50-caliber gun hand-operated in the tail, swung 60 degrees in horizon and 107 degrees in the vertical; the first real tail gun on an American plane, although Igor Sikorsky had put them on Czarist bombers over 20 years earlier. Side-by-side waist hatches had two .30 or .50-caliber guns.

Sikorsky's boat soon had a rival, Consolidated's Model 29 designed by Isaac Laddon. The XPB2Y-l had four R-1830-66 Twin Wasps and 11-foot propellers, similar crew accommodations and a cleaner appearance gained by PBY-style retractable wing-tip floats. Eight cells within the wings carried 1,000-pound bombs and racks beneath the outboard engines could add four more bombs, or two torpedoes. Single .50-caliber guns were mounted in the bow turret and tail position, while .30 or .50-caliber guns were provided for the twin waist hatches and a tunnel mount firing downward.

Mfr

CONSOLIDATED XPB2Y-1 with single rudder

On December 17, 1937, the same day the 100th PBY was delivered, the XPB2Y-l was flown at San Diego, but the area of the single fin was too small for directional stability. After three flights, it was beached to add a pair of elliptical fins on the stabilizer by February 2, 1938.

Mfr

CONSOLIDATED XPB2Y-1 with added fins

Stability and water behavior were still unsatisfactory so, on June 30, it was tested with twin rudders placed at the ends of a new stabilizer with dihedral. In July, the hull's step locations were changed and the power plant changed to new R-1830-72 (PBY-4 type) Wasps with 12-foot props. This worked, and the aircraft was turned over to the Navy on August 24, 1938. Empty weight had increased from 25,496 to 26,847 pounds.

The XPB2Y-l became the first official "Flagplane" when a special cabin was provided in August 1939 for Admiral A.B. Cook, of the Aircraft Scouting Force. For the next six years the "Blue Goose" served as a VIP transport carrying senior Navy leaders around the Pacific.

Mfr

CONSOLIDATED XPB2Y-1
Four Pratt & Whitney R-1830-72, 1050 hp takeoff, 900 hp at 12,000'
DIMENSIONS: Span 115', Lg. 79'3", Ht. 27'4", Wing Area 1780 sq. ft.
WEIGHT: Empty 26,847 lb., Gross 49,754 lb., Max. 52,994 lb. Fuel 2300-3500 gal.
PERFORMANCE: Speed- Top 206 mph at s. l., 230 mph at 12,000', Stalling 65 mph. Service ceiling 22,000', Climb 830'/ 1 min. Range 4390 miles normal, 3420 miles/4000 lb. bombs, 4950 miles max.

Despite their advanced performance, these giants did not win generous orders, for budget-limited admirals looked askance at their high cost and complexity, and reflected that "a large plane over a given area of sea is not, necessarily, any more effective as an observation post than is a small plane ...the small plane may have an advantage in that the facilities which made it and maintain it can make and maintain more units." With so much money already invested in the PBYs, the Navy bought no patrol bombers at all in 1938, and during the following year concentrated funds on twin-engine types that could be obtained in quantity.

Six Consolidated PB2Y-2s were ordered March 31, 1939. They had a new deeper hull, R-1830-78 Wasps with two-stage superchargers, and a crew of nine. Six .50-caliber guns were distributed among the nose turret, top tear-drop blister, circular side windows, tunnel orifice, and tail post. The first was flown on November 22, 1940, delivered to VP-13 at San Diego on December 31, and five were accepted by July 1941.

The sixth was delayed to become the XPB2Y-3 configuration, preparing for the 200 heavier production versions ordered November 19, 1940, at a cost, $311,000 each, three times that of a PBY. On November 11, 1941, Richard

Mfr

CONSOLIDATED PB2Y-2
Four Pratt & Whitney R-1830-88, 1200 hp takeoff, 1000 hp at 19,000'
DIMENSIONS: Span 115', Lg. 79', Ht. 27'6", Wing Area 1780 sq. ft.
WEIGHT: Empty 34,315 lb., Gross 60,441 lb., Max. 63,700 lb. Fuel 4400 gal.
PERFORMANCE: Speed- Top 224 mph at s. l., 255 mph at 19,000', Cruising 141 mph, Stalling 71 mph. Service ceiling 24,100', Climb 830'/1 min. Range 3705 miles normal, 1330 miles/12,000 lb. bombs, 4275 miles max.

McMachin began XPB2Y-3 flight tests, and this aircraft, #1638, also became the XPB2Y-4 when flight tests with 1,700-hp Wright R-2600-10 Double Cyclones began April 27, 1943.

Mfr

CONSOLIDATED XPB2Y-3

The first PB2Y-3, #7043, was flown on April 29, 1942, and accepted June 4. Now called the Coronado, it had R-1830-88s, self-sealing fuel tanks, about 2,000 pounds of armor, eight .50-caliber guns, and 4,840 rounds of ammunition. The wartime increase in firepower over the XPB2Y-1 prototype was great.

Instead of a single gun with 200 rounds in the manual bow turret, there were two with 800 rounds in an armored, power-operated Martin turret. Instead of the single hand-held tail gun with 200 rounds, there were two with 2,000 rounds in the Convair tail turret, adopted from the B-24, which swung 122 degrees side-to-side and 112 degrees up

Mfr

CONSOLIDATED PB2Y-3 Coronado
Four Pratt & Whitney R-1830-88, 1200 hp takeoff, 1000 hp at 19,000'
DIMENSIONS: Span 115', Lg. 79'3", Ht. 27'6", Wing Area 1780 sq. ft.
WEIGHT: Empty 39,662 lb., Gross 66,000 lb., Max. 72,500 lb. Fuel 2041-3730 gal.
PERFORMANCE: Speed- Top 204 mph at s. l., 221 mph at 13,700', 217 mph at 19,000', Cruising 164 mph, Stalling 81 mph. Service ceiling 20,800', Climb 550'/1 min. Range 2540 miles/1000 lb. bombs, 1550 miles/12,000 lb. bombs, 3250 miles max.

and down. Amidships was another two-gun Martin turret on top and one gun at each side opening. Up to 12,000 pounds of bombs could be carried when the external racks were added.

Hoping to replace the vulnerable PBYs, the Navy pressed the company early in 1942 to speed Coronado production. In addition, a transport role for deep-hulled flying boats was foreshadowed when the Sikorsky prototype made an emergency dash across the Pacific with high-priority cargo in January, 1942. It was joined by the PB2Y-2s of VP-13, which also lacked the armor protection needed for combat.

After the first three PB2Y-3s were accepted and joined VP-13, four Coronados were delivered in August 1942 as transports used on Pan American Airways wartime routes, and temporarily called JRF-1s. Consolidated delivered 30 PB2Y-3s to the Navy by December 1942, followed by 25 more transports, now designated PB2Y-3R, for the Naval Air Transport Service (NATS).

Britain had been scheduled on May 3, 1942, to get 50 lend-lease PB2Y-3Bs, and the first, actually the 60th PB2Y-3, #7102, (JX470) crossed the Atlantic in April 1943. But later, only nine more Coronados reached the RAF and these were used as Atlantic and West African transports.

Another 53 PB2Y-3 patrol bombers were accepted from February to May, 1943, and four U.S. Navy squadrons deployed with these Coronados. From January 30 to February 9, 1944, 50 sorties were flown from Midway Island to bomb enemy forces on Wake Island.

While far better armed than the PBYs, Coronados were slower than the PB4Y-1 Liberators the Navy was get-

CONSOLIDATED PB2Y-5 Coronado
Four Pratt & Whitney R-1830-92, 1200 hp takeoff, 1050 hp at 7,000'
DIMENSIONS: Span 115', Lg. 79'5", Ht. 27'6", Wing Area 1780 sq. ft.
WEIGHT: Empty 41,180 lb., Gross 68,000 lb., Max. 72,500 lb. Fuel 3017-3796 gal.
PERFORMANCE: Speed- Top 198 mph at s. l., 211 mph at 7,000', Cruising 154 mph, Stalling 76 mph. Service ceiling 13,100', Climb 490'/1 min. Range 2507 miles/four 325 lb. depth charges, 1640 miles/8,000 lb. bombs.

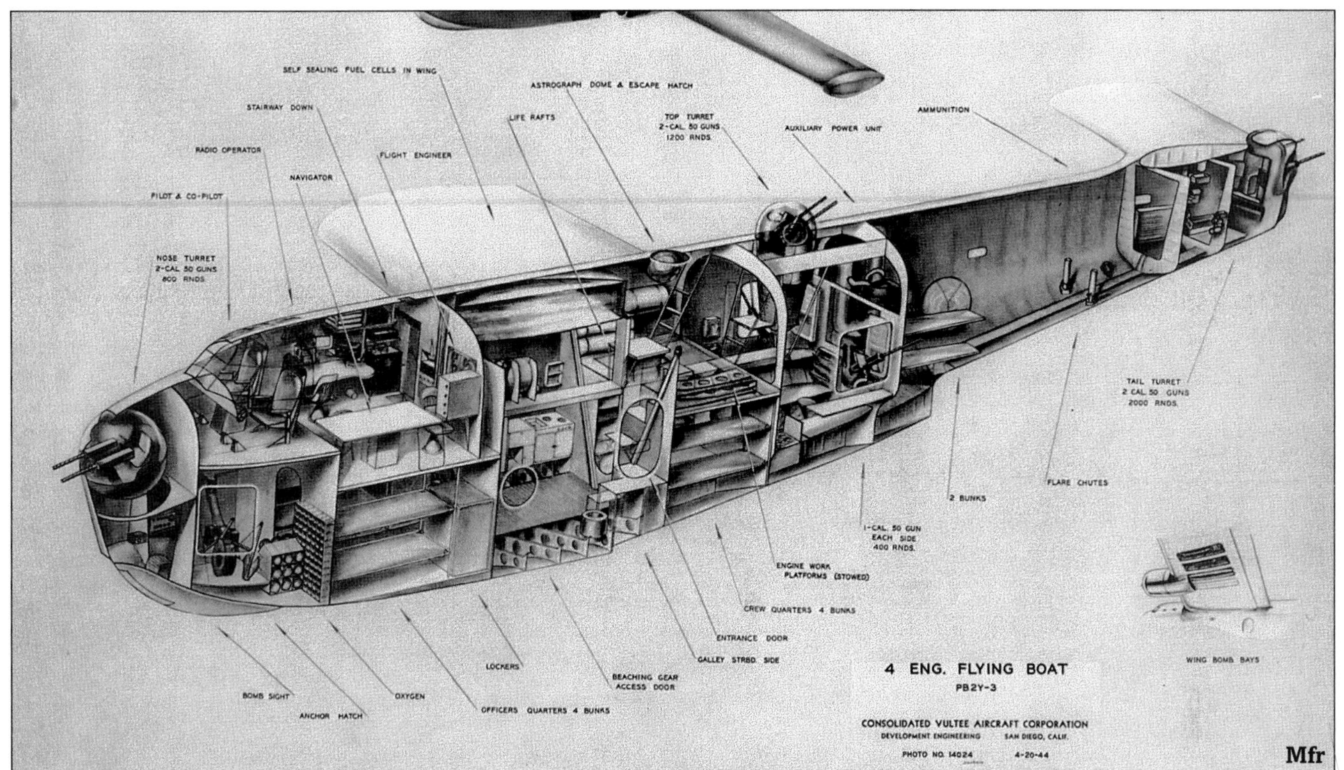

CONSOLIDATED PB2Y-3 Coronado interior

ting, and suffered from fuel tank leaks and numerous problems. On May 6, 1943, the Navy decided to terminate Coronado production after 210 were built, instead of the 626 planned in 1942.

The boats remaining to be delivered became PB2Y-3Rs, which reverted to the PBY's R-1830-92 engines with single-stage superchargers, were stripped of weapons and armor, and fitted with benches and shelves for up to 44 passengers or 16,000 pounds of cargo. Four-bladed 12'2" propellers were provided on the inboard engines, while the outboard engines had 12'6" three-bladed props. Convair delivered 56 from July to October 1943 and the last 41 Coronados were completed as PB2Y-3R transports by Convair sub-contractor Rohr Aircraft from January to September 1944.

Eighty Coronados were returned to Convair for overhaul and refurbishment with the R-1830-92 engines to become PB2Y-5s with less speed, but more range. APS-15 radar was installed above the flight deck, and six JATO bottles could be added to assist takeoffs. Beginning in November 1944, enough PB2Y-5 bombers were provided to resupply three patrol squadrons in 1945, along with PB2Y-5R transports, seven PB2Y-5H boats for medical evacuations, and four PB2Y-5Z staff transports.

Martin Mariners

During 1937, Martin engineers designed a new twin-engine patrol bomber called the Model 162, and tested its air and sea behavior on a three-eighth scale two-passenger flying model. An XPBM-1 prototype was ordered June 30, 1937, together with 21 PBMs on December 28. The XPBM-l was first flown February 18, 1939, with Wright R-2600-6 Double Cyclones mounted high on wings gulled to keep the three-bladed propellers clear of the water. Outboard floats retracted into the wings and twin rudders were perched behind the all-metal hull.

MARTIN XPBM-1
Two Wright R-2600-6, 1600 hp takeoff, 1275 hp at 12,000'
DIMENSIONS: Span 118', Lg. 77'2", Ht. 24'6", Wing Area 1405 sq. ft.
WEIGHT: Empty 24,006 lb., Gross 40,814 lb., Max. 56,000 lb. Fuel 1338-2800 gal.
PERFORMANCE: Speed- Top 213 mph at 12,000', Cruising 128 mph, Stalling 64 mph. Service Ceiling 20,600', Climb 840/ 1 min. Range 3450 miles/1000 lb. bombs.

Twenty PBM-ls accepted from September 1940 to March 1941 could be distinguished from the prototype by the dihedral on the stabilizers. The crew of seven operated five .50-caliber guns mounted in Martin power-operated nose and top turrets, circular waist fixtures and prone tail position. Two tons of bombs or depth charges could be carried within the engine nacelles. The first squadron to get the PBM-1 was VP-55 at Norfolk, which became the VP-74 whose Bermuda-based aircraft sank U-158 on June 30, 1942.

USN

MARTIN PBM-1
Two Wright R-2600-6, 1600 hp takeoff, 1275 hp at 12,000'
DIMENSIONS: Span 118', Lg. 77'2", Ht. 27'6", Wing Area 1408 sq. ft.
WEIGHT: Empty 24,143 lb., Gross 41,139 lb., Max. 56,000 lb. Fuel 2700 gal.
PERFORMANCE: Speed- Top 197 mph at s. l., 214 mph at 12,000', Cruising 128 mph, Stalling 65 mph. Service Ceiling 22,400', Climb 640'/1 min. Range 3434 miles/1000 lb. bombs, 2590 miles/4000 lb. bombs.

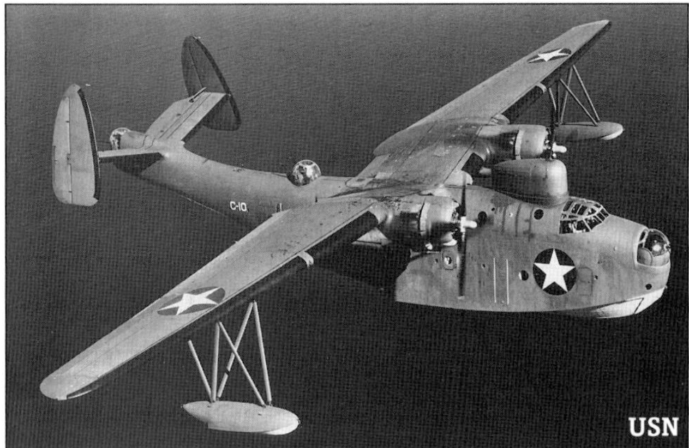

MARTIN PBM-3C Mariner
Two Wright R-2600-12, 1700 hp takeoff, 1350 hp at 13,000'
DIMENSIONS: Span 118', Lg. 80', Ht. 27'6", Wing Area 1408 sq. ft.
WEIGHT: Empty 32,378 lb., Gross 52,665 lb., Max. 58,000 lb. Fuel 1751+788=2539 gal.
PERFORMANCE: Speed-Top 182 mph at s. l., 198 mph at 13,000', Stalling 76 mph. Service Ceiling 16,900', Climb 410'/1 min. Range 2137 miles/eight 325-lb. depth charges, 3074 miles patrol.

In April 1941, an XPBM-2 was accepted with the fuel capacity increased from 2,700 to 4,815 gallons and the hull strengthened. This huge overload was planned to be launched from a big catapult ordered from Philadelphia's Naval Aircraft Factory on November 8, 1938. But the AVC-1 catapult-barge was not ready to make the first live XPBM-2 launch until May 19, 1942. Interest in giant catapults ended with the success of practical jet-assisted takeoff rockets (JATO).

Contracts made November 1, 1940, and August 20, 1941, ordered 379 PBM-3 and 180 PBM-4 Mariners, as the Martin boat was named, but war changed this program. The first PBM-3 from a new Middle River, Maryland, factory was flown early in 1942 with 1,700 hp R-2600-12 Cyclones, and larger non-retractable floats. Armament included Martin power-operated two-gun bow and top turrets, and single hand-operated .50-caliber guns at the waist doors and a tail position. The second PBM-3 became the XPM-3E radar test ship, and VP-74 flew the first of 50 PBM-3s accepted from April to October 1942.

MARTIN PBM-3 Mariner
Two Wright R-2600-12, 1700 hp takeoff, 1350 hp at 13,000'
DIMENSIONS: Span 118', Lg. 80', Ht. 27'6", Wing Area 1408 sq. ft.
WEIGHT: Empty 30,466 lb., Gross 50,664 lb., Max. 56,094 lb. Fuel 1750+788=2538 gal.
PERFORMANCE: Speed- Top 205 mph at 13,000', Cruising 130 mph, Service Ceiling 17,700', Range 2300 miles/eight 325-lb. depth charges, 3320 miles patrol.

Since the most urgent need in 1942 was for transports, 49 of those PBM-3s were converted to unarmed PBM-3R transports for NATS Atlantic routes, and some of their gun turrets were made available to the PB2Y-3. In October 1942 deliveries began on 272 PBM-3Cs with four-bladed propellers. They had 1,178 pounds of armor, self-sealing tanks, and eight .50-caliber guns with 4,840 rounds in the bow, top, and tail power turrets, and manual waist guns.

Enlarged bomb bays could hold eight depth charges or 1,000-pound bombs. Two torpedoes could be carried beneath the wings, but this was not tried in combat. Two pilots, two radio and radar operators, a flight engineer, and a navigator were on the flight deck, and below them was a galley and lavatory. Most of the fuel was in the hull, below the six bunks and gunner's deck. APS-15 search radar installed behind the pilot's cabin enabled the Mariner to catch surfaced submarines at night or in bad weather.

Two more Mariners became the prototype XPBM-3D in March 1943 and the XPBM-3S in May. From July to October 1943, Martin delivered 94 of a special anti-submarine version. Intended for areas beyond the risk of enemy fighters, the PBM-3S gained longer range by omitting heavy power turrets, limiting protection to two hand-held .50-caliber nose guns, another in the waist, and a fourth in the tail, with but 1,000 rounds total, and 261 pounds of armor.

During 1943, PBM squadrons deployed against U-boats increased from one to 17. Most patrols were uneventful, but knowing where the foe is not, is also necessary to allow concentration on active threats. Eight U-boats were sunk and others hurt from July 15 to September 27 by Mariners flying from Haiti, Brazil, and Trinidad. Surfaced subs sometimes fought back, and three PBMs were lost to their guns.

Britain was to get 42 Mariners, beginning in August 1943, but only two PBM-3C and two PBM-3S boats were flown to the UK for short trials, while the rest remained with the U.S. Navy. Unlike the USN, the RAF preferred to keep the Catalina to the war's end, rejecting the Coronado and Mariner, but 12 PBM-3R Mariners did go to Australia in November 1943.

From October 1943 to June 1944, 259 PBM-3Ds were delivered with R-2600-22 Cyclones and four-bladed propellers. Armament was the same as the PBM-3C, but armor was 1,058 pounds, and Mareng leakproof tanks added another 1,321 pounds. They were used by the 12 squadrons deployed to the Pacific, where their targets were surface vessels more often than subs.

MARTIN PBM-3S Mariner
Two Wright R-2600-12, 1700 hp takeoff, 1350 hp at 13,000'
DIMENSIONS: Span 118', Lg. 79'10", Ht. 27'6", Wing Area 1408 sq. ft.
WEIGHT: Empty 29,915 lb., Gross 51,860 lb., Max. 54,525 lb. Fuel 2350+788=3138 gal.
PERFORMANCE: Speed- Top 194 mph at s. l., 209 mph at 13,000', Cruising 134 mph, Stalling 76 mph. Service Ceiling 17,600', Climb 550'/1 min. Range 2725 miles/four 650-lb. depth charges, 3130 miles/four 325-lb. depth charges, 3530 miles max.

The PBM-4 ordered in 1941 was to use the big Wright R-3350, but when this engine's supply was absorbed by the B-29, the next version became the two XPBM-5s reworked from -3Ds in May 1944 with the 2,100-hp Pratt & Whitney R-2800-22 Double Wasp.

Production continued after June 1944 with the PBM-5, using the R-2800-22, eight .50-caliber guns, 1,067 pounds of armor, APS-15 radar and JATO provisions. By March 31, 1945, the Navy had 29 active PBM squadrons, along with 17 PBY amphibian, three PB2Y-5, and one PBY-5 squadron, as well as 52 with PB4Y and PV landplanes.

Pacific operations climaxed at Okinawa, where six squadrons sank ships day and night, and located the giant battleship *Yamato*'s final sortie. Four rescue (VH) squadrons made 108 open-sea landings to save endangered people.

MARTIN PBM-3D Mariner
Two Wright R-2600-22, 1900 hp takeoff, 1350 hp at 15,400'
DIMENSIONS: Span 118', Lg. 79'10", Ht. 27'6", Wing Area 1408 sq. ft.
WEIGHT: Empty 32,848 lb., Gross 51,608 lb., Max. 58,000 lb. Fuel 1950-2744 gal.
PERFORMANCE: Speed-Top 192 mph at s. l., 202 mph at 15,900', Cruising 135 mph, Stalling 76 mph. Service Ceiling 20,800', Climb 740'/1 min. Range 2260 miles patrol, 2580 miles/four 325-lb. depth charges, 3000 miles max.

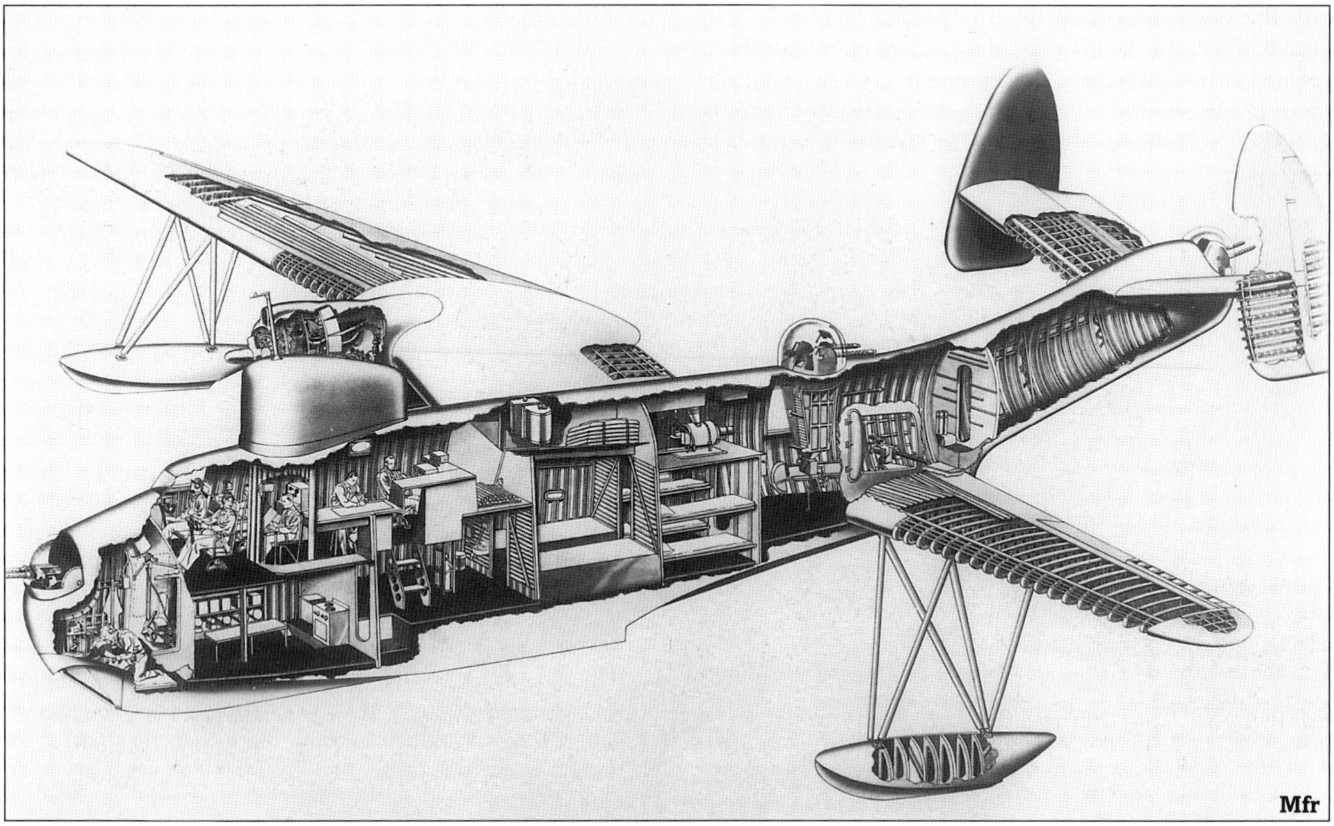

MARTIN PBM-5 Mariner cutaway

MARTIN PBM-5 Mariner
Two Pratt & Whitney R-2800-22, 2100 hp takeoff, 1700 hp at 8500'
DIMENSIONS: Span 118', Lg. 79'10", Ht. 27'6", Wing Area 1408 sq. ft.
WEIGHT: Empty 33,200 lb., Gross 55,968 lb., Max. 58,000 lb. Fuel 2702+786 gal.
PERFORMANCE: Speed-Top 197 mph at s. l., 215 mph at 9,700', Cruising 138 mph, Stalling 80 mph. Service Ceiling 15,800', Climb 500'/1 min. Range 2100 miles/eight 650-lb depth charges, 2760 miles/four 325-lb. depth charges, 3463 miles max..

Production and service continued after the war ended, with 592 PBM-5s completed by the end of 1945 and 629 built by June 1947. About 24 were modified to PBM-5Gs for the Coast Guard. Post-war boats were often fitted with APS-31 radar and new R-2800-34 engines, while the PBM-5S added MAD and sonobuoy gear, and deleted the top turret. After tests of a modified XPBM-5A begun on wheels December 4, 1945, 36 PBM-5A amphibian models with retractable tricycle gear were added from April 1948 to March 1949, bringing the Mariner production to 1,366.

When the Korean War began in 1950, the Navy had three PBM squadrons in the Pacific and three in the Atlantic. Three more Naval Reserve squadrons were activated, so that six could remain on station in the Korean area until after the war ended in 1953.

MARTIN PBM-5A Mariner
Two Pratt & Whitney R-2800-34, 2100 hp takeoff, 1700 hp at 9400, 1850 hp at 15,500œ

While the last Navy Mariners retired in July 1956, the Dutch purchased 17 surplus PBM-5A amphibians in November 1954. Most served 321 Squadron in the Netherlands New Guinea from 1956 until 1959.

Experimental Boats

Navy interest in testing very large flying boats increased

with the development of the 18-cylinder Wright R-3350 Duplex Cyclone, who's promised 2,000 hp could lift a mighty load off the water. As early as January 1937, Consolidated prepared plans of the first version of a four-engine XPB3Y-1, essentially a single-tail XPB2Y-1 with a 180-foot wing span.

Mfr

CONSOLIDATED XPB3Y-1 (1938 design)
Four Wright XR-3350-4, 2000 hp takeoff, 1700 hp at 6200'
DIMENSIONS: Span 190', Wing Area 3200 sq. ft.
WEIGHT: Empty 57,258 lb., Gross 124,700 lb. Fuel 3350-8400 gal.
PERFORMANCE: Speed- Top 229 mph at s. l., 246 mph at 6500'. Stalling 76 mph. Service Ceiling 21,750', Climb 5000'/6.9 min. Range 8200 miles/4000-lb. bombs.

By April 1938 Model 30, a 62-ton XPB3Y-1 design, was offered to the Navy with four XR-3350-4 engines, 190-foot wing span, twin rudders, retractable floats, and a capacity of from four to 36 1,000-lb. bombs. Fifteen crewmen flew the plane and manned ten gun emplacements. Power-operated turrets were placed at the nose, top waist, and stern, while manual mounts were planned for the sides and behind the step. Gunners were also placed in the leading edge of each wing fillet, and passageways led outboard of the engines to two cupolas whose guns could fire up or down.

Martin's more conservative Model 170 design with the same power plants was chosen by the Navy for a prototype XPB2M-1 ordered on August 23, 1938. During that giant's protracted construction, Consolidated offered the Model 34, a smaller XPB3Y-1 version designed in September 1941 as a nine-place flying boat with either four Wright R-3350 or Pratt & Whitney R-2800 engines, leak proof tanks, and armor. Turbosuperchargers and pressurized crew cabins were supposed to give the Wright-powered version a top speed of 308 mph at 25,000 feet with a 132,500-pound gross weight.

An XPB3Y-1 prototype was ordered April 2, 1942, looking like a bigger PB2Y-3 with a 169-foot span and "collapsible" floats retracting behind the engine nacelles. Eight .50-caliber guns were paired in Erco nose and top ball turrets, along with twin waist blisters, and a Convair tail turret. But on September 9, designer I.M. Laddon urged the Navy to cancel the XPB3Y-1 in favor of land bomber development, and the Navy agreed by October 20. Glenn L. Martin, however, continued to press for large flying boats.

Mfr

MARTIN XPB2M-1
Four Wright XR-3350-4, 2000 hp takeoff, 1700 hp at 4000'
(R-3350-8, 2300 hp takeoff on XPB2M-1R)
DIMENSIONS: Span 200', Lg. 117'3", Ht. 38'5", Wing Area 3685 sq. ft.
WEIGHT: Empty 70,684 lb., Gross 140,000 lb. Fuel 9113 gal. (75,573-144,000 lb. on XPB2M-1R)
PERFORMANCE: Speed- Top 205 mph at s. l., 221 mph at 4500', Stalling 83 mph. Service Ceiling 14,600', Climb 440'/1 min. Range 6200 miles/4000 lb. bombs, 4945 miles/10,000 lb.

Martin Mars

The largest of all Navy patrol planes was the Martin XPB4M-1 Mars, originally powered by four 2,000-hp XR-3350-4 Cyclones. The aircraft's size inspired Martin to arrange formal ceremonies at the launching on November 5, 1941, but an accidental fire delayed the first flight to July 3, 1942.

The spacious hull contained two full decks and all the room the 11-man crew needed. Below the flight deck was the officers' quarters, wardroom, lavatory, and private cabin for the captain. Amidships was the bomb bay for ten 1,000-lb bombs that could be dropped from an opening on each side, and next came the crew quarters, mess, and lavatory.

Five of the six .50-caliber guns were in 54-inch diameter ball power turrets in the nose, tail, and three hidden in the waist until extended out the top and sides. Another flexible gun was mounted behind the bottom step. The Mars had been designed too early to include armor and fuel tank protection.

USN

MARTIN XPB2M-1R on October 17, 1944

As a patrol bomber, the Mars was far less practical than the much larger number of PBMs that could be obtained with the same productive effort. Instead, it was decided to strip the armament and remodel the Mars as a transport with new R-3350-8 engines. After company flight tests were completed on October 5, 1942, the Mars was returned to the shop for rework.

Flight tests as the PB2M-1R began on May 5, 1943, and ended with a 33-hour endurance flight in October. The Mars served the Navy on the east coast and then flew the Alameda to Honolulu route. Twenty cargo versions (JRM-l) were ordered in June 1944, and six of these would be completed after the war's end cut back the contract. Fifty years later, two would still be flying for a Canadian fire-fighting company.

Consolidated Corregidor

Consolidated Aircraft wanted to replace its PBY with an entirely new project, the Model 31. This twin-engine design by I.M. Laddon was going to be the world's fastest flying boat, with everything new- wing, power plant, and hull shape.

The long narrow wing used an airfoil invented by David R. Davis, and Consolidated's exclusive property for a limited time. The Model 31 was the first aircraft to fly with the 2,000-hp Wright l8-cylinder R-3350, which became the B-29's future power plant. The deep double-deck hull had room for retractable tricycle beaching gear, and the outboard floats retracted inwards, instead of to the wingtips. Twin rudders were added, and like the Davis wing, would be adopted for the B-24 design in 1939.

CONSOLIDATED Model 31 on March 7, 1941
Two Wright R-3350-A71, 2000 hp takeoff, 1900 hp at 16,000'
DIMENSIONS: Span 110', Lg. 73'10", Ht. 24'10", Wing Area 1048 sq. ft.
WEIGHT: Empty 26,046 lb., Gross 40,000 lb., Max. 46,000 lb. Fuel 1470-2395 gal.
PERFORMANCE: Speed- Top 242 mph at s. l., 271 mph at 16,000', Cruising 185 mph, Stalling 76 mph. Service Ceiling 29,500', Climb 1830'/1 min. Range 2800 miles/1000-lb. bombs, 4220 miles max.

Prototype construction began on July 6, 1938, and although both patrol bomber and airliner versions were designed, the hull was bare of fittings when first flown on May 5, 1939. Tests in light weight did show the predicted 270-mph top speed at 15,000 feet, but the horizontal tail had to be raised and increased from 22 to 26 feet in width.

Navy trial board flight tests were not begun until March 25, 1940, and high speed, with 46,620 pounds weight, was measured from 230 mph at sea level to 258 mph at 16,600 feet. But the proposed 8-place patrol configuration with armor and power turrets was discarded by the Navy in favor of buying Boeing's proposed XPBB-1, using the same Cyclone engines.

The prototype was provided with dummy gun turrets, but another effort to sell it to the Navy failed during April 1941 trials. Yet the war opened another sales opportunity, and the prototype was accepted April 13, 1942, for conversion to the XP4Y-l. On July 8, 1942, a Navy contract scheduled 200 P4Y-1 Corregidor boats to be built at a new factory in New Orleans.

CONSOLIDATED XP4Y-1 (1943)
Two Wright R-3350-8, 2300 hp takeoff, 1800 hp at 13,600'
DIMENSIONS: Span 110', Lg. 74'1", Ht. 25'2", Wing Area 1048 sq. ft.
WEIGHT: Empty 29,334 lb., Gross 46,000 lb., Max. 48,000 lb. Fuel 1545-3000 gal.
PERFORMANCE: Speed- Top 247 mph at 13,600', 231 mph at s.l., Cruising 136 mph, Stalling 89 mph. Service Ceiling 21,400', Climb 1230'/1 min. Range 2300 miles/eight 325-lb. depth charges, 1745 miles/two torpedoes, 2695 miles/1845 gal., 3280 miles max.

The new boats were powered by two 2,300-hp R-3350-8 Cyclones, and have radar above a movable 37-mm M-9 gun with 120 rounds in the bow, twin .50-caliber guns in a top Erco power turret with 2,000 rounds, and another pair for a tail gunner. Eight 325-pound depth charges or four 1,000-pound mines inside the hull were moved out on tracks under the wings for release. Since no provisions were made for conventional bombing, the usual PB designation became simply P.

On July 28, 1943, flight tests began on the rebuilt XP4Y-1, but on September 11 the P4Y-1 program was canceled because B-29 production required the entire R-3350 engine supply and so the New Orleans plant was instead given a contract for 450 Catalinas.

Mfr

BOEING XPBB-1
Two Wright R-3350-8, 2300 hp takeoff, 1800 hp at 13,600'
DIMENSIONS: Span 139'8", Lg. 94'9", Ht. 34'2", Wing Area 1826 sq. ft.
WEIGHT: Empty 41,531 lb., Gross 62,000 lb., Max. 101,130 lb. Fuel 2490 gal. in self-sealing tanks, 7400 gal. max.
PERFORMANCE: Speed- Top 214 mph at s. l., 228 mph at 14,200', Cruising 127 mph, Stalling 67 mph. Service Ceiling 22,400', Climb 980'/1 min. Range 2320 miles/1000-lb. bombs, 7300 miles max.

Boeing XPBB-1

The Navy's largest twin-engine flying boat was the Boeing XPBB-1 Sea Ranger ordered June 20, 1940, and first flown July 5, 1942. Powered by two R-3350-8 Cyclones, it had the wing shape later used on all the B-29s, large fixed floats, a high fixed rudder, and a crew of ten.

The normal takeoff with 1,479 gallons and 1,000-pound load was for a 62,000-pound design weight. But if the big catapult-barge (AVC-1) tested with the XPBM-2 would be available, the Boeing could take flight weighing 101,129 pounds, including 7,243 gallons. Design range would be increased from 1,940 to 7,090 miles, or the bomb load increased to 20,000 pounds with 4,263 gallons.

Eight .50-caliber guns with 32,000 rounds were placed in new Erco power turrets: two guns in nose, top, and tail, and one in each tear-shaped side blister. A new Boeing factory at Renton, Washington, was to begin with an order for 57 PBB-1s, but the PBB-1 was canceled in favor of the B-29A when the Navy exchanged its program for immediate deliveries of PB4Y-1 Liberators. Yet the lone Ranger's gun turret designs would later become an important part of the PB4Y production.

Borrowed Bombers

The Navy's exclusive reliance on flying boats for patrol missions was rooted in traditional national policies that gave naval aircraft responsibility for fleet support and overseas scouting, and Army aircraft responsibility for coastal defense, and cooperation with land forces. Land-based aircraft were employed by the Army, and the Navy was limited to water-based and ship-based aircraft.

The unfortunate result was that the superior performance of landplanes for long-distance flights was not used by the Navy. But, since most attacks began when submarines were seen on the surface, faster planes were needed to catch them before they dived to safety.

Acquisition of bases in Iceland and Newfoundland for the Neutrality Patrol, however, required land-based planes, for water-based operations in those areas suffered from winter ice conditions. This requirement led to procurement of amphibian Catalinas, but in the meantime the Lockheed Hudson built for the RAF was available.

Lockheed Hudson

Lockheed has built all of the Navy's patrol planes for many years, but the first Lockheed patrol type began as a modest twin-engine airliner until a British Purchasing Commission came to the United States in April 1938 looking for a twin-engine trainer.

Lockheed quickly put together at Burbank a military mockup based on the Model 14 transport and offered a specification that was far superior to the current RAF coastal reconnaissance type, the Anson. Various changes were made to fit British plans; instead of the two pilots of American practice, there was a single pilot, and a navigator's post in the nose.

After designer Kelly Johnson visited London to finalize details, the British ordered 200 on June 23, 1938, and the first Hudson I flew on December 10, 1938. War brought more orders and 351 Hudson Is were built, followed by 20 Hudson IIs, alike but for improved Hamilton propellers. Canada received 28 of the Hudson Is and one Mk. II after the war began.

The Hudson I (Model B14L) had 1,100-hp Wright R-1820-G102A Cyclones and had the tapered wings with Fowler flaps, twin rudders, and tail-down landing gear of previous Lockheed transports. Four crewmen were carried along with enough fuel for patrols up to 11 hours. Hudson I armament consisted of four 250 or ten 100-pound bombs, two fixed .303 Brownings in the nose above the bombardier's windows, and two in the rear Boulton Paul power turret, which was installed after the aircraft reached Britain. (No power turrets were yet in American production.)

LOCKHEED Hudson I
Two Wright R-1820-G102A, 1100 hp takeoff, 900 hp at 6700'
DIMENSIONS Span 65'6" Lg. 41'4", Ht. 11'10", Wing Area 551 sq. ft.
WEIGHT: Empty 11,630 lb., Gross 17,500 lb. Fuel 644 gal.
PERFORMANCE: Speed- Top 246 mph at 6,500', Cruising 170 mph, Landing 70 mph. Service Ceiling 25,000', Climb 2180'/1 min. Range 1,020 miles normal, 1960 miles max.

The first Hudsons arrived by ship at Liverpool on February 15, 1939, and No. 224 squadron was operational in time to become the first RAF plane to exchange shots with the Luftwaffe on the war's second day. The Hudson's first victory was a Do 18 flying boat downed on November 10, 1939, and by April 1940, five Hudson squadrons operated over the North Sea. That month, the normal routine of open-sea patrolling was broken by bombing raids against the German invaders of Norway. Hudsons covered the evacuation of Dunkirk in June, even attacking enemy dive-bombers.

Australia had announced an order for Hudson Model B14S with twin-row 1,050-hp Pratt & Whitney SC3G Wasps on November 2, 1938, but delivery didn't begin until January 1940. One hundred were shipped to Melbourne by June, and were listed as Hudson Mark IV by the RAF, which had already ordered the Mark III version. These became the principal Australian combat aircraft facing the Japanese advance in December 1941 and were the first Hudsons heavily engaged in the Pacific.

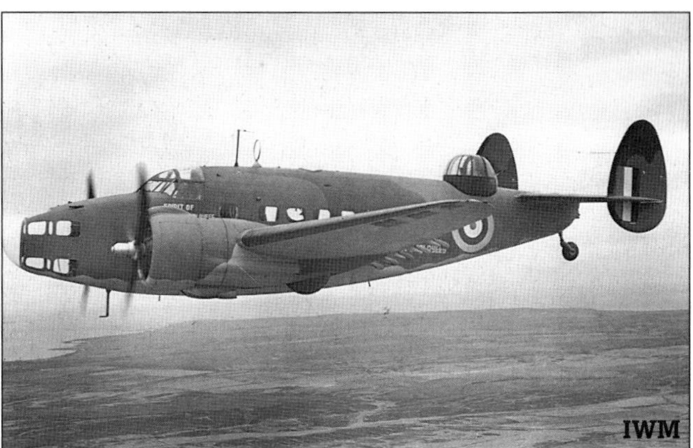

LOCKHEED Hudson III
Two Wright R-1820-G205A, 1200 hp takeoff, 900 hp at 15,200'
DIMENSIONS: As Hudson I
WEIGHT: Empty 12,536 lb., Gross 18,500 lb., Max. 20,000 lb. Fuel 644+384 gal.
PERFORMANCE: Speed- Top 255 mph at 15,000', Cruising 223 mph. Service Ceiling 24,500'. Range 2160 miles max.

LOCKHEED Hudson IV

Anti-submarine patrols would became the main Hudson mission in the Atlantic, but despite installation of the first few ASV Mark I radar sets in January 1940, confirmed successes were slow in coming. On October 25, a direct hit with a Hudson's 100-pound bomb was not enough to sink the U-46; it would take 250-pound Mk VIII depth charges to sink subs.

More powerful Wright G-205A Cyclones, giving 1,200 hp at takeoff, powered the 428 Hudson IIIs that began to appear in August 1940. Labeled Lockheed 414-56s by the company, this five-place model added a retractable .303-caliber ventral gun, provisions for a gun on each side, up to 1,600 pounds of bombs, armor, and extra fuel capacity in the wings. The added tankage enabled the remaining

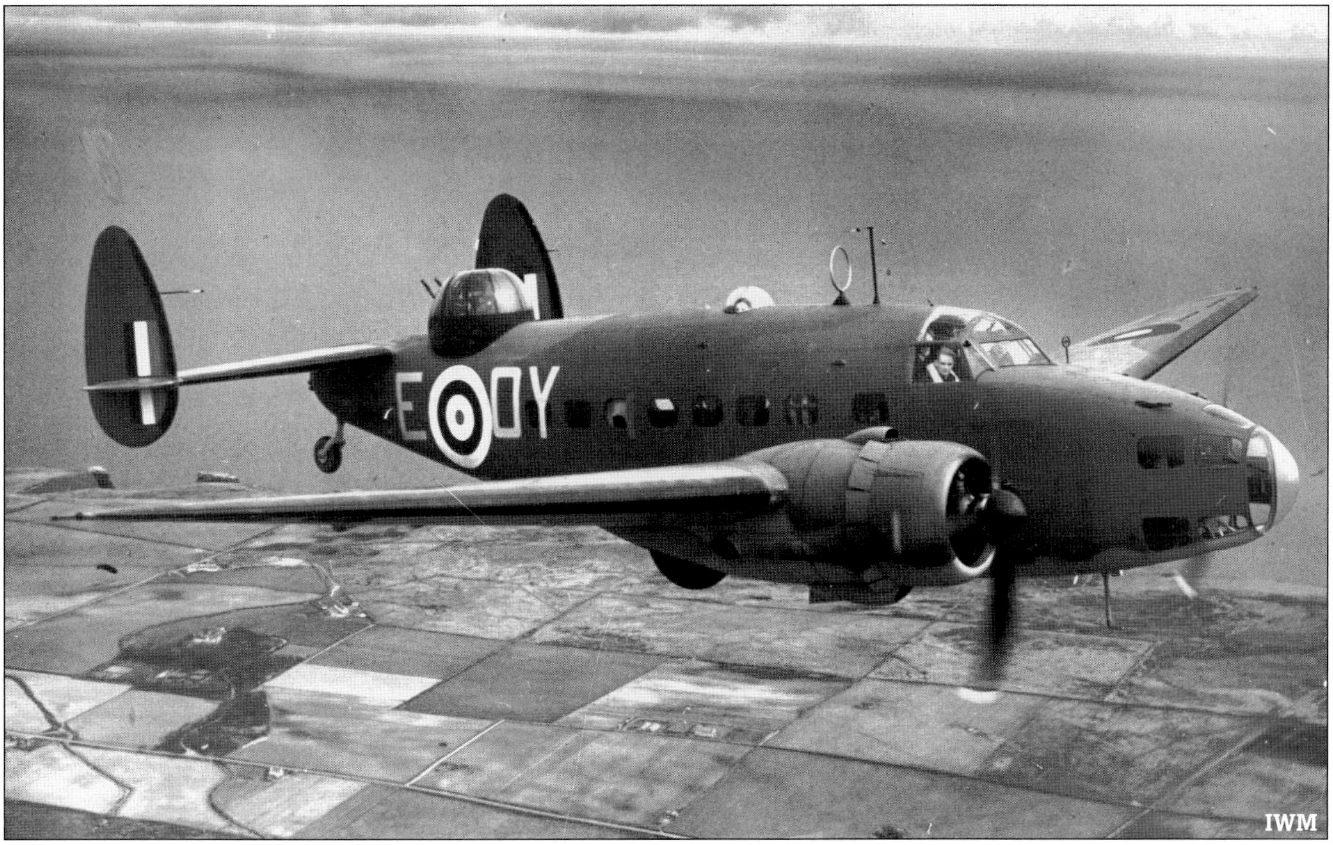

LOCKHEED A-28 (Hudson V)
Two Pratt & Whitney R-1830-45, 1050 hp takeoff, 1000 hp at 11,500'
DIMENSIONS: Span 65'6", Lg. 41'4", Ht. 11'11", Wing Area 551 sq. ft.
WEIGHT: Empty 12,810 lb., Gross 18,500 lb., Max. 20,500 lb. Fuel 644 gal.
PERFORMANCE: Speed- Top 260 mph at 12,500', Cruising 206 mph, Landing 68 mph. Service Ceiling 26,000', Climb 10,000'/7.8 min. Range 1500 miles/four 325-lb. bombs, 1800 miles max.

Hudsons for Britain to be delivered by air, beginning with the first transatlantic ferry on November 10, 1940.

Thirty Hudson IIIs went to New Zealand (RNZAF) in 1941, three went to Canada, and another 17 were lost before delivery to the RAF. With the aid of ASV Mk. II radar and its operator, anti-submarine patrols became more effective, and an Iceland-based Hudson crippled U-570, which on August 27, 1941, became the first U-boat to surrender to an aircraft.

Parallel production of Wasp-powered Hudsons for the RAF continued in 1941 along with the Cyclone versions, including 30 Mark IV (Model 414-08) with SC3G Wasps and 409 Hudson Vs with 1,200 hp S3C4G Wasps and the IIIA's armament provisions. Of these, 43 went to Canada, six to the RNZAF, and 14 were lost before reaching service.

The Lend-lease Act made American funds available for Allied contracts, which were then given Army Attack designations despite their maritime role. Thus, on May 29, 1941, Defense Aid contract DA 5 ordered 52 A-28 (Mark IVA) Hudsons delivered to Australia in December 1941 with 1,050 hp R-1830-45 Wasps, and 417 A-29 (Mark IIIA) Hudsons with 1,200 hp R-1820-87 Cyclones for the RAF.

Later Lend-lease contracts added 383 A-29As and 450 A-28A (Hudson VI) models with 1,200-hp R-1830-67 Wasps. Provisions had been made in both the A-28A and A-29A models for conversions to transport work. When the last A-29A came off the Burbank production line in May 1943, Lockheed had delivered 2,640 Hudson bombers, plus 300 AT-18 and AT-18A training and target towing versions, the former with Martin twin .50-caliber gun turrets.

LOCKHEED A-28A (Hudson VI)
Two Pratt & Whitney R-1830-67, 1200 hp takeoff
DIMENSIONS: Span 65'6", Lg. 44'4", Ht. 11'11", Wing Area 551 sq. ft.
WEIGHT: Empty 13,195 lb., Gross 18,500 lb., Max. 22,360 1b. Fuel 644+384 gal.
PERFORMANCE: Speed- Top 261 mph at 18,500', Cruising 215 mph, Landing 68 mph. Service Ceiling 28,000', Climb 10,000'/7.8 min. Range 1300 miles/four 325-lb. bombs, 2600 miles max.

LOCKHEED Hudson VI with radar and rockets

As it happened, the first 20 A-29s went to the U.S. Navy as PBO-ls on October 29, 1942, serving with VP-82 at Argentina, Newfoundland, the Navy's first landplane patrol squadron. Powered by two R-1820-40 Cyclones, they were armed with four 325-pound depth charges, two fixed and three flexible 30-caliber guns.

Unlike Catalinas, they were fast enough to catch surfaced submarines before they crash-dived, so despite the efforts of four flying boat squadrons and many surface ships, these PBO-ls sank the first two U-boats, U-656 and 503, killed by American forces on March 1 and 15, 1942.

LOCKHEED PBO-1 Hudson
Two Wright R-1820-40, 1200 hp takeoff, 900 hp at 14,000'
DIMENSIONS: Span 65'6", Lg. 44'4", Ht. 11'10", Wing Area 551 sq. ft.
WEIGHT: Empty 12,680 lb., Gross 18,837 lb., Max 20,203 lb. Fuel 644 gal.
PERFORMANCE: Speed- Top 237 mph at s.l., 262 mph at 15,300', Cruising 129 mph. Service Ceiling 26,200', Climb 1450'/1 min. Range 1750 miles/four 325-lb. depth charges, 1890 miles max.

In 1942, the Army Air Force also requisitioned 153 A-29s to fill out its own bomber units for anti-submarine patrols and one from the 396th Bomb Squadron at Cherry Point, North Carolina, hit the first U-boat (U-701) destroyed by the Army Air Forces on July 7, 1942. They were also used on the West Coast by the 30th, 41st, and 42nd Bomb Groups. Air Force A-29s usually replaced the power turret with a .50-caliber gun in an open pit, and 24 fitted with four cameras for the 1st Mapping Group were redesignated A-29B.

Canada had 248 Hudsons, beginning in September 1939: 28 Mark Is, one II, three IIIs, 137 IIIAs, 43 Vs and 36 Vs, and the RCAF sank two U-boats on July 31 and October 30, 1942.

RAF Hudsons knocked out 18 U-boats from May 1942 to October 1943, including three sunk by under wing rockets, and joined the 1,000 plane night raids over Germany in 1942, and even fought Zeros over the Bay of Bengal. While most Hudsons went to the RAF, Australia received 247: 100 IV, 52 IVA, and 95 A-29 Hudsons, from January to May 1942. New Zealand had 94: 30 IIIs, 54 IIIAs, six Vs and four VIs. while Brazil got 28 A-28A Hudsons from December 1942 to March 1943 to patrol South Atlantic waters.

LOCKHEED A-29 (Hudson IIIA)
, 1200 hp takeoff, 1000 hp at 14,200'
DIMENSIONS: Span 65'6", Lg. 44'4", Ht. 11'11", Wing Area 551 sq. ft.
WEIGHT: Empty 12,825 lb., Gross 20,500 lb., Max. 21,300 lb. Fuel 644-1028 gal.
PERFORMANCE: Speed- Top 253 mph at 15,000', Cruising 205 mph, Landing 68 mph. Service Ceiling 26,500', Climb 10,000'/6.3 min. Range 1,550 miles/four 325-lb. depth charges, 2,800 miles max.

China had been promised 33 in 1941 to be used by a second AVG volunteer group, but this plan was dropped and 26 A-29s began a hazardous trip with ferry pilots in June 1942. Of 19 A-29s turned over to replace the Tupolev SBs of China's 2nd Bomb Group from August 12 to October 25, ten suffered accidents within three months, and the remainder became transports, while the group's airmen were sent to the U.S. for B-25 training.

Navy Liberators

Early in the war, as flying boats suffered grievous losses to the Zero's guns, the weakness of big boats became painfully obvious. As the hull design's performance handicap was often proving fatal, the ability to land on water was losing tactical importance. When prepared landing fields increased in number, faster and better armed landplane patrol bombers could attack or escape their enemies more quickly.

The Navy became eager to acquire land-based patrol planes and in February 1942 requested a reallocation of bomber production, especially of the long-range B-24 Liberators already being used by the British for patrol work. But the Army wanted every bomber it could get, so it took much negotiation before Chief of Staff George C. Marshall agreed to a Navy share on July 7, 1942. The Navy relinquished the Boeing Renton plant's PBB-1 flying boat program to expand future B-29A production.

Consolidated B-24Ds were scheduled for Navy use on July 11, 1942, redesignated PB4Y-l, and the first seven from San Diego arrived in September. Liberator deliveries began slowly, but gathered volume and were joined in 1943 by the entire Lockheed Ventura production, so that

Mfr

LOCKHEED A-29 with turret

CONSOLIDATED PB4Y-1 (1942)

the majority of Navy patrol planes during the latter part of the war were land planes.

A Marine Photo squadron, VMD-254 was the first to take the PB4Y-1 to the South Pacific, and was joined by VP-51 (later designated VB-101) in January 1943. Deployed PB4Y-1 squadrons increased from two in March 1943 to 12 by December 31, 1943.

Until more Navy Liberator squadrons became combat-ready, Army squadrons were deployed against German submarines. Army B-24Ds operating from Morocco, the Canary Islands, and Britain, sank eight U-boats from February 10 to August 2, 1943. A Navy PB4Y-1 from VB-107 on Ascension Island made its first kill on July 23, 1943, and Navy Liberators sank 13 U-boats by April 25, 1945.

The first PB4Y-1s from San Diego were 278 B-24Ds with Navy paint, but modification centers began adding features such as APS-15 surface-search radar instead of the belly gun turret. A new Erco ball turret, originally designed for the Boeing PBB-1, was installed in the bow of the 112th PB4Y-1 (a B-24D-70-CO) in May 1943. Heavier armor and a better fire field with a 170-degree horizontal and 165-degree lateral turn, compared to the older Convair turret's 143 and 104-degree swing, improved the Erco's effectiveness.

This front power turret and ASV radar under the wings distinguish the later PB4Y-1s from their AAF origin as 368 B-24J, 186 L, and 145 M models. Eight .50 caliber guns with 3,770 rounds, 1,318 pounds of armor, 2,110 pounds of fuel tank protection, and up to eight 1,000-pound bombs, mines, or 650-pound depth charges could be carried. Cameras were provided on those supplied to four photographic squadrons.

The Navy received 977 PB4Y-l Liberators by January 1945, when all deliveries shifted to the PB4Y-2 Privateer. Unlike the massed high-altitude Air Force formations, Navy Liberators usually flew alone, or in pairs, and attacked from low altitudes. Seventeen Navy Liberator squadrons were deployed by the end of 1944, with eight in the Atlantic and nine in the Pacific, along with two Marine photo PB4Y-1P squadrons.

CONSOLIDATED PB4Y-1 (1944)
Four Pratt & Whitney R-1830-65, 1200 hp to 25,000'
DIMENSIONS: Span 110', Lg. 67'3", Ht. 17'11", Wing Area 1048 sq. ft.
WEIGHT: Empty 37,160 lb., Gross 60,000 lb., Max. 63,000 lb. Fuel 2814+800 gal.
PERFORMANCE: Speed- Top 231 mph at s. l., 287 mph at 26,700', Cruising 149 mph, Stalling 95 mph. Service Ceiling 32,600', Climb 990'/1 min., 10,000'/10.1 min Range 2065 miles/8000 lb. bombs, 3090 miles patrol, 4190 miles ferry.

Several PB4Y-1s in Britain were converted to radio-controlled drones carrying 21,248 pounds of explosives. They were to attack German V-1 sites, but only two sorties were made. The first exploded August 12, 1944, with pilot Joseph P. Kennedy still aboard. After the war, the PB4Y-1s were declared surplus except for a photographic squadron that kept the PB4Y-1P until 1956.

Vega Ventura

The Lockheed Vega Ventura (Model 37) was a mid-wing monoplane with twin rudders and tail-down landing gear developed from the Hudson light bomber and the Lodestar Model 18 airliner. After the RAF studied a Lockheed proposal for a faster and better armed bomber with two big Pratt & Whitney Double Wasp engines, engineering began May 13, 1940, on an order for 300 that was increased to 675 in September.

These planes were built in a new factory by Lockheed's Vega subsidiary nearby in Burbank. Lend-lease contracts in August 1941 added 200 more that were designated as B-34s and another 550 expected to be built in the Lockheed plant as the O-56.

The Ventura I was first flown with 1,850-hp R-2800-SIA4-G Wasps on July 31, 1941, and was accepted in September. Armament included 2,500 pounds of bombs, two fixed .50-caliber guns in the nose, a pair of .303-caliber guns in a power-operated British top turret, and another pair at a rear ventral opening. Two more .303-caliber guns in the tip of the nose could be fired forward or slanted 25 degrees downwards.

LOCKHEED-VEGA Ventura I
Two Pratt & Whitney R-2800-SlA4-G, 1850 hp takeoff, 1450 hp at 13,000'
DIMENSIONS: Span 65'6", Lg. 51'5", Ht. 11'11", Wing Area 551 sq. ft.
WEIGHT: Empty 17,233 lb., Gross 22,500 lb., Max. 26,000 lb. Fuel 565 gal.
PERFORMANCE: Speed- Top 312 mph at 15,500', Cruising 272 mph Landing 80 mph. Service Ceiling 25,200', Climb 2035'/ 1 min. Range 925 miles/2500 lb. bombs.

Of the 25 Ventura Is accepted by the end of 1941, 18 went to Canada and one was kept by Lockheed for engine development. Deliveries began by ship to Liverpool in April 1942, and RAF Bomber Command Squadrons No. 21, 464, and 487 readied the type for action.

LOCKHEED-VEGA Ventura II of No. 464 Squadron RAAF

The 188 Ventura Is were followed by 487 Ventura IIs with 2,000-hp R-2800-31 engines. Of the 675 direct-purchase Venturas built by September, 1942, 162 went to the RAF, 69 remained in Canada, 135 reached the South African Air Force, 28 were lost in transit, one was sold back to Lockheed, and 280 were requisitioned by the AAF, which turned over the last 27 Ventura IIs as the PV-3 to the U.S. Navy in September 1942 as an advance on all future Ventura production.

LOCKHEED-VEGA B-34A (Ventura IIA)
Two Pratt & Whitney R-2800-31, 2000 hp takeoff, 1600 hp at 13,500'
DIMENSIONS: Span 65'6", Lg. 51'5", Ht. 11'11", Wing Area 551 sq. ft.
WEIGHT: Empty 17,275 lb., Gross 25,600 lb., Max. 27,750 lb. Fuel 565+800 gal.
PERFORMANCE: Speed- Top 315 mph at 15,500', Cruising 230 mph, Landing 80 mph. Service Ceiling 24,000', Climb 15,000'/ 8.2 min. Range 950 miles/3000 lb. bombs, 2600 miles max.

Beginning on May 26, 1942, the AAF held 9 Ventura I and 239 Ventura IIs, which were called R-37s in Air Force service, and all 200 Lend-Lease Ventura IIAs, or B-34A-VEs, completed by November 1942. They were not used by operational squadrons, but were scattered about for various service and training roles, and Canada got 60. Beginning in May 1943, Australia was sent 20 B-34 and 41 R-37 Venturas and New Zealand got 23 B-34s from AAF stocks.

LOCKHEED-VEGA B-37 (VENTURA III)
Two Wright R-2600-31, 1700 hp takeoff, 1450 hp at 12,000'
DIMENSIONS: As B-34A
WEIGHT: Empty 18,615 lb., Gross 27,000 lb., Max. 29,500 lb. Fuel 565+735 gal.
PERFORMANCE: Speed- Top 298 mph at 13,500', Cruising 198 mph, Landing 77 mph. Service Ceiling 22,400', Climb 10,000'/ 5.5 min. Range 1300 miles/2000-lb. bombs, 2700 miles max.

Since the British turret was unavailable, most B-34As used a Martin turret with twin .50-caliber guns, and had mounts for two .50-caliber guns in the nose and six flexible .30-caliber guns; two in the nose, two at the ventral post, and one on each side of the cabin. Five crewmen and six 500-pound bombs or two 390-gallon bomb bay tanks could be carried. Designations for aircraft modified for specific training missions were B-34A-2 bombardier, B-34A-3 gunnery, B-34A-4 tow-target, and B-34B-l navigation trainers.

The three RAF bomber squadrons used the Ventura for cross-Channel daylight attacks from November 3, 1942, to September 8, 1943. Losses were heavy, so the Ventura was replaced by Mosquitoes in Bomber Command and passed to Coastal Command and weather units.

The Ventura III model began with an order on August 8, 1941, for 550 Lockheed O-56 aircraft powered by Wright R-2600-13 Cyclones and redesignated B-37-LO before the first flight on September 21, 1942. The order was cut back to only 18 aircraft accepted from January to April 1943. Armed with two .50-caliber fixed and two .50-caliber turret guns, and twin .30-caliber tunnel guns, the B-37 could be recognized by oval windows in the lower waist for two additional .30-caliber guns. All remained with the AAF.

LOCKHEED-VEGA PV-1
Two Pratt & Whitney R-2800-31, 2000 hp takeoff, 1600 hp at 11,900'
DIMENSIONS: Span 65'6", Lg. 51'9", Ht. 13'2" Wing Area 551 sq. ft.
WEIGHT: Empty 20,197 lb., Gross 26,500 lb., Max. 31,077 lb. Fuel 981+790 gal.
PERFORMANCE: Speed- Top 296 mph at s. l., 312 mph at 13,800', Cruising 166 mph, Stalling 91 mph. Service Ceiling 26,300', Climb 2230'/1 min., 10,000'/5.4 min. Range 1660 miles/six 325-lb. depth charges, 1360 miles/torpedo.

Navy Venturas

As a short-range supplement to long-range Liberators, the Vega Ventura was allocated to the Navy on July 24, 1942. The PV-1 modified for Navy equipment and a larger PV-2 design begun to Navy requirements were preceded by the 27 PV-3s drafted, minus turrets, from the Ventura II contract in October 1942 to replace the Hudsons of VP-82 and begin the Navy training program.

The PV-1 was first flown November 3, 1942, and 1,600 were delivered from December 1942 to May 1944. Since they were intended for low-level attacks, they needed no Norden bombsight or oxygen gear, and a simple patrol label replaced the patrol-bomber (PB) appellation. An ASD-1 search radar dish was concealed behind the plastic nose cone.

Powered by R-1830-31 Wasps, the PV-1 had fuel tanks enlarged for 823 gallons protected by 1,055 pounds of self-sealing, and could add 490 gallons in droppable bomb-bay tanks and two 150-gallon drop tanks under the wings.

Six crewmen were protected by 762 pounds of armor, and the bomb bay could hold up to six 325-pound depth charges or 500-pound bombs, or a Mk. 13 torpedo. Twin .50-caliber guns were in the Martin top turret with 400 rpg, twin .30-caliber guns with 1,000 rpg were in the ventral tunnel, while the nose had two of the heavy guns on top and could add three more underneath for a total of five fixed guns together with 1,250 rounds.

VP-93, which had replaced its PBYs by PV-1s in January 1943 and became VB-126 at Argentina, Newfoundland, was joined in April 1943 by VP-82, now also with the PV-1, which became VB-125 and sank U-174 on April 27, 1943. U-591 and U-761 were lost to VB-127, the first of five squadrons stationed in Brazil, and VB-128 on Iceland sank U-336 in 1943. By 1944, 15 Ventura squadrons based around the Atlantic joined surface forces and other Navy air to frustrate the U-boat's war.

The Ventura appeared in the Pacific when VB-135 and VB-136 began operations from the Aleutians in May 1943, and began attacks on the Kuriles from Attu in November. There were 15 PV-1 squadrons (redesignated VPB) deployed around the Pacific in 1944 with Fleet Air Wings Two, Four, Six, Eight, Ten, and 17. Their targets were Japanese surface shipping and land establishments.

Marine Aviation's first night fighter squadron, VMF(N)-531, received three-place Venturas with Mark IV radar and six nose guns in April 1943, moved to the South Pacific by October and downed six bombers from November 13, 1943, to May 11, 1944.

The RAF was allocated 386 PV-1s, called the Ventura G.R. V, of which 15 were lost in transit and 108 went to the South African Air Force. The Ventura G.R. V joined No. 459 and 500 Squadrons in December 1943 and served in Italy along with three SAAF squadrons. Canada received 20 PV-1s from the RAF and 137 from the U.S. Navy. Australia added 14 PV-ls to its 61 older Venturas and New Zealand got 116 PV-ls and four PV-2s.

Five hundred Lockheed PV-2 Harpoons were ordered on June 30, 1943. A larger and longer range development of the PV-l, the Harpoon had greater span, larger fins, 714 pounds of armor, five .50-caliber fixed nose guns, and two in the power turret. Eight 5-inch rockets could be added, while ventral guns were omitted. The bomb bay could hold six 325-pound or four 650-pound depth charges, or four 1,000-pound bombs or mines, and a pair of drop tanks or 1,000-pound bombs could be added on under wing pylons.

First flown on December 3, 1943, the PV-2 had wing problems that delayed acceptance until March 1944, and VPB-139 did not fly its first strikes from Attu against the Kuriles with bombs and rockets until April 1945. VPB-142, VPB-148, and VPB-153 fought in the central Pacific.

Another contract was placed in October 1944 for the PV-2D, with the first accepted in July 1945. This model had eight fixed .50-caliber guns grouped around the nose radar, as well as the eight rockets and 4,000-pound bomb load of the previous model. Production of both the PV-2 and PV-2D concluded in December 1945, with 500 PV-2 and 35 PV-2D Harpoons built and 379 Ds canceled.

At the war's end, there were 16 Lockheed PV-1 and five PV-2 squadrons in service. Brazil got 14 PV-1 and six PV-2s in 1944.

Although replaced in first-line units by P2V Neptunes by August 1948, Harpoons served 11 post-war Navy Reserve squadrons and were supplied to allied nations during the Korean War. No longer an enemy, the Japanese Navy received 17 in 1951, while the Dutch Navy got 18, which were transferred to Portugal in 1954. Italy and Peru also used PV-2s.

LOCKHEED-VEGA PV-2
Two Pratt & Whitney R-2800-31, 2000 hp take-off, 1600 hp at 11,900'
DIMENSIONS: Span 75', Lg. 52'1", Ht. 13'3", Wing Area 686 sq. ft.
WEIGHT: Empty 21,028 lb., Gross 33,668 lb., Max. 36,000 lb. Fuel 1149+714 gal.
PERFORMANCE: Speed- Top 271 mph at s. l., 282 mph at 13,700', Cruising 171 mph, Landing 83 mph. Service Ceiling 23,900', Climb 1630'/1 min., 10,000'/7.6 min. Range 1790 miles/six 325-lb. depth charges, 2930 miles ferry.

Five hundred North American Mitchells allotted to the Navy January 14, 1943, were designated PBJ-l although they actually were used by the Marine Corps for medium bombing rather than patrol missions. Since they were similar to Army Mitchells, the reader is referred to the B-25 description in Chapter 15.

Convair Privateer

Meanwhile, experience with Liberators indicated that a superior patrol plane could be obtained by redesigning the Consolidated ship especially for naval tasks, and replacing both the PB2Y-3 flying boat and PB4Y-1 with the new type.

On May 8, 1943, three XPB4Y-2 prototypes were ordered converted from PB4Y-ls. The wings and tricycle

Mfr

CONSOLIDATED XPB4Y-2 (3-30-44)

landing gear were those of the B-24, but more fuel, guns and radar were to be added,

The first XPB4Y-2 Privateer flown September 20, 1943, tested the drag of dummy turrets but retained the B-24's twin rudders and turbosuperchargers. The second XPB4Y-2 was flown on October 30 with a lengthened fuselage and live turrets but was returned to the shop for a new single tail and redelivered February 2, 1944. The third prototype, flown December 15 by Phil Prophett, was the production prototype but stability problems required a higher tail fin and the final configuration was not accepted until March 29.

Meanwhile work went ahead on the contract placed October 15, 1943, for 660 PB4Y-2 Privateers. Although the first flew on February 15, 1944, changes delayed the first acceptance to March 31, the same day San Diego delivered its last PBY-5A. One more was accepted in April, and only five in May. Since patrol planes work at low altitudes, the turbosuperchargers were omitted on the four R-1830-94 Wasps, giving the Privateer a higher sea-level speed at a cost in high-altitude performance.

A crew of eleven, including two electronics operators for the APS-15B radar, and 1,171 pounds of armor were carried. Up to eight 1,000-pound bombs, mines, or 650-pound depth charges, or four 400-gallon fuel tanks could be carried in the bomb bays.

Mfr

CONSOLIDATED PB4Y-2
Four Pratt & Whitney R-1830-94, 1350 hp takeoff, 1100 hp at 13,400'
DIMENSIONS: Span 110', Lg. 74'7", Ht. 29'2", Wing Area 1048 sq. ft.
WEIGHT: Empty 37,405 lb., Gross 64,000 lb., Fuel 2364+ 1600 gal.
PERFORMANCE: Speed- Top 238 mph at s. l., 247 mph at 14,000', Cruising 158 mph, Stalling 96 mph. Service Ceiling 19,500', Climb 990'/1 min., 10,000'/13.2 min. Range 2630 miles/4000 lb. bombs, 3530 miles ferry.

Twelve .50-caliber guns were disposed in six power turrets: Convair nose and tail, two Martin top domes, and tear-shaped Erco side blisters. A great improvement on the hand-held side guns, the blisters could point downwards 95 degrees and up 60 degrees. The Convair nose turrets on the first 100 were replaced on the rest with better Erco nose turrets, beginning with the 101st PB4Y-2 delivered September 23, 1944.

Overseas deployment began in January 1945 as VPB-118 arrived in the Marianas. There were 14 PB4Y-2 squadrons equipped by July 1, 1945, with ten PB4Y-1 units awaiting conversion. Three squadrons had special PB4Y-2Bs with a Bat anti-shipping missiles below each wing; they were 1,600-pound radar-homing glide bombs with a 12-foot wing and 1,000-pound warhead. On April 23, they became the first and only automatic homing missiles used in the war by the Navy. The PB4Y-2S was an anti-sub version with 36 sonobouys.

While 710 more Privateers had been ordered on October 19, 1944, cancellations ended PB4Y-2 production in October 1945 after 739 were completed. Privateers remained in squadron service for several years after the war; and 28 modified as PB4Y-2M weather planes, without gun turrets to track hurricanes in 1946. The French Navy was supplied with 24 PB4Y-2S models.

A PB4Y-2 became the first Navy loss of the Cold War when a VP-26 Privateer on an ELINT mission near the Baltic coast of Latvia was shot down by four La-11 fighters on April 4, 1950. Eight Privateer squadrons remained when the Korean War began in June 1950. In 1951 they were redesignated P4Y-2, P4Y-2B, and P4Y-2S, and remained in service until 1954. The Chinese air force on Taiwan received 38 in 1953-55 to fight in the Formosa Straits.

Landplanes like these reduced flying boats to a minority of the patrol force. On December 31, 1941, the Navy had 466 patrol bombers, including 423 Catalina and 20 Mariner twin-engine flying boats, five four-engine boats, and only 18 twin-engine landplanes. Of 4,054 Navy patrol planes on hand June 30, 1945, there were 1,629 twin-engine and 55 four-engine flying boats, and 1,374 twin-engine and 996 four-engine landplanes.

CHAPTER 20

NAVY SCOUT AND OBSERVATION AIRCRAFT, 1932-1946

The *USS Honolulu's* flight of SOC-3s on November 14, 1940, the most common cruiser catapult-launched seaplane.

Vought SU Corsairs

Putting monoplanes on Navy ships was a good deal more difficult than putting them on Army airfields, for shipboard aircraft had strict size and weight limitations. This is why each carrier's scouting squadron still used Vought biplanes with fixed landing gear until 1939, and why biplanes remained aboard some cruisers until 1945.

In 1931, the three scouting squadrons on Navy carriers were using the same Vought Corsair design as the seaplane units aboard battleships and cruisers. To improve their performance with more engine power, they would have to transcend the limits of catapult launching weights and the modest R-1340 Wasp engines. Such new types would be classified VS for Scouting in June 1932.

The answer for the carrier-based squadrons was the Vought SU-l, sporting a new look with its 600-hp Pratt & Whitney R-1690 Hornet in a ring cowl, straight-axle landing gear, and a tail wheel. While the wing bomb racks and fixed .30-caliber gun in the upper wing remained, the observer now had a .30-caliber Browning on a new post-mount, instead of the Lewis gun and Scarff ring used since World War I. A tail hook was provided for deck landings and metal covers on the fuselage sides indicated emergency flotation gear.

Despite these changes from the first O3U type, the SU-1 had been ordered in March 1931 and delivered from October 1931 to April 1932 with an O3U-2 designation, and the similar O3U-4 was first flown May 12, 1932, at the East Hartford, Connecticut, factory. They became the SU-l and SU-2 in June 1932, while the camera-equipped SU-3 began flying as such on August 31, 1932.

Twenty-nine SU-ls were built, serving on the *Lexington* in 1932 with VS-2B and a Marine detachment, VS-14M, and on the *Langley* in 1933 with VS-lB. When 44 SU-2 and

VOUGHT SU-1
Pratt & Whitney R-1690-40, 600 hp
DIMENSIONS: Span 36', Lg. 26'3", Ht. 11'6;, Wing Area 325.6 sq. ft.
WEIGHT: Empty 2949 lb., Gross 4467 lb., Max. 4587 lb. Fuel 110 gal.
PERFORMANCE: Speed- Top 170 mph at s. l., 168 mph at 5000', Stalling 60.5 mph. Service Ceiling 19,900', Climb 5000'/4 min. Range 654 miles normal, 770 miles max.

VOUGHT SU-3
Pratt & Whitney R-1690-40, 600 hp
DIMENSIONS: Same as SU-l
WEIGHT: Empty 2978 lb., Gross 4522 lb., Max. 4642 lb. Fuel 110 gal.
PERFORMANCE: Speed- Top 171 mph at s. l., 168 mph at 5000', Stalling 60.4 mph. Service Ceiling 19,900', Climb 5000'/3.9 min. Range 694-814 miles.

VOUGHT SU-2
Pratt & Whitney R-1690-40, 600 hp
DIMENSIONS: Same as SU-1
WEIGHT: Empty 2966 lb., Gross 4481 lb., Max. 4601 lb. Fuel 110 gal.
PERFORMANCE: Speed- Top 171 mph at s. l., 168 mph at 5000', Stalling 60 mph. Service Ceiling 19,500', Climb 5000'/3.9 min. Range 674-788 miles.

20 SU-3 Corsairs arrived, these Voughts could also be used by VS-3B and VS-15M on the *Saratoga*, VO-8M at San Diego, and VO-9M in Haiti until it returned to Quantico. These Corsairs were also popular with admirals as brightly painted blue "command" ships.

The XO3U-5 was the second aircraft of the O2U-4/SU-2 contract flown in April 1932 as a test bed for Pratt & Whitney's new 625-hp R-1535 Twin Wasp, Jr. in an enclosed cowling designed by Dr. Michael Watters.

While the scouts dashed from carrier decks to seek distant hostile ships, battleships still used floatplanes to spot for their big guns. A seaplane Corsair light enough for the catapults was still needed, so the O3U-3 reverted to the R-1340-12 Wasp and pontoons, but introduced a new rounded, longer rudder. Seventy-six were built, with the first example flown with wheels on May 20, and with pontoons on July 1, 1932. Easily convertible from floats to wheels, O3U-3s did most of their flying from warship catapults until 1938.

The Corsair story can be confusing, because of the shifts in designations and missions. For example, the XO4U-2 was apparently fitted for the scout mission, and has nothing in common with the XO4U-1 of 1931 except the serial number. This number was retained as this aircraft replaced the first prototype, which had been destroyed in a crash. The XO4U-2 was first flown June 5, 1932 with a Pratt & Whitney twin-row Twin Wasp, Jr. under a neat cowling, the O3U-3's rounded rudder, and a metal wing structure. When a supercharger and controllable-pitch propeller was fitted to the 700-hp R-1535-64, this became the fastest Corsair to date.

One SU-2 was modified and grandly provided with a cowled R-1690D Hornet, enclosed cockpits, and wheel pants. Flown on May 1, 1933, as the XSU-4, it remained at

VOUGHT XO3U-4/5

VOUGHT O3U-3
Pratt & Whitney R-1340-12, 550 hp
DIMENSIONS: Span 36', Lg. 31', Ht. 13'2", Wing Area 325 sq. ft.
WEIGHT: Empty 3100 lb., Gross 4585 lb. Fuel 110 gal.
PERFORMANCE: Speed- Top 156 mph at s. l., 153 mph at 5000', Stalling 61.6 mph. Service Ceiling 16,600', Climb 5000'/4.9 min. Endurance 4.58 hr.

VOUGHT XO4U-2
Pratt & Whitney R-1535-64, 700 hp at 8900'
DIMENSIONS: Span 36', Lg. 27'2", Ht. 11'6", Wing Area 325.6 sq. ft.
WEIGHT: Empty 3155 lb., Gross 4669 lb., Max. 4984 lb. Fuel 110 gal.
PERFORMANCE: Speed- Top 196 mph at 8900', Stalling 60.6 mph. Service Ceiling 27,100', Climb 5000'/4.2 min. Range 646-916 miles.

Anacostia, but without the wheel pants. Vought did build 20 SU-4s in 1933 for VS-l on the *Ranger*, but they were identical to the open cockpit SU-3 series except for the O3U-3 rudder. The SU-4 Corsairs then went to the *Langley's* VS-4 until the oldest carrier was retired from first-line service in 1936.

Last of the Navy's biplane Corsairs was the O3U-6 series, which began when the last aircraft on the O3U-3 contract was modified as an XO3U-6 with a deep cowl and enclosed cockpits and flown June 13, 1934. A production contract was made October 23, 1934, and the first O3U-6 flew February 27, 1935. Thirty-two delivered by July were the last pre-war Navy planes designated as pure observation types, replacing the Curtiss O2C-ls of the Marine's VO-7M and VO-8M squadrons at Quantico and San Diego. Standard O3U-6 armament included two Browning guns with 1,100 .30-caliber rounds and wing racks for four 116-pound bombs.

VOUGHT XSU-4

VOUGHT SU-4
Pratt & Whitney R-1690-42, 600 hp
DIMENSIONS: Span 36', Lg. 27'11", Ht. 11'5", Wing Area 337 sq. ft.
WEIGHT: Empty 3307 lb., Gross 4773 lb., Max. 4913 lb. Fuel 110 gal.
PERFORMANCE: Speed- Top 167.5 mph at s. 1., Stalling 62 mph. Service Ceiling 18,600', Climb 5000'/3.5 min. Range 611 miles.

Corsairs for export

Vought had much success selling these Corsairs to foreign countries as land-based military types. Beginning in September 1932, Brazil's Army received 37 Hornet-powered V-65B two-seaters, and her Navy eight Wasp-powered V-66Bs convertible to seaplanes. These aircraft were similar to the SU-l in most respects, but had Lewis guns and Scarff rings for the rear cockpits.

The 500-hp R-l340D Wasp was used on the V-66E, first flown November 17, 1932, and shipped to England in January 1933 for evaluation by the British Air Ministry in both sea and land plane configurations. A single V-66F for Argentina was similar.

The Vought V-70A was an attack version of the SU-l with a 600-hp R-1690D Hornet, wheel pants and four fixed

USN

VOUGHT O3U-6
Pratt & Whitney R-1340-18, 550 hp
DIMENSIONS: Span 36', Lg. 27'3", Ht. 11'5", Wing Area 342 sq. ft.
WEIGHT: Empty 3300 lb., Gross 4743 lb., Max. 4875 lb. Fuel 110 gal.
PERFORMANCE: Speed- Top 164 mph at s. l., 160 mph at 5000', Stalling 53 mph. Service Ceiling 17,800', Climb 5000'/4.8 min. Range 688-806 miles.

Mfr

VOUGHT V-66E
Pratt & Whitney R-1340D1 Wasp, 500 hp at 7500'
DIMENSIONS: Span 36', Lg. 26'2", Ht. 10'8", Wing Area 326 sq. ft.
WEIGHT: Empty 2841 lb., Gross 4040 lb. Fuel 100 gal.
PERFORMANCE: Speed- Top 144 mph at s. l., 150 mph at 10,000', Cruising 99 mph, Landing 58 mph. Service Ceiling 21,400', Climb 1320'/1 min.

NASM

VOUGHT V-70A
Pratt & Whitney R-1690C, 600 hp
DIMENSIONS: Span 36', Lg. 26'2", Ht. 10'8", Wing Area 326 sq. ft.
WEIGHT: Empty 3156 lb., Gross 5300 lb., Max. 5600 lb. Fuel 130-180 gal.
PERFORMANCE: Speed- Top 193 mph at s. l., Cruising 157 mph, Landing 63 mph. Service Ceiling 19,000', Climb 1425'/1 min. Range 610-840 miles.

guns (two in the upper wing and two under the cowl) with a flexible observer's gun and racks for four 116-pound bombs. First flown February 8, 1933, it was offered to the U.S. Army and for export, but found no buyers. Four-gun fixed armament and bomb racks were also provided on the V-80P single-seat fighter, with a Hornet engine and cockpit canopy. The first of three for Peru was flown May 19, 1933.

China got 42 V-65C two-seaters with the R-1690 Hornet, split-axle gear, round rudder, and a cockpit canopy. They also had a fixed and a flexible gun and bombs, which were often used in China's civil warfare. First flown by Vought on July 11, 1933, they went into action with the bombing of the Fukien rebels in January 1934, and of the Communists on the famous Long March.

VOUGHT V-80P
Pratt & Whitney Model SD Hornet, 675 hp at 6000'
DIMENSIONS: Span 36', Lg. 27'7", Ht. 10'6", Wing Area 337 sq. ft.
WEIGHT: Empty 3287 lb., Gross 4373 lb. Fuel 110-150 gal.
PERFORMANCE: Speed- Top 178 mph at s. l., 197 mph at 6000', Cruising 163 mph, Stalling 61 mph. Service Ceiling 27,800', Climb 1850'/1 min. Range 760 miles max.

VOUGHT V-65C for China

Next came 12 V-65F Corsairs for Argentina, which were similar to the SU-4 except for the addition of a sliding cockpit enclosure and an auxiliary fuel tank; they were armed with one fixed and one flexible 7.65-mm gun. The first V-65F was flown October 18, 1933, followed by a single Argentine V-80F single-seat fighter flown April 10, 1934, with an extended cockpit enclosure and deep cowl. Six V-85G "Kurier" single-seaters for Germany were intended for a ship-to shore mail project, not military operations, however.

China received 21 V-92C two-seaters in 1934 which were like the SU-4/V-65F types with Hornet and ring cowl, and were armed with a .30-caliber Browning in the upper wing, another in the rear cockpit, and racks for four 116-pound bombs. They fought in civil warfare and against Japan in August 1937.

Twelve V-93S two-seaters with 625-hp Hornets were shipped from July 26 to September 13, 1934, to Siam (now called Thailand), which adopted the Corsair as its principal army type, and built a reported 72 in Bangkok. An 8-mm Vickers gun was mounted in the rear cockpit, two more on the upper wing, while bomb racks and optional fixtures for two guns more were provided under the lower wings. Beginning on November 28, 1940, six Vought squadrons

VOUGHT V-65F for Argentina

VOUGHT V-80F

VOUGHT V-93S in Siam
Pratt & Whitney R-1690SD 675 hp at 6000'
DIMENSIONS: Span 36', Lg. 27', Ht. 11'1", Wing Area 337 sq. ft.
WEIGHT: Gross 4561 lb. Fuel 115 gal.
PERFORMANCE: Speed- Top 176 mph at s. l., 191 mph at 6000', Cruising 158 mph, Landing 60 mph. Service Ceiling 24,300', Climb 1670'/1 min., 14,000'/10 min. Range 736 miles.

VOUGHT V-99M for Mexico
Pratt & Whitney R-1340, 550 hp at 8000'
DIMENSIONS: Span 36', Lg. 27'6", Ht. 9'10", Wing Area 342 sq. ft.
WEIGHT: Empty 3245 lb., Gross 4645 lb. Fuel 115 gal.
PERFORMANCE: Speed- Top 176 mph at 8000', Landing 61 mph. Service Ceiling 23,900'. Range 803 miles.

Tien

VOUGHT V-92C in China
Pratt & Whitney R-1690SD, 675 hp at 6000'
DIMENSIONS: Span 36', Lg. 27'3", Ht. 10'5", Wing Area 337 sq. ft. WEIGHT: Empty 3090 lb., Gross 4490 1b. Fuel 115 gal.
PERFORMANCE: Speed- 169 mph at s. l., Top 184 mph at 6000', Climb 13,000'/10 min. Range 709 miles.

fought French forces on the Indochina's border until January, 1941.

The last of these two-seater Corsairs to be exported were ten V-99Ms for Mexico in December 1937 with supercharged 550-hp TlH-l Wasps. Company statements say Vought built 769 Corsair biplanes, including 185 for export and civilian customers.

Navy Scouts in Transition

The Navy found the task of replacing the Corsairs of the scouting squadrons complicated by uncertainty as to the role future scouts would play. Scouting had been a designation applied alike to carrier-based reconnaissance, shore-based Marine observation, and cruiser-based seaplane squadrons. While in 1931-35 the Corsairs had filled all three roles, advanced performance requirements made continued commonality impossible.

There was a hope that an amphibian would be compatible with these combat requirements, and the Great Lakes XSG-l, Grover Loening XS2L-l, and Sikorsky XSS-l prototypes were ordered June 30, 1931, as two-seat scout amphibians with arresting gear for carrier landings, limited weight for catapults, and folding wings to fit in the hangars of the new cruisers planned for 1930-39. A single flexible .30-caliber M-1 gun was provided, but a requirement for two 250-pound bombs was deleted.

The XSG-1 biplane flew first, beginning tests at Cleveland on September 15, 1932, and after many difficulties, the XSG-1 was delivered to Anacostia on November 27. An enclosed gunner's position was behind and below the open pilot's cockpit. The expected speed of 136 mph was reduced to barely 124 mph when the weight proved too much for the 400-hp R-985-38 Wasp, Jr.

Both crewmen were completely enclosed below and behind the R-985A on the XS2L-2, first flown on October 30, 1932, at Roosevelt Field, New York, and flown to Anacostia on November 21. While less troubled than the Great Lakes offering, it was still too underpowered for satisfactory performance.

LOENING XS2L-1
Pratt & Whitney R-985-38, 400 hp
DIMENSIONS: Span 34/6", Lg. 30'7", Ht. 14'7", Wing Area 355 sq. ft. WEIGHT: Empty 2833 lb., Gross 4053 lb., Max. 4317 lb. Fuel 80 gal.
PERFORMANCE: Speed- Top 130 mph at s. l., 126 mph at 5000', Stalling 60 mph. Service Ceiling 12,400', Climb 5000'/7.1 min. Range 432-633 miles.

NASM

GREAT LAKES XSG-1
Pratt & Whitney R-985-38, 400 hp
DIMENSIONS: Span 35' (13'3" fld.), Lg. 35'7", Ht. 14'1", Wing Area 358 sq. ft.
WEIGHT: Empty 3239 lb., Gross 4760 lb., Max. 5078 lb. Fuel 120-170 gal.
PERFORMANCE: Speed- Top 124 mph at s. l., Stalling 70 mph.
Service Ceiling 8,400'. Climb 4800'/10 min. Range 892 miles.

Arc

SIKORSKY XSS-2
Pratt & Whitney R-1340-12, 550 hp
DIMENSIONS: Span 42', Lg. 33'1", Ht. 14'7", Wing Area 285 sq. ft.
WEIGHT: Empty 3274 lb., Gross 4526 lb., Max. 4790 lb. Fuel 80 gal.
PERFORMANCE: Speed- Top 154 mph at s. l., 149 mph at 5000', Stalling 63 mph. Service Ceiling 14,800', Climb 5000'/5.8 min., Range 417-618 miles.

Sikorsky was allowed to replace the R-985A with a 550-hp R-1340-12 above the hull of the XSS-1, which then became the XSS-2. This monoplane with the crew cockpits in the hull behind the folding wing was actually designed by the Navy itself. It was flown in April 1933 and arrived at Anacostia on May 22. Test difficulties confirmed the opinion that amphibian performance was too limited for cruiser work.

However, one amphibian that year would be very successful. Produced by former Loening employees who had formed Grumman Aircraft, the XFJ-1 was first flown April 24, 1933. Although there was provision for a flexible gun, the XFJ-1 was intended to be a utility type with no need for catapulting, so a 700-hp R-1830 Twin Wasp could be used.

Arnold

GRUMMAN J2F-2A
Wright R-1820-30, 790 hp takeoff, 750 hp at 3200'
DIMENSIONS: Span 39', Lg. 34', Ht. 12'4", Wing Area 409 sq. ft.
WEIGHT: Empty 4300 lb., Gross 6180 lb. Fuel 190 gal.
PERFORMANCE: Speed- Top 179 mph at s. l., Cruising 150 mph, Stalling 64 mph. Service Ceiling 21,600', Climb 1500'/ 1 min. Range 780 miles.

BELLANCA XSE-2
Wright R-1510-92, 650 hp
DIMENSIONS: Span 49'9", Lg. 29'8", Ht. 12'2", Wing Area 373 sq. ft.
WEIGHT: Empty 3789 lb., Gross 6100 lb. Fuel 250 gal.
PERFORMANCE: Speed- Top 174 mph at s. l., 170 mph at 5000', Stalling 64 mph. Service Ceiling 18,400', Climb 5000'/4.9 min. Range 1455 miles.

Over 600 of the Grumman "Duck" series were built from 1934 to 1945. As unarmed utility aircraft, they are outside this history of combat planes, but it can be mentioned that a few carried depth charges and flexible guns during the war, beginning with nine Cyclone-powered J2F-2As used by the Marines' VMS-3 in the Virgin Islands in 1939-1941.

Later experimental aircraft tested as scouts were landplanes without any provision for floats. The big Bellanca XSE-l monoplane was based on that firm's civilian transport designs with enclosed crew cockpits below the high wing, which was supported by thick fairings from stub wings and wheel pants. Ordered October 19, 1931, it appeared in December 1932 with a Wright R-1820 Cyclone and a fuel capacity for long-range reconnaissance, but crashed before delivery to the Navy.

BELLANCA XSE-l
Wright R-1820F, 650 hp at s.1.
DIMENSIONS: Span 49'9", Lg. 29'11", Wing Area 373 sq. ft.
WEIGHT: Empty 3054 lb., Gross 5526 lb. Fuel 250 gal.
PERFORMANCE: Speed- Top 171 mph at s.1., Stalling 61 mph. Service Ceiling 21,200'. Range 1392 miles.

Bellanca rebuilt the two-seater as the XSE-2 with a Wright R-1510 Twin Whirlwind, larger tail, and reworked rear cockpit. A tail hook and folding wings was provided for carrier service. Tests begun April 22, 1934, at Anacostia proved that the aircraft could not be accepted as a Navy type and the contract was terminated.

Curtiss built two prototypes with Navy scout designations; the XS2C-1 monoplane ordered on December 13, 1932, and the XS3C-l biplane originally ordered as an O2C-2 and described in Chapter 9. The XS2C-1 was essentially similar to the Army's YA-10 attack, with wire-braced metal wings, wheel pants, and a Wright R-1510 Twin Whirlwind. Delivered in June 1933 without guns or tail hook, it was bought so the Navy could test its elaborate system of leading-edge slots, licensed from Handley-Page,

CURTISS XS2C-1
Wright R-1510-28, 625 hp
DIMENSIONS: Span 44', Lg. 31'3", Ht. 12'2", Wing Area 285 sq. ft.
WEIGHT: Empty 3677 lb., Gross 4822 lb., Max. 5180 lb. Fuel 104+52 gal.
PERFORMANCE: Speed- Top 186 mph at s. l., Landing 71 mph. Service Ceiling 18,900', Climb 5000'/4.4 min. Range 640 miles/488 lb. bombs, 912 miles max.

and split trailing edge flaps. This system would be used on the successful SOC series, as well as on the unsuccessful SO3C type.

The only successful new scout prototype tested in this period was developed from a two-seat fighter. Grumman's XFF-l was the first Navy fighter with retractable wheels and a 200-mph speed, so a second prototype fitted as an XSF-l scout was ordered June 9, 1931, and first flew August 20, 1932. The XSF-l had a 750-hp R-1820-78, and the two synchronized cowl guns of the XFF-l were removed to allow a larger fuel tank, while the pilot was given a fixed gun in the upper wing and another .30-caliber gun was handled by the observer.

SDAM

GRUMMAN XSF-l

SDAM

GRUMMAN SF-l
Wright R-1820-84, 725 hp at 3000'
DIMENSIONS: Span 34'6", Lg. 24'11", Ht. 11'1", Wing Area 310 sq. ft.
WEIGHT: Empty 3259 lb., Gross 5073 lb. Fuel 165 gal.
PERFORMANCE: Speed- Top 206 mph at 4000'. Service Ceiling 23,100', Climb 1650'/1 min. Range 800 miles.

The production SF-l had an R-1820-84, larger cowl, and controllable-pitch propeller. Ordered December 4, 1933, 33 SF-ls were delivered from February to July 1934, and served on the *Lexington* with VS-3B, replacing Vought SU-2 Corsairs. Armament was two .30-caliber guns and, when needed, two 116-pound bombs.

The 34th and last Grumman on this contract was completed with a twin-row R-1535 Wasp in a full cowl, and fixed gun mounted on the right side behind the engine. The XSF-2 was first flown November 26, 1934; the last pre-war Navy purely scout type. Future scouting aircraft would be either carrier-based SB scout-bombers or catapult-launched SO scout-observation types

Arc

GRUMMAN XSF-2
Pratt & Whitney R-1535-72, 700 hp at takeoff, 650 hp at 7500'
DIMENSIONS: Span 34'6", Lg. 24'8", Ht. 10'11", Wing Area 310 sq. ft.
WEIGHT: Empty 3259 lb., Gross 4783 lb. Fuel 120 gal.
PERFORMANCE: Speed- Top 215 mph at 8900', Stalling 63 mph., Service Ceiling 24,100', Climb 5000'/3.2 min. Range 934 miles.

SCOUT-OBSERVATION TYPES, 1935-45

Curtiss Seagull

While American impressions of World War II are dominated by monoplanes, the most widely used Navy type in 1940 was the Curtiss SOC Seagull biplane. Despite the rapid obsolescence of its contemporaries, the SOC still operated in 1944, even replacing the type that was supposed to replace it.

The prototype was the Curtiss XO3C-l, designed to a Navy specification for a two-place biplane with folding wings, tail hook, and a large central float with retracting wheels. A weight limit dictated by catapult launching and a low stalling speed for water landings confined the power plant to a 550-hp R-1340 Wasp and 140-gallon fuel capacity. A forward fixed and a rear flexible .30-caliber gun would be carried.

Ordered June l9, 1933, the XO3C-1 was first flown by H. L. Child at Buffalo on March 5, 1934. The prototype's cockpits were open, and the upper wing had full-length flaps and leading-edge automatic slots. When the wings were folded for storage in cruiser hangers, width was only 14 feet, 6 inches, an important advantage over the old Corsairs.

Two rival prototypes were built to the same specification: the Douglas XO2D-l and Vought XO5U-l. The Douglas ship ordered May 29, 1933, first flew on March 27, 1934. with a more modern-looking cockpit canopy. Vought's XO5U-l, first flown May 8, 1934, also had a cockpit canopy and its most distinctive feature was a swept-back upper wing with flaps. Both prototypes went to Anacostia for trials.

The fastest amphibian in the world then was the Seversky Sev-3, considered by the Navy in March 1934, but this all-metal low-wing monoplane with twin floats did not fit the Navy concept of a shipboard aircraft. The Navy relented on the amphibian aspect of its requirements, for the wheel retraction weight penalty was undesirable, so all of these biplane prototypes were converted to a plain pontoon configuration.

A new specification dated December 5, 1934, introduced the VSO class. Combining the Scout-Observation

CURTISS XO3C-1
Pratt & Whitney R-1340-12, 550 hp
DIMENSIONS: Span 36', Lg. 30'2", Ht. 15'8", Wing Area 347.8 sq. ft.
WEIGHT: Empty 3582 lb., Gross 5236 lb. Fuel 140 gal.
PERFORMANCE: Speed- Top 159 mph at s. l., 155 mph at 5000', Stalling 62 mph. Service Ceiling 16,100', Climb 5000'/5.6 min. Range 770 miles.

designation indicated that the same catapult-launched aircraft could fit two roles. Floatplanes on battleships were organized in observation squadrons whose primary duty was spotting for the big guns, but cruiser floatplanes were flown by scouting squadrons for more distant reconnaissance. An alternate wheeled undercarriage was used when the aircraft were on shore, but no deck-landing tail hook was provided.

DOUGLAS XO2D-1
Pratt & Whitney R-1340-12, 550 hp
DIMENSIONS: Span 36', Lg. 32', Ht. 16'4", Wing Area 302.8 sq. ft.
WEIGHT: Empty 3460 lb., Gross 5109 lb., Fuel 140 gal.
PERFORMANCE: Speed- Top 162 mph at s.1., 158 mph at 5000', Stalling 58.6 mph. Service Ceiling 14,300', Climb 5000'/6 min., Range 798 miles.

VOUGHT XO5U-1
Pratt & Whitney R-1340-12, 550 hp
DIMENSIONS: Span 36', Lg. 32'6", Ht. 15'6", Wing Area 337 sq. ft.
WEIGHT: Empty 3563 lb., Gross 5213 lb., Fuel 138 gal.
PERFORMANCE: Speed- Top 157 mph at s. l., 153 mph at 5000', Stalling 56.5 mph. Service Ceiling 16,300', Climb 5000'/5.6 min. Range 751 miles.

USN

CURTISS SOC-1 as seaplane
Pratt & Whitney R-1340-18, 550 hp
DIMENSIONS: Span 36', Lg. 32'3", Ht. 14'10", Wing Area 342 sq. ft.
WEIGHT: Empty 3648 lb., Gross 5302 lb., Max. 5490 lb. Fuel 140-170 gal.
PERFORMANCE: Speed- Top 159 mph at s. l., 154 mph at 5000', Cruising 95 mph, Stalling 55.5 mph. Service Ceiling 14,200', Climb 960''/1 min. Range 840-1003 miles.

Equipment included a forward fixed .30-caliber M-2 with 500 rounds in front of the pilot, the observer's rear flexible M-2 with 600 rounds, a 146-pound radio and a life raft. The normal 140-gallon fuel load was reduced to 100 gallons if two 116-pound bombs were carried under the wings, and 30 more gallons could be added in the main float.

Curtiss received the largest Navy contract in many years- for 135 SOC-1 aircraft on March 23, 1935. The prototype itself had been returned to the Buffalo factory and redesignated XSOC-l when the production contract was made. It was flown again April 5, 1935, modified to production configuration with enclosed cockpits and neatly faired wheeled landing gear. The first production SOC-1, fully convertible from floats to wheels, was flown August 8, 1935.

Fleet service began on November 12, 1935, when two SOC-ls replaced the OJ-2s on the *USS Marblehead*, first cruiser to use the type. By June 1936, the SOC-l contract was filled, and in October 1936, delivery began on 40 more aircraft redesignated SOC-2 on November 9, 1936, although nearly identical to the SOC-l.

Meanwhile, two experimental VSO projects of this period passed almost unnoticed. The Bellanca XSOE-l had a 725-hp R-1820-84, folding wings, enclosed pilot's cockpit ahead of the gulled upper wing and a deep fairing between fuselage and pontoon. When offered in May 1934, this design had attracted Navy approval because of its large float affording protection to propeller and tail, rugged built-up structure between float and fuselage, excellent pilot's visibility, and promised low landing speed.

PMB

CURTISS SOC-1
Pratt & Whitney R-1340-18, 550 hp at s. l.
DIMENSIONS: Span 36', Lg. 27'5", Ht. 13'1", Wing Area 342 sq. ft.
WEIGHT: Empty 3442 lb., Gross 5130 lb., Fuel 140 gal.
PERFORMANCE: Speed- Top 162 mph at s. l., 158 mph at 5000', Cruising 95 mph, Stalling 54.6 mph. Service Ceiling 14,600', Climb 1055'/1 min. Range 878 miles.

USN

CURTISS SOC-3
Pratt & Whitney R-1340-22, 550 hp
DIMENSIONS: Span 36', Lg. 31'8", Ht. 14'10", Wing Area 342 sq. ft.
WEIGHT: Empty 3633 lb., Gross 5306 lb., Max. 5495 lb. Fuel 140-170 gal.
PERFORMANCE: Speed- Top 162 mph at s.l., 164 mph at 800', Cruising 97-121 mph, Stalling 57.4 mph. Service Ceiling 14,400', Climb 880'/1 min. Range 859-1027 miles.

The XSOE-l was ordered October 11, 1934, but by the time the prototype was completed on March 28, 1936, the empty weight had increased from the estimated 3,821 pounds to over 4,500 pounds. This threatened landing and catapult launch speeds so much that the Navy inspector called the XSOE-l a "decidedly bad airplane." When the insurance was canceled, both company and Navy lost interest in flight tests. The aircraft was taxied up the Delaware River from the Wilmington factory to delivery at the Philadelphia NAS on July 13, 1936. Accepted as is, without ever being flown, it was stripped of equipment, stored and forgotten.

Even less progress was made by another proposal made at the same time. The Fairchild XSOK-l was based on a civil monoplane flying boat, and powered by a Pratt & Whitney R-1510 over the wing. It was ordered September 27, 1934, but the contract was canceled August 15, 1935, with only the mockup in evidence.

On January 24, 1937, Curtiss first flew the XSO2C-l, which was an SOC with a longer fuselage and ailerons on both upper and lower wings. The standard configuration, however, was preferred for 83 SOC-3s ordered May 18, 1937. Powered by the R-1340-22, and delivered from December 1937 to May 1938, they were the first model to go aboard battleships, replacing the O3U-3 Corsair. Three similar SOC-4s without weapons went to the Coast Guard.

The last Seagulls were built by the Naval Aircraft Factory at Philadelphia because Curtiss had become too busy with other projects. Ordered on June 10, 1937, as the SON-l, but identical to the SOC-3, the first of 44 SON-ls was flown on September 15, 1938, and the rest were accepted from March to August 1939. A total of 307 Seagulls had been built, and it was the most widely used U.S. Navy aircraft when World War II began. They were the last Navy combat types with fabric-covered wings and rear fuselage.

Three were usually carried on each of the 15 battleships organized into five divisions of three ships. Each division had an observation squadron bearing its division number, VO-l to VO-5. Two were carried by each of the

BELLANCA XSOE-1
Wright R-1820-84, 725 hp at 3000'
DIMENSIONS: Span 41', Lg. 34'7", Ht. 14'1", Wing Area 398 sq. ft.
WEIGHT: Empty 4508 lb., Gross 6031 lb., Max. 6552 lb. Fuel 150-226 gal.
PERFORMANCE: Speed- Top 168 mph at s. 1., 176 mph at 3000', Landing 51 mph. Service Ceiling 21,400', Climb 5000'/3.6 min. Range 752-1104 miles. (Pre-flight estimates)

CURTISS XSO2C-l
Pratt & Whitney R-1340-36, 550 hp
DIMENSIONS: Span 36', Lg. 31'11", Ht. 14'8", Wing Area 342 sq. ft. WEIGHT: Gross 5479 lb.
PERFORMANCE: Speed- Top 165.7 mph. Service Ceiling 13,900'.

NAVAL AIRCRAFT FACTORY SON-1

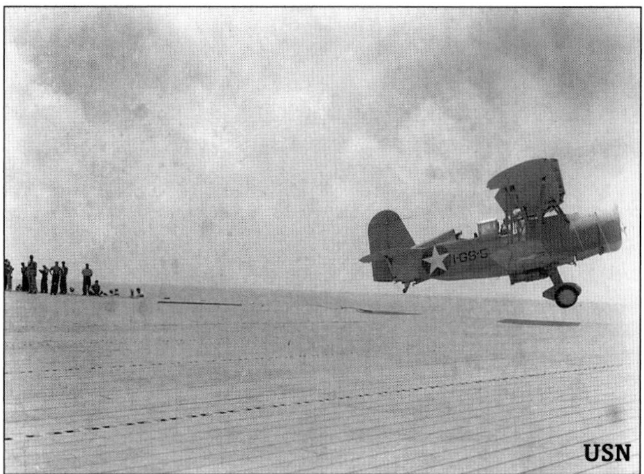

CURTISS SOC-3A takeoff with depth charge from CVE-1
Pratt & Whitney R-1340-22, 550 hp
DIMENSIONS: Span 36', Lg. 27'5", Ht. 13'1", Wing Area 342 sq. ft.
WEIGHT: Empty 3510 lb., Gross 4977 lb., Max. 5600 lb. with two 325 lb. depth charges. Fuel 110 gal.
PERFORMANCE: Speed- 167 mph at s. l., Top 171 mph at 800', Cruising 125 mph, Stalling 55 mph. Service Ceiling 15,900', Climb 1080'/1 min. Range 512-620 miles as scout, 468-530 miles with 2/325 lb. bombs.

ten older Omaha-class light cruisers, and four by each of the 27 larger cruisers. Most operated in Cruiser Divisions of four or five ships, each with a Cruiser Scouting Squadron numbered accordingly as VCS-3 to VCS-9. A few unattached cruisers and smaller ships also carried SOCs. The Marine's VMS-2 at San Diego also had 12 SOC-3 landplanes, and others served on every carrier and shore station.

When the first escort carrier, *USS Long Island,* was commissioned in June 1941, its complement comprised VS-201 (later VSG-l) with 12 SOC-3A and seven F2A-2 aircraft. These Seagulls were former battleship aircraft modified for carrier use with a tail hook and a 325-pound depth charge under the fuselage, or two under the wings.

Similar Escort Scouting Squadrons were organized in 1942 as more escort carriers joined the fleets, and several

NAVAL AIRCRAFT FACTORY XOSN-l
Pratt & Whitney R-1340-36, 600 hp at takeoff, 550 hp at 6000'
DIMENSIONS: Span 36', Lg. 34' (28'2"), Ht. 15'5", (14'2") Wing Area 378 sq. ft. (landplane data also)
WEIGHT: Empty 3771 lb. (3475 lb.), Gross 5516 lb. (5250 lb.) Fuel 173 gal.
PERFORMANCE: Speed- Top 147 mph (149 mph) at s. l.,160 mph (l62 mph) at 6000', Cruising 103 mph (101 mph), Stalling 54 mph (53 mph). Service Ceiling 14,900' (15,90"). Range 925 (978) miles.

SOC-1A and SON-1A conversions were added. Although all battleship SOCs had been replaced with Vought monoplanes by December 1941, all cruisers still used Seagulls through 1942, and 27 cruisers still used them in August 1943.

The program to replace the SOCs with the SO3C was a failure, and when that monoplane was withdrawn from service in 1944, SOCs were returned to their ships. This may be the only case in which an aircraft replaced the newer aircraft intended to replace itself. Not until sufficient SC-ls were available in 1945 could the SOC retire!

Vought Kingfisher

The Observation-Scout specification was developed in 1937 to provide a two-seat aircraft small enough to operate from battleships, without the use of folding wings, while easily convertible to wheeled operations.

The first such prototype was the XOSN-l ordered from the Naval Aircraft Factory on May 11, 1936, and tested at Anacostia in May 1938. Powered by an R-1340-36 giving 550 hp at 6,000 feet, it had automatic slots and I struts between the wings. The same engine and the same 36-foot wingspan common to the O3U-3 and SOC aircraft was also specified for the Stearman XOSS-l, ordered May 6, 1937. First flown May 19, 1938, at Wichita as a landplane and tested at Anacostia as both a land and seaplane from July to September 1938, its most distinctive feature was the full-length flaps on the upper wing, but the XOSS-1 was less attractive to the Navy than the new Vought monoplane.

USN

STEARMAN XOSS-1
Pratt & Whitney R-1340-36, 600 hp at takeoff, 550 hp at 6000'
Dimensions: Span 36', Lg. 29'10", Ht. 12'7", Wing Area 377.6 sq. ft.
Weight: Empty 3440 lb., Gross 5026 lb. Fuel 133 gal.
Performance: Speed- Top 150 mph at s. l., 164 mph at 6000', Stalling 55 mph. Service Ceiling 17,500', Climb 800'/1 min. Range 832 miles.

Vought had had a little experience with the OS requirement when the last O3U-6 was returned to the factory to be rebuilt with full-span ailerons and flaps on both wings and flown as the XOSU-1 on October 20, 1936. Afterwards the aircraft was returned to the normal O3U-6 configuration.

In 1937, designer Rex Beisel boldly proposed a Navy observation plane designed as an all-metal monoplane. Full-span flaps and spoiler lateral control would be utilized, along with spot-welding of the metal structure.

USN

STEARMAN XOSS-1 seaplane
Pratt & Whitney R-1340-36, 600 hp at takeoff, 550 hp at 6000'
DIMENSIONS: Span 36', Lg. 34'6", Ht. 14'6", Wing Area 377.6 sq. ft.
WEIGHT: Empty 3826 lb., Gross 5612 lb. Fuel 133-170 gal.
PERFORMANCE: Speed- Top 148 mph at s. 1., 162 mph at 6000', Stalling 56.7 mph., Service Ceiling 16,900', Climb 698'/1 min. Range 986 miles.

SDAM

VOUGHT XOSU-l

Staying within the 36-foot wing span, catapult weight limitations, and low stalling speed, meant stepping down to a smaller engine size, the 450-hp Pratt & Whitney R-985-4.

The XOS2U-1 prototype was ordered March 19, 1937, and made its first flight on March 1, 1938, as a landplane, and on May 19 as a seaplane. Paul S. Baker was the test pilot, as he had been for the other Vought types since 1932. After the first tests, wing dihedral was added for final trials in October.

NASM

VOUGHT XOS2U-l as landplane
Pratt & Whitney R-985-4, 450 hp at takeoff, 400 hp at 5500'
DIMENSIONS: Span 36', Lg. 30'1", Ht. 12'11", Wing Area 262 sq. ft.
WEIGHT: Empty 2950 lb., Gross 4611 lb. Fuel 144 gal.
PERFORMANCE: Speed- Top 169 mph at s. l., 177 mph at 5000', Cruising 112 mph, Stalling 54 mph. Service Ceiling 20,300', Climb 1020'/1 min. Range1270 miles.

USN

VOUGHT OS2U-1 seaplane
Pratt & Whitney R-985-48, 450 hp at takeoff, 400 hp at 5500'
DIMENSIONS: Span 35'11", Lg. 33'7", Ht. 15'1", Wing Area 262 sq. ft.
WEIGHT: Empty 3432 lb., Gross 4926 lb., Max. 5077 lb. Fuel 144 gal.
PERFORMANCE: Speed- Top 167 mph at s. l., 175 mph at 5500', Cruising 114 mph, Stalling 56 mph. Service Ceiling 19,000', Climb 890'/1 min. Range 982 miles.

Arc

VOUGHT XOS2U-1 as seaplane
Pratt & Whitney R-985-4, 450 hp at takeoff, 400 hp at 5500'
DIMENSIONS: Span 36', Lg. 33'10", Ht. 15'3", Wing Area 262 sq. ft.
WEIGHT: Empty 3213 lb., Gross 4711 lb., Max. 4862 lb. Fuel 144 gal.
PERFORMANCE: Speed- Top 167 mph at s. l., 175 mph at 5000', Cruising 114 mph, Stalling 55.6 mph. Service Ceiling 19,900', Climb 970'/1 min. Range 1015 miles.

USN

VOUGHT OS2U-1
Pratt & Whitney R-985-48, 450 hp at takeoff, 400 hp at 5500'
DIMENSIONS: Span 35'11", Lg. 30'1", Ht. 12'11", Wing Area 262 sq. ft.
WEIGHT: Empty 3105 lb., Gross 4780 lb. Fuel 144 gal.
PERFORMANCE: Speed- Top 169 mph at s. l., 177 mph at 5500', Cruising 116 mph, Stalling 55 mph. Service Ceiling 19,600', Climb 950'/1 min. Range 1233 miles.

When the new Vought proved to be practical for catapult work, 54 OS2U-ls were ordered May 22, 1939, and delivered from May to November 1940, beginning operations from the battleship *Colorado* in August. Armament was the two .30-caliber guns and two 116-pound bombs traditionally on Navy observation planes, but a radio direction loop had been added to the equipment. While the small engine kept performance quite modest, the sturdy seaplanes, soon named Kingfishers, proved to be reliable types.

The OS2U-2 model added leak proof fuel tanks and armor protection, and used the R-985-50. Of 158 OS2U-2s ordered December 4, 1939, 45 were delivered as seaplanes, beginning in November 1940, while the rest were delivered as landplanes with 70 extra Edo float sets. The new battleship, *North Carolina*, had the OS2U-2, while many went to shore stations for the Navy's new Inshore Patrol Squadrons, the first organized in September 1940. In the anti-submarine role, 325-pound depth charges were carried. Two OS2U-2s were redesignated XOS2U-4s when testing special wings with Northrop "Zap" flaps.

The mass-production version, OS2U-3, was identical to its predecessor, with 220 pounds of armor and the engine redesignated R-985-AN2. The first production contract was made October 31, 1940, and the first OS2U-3 flew May 17, 1941. They replaced the OS2U-2 on the production line in July 1941, with 1,006 completed by September 1942 (175 as seaplanes and 831 as landplanes with 157 extra float sets).

VOUGHT OS2U-2
Pratt & Whitney R-985-50, 450 hp at 5000'
DIMENSIONS: Span 35'11", Lg. 30'1", Ht. 12'11", Wing Area 262 sq. ft.
WEIGHT: Empty 3549 lb., Gross 4883 lb. Fuel 100-240 gal.
PERFORMANCE: Speed- Top 168 mph at s. l.,177 mph at 5500', Cruising 117 mph, Stalling 56 mph. Service Ceiling 17,100', Climb 910'/1 min., 10,000'/12.1 min. Range 825 miles.

VOUGHT OS2U-2 seaplane
Pratt & Whitney R-985-50, 450 hp to 500', 400 hp at 5500'
DIMENSIONS: Span 35'11", Lg. 33'7", Ht. 15'1", Wing Area 262 sq. ft.
WEIGHT: Empty 3925 lb. Gross 5229 lb., Max. 6108 lb. Fuel 100-240 gal.
PERFORMANCE: Speed- Top 161 mph at s. l., 170 mph at 5500', Cruising 116 mph, Stalling 58 mph. Service Ceiling 16,000', Climb 760'/1 min., 10,000'/14.7 min. Range 745-1320 miles.

To enable Vought to change over to F4U-1 fighters sooner, the Naval Aircraft Factory was directed on January 30, 1941, to build 300 OS2N-1 Kingfishers. Nearly identical to the OS2U-3, but lighter, the first OS2N-1 was completed in January 1942, and all 300 were accepted from February to November. They mingled with the Voughts on battleships and cruisers and also served with VMS-3 at St. Thomas.

Lend-lease allocated 100 Voughts to the British Navy for use aboard armed merchant cruisers and light cruisers. From March to July 1942, 45 were shipped to the UK, 35 to South Africa, and 20 to the West Indies. Australia got 18 originally intended for the Dutch East Indies, while 12 went to Mexico beginning in March 1942, 15 went to Chile and six to Uruguay by September, and Cuba got three in July. Two Kingfishers were aboard the cruiser *Milwaukee*, which was loaned to the Soviet Navy on April 20, 1944, and several of the British lot also reached the VVS-VMF.

VOUGHT OS2U-3 of VMS-3
Pratt & Whitney R-985-AN2, 450 hp.
DIMENSIONS: same as OS2U-2 landplane.
WEIGHT: Empty 3749 lb. Gross 5265 lb., Max. 5936 lb. Fuel 240 gal.
PERFORMANCE: Speed- Top 165 mph at s. l., 172 mph at 5500', Service Ceiling 15,500', Climb 10,000'/17 min. Range 790 miles.

The United States Navy had these Voughts aboard all its battleships in December 1941, and on many aircraft tenders and carriers as utility types. Four Inshore Patrol squadrons with Kingfishers in December 1941 were increased to 30 during 1942. Two Kingfishers from VS-9 helped sink U-576 on July 15, 1942. After most Inshore Patrol squadrons got SBDs, eight still had OS2Us in July 1944, and two remained until the war's end.

NAVAL AIRCRAFT FACTORY OS2N-1

VOUGHT OS2U-3 seaplane
Pratt & Whitney R-985-AN2, 450 hp at takeoff, 400 mph at 5500'
DIMENSIONS: Span 35'11", Lg. 33'10", Ht. 15'1", Wing Area 262 sq. ft.
WEIGHT: Empty 4123 lb. Gross 5600 lb., Max. 6000 lb. Fuel 141-241 gal.
PERFORMANCE: Speed- Top 157 mph at s. l., 164 mph at 5500', Cruising 119 mph, Stalling 62 mph. Service Ceiling 13,000', Climb 10,000'/29 min. Range 805-1155 miles.

The Coast Guard used 53 Voughts, and five destroyers were commissioned with catapults for OS2Us in 1942/43. The Voughts had not been intended for cruiser hangars because of their rigid wings (battleship floatplanes were carried in the open), but some were pressed into cruiser service in 1943 when the SO3C program failed.

During the war the Kingfishers were to be seen on every ocean. Pre-war squadron organizations were abandoned, and the aircraft functioned as part of each ship or shore station's company. Spotting for big guns became a job for ship's radar, and the floatplanes had other duties, such as anti-submarine warfare. One OS2U was even credited with downing a Zero fighter with its forward gun at Iwo Jima on February 16, 1945.

Yet of all the missions flown by the 1,519 Kingfishers built, the best remembered by fliers are the rescue missions in which the seaplanes landed in rough waters and under enemy fire saved downed airmen. On one day an OS2U-3 from the *North Carolina,* flown by Lt. John A. Burns, rescued ten downed airmen near Truk, carrying seven at one time while he taxied to a waiting submarine.

Curtiss Scouts

To replace the SOC biplane aboard cruisers the Navy proposed a specification for a "high speed scout", BuAer Design No. 403 for an all-metal, mid-wing monoplane with interchangeable wheels and pontoons. While battleship-based aircraft were classed as VOS, the cruiser scouts would be rated as VSO.

Besides the limits on catapult weight and landing speed (no more than 6,350 pounds gross, or 56 mph), the VSO had to have wings no greater than 38 feet span, folding to 15 feet for cruiser hangars, carry more radio gear, be strengthened to 7.5Gs for dive-bombing, and hopefully have better speed and pilot visibility than the SOCs. The two-seater would be powered by the new 12-cylinder, inverted-V air-cooled Ranger XV-770-4 developed for the Navy.

In August 1937 Curtiss designed a monoplane using either the R-985 radial or an inline XV-770, and the Navy preferred the latter. Contracts were made on May 9, 1938, for the Curtiss XSO3C-1 and June 21 for the Vought XSO2U-l prototypes. In both types the pilot sat ahead of the wing and the observer near the tail. Vought finished their prototype first with wheels in July 1939, and with floats in December 1939.

VOUGHT XSO2U-l
Ranger XV-770-4, 500 hp at takeoff, 450 hp at 9000'
DIMENSIONS: Span 38'2", Lg. 34'2", Ht. 15'1", Wing Area 299.8 sq. ft.
WEIGHT: Empty 3713 lb., Gross 5186 lb. Fuel 128 gal.
PERFORMANCE: Speed- Top 185 mph at s. l., 201 mph at 9000', Cruising 129 mph, Stalling 53 mph. Service Ceiling 24,000', Climb 1010'/1 min. Range 872 miles.

VOUGHT XSO2U-l as seaplane
Ranger XV-770-4, 500 hp at takeoff, 450 hp at 9000'
DIMENSIONS: Span 38'2", Lg. 36'1", Ht. 15'11", Wing Area 299.8 sq. ft.
WEIGHT: Empty 4016 lb. , Gross 5439 lb., Max. 5634 lb. Fuel 128 gal.
PERFORMANCE: Speed- Top 175 mph at s. l., 190 mph at 9000', Cruising 127 mph, Stalling 54.7 mph. Service Ceiling 22,200', Climb 890'/1 min. Range 778 miles, Max. 984 miles.

The Curtiss prototype flew October 6, 1939, with wheels, and demonstrated its seaplane capability in December. The wings had leading-edge slots, and folded backwards for storage. Both prototypes were longer and more streamlined than the OS2U-ls, and seemed to be a step forward. Although the Vought XSO2U-1 had slightly better performance, that company was preoccupied with the OS2U and F4U programs.

Curtiss received a contract for production of 300 in a new Columbus, Ohio, factory on September 10, 1940, and a lend-lease program for the Royal Navy was added October 21, 1941. A Letter of Intent to San Diego's Ryan company in December 1941 added 72 aircraft designated SOR-1 to be built to the SO3C specification, and the contract made June 30, 1942, called for 1,072 SOR-1s.

The first Curtiss SO3C-1 completed in April 1942 had lost the prototype's light weight and streamlined appearance. Armor, self-sealing for the fuselage fuel tank, and wing tanks had been added, severe stability problems had been treated with blunt, upturned wingtips and enlarged dorsal fin, and cooling problems had broken the cowl lines. Empty weight of the seaplane version increased from 4,250 pounds on the XSO3C-1 to 4,713 pounds on the first production aircraft, and later grew past 4,900 pounds.

CURTISS XSO3C-1
Ranger XV-770-4, 500 hp at takeoff, 450 hp to 9000'
DIMENSIONS: Span 38', Lg. 34'3", Ht. 14', Wing Area 290 sq. ft.
WEIGHT: Empty 4049 lb., Gross 5489 lb. Fuel 96 gal.
PERFORMANCE: Speed- Top 182 mph at s. l., 198 mph at 9000', Stalling 54.4 mph. Service Ceiling 18,200', Climb 890'/1 min. Range 782 miles.

All the aircraft were delivered with panted wheel gear, convertible to Edo center floats on pedestals when needed. Armament included the usual two .30-caliber guns with 1,100 rounds plus two 325-pound depth bombs, and 144 pounds of crew armor was fitted.

CURTISS XSO3C-1 as seaplane
Ranger XV-770-4, 500 hp at takeoff, 450 hp to 9000'
DIMENSIONS: Span 38', Lg. 37', Ht. 15'3", Wing Area 290 sq. ft.
WEIGHT: Empty 4250 lb., Gross 5660 lb., Max. 5855 lb. Fuel 96-126 gal.
PERFORMANCE: Speed- Top 173 mph at s. l., 189 mph at 9000', Stalling 55 mph. Service Ceiling 17,800', Climb 810'/1 min. Range 722 miles, max. 933 miles.

The SO3Cs went aboard the new *Cleveland*, first cruiser of its class, on July 15, 1942, but the operational difficulties indicated the aircraft was too heavy for its power plant, and when the *Cleveland* sailed for the North African invasion in November 1942, SOC biplanes had replaced the unlucky Curtiss monoplanes.

Other models followed the SO3C-1. The SO3C-2, which appeared in October 1942, had a tail hook for escort carrier operations and could carry a 500-pound bomb

USN

CURTISS SO3C-1 as seaplane
Ranger V-770-6, 530 hp at takeoff, 450 hp at 11,800'
DIMENSIONS: Span 38', Lg. 35', Ht. 14'1", Wing Area 293 sq. ft.
WEIGHT: Empty 4995 lb., Gross 6600 lb., Max. 7000 lb. Fuel 120-300 gal.
PERFORMANCE: Speed- 150 mph at s. l., Top 167 mph at 11,800', Cruising 117 mph, Stalling 56 mph. Service Ceiling 16,500', Climb 380'/1 min. Range 640 miles as scout, 540 miles with 2/325 d/c, 980 miles ferry.

under the fuselage with the wheeled configuration, while the SO3C-2C appeared in December 1942 with the slightly more powerful V-770-8, new radio, and 24-volt system. While the SO3C-1s had been removed from four new light cruisers, three inshore patrol squadrons used the Curtiss monoplanes in 1943. The SO3C-3 of June 1943 also had the V-770-8, but no tail hook.

USN

CURTISS SO3C-1

The Ryan contract was canceled in December 1942 before any SOR-1s were built, when it was realized that the S03C's power plant was inadequate and the aircraft could not fulfill its mission. Denounced by Navy pilots as useless, SO3C contracts were cut back by 200 on September 21, 1943, and in the following month work began on converting 125 aircraft to radio-controlled target drones.

The Royal Navy had begun to receive 250 SO3C-2C Seamews, as they called them, in December 1942, but used them only for training and drone work. Of these, the UK got 170, Canada's Dartmouth Station had 72, six were lost in accidents, and Cuba got the last two.

USN

CURTISS SO3C-2
Ranger V-770-6, 530 hp at takeoff, 450 hp at 11,800'
DIMENSIONS: Span 38', Lg. 33'9", Ht. 10'2", Wing Area 293 sq. ft.
WEIGHT: Empty 4785 lb., Gross 6350 lb., Max. 7000 lb. Fuel 120-320 gal.
PERFORMANCE: Speed- Top 164 mph at s.l., 182 mph at 11,800', Cruising 121 mph, Stalling 53 mph. Service Ceiling 18,200', Climb 520'/1 min. Range 630-1165 miles as scout, 690 miles/500 lb. bomb, 1600 miles ferry.

The Seamew's name in the U.S. Navy was Seagull, the same as the SOC. Curtiss built 800 of these two-seaters: 141 SO3C-ls, 150 SO3C-2s, 309 SO3C-2Cs, and 200 SO3C-3s, the last 43 delivered in January 1944. By that time, the Navy had already begun withdrawing the type from operating units, and the last to report an SO3C-3 on

CURTISS SO3C-3
Ranger V-770-8, 550 hp at takeoff, 500 hp at 8100'
DIMENSIONS: Span 38', Lg. 33'9", Ht. 10'2", Wing Area 293 sq. ft.
WEIGHT: Empty 4800 lb., Gross 6370 lb., Max. 7000 lb. Fuel 120- 320 gal.
PERFORMANCE: Speed- Top 171 at s. l., 183 mph at 8100', Cruising 121 mph, Stalling 53 mph. Service Ceiling 17,400', Climb 860'/1 min. Range 630-1150 miles as scout, 1200 miles ferry.

hand was the shore-based VS-42 on March 31, 1944. SOC biplanes were reinstated in service, together with OS2Us, until the new SC-ls would become available.

Curtiss Seahawk

The last float plane in service on Navy warships was the Curtiss SC-1 Seahawk, developed to meet the need for a more powerful shipboard scout. German warships had the Arado 196 with twice the Kingfisher's horsepower, and float versions of Japan's Zero fighter were active in the Pacific. In June 1942, the Navy requested proposals for a single-seat monoplane convertible from wheels to floats.

Curtiss submitted the Model 97 design and received a Letter of Intent for XSC-l and SC-l aircraft, dated October 30, 1942. Contracts were approved for two prototypes on March 31 and for 500 aircraft on June 30, 1943. (The SC-l designation duplicated that of 1925's torpedo biplane.)

CURTISS XSC-1
Wright R-1820-62, 1350 hp at takeoff, 1300 hp to 26,800'
DIMENSIONS: Span 41', Lg. 30'10", Ht. 14'2", Wing Area 280 sq. ft.
WEIGHT: Empty 5970 lb., Gross 7590 lb., Max. 8090 lb. with 2/325 lb. depth charges. Fuel 120 gal.
PERFORMANCE: Speed- Top 254 mph at s. l., 334 mph at 28,700', Cruising 136 mph, Stalling 60 mph. Service Ceiling 38,200', Climb 2,650'/1 min., 10,000'/3.8 min. Scouting Radius 172 miles, Range 710 miles as scout, 760 miles ferry.

The power plant was the Wright R-1820-62 with 1,350 hp for takeoff and turbosupercharged to give 1,300 hp up to 26,800 feet. Anticipated top speed of the wheeled version would rise from 254 mph at sea level to 334 mph at 28,700 ft., making Seahawk an equal to the F4F-4 Wildcat, and the seaplane model was expected to do 313 mph.

The prototype first flew at Columbus, Ohio, on February 16, 1944, and four XSC-ls were accepted in April 1944, with another deferred to 1945 for developmental testing. Curtiss delivered the first 119 SC-ls from July to December 1944. All appeared with wheeled gear, the Navy adding the Edo float and pedestal as needed, that conversion taking about six hours. First ship to get Seahawks was the new 12-inch-gun large cruiser *Guam* on October 22, 1944, and its sister ship, *Alaska*, followed.

CURTISS SC-l
Wright R-1820-62, 1350 hp at takeoff, 1300 hp to 22,800'
DIMENSIONS: Span 41', Lg. 36'4", Ht. 15'4", Wing Area 282 sq. ft.
WEIGHT: Empty 6613 lb., Gross 7997 lb., Max. 8740 lb., Fuel 116+95 gal.
PERFORMANCE: Speed- Top 228 mph at s. 1., 284 mph at 23,700', Cruising 125 mph, Stalling 61 mph. Service Ceiling 35,200', Climb 2200'/1 min., 10,000'/4.9 min. Range 500-830 miles.

Weapons included two .50-caliber guns in the wings with 400 rounds while the pilot had 110 pounds of back armor, an armor-glass windshield, and a canopy with all-around vision. The wings had slots and folded backwards, with racks that could accommodate an APS-4 radar under the right wing and a 325-pound depth charge under the left. The central pontoon was originally designed with a bomb bay in the center, but this feature was replaced by an extra 95-gallon fuel tank.

Seahawk production continued to September 1945, with 568 delivered and 384 canceled by VJ Day. Of the 23 Navy battleships when the war ended, seven had Seahawks and 16 the older Kingfishers. Of 70 cruisers then assigned floatplanes, 43 had Seahawks, 20 Kingfishers, and seven still used prewar Seagull biplanes. Replacement training units were based at Alameda, Pearl Harbor, and Norfolk.

One SC-1A had been modified to the XSC-1A with the more economical XR-1820-68 without a turbo. In July 1946, this aircraft was again accepted as the XSC-2 with an R-1820-76 and two-speed supercharger. This engine and

PMB

CURTISS XSC-1 as seaplane
Wright R-1820-62, 1350 hp at takeoff, 1300 hp to 26,800'
DIMENSIONS: Span 41', Lg. 36'4", Ht. 16'9", Wing Area 280 sq. ft.
WEIGHT: Empty 6320 lb., Gross 7936 lb., Max. 8612 lb. with 2/325-lb. depth charges. Fuel 120+112 gal.
PERFORMANCE: Speed- Top 238 mph at s. l., 313 mph at 28,700', Cruising 125 mph, Stalling 62 mph. Service Ceiling 37,300', Climb 2,500'/1 min., 10,000'/4.1 min. Scouting Radius 152-311 miles, Range 625-1090 miles as scout, 1200 miles ferry.

Mfr

CURTISS SC-2
Wright R-1820-76, 1425 hp to 1000', 1100 hp at 11,600'
DIMENSIONS: Same as SC-l
WEIGHT: Empty 6442 lb., Gross 8000 lb., Max. 8770 lb. Fuel 116+100 gal.
PERFORMANCE: Speed- Top 235 mph at s. l., 241 mph at 12,700', Cruising 137 mph, Stalling 75 mph. Service Ceiling 28,800', Climb 2480'/1 min. Range 515-925 miles. Data is for seaplane; landplane was for ferry only.

refinements like a one-piece canopy and new cowl were incorporated in 240 SC-2s ordered May 16, 1945. Cancellations reduced this number to nine delivered August/ October 1946 and a tenth SC-2 accepted in March 1948, as scout-rescue aircraft with a jump seat in the fuselage behind the pilot. Wing racks could accommodate a choice of two depth bombs, or rescue cells, four rockets, or radar, and the landplane version could handle a 100-gallon external ferry tank. Rescue equipment was also fitted to SC-1s that remained on the post-war warships.

Edo XOSE-1

Edo, the College Point, New York, company that had built most of the Navy's floats, also designed a seaplane of its own. The idea was to build a light, single-seater with the S03C-3's dimensions and Ranger engine. Edo XOSE-l prototypes were ordered January 11, 1944, and the first flew on December 28, 1945. (Originally XSO2E-l, following Bellanca's XSOE-l of 1938, but then changed to XOSE-1.)

EDO XOSE-1
Ranger V-770-8, 550 hp at takeoff, 500 hp at 8000'
DIMENSIONS: Span 37'11", Lg. 31'1", Ht. 14'11", Wing Area 237 sq. ft.
WEIGHT: Empty 3973 lb., Gross 5316 lb., Max. 6064 lb. Fuel 120+58 gal.
PERFORMANCE: Speed- Top 188 mph at s. l., 198 mph at 8800', Cruising 111 mph, Stalling 61 mph. Service Ceiling 22,300', Climb 1210'/1 min. Range 900-1150 miles.

Folding wings, 135 pounds of armor and a self-sealing fuel tank, two .50-caliber guns, and two depth charges were provided, along with a central float that could be replaced by wheels for ferry flights. A two-seat version with just one gun was flown as the XOSE-2 July 24, 1947, but both versions showed serious flying problems.

The development program was cut back and acceptances were limited to six XOSE-l single-seaters in April 1948 and two XOSE-2 two-seaters in August, along with two unarmed dual-control TE-1 trainers. None went aboard warships.

After the war, the warships were gradually demobilized or had their catapult gear replaced by utility helicopter provisions. The last shipboard seaplane squadrons were disbanded in June 1949, and the shore-based SC-ls were last reported with a utility unit, HU-2, in October 1949. The age of the Navy float plane was over; the catapult launches and often hectic recovery operations were at an end.

CHAPTER 21

NAVY ATTACK PLANES, 1931-1945

SBD dive-bombers would win the battle of Midway

The U.S. Navy and Marines had 20 dive-bomber or torpedo plane squadrons when World War II began in 1939. Seven years earlier its carrier-based attack force had consisted of only two squadrons of open-cockpit biplanes; one the Martin dive-bombers aboard the *Lexington* and the other the Great Lakes torpedo planes on the *Saratoga*. The story of this ten-fold expansion can be begun in 1931 when development of the next attack plane generation began.

Navy Bombers, 1931-35

The first all-metal monoplane bomber obtained by the Navy bore little resemblance to the carrier-based types used in World War II. In fact, the Consolidated XBY-l was based on the commercial Fleetster cabin plane designed in 1929 by I. M. Laddon with a high cantilever wing and wheel pants. The first metal monocoque fuselage on an American production plane contained the passenger cabin with the pilot's enclosure streamlined into the wing's center section on top of the fuselage.

CONSOLIDATED XBY-l
Wright R-1820-78, 600 hp at 8000'
DIMENSIONS: Span 50', Lg. 33'8", Ht. 10'6", Wing Area 361 sq. ft.
WEIGHT: Empty 3879 lb., Gross 6635 lb. Fuel 130 gal.
PERFORMANCE: Speed- Top 154 mph at s. l., 170 mph at 8000' Stalling 64 mph. Service Ceiling 20,500', Climb 7600'/10 min. Range 634 miles.

In the two-seat XBY-l, this cabin contained a bomb bay whose door folded left and upwards on the rounded fuselage. Behind a 1,000 (actually 989) pound bomb, the second crewman operated the 78-pound Norden Mark XI bombsight, the radio, and a .30-caliber flexible gun deployed by opening a sliding panel in the roof behind the wing. Two integral fuel tanks, another first for the Navy, were in the wing's leading edges, inboard of the flotation bags.

Ordered April 9, 1931, the XBY-l was first flown on September 17, 1932, by William Wheatley. When flight delivered from Buffalo to Anacostia on September 26, the XBY-1 had a 575-hp R-1820-70, but a 600-hp R-1820-78 Cyclone F-2 replaced it for new flight tests begun January 10, 1933. Tests ended after the landing gear collapsed on April 13. By that time, Navy experience demonstrated that horizontal bombing was much less accurate than dive-bombing on moving ships.

CONSOLIDATED XB2Y-1
Pratt & Whitney R-1535-64, 700 hp at 8900'
DIMENSIONS: Span 36'6", Lg. 27'10", Ht. 10'10", Wing Area 362 sq. ft.
WEIGHT: Empty 3538 1b., Gross 6010 lb. Fuel 153+60 gal.
PERFORMANCE: Speed- Top 187 mph at 8900', Stalling 66 mph. Service Ceiling 21,000', Climb 5000'/4.2 min. Range 487 miles.

BuAer Design No. 110, dated October 30, 1931, for a dive-bomber aimed by the pilot with a simple telescopic sight and stressed for a 9G pullout, called for a traditional biplane with a 36-foot wing span and a 700-hp Pratt &

Arc

GREAT LAKES BG-1
Pratt & Whitney R-1535-82, 750 hp takeoff, 700 hp at 8900'
DIMENSIONS: Span 36, Lg. 28'9", Ht. 11', Wing Area 384 sq. ft.
WEIGHT: Empty 3903 lb., Gross 6123 lb., Max. 6347 lb. Fuel 165+60 gal.
PERFORMANCE: Speed- Top 188 mph at 8900' as scout, 187 mph as bomber, Stalling 66 mph. Service Ceiling 20,100', Climb 5000'/5.5 min. Range 519 miles/1000-lb. bomb, 1345 miles as scout.

Arc

GREAT LAKES XBG-l
Pratt & Whitney R-1535-64, 700 hp at 8900'
DIMENSIONS: Span 36', Lg. 28'9", Ht. 11'10", Wing Area 380 sq. ft.
WEIGHT: Empty 3474 lb., Gross 5892 lb. Fuel 165+60 gal.
PERFORMANCE: Speed- Top 185 mph at 8900', Stalling 64 mph. Service Ceiling 22,300', Climb 5000'/4.2 min. Range 501 miles.

Whitney twin-row Wasp. Specified construction was steel tubing with mostly fabric covering, aluminum alloy tail surfaces, and open cockpits. Required armament was a Mark V 989-pound bomb with a displacement crutch to eject the bomb clear of the propeller in a dive. One fixed and one flexible .30-caliber gun, with 500 rounds each, were carried, and a 60-gallon drop tank could replace the bomb for scouting missions. A radio, tail hook, flotation bags, and a life raft for the two crewmen must be included.

The Navy ordered prototypes from two companies on June 22, 1932. Both the Consolidated XB2Y-1 and Great Lakes XBG-l were powered by 700-hp R-1535-64 Wasps with neat NACA cowls, open cockpits, and metal N struts between the wings. The last design engineered by B. D. Thomas, the XB2Y-1 was flight delivered from Buffalo to Anacostia on June 28, 1933.

Designed by P. B. Rogers, the Great Lakes XBG-1 had been flight delivered from Cleveland to Anacostia on June 12, 1933, and won a contract on November 22, 1933, for 27 BG-ls. The first BG-1 was received on September 28, 1934, with a sliding canopy over the two cockpits. They went first to VB-3, organized for the new carrier *Ranger.* Later contracts expanded production to 60 delivered by November 1935 to provide a Marine dive-bomber squadron on each coast until they were replaced by SBD-1s in 1940.

The First Scout-Bombers

As a carrier's dive-bomber squadron could also be used as scouts, so the scout squadron's two-seaters could combine scout and dive bomber roles. Slightly smaller and faster aircraft fitted with displacement gear for a Mark III 500 (actually 474) pound bomb were designated scout-bombers in January 1934. The first of the scout-bomber class, the Vought SBU-l is also the last biplane with non-retractable landing gear used in squadron strength on the Navy's carriers before the arrival of the dive-bomber monoplanes of World War II.

This two-seater first flew in May 1933 as the XF3U-l, but the Navy had decided against further two-seat fighter development. Vought received a contract February 23, 1934, to rebuild the XF3U-l prototype as the XSBU-l scout-bomber. First flown May 29, 1934, the XSBU-l had a 700-hp R-1535-80 in a new cowling with adjustable cooling gills, more wing area and fuel, and could carry a 500-pound bomb under the fuselage.

Mfr

VOUGHT XSBU-1
Pratt & Whitney R-1535-80, 750 hp takeoff, 700 hp at 8900'
DIMENSIONS: Span 33'3", Lg. 27'10", Ht. 12', Wing Area 327 sq. ft.
WEIGHT: Empty 3558 lb., Gross 5297 lb., Max. 5520 lb. Fuel 100-145 gal.
PERFORMANCE: Speed- Top 208 mph at 8900', 201 mph/500-lb. bomb, Stalling 65 mph. Service Ceiling 25,300', Climb 5000'/ 3.7 min. Range 561 miles/500-lb. bomb, 902 miles as scout.

Eighty-four production SBU-ls were ordered January 3, 1935, enough for all three carrier scouting squadrons. The SBU-1's cowling was so efficient that it became the model for all new Navy planes with twin-row radials. Armament included the usual fixed .30-caliber gun, mounted under the cowl's right side, and a flexible gun. Top speed was 205 mph as a scout, or 198 mph when a bomb was carried between the wheels, or two 116-pound bombs hung on wing racks.

The first SBU-1 was flown August 9, 1935, and the others were delivered from November 1935 to May 1936 to serve with VS-1B, VS-2B, and VS-3B. Fourteen SBUs were also built for Argentina as the V-142A, the first flown on December 1, 1936. Forty SBU-2s ordered in November

Arc

VOUGHT SBU-1
Pratt & Whitney R-1535-82, 750 hp takeoff, 700 hp at 8900'
DIMENSIONS: Span 33'3", Lg. 27'9", Ht 12', Wing Area 327 sq. ft.
WEIGHT: Empty 3645 lb., Gross 5394 lb., Max. 5618 lb. Fuel 100-145 gal.
PERFORMANCE: Speed- Top 180 mph at s. l., 205 mph at 8900', 174 -198 mph/500 lb. bomb, Cruising 122 mph, Stalling 66 mph. Service Ceiling 24,400', Climb 1180'/1 min. Range 548 miles/500-lb. bomb, 862 miles as scout.

Mfr

VOUGHT V-142A for Argentina

Mfr

VOUGHT SBU-2

1936, similar but for a R-1535-98 of equal power, were delivered minus tail hooks from April to August 1937 to naval reserve stations.

The last carrier to use SBU-ls was the *Ranger*, which moved to the Atlantic in 1939 with VS-41 and VS-42, flying the Neutrality Patrol until most SBU-ls were retired by April 1941 to Pensacola as trainers.

The torpedo comes back on one wing

While the Navy operated only one torpedo-plane squadron (VT-2 with TG-2s) from 1932 to 1937, development of this attack style wasn't forgotten. Three different prototypes ordered June 30, 1934, got the new torpedo-bomber (TB) designation and the 800-hp Pratt & Whitney XR-1830-60 Twin Wasp: the carrier-based XTBG-1 and TBD-l, as well as the water-based VPTBH-l. (See Chapter 19.)

The Great Lakes XTBG-1 was the last torpedo biplane, and first flew at Cleveland on August 18, 1935. Wheels retracted into the all-metal fuselage ahead of tapered fabric-covered wings. A torpedo-man sat under a low canopy behind the Twin Wasp with a bomb-aiming window between the wheel wells. Pilot and gunner behind the wings were covered by a sliding canopy. A torpedo or 1,000-pound bomb and two .30-caliber guns were carried, but flight characteristics were unstable and performance was inferior to the XTBD-l.

GREAT LAKES XTBG-1
Pratt & Whitney XR-1830-60, 800 hp at 7,000'
DIMENSIONS: Span 42', Lg. 35'1", Ht. 15'1", Wing Area 547 sq. ft.
WEIGHT: Empty 5323 lb., Gross 8924 lb., Max. 9275 lb. Fuel 220 gal.
PERFORMANCE: Speed- Top 171 mph at s.l. with torpedo, 185 mph at 7,000' as bomber. Stalling 60 mph. Service Ceiling 16,400', Climb 5000'/6.2 min. Range 586 miles/torpedo, 998 miles/1000-lb. bomb.

The Douglas XTBD-l was an all-metal, low-wing monoplane with the crew of three under a long enclosure, and wheels retracting backward into the wing, left partially protruding for emergency landings. So that the big plane could be stored aboard carriers, the 50-foot wings folded upward, reducing span to 25 feet, 8 inches.

The prototype was first flown at Santa Monica April 15, 1935, and reached the Anacostia test station on April 24. This Douglas became the first monoplane chosen for carrier service when 114 TBD-ls were ordered on February 3, 1936. The first was delivered June 25, 1937, with an R-1830-64, higher pilot's canopy, modified rudder, and the oil cooler moved under the starboard wing root.

The pilot himself sighted the 1,935-pound Mk. 13 torpedo carried with about four feet of its 15-foot length exposed. When bombs replaced the torpedo, the bombardier sitting between the pilot and gunner when acting as navi-

DOUGLAS XTBD-1
Pratt & Whitney XR-1830-60, 800 hp at 8,000'
DIMENSIONS: Span 50', Lg. 35', Ht. 14'2", Wing Area 420 sq. ft.
WEIGHT: Empty 5046 lb., Gross 8385 lb., Max.. 8773 lb. Fuel 180 gal.
PERFORMANCE: Speed- Top 188 mph at s.l., 205 mph at 8000', 201 mph/torpedo. Stalling 63 mph. Service ceiling 20,800', Climb 5,000'/4.8 min. Range 449 miles/torpedo, 907 miles/1000-lb. bomb.

gator, knelt down to use a Norden Mk. XV sight through a window behind the engine. One 1,000 or three 500-pound bombs could be carried under the fuselage, or 12 116-pound bombs under the wings. A .30-caliber M-2 flexible gun with 600 rounds was provided at the rear cockpit and the .30-caliber fixed gun on the cowl's right side was sometimes replaced by a .50-caliber weapon.

DOUGLAS TBD-1
Pratt & Whitney R-1830-64, 900 hp at takeoff, 850 hp at 8,000'
DIMENSIONS: Span 50', Lg. 35', Ht. 15'1", Wing Area 420 sq. ft.
WEIGHT: Empty 6182 lb., Gross 9862 lb., Max.. 10,194 lb. Fuel 180 gal.
PERFORMANCE: Speed- Top 192 mph at s.l., 206 mph at 8000', 201 mph/torpedo, Cruising 128 mph. Stalling 68 mph. Service ceiling 19,700', Climb 720'/1 min. Range 435 miles/torpedo, 716 miles/1000-lb. bomb.

As was customary, the first TBD-1 remained at Anacostia for type testing. In August 1939 it became the TBD-lA when twin floats were fitted and the aircraft went to the Naval Torpedo Station at Newport, Rhode Island. The remaining TBD-ls delivered from September 1937 to June 1938 began to replace the *Saratoga's* TG-2s on October 5, 1937, and equipped all four Pacific Fleet torpedo squadrons. Another 15 were delivered from June to

WES

DOUGLAS TBD-1A

November 1939, and some TBD-ls were stationed at Norfolk on the east coast, where they were issued to VT-8 in October 1941, with a few to the *Ranger* and *Wasp*.

The world's best torpedo plane when introduced, the TBD-l was named the Devastator in 1941 and 100 remained to be the fleet's only torpedo type at the start of 1942. On February l, a series of raids on enemy islands by TBDs and SBDs began, and on May 7, the types worked together- TBDs with torpedoes at low level, and SBDs dive-bombing from above- and hit *Shoho,* the first Japanese carrier sunk in the war.

The failure of the next day's torpedo attack on a larger enemy carrier pointed out the TBD's weakness. The unsatisfactory Mk. 13 torpedo required that runs be made below 100 feet at no more than 100 knots (111 mph), with release no more than 1,000 yards from the target, and even then the slow torpedo often failed to work properly. Enemy fighters and antiaircraft soon made such attacks nearly suicidal, and at the Midway battle, only four of 41 Devastators launched on June 4 returned to land on their carrier. Altogether, the TBDs flew 178 combat sorties in the Pacific, including 132 with torpedoes that scored only about nine hits.

The last of the biplanes

Two types of Navy dive-bombers were planned in 1934, the VB class with a 1,000-pound bomb and a .50-caliber fixed gun, and the VSB class with a 500-pound bomb and .30-caliber fixed gun. That distinction that would soon disappear with heavier aircraft, and all were two-seaters protected by a single .30-caliber flexible gun for the gunner.

USN

GREAT LAKES XB2G-1
Pratt & Whitney R-1535-82, 750 hp takeoff, 700 hp at 8900'
DIMENSIONS: Span 36', Lg. 28'9", Ht. 11'1", Wing Area 384 sq. ft.
WEIGHT: Empty 4248 lb., Gross 6394 lb., Max. 6802 lb. Fuel 165+60 gal.
PERFORMANCE: Speed- Top 197 mph at 8900'. Stalling 61 mph. Service Ceiling 19,500', Climb 5000'/6.3 min. Range 582 miles/1000-lb. bomb, 1115 miles as scout.

First to appear was the Great Lakes XB2G-l, with an R-1535-82, ordered on June 30, 1934. Similar to the BG-l except for a deep belly containing wells for retracting wheels, and an internal bay for a 1,000-pound bomb, the XB2G-l had four pairs of dive brakes on the wings and was armed with the .50-caliber M1921 fixed gun ahead of the pilot and a .30-caliber M 1922 flexible gun. Completed in November 1935, the XB2G-1 was delivered to Anacostia on January 24, 1936, and eventually became a Marine Command plane at Quantico, but was found not satisfactory as a dive bomber and the Cleveland firm went out of business in 1936.

The smaller Grumman XSBF-l ordered March 26, 1935, was first flown December 24 at Farmingdale and delivered for tests on February 12, 1936. Powered by an R-1535-72, the XSBF-l was a development of the SF-2 two-seat biplane with wheels retracting into the fuselage, enclosed cockpits, two .30-caliber guns and displacement gear for a 500-pound bomb under the fuselage. But since Grumman was already busy with fighter production, the Navy preferred to turn to Curtiss for its next scout-bomber contract.

PMB

GRUMMAN XSBF-1
Pratt & Whitney R-1535-72, 700 hp takeoff, 650 hp at 7,000'
DIMENSIONS: Span 31'6" Lg. 25'9" Ht. 11'3" Wing Area 310 sq. ft.
WEIGHT: Empty 3395 lb., Gross 5002 lb., Max. 5442 lb., Fuel 130 gal.
PERFORMANCE: Speed- Top 215 mph at 15,000', 209 mph/500 lb. bomb, Stalling 65 mph. Service ceiling 26,000', Climb 5000'/ 3.2 min. Range 688 miles/500-lb. bomb, 987 miles as scout.

The last combat biplanes built in the United States, the SBC series was actually the culmination of a 1932 contract made for the XF12C-1 two-seat, high-wing monoplane. On December 7, 1933, this type was redesignated XS4C-1 and a Wright R-1820-80 with a two-bladed propeller was installed. With the addition of gear for a 500-pound bomb,

Mfr

CURTISS XSBC-1

this aircraft was labeled XSBC-l in January 1934. Before it could be delivered to the Navy, the XSBC-1 crashed on June 14, 1934, during dive tests at the Buffalo factory.

On July 6, Curtiss proposed building a replacement prototype with a rigid 34-foot biplane structure instead of the 41-foot span folding wing, and with full-span flaps on the lower wing instead of leading edge slats. The prototype was reordered in April 1935 as the XSBC-2 with an XR-1510-12 with a three-bladed Curtiss propeller, a new cockpit canopy, and new tail. That XSBC-2 version began tests December 9, 1935, and in April 1936 reappeared as the XSBC-3 with an R-1535-82 and Hamilton propeller.

NASM

CURTISS XSBC-2
Wright R-1510-12, 700 hp at 7000'
DIMENSIONS: Span 34', Lg. 28'4", Ht. 12'7", Wing Area 317 sq. ft.
WEIGHT: Empty 3769 lb., Gross 5453 lb., Max. 5790 lb. Fuel 140 gal.
PERFORMANCE: Speed- Top 217 mph at 7000'/scout, 210 mph/ bomber, Stalling 63 mph, Service ceiling 24,900', Climb 5000'/ 3.5 min. Range 612 miles/500-lb. bomb, 944 miles as scout.

Mfr

CURTISS XSBC-3

This long development was rewarded August 29, 1936, with a contract for 83 SBC-3s powered by R-1535-94 Wasps. First delivered on July 17, 1937, the SBC-3 was similar to its prototype, with wheels retracting by hand crank into an all-metal fuselage and with a sliding canopy for pilot and observer. The wings were connected by "I" struts, the metal swept-back upper wing with the ailerons and the fabric-covered straight lower wing utilizing flaps for landing and as dive brakes. Armament included a .30-caliber gun under the cowl and another in the rear cockpit, while a 500-pound bomb or a drop tank could be carried beneath the fuselage, or two 116-pound bombs hung on wing racks.

USN

CURTISS SBC-4
WRIGHT R-1820-34, 950 hp takeoff, 750 hp at 15,000'
DIMENSIONS: Span 34' Lg. 27'6", Ht. 13'2" Wing Area 317 sq. ft.
WEIGHT: Empty 4552 lb., Gross 6260 lb., Max. 7141 lb. Fuel 135+45 gal.
PERFORMANCE: Speed- 218 mph at s.l., Top 237 mph at 15,200', Cruising 127 mph, Stalling 68 mph, Service ceiling 27,300', Climb 1860'/1 min. Range 555 miles/1000-lb. bomb, 590 miles/500-lb. bomb, 876 miles/scout, 1090 miles max.

CURTISS SBC-3
Pratt & Whitney R-1535-94, 825 hp takeoff, 750 hp at 9500'
DIMENSIONS: Span 34' Lg. 28'1", Ht. 13'2" Wing Area 317 sq. ft.
WEIGHT: Empty 4324 lb., Gross 6023 lb., Max. 6904 lb. Fuel 135+45 gal.
PERFORMANCE: Speed- Top 203 mph at s.l., 220 mph at 9500', Stalling 67 mph. Service ceiling 23,800' Climb 1340'/1 min. Range 635 miles/500-lb. bomb, 940 miles/scout, 1190 miles max.

All were accepted by December 1937 and served three scouting squadrons. The *Saratoga* got SBC-3s in September 1937, replacing the SBU-1s of VS-3, while VS-5 and VS-6 were equipped for the new carriers *Yorktown* and *Enterprise*.

One aircraft on this contract was completed in March 1938 as the XSBC-4 with a Wright R-1820-22 Cyclone, and these single-row engines had been chosen for 58 SBC-4s first ordered January 5, 1938. When delivery began in March 1939, the SBC-4s were distinguished from the earlier models by their wide-diameter engines, a 1,000-pound bomb capacity, and a .50-caliber nose gun. Pilots especially appreciated the hydraulic-powered wheel retraction that replaced the old manual gear.

Additional orders brought the total to 124 completed by April 1940, these planes going to VS-2 on the *Lexington* and to several Naval Reserve bases. On June 6, 1940, 50 SBC-4s were returned to the company for transfer to France. They were refurbished to French standards, painted in green and gray, and reached Halifax on June 10 with one lost on the way, 44 loaded on the carrier *Bearn* and five on the British *Furious*.

The *Bearn* left Halifax on June 16, but was diverted to Martinique, while the others got to Britain as the Curtiss Cleveland I. In neither case did they do any fighting, for the French aircraft were interned, while the Clevelands were used for mechanics' practice. Fifty more SBC-4s, originally ordered by France as Model 77F, were built between February and May 1941 to replace those sent abroad. Except for a 126-gallon self-sealing tank replacing the unprotected 135-gallon fuselage tank, they were similar to their predecessors.

Two SBC-4 squadrons served on the new *Hornet* in December 1941, but fortunately were replaced by SBDs when that carrier reached the West Coast in March 1942, so that the Navy did not have to take these biplanes into battle. A Marine observation squadron, VMO-151, did have them on Samoa from May 1942 to June 1943.

Vought Vindicator

With the expanding number of carrier-based dive-bomber squadrons came the opportunity to introduce new monoplanes to the fleet Three new prototypes, the Vought XSB2U-1, the Northrop XBT-1, and the Brewster XSBA-1, competed for production contracts with the more traditional biplanes.

VOUGHT XSB2U-1
Pratt & Whitney R-1535-78, 700 hp at 8900'
DIMENSIONS: Span 42', Lg. 33'2", Ht. 9'8", Wing Area 305 sq. ft.
WEIGHT: Empty 4392 lb., Gross 6070 lb., Max. 6855 lb. Fuel 130 gal.
PERFORMANCE: Speed- Top 246 mph at 8900', Stalling 64 mph. Service ceiling 28,900', Climb 5000'/3.7 min. Range 532 miles/1000-lb. bomb, 564 miles/500-lb. bomb, 892 miles max.

Two Wasp-powered scout bombers offered by Vought to the Navy illustrate the dispute between biplanes and monoplanes for carrier service. The XSB2U-l ordered October 11, 1934, was a low-wing monoplane with an R-1535-72, while the XSB3U-1 ordered February 7, 1935, was a biplane similar to the SBU-l, but for wheels retracting backward into the wing roots.

The XSB2U-1 first flew January 4, 1936, and the XSB3U-1 on March 13, but the monoplane's superior performance was demonstrated by Navy tests in April. Folding the wings upwards, as on the TBD, solved the shipboard stowage problem by reducing width to 16 feet, four inches.

VOUGHT XSB3U-1
Pratt & Whitney R-1535-82, 750 hp takeoff, 700 hp at 8900'
DIMENSIONS: Span 33'3", Lg. 28'2", Ht. 11', Wing Area 327 sq. ft.
WEIGHT: Empty 3876 lb., Gross 5627 lb., Max. 5837 lb. Fuel 145 gal.
PERFORMANCE: Speed- Top 214.5 mph at 8900', 209 mph/500-lb. bomb, Stalling 66.5 mph. Service ceiling 26,500' Climb 5000'/4.2 min. Range 590 miles/500-lb. bomb, 926 miles as scout.

Vought designer Rex Beisel used all-metal construction on the XSB2U-l, except for fabric-covering on the rear fuselage, control surfaces, and part of the wings. Wheels retracted backwards, rotating to fit flat within the wing. A

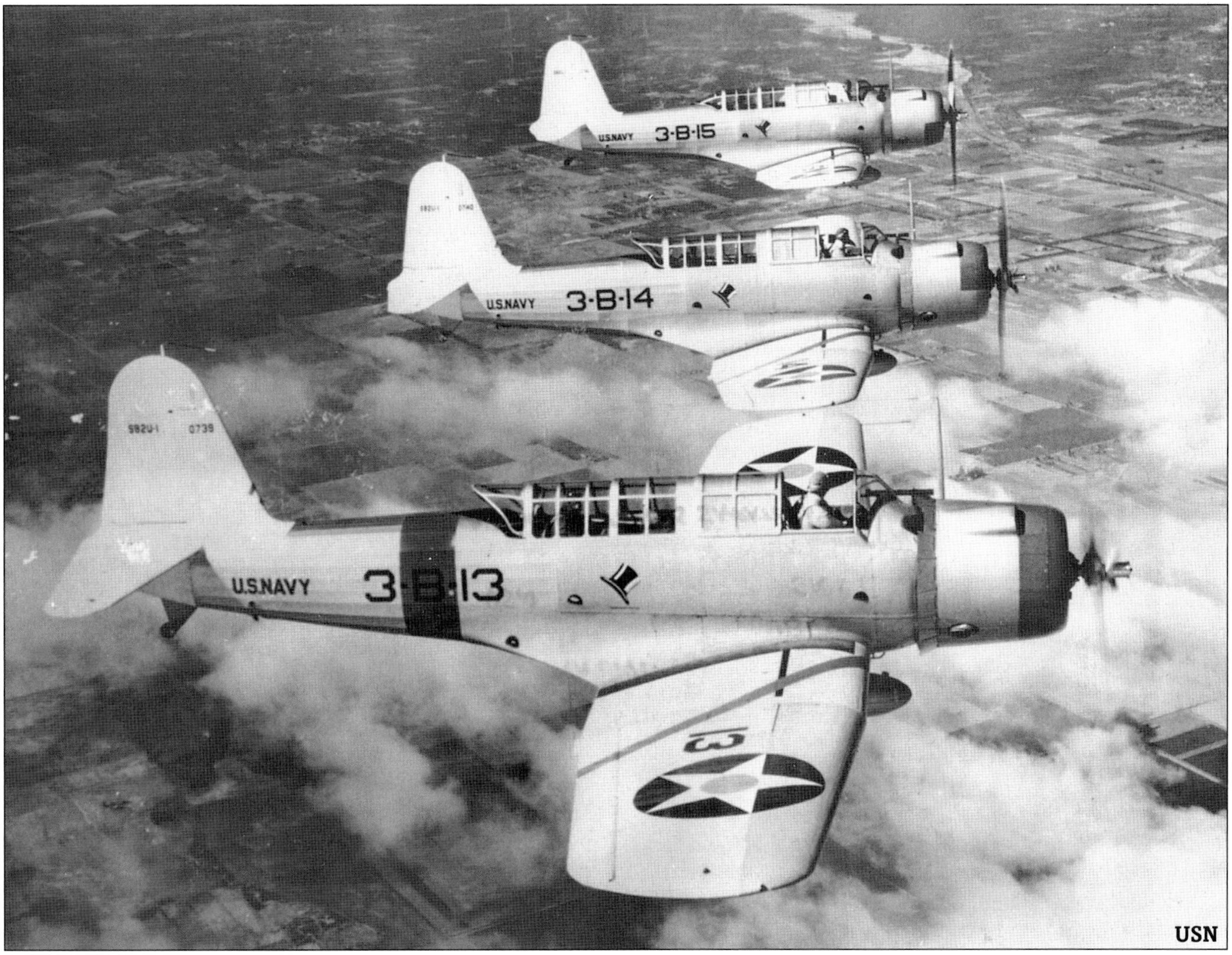

USN

VOUGHT SB2U-1
Pratt & Whitney R-1535-96, 825 hp takeoff, 750 at 9500'
DIMENSIONS: Span 42', Lg. 34', Ht. 10'3", Wing Area 305 sq. ft.
WEIGHT: Empty 4676 lb., Gross 6323 lb., Max. 7278 lb. Fuel 130+50 gal.
PERFORMANCE: Speed- Top 231 mph at s.l., 250 mph at 9500', 241 mph/500 lb. bomb, Cruising 143 mph, Stalling 66 mph. Service ceiling 27,400', Climb 1500'/1 min. Range 635 miles/1000-lb. bomb, 699 miles/500-lb. bomb, 1004 miles as scout.

long enclosure covered both crewmen, who had a .30-caliber fixed gun with 500 rounds in the right wing and a .30-caliber flexible gun with 600 rounds in the rear cockpit. Gear beneath the fuselage could handle a 500 or 1,000-pound bomb or 50-gallon drop tank, or two 116-pound bombs hung on wing racks.

Fifty-four SB2U-ls were ordered October 26, 1936. (Providing two 18-plane squadrons with 50% reserves, this order size was common in the pre-war period.) The first SB2U-1 flew May 21, 1937, and the rest were accepted from December 1937 to June 1938. On December 22, 1937, they became the second carrier-based monoplane in service when they began replacing VB-3's single-seat BFC-2 biplanes on the *Saratoga*, and then joined the *Lexington's* VB-2.

Similar to the prototype except for a new intake on the upper right cowl over the 1535-96 Wasp, their use of reversible Hamilton propellers to limit diving speeds was not very reliable. Only minor changes distinguished 58 SB2U-2s ordered January 27, 1938, first flown August 11, and completed by July 1939. Along with the earlier model, they were flown by VB-2, VB-3, VB-4, and in 1940 by VS-72 on the new *Wasp*.

Shertzer

VOUGHT SB2U-2
Pratt & Whitney R-1535-96, 825 hp takeoff, 750 at 9500'
DIMENSIONS: As SB2U-1
WEIGHT: Empty 4713 lb., Gross 6379 lb., Max. 7332 lb. Fuel 130+50 gal.
PERFORMANCE: Speed- Top 232 mph at s.l., 251 mph at 9500', Stalling 66 mph. Service ceiling 27,500', Climb 1340'/1 min. Range 630 miles/1000-lb. bomb, 1002 miles as scout.

An October 13, 1938, contract had the last SB2U-1 rebuilt with long-range fuel tanks as the XSB2U-3 and tested

VOUGHT XSB2U-3
Pratt & Whitney R-1535-96, 825 hp takeoff. 750 hp at 9500'
DIMENSIONS: Span 42', Lg. 36'9", Ht. 16'1", Wing Area 305 sq. ft.
WEIGHT: Empty 5400 lb., Gross 7218 lb., Max. 8036 lb. Fuel 130+355 gal.
PERFORMANCE: Speed- Top 210 mph at 9500',194 mph/1000-lb. bomb, Stalling 67 mph. Service ceiling 21,800'.

as a landplane in May 1939. Twin pontoons were fitted for tests begun August 9 that demonstrated that top speed was reduced from 246 mph with retractable wheels to 210 mph with the pontoons.

After Vought sent a V-156 demonstrator to the Paris air show in November 1938, the French Navy ordered 40 V-156Fs on February 22, 1939; similar to the SB2U-2 except for dive brakes on the wings, pilot armor, and armament. Two 7.5-mm Darne guns were in the wings with a third in the rear pit, and since the Navy's centerline yoke was then not for export, simple wing racks accommodated two 150-kg. (330-pound) bombs. The first V-156F appeared in April 1939, and was shipped to France in July, and the Voughts equipped two squadrons on the Channel coast. Most were lost in the bitter fighting of May 1940, while a third squadron fought Italy in June.

VOUGHT V-156F

Fifty-seven SB2U-3 Vindicators with standard retractable gear had been ordered by the Navy on September 25, 1939, while 50 more ordered March 28, 1940, by France were transferred to Britain as the V-156B Chesapeake. The first SB2U-3 flew January 10, 1941, and the first V-156B on February 26, with deliveries on both contracts made from March to July 1941. SB2U-3s had additional fuel capacity, a self-sealing main tank, and two .50-caliber wing guns. British Voughts had four .303-caliber wing guns, three 500-pound bombs, and more armor, but never saw combat because their takeoff run was too long for small aircraft carriers.

VOUGHT SB2U-3
Pratt & Whitney R-1535-02, 825 hp takeoff. 750 hp at 9500'
DIMENSIONS: As SB2U-1
WEIGHT: Empty 5634 lb., Gross 7474 lb., Max. 9421 lb. Fuel 370+50 gal.
PERFORMANCE: Speed- Top 222 mph at s.l., 243 mph at 9500', Cruising 152 mph Stalling 71 mph. Service ceiling 23,600', Climb 1070'/1 min. Range 1120 miles/1000-lb. bomb, 2450 miles ferry.

When America entered the war, the Marines had two SB2U-3 squadrons while older Vindicators served the four scout squadrons on the *Ranger* and *Wasp* in the Atlantic.

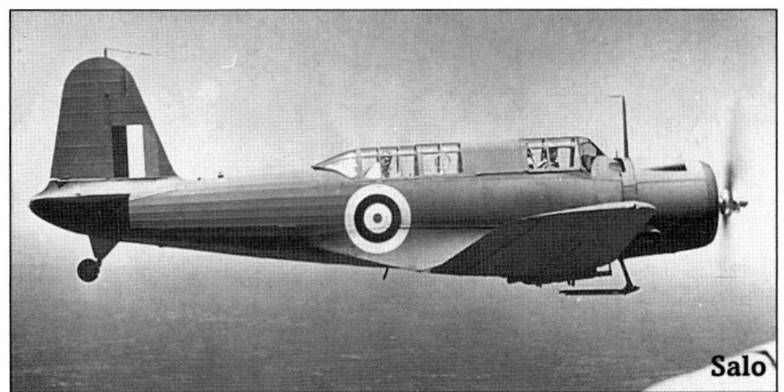

VOUGHT V-156B Chesapeake
Pratt & Whitney R-1535-SB4-G, 825 hp takeoff. 750 hp at 9500'
DIMENSIONS: As SB2U-1
WEIGHT: Empty 6500 lb., Gross 8360 lb., Max. 9763 lb. Fuel 255+50 gal.
PERFORMANCE: Speed- Top 225 mph at s.l., 247 mph at 9500', (198-222 mph/500-lb. bombs), Cruising 215 (181) mph. Service ceiling 22,700' (16,400'), Climb 1050' (600')/1 min. Range 1170 miles/500-lb. bomb, 1340 miles as scout.

The Marine's VMSB-231 was hit on December 7 at Ewa, but on December 11, flew 1,137 miles to Midway Island where it became the only Navy Vindicator unit to fight in a major battle.

Northrop BT-1

The third carrier-based monoplane in Navy service, the Northrop XBT-1 ordered November 18, 1934, was the predecessor of the famous SBD series. First flown August 19, 1935, by Vance Breese, the XBT-1 was a two-seat low-wing monoplane resembling the A-17 attack type, and reached Anacostia on December 12.

NORTHROP XBT-1
Pratt & Whitney R-1535-66, 700 hp at 8900'
DIMENSIONS: Span 41'6", Lg. 31'10", Ht. 12'6", Wing Area 315 sq. ft.
WEIGHT: Empty 4183 lb., Gross 6156 lb., Max. 6718 lb., Fuel 183 gal.
PERFORMANCE: Speed- Top 222 mph at 8900', 212 mph/1000-lb. bomb, Stalling 62 mph. Service ceiling 25,800', Climb 5000'/4.1 min. Range 564 miles/1000-lb. bomb, 1063 miles max.

The all-metal construction, except for fabric-covered control surfaces and Plexiglas cockpit covers, would become standard on all Navy bombers, but the multi-cellule wing structure prevented the usual folding for carrier stowage. Another feature was retraction of the wheels back into fairings under the wings, which had split flaps at the trailing edge. These flaps were opened in dives to limit dangerous high-speed pullouts, and were perforated after tests showed this would prevent buffeting from spoiling the aim.

NORTHROP BT-1
Pratt & Whitney R-1525-94, 825 hp takeoff, 750 hp at 9500'
DIMENSIONS: Span 41'6", Lg. 31'8", Ht. 9'11", Wing Area 319 sq. ft.
WEIGHT: Empty 4606 lb., Gross 6650 lb., Max. 7197 lb. Fuel 180 gal.
PERFORMANCE: Speed- Top 222 mph at 9500', 212 mph/1000-lb. bomb, Cruising 192 mph, Stalling 66 mph. Service ceiling 25,300', Climb 1270'/1 min. Range 550 miles/1000-lb. bomb, 1150 miles as scout.

Armament included a .50-caliber fixed gun in front of the pilot and the observer's .30-caliber flexible gun, as well as a 1,000-pound bomb carried below the fuselage, and wing racks were provided for a pair of 116-pound bombs. The original 700-hp R-1535-66 was replaced in April 1936 by the R-1535-94 to be used on 54 BT-1s ordered September 16, 1936. The first BT-1 was delivered on November 16, 1937, but a strike delayed the next delivery to March 21, 1938. By August 5, 52 had been delivered and they joined VB-5 on the *Yorktown* in April, and afterwards VB-6 on the *Enterprise*.

The last BT-1 was flown on October 12, 1938, with fixed tricycle gear to test that configuration for carrier landings. After crash damages it remained with the company, which restored it to normal configuration, called it the DB-19, and sold it to Japan.

NORTHROP XBT-2
(Shown before change to SBD configuration)
Wright XR-1820-32, 1000 hp takeoff, 800 hp at 16,000'
DIMENSIONS: Span 41'6", Lg. 31'9", Ht. 12'10", Wing Area 320 sq. ft.
WEIGHT: Empty 5093 lb., Gross 7231 lb., Max. 7593 lb. Fuel 210 gal.
PERFORMANCE: Speed- Top 243 mph at s.l., 265 mph at 16,000', 252 mph/1000-lb. bomb, Cruising 155 mph, Stalling 67 mph, Service ceiling 30,600', Climb 1450'/1 min. Range 604 miles/1000-lb. bomb, 1458 miles as scout.

A contract change dated November 28, 1936, lead to completion of the 38th aircraft as the XBT-2 with wheels retracting inwardly flush into the wing roots. By the time the XBT-2 first flew on April 22, 1938, the original Northrop firm had become the Douglas El Segundo division, while Ed Heinemann remained as chief designer. On June 21, he was authorized to replace the original Wasp engine with a 1,000-hp Wright R-1820-32 Cyclone and three-bladed propeller.

Delivered to the Navy on August 24, 1938, the XBT-2 reached a top speed of 265 mph. In December 1938, tests begun in NACA's full-scale wind tunnel at Langley Field lead to many changes, especially in the tail, that became the configuration of the SBD series.

USN

DOUGLAS SBD-1
Wright R-1820-32, 1000 hp takeoff, 800 hp at 16,000'
DIMENSIONS: Span 41'6", Lg. 32'2", Ht. 13'7", Wing Area 325 sq. ft.
WEIGHT: Empty 5903 lb., Gross 8138 lb., Max. 9190 lb. Fuel 180-210 gal.
PERFORMANCE: Speed- Top 232 mph at s.l., 253 mph at 16,000' (226-246 mph with 1000-lb. bomb), Cruising 142 mph, Stalling 70.5 mph. Service ceiling 29,600', Climb 1730'/1 min. Range 860 miles/1000-lb. bomb, 985 miles as scout, 1165 miles ferry.

Douglas Dauntless

When World War II began in September 1939, there were 385 dive bombers for 16 Navy and Marine squadrons, not including the Reserves. This force was comparable to the 366 land-based Stukas with which Germany began the war.

Seven types were included: three squadrons each of BG-l, SBU-l and SBC-3 biplanes, two squadrons each of BT-l, SB2U-l and SB2U-2 monoplanes, and one with the Cyclone-powered SBC-4. All these aircraft would be replaced within three years by Ed Heinemann's design for Douglas.

On April 8, 1939, Douglas received a contract for 57 SBD-ls and 87 SBD-2s, developed from the XBT-2 with a high tapered fin, and powered by an R-1820-32 Cyclone. The SBD-l first flew on May 1, 1940, and replaced the BG-l in both Marine bomb squadrons by December. Perforated trailing edge flaps and slots on the leading edge contributed to the SBD's excellent handling qualities, especially in 70-degree dives.

A yoke under the center held a 500 or 1,000-pound bomb and wing racks were provided for two 100-pound bombs. Two .50-caliber guns with 360 rounds were in front of the pilot, and the gunner had the usual .30-caliber M-2 with 600 rounds.

Designed to operate aboard carriers, the SBD-2 was first flown December 18, 1940, with fuel capacity increased from 210 to 310 gallons, and with a smaller air intake. One of the forward guns was usually omitted from this model, which first served both VB-6 and VS-6 on the *Enterprise* and the *Lexington's* VB-2 and VS-2.

Mfr

DOUGLAS SBD-2
Wright R-1820-32, 1000 hp takeoff, 800 hp at 16,000'
DIMENSIONS: As SBD-1
WEIGHT: Empty 6293 lb., Gross 9061 lb., Max. 10,360 lb. Fuel 260-310 gal.
PERFORMANCE: Speed- Top 232 mph at s.l., 252 mph at 16,000', Cruising 148 mph, Stalling 75.5 mph. Service ceiling 26,000', Climb 1080'/1 min. Range 1225 miles/1000-lb. bomb, 1370 miles as scout.

Self-sealing tanks that reduced fuel capacity to 260 gallons and 167 pounds of cockpit armor were provided on the 174 SBD-3s ordered on September 27, 1940. The first was delivered on March 18, 1941, and the Douglas bombers were named the Dauntless in October. Along with 78 similar SBD-3As (A-24) for the Army, they introduced the R-l820-52 and were armed with two .50-caliber front guns and one .30 caliber gun in the rear cockpit.

SDAM

DOUGLAS SBD-3
Wright R-1820-52, 1000 hp takeoff, 800 hp at 16,000'
DIMENSIONS: Span 41'6", Lg. 32'8", Ht. 13'7", Wing Area 325 sq. ft.
WEIGHT: Empty 6345 lb., Gross 9407 lb., Max. 10,400 lb. Fuel 260 gal.
PERFORMANCE: Speed- Top 231 mph at s.l., 250 mph at 16,000' as scout (224-241 mph/1000 lb. bomb), Stalling 78 mph. Service ceiling 27,100', Climb 1190'/1 min., 10,000'/9 min., Range 1205 miles/1000-lb. bomb at 152 mph., 1415 miles as scout.

Dauntless production might have ended when the last SBD-3 of that contract was delivered on January 4, 1942, but the Pearl Harbor attack created a demand for all the dive-bombers Douglas could build. On March 4, 1942, the El Segundo factory delivered the first of 412 additional SBD-3 and 90 SBD-3A aircraft. Twin-.30-caliber M-2s with 2,000 rounds replaced the single flexible gun that had been standard dive-bomber defense for a decade and the bomb gear was strengthened for bigger

USN

DOUGLAS SBD-6
Wright R-1820-66, 1350 hp takeoff, 1000 hp at 15,600'
DIMENSIONS: Span 41'6", Lg. 33', Ht. 12'11", Wing Area 325 sq. ft.
WEIGHT: Empty 6544 lb., Gross 9602 lb., Max. 11,770 lb. Fuel 284+116 gal.
PERFORMANCE: Speed- Top 247 mph at s.l., 262 mph at 15,600', (232-244 mph/1000-lb. bomb) Cruising 144 mph, Stalling 75 mph. Service ceiling 28,600', Climb 1710'/1 min. Range 1230 miles/1000-lb. bomb, 1700 miles as scout.

loads. A 1,600-pound armor-piercing bomb, developed from the 14-inch gun shell, could be attached to the center rack, or wing racks could accommodate two 325-pound depth charges for anti-sub patrols.

These protection and weapons improvements were retrofitted to some SBD-2s, including 19 sent to Midway island Marines in May 1942. In October acceptances began on 780 SBD-4 and 170 Army A-24As. They were similar to the SBD-3 except for a new 24-volt electrical system and Hamilton propeller. The SBD-2P, SBD-3P, and SBD-4P were some 40 fitted with camera mounts after delivery.

Since development of the Curtiss SB2A as the SBD replacement had been too slow, Douglas received an order on December 1, 1942, for the SBD-5, which was first delivered on February 21, 1943. The basic SBD airframe remained the same, but an R-1820-60 engine was in a new cowl omitting the top intake. Two 58-gallon drop tanks could be attached under the wings. Another improvement in the 3,025 SBD-5s built by April 1944 was the reflector sight that replaced the 3-power telescopic sight of previous dive-bombers.

One SBD-5 fitted with an R-1820-66 Cyclone and new fuel tanks became the XSBD-6 accepted on February 8, 1944, and the last 450 Dauntless bombers were SBD-6 models with the ASV radar fitted on some earlier aircraft. The last of 5,938 SBDs built, including Army models, was delivered on July 22, 1944.

NASM

DOUGLAS SBD-5
Wright R-1820-60, 1200 hp takeoff, 1000 hp at 13,800'
DIMENSIONS: Span 41'6", Lg. 33', Ht. 12'11", Wing Area 325 sq. ft.
WEIGHT: Empty 6533 lb., Gross 9352 lb., Max. 10,700 lb. Fuel 254+116 gal.
PERFORMANCE: Speed- Top 229 mph at s.l., 255 mph at 15,700', Cruising 153 mph, Stalling 80 mph. Service ceiling 25,000', Climb 1550'/1 min. Range 1115 miles/1000-lb. bomb, 1565 miles as scout.

In December 1941, the three Navy carriers in the Pacific had 113 SBDs aboard for six scout and bomber squadrons, and the Marines had an SBD-1 squadron at Ewa. The carriers were fortunate enough not to be at Pearl Harbor, but seven SBD-2 pilots from the *Enterprise* were shot down when they flew unaware into the December 7 attack and another 17 Marine SBD-ls were destroyed on the ground. One of pilots downed that day, Clarence E. Dickinson, sank a Japanese submarine, *I-170*, on December 10, the first enemy warship sunk by Navy SBDs in the war.

Joined by the *Yorktown's* air group in February 1942, the Dauntless dive-bombers, Devastator torpedo planes, and Wildcat fighters, struck repeatedly at the Japanese Navy. At the Battle of Midway, 101 SBD-3s from three carriers destroyed all four enemy carriers and turned the tide of the Pacific war. By that time, two SBD squadrons were embarked on each large U.S. carrier, and fought in every carrier action of the next two years. Since it did not have folding wings, the SBD was not used on escort carriers.

Although the Dauntless was phased out of attack carrier operations after July 1944, it continued operating in land-based dive-bomber squadrons until the war's end. The Marines had 17 SBD squadrons by August 1943, and the first Navy inshore SBD squadron was deployed in 1942. By July 1944, five SBD-4 and 19 SBD-5 inshore squadrons were added to replace the Vought Kingfishers and four squadrons remained in July 1945.

New Zealand operated 68 between July 1943 and May 1944: 18 SBD-3s, 27 SBD-4s, and 23 SBD-5s; and Britain's Navy received nine SBD-5s by October 1944. Two French Navy *escadrilles* received 32 SBD-5s in November 1944.

During its successful career, the Douglas was credited with sinking 18 warships, including six carriers and a battleship in 1942, often with torpedo-bomber help. Rather surprising is that SBD pilots and gunners were also credited with 138 Japanese planes in the brisk fights that often followed the bomb drops.

Brewster's Bombers

In contrast with the success of the Douglas Dauntless is the failure of the Brewster Company's dive-bomber production. This firm's first airplane was the XSBA-1 designed by Dayton T. Brown and ordered by the Navy on October 15, 1934. A mid-wing, two-place monoplane, it was not flown until April 1, 1936, and Anacostia tests began April 15.

Powered by a 725-hp Wright R-1820-04 with a two-bladed propeller, the XSBA-1 had wheels retracting into the metal fuselage ahead of the internal bay for a 500-pound bomb, and had fittings for a fixed 30-caliber gun behind the engine and a .30-caliber flexible gun in the rear cockpit.

In its original form, the Brewster weighed 3,695 pounds empty and 5,569 pounds with the bomb, and did 242 mph. It was returned to the factory for installation of an XR-1820-22 with a short cowl and three-bladed propeller. The revised prototype was flown January 17, 1937, with a higher cockpit for the pilot and gunner and perforated split flaps to limit dive speeds.

While this was the fastest dive-bomber of 1937, the Navy preferred that the small new company concentrate on its XF2A-1 fighter. To provide work for the Naval Aircraft Factory in Philadelphia, an order was placed on September 28, 1938, for 30 to be designated SBN-1.

Although the XSBA-1 was sent to the NAF as a pattern aircraft, the SBNs took uncommonly long to build. The first was not delivered until November 1940, the next 22 were not accepted until June and July 1941, and the last were not completed until March 1942.

BREWSTER XSBA-1 (original 1936 form)

SBN refinements included an R-1820-38, a taller rudder, improved crew canopies, and a .50-caliber fixed gun, but the 500-pound bomb load remained. Had the SBN served in 1939, it might have been impressive, but in 1941 it became only an operational trainer at Norfolk for the new *Hornet* air group, including VT-8. All were replaced before that carrier was deployed.

Brewster received a contract for the larger SB2A-1 on April 4, 1939. Like the Curtiss XSB2C-1 designed at the same time, it had a twin-row Wright XR-2600-8, a 1,000-pound bomb in the internal bay, and wheels that retracted inwards into the wings. Armor and self-sealing fuel tanks were added by a July 1940 order.

BREWSTER XSBA-1 (1937)
Wright XR-1820-22, 950 hp takeoff, 750 hp at 15,200'
DIMENSIONS: Span 39', Lg. 28'3", Ht. 11'1", Wing Area 259 sq. ft.
WEIGHT: Empty 4081 lb., Gross 5736 lb., Max. 5972 lb. Fuel 136 gal.
PERFORMANCE: Speed- Top 263 mph at 15,200', Stalling 69 mph. Service ceiling 28,500', Climb 1970'/1 min. Range 573 miles/500-lb. bomb, 890 miles as scout.

After France surrendered, the RAF launched a program in 1940 to buy 1,200 dive-bombers in America: 700 from

Arc

N.A.F. SBN-1
Wright R-1820-38, 950 hp takeoff, 750 hp at 15,200'
DIMENSIONS: Span 39', Lg. 27'8", Ht. 12'5", Wing Area 259 sq. ft.
WEIGHT: Empty 4503 lb., Gross 6245 lb., Max. 6759 lb. Fuel 136 gal.
PERFORMANCE: Speed- Top 231 mph at s. l., 254 mph at 15,200', Cruising 117 mph, Stalling 68 mph. Service ceiling 28,300', Climb 1970'/1 min. Range 1015 miles/500-lb. bomb, 1110 miles as scout.

Vultee, and 450 from Brewster, preceded by the 50 Voughts first ordered by France. The RAF named a land-based version of the SB2A, the Brewster 340-14, the Bermuda. The Dutch East Indies ordered 162 examples of model 340-17, similar except for bomb and radio provisions.

On the day before Christmas, 1940, the Navy ordered 203 SB2A-1s with folding wings and powered gun turret. This specification (model 340-20) called for two .50-caliber guns in the nose, two in the wings, and two in the turret. Promised top speed was to be 308 mph with a gross weight of 13,321 pounds. Since the company's Long Island City factory could not handle production of so many dive-bombers, a new assembly plant was built in Johnsville, PA.

On June 17, 1941, the XSB2A-1 was flown at Newark. A metal shell simulated the promised Maxson power turret for a .50-caliber gun, and the four fixed guns were also omitted, but the gross weight had increased and numerous flight problems were discovered.

The first Bermuda was flown late in November 1941 with the long Plexiglas enclosure seen on all production models. Unwilling to wait for perfection of the turret, the RAF and Dutch planes chose twin .30-caliber flexible guns in the rear cockpit and six fixed .30-caliber forward guns; two in the nose and four in the wings.

Mfr

BREWSTER XSB2A-1
Wright R-2600-8, 1700 hp takeoff, 1350 hp at 13,000'
DIMENSIONS: Span 47', Lg. 38', Ht. 16'1", Wing Area 379 sq. ft.
WEIGHT: Empty 7208 lb., Gross 10,409 lb., Max. 11,200 lb. Fuel 304-395 gal.
PERFORMANCE: Speed- Top 311 mph at 15,000', Cruising 157 mph, Stalling 70 mph. Service ceiling 27,000', Climb 2310'/1 min. Range 980 miles/1000-lb. bomb, 1570 miles as scout.

Flight tests of the turret on the XSB2A-1 begun in March 1942 were so unsatisfactory and production so slow that the original Navy schedule was replaced with one SB2A-1, 80 SB2A-2s, and 59 SB2A-3s. Called the Buccaneer by the Navy, they were to be built alongside the

Arc

BREWSTER SB2A-2
Wright R-2600-8, 1700 hp takeoff, 1450 hp at 12,000'
DIMENSIONS: Span 47', Lg. 39'2", Ht. 15'5", Wing Area 379 sq. ft.
WEIGHT: Empty 9924 lb., Gross 13,068 lb., Max. 14,289 lb. Fuel 174-421 gal.
PERFORMANCE: Speed- Top 259 mph at s. l., 274 mph at 12,000', Cruising 161 mph, Stalling 87 mph. Service ceiling 24,900', Climb 2080'/1 min. Range 720 miles/500-lb. bomb, 1675 miles as scout.

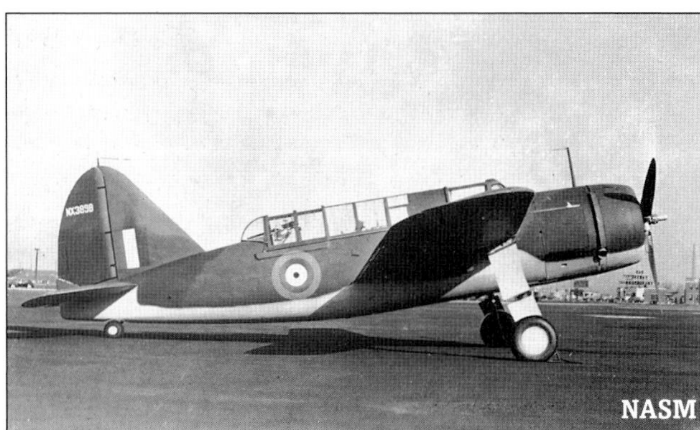

BREWSTER BERMUDA I (A-34)
Wright R-2600-8, 1700 hp takeoff, 1450 hp at 12,000'
DIMENSIONS: Span 47', Lg. 39'2", Ht. 15'5", Wing Area 379 sq. ft.
WEIGHT: Empty 8173 lb., Gross 12,700 lb., Max. 13,062 lb., Fuel 174-271 gal.
PERFORMANCE: Speed- Top 304 mph at 12,000', Cruising 161 mph, Stalling 75 mph. Service ceiling 27,230', Climb 15,000'/8.3 min. Range 750 miles/1000-lb. bomb, 1150 miles/500-lb. bomb.

BREWSTER SB2A-4
Wright R-2600-8A, 1700 hp takeoff, 1450 hp at 12,000'
DIMENSIONS: As SB2A-2
WEIGHT: Empty 9785 lb., Gross 12,663 lb., Max. 13,811 lb. Fuel 174-421 gal.
PERFORMANCE: Speed- Top 275 mph at 12,000', Cruising 155 mph, Stalling 86 mph. Service ceiling 25,400', Climb 2190'/1 min. Range 750 miles/500-lb. bomb, 1750 miles as scout.

Bermudas in 1943 and would be similar to the export models except for folding wings on the SB2A-3.

Acceptances of the Bermuda finally began in July 1942, but the overweight aircraft did not achieve the expected 304 mph. Dutch 340-17s were transferred to the Navy and became the SB2A-4. Acceptances began in October, and Navy SB2A-4s were used for operational training at Vero Beach, Florida. By 1942's end, 140 Bermudas and 28 SB2A-4s had been delivered.

During 1943, the Maxson turret was discarded and the XSB2A-1 accepted as a single-seater on November 9, 1943. An SB2A-1 was reported at Anacostia in April 1942, but was not formally accepted until May 1944. Acceptances of the SB2A-2 (340-26) began in February 1943 and of the SB2A-3 in June. They were armed with two .30-caliber guns in the nose, two .30-caliber guns in the wings, and twin .30-caliber flexible guns.

During 1943, the RAF got 314 Bermudas while the Navy got 25 SB2A-2s, 44 SB2A-3s, and 132 SB2A-4s. Some of the latter trained Marine night fighter pilots in 1943. The last 14 Bermudas, five SB2A-2s and two SB2A-4s, as well as 11 SB2A-3s, were accepted in January 1944, followed by the last two SB2A-3s in February. The Navy had received 303 Buccaneers, but on June 23, 1944, "all SB2A airplanes were requested to be stricken from the Navy list."

Of 468 Bermudas built, British records say 206 came to the United Kingdom, but 98 were kept by the U.S. Army and designated the A-34. Six Bermudas were lost, three went to Canada and three to the West Indies, and the remaining152 simply "reduced to produce." None ever served in a regular bombing squadron. The whole Brewster program must be described as a wasteful example of bad management and planning. A sad end for a handsome aircraft.

Helldivers at War

The dive-bomber expected to replace the SBD was the Curtiss design by Raymond Blaylock judged superior to Brewster's in a December 1938 competition and ordered as the XSB2C-1 on May 15, 1939. Before prototype flight tests began, a production contract for 370 was placed November 19, 1940, and plans called for the first production SB2C-1 to be delivered by December 31, 1941.

CURTISS XSB2C-1
Wright R-2600-8, 1700 hp takeoff, 1450 hp at 12,000'
DIMENSIONS: Span 49'9", Lg. 35'4", Ht. 15'5", Wing Area 422 sq. ft.
WEIGHT: Empty 7122 lb., Gross 10,261 lb., Max. 10,859 lb. Fuel 270-400 gal.
PERFORMANCE: Speed- Top 290 mph at s. l., 322 mph at 14,600', Cruising 155 mph, Stalling 69 mph. Service ceiling 29,975', Climb 2380'/1 min. Range 996 miles/1000-lb. bomb, 1620 miles as scout, 2260 miles ferry.

First flown on December 18, 1940, at Buffalo by Lloyd Child, the prototype mid-wing monoplane powered by an R-2600-8 inherited the name Helldiver from the earlier Curtiss biplane. Delivered six months before the Brewster, the XSB2C-1 was faster and its short fuselage would better fit carrier elevators. Severe weight and stability problems appeared, and the prototype crashed February 9, 1941, was modified and rebuilt, but then completely destroyed in a December 21 dive test.

Over 800 changes, including a larger tail, longer nose, self-sealing fuel tanks of increased capacity, and addition of 195 pounds of armor, had to be incorporated into production aircraft before flight tests were made. The new Curtiss factory at Columbus, Ohio was also building the SO3C series with a very inexperienced labor force and the first SB2C-l began flight tests six months behind schedule, on June 30, 1942. Contracts to build 3,865 had been made June 4.

CURTISS SB2C-1

A 1,700 hp Wright R-2600-8 Cyclone turned a spinnered three-bladed Curtiss propeller, and the wings had leading edge slats and folded upward for carrier stowage. The internal bay could hold a 1,000-pound M-59 DAP bomb, or one of the new 1,600-pound Mk 1, or two 1,000-pound M-33 armor-piercing bombs, or a 130-gallon auxiliary tank. Wing racks could accommodate two 325-pound depth charges or 58-gallon drop tanks for special missions.

While one SB2C-1 was tested from November 30, 1942, to January 30, 1943, as a torpedo-bomber, this was not done in actual combat. More trials in May proved that conversion of standard types would require several hours each on the busy carriers, and the flow of TBF-1 Avengers to the fleet made that project unnecessary

Fifty SB2C-1s were accepted by December 31, and Helldivers were issued in December to two squadrons for the first new *Essex* class carrier. Too many mechanical faults were found to allow them to begin operations, and the *Essex* (CV-9) went to sea in March with SBD-4s instead. The next SB2C-1 batch went to the new *Yorktown* (CV-10) group, but carrier qualification trials went so badly that the aircraft were replaced by SBD-5s when that ship also sailed for the war zone. The *Bunker Hill's* VB-17 became the next squadron to try the SB2C-1.

Senator Truman's Congressional investigation found the program "hopelessly behind schedule" and reported that Curtiss in April 1943, "had not succeeded in producing a single SB2C...useable as a combat airplane" despite expensive self-praise in advertising. In fact, SB2A-1s on hand had been returned to the factory for many modifications. Empty weight increased from the original contract guarantee of 7,868 pounds to 10,114, and the 313-mph top speed guarantee was reduced to 281 mph with military power.

The first 200 SB2C-ls completed by May 1943 had five .50-caliber guns. Instead of the two fixed guns on the prototype's nose with a telescopic sight, a reflector sight aimed four in the wings. At first a .50-caliber gun on a hydraulic-powered mount protruded from the folding fairing at the rear of the cockpit enclosure, but this had to be replaced by the same twin .30-caliber flexible guns used on the Douglas SBD.

Later Helldivers, beginning with the SB2C-lC, had two 20-mm belt-fed wing guns with 400 rounds. This arrangement of two cannon and twin flexible guns with 2,000 rounds remained on all but those first 200 Helldivers. From May 1943 to March 1944, 778 SB2C-lCs were built at Columbus. These changes did work well enough so that on August 20, 1943, *Bunker Hill's* VB-17, replaced its older models with a new set of 36 SB2C-lCs. On November 11, that squadron attacked enemy warships at Rabaul, and it soon appeared that the numerous modifications had succeeded.

USN

CURTISS SB2C-1C
Wright R-2600-8, 1700 hp takeoff, 1450 hp at 12,000'
DIMENSIONS: Span 49'9", Lg. 36'8", Ht. 13'2", Wing Area 422 sq. ft.
WEIGHT: Empty 10,114 lb., Gross 14,720 lb., Max. 16,607 lb. Fuel 320+246 gal.
PERFORMANCE: Speed- Top 265 mph at s. l., 281 mph at 12,400', Cruising 158 mph, Stalling 79 mph. Service ceiling 24,700', Climb 1750'/1 min. Range 1110 miles/1000-lb. bomb, 1895 miles max.

The fifth SB2C-1 had become the XSB2C-2 tested March 1943 with twin floats for the Marines and was also the first with the twin flexible guns. A production program was canceled when it was realized the Marines would use land-based aircraft only, and the SB2C-lA from St. Louis was substituted; these were actually 410 surplus Army A-25As with more armor and without folding wings. None actually entered combat, however, but were used for operational training of eight Marine squadrons.

Mfr

CURTISS XSB2C-2

A 1,900 hp R-2600-20 Cyclone, using a four-bladed Curtiss propeller with no spinner, was tested on an XSB2C-3 converted from the 8th SB2C-1, and this engine powered the first production SB2C-3 in December 1943 and the rest of 1,112 delivered by July 1944. Numerous detail refinements were included. By October 1944, every large carrier in the U.S. Fleet had a Helldiver bombing squadron.

Perforated diving flaps and under wing studs for eight 5-inch rockets introduced on some later SB2C-3s were standard on the SB2C-4, which also added a spinner to the four-bladed prop, a 35-pound armor plate under the engine, and wing racks for two 500-pound bombs. From June 1944 to March 1945, 2,045 SB2C-4s were delivered, including some designated SB2C-4E with an APS-4 radar pod under the right wing to replace the older ASB Yagi system.

PMB

CURTISS XSB2C-3

Delivery began in February 1945 on 970 SB2C-5s with a larger fuel capacity and standard APS-4 radar provisions. Two XSB2C-6s, ordered February 9, 1944, were converted from SB2C-1Cs, but appeared with the 2,100-hp R-2600-22 and revised fuselage in August 1945.

The war's end terminated plans for 1,560 more SB2C aircraft. When Helldiver deliveries ended on October 29,

CURTISS SB2C-5 with APS-4
Wright R-2600-20, 1900 hp takeoff, 1450 hp at 15,000'
DIMENSIONS: As SB2C-1
WEIGHT: Empty 10,589 lb., Gross 14,415 lb., Max. 16,287 lb. Fuel 355+300 gal.
PERFORMANCE: Speed- Top 267 mph at s.l., 290 mph at 16,500', Cruising 161 mph, Stalling 92 mph. Service ceiling 27,600', Climb 1850'/1 min. Range 1162 miles/500-lb. bomb, 1323 miles as scout.

CURTISS SB2C-3
Wright R-2600-20, 1900 hp takeoff, 1450 hp at 15,000'
DIMENSIONS: As SB2C-1
WEIGHT: Empty 10,400 lb., Gross 14,042 lb., Max. 16,471 lb. Fuel 320+246 gal.
PERFORMANCE: Speed- 269 mph at s. l., Top 294 mph at 16,700', (260-284 mph/1000-lb. bomb), Cruising 158 mph, Stalling 79.5 mph. Service ceiling 29,300', Climb 1830'/1 min. Range 1165 miles/1000-lb. bomb, 1925 miles max.

CURTISS SB2C-4
Wright R-2600-20, 1900 hp takeoff, 1450 hp at 15,000'
DIMENSIONS: As SB2C-1
WEIGHT: Empty 10,547 lb., Gross 14,189 lb., Max. 16,618 lb. Fuel 320+246 gal.
PERFORMANCE: Speed- 270 mph at s. l. Top 295 mph at 16,700', (261-285 mph/1000-lb. bomb), Cruising 158 mph, Stalling 84 mph. Service ceiling 29,100', Climb 1800'/1 min. Range 1165 miles/1000-lb. bomb, 1235 miles normal, 1920 miles max. as scout.

1945, 5,106 had been finished at Columbus, and 900 A-25As had been built for the Air Force at St. Louis.

In addition, two Canadian factories had produced Helldivers beginning with a contract placed on May 23, 1942, with the Canadian Car and Foundry company at Fort William, Ontario, for 1,000 dive-bombers designated SBW, including 450 scheduled for Britain's Fleet Air Arm (FAA). The first SBW-1 accepted in September 1943 was identical to the SB2C-1C.

Only 26 SBW-1B versions were turned over to the Royal Navy by February 1944, when the United States Navy required all the remaining Canadian dive-bombers. One FAA squadron, No. 1820, was formed in the United States in April 1944, and trained at NAS Squantum until shipped with ten planes to Britain in July, but was dissolved in December without any combat use.

The U.S. Navy took delivery of 40 SBW-1, 413 SBW-3, 270 SBW-4, and 85 SBW-5 bombers built by September 1945. In addition, Fairchild of Canada built 50 SBF-1, 150 SBF-3, and 100 SBF-4E airplanes, for a total of 1,134 Helldivers built in Canada.

CANADIAN Car and Foundry SBW-5

Helldiver squadrons served on each of the 20 large carriers in commission by July 1, 1945, but were not used by any of the light or escort carriers. Three shore-based squadrons had the SB2C-4E and several Marine squadrons had the SB2A-5. Post-war Navy SB2A-5s were gradually replaced by the Douglas AD-1, the last, from squadron VA-54, was not retired from service until June 1949.

Greece was given 49 SB2A-5s in August 1949 for use in the civil war, while Italy got 42 in 1950, as well as another 46 Helldivers intended for the Italian Navy in September 1953 that never actually entered service. Portugal also got 24 in 1950 and Thailand was shipped six in June 1951.

The fiercest combat, however, was seen by 48 SB2A-5s sold to the French Navy and sent to Vietnam on the carrier *Arromanches* in 1951. Although there was no enemy air force, they bombed the Viet Cong until the final French defeat at Dien Bien Phu in May 1954.

The Avengers

Grumman's Avenger was the most versatile and widely-used carrier attack aircraft of World War Two, and the standard torpedo-bomber through all but the war's first six months. The Navy requested design proposals for a TBD-1 replacement on March 29, 1939, and the Grumman design submitted on August 24 by William Schwendler was favored.

Two XTBF-l prototypes were ordered April 8, 1940, and 286 production TBF-ls purchased on December 23, for the need for a better torpedo-bomber could not await the prototype's first flight by Bob Hall on August 7, 1941. Although the first XTBF-1 was destroyed November 28, the second flew December 20 with a new dorsal fin and extended engine mount.

Grumman flight delivered the first TBF-l to Anacostia on January 30, 1942, and 645 were accepted by the end of 1942. This production success at Bethpage contrasts with the only 50 Helldivers delivered by Curtiss that year.

A fat-bodied mid-wing monoplane with a 1,700-hp R-2600-8, the TBF had wheels retracting outwards into the wings, which the pilot could fold backwards to ease shipboard stowage. Instead of hand-held light guns, the gunner had a .50-caliber gun with 400 rounds in an electric-powered ball turret. The pilot had a single .30-caliber gun with 500 rounds on the cowl's right side, and behind him the navigator could drop down behind the bomb bay to set the torpedo, use the bombsight, or fire the .30-caliber ventral gun with 500 rounds. Self-sealing fuel tanks and 331 pounds of armor were standard.

GRUMMAN XTBF-1

The capacious internal weapons bay contained the new Mod. 1 version of the Mk 13 torpedo, whose warhead was increased from 400 to 600 pounds. Total weight of the 22-inch diameter, 22.5-foot long Mk13-1 was 2,216 pounds. It could be launched from up to 300 feet high and as fast as the TBF could go, but careful attention to speed, height, and distance from target were required for success, since the water entry angle and underwater run had to be correct. Later Mods 13-2 and 13-3 improved launching.

Alternate loads included one 1,600 or 1,000-pound bomb, or four 500-pound bombs or 325-pound depth charges, or 12 100-pound bombs, or an auxiliary fuel tank. Combat experience soon favored low-level glide or skip bombing tactics, instead of the traditional horizontal run, making the Norden bombsight unnecessary.

The Avenger's first combat deployment was the VT-8 detachment with 20 TBF-ls shipped to Pearl Harbor by May 29, 1942. On June 1, six of the VT-8 planes were flown to Midway Island and on June 4 these six, without fighter escort, attacked Japanese ships; none were hit and only one TBF returned.

Sustained TBF operations began with the squadrons aboard the three carriers (*Saratoga, Enterprise, and Wasp)* near Guadalcanal on August 7, and sank the carrier *Ryuyo* on August 24. The Navy's first aerial mine-laying operation of the war was by 42 TBF-1s near Bougainville on March 20, 1943.

Even though Grumman had received another TBF order on January 2, 1942, the fighter programs had top priority, so the automobile industry's resources were brought in on March 23, 1942, when General Motors contracted to build 1,200 Avengers. Designated TBM-1, they were assembled at the Eastern Aircraft Division in Trenton, New Jersey, where the first TBM-l was delivered on November 12, 1942.

Grumman completed one XTBF-2, flown May 1, 1942, with an XR-2600-10 Cyclone, but this two-stage engine was unnecessary for the low-altitude work of Navy attack planes. On July 2, Grumman was authorized to convert one TBF to a single-seat long-range fighter & torpedo configuration. First flown on July 26, it deleted all the guns and fittings for two crewmen and was armed with two .50-caliber wing guns, but was too slow for real fighter work.

USN

GRUMMAN TBF-1
Wright R-2600-8, 1700 hp takeoff, 1450 hp at 12,000'
DIMENSIONS: Span 54'2" (19' fld.), Lg. 40', Ht. 16'5", Wing Area 490 sq. ft.
WEIGHT: Empty 10,080 lb., Gross 13,667 lb., Max. 15,905 lb. Fuel 335+60 gal.
PERFORMANCE: Speed- Top 251 mph at s. l., 271 mph at 12,000', (269 mph/torpedo), Cruising 145 mph, Stalling 76 mph. Service ceiling 22,400', Climb 1430'/1 min. Range 1215 miles/torpedo, 1450 miles as scout.

USN

GENERAL MOTORS TBM-1C
Wright R-2600-8, 1700 hp takeoff, 1450 hp at 12,000'
DIMENSIONS: As TBF-1
WEIGHT: Empty 10,555 lb., Gross 16,412 lb., Max. 17,364 lb. Fuel 335+391 gal.
PERFORMANCE: Speed- Top 249 mph at s. l., 257 mph at 12,000', Cruising 153 mph, Stalling 77 mph. Service ceiling 21,400', Climb 10,000'/13 min. Range 1105 miles/torpedo, 2335 miles as scout.

USMC

GENERAL MOTORS TBM-1D

The next production model, the TBF-lC introduced in July 1943, deleted the cowl gun, had two .50-caliber wing guns with 600 rounds and added bullet-proof glass in the turret. A 275-gallon auxiliary fuel tank could replace the bomb load, and two 58-gallon drop tanks could be attached below the wings. Eight 5-inch rockets could be launched from under the wings of the last ones built.

Search radar (ASB-3) was first installed on five TBF-ls and five SBD-4s in October 1942, and in January 1944, the first carrier-based night bombing attack were made by radar-equipped TBF-1Cs of the *Enterprise*'s VT-10 in the Pacific. By December 31, 1943, 1,524 TBF-l and 764 TBF-1C Avengers were completed at Bethpage, after which all Avenger production was at Trenton, so Grumman could concentrate on fighters.

Grumman also flew the first of two XTBF-3 Avengers on June 20, 1943, distinguished by a 1,900-hp R-2600-20 engine with multiple cowl flaps. Eastern Aircraft began delivering TBM-3 models in April 1944 with 495 pounds of armor and eight 5-inch rocket launchers under the wings. Fittings were provided for 100-gallon drop tanks or 1,000-pound bombs under the wings and a 2,000-pound bomb or mine in the bomb bay.

Trenton-built Avengers parallel Grumman models, proceeding through 550 TBM-1s, 2,332 TBM-1Cs, and 4,661 TBM-3s by September 1945. Some of these became TBM-1Ds and TBM-3Ds when fitted with APS-3 radar on the starboard wing's leading edge. The Navy's first Night Air Group, for the *Independence* in August 1944, included four TBM-1Ds of VTN-41, and was joined in December by VTN-90's 21 TBM-3Ds on the *Enterprise*.

The numerous TBM-3E modifications had an APS-4 radar pod below the right wing, deleted the tunnel gun, and reduced armor to 248 pounds. Three XTBM-4s were added with wing structures strengthened for dive bombing.

Every new fast carrier and escort carrier that joined the Pacific fleet from 1943 to the war's end had an Avenger squadron, and they participated in every major battle and sank 12 Japanese submarines. Teamed with dive-bombers, they destroyed both of the world's largest battleships, *Musashi* and *Yamato*. The *Musashi* was sunk during the recapture of the Philippines begun in October 1944, a campaign involving 236 Avengers on fast carriers and 199 on the escort carriers. Avengers were 98 of the 280 planes attacking the *Yamato* and her escorts on April 7, 1945. The loss that day of 3,365 Japanese seamen at a cost of 12 American airmen and 10 planes was convincing evidence that the strongest surface vessels, without air cover, could not survive heavy air attack.

The Marine Corps began land-based operations with TBF-1s at Guadalcanal in November 1942. The first Marine attack squadrons in combat in the Pacific had begun as SBD units, but by 1945, 23 Marine squadrons, land-based or on four escort carriers, used TBMs.

In the Atlantic, Avengers served on escort carriers (CVE), first in support of the North African invasion, and then with the anti-submarine squadrons (VC) being formed

GENERAL MOTORS TBM-3
Wright R-2600-20, 1900 hp takeoff, 1450 hp at 15,000'
DIMENSIONS: As TBF-1
WEIGHT: Empty 10,960 lb., Gross 16,940 lb., Max. 18,440 lb. Fuel 335+475 gal.
PERFORMANCE: Speed- Top 254 mph at s. l., 272 mph at 16,500', Cruising 163 mph, Stalling 79 mph. Service ceiling 28,900', Climb 1480'/1 min. Range 1065 miles/torpedo, 1510 miles/drop tanks, 2550 miles max. ferry.

with 12 Avengers and 9 Wildcat fighters. They made their first kill, U-569, on May 22, 1943, and soon became the most important force to defeat U-boats in the mid-Atlantic areas beyond the reach of land-based bombers. The first American plane to be fitted with forward-firing rockets (the 5-inch HVAR), the TBM-1C first used them in combat against a U-boat on January 11, 1944. Avengers on 14 escort carriers shared in the 53 U-boat kills and one capture by the hunter carrier and destroyer groups, the last on May 6, 1945.

Britain's Royal Navy had rejected the SBD dive-bomber, but received 401 TBF-l (Avenger I), 334 TBM-1C (Avenger II), and 222 TBM-3 (Avenger III) aircraft, beginning on January 1, 1943, and they served carriers in the Atlantic, Arctic, and Pacific. New Zealand also received six TBF-l and 42 TBF-lCs for bombing from March to July 1944.

An important post-delivery project was the TBM-3W, the Navy's first airborne early warning (AEW) aircraft. Developed by Project Cadillac, it had a large APS-20 radar antenna underneath the fuselage that could detect enemy aircraft far beyond the line-of-sight of surface vessels. A circular area 200 miles in every direction could be scanned from 20,000 feet and relayed to ships. All armament had to be removed to accommodate the electronics and its operator, located with his console within the fuselage, and the XTBM-3W flew on August 5, 1944.

In March 1945, deliveries began on the first 27 being rebuilt at the Johnsville Navy facility, and trials were made on the *Ranger* in May 1945. Four-plane TBM-3W units were first deployed with AEW installations on the *Enterprise, Hornet,* and *Bunker Hill,* late in 1945.

Altogether, there were 9,839 Avengers built, 2,293 by Grumman and 7,546 by General Motor's Eastern Aircraft Division. Together with the dive-bombers, they gave the Navy a striking power and reach far beyond that of the traditional warship fleets.

The number of Navy attack planes grew from 709 scout bombers and 100 torpedo bombers in December

GENERAL MOTORS TBM-3E
Wright R-2600-20, 1900 hp takeoff, 1450 hp at 15,000'
DIMENSIONS: Span 54'2", Lg. 40'11", Ht. 16'9" Wing Area 490 sq. ft.
WEIGHT: Empty 10,545 lb., Gross 14,160 lb., Max. 17,895 lb. Fuel 335+475 gal.
PERFORMANCE: Speed- 251 mph at s. l., Top 276 mph at 16,500', (235-259 mph/torpedo), Cruising 142 mph, Stalling 81 mph. Service ceiling 30,100', Climb 2060'/1 min. Range 1010 miles/torpedo, 1145 miles normal, 1920 miles as scout, 2480 miles ferry.

1941 to a total of 5,101 scout bombers and 4,937 torpedo bombers on June 30, 1945. These attack planes sank six of the ten Japanese battleships sunk during the war, as well as 11 of the 15 carriers and ten of 14 heavy cruisers lost.

GENERAL MOTORS TBM-3S (1950)
Wright R-2600-20, 1900 hp takeoff, 1450 hp at 15,000'
DIMENSIONS: Span 54'2", Lg. 41', Ht. 15'7", Wing Area 490 sq. ft.
WEIGHT: Empty 11,055 lb., Gross 17,280 lb., Max. 17,377 lb. Fuel 335+150 gal.
PERFORMANCE: (at 15,097 lb. combat weight) Speed- 236 mph at s. l., Top 257 mph at 16,400', Cruising 145 mph, Stalling 81 mph. Service ceiling 25,600', Climb 1860'/1 min. Range 1110 miles/torpedo.

Of the 12 remaining large Japanese ships, submarines sank eight and surface ships sank four. None were lost to horizontal bombing by Army planes.

After the war, the Navy's carrier-based Avengers had no foreign surface fleets to oppose, and the attack forces shrunk. Submarines remained the only potential naval threat, so some TBMs were modified to the TBM-3S configuration, whose turret was removed. An acoustic torpedo, the 1,160-pound Mk 34, became the main weapon for the ASW squadrons, who were guided to targets by APS-4 radar, a searchlight, and sonobuoys. Eight rockets and the two wing guns could hit surface targets.

Airborne early warning became a top priority, and by June 1948, the first AEW squadron, VC-2, was formed with TBM-3Ws, as additional conversions were made until 156 were in the fleet by 1953. Radar countermeasures were tested by TBM-3Q version. The last TBM-3E left squadron (VS-27) service in October 1954, but many Avengers also filled utility and non-combat roles.

When the Mutual Defense Assistance Program (MDAP) was established, second-hand TBM-3s of various modifications were sent to allied powers, including 117 to Canada in 1950, 19 to Uruguay in 1949/50, and 140 to France, beginning in May 1951. Shipments of 100 TBM-3Es began in March 1953 for the Royal Navy, where they served ASW squadrons as Avenger AS.4, AS.5, or ECM.6, depending on what electronics was fitted. After their replacement by the Fairey Gannet in 1955, 47 were passed to France, and another 19 to the Netherlands were added to 58 gotten earlier from the United States.

Twenty became the first combat planes of the new Japanese Navy (called the Maritime Self-Defense Force) in 1954/55. These became the last TBMs remaining in military service until retirement in 1962, but civilian TBMs worked as forest firefighters in North America for many years afterwards.

The Sea Wolf

Shortly after Grumman's XTBF had been ordered, a second torpedo-bomber design was chosen as a backup. Vought's XTBU-l had a Pratt & Whitney XR-2800-6 Wasp, and a single prototype was ordered April 22, 1940.

First flown December 22, 1941, it was a three-place mid-wing monoplane like the Avenger, but with a longer fuselage, high tail fin, and rounded wing tips. The wheels retracted back into the wings, which folded upwards for carrier stowage. Armament included a .50-caliber gun in the nose, another in a power-operated turret, and a .30-caliber ventral gun, as well as the torpedo or bomb load.

The XTBU's high speed made it an attractive alternate to the Avenger, but Vought was too occupied with Corsair fighters to undertake its production. Instead, Consolidated-Vultee was given a contract on September 6, 1943, for 1,100 aircraft to be designated the TBY-1 Sea Wolf.

After a landing accident tore off the prototype's rear end, the XTBU-1 was reworked to use an R-2800-20 and relocate the tail wheel and tail hook. These changes altered the planned TBY-1 to the TBY-2 as production was

Mfr

VOUGHT XTBU-1
Pratt & Whitney R-2800-20, 2000 hp takeoff, 1600 hp at 13,500'
DIMENSIONS: Span 57'2", Lg. 39', Ht. 18'7", Wing Area 439 sq. ft.
WEIGHT: Empty 10,504 lb., Gross 16,247 lb. Fuel 317+270 gal.
PERFORMANCE: Speed- Top 295 mph at s. l., 311 mph at 14,700', Cruising 165 mph, Stalling 77 mph. Service ceiling 27,900', Climb 1820'/1 min. Range 1400 miles/torpedo.

getting underway at a former truck factory in Allentown, Pennsylvania, but the plant's inexperienced labor was unable to meet the original schedule of 504 deliveries by the end of 1944.

The first TBY-2 was flown in August 20, 1944, by Philip Prophett, and was accepted on November 7. Flight tests began on the second TBY-2 on December 19, and the next eight were accepted in January 1945.

Mfr

CONSOLIDATED TBY-2
Pratt & Whitney R-2800-22, 2100 hp takeoff, 1600 hp at 16,400'
DIMENSIONS: Span 56'11" (27'6" fld.), Lg. 39'2", Ht. 15'6", Wing Area 440 sq. ft.
WEIGHT: Empty 11,336 lb., Gross 17,491 lb., Max. 18,940 lb., Fuel 317+200 gal.
PERFORMANCE: Speed- Top 292 mph at s. l., 312 mph at 17,700', Cruising 156 mph, Stalling 80 mph. Service ceiling 29,400', Climb 1770'1 min. Range 1025 miles/torpedo, 1615 miles max. as scout.

Similar in appearance to its prototype, the TBY-2 had one .50-caliber gun with 400 rounds in the power turret, a .30-caliber ventral gun, and three .50-caliber fixed guns: two under the wings with 220 rounds each and one in the nose. A Mk 13-2A torpedo or two 1,600 or 1,000-pound bombs could fit in the fuselage bay, while two 1,000-pound bombs, 100-gallon fuel tanks, or eight rocket launchers could be added below the wings. The crew was protected by 390 pounds of armor, and had an APS-3 radar on the right wing.

An R-2800-34 was tested on March 23 on the 7th aircraft for the proposed TBY-3 version, but Sea Wolf production was canceled on August 14, 1945, and none of the 180 completed by August 24 were ever used in combat. Only one squadron, VT-154, actually trained on the TBY, but was disbanded after the war ended.

Douglas Destroyer

Douglas planned to replace the SBD series with the XSB2D-1 two-seat scout-bomber, which had a 2,300-hp Wright R-3350-14 and the first retractable tricycle landing gear designed for a carrier aircraft. In response to a Navy design competition dated February 3, 1941, Douglas had submitted its DS-103 proposal, and two XSB2D-1 prototypes were ordered on June 30, 1941, the first to be delivered 12 months later.

The mockup inspected at El Segundo in August 1941 featured a laminar-flow low-drag wing with an inverted gull planform to reduce wing span. An internal bomb bay enclosed two 1,600-pound bombs, while the rear gunner's

DOUGLAS XSB2D-1
Wright R-3350-14, 2300 hp takeoff, 1900 hp at 14,000'
DIMENSIONS: Span 45' (20'4" fld.), Lg. 38'7", Ht. 16'11", Wing Area 375 sq. ft.
WEIGHT: Empty 12,458 lb., Gross 16,273 lb., Max. 19,140 lb. Fuel 350+200 gal.
PERFORMANCE: Speed- Top 346 mph at 16,100', Cruising 180 mph, Stalling 88 mph. Service ceiling 24,400', Climb 1710'/ 1 min. Range 1480 miles/1000-lb. bomb.

periscopic sights aimed one .50-caliber gun in an upper remote-controlled power-operated turret, and another in a turret beneath.

Curtiss offered a rival two-seat XSB3C-1 design in the same competition with similar R-3350-8 engine and tricycle gear, two .50 fixed guns and two in a powered turret. This low mid-wing monoplane was of conventional SB2C style. A mockup board inspection was held in December 1941, but promised performance was less than that of the Douglas, so the Curtiss project was canceled in 1942.

On April 9, 1942, a contract for 358 SB2D-1s was placed and in May the .50-caliber fixed guns were replaced by a pair of 20-mm guns at the bends of the gulled wings, which folded upwards. But the weight grew heavier and development of the complicated innovations delayed the first XSB2D-1, which flew April 8, 1943, with dummy turrets. The second prototype, with larger tail surfaces and outer wing dihedral reduced from 14 to 10 degrees, flew on August 11, but takeoff from a carrier was judged be "marginal."

The Navy now wanted to combine the dive-bombing and torpedo attack roles in one single-seat aircraft. This was possible because the single-seater's increasing power permitted accommodation of either bombs or torpedoes, and because the weight handicap of a gunner and his weapons seemed to have been made unnecessary by American fighters' control of the air.

Responding to the Navy's new specification, Douglas redesigned the XSB2D-l by removing the rear gunner and his turrets and providing racks under the bomb bay to accommodate two 2,200-pound torpedoes instead of two 1,600-pound bombs or added fuel tankage. The pair of 20-mm guns with 200 rpg in the gulled wings was retained, along with the R-3350-14, the prop spinner, and tricycle gear.

Although the original Douglas contract had been increased by August 31, 1943, to 623 SB2D-l Destroyers to be delivered from November 1943 to February 1945, a telephone call on September 7, 1943, ordered Douglas to change the whole program to the single-seat configuration. Designer Heinemann urged his staff to push the BTD-1 as an essential SBD replacement, and the first, BuNo 04959, was flown on December 15, 1943.

The second, 04960, flew on March 5, 1944, but only four BTDs were actually accepted in 1944, because the BTD program had been curtailed in June in favor of completely redesigning the type as the BT2D-1, which became the famous post-war AD series. Another 24 BTDs were accepted from February to October 1945, and they were used for miscellaneous tests. Beginning with the 6th aircraft, dive brakes on the wings were joined by a six-panel spray on the fuselage. Two aircraft became XBTD-2s in May 1944 when fitted with a 1,550-pound thrust Westinghouse booster jet in the tail, but tests were unsatisfactory.

DOUGLAS BTD-1
Wright R-3350-14, 2300 hp takeoff, 1900 hp at 14,000'
DIMENSIONS: Span 47'11" (20'4" fld.), Lg. 39'2", Ht. 13'7", Wing Area 373 sq. ft.
WEIGHT: Empty 12,900 lb., Gross 18,140 lb., Max. 19,000 lb. Fuel 460+180 gal.
PERFORMANCE: Speed Top 319 mph at s. l., 344 mph at 16,100', 340 mph/torpedo, Cruising 188 mph, Stalling 91.5 mph. Service ceiling 23,600', Climb 1650'/1 min. Range 1480 miles/torpedo, 2140 miles max.

The largest Douglas torpedo bomber was the three-place XTB2D-1 initiated by a November 1942 Navy Letter of Intent, and ordered on October 31, 1943. A company analysis said it could carry two torpedoes or bombs from an *Essex* class carrier deck or four torpedoes from a shore base. Powered by a Pratt & Whitney XR-4360-8 Wasp Major turning eight-bladed counter rotating propellers, the two XTB2D-l prototypes had tricycle landing gear, and a low wing with a flat center section and dihedral on the outer panels. Dual nose wheels retracted backwards beneath the pilot and main wheels retracted outwards into the wings, which folded upwards.

The heavy Douglas could mount four .50-caliber fixed guns in the wings, two .50-caliber guns in an upper rear power-turret, a lower gondola for a Mk 15 bombsight and another gun, and 527 pounds of armor. Four under wing racks carried either Mk 13-2 torpedoes, 2,000 pound bombs, or smaller loads. Two 300-gallon drop tanks could be hung on the outer pylons, and APS-4 radar was fitted.

The XTB2D-1 was rolled out for photos on February 28, 1945, less than ten years after the first XTBD-1, but the reader can see the enormous increase in firepower and

DOUGLAS XTB2D-1
Pratt & Whitney XR-4360-8, 3000 hp takeoff, 2400 hp at 13,500'
DIMENSIONS: Span 70' (36'8" fld.), Lg. 46', Ht. 22'7", Wing Area 605 sq. ft.
WEIGHT: Empty 18,405 lb., Gross 28,545 lb., Max. 34,760 lb. Fuel 774+600 gal.
PERFORMANCE: Speed- Top 292 mph at s. l., 340 mph at 15,600' (312 mph/torpedo), Cruising 162 mph, Stalling 75 mph. Service ceiling 24,500', Climb 1,390"1 min. Range 1250 miles/torpedo, 2880 miles max.

GRUMMAN XTB2F-1 (mockup)
Two Pratt & Whitney R-2800-22, 2100 hp takeoff, 1600 hp at 16,000'
DIMENSIONS: Span 74' (33' fld.), Lg. 52', Ht. 17', Wing Area 777 sq. ft.
WEIGHT: Empty 23,650 lb., Gross 31,777 lb. Max. 43,937 lb. Fuel 490-960+600 gal.
PERFORMANCE: Speed- Top 311 mph at s.l., 336 mph at 18,000'. Stalling 81 mph. Service ceiling 30,400', Range 1,137-2063 miles, ferry 3700 miles.

performance developed in that decade. Yet this formidable attack type was considered less promising than that of the simpler BT2D, and a 23-plane initial production order had been dropped before flight tests began on May 8.

Even larger would have been Grumman's XTB2F-l, the only twin-engine design in this class. Two R-2800-22 Wasps were mounted on a 74-foot span high-wing, folding for stowage, and tricycle gear was provided. Armament included up to two Mk 13 torpedoes or four 2,000-pound bombs, while the nose had a 75-mm cannon on the right side and two .50-caliber guns on the left, with four more fixed guns in the wing roots and APS-6 radar on the port side. Two .50-caliber guns were in a top rear turret and another pair were underneath in a Sperry retractable ball turret.

Grumman had submitted Design 55 on December 21, 1942, and won an engineering and prototype contract on August 6, 1943. After a mockup inspection, the XTB2F-l project was canceled on June 14, 1944, as too heavy for the carriers of that time. It was realized that since few such aircraft could be operated from even the largest carrier, more bombs could be delivered by a greater number of smaller aircraft.

Single-seat Bombers

Using one man and one aircraft to do work previously assigned to two different types of planes, each with two or three crewmen, had obvious advantages for carrier operations, despite the increase of the pilot's workload. Elimination of defense guns seemed justified by the protection of superior Navy fighters.

By 1944, four single-seat bomber-torpedo designs were begun with conventional tail-down landing gear. In the order that contracts were made, they were the Curtiss XBTC, Kaiser XBTK, Martin XBTM, and Douglas XBT2D.

The Navy Bureau of Aeronautics on February 9, 1942, had requested Curtiss to design a single-seater that could carry two 1,000 or 1,600-pound bombs in an internal bomb bay or a Mk 13-2 torpedo below the fuselage. Range would be 1,000 miles with one 1,000-pound bomb and fuel in protected tanks, or 1,500 miles with added drop tanks. Four 20-mm fixed guns and pilot armor were required, along with folding wings.

The Curtiss response won a June 26, 1942, letter contract for two XBTC-1 airplanes with the 2,300-hp Wright R-3350, and two XBTC-2s using the largest engine then being developed, the 3,000-hp Pratt & Whitney XR-4360-8A Wasp Major. The latter version would require dual-rotation six-bladed propellers and larger wings.

While the XBTC-1 attracted Army interest in an XA-40 version, the complicated situation of the Curtiss Columbus factory's SO3C, SB2C, and SC programs led the Navy to cancel the XBTC-1 by December 1943 and delay the XBTC-2. The first XBTC-2 flew on January 20, 1945, with a straight leading edge and tapered trailing edge on the low mid-wing.

On the second XBTC-2 the wing had a sweptback leading edge, a straight trailing edge, and full-span duplex flaps. Four 20-mm guns were on the leading edge with racks underneath for two 500-pound bombs, or a drop tank on one side and an APS-4 radar on the other.

CURTISS XBTC-2
Pratt & Whitney XR-4360-8A, 3000 hp takeoff, 2400 hp at 13,500'
DIMENSIONS: Span 50', Lg. 38'7", Ht. 16'8", Wing Area 406 sq. ft.
WEIGHT: Empty 14,288 lb., Gross 20,563 lb. Fuel 540+150 gal.
PERFORMANCE: Speed- Top 321 mph at s.l., 362 mph at 16,900', Cruising 180 mph, Stalling 88 mph. Service ceiling 25,000', Climb 1620'/1 min. Range 1245 miles/torpedo.

Weight had increased from an estimated 17,910 pounds in 1944 to 20,563 pounds, reducing top speed clean from 386 to 362 mph. Since the prototypes were troubled with propeller problems and the Martin BTM-1 with the same engine had been accepted for production, the Curtiss project was canceled and both aircraft accepted in July 1946.

To offset the trend towards larger dive-bombers, BuAer decided to build a relatively light single-seater for escort carriers, and a promising design was offered in January 1944 by the Fleetwings plant in Bristol, Pennsylvania, which had been bought by the Kaiser Cargo Company. Two XBK-1 prototypes with the R-2800-22W Wasp were ordered by a Letter of Intent on February 23, 1944, and a contract on March 31.

Three center and under wing racks were provided for a 1,000-pound bomb, drop tanks or APS-4 radar, and on February 9, 1945, the designation was changed to XBTK-1 to reflect a new centerline rack carrying a Mk 13-2 torpedo or 2,000-pound bomb. Two 20-mm wing guns with 200 rpg, 230 pounds of armor, a self-sealing fuel tank behind the pilot, and eight rocket stations were included.

KAISER-FLEETWINGS XBTK-1
Pratt & Whitney R-2800-34W, 2100 hp takeoff, 1850 hp at 16,000'
DIMENSIONS: Span 48'8" (21' fld.), Lg. 38'11", Ht. 15'8", Wing Area 380 sq. ft.
WEIGHT: Empty 9959 lb., Gross 12,728 lb., Max. 15,782 lb. Fuel 275+100 gal.
PERFORMANCE: Speed- Top 342 mph at s.l., 373 mph at 18,000' (258-297/torpedo), Cruising 158 mph, Stalling 80 mph. Service ceiling 33,400', Climb 3550'/1 min. Range 1250 miles/torpedo, 1370 miles/1000-lb. bomb.

Although the contract had been increased to 22 aircraft on October 7, 1944, to be delivered from November 1944 to August 1945, the first example would be six months late. When first flown on April 12, 1945, the XBTK-1 used a Pratt & Whitney R-2800-22W, but that was soon replaced by the improved R-2800-34W with a four-blade Hamilton propeller.

Balanced picket type dive brakes opened from the top and bottom of the trailing edge and instead of cowl flaps the engine used exhaust gases discharged from ducts on each side of the fuselage. The war's end and vibration problems reduced deliveries to four flying and one static aircraft before the program was halted on September 3, 1946.

The Martin Mauler

The Martin company offered the Navy Model 210 for a dive-bomber using the same big Wasp Major as the Curtiss XBTC-2, but with a less complicated layout and the chance to replace the B-26 in the Baltimore factory production line. The Navy response was a Letter of Intent on January 15, 1944, followed by a mockup inspection in February and a May 31 contract for two XBTM-l prototypes and a static test article.

The XBTM-l had a 3,000-hp Pratt & Whitney XR-4360-4 and four-bladed Curtiss propeller, four 20-mm guns with 200 rpg in the wings, armor, APS-4 radar, and picket-type dive brakes. A torpedo or 2,000-pound bomb could be carried below the fuselage and two under wing stations could hold 1,000-pound bombs or 150-gallon drop tanks, while small stations allowed eight rockets.

Remarkably soon, the first XBTM-l flight was on August 26, 1944, by O. E. Tibbs; this was the shortest time

MARTIN XBTM-1
Pratt & Whitney XR-4360-4, 3000 hp takeoff, 2400 hp at 13,500'
DIMENSIONS: Span 50' (24' fld.), Lg. 41'2", Ht. 16'10", Wing Area 496 sq. ft.
WEIGHT: Empty 14,296 lb., Gross 19,000 lb., Max. 23,000 lb. Fuel 500+300 gal.
PERFORMANCE: Speed- Top 341 mph at s.l., 367 mph at 16,000', Cruising 178 mph, Stalling 88 mph. Service ceiling 26,800', Climb 2480'/1 min. Range 1200 miles/torpedo, 2350 miles max.

in which an airplane company had ever built an experimental dive-bomber for the U.S. Navy.

On January 15, 1945, 750 production BTMs were ordered. After early flight and static tests, changes including a new fin and rudder were made to the second prototype, which was flown on May 20, 1945. The war's end cut back the production contract to 99 planes, redesignated AM-l in the April 1946 Attack series. Another 50, with Hamilton instead of Curtiss propellers, was added in 1948.

Delivery of the Martin AM-l Mauler began in March 1947, but extensive testing of control problems preceded entry into service with VA-17A of the Atlantic Fleet in March 1948. Redesignated VA-174, that squadron didn't begin carrier qualification (CarQuals) exercises on the *Kearsarge* until December 27. Numerous structural modifications delayed carrier operations of four more squadrons in 1949, although the Martins could easily carry the heaviest attack load yet.

In service the Maulers proved remarkable weight lifters, since all three pylons could handle 2,000-pound bombs, mines, or torpedoes, and 12 rocket stations had been added. APS-4 radar and 246 pounds of armor were also provided. On March 30, 1949, one AM-1 carried three 2,200-pound torpedoes and 12 250-pound bombs. Gross weight on that widely published flight was 29,332 pounds.

The last AM-l was delivered in October 1949, including 18 as AM-IQ radar counter-measures versions with a second crewman and his controls inside the fuselage behind the pilot. Maulers remained in Fleet service only until 1950 before transfer to reserve units, for the Navy decided to standardize on the Douglas AD series. That story will be told in the chapter on post-war Attack planes.

MARTIN AM-1
Pratt & Whitney R-4360-4, 3000 hp takeoff, 2400 hp at 16,200'
DIMENSIONS: Span 50' (23'5" fld.), Lg. 41'3", Ht. 16'10", Wing Area 496 sq. ft.
WEIGHT: Empty 15,257 lb., Gross 21,141 lb. (scout), 22,323 lb. (bomber), Max. 25,737 lb., Fuel 510+300 gal.
PERFORMANCE: Speed- Top 310 mph at s. l. as scout, 334 mph at 15,400' (304-323 mph as bomber), Cruising 189 mph, Stalling 108 mph. Service ceiling 27,000', Climb 10,000'/5.9 min. Range 1800 miles/2000-lb. bombs. max. full.

The last Curtiss Navy bomber

Another Curtiss bomber-torpedo type, using the same R-3350-24 as the BT2D, was also eclipsed by that type's success. Ten Curtiss XBT2C-ls were ordered March 27, 1945. First flown on August 7, 1945, half of their parts were common with those of the SB2C-5. Although four were flown in 1945, only nine of the Navy's last Curtiss type were actually delivered by October 1946.

They had two 20-mm wing guns, a 2,000 pound bomb or Mk 13-3 torpedo in the bomb bay and two 1,000-pound bombs under the wings, eight rocket stations, 182 pounds of armor, and APS-4 radar. The pilot sat under a bubble canopy and a radarman could be accommodated behind him within the fuselage.

CURTISS XBT2C-1
Wright R-3350-24, 2500 hp takeoff, 1900 hp at 14,800'
DIMENSIONS: Span 47'7", Lg. 38'8", Ht. 16'5", Wing Area 416 sq. ft.
WEIGHT: Empty 12,268 lb., Gross 15,975 lb. as scout, 16,938 lb./1000 lb. bomb. Max. 19,022 lb. Fuel 410+300 gal.
PERFORMANCE: Speed- Top 319 mph at s.l., 338 mph/1,000 lb. bomb at 16.900', 349 mph at 17,000' as scout, 313 mph/ torpedo, Cruising 175 mph, Stalling 90 mph. Service ceiling 28,100', Climb 2590'/1 min. Range 1435 miles/torpedo.

CHAPTER 22
NAVY FIGHTERS, 1931-1939

A Marine F3F-2 flight from San Diego shows prewar colors.

Two-seaters

Up to 1931 naval aircraft used the open cockpits and fixed landing gear traditional on combat planes since the First World War. Gradually, however, metal was replacing fabric for airframe covering, and efforts to decrease drag led to retractable landing gear and enclosed cockpits. From 1931 to 1938, Navy fighters advanced performance to a new level.

Retractable landing gear was used for the first time by a Navy fighter on the Grumman company's first aircraft, the XFF-l ordered March 28, 1931. The wheels were folded by 35 hand-crank turns into a bulge in the deep aluminum fuselage behind a cowled Wright Cyclone, ahead of fully enclosed cockpits. Fabric covered the metal ribs and spars of the biplane's wings. Two .30-caliber M-2 guns in the nose and a third in the rear cockpit were provided.

Although a two-seater, the XFF-l was faster than any single-seater carrier-based type then available. When first flown by William McAvoy on December 29, 1931, it did 195 mph with a 616-hp R-1820E. In October 1932, the Grumman reappeared with a 700-hp R-1820F, which raised speed to 201 mph. A second prototype equipped for scouting missions was the Grumman XSF-l described in Chapter 10.

GRUMMAN FF-1
Wright R-1820-78, 700 hp at 4000'
DIMENSIONS: Span 34'6", Lg. 24'6", Ht. 11'1", Wing Area 310 sq. ft.
WEIGHT: Empty 3098 lb., Gross 4677 lb., Max. 4888 lb. Fuel 120 gal.
PERFORMANCE: Speed- Top 207 mph at 4000', Stalling 64 mph., Service Ceiling 22,100', Climb 5000'/2.9 min. Range 685 miles normal, 800 miles max.

Twenty-seven FF-ls ordered December 19, 1932, from the Farmingdale factory were delivered from April 24 to November 1, 1933, and 25 served on the *Lexington* with VF-5B and the 33 SF-ls delivered for VS-3B in 1934. After the FF-l's retirement from fleet service, 22 were modified to FF-2s with dual controls in 1936 for the Reserves.

The Grumman two-seater got a taste of war when the Canadian Car and Foundry Company decided in October 1936 to open an aircraft factory at Fort William by producing 50 aircraft for the Spanish Republic. Direct sales to Spain by Americans was forbidden by the U.S. government, but Grumman provided a prototype (CG-l, registered NR12V) in November 1936 and supplied 52 fuselages.

Known as the G-23, and powered by an R-1820F-52 of 775 hp at 5,800 feet, the first Canadian example was not flown until February 5, 1938, and was delivered to Nicaragua on March 21, while the second was sold to Japan. Thirty-four did reach *Grupo* No. 28 in Spain by May 7, 1938, to be used for attack and reconnaissance. Although obsolete in most respects, they were better than the Soviet R-5s previously available. After the Civil War, nine survivors served the Nationalist *Grupo* 5W in Morocco as the R6 "Delphin."

Shipment to Spain of 16 more in May 1938 was blocked by the Canadian government, which had learned that their true destination was not Turkey, as had been falsely claimed. One was sent to Mexico, and 15 remained in crates until they were acquired in September 1940 by the Royal Canadian Air Force. The Canadian company also utilized some of the structural and landing gear design for a single-seat fighter prototype designed by Michael Gregor and flown in December 1938.

The next two-seat fighter biplane was the Berliner-Joyce XF2J-l, which had the upper wing gulled into the fuselage behind a 625-hp Wright R-1510-92. Ordered June 30, 1931, the XF2J-1 was based on the Army's Y1P-16, but had an all-metal monocoque fuselage and fixed tail surfaces and was armed with a pair of fixed guns in the upper wing roots, a flexible gun, and two 116-pound bombs.

When delivered in May 1933, a low cockpit enclosure was installed, but was replaced by ordinary windshields as

Arc

GRUMMAN XFF-1
Wright R-1820E, 616 hp (modified with R-1820F, 675 hp)
DIMENSIONS: Span 34'6", Lg. 24'6", Ht. 9'8", Wing Area 310 sq. ft.
WEIGHT: Empty 2667 lb., Gross 3933 lb. (4565 lb.). Fuel 120 gal.
PERFORMANCE: Speed- Top 195 mph at s. l. (201 mph with R-1820F), Stalling 60 (63) mph. Service Ceiling 23,600' (20,700'), Climb 5000'/4.3 min. Range 818 miles.

Arc

BERLINER-JOYCE XF2J-1
Wright R-1510-92, 625 hp at 6000'
DIMENSIONS: Span 36', Lg. 28'10", Ht. 9'6", Wing Area 303.5 sq. ft.
WEIGHT: Empty 3211 lb., Gross 4539 lb., Max. 4851 lb. Fuel 80-160 gal.
PERFORMANCE: Speed- Top 193 mph at 6000', Stalling 66 mph. Service Ceiling 21,500', Climb 5000'/3.1 min. Range 522 miles normal, 1015 miles max.

Mfr

DOUGLAS XFD-1
Pratt & Whitney R-1535-64, 700 hp at 8900'
DIMENSIONS: Span 31'6", Lg. 25'4", Ht. 11'1", Wing Area 295 sq. ft.
WEIGHT: Empty 3227 lb., Gross 4745 lb., Max. 5000 lb. Fuel 110 gal.
PERFORMANCE: Speed- Top 204 mph at 8900', Stalling 64 mph., Service Ceiling 23,700', Climb 5000'/3.3 min. Range 576 miles.

Mfr

VOUGHT XF3U-1
Pratt & Whitney R-1535-64, 700 hp at 8900'
DIMENSIONS: Span 31'6", Lg. 31'6", Ht. 10'11", Wing Area 294 sq. ft.
WEIGHT: Empty 3078 lb., Gross 4616 lb. Max. 4871 lb. Fuel 110+40 gal.
PERFORMANCE: Speed- Top 201 mph at s. l., 214 mph at 8900', Stalling 67 mph. Service Ceiling 24,600'. Range 570-800 miles.

tests proceeded. With fixed landing gear, XF2J-1 performance was below that of the fast Grumman ships, and there was no production.

Three more two-seat fighters were ordered on June 30, 1932. The Douglas XFD-l and Vought XF3U-1 were both developed from BuAer Design 113, with a conventional biplane layout, fixed landing gear, enclosed cockpits, and a 700-hp Pratt & Whitney R-1535-64 Twin Wasp. Armament consisted of two synchronized .30-caliber guns under the cowling, the observer's .30-caliber flexible Browning, and two 116-pound bombs.

The Douglas ship had a fabric-covered metal structure and a spreader bar between the wheels, and was delivered to Anacostia on June 18, 1933, six days ahead of Vought's XF3U-1, which had first flown on May 3, 1933. But the Navy decided that its two-seat fighters should become scout-bombers, and returned the Vought to the factory for rebuilding and redesignation as the XSBU-l in February 1934.

Although ordered the same day as the Douglas and Vought biplanes, the Curtiss XF12C-l was an all-metal high-wing monoplane with slats and flaps on a swept-back wing braced by V main struts; the wing folded backwards for shipboard stowage. Like the Grummans, the XF12C-l had wheels retracting into the fuselage behind the engine. This was the last two-seat fighter of that period, for like the XF3U-1, the Curtiss became a scout-bomber. First built in July 1933 with a 625-hp Wright GR-1510-92 Twin Whirlwind, the XF12C-l got an SR-1820-80 Cyclone in October, became the XS4C-l on December 7, 1933, and was redesignated SBC-l in January 1934. A long and often painful development remained, as was described in the previous chapter.

CURTISS XF12C-1
Wright R-1510-92, 625 hp at 6000'
DIMENSIONS: Span 41'6", Lg. 29'1", Ht. 12'11", Wing Area 272 sq. ft.
WEIGHT: Empty 3884 lb., Gross 5461 lb., Max. 5840 lb. Fuel 110+60 gal.
PERFORMANCE: Speed- Top 217 mph at 6000', Stalling 64 mph., Service Ceiling 22,500'. Range 738 miles normal, 1074 miles max.

Mfr

CURTISS XF11C-2
Wright R-1820-78, 700 hp at 8000'
DIMENSIONS: Span 31'6", Lg. 25', Ht. 10'7", Wing Area 262 sq. ft.
WEIGHT: Empty 3000 lb., Gross 4132 lb. Max. 4601 lb. Fuel 94 gal.
PERFORMANCE: Speed- Top 202 mph at 8000', Landing 65 mph. Service Ceiling 25,100', Climb 10,400'/10 min. Range 303 miles at top speed.

The Bomber-Fighter Idea

The success of dive-bombing had led the Navy to include this capability on single-seat fighters and two-seat scouts. One of the two fighter squadrons on each carrier were to be redesignated bomber units, and so the next Boeing and Curtiss single-seaters were redesignated BF (bomber-fighter) types.

Boeing's last effort to develop a biplane fighter was the XF6B-1 which had a twin-row 625-hp R-1535-44, equal-span biplane wings with a metal structure, ailerons only on the lower wing, and faired wheel struts. Armament comprised the usual two .30-caliber guns under the cowl and a 500 (actual weight 474) pound bomb under the fuselage, or two 116-pound bombs under the wings.

Arc

BOEING XF6B-1 (XBFB-1)
Pratt & Whitney R-1535-44, 625 hp at 6000'
DIMENSIONS: Span 28'6", Lg. 22'2", Ht. 10'6", Wing Area 252 sq. ft.
WEIGHT: Empty 2823 lb., Gross 3705 lb., Max. 4007 lb. Fuel 64+45 gal.
PERFORMANCE: Speed- Top 195 mph at 6000', Landing 64 mph., Service Ceiling 20,700', Climb 5000'/4.2 min. Range 437miles normal, 737 miles max.

Ordered June 30, 1931, the XF6B-1 first flew February 1, 1933, was delivered to the Navy in April, and was redesignated as XBFB-1 (Bomber-fighter Boeing) on March 21, 1934. By then, traditional open-cockpit biplanes were becoming outmoded.

More successful was the Curtiss design called the Goshawk, whose basic airframe was similar to that of the Army P-6Es, except for a radial engine. Fabric covered the fuselage's welded steel tubular frame and the wooden frame of the tapered Hawk wings. Two prototypes were purchased by the Navy April 16, 1932. One had been flying since March 25, as it was built as a private demonstrator with a single-row Wright SR-1820-78 Cyclone and two-bladed propeller. This aircraft was delivered to Anacostia on May 2 as the XF11C-2, while the XF11C-1 was built to Navy specifications by September with a twin-row R-1510-98 Whirlwind, three-bladed propeller and different wheels at the end of the streamlined struts.

The armament included two .30-caliber synchronized Brownings in the nose with 1,200 rounds and a 474-pound bomb beneath the fuselage with the Navy's displacement gear to swing that bomb clear of the propeller in a dive. A streamlined 50-gallon drop tank could replace that bomb, or wing racks could hold two 116-pound bombs. Radio, tail hook, and flotation gear were standard Navy equipment.

Mfr

CURTISS XF11C-1
Wright R-1510-98, 600 hp at 6000'
DIMENSIONS: Span 31'6", Lg. 23'1", Ht. 10', Wing Area 262 sq. ft.
WEIGHT: Empty 3290 lb., Gross 4368 lb. Fuel 94 gal.
PERFORMANCE: Speed- Top 203 mph, Landing 67 mph. Service Ceiling 23,800', Climb 5000'/8.2 min. Range 530 miles.

Cyclone engines were chosen for 28 F11C-2s ordered October 18, 1932, and first delivered March 11, 1933. They served aboard the *Saratoga* with the "High Hat" squadron from April 1933 until SB2U-1 two-seaters began arriving in December 1937.

SDAM

CURTISS BFC-2 (F11C-2)
Wright R-1820-78, 700 hp at 8000'
DIMENSIONS: Span 31'6", Lg. 25', Ht. 10'7", Wing Area 262 sq. ft.
WEIGHT: Empty 3037 lb., Gross 4120 lb. Max 4638 lb. Fuel 94+50 gal.
PERFORMANCE: Speed- Top 205 mph as fighter, 198 mph as bomber, Landing 65 mph. Service Ceiling 24,300', Climb 5000'/2.6 min. Range 560 miles normal, 628 miles max.

One Curtiss was delivered on May 27, 1933, as the XF11C-3 with hand-cranked landing gear retraction into the fuselage. Twenty-seven production models ordered February 26, 1934, had 700-hp R-1820-04s and two-bladed propellers. In recognition of their dive-bombing capabilities, on March 21, 1934, the F11C-2 was redesignated BFC-2 and the F11C-3s on order became BF2C-1s. Both were modified behind the cockpit with a partial sliding canopy and higher turtleback containing a life raft. First delivered on October 7, 1934, the BF2C-1 was the first single-seater assigned to the new light carrier *Ranger*.

Unfortunately, the BF2C-1 had departed from the spruce wing framework usual to the Curtiss Hawks for a metal framework, whose periodic vibration coincided with the engine vibrations of the Cyclone. These aircraft had to be withdrawn from service by February 1936, although the wooden-winged BFC-1s remained until 1938.

USN

CURTISS XF11C-3 (XBF2C-1)
Wright R-1820-80, 700 hp at 8000'
DIMENSIONS: Span 31'6", Lg. 23', Ht. 10'7", Wing Area 262 sq. ft.
WEIGHT: Empty 3230 lb., Gross 4495 lb. Max. 5020 lb. Fuel 98+50 gal.
PERFORMANCE: Speed- Top 229 mph at 8000', Landing 69 mph. Service Ceiling 26,000', Climb 11,600'/10 min.

Curtiss also sold 132 Hawk IIs, the F11C-2 export version with the R-1820F-3, fixed gear, but omitting Navy equipment, and usually armed with two 7.7-mm guns and wing racks for four 110-pound bombs. Turkey was the first customer, getting 24 Hawk IIs in September 1932, and Colombia acquired 26 Hawk II twin-float seaplanes from October 1932 to July 1934.

Eight Hawk II landplanes and one seaplane were delivered to Bolivia from December 1932 to July 1934 and fought in the Gran Chaco War against Paraguay, downing a Potez 25 on December 11, 1934, and flying many fighter-bomber missions. Cuba got four Hawk IIs in January 1933, and China was the best American aircraft customer in that period, getting 50 Hawk IIs from March to September 1933 for China's first fighter squadrons.

Arc

CURTISS BF2C-1 (F11C-3)
Wright R-1820-04, 700 hp at 8000'
DIMENSIONS: Span 31'6", Lg. 23', Ht. 10'10", Wing Area 262 sq. ft.
WEIGHT: Empty 3329 lb., Gross 4555 lb., Max. 5086 lb. Fuel 110+50 gal.
PERFORMANCE: Speed- Top 225 mph at 8000' (210 mph/474-lb. bomb), Landing 69 mph. Service Ceiling 27,000', Climb 5000'/2.6 min. Range 797 miles normal, 1054 miles max.

Two sold to Germany in October 1933 for Ernst Udet were the first modern fighters in Nazi hands, and influenced German dive-bombing development. Norway also acquired a single Hawk II in July 1934, Siam (now Thailand since 1939) got 12 by September 1934, and four in January 1935 ordered by Chile, actually went to Peru.

A Hawk III demonstrator with an SR-1820-F53, three-bladed propeller, retractable wheels, and partial cockpit cover appeared in October 1934 and 137 were quickly sold abroad. While they lacked the radio, Navy equipment, and center bomb displacement gear of the BF2C-1, they had two 7.7-mm guns and wing racks for four 110-pound bombs.

Turkey wanted 40, so a single Hawk III was sent in April 1935 as a pattern for the rest, which were license-built at a new Turkish factory at Kayseri. Siam acquired 24 Hawk IIIs from August 1935 to February 1936, and 25 more were to be built there under license.

SDAM

CURTISS HAWK II for China
Wright SR1820F-3, 710 hp at 7000'
DIMENSIONS: Span 31'6", Lg. 22'4", Ht.9'9", Wing Area 252 sq. ft.
WEIGHT: Empty 2903 lb., Gross 3876 lb. Fuel 94+50 gal.
PERFORMANCE: Speed- Top 187 mph at s. l., 208 mph at 6900', Cruising 179 mph, Stalling 63 mph. Service Ceiling 26,400', Range 414 miles normal, 635 miles max.

Mfr

CURTISS HAWK II for Turkey

China was shipped 72 Hawk IIIs from March to August 1936. When Japan's invasion began anew in 1937, China had three fighter groups; two with Hawk IIIs and the third mixed Hawk IIs, Boeing 281s, and Fiats. The 4th Fighter Group began the fight on August 14 by successfully intercepting an attack on Hangchow by Navy G3M bombers.

In general, the Hawks did well against Japanese bombers, but were badly outclassed by the A5M fighters. Thirty Hawk III replacements were sent from April to June 1938,

Mfr

CURTISS HAWK II seaplane for Colombia
Wright SR-1820F-3, 710 hp at 7000'
DIMENSIONS: Span 31'6", Lg. 25'7", Ht. 12'6", Wing Area 252 sq. ft.
WEIGHT: Empty 3293 lb., Gross 4266 lb. Fuel 94 gal.
PERFORMANCE: Speed- Top 173 mph at s. l., 192 mph at 6900', Cruising 163 mph, Stalling 66 mph. Service Ceiling 24,900', Range 377 miles.

Mfr

CURTISS HAWK III for China
Wright R-1820F-53, 740 hp at 9000'
DIMENSIONS: Span 31'6", Lg. 23'6", Ht. 9'11", Wing Area 262 sq. ft.
WEIGHT: Empty 3213 lb., Gross 4317 lb. Fuel 110+50 gal.
PERFORMANCE: Speed- Top 202 mph at s. l., 240 mph at 11,500', Cruising 203 mph, Stalling 68 mph. Service Ceiling 25,800', Climb 2280'/1 min. Range 611 miles.

Mfr

CURTISS HAWK IV
Wright R-1820F-56, 745 hp at 12,000'
DIMENSIONS: Span 31'6", Lg. 23'5", Ht. 9'9", Wing Area 262 sq. ft.
WEIGHT: Empty 3404 lb., Gross 4598 lb. Fuel 110 gal.
PERFORMANCE: Speed- Top 204 mph at s. l., 248 mph at 12,500', Cruising 211 mph, Stalling 69 mph. Service Ceiling 29,700', Range 577 miles.

but most Chinese fighters were then coming from Russia. Argentina's Army received ten Hawk IIIs, beginning in

NASM

CURTISS HAWK III demonstrator, 1934

May 1936, and a single Hawk IV with a modified canopy and supercharger in July.

Three squadrons of Thai Hawk IIIs were involved in the fighting with France on the Indochina's border from November 28, 1940 to January 24, 1941. On the day Japan invaded Thailand, December 8, 1941, four Hawks were shot down before the government capitulated. The air museum at Bangkok has the only surviving Hawk III.

Streamlined Biplanes

The last biplane fighter with old-fashioned fixed landing gear was the Berliner-Joyce XF3J-1 ordered June 30, 1932. First flown January 23, 1934 and tested in April by the Navy, it was a handsome aircraft with elliptical wings tapered at the tips and roots, and a turtleback running from the enclosed cockpit to the rounded rudder. Powered by an SR-1510-26, the XF3J-1 had two .30-caliber cowl guns and could carry two 116-pound bombs under the wings. During its long construction, it was surpassed by more advanced types and with its failure to win a production contract, the Berliner-Joyce firm retired from business, its assets acquired by North American Aviation.

BERLINER-JOYCE XF3J-1
Wright R-1510-26, 625 hp at 6000'
DIMENSIONS: Span 29', Lg. 22'11", Ht. 10'9", Wing Area 240 sq. ft.
WEIGHT: Empty 2717 lb., Gross 4016 lb., Max. 4264 lb. Fuel 120 gal.
PERFORMANCE: Speed- Top 191 at s. l., 209 mph at 6000', Stalling 66 mph. Service Ceiling 24,500', Climb 5000'/2.7 min. Range 719 miles/232 lb. bombs.

GRUMMAN XF2F-1
Pratt & Whitney XR-1535-44, 625 hp at 8400'
DIMENSIONS: Span 28'6", Lg. 21'1", Ht. 8'6", Wing Area 230 sq. ft.
WEIGHT: Empty 2525 lb., Gross 3490 lb., Max. 3690 lb. Fuel 80-110 gal.
PERFORMANCE: Speed- Top 229 mph at 8400', Cruising 198 mph, Stalling 64 mph. Service Ceiling 29,800', Climb 3080'/1 min. Range 543 miles normal, 750 miles max.

Although the aviation business has resulted in many such failures, it has also produced such successes as

USN

BOEING XF7B-1
Pratt & Whitney R-1340-30, 550 hp at 10,000'
DIMENSIONS: Span 31'11", Lg. 27'7", Ht. 10', Wing Area 213 sq. ft.
WEIGHT: Empty 2697 lb., Gross 3579 lb. Fuel 112 gal.
PERFORMANCE: Speed- Top 214 mph at s. l., 239 mph at 10,000', Stalling 70 mph. Service Ceiling 29,200', Climb 2180'/1 min., 10,000'/4.2 min. Range 824 miles.

Grumman, whose chunky little XF2F-1 biplane single-seater ordered November 2, 1932, and first flown on October 18, 1933, won quick recognition. Fabric covered the wings, and metal covered a tear-drop shaped fuselage with an enclosed cockpit. Wheels retracted into a bulge behind a Pratt & Whitney XR-1535-44 Twin Wasp Jr. encircled by a cowl so tight that small blisters covered the cylinder rocker arms. Armament included two .30-caliber synchronized guns with 1,200 rounds, but no bombs. While a radio and life raft were standard, the watertight fuselage made flotation bags unnecessary.

USN

GRUMMAN F2F-1
Pratt & Whitney R-1535-72, 700 hp takeoff, 650 hp at 7500'
DIMENSIONS: Span 28'6", Lg. 21'5", Ht. 9'1", Wing Area 230 sq. ft.
WEIGHT: Empty 2691 lb., Gross 3847 lb. Fuel 110 gal.
PERFORMANCE: Speed- Top 203 mph at s. l., 231 mph at 7500', Stalling 66 mph. Service Ceiling 27,100', Climb 2052'/1 min., 5000'/2.1 min. Range 985 miles max.

Fifty-four F2F-1s with R-1535-72 Twin Wasps were ordered May 17, 1934, and another was added later, so that 55 were delivered from January 19 to August 2, 1935, at a cost of $12,000 each. These Grumman biplanes began a long tradition by this company, which has had fighters with the Navy ever since. The first F2F-1 went to Anacostia, as was usual, and others flew from Farmingdale to San Diego to join *Lexington*'s VF-2 in February and served with that squadron until September 1940. VF-3 on the *Ranger* was the second squadron to get F2F-1s in 1935.

Premature Monoplanes

Although by 1933, monoplanes were in production for all classes of Army Air Corps aircraft, the Navy had hesitated to adopt the more streamlined aircraft for carrier operation. Only the high-wing XF5B-1 and XF12C-1 had attempted to utilize the speed offered by monoplane configurations, but problems of shipboard stowage, structural strength, and relatively high landing speed had barred adoption of those types.

Boeing's XF7B-1, ordered March 20, 1933, and powered by a 550-hp Pratt & Whitney R-1340-30, was the first low-wing monoplane fighter ever tested by the Navy. Of all-metal construction, the Boeing had wheels folding back partially into a cantilever wing, and had a long turtleback running from the enclosed cockpit to the tail. Two .30-caliber synchronized guns in the nose were provided with 1,000 rounds,

The first flight was at Seattle on September 14, 1933, and the XF7B-1 was delivered to the Navy on November 11. Despite the fastest speed of any Navy fighter to date, the plane was criticized for excessively long takeoff runs, high landing speed, poor maneuverability, and general instability. Visibility from the enclosed cockpit was especially bad during landings. The aircraft was sent back to the factory in April 1934, modified with an open cockpit and landing flaps, and returned to Anacostia on March 5, 1935. Weight was increased to 3868 pounds, top speed reduced to 231 mph, and landing speed to 66 mph, but during a March 9 dive the plane was so over-stressed that repair was impractical.

NASM

CURTISS XF13C-1
Wright XR-1510-94, 600 hp at 10,000'
DIMENSIONS: Span 35', Lg. 25'8", Ht. 12'9", Wing Area 205 sq. ft.
WEIGHT: Empty 3238 lb., Gross 4400 lb. Fuel 110 gal.
PERFORMANCE: Speed- Top 236 mph at 10,000', Stalling 67 mph. Service Ceiling 23,800', Climb 5000'/3.5 min. Range 864 miles.

Mfr

CURTISS XF13C-2
Wright XR-1510-94, 600 hp at 10,000'
DIMENSIONS: Span 35', Lg. 25'8", Ht. 12'9", Wing Area 282 sq. ft.
WEIGHT: Empty 3183 lb., Gross 4343 lb. Fuel 110 gal.
PERFORMANCE: Speed- Top 218 mph, Stalling 68 mph. Service Ceiling 23,900', Climb 5000'/3.6min. Range 863 miles.

Curtiss developed the XF13C-1 ordered November 23, 1932, with a Wright XR-1510-94, wheels retracting into a clean metal fuselage, a pilot's cabin and a remarkable configuration. The Curtiss could be a high-wing monoplane, or use a spare set of biplane wings. The 35-foot high wing had slots and flaps to reduce the landing speed, but the alternate arrangement had narrower chord wings without the lift devices, utilizing instead the added area of a 24-foot lower wing. As a biplane the type was known as XF13C-2, although the original type number was retained on the tail fin.

The XF13C-1 was first flown at Buffalo in December 1933 as a biplane, next as a monoplane on January 7, 1934, and then delivered to the Navy on February 10. Comparative tests showed the monoplane faster, but the biplane had quicker takeoffs and slower landings. Returned to Buffalo, the aircraft appeared on May 14, 1935, with a new vertical fin, an XR-1510-12, and was redesignated XF13C-3. One of the twin .30-caliber guns in the nose was replaced by a .50-caliber gun.

Mfr

CURTISS XF13C-3
Wright XR-1510-12, 700 hp at 7000'
DIMENSIONS: Span 35', Lg. 26'3", Ht. 12', Wing Area 205 sq. ft.
WEIGHT: Empty 3553 lb., Gross 4772 lb. Fuel 110 gal.
PERFORMANCE: Speed- Top 222 mph at s. l., 241 mph at 7000', Cruising 145 mph, Stalling 70 mph. Service Ceiling 24,500', Climb 5000'/2.5 min. Range 774 miles.

The Northrop XFT-1 ordered May 8, 1933, was a smaller derivative of the Gamma low-wing monoplane series. Jack Northrop's company included Chief Engineer Don Berlin and the Project Engineer was 25-year-old Ed

Mfr

NORTHROP XFT-1
Wright R-1510-26, 625 hp at 6000'
DIMENSIONS: Span 32', Lg. 21'1", Ht. 9'5", Wing Area 177 sq. ft.
WEIGHT: Empty 2469 lb., Gross 3756 lb., Max. 4003 lb. Fuel 120 gal.
PERFORMANCE: Speed- Top 235 mph at 6000', Stalling 63 mph. Service Ceiling 26,500', Climb 6000'/2.6 min. Range 976 miles normal, 902 miles/232-lb. bombs.

Heinemann. First flown on January 18, 1934, by Vance Breese and tested at Anacostia in March, it was powered by a 625-hp Wright R-1510-26.

An all-metal single-seater with a long turtleback from the enclosed cockpit to the tail, it had the deep wheel pants characteristic of early Northrops. A .30 and a .50-caliber gun were mounted in front of the cockpit, two 116-pound bombs could be carried under the wings, and a radio, tail hook, and life raft were provided, along with 120 gallons of fuel in integral wing tanks.

On August 10, 1935, the Navy ordered the aircraft reworked as the XFT-2 with the 650-hp Pratt & Whitney R-1535-72 Twin Wasp Jr. used by the Grumman fighters, for BuAer had finally given up hope for the Wright R-1510 series. Delivered in March 1936, the XFT-2 had a new cowling, modified landing gear, and only 80 gallons of fuel, but a July 21 crash ended development.

NORTHROP XFT-2
Pratt & Whitney R-1535-72, 650 hp at 7500'
DIMENSIONS: As XFT-1
WEIGHT: Empty 2730 lb., Gross 3770 lb., Max. 4017 lb., Fuel 80 gal.
PERFORMANCE: Speed- Top 240 mph at 7500', Stalling 67 mph. Service Ceiling 27,500', Climb 5000'/2.2 min.

Failure of these monoplanes to win Navy contracts has been attributed to their high landing speed and stowage difficulties, although all had wing flaps and were relatively small. In any case, the Navy chose to stick to biplanes, even though the Army was now concentrating on faster monoplanes. Discouraged by their unsuccessful efforts, neither Boeing, Curtiss, nor Northrop was to offer a Navy fighter for many years.

Grumman F3F Biplanes

Grumman's first single-seater, the F2F-1, had been successful but Navy engineers desired better directional stability, maneuverability, and a bombing capability. The XF3F-1, which had the same R-1535-72, but with more wing area and longer fuselage, was ordered October 15, 1934. Reduction of the wheel diameter from 30 to 26 inches eliminated the bulge behind the engine and allowed a more streamlined shape.

Grumman had to build three aircraft before the contract was completed. The first was flown by Jimmy Collins on March 20, 1935, but he was killed two days later when the XF3F-1 broke up coming out of a terminal velocity dive. A replacement flown May 9 was destroyed in a spin

GRUMMAN XF3F-1
Pratt & Whitney R-1535-72, 700 hp at takeoff, 650 hp at 7500'
DIMENSIONS: Span 32', Lg. 23', Ht. 10'6", Wing Area 261 sq. ft.
WEIGHT: Empty 2868 lb., Gross 4094 lb., Max. 4327 lb. Fuel 110 gal.
PERFORMANCE: Speed- Top 226 mph at 7500', Stalling 64.5 mph. Service Ceiling 29,500', Climb 5000'/2.5 min. Range 910 miles.

GRUMMAN F3F-1
Pratt & Whitney R-1535-84, 700 hp takeoff, 650 hp at 7500'
DIMENSIONS: Span 32', Lg. 23'3", Ht. 9'4", Wing Area 261 sq. ft.
WEIGHT: Empty 2952 lb., Gross 4170 lb., Max. 4403 lb. Fuel 110 gal.
PERFORMANCE: Speed- Top 215 mph at s. l., 231 mph at 7500', Stalling 66 mph. Service Ceiling 28,500', Climb 1900'/1 min. Range 882 miles normal, 1000 miles max.

GRUMMAN XF3F-2
Wright XR-1820-22, 1000 hp takeoff, 820 hp at 12,000'
DIMENSIONS: Span 32', Lg. 23'2", Ht. 10'4", Wing Area 260 sq. ft.
WEIGHT: Empty 3170 lb., Gross 4438 lb., Max. 4700 lb. Fuel 110-140 gal.
PERFORMANCE: Speed- Top 229 mph at s. l., 255 mph 12,000', Stalling 70 mph. Service Ceiling 31,500', Climb 5000'/2.3 min.

on May 17. A third prototype delivered June 20 was accepted and won the production contract on August 24.

Powered by a 650-hp R-1535-84, 54 F3F-1s were delivered from January 29 to September 21, 1936, and went

Mfr

GRUMMAN F3F-3
Wright R-1820-22, 950 hp takeoff, 750 hp at 15,200'
DIMENSIONS: Same as F3F-2
WEIGHT: Empty 3285 lb., Gross 4543 lb., Max. 4795 lb. Fuel 130 gal.
PERFORMANCE: Speed- Top 239 mph at s. l., 264 mph at 15,200', Stalling 68 mph. Service Ceiling 33,200', Climb 2750"1 min. Range 980 miles normal, 1150 miles max.

USN

GRUMMAN F3F-2
Wright R-1820-22, 950 hp takeoff, 750 hp at 15,200'
DIMENSIONS: Span 32', Lg. 23'2", Ht. 9'4", Wing Area 260 sq. ft.
WEIGHT: Empty 3254 lb., Gross 4498 lb., Max. 4750 lb. Fuel 130 gal.
PERFORMANCE: Speed- Top 234 mph at s. l., 260 mph 17,250', Stalling 69 mph. Service Ceiling 32,300', Climb 2800'/1 min. Range 975 miles at 123 mph, 1130 miles max.

to VF-5 on the *Ranger* and VF-6 on the *Saratoga*.. Weapons included the usual .30-caliber gun under the left side of the cowl with 500 rounds, but the other gun was a .50-caliber M2 with 200 rounds. A 116-pound Mk IV bomb could be attached below each wing and was aimed by the same three-power telescopic sight used for the guns. Radio, oxygen, tail hook, and life raft were standard.

Instead of the twin-row Wasps and two-bladed propellers of earlier models, the XF3F-2 had a single-row 750-hp Wright XR-1820-22 Cyclone and three-bladed propeller. This aircraft was flown July 21, 1936, delivered to Anacostia on July 27 and could be distinguished from the F3F-1 by the wider-diameter engine and modified rudder.

Eighty-one production F3F-2s were ordered March 23, 1937, accepted from November 1937 to May 1938, joined VF-6 on the *Enterprise* and the Marine fighter squadrons on the East and West coasts. They were followed by 27 refined F3F-3s ordered June 21, 1938, delivered from December 16, 1938, to May 10, 1939, and used by the *Yorktown's* VF-5 until June 1941. These were the last biplane fighters built in the United States, and all F3Fs were armed with one .30-caliber and one .50-caliber gun and two 116-pound bombs. The wheels required 31 complete turns of the hand crank to retract.

Grumman biplanes then equipped all six Navy and both Marine fighter squadrons, but the drag of their strut-braced wings prevented performance comparable to the Army's monoplanes. The F3Fs remained on carriers until June 1941, and the Marines did not turn in their last Grumman biplanes until October 11, 1941.

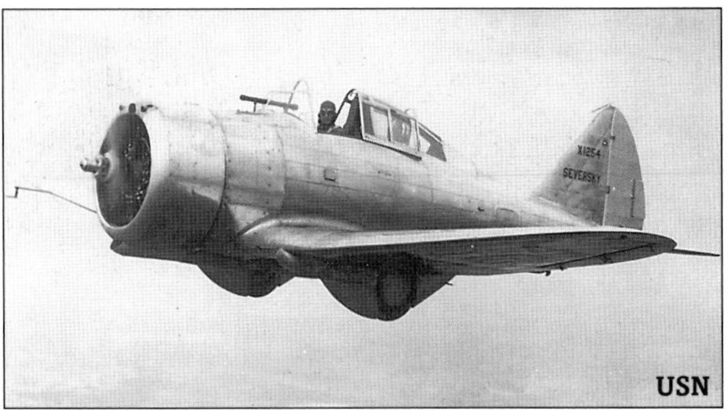

SEVERSKY NF-1
Wright R-1820-22, 950 hp takeoff, 750 hp at 15,200'
DIMENSIONS: Span 36', Lg. 25'2", Ht. 9'1", Wing Area 220 sq. ft.
WEIGHT: Empty 4020 lb., Gross 5231 lb. Fuel 90-200 gal.
PERFORMANCE: Speed- Top 267 mph at 15,000', Stalling 69 mph. Service Ceiling 30,700', Climb 2760'/1 min.

USN

The Navy tried the monoplanes then on order for the Army to see if carrier-based adoptions would be practical. In July 1936, Curtiss Design 75B, the P-36's prototype, was tested at Anacostia. Powered by an 840-hp Wright R-1820G-5, it did 277 mph at 5265 pounds gross, better than the Grumman biplanes. A naval version of the Seversky P-35 was called the NF-1 (Naval Fighter One) by the company, but never received a Navy designation or contract. Powered by a Wright R-1820-22 Cyclone instead of the Wasps on the Army versions, it had the AP-1's enclosed wheels and large windshield. Completed about June 3, 1937, it was flown to Anacostia on September 24.

The Navy did not consider either of these aircraft suitable for carrier use, but knew it had to develop monoplane fighters of its own to match the performance of land-based types. Landing speeds thought too dangerous in the '30s were to become commonplace during the war years, and ingenious methods of wing folding would solve the stowage problem.

CHAPTER 23
NAVY FIGHTERS AGAINST JAPAN

These F4U-1s began the Corsair's combat career, the longest of WW II Navy fighters. NASM

Brewster Buffalo

During World War Two, the Navy's Buffalo, Wildcat, Corsair, and Hellcat fighters did nearly all of their fighting against Japanese aircraft. All of these monoplanes used air-cooled engines and were designed to operate from aircraft carriers.

The first monoplane fighter actually used by Navy squadrons was the barrel-shaped Brewster Buffalo. This mid-wing single-seater designed by Dayton T. Brown was all-metal, except for fabric-covered control surfaces and Plexiglas canopy, the construction style of every Navy wartime fighter. The XF2A-l prototype was ordered June 22, 1936, and began tests on December 2, 1937, at Roosevelt Field, New York.

USN

BREWSTER XF2A-1
Wright XR-1820-22, 950 hp takeoff, 750 hp at 15,200'
DIMENSIONS: Span 35', Lg. 25'6", Ht. 11'9", Wing Area 209 sq. ft.
WEIGHT: Empty 3711 lb., Gross 5059 lb. Fuel 110-164 gal.
PERFORMANCE: Speed- Top 295 mph at 15,200', Stalling 69 mph. Service Ceiling 30,900', Climb 2750'/1 min. 21,000'/10 min.

Like the Grumman F3F-2 biplanes, the Brewster was powered by a Wright R-1820-22 Cyclone and armed with one .30-caliber and one .50-caliber gun in the nose and two 116-pound bombs under the wings. Provisions were made to accommodate one .50-caliber or even a 20-mm gun in each wing, but this option was not installed during tests.

The wing introduced the NACA 230 airfoil on Navy fighters, and contained fuel tanks that allowed the normal 110-gallon load to be increased to 164 gallons. Wheel retraction into the fuselage was powered by hydraulics, instead of by the hand cranks of previous Navy fighters. The life raft and tail hook of Navy models would be omitted on export versions.

Speed on Anacostia tests begun January 14, 1938, was a disappointing 277 mph, so in April 1938 the prototype became the first full-size aircraft to be tested in NACA's new wind tunnel. Refinements to reduce drag were made, increasing top speed to 295 mph. Fifty-four F2A-ls were ordered June 11, 1938, for $1,910,395, not including the R-1820-34 engines.

Brewster purchased an old four-story auto factory in Long Island City to build the F2A-1, which had a 9-foot Hamilton propeller with spinner, an enlarged fin, more dihedral, and added two .50-caliber guns in the wings to the two nose guns. The first was delivered on May 18, 1939, and

USN

BREWSTER F2A-1
Wright R-1820-34, 950 hp takeoff, 750 hp at 17,000'
DIMENSIONS: Span 35', Lg. 25'7", Ht. 11'8", Wing Area 209 sq. ft.
WEIGHT: Empty 3785 lb., Gross 5055 lb., Max. 5370 lb. Fuel 110-160 gal.
PERFORMANCE: Speed- Top 271 mph at s.l., 301 mph at 17,000', Stalling 69 mph. Service Ceiling 32,500', Climb 3060'/1 min. Range 1095 miles normal, 1545 miles max.

NASM

BREWSTER F2A-2
Wright R-1820-40, 1200 hp takeoff, 900 hp at 14,000'
DIMENSIONS: Span 35', Lg. 25'7", Ht. 12', Wing Area 209 sq. ft.
WEIGHT: Empty 4576 lb., Gross 5942 lb., Max. 6890 lb. Fuel 110-240 gal.
PERFORMANCE: Speed- Top 285 mph at s.l., 323 mph at 16,500', Cruising 157 mph, Stalling 78 mph. Service Ceiling 34,000', Climb 2500'/1 min., 10,000'/4 min. Range 1015 miles normal, 1670 miles ferry with 180 gal.

displayed at the New York World's Fair to promote foreign sales, and the second went to Anacostia on July 18. Nine more were accepted by December 11, and served with VF-3 as the *Saratoga*'s first 300-mph monoplane fighters.

Salo

BREWSTER B-239 (Finland)
Wright R-1820-G5, 950 hp takeoff, 750 hp at 15,200'
DIMENSIONS: As F2A-1
WEIGHT: Empty 3744 lb., Gross 5014 lb., Max. 5820 lb., Fuel 110-160 gal.
PERFORMANCE: (at 5820 lb.) Speed- Top 297 mph at 15,580', Cruising 236 mph. Service Ceiling 32,480', Climb 9840'/4.2 min.

Stalin's invasion of Finland had aroused American sympathy and on December 16, the Navy agreed to release the remaining aircraft. By February 1940, 44 were completed with commercial R-1820-G5 engines, and shipped via Sweden. They arrived too late for the Winter War that ended on March 13, but were issued to the most experienced Finnish pilots and were provided with seat armor and a reflector gun sight, instead of the Navy's telescopic sight. Brewsters won their first battle on June 25,

USN

BREWSTER XF2A-2
Wright R-1820-40, 1200 hp takeoff, 900 hp at 14,000'
DIMENSIONS: Span 35', Lg. 25'7", Ht. 12'1", Wing Area 209 sq. ft.
WEIGHT: Empty 4131 lb., Gross 5409 lb., Max. 5643 lb. Fuel 110-164 gal.
PERFORMANCE: Speed- Top 290 mph at s.l., 325 mph at 16,100', Cruising 144 mph, Stalling 70 mph. Service Ceiling 35,000', Climb 3100'/1 min. Range 1015 miles max.

BREWSTER B-339D
Wright GR-1820-G105A, 1100 hp takeoff, 800 hp at 17,100'
DIMENSIONS: Span 35', Lg. 26', Ht. 12'1", Wing Area 209 sq. ft.
WEIGHT: Empty 4282 lb., Gross 6095 lb., Max. 6800 lb. Fuel 110-160 gal.
PERFORMANCE: (at 6000 lb.) Speed- Top 275 mph at s.l., 296 mph at 18,500', Cruising 232 mph. Service Ceiling 33,000', Climb 15,000'/7.4 min. Range 875 miles at 232 mph, max. 1165 miles at 170 mph.

1941, by claiming ten Tupolev SB bombers downed when the war reopened.

The Navy was willing to release those fighters because a superior model had become available. On March 22, 1939, the Navy had ordered the original prototype modified to an XF2A-2, using a 1,200-hp R-1820-40 with a 10-foot 3-inch Curtiss propeller, large spinner, and modified tail fin. This version began tests on July 10, 1939, and its improvements included on 43 F2A-2s ordered December 18, 1939, to replace the Finnish lot.

With an R-1820-40, four .50-caliber guns with 900 rounds, wing racks for two 116-pound bombs, and cockpit armor, they were completed from September to November 1940. Fuel capacity was increased to 240 gallons with partial self-sealing. The Navy deployed them on the *Lexington*, replacing VF-2's F2F-1 biplanes in October, and then *Saratoga*'s VF-3 got F2A-2s, turning back eight F2A-1s. These were returned to the factory to be modernized in May 1941 to F2A-2 configuration for VS-201 on the first escort carrier, the *Long Island*.

Belgium had ordered 40 Model B-339B Brewsters on December 11, 1939, and they were allowed to precede the F2A-2s, being completed from April to July 1940 with R-1820-G105A Cyclones and Curtiss propellers. They were shipped without guns, which were to be fitted by the customer. After Belgium was overrun, one B-339B did reach France, but fell into German hands, six on the *Bearn* were diverted to Martinique, and 33 reached Britain. After tests, including some on the carrier *Eagle*, they were used only for training.

Since 1939, the RAF had considered Brewsters too slow to fight Germans, but on January 25, 1940 they were ordered to protect British possessions in the Far East. While the better RAF fighters were needed at home, the Brewster seemed adequate to match Japanese airpower.

Known as the Buffalo I, these 170 B-339Es had R-1820-G105A Cyclones, Hamilton propellers, fixed tail wheel, four .50-caliber guns, reflector sight, armor, and their fuel tanks had Linatex protective covering. Heavier than previous models, they were rated at only 294 mph by rigorous British tests. Completed from December 1940 to May 1941, two went to England for tests, and 168 began arriving in Singapore in February. After 32 moved up to Rangoon, and some accidental losses, 113 remained to defend Malaysia on December 7, 1941.

Seventy-two similar Buffaloes (339D) for the Dutch East Indies were completed from March to June 1941, and were armed with two .303-caliber guns in the nose, two

BREWSTER B-339E Buffalo I
Wright GR-1820-G105A, 1100 hp takeoff, 800 hp at 17,100'
DIMENSIONS: Span 35', Lg. 26', Ht. 12'1", Wing Area 209 sq. ft.
WEIGHT: Empty 4479 lb., Gross 6430 lb., Max. 6840 lb. Fuel 110-160 gal.
PERFORMANCE: (at 6430 lb.) Speed- Top 294 mph at 18,200', Service Ceiling 31,800', Climb 2240'/1 min., 15,000'/6.5 min.

.50-caliber guns in the wings, and two 110-pound bombs. R-1820-G105A, or G205 engines, and Curtiss propellers were fitted.

The Navy ordered 108 F2A-3s on January 21, 1941, and they were delivered from July to December 1941. Fuel capacity was 240 gallons, the .50-caliber rounds were increased to 1,300, and the nose was longer. The first replaced VF-2's F2A-2s in October 1941, but VF-3 shifted from Brewster to the newer Grumman F4Fs in September.

BREWSTER F2A-3
Wright R-1820-40, 1200 hp takeoff, 900 hp at 14,000'
DIMENSIONS: Span 35', Lg. 26'4", Ht. 12', Wing Area 209 sq. ft.
WEIGHT: Empty 4732 lb., Gross 6321 lb., Max 7159 lb. Fuel 110-240 gal.
PERFORMANCE: Speed- Top 284 mph at s.l., 321 mph at 16,500', Cruising 161 mph, Stalling 81 mph. Service Ceiling 33,200', Climb 2290'/1 min., 10,000'/4.4 min. Range 965 miles normal, 1680 miles ferry with 180 gal.

Total Buffalo production reached 509 by March 1942, ending with 20 more built for the Dutch. But the latter were shipped to Australia, where 17 were taken on hand by the RAAF.

In December 1941, there were F2A-3s with VF-2 and seven with VS-201 on the *Long Island*, but VF-2 passed them to VMF-211 in February 1942. Only the Marines of VMF-221, at San Diego on December 7 with F2A-3s and brought to Midway island on Christmas Day, used them in combat. On March 10, 1942, a Japanese flying boat was shot down and on June 4, 16 of 19 Buffaloes sent up were downed by attacking Japanese fighters.

This was the last fight by Allied Brewsters, which had been badly beaten in nearly every encounter with the enemy since December over Malaysia, Burma, and the East Indies. Additions to later models had increased weight so much that climb and maneuverability had been badly hurt.

In contrast, the Brewsters operated by Finland in their war with Russia from June 1941 to August 1944, were remarkably successful, Captain Hans Wind being credited with 39 of the 485 victories claimed by the type's Finnish pilots in that period. This was the lighter original model, operated by very experienced pilots against an inadequately trained enemy, the opposite of the situation prevailing in the Far East.

Grumman Wildcats

Grumman's first monoplane fighter actually began as a biplane, the XF4F-1 ordered March 2, 1936. After the Brewster XF2A-1 monoplane and more powerful engines became available, the XF4F-1 contract was replaced by Grumman's XF4F-2 monoplane design on July 28, 1936. The original specification promised a top speed of 257 mph at sea level and 280 mph at 9,000 feet.

GRUMMAN XF4F-2
Pratt & Whitney R-1830-66, 1050 hp takeoff, 900 hp at 12,000'
DIMENSIONS: Span 34', Lg. 26'5", Ht. 11', Wing Area 232 sq. ft.
WEIGHT: Empty 4036 lb., Gross 5535 lb. Max. 5737 lb. Fuel 110 gal.
PERFORMANCE: Speed- Top 288 mph at 12,000', Cruising 210 mph, Stalling 72 mph. Service Ceiling 29,700', Climb 15,000'/6.2 min. Range 650 miles.

Powered by a 900-hp Pratt & Whitney R-1830-66 with a single-stage supercharger, the XF4F-2 was first flown September 2, 1937, by Robert Hall at Bethpage and was delivered to Anacostia on December 23. Like the Brewster, it was an all-metal mid-wing monoplane using the new NACA 230 airfoil section and rounded tips. The wheels, however, were retracted by 30 turns of a hand crank, as on the older biplanes. Two .50-caliber guns protruded from the cowling top with provisions for two more in the wings and two 116-pound bombs could be hung under the wings.

Although the XF4F-2 in its original form made a crash landing in April and lost the 1938 production contract to Brewster, in October 1938 the aircraft was ordered rebuilt with the Navy's first engine with a two-stage, two-speed supercharger, the XR-1830-76 developing 1,000 hp at 19,000 feet with 100-octane fuel. Redesignated XF4F-3 and fitted with a larger, square-tipped wing and redesigned tail, that Grumman flew on February 12, 1939. A Curtiss

GRUMMAN XF4F-3
Pratt & Whitney XR-1830-76, 1200 hp takeoff, 1000 hp at 19,000'
DIMENSIONS: Span 38', Lg. 28'10", Ht. 11'11", Wing Area 260 sq. ft.
WEIGHT: Empty 4907 lb., Gross 6103 lb., Max. 6404 lb. Fuel 110-160 gal.
PERFORMANCE: Speed- Top 278 mph at s.l., 336 mph at 17,500', Cruising 210 mph, Stalling 69 mph. Service Ceiling 33,500', Climb 15,000'/4.5 min. Range 735 miles normal, 1270 miles max.

propeller replaced the original Hamilton, with two .30-caliber guns in the nose and a pair of .50-caliber guns added in the wings.

In June 1939, the XF4F-3 was tested in NACA's full-scale wind tunnel and the raised stabilizer and squared tail of the production shape was established. A new specification for the production F4F-3 promised a top speed of 343 mph and a contract for 54 (later 78) was placed on August 8, just before World War II began. In October, the French Navy was allowed to order 81 Grummans, but with a commercial Cyclone engine.

GRUMMAN F4F-3 (first production aircraft)
Pratt & Whitney R-1830-76, 1200 hp takeoff, 1000 hp at 19,000'
DIMENSIONS: Span 38', Lg. 28'9", Ht. 11'10", Wing Area 260 sq. ft.
WEIGHT: Empty 4966 lb., Gross 6158 lb., Max. 6735 lb. Fuel 110-160 gal.
PERFORMANCE: Speed- Top 274 mph at s.l., 343 mph at 19,000', Cruising 258 mph, Stalling 69 mph. Service Ceiling 35,000', Climb 15,000'/6 min. Range 900 miles normal, 1200 miles max.

The first F4F-3 was delivered on February 24, 1940, with a twin-row R-1830-76 and Curtiss propeller, and the second F4F-3 tried a nose spinner. Both were armed with two .30-caliber nose guns and two .50-caliber wing guns aimed with a telescopic sight. An order issued in April had the third and fourth aircraft delivered on July 2 as XF4F-5s with single-row Wright R-1820-40 Cyclones, the same engine used on the Brewster fighters.

GRUMMAN XF4F-5
Wright R-1820-40, 1200 hp takeoff, 900 hp at 14,000'
DIMENSIONS: Span 38', Lg. 28'10", Ht. 11'10", Wing Area 260 sq. ft.
WEIGHT: Empty 4942 lb., Gross 6134 lb. Max. 6711 lb. Fuel 160 gal.
PERFORMANCE: Speed- Top 279 mph at s.l., 312 mph at 15,250', Cruising 148 mph, Stalling 68 mph. Service Ceiling 34,000', Climb 2240'/1 min. Range 910 miles normal, 1250 miles max.

Just as the Navy allowed Brewsters to go to Finland in exchange for later models, the G-36A model ordered for the French Navy was allowed to precede the rest of the F4F-3 order. Powered by a Wright R-1820-G205A Cyclone, the G-36A first flew on May 11, 1940, with French markings, and provisions for cockpit armor and six 7.5-mm Darne guns, two in the nose and four in the wings, to be fitted in France.

GRUMMAN G-36A (Martlet I)
Wright R-1820-205A, 1200 hp takeoff, 900 hp at 15,200'
DIMENSIONS: Span 38', Lg. 28'10", Ht. 11'10", Wing Area 260 sq. ft.
WEIGHT: Empty 4887 lb., Gross 6063 lb. Max. 6607 lb. Fuel 160 gal.
PERFORMANCE: Speed- Top 306 mph at 15,000', Cruising 247 mph, Stalling 70 mph. Service Ceiling 31,000', Climb 2300'/1 min. Range 930 miles.

Britain took over the contract in June, named the G-36A the Martlet I, and installed four .50-caliber wing guns and reflector sights. From July to October, 81 Martlets, less 10 lost at sea, were sent to the Royal Navy, where the first replaced No. 804 Squadron's Gladiator biplanes. Their first German Ju 88 bomber kill scored on Christmas Day was also the first by American fighters flown by British pilots.

Deliveries resumed on the F4F-3, now with four .50-caliber wing guns and 1,720 rounds, and nose guns deleted. The usual wing racks for two 116-pound bombs remained, and 155 pounds of 3/8-inch pilot armor were authorized in December 1940, to be added when available.

IWM

GRUMMAN G-36B (Martlet II)
Pratt & Whitney R-1830-S3C-G, 1200 hp takeoff, 1000 hp at 14,500'
DIMENSIONS: As F4F-3
WEIGHT: Empty 5345 lb., Gross 7512 lb., Max. 7790 lb. Fuel 147 gal.
PERFORMANCE: (at 7790 lb.) Speed- Top 293 mph at 13,000', Cruising 165 mph, Stalling 75 mph. Service Ceiling 31,000', Climb 1940'/1 min. Range 890 miles.

The first standardized, heavier, F4F-3 was delivered November 26, 1940, and 18 went to a *Ranger* squadron, VF-4 (later VF-41), and the rest to VF-72 and VF-71 on the new *Wasp*. All 78 F4F-3s on this contract were completed by February 1941 and served on the Navy's Atlantic side.

Arc

GRUMMAN F4F-3 (Early 1941 version)
Pratt & Whitney R-1830-76, 1200 hp takeoff, 1000 hp at 19,000'
DIMENSIONS: Span 38', Lg. 28'9", Ht. 11'10", Wing Area 260 sq. ft.
WEIGHT: Empty 5264 lb., Gross 6862 lb., Max. 7652 lb. Fuel 110-147 gal.
PERFORMANCE: Speed- Top 281 mph at s.l., 331 mph at 21,100', Cruising 148 mph, Stalling 75 mph. Service Ceiling 37,700', Climb 2300'/1 min, 10,000'/4.4 min. Range 860 miles normal, 1190 miles ferry.

Mass production had been ordered by the Navy on August 8, 1940, and 100 G-36Bs (Martlet II) were ordered for Britain on October 1. These contracts added a 25-pound bullet-proof windshield and a self-sealing main tank, which reduced fuel capacity from 160 to 147 gallons. A 62-pound radio, oxygen, and a life raft were provided, but the old flotation bags were gone.

NASM

GRUMMAN F3F-3A
Pratt & Whitney R-1830-90, 1200 hp takeoff, 1000 hp at 14,500'
DIMENSIONS: As F4F-3
WEIGHT: Empty 5184 lb., Gross 6783 lb., Max. 7573 lb. Fuel 110-147 gal.
PERFORMANCE: Speed- Top 282 mph at s.l., 320 mph at 16,100', Stalling 75 mph. Service Ceiling 34,300', Climb 10,000'/4.2 min. Range 830 miles normal, 1210 miles ferry.

Sufficient two-stage supercharged engines were lacking, so a substitute was found in the single-stage R-1830-90 Wasp on the XF4F-6 first tested on October 26. Despite a sacrifice of high-altitude performance, this engine was used in the new Navy contract's first 95 aircraft, designated F4F-3A and delivered from March 8 to May 28, 1941, and on the G-36B. The F4F-3A served VMF-111 at Quantico and VF-6 on the *Enterprise*, but the first 30 were shipped as lend-lease for Greece.

When that country was overrun in April, the shipment was halted at Gibraltar and those F4F-3As became the Royal Navy's Martlet III and were first used in North Africa by 805 Squadron on July 23, 1941. The first ten G-36Bs (Martlet II) for the Royal Navy were also completed in March, but 90 were delayed until they could have the folding wings of the F4F-4 model.

From May to September 1941, 107 more F4F-3s followed with the two-stage R-1830-86 Twin Wasps in modified cowls with more flaps, but without the upper air intake. Most F4F-3 aircraft had to be delivered without tank protection, until enough sealing bags became available in December. Not until December 1941 did the Navy replace the old telescopic sight with the reflector sight on all Navy fighters. Officially named the Wildcat by the Navy on October 1, these Grummans equipped 10 of the 13 Navy and Marine fighter squadrons in December 1941.

GRUMMAN F4F-3 (Late 1941 version)
Pratt & Whitney R-1830-86, 1200 hp takeoff, 1040 hp at 18,400'
DIMENSIONS: Span 38', Lg. 28'11", Ht. 11'11", Wing Area 260 sq. ft.
WEIGHT: Empty 5381 lb., Gross 7556 lb., Max. 8361 lb. Fuel 144+116 gal.
PERFORMANCE: Speed- Top 290 mph at s.l., 329 mph at 21,100', Cruising 150 mph, Stalling 75 mph. Service Ceiling 36,400', Climb 2450'/1 min, 10,000'/4.4 min. Range 860 miles normal, 1190 miles ferry.

Folding wings, reducing span from 38 to 14 feet, enabled the Navy to double the number of Wildcats placed on a carrier and the first with this feature was the XF4F-4, the 54th aircraft from the first F4F-3 contract. Flown April 14, 1941, it had the R-1830-76, six wing guns, and power folding. Lighter manual folding wings with six .50-caliber guns, were next built on the 90 Martlet IIs delivered with R-1830-S3C4G Wasps and Hamilton props from August 1941 to April 1942. The first 35 were sent to the United Kingdom, 19 were lost at sea, and 26 were shipped to a Royal Navy station in India. Six embarked on *HMS Audacity*, the first British escort carrier, destroyed five Fw 200C bombers from September 20 to December 21, 1941.

GRUMMAN XF4F-4
Pratt & Whitney R-1830-76, 1200 hp takeoff, 1000 hp at 19,000'
DIMENSIONS: Span 38', Lg. 28'9", Ht. 11'10", Wing Area 260 sq. ft.
WEIGHT: Empty 5776 lb., Gross 7489 lb. Fuel 110-147 gal.
PERFORMANCE: Speed- Top 282 mph at s.l., 326 mph at 19,500', Cruising 200 mph, Stalling 77 mph. Service Ceiling 34,400', Climb 2050'/1 min. Range 1200 miles max.

The first production F4F-4 was delivered to Anacostia on November 25, 1941, with the R-1830-86, Curtiss propeller, and the air intake on the upper cowl. Six .50-caliber guns with 1,440 rounds were in the manual folding wings, and 164 pounds of cockpit protection were installed. By December 31, 1942, 1,169 had been delivered. Two 58-gallon drop tanks could be attached under the wings of late examples, instead of the two bombs. Grumman also delivered 220 F4F-4Bs (Martlet IV) for the Royal Navy from February 27 to November 23, 1942, with folding wings and six guns, but these used the Wright R-1820-40B Cyclone and Hamilton propeller.

GRUMMAN F4F-4
Pratt & Whitney R-1830-86, 1200 hp takeoff, 1040 hp at 18,400'
DIMENSIONS: As F4F-3
WEIGHT: Empty 5895 lb., Gross 7975 lb., Max. 8762 lb. Fuel 144+116 gal.
PERFORMANCE: Speed- Top 284 mph at s.l., 320 mph at 18,800', Cruising 161 mph, Stalling 81 mph. Service Ceiling 34,000', Climb 10,000'/5.6 min. Range 830 miles normal, 1275 miles max.

December 30, 1941, saw the first flight of the F4F-7, a long-range photographic version that had two cameras and replaced the guns with unprotected wing tanks that increased fuel capacity to 672 gallons. Weighing 10,328 pounds loaded, it was expected to have a 3,700-mile range. Twenty more were accepted by December 18, 1942, while ten F4F-3P camera planes had been converted from early Wildcats by Navy shops to fill out VMO-251 in the South Pacific until the -7s arrived.

Another 100 F4F-7s had been ordered, but were completed as fixed-wing F4F-3s from January to May 1943, the last of 1,978 Wildcats built by Grumman. They were used for training, except for one flown February 28, 1943, as the F4F-3S seaplane with twin floats. Although seaplane fighters were widely used by Japan, they were finally considered too slow and unnecessary by the U.S. Navy.

PMB

GRUMMAN F4F-3S seaplane
Pratt & Whitney R-1830-76, 1200 hp takeoff, 1000 hp at 19,000'
DIMENSIONS: Span 38', Lg. 39'1", Ht. 11'10", Wing Area 260 sq. ft.
WEIGHT: Empty 5804 lb., Gross 7506 lb.
PERFORMANCE: Speed- Top 266 mph at 20,300', Cruising 132 mph. Service Ceiling 33,500', Climb 10,000'/4.5 min. Range 600 miles.

The growing escort carrier fleet led to Wildcat production by General Motors' Eastern Aircraft Division at Linden, New Jersey. An April 18, 1942, contract provided the FM-1, identical to the F4F-4 except for having four 50-caliber wing guns with 1,720 rounds. First flown August 30, the 1,150 FM-1s delivered by December 1943 included 312 (of which 297 arrived at destinations) lend-leased to Britain as the Martlet V, then renamed Wildcat V in 1944 to fit the American system.

USN

GENERAL MOTORS FM-1

Hellcats replaced the Wildcats at Grumman, but the older type was still needed for the escort carrier's small decks. Efforts to improve Wildcat performance included fitting the first XF4F-5 with a turbosupercharged R-1820-54 and achieving 340 mph at 26,400 feet by February 1943. More practical was the lighter R-1820-56 on the XF4F-8 first flown November 8, 1942; a second example had a larger vertical fin.

Mfr

GENERAL MOTORS Wildcat V

The production version of the XF4F-8 was the General Motors FM-2, which became the most widely used Wildcat, with an R-1820-56W, high fin, four 50-caliber wing guns and 1,720 rounds, 142 pounds of armor, and fittings for two 250-pound bombs or six 5-inch rockets. Takeoff distance with a 15-knot headwind was 301 feet, compared to 428 feet for an F6F-5 Hellcat, so the FM-2 served escort carriers until the war ended.

USN

GENERAL MOTORS FM-2
Wright R-1820-56W, 1350 hp takeoff, 1000 hp at 14,700'
DIMENSIONS: Span 38', Lg. 28'11", Ht. 11'5", Wing Area 260 sq. ft.
WEIGHT: Empty 5448 lb., Gross 7487 lb., Max. 8271 lb. Fuel 126+116 gal.
PERFORMANCE: Speed- Top 306 mph at s.l., 332 mph at 20,800', Cruising 164 mph, Stalling 76 mph. Service Ceiling 34,700', Climb 3650'/1 min.,10,000'/3.2 min. Range 900 miles normal, 1310 miles max.

From September 1943 through August 1945, 4,777 FM-2s were built, including 340 Wildcat VIs for Britain (of which 338 arrived at destinations). An XF2M-1 project with a turbosupercharged Wright R-1820-70W was canceled.

Wildcats in Combat

The first U.S. Wildcats to fight were the Marine F4F-3s of VMF-211 on Wake Island. Although seven of its 12 planes were lost on the ground, the remaining pilots claimed eight

GRUMMAN XF5F-1
Two Wright R-1820-40, 1200 hp takeoff, 900 hp at 14,000'
DIMENSIONS: Span 42', Lg. 28'11", Ht. 12', Wing Area 303 sq. ft.
WEIGHT: Empty 7990 lb., Gross 10,021 lb., Max. 10,892 lb. Fuel 178-277 gal.
PERFORMANCE: Speed- Top 312 mph at s.l., 358 mph at 17,300', Stalling 72 mph. Service Ceiling 34,500', Climb 10,000'/4.2 min. Range 780 miles normal, 1170 miles max.

enemy planes and their small bombs sank a destroyer before Wake was captured. On February 20, 1942, on the *Lexington's* first intrusion into enemy waters, Lt. Edward H. O'Hare became the first Navy ace by shooting down five G4M bombers attacking his ship.

While four-gun F4F-3s flew the combat sorties of the first five months, they were replaced by the folding-wing, six-gun F4F-4s, with 81 aboard the three carriers that won the battle of Midway on June 3-6, 1942. Wildcats were flown by every carrier fighter squadron in 1942, and were our only carrier fighter in action for the first half of the war, fighting in all the major naval battles. Royal Navy Grummans protected their carriers in 1942-44, and remained on the escort carriers to the war's end.

Of all of the American wartime fighters, the Wildcats were the slowest, even among carrier-based types, yet the Wildcat was often successful, for the generous wing's low loading permitted better maneuverability than some faster types. Inferior to the Mitsubishi Zero in performance, but possessing internal protection and more firepower, the Wildcat's victories were due to the superior tactics of U.S. fighter pilots. Using their own strong points against the enemy's weaknesses, American pilots used two-plane elements to dive, fire, and dive away, avoiding any attempt to turn and twist with the lighter Zeros.

Top Wildcat ace was Marine Major Joseph J. Foss, whose F4F-4 scored 26 victories near Guadacana1 from October 13, 1942, to January 15, 1943. At the war's end, Navy figures claimed Wildcats destroyed 1,327 enemy aircraft for a loss of 191 Wildcats in combat, a ratio of almost seven to one. Of these victories, 377 were claimed during the war's last year, for the combat loss of only nine FM-2s.

Vought Corsair

With its distinctive gull-wing, the Corsair was in production so long that it became the last American propeller-driven fighter to roll out of the factory. It was the most successful of three new fighter projects launched in 1938 to bring carrier-based performance up to the level of land-based contemporaries. The Navy evaluated proposals from five companies in April 1938 that offered increased power and weaponry, including anti-aircraft bombs.

The Grumman XF5F-1 and Vought XF4U-1 were ordered June 30, 1938, and the Bell XFL-1 was ordered November 8. The first twin-engine single-seater built for the Navy, the XF5F-1 was first flown on April 1, 1940, by B. A. Gillies with Wright Cyclones slung ahead and below the leading edge of stubby square-cut wings. Rotating in opposite directions, the R-1820-40 and -42 engines could be close together since the short fuselage began behind the wing's leading edge and extended back to twin rudders. Main wheels folded back into the engine nacelles, while the tail wheel was fixed and the wings folded upwards for carrier stowage.

GRUMMAN XF5F-1 in final configuration
Two Wright R-1820-40, 1200 hp takeoff, 900 hp at 14,000'
DIMENSIONS: Span 42', (21' folded) Lg. 28'8", Ht. 11'4", Wing Area 303 sq. ft.
WEIGHT: Empty 8107 lb., Gross 10,138 lb., Max. 10,892 lb. Fuel 178 gal.
PERFORMANCE: Speed- Top 380 mph at 16,500'. Stalling 72 mph. Service Ceiling 34,200', Climb 4,000'/1 min. Range 1200 miles/210 mph.

Four guns ahead of the pilot's cockpit were originally to be imported 23-mm Madsen cannons, but in February 1939, two .30-caliber and .50-caliber guns were specified, as then planned for the F4F-3. Four .50-caliber guns were scheduled in July 1940. The most unusual armament planned for all three new types was 20 5.2-pound anti-aircraft bombs in five containers outboard within each wing; they were to be released in salvos at a fixed distance above an enemy formation.

Delayed by cooling troubles, the prototype did not complete tests until February 1941, and was returned to the factory for rework with an extended nose and engine nacelles, wing fillets, and prop spinners added to reduce drag. By that time the XF5F-1 returned to Anacostia on July 24, 1941, the Navy's interest had shifted to the XF7F-1, and like the XP-50 Army version, the project ended without production.

BELL XFL-1
Allison XV-1710-6, 1150 hp takeoff, 1000 hp at 10,000'
DIMENSIONS: Span 35', Lg. 29'9", Ht. 11'5", Wing Area 232 sq. ft.
WEIGHT: Empty 5352 lb., Gross 6742 lb. Fuel 126-200 gal.
PERFORMANCE: Speed- Top 281 mph at s.l., 333 mph at 12,000', Cruising 161 mph, Stalling 75 mph. Service Ceiling 33,000', Climb 10,000'/4.2 min. Range 1127 miles.

First flown May 13, 1940, the Bell XFL-1 was a carrier version of the XP-39 Airacobra, with an 1,150-hp Allison XV-1710-6 placed behind the pilot and turning the propeller by a drive shaft extended to the nose. Instead of tricycle wheels, the Navy insisted on conventional tail-down landing gear, with an arrestor hook added for carrier landings. Radiators below the wing cooled the only inline engine on a post-1927 Navy fighter.

Known as the Bell Model 5 Airabonita by the company, it had provisions for a 37-mm cannon and two .30-caliber guns in the nose with a telescopic sight, and wing cells for 20 anti-aircraft bombs aimed through a small window beneath the cockpit. However, the cannon was unavailable and would be replaced by a .50-caliber gun, although no weapons were ever tested on the XFL-1. Delivered from Buffalo to Anacostia on February 27, 1941, the XFL-1 never was a successful fighter, even if its performance had not been surpassed by the Vought XF4U-1.

VOUGHT XF4U-1
Pratt & Whitney XR-2800-4, 1850 hp takeoff, 1460 hp at 21,500'
DIMENSIONS: Span 41' (16'8" fld.), Lg. 32'6", Ht. 15', Wing Area 314 sq. ft.
WEIGHT: Empty 7460 lb., Gross 9316 lb., Max. 10,034 lb. Fuel 175-273 gal.
PERFORMANCE: Speed- Top 312 mph at s.l., 397 mph at 23,000', Stalling 75 mph. Service Ceiling 39,900', Climb 15,000'/5.9 min. Range 940 miles, 1620 miles max.

Designed by Rex Beisel, who had designed the Navy's little TS biplane in 1922, the Vought Corsair was first Navy plane built around the Pratt & Whitney 1,850-hp XR-2800-4 Double Wasp. In order to give the 13-foot,4-inch diameter three-bladed propeller sufficient ground clearance without making the landing gear too stilted and heavy, the wing was gulled downward, a technique that also promised reduced drag at the juncture of wing and body. The wheels retracted backward and swiveled 90 degrees flat into the wing, which folded upward for stowage.

Finished with a smooth spot-welded skin, the XF4U-1 was first flown on May 29, 1940, at Stratford by Lyman A. Bullard. Two .30-caliber guns were mounted above the engine with 500 rpg, and two .50-caliber wing guns were provided with 200 rpg. Like the XF5F-l and XFL-1, the XF4U-1 had wing cells for anti-aircraft bombs; up to forty 5-pound bombs might be dropped on bomber formations from above. A window for aiming was provided in the Vought's cockpit bottom, but these bombs were not included on any production aircraft.

The contract specification called for 390 mph at 24,000 feet, but the company claimed that this was the first American fighter to surpass 400 mph. The Army Air Corps chief was told that the XF4U-1 had shown a speed of 397 mph, by Army officers who had inspected it on October

VOUGHT F4U-2
Pratt & Whitney R-2800-8, 2000 hp takeoff, 1650 hp at 21,000'
DIMENSIONS: As F4U-1
WEIGHT: Empty 9170 lb., Gross 11,446 lb., Max. 13,112 lb. Fuel 178+175 gal.
PERFORMANCE: Speed- Top 325 mph at s.l., 381 mph at 23,500', Cruising 187 mph, Stalling 82 mph. Service Ceiling 33,900', Climb 2970'/1 min. Range 955 miles normal, 1790 miles max.

29. On November 28, 1940, the Navy requested Vought to propose a production configuration with increased firepower, fuel capacity, and internal protection.

An initial production contract for 584 F4U-ls was placed June 30, 1941, but expanded requirements began the VGB program in November to pool the resources of Vought, Goodyear, and Brewster to produce Corsair fighters. On June 25, 1942, the first production F4U-1 was flown by Boone T. Guyton with a 2,000-hp R-2800-8 and longer fuselage. To make room for a 237-gallon self-sealing fuel tank, the cockpit was moved back and provided with 150 pounds of armor.

Like most American World War II fighters, the F4U-1 had six .50-caliber M-2 guns in the wings, with 2,350 rounds of ammunition. Instead of the bomb cells in the wings, there were a pair of unprotected 62-gallon fuel tanks, and the usual racks for two 116-pound bombs could be added.

By the end of 1942, 178 F4U-1s had been accepted and the first squadron to begin receiving them, on October 26, 1942, was VMF-124 of the Marines at San Diego.

USN

VOUGHT F4U-1
Pratt & Whitney R-2800-8, 2000 hp takeoff, 1650 hp at 21,000'
DIMENSIONS: Span 41' (17'1" fld.), Lg. 33'4", Ht. 15'3" Wing Area 314 sq. ft.
WEIGHT: Empty 8763 lb., Gross 11,156 lb., Max 12,676 lb. Fuel 237-363 gal.
PERFORMANCE: Speed- Top 343 mph at s.l., 396 mph at 23,900', Cruising 182 mph, Stalling 87 mph. Service Ceiling 39,800', Climb 10,000'/3.8 min. Range 1015 miles normal, 2220 miles ferry.

VFM-124 arrived on Guadacanal on February 12, 1943, with 24 Corsairs nearly 80-mph faster than the F4F-4s previously used.

The second Corsair squadron was the Navy's VF-12 with 22 F4U-1s by January 1943, but efforts to qualify for aircraft carrier operations were frustrated by poor landing behavior, worsened by bad downward visibility and a severe bounce. VF-12 lost 14 pilots while training and changed to Grumman Hellcats in April 1943. Another Navy squadron, VF-17 at Norfolk, continued to try to perfect F4U-1 operations from a carrier.

But the Corsair was satisfactory for land-based operations and Marines established a definite superiority over enemy fighters. By July 2, 1943, all eight Marine fighter squadrons in the South Pacific used Corsairs.

Goodyear's first FG-l flew at Akron on February 25, 1943, and the first Brewster's F3A-1 Corsair flew at Johnsville on April 26; they were identical to the F4U-1. Beginning in May 1943, the Royal Navy got 95 F4U-1s as the Corsair I, training Fleet Air Arm (FAA) squadrons at Quonset Point.

A night fighter version had been proposed as early as November 8, 1941, and the first production F4U-1 was converted to an F4U-2 with an Aircraft Intercept (AI) radome on the starboard wingtip, an outboard gun deleted, and flown for tests to Quonset by January 7, 1943. The Naval Aircraft Factory converted 32 F4U-ls to the F4U-2 configuration by September and the first were issued to VF(N)-75 which made the first kill by a radar-equipped Navy fighter on the night of October 31, 1943.

USN

VOUGHT F4U-1A
Pratt & Whitney R-2800-8W, 2000 hp takeoff, 1975 hp at 16,900'
DIMENSIONS: Span 41' (17' fld.), Lg. 33'4", Ht. 15'1", Wing Area 314 sq. ft.
WEIGHT: Empty 8982 lb., Gross 12,039 lb., Max, 14,000 lb. Fuel 361+175 gal.
PERFORMANCE: Speed- Top 359 mph at s.l., 417 mph at 19,900', Cruising 182 mph, Stalling 87 mph. Service Ceiling 36,900', Climb 2890'/1 min. Range 1015 miles normal, 2220 miles ferry.

Up to this point, night fighters had always carried a radar operator to assist the pilot, so the Corsair was the first to attempt the mission with the pilot using his own three-inch radar scope. The first Marine night fighter squadron was VMF(N)-514 on Roi island and the only F4U-2 squadron on a carrier was the *Enterprise's* VF(N)-101.

Numerous improvements were gradually introduced on the F4U-1 production line without changing the official designation, and parallel Brewster and Goodyear aircraft reflected these changes. The first 949 F4U-1s had a low, framed "birdcage" canopy, while a new cockpit canopy and pilot's seat raised seven inches to improve vision was introduced on Corsair #950 on August 9, 1943; these were styled F4U-lA in unofficial reports. The first 36 went to VF-17, which began a South Pacific combat tour in October 1943, based in the Solomons after being removed from a carrier. Capt. John T. Blackburn's squadron claimed 127 victories in 75 days, considered to be the most successful Navy squadron record.

Beginning with F4U-1 #1302 on October 5, a center-line rack for a 175-gallon drop tank or 1,000-pound bomb was installed, allowing the Corsairs to become dive-bombers. With each wingtip clipped 8 inches so they could fold inside the smaller hangars on British carriers, they became the Corsair II.

USN

VOUGHT F4U-1D
Pratt & Whitney R-2800-8W, 2250 hp takeoff, 2075 hp at 1800', 1975 hp at 16,900'
DIMENSIONS: Span 41' (17' fld.), Lg. 33'4", Ht. 15'4" (16'4" fld.) Wing Area 314 sq. ft.
WEIGHT: Empty 8923 lb., Gross 12,059 lb., Max. 14,181 lb. Fuel 237+300 gal.
PERFORMANCE: Speed- Top 358 mph at s.l., 409 mph at 19,900', Cruising 182 mph, Stalling 87 mph. Service Ceiling 40,000', Climb 3400'/1 min., 10,000'/3.3 min. Range 990 miles normal, 1915 miles max.

The R-2800-8W with water injection for emergency power appeared with the 1,551st Vought Corsair on November 25, 1943. These engines were also standardized on the 101st FG-1, the last 86 F3A-1s, and all the F4U-1D models. Using water injection, allowed for no more than five minutes, increased F4U-1D speed with military power at sea level from 343 to 358 mph, with similar gains to 20,000 feet.

The F4U-1D and FG-1D added twin pylons under the gulled wings for two 1,000-pound bombs or 150-gallon drop tanks. The internal wing tanks were eliminated, and the last six hundred added eight 5-inch rockets. With improved landing gear, the first F4U-1D was accepted April

Mfr

VOUGHT F4U-4
Pratt & Whitney R-2800-18W, 2100 hp takeoff, 2050 hp at 23,300'
DIMENSIONS: Span 41' (17' fld.), Lg. 33'8", Ht.15'1", Wing Area 314 sq. ft.
WEIGHT: Empty 9205 lb., Gross 12,420 lb., Max. 14,670 lb. Fuel 234+300 gal.
PERFORMANCE: Speed- Top 381 mph at s.l., 446 mph at 26,200', Cruising 215 mph, Stalling 89 mph. Service Ceiling 41,500', Climb 3870'/1 min., 10,000'/2.9 min. Range 1005 miles normal, 1560 miles max.

22, 1944, and the last of 1,685 F4U-1Ds was delivered February 2, 1945. Beginning in July 1944, Vought also built concurrently 200 F4U-1Cs armed with four 20-mm guns and 924 rounds instead of the usual .50-caliber guns.

Altogether, Vought built 4,699 F4U-1 series Corsairs including 95 Corsair Is and 510 Corsair IIs (new canopy) for the British Navy, of which 416 were actually exported, the others training British pilots at U.S. Naval Air Stations. New Zealand received another 238 F4U-1As and 126 F4U-1Ds.

USN

GOODYEAR FG-1D

The Navy had closed the badly managed Brewster factory in July 1944 after 735 F3A-ls were finished, including 430 British Corsair IIIs, of which 361 were exported. Goodyear continued production until the war's end, completing 4,007 FG-l series Corsairs, with the Royal Navy allocated 932 FG-1Ds as the Corsair IV, of which 823 were exported, and 60 more delivered for New Zealand from January to April 1945.

Three high-altitude XF4U-3s with a turbosupercharged R-2800-16 fed by a belly intake were ordered in March 1942 as F4U-1 conversions, with the first flown April 22, 1944, but the adaptation was unsuitable. Vought began the conversion of two F4U-ls to an F4U-4X configuration on May 20, 1943, and five fresh XF4U-4 prototypes and 1,414 F4U-4s were ordered January 25, 1944.

Mfr

VOUGHT XF4U-3
Pratt & Whitney XR-2800-16, 2000 hp at 30,000'
DIMENSIONS: as F4U-1
WEIGHT: Empty 9039 lb., Gross 11,623 lb., Max. 13,143 lb. Fuel 178-310 gal.
PERFORMANCE: Speed- Top 314 mph at s.l., 412 mph at 30,000', Cruising 180 mph, Stalling 83 mph. Service Ceiling 38,400', Climb 2990'/1 min. Range 780 miles normal, 1430 miles max.

Powered by an R-2800-18W and four-bladed propeller, and recognizable by the air intake added under the cowl, the first F4U-4X flew May 19, 1944, the first XF4U-4 on September 20, and the first three F4U-4s were accepted in December. Six .50-caliber guns, 212 pounds of armor and two 1,000-pound bombs or eight 5-inch rockets were carried.

Corsair combat operations from U.S. aircraft carriers were finally begun January 3, 1945, by Marine F4U-1D squadrons VMF-124 and VMF-213 on the *Essex*. Additional Marine Corsair squadrons doubled the single-seat fighter strength on carriers *Wasp, Bunker Hill*, and *Franklin*. The *Bennington* had 35 F4U-1Ds of VMF-112 and -123, along with 37 Hellcats of VF-82, 15 Helldivers, and 15 Avengers when the battle for Okinawa opened in March. Marines were also assigned four new escort carriers to provide mixed Corsair/Avenger units for close support.

Marine successes made previous reluctance to operate Corsairs from flight decks seem timid. Navy bomber-fighter squadrons (VBF) joined the battle from the big carriers, while land-based Marine squadrons continued the ground-support role, introducing napalm bombs on April 18 on Okinawa. VBF-83's 36 F4U-1D Corsairs replaced the Marines on the *Essex* and VBF-86 Corsairs went on the *Wasp*. By August 1945, there were 1,236 Corsairs with Navy fighter-bomber squadrons, and 874 with 34 Marine units.

Nineteen Fleet Air Arm squadrons formed on Corsairs at U.S. Navy bases from June 1943 to April 1945, and fought from Norway to Japan. New Zealand's 13 fighter squadrons replaced their Kittyhawks with 424 Corsairs in 1944/45.

At the war's end, Corsairs had flown 64,051 action sorties, and shot down 2,140 Japanese aircraft at a loss of 768 F4Us, including only 189 in air combat, 341 to anti-aircraft fire, 98 on ships or fields, and 230 operational. Its most successful pilots were Marines: Gregory Boyington, who flew Corsairs for 22 of his 28 victories, Robert M. Hanson with 25 victories, and Kenneth A. Walsh with 21 victories.

The F4U-4 scored its first victory on June 10, 1945, with VMF-212 and production peaked when 303 were delivered in July. By the end of August 1945, 1,859 F4U-4s had been accepted, but victory cancellations reduced contracts from 3,149 to 2,196, the rest delivered as 21 planes each month until April 1946. They were followed by 287 F4U-4Bs with four 20-mm guns, one XF4U-4N with APS-6 radar, and 11 F4U-4P photo ships completed by August 1947.

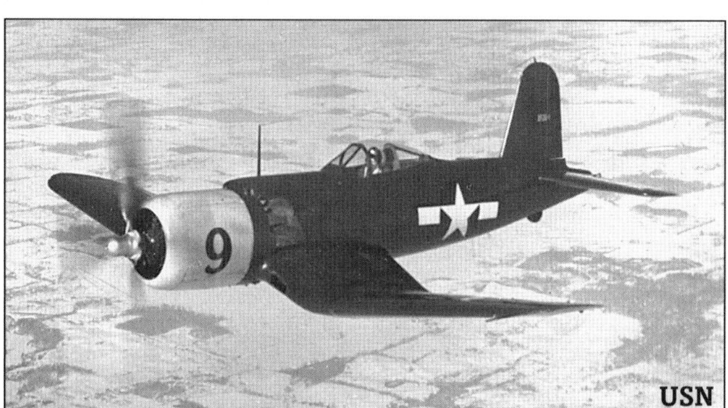

GOODYEAR F2G-1 (Data for F2G-2)
Pratt & Whitney R-4360-4, 3000 hp takeoff, 2400 hp at 13,500'
DIMENSIONS: Span 41' (17' fld.), Lg. 33'10", Ht. 16'1", Wing Area 314 sq. ft.
WEIGHT: Empty 10,249 lb., Gross 13,346 lb., Max. 15,422 lb. Fuel 309+300 gal.
PERFORMANCE: Speed- Top 399 mph at s.l., 431 mph at 16,400', Cruising 190 mph, Stalling 92 mph. Service Ceiling 38,800', Climb 4400'/1 min. Range 1190 miles normal, 1955 miles max.

Goodyear's contracts for 2,500 FG-4s was also canceled, but they had designed the F2G-1 with the big 3,000-hp Wasp Major and higher tail. Eight FG-ls were diverted to the XF2G-l program, the first flying May 31, 1944. A March 22, 1944, contract called for 418 F2G-ls, and ten F2G-2s with carrier gear and folding wings, the first flown October 15. But only five of each were actually accepted; one in June 1945, the rest from August 1945 to February 1946.

Faster at low altitudes than the standard Corsair, they had a bubble canopy and an intake above the engine. Four .50-caliber guns with 1,200 rounds were carried in the wings together with fittings for two 1,600- pound bombs. All F2Gs were eventually sold as surplus and some were successful as private racers.

Since the remainder of the Corsair story is in the Cold War period, we now turn to the Grumman fighters and other wartime efforts.

Hellcats

Since the Corsair was not accepted for carrier operations earlier in the war, it is fortunate that another type more suitable for flight deck work was available. The Grumman Hellcat also had a 2,000-hp Pratt & Whitney Wasp and six wing guns, but sacrificed speed for better maneuverability, climb, and pilot visibility.

A mockup of Grumman 's Design 50 was inspected by the Navy on January 12, 1941, and an enlarged development with 1,700 hp Wright R-2600-16 Cyclones was specified for two XF6F-1 prototypes ordered June 30, 1941, and for the F6F-1 production contract made January 7, 1942. This contract originally called for 434 aircraft, plus a lend-lease allotment for Britain, establishing a completely standardized Hellcat for both navies.

GRUMMAN XF6F-1

An XF6F-2 version with a turbosupercharged XR-2600-10 was projected by April 29, but Grumman was also studying the 2,000-hp Pratt & Whitney Double Wasp for an XF6F-3 model given priority and chosen for the second prototype.

By June 3, 1942, the Navy decided that all production Hellcats would have Double Wasp, so the XF6F-1 flown June 26 by Robert Hall was the only Cyclone-powered

Hellcat completed, and had a Curtiss propeller in a large spinner, bulky landing gear, and no guns. The XF6F-3 was flown July 30 with a 2,000 hp R-2800-10.

Mfr

GRUMMAN XF6F-3

The first prototype was also fitted with an R-2800-10 in September, while the second became the XF6F-4 flown October 3 with a single-stage R-2800-27 rated at 1,600 hp at 13,500 feet, and in April 1943 tested a wing with four 20-mm guns. A turbosupercharged XF6F-2 finally appeared in January 1944 with an XR-2800-16 Wasp, but was no longer desired.

Meanwhile, the expedited production contract had been changed to the F6F-3 model, the first flying October 3 with an R-2800-10, three-bladed Hamilton propeller without spinner, a simplified landing gear, and six guns. Ten F6F-3s were delivered by 1942's end, and production accelerated rapidly, the 2,545 Hellcats delivered in 1943 being enough to equip every fighter squadron on the fast carriers. There was little change in the basic configuration, although the R-2800-l0W with water injection for emergency power was introduced in January 1944.

Mfr

GRUMMAN F6F-3
Pratt & Whitney R-2800-10W, 2000 hp takeoff, 1975 hp at 16,900'
DIMENSIONS: Span 42'10" (16'2" fld.), Lg. 33'7", Ht. 13'1", Wing Area 334 sq. ft.
WEIGHT: Empty 9101 lb., Gross 12,445 lb., Max. 15,487 lb. Fuel 250+150 gal.
PERFORMANCE: Speed- Top 335 mph at s.l., 375 mph at 17,300', Cruising 160 mph, Stalling 84 mph. Service Ceiling 37,200', Climb 3500'/1 min., 20,000'/7 min. Range 1090 miles normal, 1590 miles max.

To keep wing loading low, the Hellcat had the largest wing area of any U.S. single-engine service fighter. The wheels folded backward flat into the wings, which folded backward aboard ship. Seating the pilot high on top of the fuel tanks gave him fine visibility. A downward angle given the engine thrust line enhanced his view, and keeping the tail down in relation to the thrust line made climb the aircraft's natural tendency.

IWM

GRUMMAN Hellcat I

Installations on the F6F-3 included six .50-caliber guns with 2,400 rounds in the wings, 212 pounds of armor, and the self-sealing fuel tanks standard on wartime Navy types. An 150-gallon drop tank was added in August 1943. In September 1943, acceptances began on F6F-3N night fighters with Sperry APS-6 radar on the starboard wing, while the F6F-3E was delivered in January 1944 with the lighter Westinghouse APS-4 radar below the wing. A total of 4,156 F6F-3, 229 F6F-3N, and 18 F6F-3E Hellcats were completed by April 20, 1944.

Mfr

GRUMMAN F6F-3N
Pratt & Whitney R-2800-10W, 2000 hp takeoff, 1975 hp at 16,900'
DIMENSIONS: As F6F-3
WEIGHT: Empty 9331 lb., Gross 13,015 lb., Max. 14,074 lb. Fuel 250+150 gal.
PERFORMANCE: Speed- Top 305 mph at s.l., 360 mph at 18,000', Cruising 161 mph. Stalling 89 mph. Service Ceiling 38,100', Climb 3090'/1 min. 20,000'/7.4 min. Range 865 miles normal, 1235 miles max.

First flown April 4, 1944, the F6F-5 had a modified cowl and windshield, armor increased to 232 pounds, could substitute 20-mm guns for the two inner wing weapons, and fittings for six rockets under the wings or two 1,000-pound bombs under the fuselage were provided. Contracts for 6,436 F6F-5s and 1,432 F6F-5Ns were completed, bringing Hellcat totals to 12,275 when deliveries ended November 21, 1945. Two XF6F-6s with the 2,100-

hp R-2800-18W and four-bladed propeller were first flown July 6, 1944, but this advanced power plant was reserved for the F4U-4.

GRUMMAN F6F-5
Pratt & Whitney R-2800-10W, 2000 hp takeoff, 1975 hp at 16,900'
DIMENSIONS: As F6F-3
WEIGHT: Empty 9238 lb., Gross 12,740 lb. Max. 15,413 lb. Fuel 250+150 gal.
PERFORMANCE: Speed- Top 318 mph at s.l., 380 mph at 23,400', Cruising 159 mph, Stalling 88 mph. Service Ceiling 37,300', Climb 2980'/1 min., 10,000'/3.5 min. Range 945 miles normal, 1355 miles max.

GRUMMAN F6F-5E

Hellcats joined the Navy at the same time as the new carriers begun in 1941; the *Essex*, name-ship of the class, got the first F6F-3 squadron in January 1943. The new ship and fighter went into action together, along with its sister ship, the new *Yorktown*, and the *Independence*, first of the new light carriers, with an attack on Marcus Island August 31, 1943. This was only 14 months after the prototype's first flight. (Corresponding time on the Corsair was over 32 months.)

High mark of the Hellcats' success was the battle of the Philippine Sea in June 1944 when the Grummans smashed the Japanese attack with very small losses to themselves, in the famous "Turkey Shoot." Each *Essex*-class carrier carried 36 Hellcats, 36 dive-bombers and 18 torpedo bombers at first, but the fighter number increased to 72 at the expense of the bombers as the war went on. Night fighters operated as detachments with regular carriers, as a squadron on special night-carriers, or as land-based Marine squadrons.

By the war's end, Hellcats were credited with 5,156 of the total of 9,282 enemy aircraft destroyed in aerial combat by Navy and Marine planes, although only 270 Hellcats were lost to enemy aircraft in combat. Leading Hellcat ace, and top Navy ace, is Captain David McCampbell with 34 victories, including nine confirmed on one mission from the *Essex*. The Navy's second-ranking ace, Commander Cecil E. Harris, scored 23 victories in his Hellcat, and Commander Eugene Valencia got 23. After the war, Hellcats were widely used by reserve squadrons, and in Korea a guided missile unit attacked bridges with six F6F-5K drones, beginning August 26, 1952.

GRUMMAN F6F-5N
Pratt & Whitney R-2800-10W, 2000 hp takeoff, 1975 hp at 16,900'
DIMENSIONS: As F6F-3
WEIGHT: Empty 9421 lb., Gross 13,190 lb., Max. 14,250 lb. Fuel 250+150 gal.
PERFORMANCE: Speed- Top 309 mph at s.l., 366 mph at 23,200', Cruising 166 mph, Stalling 89 mph. Service Ceiling 36,700', Climb 2840'/1 min., 20,000'/8.1 min. Range 880 miles normal, 1260 miles max.

Britain's Royal Navy was given 251 F6F-3s as the Hellcat I, 848 F6F-5s as the Hellcat II, and 78 F6F-5Ns as the Hellcat NF. II. Delivery began in May 1943, and 12

GRUMMAN XF6F-6
Pratt & Whitney R-2800-18W, 2100 hp takeoff, 1800 hp at 21,900'
DIMENSIONS: as F6F-3
WEIGHT: Empty 9526 lb., Gross 12,768 lb., Max. 13,823 lb. Fuel 250+150 gal.
PERFORMANCE: Speed- Top 417 mph at 21,900', Cruising 171 mph, Stalling 85 mph. Service Ceiling 39,000', Climb 3070'/ 1 min. Range 1170 miles normal, 1730 miles max.

IWM

GRUMMAN Hellcat II

squadrons formed from July 1943 to June 1945 served aboard British carriers from the North Sea to the Pacific.

French Army and Navy squadrons received 179 surplus Navy Hellcats flying their last combat actions in Indochina from 1950 to 1954. Argentina and Uruguay each received ten F5F-5s in 1952.

Too Late For The War

The Navy launched several new fighter projects from 1941 to 1944, but none actually was in time to fight the war against Japan. On the same day, June 30, 1941, that the Navy ordered the Hellcat prototypes, it also ordered two prototypes each of the Curtiss XF14C-1 and the Grumman XF7F-l.

Grumman's twin-engine XF7F-l Tigercat began with Wright XR-2600-14 Cyclones like the Hellcat, but shifted to Pratt & Whitney engines.

Mfr

GRUMMAN XF7F-1

The first Navy fighter with tricycle landing gear first flew November 2, 1943, with short shoulder-high square-tip wings that folded upwards outboard of two R-2800-27 Wasps rated as 1,600 hp at 13,500 feet. Large spinners were fitted to the three-blade Hamilton props.

The second XF7F-1 was flown March 2, 1944, with R-2800-22 Wasps giving 1,600 hp at 16,000 feet. Production aircraft would get the R-2800-22W whose water injection would yield 1,850 hp and raise the expected top speed from 412 to 427 mph. While the prototypes had no guns, production F7F-1 Tigercats had the heaviest armament yet seen on a Navy fighter.

The pilot sat ahead of the wings with four .50-caliber guns mounted low in the pointed nose with 1,200 rounds. Four 20-mm guns with 800 rounds were in the wing roots. Armor protection included 283 pounds for the pilot and 94 pounds for the oil system. Fittings under the wings could carry two 1,000-pound bombs or 150-gallon drop tanks. An alternative rack under the fuselage was available for a 300-gallon tank, 2,000-pound bomb, or even a standard Mk 13-3 torpedo. This weapon had been tested for the first time on an F6F-3 fighter in June 1943, but no service fighter ever launched a torpedo in combat.

Because of concerns about how the twin-engine fighter's weight and nose wheel would actually work on carriers, the 500 Tigercats on order were intended for land-based Marine Corps squadrons. The first of 34 F7F-1 single-seaters was delivered on April 29, 1944. Since all were provided with APS-6 radar in the nose, they were redesignated F7F-1N by the time deliveries were completed in October. Actual top speed was increased from 412 to 422 mph with War Emergency power. Performances given here from Navy documents are much more conservative than those supplied by the company.

GRUMMAN F7F-3
Pratt & Whitney R-2800-34W, 2100 hp at takeoff, 1850 hp at 15,500'
DIMENSIONS: Span 51'6" (32'2" fld.), Lg. 45'4", Ht. 16'7", Wing Area 455 sq. ft.
WEIGHT: Empty 16,270 lb., Gross 21,720 lb., Max. 25,075 lb. Fuel 455+300 gal.
PERFORMANCE: Speed- Top 367 mph at s.l., 435 mph at 22,200', Cruising 180 mph, Stalling 91 mph. Service Ceiling 40,700', Climb 4530'/1 min., 20,000'/5.4 min. Range 1200 miles normal, 1830 miles max.

GRUMMAN F7F-1
Pratt & Whitney R-2800-22W, 2100 hp takeoff, 1850 hp at 14,000'
DIMENSIONS: Span 51'6" (32'2" fld.), Lg. 45'4", Ht.15'2", Wing Area 455 sq. ft.
WEIGHT: Empty 15,906 lb., Gross 21,523 lb., Max. 25,852 lb. Fuel 426+300 gal.
PERFORMANCE: Speed- Top 363 mph at s.l., 422 mph at 20,000', Cruising 182 mph, Stalling 85 mph. Service Ceiling 40,000', Climb 4600'/1 min., 20,000'/5.2 min. Range 1115 miles normal, 1740 miles max.

The third Tigercat was accepted as an XF7F-2N two-seater in July 1944 with a radar operator seated behind the pilot, reducing fuel capacity. Then delivery of 65 F7F-2Ns two-seaters began October 31, 1944, with armor protection increased to 487 pounds for the crew and 101 pounds for the oil system, and eight 5-inch rockets could be added below the wings.

New R-2800-34W Wasps and a higher fin appeared on the single-place F7F-3 first flown on March 10, 1945, with

GRUMMAN F7F-2N
Pratt & Whitney R-2800-22W, 2100 hp takeoff, 1850 hp at 14,000'
DIMENSIONS: As F7F-1
WEIGHT: Empty 16,321 lb., Gross 21,857 lb., Max. 26,194 lb. Fuel 375+300 gal.
PERFORMANCE: Speed- Top 362 mph at s.l., 421 mph at 20,600', Cruising 183 mph, Stalling 84 mph. Service Ceiling 39,800', Climb 4540'/1 min., 20,000'/5.2 min. Range 960 miles normal, 1580 miles max.

APS-6 radar, 488 pounds of armor, eight guns, and eight rockets or up to 4,000 pounds of bombs or 300 gallons in drop tanks. Cancellations limited deliveries to 144 F7F-3s by January 1946, including 61 modified in 1945 to the F7F-3P camera configuration, and one that became the XF7F-4.

Another 106 were completed from May 15, 1945, to June 20, 1946, as the two-place F7F-3N. The enlarged nose held the heavier SCR-720 radar whose reflector diameter was 29 inches, instead of the 17-inch APS-6 reflector, and the nose guns had to be omitted. Armament included the four 20-mm wing root guns, eight 5-inch rockets, or up to 4,000 pounds of bombs, with 588 pounds of armor.

Production of 364 Tigercats ended November 7, 1946, with the last 12 being F7F-4N two-seaters with APS-19 radar in the pointed nose and a structure strengthened for carrier operations. Two F7F-1s loaned to the Royal Navy for carrier tests were the only examples in foreign service.

Although an F7F-1 completed carrier qualification trials on the new *Shangri-La* in November 1944, no full Tigercat squadron was deployed aboard ship, although post-war operations by night fighter detachments were seen. The first Marine F7F-1 squadron, VMF-911 at Cherry Point in 1944, did not go overseas, but VMF(N)-533, with the F7F-2N, arrived at Okinawa the day before Japan's surrender. VMD-354, with the F7F-3P, was shipped to Guam in May 1945, in time for photo missions in the West Pacific. VF(N)-52 was the only Navy F7F-2N unit in 1945.

After the war, Marine Tigercat units included three day fighter, two photo, and four night fighter squadrons. Most were replaced by 1950, and all the F7F-2Ns became F7F-2D directors for drone aircraft in 1948.

While the Tigercat was too late for World War II, VMF(N)-542 still had the F3F-3N when the Korean War began, and arrived in Korea in September 1950, flying night and day close support missions until March 1951, when its planes were turned over to VMF(N)-513, which continued vigorous ground attacks and also downed two Po-2 biplane light night bombers before the Tigercat's retirement in April 1952, when F3D-2 jets replaced them.

Mfr

GRUMMAN F7F-3N
Pratt & Whitney R-2800-34W, 2100 hp takeoff, 1850 hp at 15,500'
DIMENSIONS: As F7F-3
WEIGHT: Empty 16,400 lb., Gross 21,476 lb., Max. 25,846 lb. Fuel 375+300 gal.
PERFORMANCE: Speed- Top 359 mph at s.l., 423 mph at 21,900', Cruising 170 mph, Stalling 91 mph. Service Ceiling 40,800', Climb 4580'/1 min., 20,000'/5.2 min. Range 960 miles normal, 1595 miles max.

The first Curtiss Navy fighter since 1935 was ordered the same day as the XF7F-1 but failed to have any impact on the war. The XFl4C-1 was to be powered by a 2,200-hp Lycoming H-2470-4, and the second prototype was redesigned to take a 2,300-hp Wright R-3350-16 Cyclone.

When the inline Lycoming proved unsatisfactory, the XFl4C-1 was canceled in December 1943, but the second prototype was first flown in September 1943 and accepted as the XF14C-2 in July 1944. Co-axial contrarotating propellers were provided for the big Cyclone, along with an intake under the cowl for the turbosupercharger. The wheels folded inwards into the roots of the low wing, which could fold upwards for stowage. Four 20-mm guns protruded from the wing's leading edge.

Mfr

GRUMMAN F7F-4N
Pratt & Whitney R-2800-34W, 2100 hp at takeoff, 1850 hp at 14,000'
DIMENSIONS: Span 51'6" (32'2" fld.), Lg. 46'10", Ht. 16'7", Wing Area 455 sq. ft.
WEIGHT: Empty 16,954 lb., Gross 21,960 lb., Max. 26,167 lb. Fuel 375+300 gal.
PERFORMANCE: Speed- Top 360 mph at s.l., 430 mph at 21,900', Cruising 235 mph, Stalling 92 mph. Service Ceiling 40,450', Climb 4385'/1 min. Range 810 miles normal, 1360 miles max.

Mfr

CURTISS XF14C-2
Wright XR-3350-16, 2300 hp takeoff, 2250 hp at 32,000'
DIMENSIONS: Span 46', Lg. 37'9", Ht.17', Wing Area 375 sq. ft.
WEIGHT: Empty 10,582 lb., Gross 13,405 lb., Max. 14,582 lb. Fuel 230+150 gal.
PERFORMANCE:* Speed- Top 317 mph at s.l., 424 mph at 32,000', Cruising 172 mph. Service Ceiling 39,500', Climb 2700'/1 min. Range 950 miles normal, 1355 miles max.
*Design estimates.

The Curtiss design was as unsuccessful as the parallel XP-62 for the Air Force. Actual speed in tests is reported as only 398 mph, instead of the 424 mph promised, and the type was inferior to the F4U-4 already in production.

Bearcats

The Grumman Bearcat was designed by William T. Schwendler as a Hellcat replacement that would have better climb and maneuverability and be able to operate from even the smallest carriers, the opposite of the heavy Tigercat concept. Two XF8F-l prototypes ordered November 27, 1943, had a Pratt & Whitney R-2800-22W with a four-bladed propeller, a bubble canopy, and low square-

GRUMMAN F8F-1
Pratt & Whitney R-2800-34W, 2100 hp takeoff, 1850 hp at 15,500'
DIMENSIONS: Span 35'10" (23'3" fld.), Lg. 27'6", Ht. 13'8", Wing Area 244 sq. ft.
WEIGHT: Empty 7077 lb., Gross 9386 lb., Max. 12,447 lb. Fuel 183+150 gal.
PERFORMANCE: Speed- Top 382 mph at s.l., 421 mph at 19,700', Cruising 163 mph, Stalling 92 mph. Service Ceiling 38,700', Climb 4570'/1 min., 20,000'/5.7 min., Range 1150 miles normal, 1965 miles max.

tipped wings that could be folded upwards. First flown August 31, 1944, the XF8F-l lacked the fin fillet of production jobs.

GRUMMAN XF8F-1
Pratt & Whitney R-2800-22W, 2100 hp takeoff, 1600 hp at 16,000'
DIMENSIONS: Span 35'6" (23'3" fld.), Lg. 28'8", Ht. 13'8", Wing Area 244 sq. ft.
WEIGHT: Empty 6733 lb., Gross 8788 lb., Max. 9537 lb. Fuel 150+100 gal.
PERFORMANCE: Speed- Top 393 mph at s.l., 424 mph 17,300', Cruising 170 mph. Service Ceiling 33,700', Climb 4800'/1 min. Range 955 miles normal, 1450 miles max.

Small and strictly limited in weight, the Bearcat was armed with four .50-caliber guns and 1,200 rounds in the wings, had 169 pounds of armor, and fittings for a 150-gallon drop tank, two 1,000-pound bombs, or four rockets. Contracts for 2,023 Bearcats were approved October 6, 1944, and General Motors received a February 5, 1945, order for 1,876 Bearcats to be designated F3M-l.

The first production F8F-l, with the R-2800-34W and more fuel, was delivered December 31, 1944, and accepted in February 1945. VF-l9 became the first Bearcat squadron in May and was embarked on the light carrier *Langley*, but the war ended before combat deployment, cutting back Grumman's contracts and eliminating the F3M program. Grumman had furnished 151 Bearcats by the end of August 1945 and completed 658 F8F-ls by August 1947. Four 20-mm M-3 cannon were provided on 226 F8F-lB Bearcats accepted from February 1946 to January 1948 and APS-l9 radar was provided on 12 F8F-lN night fighters accepted from August to November 1946. An XF8F-2 accepted in February 1947 tested the modified fin and cowl that distinguished the F8F-2 ordered June 28, 1946, and first flown October 11, 1947, with an R-2800-30W. By May 1949, Grumman delivered 1,263 Bearcats, including 293 F8F-2s and a dozen F8F-2Ns. Four 20-mm guns, 820 rounds, and 173 pounds of armor were carried. Sixty F8F-2P photo jobs had cameras and only two 20-mm. guns. Two G-58A civilian models are not included in the total.

Many Navy pilots considered Bearcats the best of the propeller-driven fighters, but no opportunity to prove this occurred. After serving about 30 Navy squadrons from

GRUMMAN F8F-2
Pratt & Whitney R-2800-30W, 2300 hp takeoff, 1600 hp at 22,000'
DIMENSIONS: Span 35'6" (23'3" fld.), Lg. 27'6", Ht. 13'8", Wing Area 244 sq. ft.
WEIGHT: Empty 7690 lb., Gross 10,426 lb., Max. 13,494 lb. Fuel 185+150 gal.
PERFORMANCE: Speed- Top 387 mph at s.l., 447 mph at 28,000', Cruising 182 mph, Stalling 105 mph. Service Ceiling 40,700', Climb 4420'/1 min. Range 865 miles normal, 1435 miles max.

1945 to 1949, the Grumman missed the Korean War because it lacked a Corsair's load and a jet's speed.

Conflict in South Asia did bring the F8F action when about 140 Bearcats were used by the French in Indochina from February 1951 to January 1956. Their war was strictly ground attack, for there were no enemy aircraft. In June 1956 the first combat squadron of the new Republic of Vietnam was activated with 28 F8F-1s received from the departing French. Thailand was also supplied 100 F8F-1s and 29 F8F-lBs for its Air Force in 1953-55 from American and French stocks.

A few Bearcats were used for private racing, and one F8F-2 highly modified by Darryl Greenamyer, broke the World's Speed Record for propeller-driven aircraft. Previously held for over 30 years by the Messerschmitt Bf 209, the new record was 483 mph made on August 16, 1969. Modified "round engine" Bearcats rivaled sleek Mustangs at the air races for many years and Lyle Shelton's "Rare Bear", with a 3,800-hp R-3350, set another prop-driven record at 528 mph on August 21, 1989.

Ryan Fireball

Wartime development of gas-turbine engines greatly interested the Navy, but adoption of jet-powered aircraft for carrier service presented many difficulties. Jet aircraft required large quantities of fuel and tricycle landing gear, which had not yet been used on flight decks. The long takeoff run required by jet types made catapult launching desirable, and their high landing speed required improved arresting and barrier systems.

Facing such difficulties, it is not surprising that the first approach should be via composite aircraft using a normal engine and propeller for cruising, and a jet unit only for quick climb and high speed. Such a machine was first proposed by the Navy in December 1942, and on December 17, Ben T. Salmon, Chief Engineer of San Diego's Ryan company, met with the Navy's Fighter-Design Class Desk chief, Comdr. J. B. Pearson, to work out the feature of a hybrid fighter able to operate from the smaller carriers.

Three Ryan XFR-l prototypes were ordered by a letter contract February 11, 1943, of the Model 28 Fireball, as it was called by the company. The mockup approved March 23, at first glance resembled the usual single-seat low-wing monoplane powered by a Wright R-1820-56. Behind the pilot, however, was a General Electric I-16 jet, like that of the XP-59, fed by intakes in the wing roots, and providing 1,600-pounds thrust through a tail nozzle.

RYAN XFR-1
Wright R-1820-56, 1350 hp takeoff, 1000 hp at 17,500', and General Electric I-16, 1610 lb. st at s.l.
DIMENSIONS: Span 40' (15'10" fld.), Lg. 32'4", Ht. 12'3" (16'5" fld.), Wing Area 275 sq. ft.
WEIGHT: Empty 6190 lb., Gross 8061 lb., Max. 8608 lb. Fuel 135+75 gal.
PERFORMANCE: (prop. only) Speed- Top 307 mph at s.l., 326 mph at 18,500', Cruising 189 mph, Stalling 70 mph. Service Ceiling 30,400', Climb 2990'/1 min., 10,000'/3.8 min., 20,000'/9.9 min. Range 966 miles normal, 1430 miles max.
With jet added: Speed- Top 395 mph at s.l., 426 mph at 22,000', Service Ceiling 42,000', Climb 5910'/1 min., 10,000'/1.9 min., 20,000'/4.35 min.

Jet propulsion required tricycle landing gear, and the laminar flow wings could fold upward. Even the control surfaces had flush-riveted metal skin. Four .50-caliber wing guns with 300 rpg and a 75-gallon drop tank were specified for the prototype. A production order for 100 FR-ls was added December 2, and William Immenschuh became Project Engineer as the San Diego factory, across Lindbergh Field from the Convair plant, shifted from building trainers to the Navy's first combination prop-jet fighter.

To show the Fireball concept's growth, the original specification for the XFR-1 is contrasted with the heavier FR-1's characteristics under their photos. The first XFR-1 was flown June 25, 1944, by Robert Kerlinger, and the second on September 20. While the power plants worked well, changes to the tail design were needed. The first prototype was lost October 13, but the other two had their tails rebuilt to the production configuration.

FR-l deliveries began January 1945 with an R-1820-72W Cyclone and the I-16 jet. The four 50-caliber guns and 189 pounds of armor were joined by fittings for two 1,000-pound bombs or 150-gallon drop tanks, or four 5-inch rockets could be carried. Top speed was 295 mph with the propeller only, but increased to 404 mph for the expected 11 minutes that the jet unit would also be running.

USN

RYAN FR-1 test on the *USS Ranger*

By January 1945 1,200 more Fireballs were ordered, but were canceled by the war's end, so only 66 Fireballs were delivered by November 1945. VF-66 had been scheduled to introduce the FR-1 to the fleet, replacing FM-2s. Takeoffs from the deck of the carrier *Ranger* began in May 1945, and the squadron was renamed VF-41 in October. Several fatal accidents marred postwar operations from escort carriers and the FR-1 was withdrawn from service by July 1947.

Proposed FR-2 and FR-3 modifications with new engines were not completed, but one FR-1 became the XFR-4 in 1946 with an R-1820-74W and new flush fuselage intakes for a 4,200-pound thrust Westinghouse J34 in a longer tail section. Another FR-1 became the Navy's first turboprop aircraft when it was rebuilt with a General Electric XT-31 giving 1,700 hp to a four-bladed Hamilton propeller and adding 550-pound residual thrust to the 1,600 pounds of the I-16 in the tail.

Called the XF2R-1 "Darkshark", this prototype was similar to the FR-1 except for the long nose. First flown on November 1, 1946, at Muroc Dry Lake by Al Conover, the XF2R-1 flew well, but its power plant was far from ready for production. A mockup of a proposed XF2R-2 had been inspected in February 1946, proposing a Westinghouse 24C jet in the rear and four 20-mm guns in the wings, but two prototypes were canceled.

Another composite engine fighter begun in December 1943 was larger, intended for the *Essex* class carriers. The

RYAN FR-1
Wright R-1820-72W, 1350 hp takeoff, 1000 hp at 14,800', and General Electric I-16, 1610 lb. st at s.l.
DIMENSIONS: Span 40' (15'11" fld.), Lg. 32'3", Ht. 13'11" (16'9" fld.), Wing Area 275 sq. ft.
WEIGHT: Empty 7689 lb., Gross 9958 lb., Max. 11,652 lb. Fuel 180+200 gal.
PERFORMANCE: (prop. only) Speed- Top 287 mph at s.l., 295 mph at 16,500', Cruising 160 mph, Stalling 91 mph. Service Ceiling 29,000', Climb 2390'/1 min., 10,000'/5 min., 20,000'/12.6 min. Range 930 miles normal, 1620 miles max.
With jet added: Speed- Top 378 mph at s.l., 404 mph at 17,800', Service Ceiling 43,100', Climb 4650'/1 min., 10,000'/2.5 min., 20,000'/5.7 min.

Curtiss XF15C-1 was also a low-wing monoplane with tricycle gear, but used the popular Pratt & Whitney R-2800-34W with a four-bladed propeller and a De Haviland Halford jet of 2,700-pound thrust under the tail. Three prototypes ordered April 7, 1944, were to be armed with four 20-mm guns in the wings and two 1,000-pound bombs.

SDAM

RYAN XFR-4

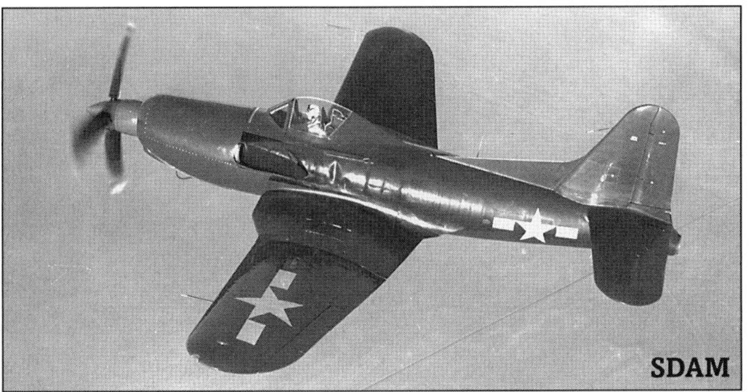
SDAM

RYAN XF2R-l
General Electric XT31-GE-2, 1700 hp+550 lb.; J31-GE-3, 1600 lb. st
DIMENSIONS: Span 40', Lg. 36', Ht. 14', Wing Area 275 sq. ft.
WEIGHT: Gross 11,000 lb.
PERFORMANCE: (Approx.) Speed- Top 500 mph at s.1. Service Ceiling 39,100', Climb 10,000'/2 min.

SDAM

RYAN XF2R-2 Mockup *(Design estimates)*
General Electric TG100, 1700 hp+550 lb.; Westinghouse 24C, 3000 lb. st
DIMENSIONS: Span 42', Lg. 37'5", Ht. 13'10", Wing Area 305 sq. ft.
WEIGHT: Empty 9700 lb., Gross 13,043 lb., Max. 17,763 lb. Fuel 250+300 gal.
PERFORMANCE: (prop. only) Speed- Top 337 mph at 20,000's, Cruising 289 mph, Stalling 91 mph. Range 785 miles normal, 1280 miles max.
With jet added: Speed- Top 515 mph at 20,000', Service Ceiling 50,900', Climb 6450'/1 min.

The first XF15C-1 was flown February 28, 1945, at Buffalo, NY, by Lloyd Child with only an R-2800-22W installed. The imported jet unit wasn't flown until May 3, but tests were interrupted by a crash on May 8. Tests resumed July 9 on the second prototype, which had the R-2800-34W and an Allis-Chalmers H-lB jet unit (U.S. copy of Halford), while the third XF15C-l was flown with a new tail on March 13, 1946. The horizontal tail service was raised to the vertical fin's top, a change also made to the second prototype by August. Development of pure jet types, however, led the Navy to cancel its last Curtiss fighter program on October 10, 1946.

Mfr

CURTISS XF15C-1
Pratt & Whitney R-2800-34W, 2100 hp takeoff, 1850 hp at 15,500', and De Havilland Halford, 2700 lb. st
DIMENSIONS: Span 48', Lg. 44', Ht. 15'3", Wing Area 400 sq. ft
WEIGHT: Empty 12,648 lb., Gross 16,630 lb., Max. 18,698 lb. Fuel 376+150 gal.
PERFORMANCE: (prop. only) Speed- Top 322 mph at s.1., 373 mph at 22,000'; Cruising 163 mph. Range 1385 miles max.
With jet added: Speed- Top 432 mph at s.1., 469 mph at 25,300'. Service Ceiling 41,800', Climb 5020'/1 min.

Mfr

CURTISS XF15C-1 (with T tail)

Boeing's last fighter

Boeing interrupted its retirement from fighter design with the XF8B-l. A large low-wing monoplane built around a 3,000-hp Pratt & Whitney R-4360-10 with Aeroproducts contrarotating six-blade propellers, the Boeing's wheels rotated 90° to retract backward into the wing. Armament included six .50-caliber wing guns, two 1,600-pound bombs in an internal bay, or two more on external racks, which could also be used for 2,000-pound bombs, torpedoes or drop tanks. Recognition features included the large scoop below the engine and a bubble canopy.

Three long-range fighter-bomber prototypes contracted April 10, 1943, were built, the first flying November 27, 1944, and delivered to the Navy on March 10, 1945. The second XF8B-l, which flew a year after the first, was tested by the Air Force in 1946, but the Navy had lost interest in the type after the war.

A "Flying Saucer"?

The last propeller-driven fighter Vought offered the Navy was also the oddest. The XF5U-l was based on a proposal by Charles H. Zimmerman for a circular flying wing aircraft designed to be capable of hovering by standing on its tail and using twin propellers on wingtips as helicopter rotors. A full-scale wood and fabric flying model with panted fixed landing gear, the V-173 was flown November 23, 1942, by Boone Guyton, and construction began on a single-place fighter development known as the XF5U-l.

Mfr

VOUGHT XF5U-1
Pratt & Whitney R-2000-7, 1600 hp at 23,000'
DIMENSIONS: Width 36'5", Lg. 28'7", Ht. 14'9", Wing Area 475 sq. ft.
WEIGHT: Empty 14,000 lb., Gross 16,802 lb., Max. 18,917 lb. Fuel 261+300 gal.
PERFORMANCE: (Design estimates) Speed- Top 394 mph at s. l., 504 mph at 28,900', Cruising 236 mph. Stalling 105 mph. Service Ceiling 32,000', Climb 3950"1 min., 10,000'/4.9 min. Range 910 miles.

This was to be powered by two 1,600-hp turbo-supercharged Pratt & Whitney R-2000-7 radials buried inside the thick circular wing on each side of the cockpit and driving two large four-bladed propellers located at the wingtips. Twin rudders were mounted at the wing's trailing edge, and horizontal controls extended outboard of the weird saucer-shaped airframe. Dual main wheels and a tail wheel retracted backwards.

Mfr

BOEING XF8B-1
Pratt & Whitney XR-4360-10, 3000 hp takeoff, 2540 hp at 22,000'
DIMENSIONS: Span 54', Lg. 43'3", Ht. 16'3", Wing Area 489 sq. ft.
WEIGHT: Empty 14,190 lb., Gross 20,508 lb., Max. 22,960 lb., Fuel 384+570 gal.
PERFORMANCE: (at 19,523 lb. combat) Speed- Top 340 mph at s.l., 432 mph at 26,500', Cruising 225 mph, Stalling 82 mph. Service Ceiling 37,500', Climb 3660'/1 min. Range 2300-3500 miles.

Armed with six .50-caliber guns in the wing roots and two bombs or drop tanks, the aircraft had a span of 23 feet, 4 inches at the wingtips and 36 feet, 4 inches at the propeller tips. While vertical takeoff was beyond power capacity, a short takeoff combined with a high top speed seemed possible.

On September 17, 1942, a letter of intent was issued for the XF5U-l, a mockup inspected in June 1943, and the contract dated July 15, 1944. The prototype was completed by August 20, 1945, with 1,350-hp R-2000-7 engines, since the planned XR-2000-2 units and special propellers were not ready.

Mfr

VOUGHT XF5U-1

With the temporary power plant, expected top speed was 388 mph at 15,000 feet and a 14,550-pound gross weight. (Characteristics of the XR-2000-2 version are given in the accompanying picture caption.) Initial flight tests required transportation by sea to Muroc test base in California, an expense the post-war Navy was unwilling to meet. On March 17, 1947, the XF5U-l contract was terminated and the aircraft was demolished for scrap without ever being flown.

CHAPTER 24

VERY HEAVY BOMBERS END THE WAR

BOEING B-29s of 468th Group in February 1945.

AF

Superfortress over Japan

Had the war ended on V-E Day there could have remained doubt as to the decisive effects of strategic bombardment. Postwar study revealed that German production actually increased during 1944, and had the Nazi jet fighter program not foundered, defeat of Hitler might have depended entirely on Allied ground forces.

But war against Japan demonstrated air power's full weight. Japan, whose armed forces suffered 780,000 combat casualties in the entire war, sustained in nine months 806,000 civilian casualties, including 330,000 dead. All were victims of the Boeing B-29 Superfortress, which had proved itself a weapon of war without equal in the history of mankind. A high price had been paid for Japan's invasions of China and the attack on America.

The bomber which accomplished this feat, making the Kaiser's Gothas, Hitler's Heinkels, Japan's Mitsubishis, and our own B-17s seem rather primitive, was the first Very Heavy Bomber (VHB) class aircraft. Boeing's B-29 was based on B-15, B-17 and B-19 developments, but added a pressurized crew cabin so attacks could be made above the effective reach of anti-aircraft fire. Manual turrets seemed incompatible with pressurization, so a remote-control firing system was provided.

On November 10, 1939, General Arnold asked War Department permission to initiate development of a four-engine bomber of 2,000 mile radius "superior in all respects to the B-17B and the B-24." Permission was granted, and on January 29, 1940, Request for Data R-40B was issued to leading aircraft builders.

When R-40B, which called for a range of 5,333 miles with a ton of bombs, reached Boeing, the Seattle engineers lead by Ed Wells completed a design already under way. Sent to Wright Field by March 5, 1940, Model 341 offered a 76,000 pound design gross weight, 124 feet 7 inches span, 405-mph speed, a capacity of 4,120 gallons of fuel or five tons of bombs, and six hand-operated .50-caliber guns.

But the Air Corps made even higher demands on April 8, 1940, with Type Specification XC-218-A that, along with leak proof tanks and heavier armament, called for a 5,333 mile range with 2,000-pound bomb load, and a bomb capacity, in lieu of fuel, of eight tons. A 300-mph top speed at 25,000 feet and a 30,000-foot service ceiling was the minimum required. While 450 mph and 40,000 feet were "desired", they proved beyond the reach of conventional power plants.

Boeing replied on May 11,1940, with Model 345, with a 97,700 pound design gross, 141 feet 2 inch span, 382-mph speed, 5,140 gallon fuel capacity, and ten .50-caliber and one 20-mm. gun in remote-controlled turrets. The four engines would be the new 2,200 hp Wright R-3350-13 Duplex Cyclones also used by Lockheed's entry, Model 51, in the design competition.

"An evaluation board appraised the designs and rated the four competitors in this order of preference: Boeing, Lockheed, Douglas, Consolidated. Contracts for preliminary engineering data were issued to the firms on June 27 and their planes were designated, respectively, the XB-29, XB-30, XB-31, XB-32." The Lockheed design was simply an armed version of the future Constellation airliner, while the Douglas XB-31 idea was a 99-ton giant with a 207-foot span and four R-4360 Wasp Majors.

Based on comparison of that engineering data, Boeing won a $3,615,095 contract for two XB-29 prototypes on September 6, 1940. A similar contract went to the XB-32 at the same time, while a third prototype machine was added to each in December.

Even before flight testing began, the pressures of war led the Air Force to program 1,644 production aircraft in a three-billion dollar effort that finally produced 3,957 B-29s from four different factories.

So that the B-17 program would not be obstructed, a new factory was built at Wichita, Kansas, utilizing Midwestern labor reserves. An order for fourteen YB-29s, approved on June 6, 1941, was followed on September 6 by a contract for 250 B-29s, and 500 more were added on January 31, 1942. Later, Bell Aircraft was enlisted to build others at a

BOEING XB-29
Four Wnght R-3350-13, 2200 hp to 25,000'
DIMENSIONS: Span 141'3", Lg. 98'2", Ht. 27'9", Wing Area 1739 sq. ft.
WEIGHT: Empty 66,120 lb., Gross 105,000 lb., Max. 120,000 lb. Fuel 5155-7494 gal.
PERFORMANCE: Speed- Top 284 mph at s. l., 368 mph at 25,000', Cruising 247 mph, Landing 105 mph. Service Ceiling 32,100', Climb 25,000'/27 min. Range 4525 miles/2000-lb. bombs. At 120,000 lb. gross: 4100 miles/16,000-lb. bombs, 5850 miles ferry.

Marietta, Georgia, facility, the first aircraft plant in the old South. A Renton, Washington, plant built for Boeing flying boats was released by the Navy for B-29A production in exchange for Mitchell medium bombers. Finally, Martin's Omaha factory then building B-26Cs was also, after a short reservation for 400 stillborn B-33As, assigned to B-29s.

BOEING XB-29 (3rd prototype)

BOEING YB-29 (1943)

Three XB-29s were built at Seattle, using four Wright R-3350-13 Cyclones, each with double turbosuperchargers and 2,200 hp at 25,000 feet. The first, flown September 21, 1942, by Edmund T. Allen, had three-bladed propellers and four teardrop blisters for the periscopic sights of a Sperry fire-control system. These were replaced in the third prototype by hemispheric blisters for the General Electric fire-control system adopted for production aircraft. Only these prototypes had an astrodome behind the pilot's cockpit.

BOEING YB-29 as escort fighter

Problems with the big new engines were the main threat to B-29 tests; 16 engine changes were made in the XB-29's first 27 test hours. An engine fire interrupted the second XB-29's maiden flight December 30, 1942, and another caused a crash that killed everyone aboard on February 18, 1943. Flight tests were halted and the big gamble of industrial resources on an untested aircraft and power plant was in doubt, but after hasty engine improvements, the third prototype was airborne on June 6.

Production Superfortresses were similar in appearance, with a single tail and a narrow high-aspect ratio wing whose area was increased by 19% when the Fowler flaps were extended. The retractable tricycle gear used double main wheels of B-17-size.

The crew of eleven sat in pressurized compartments, beginning with the bombardier in the circular nose with his bomb and gun sights, pilot and co-pilot protected by panels of armor and bulletproof glass, then the flight engineer, radio operator, and navigator. That front compartment was connected by a 33-foot long tunnel over the double bomb bays to the rear compartment containing three gunners and the radar man, all protected by an armor bulkhead.

Like the main cabins, the separate tail gunner's compartment was also protected and pressurized to maintain an internal altitude of 8,000 feet up to an actual altitude of 30,000 feet. Up to forty 500 or sixteen 1,000-pound bombs could be carried in the tandem bomb bays, or replaced by up to four 640-gallon drop tanks. An APQ-13 radar dome could be extended below between the bomb bay doors.

The distinguishing armament feature was an elaborate General Electric fire-control system with computing sights in the nose and in rear top and side blisters directing four remote-controlled turrets turning a full 360-degrees. Each had two .50-caliber guns, and the tail gunner had two .50-caliber and one 20-mm gun moving in a 30-degree arc.

The first YB-29-BW flew on June 26, 1943, in Kansas with the R-3350-21, three-bladed propellers, and a full armament system. R-3350-23 engines and Hamilton Hydromatic four-bladed propellers were introduced on the first production B-29-1-BW Superfortress accepted on September 21, 1943, and by the year's end at Wichita, 40 B-29-1 and 33 B-29-5-BW had been accepted, the latter omitting camouflage paint. In 1944, 722 rolled out of the plant, taking block numbers to B-29-55-BW.

Unfortunately, acceptance didn't mean combat-ready, for the heaviest plane in mass production had a multitude of minor mechanical items that needed fixing. The engines were a constant cause of concern; and the R-3350-23 had to be replaced with -23A models before going overseas. Newer Cyclone engine models with fuel injection, the R-3350-41 and -57, were introduced in 1945. Aircraft complexity had increased factory man-hours from 200,000 on each B-17 to three million on the B-29, and average fly-away cost per B-29 during the war was $639,188.

A new factory near Atlanta managed by Bell Aircraft began in November 1943 by assembling five B-29-1-BA bombers from Wichita parts and adding 200 of its own in 1944. Martin's Omaha factory also began in December 1943 with five B-29-1-MO bombers from Wichita parts and added 95 from May to December 1944. Boeing's Renton plant began B-29A-1-BN deliveries in January 1944 with a new wing center section structure, and completed 139 in 1944.

The first 415 B-29s from Wichita (blocks 1 to 40-BW) had ten .50-caliber guns with 5,000 rounds, and 100 rounds for the 20-mm gun. In July 1944, beginning in the B-29-40-BW, B-29-15-BA, B-29-5-MO, and B-29A-20-BN blocks, there were four guns in the upper front turret. The 20-mm gun, unpopular with crews, was omitted after blocks B-29-50-BW, B-29-15-BA, B-29-20-MO, and B-29A-10-BN, leaving just the twin fifties. These were the only guns remaining when all four turrets were removed to improve the range and speed of those aircraft selected for night raids later in the war.

Although B-29 production closed with the cancellation of 5,092 planes after the war ended in September 1945,

BOEING B-29-25-BW (1944)
Four Wright R-3350-23, 2200 hp takeoff, 2430 hp WE at 32,000'.
DIMENSIONS: Span 141'3", Lg. 99', Ht. 27'9", Wing Area 1736 sq. ft.
WEIGHT: Empty 70,140 lb., Gross 110,000 lb, Max. 134,000 lb. Fuel 5638-8198 gal.
PERFORMANCE: Speed- Top 295 mph at 5000', 358 mph at 25,000', Cruising 230 mph, Landing 105 mph. Service Ceiling 31,850', Climb 20,000'/38 min. Range 3250 miles/20,000-lb. bombs, 5600 miles ferry.
(Data for blocks B-29-1 to B-29-20-BW, at military power.)

BOEING B-29A-5-BN
Four Wright R-3350-23, 2200 hp takeoff, 2430 hp WE at 32,000'.
DIMENSIONS: Span 142'3", Lg. 99', Ht. 27'9", Wing Area 1736 sq. ft.
WEIGHT: Empty 70,975 lb., Gross 110,000 lb, Max. 140,000 lb. Fuel 6738-9298 gal.
PERFORMANCE: Speed- Top 358 mph at 25,000', Cruising 223 mph, Landing 105 mph. Service Ceiling 31,850', Climb 20,000'/ 38 min. Range 3900 miles/17,500-lb. bombs, 5800 miles ferry.

Renton was allowed to resume deliveries in November with another 50 B-29A-70-BNs and, with new forward upper turrets, 19 B-29A-75-BNs. The last was delivered on June 10, 1946, for a total of 1,119 B-29As. There were 1,634 B-29s from Wichita, and Martin delivered 536 B-29-MO.

Bell alternated between 357 B-29-BA and 311 B-29B-BA models. The B-29B was a night-bomber with APQ-7 Eagle bombing radar instead of the APS-13, no turrets, and APG-15 radar for the tail guns; two .50-caliber, or three in the last 260 planes. The B-29B was used entirely by the 315th Bomb Wing's attacks on the oil industry. Altogether, 3,960 B-29s of all models were accepted by the AAF.

Six cameras were fitted in the rear section of 118 photo-recon versions known as the F-13 and F-13A and the first, converted from a B-29-40-BW, flew on August 4, 1944. Some retained turrets and others did not. An F-13A flew over Tokyo on November 1, 1944, locating targets for the B-29 bombing campaign soon to begin. Many such vital sorties were made and followed by others to evaluate damage.

Mfr

BOEING B-29-90-BW (1945)
Four Wright R-3350-41, 2320 hp takeoff, 2430 hp WE at 32,000'.
DIMENSIONS: Span 141'3", Lg. 99', Ht. 27'9", Wing Area 1736 sq. ft.
WEIGHT: Empty 71,360 lb. Gross 138,500 lb., Max 141,100 lb., Fuel 6988-9548 gal.
PERFORMANCE: (at 110,000 lb.) Speed- Top 302 mph at 5000', 361 mph at 25,000' (WE), Cruising 230 mph, Stalling 105 mph, Service Ceiling 31,850', Climb 20,000'/38 min. Range 3800 miles/16,000-lb. bombs, 5500 miles ferry. Data for blocks B-29-25 to B-29-90-BW.

BOEING B-29-30-MO (Martin) of 19th Group

Extra armament had been fitted to the fourth YB-29 to test it as an escort fighter, like the B-40. Two .50s were mounted in a nose turret and in each of four side blisters. The top and bottom turrets were retained with a 20-mm gun added to the lower turret and a 37-mm gun in the tail, for a total of 22 guns.

BOEING B-29B-60-BA (Bell)
Four Wright R-3350-41, 2320 hp takeoff, 2430 hp WE at 32,000'.
DIMENSIONS: As B-29
WEIGHT: Empty 69,000 lb., Gross 110,000 lb., Max. 137,500 lb.
PERFORMANCE: Speed- Top 306 mph at 5,000', 367 mph at 25,000' WE, Cruising 228 mph, Landing 105 mph. Service Ceiling 32,000' Climb 20,000'/38 min. Range 3875 miles/18,000-lb. bombs, 5725 miles ferry.

One experimental B-29-25-BW tested in October 1944 replaced the remote-controlled system with two conventional Martin top turrets, two Sperry "ball" turrets underneath, a one-gun Emerson barrette on each side of the nose, and a manual gun at each side blister. Production aircraft, however, kept the 12-gun configuration, except for the two-gun night bombers.

The XB-39

An alternative power plant proposed for the B-29 was the liquid-cooled inline Allison V-3420-11. A contract was awarded in May 1942 to develop a turbosupercharged version and the new engine installations were tested on the XB-19A. The first YB-29 was flown to Cleveland in November 1943, stripped of its Cyclones, but retaining guns and war paint so that performance could be accurately compared. After engine delays to aid the P-75 program, the redesignated XB-39 was first flown on December 9, 1944. By

BOEING XB-39
Four Allison V-3420-11, 3000 hp takeoff, 2600 hp at 25,000'
DIMENSIONS: Span 141'3", Lg. 99', Ht. 27'9", Wing Area 1739 sq. ft.
WEIGHT: Empty 75,120 lb., Gross 105,000 lb., Max. 135,000 lb. Fuel 3000-6988 gal.
PERFORMANCE: Speed- Top 312 mph at s. l., 405 mph at 35,000', Cruising 282 mph, Service Ceiling 39,000', Climb 30,000'/29 min. Range 2550 miles/2000-lb. bombs.

that time, AAF attention was looking forward to the XB-44 project with even larger Wasp Majors.

B-29 Operations, 1944-45

Although the first Superfortress to go overseas was a YB-29 flown to England on March 8, 1944, this was just a feint to obscure the concentration against Japan. Four groups began moving to India on March 26 and on June 5, 77 B-29s raided Bangkok, the longest (2,261 miles) bombing mission to that date. The first attack on southern Japan itself was by 47 B-29s staged through China on June 15. These and all future B-29 missions were made by the Twentieth Air Force, created solely to use the big Boeings. The longest American air raid of the war was a 4,030-mile, 19-hour mission from Ceylon to Sumatra on August 10, 1944.

When Chinese bases proved too difficult to supply and defend, the B-29s shifted to the newly-captured Mariana Islands. From there, beginning with a raid on Tokyo on November 24, 1944, they bombed the war economy on the main Japanese islands. Japanese weather frustrated the precision bombing technique used in Europe, and engine failure caused many aborted sorties. General Curtis E. LeMay shifted his method to night low-level incendiary attacks on Japanese cities. The first of these on Tokyo, March 10, 1945, caused more casualties than either of the atomic bombs.

On March 27, the B-29s added Operation Starvation to their missions, eventually dropping 12,035 mines in coastal waters to destroy Japanese shipping. Even without the atomic bomb, these fire bomb and mining attacks crippled Japan. The largest single-day effort with conventional bombs was the 836 B-29s dispatched on August 1.

Silverplate

In his letter to President Roosevelt on August 2, 1939, suggesting the atomic bomb, Albert Einstein had feared "such bombs might very well prove too heavy for transport by air". But the length of the uranium-gun "Little Boy" and diameter of the plutonium "Fat Man" weapons completed at Los Alamos were tailored to fit the bomb bay of the B-29,

BOEING B-29-45-MO (Martin) Enola Gay

which in September 1943 had been selected as their carrier, and the very secret operation was code-named Silverplate on December 1, 1944.

Seventeen B-29s with modified bomb bays for training and drop tests preceded the 26 Silverplate B-29s built in the Omaha factory in 1945 with special fittings in the front bomb bay, fuel cells in the rear bay, fuel injection engines, Curtiss electric propellers, and accommodations for the weapons specialist in the front compartment. No turrets were fitted, except for the two .50-caliber tail guns.

Fifteen went to the specially-trained 509th Composite Group in May 1945, and flew to Tinian in the Marianas in June. There they flew practice bombing missions while awaiting the test-firing of the implosion prototype on July 16 in New Mexico, and the rush of the first two bomb cores to Tinian by cruiser in time for the August 6 strike on Hiroshima.

The 8,900-pound uranium bomb was dropped from Enola Gay, an Omaha-built B-29-46-MO, flying 328 mph at 31,600 feet, on its third mission over Japan. On August 9, the USSR began its offensive against Japan and a B-29-36-MO dropped a 10,300-pound prototype Mk 3 plutonium weapon on Nagasaki. Another atomic bomb wasn't yet available, so the B-29s continued their campaign until 809 made their last attack of the war on August 14, 1945. Japan's surrender was announced as they returned to their bases.

By the war's end, there were about 2,865 B-29s on hand, and 40 VHB groups, of which 21 had been deployed in the Pacific. They flew 38, 808 sorties, dropped 171,000 tons of bombs or mines, claimed 914 enemy fighters, and lost 512 B-29s on combat missions. Another 260 were destroyed in the U.S. on training missions.

Before reading about the B-29's Cold War activities, the little-known story of the other wartime AAF long-range bomber programs will be told.

The B-32

The success of the Superfortress made the parallel heavy bomber development by Convair superfluous. The first XB-32 had the same engines and pressurization of the B-29, with the high wing and twin tails of its B-24 ancestors. Issac B. Laddon designed a smaller wing area using the Davis airfoil and Fowler flaps, a circular fuselage, and dual main and nose wheels on the retractable tricycle gear.

Convair XB-32
First prototype begins test flights at San Diego's Lindbergh Field.

Prototypes were ordered September 6, 1940, and 13 YB-32s were added on June 30, 1941. The first XB-32 was flown on September 7, 1942, two weeks ahead of the B-29, by Russell Rogers at San Diego. Powered by R-3350-13 Duplex Cyclones with Hamilton three-blade propellers and dual turbosuperchargers, it had extensive test instrumentation and no armament. While that plane crashed

AF

Mk. I "Little Boy" used at Hiroshima
Length 126", Diameter 29", Weight 8900 lb.

when taking off on May 10, 1943, the second XB-32 flew July 2, 1943, and after 30 flights went to Muroc (now Edwards) for acceptance tests in February 1944.

Range was calculated as 5,030 miles with a one-ton bomb load, which could be increased to ten tons if fuel load was cut down. Since no fighter escort could go so far, remarkably heavy protection was planned, including 1,221 pounds of armor for the crew, with 14 .50-caliber and two 20-mm guns in remote-control stations.

The "cannons" and a pair of fifties were installed in the rear of each outboard engine nacelle, and could be swung out to 70 degrees outboard and aimed 16 degrees up and 30 degrees down. Four guns placed in a retractable top turret behind the wing covered the upper hemisphere, while four more were in a retractable bottom turret underneath.

All this firepower would be concentrated on planes attacking from the rear by the tail gunner's computer sight. Most unusual was the installation of two .50-caliber guns on the leading edge of the wings; one outboard of each side's propeller disks! Each could be aimed up or down 13 degrees, or swung 60 degrees sideward to cover the forward area blocked from the main turrets by propeller disks.

A fire-control officer sat under a scanner dome behind the flight deck, with top and bottom periscope sights. His computer was linked to the tail gunner's, and a third gunner behind the bottom turret had a periscopic sight. But by October 17, 1942, Convair engineers raised doubts about the Sperry company's success in perfecting an accurate fire control system and favored a single vertical tail for the production version.

Mfr

CONVAIR XB-32 (2nd prototype)
Four Wright R-3350-13, 2200 hp to 25,000'
DIMENSIONS: Span 135', Lg. 83', Ht. 20'10", Wing Area 1,422 sq. ft.
WEIGHT: Empty 65,449 lb., Gross 102,428 lb., Max. 113,500 lb. Fuel 5226 gal.
PERFORMANCE: Speed- Top 379 mph at 25,000', Cruising 250 mph, Landing 96 mph. Service Ceiling 30,700', Climb 25,000'/22.6 min. Range 1610 miles /20,000-lb., 4450 miles/2000-lb. bombs.

Mfr

CONVAIR XB-32 (2nd prototype)
Four .50-caliber guns in retractable turrets

On March 17, 1943, a contract was approved for 300 B-32 bombers to be delivered at Fort Worth, instead of the busier San Diego factory, from September 1943 to October 1944. But drastic changes made in the production design put back that schedule a year. These changes included elimination of the pressurized fuselage and remote control turrets in favor of conventional manned turrets, and cancellation of the YB-32 version.

The tall single tail was introduced on the third XB-32, first flown by Beryl Erickson with twin fins on September 17, 1943, and then with a single fin from the Boeing B-29 on January 6, 1944. Convair engineers then designed their own taller fin for that prototype. By June 1944, contract changes called for 1,213 production ships, including 500 to be built in San Diego, instead of Fort Worth.

The first production B-32-1-CF Dominator was flown August 5, 1944 at Fort Worth by Beryl Erickson. Powered by R-3350-23A Duplex Cyclones with Curtiss 16-foot, 8-inch, four-blade propellers, a B-32 could hold forty 500, or twelve 1,000, or eight 2,000, or four 4,000-pound bombs in the double bay. Ten .50-caliber guns with 5,450 rounds were paired in power-operated turrets: two Martin turrets on top, Sperry ball turrets in the nose and in the tail, and another as a retractable belly turret. Armor protection was limited to turrets and 520 pounds on engine nacelles.

Fourteen B-32s accepted for service tests were followed by 40 TB-32s completed without turrets by March 24, 1945, for the transitional training unit at Fort Worth. On April 17, acceptances began on combat-ready B-32-20-CFs, whose nine crewmen included an operator of the APQ-5B and -13 radar, with a retractable radome in front of the bomb bays. San Diego's first B-32-20-CO flown on March 17, 1945, became the only one accepted from there.

Since only 14 Dominators had been accepted by the end of 1944, they were too late to replace the B-24 in the war in Europe, and only General George C. Kenney of the Fifth Air Force had requested the B-32s. After Germany surrendered in May, the contract was cut back to only

Mfr

CONVAIR XB-32 (3rd prototype)
With new single tail and left-hand props feathered on July 1, 1944.

Mfr

CONVAIR B-32-1-CF

214 bombers from Fort Worth to supply Kenny's forces. Convair's Laddon protested the decision, arguing that the B-32 was a very superior replacement for the B-24 in the Pacific, but official opinion was that B-32s were no longer needed as "insurance against failure of the B-29".

Dominators (later renamed Terminators to avoid political inference) were sent to the 312th Bomb Group on Luzon, where two flew the first mission May 29, 1945. Nine B-32s had arrived in the Far East by August 17, when a photographic sweep near Tokyo to confirm Japan's surrender was the first to encounter enemy fighters. The following day, B-32 gunners got the last Japanese fighter to be downed by American aircraft.

Only 114 B-32s had been accepted at Fort Worth by August 10, and on August 15 Convair was ordered to halt production, sending eight more flyable planes to be scrapped at a disposal center, and also to dispose of two more at San Diego, and 49 nearly-finished aircraft. By the month's end all B-32 training was halted.

Martin's XB-33

Another heavy bomber design of this period never reached the flying stage. The Martin Model 189 was designed with two Wright R-3350s in response to an AAF medium bomber specification dated October 15, 1940, and on February 11, 1941, Martin was sent an Air Corps Letter of Intent to buy it as the XB-33.

But on April 20, the Model 190 heavy bomber was proposed and the Air Corps contract was made on June 11 for two XB-33 prototypes with four 1,750-hp turbosuper-

Mfr

CONVAIR B-32-25-CF *Four Wright R-3350-23A, 2200 hp to 25,000'*
DIMENSIONS: Span 135', Lg. 83'1", Ht. 32'2", Wing Area 1422 sq. ft.
WEIGHT: Empty 60,465 lb., Gross 100,000 lb., Max 121,000 lb., Fuel 5460 gal. (+1500 gal. on block B-32-25-CF)
PERFORMANCE: Speed- Top 281 mph at 5000', 357 mph at 25,000', Cruising 248 mph, Landing 96 mph.
Service Ceiling 29,600', Climb 25,000'/38 min. Range 2400 miles/20,000-lb. bombs, 4421 miles/2000-lb. bombs.

charged Wright R-2600-15s and twin tails. A mockup was inspected in October and after America went to war, an order to build 400 B-33As at the Omaha factory received a Letter of Intent on December 26, and a contract approved January 17, 1942.

Called the Super Marauder by the company, the B-33 had a 134-foot span high wing configuration like the XB-32 and remote-control for ten .50-caliber guns; four in the top turret and two each in the tail and both bottom turrets. Top speed was estimated at 345 mph at 35,000 feet and range 2,000 miles with a 2,000-pound bomb load.

These estimates were not impressive when compared to the B-29 program, and by November 9, 1942, the Air Force had decided to use the Omaha plant for the B-29, or even the promising B-35 flying wing. All B-33 work was stopped by a December 14 order, so the prototypes were never completed. The B-29 was all the bomber needed to end that war.

The war with Japan was over, but the B-29 had another atom bomb to drop. At Bikini atoll, Operation Crossroads tested the effects of a Mark 3 bomb on a target array of ships. On July 1, 1946, a B-29-40-MO supported by eight other B-29s and eight F-13As dropped the weapon in an elaborately monitored and photographed assessment of nuclear warfare.

The Cold War would extend the service life of the B-29s for another decade and another war, and that story will be told in Chapter 26.

PART THREE

AIR WEAPONS FOR THE COLD WAR, 1946 TO 1962

CHAPTER 25

NUCLEAR BOMBS AND THE COLD WAR

Air Force strategic power in 1950-55 is represented by this RB-36 escorted by Marine F9F-5P Panthers. The turrets may safely be retracted, for these Marines carry cameras, not guns.

While American occupation troops thoughtfully examined the burned-out heart of Tokyo and the flattened wasteland at Hiroshima, United States policy makers considered the postwar military establishment. Adherence to the United Nations implied a world security system in which armed forces might be dispatched anywhere. Continental defense, center of prewar plans, became secondary to offensive capabilities of global range.

As the United States had the world's only atomic weapons and, in its B-29 fleet, by far the world's best agency to deliver them, it appeared to some that the nation was able to fill the role of world policeman, with little aid from other nations, or even from its own land armies. Long-range nuclear bombing was seen by many as a magic weapon that had ended the war with Japan, would deter any future aggression, and established American leadership in world affairs.

In the years following World War II, most of the world polarized into two camps as hostility and tension increased between the United States and the Soviet Union. Nearly all the remaining sea power was American, but Soviet land forces were overwhelmingly larger than those of the United States. Air power seemed to hold the balance, and since the Soviet air force role was almost entirely tactical support for the Red Army, the Strategic Air Force (SAC) became America's main military asset. Nuclear bombs and SAC bombardment capacity was a major weight in the balance of power.

Metal resources largely determine a nation's potential air power and weapons production. During World War Two's most intense year, 1944, steel production in the USSR was 10.9 million tons, compared to 85.1 million tons for the United States. Aluminum production that year in USSR was only 82.7 thousand metric tons, compared to 1,092.9 thousand metric tons for the United States.

The Soviets had tried to compensate for their limitations in aircraft production by using as little metal and as much wood as possible in the smaller aircraft for close support preferred to the heavy strategic bombers and their escort fighters built in America. Aircraft production during 1944 was 40,245 for the USSR, and 96,369 for the United States.

When 1946 began, the Soviet Union lacked the main elements seen in American air power, having no atomic bombs, long-range bombers, aircraft carriers or jet fighters. Soviet wartime losses, including nearly 27 million people, and its naval weakness, made an attack by the USSR on the United States very unlikely for many years.

Clearly, it would take a generation of Soviet forced economic expansion to approach American resources, but by giving first priority to air defense and strictly limiting civilian allocations, a credible response to American air power was made. Gradually the USSR's industry would expand steel output to a close second to America's, and aluminum production to a million tons, but at a cost of prolonging civilian poverty. Only a strict dictatorship could require such sacrifices, while propaganda promoting communist society might win support from the outside.

Air power in America achieved equal status with the Army and Navy through creation of the National Military Establishment on September 18, 1947, with Secretaries of Air, Army, and Navy, under a Secretary of Defense. On July 18, 1947, President Truman appointed an Air Policy Commission headed by Thomas K. Finletter to formulate "an integrated national aviation policy."

The Commission's report submitted on December 30 called for an Air Force of 70 groups: 20 strategic bomber, 5 light bomber, 22 day fighter, 3 all-weather fighter, 6 strategic and 4 tactical reconnaissance, and 10 troop carrier.

Resistance arose to the program as the Navy demanded renewed recognition for carrier and anti-submarine aviation, the Army charged neglect of tactical air, and development of Soviet atomic weapons raised concern over continental defense.

The Finletter report was made at a time when "no possible enemy could make a (sustained) assault" on the American mainland, but suggested January 1, 1953, as a target date for the Air Force to be capable of dealing with

The changing shape of the Cold War Air Force in 1950; the swept wings and J47 turbojet-powered B-47A and F-86A.

a possible atomic attack on the U.S. Establishment of a Scientific Advisory Board, headed by Theodore von Karman, gave the Air Force a long-range technological outlook.

Just as American war plans like Rainbow Five had been prepared for attack on Germany, so plans were made for the new adversary. Only 51 days after Japan surrendered, the vulnerability of Russian cities to a "limited air attack" with atomic bombs had been analyzed by a Joint Intelligence Staff study. By 1948, Cold War tensions produced an American war plan, **Charioteer**. Strategic Air Command had the leading role, to deliver 133 atomic bombs on 70 Soviet vital centers in thirty days, including eight on Moscow and seven on Leningrad.*

But the Soviet Army was strong enough to occupy western Europe, probably within twenty days, and could threaten the bases in Britain and the Middle East necessary for B-29/B-50 attacks. Soviet technical progress gradually began to reduce the substantial lag behind American long-range weapons. By 1949's end, atomic bombs, long-range bombers, and MiG-15 jet fighters began joining the Soviet inventory.

While the capability for a sustained attack on the United States did not yet exist, the capability was there to overrun all of Continental Europe and the Near East, which would be an "unacceptable threat" to United States security. Fear of a "nuclear Pearl Harbor" promoted PARPRO, the Peacetime Airborne Reconnaissance Program designed to measure Soviet strength and preparations. Electronic intelligence (ELINT) became a central concern, leading to the aircraft modifications described in later chapters.

A new global war plan, **Dropshot,** was developed in 1949 by the Joint Chiefs of Staff on the basic assumption that war could be "forced upon the United States by an act of aggression of the USSR and/or her satellites, " on or about January 1, 1957, the date selected for planning purposes. The USAF would be built up to the level wanted to sustain a strategic air offensive, ward off attack on the Western Hemisphere, support allies (like NATO and CENTO) overseas, and begin a counteroffensive.

These war plans, however, were for big, relatively short, nuclear wars, but the future actually brought small, long,

*Anthony C. Brown, *Dropshot, the American Plan for World War III,* (New York: 1978) 3-6.

non-nuclear struggles. Skyrocketing costs of air weapons limited procurement, and thus the Air Force on January 1, 1950, had 48 groups with some 17,000 aircraft (8,000 combat), about half of which were Second World War types held in storage. Naval Air had 4,900 planes attached to the fleet, plus 1,900 in the Reserve and 550 in storage.

DOUGLAS B-26B in Korea, 1953
Two Pratt & Whitney R-2800-79, 2000 hp takeoff, 2350 hp WE
DIMENSIONS: Span 70', Lg. 50'9", Ht. 18'6", Wing Area 540 sq. ft.
WEIGHT: Empty 22,362 lb., Combat 31,775 lb., Gross 40,015 lb. Max. 41,811 lb. Fuel 1235+800 gal.
PERFORMANCE: Speed-Top 360 mph at s.l., 371 mph at 10,000', Cruising 230 mph, Stalling 113 mph. Combat Ceiling 21,800', Climb 2515/1 min. Range 966 miles/4000-lb. bombs, 3350 miles ferry.

DOUGLAS B-26C in 1951 (former A-26B-55-DL before rework)
Two Pratt & Whitney R-2800-79, 2000 hp takeoff, 2350 hp WE
DIMENSIONS: Span 70', Lg. 51'3", Ht. 18'6", Wing Area 540 sq. ft.
WEIGHT: Empty 22,690 lb., Combat 29,920 lb., Gross 37,740 lb. Fuel 1235+675 gal.
PERFORMANCE: Speed-Top 361 mph at s.l., 372 mph at 10,000', Cruising 226 mph, Stalling 109 mph. Combat Ceiling 23,100', Climb 2745/1 min. Range 892 miles/4000-lb. bombs, 3367 miles ferry.

Douglas Invader light bombers from 1948 to 1969

Concentrating on strategic bombing, not close support of ground forces, the USAF had built no light bombers after the war, and had even dropped the A designation for attack bombers in June 1948, changing the Douglas Invader from A-26 to B-26. Many were relegated to non-combat duties, like 152 A-26Cs that in 1945-1947 became the Navy's JD-l and JD-1D unarmed target-towing and drone-control planes, redesignated UB-26J and DB-26J in 1962.

Surplus Invaders left over after World War II appeared in many countries around the world involved in Cold War rivalries. The first of these exports resulted from the Truman Doctrine opposing Soviet pressure on Turkey, which inspired the transfer of 45 B-26s to the Turkish Air Force, beginning in March 1948.

The unexpected war begun in Korea on June 25, 1950, confronted America with the need for immediate support of ground troops. While the small North Korean air force was easily demolished soon after fighting began, stronger ground forces were not routed until September. North Korea was defeated in three months, but China entered the war in October, extending that war to a 37-month stalemate.

When war began, there were 1,054 B-26s in the USAF inventory. All were in reserve units or storage except for 26 B-26Bs in Japan with the 3rd Bombardment Wing (Light), and 46 RB-26C night reconnaissance aircraft serving with Tactical Reconnaissance wings (TRW).

The 3rd Bomb Wing flew the first American bombing mission into Korea on June 28, 1950, against a railway supplying enemy forces, and the following day, 18 B-26Bs struck North Korea with a successful attack on the principal enemy air base. That same unit dropped the last American bombs in Korea on July 27, 1953, and an RB-26C flew the last combat sortie of the Korean War the same evening. Other B-26 Wings in Korea were the 452nd reserve Wing in October 1950, replaced by the 17th Bomb Wing in 1952.

During that war, 60,096 B-26 and 11,944 RB-26 sorties were made, the majority at night, with 226 aircraft lost, including 56 to enemy action. In 1954, there were four B-26 and two RB-26 active wings in the USAF. They were replaced by B-57 and RB-66 jets by 1956.

Another war was going on at the same time in Vietnam, and the French asked to borrow Douglas Invaders, then the only bomber type available to form their first post-WW II bomber force. On January 1, 1951, GB 1/19 was formed with 17 B-26B and 8 B-26C bombers and was soon joined by four RB-26C Invaders of a reconnaissance unit. By July 1954, four groups had received 111 B-26s, but French defeat at Dien Bien Phu halted the fighting with a cease-fire signed July 21, and surviving planes were returned to the USAF in 1955.

French B-26s were also at war in Algeria where, from 1957 to 1962, they were being used by *escadrons* GB.1/91, 1/25 and ERP.1/32 (RB-26). Saudi Arabia's first combat planes were nine B-26Bs received in 1955, establishing an air force that would be helpful in 1991's desert war.

After the Korean War ended, American B-26s were supplied to various small air forces and used in several covert operations arranged by the Central Intelligence Agency (CIA). An excellent book by Hagedorn and Hellstrom* describes the operations in these countries in such detail that only a brief survey shall be made here.

Latin American deliveries began when Peru acquired eight B-26Cs in October 1954, followed by ten for Chile in

*Dan Hagedorn & Leif Hellstrom, *FOREIGN INVADERS* Midland, Leicester: 1994.

November, as well as allotments to Colombia and Brazil, and later replenishments for each of them. Guatemala got eight B-26s, its first bombers, in 1961.

Cuba became an Invader combat area when the Batista government used 16 B-26Cs received in November 1956 against Castro's rebels. After Castro won power, most remained for his FAR (Revolutionary Air Force). When the anti-Castro Cuban exiles prepared for the Bay of Pigs invasion attempt, the CIA took about 20 B-26s out of USAF storage for the exiles based in Nicaragua. Painted in false FAR markings, they launched the attack on April 15, 1961. B-26s fought on both sides, but Castro forces defeated the exiles by April 20, and seven surviving B-26s were left to the Nicaraguan air force.

Four USAF B-26Bs joined the "Farm Gate" detachment in Vietnam in December 1961 and two RB-26Cs were added in May 1962, along with about ten more B-26Bs by January 1963. They served the 1st Air Commando Squadron on attack missions until February 11, 1964, when all the B-26s were grounded because of inflight structural failures due to age.

There was still a demand for the Invader's services if a safe remanufacture could be arranged. On Mark Engineering, a firm experienced in modification of B-26s to custom executive transports, had started rebuilding a B-26C in October 1962 to become the YB-26K prototype. First flown January 28, 1963, it had completely rebuilt wings and fuselage, 2,500-hp water-injection Pratt & Whitney R-2800-103W engines with reversible propellers, permanent wingtip tanks, eight wing weapons pylons, and 14 fixed guns, but turrets were omitted.

ON MARK YB-26K prototype

Forty more conversions were ordered by the USAF in November 1963, the first B-26K flying May 26, 1964 with R-2800-52Ws. Similar to the YB model but for deletion of prop spinners and six wing guns, the B-26K was armed with eight .50-caliber nose guns and 4,000 pounds of bombs in the bay, or up to 8,000 pounds on the wing pylons. Besides the fixed-wing tip tanks, two 230-gallon drop tanks or a 675-gallon bomb bay tank could be carried.

Most of the remodeled aircraft completed by April 15, 1965, went to the 1st Air Commando Wing at Hurlburt Field, Florida. Five had been sent to the Congo, beginning in August 1964, to be flown by Cuban exile pilots against the so-called Simba rebels.

ON MARK B-26K (A-26A)
Two Pratt & Whitney R-2800-52W, 2500 hp takeoff, 1900 hp at 15,700'
DIMENSIONS: Span 71'6", Lg. 51'7", Ht. 19', Wing Area 541 sq. ft.
WEIGHT: Empty 25,130 lb., Combat 30,809 lb. Gross 38,311 lb., Max. 39,250 lb. Fuel 1230+1135 gal.
PERFORMANCE: Speed-Top 291 mph at s.l., 323 mph at 17,000', Cruising 169 mph, Stalling 111 mph. Service Ceiling 28,600', Combat Ceiling 24,400' Climb 2050'/1 min. Combat Radius 700 miles/3518-lb. bombs. Ferry Range 2700 miles.

In 1967, B-26K aircraft were redesignated A-26A, supposedly because bombers could not be stationed in Thailand at that time. The A-26As came to Thailand in June 1966 with the 609th Special Operations Squadron (originally the 606th Air Commando). Operating on night interdiction missions against trucks on the Ho Chi Minh Trail in Laos, the squadron made the last American combat sorties with the A-26A on November 9, 1969.

Nearly 25 years had passed since the first major A-26 combat mission. In between the major sorties into Germany and Laos had been many obscure actions in Indonesia, Angola, and Biafra. The Invader's long life was due to being the best of its generation of attack bombers, with no rivals in sight for more than a decade.

Air war over MiG Alley

Mao Zedong had asked Stalin for air cover when China entered the Korean War. His own PLAAF had established its first four combat regiments as a mixed brigade in June 1950 and began training enough personnel to organize 16 air divisions in only one year. In the meantime, three Soviet air divisions, with 62 MiG-15s each, arrived to cover Manchuria and the Yalu river area, beginning operations on November 1, 1950.

Chinese MiG-15 divisions joined steady Korean combat in September 1951, and like the Soviets, were rotated to give combat experience to many units. Four VVS and six PLAAF MiG divisions as well as two North Korean air divisions, faced American forces during the war's last months in 1953.

But for America, this was "the wrong war, at the wrong place, at the wrong time, and with the wrong enemy" so only a limited containment struggle continued. Most USAF missions continued to be for close support and interdiction, while the Korean war did make funds available for a new rearmament that increased the Air Force to 134 Wings (replacing the old group organization) with 24,949 aircraft by December 31, 1956. Along with expansion came an enormous increase in performance and firepower, fruits of vigorous development since 1945.

War in Korea did show that tactical air power, long neglected for strategic air power, had to be revitalized. After 1957, the number of aircraft declined, especially when ballistic missiles began replacing bombers, thus reducing the need for defensive fighters. An Air Force built for massive retaliation had to adapt itself to limited warfare. Table 8 details Air Force expansion in this period.

Table 8 • USAF Combat Wings 1951–1957

Type	10 July 1951	30 June 1952	30 June 1953	30 June 1954	30 June 1955	30 June 1956	30 June 1957
F-47N	2	2	—	—	—	—	—
F-51	10	8	2	—	—	—	—
F-80	6	2	2	—	—	—	—
F-82	1	—	—	—	—	—	—
F-84	9	11	14	9	12	11	5
F-86A,E,F	5	7	13	19	13	7	3
F-86D	—	—	3	13	19	20	15
F-86H	—	—	—	—	3	3	1
F-89	—	—	1	3	6	7	7
F-94	3	4	7	6	3	3	1
F-100	—	—	—	—	1	6	16
F-102	—	—	—	—	—	—	4
Fighter total	36	34	42	50	57	57	52
B-26	3	3	3	4	4	—	—
B-29	9	14	10	3	—	—	—
B-36	2	3	5	6	6	9[1]	5
B-45	1	1	1	1	1	1	1
B-47	—	1	4	13	21	27	28
B-50	4	5	5	2	—	—	—
B-52	—	—	—	—	—	1	3
B-57	—	—	—	—	1	4	4
B-66	—	—	—	—	—	—	1
Bomber total	19	27	28	29	53	42	42
Reconnaissance	8	9	10	12[2]	14[3]	11[4]	9[5]
Troop Carrier, etc.	24	25	26	24	17	21	20
Total Wings	87	95	106	115	121	131	123

1) Includes 3 RB-36 wings previously carried as reconnaissance wings.
2) 4 RB-47, 4 RB-36, 2 RB-26, and 2 RF-80s.
3) 5 RB-47, 4 RB 36, 2 RB-26, 2 RF-80, and 1 RF-84.
4) 5 RB-47, 1 RB-26, 1 RB 66, and 4 RF-84.
5) 5 RB-47, 2 RB-66, and 2 RF-84.

Naval Air Power growth in the Cold War

During the cold war period, Navy aviation's greatest constraint was the competition with the Air Force and Army for defense funds. The huge surface fleet inherited from World War II seemed sufficient for its time, and Air Force needs in the '50s had greater priority. Three *Midway*-class carriers could handle 133 planes each, and 97 planes were on each *Essex*–class CV.

Of 15 commissioned aircraft carriers when the Korean War began, only the *Valley Forge* was in the Far East. This deployment reflected the national strategy of facing Stalin's potential threat to Europe and to Middle East oil fields. That carrier's air group of two Corsair, two Panther, and one Skyraider squadron, plus special detachments, would be so important in defeating the first North Korean invasion, that expanding the Navy carrier force's power became a national priority.

Corsairs for the Korean War

Just as the B-26 represented World War USAF Two aircraft active in Korea, the Vought F4U Corsair's story also continued through that war. Since early jet types could not meet Navy close-support and night-fighter requirements, the World War Two propeller-driven fighter continued in production until 1952.

When the Korean War began, the Navy still relied mainly on propeller-driven aircraft, like the F4U-4, operating from World War II *Essex*-class carriers.

VOUGHT F4U-5

Pratt & Whitney R-2800-32W, 2300 hp at takeoff and 26,200'

DIMENSIONS: Span 41' (17' fld.), Lg. 34'6", Ht. 14'9" (16'4" fld.) Wing Area 314 sq. ft.

WEIGHT: Empty 9583 lb., Gross 12,902 lb., Max. 15,079 lb. Fuel 234+300 gal.

PERFORMANCE: Speed- Top 403 mph at s.l., 462 mph at 31,400', Cruising 190 mph, Stalling 91 mph. Service Ceiling 44,100', Climb 4230'/1 min., 10,000'/2.6 min. Range 1036 miles normal, 1532 miles max.

USN

USS Midway (CVB-41) was the first of the three largest carriers in the post-war Navy.

Post-war Corsair development began with two XF4U-5s converted from F4U-4s by installation of the two-stage R-1830-32W Wasp, and the first flew April 4, 1946. Production F4U-5s could be recognized by two cheek inlet ducts, and metal-covered control surfaces. Four 20-mm M-3 guns with 924 rounds were in the wings, a new centerline pylon could hold a 2,000-bomb or 150-gallon drop tank, two wing pylons could hold 1,000-bombs or drop tanks, and eight 5-inch rockets might be carried under the outer wings.

The first of 223 F5U-5s ordered July 19, 1946, was flown September 7, 1947, and deliveries were completed in September 1948. Water injection increased top speed from 424 to 462 mph, and the cockpit was rearranged for better pilot comfort. Carrier service began on the *Franklin D. Roosevelt.*

Most of the remaining Corsairs became night-fighters with APS-19 radar on the right wing. In May 1948, delivery began on 75 radar-equipped F4U-5N Corsairs and on 30 F4U-5Ps fitted with three cameras and four cannon. Production then shifted from Hartford, Connecticut, to Dallas, Texas, where deliveries on 240 more F4U-5N Corsairs began in May 1949 and were finished on October 22, 1951. The last 101 Corsair night fighters were delivered as winterized F4U-5NLs for the Korean War with deicer boots on the wings.

When the Korean War began, the Navy had 370 Corsairs in 20 fleet squadrons, and the Marines had 223 in ten squadrons. Navy units with F4U-5s included VF-13 & 14 at Jacksonville and VF-173/174 on the *Coral Sea,* while 14 other squadrons still used F4U-4s, as did eight reserve squadrons deployed on carriers during the war.

Mfr

VOUGHT AU-1

Pratt & Whitney R-2800-83W, 2300 hp takeoff, 2800 hp WE at s.l.

DIMENSIONS: Span 41' (17' fold.), Lg. 34'6", Ht. 14'10" (16'4" fold.) Wing Area 314 sq. ft.

WEIGHT: Empty 9835 lb., Combat 13,343 lb., Gross 18,979 lb., Max 19,398 lb. Fuel 234+300 gal.

PERFORMANCE at combat weight: Speed- Top 361 mph at s.l., 389 mph at 14,500', Cruising 184 mph, Combat Ceiling 28,800', Climb 4620'/1 min. Range 484 miles/4,600 lb. bombs, 1277 miles/10-5" VAR.

USN

VOUGHT F4U-5N
Pratt & Whitney R-2800-32W, 2300 hp at takeoff and 26,200'
DIMENSIONS: Span 41' (17' fold.), Lg. 34'6", Ht. 14'9" (16'4" fold.), Wing Area 314 sq. ft.
WEIGHT: Empty 9683 lb., Gross 12,901 lb., Max. 14,106 lb. Fuel 234+300 gal.
PERFORMANCE: Speed- Top 379 mph at s.l., 460 mph at 26,800', Cruising 227 mph. Service Ceiling 41,400', Climb 3780'/1 min. Range 1120 miles.

VOUGHT F4U-7 for France

F4U-5N night fighters of VC-3/4 usually operated from carriers in four-plane detachments, and the photo F4U-5Ps of VC-61/62 were scattered as needed.

Valley Forge F4U-4Bs from VF-53/54 began attacks on July 3, 1950, and two Marine squadrons arrived in August to provide close air support. An F4U-5N squadron, VMF(N)-513 performed interdiction missions, and Navy fighters of VC-3 came in June 1953 to interrupt enemy night intruders, when Lt. Guy Bordelon became the only Navy night fighter ace.

A new requirement for a close-support Corsair version was created by that war, and the XF4U-6, later designated XAU-l, was designed for that purpose. First flown December 19, 1951, it had a narrow cowl with the oil coolers moved back into the wing roots for protection. An R-2800-83W with a single-stage supercharger provided low-altitude power, and 378 pounds of armor was placed under the cockpit, fuel tank, and engine accessory compartment.

Fuel and 20-mm M-3 armament was the same as that of the F4U-5, but external racks could handle up to 4,600 pounds of bombs or ten rockets. Data on our table shows performance when loaded with two 1,000 and ten 250-pound bombs, and a 150-gallon drop tank! Marine squadrons received 111 AU-1s by October 10, 1952.

At the Korean War's end in 1953, there were three Marine attack squadrons and four Navy fighter squadrons using Corsairs. These squadrons retired their aircraft by 1955, but Corsairs remained with the Navy Reserves until 1957.

The final Corsair model was the F4U-7 built for the French Navy with R-2800-43W two-stage supercharged engines and a scoop on the cowl's bottom, like the F4U-4B, and the AU-1's armament. Ninety-four were built, the first flying July 2, 1952. They were used aboard the carrier *Lafayette* and joined in April 1954 by 25 second-hand AU-ls, which were used in Indochina. After France left

USS Bennington illustrates a modernized *Essex*-class carrier in 1957 with an AJ-2, AD-6, F2H-3 and FJ-4B Air Group.

Vietnam, French Corsairs served in the Mediterranean and Algeria until 1962, and were decommissioned in 1964.

When the last F4U-7 was accepted on January 31, 1953, production of the last propeller-driven fighter built in the United States was complete with a total of 12,571 Corsairs built. In length of time in production, the Corsair surpassed any propeller-driven fighter in America.

The Corsair's last service was in Latin America, beginning with the Argentine Navy's purchase of ten second-hand F4U-5NLs in 1956. Another 12 F4U-5 Corsairs were acquired in 1958 to fly from the ex-British light carrier *Independencia,* and served until 1965.

Honduras bought 10 F4U-4s in March 1956 and added ten more of various models in 1960, while neighboring Salvador got 19 FG-1Ds in 1957. During the so-called "Soccer War," these Corsairs fought each other and on July 17, 1969, a Honduran F4U-5 shot down a Salvadorian FG-1D. The Corsair's last fight was against another Corsair, and was probably the last kill claimed by a piston-engine fighter anywhere!

During the Korean war, the Navy was able to expand and modernize its air power. The major cost factor was modernizing the World War II carriers and replacing them with the giants of post-war design. Nine *Essex*-class carriers were provided with nuclear weapons facilities and new flight decks by the Project 27A conversions from 1950 to 1953. Another six were more completely modernized by Project 27C to add angled decks, steam catapults and other improvements in 1954/56. Eight conventionally powered super-carriers were commissioned, from the *Forrestal* in October 1955 to the *John F. Kennedy* in September 1968, and the first nuclear carrier, the *Enterprise,* joined the fleet in November 1961.

Navy aircraft also increased in performance and efficiency and their inventory during the Korean war rose from 14,036 (9,422 combat) on July 1, 1950, to 16,440 (8,884 combat) on July 1, 1955. That inventory would decline to 10,586 (5,420 combat) in 1964.

The U-2 story

Combat planes were also influenced by major developments of non-combat types. Tankers built for inflight refueling greatly extended the reach of the bomber, as told in the following chapters. And development of the U-2 high altitude reconnaissance plane changed the strategic bombing situation.

First of the super-carriers, the *USS Forrestal,* commissioned in July 1955, could handle the most advanced jet aircraft. CV-59 carried over three times the aircraft fuel of earlier types, and its broad decks and new equipment cut the accident rate in half. Overhead are an RF-8A and two F-8D Crusaders.

During World War II and the Korean War, modified bombers and long-range fighters did strategic reconnaissance. The idea of a type designed only for that mission did result in the Hughes XF-11 and Republic XF-12, but both ended in the prototype stage. Air Force leaders limited by post-war budgets rejected investment in aircraft types that were only able to take pictures, and not have any fighting potential. But the best of bombers cannot bomb until they know where their targets are.

President Dwight Eisenhower met with scientific advisors on March 27, 1954, about his concern that Soviet H-bomb and Myasishchev M-4 bomber development created the possibility of a surprise attack. Only actual overflight photography could assess the situation, but escaping interception would require flying over 70,000 feet. No aircraft then planned for the Air Force could do that.

Lockheed designer Kelly Johnson had offered the USAF a remarkable "super glider" design the previous year, but General LeMay rejected the frail project as unsuitable, and the Martin RB-57 was ordered instead. But other presidential advisors recognized the Lockheed's possibilities. Eisenhower insisted that the flights be made secretly, assigning the program to the CIA.

An FJ-4B Fury of VA-116 landing on the *Ranger,* January 16, 1959.

Mfr

LOCKHEED U-2C
Pratt & Whitney J75-P-13, 15,800 lb. st
DIMENSIONS: Span 80'2", Lg. 49'8", Ht. 15'2", Wing Area 565 sq. ft.
WEIGHT: Empty 13,870 lb. Gross 23,970 lb. Fuel 1320+200 gal.
PERFORMANCE: Speed- Cruising 450 mph. Ceiling over target, 73,000'. Range 2460-3900 miles.

Four different wing styles are seen on single-seat Navy in 1961: clockwise from the front, an FJ-4B, A4D-2, F8U-1 and F4D-l.

Lockheed received a secret CIA letter contract December 22, 1954, for 20 aircraft, and the order was increased to 49 by a January 1956 Air Force contract to provide a SAC squadron. The first example, designated U-2 to disguise its real role, made its first flight from the secret Groom Lake base on August 4, 1955, piloted by Tony LeVier.

Essentially, the U-2 was a single-seat long-range sailplane built as light as possible. The first were powered by a 10,200-pound thrust Pratt & Whitney J57-P-37, but those engines were replaced by the 13,000-pound thrust J57-P-31. Redesignated U-2B, the aircraft had another upgrade in 1959 with a J75-P-13 and newer cameras, resulting in the U-2C model.

Two F-8Es in *Bon Homme Richard's* elevator show the importance of aircraft size for aircraft designed for carriers.

The wide-winged U-2B lifted its special A-2 camera system up to 70,600 feet at the beginning of its cruise, rising to 73,100 feet as fuel was burned off. During tests a

74,500-foot ceiling was reached, and fuel was provided for ten hours flying. Because of the delicate construction, it was limited to Mach 0.8 (453 mph) at high altitudes and less than half that at low levels. Yet the U-2 had to stay quite close to those speeds to avoid stalling.

After a U-2B detachment in Germany flew three overflights of Eastern Europe beginning June 20, 1956, the first five overflights of the Soviet Union were made from the 4th to the 10th of July. Covering Leningrad, Moscow, and major bomber bases, they were detected, but MiG-17s were unable to fly high enough to intercept the U-2s.

By the time presidential authorization of overflights was suspended in December, it was proven that the M-4 threat had been greatly exaggerated. In August 1957, overflights resumed from Turkish and Pakistan bases to study intercontinental missile and nuclear test sights in Central Asia. Most U-2 missions, however. were peripheral ELINT flights and extensive Middle East observations.

There were 23 successful deep penetrations of the USSR before May 1, 1960, when Gary Powers' U-2C became the first downed by a SA-2 (surface-to-air missile). Afterwards, surveillance of the USSR became the responsibility of the **Corona** satellite program.

Chinese pilots usually made overflights of China from the Nationalist Air Force on Taiwan. Their borrowed U-2s made 102 overflights on routes usually selected by Americans, as well as 118 coastal missions, from January 13, 1962, to April, 1974, despite the loss of five U-2s to SA-2 missiles.

By the time John F. Kennedy became President in January 1961, early war plans had been replaced by the SIOP (Strategic Integrated Operating Plan) a continually updated force deployment program. This system required an accurate assessment of targets and hostile forces.

The 4080th Strategic Reconnaissance Wing operated Air Force U-2s on many missions over the Middle East, Asia, and Latin America, but the most important accomplishment was revealing the threat posed by the Cuban Missile Crisis in October 1962. Instead of the purported defensive systems, the secret Soviet buildup in Cuba included 60 ballistic missiles, accompanied by Il-28 jet bombers, 134 nuclear warheads, and 40,000 troops.

This unacceptable threat brought a catastrophic nuclear war closer than at any other time in history. The crisis ended with an agreement to remove offensive weapons from Cuba in exchange for a promise not to invade Cuba and to withdraw Jupiter missiles from Turkey.

Improved models of Lockheed's U-2 would continue to provide information on international situations for the rest of the century. As a non-combat type, its detailed history is not part of this book, but interested readers should see Norman Polmar's excellent study, *SPYPLANE,* (MBI Publishing: 2001).

The Cold War reached a climax in 1962 with the Cuban Missile crisis. Other air power events that year included the end of Boeing bomber production, and establishment of the aircraft designation system that would be used for the remainder of the century. This book's last section will complete the story of Cold War air power development.

Cold War Aircraft and Weapons development

From 1946 to 1962, combat planes evolved into the shape of contemporary aircraft, with gas turbine power plants, wings swept back for high speeds, and extensive electronics. These aircraft became much heavier and more expensive than their ancestors, consumed enormous amounts of fuel, but did have a much longer service life.

A new system of stating aircraft performance was required by the increase in fuel weight. Combat weight, after fuel has been consumed to reach combat area, was selected as the point of measurement. At that weight, combat ceiling is that at which a fighter can climb at a rate of 500 feet per minute, or a bomber at 200 feet per minute.

Wartime research indicated that propeller-driven aircraft could not be expected to achieve speeds much beyond 500 mph. When information was received in 1941 on the British Whittle jet engine, General Electric began developing this centrifugal-flow gas turbine into the J31 and J33 units . Meanwhile, Westinghouse in 1943 developed an axial-flow turbine, the J34. Axial-flow units are smaller in diameter, but longer than the centrifugal-flow types. Their development led in 1953 to the Pratt & Whitney J57 used in the B-52 and in the F-100, the world's first supersonic fighter. By 1973, the same company was producing the F-100 turbofan power plant for Air Force fighters.

When a long endurance was required, such as the Navy's patrol and early warning types, propellers retained their place, now powered by turbojet engines with the propeller driven from the turbine shaft. The Allison T56 used on the P-3 Orion is the most successful example of these turboprop engines.

Weapons

The most prominent weapons of the new generation were, of course, the atomic bombs. First tested at Alamogordo July 16, 1945, with a yield of 19 kilotons, was the "Fat Man," actually the 10,300-pound plutonium bomb used at Nagasaki.

The Mk III production version had so many faults that, after about 120 examples, it was replaced by the improved Mk 4 in 1949/50. A family of nuclear weapons developed in two directions; one to increase blast, and the other to provide smaller packages for smaller aircraft. Thus the first lightweight bomb, the 3,175-pound Mk 5, and the powerful 8,500-pound Mk 6 mass-produced for the heavy bombers. The basic Mk 6 shape evolved by 1954 into the 8,600-pound Mk 18, with 25 times the kiloton yield of the original "Fat Man."

The next step was a smaller bomb shaped to be carried beneath fighters, the 1,680-pound Mk 7 of 1952. Also produced as the W-7 warhead, it became a multi-purpose weapon usable on missiles and a variety of shapes that remained in service until 1967. To attack underground facilities, the Navy developed the 3,230-pound Mk 8 with delayed action detonation, instead of the airbursts of the earlier weapons. No longer were nuclear weapons a SAC monopoly, as the other forces demanded warheads to fit their needs.

Early nuclear weapons
Mk III The 10,300-pound production version of Nagasaki's "Fat Man."

Mk5 The first smaller-size shape, weighing 3,175 pounds, with the front opened for inflight setting.

Mk 6 Same size as Mk III, but more efficient and lighter.

Just as the first atomic explosion in 1945 had begun a new level of warfare, development of the "H-bomb" was a massive increase in the possibilities of mass destruction. A thermonuclear device yielding over ten megatons was exploded October 31, 1952, and led to tests of weaponized H-bombs by the U.S. in February 1954, and by the USSR on August 12, 1953. A Soviet Tu-95V Bear dropped a huge 20-ton bomb on October 30, 1961, that was estimated at 58-megatons, but more practical thermonuclear warheads were among thousands of weapons stockpiled in many shapes.

Mk 7 Shown below A-4A, this was the first A-bomb for fighters.

Mk 8 A 3,250-pound Navy weapon designed for penetration.

Thermonuclear weapons expanded the threat of mutual destruction and leaders on both sides of the cold war seriously questioned the path to a world war that would put civilization itself at risk. The Limited Nuclear Test Ban Treaty of 1963 was the first step to contain that threat.

Table 9 • Major Nuclear Air Weapons of 1945–1962

	Weight (lb)	Length	Diameter	Dates in Stockpile
Mk III:	10,300	10'8"	5'	1945-1950
Mk 4	10,800	10'8"	5'	1949-1953
Mk 5	3175	11'	3'8"	1952-1963
Mk 6	8500	10'8"	5'	1951-1962
Mk 7	1680	15'3"	2'6"	1952-1967
Mk 8	3250	9'8"	1'2"	1951-1957
Mk-12	1100	12'11"	1'10"	1954-1962
Mk 15	7600	11'7"	2'11"	1955-1965
Mk 17	41,400	24'8"	5'1"	1954-1957
Mk 27	3150	11'10"	2'6"	1957-1964
Mk 28	2040	14'2"	1'8"	1958-1984*
	1980	8'	"	(Internal version)
Mk 36	17,400	12'6"	4'10"	1956-1962
Mk 39	10,000	11'7"	4'7"	1957-1966.
Mk 43	2120	13'8"	2'8"	1961-1972

*Various models long active. All Table 9 data extracted from Chuck Hansen, *U.S. Nuclear Weapons: The Secret History.* Arlington: Aerofax, 1988.

AF

Mk 15. Two 7,600-pound weapons for a B52's bomb bay

Iron Bombs

Despite the growing stock of nuclear weapons, the need for conventional munitions continued. The most important development was the appearance of new low-drag shapes suitable for external pylons of high-speed jet aircraft. A weapons family with nominal (A) and actual (B) weights became standard.

	A	B
Mk 81	250	260 pounds
Mk 82	500	531 pounds
Mk 83	1000	985 pounds
Mk 84	2000	1970 pounds

New Fighter Weapons

Such weapons on bombers made it all the more necessary to arm fighters with weapons most likely to destroy the bomber on the first pass. Fifty-caliber guns were soon replaced by the fast-firing 20-mm M-39, and then the M-61 Vulcan became the standard weapon for the next generation. Six rotating barrels gave the Vulcan a rate of fire equal to four of the earlier weapons

Bulinski

Jet-propelled bombers just needed defense from the rear, so only tail guns were installed. APG-41 radar directed the fire of two 20-mm M-24A guns on early B-52B.

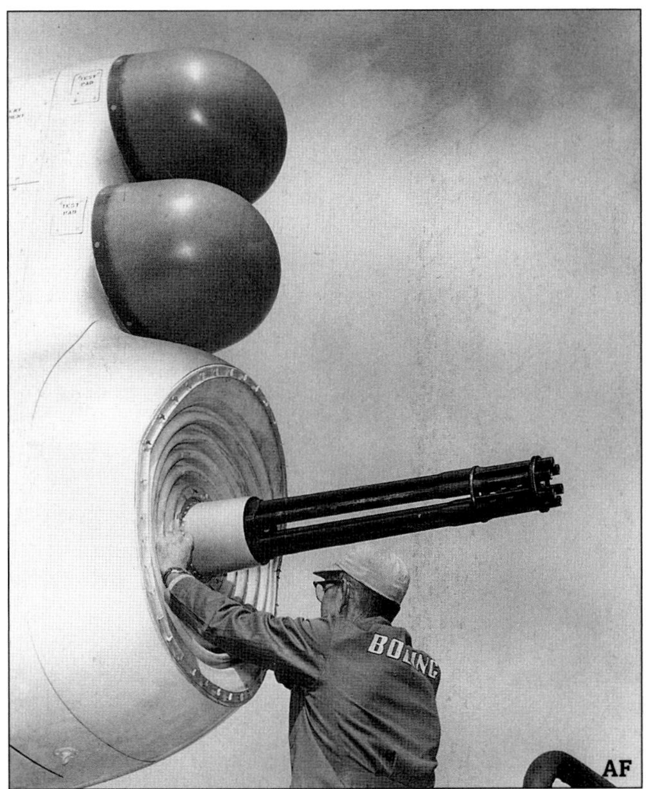

Six-barreled 20-mm M-61A Vulcan on B-52H had the firepower of four earlier guns.

Table 10 • American Aircraft Guns After 1945

Type	Length (inches)	Gun (lb.)	Weight of Bullet (ounces)	Muzzle Velocity (ft./sec)	Rate of Fire (rds/min)	Range (yards)
.50-cal. M-3	57.2	63	3.92	2840	1200	7400
20-mm M-39	72.3	179	8.96	3350	1500	4270
20-min M-61	73	265	8.96	3400	6000	4270

For bomber interception, the favored weapons soon became the air-to-air missile. Salvos of small unguided rockets used by jet fighters in the 1950's proved too inaccurate, so radar-directed Falcon and Sparrow missiles were developed.

The heat-seeking AIM-9 Sidewinder developed by the U.S. Navy has become the most widely used missile used against aircraft. The Sidewinder's first successful direct hit was on September 11, 1953, when future astronaut Wally Schirra fired a test shot from an AD-4 at a QB-17 drone. Sidewinders were first deployed with the F9F-8s of VA-46 in July 1956. Steady development of the AIM-9 would result in new models for each generation of fighters.

The first small ground attack missile was the Bullpup A deployed with VA-212 FJ-4Bs in April 1958. A 250-pound bomb with a solid-fuel rocket and radio control, it was replaced by the Bullpup B (AGM-12C) with a 1,000-pound warhead and liquid-fuel for a ten-mile range limited by visual guidance and adopted by the Air Force as AGM-12D.

Salvo of 2.75" rockets is fired from Convair F-102A in this picture sequence. Twenty-four rockets from 12 tubes in four missile bay doors are fired in less than half a second, leaving in 12 rapid pulses, two at a time.

Table 11
Air-to-Air Guided Missiles Deployed in 1956-1962

Popular Name	Maker	Former Designation	Current Designation	Approximate Weight	Long	Type
Falcon	Hughes	GAR-lD	AIM-4A	120 lb.	6.5'	homing
Falcon	Hughes	GAR-2A	AIM-4C	120 lb.	6.5'	infrared
Falcon	Hughes	GAR-3A	AIM-4E	150 lb.	7.2'	homing
Falcon	Hughes	GAR-4A	AIM-4F	145 lb.	6.7'	infrared
Falcon	Hughes	GAR-9	AIM-47A	800 lb.	12.5'	nuclear
Falcon	Hughes	GAR-l1	AIM-26A	203 lb.	8'	nuclear
Genie	Douglas	MB-l	AIR-2A	830 lb.	9.6'	nuclear
Sidewinder	Philco	GAR-8	AIM-9B	155 lb.	9.4'	infrared
Sparrow I	Sperry	AAM-N-2	AIM-7A	300 lb.	12.5'	beam
Sparrow III	Raytheon	AAM-N-6	AIM-7C	350 lb.	12'	homing
Sparrow III	Raytheon	AAM-N-6B	AIM-7E	400 lb.	12'	homing

Air-to-air Falcon missiles. From left to right, the Hughes AIM-26A (with a nuclear W54 warhead), radar-guided conventional AIM-4A, infrared AIM-4C and AIM-4F, and supersonic AIM-4E. Before 1962, they were known as the GAR-1l, GAR-1D, GAR-2A, GAR-4A, and GAR-3A.

By the 1960s, the warplane's electronic and weapons systems were far more sophisticated than the eyeball and brain-directed aircraft that began World War II, and the expense of these aircraft have risen accordingly. The high initial costs have been balanced by a long production and service life, as witnessed by the A-4, B-52, and F-4 series.

Bullpup missiles on a Navy FJ-4B on April 16, 1958.

A Bullpup missile is launched from an F-105 in an August 11, 1961, Air Force test.

An F-101A's retractable probe is inserted into the drogue from an F-84F-35 external tank.

Mfr

Air refueling an F-105D by Boeing's flying boom method gave USAF fighters a worldwide reach.

Designations

Most Air Force combat types after June 11, 1948, have had two designations: "F" for fighter, and "B" for Bomber, as in the F-86 and B-52. Reconnaissance versions are prefixed by "R" as in the RF-80 and RB-45C.

Navy combat aircraft are known as "A" for attack, "F" for fighter, "P" for patrol, and "S" for Search, since 1946. Official Standard Aircraft Characteristics charts are available for each aircraft in service since 1947, except for any types still classified at this writing.

A new joint Department of Defense designation system was established in 1962. Since then, fighters of both services are numbered in the same series. Although the system did not change most Air Force combat aircraft then in service, all Navy types did change. The manufacturer's letter was dropped in favor of block letters showing factory of origin. Thus the A3D-2 became the A-3B-DL. Other changes are shown in the appropriate chapters.

Department of Defense designations for combat aircraft since 1962.

A=	Attack types formerly	Name	B=	Bomber All retained former USAF numbers
A-1	AD	Skyraider		
A-2	AJ	Savage	E=	Early warning
A-3	A3D	Skywarrior	F=	Fighter (See Chapter 31)
A-4	A4D	Skyhawk	H=	Helicopter
A-5	A3J	Vigilante	O=	Observation
A-6	A2F	Intruder	P=	Patrol
A-7	——	Corsair II	S=	Search

CHAPTER 26

STRATEGIC AIR COMMAND'S FIRST BOMBERS

Strategic Air Command began in 1946 with a fleet of wartime B-29s and the first XB-36.

B-29s in the Cold War

Strategic Air Command (SAC) began on March 21, 1946, with the mission of conducting long range combat operations with the latest and most advanced weapons. After post-war reductions, six B-29 bomb groups (45 a/c each) remained for the Strategic Air Command, with only the 509th Group configured for nuclear bombs by the "Silverplate" program.

By October 1946, the US Joint Chiefs of Staff Intelligence Committee began drafting a plan for a first strike against the Soviet Union of 20 to 30 atomic bombs, and the 509th Group's B-29s would be the only means available to deliver the bombs for several years. But little was done to bring that group to combat proficiency until General Curtis E. LeMay became SAC commander in October 1948.

BOEING B-29-90-BW of 509th Bomb Wing

By April 1947, 46 Silverplate modifications had been completed, with another 180 nuclear-capable B-29s to be modified in 1947-1950 by the Saddletree program. In December 1947, there were 319 B-29s in SAC, including 35 Silverplate versions with the 509th. But many Boeings remained in storage and some tested post-delivery modifications.

The F-13 reconnaissance version was redesignated RB-29 in 1947 and fitted with new oblique cameras and ECM (electronic counter-measures) gear. A B-29-96-BW, the first fitted with ELINT (electronic intelligence) gear operated by six specialists in the rear compartment, began flights from Alaska to the Siberian seacoast in June 1947. Many more such "Ferret" missions would follow.

Early sets of engines were replaced with modernized R-3350-79 or -81s and cruise control experience improved range capabilities. Post-war performances were calculated on a different basis than before. Speed was measured with "combat weight"; defined as with the fuel load still remaining when the bomber was over the target area. In 1945, the B-29 was credited with a top speed of 358 mph at 25,000 feet with military power, or 361 mph with war emergency power. That was at 110,000 pounds, but in 1952 the B-29, with new engines and a 101,082-pound combat weight, could be credited with 399 mph at 30,000 feet.

BOEING B-29A-75-BN
Four Wright R-3350-57, 2320 hp takeoff, 2500 hp WE
DIMENSIONS: Span 142'3", Lg. 99', Ht. 27'9", Wing Area 1739 sq. ft.
WEIGHT: Empty 72,208 1b., Gross 140,000 1b. Fuel 7748-9150 gal.
PERFORMANCE: (at 101,480 lb. combat weight) Speed- Top 399 mph at 30,000', Cruising 253 mph, Stalling 119 mph. Service Ceiling 23,950' with full load, Combat Ceiling 36,150', Climb 1620'/1 min. Combat Radius 1930 miles, ferry range 5418 miles. Data for 1952 configuration.

Other configurations, like 16 SB-29 rescue versions with a lifeboat, and the WB-29 weather version were converted from standard planes from 1946 to 1952. Four B-29-95-BWs given to the Navy in April 1947 were redesignated P2B-1s for special tests, and an EB-29B lifted the Bell X-1 for the first supersonic flight on October 14, 1947.

Strategic Air Command needed inflight refueling to extend bomber range. Otherwise, attaining the built-in 10,000-mile range with 10,000-pound bomb load of the 1941 specification for the B-36, required too large and slow an aircraft for a high-speed era. This would be especially true for the high fuel consumption of jet propelled aircraft.

An Air Refueling Squadron was formed for each B-29 group to extend range. The first was activated in June 1948 as 92 KB-29M tankers were converted at Wichita to the British method with trailing hoses. Another 72 B-29MR receivers were provided with receptacles and a fuel tank in the rear bomb bay. Boeing's own flying boom system, however, was a faster and more practical method, and began SAC service in September 1950 with the first of 116 KB-29P tankers converted at Renton. Both SAC B-50 bombers and F-84 fighters could be refueled in flight,

By January 1, 1949, the stockpile of 56 Mark III bombs could be carried by the 124 of 486 active SAC's B-29s that had been modified for nuclear weapons, and the new B-36 and B-50 aircraft were entering squadron service. Preparations for an air offensive across the Arctic Ocean had been made by RB-29 and WB-29 reconnaissance units, and close flights around Soviet borders were made for photographic and electronic intelligence.

SDAM

BOEING RB-29-100-BW
With drift sight under the nose and camera windows in rear compartment.

Stalin's air defense capabilities were still weak, according to USAF Chief of Staff General Hoyt Vandenberg. But a WB-29 flying east of Kamchata brought back proof of the first Soviet A-bomb test on August 29, 1949, and a modern radar and jet fighter defense was rapidly being built in the Soviet Union.

When the Korean War began in June 1950, the USAF inventory included 1,787 B-29 bomber and 162 RB-29 recon aircraft in storage or service with eight Bomb Groups and one Strategic Reconnaissance Group. Five groups were transferred to the Far East Air Forces and the 19th BG began flying combat missions from Okinawa on June 28, 1950. The 22nd and 92nd Groups joined in July, followed by the 98th and 307th in August.

Although interdiction and tactical support accounted for most missions, these five groups had accomplished the destruction of all scheduled strategic targets in Korea by September 15. While the 22nd and 92nd were returned to SAC, the others and the 91st Strategic Reconnaissance Squadron were retained to attack enemy supply lines and troop concentrations. Bridges were also the most likely targets of 489 1,000-pound Razon and 30 12,000-pound Tarzon guided bombs. After MiG-15 interceptions on daylight missions in October 1951 became too costly, B-29s often changed to night bombing.

During the war, 21,328 effective combat sorties were flown, 167,100 tons of bombs dropped, and 20 B-29s lost to enemy action. SAC's newer bombers and nuclear capable planes were not used because the main force was held back in case a major war with Stalin actually began, although nine B-29s with Mk 4 weapons were positioned at Guam. (A 10th plane, carrying another Mk 4 and General Robert Travis had crashed on takeoff on August 5, 1950) Two RB-29s on intelligence missions, however, were shot down north of Japan in 1952.

SDAM

BOEING RB-29A-70-BN for electronic intelligence.

Although 417 B-29s served 14 bomber groups in December 1952, and 179 KB-29s served ten refueling squadrons, the bombers were replaced with B-47s by 1954, and the tankers with KC-97s by 1957. The last USAF Superfortress in bomber service was a B-29A retired from the 307th Bomb Wing on November 4, 1954, but several were used by a Radar Evaluation squadron until June 1960. Built for World War II, the B-29s had played a leading role in the opening years of the Cold War.

B-29s in Foreign Service

American strategic bombing power was obvious to the Soviet Union, which had built only 91 four-engine bombers during the World War II, compared to 35,654 four-engine bombers for the AAF. The nuclear weapons program being pushed in Russia would have little impact without a means of long-range delivery.

On July 7, 1944, the second B-29-5-BW (42-6256) had made a forced landing at Vladivostok, after a raid into Manchuria. A B-29A-1-BN crashed in Siberia in August and in November two B-29-15-BWs also reached Vladivostok. The aircraft and their crews were interned according to neutrality rules, but the airmen were allowed to "escape" to Iran on January 30, 1945, while their planes were being examined and tested by the VVS.

Soviet test flights on the B-29-5 begun January 9,1945, demonstrated the potential value this strategic bomber offered, and by June 22, Stalin demanded that Russia's leading designer of larger planes, Andrei Tupolev, reproduce the B-29 at the Kazan bomber factory. He wanted this

BOEING KB-29P refueling F-84F

done in two years, so a tried bomber could be in service without waiting for the lengthy development of Tupolev's own heavy bomber design. The same philosophy of using foreign technology to hasten production was also applied to the first Soviet nuclear weapon and to jet engines.

The B-29A was also sent to Moscow, and completely stripped down in a remarkable effort at reverse engineering. Changing inches to millimeters for all the metal pieces and wires was only part of the difficulty in duplicating such a sophisticated aircraft and all of its complicated electronics. Tupolev's deputy project engineer, Dimitri Markov, had been in charge of the Vultee V-11 work in 1938, and had joined Tupolev in prison during the great purge.

A new fuselage was built on to the restored B-29A parts, which became the Tu-70 transport flown on November 27, 1946. The first bomber replica built at Kazan was called the Tu-4 and first flew on May 19, 1947. Production proceeded with gradual improvements, like the use of 20 and 23-mm guns. When the Kazan factory shifted to Tu-16 jet bombers in 1952, 847 Tu-4s had been built. This program provided an interim strategic bomber without expensive development costs, so that Russian efforts could be concentrated on advanced jet types.

The Royal Air Force could be more direct, by borrowing 87 B-29s, beginning in March 1950. Called the Boeing Washington, they served Bomber Command until the jet-powered V-bombers became available by 1955. China joined the Superfortress club when 30 Tu-4s were received in 1953 to form the only PLAAF long-range bombing regiment.

Northrop's Flying Wing

Strategic Air Command (SAC) inherited a trio of bomber projects developed during World War II period. A radical Northrop flying wing, a six-engine Consolidated giant, and a more conventional Boeing all took advantage of the 3,000-hp Pratt & Whitney R-4360 Wasp Major.

NORTHROP XB-35
Four Pratt & Whitney R-4360-17/21, 3000 hp takeoff and 35,000'
DIMENSIONS: Span 172', Lg. 53'1" Ht. 20'1", Wing Area 4000 sq. ft.
WEIGHT: Empty 89,560 lb., Gross 162,000 lb. Max. 209,000 lb. Fuel 5000 gal.
PERFORMANCE: (estimated) Speed- Top 391 mph at 35.000', Cruising 183 mph, Service Ceiling 39,700', Climb 35,000'/ 5.7 min. Range 7500 miles max., 720 miles/51,070-lb.

The most unconventional bomber of this era was the XB-35 flying wing, designed by John K. Northrop. His light

NORTHROP YB-35

wooden experimental twin-engine N-1M, first flown in July 1940, had demonstrated the possibilities of aircraft carrying all loads and controls within the wing and dispensing with fuselage and tail sections. The larger the aircraft, the greater the savings in weight and drag reduction, so an Air Force request on April ll, 1941, for bomber designs that could carry a 10,000-pound load halfway across a 10,000-mile range gave Northrop a chance for a bold step.

Encouraged by Air Force leaders, his company proposed a four-engine flying wing bomber, design NS-9E, and procurement was endorsed in a September 9 conference with General Oliver P. Echols, AMD Chief. A contract for a 1/3-scale flying model (N-9M) was approved October 3, 1941, to test the configuration's characteristics before XB-35 construction actually began. The prototype contract approved November 22, 1941, ordered an XB-35 to be delivered in two years. A second XB-35 prototype added to that contract on January 2, 1942, was expected to be delivered in April 1944.

Engineers of Northrop's small new factory at Hawthorne, California, began 1942 with three quite radical projects: the single-engine XP-56 interceptor, the twin-engine XP-61 night fighter, and the four-engine XB-35. Although Northrop would not guarantee any performance levels before the small-scale model was flight tested, the AAF was confident enough to order 13 YB-35 service-test aircraft on December 17, 1942.

The first N-9M flew on December 27, 1942, powered by two Menasco engines. Although it crashed on its 45th flight, three more were built, resuming the flight program on June 24, 1943. Optimism about the early results led to a June 30, 1943, contract to have Martin engineer and build 200 B-35Bs at the Omaha plant, but this was canceled May 26, 1944, when it was realized that the flying wing could not be ready in time for that war. Despite many technical delays, the radical design's potential continued to spark Air Force interest.

The XB-35 was first flown by Max R. Stanley from Hawthorne to Muroc on June 25, 1946, 55 months after the contract was approved. The power plant consisted of Pratt & Whitney Wasp Majors (two R-4360-17s outboard and two R-4360-21s inboard) with double turbosuperchargers and extended drive shafts for co-axial counterrotating Hamilton four-bladed pusher propellers. These dual propellers proved unsatisfactory, and after 3 flights, the XB-35 was grounded until March 1947.

The second XB-35 began test flights on June 26, 1947, but after only 11 flights by the first prototype and four by the second, the big Northrops were grounded in August 1947 to replace the dual-rotation system with Curtiss single-rotation propellers. Seven more flights were made by the first XB-35 from February 12 to April 1, 1948, but it wasn't flown again until its return to the factory on October 7 for scrapping after less than 24 flight hours.

Single-rotation propellers were also fitted to the second XB-35 and to the first YB-35 flown May 12, 1948, which was the only flying wing actually fitted with gun turrets. The crew consisted of nine men in the pressurized center section (two pilots, with a bombardier, engineer, navigator, radioman, and three gunners), plus accommodations for six relief men. Northrop's control system was the first fully-powered hydraulic system on an American airplane, and the NACA 65 wing section was thick enough (seven feet at the apex) to enclose the retracted double-wheel landing gear and all of the equipment.

The eight bomb bays held from 10,498 to 51,200 (thirty-two 1,600-pound) pounds of bombs, but none of those bays was large enough for an atomic bomb. Twenty .50-caliber M-2 guns were in seven remote-controlled turrets aimed from central sighting stations behind the pilot, on top and beneath a cone protruding from the trailing edge. Four-gun turrets were spotted above and below the center section, two-gun turrets were visible outboard of the engines, one pair on top, another below, and four guns could be placed in the tail cone.

All test flights had been made from Muroc, now Edwards Air Force Base, by company pilots, and the pretest performance estimates were not verified. Jet propulsion had rendered the original concept obsolete, but interest in the flying-wing principle with jet propulsion continued. To save enough funds for that YB-49 program, both XB-35s and the YB-35 were scrapped in August 1949.

Boeing B-50

Development of the Pratt & Whitney R-4360 Wasp Major gave Boeing an opportunity to improve their own bomber, and these 3,000-hp radials were installed on a B-29A; which became the XB-44. Ordered in July 1944, the XB-44 began tests in May 1945 with redesigned engine nacelles.

This became the prototype for the next Boeing series, originally designated B-29D when first 200 were ordered in July 1945, but renamed B-50 in December 1945, when the order was cut to 60. The new designation emphasized that this was a B-29 replacement, not a mere modification, and had a 75% new structure, including a stronger grade of aluminum. First flown June 25, 1947, by A. Elliott Merrill, the B-50A-1 had 3,500-hp R-4360-35s, a crew of 11 and could be distinguished from B-29s by their engine nacelles and tall tail, which folded for hangar storage. Armament was similar to late B-29A models, with thirteen .50-caliber guns and a double bay for 20,000 pounds of bombs, or a Mk III nuclear bomb in the forward bay.

BOEING XB-44
Four Pratt & Whitney R-4360-33, 3000 hp takeoff, 2500 hp at 25,000'
DIMENSIONS: Span 142'3", Lg. 99', Ht. 27'9", Wing Area 1728 sq. ft.
WEIGHT: Empty 75,035 1b., Gross 105,000 1b.
PERFORMANCE: Speed- Top 392 mph at 25,400', Cruising 282 mph. Range 2400 miles.

Before entering service with SAC's 43rd Bomb Wing on February 20, 1948, they had to be modified with winterization provisions for arctic operations, and to handle new Mk 4 nuclear weapons. Of 79 B-50As, 57 were fitted for air refueling from the KB-29M hose system. This was demonstrated when the B-50A-5 "Lucky Lady II", made the first nonstop flight around the world, 23,452 miles, arriving back at Carswell AFB, Texas, on March 2, 1949, after 94 hours and refueling from eight KB-29M tanker planes.

On January 18, 1949, the last B-50A was followed by the first of 45 B-50Bs with two 700-gallon fuel tanks under strengthened wings, and the hose refueling system. All but the first B-50B were modified with nine cameras to become ten-place RB-50Bs and issued to a strategic reconnaissance group. Fourteen were reconfigured as RB-50E at the Wichita factory and redelivered, beginning in May 1950, followed by 14 RB-50F rebuilds with Shoran radar.

Mfr

BOEING B-50D
Four Pratt & Whitney R-4360-35, 3500 hp takeoff
DIMENSIONS: Span 141'3", Lg. 99', Ht. 32'8", Wing Area 1720 sq. ft.
WEIGHT: Empty 80,609 lb., Combat 121,850 lb., Gross 173,000 lb. Fuel 11,685 gal.
PERFORMANCE: Speed- Top 395 mph at 30,000', Cruising 244 mph, Stalling 137 mph. Combat Ceiling 35,650', Service Ceiling 36,900', Climb 2200'/1 min. Combat Radius 2398 miles/10,000-lb., Max. range 5762 miles.

PMB

BOEING B-50A
Four Pratt & Whitney R-4360-35, 3500 hp
DIMENSIONS: Span 141'3", Lg. 99', Ht. 32'8", Wing Area 1720 sq. ft.
WEIGHT: Empty 81,050 lb., Combat 120,500 lb., Gross 168,000 lb. Fuel 10,772 gal.
PERFORMANCE: Speed- Top 391 mph at 30,000', Cruising 244 mph, Stalling 136 mph. Combat Ceiling 36,000', Service Ceiling 37,300'. Climb 2260'/1 min. Combat Radius 2190 miles, Max. range 5230 miles.

Mfr

BOEING B-54A (project)

Electronic reconnaissance was the mission of 15 16-place RB-50G conversions delivered from June to October 1951.

A YB-50C was proposed with Pratt & Whitney R-4360-51 compound VDT engines, but this change required complete airframe redesign. Forty-three were ordered in May 1948 as the Boeing B-54A, but on April 5, 1949, they were canceled in favor of the B-36D.

The B-50D introduced a modified plastic nose cone, more fuel space including two underwing drop tanks, and APQ-24 bombing radar. Between May 1949 and December 1950, 222 B-50Ds were delivered, and beginning with 16th B-50D, receptacles were installed for the boom air refueling system on the KB-29P. They could accommodate the 10,800-pound Mk 4 nuclear bomb that replaced the Mk III by 1950

Production was completed with 24 unarmed TB-50Hs built by February 1953 built to train future B-47 jet crews to use the K-system of radar navigation and bombing. As the B-50s retired from their five SAC bomber wings in 1953/55, they were recycled as TB-50D trainers, WB-50D weather reconnaissance types, and KB-50J and KB-50K tanker aircraft. These supported the B-47 jets that had replaced the older types.

The Intercontinental Bomber

The B-36, which became the most controversial American combat type since the DH-4, began its career before the attack on Pearl Harbor. The world's largest bomber owed its size to the desire to achieve intercontinental range, for in 1941 the United States faced the possibility that Nazi Germany would control all of Europe, and that only bases in America would be available for strikes at enemy strategic targets.

A design competition for a heavy bomber was opened on April 11, 1941. That specification was refined in August to include a 10,000-pound load carried halfway across a 10,000-mile range, and Consolidated Aircraft submitted designs dated September 19. A proposal with six pusher engines seemed superior to Boeing and Douglas offerings, and a contract approved November 15, 1941, ordered two XB-36 prototypes to be delivered about May 15 and November 15, 1944.

CONVAIR XB-36
Six Pratt & Whitney R-4360-25, 3000 hp takeoff
DIMENSIONS: Span 230', Lg. 163', Ht. 46'10", Wing Area 4772 sq. ft.
WEIGHT: Empty 133,370 lb. Design Gross 265,512 lb., Max. 278,000 lb. Fuel 18,881 gal normal, 21,116 gal. max.
PERFORMANCE: Speed- Top 323 mph at 30,000', Cruising 225 mph. Service Ceiling 38,200'. Max. range 9360 miles/ 10,000-lb. bombs.

The project was moved from San Diego to Fort Worth, Texas, in August 1942, but progress was slow due to the company's concentration on B-24 production and B-32 development. General Arnold saw that the B-36 might be needed for attacking Japan if bases near enough for the B-29 strikes were not secured. The company's president complained that it was difficult to get subcontractors for a two-plane order; but they would be interested if large-scale production was promised. A letter of intent for 100 B-36 bombers was issued July 23, 1943, at which time company officials planned to fly the XB-36 in September 1944 and begin production deliveries in March 1945, with 29 expected by the end of August.

Engineering changes like the shift from twin tails to a stronger single fin in October 1943, the change to the NACA 63 airfoil, and the complexity of the huge aircraft caused more delay. By the time a firm contract was approved on August 19, 1944, expecting delivery for 100 B-36s to begin in August 1945, capture of the Marianas Islands, from which B-29s could bomb Japan, had made the B-36 unnecessary for that war. Again the B-36 program was neglected in favor of the B-32.

Defensive armament designed for the XB-36 included four remote-controlled retractable turrets and a radar-directed tail turret. Each upper and lower forward turret had two 37-mm guns and each upper and lower rear turret had four .50-caliber guns, like those planned for the XB-32. The tail turret, like the B-29, would have one 37-mm and two .50-caliber guns.

This system was replaced in production aircraft by a new arrangement planned in 1944. The most formidable armament of any warplane would have sixteen 20-mm guns, with 9,200 rounds, paired in eight General Electric remote-controlled turrets. Computing sights at blisters in the nose and six side spots aimed the front turret and six retractable turrets which disappeared under sliding panels, while APG-3 radar aimed the tail guns.

A new pilot's canopy, raised over the redesigned flight deck was chosen in October 1944 for the second prototype, which was designated YB-36. The prototype's single 110-inch wheels on each side required runways twice as thick as usual, so only Fort Worth and two other fields could handle the test aircraft. Production models would spread the weight over four 56-inch wheels on each side, along with the dual nose wheels, so the B-36 could use most B-29 bases.

A major problem was the loss of speed due to added weight and engine problems. Guaranteed top speed in April 1944 of 369 mph at 30,000 feet was reduced to 347 mph in July 1945 and to 323 mph in the July 1946 estimate. But the lifting power of six 3,000-hp R-4360-25 radials and the enormous bays were undeniable: 72 1,000-pound bombs could be carried half-way for 4,600 miles, or 20 500-pound bombs for 9,360 miles.

Japan's surrender, and the new importance the atomic bomb gave strategic bombing, once again revived the giant bomber program. An air staff conference on August 9, 1945, recommended that four B-36 groups be included in the postwar Air Force.

Delayed by manpower shortages, and late engine delivery, the XB-36 made its first flight nearly five years after it had been ordered, instead of the 30 months originally planned. Beryl A. Erickson and G. S. Green piloted the takeoff on August 8, 1946, of the heaviest, 100 tons, and largest plane ever to fly up to that time.

A new canopy, raised over the flight deck, and the four-wheel main landing gear was installed on the first aircraft from the production line, which was designated YB-36A and first flew on August 28, 1947, in unfinished condition. It was flown from Fort Worth to Wright Field two days later to be stripped and demolished in static tests.

The second prototype, the YB-36, had the new nose, but retained the large single main wheels. Delayed by the installation of equipment, it flew on December 4, 1947, and

Mfr

CONVAIR B-36B
Six Pratt & Whitney R-4360-41, 3500 hp at 40,000'
DIMENSIONS: As B-36A
WEIGHT: Empty 140,640 lb., Combat 227,700 lb., Gross 328,000 lb. Fuel 26,217 gal.
PERFORMANCE: Speed- Top 354 mph at 25,000', 381 mph at 34,500', Cruising 203 mph, Stalling 115 mph. Combat Ceiling 38,800', Service Ceiling 42,500'. Combat Radius 4300 miles/10,000-lb., Ferry Range 8174 miles.

better dual superchargers immediately improved high altitude performance. Yet the bomber's large size and slow speed raised doubts of its ability to survive in enemy air space.

Doubts about the B-36s were shared by the first SAC commander, General George C. Kenney, who in December 1946 had suggested cancellation of B-36 production in favor of the faster and smaller B-50. In that case, strategic bombing would require advanced bases or aerial refueling. Increased B-36 over-the-target speed was needed, so in March 1947 Convair proposed the installation of Pratt & Whitney's proposed experimental VDT engines with tractor propellers.

That project, designated B-36C, was approved December 4, 1947, and the last 34 bombers on order were to get the VDT engines. Top speed might be increased to 410 mph, and increased costs were met by reduction of the total program from 100 to 95 planes. Those engines, however, did not reach anticipated levels of development, so the B-36C was abandoned on May 21, 1948.

Production was underway with 21 B-36As delivered to the Air Force from May to September 1948 and first used for testing. On June 26, the 7th Bomb Group got their first B-36A. The 8,000-foot takeoff run was accommodated by the runway at Carswell AFB, Texas, adjoining the Fort Worth factory. Training began preparing the crews for 35-hour high-altitude missions and use of special equipment like the APQ-23 radar protruding behind the nose wheels.

Mfr

CONVAIR B-36A
Six Pratt & Whitney R-4360-25, 3000 hp at 40,000'
DIMENSIONS: Span 230', Lg. 162'2", Ht. 46'10", Wing Area 4772 sq. ft.
WEIGHT: Empty 135,020 lb., Combat 212,800 lb., Gross 310,380 lb. Fuel 21,010+5675 gal.
PERFORMANCE: Speed- Top 345 mph at 31,600', Cruising 218 mph, Stalling 113 mph. Combat Ceiling 35,800', Service Ceiling 43,000'. Climb 20,000'/53 min. Combat Radius 3880 miles/10,000-lb., 2170 miles/72,000-lb. Ferry range 9136 miles.

The 15-man crew was contained in two pressurized compartments: two pilots, bombardier, navigator, flight engineer, two radar & radiomen, and three gunners forward were separated from five gunners in the rear compartment by four 16-foot long bomb bays. Four rest bunks were provided for relief, and personnel shifted between compartments by rolling on a little dolly in a tunnel through the bomb cells.

The first newsworthy major flights were those demonstrating the long range. Combat radius (3/8 of range) was 3,880 miles with a 10,000-pound bomb load, or 2,100 miles with 72,000 pounds. The bomb bay was not originally configured to handle nuclear weapons, and no armament had been installed in the B-36As.

That lack of combat capability was not mentioned in Air Force publicity, for the B-36 was hoped to be seen as a deterrent to Stalin's policies. But on June 18, 1948, all traffic into Berlin was stopped by the Soviet blockade, and June 25 the Air Force decided to go ahead with all 95 B-36s in the original contract.

The first armed model was the B-36B, first flown July 8, 1948, and delivered November 25. Sixty-two were delivered by September 1950. Power plants were the 3,500-hp R-4360-41 Wasp Majors with fuel injection, and APQ-24 bomb-navigation radar was provided, while bomb bays could handle two 43,000-pound "Grand Slam" conventional bombs if needed. Those bays was large enough to handle the 10,800-pound Mk 4 nuclear bomb, which was replacing the Mk III nuclear weapons. Combat radius with a 10,000-pound bomb load was up to 4,300 statute miles, and total mission time was 42.43 hours.

Sixteen 20-mm M-24A-1 guns paired in eight turrets were provided with 600 rounds each, except for the nose turret's 400 rpg. Unfortunately the fire control system was not ready for dependable service. Although B-36B guns were first fired on April 12, 1949, B-36 full operational capability was not achieved before 1952.

But if the B-36s were to be a believable strategic deterrent, more speed and altitude was still needed to improve survival over enemy territory. On October 5, 1948, Convair proposed adding a pair of turbojet engines under each wing, using the General Electric engines and the nacelles or "pods" already available on the Boeing B-47.

Conversion of a B-36B was authorized January 4, 1949, the modified aircraft flew with J35 jets on March 26, and on July 11, tests began with J47 jets. The improved performance led the Air Force to contract for more bombers on November 2 as B-36Ds and to plan future modifications of all B-36A and B-36B models to jet pod configuration. The jets shortened takeoff runs and gave short bursts of speed over the target at a moderate cost of range. Money for the program was obtained by canceling contracts for smaller planes, including the RB-49 flying wing.

As a strategic deterrent, the B-36 could threaten any industrial center in the world with nuclear attack. The key to any estimate of the big bomber's value was its ability to escape destruction by hostile fighters. Supporters of the B-36 argued that current jet fighters could not climb to high altitudes in time to intercept the bomber. Once in position, the fighter's limited speed advantage might permit only slow tail cone passes in the face of heavy defensive gunfire.

Others challenged the B-36's ability to penetrate an effective defense system. Critics insisted that radar would detect the big ship soon after it began its approach, and that the latest jet fighters could indeed reach high altitudes quickly enough to stop it.

On May Day (May 1) in 1949 the Russians first displayed formations of the MiG-15 jet interceptor. MiG-15 fighter production amounted to 729 in 1949, 1,111 in 1950, and 9,698 from Russian factories by 1952, when the MiG-17 began replacing that model.

American tests in 1953 demonstrated a climb in 6.4 minutes to 40,000 feet, where top speed was 620 mph, and a 51,000-foot service ceiling. The MiG-15 capabilities would make daylight flying over Russia dangerous for hostile bombers. Its heavy guns may have been less of a threat than the propensity of zealous Soviet pilots to ram enemy aircraft.

Official controversy suddenly exploded into the open with a congressional investigation of charges that political favoritism had influenced procurement of a costly sitting duck. Secretary of Defense Louis A. Johnson (a former Convair director) was blamed. More serious were the technical issues raised by the Navy, which resented Johnson's cancellation, on April 23, 1949, of the supercarrier ordered by his predecessor, James V. Forrestal. That ship had been seen as a way of giving the Navy a strategic bombing capability, but the Air Force leaders insisted that strategic bombing was an Air Force function. Available defense budget funds could provide new strategic bombers or a new carrier force, but not both.

The B-36 was expensive, for the prototypes had cost $39 million, and the first 95 $6,248,686 each. Average price would drop below four million as production flowed. Investigations held in August and October 1949, however, found the Air Force defending its bomber's capabilities against both political and Navy critics. Despite the so-called "Revolt of the Admirals," the B-36 program survived that investigation. War in Korea would make funds available for both strategic bombers and big carriers. When that war began, SAC had two Wings, the 7th and 11th with B-36Bs, but the 28th Strategic Reconnaissance Wing had received its first jet- boosted RB-36D on June 3, 1950.

CONVAIR B-36D

Six Pratt & Whitney R-4360-41, 3500 hp at 40,000' & four J47-GE-19, 5200 lb. st.

DIMENSIONS: Span 230', Lg. 162'2", Ht. 46'10", Wing Area 4772 sq. ft.
WEIGHT: Empty 161,371 lb, Combat 250,300 lb., Gross 370,000 lb. Fuel 26,995-30,716 gal.
PERFORMANCE: Speed- Top 406 mph at 32,200', Cruising 222 mph, Stalling 123 mph. Combat Ceiling 40,700', Service Ceiling 43,800'. Combat Radius 3530 miles/10,000-lb., 1300/86,000-lb. Ferry Range 8800 miles.

Penetration capabilities of the B-36D were increased by the added boost of J47 jet pods, but the 444 mph esti-

Bodie

CONVAIR RB-36E

Six Pratt & Whitney R-4360-41, 3500 hp at 40,000' & four J47-GE-19, 5200 lb. st.

DIMENSIONS: Span 230', Lg. 162'2", Ht. 46'10", Wing Area 4772 sq. ft.

WEIGHT: Empty 164,238 lb, Combat 238,300 lb., Gross 370,000 lb. Fuel 28,806-33,060 gal.

PERFORMANCE: Speed- Top 401 mph at 36,500', Cruising 219 mph, Stalling 123 mph. Combat Ceiling 40,000', Combat Radius 3520 miles / 10,000-lb.

mated earlier by the company became 406 mph. Yet the real measure of B-36 success was an ability to attack in night and bad weather, the tactic most difficult for an enemy to block. The elaborate 1,700-pound K-1, and later the K-3A, bombing-navigation system could find targets in the worst weather conditions, and combined the tasks of bombardier and radar operator in one man. Bomb racks were modified to hold the differences in shape among the nuclear Mk 4, 5, 6, or 8 models, and new bomb doors could snap open or shut in two seconds. An APG-32 radar aimed the tail guns.

Convair provided 26 B-36Ds accepted from August 1950 to August 1951. Fifty-nine of the 62 B-36Bs accepted earlier were returned to the company for conversion to B-36Ds, and were redelivered with jets from November 1950 to February 1952. The RB-36D reconnaissance model was first flown December 18, 1949, and 24 were accepted from June 1950 to May 1951.

The RB-36D and RB-36E reconnaissance versions increased the crew from 15 to 22, had 14 cameras in the pressurized front bomb bay and 80 flash bombs in the second bay. Behind them the bays could hold an auxiliary fuel tank or bombs, followed by three protruding ECM (electronic countermeasure) antennas. All 16 guns were retained. Twenty-one B-36As and the YB-36 were converted to RB-36E jets, and delivered from July 1950 to July 1951.

On November 18, 1950, the first B-36F was flown with the 3,800-hp R-4360-53 engines and K-3A radar. From March to December 1951, 34 B-36Fs and 24 RB-36Fs were delivered. The B-36H, first flown April 5, 1952, had an APG-41A twin-radar tail defense, allowing search and gun aiming at separate attackers, while 1,400 pounds of chaff were carried to jam enemy radar. The flight deck was modified to include a second engineer. From December 1951 to July 1953, 83 B-36Hs and 73 RB-36Hs were delivered.

SDAM

CONVAIR B-36F

Six Pratt & Whitney R-4360-53, 3800 hp at 40,000' & four J47-GE-19, 5200 lb. st.

DIMENSIONS: Span 230', Lg. 162'2", Ht. 46'10", Wing Area 4772 sq. ft.

WEIGHT: Empty 167,646 lb., Combat 264,300 lb., Gross 370,000 lb. Fuel 29,017-33,626 gal.

PERFORMANCE: Speed- Top 417 mph at 37,100', Cruising 235 mph, Stalling 123 mph. Combat Ceiling 40,900', Service Ceiling 44,000', Combat Radius 3230 miles/10,000 lb. Ferry Range 7740 miles.

A B-36H made a live drop of the largest pure-fission bomb on November 16, 1952, when an 8,600-pound Mk 18, released from 40,000 feet, exploded at 8,000 feet with a 500-kiloton blast. Only the B-36 could carry the largest thermonuclear bomb, the 41,400-pound Mk 17, which

CONVAIR B-36H
Six Pratt & Whitney R-4360-53, 3800 hp at 40,000' & four J47-GE-19, 5200 lb. st.
DIMENSIONS: Span 230', Lg. 162'2", Ht. 46'10", Wing Area 4772 sq. ft.
WEIGHT: Empty 168,487 lb., Combat 253,900 lb., Gross 370,000 lb. Fuel 28,688-33,626 gal.
PERFORMANCE: Speed- Top 416 mph at 36,700', Cruising 234 mph, Stalling 123 mph. Combat Ceiling 40,800', Service Ceiling 44,000'. Combat Radius 3110 miles/10,000-lb. Ferry Range 7690 miles.

yielded 13.5 megatons when tested in 1954. A large parachute was installed on the bomb to slow the fall enough to allow the aircraft to escape the blast.

Two hundred Mk 17 and 105 similar Mk 24 bombs were made by November 1955, and the last retired by August 1957. One was accidentally dropped on New Mexico when a B-36 crewman leaned against a release, but since the nuclear element was not then installed, there was no catastrophe. No live H-bomb drop was ever made from a B-36, as the B-52's speed allowed a safer distance from the blast. Readers can find a very detailed study of B-36 weaponry by Chuck Hansen in the Jacobsen anthology cited in the chapter notes.

Mark 17
The largest bomb ever carried on the B-36 was this thermonuclear Mk 17. Length 24'8", Diameter 5'1", Weight 41,400 lb.

Last was the B-36J model, first flown September 3, 1953, with an additional 2,770 gallons of fuel, and 19 were accepted by March 1954. The last 14, however, were completed in the B-36J (III) Featherweight configuration from May to August. All turrets but the tail turret removed, just 13 crewmen retained, and flush windows replaced sighting blisters.

Project Featherweight was a program to reduce airframe weight to balance this extra fuel. Class II Featherweights kept their guns, but some of the older B-36D, B-36F, B-36H, and B-36J aircraft adopted the Featherweight (III) configuration when overhauled in 1954. Abandonment of the multi-turret system was the end of the World War II concept of the heavy bomber formation shooting its way to the target. Protection was the task of the single gunner using his APG-41 tail radar to search backwards, shifting to the gun-laying mode when a target enters the 90-degree horizontal and 74-degree vertical cone of fire.

Delivery of the final B-36J (III) on August 14, 1954, brought the Convair total to 382, not including two B-36Gs redesignated YB-60 or the unarmed NB-36H, flown September 17, 1955, with the world's only airborne nuclear reactor. There was also the single transport version, the XC-99 flown from San Diego in 1947, that never was sold to the commercial airlines.

Ten SAC Wings used B-36s from 1953 to 1955, until replacement by B-52s was finally completed with the retirement of the last B-36J from SAC on February 12, 1959. Considered as a strategic deterrent, the B-36 never had to fight.

CONVAIR B-36J-75 (III) Featherweight
Six Pratt & Whitney R-4360-53, 3800 hp at 40,000' & four J47-GE-19, 5200 lb. st.
DIMENSIONS: Span 230', Lg. 162'2", Ht. 46'10", Wing Area 4772 sq. ft.
WEIGHT: Empty 166,165 lb. Combat 262,500 lb., Gross 410,000 lb. Fuel 33,400+2996 gal.
PERFORMANCE: Speed- Top 418 mph at 37,500', Cruising 227 mph, Stalling 129 mph. Combat Ceiling 39,500', Service Ceiling 43,600'. Climb 20,000'/34 min. Combat Radius 3990 miles/10,000-lb.,2500 miles/72,000-lb. Ferry Range 9440 miles.

FICON (FIghter-CONveyor) was a plan intended to carry a fighter aircraft on the B-36. The first such project was the XF-85 (see Chapter 27). All of its tests were made from a B-29B. On January 19, 1951, Convair was ordered to modify an RB-36F to carry and recover an F-84E, and redesignated GRB-36F, it began its first retrieval and launch tests January 9, 1952. In May 1953, a swept-wing YF-84F modified to fit the cradle below the GRB was successfully tested. Ten GRB-36Ds (III) with cradles for

SDAM

CONVAIR GRB-36F FICON

RF-84K reconnaissance jets were delivered to SAC in February/March 1955. They could carry the RF-84K out to a 2,810-mile radius, launching the 29,500-pound parasite at 25,000 feet for its dash over the target area. The partnership lasted less than a year's service with the 99th Reconnaissance Wing.

Another range-extension program was Project Tom-Tom, which attempted to have the jets attach themselves to each wing tip. In 1953 the same GRB-36F previously mentioned was fitted with wing tip mechanisms to mate with two RB-84Fs. But a similar system tried with a B-29A and two F-84Bs resulted in a fatal crash of all three aircraft on April 24, 1953, and dangerous test experiments with the GRB-36F soon led to the program's termination.

Three B-36Hs became DB-36H models when modified to carry the Bell GAM-63 "Rascal," a 32-foot, 18,200-pound air-to-ground missile launched at a target up to 75 miles away. These conversions were begun in March 1953, but the system was deleted from B-36 plans by the time the last was completed in July 1955.

CHAPTER 27

AIR FORCE FIGHTERS FROM P-79 TO F-94

A flight of very polished F-80As display the new jet age in 1946.

The end of the Second World War also ended production of propeller-driven single-seaters for the Army Air Force. Development of jet propulsion made most existing fighters obsolescent, and the postwar period saw production of new jet types to re-equip the world fighter units.

Nuclear bombs, and strategic elements of the growing cold war between America and Russia tended to center Air Force attention on bombers rather than fighters, and not until the unexpected appearance of Soviet atomic weapons in 1949 did jet fighter production reach really large numbers. The terrible destructive capability of bombardment now lent a new urgency to development of defensive weapons. Only the ability to clear skies of enemy intruders seemed to offer any shield against annihilation.

Although the United States had no jets ready in time for combat during the big war, wartime development had begun projects from the XP-79 to the XP-86, and had gotten the P-80 Shooting Star into successful production. At the opening of the Korean War in 1950, Air Force fighters in actual service still consisted almost entirely of types begun before the end of World War II.

NORTHROP XP-79B
Two Westinghouse l9B, 1365 lb. st
DIMENSIONS: Span 38', Lg. 11', Ht. 7'6", Wing Area 778 sq. ft.
WEIGHT: Empty 5840 lb., Gross 8670 lb. Fuel 300 gal.
PERORMANCE: Speed- Top 547 mph at s.1., 508 mph at 25,000', Cruising 480 mph. Climb 25,000'/4.7 min. Range 993 miles cruising on one engine.

Even before the first American jet, the Bell XP-59, flew, Jack Northrop proposed on September 15, 1942, a tailless flying wing "jet-driven interceptor". By December 1942 that design became his NS-14, to be operated by a pilot lying prone in the cockpit. It was hoped that this prone position would reduce strain on the pilot during violent maneuvers and sudden pullouts, and present a minimum target to enemy gunners.

On January 12, 1943, the Air Force authorized purchase of three XP-79 prototypes to be built under Northrop subcontract by Avion, Inc., since Northrop's factory was too busy to undertake more work. They were designed for 2,000-pound static thrust Aerojet rockets, but in March the more certain availability of the Navy's Westinghouse l9-B axial-flow jet engines led to a decision to use two jets in the third ship, designated XP-79B.

The radical layout required tryouts in the form of towed gliders with fixed tricycle gear. One, the MX-324, was towed into the air by a P-38 and became the first rocket-powered U.S. aircraft to fly on July 5, 1944. Aerojet was unable, however, to perfect a rocket motor suitable for the XP-79, so both prototypes were canceled in September.

This left only the XP-79B, which was trucked to the Dry Lake near Muroc for testing in June 1945. Sitting low on the ground, it had four retractable wheels and twin vertical fins atop the jet exhaust. The welded magnesium flying wing had air bellows-operated split-flap wingtip rudders outboard elevons, as on the XP-56, and was armed with four .50 caliber guns.

The wing itself was constructed of a heavy gauge to provide some protection for the fuel tanks and prevent a dangerous mix of the two rocket fuels originally planned. On its first test flight at Muroc Army Airfield, delayed to September 12, 1945, the XP-79B crashed, test pilot Harry Crosby was killed, and the project ended.

Shooting Stars

The most successful jet fighter to come out of the war began when Lockheed was asked by the Air Force on May 17, 1943, to build a single-seater around a De Havilland

Halford jet engine imported from England. By June 24, a letter contract was issued, and 23 engineers and 105 mechanics led by Kelly Johnson were gathered in a temporary building to quickly build prototypes in secret.

Given nearly complete authority and independence from the rest of the Burbank company, that organization became known as the "Skunk Works" and was so successful that this system was used for the most important future Lockheed projects begun in secret, such as the XF-104, U-2, and A-12/YF-12.

In 143 days a neat dark green prototype was finished and the engine installed. But an accident during the run-up damaged that engine, and another had to be imported so that Milo Burcham could make the first XP-80 flight on January 8,1944, from Muroc (Edwards AFB since 1949). Although the engine developed only 2,460-pound static thrust, instead of the 3,000-pounds expected, the Lockheed XP-80 did 502 mph, and became the first American plane that fast.

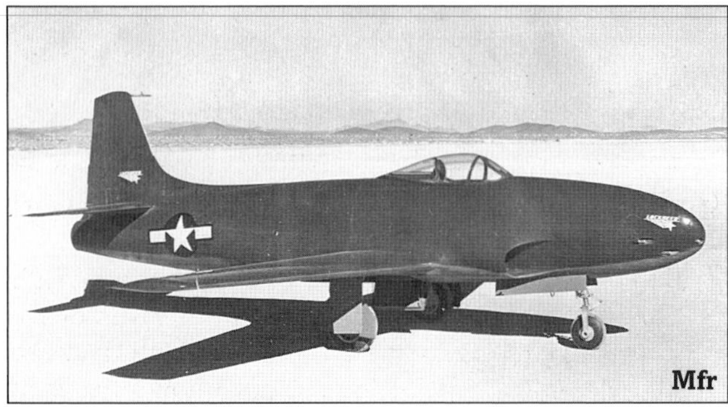
Mfr

LOCKHEED XP-80
De Havilland Halford H-lB, 2460 lb. actual static thrust
DIMENSIONS: Span 37', Lg. 32'10", Ht. 10'3", Wing Area 240 sq. ft.
WEIGHT: Empty 6287 lb., Gross 8916 lb. Fuel 200-285 gal.
PERFORMANCE: Speed- Top 502 mph at 20,480'. Service Ceiling 41,000', Absolute Ceiling 41,800', Climb 3000'/1 min., 10,000'/3.7 min.

Propelled by the jet exhaust from the tail, the fighter had the engine behind the pilot fed by twin air intakes ahead of the wing roots. There was a clear plastic canopy, and six .50-caliber guns with 1,200 rounds low in the nose. Like all future jet fighters, the XP-80 sat low on retractable tricycle landing gear.

General Electric had prepared a larger jet engine, the I-40 (became J33 in April 1945), so two more prototypes were ordered on February 16, to be followed by 13 service examples ordered March 10, and the first production letter contract was made on April 2, 1944. First flown June 1, 1944, by Tony LeVier, the GE-powered XP-80A introduced the similar, but heavier, airframe followed on production models. While the first American jets, the Bell P-59s, had been less agile than regular fighters, the Air Force now had a fighter worthy to meet Germany's Me 262.

The first of 13 YP-80As flew on September 13, 1944, powered by the J33-GE-11, and as the fastest wartime AAF fighter, the Shooting Star won orders for 3,548 P-80A copies. One thousand were to be built at North American's Dallas plant, the remainder by Lockheed, who began P-80A deliveries in April 1945. Two YP-80As were shipped in December to AAF bases in Italy and two to England, but the war ended before the Shooting Star could be tested in action. Lockheed's contract was reduced to 917 and the Dallas order dropped, leaving the P-80A the only Air Force single-seater in production after V-J Day, with 231 delivered in 1945.

Mfr

LOCKHEED P-80A-1
General Electric J33-GE-11 or Allison J33-A-9, 4000 lb. st
DIMENSIONS: Span 38'10", Lg. 34'6", Ht 11'4", Wing Area 238 sq. ft.
WEIGHT: Empty 7920 lb., Gross 11,700 lb., Max. 14,500 lb. Fuel 425+330 gal.
PERFORMANCE: Speed- Top 558 mph at s.1., 533 mph at 20,000', 508 mph at 30,000', Cruising 410 mph. Service Ceiling 45,000', Climb 4580'/1 min., 20,000'/5.5 min. Range 540 miles normal, 1440 miles max.

Allison produced the GE-designed 4,000-pound thrust J33-A-9 engine after 1945, and 1,800 rounds were provided for the six M-2 .50-caliber guns in the nose, while a 165-gallon drop tank below each wing tip extended the range, and a fuselage dive brake limited dive speed for safety.

Wanting a photo-recon jet with the P-80's speed, the Air Force had, on September 23, 1944, ordered that the second YP-80A be completed as the XF-14 with three cameras replacing the guns in a longer nose. First flown October 15, 1944, that aircraft was destroyed by collision

Mfr

LOCKHEED XP-80A
General Electric I-40, 4000 lb. st
DIMENSIONS: Span 38'10", Lg. 34'6", Ht. 11'4", Wing Area 238 sq. ft.
WEIGHT: Empty 7225 lb., Gross 9600 lb., Max. 13,750 lb. Fuel 485+330 gal.
PERFORMANCE: Speed- Top 553 mph at 5700', Cruising 410 mph, Landing 95 mph. Service Ceiling 48,500', Climb 20,000'/4.6 min. Range 560 miles normal, 1200 miles max.

LOCKHEED P-80B
Allison J33-A-21, 4500 lb. st WE
DIMENSIONS: Span 38'9", Lg. 34'5", Ht 11'3", Wing Area 238 sq. ft.
WEIGHT: Empty 8176 lb., Gross 11,975 lb., Max. 16,000 lb. Fuel 425+330 gal.
PERFORMANCE: Speed- Top 577 mph at 6000', 497 mph at 35,000', Cruising 386 mph, Stalling 122 mph. Service Ceiling 36,800', Climb 6475'/1 min. Range 1210 miles.

on December 6, but the concept was proven, and an interchangeable camera nose was substituted in 1946 on production FP-80As (RF-80 after 1948).

Lockheed delivered 525 P-80A and 152 FP-80A jets by December 1946, but the accident rate was more than twice that of the prop-fighters. Early crash victims of engine failures included Milo Burcham and top war ace Richard Bong. In 1945, P-80As flew with the 412th Fighter Group, which had trained on P-59s, and was redesignated the 1st FG in 1946. The 4th, 36th, and 56th groups followed, while a single squadron became the first to be deployed overseas in Germany in 1946, followed by the 36th FG during 1948's Berlin crisis.

From March 1947 to March 1948, Lockheed delivered 240 P-80Bs with a much-needed ejector seat for the pilot, under wing rocket racks, new M-3 .50-caliber guns (firing 1,200 rounds per minute, instead of the 800 rpm of the wartime M-2) and a water-alcohol injection system giving the engine bursts of emergency power. Most of the P-80As on hand were retroactively brought up to B standards, using several models of the J33 engine (A-9B, -11B, -17A, or -21). Air National Guard units at stations with the necessary 7,000-feet runways also had P-80s in 1948.

On March 1, 1948, the first P-80C was flown, and 670 were delivered between October 1948 and June 1950. Since F for fighter replaced the old P for pursuit in June 1948, they became known as F-80Cs, and had an Allison J33-A-23 rated at 4,600-pound thrust. Besides the two 165-gallon drop tanks, wing racks could handle 16 rockets or two 1,000-pound bombs.

The most widely used Shooting Star version was the two-place T-33 trainer, originally seen in 1948 as the TF-80C. Lockheed built 5,691 for the USAF, the Navy and allied nations by August 1959. The Navy began testing three P-80As June 29, 1945, and acquired 50 F-80C and 699 T-33 jets for training as the TO-l and TO-2 (later TV-l and TV-2).

Other versions included the XP-80R, a P-80A with modified wings, canopy and J33-A-23 engine, which established a 623.8-mph world's speed record in June 1947; the first won by America since 1923. Another P-80A tested in 1947 had an automatic rocket launcher protruding from the nose. Numerous F-80s later became drones (QF-80), directed by DT-33As.

Air Force Groups became Wings in January 1950, and on June 27, 1950, F-80Cs of the 8th Fighter-Bomber Wing shot down four North Korean Il-10 attack planes. The 35th and 49th Fighter-Bomber Wings joined the Korean war in July. Most F-80C missions were ground attacks, but the radius of action with rockets was only 225 miles. This increased to 325 miles when improvised 265-gallon tip tanks replaced the standard 165-gallon size.

LOCKHEED P-80C
Allison J33-A-23, 4600 lb. st, 5400 lb. st WE
DIMENSIONS: As P-80B
WEIGHT: Empty 8240 lb., Combat 12,330 lb., Gross 15,336 lb., Max. 16,856 lb. Fuel 425+330 gal.
PERFORMANCE: Speed- Top 580 mph at 7000', 543 mph at 25,000'. Cruising 439 mph, Stalling 122 mph. Service Ceiling 42,750', Climb 6870'/1 min. Range 1127-1380 miles.

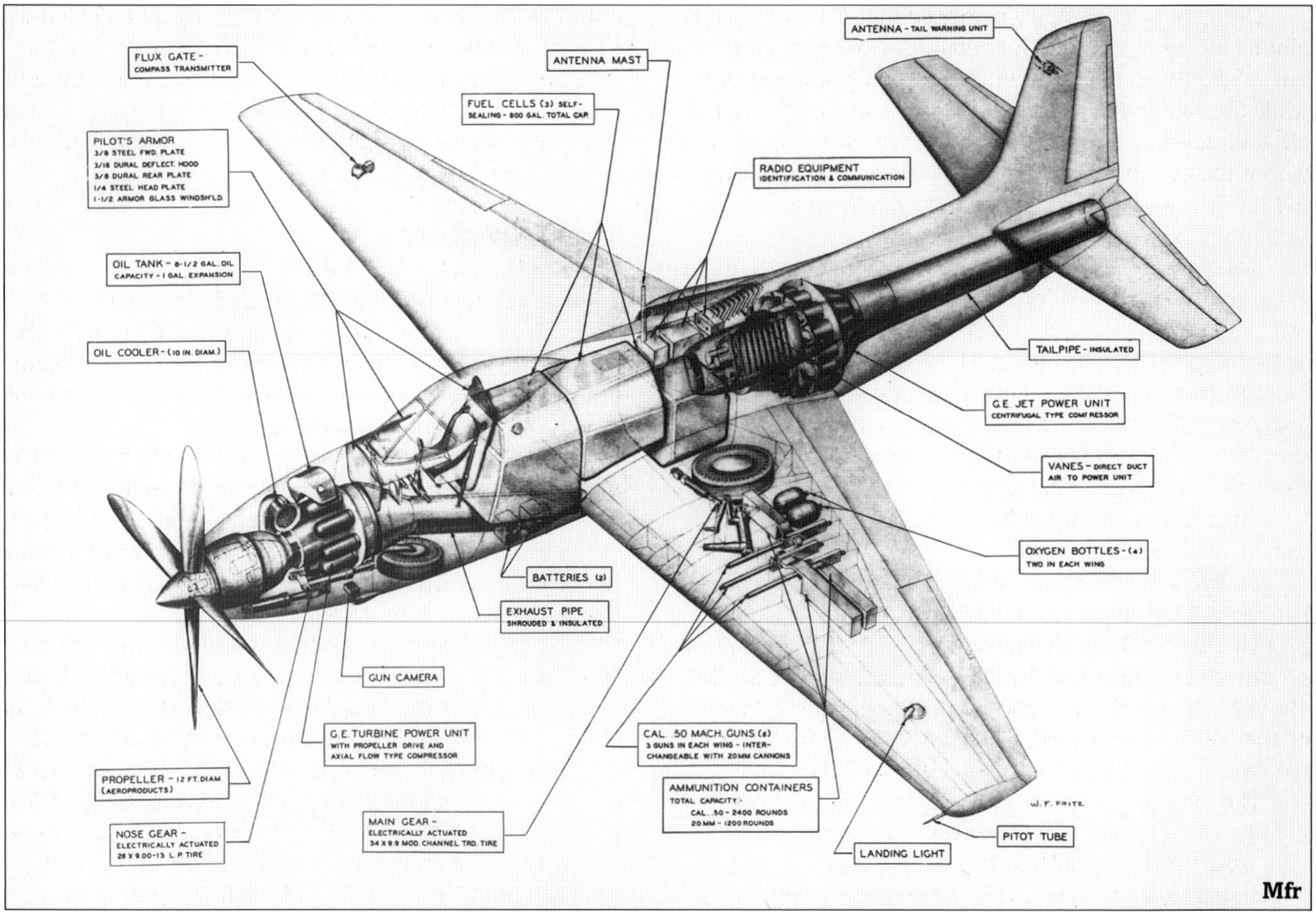

Mfr

XP-81 interior shows mixed power plant, with both XT-31 turboprop and J33 jet, fueled by kerosene.

RF-80s of the 15th and 45th TRS made most of the war's photo missions. History's first all-jet air battle occurred on November 8, 1950, when an F-80C pilot claimed a Russian-piloted MiG-15. But later fights were more often won by MiGs.

Six MiGs and 31 prop-aircraft were downed in air-to-air combat for a loss of 14 F-80s during the Korean war. The F-80Cs flew 98,515 sorties, with 143 losses to enemy action, mostly anti-aircraft, compared to 62,607 sorties and 194 losses for the F-51 Mustangs.

In 1958, F-80Cs retired from the USAF and ANG were supplied to Latin America under the MAP (Military Assistance Program). These included 33 for Brazil, 18 for Chile, 16 each for Colombia, Ecuador, and Peru, as well as 14 for Uruguay.

Reaching for Range

Short range was the most obvious limitation of early jet types, so in 1943 the USAF began reaching for designs that might combine jet speeds with the range necessary to escort B-29s to their targets. The goal was a 1,250-mile combat radius with a 250-mph cruising speed and 500-mph top speed. Such a combination seemed beyond the contemporary state of the art, but three twin-engine escort fighter designs were ordered to address this problem.

First was the XP-81 single-seater proposed in September 1943 by Consolidated's Vultee division, as a combination of jet propulsion for high speeds with propeller-driven power for cruising. Two prototypes ordered February 11 were powered by a J33-GE-5 installed behind the pilot, while the first turboprop engine used in America, a General Electric TG-100 (later called XT-31), turned a four-bladed propeller in the nose.

Mfr

CONSOLIDATED-VULTEE XP-81

General Electric XT-31-GE-1, 2300 hp and J33-GE-5, 4000 lb. st

DIMENSIONS: Span 50'6", Lg. 44'8", Ht. 13'10", Wing Area 425 sq. ft.

WEIGHT: Empty 12,954 lb., Design Gross 19,500 lb., Max. 23,943 lb. Fuel 752+600 gal.

PERFORMANCE: Design Speed- Top 494 mph at s.l., 510 mph at 20,000', 498 mph at 30,000', (Actual speed 494 mph at 20,000', 486 mph at 30,000') Cruising 315 mph. Service Ceiling 44,500', Climb 5000'/1 min. 30,000'/9.6 min. Actual range 1450 miles/752 gal., 1740 miles full load.

Designer Charles R. Irvine hoped that TG-100 gas turbine's kerosene consumption would be low enough to allow a 2,500-mile range when only the propeller was used, while the J33's tail thrust would be turned on only for takeoff and combat. Ryan's FR-1 fighter was also being built with a mixed power plant, but that Navy project's Wright R-1820 was a standard type, not the totally new untested turboprop experiment.

Delays in building a TG-100 forced the substitution of a Packard V-1650-7 Merlin in the nose when the XP-81 was built at Downey and first flown on February 11, 1945, at Muroc. Not until December 21 could flight tests with the TG-100 begin. Tricycle landing gear and a pressurized cockpit with 3/8-inch armor and an ejection seat were provided. The low squared-off laminar-flow wing had room for the usual six .50-caliber guns with 1,800 rounds, while under wing fittings carried two 300-gallon drop tanks or two 1,600-pound bombs.

As the first turboprop aircraft in America, the XP-8l had many mechanical difficulties with its power plant and propeller. The TG-100 delivered only 1,700 of the 2,300 hp promised. Top speed, 462 mph with the Merlin, tested at 494 mph with both the turboprop and jet running, instead of the 510-mph expected. The promised 2,500-mile combat range with full tanks was reduced to 1,740 miles.

The second prototype delivered in March 1947 had modified tail surfaces, but a reliable turboprop combination would not be available for several years. A contract negotiated in November 1946, for 13 service test YP-81s with improved engines, was stopped two months later.

The last Bell fighter, Model 40, was proposed on March 29, 1943, as an interceptor, but the design was redone in April as a long-range escort fighter, and a letter contract for two XP-83 prototypes issued March 29, 1944, was approved July 31. An enlarged P-59 with two J33-GE-5s and bubble canopy, the XP-83 had large fuselage fuel tanks supplemented by two 150-gallon drop tanks, or two 1,000-pound bombs.

Mfr

BELL XP-83
Two General Electric J33-GE-5, 3750 lb. st
DIMENSIONS: Span 53', Lg. 44'10", Ht. 15'4" Wing Area 431 sq. ft.
WEIGHT: Empty 14,105 lb., Design Gross 21,950 lb., Max. 24,090 lb. Fuel 1150+300 gal.
PERFORMANCE: Speed- Top 522 mph at 15,660', Cruising 441 mph. Service Ceiling 42,300', Climb 3750'/1 min., 20,000'/6.8 min. Range 1750 miles/1450 gal.

Six .50-caliber guns in the nose with 1,800 rounds armed the first XP-83, flown February 27,1945. The second flew on October 19, had a wider tail fin, and tested a new installation of six .60-caliber T17E3 guns.

But neither the XP-81 or XP-83 would enter production, for the Air Force had decided that the escort fighter mission could be accomplished sooner by the P-82, the last fighter with piston engines.

Twin Mustangs

The last propeller-driven fighter purchased by the Air Force began as a sketch made by North American Aviation chief designer Edgar Schmued on October 21, 1943. His preliminary design group prepared a proposal that became the NA-120 approved on January 7, 1944, by General Arnold on his visit to the factory.

This twin-engine long-range fighter joined twin fuselages based on the P-51F together on a single wing and stabilizer to provide a pilot on the left side and a relief pilot to aid navigation on the other. The last tail-down landing gear on an Air Force fighter had a retractable main wheel and tail wheel underneath each fuselage.

Two XP-82 and two XP-82A prototypes were ordered by a February 8, 1944, letter contract, followed by a production contract on June 30 for 500 P-82Bs capable of bomber escorts or ground attacks. Armament included six .50-caliber M-2 guns with 400 rpg in the wing center section. Wing racks held two drop tanks, or up to 6,000 pounds of bombs or 25 5-inch rockets, and a center pod containing eight more guns was tested, but not adopted.

Powered by Packard Merlins with opposite inward-rotating propellers, the XP-82 was completed May 25, 1945, but had difficulty lifting off until June 16, when Joseph Barton took off from Mines Field. After prop rotation was reversed, Robert Chilton resumed tests on June 26.
The second XP-82 flew on August 30, but the Allison V-1710-119 intended for the XP-82A malfunctioned, so those prototypes were canceled.

After V/J Day, the P-82B schedule was cut back to 20, and the first was flown October 19, 1945. Delivered by March 1946, they were similar to the XP-82, except for the 10th and 11th aircraft equipped as night fighters. The P-82C was flown March 27, 1946, with SCR-720 radar in a center pod, and the P-82D flew later with an APS-4 radar. One P-82B with extra tanks flew 4,968 miles nonstop from Hawaii to New York on February 28, 1947, setting a distance record for fighters, and another began tests with a camera pod for reconnaissance on November 15, 1948.

Olmstead

NORTH AMERICAN P-82B

Mfr

NORTH AMERICAN XP-82

Two Packard V-1650-23, -25, 1380 hp takeoff, 1830 hp WE at 18,500'

DIMENSIONS: Span 51'3", Lg. 39', Ht. 13'6", Wing Area 408 sq. ft.

WEIGHT; Empty 13,402 1b., Gross 19,170 lb., Max. 22,000 1b. Fuel 600+445 gal.

PERFORMANCE: Speed- Top 468 mph at 22,800', Landing 130 mph. Service Ceiling 40,000', Climb 4900'/1 min., 25,000'/6.4 min. Range 1390 miles normal, max. 2600 miles

Mfr

NORTH AMERICAN P-82D

Revision of the wartime contract on December 12, 1945, called for 250 more Twin Mustangs to be powered by Allison V-1710-143/-145 engines, and as approved on October 10, 1946, provided that the last 150 would be night fighters with a radar man in the right cockpit. The first flew February 17, 1947, but engine difficulties soon showed that switching from the Merlins had been unfortunate.

By the year's end, only four had been accepted as P-82As, while 130 empty airframes awaited satisfactory power plants. Allison finally got engine production underway, so that from January to July 1948, 96 P-82Es were accepted and in May began service with the only SAC fighter escort group. They were redesignated as F-82Es in June, and were armed with six 50-caliber M-3 guns with 400 rpg. Wing racks held two 310-gallon drop tanks, 25 5-inch rockets, or four 1,000-pound bombs.

APG-28 radar had been chosen for the F-82F, but since older SCR-720C radar used on the P-61 was already available, that was installed on the first F-82G version flown on December 8, 1947. As engines and radars appeared, an F-82F flew March 11, 1948, and the USAF accepted 91 F-82Fs and 45 F-82Gs. Weapons included the usual six guns, 20 5-inch rockets, or two 1,000-pound bombs. Fourteen F-82Hs winterized for Alaskan duty ended Twin Mustang deliveries in March 1949, as the type replaced the P-61.

SAC's 27th Fighter-Escort Group used the F-82E until August 1950. Beginning in September 1948, the all-weather versions went to the 52nd Fighter Group at Mitchel Field to protect the northeastern states, the 325th

Mfr

NORTH AMERICAN P-82E
Two Allison V-1710-143, -145, 1600 hp takeoff, 1700 hp WE at 21,000'
DIMENSIONS: Span 51'3", Lg. 39'1", Ht. 13'10", Wing Area 417 sq. ft.
WEIGHT: Empty 14,914 lb., Combat 20,741 lb., Gross 24,864 lb. Fuel 576+620 gal.
PERFORMANCE: Speed- Top 465 mph at 21,000', Cruising 304 mph, Stalling 124 mph. Combat Ceiling 38,400', Service Ceiling 40,000', Climb 4020'/1 min. Combat radius 1235 miles. Range 2504 miles normal, ferry 2708 miles.

Mfr

NORTH AMERICAN P-82F
Two Allison V-1710-143, -145, 1600 hp takeoff, 1700 hp WE at 21,000'
DIMENSIONS: Span 51'7", Lg. 42'2", Ht. 13'10", Wing Area 417 sq. ft.
WEIGHT: Empty 16,309 lb., Combat 21,116 lb., Gross 26,208 lb. Fuel 576+620 gal.
PERFORMANCE: Speed- Top 460 mph at 21,000', Cruising 288 mph, Stalling 128 mph. Combat Ceiling 36,800', Service Ceiling 38,700', Climb 3690'/1 min. Combat radius 1000 miles. Range 2200 miles, ferry 2400 miles.

FG at McChord AFB to protect the northwest, and the 347th FG in Japan.

The latter group's F-82Gs became the first American planes to down North Korean aircraft on June 27, 1950. These Twin Mustangs flew 1,868 sorties in the Korean War, including fighter patrol, close support, and night intrusion missions. The last USAF squadron to use the type was the 449th, whose P-82Hs protected Alaska and flew sorties over the Russian coast. Their last Twin Mustang retired in November 1953.

Thunderjets

The first new fighter of the postwar period was Republic's XP-84, a response to a September 11, 1944, Air Force requirement for the best speed and range obtainable from jet propulsion. Alexander Kartveli offered his AP-23 design on November 2 and a November 11 letter contract ordered three prototypes.

General Electric's TG-180 (called J35 since 1945) axial-flow engine permitted a long narrow fuselage whose streamlining contributed to the expected 600-mph speed and 1,300-mile range. The first nose air intake on an American jet permitted straight-through air flow. Fuel was carried within the fuselage and in wings thick enough to contain the retracted main wheels of the tricycle landing gear.

AF

REPUBLIC XP-84
General Electric J35-GE-7, 3750 lb. st
DIMENSIONS: Span 36'5", Lg. 37'2", Ht. 12'10", Wing Area 260 sq. ft.
WEIGHT: Empty 9080 lb., Gross 13,400 lb., Max. 16,200 lb. Fuel 440 gal.
PERFORMANCE: Speed- Top 592 mph at s.1., 378 mph at 35,000', Cruising 425 mph. Climb 35,000'/13 min. Range 1300 miles normal.

The mid-wing single-seater was built in Farmingdale, New York, and flown aboard an XC-97 to Muroc. When Major Wallace Lien made the first XP-84 flight on February 28, 1946, it had already earned a 100-plane contract on January 5. The second XP-84 prototype was stripped to set a United States speed record of 611 mph on September 7, but this could not be matched under service conditions.

Production began with 15 YP-84As delivered in February 1947; similar to the prototypes, but with J35-A-15 engines now made by Allison, and 165-gallon wing-tip drop tanks were added. Four .50-caliber M-2 guns were mounted above the nose air intake and two more were in the wing roots. Successful tests added another 486 planes to the contracts by October 1947, and the 14th Fighter Group was chosen to be the first P-84 unit.

AF

NORTH AMERICAN P-82G

Two Allison V-1710-143, -145, 1600 hp takeoff, 1700 hp WE at 21,000'

DIMENSIONS: Span 51'7", Lg. 42'5", Ht. 13'10", Wing Area 417 sq. ft.

WEIGHT: Empty 15,997 lb., Combat 21,810 lb., Gross 25,891 lb. Fuel 576+620 gal.

PERFORMANCE: Speed- Top 460 mph at 21,000', Cruising 288 mph, Stalling 127 mph. Combat Ceiling 37,200', Service Ceiling 38,900', Climb 3770'/1 min., 25,000'/7.8 min. Combat radius 1015 miles. Range 2240 miles, ferry 2495 miles.

Mfr

REPUBLIC YP-84A

P-84B Thunderjets appearing in June 1947 also had J35A-15s, but standardized the faster-firing M-3 guns, with 300 rpg, and ejector seats. The first 85 did not have the eight retractable under wing rocket racks of the last 141. Just as deliveries were being completed, these fighters were grounded on May 24, 1948, due to a host of maintenance and safety problems. The waiting planes were redesignated F-84B on June 11.

PMB

REPUBLIC F-84B

Allison J35-A-15, 3750 lb. st

DIMENSIONS: Span 36'6", Lg. 37'6", Ht. 12'10", Wing Area 260 sq. ft.

WEIGHT: Empty 9538 lb., Combat 13,465 lb., Gross 16,475 lb., Max. 19,689 lb. Fuel 416+370 gal.

PERFORMANCE: Speed- Top 587 mph at 4000', Cruising 436 mph, Stalling 132 mph. Service Ceiling 40,750', Climb 4210'/1 min. Range 1282 miles.

Production resumed with J35-A-13 engines found more dependable than the A-15. From May to November 1948, 191 F-84Cs were delivered, and 154 F-84Ds followed by April 1949. Only internal mechanical changes distinguished the D from the C, and the Air Force came close to canceling the troubled Thunderjet program until a major modification program was approved in May 1949. Thunderjets served the 20th, 31st, 33rd, 34th, and 78th Fighter Groups, but mechanical problems persisted.

Arnold

REPUBLIC F-84C
Allison J35-A-13, 3750 lb. st
DIMENSIONS: As F-84B
WEIGHT: Empty 9662 lb., Combat 13,574 lb., Gross 16,584 lb., Max. 19,798 lb. Fuel 416+370 gal.
PERFORMANCE: Speed- Top 587 mph at 4000', Cruising 436 mph, Stalling 132 mph. Service Ceiling 40,600', Climb 4180'/1 min. Range 1274 miles.

Arnold

REPUBLIC F-84D
Allison J35-A-13, 3750 lb. st.
DIMENSIONS: As F-84B
WEIGHT: Empty 9860 lb., Combat 13,894 lb. Gross 16,862 lb., Max. 20,076 lb. Fuel 416+370 gal.
PERFORMANCE: Speed- Top 587 mph at 4000', Cruising 441 mph, Stalling 133 mph. Service Ceiling 39,300', Climb 4060'/1 min. Range 1198 miles.

The improved performance of the F-84E, with a 4,900-pound thrust J35-A-17 and increased JP-1 fuel capacity in a longer fuselage, restored confidence in Republic fighters. Ordered December 29, 1948, and first flown May 18, 1949, the F-84E-1 added inboard pylons under the wings for two 1,000-pound bombs or 11.75-inch rockets for ground-attack missions. These pylons could add two 230-gallon drop tanks to the two 230-gallon wingtip tanks. Sperry APG-30 radar-ranging for an A-1B gun sight became standard.

The 27th, 12th, and 31st Fighter-Escort Wings were the first to use the E model. Republic delivered 843 F-84Es by June 1951, the last 270 (F-84E-25/-30) with a J35-A-17B and new tail pipe ejector.

Mfr

REPUBLIC F-84E-1
Allison J35-A-17, 4900 lb. st
DIMENSIONS: Span 36'5", Lg. 38'6", Ht. 12'7", Wing Area 260 sq. ft.
WEIGHT: Empty 10,121 lb., Combat 14,850 lb, Gross 18,170 lb., Max. 21,384 lb. Fuel 452+460 gal.
PERFORMANCE: Speed- Top 626 mph at s.l., 547 mph at 35,000, Cruising 479 mph, Stalling 140 mph. Combat Ceiling 42,800', Service Ceiling 45,100', Climb 5370'/1 min., 20,000'/4.94 min. Combat radius 780 miles/two 230 gal. drop tanks, 447 miles/6214-lb. stores. Range 1819 miles/two drop tanks.

The F-84E's increased power brought the Thunderjet close to the straight wing's speed limit (Mach .82), and Republic offered a swept-wing version on November 10, 1949. A February 24, 1950, contract change ordered the last (409th) F-84E-15 built as the YF-96A, with a 5,200-pound thrust XJ35-A-25, and 40° sweep on wings and tail. First flown on June 3, 1950, at Edwards AFB, that prototype became the YF-84F on September 8, since tooling was then expected to be 55% the same as that of the F-84E. Actually, barely 15 per cent of the straight-wing F-84E components could be used in the final F-84F model.

Alarm over the Korean War led in July to an order for production models to be powered by 7,200-pound thrust Wright J65s, an American-built version of the British Armstrong-Siddeley Sapphire engine. General Motors was chosen to manage a second production line in a Kansas City factory once used to make B-25s.

F-84F production was delayed by complexities of the new wing structure and the engine, so delivery began in July 1951 of an interim type designated F-84G with the straight wing, a 5,600-pound thrust J35-A-29, and reinforced canopy. Essentially an F-84E fitted for long-range flying, the F-84G had an automatic pilot and a receptacle on the left wing for air refueling by a flying boom of a Boeing KB-29P or KC-97E tanker, instead of the probe and drogue technique tested with tip tanks on modified F-84Es, and used on F-84G missions when only older tankers were available.

The value of air refueling was demonstrated in July 1952 by nonstop deployment of the 31st Fighter-Escort Wing from Turner AFB, Georgia, to Japan. Jet squadrons could now fly to any point in the world, refueling from flying tankers at prearranged rendezvous. Six F-84G wings served SAC by 1954, the last replaced in August 1955 by the F-84F, and eight wings served other commands.

The F-84G-5 was also the first USAF jet fighter to handle a 1,680-pound Mk 7 nuclear weapon under the left wing. Beginning in 1953, it was released by a low-altitude

REPUBLIC F-84E-15 of 136th FBW, Korea
Allison J35-A-17B, 4900 lb. st
DIMENSIONS: As F-84E-1
WEIGHT: Empty 10,300 lb., Combat 14,805 lb. Gross 18,151 lb., Max. 22,500 lb. Fuel 452+920 gal.
PERFORMANCE: Speed- Top 619 mph at s.l., 543 mph at 35,000', Cruising 490 mph, Stalling 140 mph. Combat Ceiling 42,600'. Service Ceiling 43,220', Climb 5160'/1 min., 35,000'/9.2 min. Combat radius 544 miles/2,000- lb., 1,000 miles/1372 gal. Ferry range 2057 miles.

bombing system (LABS). Racing in under 1,000 feet over the ground to the target, making a half loop up, and releasing the bomb, the F-84 escaped with a turn. Release altitude varied from 1,400 to 5,100 feet, depending on approach to target and bomb fusing.

REPUBLIC F-84G-5
Allison J35-A-29, 5600 lb. st
DIMENSIONS: Span 36'5", Lg. 38'1", Ht. 12'7", Wing Area 260 sq. ft.
WEIGHT: Empty 11,095 lb., Gross 18,645 lb., Max. 23,525 lb. Fuel 442+920 gal.
PERFORMANCE: Speed- Top 622 mph at s.1., 540 mph at 35,000', Cruising 483 mph, Stalling 142 mph. Combat Ceiling 40,500', Service Ceiling 42,100'. Climb 35,000'/7.9 min. without tanks. Range 670 miles/442 gal., 1330 miles/982 gal., 2000 miles max.(at 21,700 lb.)

The 20th Fighter-Bomber Wing received the first F-84Gs in November 1951, and this TAC unit was transferred to England in May 1952. Pilots practiced LABS techniques, but F-84 wings never actually possessed nuclear weapons, which remained in Atomic Energy Commission custody.

F-84s in combat

Thunderjets first entered combat with the 27th Fighter-Escort Wing, whose F-84Es had replaced F-82Es Twin Mustangs in 1950. That Wing began Korean missions on December 6, scoring its first MiG kill on January 21, 1951. The 49th, 58th, 116th, 136th, and 474th Fighter-Bomber Wings also used F-84s as they replaced F-80s in the fighter-bomber role, including refurbished F-84Ds provided in 1952 and new F-84Gs.

As an air-to-air fighter, the F-84 downed nine enemy aircraft for a loss of 18; it was too slow to do well against swept-wing MiGs. Most of the 86,408 F-84 sorties were used to deliver 55,987 tons of bombs, losing 122 planes to antiaircraft fire, 13 to unknown causes on combat missions, and 182 in non-combat accidents.

Due to the delayed swept-wing F-84F production, deliveries of the F-84G continued until the Korean war's last day, July 27, 1953. Of 4,302 straight-wing Thunderjets built, including 3,025 F-84Gs, Allied nations overseas joined in the Mutual Defense Assistance Program (MDAP - later MAP) were allocated 100 F-84Es and 2,236 F-84Gs.

Straight-wing Thunderjets were flown in 1953 by fourteen USAF Wings (about 75 a/c each) and 21 smaller NATO units. Beginning in March 1951, the Netherlands received 21 F-84Es and 170 F-84Gs to form two Wings and a

Mfr

REPUBLIC YF-84F (YF-96A)
Allison J35-A-25, 5200 lb. st
DIMENSIONS: Span 33'7" Lg. 43'1" Ht. 15'2", Wing Area 325 sq. ft.
WEIGHT: Empty 12,150 lb., Max. 23,230 lb. Fuel 605+900 gal.
PERFORMANCE: Speed- Top 693 mph at s.l., Cruising 514 mph, Stalling 140 mph. Service Ceiling 38,300'. Climb 35,000'/14.8 min. Range 1716 miles.

reconnaissance squadron. Denmark and Norway each organized two Wings of F-84E and F-84G aircraft, while France and Turkey had enough for four Wings.

Mfr

REPUBLIC F-84F-20-RE
Wright J65-W-3, 7200 lb. st
DIMENSIONS: Span 33'7", Lg. 43'5"', Ht. 14'4", Wing Area 325 sq. ft.
WEIGHT: Empty 13,645 lb., Combat 18,700 lb. Gross 25,226 lb., Ferry 27,000 lb. Fuel 579+900 gal.
PERFORMANCE: Speed- Top 685 mph at s.1., 608 mph at 35,000', Cruising 539 mph, Stalling 151 mph. Combat Ceiling 42,250', Service Ceiling 44,300'. Combat radius 860 miles, Ferry range 2314 miles.

Belgium, Italy, and Greece would each form three F-84 Wings. Portugal acquired 119 F-84Gs and some served in Africa. After the Korean war ended, more F-84Gs were available, so 150 could be sent to Taiwan in 1953 for two groups, while 169 for Yugoslavia, 75 for Iran, and 40 for Thailand were the first jet fighters owned by those countries.

Thunderstreaks

The first aircraft completed on Republic's swept-wing contract was a pre-production YF-84F flown February 14, 1951, with an imported Sapphire engine. The fuselage was deepened for the new power plant, but the sliding canopy and belly speed brake of previous models were retained.

The definitive production contract approved June 8, 1951, produced the first F-84F-1 Thunderstreak, flown a year behind schedule on November 22, 1952. Four store points could hold a pair of 450-gallon drop tanks, four 225-gallon tanks, bombs, or 24 5-inch rockets to add punch to the six M-3 guns with 1,800 rounds.

While the first 275 (F-84F-1 to F-20) had the Wright YJ65-W-1, these had to be replaced with the 7,200-pound thrust J65-W-3. Deliveries were delayed by so many problems that not until January 1954 did TAC's 506th Fighter-Bomber Wing get its first F-84F, and SAC's 27th Strategic Fighter Wing got F-84Fs with the new engines in June.

REPUBLIC F-84F-30

These swept-wing fighters were so different from the straight-wing versions that it is regrettable that the F-96 designation was not kept. The cockpit canopy now swung upwards, while an automatic pilot, leading edge slats, twin fuselage perforated speed brakes, and an air-refueling receptacle in the left wing were provided. A low-altitude bombing system (LABS) released a Mk. 7 nuclear bomb under the left wing. Less impressive was the nickname "Hog" given the F-84F for it's excessively long takeoff runs.

A movable one-piece horizontal tail (stabilator) was introduced on the F-84F-25, and the 7,800-pound thrust J65-W-7 was standard on the F-84F-50 in March 1955. By August 1957, 2,713 Thunderstreaks were built, including 237 F-84F-GKs from the Kansas City plant managed by General Motors.

REPUBLIC F-84F-56
Wright J65-W-7, 7800 lb. st
DIMENSIONS and WEIGHT: as F-84F-25
PERFORMANCE: Speed- Top 685 mph at s.1., 612 mph at 35,000', Cruising 539 mph, Stalling 151 mph. Combat Ceiling 44,850'. Combat radius 856 miles, Ferry range 2343 miles.

The F-84Fs went to six Strategic Air Command escort-fighter wings and six Tactical Air Command fighter-bomber wings, but by July 1957, the SAC wings were also transferred to TAC. After being replaced in front-line service by F-l00s, the F-84F was given to Air National Guard squadrons, but four F-84F Tactical Fighter Wings were reactivated in 1961 and served until replaced by F-4Cs by July 1964.

REPUBLIC F-84F in Netherlands

NATO received 1,305 F-84F fighter-bombers to replace the F-84Gs, beginning in June 1955 with 180 for six Dutch squadrons, 197 for Belgium's two Wings, 328 for five French *Escadres*, and 150 for Italy's three *Aerbrigata*. The Thunderstreak was the first combat type to go to the revived German Air Force which, beginning in November 1956, received 450 F-84Fs.

The French Thunderstreaks were the only ones to enter combat, during the Suez Crisis. *Escadres* based in Cyprus and Israel successfully attacked the Egyptian Air Force on the ground in November, 1956. Greece and Turkey each were supplied two wings from former German and Dutch aircraft. Republic Thunderjets served NATO until Belgium retired its last F-84F in May 1972.

Thunderflash

Republic proposed a reconnaissance version on August 15, 1949, a contract was made on June 12, 1951, and a YRF-84F flown in February 1952 had twin wing root intakes and a solid cover on the nose, resulting in a small thrust loss, but making space for cameras. While the old sliding canopy remained on that aircraft, production RF-84Fs used standard hinged covers and J65-W-3 engines on the first 11, J65-W-7s on the rest.

REPUBLIC YRF-84F

The first RF-84F Thunderflash flew September 9, 1953. Up to 15 cameras could be placed in the nose, with four .50-caliber guns in the lower lips of each intake and two 450-gallon drop tanks or bombs. Dual fences on each wing were added later.

Many F-84F problems also delayed RF-84F squadron service until March 1954, and further production was halted until November 1955. Four USAF reconnaissance wings used the RF-84F. Of 715 Thunderflashes built by

REPUBLIC XF-84H
Allison XT40-A-1, 5332 hp takeoff, and 1296 lb. st
DIMENSIONS: Span 33'6", Lg. 51'4", Ht. 15'4", Wing Area 325 sq. ft.
WEIG HT: Empty 17,389 lb., Combat 23,000 lb., Gross 29,700 lb. Fuel 800+900 gal.
PERFORMANCE: (estimated) Speed- Top 670 mph at 10,000, 639 mph at 30,000', Cruising 456 mph, Stalling 165 mph. Combat Ceiling 39,800', Climb 5230'/1 min., 35,000'/12 min. Combat Radius 1027 miles, Ferry range 2356 miles.

REPUBLIC RF-84F
Wright J65-W-7, 7800-lb. st
DIMENSIONS: Span 33'6", Lg. 47'6", Ht. 15', Wing Area 325 sq. ft.
WEIGHT: Empty 14,014 lb., Combat 20,091 lb., Gross 25,390 lb. Fuel 575+900 gal.
PERFORMANCE: Speed- Top 629 mph at 5000', 582 mph at 35,000', Cruising 542 mph, Stalling 166 mph. Combat Ceiling 39,200', Service Ceiling 45,600'. Climb 5820'/1 min., 35,000'/ 11.6 min. Combat radius 840 miles, Ferry range 1800 miles.

Republic by January 1958, 327 were built new for MDAP, plus 134 used USAF RF-84Fs also exported for MAP.

Nine NATO countries with RF-84 squadrons included Belgium, Denmark, France, Greece, the Netherlands, Norway, and Turkey. Germany had 108 RF-84Fs and Italy 78. Nationalist China also acquired 20 new RF-84Fs in February 1956, plus five used USAF examples in 1958, and flew them over the mainland.

The FICON (Fighter CONveyor) project was an effort to extend the range of fighter and reconnaissance jets by teaming F-84s with giant B-36s. Chapter 26 mentioned the 1953 tests of an F-84E and the YF-84F with the GRB-36F. Hoping to add 2,000 miles to the jet's radius of action, 25 RF-84F-17s were redesignated RF-84K and completed with a retractable hook ahead of the cockpit and down turned horizontal tail fins. Equipping the 91st Strategic Reconnaissance Squadron in July 1955, they operated with SAC's GRB-36Ds until the last launch on May 22, 1957.

REPUBLIC RF-84K

Designed to explore the possibilities of a turbo-prop strike fighter, the XF-84H had an Allison XT-40-A-l with 5,332 hp for its three-bladed Aeroproducts propeller, plus added jet thrust, an anti-torque fin behind the cockpit, and a high Tee tail. Design armament included a single .60-caliber T-45 gun with 1,200 rounds and 4,000 pounds of bombs.

The mockup inspection was in May 1952 and a contract for two prototypes was approved December 18, 1952. Only eight flights with the first prototype, and four flights with the second, were made by company test pilots at Edwards AFB from July 22, 1955, to October 9, 1956; all but one flight ending in emergency landings after engine problems.

The project was a failure, and was never flown by an Air Force pilot. One of the noisiest aircraft ever heard, it never flew more than some 520 mph of the 670-mph design speed. Originally, the Navy had been interested in the project, but development of steam catapults, angled deck and air refueling made propeller-driven substitutes for jet fighters unnecessary. As the Navy lost interest and mechanical difficulties persisted, the project was abandoned.

Mfr

NORTH AMERICAN XP-86
Allison J35-A-5, 4000 lb. st
DIMENSIONS: Span 37'1", Lg. 37'6", Ht. 14'9", Wing Area 288 sq. ft.
WEIGHT: Empty 9730 lb., Gross 13,790 lb., Max. 16,438 lb. Fuel 435+413 gal.
PERFORMANCE: Speed- Top 599 mph at s.1., 618 mph at 14,000', 575 mph at 35,000'. Service Ceiling 41,300', Climb 4000'/1 min., 30,000'/12.1 min. Combat radius 660 miles, Ferry range 2015 miles.

Mfr

REPUBLIC YF-84J

Two F-84F-25s were completed with the 8,920-pound General Electric YJ73-GE-7 in a deeper fuselage and designated YF-84J. First flown May 7, 1954, the type wasn't accepted for production. The YF-84J reached Mach 1.09, but the Air Force rejected the expense involved in changing engines on the production line and canceled the second example in June and the whole F-84J program on August 31.

Sabres

The North American F-86 Sabre has become a historic landmark among combat planes. The first American jet fighter with swept wings, it was the most effective weapon to win the air war in Korea.

Shortly after Hitler's defeat, captured German scientific data indicating the advantages of sweptback wings arrived in the United States. At that time, aircraft speeds were becoming limited less by power than by compressibility effects; as sonic speeds were approached, shock waves built up over airframe projections caused buffeting and other phenomena. Sweeping wing and tail surfaces back toward their tips delays the onset of compressibility troubles, and permits higher speeds.

American aerodynamicists were aware of these effects, and NACA investigators had alerted the North American company, who's NA-140 had been ordered as the XP-86 on May 18, 1945. That single-seater's mockup had been approved on June 20 with conventional straight wings and an estimated top speed of 582 mph at 10,000 feet. Larry P. Greene, the project aerodynamicist, proposed sweeping the wings and tail back 35 degrees , and a new design study was ordered August 14. On November 1, the Air Force accepted the idea.

The first of three low-wing XP-86s was flown on October 1, 1947, by George S. Welch at Muroc (now Edwards Air Force Base). First powered by a Chevrolet-built J35-C-3 behind the pilot, it changed to a 4,000-pound thrust Allison J35-A-5 and reached 618 mph at 14,000 feet. Features included a nose air inlet, pressurized cockpit, twin fuselage dive-brakes, and leading edge slats to reduce the swept wing's stalling point. After the third prototype was fitted with a J47 engine, Welch reached Mach 1 on April 26, 1948.

Thirty-three production aircraft had been ordered December 20, 1946, designated P-86A (F-86A-l Sabre after June 1948), and 188 P-86B (F-86A-5) were added by December 1947. After the first F-86A-1 flew on May 20, 1948, 333 more Sabres were purchased on May 29. Power plants were the General Electric J47-GE-3 and GE-7, until sufficient GE-13s were available. The 5,200-pound thrust offered enabled the third F-86A-1 to set a world's speed record of 670.98 mph on September 15, 1948.

NORTH AMERICAN F-86A-5
General Electric J47-GE-13, 5200 lb. st
DIMENSIONS: Span 37'1", Lg. 37'6", Ht. 14'9", Wing Area 288 sq. ft. WEIGHT: Empty 10,093 lb., Combat 13,791 lb., Gross 15,876 lb. Fuel 435+240 gal.
PERFORMANCE: Speed- Top 679 mph at s.1., 601 mph at 35,000', Cruising 533 mph, Stalling 121 mph. Service Ceiling 48,000', Climb 7470'/1 min., 40,000'/10.4 min. Combat radius 330 miles, Ferry range 1052 miles.

Six .50-caliber M-3s with 267 rpg at the sides of the nose intake were aimed using range-finding APG-30 radar in the intake's upper lip. External racks handled two 120-gallon drop tanks, 1,000-pound bombs, or up to 16 5-inch rockets.

The first swept wing fighters were extensively tested before replacing the F-80s of the First Fighter Group at March AFB, which received 83 F-86As from February to May 1949. Next came the 4th Fighter Group at Langley AFB, and the 81st at Kirtland AFB. Air Force Groups became Wings in January 1950, and Sabres were then supplied to the 33rd and 56th Fighter-Interceptor Wings. Production of 554 F-86As ended in December 1950.

A new threat calls Sabres to war

On February 22, 1949, the first swept wing MiG-15s arrived for the 29th GvIAP (Guards Fighter Air Regiment) near Moscow, the same month that Sabres first arrived at March AFB. That pioneer regiment moved to China in March 1950, and was based near Shanghai to protect the mainland from RoC planes on Taiwan. An F-5G Lightning became the first MiG victory claim on April 28.

In October, the Soviet pilots were about to leave China after turning over their 39 MiGs to the PLAAF's 10th Combat Regiment. But Mao Zedong had decided to send his army into Korea, and asked Stalin for air cover. The 29th GvIAP was sent new MiGs and relocated to Antung, on the Chinese side of the Yalu river. They were joined by the 72nd GvIAP, which first engaged F-51Ds on November 1, 1950, while pilots from the 29th fought the first skirmish with 51st FIS F-80Cs on November 8.

Six Soviet fighter regiments in Manchuria that winter were paired in the three divisions of the 64th IAK (Fighter Air Corps). Their mission was to intercept United Nations aircraft between the Yalu River and a line from Pyongyang to Wonsan. MiG pilots were forbidden to fly south of that line, which meant there was no air cover for Chinese troops at the front.

Russian pilots were ordered to pretend to be Chinese, and their MiGs wore PLAAF markings. Chinese pilots of the Joint Air Army were unready to fly MiGs in combat before June 1951, and North Korean pilots flew only a few propeller-driven Yak-9 and small Po-2 biplane sorties.

When the MiG-15 appeared over Korea, the 4th Fighter-Interceptor Wing was ordered on November 8 to move from Wilmington, Delaware, to Korea. They flew their F-86A-5s to San Diego and an escort carrier took them to Japan. A detachment of veteran pilots went to the Korean Kimpo base and on December 17, four Sabres flew their first combat mission and won their first victory.

In March 1951, the first Soviet air regiments were rotated out of Manchuria and replaced by new air divisions with newcomer pilots. Operations begun by the 51st Fighter Wing with new F-86Es in December 1951 increased American strength to 127 Sabres in Korea, but they remained outnumbered by enemy jets. During 1952, the VVS in Korea expanded to 17 MiG regiments, supported by some 12 MiG regiments of the Chinese-North Korean Joint Air Army.

When MiGs operated against straight-wing Americans, they were fairly successful during the war, downing 42 F-51s, -80s, and -84s for a loss of 15 MiGs, as well as 23 B-26 and B-29 bombers against 16 MiGs claimed by bomber gunners. But, although the F-86A was inferior to the lighter Soviet type in climb and ceiling, American pilots proved superior in air-to-air combat, especially against less experienced Chinese. Under orders to concentrate on bomb carriers, MiG pilots tended to avoid F-86s except when they had tactical advantages.

"Operation Ashtray" modifications began with two RF-86As with two guns on the right side replaced by a K-25 camera. Another six with guns replaced by various multi-camera arrangements were designated RF-86A-7, and began flying with the 15th TRS in Korea in 1952.

Work proceeded on improved Sabre versions. The F-86C became the YF-93 penetration fighter described later, while the F-86D designation was given the night fighter project known until July 24, 1950, as the F-95. That aircraft, with its radar, air-to-air rockets, and afterburner, is so different in operation from day-fighting Sabres that this night-fighter Sabre is considered in the next section on all-weather fighters.

NORTH AMERICAN F-86E-6
General Electric J47-GE-13, 5200 lb. st
DIMENSIONS: As F-86A
WEIGHT: Empty 10,555 lb., Combat 14,255 lb. Gross 16,346 lb. Fuel 435+240 gal.
PERFORMANCE: Speed- Top 679 mph at s.1., 601 mph at 35,000', Cruising 537 mph, Stalling 123 mph. Combat ceiling 45,000', Service Ceiling 47,200', Climb 7250'/1 min., 30,000'/6.3 min. Combat radius 320 miles, Ferry range 1022 miles.

The next Sabre version in production was the F-86E, which introduced the power-operated all-movable horizontal tail surface, but was otherwise identical to late F-86As with J47-GE-13s. Beginning in February 1951, the USAF accepted 336 F-86Es, plus 60 F-86E-6-CANs from Canadair by July 1952.

A 5,910-pound thrust J47-GE-27 was used by 1,159 F-86Fs, first flown March 19, 1952, and rushed to Korea in June 1952. The first 78 F-86F-1, had two 120-gallon drop tanks, but 200-gallon tanks could be carried on 57 F-86F-5 to F-15 models. Beginning with the F-86F-10, the six .50-caliber guns used an A-4 sight linked to APG-30 radar.

Most Sabres were built in Los Angeles, but North American had leased a Columbus, Ohio, plant in September 1950, and delivered 100 F-86F-20-NH and 600 F-86F-25-NH from September 1952 to March 1954. The F-86F-25-NH introduced fittings for two 200-gallon plus two 120-gallon drop tanks, or two 200-gallon tanks and two 1,000-pound bombs. They were followed by the Sabre's Navy version, the FJ-2 Fury.

In Los Angeles, deliveries began in October 1952 on 859 F-86F-30-NAs, the first to replace the slatted wing with an extended leading edge to improve speed and maneuverability and had enough combat radius to deliver bombs effectively. This model arrived in Korea in January 1953, serving the 18th and 8th Fighter-Bomber Wings. Kits were shipped to Korea to equip all older F-86s in hand to the new wing shape.

A South African squadron in Korea borrowed 22 USAF F-86F-30s in 1953.

NORTH AMERICAN F-86F-30
General Electric J47-GE-27, 5910 lb. st
DIMENSIONS: Span 37'1", Lg. 37'6", Ht. 14'9", Wing Area 302 sq. ft.
WEIGHT: Empty 10,890 lb., Combat 13,076 lb., Gross 17,921 lb., Max. 20,357 lb. Fuel 435+640 gal.
PERFORMANCE: Speed- Top 695 mph at s.1., 608 mph at 35,000', Cruising 486 mph, Stalling 144 mph. Service Ceiling 48,000', Climb 9300'/1 min., 35,000'/7.5 min. Combat radius 458 miles, 316 mph/2,000 lb., Ferry range 1615 miles.

Five F-86E-10 and six F-86F-1s armed with four 20-mm T-60 guns were redesignated F-86F-2s, while two F-84F-1s modified for Oerlikon guns became F-86F-3 airplanes. Called the "Gun-Val" project, they were combat tested in March 1953, and proved the value of heavier gun calibers.

In 87,177 sorties from December 1950 to July 1953, Sabres were credited with 792 MiGs and 13 older aircraft, losing 78 F-86s to the MiGs, 19 to ground fire, 13 to unknown causes, and 114 to non-enemy or non-operational causes. Much of this success was due to the superior experience and skill of American pilots, and in some part to improvements made on the F-86F. Readers can contrast the American and Russian fighter experiences in the detailed books by Dorr and Gordon cited in the chapter notes.

By June 1954, the USAF had 14 F-86F wings in service including the four (lst, 8th, 18th, and 51st) with Korean combat experience. The top aces of that war were Capt. Joseph McConnell, Jr. with 16 victories, Maj. James Jabara (15), Capt. Manuel J. Fernandez (14), and Major George A. Davis, Jr. (14).

More powerful Sabres

The first models fitted to carry a 1,200-pound Mk 12 nuclear bomb under the port wing, released by a Low Altitude Bombing System (LABS), were 265 F-86F-35-NAs delivered from January to June 1954. The 48th FBW based in Chaumont, France, had 89 of these in July 1954. Two F-86Fs were completed in December 1953 and August 1954 as two-place TF-86F trainers.

Three RF-86F-30 planes modified in Japan with five cameras were followed by eight factory modified with all guns replaced by three newer cameras. These were used by the 15th TRS to secretly photograph Soviet air bases near Vladivostok, beginning on March 22, 1954. Each had two 200-gallon and two 130-gallon drop tanks, and the deepest and last mission was flown to photograph the Khabarosvsk area on February 19, 1955. Another 18 RF-86F camera planes were converted by Mitsubishi for the Japanese and Republic of China forces.

NORTH AMERICAN F-86F-5
General Electric J47-GE-27, 5910 lb. st
DIMENSIONS: As F-86A
WEIGHT: Empty 10,815 lb., Combat 14,857 lb. Gross 17,772 lb., Fuel 435+400 gal.
PERFORMANCE: Speed- Top 688 mph at s.1., 604 mph at 35,000', Cruising 513 mph, Stalling 128 mph. Service Ceiling 48,000', Climb 9300'/1 min., 35,000'/7.5 min. Combat radius 463 miles, Ferry range 1317 miles.

NORTH AMERICAN F-86F-10/25
Extended wing modification on 4th FIW Sabres at Kimpo, Korea in 1953.

The first Sabre actually designed as a fighter-bomber was the F-86H begun March 16, 1951, which used a larger intake and fuel capacity for a J73-GE-3 engine. A mockup was inspected in July 1951, and the first of two F-86H-1-NAs built at Los Angeles flew May 9, 1953. The Columbus Ohio plant flew its first F-86H-1-NH September 4, and delivered 113 F-86H-ls armed with six .50-caliber guns with 300 rpg, an LABS for a Mk 12 nuclear weapon, or conventional stores. Extended wing tips and leading edges were added, beginning with the 15th aircraft.

NORTH AMERICAN F-86H-10
General Electric J73-GE-3D, 8920 lb. st
DIMENSIONS: Span 39'1", Lg. 38'10", Ht. 15', Wing Area 313 sq. ft.
WEIGHT: Empty 13,836 lb., Combat 18,683 lb. Gross 21,852 lb., Max. 24,296 lb. Fuel 562+400+240 gal.
PERFORMANCE: Speed- Top 692 mph at s.1., 617 mph at 35,000, Cruising 552 mph, Stalling 138 mph. Service Ceiling 50,800', Climb 12,900'/1 min. Combat radius 519 miles, 400 mies/2000 lb. bombs, Ferry range 1810 miles.

Four 20-mm M-39s with 150 rpg armed 360 F-86H-5-NHs and H-10s delivered at Columbus from January 1955 to April 1956. The F-86H entered operational service with the 312th FBW in October 1954, and was used by three wings (50th, 83rd, & 312th) until passed to the Air National Guard by June 1958. Despite the increase in power, air-frame limits prevented much increase in speed over the F-86F, but acceleration and climb were better.

Sabres in foreign service

At least 26 foreign nations used the Sabre, beginning with those made near Montreal by Canadair. The first Canadair Sabre was a single Mark 1, assembled from NAA F-86A-5 parts and flown August 9, 1950, a year after the contract. Then 350 Mk 2 (F-86E-6) and 438 similar Mk 4s followed by 1953. Twelve RCAF squadrons were flown across the ocean to back NATO, and the first swept-wing fighters with the RAF were three Mk 2 and 428 Mk 4 Sabres delivered for 12 squadrons, formed beginning in May 1953.

When Turkey began receiving 105 Mk 2 Sabres from Canada in July 1954, they were balanced by 104 ex-RAF Sabres for Greece. After RAF Mk 4 Sabres were replaced by new Hunters in 1956, 180 were passed on to Italy and 121 to Yugoslavia.

Canadian Avro Orenda engines used on the remaining Canadair Sabres were tested first on a NAA F-86J (modified F-86A) in October 1950 and on a single Canadair Sabre Mk 3. Beginning in July 1953, 370 Mk 5 (6,355-pound thrust Orenda 10) and 655 Mk 6 (7,275-pound thrust Orenda 14) were built, with a total of 1,815 Canadair Sabres by October 9, 1958. Most went to the RCAF, but 34 Mk 6s went to South Africa in April 1956, and six to Colombia in June. West Germany got 75 Mk 5s, beginning in May 1957, and the last 225 Mk 6 Sabres.

CANADAIR SABRE Mk 6

Other European allies got second-hand USAF F-86Fs, beginning with five allocated to Belgium in June 1955. Spain began receiving 244 in September 1955, Norway got 115 F-86Fs beginning in March 1957, and Portugal 50 in 1958. South American countries sent ex-USAAF F-86Fs were Peru (26 in 1955) and Venezuela (30 from 1955 to 1960), while Argentina got 28 in 1960.

Australia's Commonwealth Aircraft was chosen in February 1951 to build their own Sabre version, with a 7,500-pound thrust Rolls-Royce Avon and two 30-mm Aden guns. A prototype built of U.S. components was flown August 3, 1953, and 111 production CA-27 Sabres followed from July 1954 to December 1961. They served five RAAF fighter squadrons until 1969, when 16 were sold to Malaysia, and Indonesia got 18 in 1973.

Chinese Nationalists (the RoC) on Taiwan got 320 F-86F and seven RF-86F Sabres beginning on November 29, 1954, and these second-hand USAF jets found themselves engaging MiGs again on October 15, 1955, fighting over off-shore islands. Sidewinder infrared homing missiles were first used in combat by the Sabres on September 24, 1958, destroying ten enemy jets and ending the seven-week battle.

Japan used the Sabres in the greatest numbers. An agreement made July 13, 1954, provided for joint production of a new model, F-86F-40, by North American and Mitsubishi, maker of the wartime Zero fighter. With both new extended wing tips and leading edge slats, this model, flown in October 1955, had greatly improved handling qualities and lower stalling speeds than earlier models, which were often modified to the new standards.

North American delivered the last of 280 F-86F-40s on December 28, 1956, 6,210 Sabres having been built in the United States and 300 sets of parts forwarded to Mitsubishi in Japan. Japan received 29 second-hand F-86F-25/30s and 180 new F-86F-40s by June 1957, but returned 45 of the latter to the USAF. Mitsubishi's first F-86F-40 was flown

August 9, 1956, but a 1959 typhoon delayed the contract's completion to February 1961. Mitsubishi also modified 18 F-86Fs to RF-86F camera planes.

NORTH AMERICAN F-86F-40
General Electric J47-GE-27, 5910 lb. st
DIMENSIONS: Span 39'1", Lg. 37'7", Ht. 14'9", Wing Area 313 sq. ft.
WEIGHT: Empty 11,125 lb., Combat 15,352 lb., Gross 18,152 lb., Max. 20,611 lb. Fuel 437+640 gal.
PERFORMANCE: Speed- Top 678 mph at s.l., 599 mph at 35,000', Cruising 529 mph, Stalling 124 mph. Service Ceiling 47,000', Climb 30,000'/5.2 min. Combat radius 463 miles. Ferry range 1525 miles.

But the Sabre next saw combat with Pakistan, who received 102 F-86F-40s in 1956-57. These served seven of the ten Pakistani Air Force squadrons (the rest had B-57Bs and F-104As) during the September 1965 war with India. Again, Sidewinders were used successfully, this time against Hawker Hunters. This conflict halted U.S. supplies to Pakistan, who, nevertheless, managed to obtain 90 ex-German Canadair Mk 6 Sabres in 1966.

South Korea got 112 F-86Fs and ten RF-86As, beginning in June 1955, and the Philippine Air Force got 40 F-86Fs in 1957. Saudi Arabia received ten F-86F Sabres in 1957 and eight more in 1969, Thailand got 40 by April 1962, and Tunisia, 12 ex-Japanese F-86Fs in 1969.

All-weather Fighters

Shortly after the war with Japan ended, the Air Technical Service Command (ATSC) issued requirements for three kinds of specialized fighters, described as All-weather, Penetration, and Interceptor types. The largest of these would be the "all-weather fighter" with room for radar and an electronics operator to operate in darkness or any bad flying weather.

Tentative characteristics issued November 23, 1945, included a 550-mph top speed, 1,000-mile radius of action, heavy weapons, and ground attack capability. Curtiss received authorization on December 26 to go ahead with its Model 29A night fighter design by using funds remaining from an aborted XA-43 contract. An amended contract for two XP-87 prototypes was issued March 22, 1946.

The mockup officially inspected July 16, 1946, provided for four Westinghouse J34 jets paired under the wings, double-wheels for the tricycle gear, 600-gallon wingtip tanks, and side-by-side seats for the pilot and radar operator. Armament was to include four 20-mm guns in a Martin conical nose turret that could swing the barrels in a 60-degree arc around the nose, and was aimed by a periscope sight or by APG-3 radar. A planned remote-control tail turret with two .50-caliber guns was eliminated to save weight.

When it was realized that the Martin turret would not be available until 1949, the prototype was completed without any guns at the Columbus, Ohio, factory in October 1947. Shipment by road to the Muroc test base met with accidents and flight tests were delayed until March 1, 1948.

Although the overweight Curtiss XP-87 Blackhawk (soon redesignated XF-87) did not reach the 600-mph speed promised, a contract for 58 F-87s and 30 RF-87As was authorized June 1, 1948. They were to use the two 6,000-pound thrust J47 engines planned for the uncompleted second prototype, but on October 19, 1948, that contract was canceled to free funds for other projects, and the famous Curtiss name was never again used on a new combat plane.

The first Scorpions

The Curtiss design was defeated by the more successful F-89 long-range all-weather fighter. Responding to the same November 23, 1945, requirement, Northrop offered four different proposals, of which the Air Force chose the most conventional, avoiding more problematic tailless layouts.

Northrop received a letter contract approved on June 13, 1946, for two prototypes of its NS-24 specification, and the mockup was inspected in September. That contract was formalized December 18 and approved on May 21, 1947. On August 16, 1948, the first XF-89 prototype was flown at Muroc by Fred Bretcher.

NORTHROP XF-89
Two Allison J35-A-15, 4000 lb. st
DIMENSIONS: Span 52', Lg. 50'6", Ht. 17'8", Wing Area 606 sq. ft.
WEIGHT: Empty 25,864 lb., Gross 43,910 lb. Max. 48,936 lb. Fuel 1160+1200 gal.
PERFORMANCE: Speed- Top 603 mph at 2500', Cruising 497 mph, Stalling 127 mph. Service Ceiling 35,500', Climb 35,000'/21 min. Range 1750 miles.

Powered by two 4,000-pound thrust J35-A-9 jets tucked against the fuselage under the thin wing, the XF-89 had split-edge full-span flaps lining the trailing edge out to 600-gallon wingtip fuel tanks. The outer panels of these flaps acted as both ailerons and speed brakes. Pilot and radar man sat in tandem ejection seats. A high tail and the black finish inspired the name Scorpion.

Originally, the rounded nose was designed for four 20-mm guns in a turret that could swing the barrels in a 30-

Mfr

CURTISS XF-87
Two Westinghouse XJ34-WE-7/9, 3000-lb. st
DIMENSIONS: Span 60', Lg. 62'10", Ht. 20'6", Wing Area 600 sq. ft.
WEIGHT: Empty 27,935 lb., Gross 39,875 lb., Max. 49,900 lb. Fuel 1380+1200 gal.
PERFORMANCE: Speed- Top 584 mph at s.l., 532 mph at 29,300'. Service Ceiling 45,500', Climb 5500'/1 min. Ferry range 2175 miles.

degree arc, but in August 1947 that Northrop design had been replaced by the Martin conical nose turret planned for the XP-87. By September, it was decided to complete the XF-89 without guns and fit the second prototype and production aircraft with six 20-mm fixed guns.

That second aircraft became the pre-production prototype, YF-89A, flown on June 27, 1950. It introduced a pointed nose, 5,200-pound thrust J35-A-21s with afterburners added, fixed 306-gallon wingtip fuel tanks and dispensed with the solid black paint previously the night owl's uniform.

Mfr

NORTHROP YF-89A

A contract approved July 14, 1949, had ordered 48 similar F-89As and deliveries began in September 1950. When a new autopilot and instrument landing system was installed, beginning with the 12th aircraft in February 1951, they became F-89Bs. Powered with J35-A-21 engines, these Northrops had APG-33 radar in the nose with six 20-mm guns and 200 rpg, and under wing fittings could accommodate two 1,600-pound bombs or 16 5-inch rockets. Northrop Scorpions first went into service with the 78th Fighter-Interceptor Group at Hamilton AFB in June 1951, but the high-performance fighters were so complex that they would take a long time to become fully operational.

A refined version, the F-89C, ordered June 20, 1950, and first flown September 18, 1951, replaced the external elevator mass balances with internal ones. Of 163 F-89Cs, the first 64 were delivered with J35-A-21A engines, the next 45 (beginning February 1952) with J35-A-33s, and the rest completed with J35-A-35s by November 1952. The F-89C entered service in January 1952, but after several aircraft were lost to fatigue failure of wing fittings due to aero elasticity, all Scorpions were grounded September 22, 1952, until the wing structure could be changed. All had to be returned to the factory to be reworked, until 194

NORTHROP F-89A
Two Allison J35-A-21, 5200 lb. st (6800 lb. AB)
DIMENSIONS: Span 56', Lg. 53'6', Ht. 17'6", Wing Area 606 sq. ft.
WEIGHT: Empty 23,645 lb., Combat 31,680 lb., Gross 36,400 lb., Max. 42,026 lb. Fuel 1004+612 gal.
PERFORMANCE: Speed- Top 642 mph at s.1., 570 mph at 35,000', Cruising 497 mph, Stalling 113 mph. Combat Ceiling 50,200', Service Ceiling 51,400', Climb 10,800'/1 min. Combat radius 425 miles, Ferry range 1300 miles.

NORTHROP F-89C
Two Allison J35-A-33, 5600 lb. st (7400 lb. with AB)
DIMENSIONS: Span 56', Lg. 53'6", Ht. 17'6", Wing Area 606 sq. ft.
WEIGHT: Empty 24,570 lb., Combat 33,100 lb., Gross 37,348 lb. Fuel 947+612 gal.
PERFORMANCE: Speed- Top 650 mph at s.1., 562 mph at 40,000', 531 mph at 47,800', Cruising 489 mph, Stalling 122 mph. Combat Ceiling 47,800', Service Ceiling 50,500', Climb 12,300'/1 min., 50,000'/24.5 min. Combat radius 389 miles, Ferry range 905 miles.

F-89A/B/Cs were returned to service beginning on February 23, 1953.

Lockheed F-94

The first all-weather jet fighter actually in Air Force service was the Lockheed F-94, a less sophisticated single-engine type that could be obtained more quickly because 75% of its parts were included in F-80Cs in current production. Lockheed was told to go ahead on the YF-94 on October 14, 1948, and a November 10 letter contract ordered 110 similar F-94As. Two YF-94 prototypes were rebuilt from TF-80C two-seat trainers, the first was tested April 16, 1949, and the first F-94A flew July 1, 1949.

The wings, tail, and landing gear were those of the F-80; only the fuselage was new. There were 940 pounds of APG-33 radar in the nose and a radar operator sitting behind the pilot. Four .50-caliber guns were directed by the Hughes E-1 fire control, and two 1,000-pound bombs could be added. An Allison J33-A-33 of 4,600-pounds dry thrust had a Solar afterburner to boost this to 6,000-pounds for brief moments of climb and dash, but that devoured fuel so fast that it could be used only sparingly. The F-94A was the first production job with an afterburner; which have since become standard on fighters in which short bursts of power are more important than range.

LOCKHEED F-94A-5
Allison J33-A-33, 4600 lb. st (6000 lb. AB)
DIMENSIONS: Span 38'11", Lg. 40'1", Ht. 12'8", Wing Area 238 sq. ft.
WEIGHT: Empty 9557 lb., Gross 12,919 lb., Max. 15,330 lb. Fuel 318+330 gal.
PERFORMANCE: Speed- Top 606 mph at s.l., 546 mph at 35,000', Cruising 443 mph, Landing 122 mph. Service Ceiling 49,750', Climb 11,274'/1 min. Range 1079 miles.

One F-94A was modified to the YF-94B configuration in September 1950, and 356 F-94Bs first ordered March 3, 1950, were delivered from January 1951 to January 1952 and appeared with center-mounted 230-gallon tanks on each wing tip, instead of the 165-gallon tanks on the F-94A. A Sperry Zero Reader instrument was added to aid blind landings.

Lockheed F-94s entered USAF service in May 1950 with the 325th Fighter-Interceptor Group at McChord AFB, and then with the 52nd Group at McGuire AFB in New Jersey. The former group's 319th Squadron was transferred to Korea in March 1952.

At first its missions were limited to local defense, so the radar equipment would not be captured, but more aggressive tactics were allowed in 1953 to support B-29 operations. An F-94B made the first night kill, a prop-driven La-11, on January 30, 1953, and the squadron claimed two MiGs and a Po-2 biplane in the spring, while an F-94B collided with a Po-2 on June 12, destroying both aircraft. Three F-94s were lost in action and six to non-enemy operational causes.

Penetration Fighters

While some engineers wrestled with the problem of stopping the bombers, others tried to build fighters to protect

LOCKHEED F-94B interior
Allison J33-A-33, 4600 lb. st (6000 lb. AB)
DIMENSIONS: Span 38'11", Lg. 40'1", Ht. 12'8", Wing Area 235 sq. ft.
WEIGHT: Empty 10,064 lb., Combat 13,474 lb., Max. 16,844 lb. Fuel 318+460 gal.
PERFORMANCE: Speed- Top 588 mph at s.l., 490 mph at 35,000', Cruising 452 mph, Landing 122 mph. Combat ceiling 45,700', Service ceiling 47,260', Climb 7800'/1 min. Combat radius 332 miles, Range 905 miles.

bombers from enemy interception. Heavy losses of bombers on daytime sorties had made escort missions penetrating deep into enemy territory the main concern of wartime Air Force fighters, and postwar designers did not forget the problem.

The most specialized escort fighter was the McDonnell Model 27D, offered March 19, 1945, as a parasite fighter to be carried inside a B-36. On October 9, a letter contract ordered two XP-85 prototypes. When big bombers on a mission were menaced, the concept was that some might open their bomb bay, lower parasites on a trapeze, launch them and at the end of the engagement recover any survivors. These fighters would have to be small enough to fit inside bomb bays, yet equal enemy interceptors in performance.

McDonnell's answer to the unique problem was short enough to fit a 16-foot long bay, and its swept wings folded to only 5 feet,5 inches in width, and 10 feet,3 inches in height. The pilot straddled a 3000-pound thrust Westinghouse J34-WE-22 with about 32 minutes of fuel, and preliminary estimates promised a top speed of 664 mph. Four .50-caliber guns were grouped about the nose intake. Instead of landing wheels, there was a retractable hook for the trapeze of the carrier plane. Tail span was reduced by dividing the tail into six odd-shaped surfaces.

A mockup of the parasite fighter and the B-36 bay and trapeze was inspected at St. Louis in June 1946, and a definitive contract approved February 5, 1947. Since a B-36 would not be available on time, an EB-29B was modified as a carrier plane. As the XF-85 Goblin descended on its trapeze from the mother plane, it looked like a fat little bug.

Edwin F. Schoch made the first XF-85 test flight on August 23, 1948, but when he attempted to return to the mother plane, the trapeze smashed the canopy, and he was forced to make an emergency landing on a belly skid. Another attempt on October 14 succeeded, but the difficulty of recovering the parasites had been demonstrated.

After Schoch made seven free flights, the test program terminated on October 24, and a service test contract was forgotten. The parasite fighter concept, first seen in the Navy's Sparrowhawks, was tried again with the RF-84F

McDONNELL XF-85
Westinghouse J34-WE-22, 3000 lb. st
DIMENSIONS: Span 21'1", Lg. 16'4", Ht. 8'4", Wing Area 100.5 sq. ft.
WEIGHT: Empty 3984 lb., Combat\Gross 5600 lb. Fuel 115-201 gal.
PERFORMANCE: Speed- Top 648 mph at s.l., 581 mph at 35,000', Combat Ceiling 46,750', Service Ceiling 48,000', Climb 12,500'/1 min, 35,000'/5.1 min. Combat Endurance 20 min. full power, 32 min. cruising.

FICON system, but did not earn the Air Force's confidence as feasible for actual combat.

A more practical approach to the escort fighter was the Air Force request in August 1945 for penetration fighter designs with two engines, a 2,000-mile range, and 630-mph top speed. This requirement resulted in the XF-88 and XP-90, built with two Westinghouse J34 jets buried within the fuselage, large fuel tanks, 35-degree swept wings, and six 20-mm guns.

McDonnell's Model 36 design begun April 1, 1946, received a letter of intent May 7, and won a contract approved February 14, 1947, for two prototypes. The first XF-88 flew October 20, 1948, at Muroc with 3,000-pound thrust XJ34-WE-13s. A second, the XF-88A, flew April 26, 1949, with 3,600-pound thrust XJ34-WE-15s that added short afterburners to boost thrust to 4,825 pounds, and mounted the six 20-mm M-24 guns. Top speed increased from 641 t0 718 mph, but even without the two planned 350-gallon drop tanks, which proved unsafe, or a bomb load, weight was too high.

After 265 test flights, both aircraft were retired in August 1950, but the XF-88 was later reworked for NACA as a unarmed test bed for the Allison XT38 turboprop engine. Known as the XF-88B, it flew in that three-engine configuration from April 24, 1953, to January 1958.

Lockheed's XF-90, first ordered June 20, 1946, and flown June 6, 1949, was distinguished by a needle-nose, jet exhausts running back to the tail, and wings flush with fuselage bottom. The six 20-mm guns were mounted under the air intakes, and a pair of 1,000-pound bombs under the wings, or a 220-gallon drop tank could be carried on each wingtip.

Westinghouse XJ34-WE-11s on early flights were replaced by the XJ34-WE-15 with an afterburner on both prototypes, which then became the XF-90A in 1950. During the test flights at Edwards AFB, Tony LeVier reached Mach 1.12 in a dive. Using stronger 75ST aluminum made Lockheed's design so much heavier than the XF-88, that the F-90s were soon discarded.

McDONNELL XF-85 (launch from B-29)

A third penetration fighter was begun at North American on December 17, 1947, as the NA-157. As a Sabre development, it was first called the F-86C, and while 120 scheduled in June 1948 were canceled in January 1949 to provide more funds for bombers, two were ordered by the Air Force as the YF-93A on February 25, 1949.

AF

McDONNELL XF-88
Two Westinghouse J34-WE-13, 3000 lb. st
DIMENSIONS: Span 39'8", Lg. 54'2", Ht. 17'3", Wing Area 350 sq. ft.
WEIGHT: Empty 12,140 lb., Gross 18,500 lb., Max. 23,100 lb. Fuel 734+700 gal.
PERFORMANCE: Speed- Top 641 mph at s.1., Cruising 527 mph, Stalling 140 mph. Service Ceiling 36,000', Climb 35,000'/14.5 min. Range 1737 miles.

AF

McDONNELL XF-88A

Mfr

LOCKHEED XF-90
Two Westinghouse XJ34-WE-11, 3000 lb. st (later WE-15, 4200 lb. st AB)
DIMENSIONS: Span 40', Lg. 56'2", Ht. 15'9", Wing Area 345 sq. ft.
WEIGHT: Empty 18,520 lb., Gross 27,200 lb., Max. 31,060 lb. Fuel 1225+440 gal. max.
PERFORMANCE: Speed- Top 668 mph at 1000', Cruising 473 mph, Stalling 145 mph. Service Ceiling 39,000', Climb 25,000'/4.5 min. Range 1050 miles normal, 2300 miles max.

First flown January 25, 1950, the YF-93A was larger than the Sabres, and had a long solid nose, side intakes, wider fuselage for the centrifugal-flow J48 with afterburner, and dual main wheels. Automatic wing slots were provided and the armament included six 20-mm guns and two 1,000-pound bombs when desired. After Air Force tests, both prototypes went to the NACA for study of various intake arrangements.

Mfr

NORTH AMERICAN YF-93
Pratt & Whitney J48-P-1, 6000 lb. st (8000 lb. AB)
DIMENSIONS: Span 38'11", Lg. 44'1", Ht. 15'8", Wing Area 306 sq. ft.
WEIGHT: Empty 14,035 lb., Combat 21,610 lb., Gross 26,516 lb. Fuel 1581 gal.
PERFORMANCE: Speed- Top 708 mph at s.1., 622 mph at 35,000', Cruising 534 mph, Stalling 150 mph. Combat Ceiling 45,500', Service Ceiling 46,800', Climb 11,960'/1 min. Range 1967 miles.

Shortages of funds, and improvement of the F-84 series prevented procurement of one of these penetration fighters, even the XF-88, seen as the best in comparative tests. Strategic Air Command had six F-84G Strategic Fighter wings attached by 1953, but they were reequipped with swept wing F-84Fs (ex F-96s).

Interceptors

The Air Force developed a requirement in December 1945 for a bomber interceptor that could climb to 47,500 feet in 2.5 minutes, cruise for 15 minutes, fight for three minutes at supersonic (792 mph) speeds and descend to land in five minutes. Partly inspired by the rocket-powered Messerschmitt Me 163, this interceptor would need a power plant allowing rapid acceleration for a short range.

Republic presented its AP-31 design, the first fighter designed for supersonic speeds, and a contract for two XP-91 interceptors was made May 29, 1946, but engineering and government paperwork took so long that final contract approval was delayed to January 27, 1949.

To avoid tip stalls at low speeds, the XP-91 had unique inverse tapered wings that were wider at the tips than at the roots. Swept back 35°, they had variable incidence to provide a low angle of attack for flight and a higher angle for extra lift on takeoff and landings. A pair of tandem main wheels was kept small enough to fit in the thin wings.

The intended power plant was a General Electric J47 with afterburner supplemented by a 90-second blast from four Curtiss-Wright XLR-27 rocket units in the tail. Liquid oxygen (LOX) fuel, cooled by water/alcohol (WALC), was expected to add 2,100-pound thrust from each unit.

But that original power plant was not perfected, and only a J47-GE-3 with 559 gallons of jet fuel (JP) in the fuselage powered the first flight on May 9, 1949. Now called the XF-91 Thunderceptor, it was tested at Muroc by Carl Bellinger. The second XF-91 was flown October 14 with a J47-GE-17, but the proposed armament of four 20-mm guns in the nose was never fitted to the prototypes.

REPUBLIC XF-91
General Electric J47-GE-9, 5000 lb. st (6800 lb. AB) and four Curtiss-Wright XLR-27-CW-1, 2100 lb st each.
DIMENSIONS: Span 31'3", Lg. 43'3", Ht. 18'1", Wing Area 320 sq. ft.
WEIGHT: Empty 14,140 lb., Combat 18,600 lb. Gross 28,300 lb., Fuel 1568 gal.
PERFORMANCE: Speed- Top 918 mph at 35,000', 984 mph at 47,500' (with 2 rockets), Stalling 138 mph. Combat Ceiling 47,500', Service Ceiling 48,700', Climb 47,500'/2.5 min., Cruise 15 min. at 560 mph, 3 min. of combat, 5 min. for descent. Total mission time- 25.5 min.
[Planned data for completed aircraft as estimated November 1950]

Reaction Motors XLR-11-RM-9 1,500-pound thrust rockets became available in 1952, and fuselage tanks were arranged for 331 JP gallons, 137 gallons of LOX, and 141 gallons of water/alcohol. Two external tanks could be provided under wings, each with 60 gallons of JP, 218 of LOX, and 265 of WALC.

On December 9, 1952, Republic test pilot Russell Roth made the first supersonic rocket-powered flight by an American combat plane, reaching Mach 1.07 at 35,000 feet over Edwards AFB. Republic also planned that a XF-9lA version with a 5,200-pound thrust J47-GE-21 and four XLR-RM-9 rockets totaling 6,000-pounds of thrust would reach 1,126 mph at 50,000 feet, but this configuration was not actually tested. The concept of rocket-powered point defense was not accepted by the Air Force.

The First American delta wing aircraft

When the Air Force announced a design competition in August 1945 for a supersonic interceptor capable of climbing to 50,000 feet in four minutes and reaching 700 mph, Convair submitted a specification on November 15.

An Air Force Letter of Intent to purchase dated May 2, 1946, was followed by a contract signed June 28 for two XP-92 rocket-propelled prototypes with wings swept back 45 degrees, a V-tail, and a power plant composed of a ramjet, four 1,500-pound thrust Reaction Motors XLR-11 rocket motors for acceleration, and a Westinghouse turbojet for cruising.

After wind tunnel tests indicated a delta wing configuration would be more successful in approaching supersonic flight, Convair engineers met with Dr. Alexander Lippisch in July 1946. Designer of World War II's fastest fighter, the Me 163 rocket-powered interceptor, Dr. Lippisch's next step had been to design of a tailless delta-wing fighter, preceded by a delta glider for test work. The preliminary design, glider, and the engineer himself were brought to the U.S. after the war.

A thin delta-shaped wing with a 60° sweepback on the leading edge was chosen, and the contract amended November 7, 1946, to authorize construction of a full-scale flying model with a conventional J33 engine to test the actual flight characteristics of the delta wing.

Development of the XP-92 itself continued with novelties like a high triangular fin, a pressurized cockpit pod within the ramjet intake duct at the front of the barrel-shaped fuselage, and a takeoff trolley. Armament was to be four 20-mm guns, and projected performance was a four-minute climb to 50,000 feet where top speed was to be 1,165 mph.

But the project was delayed by moving from Downey to San Diego in 1947, and because of the undeveloped nature of the power plant and other features the AAF terminated the XF-92 on 5 August 1948. but the full-scale flying model continued as the XF-92A.

Using an Allison J33-A-21, and some parts from other aircraft the XF-92A arrived at Muroc Dry Lake April 9, 1948. During a taxi test on June 9, test pilot E. D. Shannon lifted it a few feet off the ground for a short run, but he made the first official flight of an American delta-wing

CONVAIR XF-92A with afterburner
Allison J33-A-29, 5600 lb. st (7500 lb. AB)
DIMENSIONS: Span 31'4", Lg. 42'10", Ht. 17'6", Wing Area 425 sq. ft.
WEIGHT: Empty 11,808 lb., Gross 15,560 lb., Fuel 560 gal.
PERFORMANCE: Speed- Top 718 mph at s.1., 655 mph at 35,000'. Combat Ceiling 50,750', Climb 13,000'/1 min., 35,000'/4.3 min.

CONVAIR XF-92A
Allison J33-A-23, 5400 lb. st with WE
DIMENSIONS: Span 31'4", Lg. 42'6", Ht. 17'9", Wing Area 425 sq. ft.
WEIGHT: Empty 9,078 lb., Combat 13,000 lb. Gross 14,608 lb., Fuel 300 gal.
PERFORMANCE: Speed- Top 552 mph at s.1., 631 mph at 35,000'. Climb 30.000'/12.9 min.

aircraft September 18, 1948, after a 4,250-pound thrust J33-A-23 had been fitted.

After 47 flights by company pilots proved the XF-92As practical qualities, Major Charles Yeager, who had made the first supersonic flight, began Air Force tests. There wasn't enough power for supersonic speeds, except in very steep dives, so the XF-92A returned to San Diego in 1950 to get a J33-A-29 with afterburner. Tests resumed July 20, 1951, but the aircraft remained sub-sonic, although 118 research flights did validate the wing design and clear the way for the successful F-102 and B-58 designs.

Rocket-firing interceptors

Detonation of the first Soviet atomic bomb on August 29, 1949, spurred American interceptor development as the Air Defense Command was directed to prepare a defense against the probability that the long-planned Strategic Air Command attack on the adversary would be matched by a counterstroke from enemy long-range bombers.

There were 293 U.S. facilities defined by a May 1949 JCS study as *vital*; that is, those whose "loss would mean the elimination of our ability to retaliate with strategic air power...and would delay for several years the development of our war potential to fight offensively in enemy-held territories." War plan Dropshot projected a Soviet long-range force by 1957 of 1,800 bombers directed against the United Kingdom and the United States. The Air Defense Command had to anticipate that enemy radar development by then would enable all attacks to be made at night, and therefore all U.S. interceptors should have all-weather capability.

Atomic weapons place exceptional demands on defense systems. No longer will prospects of heavy losses discourage an attacker when his surviving bombers may inflict fatal injuries on an enemy. Fighters may fail to stop an attack if their guns are poorly aimed, or if the enemy bombers endure damage long enough to reach their targets. Defense now requires weapons systems capable of guaranteeing destruction of bombers at first contact.

NORTH AMERICAN YF-86D firing air-to-air rockets

One answer to this problem was a new weapons system, largely replacing guns on Air Defense Command fighters, consisting of 2.75-in. air-to-air rockets aimed and fired in salvo by a radar-directed automatic computer. With that system, an interceptor takes off and is vectored by directions from ground radar to a lead collision course at right angles to the bomber's path, instead of approaching from the rear in the pursuit-curve attack of the past. After the target is picked up by the fighter's radar, the pilot directs his plane so as to center the target on his scope. When a certain range is closed, the Hughes electronic computer takes over flight control through an autopilot and at the proper moment automatically fires a salvo of rockets. The pilot only monitors the actual attack, resuming control to return to his base.

The system had several advantages. Exposure of the fighter to bomber defense guns is brief, accuracy is greater in all kinds of weather, and only one of the rockets need strike the target to destroy it. The four-foot, eighteen-pound FFAR (Folding Fin Aircraft Rocket) was called Mighty Mouse. Firing a salvo of mice at an invisible aircraft presumes one too large and steady to evade the missiles; one pilot shot down by mistake the B-17 guide plane instead of his radio-controlled target.

The first plane designed for the new weapon was the swept wing North American YF-95A. This plane was begun March 28, 1949, as an all-weather interceptor version of the F-86, with radar and afterburner added and became the first single-seat all-weather jet fighter in any country. A letter contract for two YF-95Ds and 122 F-95Ds was prepared by October 7, 1949, and the first prototype was flown December 22, without armament provisions.

In February 1950, a choice of rocket armament was made and a Hughes fire control system specified, and a formal production contract for 153 aircraft approved June 2, 1950. These aircraft (NA-165) were known as F-95As until July 24, 1950, when the designation reverted to F-86D, so that funds budgeted for the F-86 could be used and a new appropriation by Congress would not be needed. This consideration also affected the Republic F-96 and Lockheed F-97 projects.

The second prototype went to Hughes Aircraft in October 1950 to prove out the E-3 fire control system, while the initial YF-86D became the first American fighter to fire air-to-air (not air-to-surface) rockets in February 1951. Twenty-four 2.75-inch rockets were carried in a retractable tray that popped out of the belly just long enough to launch them at targets about 500 yards away.

The Sabre-Dog's effectiveness, however, depended on its fire control system, and this development fell behind schedule. The first 37 F-86D-ls were to have simplified E-3 systems, but these were not finished when delivery began in March 1951, and all 37 could not be accepted until October 1952, three years after the original letter contract.

As for the more complex E-4 system needed for a lead collision attack course, the one installed in the first F-86D-5 delivered in July 1952, still required work. By 1953, more than 320 F-86Ds were parked at the factory waiting for various electronic items to appear. Yet the Air Defense Command (ADC) depended on the F-86D and so it entered squadron service in April 1953 despite unsolved problems.

New contracts had been approved in April 1951, for 188 more F-86Ds, and 638 in July; the latter were briefly known as F-86Gs, but were returned to the F-86D series.

By June 1953, production orders reached 2,504 aircraft, and three ADC wings flew them along with seven F-94 wings and an F-89 wing. General Electric J47-GE-17 engines were replaced by -17B engines on 1,517 F-86D-1 to D-40s and improved J47-GE-33s powered the last 987, beginning with F-86D-45.

NORTH AMERICAN F-86D-1
General Electric J47-GE-17, 5425 lb. st (7500 lb. AB)
DIMENSIONS: Span 37"1", Lg. 40'3", Ht. 15', Wing Area 288 sq. ft.
WEIGHT: Empty 13,518 lb., Combat 16,068 lb. Gross 18,183 lb., Max. 19,975 lb. Fuel 608+240 gal.
PERFORMANCE: Speed- Top 692 mph at s.l., 612 mph at 40,000', Cruising 550 mph, Stalling 130 mph. Service Ceiling 49,750', Climb 12,150'/1 min., 40,000'/7.2 min. Combat radius 277 miles, Ferry range 769 miles.

When the last F-86D-60 was completed in September 1955, the ADC could fill twenty 75-plane wings, along with six F-89 wings and three with F-94Cs. In 1957-58, the Air National Guard received 25 F-86Ds for each of nine squadrons.

NORTH AMERICAN F-86D-5

For export to NATO nations, a less complicated weapons system was installed in the F-86K all-weather interceptor. In May 1953, two YF-86Ks were ordered and a license agreement was made for assembly by Fiat in the hope of improving morale in Italy. Four 20-mm M-24A-1 guns with 132 rpg and MG-4 fire control (lead-pursuit instead of lead collision course) distinguished the K from the D-40 model. The YF-86K flew July 15, 1954, with both

NORTH AMERICAN F-86D-60
General Electric J47-GE-33, 5550 lb. st (7650 lb. AB)
DIMENSIONS: As F-86D-1
WEIGHT: Empty 13,498 lb., Combat 15,956 lb., Gross 18,160 lb., Max. 19,952 lb. Fuel 610+240 gal.
PERFORMANCE: Speed- Top 693 mph at s.1., 616 mph at 40,000', Cruising 550 mph, Stalling 129 mph. Service Ceiling 49,750', Climb 12,000'/1 min., 40,000'/6.9 min. Combat radius 270 miles. Ferry range 769 miles.

YF-86Ks being shipped to join 221 F-86Ks assembled by Fiat for the Italian, French and German air forces. North American itself completed, from March to December 1955, 120 divided between Norway and the Netherlands.

NORTH AMERICAN F-86K
General Electric J47-GE-17B, 5425 lb. st (7500 lb. AB)
DIMENSIONS: Span 37'1", Lg. 40'11", Ht. 15', Wing Area 288 sq. ft.
WEIGHT: Empty 13,367 lb., Combat 16,252 lb., Gross 18,379 lb., Max. 20,171 lb. Fuel 608+240 gal.
PERFORMANCE: Speed- Top 692 mph at s.1., 612 mph at 40,000', Cruising 550 mph, Stalling 130 mph. Combat Ceiling 47,700', Service Ceiling 49,100'. Climb 12,000'/1 min., 40,000'/7.3 min. Combat radius 272 miles. Ferry range 744 miles.

The F-86L versions were converted from 576 Ds beginning in May 1956 by extending the wing tips and leading edge, adding engine cooling ducts, and a "Data Link" receiver. Although performance was little changed, the interceptor was now fitted into the SAGE system of semi-automatic ground control by computers. Entering ADC service in October 1956, this improvement extended the Sabre Dog's life until it was replaced by the supersonic,

Mfr

LOCKHEED F-94C
Pratt & Whitney J48-P-5, 6350 lb. st (8750 lb. AB)
DIMENSIONS: Span 37'4", Lg. 44'6", Ht. 14'11" Wing Area 233 sq. ft.
WEIGHT: Empty 12,708 lb., Combat 16,689 lb., Gross 20,324 lb., Max. 24,184 lb. Fuel 366+500+460 gal.
PERFORMANCE: Speed- Top 640 mph at s.l., 578 mph at 40,000', Cruising 493 mph, Stalling 152 mph. Combat ceiling 49,700', Service Ceiling 51,400'. Climb 10,800'/1 min., 49,700'/19 min. Combat radius 240 miles, Ferry range, 1275 miles.

delta-wing F-102, and the F-86Ls were transferred to 24 Air National Guard squadrons in 1959-60, where they served until retirement in 1965.

After the E-4 fire-control system was no longer secret, 56 ex-USAF F-86Ds were transferred to Denmark, beginning on June 26, 1958, 122 went to Japan in 1958-60, 40 to South Korea, and 130 were sold to Yugoslavia in 1961.

Starfires with rockets

The Lockheed F-94C Starfire was the second "nearly automatic" night fighter using Mighty Mouse rockets to be purchased by the Air Defense Command. Essentially, it was similar to the earlier F-94 two-seater, but replaced the J33 with a Pratt & Whitney J48-P-5 with afterburner, had increased dihedral, and used a thinner wing and swept horizontal tail to increase the critical Mach number.

The most important innovation was the armament of twenty-four 2.75-inch rockets ringed around the nose in launching tubes concealed by snap doors. Each wing carried 250-gallon drop tanks at the tips, and a pod for 12 more rockets could be added on the leading edge, or a 230-gallon ferry tank or bomb carried underneath. A bullet-shaped nose replaced the original rounded plastic cover for the APG-40 radar directing the Hughes E-5 fire control system. An automatic pilot was added, with a drag chute in a tail fairing to slow landings.

A modified F-94B, flown January 18, 1950, with the new airframe, and a second prototype had been designated YF-97A until September 12, when the YF-94C label was chosen. Production F-94C Starfires were ordered July 21, 1950, but 112 single-place F-94D ground support versions with eight guns ordered January 4, 1951, were canceled on October 15.

Although nine F-94Cs were completed by June 1952, they did not enter ADC service with the 437th FIS until March 7, 1953. Reliability problems with missiles and en-

NORTHROP F-89D
Two Allison J35-A-35, 5440 lb. st (7200 lb. AB)
DIMENSIONS: Span 59'8", Lg. 53'10", Ht. 17'6", Wing Area 606 sq. ft.
WEIGHT: Empty 25,194 lb., Combat 37,190 lb., Gross 42,241 lb. Fuel 2434+400 gal.
PERFORMANCE: Speed- Top 635 mph at 10,600', 558 mph at 40,000', Cruising 467 mph, Stalling 136 mph. Combat Ceiling 46,500', Service Ceiling 49,200'. Climb 8360'/1 min., 46,500'/ 18.1 min. Combat radius 382 miles, Ferry range 1367 miles.

gines had put the F-94C nearly two years behind schedule; on early tests the engine flamed out when the nose rockets were salvoed over 25,000 feet. While the problems were solved, the contract was cut back from 617 to 387 accepted from May 1952 to May 1954, for the interceptor could handle no bomber more advanced than a Tu-4 (Soviet B-29). Seven ADC wings used F-94B/Cs in June 1953, but only three F-94C wings served through 1955/56, and the last unit remained until February 1959.

Scorpions with a heavy punch

The third USAF fighter type with Mighty Mouse rockets was the Northrop F-89D ordered April 1951, and preceded by a YF-89D first flown October 23, 1951. In June 1952, delivery began on F-89D Scorpions, providing the ADC with a fighter carrying 104 2.75-in. rockets. No guns were carried, but wingtip pods each contained 52 rockets and 308 gallons of fuel, with additional fuel in the fuselage, and the nose was enlarged for APG-40 radar, E-6 fire control, and an E-11 autopilot. Most of the 682 P-89Ds built used J35-A-35s.

Again ADC hopes for early deployment of rocket-firing fighters were disappointed when the entire F-89 force was grounded on September 22, 1952, just as F-89D deliveries were getting underway, and full production did not resume until November 1953 and was completed in March 1956. The F-89D entered operational service with the 18th FIS in January 1954.

A pair of Allison YJ71-A-3s were tested on the lone YF-89E accepted in August 1954, a converted F-89C. No F-89F or G model was produced, but the F-89H was the first USAF plane to enter service with the Hughes Falcon (GAR-l, later AIM-4A) semi-active radar guided missile,

AF

NORTH AMERICAN F-86L
General Electric J47-GE-33, 5550-lb. st (7650 lb. AB)
DIMENSIONS: Span 39'1", Lg. 40'3", Ht. 15', Wing Area 313 sq. ft.
WEIGHT: Empty 13,822 lb., Combat 16,252 lb., Gross 18,484 lb., Max 20,276 lb. Fuel 610+240 gal.
PERFORMANCE: Speed- Top 693 mph at s.l., 616 mph at 40,000', Cruising 550 mph, Stalling 130 mph. Combat ceiling 48,250', Service Ceiling 49,600', Climb 12,200'/1 min., 40,000'/7 min., Combat radius 260 miles, Ferry range 750 miles.

Mfr

NORTHROP F-89H
Two Allison J35-A-35, 5440 lb. st (7200 lb. AB)
DIMENSIONS: Span 59'8", Lg. 53'10", Ht. 17'6", Wing Area 606 sq. ft.
WEIGHT: Empty 29,419 lb., Gross 39,200 lb., Max. 47,400 lb. Fuel 2434+400 gal.
PERFORMANCE: Speed- Top 625 mph at 9,750', 547 mph at 40,000', Combat Ceiling 44,600', Service Ceiling 46,400'. Climb 7200'/1 min. Combat radius 350 miles.

which had a five-mile range. The Falcon made its first live fire kill when fired from a modified Scorpion on January 27, 1955. Ordered February 24, 1955, and first accepted in September 1955, the 156 F-89Hs had redesigned tip pods each with three Falcons and 21 2.75-inch rockets, and became operational in March 1956.

When Scorpion production ended in August 1956, 1,052 had been delivered and seven ADC wings used them. While slower than the F-86D single-seaters, they provided more range and firepower and were posted at the outer edges of the continental defenses, in Alaska and Greenland.

The first air-to-air rocket with a nuclear warhead, the Douglas MB-1 (AIR-2) Genie, an unguided, 830-pound rocket, was fired from a F-89J at 20,000 feet on July 19, 1957, the first and only live shot of that two-kiloton weapon. Northrop modified 350 F-89Ds to the F-89J configuration, with J35-A-35 engines, MG-12 fire control, under wing racks for two Genies and four GA-2 infrared-homing Falcons and wingtip pods interchangeable with 600-gallon tanks or standard rocket pods. The remodeled aircraft were delivered from November 1956 to February 1958, entering service in January 1957.

When the Northrops were replaced by supersonic F-101Bs, they were passed to the ANG, which retired the last squadrons in 1969. From 1950 to 1956, 4,412 all-weather jet interceptors of the first generation had been produced for the USAF, but except for the few F-94B skirmishes in Korea, none were used in combat. The Soviet bombers were never built in the numbers feared, and when Air Defense Command strength peaked, the anticipated war situation was changing, and a new generation of supersonic interceptors rapidly retired these sub-sonic jets to obsolescence and scrap metal.

CHAPTER 28
AIR FORCE JET BOMBERS, 1946-1962

Mfr

Boeing's B-52 would have the longest service of any American jet bomber.

The first American jet bombers

Adapting jet propulsion to bombers was no easy task. The first gas turbine units made in America were centrifugal-flow units whose wide diameter and fuel consumption was too great to guarantee the endurance needed for bomber missions.

By April 1944, General Electric's TG-180 (later called the J35) had made its bench run, providing an axial-flow turbojet engine whose narrow diameter and smaller fuel needs recommended it for bomber use. The first American bomber to use jet engines became the Douglas XB-43.

Mfr

DOUGLAS XB-43
Two General Electric J35-GE-3, 3820 lb. st
DIMENSIONS: Span 71'2", Lg. 51'5", Ht. 24'3", Wing Area 563 sq. ft.
WEIGHT: Empty 22,890 lb. Combat 35,900 lb. Gross 40,000 lb. Fuel 1209+900 gal.
PERFORMANCE: Speed- Top 503 mph, Cruising 420 mph. Combat Ceiling 41,800', Service Ceiling 38,200'. Climb 2470'/ 1 min., Combat radius 540 miles. Range 1100 miles normal.

Two prototypes were ordered on a contract approved March 31, 1944, but a production program was canceled August 18, 1945, when superior designs had become available. The XB-43 replaced the Allisons of its predecessor with two J35s fed by air intakes behind the pilots and delivering 3,820 pounds static thrust each from jet exhausts in the tail. Like the XB-42, it was a three-place, high-wing monoplane with an 8,000-pound bomb capacity, but no guns were installed on either XB-43 prototype.

Built in Santa Monica, the XB-43 was trucked to the desert Muroc Army Air Field and first flown on May 17, 1946 by Bob Brush. Nearly a year later, tests began on the second XB-43, which replaced the twin canopies with a more conventional cockpit enclosure, and the Plexiglas nose with a plywood cover. Later it became a test bed for the new J47 engine, and had an enlarged tail fin.

PMB

2nd DOUGLAS XB-43

Early in the study of bomber jet propulsion, it became apparent that more than two engines would be required for the capabilities needed. As early as January 1944, Boeing offered its model 413 photo-reconnaissance design to the Air Force. Basically a B-29 powered by four turbojets paired in nacelles on the wings, the 413 was not accepted. Shortly after the J35 engine was satisfactory in April tests, the Air Force invited bids on jet-powered bombers capable of a speed of 500 mph, a service ceiling of 40,000 feet, and a 1,000-mile tactical radius.

By December 1944, each of the four Air Force bomber manufacturers responded with proposals, all of which were accepted and ordered as design studies. The North American NA-130 design begun September 13, 1944, was ordered as the XB-45, and the Consolidated Model 109 became the XB-46, also with four J35s. Six engines were provided on the Boeing Model 432 and the Martin Model 234, which became the XB-47 and XB-48.

Mfr

NORTH AMERICAN XB-45
Four Allison/GE J35-A-7, 3820-lb. st
DIMENSIONS: Span 89', Lg. 74'1", Ht, 25'2", Wing Area 1175 sq. ft.
WEIGHT: Empty 41,876 lb., Combat 67,235 lb. Gross 82,600 lb. Fuel 3400+2284 gal.
PERFORMANCE: Speed- Top 494 mph at s.l., 516 mph at 14,000', 483 mph at 30,000'. Service Ceiling 37,600'. Climb 2070'/1 min., 30,000' /19min. Range 1700 miles /14,000 lb., 2236 miles/8350 lb., Ferry range 2921 miles.

All types ordered were high-wing monoplanes with a pressurized compartment for a bombardier-navigator in the nose and tandem pilot and copilot seats under a fighter-style tear-drop canopy. Production of their J35 engines was transferred from General Electric to Allison in September 1946. Drag was minimized by eliminating protruding turrets. Since it was believed that the bomber's high speed would permit enemy fighters to make only tail cone passes, planned armament was limited to a pair of .50-caliber tail guns trained by an Emerson APG-7 radar and fired by the co-pilot. With gunners unnecessary and endurance short, the crew was kept small and weight was saved for fuel.

Mfr

CONVAIR XB-46
Four General Electric J35-GE-3, 3820 lb. st
DIMENSIONS: Span 113', Lg. 105'9". Ht. 27'11", Wing Area 1285 sq. ft.
WEIGHT: Empty 48,018 lb. Combat 75,200 lb., Gross 94,400 lb. Fuel 4280-6682 gal.
PERFORMANCE: Speed- Top 491 mph at s.l., 489 mph at 40,000', Cruising 439 mph. Service Ceiling 36,500'. Climb 35,000'/19 min. Combat radius 694 miles/8000-lb. Max. range 2870 miles.

The normal bomb load was 8,000 pounds (16 x 500 pounds), but in March 1945 designers were told to lengthen the bomb bay to hold a single 22,000-pound "Earthquake" bomb developed in Britain. At that time the secret atomic bomb was unknown to the designers, and the actual weights and measurements necessary to properly prepare the bomb racks were concealed until 1949.

All of these prototypes first flew in 1947. Three XB-45s were built on a contract approved May 2, 1946, and the first flew at Muroc on March 17, piloted by George Krebs. Nacelles under each laminar-flow wing held a pair of J35s, and a pressurized tail gunner's cabin had been added to replace the delayed APG-7 system.

The last bomber built by I.M. Laddon's San Diego design team began with a preliminary design offered the Air Force on November 6, 1944, and a January 17, 1945, letter contract for three XB-46 aircraft. To save funds for the XA-44 proposal, just one prototype survived on the contract finally approved June 7, 1946. Slim and graceful, the carefully streamlined XB-46 had a Davis wing section, Fowler flaps, and 32-foot long bomb bay, but no APG-7 or other tactical equipment was ever installed.

On April 2, 1947, Convair's XB-46 was flown from San Diego to Muroc by E.D. Shannon. But the smaller, lighter, and faster North American design had already been chosen for production.

Mfr

MARTIN XB-48
Six General Electric J35-GE-7, 3820-lb. st
DIMENSIONS: Span 108'4", Lg. 85'9", Ht. 26'6", Wing Area 1330 sq. ft.
WEIGHT: Empty 72,000 lb., Combat 92,600 lb. Gross 102,600 lb. Fuel 4150-4968 gal.
PERFORMANCE: Speed- Top 486 mph at s.l., 516 mph at 20,000', 479 mph at 35,000', cruising 453 mph. Service Ceiling 39,000'. Combat radius 498 miles/22,000 lb. Range 900 miles.

Martin's XB-48, the third to appear, had six J35s in nacelles under the wings. Although larger than a B-24, it needed only three crewmen, like the XB-46. Fourteen 1,000-pound or one 22,000-pound bomb could be accommodated, but the APG-7 gun system was not installed.

Martin had submitted their design on December 9, 1944, the mockup was inspected on April 19, 1945, and a contract for two approved at last on December 13, 1946. On June 22, 1947, the XB-48 was flown from Baltimore to Patuxent River NAS by E.R. Gelvin. The most unusual feature was the retractable bicycle landing gear: a pair of large wheels forward, another pair aft, and a smaller outrigger wheel under each wing. That tandem gear had been tested two years before on a converted Marauder called the XB-26H.

Unfortunately, empty weight had risen from 58,000 to 72,000 pounds, and drag reduced guaranteed speed from

Mfr

NORTHROP YRB-49A
Six Allison J35-A-15, 3750-lb. st
DIMENSIONS: Span 172' Lg. 53'1" Ht. 15'2", Wing Area 4000 sq. ft.
WEIGHT: Empty 84,000 lb., Gross 206,000 lb. Fuel 15,231 gal.
PERFORMANCE: Speed- Top 381 mph at 35,000', Cruising 340 mph. Service Ceiling 45,500'. Range 2250 miles.

552 to 516 mph. Outclassed by the XB-47, the two XB-48 prototypes were used to test the landing gear and equipment for the more advanced Boeing.

Jet propulsion had rendered the original Northrop B-35 flying-wing concept obsolete, but a June 1, 1945, contract had the 2nd and 3rd YB-35 aircraft completed with eight Allison J35-A-15 jets. First flown October 21, 1947, from Northrop Field to Muroc by Max Stanley, the six-place YB-49 fed eight 3,750-pound thrust engines through leading-edge intakes, added four wing fences and vertical stabilizing fins, and eliminated turrets and guns. Twelve 1,000-pound bombs could be carried less than half the range of the B-35, but the jets added 100 mph to the speed.

A second YB-49 was flown January 13, 1948, but crashed mysteriously on June 5. Among the five dead crewmen was Captain Glen W. Edwards, for whom Muroc Air Force Base was renamed.

Nevertheless, contracts were placed August 12 for 30 RB-49As to be built by Convair at Fort Worth, and conversion by Northrop of the remaining ten YB-35 airframes to RB-35B strategic reconnaissance types.

Many deficiencies turned up in the second phase of YB-49 tests. Air force test reports complained that the aircraft was unstable, difficult to fly and since it could not hold a steady course, was unsuitable as a bombing platform. Computerized fly-by-wire systems were still unknown. Cancellations ended the RB-49 program in April 1949 in favor of the B-36, and the RB-35B program was scrapped by November.

Only one more flying wing was completed, the YRB-49A flown May 4, 1950. Four 5,000-pound thrust

Mfr

NORTHROP YB-49
Eight Allison J35-A-15, 3750-lb. st
DIMENSIONS: Span 172' Lg. 53'1", Ht. 15'2", Wing Area 4000 sq. ft.
WEIGHT: Empty 88,442 lb., Combat 133,569 lb., Gross 193,938 lb. Fuel 12,752-14,542 gal.
PERFORMANCE: Speed- Top 493 mph at 20,800', 464 mph at 35,000', Cruising 420 mph. Stalling 104 mph. Combat Ceiling 40,700', Service Ceiling 45,700'. Climb 33785'/1 min. Combat radius 1615 miles/10,000 lb., Ferry range 3575 miles.

Mfr

NORTH AMERICAN B-45C
Four General Electric J47-GE-7/-9. 5200-lb. (5820-lb WE) st
DIMENSIONS: Span 89', Lg. 75'4", Ht. 25'2", Wing Area 1175 sq. ft.
WEIGHT: Empty 48,969 lb. Combat 73,715 lb., Gross 110,050 lb. Fuel 6933+1200 gal.
PERFORMANCE: Speed- Top 573 mph at s.l., 509 mph at 32,500', Cruising 466 mph, Stalling 153 mph. Combat Ceiling 37,550', Service Ceiling 41,250'. Climb 4550'/1 min. Combat radius 1008 miles/10,000 lb. Ferry range 2426 miles.

Allison J35-A-19 engines were in the wing, and two more in outside pods below it, leaving more fuel space.

Photographic equipment was installed in a bulge below the center section. The first YB-49 had been demolished in an accident in March 1950, and when the YRB-49 was retired in 1951 the dream of the giant all-wing aircraft was over for that generation.

Jet Bombers enter USAF service

North American's B-45A Tornado became the first U.S. jet bomber to go into production. Begun as NA-147 on June 13, 1946, 96 were ordered January 20, 1947, and the first B-45A-1 flew on February 24, 1948. After 22 were built with J35 engines, 74 B-45A-5 models with new J47 engines were completed by March 1950. These power plants had been tested on the first prototype, whose fatal crash on September 20, 1948, demonstrated the need for pilots' ejection seats on production aircraft.

NORTH AMERICAN B-45A-1

The four-place B-45A was classed as a light bomber, since combat radius, not weight, now defined bombers. Less than 1,000 miles was considered light, over 2,500 miles heavy, like the B-36, and in between were medium bombers like the B-50. An APQ-23 radar-bombing system and visual Norden sight was provided until the APQ-24 became available in 1950. Fourteen 1,000-pounds was a normal load, but the 22,000-pound Grand Slam could be carried. Since the radar gun direction originally planned was not yet perfected, a tail gunner's cockpit was provided with twin .50-caliber M-3 guns and 1,200 rounds.

The 47th Bomb Wing at Barksdale AFB became the first USAF unit with jet bombers in November 1948, replacing B-26Cs as part of the Tactical Air Force (TAC). When TAC was authorized on November 27, 1950, to add nuclear weapons to its program, 40 B-45As received "Backbreaker" modifications carrying Mk 4, 5, or 6 nuclear weapons, as well as APQ-24 radar, and APG-30 tail gun radar. More fuel increased combat radius from 533 to 880 miles. The 27th Wing flew its modernized Tornadoes to Britain in May 1952, becoming part of NATO forces.

Another version began as the NA-153 on October 17, 1947, was ordered November 11, 1947, and first flown May 3, 1949 as the B-45C.

NORTH AMERICAN B-45A-5
Four General Electric J47-GE-7/-9. 5200-lb. st
DIMENSIONS: Span 89', Lg.75'4", Ht. 25'2", Wing Area 1175 sq. ft.
WEIGHT: Empty 45,694 lb. Combat 58,548, Gross 91,775 lb. Fuel 5746 gal.
PERFORMANCE: Speed- Top 571 mph at 33,500', 503 mph at 37,000', Cruising 470 mph, Stalling 125 mph. Combat Ceiling 42,800' Climb 5950'/1 min. Combat radius 533 miles/10,000 lb.

No B-45B was built, but 600-gallon wingtip drop tanks and water injection was added to the ten B-45Cs. The company did propose a ground attack version in July 1949, but the Air Force canceled 51 Tornadoes, and allowed completion of 33 RB-45Cs, first flown January 30, 1950, by October 1951.

Provided with up to 12 cameras, 25 photo flash bombs, and a receptacle for in-flight refueling, the RB-45C was first delivered to the 91st SRW on August 26, 1950. Three planes from this unit based in Japan began missions over Manchuria and Soviet Siberia on November 2, 1950, and on December 4, one became the first jet bomber shot down by a MiG-15. The first air refueling of a jet bomber from a KB-29P was demonstrated on June 22, 1951.

NORTH AMERICAN RB-45C
Four General Electric J47-GE-7/-9. 5200-lb. (5820-lb WE) st
DIMENSIONS: Span 89', Lg. 75'4", Ht. 25'2", Wing Area 1175 sq. ft.
WEIGHT: Empty 50,687 lb. Combat 73,200 lb., Gross 110,721 lb. Fuel 6933+1200 gal.
PERFORMANCE: Speed- Top 570 mph at 4,000', 502 mph at 35,000', Cruising 465 mph, Stalling 153 mph. Combat Ceiling 37,800', Service Ceiling 41,500'. Combat radius 1055 miles.

Four RB-45Cs were loaned to the RAF to prepare a very secret overflight of the Soviet Union. On the night of April 17, 1952, three began separate penetrations reaching in to 1,000 miles deep, while MiG-15s were unable to find them in the darkness. RAF pilots repeated these missions on April 28, 1954. RB-45Cs were phased out in 1958 as they were replaced by RB-47s.

Boeing B-47

Boeing's B-47 Stratojet was built in larger numbers than any other multi-engine jet bomber and had a revolutionary influence on aircraft design. The Seattle company was the only bomber builder with its own high-speed wind tunnel, giving Boeing an advantage in adopting new aerodynamic technology.

Model 432, submitted in the Air Force bomber competition in December 1944, had a conventional straight wing with jet engines buried within the fuselage, and won a letter contract for design development on February 1, 1945. Captured German research data on the high-speed advantages of swept-back wings was verified and incorporated in the layout of Boeing's Model 448. That September 1945 proposal had a swept-back wing and six engines, but the enclosed engines were unsatisfactory.

Model 450 replaced this project in October, with four engines paired in pods below and forward of the wing, where interference with airflow over the wing would be minimized. The other two engines were in individual pods near the wing tips. After the mockup was approved in April 1946, construction of two XB-47 prototypes began in June, although contract negotiations were not approved until July 10, 1947.

The XB-47 wing had a Boeing 145 laminar airfoil, a sweepback of 35 degrees, and an aspect ratio of 9.6. Like the XB-48, there were six J35 engines, tandem landing gear with four main wheels, and the pilot and co-pilot sat in tandem under a bubble canopy. A bombardier-navigator in the nose was to get a radar bombing system whose an-

BOEING XB-47
Six Allison/GE J35-A-7/-9, 3820-lb. st
DIMENSIONS: Span 116', Lg. 107'6", Ht. 27'9", Wing Area 1428 sq. ft.
WEIGHT: Empty 74,623 lb., Combat 115,000 lb. Gross 162,500 lb. Fuel 6050-11,550 gal.
PERFORMANCE: Speed- Top 568 mph at s.l., 578 mph at 15,000', 545 mph at 35,000', Cruising 466 mph, Stalling 148 mph. Service ceiling 41,000'. Range 2650 miles/10,000 lb.

Mfr

BOEING B-47A
Six General Electric J47-GE-11, 5200 lb. st
DIMENSIONS: Span 116', Lg. 106'10", Ht. 27'9", Wing Area 1428 sq. ft.
WEIGHT: Empty 73,250 lb., Combat 106,000 lb. Gross 157,500 lb. Fuel 9789 gal.
PERFORMANCE: Speed- Top 599 mph at 8800', Cruising 488 mph. Service ceiling 38,100'. Combat radius 1546 miles/10,000 lb.

tenna bulged below in a plastic fairing, and the bomb bay could accommodate up to 16 1,000-pound or one 22,000-pound bomb. As was customary, no tactical equipment was provided in the prototypes.

Flight tests on the XB-47 began on December 17, 1947, the 44th anniversary of the Wrights' first flight. Robert Robbins flew the prototype from Boeing Field to Moses Lake AFB. Tests continued at Muroc proved the Stratojet the fastest bomber in the world, even if the expected 635 mph wasn't reached. When the second XB-47s was flown July 21, 1948, with J47-GE-3 power plants, top speed did pass the 600-mph level. Eighteen JATO rockets in the rear fuselage accelerated takeoff, and a 32-foot diameter ribbon parachute was used to slow landings.

Cautiously, the USAF put the Stratojet into production at Wichita, Kansas, while reserving its main funds for the B-36. Ten B-47As were ordered October 28, 1948, and the first 88 B-47B aircraft were added to the contract November 14, 1949. First flown June 25, 1950, the day the Korean war began, the B-47A had 5,200-pound-thrust J47-GE-11s, increased takeoff weight, and was used for service tests and training. Only four had K-2 bombing systems, and two had a pair of .50-caliber guns mounted in the tail cone; one testing an Emerson A-2 radar aiming system, and the other the General Electric A-5 system.

The Korean War opened the national purse and the North Atlantic Treaty provided bases abroad to encircle the potential enemy. To carry out the largest bomber-production program since World War II, Stratojet production by Boeing-Wichita was joined in December 1952 by B-47s from the factories in Tulsa, Oklahoma, and Marietta, Georgia, reopened under the management of Douglas and Lockheed. Far more complex than the B-29, the B-47 required major innovations in metal work and wiring.

BOEING B-47B
Six General Electric J47-GE-23, 5910 lb. st.
DIMENSIONS: Span 116', Lg. 106'10", Ht. 27'9", Wing Area 1428 sq. ft.
WEIGHT: Empty 78,102 lb., Combat 122,650 lb. Gross 184,908 lb. Fuel 13,900-15,213 gal.
PERFORMANCE: Speed- Top 608 mph at 16,300', 565 mph at 35,000', Cruising 498 mph, Stalling 177 mph. Combat ceiling 40,900', Climb 4775'/min. Combat radius 1960 miles/10,000 lb. Ferry range 4440 miles.

BOEING B-47E-IV refueling
Six General Electric J47-GE-25, 7200 lb. st
DIMENSIONS: Span 116', Lg. 107'1", Ht. 28', Wing Area 1428 sq. ft.
WEIGHT: Empty 79,074 lb., Combat 133,030 lb. Gross 225,958 lb. Fuel 14,610+3390 gal.
PERFORMANCE: Speed- Top 608 mph at 16,300', 556 mph at 37,350', Cruising 500 mph, Stalling 191 mph. Combat ceiling 39,300'. Combat radius 2360 miles/10,845 lb. Ferry range 4995 miles.

Extending the B-47B's range was the first task, for the Stratojet needed more than twice the fuel to cover the same distance as a B-29. A pair of 1,780-gallon drop tanks under the wings increased fuel capacity to 15,213 gallons, and a receptacle for in-flight refueling from a flying boom tanker was provided in the nose. A periscope sight for a K-4A bombing system replaced the B-47A's Plexiglas nose. A shorter bomb bay allowed more fuel space, but still accommodated 18,000 pounds of Mk 6 nuclear, or conventional bombs, although tactical plans emphasized the former.

The B-47B first flown April 26, 1951, had the same J47-GE-11s, but J47-GE-23s were used after the first 88 aircraft. Early B models were mostly used for training, and lacked the B-4 radar system for the two .50-caliber M-3 guns with 1,200 rounds provided for rear defense. Since these jet bombers had much longer takeoff and landing runs than the B-29s they replaced, they needed 18 solid-fuel JATO rockets to reduce the takeoff ground run from 9,100 to 7,200 feet.

Strategic Air Command's 306th BW received its first B-47B on October 23, 1951, but that Wing would not become operational for another year. B-47s were to be deployed in 45-plane medium-bomber Wings, each accompanied by an air-refueling squadron with 20 KC-97 tankers. Air refueling transformed the B-47 into an intercontinental bomber.

The three-man crews had to learn entirely new and more complicated skills than those required for the B-29. Until 1958, Air Training Command had the task of preparing those men for their new roles in unarmed B-47Bs.

Of 397 B-47Bs delivered by June 1953, Lockheed assembled eight, and Douglas ten. Many B-47Bs were modified to B-47E standards (as the B-47B-II or III) in 1953/54, 66 became TB-47B trainers, and 24 became RB-47Bs when camera pods were installed in bomb bays. The first YRB-47B joined the 91st Strategic Reconnaissance Wing in April 1953.

The 88th B-47B was first redesignated XB-56, and then YB-47C, based on a January 1950 design to increase range by replacing the six jet engines with four Allison T71-A-5 engines. That aircraft was canceled in December 1952 before its completion because the power plants were unready.

Two XB-47Ds were actually B-47Bs completed as unarmed test-beds for a pair of 9,710-hp Curtiss-Wright YT49-W-1 turboprops in the inboard engine pods, while the outboard pods kept their J47s. First flown on August 26, 1955, and reported to have a 597-mph top speed at 13,500 feet, it may have been the fastest propeller-driven USAF aircraft.

BOEING B-47E
Six General Electric J47-GE-25, 7200 lb. st
DIMENSIONS: Span 116', Lg. 107'1", Ht. 28', Wing Area 1428 sq. ft.
WEIGHT: Empty 80,756 lb., Combat 124,875 lb. Gross 198,180 lb. Fuel 14,610+3390 gal.
PERFORMANCE: Speed- Top 607 mph at 16,300', 557 mph at 38,550', Cruising 498 mph, Stalling 178 mph. Combat ceiling 40,500', Climb 4660'/min. Combat radius 2010 miles/10,845 lb. Ferry range 4035 miles.

The principal Stratojet model was the B-47E, which had engine water injection to increase their J47-GE-25A's thrust and 33 jettisonable JATO units for takeoff. Ejection seats, K-4A bombing system and a stronger landing gear were provided. First flown January 30, 1953, the E added 845 pounds of chaff, to confuse hostile radar, to the 18,000-pound bomb load.

Two 20-mm M-24A-1 guns and 700 rounds with General Electric APG-32 gun-laying radar tail turret replaced the twin .50s and A-5 system of earlier models. The co-pilot turns his seat to the rear, when the warning radar indicates hostile aircraft. The search radar computer is provided with air temperature, altitude and air speed information. When a bright spot on the screen shows that the radar has picked up an attacking plane, the gunner can locked on

BOEING RB-47K-BW

to the target, which is tracked automatically until the hostile aircraft enters gun range and the guns can fire.

The RB-47E first flew on July 3, 1953, with elongated nose, 11 cameras, twin 20-mm guns and A-5 fire control, but no bombs. Beginning with the 862nd Stratojet in February 1955, MA-7A bombing radar was installed, and this model became the B-47E-IV. Heavier landing gear permitted an increase in takeoff weight from 99 to 113 tons, giving a 2,360-mile combat radius with full tanks.

Production included 691 B-47E-BWs, 386 B-47E-LMs, 264 B-47E-DTs, and 240 RB-47E-BWs. The YB-47F receiver and KB-47G tanker, however, were B-47Bs modified to test the probe-drogue in-flight refueling system.

Cold War Overflights

By 1956, the nuclear bomb stockpile held over 3,500 warheads, including Mk. 15, 28, 36 and 43 models that could fit the B-47 bomb bay. But the B-47 never had to drop a bomb in combat. Instead, it made some of the Cold War's most dangerous missions; actual overflights over the USSR. President Truman had authorized prehostility strategic reconnaissance during the Korean War, fearful that Tu-4s with atomic weapons might be grouped in Siberia for a surprise attack on America. Since overflights were a deliberate violation of international law, they were kept secret for many years.

The fourth B-47B was provided with a bomb bay camera pod and special instruments and flown to Alaska, but before its mission, was destroyed by an accidental fire on August 15, 1951. Two more B-47Bs were modified in 1952 and, accompanied by KC-97 tankers, moved to Alaska by 306th BW crews. On October 15, 1952, they photographed bases in Eastern Siberia, and discovered no bomber threat.

In 1954, concern about a possible M-4 jet bomber concentration led to a bold RB-47E sortie from Britain over the Kola Peninsula on May 8. Despite damage from MiG-17 interceptors, the crew completed their mission. More SAC RB-47E overflights were accomplished from Alaska in Project Seashore, starting on March 30, 1955.

Beginning in June 1955, 35 RB-47H models were completed as electronic reconnaissance aircraft. These aircraft carried an additional three men (called Crows!) in the bomb bay, with equipment to locate and analyze enemy radar. **Project Homerun,** flying from Thule, Greenland, over the Arctic to the Soviet coast from March 21 to May 16, 1956, used 16 RB-47Es from the 10th SRS and five RB-47Hs from the 343rd SRS. SAC's 156 **Homerun** sorties included a bold formation of six RB-47Es on May 6.

However, an RB-47H shot down by MiG-19s over the Barents Sea on July 1, 1960, was on an ELINT mission, not an overflight. These sorties were intended to provoke VVS reaction, so that hostile radar could be analyzed. About 40 RB-47Es became EB-47Es when fitted with elaborate radar jamming antennae; they were planned to divert an enemy from any SAC bomber thrusts.

Cold war tensions reached the point where part of the B-47 squadrons dispersed around the world were kept on a 15-minute alert. To evade enemy radar, new mission profiles focused on low-altitude penetration, with nuclear bombs delivered by "pop up" or LABS techniques.

Many Stratojet modifications were tried. One YDB-47B and two YDB-47Es were modified to carry a radio-controlled Bell Rascal (GAM-63) air-to-surface missile on the fuselage starboard side. The first successful launching of the ten-ton missile with a 100-mile range was made February 17, 1955, but the Rascal was canceled November 29, 1958, in favor of the Hound Dog program.

BOEING RB-47H-1-BW
Six General Electric J47-GE-25, 7200 lb. st
DIMENSIONS: Span 116', Lg. 108'8", Ht. 28', Wing Area 1428 sq. ft.
WEIGHT: Empty 83,642 lb., Combat 136,955 lb. Gross 213,491 lb. Fuel 18,370 gal.
PERFORMANCE: Speed- Top 602 mph at 15,600', 551 mph at 37,350', Cruising 489 mph, Stalling 186 mph. Combat ceiling 37,900'. Climb 3960'/min. Combat radius 2235 miles. Ferry range 4529 miles.

A single YB-47J was modified to test an MA-2 radar system and 15 RB-47Ks were the last RB-47Es modified for inflight transmissions of weather data and collecting samples from foreign nuclear blasts. The first was delivered in January 1955. The EB-47Ls were "post-attack communication relay stations" converted from 36 B-47Es in 1962-63.

A total of 2,041 Stratojets were built. When SAC received its last production-line Stratojet, a B-47E, on February 18, 1957, it had 28 Medium Bomb and five Medium Strategic Reconnaissance Wings, with about 1,306 B-47 and 254 RB-47 aircraft. SAC retired its last B-47E in February 1966 and its last RB-47H in December 1967, although a few remained in non-combat roles elsewhere. The B-47's most important legacy was the technical experience that enabled Boeing to lead the world in jet airliners, and to produce the B-52 bomber.

Light Bombers Revived

When the Korean War ended in 1953, the 29 USAF bomber wings included ten with B-29 and five with B-50 medium bombers, five with intercontinental B-36s, and four with the new B-47. Propeller-driven Douglas B-26 Invaders filled the three wings assigned to short-range light bombing, and Tactical Air Command (TAC) had only one B-45 jet bomber wing with nuclear weapons.

Two such projects had been started under the old "Attack" category: Convair's XA-44 and Martin's XA-45. Redesignated XB-53 in 1948, the Convair was an odd canard design with three J35 jets and a swept-forward wing that was canceled before completion. Martin's XA-45 had been proposed on April 1, 1946, as a straight-winged, six-place bomber with two TG-110 turboprop and two I-40 turbojets, but by February 1947 that design had been replaced by a smaller swept-wing, two-place design with three jet engines.

This became the XB-51, whose mockup was inspected in February 1948 by the Air Force, which directed Martin to go ahead with two prototypes on April 23, 1948. Two J47-GE-13s were attached below the fuselage, with a third in the tail. Wings were swept back 35 degrees, had a 6-degree cathedral (droop), and their incidence could be increased for takeoff and landing. Instead of ailerons, spoilers were used along with leading-edge slats and full-span slotted flaps. Tandem dual main wheels, like those on the B-47, were provided, along with a high T-tail. The pilot sat under a bubble canopy and the navigator was placed behind and below him within the fuselage.

MARTIN XB-51
Three General Electric J47-GE-13, 5000 lb. st
DIMENSIONS: Span 53'1", Lg. 85'1", Ht. 17'4", Wing Area 548 sq. ft.
WEIGHT: Empty 29,584 lb. Combat 41,457 lb. Gross 55,923 lb. Max. 62,452 lb. Fuel 2835 +700 gal.
PERFORMANCE: Speed- Top 645 mph at s.l., 579 mph at 35,900', Cruising 532 mph, Stalling 253 mph. Service Ceiling 41,400'. Climb 6980'/1 min. Combat radius 435 miles/4000-lb. bombs, Ferry range 1613 miles.

Eight 20-mm nose guns had 160 rpg and up to 10,400 pounds of bombs could be carried in a unique rotary bomb bay door, with the basic mission the delivery of 4,000 pounds over a 435-mile radius. Flight tests began October 28, 1949, with the second, slightly modified, example flown the following April 17. But in 1951 the Air Force decided to terminate the XB-51 in favor of another program.

The Canberra

Another two-seat jet bomber of very different design philosophy, the English Electric Canberra, had been flown in Britain on May 13, 1949, and put into production for the Royal Air Force. Although not as fast or well armed as the XB-51, it had advantages in endurance, range, and maneuverability, and two Canberra B Mk. 2s were obtained for the USAF, the first flying across the Atlantic on February 21, 1951. The Korean War created the need for a B-26 replacement for night intruder operations, and tests of the XB-51, B-45, and the Navy's AJ-1 indicated that they were less suitable than the British aircraft for these missions.

Mfr

2nd MARTIN XB-51

To the surprise of the American industry, Martin received a letter contract March 24, 1951, for the first 250 Canberras, to be delivered in the year beginning in November 1952. But the difficulties in producing the foreign aircraft and engines were greater than expected. Not until July 20, 1953, when the Korean War was about over, was Martin's first B-57A Canberra flown by O. E. Tibbs from Middle River factory in Maryland.

Mfr

MARTIN B-57A

The power plants were two J65-BW-5 Sapphires, a British engine built under license first by Buick and then by Wright. The short, wide wings had an aspect ratio of only 4.27, the pilot had a clear bubble canopy, and the second crew member sat behind him within the fuselage. Added to the original design was the rotary bomb bay door Martin introduced on the XB-51, and eight .50-caliber guns with 300 rpg in the wings. Wing-tip 320-gallon drop tanks extended the range.

Eight B-57As accepted by December 1953, were for test work and not for tactical units. They were followed by 67 RB-57As completed from January to October 1954 with black paint and cameras, but no guns. They served the 363rd Tactical Reconnaissance Wing and the 10th and 66th TRWs based in Germany until replaced by the RF-84F in 1958.

Mfr

MARTIN RB-57A
Two Wright J65-W-5, 7220 lb. st
DIMENSIONS: Span 64', Lg. 65'6", Ht. 14'10", Wing Area 960 sq. ft.
WEIGHT: Empty 24,751 lb., Combat 34,917 lb., Gross 48,847 lb. Fuel 2252+640 gal.
PERFORMANCE: Speed- Top 609 mph at 4,500', 534 mph at 45,700', Cruising 495 mph, Stalling 119 mph. Combat Ceiling 48,350'. Climb 7180'/1 min. Combat radius 1267 miles, Ferry range 2568 miles.

A new tandem double-canopy distinguished the B-57B, first flown June 24, 1954, and the eight .50-caliber guns in the first 90 were replaced by four 20-mm M-39s with 200 rpg. Four under wing pylons for 750-pound bombs or rocket pods were added, while the bomb bay held 5,240 pounds of bombs or a Mk 7 nuclear weapon. The night intruder mission specialty required the original black paint.

MARTIN B-57B
Two Wright J65-W-5, 7220 lb. st
DIMENSIONS: Span 64', Lg. 65'6", Ht. 14'10", Wing Area 960 sq. ft.
WEIGHT: Empty 27,091 lb., Combat 38,689 lb., Gross 53,721 lb. Fuel 2252+1188 gal.
PERFORMANCE: Speed- Top 598 mph at 2500', Cruising 476 mph, Stalling 124 mph. Combat Ceiling 45,100', Climb 6180'/ 1 min. Combat radius 948 miles, Ferry range 2722 miles.

By September 1956, 202 B-57Bs and 38 B-57Cs with dual controls had been built to replace the B-26s of four TAC bomb wings: the 345th and 463rd in the United States, the 3rd in Japan, and the 38th in France.

Similar to the B-57B, 68 B-57Es were the only USAF types built as target tugs, and could be changed to combat configurations. Some were later changed to unarmed EB-57E and RB-57E versions.

The Air Force desire for a high-altitude reconnaissance aircraft resulted in a June 21, 1954 contract for the unarmed single-seat RB-57D. Powered by J57 engines, the RB-57D had more fuel, four cameras, and a 106-foot wingspan. Combat ceiling was up to 59,700 feet. The first of 20 RB-57Ds was flown November 3, 1955, deliveries including an RB-57D-1 with APG-56 side-looking radar, and six RB-57D-2s with an ECM operator and equipment

SAC's new 4080th Light Strategic Reconnaissance Wing began receiving the RB-57D on May 30, 1956, and the Lockheed U-2 on June 11, 1957. On December 11, 1956, three RB-57Ds made a daylight overflight of Vladivostok

MARTIN RB-57D
Two Pratt & Whitney J57-P-27, 10,500 lb. st
DIMENSIONS: Span 106', Lg. 65'6", Ht. 15'7", Wing Area 1505 sq. ft.
WEIGHT: Empty 27,275 lb. Combat 35,357 lb. Gross 45,085 lb. Fuel 2740 gal.
PERFORMANCE: Speed- Cruising 475 mph. Ceiling over target, 59,700'. Range 1560 miles.

that led to a vigorous Soviet protest. President Eisenhower decided that such flights seemed too aggressive when made by the USAF, and turned overflight missions to the CIA and its own U-2s.

Martin completed 403 Canberras by March 1957 with the last RB-57D and B-57E aircraft. The Canberra TAC bomb wings' mission changed in 1957 from night intrusion to nuclear bombing, so the black paint was scraped off and a LABS (Low-altitude Bombing System) was installed. The Canberra began retirement from TAC bomber service in 1958, and SAC retired its reconnaissance Canberras in April 1960.

Two RB-57As loaned the Chinese on Taiwan began spy flights over mainland China on December 6, 1957, but F-6 (Chinese MiG-19) fighters soon shot one down. They were replaced by three RB-57Ds and on October 7, 1959, near Peking, one became the first American-built aircraft downed by a Soviet-made SA-2 missile. Pakistan received 22 B-57Bs and 3 B-57Cs in June 1959 that fought in the September 1965 Kashmir war, a dispute continued for the rest of the century.

Another non-combat modification was the WB-57F weather aircraft, rebuilt from 21 older models by General Dynamics at Fort Worth, with two TF-33-P-11A turbofans, and two J60 auxiliary jets could be added below the 122-foot wing. The first was originally designated RB-57F when first flown on June 23, 1963, and 21 of these two-seaters were delivered by March 1967. Combat altitude was 63,200 feet and combat radius was 1474 miles. Their work included gathering air samples from nuclear tests before retirement from Air Force service in June 1974.

Just as an American version of a British design was the first Army plane to bomb enemy soldiers in 1918, the first USAF jet bombers to hit enemy troops were also of British design. Only two Canberra squadrons, the 8th and 13th, of the 3rd Bomb Wing remained active when war in Vietnam revived the need for light bombers, and in April 1964 they moved 47 aircraft to Clark Field in the Philippines.

The first Canberras actually in Vietnam were two RB-57Es provided for the "Patricia Lynn" reconnaissance missions begun May 2, 1963, and, with three additional planes, continued until August 1971 by the 460th TRW. On August 5, 1964, the day after the Tonkin Bay incident, 20 B-57Bs were sent from Clark Field to Bien Hoa, near Saigon. They seemed to be positioned as a threat, for only a few road reconnaissance flights were made, but a November 1 mortar attack destroyed five and damaged 15 of the 20 bombers present, and caused 76 American casualties.

President Johnson decided to commit the USAF to direct intervention, and on February 19, 1965, 24 B-57Bs made the first heavy attack on a Viet Cong base. The Rolling Thunder bombing campaign against North Vietnam began March 2 with an attack including by 20 B-57s.

Strong AAA fire was dangerous enough, but the worse experience was destruction of ten B-57s on May 16, by runway explosions at Bien Hoa. Canberra missions were moved to Da Nang in June. Vietnam Air Force pilots had begun training at Clark Field in May 1964, and four B-57s were provided them in August 1965. That program was ended in April 1966, after discouraging accidents. Of 96 Canberras deployed in Southeast Asia by 1968, only 32 survived.

The Canberras shifted to their original planned role of night intrusion, but target location provided quite difficult. To solve this problem, 16 aircraft were returned to Martin for conversion to the B-57G. The nose was reshaped to house APQ-139 radar, a low-light-level television, and laser range finder, with an infrared detection system under the left wing. No wing guns, but four laser-guided 500-pound Mk-82 bombs, four 750-pound M-117A-1 bombs and 3,950 pounds of canister ordinance were available. A downward firing 20-mm M61A turret was added to the B-57G below.

Arc

MARTIN B-57G
Two Wright J65-W-5D, 7650 lb. st
DIMENSIONS: Span 64', Lg. 68'1", Ht. 14'10", Wing Area 960 sq. ft.
WEIGHT: Empty 32,291 lb., Combat 52,640 lb., Gross 58,800 lb. Fuel 2482+836 gal.
PERFORMANCE: Speed- Top 479 mph at 5000', 465 mph at 15,000', Cruising 354 mph, Stalling 135 mph. Combat Ceiling 28,600', Service Ceiling 32,500'. Climb 3320'/1 min. Combat radius 223 miles/ 8276 lb. Ferry range 1770 miles.

The first B-57G was delivered to TAC on May 22, 1970, and 11 arrived in Thailand with the 13th Bomb Squadron in September. They operated against trucks on the Ho Chi Minh Trail until 1972, when the aircraft returned to the United States for a Kansas ANG squadron until retiring in 1974.

Despite withdrawal from combat units, the Canberra continued in many utility roles, especially in weather investigations. Two Defense System Evaluation squadrons (DSES) were established, using modified EB-57s to simulate enemy attempts to penetrate our airspace.

Douglas B-66

The next tactical bomber began as the Navy's carrier-based Douglas A3D Skywarrior, but on January 12, 1952, even before the Navy version flew, the Air Force decided to purchase a development called the B-66. Contracts were signed for five test RB-66As on December 4, 1952, and for 99 RB/B-66Bs approved on August 24, 1953.

A three-place high-wing monoplane with two Allison YF-71-A-9s under 35 degree swept-back wings, the RB-66A-DL first flew June 28, 1954, at Long Beach, California. Naval features like folding wings and tail hooks were omitted, but numerous other changes had been made, including ejection seats, and early flight tests were unsatisfactory.

Various detail improvements were made on the RB-66B-DL, first flown January 4, 1955, like two pylons for

Mfr

DOUGLAS RB-66A

450-gallon drop tanks, a flight refueling receptacle, and J71-A-13 engines when they became available in 1956. Up to 15,000 pounds of conventional bombs or Mk 28 nuclear bombs were aimed by a K-5 radar system in the nose. MD-1A fire control aimed two M-24A-1 guns, with 1,000 rounds, in a General Electric tail turret similar to that of the B-47.

Seventy-two B-66Bs, named the Douglas Destroyer, were delivered by October 1957 and used by TAC's 17th Bomb Wing in Florida until transferred in 1958 to the 47th Bomb Wing in Britain, where they served until that unit was inactivated in June 1962.

AF

DOUGLAS B-66B
Two Allison J71-A-13, 9,700 lb. st military, 10,200 lb. max.
DIMENSIONS: Span 71'6", Lg. 75'2", Ht. 23'7" Wing Area 780 sq. ft.
WEIGHT: Empty 42,549 lb. Combat 57,800 lb. Gross 83,000 lb. Fuel 4487+900 gal.
PERFORMANCE: Speed- Top 631 mph at 6000', 577 at 35,000', Cruising 528 mph, Stalling 153 mph. Combat Ceiling 39,400', Service Ceiling 41,500'. Climb 5000'/1 min. Combat radius 900 miles /10,000 lb. Ferry range 2468 miles.

Douglas also built, at the same time, 145 RB-66B-DLs for night reconnaissance, which entered service in 1956 with the 12th TRS in Japan and in 1957, the 66th and 10th TRW in Europe. The RB-66B had four K-47 cameras and 8,044 pounds of photoflash bombs. During 1958-1960, the RB-66s were modernized with new cameras and by replacing the tail guns with a tail cone housing electronic countermeasure (ECM) devices.

The Douglas Tulsa factory added 30 RB-66B-DTs and six RB-66C-DTs, a seven-seat, radar-reconnaissance version flown October 29, 1955, with radomes at the wing tips and an ECM compartment that replaced the former bomb bay. Finally, Tulsa delivered 36 WB-66D five-place weather reconnaissance models from June 1957 to January 1958, bringing the B-66 total to 294.

AF

DOUGLAS RB-66B
Two Allison J71-A-13, 9,700 lb. st military, 10,200 lb. max.
DIMENSIONS: Span 71'6", Lg. 75'2", Ht. 23'7" Wing Area 780 sq. ft.
WEIGHT: Empty 43,476 lb. Combat 59,550 lb. Gross 83,000 lb. Fuel 4489+900 gal.
PERFORMANCE: Speed- Top 631 mph at 6000', 575 at 35,200', Cruising 527 mph, Stalling 151 mph. Combat Ceiling 38,900'. Service Ceiling 40,900'. Climb 4840'/1 min. Combat radius 925 miles /8,044 lb. Ferry range 2428 miles.

Mfr

DOUGLAS RB-66C
Two Allison J71-A-13, 9,700 lb. st military, 10,200 lb. max.
DIMENSIONS: Span 71'6", Lg. 75'2", Ht. 23'7" Wing Area 780 sq. ft.
WEIGHT: Empty 44,771 lb. Combat 65,360 lb. Gross 83,000 lb. Fuel 4385+900 gal.
PERFORMANCE: Speed- Top 613 mph at 8000', 544 at 35,500', Cruising 502 mph, Stalling 153 mph. Combat Ceiling 35,500'. Service Ceiling 37,700'. Climb 4320'/1 min. Combat radius 1090 miles, Ferry range 2228 miles.

J. Sullivan

DOUGLAS EB-66B
Two Allison J71-A-13, 9,700 lb. st military. 10,200 lb. max.
DIMENSIONS: Span 71'6", Lg. 75'2", Ht. 23'7" Wing Area 780 sq. ft.
WEIGHT: Empty 43,476 lb. Combat 59,300 lb. Gross 77,072 lb. Fuel 4483 gal.
PERFORMANCE: Speed- Top 644 mph at 8000', 576 at 35,500', Cruising 525 mph, Stalling 147 mph. Combat Ceiling 40,000'. Service Ceiling 41,900'. Climb 5250'/1 min. Combat radius 1100 miles/ 2492 lb. chaff.

When the Douglas Destroyer did go to war from 1965 to 1972, it was as an electronic countermeasures aid to the bomber offensive against North Vietnam. Modified B-66Bs, RB-66Bs, and RB-66Cs become the EB-66B, EB-66E, and EB-66C respectively, with bomb bay radar pallets, dispensers for 2,492 pounds of chaff, and an ECM fairing to replace the tail gun turret.

Although they were unarmed, they became indispensable to Air Force operations in Southeast Asia by warning Air Force crews when they were tracked by hostile radar or by jamming SAM missile guidance.

Designing the B-52

'The most formidable expression of air power in the history of military aviation" was how Air Force Secretary Donald A. Quarles described the B-52. "Its range, which can be augmented by refueling techniques, its bomb load, its highly skilled crews, coupled with electronic equipment which makes it possible to find and hit any target anywhere in the world in any weather, constitute a weapons system which no other nation can match."

When that evaluation was made in 1955, American bombers looked back on some 38 years of continuous development, each type being succeeded by a better one in a few years. No one imagined that B-52s would retaliate 46 years later against a terrible attack from an enemy not yet visible in 1955.

Boeing's Stratofortress was to serve in front-line squadrons longer than any other USAF type, although its combat experience was to be very different than expected. The B-52 was designed to carry H-bombs, and the first thermonuclear weapon to be dropped from an American plane was a Mk 15 released from a B-52B on May 21, 1956, at Bikini Island. Its intended mission was to deter any such attack on America.

The B-52 story starts with an Army Air Force requirement dated November 23, 1945, for a heavy bomber with a 5,000-mile operating radius with a 10,000-pound bomb load and a 300-mph speed at 34,000 feet. Boeing, Convair and Martin responded to a Request for Proposals made February 13, 1946. Boeing's Model 462, a 180-ton project incorporating six 5,500-hp Wright XT35 turboprops on a straight, 221-foot span, wing won a design contract on June 28, 1946.

Engineers began another struggle to combine long range with speed, and many revisions were made before Boeing offered another concept, Model 464-29 with four turboprops, 20 degree sweepback, and a 445 mph estimate. But Air Force doubts that any propeller-driven bomber could meet its performance goals almost caused the project's cancellation, despite more revisions. Boeing engineers led by Edward Welles and George Schairer were called to AMC headquarters at Wright Field to defend their project. Learning that Pratt & Whitney was working on a new XJ57 jet engine, the Boeing men quickly produced a design in their Dayton hotel based on their XB-47 experience.

This configuration, Model 464-49, with eight J57s paired on pods suspended below a wing swept back 35 de-

BOEING XB-52
Eight Pratt & Whitney J57-P-3, 8700 lb. st
DIMENSIONS: Span 185', Lg. 152'8", Ht. 48'3", Wing Area 4000 sq. ft.
WEIGHT: Empty 155,200 lb., Combat 256,800 lb. Gross 390,000 lb. Fuel 36,540 +2000 gal.
PERFORMANCE: Speed- Top 611 mph at 20,000', 594 mph at 35,000', Cruising 519 mph, Stalling 146 mph. Combat Ceiling 46,500'. Combat radius 3535 miles/10,000 lb., Ferry range 7015 miles.

grees, was presented October 27, 1948. Impressed, the Air Force approved a contract for two XB-52 prototypes on November 17. After mockup approval in April 1949, construction of the prototypes proceeded.

Meanwhile, Boeing also offered a propeller-driven Model 474 to the USAF in 1948. Powered by four 5,643-hp Allison T40-A-2 turboprops slung below a slightly swept high wing, and designated XB-55, the 153,000-pound design had twelve 20-mm guns in three turrets. Since only 490 mph was expected from the six-bladed contrarotating propulsion, the XB-55 was abandoned in favor of the faster turbojet B-52 layout. A four turboprop bomber, called the Bear, was very successful in Soviet service.

Although identical in appearance to the first XB-52, the second prototype was designated YB-52 for fiscal reasons. On April 15, 1952, it was first flown from Seattle's Boeing field by A.M."Tex" Johnson and Lt Col. Guy M. Townsend. The XB-52's flight was delayed by mechanical problems until October 2. Both aircraft had a narrow canopy over tandem pilot seats, four pairs of main wheels retracting into the fuselage, small outrigger wheels at the wing tips, and a tall fin.

Eight YJ-57-P-3s were paired below the 36.5-degree swept wings whose airfoil sections had been developed in Boeing's own wind tunnel. Neither the Sperry K-1A bombing system intended to go under the nose nor the radar-aimed two .50-caliber guns in the tail were ever installed in the prototypes.

Boeing's competitor in jet-bomber development, was Convair's Fort Worth factory, which became part of General Dynamics in 1953. Convair had proposed a B-36G on August 27, 1950, using 72 percent of the older type's parts, but with a 37-degree swept wing and tail. On March 5, 1951, the Air Force ordered that two prototypes be modified from production B-36s and redesignated YB-60.

Eight J57-P-3 jets were paired in pods, like those of the B-52, and fuel capacity increased. While the 72,000-pound bomb capacity remained, all the turrets were

CONVAIR XB-60
Eight Pratt & Whitney J57-P-3, 8700 lb. st
DIMENSIONS: Span 206'5", Lg. 175'2", Ht. 60'5", Wing Area 5239 sq. ft.
WEIGHT: Empty 153,016 lb., Combat 260,250 lb. Gross 410,000 lb. Fuel 38,590 gal.
PERFORMANCE: Speed- Top 508 mph at 39,250', 502 mph at 43,400', Cruising 467 mph, Stalling 140 mph. Combat Ceiling 44,650'. Combat radius 2920 miles/10,000 lb., Ferry range 6192 miles.

omitted except for the twin 20-mm guns in the tail. Five crewmen sat in the pressurized front cabin, with a K-3A bombing-navigation system in the nose and APG-32 radar fire control for the gunner. An instrument probe protruded from the bow, but no ordnance was actually installed on the prototypes.

On April 18, 1952, three days after the YB-52, the YB-60 was first flown by Beryl Erickson. But since the YB-60 was much slower than the B-52, it did not replace the B-36 on Fort Worth production lines. On August 14, 1952, the B-60 program was canceled, and the second prototype left unfinished. Instead, Convair was left free to concentrate on designing the world's first supersonic bomber.

Building the B-52

Boeing's first contract for 13 production B-52s, approved December 16, 1952, introduced side-by-side pilots' seats demanded by General LeMay. Provisions for two 1,000-gallon drop tanks, inflight refueling, and J57-P-1W engines with water injection were added. Four .50-caliber M-3 tail guns with A-3A radar fire control, as well as a chaff dispensing system, provided rear defense..

The first three were B-52As, whose tests began August 5, 1954. None had bombing-navigation gear, and all stayed with Boeing for tests. In 1959, the third A was a carrier plane for the X-15 research program. The B-52 became the most thoroughly tested aircraft in the USAF. Since its design required three million engineering hours, compared to 153,000 for the B-29, it was well-prepared for its long service life.

The next 17 were originally designated RB-52B in a June 17, 1953, contract, because their bomb bay was fitted for an interchangeable pressurized capsule with cameras for reconnaissance and room for two additional crewmen. Seventeen capsules were actually built, but only once was one test flown. The others remained in storage after a January 7, 1955, order, and all of the next 50 Boeings were delivered as B-52B bombers.

BOEING B-52B
Eight Pratt & Whitney J57-P-19W, 10,500 lb. st military, 12,100 lb. Wet
DIMENSIONS: Span 185', Lg. 156'7", Ht. 48'4", Wing Area 4000 sq. ft.
WEIGHT: Empty 164,081 lb., Combat 272,000 lb. Gross 420,000 lb. Fuel 35,550 +2000 gal.
PERFORMANCE: Speed- Top 634 mph at 20,300', 598 mph at 35,000', 571 mph at 45,750', Cruising 519 mph, Stalling 146 mph. Combat Ceiling 47,500', Service Ceiling 47,700'. Climb 5500'/1 min., 20,000'/9.6 min. Combat radius 3534 miles/10,000 lb., Ferry range 7340 miles.

First flown January 25, 1955, the B-52B had a Sperry K-3A bombing system, plus five transmitters and two receivers for radar countermeasures. An MA-6A system later replaced the K-3A. While the first 11 had J57-P-1Ws, the rest used J57-P-19W or 29W engines.

The crew included two pilots and an ECM operator in the pressurized top deck, two bombardier-navigators in the lower deck behind the radar, and a lonely gunner in the tail. Armament included four .50-caliber M-3 guns with 2,400 rounds and both optical and A-3A radar fire control. A pair of 20-mm M24A1 guns and MD-5 fire control was fitted to 33 B-52Bs.

The 28-foot long bomb bay could include twenty-seven 1,000-pound bombs, or up to 43,000 pounds of various sizes. When the B-52B appeared, a 8,500-pound Mk 6 was the common nuclear load, until two 7,600-pound thermonuclear Mk 15s became standard. That was the 3.75 megaton yield weapon dropped from 40,000' in the *Cherokee* test on May 21, 1956. The larger 15,000-pound Mk 21 became available by 1957.

Boeing's B-52B joined SAC's 93rd Heavy Bomb Wing at Castle AFB, Calif. in June 1955, replacing B-47s. Deliveries were completed in August 1956, and the B model would be retired in 1966.

Over half the Stratofortress takeoff weight consisted of fuel carried in the fuselage and wings, mostly in self-sealing tanks. But the receptacle for an inflight refueling boom was the key to long-range operations. Three B-52Bs completed a 24,325-mile nonstop, round-the-world flight in 45 hours, 19 minutes, on January 18, 1957.

Relays of 78 KC-97 tankers had met the bombers at five refueling points on the route. Boeing KC-135 tankers began arriving at Castle AFB in June 1957. Jet-propelled, and carrying some 31,000 gallons of fuel, they were far more effective than the propeller-driven KC-97s they replaced.

Mfr

BOEING B-52D launching GAM-72 Quail (1966 data)
Eight Pratt & Whitney J57-P-19W, 10,500 lb. st military, 12,100 lb. Wet
DIMENSIONS: As B-52B/C
WEIGHT: Empty 177,816 lb. Combat 293,100 lb. Gross 450,000 lb. Fuel 35,598 +6000 gal.
PERFORMANCE: Speed- Top 585 mph at 20,000', Cruising 521 mph. Combat Ceiling 45,800'. Service Ceiling 46,350'. Combat radius 3470 miles/10,000 lb., Ferry range 7850 miles.

Mfr

BOEING B-52C
Eight Pratt & Whitney J57-P-19W, 10,500 lb. st military, 12,100 lb. Wet
DIMENSIONS: As B-52B
WEIGHT: Empty 164,486 lb., Combat 283,100 lb. Gross 450,000 lb. Fuel 35,550 +6000 gal.
PERFORMANCE: Speed- Top 634 mph at 20,200', 570 mph at 45,000', Cruising 521 mph, Stalling 169 mph. Combat Ceiling 46,350'. Climb 5310'/1 min. Combat radius 3800 miles/10,000 lb., Ferry range 7850 miles.

Larger 3,000-gallon drop tanks, and an MA-6A bombing system by International Business Machines Corporation (IBM) was provided on the B-52C, first flown March 9, 1956. Thirty-five B-52Cs built at Seattle by December 1956 replaced the B-36s of the 22nd Bomb Wing at March AFB. Tail defense remained four .50-caliber M-3 guns with A-3A fire control, and white thermal reflecting paint underneath would reduce blast heat.

Boeing's Wichita factory was added to the Stratofortress program by an August 1954 contract, and the first of B-52Ds was flown there on June 4, 1956, with MD-9 fire control and omission of the recon capsule capability. There were 69 B-52D-BWs from Wichita and 101 B-52D-BOs from Seattle delivered by November 1957. They replaced the B-36s of the 42nd Bomb Wing at Loring AFB, Maine, in 1956, the 92nd BW at Fairchild AFB, Washington, and the 28th Bomb Wing at Ellsworth AFB, South Dakota, in 1957. War in Vietnam required B-52D modification in 1966 to carry 42 750-pound or 84 500-pound bombs in the internal bay, and improved ECM fittings were essential.

Mfr

BOEING B-52E
Eight Pratt & Whitney J57-P-19W, 10,500 lb. st military, 12,100 lb. Wet
DIMENSIONS: As B-52B
WEIGHT: Empty 163,752 lb., Combat 282,600 lb. Gross 450,000 lb. Fuel 41,217 gal.
PERFORMANCE: Speed- Top 634 mph at 20,200', 570 mph at 45,000', Cruising 521 mph, Stalling 169 mph. Combat Ceiling 46,350'. Climb 5310'/1 min. Combat radius 3830 miles/10,000 lb., Ferry range 7875 miles.

Mfr

BOEING B-52H (1962 data)
Eight Pratt & Whitney TF33-P-3, 15,500 lb. st for 30 min.. 17,000 lb. for 5 min.
DIMENSIONS: Span 185', Lg. 160', Ht. 40'8", Wing Area 4000 sq. ft.
WEIGHT: Empty 169,822 lb., Combat 289,006 lb., Gross 450,000 lb., Max. 488,000 lb. Fuel 48,030 gal.
PERFORMANCE: Speed- Top 639 mph at 20,700', 603 mph at 35,000', 560 mph at 46,650', Cruising 525 mph, Stalling 169 mph. Combat Ceiling 47,200', Service Ceiling 47,800'. Climb 6990'/1 min., 20,000'/7.1 min. Combat radius 4480 miles/10,000 lb., Ferry range 10,195 miles.

BOEING B-52F
Eight Pratt & Whitney J57-P-43W, 13,750 lb. st. Wet takeoff, 11,200 lb. st
DIMENSIONS: Span 185', Lg. 156'6", Ht. 48'4", Wing Area 4000 sq. ft.
WEIGHT: Empty 162,685 lb., Combat 283,600 lb. Gross 450,000 lb. Fuel 41,093 gal.
PERFORMANCE: Speed- Top 636 mph at 20,500', 570 mph at 45,650', Cruising 523 mph, Stalling 169 mph. Combat Ceiling 46,600'. Climb 5680'/1 min. Combat radius 3850 miles/10,000 lb., Ferry range 7976 miles.

A more advanced ASQ-38 bombing-navigation system was used on the B-52E flown at Seattle on October 3, 1957. Forty-two B-52E-BOs and 58 B-52E-BWs were built by June 1958. New J57-P-43As were used on 44 B-52F-BOs, first flown May 6, 1958, and completed when production in Seattle ceased in November 1958. Concurrently, Wichita built 45 B-52F-BWs.

The long-lived B-52G/H models

The B-52G began with a letter contract dated August 29, 1957, for a "super-B-52" with range extended by a new wing structure allowing enlarged integral wing tanks, and fixed 700-gallon external tanks. Other B-52G innovations included the elimination of ailerons in favor of control by spoilers, and a shortened fin.

All six crewmen sat in the pressurized front cabin, including the gunner who was moved forward. He and the ECM operator faced backwards, with ASG-15 remote fire control for the four .50-caliber tail guns. Hostile radar could be detected and confused by four ECM sensors, 14 ECM jammers, 400 pounds of chaff, and up to four McDonnell ADM-20A (formerly GAM-72) Quail decoy missiles carried in the bomb bay. The 13-foot, 1,200-pound Quail reflected a radar image resembling a B-52.

An ASB-9 bombing system was provided for four Mk 28 bombs, the most widely-used USAF nuclear weapon, weighing about 2,250 pounds with a variable yield up to 1.45 megatons. Other weapons available were a 17,500-pound Mk 36 with a 10-megaton yield, or the 10,000-pound Mk 39 and Mk 41 bombs.

Production contracts had been increased to 193 B-52Gs by the time the first flew on October 26, 1958, and the B-52G joined the 5th BW in February 13, 1959, the same time SAC's last B-36 was retired. Airmen from that Wing set a world record for an unrefueled closed circuit flight of 10,078 miles completed December 14, 1960.

Even the most advanced bomber is threatened by missiles from enemy surface batteries and interceptors, so development proceeded on the "stand-off bomb," an air-

BOEING B-52G
Eight Pratt & Whitney J57-P-43W, 13,750 lb. st. Wet takeoff, 11,200 lb. st
DIMENSIONS: Span 185', Lg. 157'7", Ht. 40'8", Wing Area 4000 sq. ft.
WEIGHT: Empty 158,590 lb., Combat 281,390 lb., Gross 488,000 lb. Fuel 47,975 gal.
PERFORMANCE: Speed- Top 636 mph at 20,500', 570 mph at 46,000', Cruising 523 mph, Stalling 169 mph. Combat Ceiling 47,000', Climb 5850'/1 min.,33,400'/19 min. Combat radius 4350 miles/10,000 lb., Ferry range 8900 miles.

BOEING B-52H (1990 data)
Eight Pratt & Whitney TF33-P-3, 15,500 lb. st for 30 min. 17,000 lb. for 5 min.
DIMENSIONS: Span 185', Lg. 160'4", Ht. 40'8", Wing Area 4000 sq. ft.
WEIGHT: Empty 184,291 lb., Combat 299,596 lb., Gross 488,000 lb. Fuel 48,030 gal.
PERFORMANCE: Speed- Top 460 mph at s.l., 630 mph at 19,980', Cruising 524 mph, Stalling 176 mph. Combat Ceiling 45,950', Service Ceiling 47,450'. Climb 5812'/1 min., 20,000'/8.6 min. Combat radius with inflight refueling /14,337 lb. bombs: low mission 2547 miles, high mission 4812 miles. Ferry range 9380 miles.

to-surface missile launched from the bomber at a safer distance from the target. Structural provisions had been made on some B-52s for the Bell GAM-63 Rascal tested on the YDB-47s, but this missile was canceled in favor of a North American AGM-28 (formerly GAM-77) Hound Dog carried under each B-52G wing.

That 42-foot, 10,000-pound, air-breathing jet missile used a W-28 one-megaton warhead. Two could be released to knock out enemy defenses up to 500 miles away, so the bomber could deliver gravity weapons from its bomb bay. A prototype Hound Dog was successfully launched April 23, 1959, from a B-52E, and production Hound Dogs reached B-52G bases in August 1961.

The last Stratofortress model was the B-52H, with TF33-P-3 turbofans that reduced fuel consumption. Rear defense was a 20-mm M-61 multi-barrel Vulcan tail gun with 1,242 rounds and ASG-21 fire control, and 960 pounds of chaff for the ECM system.

Ordered by letter contract February 1, 1959, the B-52H was first flown March 6, 1961, and entered service with the 379th BW in May 1961. A world's unrefueled distance record of 12,532 miles was set by an Okinawa to Spain flight completed January 11, 1962.

There was a plan to carry four Douglas GAM-87 Skybolt missiles below the wings, but this two-stage ballistic missile was canceled December 21, 1962, and two Hound Dog cruise missiles were substituted. They weighed 20,306 pounds, and the bomb bay could bring the maximum weapons load to 35,400 pounds. Beginning in August 1962, the 8,850-pound Mk 53, with a nine-megaton yield, became available.

Production of the manned bomber came to a halt in the United States when the 102nd B-52H, last of 744 Stratofortresses, was delivered October 26, 1962. Aircraft cost had increased from $5,948,000 for the B-52E to $8,965,000 for the B-52H, but frequent modernization costs continued.

At first B-52s were concentrated in three-squadron 45-plane bomb wings on a single base, along with a KC-135 Heavy Tanker squadron, but they were gradually dispersed in 15-plane wings among many bases for greater safety from ICBM attack. As Cold War tensions increased, B-52s made 29 live drops of nuclear weapons during Operation Dominic in 1962.

During the Cuban missile crisis in October 1962, SAC launched an airborne alert, coded Chrome Dome, with 65 B-52s in the air, each with four nuclear weapons on 24-hour missions designed to keep them within reach of preset targets, and others were on 15-minute ground alert. SAC had 639 B-52s, along with 547 Hound Dog missiles, 436 Quail decoys, and 515 KC-135 tankers at the end of 1962.

The increasing effectiveness of Soviet defenses against high altitude bombers became apparent with new surface-to-air missiles (SAM) and supersonic fighters. To strengthen B-52s for beneath-radar, below 500-feet, penetrations of hostile territory, a series of overhaul programs and new electronics continuously improved SAC bombers. Terrain clearance radar, new ASG bombing navigation systems, and an Electro-optical Viewing System (EVS), ASQ-151, was added under the nose of all B-52G/H types in 1973.

Since fuel consumption was much greater at low altitudes, inflight refueling became the mode for all missions, and camouflage reduced detection from above. To illustrate the effects of those additions, B-52H characteristics for 1990 are included for a 14,337-pound bomb load. The heaviest 64,552-pound load included four B28FI bombs and eight AGM-69A missiles internally, plus 12 AGM-86B cruise missiles as external stores.

The story of the B-52's forty years of post-production combat and development will be found in Chapter 37.

Convair B-58

More than twice as fast as a B-52, the world's first supersonic bomber was the Convair B-58 Hustler built at Fort Worth. Developing that extreme advance in performance was inspired by the success of the Bell X-1 supersonic aircraft in 1947.

After flying the little XF-92A delta demonstrator in 1948, Convair used its delta experience to offer a bomber design for Air Force study. On February 17, 1951, Convair signed a letter contract to develop a parasite delta, called the MX-1626, which could be carried by a B-36, and on February 26, Boeing got a similar design contract for a more conventional MX-1712 proposal.

Revised USAF requirements issued February 26, 1952, led to Convair's MX-1964 and Boeing's MX-1965 three-place supersonic medium bomber designs, which became the XB-58 and XB-59. Boeing used four General Electric J73s and a swept wing, but when both detail designs were presented, Convair's delta was chosen on November 18. A mockup was inspected in August 1953, and the design was finalized after the J79 engine was chosen.

Development of 13 YB-58 test aircraft from Fort Worth was authorized June 29, 1954, although the definitive contract was not approved until December, 1955. Beryl Erickson flew the first YB-58 November 11, 1956, with four General Electric YJ79-GE-1 turbojets and afterburners in pods below the conical-cambered delta wing.

The narrow area-ruled fuselage had pressurized compartments for three crewmen provided with tandem ejection seats, and honeycombed wing skin panels resisted the high temperatures of supersonic air friction. Aircraft size was too small for a bomb bay. Instead, the stilted 18-wheel retractable landing gear held the narrow area-ruled fuselage high enough to clear an MB-1C pod containing a W39Y-1 nuclear warhead and 4,172 gallons of fuel. A similar pod with cameras, the LA-331, was available for reconnaissance missions.

CONVAIR YB-58

The bomb pod, slung beneath the fuselage, was carried at Mach .91 cruising speed and released on a Mach 2 dash over the target at 55,000 feet. Air refueling could increase combat radius from 1,750 to 5,590 miles. A dual pod, the BLU-2B flight-tested May 12, 1960, had a 54-foot lower 3,962-gallon fuel section released before the 35-foot upper section with a BA53-Y1 warhead. This configuration allowed a Mach .91 sea-level attack capability for that nine-megaton weapon. Hard points for four 2,065-pound, one-megaton Mk 43 weapons were added and a B-58 made the first supersonic weapons drop on June 16, 1962.

Navigation and bombing at Mach 2 presented unusual problems, which on the B-58 were to be solved by a Sperry AN/ASQ-42 system which used active radar navigation during a mission's approach phase, with inertial and star-tracking methods employed over enemy territory. Weighing 1,948 pounds, the system had an analog computer receiving data from search radar in the nose, an astro star tracker amidships, a Doppler radar in the tail, inertial sensors, and radio altimeter. Sitting at his console behind the pilot, the bombardier-navigator was provided with continuous and precise information on aircraft position, heading, ground speed, altitude, steering data, and distance to target, as well as ballistic computations for weapons release. Unfortunately, not until 1967 was the system's reliability satisfactory.

The third crewman was the defense systems operator, who, seated behind the navigator, had an Emerson MD-7 fire control for a 20-mm M-61 Vulcan with 1,120 rounds, and a 60-degree cone of fire in the tail. Electronic countermeasures, including 200 pounds of chaff in the wings were provided. Beginning with the 8th aircraft, the gun and J79-GE-5A engines were fitted, and new crew escape capsules were provided in 1962.

The first 30 Hustlers were built as test ships, but ten were modified to the B-58A tactical configuration and eight to dual-control TB-58A trainers. Eighty-six more standard B-58As with J79-GE-5Bs were delivered from September 1959 to October 26, 1962, also the B-52's last delivery day. Flyaway cost per production B-58 was listed as 12.44 million dollars, including about six million for engines, electronics, and armament. B-58 operations were said to be three times B-52 costs.

The B-58A began replacing the B-47s of SAC's 43rd Bomb Wing at Carswell AFB in March 1960, and the 305th Bomb Wing in May 1961 -the only two wings to get the type. Considering the B-58's high performance and sophisticated equipment, it was surprising that its service life was curtailed. By January 16, 1970, the last Hustlers were retired from SAC. One reason was the B-58A's high accident rate, resulting in the loss of nine of the first 30 aircraft, another the growing threat of surface and air launched missiles. And unlike the B-52, it could not be configured for a mass of conventional bombs or missiles.

CONVAIR B-58A

Four General Electric J79-GE-5B, 10,300 lb. st. 15,500 lb. (AB)

DIMENSIONS: Span 56'10", Lg. 96'10", Ht. 31'5", Wing Area 1542.5 sq. ft.

WEIGHT: Empty 55,560 lb., Combat 81,750 lb./MB-1C pod,(88,025 lb./4-Mk 43), Gross 163,000 lb., Fuel 14,850 gal., (15,499 gal. air-refueled)

PERFORMANCE: Speed- Top 608 mph at s.l., 1320 mph at 63,150', Cruising 610 mph. Combat Ceiling 64,800', Climb 17,830'/1 min. Combat radius 1750 miles (5590 with flight refueling). Ferry range 5028 miles.

CONVAIR B-58A with weapons
From left, the BLU-2 fuel tank, W53 bomb pod, four Mk 43 bombs, tail gun.

Delivery of nuclear weapons was limited by the B-58's short range, and a less expensive and more deadly launcher was the intercontinental ballistic missile (ICBM), whose entrance into SAC paralleled B-58 service. The first SAC Atlas ICBM squadron was declared operational September 2, 1960, and by 1969 enough more advanced ICBMs were on hand for an operational force stabilized at 1,000 Minuteman and 54 Titan missiles, while the Navy had 656 submarine-launched missiles.

Other Bomber Designations

In 1951 bomber designations had been assigned to five guided missiles then at various stages of development: the Martin B-61 Matador tactical cruise missile; the Northrop B-62 Snark strategic cruise missile; the Bell B-63 Rascal air-launched missile; the North American B-64 Navaho strategic supersonic cruise missile; and the Convair B-65 Atlas, the first American ICBM. All of these projects were redesignated according to a standardized missile nomenclature system and consequently fall outside the scope of this book.

The B-66 tactical bomber has already been described in an earlier section of this chapter. The Radioplane Crossbow (GAM-67) decoy missile used the B-67 designation briefly, and the XB-68 was Martin's last jet-bomber design. RB-69A was the designation allotted to seven Lockheed P2V-7U Neptunes ordered from the Navy in May 1954 for special electronics intelligence missions.

Martin's Model 316 was ordered in September 1956 as the XB-68 two-place tactical bomber powered by two Pratt & Whitney 27,500-pound thrust J75s mounted on each side on the long fuselage. Like the company's earlier XB-51, it had a high T-tail and rotary bomb door, but the 53-foot span wings were straight and short like those on an F-104. Armament included a radar-aimed 20-mm T-171, like the one on the B-58, and a 3,500-pound TX-11 nuclear bomb that was to be carried over a 688-mile combat radius. Estimated top speed was 1,589 mph at 54,700 feet, a velocity requiring evaporation cooling and a steel primary structure.

Although two prototypes and a static-test article had been planned, the XB-68 was canceled early in 1957 to save money, leaving the XB-70 as the only manned strategic-bomber prototype under way. Subsequent numbers were assigned to the SR-71 reconnaissance design and to several missile projects, but the XB-70 would be the last bomber in the series that began with a Keystone biplane in 1927.

MARTIN XB-68 proposal
Two Pratt & Whitney J75-PW, 18150 lb. st. military, 27,500 lb. max.
DIMENSIONS: Span 53', Lg. 109'10", Ht. 15'6", Wing Area 875 sq. ft.
WEIGHT: Empty 53,975 lb., Combat 72,116 lb., Gross 100,000 lb. Fuel 6231 +909 gal.
PERFORMANCE: Speed- Top 1589 mph at 54,500', Cruising 606 mph, Stalling 170 mph. Combat Ceiling 58,150'. Combat radius 688 miles/3700 lb.. Ferry range 3042 miles.

CHAPTER 29

SUPERSONIC FIGHTERS, F-100 TO F-108

Supersonic fighters: F-100A, F-102A, F-101A, and YF-105, with the F-104A in the foreground. AF

Fighter designers have always wanted to make their products faster, and American engineers were the first to produce a supersonic fighter generation. This was possible because the nation's financial and industrial resources could be called upon for a costly effort beyond the reach of most countries.

An aerodynamic research program, costing over $360 million, had produced a series of research aircraft beginning with the rocket-powered Bell X-l, which was launched from a B-29 into the world's first manned supersonic flight on October 14, 1947. Another program developed advanced propulsion systems, and even more money went into the development of new machines for shaping light-alloy metal; enormous stretch-presses, heavy presses to squeeze out large forgings, and automatic precision machinery for cutting, drilling and riveting.

A North American company statement indicates how much more design effort was needed. While 300,000 engineering man-hours had been required to produce 15,485 P-51 fighters, 1,800,000 engineering man-hours produced 6,232 F-86 jets, and 4,800,000 engineering man-hours produced 2,294 supersonic F-100s.

The F-100

The first supersonic aircraft in production anywhere in the world was the F-100 Super Sabre. North American began the design on January 19, 1951, as the NA-180, using a new Pratt & Whitney XJ57 with afterburner; a 45-degree swept low wing, and moveable "slab" horizontal tail surfaces combining stabilizer and elevator functions. A speed brake was located in the fuselage bottom and a tail drag chute reduced the landing run.

After that proposal for a Mach 1.3 fighter was submitted to the Air Force on May 14, two prototypes were ordered November 1, 1951, along with a production commitment. The YF-100A designation was finalized on the 10th anniversary of the Pearl Harbor attack, beginning the "Century" series of supersonic Air Force fighters. The F-100 or "Hundred" eventually became the "Hun" in Air Force slang. Preceding fighter designations were soon forgotten: the F-95, -96, and -97 having reverted to F-86D, F-84F, and F-94C, while the Hughes F-98 became the Falcon air-to-air missile and the Boeing F-99 became the Bomarc "pilotless interceptor," a surface-to-air missile.

Mfr

NORTH AMERICAN YF-100A
Pratt & Whitney XJ57-P-5, 8450 lb. st military, 13,200 lb. AB
DIMENSIONS: Span 36'9", Lg. 46'2", Ht. 14'5", Wing Area 376 sq. ft.
WEIGHT: Empty 18,279 lb., Combat 24,789 lb., Gross 28,965 lb. Fuel 757+550 gal.
PERFORMANCE: Speed- Top 730 mph at s.l., 660 mph at 43,350', Cruising 600 mph, Stalling 160 mph. Combat Ceiling 52,600', Climb 12,500'/1 min. Combat Radius 422 miles, Ferry range 1410 miles.

A sense of urgency impelled the F-100 program ahead of the usual time schedule. The fear that the fast MiGs

AF

NORTH AMERICAN F-100A-1 with original tail fin

would soon have a supersonic successor, the desire of fighter pilots for more speed and altitude, and the awareness at the highest levels of command that 1957- the year of danger in war plan Dropshot (see Chapter 25) -was drawing near. A letter contract for the first 23 F-100As (NA-192) was given February 11, 1952, starting a contract for 273 approved by August 1952.

Pearl Harbor veteran George Welch exceeded sonic speed on the YF-100A's first flight on May 25, 1953, at Edwards. He also flew the second YF-100A on October 14, and the first F-100A-l, which also used the J57-P-7, but had a shorter tail fin, on October 29. On the same day, LtCol. F.K. Everest flew the YF-100A to a 755-mph world speed record, the last time the rules required this record be set at less than a 100-foot altitude.

Pilots of TAC's 479th Fighter Day Wing enthusiastically received the fast fighters in September 1954, but a hard blow struck the program. Four aircraft had been lost to inflight structural failure after loss of control, and George Welch was killed when the ninth F-100A-l disintegrated in a high-speed test dive on October 12, 1954. The Air Force grounded its entire F-100 inventory, waiting for the company to find out what was wrong.

The problem was that of directional stability, and fortunately the fix was relatively easy: an enlarged fin, extended wing tips and modified controls. These changes were made to all Super Sabres in the works and to those already delivered, and by February 1955, they were back in the air. By April 1955, 203 F-100As were completed, although they were operational only with the 479th Wing. The remaining Air Force day fighter strength then consisted of 12 F-84F, 13 F-86F, and three F-86H wings. (The 28 all-weather interceptor wings' equipment has been described in Chapter 27). Top speed had risen from Mach .91 on the F-86A to Mach 1.285 (852 mph) at 35,000 feet on the F-100A.

Mfr

NORTH AMERICAN F-100A-20
Pratt & Whitney J57-P-7 or -39, 9700 lb. st military, 14,800 lb. AB
DIMENSIONS: Span 38'10", Lg. 47'10", Ht. 15'6", Wing Area 385 sq. ft.
WEIGHT: Empty 18,185 lb., Combat 24,996 lb., Gross 28,899 lb. Fuel 744+550 gal.
PERFORMANCE: Speed- Top 760 mph at s.1., 852 mph at 35,000', Cruising 590 mph, Stalling 159 mph. Combat Ceiling 51,000', Climb 23,800'/1 min. Combat Radius 358 miles, Ferry range 1294 miles.

Super Sabre armament consisted of four new 20-mm M-39 guns with 200 rpg, while two 1,000-pound bombs could replace the 275-gallon drop tanks, and two Sidewinder missiles were added in 1956. Six planes were converted to RF-100A camera versions in 1954, and four went to Taiwan in 1961. The Air Force soon found that besides higher performance, the F-100 brought costly problems.

Titanium, a rare heat-resistant metal combining strength and light weight, was used in the structure and helped raise the F-100A price past $1,014,000 per aircraft. A shortage of skilled maintenance men kept many aircraft on the ground in 1955. Accidents destroyed 287 aircraft and killed 91 men during the F-100's first 750,000 flight time hours. Introducing supersonic fighters was also difficult for a Soviet counterpart, the MiG-19 first flown on January 5, 1954.

An F-100B project was diverted into the later YF-107 design, but on December 30, 1953, the F-100C fighter-bomber configuration had been selected for future Super Sabre production. The F-100C had the J57-P-21 (beginning with 101st a/c), more fuel, an air-refueling probe on the right wing, and wings strengthened to handle six 750-pound bombs, or a 1,680-pound Mk 7 nuclear weapon under the left wing, released by an MA-2 LABS, or two pods with 42 2.75-inch air-to-air rockets.

NORTH AMERICAN F-100C
Pratt & Whitney J57-P-21, 10,200 lb. st military, 16,000 lb. AB
DIMENSIONS: As F-100A
WEIGHT: Empty 19,270 lb., Combat 27,585 lb., Gross 32,615 lb. Max. 35,696 lb. Fuel 1589+550 gal.
PERFORMANCE: Speed- Top 925 mph at 35,000', 904 mph at 39,500', Cruising 593 mph, Stalling 168 mph. Combat Ceiling 49,100', Climb 21,600'/1 min., 35,000'/2.3 min. Combat Radius 572 miles, Ferry range 1954 miles.

North American flew its first F-100C-l-NA from Los Angeles on January 17, 1955, and built 451 F-100Cs by April 1956. They entered service with TAC in July 1955. A second production source at Columbus, Ohio, began delivery of 25 F-100C-10-NH models in September 1955.

Added wing and tail area, and an autopilot, distinguished the F-100D ordered October 1954, and first flown January 24, 1956. Alternate underwing loads included either six 750-pound or four 1,000-pound bombs, two GAM-83A Bullpup missiles, a Mk 28 nuclear store, four AIM-9B Sidewinder air-to-air missiles, or two 450-gallon buddy air-refueling tanks. Production amounted to 940 F-100D-NA and 334 F-100D-NHs by August 1959, to which 339 two-seat F-100F trainers added by October 1959 brought the Super Sabre production total to 2,294.

Deliveries of F-100Ds to TAC began in September 1956. By June 1957, 16 TAC Wings used Super Sabres, and as more F-100Ds arrived, F-100A and F-100C models

NORTH AMERICAN F-100D
Pratt & Whitney J57-P-21A, 10,200 lb. st military, 16,000 lb. AB
DIMENSIONS. Span 38'10", Lg. 49'4", Ht. 16'2", Wing Area 400 sq. ft.
WEIGHT: Empty 20,638 lb., Combat 28,847 lb., Gross 34,050 lb. Max. 37,124 lb. Fuel 1589+550 gal.
PERFORMANCE: Speed- Top 910 mph at 35,000', 728 mph at 47,500', Cruising 590 mph, Stalling 169 mph. Combat Ceiling 47,700', Climb 19,000'/1 min. 35,000'/2.2 min. Combat Radius 534 miles, Ferry range 1995 miles.

were passed to ANG squadrons, beginning in February 1958. Exports of 203 F-100Ds and 45 F-100Fs began in May 1958 when France began receiving 68 Ds and seven Fs for two *escadres de chasse,* serving with them until 1967. Denmark got 48 F-100Ds and 24 F-100Fs, beginning in June 1959, and Turkey received 87 F-100Ds in the same period. Eighty modernized F-100As went to Taiwan in 1959/60, plus 38 later transfers, and a few F-100Fs, and additional transfers brought the Turkish F-100 total to 260.

In 1962, TAC began replacing its F-100s with F-4s, but ten wings remained in 1964 when war in Indochina called them into action. None of these actions involved fighting enemy aircraft, since all were attacks on surface targets. Individual F-100D squadrons of four TAC Wings, beginning in August 1964 with the 3rd TFW, rotated through the area on tours of about six months, flying more sorties than all those by P-51s in World War II.

A new dimension to the air war was added by the hostile SA-2 Guideline surface-to-air missile (SAM). After these Soviet-built SAMs became effective in Viet Nam in July 1965, electronic counter measures were needed. Seven F-100F two-seaters, modified to the "Wild Weasel I" ECM version, began operations to detect and attack enemy radar sites on December 3, 1965.

The last F-100Ds in Vietnam, belonging to the 35th TFW, left in July 1971. The last "Hun" left Air Force service when the 27th TFW retired its F-100Ds in June 1972, but of 28 ANG F-100 squadrons, ten still continued to use F-100Ds in 1978. On November 10, 1979, the last operational flight by an ANG F-100D ended the first supersonic fighter's USAF service.

The F-101 series

McDonnell's F-101A Voodoo was a long-range fighter based on the earlier XF-88. Powered by two J57-P-13 turbojets with afterburners, the Voodoo had a one-piece horizontal stabilizer set high on its fin, and mid-span ailerons on the thin 35-degree swept wing. Armament included four 20-mm M-39 guns with 200 rpg in the nose, with attachments below the fuselage for a nuclear bomb released by a LABS and 450-gallon drop tanks. Air refueling provisions were also provided.

McDONNELL F-101A
Two Pratt & Whitney J.57-P-13, 10,200 lb. st military, 15,000 lb. AB
DIMENSIONS: Span 39'8", Lg. 67'5", Ht. 18', Wing Area 368 sq. ft.
WEIGHT: Empty 25,374 lb., Combat 39,495 lb., Gross 48,001 lb. Fuel 2250+900 gal.
PERFORMANCE: Speed- Top 1005 mph at 35,000', Cruising 550 mph, Stalling 198 mph. Combat Ceiling 49,450', Climb 33,700'/ 1 min. Combat Radius 677 miles, Ferry range 2186 miles.

Developed in response to a SAC requirement dated February 6, 1951, for a fighter to escort its bombers, the McDonnell Model 36W proposed in May was designated F-101 on November 20. A letter contract for 29 F-l0lAs was placed January 3,1952, the mockup inspected in July, and the first flown September 29, 1954, by Robert Little. Orders were increased to include 77 F-101A and 47 F-l0lC Voodoos.

The first 1,000-mph fighter in production, the F-l0lAs had been intended for SAC's fighter escort units, but thorough testing of the first 40 aircraft revealed such serious problems that the Air Force suspended production from May 23 to November 26, 1956. F-101As did become operational with SAC's 27th FBW in May 1957, but in July that unit was transferred to TAC, which wanted a low-altitude fighter-bomber that could deliver Mk 7 or Mk 28 nuclear bombs.

Essentially the F-101Cs, first flown August 21 and completed by May 1958, were identical except for wings strengthened for low-altitude tactical bombing. Delivery of the F-101C to the 27th FBW began in September, overlapping completion of the last As in October 1957.

On December 12, 1957, an F-101A modified with 16,900-pound thrust J57-P-55s, and no armament, set a 1,207-mph speed record. In 1958, the Voodoo fighters were transferred to the 81st TFW in Britain, serving until January 1966, when the last F-101C left, replaced by the F-4C.

For reconnaissance, two long-nose YRF-101As, first flown May 10, 1955, 35 RF-101As from June 1956, and 166 RF-101Cs were completed from July 1957 to March 1959 with six cameras and retaining their nuclear weapon capability. This application had a longer history, although it also entered TAC service in May 1957, replacing the RF-84Fs. During the Cuban Missile crisis of October 1962, 363rd TRW Voodoos flew low-level sorties over threatening missile sites.

Four RF-101Cs were transferred to the Chinese on Taiwan in November 1959 and another four were added later. After Air Force Voodoos were transferred to the ANG, 29 F-l0lAs were rebuilt as RF-l0lG and 32 F-101s as RF-101H aircraft.

McDONNELL RF-101A
Two Pratt & Whitney J57-P-13, 10,200 lb. st military, 15,000 lb. AB
DIMENSIONS: Span 39'8", Lg. 69'3", Ht. 18', Wing Area 368 sq. ft.
WEIGHT: Empty 25,335 lb., Combat 35,751 lb., Gross 47,331 lb. Fuel 2250+1350 gal.
PERFORMANCE: Speed- Top 1008 mph at 35,000', 884 mph at 44,400', Cruising 550 mph, Stalling 198 mph. Combat Ceiling 51,450', Climb 37,500'/1 min. Combat Radius 1046 miles, Ferry range 2435 miles.

Four RF-101Cs of the 15th TRS arrived at Tan Son Nhot on October 18, 1961, becoming the first Air Force unit to operate from Vietnam, and rotating RF-101 units continued to fly there until November 1970. Sorties over North Vietnam were the most dangerous, and the first RF-101 loss was on April 3, 1965. Seven more were lost to anti-aircraft fire in 1966.

McDONNELL F-101C
Two Pratt & Whitney J.57-P-13, 10,200 lb. st military, 15,000 lb AB
DIMENSIONS: As F-101A
WEIGHT: Empty 26,277 lb., Combat 40,429 lb. Gross 48,908 lb., Max. 50,996 lb. Fuel 2250+1126 gal.
PERFORMANCE: Speed- Top 1004 mph at 35,000', Cruising 552 mph, Stalling 200 mph. Combat Ceiling 49,000', Climb 32,900'/ 1 min. Combat Radius 658 miles, Ferry range 2125 miles.

The Voodoos had no trouble evading MiG-17s, but after a MiG-21 downed one in September 1967, RF-4Cs replaced the RF-101s on missions over North Vietnam, the older type confining itself to Laos and the south. By October 1971, all RF-101s had been transferred to the ANG.

Delta-wing Interceptors

Convair developed the next century series interceptor as part of a "weapons system" (WS201A) consisting of air-to-air guided missiles, all-weather radar search and fire control, and supersonic single-seat fighter. The electronics came first, with the selection of Hughes Aircraft in October 1950 as developer of the Falcon missile and fire

Mfr

CONVAIR YF-102A

control. Known in its earlier stage as the F-98, the Falcon became the GAR-l and the AIM-4 series in 1962.

Proposals for the aircraft itself were requested by the Air Force on June 18, 1950, and Convair, Lockheed and Republic were named the winners on July 2, 1951. On September 11, 1951, Convair got a design and mockup letter contract for an enlarged development of the delta wing XF-92A and two YF-102 prototypes were added December 19, 1951. The original design had a Wright J67 engine, Hughes MA-l fire control, and Falcon missiles.

Mfr

CONVAIR YF-102
Pratt & Whitney J57-P-11, 9200 lb. st military, 14,800 lb. AB
DIMENSIONS: Span 37', Lg. 52'6", Ht. 18', Wing Area 661 sq. ft.
WEIGHT: Empty 17,954 lb., Combat 23,989 lb., Gross 26,404 lb. Fuel 1050 gal.
PERFORMANCE: Speed- top 870 mph at 35,000', Cruising 596 mph, Stalling 145 mph, Combat Ceiling 54,400', Service Ceiling 55,900', Climb 25,000'/1 min, 50,000'/7 min., Combat Radius 575 miles, Ferry Range 1550 miles. (Data from 1953 pre-test specification)

When it was seen that the J67 and MA-l could not be completed in time, a J57-P-11 and MG-3 system was substituted for the interim YF-102 and F-102A, with the more sophisticated systems planned for the ultimate F-102B. Preliminary engineering on ten YF-102s began in April 1952 and the first 32 F-102A production aircraft were ordered December 17, 1952, on a contract approved the following June 12.

Carrying 1,194 pounds of armament, 1,050 gallons of fuel, and nearly a ton of electronics, the F-102 design was half again as heavy as the F-86D at combat weight, and the promised 870 mph at 35,000 feet could never be approached in actual flight. Even before the YF-102's first flight on October 24, 1953, by Richard L. Johnson, wind tunnel tests warned that the drag hump at sonic speed was beyond the airplane's capability. The first prototype encountered severe buffet at Mach 0.9 and crashed on its seventh takeoff. The second YF-102 flew January 11, 1954, but was limited to Mach .98 on the level, and dives over this speed resulted in severe yaw oscillations.

The whole F-102 program – and with it Air Defense Command's principle weapon for the 1955-60 period – faced sudden termination at a time when American leadership was alarmed by Soviet weapons progress. A Soviet H-bomb had been tested August 12, 1953, and on May 1, 1954, the prototype of the Myasishchev M-4 "Bison" jet bomber was displayed over Moscow. By 1957-58, it was assumed, the USSR would possess a large fleet of intercontinental bombers with enough thermonuclear weapons to devastate U.S. targets. That assumption would prove false, but was the basis of U.S. planning for that period.

Convair's delta wing was saved by the application of the area rule, a system of drag reduction developed by NACA scientist Richard Whitcomb. The F-102 was redesigned with a narrowed center fuselage, lengthened nose and tail fairings, and ten F-102s were followed by four longer YF-102As built with the J57-P-41, cambered leading edges for the thin wings, and a modified canopy. Supersonic speeds were achieved on December 21, 1954, the day after the first YF-102A flight. Two-thirds of the 30,000 tools prepared for the original configuration had to be discarded in favor of the new shape.

The first F-102A flew June 24, 1955, with a J57-P-23, but the production plan provided very slow deliveries until testing and modifications were complete. Many airframe changes were made, including a three-foot addition to the tail fin tested in December 1955, and standardized on all F-102As built after number 25. A TF-102A trainer with two side-by-side seats and full armament was ordered July 19, 1954, and first flown November 8, 1955. Over 50 F-102 aircraft were involved in the largest test program then ever made on an Air Force fighter, and a new wing configuration improved performance in October 1957.

Armament on the Delta Dagger in a fuselage bay consisted of six Falcon GAR-lD (AIM-4A) radar or GAR-2A (AIM-4C) infrared homing missiles. Twenty-four 2.75-inch rockets were held in the bay doors, which snapped open when the Falcons were extended into the air stream for launching. Three missiles of each guidance system were usually carried, to use against targets up to six miles away, but the inaccurate short-range rockets were usually omitted in service. Two 215-gallon tanks could be attached for ferry missions.

CONVAIR F-102A
Pratt & Whitney J57-P-23A, 10,200 lb. st military, 16,000 lb. AB
DIMENSIONS: Span 38'2", Lg. 68'2", Ht. 21'2", Wing Area 695 sq. ft.
WEIGHT: Empty 19,350 lb., Combat 24,494 lb. Gross 28,150 lb. Max. 31,276 lb. Fuel 1085+430 gal.
PERFORMANCE: Speed- Top 780 mph at 35,000', 637 mph at 51,800', Cruising 605 mph, Stalling 154 mph. Combat Ceiling 51,800', Service Ceiling 53,400', Climb 18,700'/1 min. 51,800'/ 9.9 min. Combat Radius 386 miles, Ferry range 1492 miles.

The first F-102A delivery to an operational ADC unit, the 327th FIS, was made on May 1, 1956, almost three years behind the original program date, and the Air Force at last had a Mach 1.535 fighter in which guided missiles replaced guns or unguided rockets. Convair's San Diego factory completed 14 YF-102/As, 875 F-102As and 111 TF-102As by September 1958, serving 32 ADC squadrons. About 450 F-102As were modified by 1963 with MG-10 fire control, a 262-pound AIM-26A (W54 nuclear warhead) Super Falcon radar-guided missile with three AIM-4E/Fs, and an infrared search system. The aircraft cost $1.5 million dollars and 119 were destroyed in service.

CONVAIR F-102A firing missiles

Beginning in 1959, seven squadrons served in the Pacific Air Force and six in Europe, and while ADC Delta Darts began transferring to 23 ANG squadrons in 1960, there were still 20 ADC squadrons in 1964. From March 1962 to 1970, F-102As, mostly from the 509th FIS, were rotated to Vietnam. No enemy bombers ever appeared, but sorties were flown against ground targets, four F-102As lost to ground attack, two to ground fire, and one destroyed by a MiG-21F over Laos on February 3, 1968.

After the last transfers from the ADC in 1965, the last Air Force F-102A squadron, from July 1962 to July 1973, was the 57th FIS. Based in Iceland, it made over 1,000 non-combat intercepts of Soviet long-range aircraft flying from North Russia. The last ANG outfit to lose F-102s was Hawaii's 199th FIS in 1977.

Turkey used 35 F-102As and 10 TF-102As from 1968 to 1979, and 20 F-102As and four TF-102As served Greece from 1969 to 1978. By USAF order, 70 other Daggers were converted to PQM-102A target drones in 1974 and another 145 PQM-102B added by 1981.

Republic XF-103

Republic also proposed an interceptor with delta wings, but the AP-57 design study ordered in September 1951 had a radical shape with a dual-cycle power plant combining a 12,950-pound thrust Wright XJ67 raised to a maximum 22,350-pound thrust by an afterburner, with a ramjet cutting in after reaching 35,000 feet in a climb. Mach 3 speeds, listed in January 1954 estimates as 1,985 mph at 50,000 feet, would cause so much heat that titanium was chosen as the main structural element.

The long fuselage had the pilot's cockpit flush behind the radar nose, with an escape capsule and a periscope.

Mfr

CONVAIR F-102A painted for Vietnam

REPUBLIC XF-103 proposal
Wright XJ6 7-W-3, 22,350 lb. st, and XRJ55-W-1 ramjet, 18,800 lb. st
DIMENSIONS: Span 34'5", Lg. 76'9", Ht. 16'7", Wing Area 401 sq. ft.
WEIGHT: Empty 24,949 lb., Combat 31,219 lb., Gross 38,505 lb. Max. 42,864 lb. Fuel 1800+574 gal.
PERFORMANCE: Speed- Top 1985 mph at 50,000', Cruising 678 mph, Stalling 154 mph. Combat Ceiling 69,200', Service Ceiling 69,600', Climb 50,000'/7.1 min. Combat Radius 245 miles, Ferry range 1548 miles.

Short delta wings and separate tail surface were used, and fuselage bays contained six XGAR-1A Falcon missiles and pack of 36 2.75-in. rockets.

Although an XF-103 prototype, ordered in July 1954, was supposed to fly in February 1957, the dual power plant did not materialize. Republic proposed a larger research version, but the airframe was never completed and the contract was canceled August 21, 1957, after a six-year expenditure of 104 million dollars.

The F-101B Interceptor

A two-place long-range interceptor Voodoo was proposed by McDonnell on December 1,1954, endorsed by the Air Force on February 25, 1955, and a formal contract for the first 28 was issued on July 12. Armed with missiles instead of guns, it was temporarily called the F-109, but in August 1955 became the F-101B. (The F-109 was incorrectly identified as a Ryan VTOL project by some contemporary sources.)

McDONNELL F-101B
Two Pratt & Whitney J57-P-55, 10,700 lb. st military, 16,900 lb. with AB
DIMENSIONS: Span 39'8", Lg. 71'1", Ht. 18', Wing Area 368 sq. ft.
WEIGHT: Empty 28,497 lb., Combat 40,853 lb. Gross 45,461 lb. Max. 51,724 lb. Fuel 2084+900 gal.
PERFORMANCE: Speed- Top 1094 mph at 35,000', 610 mph at 51,000', Cruising 547 mph, Stalling 212 mph. Combat Ceiling 51,000', Service Ceiling 51,500', Climb 39,250'/1 min. Combat Radius 829 miles, Ferry range 1755 miles.

The F-101B had two J57-P-55s with afterburners and MG-13 radar fire control for six Falcon GAR-lD radar or GAR-2A infrared guided missiles on a rotary door behind and below the cockpit. A launcher available later held two 834-pound AIR-2 Genie unguided nuclear air-to-air rockets externally, retaining two 120-pound AIM-4C Falcons inside. The SAGE data-link system provided automatic ground control to direct interceptions, and two 450-gallon drop tanks could be added for ferry missions.

First flown March 27, 1957, the F-101B was issued to 17 ADC Fighter-Interceptor squadrons between January 1959 and March 31, 1961, when production of 470 ended. When fitted with dual controls, 79 F-l0lBs were redesignated F-l0lF.

MCDONNELL CF-l01B

Fifty-six F-101Bs and 10 F-101Fs went to Canada, beginning in October 1961, where they were known as the CF-101Bs and CF-101F. In 1970, they were exchanged for 66 replacements with a new infrared sensor system. The F-101B interceptors served the ANG after December 1969, including 23 converted to RF-101B recon versions, and the last ANG F-101B retired on September 21, 1982.

The F-104 Starfighter

The first Air Force fighter with Mach 2 speed was designed by C.L. "Kelly" Johnson to meet the demands of Korean War pilots for the highest possible speed and ceiling obtainable. This could be done by being the first to fly with the new J79 engine, by keeping the airframe light, avoiding heavy electronics, and done, to the surprise of many, without the swept-back wings of most contemporary types.

The smallest and thinnest wings used on an American jet distinguished the Starfighter, whose design Lockheed proposed in November 1952 as the Model 83. Two XF-104 prototypes were ordered March 11, 1953, with Wright 11,500-pound thrust XJ65-W-6 engines, and Tony LeVier made a short hop February 28, 1954, at Edwards AFB, with an official first flight on March 4. A Mach 1.79 speed was achieved March 25 by the second prototype fitted with an afterburner and a test model of General Electric's radical new 20-mm T-171 gun.

Although that aircraft was destroyed April 18, when pilot H. Salmon had to use the downward-firing ejection seat, the other prototype successfully demonstrated the essential design with the 10-percent anhedral (downward slope) wing and T-tail. Seventeen YF-104A Starfighters or-

LOCKHEED XF-104

dered October 1954 had the General Electric J79-GE-3 with afterburners and the original air inlet ramps replaced by shock-control semi-cones. Fuel was contained in the fuselage and 170-gallon wingtip tanks.

The first YF-104A, flown February 17, 1956, was 5.5 feet longer and a 1,000 pounds heavier empty than the prototypes, but did reach Mach 2 on April 27. Production contracts added 153 more F-104A and 26 F-104B Starfires completed by December 1958, the latter a gun-less two-seat trainer first flown January 16, 1957.

Armament introduced the 20-mm M-61 six revolving-barrel Vulcan (ex-T-171) with 725 rounds that could be fired in about 7.5 seconds. The 6,000-rpm rate of fire made that Gatling-type weapon the equal of four ordinary guns. This would become the standard gun for the next generation of American fighters, but so many reliability problems occurred in the first guns that Vulcans were removed from the F-104As in November 1957.

LOCKHEED F-104A

General Electric J79-CE-3A, 9600 lb. st military, 14,800 lb. AB

DIMENSIONS: Span 21'11", Lg. 54'9", Ht. 13'6", Wing Area 196 sq. ft.

WEIGHT: Empty 12,782 lb., Combat 17,768 lb., Gross 22,614 lb. Max. 24,804 lb. Fuel 897+340 gal.

PERFORMANCE: Speed- Top 1324 mph at 35,000', 1232 mph at 50,000', Cruising 599 mph, Stalling 198 mph. Combat Ceiling 55,200', Service Ceiling 64,795', Climb 36,000'/1 min. Combat Radius 403 miles/2 GAR-8, Ferry range 1585 miles.

Two GAR-8 Sidewinder infrared missiles replaced the tip tanks on combat sorties, and on January 26, 1958, the F-104A joined the 83rd Fighter-Interceptor Squadron, first of the four ADC squadrons to use the type.

The limited armament was overlooked in the amazing performance, as an F-104A became the first plane to set

LOCKHEED F-104C
General Electric J79-GE-7, 10,000 lb. st military, 15,800 lb. AB
DIMENSIONS: As F-104A
WEIGHT: Empty 12,760 lb., Combat 19,470 lb., Gross 22,410 lb. Max. 27,853 lb. Fuel 897+730 gal.
PERFORMANCE: Speed- Top 1324 mph at 35,000', Cruising 584 mph, Stalling 196 mph. Combat Ceiling 58,000', Climb 38,000'/1 min. Combat Radius 352 miles, Ferry range 1727 miles.

world's records for both altitude and speed with a zoom to 91,249 feet and a 1,404 mph dash in May 1958. An upward-firing ejection seat in the pressurized cockpit would improve pilot survival in the frequent accidents.

A 2,040-pound Mk 28EX nuclear store could be attached underneath the F-104C fighter-bomber, which also had two underwing fixtures for 1,000-pound bombs, 2.75-inch rocket pods, 195-gallon tanks, or two more AIM-4B missiles. Powered by a J79-GE-7A, and with flight-refueling probes and two wingtip tanks, the first F-104C was flown in July 1958. Beginning in September, they replaced the 479th Tactical Fighter Wing's F-l00s. Seventy-seven F-104Cs were built by June 1959, joined by 21 F-104D two-seat trainers.

The 296 Starfighters supplied the Air Force by September 1959 had the highest accident rate of any service type; 49 aircraft and 18 pilots lost in the first 100,000 hours. Lacking all-weather radar, the F-104As were retired from the ADC to three ANG squadrons in 1960.

Twenty-four became QF-104 target drones and three were converted, beginning September 1962, to rocket-powered NF-104As for training NASA astronauts. But during the Cuban crisis of 1962, one F-104A squadron was called back into ADC service to be stationed with the 479th TFW in Florida, and another squadron was placed in Texas.

TAC F-104Cs had a longer service, and acquired satisfactory M-61A-1 guns, ASG-14 fire control, and Mk 43 one-megaton bombs as these systems became available. From April 1965 to December 1966 squadrons rotated to Vietnam flew over 2,775 sorties, but their limited endurance and weapons load were handicaps. After July 1967, they were passed to the ANG, whose 198th TFS was the final American squadron to use them, retiring the last F-104C on July 31, 1975.

After a visit to Taiwan by the 83rd FIS in September 1958, the RoC received 25 F-104As and two F-104Bs in 1960, while Pakistan got ten As and two F-104Bs. Jordan acquired 32 F-104As and four F-104Bs in 1969, refitted with new J79-GE-11 engines. The only Starfighter air-to-air combat by F-104s in this period was by Pakistani F-104As fighting India in August 1965 and again in December 1971.

Lockheed was not discouraged by its USAF reception and made a very successful drive to sell their fighter abroad,* beginning with Germany's search for a supersonic multi-purpose type to do all-weather tactical bombing, interception, and even reconnaissance. A new version, the F-104G, stuffed with new electronic navigation and weapons delivery systems, was chosen by Germany over a dozen rival designs.

Contracts signed February 5 and March 18, 1959, resulted in Lockheed furnishing Germany 96 F-104Gs and 136 TF-104Gs, and launched a European consortium that would produce 1,242 planes in German, Dutch, Belgian and, by a March 1961 addition, Italian factories. Canada signed up for its own production plan on September 17, 1959.

Mfr

LOCKHEED F-104G
General Electric J79-GE-llA, 10,000 lb. st military, 15,800 lb. AB
DIMENSIONS: As F-104A
WEIGHT: Empty 13,996 lb., Combat 20,002 lb. Gross 27,300 lb. Max. 29,038 lb. Fuel 1,018+730 gal.
PERFORMANCE: Speed- Top 860 mph at s.1., 1328 mph at 35,000', 1320 mph at 46,100', Cruising 586 mph, Stalling 215 mph. Combat Ceiling 46,300', Climb 41,000'/1 min. Combat Radius 620 miles/2000 lb. bomb, 736 miles area intercept, 1875 miles ferry range.

The F-104G was similar to the F-104C, but had enlarged tail surfaces, a J79-GE-llA, LN-3 navigation system, F-15A fire control, and was strengthened for one 2,000-pound and two 1,000-pound bombs or AGM-12B Bullpup missiles. Four AIM-9B Sidewinders could be carried along with the 20-mm M-61A gun; the latter removed for RF-104G reconnaissance versions. All-weather fighter and bombing capability eclipsed the original lightweight concept.

The Mutual Aid Program (MAP) funded Lockheed contracts for the 1.42 million dollar cost per F-104G. MAP deliveries began with 30 unarmed TF-104F two-seaters for the German pilots' school established at Luke AFB, Arizona by October 1959. On October 5, 1960, the first F-104G flew at Palmdale, where final assembly of 139 F-104G, 40 RF-104G, and 172 TF-104G exports was completed, plus 48 TF-104Gs as co-production parts, and three unarmed F-104Ns for NASA chase pilots.

Canada got 38 CF-104D two-seaters from Lockheed, built 200 Canadair CF-104s for the RCAF, and exported 140 F-104Gs for the U.S. Mutual Aid Program. The first Montreal-built CF-104 flew May 26, 1961, and was essentially a F-104G with a Canadian-built engine and equipment.

Japan signed a licensed production contract January 29, 1960, for 180 similar F-104Js and 20 two-seat F-104DJs. Three of the F-104Js and the F-104DJs were completed by Lockheed, the first being flown June 30, 1961. The rest were assembled by Mitsubishi, and while similar to the G model, were armed solely as interceptors. The first of seven Japanese squadrons became operational in October 1964, and another 30 F-104Js were added before Mitsubishi finished in 1967.

Mfr

LOCKHEED F-104J for Japan

In Germany, the group led by Messerschmitt built 210, the first German-built F-104G flew on August 14, 1961, and the MBB group added 50 by 1973. Fokker completed 231 F-104G and 119 RF-104G models, while Belgium's SABCA built 188 F-104Gs.

Fiat completed 164 F-104Gs and 119 RF-104Gs, as well as a new edition with a Sparrow missile capability called the F-104S. Lockheed modified two of the Fiat F-104Gs as CL-901 Super Starfighter prototypes in November 1966 with a new 17,900-pound thrust J79-GE-l9. Fiat then built 205 F-104S aircraft for the Italian Air Force and 40 for Turkey.

On interception missions, two AIM-7 Sparrow III missiles under the wings were guided by R21G radar, along with a pair of AIM-9B Sidewinders on the wing tips. Fighter-bomber configurations provided the M61 gun and nine stations for bombs or rocket pods. The first Fiat F-104S flew December 30, 1968, and when the last was delivered in December 1978, Starfighter production had ended.

Starfighter world production of 2,578 included 741 built in California plus 48 as co-production parts. Involved transfers between the countries complicate the F-104G story, and Rene Francillon's book on Lockheed aircraft shows how these fighters were distributed.

Germany had the largest total, with 96 F-104G and 136 TF-104G from Lockheed and 653 Starfighters from the European consortium. Italian Air Force units had 320 Fiat Starfighters and 24 TF-104G from Lockheed.

The Netherlands acquired 138 Starfighters, beginning in December 1962, and Belgium, 100 SABCA F-104Gs and

*The large sales commissions paid, including a million dollars to the Netherlands' Prince Bernard, resulted in a great scandal. A company report in August 1975 stated that it had paid foreign officials 22 million dollars.

12 Lockheed TF-104Gs, beginning in February 1963. Norway had 19 Canadair F-104Gs and four TF-104Gs in 1963, and in 1974 added 18 CF-104 and four CF-104Ds.

Denmark received 25 Canadair F-104Gs and four TF-104Gs from MAP in 1964, and in 1965, Spain began accepting 18 Canadair F-104Gs and three TF-104Gs. Taiwan imported 77 F-104Gs, eight RF-104Gs, and 25 TF-104Gs.

Greece received 35 F-104G and four TF-104Gs beginning in April 1964, and later replenished its two squadrons with 25 second-hand Starfighters. Turkey first acquired 32 F-104G and four TF-104Gs, and later expanded its force with over 120 second-hand fighters from Italy, Germany, the Netherlands, and RCAF Canadair CF-104s.

Although 15 air forces operated the Lockheeds, very little combat entered the fighter's history. It is remembered as the "missile with a man in it", a very fast unforgiving aircraft with terribly high crash rates in Germany and Italy. Yet pilots in some smaller countries, like Norway, had no such high accident rate, and the Japanese lost only 10 percent (23) of their aircraft in ten years of operations. Pilot selection and training were the most important success factors.

The F-105 Thunderchief

Republic's F-105 was the first type designed from the start as a TAC fighter bomber, with Mach 2 speeds, a nuclear bomb in an internal bay, electronic navigation and target computing, and a structure stressed for low-level strikes.

The design was offered the Air Force in April 1952 as the Republic AP-63, a letter contract for engineering design was made in September, and 37 F-105As with J57s were ordered in March 1953. A mockup was inspected in October, but the contract was cut back to 15 in February 1954, and in August 1954 the J75 engine was selected for the F-105B. Only the first two aircraft were completed with the J57-P-25, as the YF-105A first flown October 22, 1955, by Russell Roth.

REPUBLIC YF-105A
Pratt & Whitney J57-P-25, 10,200 lb. st military, 16,000 lb. AB
DIMENSIONS: Span 34'11", Lg. 61'5", Ht. 17'6", Wing Area 385 sq. ft.
WEIGHT: Empty 21,010 lb., Combat 28,966 lb., Gross 40,561 lb. Fuel 1560+1290 gal.
PERFORMANCE: Speed- Top 778 mph at s.l., 857 mph at 33,000', Cruising 560 mph, Stalling 185 mph, Combat Ceiling 49,950', Climb 21,750'/1 min., Combat Radius 1010 miles/Mk 7, Ferry range 2720 miles.

Alexander Kartveli's original design was greatly improved with a J75-P-3, area-ruled fuselage, higher fin, and new variable air intakes, and became the F-105B-1. First flown at Edwards AFB on May 26, 1956, it was damaged in a wheels-up landing, but was followed by nine more F-105B-1/-6 aircraft plus three originally planned as RF-105s that became JF-105B test aircraft. By June 28, 1957, a new contract for 65 F-105B fighters had been approved and the Thunderchief name chosen.

The outstanding Thunderchief feature was the first internal bomb bay used on a fighter, but the Mk 7 weapon then current was too long, so a short 1,980-pound Mk 28IN nuclear bomb was produced for the F-105. A YF-105A made the first supersonic bomb drops.

The long fuselage also contained all the internal fuel, petal-type dive brakes behind the afterburner, and the small wings were swept back 45 degrees from root intakes with lips raked forward. Two 450-gallon drop tanks extended the combat radius, and a 390-gallon bomb bay auxiliary fuel tank could replace the special store. A probe for air refueling was provided.

A 20-mm M-61A with 1,080 rounds and MA-8 fire control was fitted, as well as underwing fittings for two 3,000-pound or four 1,000-pound bombs, or 114 2.75-inch rockets in six pods, four GAR-8 Sidewinders, or any weapons combination of six tons total weight.

While the first 27 of 65 F-105B-10/-20 fighters delivered from May 1958 to December 1959 used the J75-P-5, the rest had the J75-P-19. Operational use of the Thunderchief began with the 4th TFW, which received the single F-105B-6 from the first order on May 26, 1958, but a complete operational squadron replacing the F-100Cs would not be ready until 1960. By April 1964, the F-105Bs in this wing were replaced in turn by F-105Ds and passed to a long ANG service.

REPUBLIC F-105B
Pratt & Whitney J75-P-19, 16,100 lb. military, 24,500 lb. AB
DIMENSIONS: Span 34'11", Lg. 63'1", Ht. 19'8", Wing Area 385 sq. ft.
WEIGHT: Empty 25,855 lb., Combat 34,870 lb. Gross 46,998 lb. Fuel 1160+900+390 gal.
PERFORMANCE: Speed- Top 864 mph at s.l., 1376 mph at 36,089', Cruising 585 mph, Stalling 204 mph. Combat Ceiling 48,100', Climb 35,000'/1.7 min. Combat Radius 744 miles/Mk-28, Ferry range 2228 miles.

The F-105D first flown on June 9, 1959, by Lin Hendrix, was an all-weather model with nose lengthened for the R-14 radar, ASG-19 fire control, and APN-131 Doppler navigation radar. Other improvements included a water-injection J75-P-19W, a toss-bomb computer and a new instrument system.

Mfr

Thunderchief partners
A buddy-tank drogue on the second YF-105A refuels the third F-105B-1. Note the different tails.

Two Mk 28RE or the more powerful Mk 43 bombs could be carried under the wings, increasing nuclear capability beyond the internal bay. As the emphasis was shifting from nuclear warfare to conventional bombs, provision was made to close the internal bomb bay and install a centerline pylon with a multiple ejector rack, or a 650-gallon ferry tank.

Utilizing the four-under wing pylons, 16 750-pound bombs could be carried for a short distance, although the more usual wartime load was eight. Alternate loads were two 3,000-pound M-118 bombs, three 450-gallon tanks, four AGM-12C Bullpup or AIM-9B Sidewinder missiles, or six rocket pods. That adaptation, introduced on the F-105D-25, was retrofitted to earlier B and D models.

Operation **Look-Alike**, begun in June 1962, brought up all the Ds to the F-105D-31 standard. Receptacles for both flying boom and drogue inflight refueling were provided, although as much as 2976 gallons of useable fuel could be carried.

The 610 F-105Ds completed by January 1964 were followed by 143 F-105F two-seaters, first flown June 11, 1963, which were 5 feet longer and fitted with the gun and full external stores points, bringing the production total to 833 accepted by January 1965. No two-seat F-105C trainer, or F-105E, proposed all-weather fighter, were ever built.

Seven TAC wings used F-105Ds, beginning in May 1961, with accidents and operational problems that caused ten groundings, and earned the heavy fighter the nickname "Thud" and a questionable reputation. Cost per aircraft was reckoned at 2.14 million dollars, and numerous mechanical and electronic upgrades improved efficiency.

With twice the F-100D's bomb load, and half again as much speed, the F-105D was chosen to deliver over three-quarters of the bomb tonnage of Rolling Thunder, the air offensive against North Vietnam. Flying from Korat, Thailand, 25 F-105s opened the attack March 2, 1965, losing two aircraft to AAA. On April 3, 46 F-105Ds, supported by 21 F-100Ds from South Vietnam, struck at the bridge at Thanh Hoa, and 48 F-105Ds returned the next day.

AF

REPUBLIC F-105D
Pratt & Whitney J75-P-19W, 16,100 lb. st military, 24,500 lb. AB
DIMENSIONS: Span 34'11", Lg. 64'5", Ht. 19'8", Wing Area 385 sq. ft.
WEIGHT: Empty 26,855 lb., Combat 35,637 lb. Gross 48,976 lb. Max. 49,371 lb. Fuel 1160+1550 gal.
PERFORMANCE: Speed- Top 836 mph at s.l, 1373 mph at 36,089', Cruising 778 mph, Stalling 208 mph. Combat Ceiling 48,500', Climb 35,000'/1.75 min. Combat Radius 778 miles/Mk-28, Ferry range 2208 miles.

Four MiG-17s flying the NVAF's first successful interception downed two F-105Ds and AAA a third. As for the bridge, it survived the Bullpup missiles and 750-pound bombs and remained operating until bombing resumed in 1972 by F-4Es with 3,000-pound M-118s.

Anti-aircraft guns and SA-2 missiles caused the loss of most of 67 F-105Ds lost in 1965 and 117 in 1966, since MiGs were few in number and seldom got past the F-4 fighter cover. Refueling by KCA-135A tankers extended the F-105D's reach, and EB-66 pathfinders often led formations.

In 1966, more frequent interceptions often forced the F-105s to jettison their bombs, but F-105Ds from the 355th and 388th TFWs did claim 27 MiG-17s from June 29, 1966 to October 27, 1967. They were victims of the 20-mm Vulcan gun's 6,000 rounds per minute, although two were downed by Sidewinders. Total SEA F-105D losses reached 314 by 1968.

Wild Weasel was a weapon system with a pilot and electronic warfare officer (EWO), and ECM equipment to locate and destroy radar-directed AAA and SAM installations. This work was begun in November 1965 by EF-100F two-seaters, which introduced the 400-pound AGM-45A Shrike anti-radiation missile and hit a SAM site on April 18, 1966.

AF

REPUBLIC F-105F
Pratt & Whitney J75-P-19W, 16,100 lb. st military, 24,500 lb. AB
DIMENSIONS: Span 34'11", Lg. 69'7", Ht. 20'2", Wing Area 385 sq. ft.
WEIGHT: Empty 27,500 lb., Combat 38,637 lb. Gross 40,073 lb. Max. 54,095 lb. Fuel 1160+1550 gal.
PERFORMANCE: Speed- Top 784 mph at s.l, 890 mph at 36,000', Cruising 796 mph, Stalling 214 mph. Combat Ceiling 48,500', Climb 25,000'/1 min. Combat Radius 528 miles/Mk-28, Ferry range 2228 miles.

AF

REPUBLIC F-105G
Pratt & Whitney J75-P-19W, 16,100 lb. st military, 24,500 lb. st AB
DIMENSIONS: Span 34'11", Lg. 69'7" Ht. 20'2", Wing Area 385 sq. ft.
WEIGHT: Combat 41,637 lb. Gross 54,580 lb. Fuel 1810+1290 gal.
PERFORMANCE: Speed- Top 784 mph at s.l, 833 mph at 36,000', Cruising 792 mph, Stalling 216 mph. Combat Ceiling 43,900', Climb 25,000'/1 min. Combat Radius 540 miles/AGM-45A, Ferry range 1869 miles.

In May 1966, an EF-105F squadron with QRC-128 jammers and two AGM-45A missiles replaced the F-100Fs, for 86 two-seat F-105Fs had been equipped with Wild Weasel III equipment. Besides many attacks with rockets and Shrikes, Wild Weasels also downed two MiGs.

Most F-105Ds were withdrawn from SEA, as the F-4 took over fighter-bomber work, but the F-105Fs remained until the war's end, losing 51 aircraft. Sixty were to be modified to the F-105G configuration, first tested on a prototype September 1968, with new ALQ-105 jammer blisters under the fuselage and a 1,400-pound AGM-78B missile joining the smaller Shrikes.

Although the F-105Ds were withdrawn from SEA by October 1970, F-105Gs remained from 1970 until 1974. The ANG began getting F-105Ds in January 1971, and one F-105B and four F-105D ANG squadrons were gradually retired by 1983, while two F-105G squadrons served TAC's 35th TFW until they were replaced by F-4Gs in 1977-1980.

The F-106

Convair's F-106A Delta Dart was the result of Air Defense Command's desire for an "ultimate interceptor" that could protect America from any attack by supersonic bombers. The project began as the F-102B, utilizing a Pratt & Whitney J75-P-9, air intakes moved back behind the cockpit, squared-off fin, and dual nose wheels. Seventeen test examples ordered on a November 1955 contract approved the following April 18, were redesignated F-106A on June 17, 1956.

Mfr

CONVAIR F-106A
Pratt & Whitney J75-P-17, 16,100 lb. st military, 24,500 lb. AB
DIMENSIONS: Span 38'3", Lg. 70'9", Ht. 20'3", Wing Area 698 sq. ft.
WEIGHT: Empty 24,038 lb., Combat 30,357 lb., Gross 34,510 lb. Max. 37,772 lb. Fuel 1514+716 gal.
PERFORMANCE: Speed- Top 1328 mph at 35,000', 1308 mph at 50,000', Cruising 594 mph, Stalling 173 mph. Combat Ceiling 51,800', Service Ceiling 52,700', Climb 51,800'/6.9 min. Combat Range 364 miles area intercept, Ferry range 1809 miles.

The hard-won F-102 experience was utilized so well that the delta wing and new fuselage shape remained unchanged during F-106 production. The most remarkable feature was the Hughes MA-l fire control electronic system was linked with SAGE ground control and enabled the all-weather interceptor to be "flown automatically from wheels-up following takeoff to flare-out before touchdown."

The pilot monitored the mission on a map display projected on a cockpit screen, and could take over the controls any time he desired. When radar had selected the correct target range, the F-106A could fire an 829-pound AIR-2A Genie rocket with a nuclear warhead, two AIM-4G infrared heat seeking and two Falcon AIM-4F radar homing missiles. (Before 1962, these missiles were the MB-l, GAR-4A, and GAR-3A.)

First flown December 26, 1956, by Richard L. Johnson, the F-106A had a J57-P-9 substituting for the P-17 installed later,and lacked the MA-l system until 1958. Costing $4.7 million each, the F-106A joined ADC squadrons in May 1959 and became the first Air Force fighter to last 29 years in front-line service, adding life cycle to cost considerations. (Imagine a 1919 Thomas-Morse in 1948, or a 1939 Curtiss P-40 in 1968!) Even the 1,525 mph (Mach 2.36) world's single-engine speed record set by an F-106 on December 15, 1959, remained unbroken in that period.

San Diego built 277 F-106A and 63 two-place F-106Bs, delivering the last F-106A to the ADC on July 20, 1961, completing the Air Force's equipment with supersonic fighters. The F-106B had an ASG-25 interceptor system, but was otherwise similar in weapons and performance to the single-seat model. Most of the first 35 A and seven B models were used for testing until 1960, when a "Test-to-Tactical" modification program upgraded most to combat readiness.

CONVAIR F-106B
Pratt & Whitney J75-P-17, 16,100 lb. st military, 24,500 lb. AB
DIMENSIONS: Span 38'3", Lg. 70'9", Ht. 20'3", Wing Area 698 sq. ft.
WEIGHT: Empty 25,696 lb., Combat 32,822 lb., Gross 37,552 lb. Max. 42,720 lb. Fuel 1450+716 gal.
PERFORMANCE: Speed- Top 1328 mph at 35,000', 1254 mph at 50,000', Cruising 594 mph, Stalling 173 mph. Combat Ceiling 51,450', Climb 50,000'/6.3 min. Combat Radius 548 miles area intercept, Ferry range 1842 miles.

During their long service, many improvements were made to their electronic systems, with little change in aircraft appearance. An M-61A1 20-mm Vulcan gun below the weapons bay could replace the AIR-2A after 1972, an infrared sensor was added in the nose, and an inflight fueling receptacle and 358-gallon high-speed drop tanks were provided. Two aircraft tested a YF-106C configuration, with a larger radar dish.

A reduction in the interceptor force reflected the change in the threat. Intercontinental ballistic missiles, not bombers, composed the principle menace to the continent. The much-publicized Bison bomber (M-4/3M) had inadequate range for its mission, and only 116 had been made, with 175 of the slower, but longer-range, turboprop Bear (Tu-95). The Soviet Union converted its long-range bombers into reconnaissance aircraft, and came to rely on the Strategic Rocket Force created as a separate branch May 7, 1960. By the time the first SALT agreement was made in 1972, over 1,500 Soviet strategic missiles were in place.

Air Defense Command's total fighter strength would be reduced from 30 wings in 1956 to 34 squadrons in 1968. The F-106A served 20 ADC Fighter-Interceptor squadrons until transfers to the Air National Guard began in April 1972. By 1976, ADC had only six F-106A squadrons, supported by six squadrons in the ANG. Two Canadian CF-101B squadrons and three ANG F-101B squadrons also covered the approaches to North America, and several ANG and TAC F-4 squadrons were available for continental defense.

The last ANG F-106A squadron, the 119th FIS, retired its fighters on August 1, 1988, and conversion of 194 to QF-106A target drones began.

North American's Last Fighter

North American Aviation ended twenty years of fighter production -from the NA-50 to the F-100F in 1959- after its last two designs failed to win contracts. The first was the NA-212 project began in October 1953 as the F-l00B, but the letter contract in August 4, 1954 labeled nine prototypes YF-107A.

NORTH AMERICAN YF-107A
Pratt & Whitney J75-P-9, 15,500 lb. st military, 23,500 lb. AB
DIMENSIONS: Span 36'7", Lg. 61'8", Ht. 19'6", Wing Area 376 sq. ft.
WEIGHT: Empty 22,696 lb., Combat 30,483 lb., Gross 38,022 lb. Max. 41,537 lb. Fuel 1260+1200 gal.
PERFORMANCE: Speed- Top 891 mph at s.l., 1294 mph at 36,000', Cruising 599 mph, Stalling 183 mph. Combat Ceiling 53,100', Climb 39,600'/1 min. Combat Radius 525 miles/ 2000 lb., Ferry range 2428 miles.

Mfr

3rd NORTH AMERICAN YF-107A

Designed for Mach 2 speeds, the YF-107A fighter-bomber had a variable area intake above and behind the cockpit for the J75-P-9, and one-piece vertical and horizontal tail surfaces. Instead of an internal bomb bay, a nuclear warhead and fuel would be contained in a store shape semi-recessed underneath the fuselage. Radar fire control and four 20-mm M-39 guns in the nose were provided, along with two underwing points for drop tanks, bombs or rocket pods. For the basic nuclear mission, the ventral store and two 275-gallon drop tanks were carried, or a 500-gallon ventral tank and two 1,000-pound bombs could be used.

Only three prototypes were completed, the first flying September 10, 1956, but the design was not able to equal the F-105's success and was abandoned in February 1957, except for research work.

NORTH AMERICAN F-108A proposal
Two General Electric J93-GE-3AR, 20,900 lb. military, 29,300 lb. AB
DIMENSIONS: Span 57'5", Lg. 89'2", Ht. 22'1", Wing Area 1865 sq. ft.
WEIGHT: Empty 50,907 lb., Combat 76,118 lb, Gross 102,533 lb. Fuel 7109 gal.
PERFORMANCE: Speed- Top 1980 mph at 76,550', Stalling 107 mph. Combat Ceiling 76,550', Service Ceiling 80,100', Climb 50,000'/5.4 min., Combat Radius 1020 miles/three GAR-9, Ferry range 2488 miles.

The F-108

The USAF had sought a replacement interceptor shortly after the Delta Dart's first flight and North American began the NA-157 long-range interceptor project June 6, 1957. Designated F-108A,the big two-place delta wing had two 29,300-pound thrust J93-GE-3 engines behind variable inlets under the wing roots, and was armed with three advanced 813-pound GAR-9 missiles.

Designed for a speed of 1,980 mph at 76,550 feet the F-108A weighed 51 tons, including 7,100 gallons of fuel for a 1,020-mile combat radius. A mockup was inspected January 1959, and the first flight planned for March 1961, but the project was canceled on September 23, 1959, clearing the way for the Delta Dart's long service. Ballistic missiles had replaced strategic bombers as the primary strategic threat.

Chapter 30

NAVY PATROL PLANES FOR THE COLD WAR, 1945-90

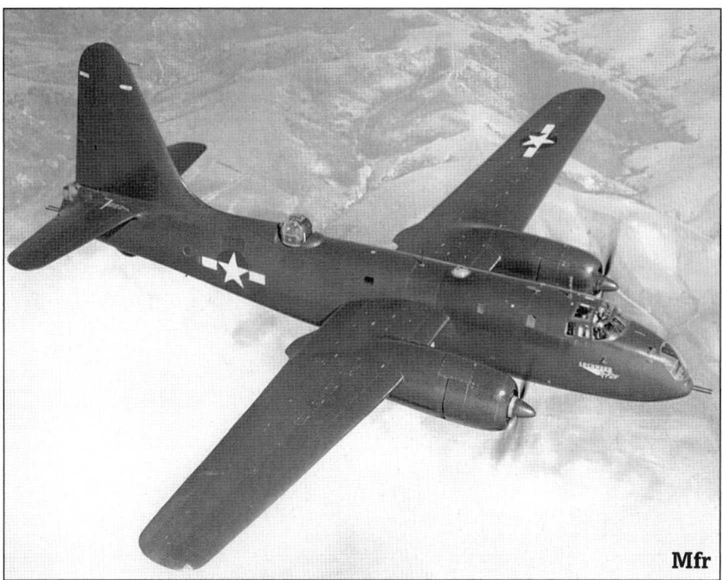

LOCKHEED XP2V-1
Two Wright R-3350-8, 2300 hp takeoff, 1900 hp at 14 000' / DIMENSIONS: Span 100', Lg. 75'4", Ht. 28'6", Wing Area 1,000 sq. ft. / WEIGHT: Empty 32,651 lb., Gross 54,527 lb., Max. 58,000 lb. Fuel 2350+1000 gal. / PERFORMANCE: Speed- Top 231 mph at s.1., 289 mph at 15,600', Cruising 163 mph, Stalling 93 mph. Service Ceiling 23,200', Climb 1120'/1 min. Range 2879 miles/eight 325-lb. depth charges, Max. range 4210 miles.

Mfr

The Neptune

Patrol plane performance had greatly advanced beyond pre World War II standards, mainly by the substitution of landplanes for flying boats. Those landplanes, however, were basically adaptations of Army bombers, and not until 1945 did a landplane designed from its inception as a patrol type become available.

Developed for the primary mission of antisubmarine and anti-surface vessel patrol work, the Lockheed Model 26 Neptune was a twin-engine high-wing monoplane with tricycle landing gear and a high single fin. Secondary missions were rocket and night torpedo attack, mine laying, bombing, and reconnaissance, although these capabilities were limited to those available after providing the best possible facilities for the primary mission. Long range, ability to operate from small fields, and high speed were listed as the desired characteristics.

After a long company study, Lockheed received a letter of intent for prototypes on February 19, 1943, two XP2V-1 and 15 P2V-ls were approved in April, 1944, and 151 more Neptunes added December 16. Powered by 2,300 hp Wright R-3350-8 Cyclones, the prototype was flown at Burbank on May 17, 1945.

Stripping off all armament, building a new streamlined nose, and adding fuselage and wingtip fuel tanks had specially modified the first P2V-l. On September 29, 1946, it took off from Australia with 8,396 gallons of gasoline and 85,500 pounds of gross weight. When the Truculent Turtle landed in Ohio, 55 hours later, it had established a world's nonstop, non-refueled, flight record of 11,236 miles (great circle distance).

Standard P2V-ls began tests on October 11, 1946, and became operational with VP-2 in March 1947. Their crew of seven operated APS-8 radar and six .50-caliber guns: two in a hand-operated bow emplacement, two in the rear deck Martin power turret, and two for the tail gunner's late-B-17G type turret. The Neptune's bomb bay could accommodate twelve 325-pound depth charges, or two 2,000-pound torpedoes for night attacks, or as much as four tons for short-distance horizontal bombing, or 1,000 gallons of additional fuel. Sixteen 5-inch or four 11.75-inch rockets could be carried on under wing studs and 581 pounds of armor were provided.

Mfr

LOCKHEED P2V-1s for VP-2
Two Wright R-3300-8A, 2300 hp takeoff, 1900 hp at 14 000'
DIMENSIONS: As XP2V-1
WEIGHT: Empty 33,720 lb., Combat 47,115 lb., Gross 61,153 lb. Fuel 2350+1000 gal.
PERFORMANCE: (At combat weight) Speed- Top 250 mph at s.1., 303 mph at 15,300', Cruising 176 mph. Stalling 77 mph. Service Ceiling 27,000'. Climb 1050'/1 min. Max. range 4133 miles.

The Truculent Turtle's longer nose was incorporated into the fifth P2V-l, along with R-3350-24W engines of 2,800 hp with water injection. That plane became the XP2V-2, which inspired 81 P2V-2 production models accepted from June 1947 to August 1948. Nose armament consisted of six 20-mm M-2 fixed guns with 1,350 rounds, and all but the first nine P2V-2s had a new Emerson tail turret with a pair of 20-mm guns and 800 rounds.

Sonobuoy launchers for underwater submarine detection became standard on all Navy patrol planes. These are

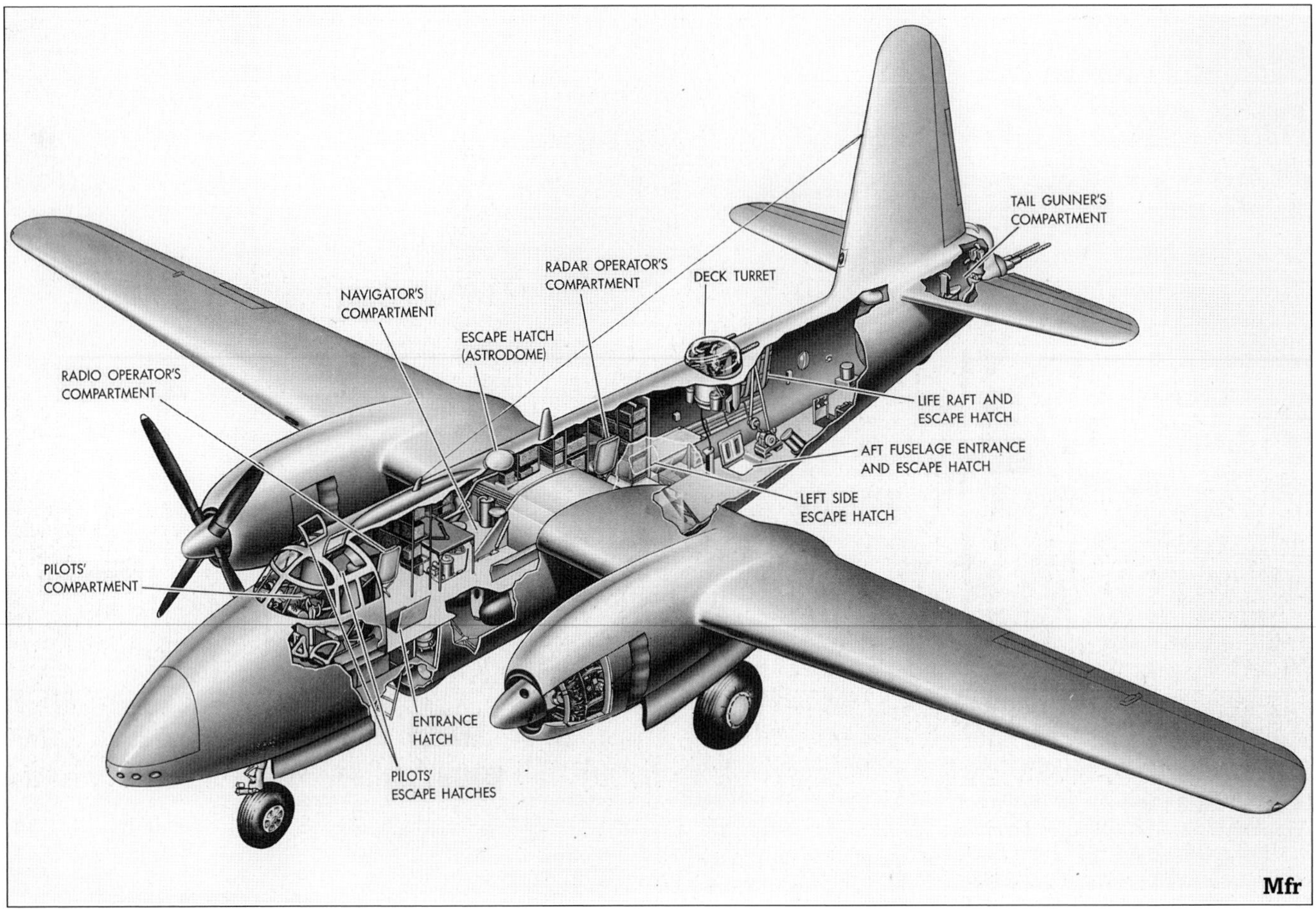

LOCKHEED P2V-2 cutaway

LOCKHEED P2V-2
Two Wright R-3350-24W, 2500 hp takeoff, 2800 hp WE
DIMENSIONS: Span 100', Lg. 77'10", Ht. 28'1", Wing Area 1,000 sq. ft.
WEIGHT: Empty 33,962 lb., Combat 49,040 lb., Gross 63,078 lb. Fuel 2350+1000 gal.
PERFORMANCE: Speed- Top 260 mph at s.1., 320 mph at 13,500', Cruising 178 mph, Stalling Landing 77 mph. Service Ceiling 26,000', Climb 810'/1 min. Range 3985 miles.

buoys dropped in a pattern to send out a sonar signal that rebounds from a submarine hull and is automatically transmitted by the buoy to the search plane. Several must be dropped if the submarine's area is to be enclosed and the vessel's position determined.

The first P2V-3 was flown on August 6, 1948, with 3,200-hp R-3350-26W Cyclones and 40 were delivered by January 1950. While nuclear bomb delivery was then a

LOCKHEED P2V-3
Two Wright R-3350-26W, 2,700 hp takeoff, 3200 hp WE
DIMENSIONS: Span 100', Lg. 77'10", Ht. 28'1", Wing Area 1,000 sq. ft.
WEIGHT: Empty 34,875 lb., Combat 50,067 lb., Gross 64,100 lb. Fuel 2350+1000 gal.
PERFORMANCE: Speed-Top 260 mph at s.1., 338 mph at 13,000', Cruising 180 mph, Stalling 77 mph. Service Ceiling 28,000', Climb 1060'/1 min. Range 3938 miles.

SAC monopoly, the Navy was anxious to demonstrate that atomic weapons could be delivered from carrier decks. An experimental squadron, VC-5, was commissioned for that mission and 11 P2V-3C Neptunes delivered from September 1948 to the following August were

Mfr

LOCKHEED P2V-4
Two Wright R-3350-30W, 2700 hp military, 3250 hp WE
DIMENSIONS: Span 101', Lg. 77'11", Ht. 28'1", Wing Area 1,000 sq. ft.
WEIGHT: Empty 42,021 lb., Gross 67,500 lb., Max. 74,129 lb. Fuel 2510+1700 gal.
PERFORMANCE: Speed- Top 312 mph at s. l., 352 mph at 9500', Stalling 109 mph. Service Ceiling 31,000'. Range 4200 miles.

modified for carrier takeoffs. Nose guns, dorsal turret, and ASW gear were removed to carry 2,400 gallons of fuel and an early nuclear bomb.

On March 7, 1949, a P2V-3C with JATO units took off from the *USS Coral Sea*, weighing 74,000 pounds with a 10,000-pound dummy atomic weapon. The heaviest aircraft then ever launched from a carrier flew 2,000 miles to a target, and 2,000 more to its landing ashore.

An early warning Neptune was the P2V-3W, with a bulging APS-20 radar in the forward bomb bay operated by two radar men who sat with the bomber-navigator and radio operator in the cabin between the pilots and the deck turret. This system had been first flown on the converted third P2V-2S on April 2, 1948, and followed by 30 P2V-3Ws accepted from August 1949 to February 1951. Two more Neptunes were converted to armored special transports (P2V-3Z) in 1950.

The P2V-4 model had increased fuel capacity, including wingtip tanks, APS-20 radar, and eight crewmen. Fifty-two were built, the first completed in November 1949, the rest delivered from January 1950 to March 1951. After delays, the R-3350-26Ws were replaced by R-3350-30W Turbo-Compound Cyclones beginning in March 1950.

The next model was P2V-5, with fixed guns in the nose replaced by an Emerson ball turret with two 20-mm guns providing a lookout and bombing station. That turret had been first tested in 1948 and its movement controlled a searchlight in the starboard tip tank. Other armament included two 20-mm tail guns, two .50-caliber guns in the deck turret, and two 1,200-pound Mk 41 homing torpedoes. The crew of nine included two pilots under a raised canopy, two radar men, navigator, a radioman, and gunners.

Mfr

LOCKHEED P2V-3W

When the Korean War began in 1950, VP-6 and VP-22 were the first Neptune squadrons to patrol nearby waters, followed by five more squadrons called up for the emergency. AAA downed a P2V-3 on August 15, 1951, and Soviet fighters shot down a P2V-3W near Vladivostok on November 6. Several other Pacific area incidents also involved Neptunes, including a P2V-5 shot down by Chinese

AAA on January 18, 1953, and two ditched after VVS MiG attacks on September 4, 1954, and June 22, 1955.

The first P2V-5 flight was on December 29, 1950, and the first 170 were accepted between April 1951 and May 1953. Fifty-two went to Britain as the Neptune M.R.1, first arriving January 13, 1952, and serving four Coastal Command squadrons until 1956. (Eight of those aircraft would be passed to Argentina and 14 to Brazil in 1958/59) Twelve new P2V-5s also went to Australia from November 1951 to January 1953.

Mfr

LOCKHEED P2V-5 (RAF)
Two Wright R-3350-30WA, 3250 hp at 3400', 2550 hp at 15,400'
DIMENSIONS: Span 104', Lg. 78'3", Ht. 28'1", Wing Area 1,000 sq. ft.
WEIGHT: Empty 43,000 lb., Combat 61,370 lb., Gross 71,400 lb., Max. 80,000 lb. Fuel 2500+1700 gal.
PERFORMANCE: Speed- Top 306 mph at 1500', 323 mph at 17,400', Cruising 207 mph, Stalling 109 mph. Service Ceiling 23,200', Climb 1820'/1 min. Range 3194 miles/2400 lb., Ferry range 3885 miles.

The mine-laying P2V-6 had four 20-mm guns with 1,600 rounds in front and tail turrets, two .50-caliber guns in the deck turret, and eight 1,000-pound mines, or 12,000 pounds of bombs, or 16 rockets. APS-33B radar and 1,092 pounds of armor were provided. The first P2V-6 (Model 726), flew October 16, 1952, and 83 delivered by November 1953 included 31 for France and 16 P2V-6B (P2V-6M) for VP-24, equipped with the Fairchild Petrel, a 3,800-pound radar-homing, anti-sub missile.

Mfr

LOCKHEED P2V-6 (P-2F)
Two Wright R-3350-30WA, 3500 hp takeoff, 3250 hp at 3500', 2550 hp at 15,400'
DIMENSIONS: Span 104', Lg. 84'10", Ht. 28'1", Wing Area 1000 sq. ft.
WEIGHT: Empty 44,383 lb., Combat 64,477 lb. Gross 80,000 lb. Fuel 2500+1700 gal.
PERFORMANCE: Speed- Top 303 mph at 1500', 318 mph at 16,500', Cruising 201 mph, Stalling 114 mph. Service Ceiling 20,200', Climb 1650'/1 min. Range 2660 miles/eight 1000-lb. mines, Ferry 4126 miles.

A magnetic anomaly detector (MAD) in a long plastic "stinger" replaced the tail turret in the next 98 P2V-5s, as well as on the last 156, called the P2V-5F model, which introduced a Westinghouse J34 jet mounted under each wing to shorten the takeoff run and increase dash speed. The P2V-5F had smaller 200-gallon tip tanks, and replaced the nose turret with a clear observer's station.

WL

LOCKHEED P2V-5F (P-2E)
Two Wright R-3350-32W, 3750 hp and
two Westinghouse J34-WE-34, 3250 lb. st
DIMENSIONS: Span 101'4", Lg. 89'4", Ht. 28'1", Wing Area 1,000 sq.ft.
WEIGHT: Empty 48,500 lb., Combat 68,020 lb. Gross 75,700 lb., Max. 84,000 1b. Fuel 2100+1400 gal.
PERFORMANCE: Speed- Top 374 mph at 1500', 398 mph at 14,000', Cruising 185 mph, Stalling 11 mph. Service Ceiling 23,000', Climb 2850'/1 min. Range 2850 miles/2 Mk 4 torpedoes.

Twelve P2V-5s with MAD tails went to the Netherlands from October 1953 to January 1954, and would be transferred to Portugal in 1960/62. Production of 424 P2V-5 series Neptunes ended in September 1954.

All Navy P2V-5s were rotated, beginning October 1954, back to Lockheed for modification to the P2V-5F standard with J34 jets and all turrets, unnecessary for anti-sub warfare, removed. Jets were also retrofitted to P2V-6F conversions.

Gann

LOCKHEED SP-2E (P2V-5S)

The final Neptune version was the P2V-7 (Model 726), first flown on April 26, 1954, with APS-20B radar, a raised pilot's canopy, two R-3350-32W Cyclones, and two J34-WE-36 jets. Although the first were completed with nose and tail turrets, it soon replaced them with a clear nose enclosure for the operator of the MAD gear in the tail. Only the twin .50s in the deck turret remained until a June 1959 order removed all turrets from P2V-7s.

Those Neptunes became strictly ASW aircraft, for a submarine generation that would not be found on the sur-

USN

LOCKHEED P-2H (P2V-7)

Mfr

LOCKHEED P2V-7 (original series)
Two Wright R-3500-32W, 3200 hp take-off, 3400 hp at 2500', 2400 hp at 18,000', and Westinghouse J34-WE-36, 3400 lb. st
DIMENSIONS: Span 101'4", Lg. 91'8", Ht. 29'4", Wing Area 1000 sq. ft.
WEIGHT: Empty 47,450 lb., Combat 68,527 lb. Gross 76,639 lb., Max. 80,000 lb. Fuel 2980+1100 gal.
PERFORMANCE: (piston only) Speed- Top 300 mph at 1500', 312 mph at 18,400', Cruising 185 mph, Stalling 111 mph. Service Ceiling 22,400', Climb 1760'/1 min. (With jet boost: Top Speed 401 mph at 19,100'. Service Ceiling 23,000', Climb 2950'/1 min.) Range 3505 miles/2400 lb., 4293 miles ferry.

face, and encounters with enemy fighters unlikely. A detection system named **Jezebel** became operational in 1958, and was joined by acoustic system **Julie** in 1960. Electronic defenses added a AVG-20 antenna in the right wingtip pod.

Known after 1962 as the P-2H, 212 P2V-7s were accepted by the Navy and the MAP provided 25 to Canada in 1955, 12 to Australia in 1962, and 15 P2V-7Bs with a gun nose for the Netherlands to use in a 1961 conflict with Indonesia. Japan got eight P2V-7s in 1956 and eight more in 1958, while France purchased 33 Neptunes, beginning in 1958.

Seven unarmed P2V-7s went to the CIA in 1957 for special ELINT work as the RB-69A. Loaded with unusual devices, they operated from bases in Germany and Taiwan. Fourteen-man RoC crews penetrated China at night and AAA downed one RB-69A on November 6, 1961. Chinese J-5A (MiG-17) fighters shot down one on June 14, 1963, another on June 11, 1964, and two more crashed for unknown reasons.*

In 1962, under the new designation system, Navy Neptunes became the P-2D (P2V-4), P-2E (P2V-5F), DP-5E (P-2E for aerial target launching) SP-2E (P-2E with Julie/Jezebel sub detection gear), P-2F (P2V-6) P-2G (P2V-6F) and P-2H (P2V-7). Several non-combat conversions to roles like polar exploration and drone control were active.

Lawson

LOCKHEED SP-2H of VP-31

*This summary of the RB-69A and other specialized models is based on the very detailed study by Wayne Mutza, *Lockheed P2V Neptune.* (Atglen, Schiffer 1996).

Lockheed delivered the last P-2H on September 11, 1962, bringing the Navy Neptune total to 1,036, of which 186 went abroad on the MAP. In Japan, Kawasaki built 48 P-2H Neptunes from 1959 to 1965, followed by 83 improved 12-place P-2Js built with turboprop engines from July 1966 to February 1979, which served until 1995.

War in Southeast Asia inspired two special modifications stripped of ASW gear, the OP-2E tactical observation aircraft, and the AP-2H night attack version. Twelve OP-2Es of VO-67 were deployed to Vietnam in November 1967 to detect enemy night movements on the Ho Chi Minh Trail. Provided with 7.62-mm SUU-11 gun pods under the wings, armor, a chaff dispenser in the tail, and APQ-131 radar, the nine-place OP-2E dropped acoustical sensors. But three planes were lost from January 11 to February 27, 1968, and that squadron ended its missions on June 25.

Olson

LOCKHEED OP-2E of VO-67

In September 1968, Heavy Attack Squadron 21 (VAH-21) was commissioned as the first multi-sensor night interdiction squadron. Four SP-2H Neptunes were converted to AP-2H versions with search radar, infrared sensors, exhaust shrouds, two 20-mm M3 guns in a tail turret, SUU-11 gun pods, M60 waist guns, an eight-barrel grenade launcher, and wing racks for eight bombs. VAH-21 hit enemy traffic on more than 200 missions without any losses until that unit closed down in June 1969.

Miller

LOCKHEED AP-2H Night Attack

Neptunes equipped 20 Navy patrol squadrons and the last SP-2H retired from a first-line squadron, VP-23, in February 1970, but they remained in Naval Reserve squadrons and in utility units until 1979. As Neptunes became surplus to Navy needs, four SP-2E and four SP-2H went second-hand to Argentina from 1966 to 1978, and two were involved with the 1982 Falklands conflict.

Lockheed's famous four-engine Constellation airliner had received a patrol designation when flown June 9, 1949, as the PO-lW with radar antennae in a dome atop the fuselage for target altitude measurements and a round search radome under the belly. But since the sole mission was providing early over-the-horizon warning of strategic bombers, and not any combat mission of patrol types, the designation was changed in production models to the WV-2 Warning Star.

Martin Mercator

Although Lockheed has dominated the patrol field since 1947, Martin offered three competing types, the first being the XP4M-l Mercator. This Baltimore-built monoplane resembled an enlarged Neptune, but behind each of the two Pratt & Whitney R-4360-4 Wasp Majors was a J33 jet for bursts of extra power.

Two prototypes were ordered July 6, 1944, and the first XP4M-l flew on September 20, 1946. The weapons bay could accommodate six tons of mines, depth charges, or bombs, or when needed, up to four extra fuel cells. Protection included 668 pounds of armor, two 20-mm guns in a Martin tail turret, two .50-caliber waist guns, and .50-caliber guns paired in a Martin rear deck power turret and a nose turret. But the nose guns were never mounted in the prototypes, replaced in the first by instrument probes, and by a radome in the stripped second XP4M-l.

USN

MARTIN XP4M-1
Two Pratt & Whitney R-1360-4, 2975 hp takeoff, 2400 hp at 16,200', and two Allison J33-A-17, 3825 lb. st
DIMENSIONS: Span 114', Lg. 82'7", Ht. 26'1", Wing Area 1311 sq. ft.
WEIGHT: Empty 45,739 lb., Gross 77,729 lb., Max. 79,657 lb. Fuel 2800+1400 gal.
PERFORMANCE: Speed- (with props) Top 273 mph at s.1., 289 mph at 17,800', Cruising 170 mph, Stalling 99 mph; (jet boost- Top 363 mph at s.1., 395 mph at 19,100'). Service Ceiling 32,800', Climb 2380'/1 min. Range 3167 miles/2 Mk 34 torpedoes, 4230 miles max.

The first of 19 P4M-ls with improved engines was flown on August 31, 1949, and the first five were accepted that December. This longer model had 20-mm guns paired in Aero bow and tail ball turrets with 400 rpg, and twin .50-caliber guns in the Martin rear deck turret. APA-5A and APA-33 radar was provided. In June 1950, they entered service with VP-21 at Patuxent NAS, replacing PB4Y-2s.

Deliveries ended in September 1950 because the less-expensive Neptune seemed more suitable to the Navy. Yet the roomier Martin could accommodate the elaborate

MARTIN P4M-1
Two Pratt & Whitney R-4360-20, 2250 hp take-off, 2500 hp at 16,800', and two Allison J33-A-23, 4600 lb. st
DIMENSIONS: Span 114', Lg. 86'2", Ht. 29'2", Wing Area 1311 sq. ft.
WEIGHT: Empty 48,536 lb., Gross 81,463 lb., Max. 83,378 lb. Fuel 2800+1400 gal.
PERFORMANCE: Speed- (with props) Top 282 mph at s.l., 296 mph at 18,700', Cruising 168 mph, Stalling 88 mph; (jet boost-Top 379 mph at s.l., 415 mph at 20,100'). Service Ceiling 34,600', Climb 2730'/1 min. Range 2840 miles/2 torpedoes, 3800 miles max.

MARTIN P4M-1Q

equipment needed for covert ELINT operations close to unfriendly coasts. A P4M-l was converted to a P4M-lQ in January 1951 by replacing all ASW gear with ECM equipment, APA-69 antennae, and increasing the crew from nine to 14 persons, while retaining the gun turrets. Gross weight increased from 83,378 to 88,378 pounds.

Mercators were removed from VP-21, which received P2V-6s in 1953, converted to P4M-lQs and issued to special covert units. After various bogus markings, 18 were assigned to Electronic Countermeasures Squadron VQ-l, commissioned in June 1955 in the Philippines, and to VQ-2 in Morocco. On August 22, 1956, Chinese fighters shot down a VQ-1 plane, and another was shot up in June 1959. Mercators were retired from those squadrons in 1960.

The Last Flying Boats

After World War II, water-based aircraft had only a small place in Navy programs. During the five years after the war, the only armed hull types accepted for service were the 36 PBM-5A amphibians built for rescue work. Before the Korean War in 1950, the Navy's patrol force consisted of eight squadrons of Neptune and six of Privateer landplanes, and six with PBM-5 flying boats. Of the Reserve Air Wings, eleven used Harpoons and nine amphibian Catalinas.

The flying boat, however, got a new lease on life by development of new hulls featuring a high ratio of length to beam and greater streamlining. These reduced the performance differential between water and land-based craft, and renewed interest in the virtues of water landing and a less destructible base.

The first to demonstrate the new look in hulls was Martin's XP5M-l, ordered June 26, 1946, which made its first flight May 30, 1948, powered by two 2,700-hp Wright R-3350-26 Cyclones. Although utilizing wings intended for the last aircraft on wartime PBM-5 contracts, the XP5M-l introduced a new longer, narrower hull with a single step and planing bottom all the way back to a high single tail. Hydroflaps were provided for quick turns on the water, radar was placed above the flight deck, and mockup gun turrets were at the nose, rear deck, and tail.

MARTIN XP5M-1
Two Wright R-3350-26, 2700 hp
DIMENSIONS: Span 118', Lg. 88', Ht. 37'11", Wing Area 1406 sq. ft.
WEIGHT: Empty 39,000 lb., Gross 60,000 lb. Fuel 1330+1433 gal.
PERFORMANCE: Speed-Top 234 mph at s. l., 249 mph at 15,700', Cruising 140 mph, Stalling 76 mph. Service Ceiling 24,000'. Range 1036 miles/four 325 lb. depth charges, 1360 miles/1330 gal.

The new hull proved successful and four P5M-ls were ordered in December 1949. Named the Marlin, the first flew June 22, 1951, and all four were accepted in December. Two 3,200-hp R-3350-30W Cyclones and new fixed floats were used, with two 20-mm guns and 600 rounds in the tail turret. Its anti-submarine warfare mission required 2,500 pounds of APS-44A radar in a bulbous nose, and homing torpedoes or depth charges in the engine nacelles. Additional Korean War contracts completed 114 P5M-ls by April 1954, plus seven P5M-lGs for the Coast Guard.

A new T-tail, with the horizontal surface atop the vertical fin, was introduced on the P5M-2, first flown in production form April 29, 1954. Other changes included a modified bow, 3,400 hp R-3350-32Ws, 813 pounds of armor, a 130-million candlepower searchlight under the starboard wingtip and magnetic detection gear high on the tail.

When the last of 119 P5M-2s was delivered on December 20, 1960, American flying boat production ended, leaving the Navy with ten squadrons of Marlin flying boats and 20 of Neptune landplanes. France had gotten 10 P5M-2s in 1959, and the Coast Guard four P5M-2Gs.

A new ASW configurations had 12 crewmen with an elaborate suite of electronics, including APS-80 search radar, ASQ-8 MAD, ECM receivers and direction finder, sonobuoy echo-sounding (Julie/Jezebel) receivers, and an

MARTIN P5M-1
Two Wright R-3350-30W, 3250 hp WE
DIMENSIONS Span 118', Lg. 90'3", Ht. 35'2" Wing Area 1406 sq. ft.
WEIGHT: Empty 47,861 lb., Gross 74,202 lb. Max. 77,399 lb. Fuel 2825+1150 gal.
PERFORMANCE: Speed-Top 269 mph at 1500', Cruising 157 mph. Service Ceiling 21,000'. Ferry Range 3600 miles.

MARTIN P5M-2
Two Wright R-3350-32WA 3700 hp takeoff, 3420 hp at 2400', 2550 hp at 16,700'
DIMENSIONS: Span 118'2", Lg. 101', Ht. 30'11", Wing Area 1406 sq. ft.
WEIGHT: Empty 48,383 lb., Combat 62,987 lb., Gross 74,302 lb., Max. 78,000 lb. Fuel 2809+1150 gal
PERFORMANCE: Speed-Top 266 mph at 1500', 276 mph at 17,000', Cruising 171 mph, Stalling 99 mph. Service Ceiling 21,900', Climb 1590'/1 min. Combat Range 2,471 miles, Ferry Range 3385 miles.

integrated display system. This modification was done on 80 redesignated P5M-lS Marlins and the P5M-2S, which became the SP-5A and SP-5B in September 1962.

Nacelle weapon bays contained two Mk 43 torpedoes, or four 2,025-pound Mk 39 mines, and eight 5-inch rockets could be carried under the wings. Tail guns were omitted, although 7.62-mm M-60 guns were installed at the four side hatches in the hull on surveillance missions off the Vietnamese coast. By 1965, only three Navy flying boat squadrons (VP-40, 48 & 50) remained, based at San Diego's North Island and rotating aircraft to the Philippines.

MARTIN SP-5A (P5M-lS of VP-46)

The First and Last Navy seaplanes: A Curtiss A-1 replica with an SP-5B of VP-42 at North Island NAS in 1961

USN

MARTIN SP-5B (P5M-2S)
Two Wright R-3350-32WA, 3700 hp takeoff, 3420 hp at 2400', 2550 hp at 16,700'
DIMENSIONS: Span 118'2", Lg. 100'2", Ht. 30'11", Wing Area 1406 sq. ft.
WEIGHT: Empty 49,218 lb., Combat 65,986 lb., Gross 76,595 lb., Max. 78,000 lb. Fuel 2843+1150 gal.
PERFORMANCE: Speed-Top 251 mph at s.l., 266 mph at 17,400', Cruising 159 mph at 1500', Stalling 112 mph, Combat Ceiling 18,200', Service Ceiling 20,600', Climb 1470'/1 min., Combat Range 2471 miles/2487 lb., Ferry Range 3060 miles.

The Navy ended 56 years of seaplane flying on November 6, 1967, with the last operational flight by an SP-5B Marlin flying boat of VP-40. Appropriately, this squadron's base in San Diego was the site of the first American seaplane flight, by Glenn Curtiss, January 26, 1911.

Convair's last boat

During the Marlin and Neptune's service, attempts were made to develop more advanced patrol planes utilizing gas turbine engines. As early as December 27, 1945, the Navy invited proposals for a turboprop flying boat using the new hull shapes under development, and Convair received a letter contract for two XP5Y-1 prototypes June 19, 1946.

This design had four Allison T-40-A-4 units yielding 5,100 hp and 830-pounds residual exhaust thrust. That powerplant joined twin T38s on the wing to twin extension shafts to six-bladed Aeroproducts contraprops, but would present serious mechanical difficulties. The streamlined hull had a 10:1 length to beam ratio, and the wing had an aspect ratio of 10, with fixed wingtip floats; retractable floats like those of the PBYs were inappropriate to the thin low-drag wing.

After many engine delays, Convair's last patrol flying boat, and the only Navy turboprop boat, took off from San Diego Bay on April 18, 1950, piloted by Sam Shannon. The XP5Y-1 was designed for an 11-man crew, APS-30 radar scanner in the nose, and four wing cells held 4,000 pounds of bombs, ASW torpedoes, or depth charges, while external racks might be added for another 8,000 pounds.

CONVAIR XP5Y-1
Four Allison XT-40-A-4, 5100 hp and 830 lb. st
DIMENSIONS: Span 146', Lg. 127'11", Ht. 44'10", Wing Area 2100 sq. ft.
WEIGHT: Empty 71,824 lb., Gross 123,500 lb., Max. 140,374 lb. Fuel 6768+1994 gal.
PERFORMANCE: Speed- Top 365 mph at s.1., 374 mph at 10,000', 383 mph at 20,000', Cruising 198 mph, Stalling 96 mph. Service Ceiling 37,500', Climb 3000'/1 min., 10,000'/3.7 min. Range 3236 miles/4000 lb. bombs, Max. Range 4200 miles

Planned protection included 721 pounds of armor for the flight deck and nacelles, and five pairs of 20-mm guns mounted on remote-controlled turrets. Four turrets were on the hull's sides: two ahead of the cockpit, and two behind the wing, and another behind the single rudder, although no guns were ever fitted. The powerplant problems

MARTIN P6M-2
Four Pratt & Whitney J75-P-2, 15,800 lb.
DIMENSIONS: Span 102'11", Lg. 134', Ht. 32'5", Wing Area 1900 sq. ft.
WEIGHT: Empty 91,284 lb. Gross 195,000 lb.
PERFORMANCE: Speed- Top 686 mph at s.l. Service Ceiling 43,900', Combat radius 863 miles/30,000 lb. of mines.

were never overcome, the second prototype was not completed, and the original aircraft crashed on July 15, 1953.

Instead of the combat plane, the Navy ordered R3Y-1 transport versions on August 16, 1950. Named the Tradewind, five were delivered in 1954, followed by six R3Y-2s with bow-loading doors. Engine troubles persisted and all Tradewinds were grounded after a January 1958 accident.

Convair did prepare a new P6Y-1 ASW flying boat design whose specification, dated May 29, 1957, proposed a mixed powerplant of three R-3350-30W and two YL85-GE-1 jets, but no contract was won.

Martin Seamaster

The only American jet-propelled flying boat began with a Navy request on July 30, 1951, that manufacturers propose designs for fast water-based aircraft that could lay mines across the paths of submarines as they sortie from Soviet bases. Left unstated was the Navy's desire to match Air Force nuclear attack capabilities.

Martin's Model 275 design was considered superior to a Convair proposal, and won a contract October 31, 1952, for two XP6M-l Seamaster flying boats. Flight tests by George Rodney of that radical design began July 14, 1955, on Chesapeake Bay.

The XP6M-l's long narrow hull with a 15 to 1 length-beam ratio had been tested on the Martin 270, actually the XP5M-1 rebuilt. Four Allison J71-A-4 turbojets were paired in nacelles atop wings swept back 40 degrees with enough anhedral to be balanced on the water by wingtip plastic floats. A high T-tail was clear of engine exhausts and hydroflaps aided control.

MARTIN YP6M-1
Four Allison J71-A-6, 9500 lb. st, 13,000 lb. st with afterburner
DIMENSIONS: Span 102'7", Lg. 134', Ht. 32'4", Wing Area 1900 sq. ft.
WEIGHT: Empty 84,685 lb., Combat 147,609 lb., Gross 167,011 lb., Max. 190,000 lb. Fuel 11,020 gal.
PERFORMANCE: Speed- Top 646 mph at 5000', Cruising 540 mph, Stalling 145 mph. Service Ceiling 35,000', Climb 3550'/1 min. Combat radius 673 miles, range 1594 miles as minelayer, 2745 miles high-altitude reconnaissance.

Pressurized compartments and ejection seats were provided for the five crewmen, along with radar in the nose, two 20-mm tail guns with 1,000 rounds, and 1,079 pounds of armor. A hull bay with a watertight rotary door and a top hatch for loading at sea, carried 30,000 pounds of mines or other stores. Weapons could include 36 504-pound Mk 50 or 15 2,030-pound Mk 25-2 mines, or two 3,500-pound Mk 91 nuclear penetration bombs.

On January 25, 1955, the Navy had committed itself to six YP6M-1 demonstrators, planned the shore bases and ships needed to sustain a Seaplane Striking Force, and ordered 24 P6M-2 Seamasters on August 29, 1956. But loss of the first XP6M-l prototype on December 7, 1955, and the second on November 9, 1956, seriously hurt hopes for the expensive program.

The YP6M-1 first flown January 20, 1958, was similar except for a slight outward cant of the J71-A-6 engines with afterburners. Pratt & Whitney J75-P-2s, whose 15,800-pounds thrust made afterburners unnecessary, powered the P6M-2, flown March 3, 1959. Only four were scarcely finished on that contract when the Navy suddenly terminated the Seamaster program on August 21.

The Navy halted American flying boat development because development of the supercarrier's attack capability and nuclear submarines with Polaris missiles, made water-based aircraft seem less needed.

The Orion

Forty years after the Lockheed Orion entered a Navy squadron, it remained the only patrol type in squadron use. Some 18 different patrol types had served in the previous 40 years, often with many alterations, but the basic P-3 airframe and powerplant remained unchanged.

That lasting success was a result of developing a patrol configuration from an airliner. Roomy passenger cabins could provide the crew comfort needed to endure long anti-sub flights. While ASW specialization had eliminated the gun turrets formerly carried to deal with enemy aircraft and surface vessels, electronic systems of growing weight had to be accommodated, along with more advanced underwater weapons.

Using the existing Electra L-188 transport with four turboprop engines saved the Navy much time and money, as was hoped when Lockheed won the design competition in April 1958 for a Neptune replacement. Since the winning design had the airliner's wing, tail, and engines, the third Electra was used in August to test the aerodynamic qualities of the new fuselage.

That aircraft became the YP3V-1 prototype ordered February 2, 1959, and flown by November 25. The first seven P3V-ls were ordered October 25, 1960, and first flown April 15, 1961; rapid development for a contemporary type. First entering service with VP-8 on July 23, 1962, the P3V-1 was redesignated P-3A in September, in time to monitor shipping to Cuba during the October crisis.

The 157 P-3As completed by December 1965 had four Allison T56-A-10W turboprops and a spacious pressurized cabin for ten crewmen. A tactical coordinator and his sensor operators searched for subs with APS-80A radar, ASQ-10 MAD gear, active and passive sonobuoys, and wingtip ECM antennae. For attack, the P-3A weapons bay contained four Mk 44 torpedoes and two 1,200-pound Mk 101 Lulu nuclear depth bombs, while under wing pylons could carry more torpedoes or 5-inch rocket pods.

More powerful T56-A-14 engines were used on the P-3B, first flown September 24, 1962. Armament now included eight 568-pound Mk 46 homing torpedoes, or two Mk 101 depth bombs, or three 1,024-pound Mk 36 mines in the bay, with 10 external pylons for torpedoes, mines, or four AGM-12B Bullpup missiles or 5-inch rockets for attacking cargo ships.

Lockheed delivered 144 P-3B Orions, including five for New Zealand in 1966, ten for Australia in 1968, and five for Norway in 1969. As they replaced Neptunes in Fleet squadrons, Orions flew "Market Time" missions monitoring water traffic near Viet Nam, and frequently upgraded their electronics. The P-3As, except for three leased to Spain in 1973 and several modified to other configurations, gradually shifted from fleet to the Naval Reserve's 19 patrol squadrons, as the last P-3As left VP-44 in November 1978 and the P-3A retired from the reserves in April 1990.

LOCKHEED P-3A (P3V-l)
Four Allison T56A-l0W, 4500 hp for takeoff, +750 lb. st
DIMENSIONS: Span 99'8", Lg. 116'10", Ht. 33'8", Wing Area 1300 sq.ft.
WEIGHT: Empty 59,201 lb., Combat 103,280 lb., Gross 127,500 lb. Fuel 9200 gal.
PERFORMANCE: Speed- Top 421 mph at s.l., 455 mph at 14,000', Cruising 357 mph, Stalling 136 mph. Combat Ceiling 27,700', Climb 2,290'/1 min., Combat Radius 1612 miles/4746 lb., Ferry Range 5570 miles.

LOCKHEED P-3B
Four Allison T56-A-14, 4880 hp military +781 lb. st, 4910 hp at take-off, +797 lb. st
DIMENSIONS: Same as P-3A
WEIGHT: Empty 61,491 lb., Combat 107,966 lb., Gross 132,990 lb., Max. 140,337 lb. Fuel 9200 gal.
PERFORMANCE: Speed- Top 430 mph at s.l., 474 mph at 14,600', Cruising 331 mph, Stalling 138 mph. Combat Ceiling 29,000', Climb 2,950'/1 min., Combat Radius 1670 miles/5527 lb., Ferry Range 5620 miles.

Although similar in appearance and armament to earlier versions, the P-3C made a major improvement in search capability. A surveillance camera was mounted in

Mfr

LOCKHEED P-3C Update II
Four Allison T56-A-14, 4880 hp military +781 lb. st, 4910 hp at takeoff, +797 lb. st
DIMENSIONS: Span 99'8", Lg. 116'10", Ht. 33'8", Wing Area 1300 sq. ft.
WEIGHT: Empty 68,900 lb., Combat 113,867 lb., Gross 138,902 lb., Max. 142,000 lb. Fuel 9204 gal.
PERFORMANCE: Speed- Top 421 mph at s.1., 465 mph at 16,000'. Cruising 402 mph, Stalling 142 mph. Combat Ceiling 27,000', Climb 2,630'/1 min. Combat Radius 1825 miles/four Mk 46 torpedoes+one B-57, Ferry Range 5207 miles.

Lawson

LOCKHEED P-3C
Four Allison T56-A-14, 4880 hp military +781 lb. st, 4910 hp at takeoff, +797 lb. st
DIMENSIONS: as P-3A
WEIGHT: Empty 66,211 lb., Combat 111,252 lb., Gross 135,000 lb., Max. 142,000 lb. Fuel 9200 gal.
PERFORMANCE: Speed- Top 412 mph at s.1., 455 mph at 12,300', Cruising 325 mph, Stalling 140 mph. Combat Ceiling 27,200'. Climb 2,750'/1 min., Combat Radius 1455 miles/six Mk 46 torpedoes, Ferry Range 5200 miles.

the nose, and the searchlight under the wing was replaced by a low-level-light television system. To integrate and store information from the new APS-115 radar, ASQ-81 MAD, navigation and ECM systems, and various acoustic sensors launched from 48 sonobuoy chutes, required naval aviation's first centralized digital computer, the ASQ-114.

While patrol aircraft performance had reached a plateau, computers had begun a generation of continuous rapid development. The basic task of locating submarines required ever-more complex electronics, so instead of airframe changes, Orions would be enhanced by a series of "Updates". Although the Orion became the only propeller-driven combat aircraft still in first-line American service, its electronics and weapons capability and twelve-hour mission endurance guaranteed a long life.

A YP-3C was converted on the P-3B assembly line and first flown September 18, 1968, and production P-3Cs were first delivered to VP-56 in October 1969. The Navy replaced earlier models by accepting 266 P-3Cs until production closed in April 1990. There were 24 first-line and two training patrol squadrons during the 1970s; including eight P-3C squadrons at NAS Moffet, California, five at

USN

LOCKHEED P-3C Update III

Barber's Point, Hawaii, seven at Jacksonville, Florida, and six at Brunswick, Maine.

Navy P-3Cs were rotated through the shops for the latest in equipment. Update I aircraft introduced in January 1975 had a seven-fold increase in the computer's memory storage and an Omega worldwide navigation system. Update II, first delivered in August 1977, introduced an AAS-36 infrared detector under the nose, a new sonobuoy reference system, and provisions for four AGM-84A Harpoon anti-ship missiles under the wings. Eight Mk 36 torpedoes could be carried in the bay, or three B-57 nuclear depth bombs, or up to ten Mk 36 mines.

Update III, delivered in 1985, entirely upgraded acoustic and computer capability and was retrofitted to earlier models. Special Orion conversions included RP-3As for research, an RP-3D magnetic surveyor, WP-3Ds for weather research, UP-3A transports and three black P-3As modified for CIA night missions from Taiwan. Twelve EP-3E Aries with ELINT devices were provided to VQ-l and VQ-2, the electronic surveillance squadrons.

Aircraft built for export increased California P-3 production to 641. Six P-3F Orions, with modest electronics, went to Iran in April 1975, while Australia got the first of 10 P-3Cs in February 1978, and added ten more in 1982. Canada ordered 18, named the CP-140 Aurora with different electronic provisions, and the first flew on March 22, 1979. The Netherlands purchased 13 P-3Cs in December 1978 and they arrived there from July 1982 to September 1984.

Lawson

LOCKHEED EP-3E

Japan signed a contract on June 9, 1978 that resulted in three P-3Cs completed by Lockheed in May 1981, four shipped in parts for assembly by Kawasaki, who built another 101 ASW Orions in Japan. Ten second-hand ex-RAAF P-3Bs were sold to Portugal in 1985, and Norway sold five of its P-3Bs to Spain in 1989, so that the RNAF could buy four new P-3Cs. Canada added three CP-140A Arcturus survey models in 1994.

Mfr

LOCKHEED P-3F (Iran)

The Cold War's end in 1991 accelerated the retirement of Navy patrol squadrons, but Korea ordered eight new P-3C Update IIIs after California P-3 production ended, so tooling was transferred to Georgia, and the first flew at Marietta on June 28, 1994. Orion total production reached 755.

While no new Orions would be built, capability upgrades continued. An AIP (Anti-surface warfare Improvement Program) system deployed with VP-9 in June 1998 provided new APS-137 radar, anti-missile flares, and imagery links. AGM-65F Maverick and AGM-84E SLAM missiles would target land targets in Kosovo and Afghanistan as VP-10 and other units acquired the new kits.

Orions remained the only American prop-driven, straight-wing combat planes to outlast the 20th century. During the summer of 2000, 226 P-3C Orions still served 12 active patrol and seven reserve squadrons, as well as one training squadron.

Squadrons VQ-1 and VQ-2 continued with the EP-3E Aries II electronic surveillance model. A collision with a Chinese fighter would remind the world in April 2001 that electronic intelligence flights remained a sensitive international issue.

CHAPTER 31
NAVY ATTACK PLANES OF THE COLD WAR

Mfr

DOUGLAS XBT2D-1
Wright R-3350-24W, 2500 takeoff, 2200 hp at 11,500'
DIMENSIONS: Span 50', Lg. 39'5", Ht. 15', Wing Area 400 sq. ft. / WEIGHT: Empty 10,093 lb. Gross 13,500 lb., Max. 17,500 lb. Fuel 365 +150 or 300 gal. / PERFORMANCE: Speed- Top 357 mph at s.1., 375 mph at 13,600' clean, 271 mph at s.1., 303 mph at 13,600' with torpedo, Cruising 185 mph, Stalling 84 mph. Service Ceiling 33,200', Climb 3680'/1 min. Range 1427 miles/torpedo/515 gal.

The A-l Skyraider

On March 11, 1946, the Navy replaced the VB and VT designations for dive and torpedo bombers, with VA for attack aircraft whose primary mission was attacking surface targets. Subsequently, the BT2D and BTM aircraft on order were redesignated AD and AM attack planes. Martin's AM-l, as described in Chapter 21, served four post-war squadrons, but was soon replaced by the Douglas Skyraider series, which became the A-l in the current designation system.

Douglas Aircraft's Chief Engineer, Ed Heinemann, wanted to overcome the troubles that crippled the BTD Destroyer. In June 1944, he proposed a simple, lighter design that used a straight high-lift wing for quicker takeoffs with heavy loads, instead of the BTD's low-drag gull wing. In place of tricycle gear and internal bomb bay, the tail-down gear and external weapons pylons of contemporary BTC, BTK, and BTM types was chosen.

Twenty-five XBT2D-l preproduction prototypes were ordered July 21, 1944, and LaVerne Brown first flew the XBT2D-l on March 18, 1945. An R-3350-8 used on the first four was replaced by the 2,500-hp R-3350-24W standard on later models. Two 20-mm wing guns with 200 rpg were carried, and three external racks could handle two tons of bombs, Mk 13-3 torpedoes, 150-gallon drop tanks, or an APS-4 radar pod. A new ejection device on the centerline rack replaced the older displacement gear used to avoid hitting the propeller.

The pilot had 208 pounds of armor, and good visibility from a bubble canopy. The wheels turned through 90° as they retracted backward into the wings, which folded upward for stowage, and dive brakes were placed at the fuselage sides and bottom. The remaining BT2D-1s were completed in 1946/47 and included two XB2D-2N night attack planes, an XBT2D-1P photo, and XB2D-1Q radar countermeasures conversion.

An order placed for 548 production Skyraiders on April 18, 1945, was reduced to 277 after V-J Day and redesignated AD-l under the new designation system. Twelve 5-inch rockets could be carried under the wings, in addition to 2,000-pound bombs on the inboard racks.

Delivery began on 242 single-seat AD-1s, first flown November 5, 1946, and from May 1947 to June 1948, 35 AD-1Q radar countermeasures versions with a technician in the fuselage behind the pilot operating devices to identify and jam hostile radar. An XAD-1W early warning prototype, converted from a BT2D-l, had a large APS-20 belly radome, two radar men in the fuselage, and no dive brakes or guns.

WL

DOUGLAS AD-1
Wright R-3350-24W, 2500 hp takeoff, 2200 hp at 11,500'
DIMENSIONS: Span 50', Lg. 38'4", Ht. 15'7" (17'6" fld.), Wing Area 400 sq. ft.
WEIGHT: Empty 10,508 lb., Gross 13,924 lb., Max. 18,030 lb. Fuel 365 +300 gal.
PERFORMANCE: Speed- Top 348 mph at s.1., 366 mph at 13,500' clean, Cruising 185 mph, Stalling 84 mph. Service Ceiling 33,000', Climb 3590'/1 min. Range 1935 miles/2000-lb. bombs/665 gal.

The AD-l began service with VA-19A in December 1946 and equipped eight carrier attack squadrons by 1948, but hard landings on carriers revealed structure weaknesses that were corrected on the AD-2. The first AD-2 was converted from an AD-l, and had stronger wings, a larger fuel tank, two more wing racks, and a 2,700-hp R-3350-26W.

AD-2 deliveries began in April 1948, enabling some AD-1s to be passed to Reserve bases. A total of 156 AD-2s and 22 AD-2Qs were purchased, followed in November by the AD-3,

DOUGLAS AD-1Q
Wright R-3350-24W, 2500 hp takeoff, 2200 hp at 11,500'
DIMENSIONS: as AD-1
WEIGHT: Empty 10,946 lb., Gross 14,718 lb., Max. 16,861 lb. Fuel 365 +300 gal.
PERFORMANCE: Speed- Top 341 mph at s.1., 356 mph at 13,300', Cruising 176 mph, Stalling 86 mph. Service Ceiling 31,900', Climb 3350'/1 min. Range 1350 miles scout, 1070 miles/2000-lb. bombs.

with a strengthened internal structure. The Navy accepted 125 AD-3, 23 AD-3Q, 31 AD-3W, and 15 AD-3N aircraft.

DOUGLAS AD-2
Wright R-3350-26W, 2700 hp takeoff, 2100 hp at 14,500'
DIMENSIONS: Span 50', Lg. 38'4", Ht. 15'5", Wing Area 400 sq. ft.
WEIGHT: Empty, 10,546 lb., Gross 16,268 lb., Max. 18,263 lb. Fuel 380 +300 gal.
PERFORMANCE: Speed- Top 321 mph at 18,300', Cruising 198 mph, Stalling 83 mph. Service Ceiling 32,700', Climb 2800'/1 min. Range 915 miles with bombs.

The Skyraider used throughout the Korean War was the AD-4, appearing in June 1949 with an automatic pilot, APS-19 radar, 186 pounds of armor, and two 20-mm guns,

DOUGLAS AD-3
Wright R-3350-26W, 2700 hp takeoff, 2100 hp at 14,500'.
DIMENSIONS: As AD-2
WEIGHT: Empty 10,812 lb., Gross 16,520 lb., Max. 18,515 lb. Fuel 380 +380 gal.
PERFORMANCE: Speed- Top 321 mph at 18,300', Cruising 200 mph, Stalling 84 mph. Service Ceiling 32,300', Climb 2760'/1 min. Range 900 miles.

but armament was increased in December 1950 to four 20-mm guns with 200 rpg on all 372 AD-4s built. Three 2,000-pound bombs, torpedoes, or drop tanks, could be carried on the main pylons, while outer wing stations were used for 500-pound bombs or rockets, with maximum capacity up to 9,900 pounds on shore or 6,500 pounds when carrier launched.

USN

DOUGLAS AD-4
Wright R-3350-26WA, 2700 hp takeoff, 2100 hp at 14,500', (3150 hp WE)
DIMENSIONS: Span 50', Lg. 39'3", Ht. 15'8", Wing Area 400 sq. ft.
WEIGHT: Empty 11,7112lb., Combat 17,818 lb., Gross 21,483 lb., Max. 25,000 lb. Fuel 380 +450 gal.
PERFORMANCE: Speed- Top 316 mph at s.1., 349 mph at 20,000', Cruising 227 mph, Stalling 81 mph. Combat Ceiling 23,300', Climb 2880'/1 min. Combat Range 620 miles. Range 1347 miles/2000-lb. bomb and 12 HVAR +2/150 gal. tanks.

Mfr

DOUGLAS AD-3N
Wright R-3350-26W, 2700 hp takeoff, 2100 hp at 14,500'.
DIMENSIONS: As AD-2
WEIGHT: Empty 11,483 lb., Gross 18,044 lb., Max. 19,664 lb. Fuel 380 +380 gal.
PERFORMANCE: Speed- Top 296 mph at 18,300', Cruising 197 mph, Landing Stalling 87 mph. Service Ceiling 28,800', Climb 2260'/1 min. Range 1175 miles.

Other versions included 39 AD-4Qs appearing in November 1949, 307 AD-4Ns beginning in February 1950, 152 AD-4Ws appearing in March, and 165 AD-4Bs first flown in August 1952. Two radar operators were carried within the fuselage of the N and W types, requiring omission of the dive brakes, but the N had an APS-31C radar pod and searchlight under the wings, while the AD-4W had the big APS-20 under the fuselage for over-the-horizon detection. Modifications for Korean winters were fitted to 63 AD-4L and 37 AD-4NL versions.

The AD-4B was the first with a low-altitude bombing system (LABS) for a tactical nuclear weapon, the fuselage rack accommodating the 1,680-pound Mk 7. Escaping the air burst required a sudden upwards loop from a 50-foot altitude, tossing the bomb at the target as the AD turned away. The 3,250-pound Mk 8 penetration "store", which exploded underground, gave the pilot a better chance of escape.

One AD-4 was converted to the AD-5 prototype first flown August 17, 1951, with a larger tail, four wing guns, a single bottom dive brake, and an expanded fuselage serving as a universal chassis on which several different conversions could be made from prepared kits. The two-man flight crew sat side by side under the canopy, and space behind them allowed flexibility.

DOUGLAS AD-5N (A-IG)
Wright R-3350-26WA, 2700 hp at takeoff,
DIMENSIONS: As AD-5
WEIGHT: Empty 12,112 lb., Combat 18,505 lb., Gross 20,517 lb., Max. 23,069 lb. Fuel 380+300 gal.
PERFORMANCE: Speed- Top 303 mph at s.1., 322 mph at 15,100', Cruising 190 mph at 5,000', Stalling 103 mph. Combat Ceiling 27,000', Climb 2580'/1 min. Combat Radius 236 miles/1100-lb. bombs, 212 miles/2700-lb bombs, 576 miles/1660-lb. store/680 gal.

DOUGLAS AD-4B
Wright R-3350-26WA, 2700 hp takeoff, 2100 hp at 14,500'
DIMENSIONS: As AD-4
WEIGHT: Empty 11,783 lb., Combat 17,757 lb., Gross 18,669 lb., Max. 24,231 lb. Fuel 380+600 gal.
PERFORMANCE: Speed- Top 303 mph at s.1., 320 mph at 15,000', Cruising 196 mph, Stalling 85 mph. Combat Ceiling 23,800', Service Ceiling 26,000', Climb 2980'/l min. Combat Radius 300 miles/Mk-7, 730 miles/Mk-7 & 2/150 gal. tanks, 725 miles/Mk-8 and 2/300 gal. tanks.

Protection for the standard day attack version included 189 pounds of pilot armor, 166 pounds of engine armor, 175 pounds of auxiliary pilot armor, and 308 pounds in an external belly armor kit. While an APS-19C radar pod could be carried under the AD-5's left wing, the AD-5N night attack put the APS-31C under the right wing and APA-69 radome near the tail, with radar operators behind the pilots. Attack loads varied from 1,100 to 2,700 pounds, or an anti-submarine load including a Mk 34 torpedo, AV-2 searchlight, and sonobuoys.

DOUGLAS AD-4N

Carrying guns, but with 300-gallon drop tanks instead of bombs, the four-place AD-5Q had electronics for detecting and jamming enemy radar. Without any weapons, the early warning AD-5W had a large APS-20B radome under the belly and two 300-gallon drop tanks, flying up to 11-hour search patterns at 1,500 feet and 185 mph. AD-5 conversions into transport and utility work were possible when up to eight passengers or four litter patients could be squeezed into the fuselage.

After the last AD-4B was delivered in June 1953, the El Segundo plant concurrently turned out three AD-5 versions and the standard AD-6 close support single-seater. Deliveries included 212 AD-5, 239 AD-5N (of which 54 became AD-5Q), one AD-5S with MAD gear, 218 AD-5W, and 713 AD-6 Skyraiders. Armor protection on the AD-6 included 186 pounds in the cockpit and an optional 618-pound external kit.

Mfr

DOUGLAS AD-6 (A-1H after 1962**)**
Wright R-3350-26WA, 2700 hp takeoff, 2100 hp @ 14,000'
DIMENSIONS: Span 50', Lg. 39'2", Ht. 15'8", Wing Area 400 sq. ft.
WEIGHT: Empty 11,902 lb., Combat 16,006 lb. (clean), Gross 18,918 lb. (2000 lb. bomb), Max. 22,602 lb. Fuel 380+600 gal.
PERFORMANCE: Speed-Top 316 mph at s.l., 341 mph at 15,400' Cruising 196 mph at 5,000', Stalling 99 mph. Combat Ceiling 28,700', Climb 3270'/1 min. Combat Radius 608 miles/2000 lb. bomb/380 gal., 783 miles/Mk 7/980 gal. (1955 data)

Mfr

DOUGLAS AD-5
Wright R-3350-26WA, 2700 hp takeoff, 2100 hp at 14,500'
DIMENSIONS: Span 50', Lg. 40', Ht. 15'10", Wing Area 400 sq. ft.
WEIGHT: Empty 12,293 lb., Combat 16,760 lb., Gross 19,672 lb., Max. 23,356 lb. Fuel 380+300 gal.
PERFORMANCE: Speed- Top 310 mph at s.1., 329 mph at 15,200', Cruising 196 mph at 5,000', Stalling 101 mph. Combat Ceiling 27,000', Climb 2980'/l min. Combat Radius 272 miles/2000-lb. bomb, 585 miles/3680 lb./680 gal.

Finally, 72 single-seat AD-7s (R-3350-26WB), the last on February 18, 1957, brought the total to 3,180 Skyraiders from El Segundo. Of these, the British Navy received the last 20 new AD-4Ws from Douglas and about 31 from Navy stocks from November 1951 to April 1953.

Lawson

DOUGLAS AD-5W (EA-lE)

USN

DOUGLAS AD-5Q (EA-1F) dispensing chaff

DOUGLAS AD-7 (A-1J)

Skyraiders in service

When the Korean War began, there were 12 Navy AD attack squadrons, plus two AD-4N night attack and two AD-3W early warning squadrons, while four AD-3/4Qs were stationed on each carrier. The *Valley Forge's* VA-55 sent its AD-4s out on July 3, 1950, for the first attack in the three-year carrier-based bombing campaign against North Korea.

Eighteen Navy AD squadrons in Korea demonstrated bomb-carrying ability, endurance over target areas, and precision bombing; the AD-4 carried a one-ton bomb and 12 rockets on a six-hour mission over a 620-mile combat radius. Eight AD-4NLs made the war's only torpedo attack on May 1, 1952, hitting the Hwachon Dam. The first of three Marine Skyraider squadrons, VMA-121, brought AD-3s to Korea in October 1951, flying from land bases through the whole war.

By the war's end in July 1953, there were 24 Navy and eight Marine Skyraider squadrons, and the "Able Dog" had been so successful that AD-5 and AD-6 aircraft replaced older models and filled out 29 Navy and 13 Marine squadrons by September 1955. A year later, replacement of each carrier's second AD squadron by A4D jet aircraft began, and in 1963 the A-6A all-weather jets started replacing the remaining squadrons.

Although most retired Skyraiders went to storage in Arizona, many would again be called to combat before long. France obtained 93 AD-4Ns in 1959 for her Algerian war, and a few of these were passed on to former colonies, like Cambodia and Chad. The Republic of Vietnam got 25 AD-6s for the small VNAF in September 1960 to replace the grounded F8F Bearcats left by the French.

On September 18, 1962, Navy Skyraiders were designated A-lE (AD-5), EA-lE (AD-5W), EA-lF (AD-5Q), A-lG (AD-5N), and the single-seat AD-6 and AD-7 became A-1H and A-1J.

American involvement in Southeast Asia found the Air Force without a proper ground attack plane of its own, so 50 A-lE Skyraiders from storage were refurbished and delivered, beginning in April 1963, to the Air Force Special Warfare Center at Eglin AFB. Another batch was delivered by December 1965. These A-lEs had dual controls for a second (side by side) crewman, four 20-mm M3 guns with 200 rpg, and 15 external stations for up to 6,500 pounds of bombs, rocket pods, or drop tanks.

DOUGLAS A-lH, VA-115 in Viet Nam
Wright R-3350-26WB, 2700 hp at takeoff,
DIMENSIONS: Span 50', Lg. 39'3", Ht. 15'8", Wing Area 400 sq. ft.
WEIGHT: Empty 12,072 lb., Combat 15,486 lb. (clean), Gross 18,398 lb. (2000 lb. bomb), Max. 24,091 lb. Fuel 380+900 gal.
PERFORMANCE: Speed- Top 319 mph at s.l., 342 mph at 15,400' clean, (312-333 mph/2000-lb bomb), Cruising 180 mph at 5,000', Stalling 102 mph. Combat Ceiling 29,400', Climb 2950'/1 min. Combat Radius 275 miles/2000- lb. bomb, 863 miles/2000-lb./980 gal. Ferry Range 3240 miles.

DOUGLAS A-1E USAF in Viet Nam
Wright R-3350-26WD, 2700 hp at takeoff, 2100 hp at 14,500'
DIMENSIONS: Span 50', Lg. 40', Ht. 15'9", Wing Area 400 sq. ft.
WEIGHT: Empty 14,721 lb., Combat 17,686 lb. Gross 22,984 lb., Max. 24,820 lb. Fuel 378+900+310 gal. aux.
PERFORMANCE: Speed- Top 295 mph at s.l., 312 mph at 12,000'. Cruising 198 mph at 10,000', Stalling 109 mph. Combat Ceiling 28,700', Service Ceiling 24,900'. Climb 2680'/1 min. Combat Radius 628 miles/3200- lb. bombs. Ferry Range 3048 miles.

In February 1964, Defense Secretary Robert McNamara decided to send 25 of these A-1Es to Vietnam to replace the First Air Commando Squadron's T-28s and B-26s, and to provide 25 A-1H (AD-6) single-seaters from Navy stocks for the VNAF. American pilots trained Vietnamese, and flew A-lE combat missions with Vietnamese observers. A second Air Commando A-1E squadron was authorized in May 1964, along with enough A-1Hs for four VNAF squadrons.

By April 1965, there were 89 VNAF A-1Hs and 54 Air Commando A-lEs in Vietnam, and in January 1966, the VNAF had about 100 A-1H and 20 A-1Gs piloted by men trained on A-lEs at Eglin. Of these aircraft, 72 remained

DOUGLAS A-lH, USAF in Viet Nam

in March 1972, and heavy losses that year were partially replaced by the remaining USAF A-lEs. At the war's end, 11 were evacuated to Thailand in 1975, and 26 A-1E/Gs were captured.

Navy Skyraiders entered the war on August 5, 1964, when the North Vietnamese coast was hit by 12 A-1Hs from VA-52 and VA-145, among the twelve Navy A-l squadrons still remaining. Strikes from the carriers continued throughout the war, until the *Coral Sea's* VA-25, the last Navy squadron with the rugged Douglas, flew its final combat sortie on February 20, 1968, and retired its aircraft on April 10.

The XA2D-1 Skyshark

Douglas made an attempt at a radical improvement in performance with the XA2D-1 Skyshark powered by an Allison XT40-A-2 turboprop engine delivering 5,035 hp to contrarotating six-bladed propellers, plus 1,225-pounds exhaust thrust. The wing plan was that of the AD, but a thinner airfoil was used. The pilot sat high above the engine and ahead of the fuel tank, which required a larger capacity than that of the AD because of higher fuel consumption. Four 20-mm guns were mounted in the wings and 8,000 pounds of bombs or 450 gallons of fuel could be carried externally.

The Navy desired a turboprop powerplant in an attack type, and had been encouraging Douglas to prepare such a design since 1945, ordering two XA2D-1 prototypes September 25, 1947. The first flight was delayed by the XT40-A-2 engine to May 26, 1950, yet the Korean War led the Navy to order ten A2D-ls on June 30, and 331 production aircraft soon afterwards.

But powerplant and propeller gear troubles were continuous, destroying the first prototype on December 19, and the second (with an XT40-A-6) could not be flown until April 3, 1952. By then, contract terminations had begun, and were made final in September 1953, with only five A2D-ls accepted between April 1953 and January 1954. The designers, however, learned from the failure and went on to produce the very successful A-4.

DOUGLAS XA2D-l
Allison XT40-A-2, 5035 hp and 1225 lb. st at 14,300'
DIMENSIONS: Span 50', Lg. 41'4", Ht. 16'11", Wing Area 400 sq. ft.
WEIGHT: Empty 14,139 lb., Combat 18,720 lb., Gross 22,966 lb. Fuel 500+450 gal.
PERFORMANCE: Speed- Top 467 mph at s.l., 501 mph at 25,000', Cruising 286 mph, Stalling 115 mph, Combat Ceiling 40,600', Climb 7290'/1 min. Combat Range 1708 miles.

The Big Punch

Versatile as the Navy's single-engine bombers were, they compared poorly with the strategic striking power of the larger Air Force aircraft. This was inherent in the limitations imposed by flight-deck operations; a carrier bomber can only be so big and so heavy, must have arresting gear, folding wings and specialized shipboard equipment, and thus can't have the tremendous power and armament of their heavier competitors.

Mfr

DOUGLAS A2D-1
Allison XT40-A-6, 5332 hp and 1225 lb. st at 14,300'
DIMENSIONS: Span 50', Lg. 41'3", Ht. 16'10", Wing Area 400 sq. ft.
WEIGHT: Empty 14,649 lb., Combat 18,452 lb., Gross 22,756 lb., Max. 27,652 lb. Fuel 500+600 gal.
PERFORMANCE: Speed- Top 445 mph at s.l., 478 mph at 28,000', Cruising 368 mph, Stalling 114 mph, Combat Ceiling 43,600', Climb 7200'/1 min., Combat Radius 240 miles/3100-lb/500 gal., 690 miles/3656-lb./1100 gal.

A larger carrier-based type was needed to enable the Navy to contribute an atomic punch to a strategic bombing offensive. and on January 25, 1946, the Navy requested aircraft builders to submit proposals on May 1. North American won a contract made June 24 for three XAJ-1 prototypes and for the first 12 AJ-1 Savages on July 1, 1947.

Mfr

NORTH AMERICAN XAJ-1

A high-wing monoplane with a crew of three in a pressurized cockpit and APS-31 radar in the nose, the AJ-1 had two Pratt & Whitney R-2800-44W Wasps under the wings and an Allison J33-A-10 jet in the fuselage to boost speeds over short distances. The wings folded up and the fin down to ease stowage.

No guns were carried, as the AJ depended on speed for protection, while the internal bomb bay was large enough for a Mk 3 or the improved 10,800-pound Mk 4 nuclear bomb. Alternative loads could include six 1,600-pound conventional bombs, or aerial mines.

The first XAJ-1 was flown on July 3, 1948, by Bob Chilton from Los Angeles International Airport, and the first AJ-1 flown on May 10, 1949, was similar, but for a reinforced canopy, and two 300-gallon tanks were on the wing tips. Composite Squadron VC-5, which had been studying nuclear delivery with P2V-3C Neptunes, received the first AJ-1s and made the first takeoff from the *Coral Sea's* deck on April 21, 1950, and the first deck landing August 31.

Mfr

NORTH AMERICAN AJ-l (A-2A)
Two Pratt & Whitney R-2800-44W, 2300 hp at 30,000', & one Allison J33-A-10, 4600 lb. st.
DIMENSIONS: Span 71'5", Lg. 64'1", Ht. 21'5", Wing Area 836 sq. ft.
WEIGHT: Empty 30,776 lb., Combat 46,352 lb. Gross 50,963 lb., Max. 54,000 lb. Fuel 1217+1240 gal.
PERFORMANCE: Speed- Top 357 mph at s.1., 449 mph at 34,000', Cruising 270 mph, Stalling 120 mph. Combat Ceiling 40,800', Climb 2900'/1 min. Combat Range 1732 miles/7600-lb. Mk-15/ 2/300 gal. tanks. Ferry Range 2993 miles.

Fifty-five AJ-l Savages were accepted from the Los Angeles plant from August 1949 to January 1952, the original APA-5 bombing director replaced by the ASB-1 for 8,500-pound Mk 6 or 3,250-pound Mk 8 nuclear bombs. Heavy Attack Wing (HatWing) One, including VC-5, -6, and -7, was established at NAS Norfolk on February 1, 1951.

Mfr

NORTH AMERICAN A-2B (AJ-2)
Two Pratt & Whitney R-2800-44W, 2300 hp at 30,000', & one *Allison J33-A-10, 4600 lb. st*
DIMENSIONS: As AJ-l
WEIGHT: Empty 30,776 lb., Combat 46,990 lb. Gross 50,580 lb., Max. 54,000 lb. Fuel 1217+1400 gal
PERFORMANCE: Speed- Top 357 mph at s.l., 449 mph at 34,000', Cruising 260 mph, Stalling 119 mph. Combat Ceiling 41,500', Climb 3050'/1 min. Combat Range 2475 miles/3200-lb. bomb, and 2/300 gal. tanks, Ferry Range 3056 miles.

NORTH AMERICAN XA2J-1
Two Allison T40-A-6, 5035 hp and 1225 lb. st at 14,300'
DIMENSIONS: Span 71'6", Lg. 70', Ht. 22'6", Wing Area 836 sq. ft.
WEIGHT: Empty 32,164 lb., Gross 43,712 lb., Max. 58,000 lb. Fuel 1802 +818 gal.
PERFORMANCE: (Design estimates) Speed- Top 451 mph at 24,000', Cruising 400 mph, Stalling 100 mph. Service Ceiling 37,500'. Range 2180 miles/8000-lb. bomb.

Four-plane detachments were deployed to the fleet's three *Midway*-class carriers, joined in 1951 by the *Oriskany*, first of the Project 27A carriers commissioned. But the AJ's suffered many mechanical difficulties, accidents, and blanket groundings, until safety changes were made.

North American leased the ex-Helldiver factory in Columbus, Ohio, for 30 AJ-2P reconnaissance models ordered February 14, 1951, and first flown March 30, 1952, followed by 55 standard AJ-2s, first flown February 18, 1953. The AJ-2P could be distinguished by its bulbous camera nose, and horizontal tail surfaces without dihedral.

Production of the North American AJ-2 Savage continued until June 1954. Most of the AJ-1 bombers were improved to AJ-2 standards. Seven heavy attack and two photo squadrons were stationed at shore bases, rotating detachments, but their large size limited their use. Composite squadrons were replaced with heavy attack squadrons (VAH).

A megaton-yield, 7,600-pound Mk 15 thermonuclear store became available in 1955, and as A3Ds began replacing the bombers in 1956, some AJs were fitted as flying tankers to refuel other aircraft in flight by a probe-and-drogue system. A photo squadron, VAP-62, continued using the AJ-2P until 1960. A few Savage survivors were redesignated A-2A/B in 1962.

Allison T40-A-6 turboprop engines with six-bladed contrapropellers were used on the XA2J-l designed by North American as an AJ replacement. Other changes included a swept tail fin, dual nose wheels, and two radar-aimed 20-mm tail guns. Two prototypes (NA-163) were begun October 1, 1948, and the first flew January 4, 1952, but the same T40 difficulties that frustrated other turboprop designs of the time halted this type.

The A-3 Skywarrior

Real progress toward a Navy strategic bomber required full jet power with all the fuel and weight that implied. The obvious answer was an aircraft carrier large enough to handle bigger bombers, but funds for this were hard to justify in the post-WW II situation. Had not the Navy a surplus of carriers already, including three *Midways* and 23 of the *Essex* class hulls, several times more than all the rest of the world put together? Besides, the Air Force felt itself perfectly capable of doing all the strategic bombing necessary, and wanted any available funds invested in its own big bombers.

A huge 65,000 ton carrier, CVA-58, had been ordered August 10, 1948, by pro-Navy Defense Secretary James V. Forrestal, but was canceled April 23, 1949, just five days after the keel was laid, by his successor in the Cabinet post, Louis Johnson. Instead, the Navy was authorized on June 21 to begin the 27A program of modernizing some *Essex*-class carriers to operate aircraft with nuclear weapons.

Douglas engineers led by Ed Heinemann had been asked to design a carrier-based bomber that could carry a 10,000-pound bomb. A Navy Request for Proposals dated August 16, 1948, indicated that the Navy thought a 100,000-pound twin-engine aircraft would be needed to accommodate in an enclosed bay the big bomb, which had to be accessible in flight to be armed by a specialist. The Douglas proposal made November 9 was favored over those of five rival companies.

Two XA3D-1 prototypes were ordered March 31, 1949, but cancellation of CVA-58 threatened the program until the Douglas Phase 1 study submitted on May 13 proved light enough to operate from *Midway*-class carriers as well as those older *Essex* ships that would be rebuilt with stronger, angled decks, and new catapults. Secrecy about atomic bombs slowed engineering; not until June 28 was Douglas informed that the 57-inch bomb bay would have to be increased to 66 inches to hold five-foot wide weapons.

DOUGLAS XA3D-1

Another opportunity came for the Navy with the Korean War, when funds became available for the first 60,000 ton super-carrier, ordered July 12, 1951, and named *USS Forrestal*, after the late Secretary. New flight decks for big jet bombers were on their way and the replacement of the World War II fleet had begun.

The first XA3D-1 was trucked from El Segundo to Edwards AFB and flown October 28, 1952, with two 7,000-pound thrust Westinghouse XJ40-WE-3 jets in pods below the wings. The A3D-l's high wing was swept back 36°, fitted with slots, and folded for stowage. The fuselage contained an ASB-1A radar bombing system in the nose, a three-place pressurized cabin, wells for the retractable tricycle landing gear, an internal bomb bay and fuel tanks, and a remote-controlled radar-aimed Aero tail turret with two 20-mm guns and 1,000 rounds.

DOUGLAS A3D-1 (to A-3A)
Two Pratt & Whitney J57-P-6, 10,000 lb. st
DIMENSIONS: Span 72'6", Lg. 74'5", Ht. 22'10", Wing Area 779 sq. ft.
WEIGHT: Empty 35,899 lb., Combat 60,250 lb., Gross 70,000 lb. Fuel 4506 gal.
PERFORMANCE: Speed- Top 621 mph at 1000', 585 mph at 35,000', Cruising 529 mph, Stalling 149 mph. Combat Ceiling 40,500'. Climb 5,270'/1 min. Combat Radius 1150 miles/7600-lb. Mk 15.

A production contract for the first 12 A3D-ls was dated October 22, 1952, and the first was flown September 16, 1953, but the Pratt & Whitney J57-P-1 jets were unsatisfactory. Delays in producing proper J57-P-6B engines, and careful testing delayed deliveries, so only 20 were ready by 1955's end, and not until March 31, 1956, did the first service squadron, VAH-l, receive their aircraft. Fifty A3D-1 Skywarriors were accepted by October, with VAH-1, VAH-2, and VAH-3 detachments first deployed in 1957 on the *Forrestal, Bon Homme Richard,* and *Franklin D. Roosevelt,* respectively.

Each A3D weighed 35 tons at takeoff, compared to the eight-ton TBMs that were 1945's heaviest carrier attack planes. When the first A3Ds arrived, the 8,500-pound Mk 6 atomic bomb was the principle strategic weapon, but by 1956, a far more potent 7,600-pound Mk 15 thermonuclear bomb could be delivered on a target 1,150 miles away at a 621 mph top speed. Smaller Mk 5, 7, 12, or 91, nuclear stores were available, while conventional loads could include four 2,000-pound bombs or Mk 25 mines.

Before long the Skywarrior became known as the "Whale", because its size took up so much deck space. Since the A3Ds were the last Navy jets without ejection seats, an escape chute was provided for the crew. Another weight-saving decision was the omission of armor plate.

First delivered in glossy sea blue, they were repainted gloss gull gray and white, the Navy color standard adopted in 1955.

On June 12, 1956, the first A3D-2 was flown with J57-P-10 engines Redesignated A-3B in 1962, 164 were delivered with bomb bay provisions for an auxiliary fuel tank and two Mk 28 nuclear weapons, or up to 12,800-pounds of bombs or mines. The twin tail guns were continued, but were replaced on the last 21 aircraft by a dovetail fairing containing ECM devices and a chaff dispenser. Those A-3B bombers were delivered from April 1960 to January 1961 with a new cambered wing leading edge, inflight refueling capability, and a new ASB-7 bombing director.

DOUGLAS A3D-2 (to A-3B)
Two Pratt & Whitney J57-P-10, 10,500 lb. st
DIMENSIONS: Span 72'6" (49'2" folded), Lg. 75'8", Ht. 22'9", Wing Area 779 sq. ft.
WEIGHT: Empty 37,077 lb., Combat 61,377 lb., Gross 73,000 lb., Max. 78,000 lb. Fuel 4338+748 gal.
PERFORMANCE: Speed- Top 643 mph at s.l., 590 mph at 35,000', Cruising 528 mph. Stalling 152 mph. Combat Ceiling 41,500', Climb 6250'/1 min. Combat Radius 1380 miles/two-2050 lb. Mk. 28s.

DOUGLAS A-3B (1963 version of A3D-2)
Two Pratt & Whitney J57-P-10, 10,500 lb. st
DIMENSIONS: Span 72'6", Lg. 74'9", Ht. 22'9", Wing Area 812 sq. ft.
WEIGHT: Empty 39,620 lb., Combat 62,089 lb., Gross 73,000 lb., Max. 78,000 lb., Fuel 4338+748 gal. (+1224 gal. tanker kit)
PERFORMANCE Speed- Top 640 mph at 2500', 585 mph at 35,000' Cruising 502 mph, Stalling 143 mph. Combat Ceiling 42,300', Climb 6510'/1 min. Combat Radius 1325 miles/two 2050-lb. Mk 28s.

DOUGLAS EKA-3B

Those changes were also made to earlier aircraft, which equipped 12 heavy attack, two electronic intelligence, two photographic, and two training squadrons. After testing photographic systems in a modified A3D-1P in 1954, Douglas delivered 30 A3D-2Ps (RA-3B) first appearing in July 1958 with 12 camera mounts. ECM modifications were made by the Navy to five A3D-1s that became A3D-1Qs in 1955, and beginning in December 1958, 24 A3D-2Qs (EA-3B) were completed with four electronic countermeasures operators in the bay, instead of bombs. Twelve A3D-2Ts (TA-3B) for training ECM operators and one A3D-2W early warning model were included in the 283 Skywarriors built by 1961.

Neither high or low altitude nuclear weapons delivery ever had to be used in war by the Skywarrior, but its value in conventional warfare was seen. On March 29, 1965, VAH-2, on the *Coral Sea* , hit targets in North Vietnam. RA-3Bs flew photo missions, and two VAH-4 A-3Bs and four VAP-61 RA-3Bs were lost in combat by January 1968.

The conversion in 1966/67 to KA-3B aerial tankers (51 aircraft) and EKA-3B aircraft (39) combined ECM and tanker capability. Those tankers saved many American crews from fuel exhaustion during the war, but lost eight tankers from July 1967 to June 1973. Squadrons VQ-l and VQ-2 still used EA-3Bs until their last carrier launch on November 28, 1987.

A-4 Skyhawks

One of the most successful aircraft in Navy service was the light, simple design called Heinemann's Hot Rod, after the Douglas Chief Engineer who insisted on reversing the trend towards constantly increasing weight and cost. Designed to deliver the new tactical nuclear weapons, the single-place A-4 had a low delta wing too small to need folding on carrier decks.

A new nuclear store designed for jet fighters like the F-84, the 1,680-pound Mk 7 had been airdrop tested in Nevada on May 1, 1952, yielding 19 kilotons. At first, the

Mfr

DOUGLAS XA4D-1

only small Navy aircraft to adopt the new store were the AD-4B and F2H-2B, but Heinemann offered to build a new jet using funds from the unsuccessful A2D program. An XA4D-1 prototype was ordered June 12, 1952, and 19 developmental aircraft added on November 28.

The XA4D-1 was first flown by Robert Rahn at Edwards AFB on June 22, 1954. While the first few A4D-ls accepted, beginning in August 1954, were powered by a Wright 7200-pound thrust J65-W-2 based on the British Sapphire, a 7,700-pound thrust J65-W-4 was used on remainder of the 165 A4D-ls.

Armed with two 20-mm Mk 12 guns in the wing roots with 100 rpg, the Skyhawk had LABS provisions for a Mk 7 or even a 3,250-pound Mk 8 penetration store under the fuselage, and two wing racks for 150-gallon drop tanks or 1,000-pound conventional bombs. An ejection seat was provided, but integral armor was limited to a 29-pound head plate and thicker dural skin around the cockpit. Pilots liked the A4D-1's performance and the Navy liked the price, down to $336,000 in 1957 compared to $1,400,000 for the big A3D-2, and the Skyhawks were so much easier to handle and service aboard ship.

USN

DOUGLAS A4D-1 (to A-4A in 1962)
Wright J65-W-4, 7700 lb. st
DIMENSIONS: Span 27'6", Lg. 39'1", Ht. 15', Wing Area 260 sq. ft.
WEIGHT: Empty 8391 lb., Combat 14,826 lb., Gross 16,826 lb./2000-lb. bombs, Max. 20,578 lb. Fuel 800+300 gal.
PERFORMANCE: Speed- Top 664 mph at s.l., 605 mph at 35,000'(clean), 650 mph at s.l., 596 mph at 35,000' (2000-lb. bombs), Cruising 472 mph, Stalling 135 mph. Combat Ceiling 42,400', Climb 9,150'/1 min. Combat Radius 190 miles/2000-lb., 635 miles/1050-lb./two 150-gal. tanks.

As the Skyhawk entered service, it was usually issued to jet fighter squadrons redesignated as attack outfits, and served alongside the prop-driven Skyraider squadron on each carrier. First was VA-72, who got A4D-ls on September 27, 1956, while VMA-224 became the first Marine Skyhawk squadron in January 1957, and VA-93 made the first carrier deployment on the *Ticonderoga* in September 1957.

A J65-W-16, flight refueling probe, and a new rudder were introduced on the A4D-2, first flown March 26, 1956. The first joined the Marines' VMA-211 in September 1957, and 542 A4D-2s were completed by August 19, 1959.

New 1,050-pound Mk 12, 2,025-pound Mk 28, and 3,500-pound Mk 91 nuclear stores became available for the center pylon, as well as standard bombs from 500 to 2,000-pounds in weight, or a 300-gallon tank. Wing racks on the A4D-2 could be used for two AGM-12 Bullpup missiles, a dozen 250-pound Mk 81 conventional bombs on multiple-ejector racks, or two 300-gallon tanks; up to 5,975 pounds of bombs could be carried.

DOUGLAS A4D-2 (to A-4B)
Wright J65-W-16, 7700 lb. st
DIMENSIONS: as A-4A
WEIGHT: Empty 9146 lb., Combat 15,359 lb., Gross 17,535 lb., Max. 22,500 lb. Fuel 800+600 gal.
PERFORMANCE: Speed- Top 593 mph at s.l., 649 mph at 4000', Cruising 496 mph, Stalling 137 mph. Combat Ceiling 41,800'/Mk 28, Climb 7950'/1 min. Combat Range 1000 miles/2025-lb. Mk 28, 1650 miles/Mk 28/two 300 gal. tanks.

Another useful application was that of tanker, carrying a centerline refueling store and two 150-gallon wing tanks, with a total of 1,400 gallons of useable fuel, including the inside tanks. A receiver A4D-2 could increase its combat radius about 50% with one air refueling.

When carrier air power was still at a peak in 1958, the Navy light attack force included 12 A4D, 10 F9F-8B, and 10 FJ-4B 14-plane squadrons with jets, and 25 with piston-engine ADs. The Marines had six A4D jet and six AD attack squadrons, with 20 planes each.

A limited all-weather capability was provided on the F4D-2N, ordered September 9, 1957, with APG-53A radar and ASQ-17W fire control package. The first example flew August 21, 1958, and production got underway with the following year with the first Marine A4D-2Ns in VMA-223 by March 1960. Production continued, with final assembly at Palmdale replacing the El Segundo plant in 1962, until 638 had been delivered by 1963. The A4D-l, A4D-2 and A4D-2N became the A-4A, A-4B, and A-4C with the current designation system.

DOUGLAS A-4C (formerly A4D-2N)
Wright J65-W-16, 7700 lb. st
DIMENSIONS: Span 27'6", Lg. 40'1", Ht. 15', Wing Area 260 sq. ft.
WEIGHT: Empty 9827 lb., Combat 14,052 lb.(clean), Gross 18,443 lb., Max. 22,500 lb. Fuel 800+900 gal.
PERFORMANCE: Speed- Top 657 mph at 4000'(clean), 633 mph at 10,000'/Mk 28, Cruising 496 mph, Stalling 140 mph. Combat Ceiling 44,000' clean, 40,100'/Mk 28. Climb 8800'/1 min. clean; 7100'/1 min., 20,000'/4.5 min./Mk 28). Combat Radius 174 miles/Mk 28, 560 miles/Mk 28/two 300-gal. Combat Range 1140 miles clean, Ferry Range 1860 miles.

No A-4D model reached flight status, but on July 30, 1959, the Navy authorized two A4D-5 aircraft to be completed with new Pratt & Whitney J52 engines. The first flew July 12, 1961, adding two more under wing pylons, each holding up to 500 pounds of bombs or rocket pods.

That new model, now designated A-4E, joined VA-23 in January 1963, and 500 production models were delivered from May 1962 to April 1966. Choice of weapons included a Mk 28 or Mk 91 bomb, three AGM-12B Bullpup missiles, or up to 8,200 pounds of weapons on multiple racks.

The A-4s combat story and the new versions that experience inspired will be described in Chapter 35.

A-5 Vigilante

The fastest, and only supersonic, bomber flying from any carrier deck was the A-5 Vigilante. This two-place Mach 2 strategic bomber was begun in July 1955 as the North American NA-233, the first bomber design to take full advantage of giant carrier decks like the *Forrestal's*.

On June 29, 1956, a letter of intent was received and two YA3J-l flight articles were ordered September 17, 1956. Named the Vigilante, the A3J was entirely a product of the Columbus, Ohio factory, and flew on August 31, 1958, powered by two General Electric J79-GE-2s of 16,150-pounds thrust. Small production contracts followed in May 1956 and again in 1959 for NA-247, or A3J-l. The first 16 entered an elaborate test program, including carrier takeoffs and landings from the second giant carrier, the *Saratoga*, in July, 1960.

A 3,020-pound Mk 27 nuclear store, or an 1,885-pound configuration of the Mk 28, was ejected rearward from an internal linear tunnel, and an ASB-12 Bombing-Navigation system guided all-weather attacks to hostile targets. Two

USN

DOUGLAS A-4E (formerly A4D-5)
Pratt & Whitney J52-P-6A, 8500 lb. st
DIMENSIONS: Span 27'6", Lg. 41'4", Ht. 15', Wing Area 260 sq. ft.
WEIGHT: Empty 9624 lb., Combat 16,135 lb/ Mk 28, Gross 18,311 lb., Max. 22,950 lb. Fuel 800+900 gal.
PERFORMANCE: Speed- Top 673 mph at s.l. (clean), 636 mph at s.l./Mk 28, Cruising 498 mph, Stalling 139 mph. Combat Ceiling 44,000' clean, 40,150' /Mk 28. Climb 10,200'/1min. clean; 8250'/1 min., 20,000'/4 min./Mk 28. Combat Radius 230 miles/Mk 28 (680 miles with 2/300-gal. tanks), Ferry Range 2130 miles.

NORTH AMERICAN A-5A (A3J-l)
Two General Electric J79-GE-8, 17,000 lb. st
DIMENSIONS: Span 53', Lg. 76'6", Ht. 19'4", Wing Area 700 sq. ft.
WEIGHT: Empty 32,714 lb., Combat 48,663 lb./Mk 27, Gross 56,293 lb., Max. 62,953 lb. Fuel 2805+800+300 gal.
PERFORMANCE: Speed- Top 806 mph at s.l., 1320 mph at 40,000', Cruising 560 mph, Stalling 156 mph, Combat Ceiling 51,500', Climb 33,100'/1 min., Combat Radius 985 miles/Mk 27, 1295 miles/Mk 27/two 400-gal. tanks. Ferry Range 1800 miles.

pylons under the wings carried 400-gallon drop tanks, bombs, or air-refueling stores. Ejection seats and pressurization were provided for the tandem cockpits, and the wings, swept 37.5° on their leading edge, had droop able landing edges, boundary layer control flaps, and folded for stowage, as did the all-movable sweptback tail.

Squadron service began in June 1961 with VAH-3, the primary A3J-l training unit. The Vigilante's first full squadron deployment was with 12 VAH-7 aircraft on the nuclear carrier *Enterprise*'s first cruise in August 1962. Most of the 57 A3J-ls, made by March 1963, used the J79-GE-8 with afterburners and all were redesignated A-5As.

Additional fuel was added to the first two A3J-2s, flown on April 29, 1962, by using a faired hump behind the bombardier-navigator's cockpit and another pair of drop tanks under the wings. Redesignated A-5B in September, that type was just a transition to the RA-5C, which had a reconnaissance pod enclosing a multi-sensor system including six cameras, passive ECM and side-looking radar in a fairing below the fuselage. Fuel tanks now filled in the bomb tunnel, but if desired, any of the four drop tanks could be replaced by Mk 28 or 43 weapons.

The RA-5C first flew June 30, 1962, deliveries of 63 began in April 1963, and in the spring of 1964 they replaced the A-5As of VAH-5, which was later assigned to the new Ranger (CVA-61). Somewhat ironically, hardly

USN

NORTH AMERICAN A-5B

had the Navy received the full strategic bombing capability it had been striving for since 1946, when the Navy's strategic mission was placed entirely with the Polaris missiles on nuclear submarines. All heavy attack squadrons were redesignated RVAH for reconnaissance missions in March 1964, and 16 A-5Bs awaiting delivery and 43 remaining A-5As were returned to the factory for conversion to RA-5C configurations.

Lawson

NORTH AMERICAN RA-5C
Two General Electric J79-GE-8, 1700 lb. st
DIMENSIONS: as A-5A
WEIGHT: Empty 37,498 lb., Combat 55,617 lb., Gross 65,589 lb., Max. 79,189 lb. Fuel 3305+1600+300 gal.
PERFORMANCE: Speed- Top 783 mph at s.l. 1290 mph at 40,000', Cruising 567 mph, Stalling 154 mph. Combat Ceiling 48,400', Climb 30,000'/7.7 min. Combat Radius 944 miles/4-400-gal. tanks. Ferry Range 2050 miles.

Ten RVAH squadrons used the RA-5C, the last becoming operational in June 1964, and each carrier detachment was reduced from six to three aircraft. No guns were carried on any Vigilante, for 1,320 mph seemed enough to evade interception, but the enemy downed 18 in Vietnam with AA guns and missiles on recon missions from October 20, 1965 and December 28, 1972.

Production was reinstated at Columbus with 36 new R-5Cs delivered with J79-GE-10s from March 1969 to November 1970. Altogether, 156 Vigilantes were built, of which 140 were finished or rebuilt as RA-5Cs. All RVAH squadrons were retired from May 1974 to November 1979.

A-6 Intruder

Grumman's Intruder was the first jet attack type designed for both limited and nuclear warfare, and its accuracy and weapons capacity enabled it to replace the last prop-driven A-l from Navy service. While only half as fast as the A-5A, which never dropped a bomb in anger during three years of operational service, the A-6 would hit targets in many conflicts during 40 years of Navy service

Of eight companies submitting designs for a May 1957 design competition, Grumman was chosen in December and awarded a development contract on February 14, 1958, and a contract for the first four aircraft approved March 26, 1959. The first A2F-1 was flown April 19, 1960, by Robert Smyth, at Calverton, New York.

Four aircraft were accepted that year, four more in 1961 and monthly production deliveries begun in April 1962 were redesignated A-6A in September. Named the Intruder, the A-6A was designed for short takeoffs and landings, long-range all-weather location of targets, and low-level attack with nuclear or conventional bombs, rockets, or missiles.

Two Pratt & Whitney J52-P-6 jets were mounted below the wing roots of wings swept back 25° with full-span leading edge slats, slotted flaps, and "flaperons"(spoilers serving as ailerons). Two crewmen sat side by side, with the bombardier-navigator operating a digital integrated attack navigation system (DIANE) including search and track (APQ-92/-88) radars, computer, and two screens for presenting both the ground below and the air ahead of the aircraft. They could attack without any outside visibility at all, but no guns were provided. The wings folded upwards, and a flight refueling boom was placed above the radar nose.

Five store stations were provided beneath the A-6A, offering several weapons choices. A Mk 28 or 2,080-pound Mk 43 nuclear bomb on the center line and four 300-gallon tanks was one, another was five 1,030-pound Mk 83 conventional bombs. Five multiple racks for up to 30 Mk 81 Snakeye bombs was a 8,850-pound load that could be carried on a 2.9 hour mission with internal fuel, or 5.8 hours with refueling from an A-6A Buddy Tanker. Four Bullpup or Shrike missiles, or rocket pods, could also be handled, as well as refueling tanks.

Numerous mechanic changes resulted from the first tests, including deletion of a tailpipe tilt option, and replacing fuselage dive brakes in favor of split wingtip devices. Beginning with the 60th aircraft, APQ-112 replaced the APQ-88 tracking radar in 1964.

In February 1963, Intruders joined fleet replacement squadron VA-42, and the first operational medium attack units, VA-75 and VA-85, reached the Atlantic Fleet. Piston-engine A-ls were gradually being replaced by A-6s for all-weather operations.

Jet-propelled A-4 Skyhawks did clear weather work, while EAK-3Bs and supersonic RA-5C Vigilantes provided tanker and reconnaissance support. Navy attack planes

Lawson

GRUMMAN A-6A
Two Pratt & Whitney J52-P-6A, 8500 lb. st
DIMENSIONS: Span 53', Lg. 54'9", Ht. 16'2", Wing Area 529 sq. ft.
WEIGHT: Empty 25,298 lb., Combat 41,675 lb./5 Mk 83, 44,831 lb./Mk 43 store; Gross 48,051 lb. (close support), Max. 53,699 lb. Fuel 2344 +1477 gal.
PERFORMANCE: (at 44,831 lb.) Speed- Top 646 mph at s.l., 555 mph at 35,900', Cruising 481 mph, Stalling 133 mph. Combat Ceiling 40,250', Combat Radius 673 miles/six Mk 83, 1585 miles/Mk 43.

were concerned almost entirely with targets on land, unlike World War II emphasis on enemy warships.

Vietnam would introduce a new era for attack aviation, and of 1963's Navy attack types, only the A-6 would outlive the Cold War. That 32-year production story will be told in chapter 35.

CHAPTER 32

NAVY FIGHTERS FROM PHANTOM I TO THE CRUSADER

GRUMMAN F9F-3 Panthers from VF-51 on the *USS Boxer* in 1949 were among the first jet fighters on Navy aircraft carriers. USN

When the Navy's first two all-jet prototypes were begun, the major aircraft producers were so involved with mass production problems that responsibility for airframe development was given the small St. Louis firm founded by James S. McDonnell (1899-1980), while Westinghouse undertook development of axial-flow turbojets.

Six small engines were originally planned for each of the prototypes ordered January 7, 1943, but fortunately, development of the 1,600-pound thrust Westinghouse 19XB-2B reduced requirements to two. Each 19-inch diameter engine was buried in the wing roots on each side of the smoothly streamlined fuselage. When first flown on January 26, 1945, the type was known as the McDonnell XFD-1, but that designation was later changed to XFH-1 to avoid confusion with Douglas types, and the engine would become the Westinghouse J30.

On March 7, 1945, the first Navy jet production contract was placed; originally for 100 planes, but cut back to 60 after the war. Production FH-ls delivered from January 1946 to May 1948 had J30-WE-20s and were similar to the prototype except for additional fuel and modified tail fin. Four .50-caliber guns with 1,600 rounds were mounted in the upper nose, 92 pounds of armor protected the cockpit, and a 295-gallon drop tank could be fitted flush with the belly.

Arc

McDonnell XFD-1 (XFH-l)
Two Westinghouse WE-l9-XB-2B, 1600 lb. st
DIMENSIONS: Span 40'9", Lg. 37'3", Ht. 14'2", Wing Area 276 sq. ft.
WEIGHT: Empty 6156 lb., Gross 8626 lb., Max. 9531 lb. Fuel 260+140 gal.
PERFORMANCE: Speed- Top 487 mph at s.1., 483 mph at 20,000', Cruising 250 mph, Landing 80 mph. Service Ceiling 43,700', Climb 4960'/ 1 min. Range 540 miles normal, max. 750 miles.

Mfr

McDonnell FH-1
Two Westinghouse J30-WE-20,1600 lb. st
DIMENSIONS: Span 40'9", Lg. 38'9", Ht. 14'2", Wing Area 276 sq. ft.
WEIGHT: Empty 6683 lb., Gross 10,035 lb., Max. 11,816 lb. Fuel 375+295 gal.
PERFORMANCE: Speed- Top 479 mph at s.1., Cruising 248 mph. Landing 87 mph. Service Ceiling 41,100', Climb 4230'/1 min. Range 695 miles normal, max. 980 miles.

On July 21, 1946, a prototype became the first jet to fly from a USN carrier, the new *Franklin D. Roosevelt.* The first Navy squadron to get FH-ls was VF-17A, in July 1947, this unit becoming the Navy's first carrier qualified fighter squadron on the *Saipan* in May 1948. Other Phantoms, as McDonnell had named the jet, were used by the Marine's VMF-122 until July 1950.

Mfr

NORTH AMERICAN XFJ-1
General Electric J35-GE-1, 3820 lb. st
DIMENSIONS: Span 38'1", Lg. 33'5", Ht. 14'1", Wing Area 221 sq. ft.
WEIGHT: Empty 8182 lb., Gross 12,135 lb., Max. 14,386 lb. Fuel 465+340 gal.
PERFORMANCE: Speed- Top 533 mph at s.1., 540 mph at 16,000', Cruising 310 mph, Landing 98 mph. Service Ceiling 47,400', Climb 4690'/1 min. Range 858 miles normal, max. 1393 miles.

The next step in jet fighters began with a September 5, 1944, Navy request for a carrier-based fighter. Grumman responded, but was left for the time being to develop its F7F and F8F prop designs. Three other respondents got prototype contracts: Vought to use a J34 engine, North American a J35, and McDonnell two J34s.

Mfr

VOUGHT XF6U-1
Westinghouse J34-WE-22, 3000 lb. st
DIMENSIONS: Span 32'10", Lg. 32'10", Ht. 11'9", Wing Area 203 sq. ft.
WEIGHT: Empty 5876 lb., Gross 9306 lb., Max. 11,125 lb. Fuel 370+280 gal.
PERFORMANCE: Speed- Top 535 mph at s.1., 530 mph at 20,000', Cruising 370 mph, Landing 98 mph. Service Ceiling 40,900', Climb 4560'/1 min. Range 783 miles normal, max. 1285 miles.

Vought's first jet type was the XF6U-l Pirate, ordered from the Stratford factory December 29, 1944, and first flown October 2, 1946, at Muroc Dry Lake. A 3,000-pound thrust Westinghouse J34-WE-22 behind the pilot was fed by wing root intakes. Four 20-mm M-3 cannon with 600 rounds were grouped in the round nose, and 140-gallon drop tanks were attached to each wing tip. Like the Phantom and subsequent Navy jet fighters, the three XF6U-ls utilized retractable tricycle landing gear. Construction was of Metalite -two thin sheets of alloy bonded to a balsa wood core.

Thirty F6U-ls ordered on February 5, 1947, were to get power plants augmented with the first American afterburners. The third prototype was flown March 5, 1948, with a J34-WE-30A, whose normal thrust was increased to 4,100-pounds thrust for short periods when using the Solar afterburner, hopefully raising the top speed from 535 mph to 600 mph. But the tail had to be redesigned, numerous engine and stability problems appeared, and that prototype was destroyed in November 1948.

The first production F6U-1 from the factory now occupied by Vought in Dallas, Texas, flew June 29, 1949. Problems persisted even after the last was accepted in February 1950. On October 13, the Pirate was pronounced so submarginal in performance that combat utilization was not feasible, and these planes were never issued to an operational squadron, or flown from a carrier.

VOUGHT F6U-1
Westinghouse J34-WE-30A, 3150 lb. st (4100 lb./AB)
DIMENSIONS: Span 32'10", Lg. 37'8", Ht. 12'11", Wing Area 204 sq. ft.
WEIGHT: Empty 7320 lb., Combat 11,060 lb., Gross 12,874 lb., Fuel 420 +280 gal.
PERFORMANCE: Speed- Top 596 mph at s.l., 550 mph at 31,000', Cruising 432 mph, Stalling 113 mph. Combat Ceiling 46,300', Climb 8060'/1 min., 30,000'/5.4 min. Combat Radius 450 miles, Max. Range 1150 miles.

North American's XFJ-1 Fury featured a nose intake for the General Electric J35-GE-1 behind the pilot in the fat fuselage. Three prototypes were ordered January 1, 1945, and 100 FJ-1s on May 18, but the production contract was cut to 30. The XFJ-1 first flew September 11, 1946, and the FJ-1 on July 8, 1947, with an Allison-built J35-A-2. Production ships retained the wing tip tanks and 119 pounds of cockpit armor, but moved the dive brakes from the wings to the rear fuselage.

NORTH AMERICAN FJ-1
Allison J35-A-2, 4000 lb. st
DIMENSIONS: Span 38'2", Lg. 34'5", Ht. 14'10", Wing Area 221 sq. ft.
WEIGHT: Empty 8843 lb., Combat 12,824 lb. Gross 15,115 lb., Max. 15,600 lb. Fuel 465+340 gal.
PERFORMANCE: Speed- Top 587 mph at s.l., 515 mph at 35,000', Cruising 432 mph, Stalling 121 mph. Combat Ceiling 38,000', Climb 5600'/1 min., 35,000'/12.7 min. Combat radius 610 miles, Range 1496 miles.

Six .50-caliber guns with 1,500 rounds were mounted at the sides of the nose scoop; the last of this caliber on Navy fighters, for 20-mm cannon have been standard since that time. The Air Force continued using the .50-caliber M-3 gun, however, until the faster-firing M-39 20-mm gun became available in 1953.

The Fury went to VF-5A in November 1947, which made its first carrier trials aboard the *Boxer* in March 1948, later became VF-51, and used the FJ-1 until October 1949. While the FJ-1 was the fastest plane yet used on carriers, it required catapult takeoffs, engine overhaul every ten flight hours, and lacked the ejection seat now so necessary for safety.

The Phantoms, Pirates, and early Furies were a transitional phase between props and jets to demonstrate that jets could operate from carriers. But the F4U Corsair's superior endurance and capacity and the F8F Bearcat's rapid climb kept propeller-driven fighters on carriers until fully capable jet fighters could join the fleet.

Navy Jet Fighters Go to War

During 1947 and 1948, four new fighter types appeared and were ordered into production. The public knew them as the Banshee, Panther, Skyknight, and Cutlass, and the Korean War outbreak found them available for Navy operations.

A twin-engine enlargement of the Phantom, the McDonnell XF2H-1 Banshee was powered by 3,000-pound thrust Westinghouse J34-GE-22s. The first of three prototypes ordered March 2, 1945, was flown January 11, 1947, at St. Louis by Robert M. Edholm.

Fifty-six F2H-1s, ordered May 29, 1947, and delivered from August 1948 to July 1949, were similar to the prototypes except for elimination of stabilizer dihedral. Four 20-mm guns with 600 rounds were mounted low in the nose, the wings folded upward for stowage, and an ejection seat was provided. They were first delivered in March 1949 to VF-171, which qualified on the *Midway* in August.

McDonnell F2H-1
Two Westinghouse J34-WE-22, 3000 lb. st
DIMENSIONS: Span 41'7", Lg. 40'2", Ht. 14'6", Wing Area 294 sq. ft.
WEIGHT: Empty 9794 lb., Combat 14,239 lb., Gross 16,200 lb., Max. 18,940 lb. Fuel 526 gal.
PERFORMANCE: Speed- Top 587 mph at s.l., 563 mph at 20,000', Cruising 351 mph, Landing 101 mph. Service Ceiling 48,500', Climb 7380'/1 min. Range 1278 miles.

In June 1948, a contract was made for the F2H-2, which had 3,150-pound thrust J34-WE-34s, more internal

Mfr

McDonnell F2H-2
Two Westinghouse J34-WE-34, 3250 lb. st military
DIMENSIONS: Span 44'10", Lg. 40'2", Ht. 14'6", Wing Area 294 sq. ft.
WEIGHT: Empty 11,146 lb., Combat 15,640 lb., Gross 17,742 lb., Max. 22,312 lb. Fuel 877+400 gal.
PERFORMANCE: Speed- Top 582 mph at s.l., 532 mph at 35,000', Cruising 501 mph, Stalling 121 mph. Combat Ceiling 49,500', Climb 7300'/1 min., 30,000'/6.7 min. Combat Radius 620 miles/drop tanks, 305 miles/1580-lb. load. Combat Range 1475 miles/ two 200 gal. drop tanks.

fuel, and a 200-gallon tank on each wing tip. In addition to the usual four 20-mm guns, two 500-pound bombs or eight 5-inch rockets could be carried. From November 1949 to April 1952, 334 F2H-2s were accepted, plus 14 F2H-2Ns with APS-19 radar added in the nose for night fighting and first flown February 3, 1950.

After the *Essex* was provided with steam catapults, VF-172's F2H-2s could join combat in Korea on August 23, 1951. Three more squadrons were involved in the war's last year, but two Marine fighter squadrons using F2H-2s did not enter combat.

First flown October 12, 1950, and last delivered on May 28, 1952, 88 F2H-2P Banshees were the Navy's first jet reconnaissance types with six cameras in an extended nose, instead of guns. The most active Banshees were the F2H-2Ps of VMJ-1 at Pohang, which flew photo missions from March 1952 to the war's end.

The F2H-2Bs were 27 F2H-2s modified to become the first Navy fighters to carry an Mk 7 tactical or Mk 8 penetration nuclear bomb under the port wing. Delivery tactics were developed with these planes by VX-3 and VX-5, and the first deployment was by four F2H-2Bs of VC-4 on the *Franklin D. Roosevelt* in August 1952.

USN

McDonnell F2H-2N

The F2H-3 was an all-weather fighter with APQ-41 radar in the nose, internal fuel, droppable tip tanks, four

McDonnell F2H-2P

McDonnell F2H-2B
Two Westinghouse J34-WE-34, 3250 lb. st
DIMENSIONS: As F2H-2
WEIGHT: Empty 11,268 lb., Combat 18,126 lb., Gross 22,409 lb. with Mk 7, 23,693 lb. with Mk 8. Fuel 1216 gal.
PERFORMANCE: Speed- Top 579 mph at s.l., 565 mph at 10,000', Cruising 465 mph, Stalling 136 mph. Combat Ceiling 40,500', Climb 5400'/1 min. Range 1209 miles/Mk 7, 1163 miles/Mk 8.

20-mm M-12 guns with 600 rounds, two pylons for 500-pound bombs, and eight for 250-pound bombs or rockets, while the F2H-4 was similar, but for Hughes APG-37 radar. Acceptances began June 1952 on 250 F2H-3s and 150 F2H-4s, with the last delivered October 31, 1953. Banshee production at St. Louis totaled 895.

McDonnell F2H-3
Two Westinghouse J34-WE-34, 3250 lb. st
DIMENSIONS: Span 41'9", Lg. 48'2", Ht. 14'6", Wing Area 294 sq. ft.
WEIGHT: Empty 13,183 lb., Combat 18,367 lb. Gross 21,013 lb. clean, Max. 25,214 lb. Fuel 1102+340 gal.
PERFORMANCE: Speed- Top 580 mph at s.1., 524 mph at 35,000', Cruising 495 mph, Stalling 132 mph. Combat Ceiling 46,600', Climb 6000'/1 min. Combat Radius 478 miles clean, 720 miles/2 drop tanks, 380 miles/1,580 lb. load. Range 1716 miles/2 drop tanks.

Banshees retired from Navy fighter squadrons in September 1959, and 39 transferred F2H-3s served the Canadian Navy from November 1955 to September 1962.

McDonnell F2H-4

Grumman Panthers

The Grumman Panther was a single-engine single-seater, but the design had begun with an April 22, 1946, contract for a two-seat XF9F-1 night fighter with four 1,500-pound thrust Westinghouse J30s. Searching for a more efficient way of getting the power required, Grumman decided to import from Britain the 5,000-pound thrust Rolls-Royce Nene (the engine also sold to Russia for the MiG-15 prototype), and in August 1946 the new Grumman G-79 design was submitted to the Navy.

The original XF9F-1 contract was changed to three single-engine prototypes on October 9, 1946. A Nene engine from Rolls-Royce arrived in time for the first XF9F-2 to fly November 21, 1947, piloted by Corwin "Corky" Meyers at Bethpage. The third prototype was flown August 16, 1948, as the XF9F-3 with an Allison J33-A-8 of 4,600-pound normal thrust. That engine was similar in size to the Nene, and was planned as a second-source engine in case the program to produce Nenes, as the J42 by Pratt & Whitney, was unsuccessful.

GRUMMAN XF9F-2
Rolls-Royce Nene, 5700 lb. st military
DIMENSIONS: Span 35'3", Lg. 37'8", Ht. 11'3", Wing Area 250 sq. ft.
WEIGHT: Empty 7107 lb., Gross 10,840 lb., Max. 12,442 lb. Fuel 357+240 gal.
PERFORMANCE: Speed- Top 594 mph at s.1., 573 mph at 20,000', Cruising 350 mph, Stalling 100 mph, Climb 7700'/1 min., Range 1100 miles max.

Grumman's first jet production contract called for 47 F9F-2s with the Pratt & Whitney J42-P-6, and 54 F9F-3s with Allison J33-A-8s. The first example flown was an F9F-3 on January 17, 1949, while the F9F-2 was not available for tests until August 17. Since the engines were interchangeable, all the F9F-3s were later converted to F9F-2s

USN

GRUMMAN F9F-3 of VF-51 on *USS Boxer*

after their completion in October 1949. One F9F-3 was flown with an experimental four gun turret, as shown in the accompanying photograph.

By August 1951, 520 more F9F-2s were made. Like the prototype, they were armed with four 20-mm M-3 nose guns with 760 rounds. Permanent 120-gallon wing tip tanks carried auxiliary fuel, which could be jettisoned in emergencies from outlets in the rear. Fuselage brakes under the nose reduced speed in descent, 140 pounds of armor and an ejection seat were provided, while wings folded upwards for stowage.

When F9F-3s replaced VF-51's FJ-ls in May 1949, that unit became the first Panther squadron, making its first operations from the *Boxer* in September. The Navy's first jet combat victories, over two Yak-9s, were scored July 3, 1950, in Korea, when 30 F9F-2s from VF-51/52 on the *Valley Forge* provided top cover for that carrier's AD-4 and F4U-4B piston-engine attack missions. On November 9, 1950, an F9F-3 of VF-111 from the *Philippine Sea* became the first Navy jet to down an enemy jet, a swept-wing MiG-15 that used the same Rolls-Royce engine design.*

When racks were added for two 1000-pound bombs and six 5-inch rockets or 250-pound bombs, the Panther became the F9F-2B. On December 10, 1950, Marine squadron VMF-311 began ground support strikes with 24 F9F-2Bs. The Navy's first bombing attack by a jet was by two VF-191 F9F-2Bs on April 2, 1951.

Mfr

GRUMMAN F9F-2

Pratt & Whitney J42-P-8, 5000 lb. st military, 5750 lb. WE

DIMENSIONS: Span 38', Lg. 37'3", Ht. 11'4", Wing Area 250 sq. ft.

WEIGHT: Empty 9303 lb., Combat 14,235 lb. Gross 16,450 lb., Max. 19,494 lb. Fuel 683+240 gal.

PERFORMANCE: Speed- Top 575 mph at s.1., 529 mph at 35,000', Cruising 487 mph, Stalling 105 mph. Combat Ceiling 43,400', Service Ceiling 44,600', Climb 6000'/1 min. Combat Radius 535 miles. Combat Range 1353 miles, 558 miles/two 1000-lb. bombs +six 5" rockets.

*Russian writers confirm LCDR William Amen's victory and the death of Capt. Mikhail Grachkov of the 139th GvIAP.

Mfr

GRUMMAN F9F-3 with gun turret

Mfr

GRUMMAN F9F-4
Allison J33-A-16, 6900 lb. st
DIMENSIONS: Span 38', Lg. 38'10", Ht. 12'3", Wing Area 250 sq. ft.
WEIGHT: Empty 10,042 lb., Combat 15,264 lb., Gross 17,671 lb., Max. 21,250 lb. Fuel 1003 gal.
PERFORMANCE: Speed- Top 593 mph at s.1., 547 mph at 35,000', Cruising 495 mph, Stalling 131 mph. Service Ceiling 43,300', Climb 5600'/1 min. Combat Range 1324 miles, 904 miles/eight 5"rockets.

WL

GRUMMAN F9F-5
Pratt & Whitney J48-P-6, 6250 lb. st military, 7000 lb./WE
DIMENSIONS: Span 38', Lg. 37'8", Ht. 12'3", Wing Area 250 sq. ft.
WEIGHT: Empty 10,147 lb., Combat 15,359 lb., Gross 17,766 lb., Max. 21,245 lb. Fuel 1003 gal.
PERFORMANCE: Speed- Top 604 mph at s.1., 543 mph at 35,000', Cruising 481 mph, Stalling 131 mph. Service Ceiling 42,800', Climb 6000'/1 min. Combat Range 1300 miles, 886 miles/six 5" rockets.

A Pratt & Whitney J48-P-2 (based on the Rolls-Royce Tay) in the F9F-5 replaced the Allison A33-A-16 used on the F9F-4. Two prototypes, both converted from F9F-2s with longer fuselages and new higher pointed tails, became an XF9F-5 flown December 21, 1949, which preceded the XF9F-4 flown July 5, 1950. They were produced in parallel after March 1951 on contracts inflated by the Korean War, with 109 F9F-4s accepted by April 1952 and 619 F9F-5s and 36 F9F-5P photo Panthers by December 1952.

The Navy accepted 1,388 Panthers, which were 715 of the 826 Navy and Marine Corps jets deployed to Korea, and flew about 78,000 combat sorties.

Douglas Skyknight

The Navy's first jet-propelled night fighter was the two-place Douglas XF3D-1 Skyknight. A mid-wing monoplane with a pair of Westinghouse 3,000-pound thrust J34-WE-22 jets low on the fuselage sides, the XF3D-l had the then usual four 20-mm guns with 800 rounds behind and below the nose scanner.

Three prototypes were ordered April 3, 1946, and the first XF3D-1 flew March 23, 1948, piloted by Russell Thaw at El Segundo. Twenty-eight F3D-ls were purchased on May 11, and the first flew February 13, 1950, with J34-WE-34 jets. They were operated by VC-3 at NAS Moffett Field and VMF(N)-542 at El Toro NATC.

USN

DOUGLAS XF3D-1

Bodie

DOUGLAS F3D-1
Two Westinghouse J34-WE-34, 3250 lb. st
DIMENSIONS: Span 50', Lg. 45'5", Ht. 16'1", Wing Area 400 sq. ft.
WEIGHT: Empty 14,890 lb., Combat 21,245 lb. Gross 24,485 lb., Max. 27,362 lb. Fuel 1350+300 gal.
PERFORMANCE: Speed- Top 443 mph at 14,000', 478 mph at 33,000', Cruising 428 mph, Stalling 117 mph. Service Ceiling 34,000', Climb 3040'/1 min. Range 1068 miles normal, max. 1318 miles.

DOUGLAS F3D-2
Two Westinghouse J34-WE-36, 3400 lb. st
DIMENSIONS: As F3D-1
WEIGHT: Empty 15,107 lb., Combat 21,904 lb. Gross 25,414 lb. clean, 27,681 lb./2 tanks, Max. 28,800 lb./4000 lb. bombs. Fuel 1350+300 gal.
PERFORMANCE: Speed- Top 549 mph at s.l., 554 mph at 10,000', 516 mph at 35,000', Cruising 463 mph, Stalling 114 mph. Combat Ceiling 39,400', Climb 4430'/1 min. Combat Radius 575 miles clean, 679 miles/2 drop tanks, 345 miles/4000 lb. load. Range 1364 miles normal, max. 1540 miles.

Over 1,000 pounds of Westinghouse APQ-35 radar included a scanner dish within the fiberglass nose and a warning device in the tail cone. The radar operator and pilot sat side by side in a pressurized cockpit from which they could escape at high speeds by bailing out through a tunnel to the fuselage's bottom. Fittings beneath the folding wings could accommodate two 150-gallon drop tanks or 2,000-pound bombs.

Larger 4,600-pound thrust Westinghouse J46s had been specified for F3D-2s ordered on September 26,1949. Since these engines were unavailable when the first F3D-2 flew February 14, 1951, the J34-WE-36 was substituted on the 237 F3D-2 Skyknights built by October 1953. Forward protection consisted of a 70-pound armor plate and a 105-pound flack-resistant windshield.

While the faster single-seat Banshee was used on carriers, the Skyknight, except for test and training work, mostly served the Marines. One Korean-based squadron, VMF(N)-513 got F3D-2s to replace the F7F-3N, and beginning on November 3, 1952, downed six enemy aircraft -the best night fighter record of the war, although this was credited more to the APQ-35 radar than to the F3Ds modest agility. Night bombing attacks on enemy positions were added in 1953.

The Navy's first intercept by a Sparrow I radar beam-riding missile was an F6F drone hit on December 3, 1952, by a Sparrow from an XF3D-1M modified from the second prototype. Two F3D-lM and 16 F3D-2M Skyknights, modified to carry APQ-36 radar and four Sparrow Is instead of guns, completed VX-4 missile tests at Point Mugu and VMF(N)-542 became the first Sparrow missile squadron in 1954.

DOUGLAS F3D-2M

Electronic countermeasures were added to 35 Skyknights modified to F3D-2Q configurations, redesignated EF-10B in 1962, and flown with a jammer pod in Vietnam patrols by VMCJ-1 from April 1965 to 1969. Other aircraft retired to trainers were designated F3D-2T. The last Marine EF-10B retired in May 1970.

Vought Cutlass

This period's most radical design was the Vought XF7U-l Cutlass, a tailless single-seater with two Westinghouse J34 units and twin rudders midway out on the 38-degree swept-back wing. Pressurized cockpit, ejection seat, and ailevators (combined ailerons and elevators) were used.

Mfr

VOUGHT F7U-1
Two Westinghouse J34-WE-32, 3370 lb. st military, 4900 lb./AB
DIMENSIONS: Span 38'8", Lg. 39'7", Ht. 11'10", Wing Area 496 sq. ft.
WEIGHT: Empty 12,837 lb., Combat 17,707 lb. Gross 20,038 lb. clean, Max. 23,387 lb./ 2 tanks. Fuel 971+500 gal.
PERFORMANCE: Speed- Top 693 mph at s.l., 626 mph at 35,000', Cruising 460 mph, Stalling 112 mph. Combat Ceiling 50,000', Climb 15,100'/1 min., 30,000'/2.8 min. Combat Radius 334 miles clean, 560 miles/2 tanks. Range 1635 miles max.

The short, stubby wings had an aspect ratio of 3:1 and leading-edge slots.

Mfr

VOUGHT XF7U-1

At rest, the Cutlass had a nose-high attitude due to the long nose wheel strut, a feature designed to maintain a high angle of attack for the wing during takeoff and landing. The Cutlass was also the first Navy fighter designed from the beginning for engine afterburners, and the first swept-wing, tailless carrier plane. Its performance was phenomenal for its design period, but it would take too many years to become operational.

Vought engineers began their design in June 1945, choosing the swept-wing tailless shape to avoid compressibility problems, and their Chief Aerodynamicist has stated that this decision was made before German research on the type was available. Six companies responded to a Navy day fighter design competition announced January 25, 1946, but the Vought V-346A design submitted April 15, 1946, won a contract on June 25 for three XF7U-1 prototypes.

First flown September 29, 1948, by Robert Baker at Patuxent, Maryland, the XF7U-1 was powered by two 3,000-pound thrust XJ34-WE-32 engines, and armed with four 20-mm guns below the cockpit. An F7U-1 contract had been awarded July 28, 1948, but delayed by Vought's move from Stratford to Dallas, the first flew March 1, 1950. Four of the 14 F7U-ls were completed that year, but two crashed before delivery, as had all three prototypes, killing three Vought test pilots. A September 1949 order for 88 F7U-2s had been canceled and serious problems discouraged the Navy from attempting any squadron use of the F7U-l.

But the Korean War led the Navy to persist in developing the high performance potential, and on August 21, 1950, the F7U-3 with J46 engines with afterburners was ordered. A heavier aircraft with more fuel, strengthened landing gear with extended front strut, and two wing pylons for 1,000-pound bombs or 250-gallon drop tanks, the F7U-3 could add a belly pack for 32 2.75-inch rockets. APG-30 radar in the nose aimed four Mk 12 20-mm guns, with 720 rounds, that had been moved to upper lips of the engine air intakes offered.

Mfr

VOUGHT F7U-3
Two Westinghouse J46-WE-8B, 3960 lb. st military, 5800 lb./AB
DIMENSIONS: Span 39'9", Lg. 44'3", Ht. 14'7", Wing Area 535 sq. ft.
WEIGHT: Empty 18,262 lb., Combat 24,741 lb., Gross 28,173 lb., Max. 35,000 lb. Fuel 1320+500 gal.
PERFORMANCE: Speed- Top 696 mph at s.1., 608 mph at 35,000', Cruising 518 mph, Stalling 137 mph. Service Ceiling 46,500', Climb 11,150'/1 min. Range 696 miles normal, max. 817 miles.

Since the Westinghouse engine deliveries were delayed, the first 16 F7U-3s were provided with Allison J35-A-29s without afterburners. The first example flew December 20, 1951, but the J46-WE-8As were not available until 1953, and accidents and mechanical problems delayed fleet introduction until February 2, 1954, when F7U-3s reached VF-81. Deliveries of 180 F7U-3s ended March 9, 1955.

Four Sparrow I beam-riding missiles, or 1,000-pound bombs, could be carried by the F7U-3M, which had APQ-51B radar and additional fuel. Two were converted from F7U-3s, and first flew July 12, 1954. Because of their bomb capacity, F7U-3M squadrons were redesignated as attack units. Vought delivered the last of 98 new F7U-3Ms August 12, 1955, and VA-83 made the first overseas deployment (on *Intrepid* to the Mediterranean) of a Navy missile squadron in March 1956, when 11 Cutlass squadrons were operating.

Twelve unarmed F7U-3P photo planes in 1954/55 never became operational, but are included in the Cutlass total of 307. Some Navy fighter squadrons had been redesigned attack (VA) units in anticipation of fighter-bomber equipment. An order for 146 A2U-l attack versions of the Cutlass, however, was canceled in November 1954, and standard fighter models were issued to three such squadrons.

PMB

VOUGHT F7U-3M
Two Westinghouse J46-WE-8, 5725 lb. st AB
DIMENSIONS: as F7U-3
WEIGHT: Empty 19,488 lb., Combat 26,968 lb. & Gross 32,975 lb. with 4 AAM, Max. 37,000 lb. Fuel 1568+520 gal.
PERFORMANCE: (with four Sparrows) Speed- Top 678 mph at s.1., 615 mph at 35,000', Cruising 449 mph, Stalling 139 mph. Combat Ceiling 45,400', Climb 10,500'/1 min. Combat Range 650 miles/four Sparrows.

Mfr

VOUGHT F7U-3P

Bedeviled with a high accident rate, the big Vought fighters were withdrawn from squadron service after November 1957, but they did serve to introduce the Fleet to the new, complex breed of airplanes that the future would bring to carrier service.

Douglas Skyray

The first new prototype to appear after the outbreak of war in Korea was the XF4D-1 Skyray, a single-engine, single-place interceptor ordered December 16, 1948, after Douglas engineers led by Ed Heinemann had developed a delta wing design influenced by Dr. Lippisch's investigations in Germany.

Mfr

DOUGLAS XF4D-l

DOUGLAS F4D-1 of VF(AW)-3 at San Diego

First flight tested on January 21, 1951, at Edwards AFB, both prototypes were temporarily powered by a 5,000-pound thrust Allison J35-A-17 until the first Westinghouse XJ40-WE-6s became available in July 1952. The unusual aircraft shape required such a long testing cycle that carrier qualification trials were not attempted on the *Coral Sea* until October 1953.

An XJ-40-WE-8 of 16,000-pounds thrust with afterburner enabled the stripped second prototype flown by LCDR James Verdin to establish a 753-mph record on October 3, 1953; the first time an aircraft designed for carriers held the world's speed record.

Because of production difficulties suffered by Westinghouse's power plant, the Navy decided in July 1953 to install Pratt & Whitney J57s in production Skyrays. Robert Rahn flew the first F4D-1 June 5, 1954, with a J57-P-2, later replaced by the J57-P-8. Armament included four 20-mm M-12 guns with 70 rounds each in the wings, four heat-seeking Sidewinders, or a volley of 56 2.75-inch rockets from four pods. Armor consisted of a single 60-pound plate in front of the pilot.

A clean F4D-1 set a climb record of 39,370 feet in 111 seconds and 49,212 feet in 156 seconds, but since a clean Skyray had only one hour of flight, takeoffs were usually made with two 300-gallon drop tanks. Modifications gradually increased combat weight from 19,100 pounds in 1956 to 22,008 in 1958. Production of 419 Skyrays was completed at El Segundo on December 22, 1958.

Douglas Skyrays were first delivered on April 16, 1956, to an operational squadron, VC-3, later redesignated VF(AW)-3. Stationed at San Diego from 1958 to 1963, VF(AW)-3 was the only Navy squadron attached to the Air Defense Command. On practice intercepts, its F4D-ls carried an electronic navigation store on a central pylon, a

DOUGLAS F4D-1
Pratt & Whitney J57-P-8 or -8B, 10,200 lb. st military, 16,000 lb./AB
DIMENSIONS: Span 33'6", Lg. 45'8", Ht. 13', Wing Area 557 sq. ft.
WEIGHT: Empty 16,024 lb., Combat 22,008 lb. clean. Gross 27,116 lb./4 AAM, 2/300-gal. tanks. Max. 28,000 lb., Fuel 640+600 gal.
PERFORMANCE: Speed- Top 722 mph at s.1., 652 mph at 35,000', Cruising 520 mph, Landing 132 mph. Combat Ceiling 52,100', Climb 18,300'/1 min. Combat Radius 174 miles/300 gal. tanks, 352 miles/600 gal tanks. Range 1150 miles max.

pair of 12 2.75-inch rocket packs, two 300-gallon drop tanks, and two Sidewinder missiles on the outer pylons.

The next unit to get F4D-ls was VMF(AW)-115, which flew them longer than any other unit. This Marine squadron's experience included crisis deployments to Taiwan (1958) and Guantanamo Bay (1962), as well as carrier service, like most Navy Skyray squadrons. Their last F4D-ls (called F-6As since 1962), retired February 29, 1964, leaving a reputation for fast climb, high ceiling, speed, and a good APQ-50A radar, but also as a difficult plane to fly.

The F4D-2N had the same Lippisch-inspired wing plan, but was designed for supersonic speeds with a thinner wing, longer fuselage, and more fuel. Two ordered October 16, 1953, and nine added March 11, 1955, were redesignated F5D-1 Skylancers before the first flight April 21, 1956. Pilot Robert Rahn reached supersonic speed using the same J57-P-8 as on an F4D.

DOUGLAS F5D-1
Pratt & Whitney J57-P-8, 10,200 lb. st military, 16,000 lb./AB
DIMENSIONS: Span 33'6", Lg. 53'10", Ht. 14'10", Wing Area 557 sq. ft.
WEIGHT: Empty 17,444 lb., Combat 25,495 lb. Max, 29,122 lb. Fuel 1333 gal.
PERFORMANCE: Speed- Top 748 mph at s.1., 790 mph at 35,000', Stalling 155 mph. Combat Ceiling 49,400', Climb 20,790'/1 min. Range 1226 miles.

Two active-homing Douglas Sparrow II (AAM-N-3) missiles under the wings, guided by APQ-64 radar and Aero X24A fire control, were the planned armament. An internal armament bay could add 72 two-inch rockets or four 20 mm guns.

Production versions with General Electric J79 engines were expected to reach a supersonic 1,098 mph, but the X24A system was unready and the F5D-ls program was canceled in November 1956 after only four were completed. All went to NACA at Moffett Field. Instead, Vought's F8U-1 Crusader was favored for the Navy fighter squadrons.

Grumman Cougar

The MiG-15's appearance in the Korean War accelerated the Navy's interest in swept wings to delay the effects of compressibility encountered at sonic or near-sonic speeds. Difficulties adapting this design style to carrier-deck landings had delayed development until Grumman's G-93 proposal to add swept back wings and tail to the standard Panther fuselage.

Three XF9F-6 prototypes were ordered converted from F9F-5s on March 2, 1951, and Fred Rowley flew the first September 20 at Bethpage. Powered by a J48-P-6, the XF9F-6 raised critical Mach number from .79 to .86, but the original ailerons had to be replaced by spoilers on the wing's top surface. Wing fences were added to smooth airflow, and all-movable horizontal tail surfaces replaced the conventional elevators.

The first swept-wing fighter actually in carrier service was the production F9F-6 Cougar first delivered December 28, 1951. Four 20-mm guns with 190 rpg, and 180 pounds of pilot armor were provided, and the power plant was a J48-P-8, although an Allison J33-A-16 was used on the F9F-7. A pair of 150-gallon drop tanks or 1,000-pound bombs could be carried under the wings.

GRUMMAN F9F-6
Pratt & Whitney J48-P-8, 6250 lb. st
DIMENSIONS: Span 34'6", Lg. 40'11", Ht. 12'4", Wing Area 300 sq. ft.
WEIGHT: Empty 11,255 lb., Combat 16,244 lb., Gross 18,450 lb., Max. 21,000 lb. Fuel 919+300 gal.
PERFORMANCE: Speed- Top 654 mph at s.l., 590 mph at 35,000', Cruising 541 mph, Stalling 128 mph. Combat Ceiling 45,000', Climb 6750'/1 min. Combat Range 932 miles.

From February 1952 to June 1954, 646 F9F-6 and 168 F9F-7 fighters and 60 F9F-6P reconnaissance models were delivered. Cougars joined VF-32 in November 1952, and Cougars became the most numerous Navy fighter, used by 20 squadrons. Most of those with J33 engines had them replaced with J48s in service.

GRUMMAN F9F-7
Allison J33-A-19, 6250 lb. st
DIMENSIONS: as F9F-6
WEIGHT: Empty 11,255 lb., Combat 16,577 lb., Gross 18,905 lb. Fuel 919+300 gal.
PERFORMANCE: Speed- Top 628 mph at s.l., 559 mph at 35,000', Cruising 509 mph, Stalling 130 mph. Range 1157 miles.

Grumman's G-99 design became the F9F-8 flown December 18, 1953, with a J48-P-8A, more internal fuel, an inflight refueling probe in the nose of a longer fuselage, and cambered leading edge extensions, instead of the slats of the previous models. Sidewinder I missiles were first successfully fired on September 11, 1953, from a F9F-6, so four

USN

GRUMMAN F9F-8
Pratt & Whitney J48-P-8A, 7250 lb. st
DIMENSIONS: Span 34'6", Lg. 41'9", Ht. 12'3", Wing Area 337 sq. ft.
WEIGHT: Empty 11,866 lb., Combat 17,328 lb., 19,738 lb./4 AIM-9B, Gross 20,098 lb., Max. 24,763 lb. Fuel 1063+300 gal.
PERFORMANCE: Speed- Top 647 mph at 2000', 593 mph at 35,000', Cruising 516 mph, Stalling 132 mph. Combat Ceiling 42,500', Climb 5750'/1 min. Combat Radius 443 miles. Range 1208 miles normal, max. 1312 miles.

could supplement the usual four 20-mm guns, and were first deployed overseas with the F9F-8s of VA-46 on the *Randolph* in July 1956.

USN

GRUMMAN F9F-8B
Pratt & Whitney J48-P-8A, 7250 lb. st
DIMENSIONS: As F9F-8
WEIGHT: Empty 11,866 lb., Combat 18,035 lb., Gross 22,575 lb., Max. 24,763 lb. Fuel 1063+300 gal.
PERFORMANCE: Speed- Top 638 mph at s.l., 640 mph at 5000', Cruising 475 mph, Stalling 142 mph. Service Ceiling 41,700', Climb 5410'/1 min. Range 1053 miles normal, 1295 miles Mk. 7 +one 150-gal. tank.

Arnold

GRUMMAN F9F-8P

Grumman delivered 601 F9F-8s from February 1954 to March 1957, many of them becoming the F9F-8B for Marine and Navy attack squadrons with an LABS for a 1,125-pound Mk 7 nuclear bomb, or six rocket pods. However, that special store was seldom fitted and their pilots practiced with conventional bombs, until those squadrons got more suitable A4Ds. The last Cougars were 110 seven-camera F9F-8Ps that served photographic squadrons until February 1960, and 400 F9F-8T two-place trainers whose completion brought Cougar production to an end in February 1960 with 1,985 delivered. That trainer version, as the TF-9J, remained in service until 1974.

McDonnell Demon

As Navy fighters increased in weight and complexity, they became more dependent on their power plants for success. The failure of the Westinghouse J40 selected for the McDonnell XF3H-1 Demon almost doomed that single-seat fighter with swept wings and tail.

MCDONNELL XF3H-1

Two prototypes ordered September 30, 1949, and a program for 150 Demon interceptors was planned as early as March 1951. Production aircraft were to be all-weather fighters, known as the F3H-1N, with larger radar and more fuel. While gross weight would increase from 20,000 to 29,000 pounds, a more powerful J40-WE-24 turbojet was expected to compensate for the increase.

McDonnell F3H-lN
Westinghouse J40-WE-22, 6500 lb. st military, 10,900 lb. /AB
DIMENSIONS: Span 35'4", Lg. 59', Ht. 14'7", Wing Area 442 sq. ft.
WEIGHT: Empty 18,691 lb., Combat 26,085 lb. Gross 29,998 lb., Fuel 1506 gal.
PERFORMANCE: Speed- Top 616 mph at s.1., 628 mph at 10,000', Cruising 553 mph, Stalling 129 mph. Service Ceiling 44,000', Climb 10,900'/1 min. Combat Range 1130 miles.

After the XF3H-1 prototype flew August 7, 1951, with a 6,400-pound thrust XJ40-WE-6, the same engine also powered the second prototype until a J40-WE-8 with afterburner became available in January 1953. A hopeful Navy had increased the production program to 528 aircraft with more to be built by Temco, but the J40 continued to suffer difficulties. In April 1952, McDonnell recommended using the Allison J71-A-2 instead, and in November the Navy decided that turbojet would be used, beginning with the 61st Demon.

By September 1953, it became apparent that the earlier F3H-lN would have to be content with the 10,900-pound thrust available from the J40-WE-22. The first F3H-lN was flown on January 24, 1953, with provisions for APG-30 radar and four 20-mm guns. The handicap of the additional weight soon became apparent, and November the contract was reduced, and in July 1955, after the fourth pilot was killed in a series of 11 accidents that had destroyed six F3H-lNs, the type was permanently grounded.

The engine's power was judged insufficient for the airframe's weight. All survivors of the first 60 Demons could be used only for mechanics' ground training, except for two converted by installation of Allison J-71s to test the F3H-2 standard. Failure of the F3H-lN had cost the Navy some $200 million, mostly expended on the unsuccessful J-40 engine.

The first converted F3H-2N, flown on January 11, 1955, had a 14,400-pound thrust Allison J71-A-2 and the wing area increased by a wider chord at the roots. An APG-51 radar was fitted in front of the cockpit between the large air intakes on each side, and four 20-mm guns with 600 rounds were below the cockpit. The wings could hold two 282-gallon drop tanks, had leading edge slats, and folded upwards.

McDonnell F3H-2N

First flown April 29, 1955, 142 F3H-2Ns entered squadron service in March 1956 with VF-14, which sailed on the giant *Forrestal*'s first overseas deployment in 1957. The first of 80 F3H-2Ms was flown on August 23, 1955, and VX-4 at Point Mugu began testing the weapons system replacing guns with four Sperry Sparrow I (AAM-N-2) beam-riding missiles aimed by APG-51B radar.

Demon development matured when delivery began in July 1957 of the 239 definitive F3H-2 configurations that introduced four Raytheon Sparrow III radar-homing missiles (AAM-N-6) for distant targets and used the four guns for

USN

McDonnell F3H-2 (F-3B after 1962**)**
Allison J71-A-2B, 10,000 lb. st military, 14,400 lb. st AB
DIMENSIONS: Span 35'4", Lg. 59', Ht. 14'7", Wing Area 519 sq. ft.
WEIGHT & PERFORMANCE: Empty 21,287 lb., Fuel 1506+564 gal. With 4 Sparrow IIIs: Combat 31,839 lb. Gross 38,997 lb. Speed- Top 693 mph at s.1., 624 mph at 35,000', Stalling 114 mph. Service Ceiling 27,150', Climb 12,410'/1 min. Combat Range 1239 miles. With 2 Sidewinders: Combat 29,020 lb., Gross 33,424 lb. Speed- Top 716 mph at s.1., 643 mph at 35,000', Stalling 112 mph. Service Ceiling 35,050', Climb 14,350'/1 min. Combat Range 1180 miles.

PMB

McDonnell F3H-2M (with Sparrow I)
Allison J71-A-2B, 14,400 lb. st AB
DIMENSIONS: Span 35'4", Lg. 59', Ht. 14'7", Wing Area 519 sq. ft.
WEIGHT: Empty 20,322 lb., Combat 27,859 lb., Gross 33,112 lb. Fuel 1506 gal.
PERFORMANCE: Speed- Top 706 mph at s.1., 662 at 35,000', Cruising 523 mph, Stalling 128 mph. Service Ceiling 47,800', Climb 14,450'/1 min. Combat Range 943 miles.

close work. Two heat-seeking Sidewinders (AAM-N-7) could replace the Sparrows if the climb advantages of light-weight condition were desired. Six underwing stations could carry bomb or rocket stores, and inflight refueling equipment allowed extended range.

McDonnell delivered the last of 519 Demons on November 17, 1959, and they served 22 fleet fighter squadrons with two training squadrons, as well as the evaluation squadrons on each coast. The F3H-2, F3H-2M, and F3H-2N were redesignated F-3B, MF-3B, and F-3C in 1962, and the last F-3B was retired from VF-161 in August 1964.

North American's Fury

In the hasty search for a quickly available swept-wing fighter, the Navy wanted a carrier version of the North American F-86 Sabrejet whose Air Force pilots had defeated MiG-15s in Korea. Contracts were approved for the NA-181, designated FJ-2, on February 10, 1951, and for three prototypes on March 8.

Built in Los Angeles as modified F-86Es, an XFJ-2B Fury was flown December 27, 1951, with four 20-mm guns, and two unarmed XFJ-2s, first flown February 19, 1952, with carrier arrestor hook and extended nose wheel. Flight deck tests from the *Coral Sea* were rather marginal, and it was decided to give the FJ-2s to the Marines, while the FJ-3 optimized for carrier work was ordered April 18, 1952.

Mfr

NORTH AMERICAN XFJ-2B

Production FJ-2s were built at Columbus, Ohio, and were heavier than the F-86F because of their folding wings, carrier gear, and four 20-mm Mk 12 guns with 600 rounds. Deliveries of 200 began in November 1952, but began so slowly that VMF-122 didn't get all their planes

USN

NORTH AMERICAN FJ-3
Wright J65-W-4B, 7650 lb. st
DIMENSIONS: Span 37'1", Lg. 37'7", Ht. 13'8", Wing Area 302 sq. ft.
WEIGHT: Empty 12,205 lb., Combat 15,669 lb., Gross 17,189 lb., Max. 21,876 lb. Fuel 559+400 gal.
PERFORMANCE: Speed- Top 681 mph (670 mph/2 AAM-9B) at s.1., 623 mph (612 mph) at 35,000', Cruising 526 mph, Stalling 133 mph. Combat Ceiling 49,000', Climb 8430'/1 min. Combat Radius 230 miles, 645 miles/two 200-gal. tanks, Combat Range 990 miles, ferry 1784 miles.

until January 1954 and was deployed on the *Coral Sea* in 1955. When production completed in September the FJ-2 served six Marine squadrons, the first common use of an Air Force fighter since the P-12/F4B series.

USMC

NORTH AMERICAN FJ-2
General Electric J47-GE-2, 6000 lb. st
DIMENSIONS: Span 37'1" (22'7" fold.), Lg. 37'7", Ht. 13'7", Wing Area 288 sq. ft.
WEIGHT: Empty 11,802 lb., Combat 15,813 lb. Gross 18,791 lb. Fuel 435+400 gal.
PERFORMANCE: Speed- Top 676 mph at s.1., 602 mph at 35,000', Cruising 518 mph, Stalling 132 mph. Combat Ceiling 41,700', Climb 7230'/1 min. Combat Radius 311 miles, Combat Range 990 miles.

A Wright J65, license-built British Sapphire engine, replaced the J47 on the first FJ-3 Fury, which was a modified FJ-2 flown with the J65 on July 3, 1953, and the production FJ-3 flew on December 11. An enlarged nose intake was provided, with four 20-mm Mk 12 guns with 648 rounds, an 88-pound front plate and a 52-pound back plate for armor. Pylons for two 200-gallon drop tanks allowed a combat radius of 645 miles, which could be extended to 1,237 miles by air refueling thru a probe on port wing.

The first Navy Fury squadron to join a Carrier Air Group was VF-173, which received FJ-3s in September 1954, and went aboard the *Bennington* the following May. Another squadron, VF-21, became the first aircraft to land on the first giant carrier, the *Forrestal,* in January 1956.

During 1955, the wing slats of earlier FJ-3s were replaced by an extended leading edge with more fuel, although no designation change was made. Four additional store stations added bomb and rocket pods to the Fury's weapons. Beginning in February 1956 with the 345th aircraft, the last 194 added two Sidewinder missiles and were labeled FJ-3M. These were first deployed in the Pacific in August 1956 with VF-211. By August 1956, 539 FJ-3 or -3Ms had been built for 18 Navy and three Marine squadrons.

NORTH AMERICAN FJ-4
Wright J65-W-16A, 7700 lb. st
DIMENSIONS: Span 39'1", Lg. 36'4", Ht. 13'11", Wing Area 339 sq. ft.
WEIGHT: Empty 13,210 lb., Combat 17,845 lb. clean, Gross 20,130 lb., Max. 23,700 lb. Fuel 840+400 gal.
PERFORMANCE: Speed- Top 680 mph at s.1., 631 mph at 35,000', Cruising 534 mph, Stalling 139 mph. Combat Ceiling 46,800', Climb 7660'/1 min. Combat Radius 518 miles, Range 1485 miles clean.

A complete redesign of the Fury, the FJ-4 had a thinner wing and larger fuel capacity. An October 1953 contract provided two prototypes (NA-208) first flown October 28, 1954, with the J65-W-4, and 150 FJ-4s (NA-209) appearing February 1955 with the J65-W-16A. Four 20-mm guns and four pylons for Sidewinders, bombs, or drop-tanks were used. A probe on the left wing allowed inflight refueling.

NORTH AMERICAN FJ-4B
Wright J65-W-16A, 7700 lb. st
DIMENSIONS: As FJ-4
WEIGHT: Empty 13,778 lb., Combat 18,936 lb, Gross 21,221 lb/4 AAM-9B, 22,396 lb./4 500-lb. bombs, Max. 23,812 lb./ /2 AAM-9B +2 200-gal. tanks.
PERFORMANCE: Speed- Top 654 mph at s.l., 617 mph at 35,000', Cruising 526 mph, Stalling 143 mph. Combat Ceiling 44,500', Climb 6890' /1 min. Combat Radius 478 miles/four AAM-9B, 489/four 500-lb. bombs, 840 miles/two AAM-9B+two 200-gal. tanks.

The FJ-4B was an attack version with an LABS system for delivering a Mk-7 weapon under the left wing and an extra pair of speed brakes beneath the tail. Six underwing stations could be used for 4,000-pounds of bombs, rocket pods, or up to five Bullpup air-to-surface missiles, first deployed overseas in April 1959. This Fury model first flew December 4, 1956, with 222 built for Pacific Fleet light attack squadrons by May 1958, when production of 1,112 Navy Furies at Columbus ended.

Seven Marine FJ-4 squadrons replaced FJ-2s and FJ-3s in 1956-57, while ten Navy and three Marine light attack squadrons got the FJ-4B, beginning with VMA-212 in April 1957 and then VA-214 on the *Hornet.* A "Buddy Tanker" method of inflight refueling was introduced in 1958, using two stores under the wing to extend drogues so another Fury's wing probe could replenish its fuel. As more compact Mk 12 and 28 nuclear weapons entered the inventory, FJ-4B pilots practiced loft bombing until they were replaced by September 1962.

GRUMMAN XF10F-1
Westinghouse J40-WE-8, 10,900 lb. st (WE-6 used on tests)
DIMENSIONS: Span 50'7" (36'8" swept), Lg. 54'5", Ht. 16'3", Wing Area 467 (450) sq. ft.
WEIGHT: Empty 20,426 lb., Gross 31,255 lb., Max. 35,450 lb., Combat 27,451 lb. Fuel 1585+600 gal.
PERFORMANCE: Speed- Top 710 mph at s.1., 632 mph at 35,000', Cruising 478 mph, Stalling 112 mph. Combat Ceiling 45,800', Climb 13,350'/1 min., 35,000'/4.5 min. Combat Radius 633 miles, 858 miles/two 300-gal. tanks, Combat Range 2090 miles.

Navy's fighter strength had reached a peak at the end of 1956, when 79 Navy and Marine squadrons protected the Fleet and its bases. Only one stray fighter squadron still used the straight-wing F9F-5, although most F9F-6s had already been relegated to the Reserves, replaced by seven F9F-8, 16 F9F-8B, five F7U-3 , three F7U-3M, three FJ-2, eight FJ-3, 12 FJ-3M, and one FJ-4 squadron.

All-weather fighter squadrons on December 31, 1956, still included nine F2H-3 and five F2H-4 straight-wing Banshee squadrons, while two F3H-2M, four F3H-2N, and four F4D-l squadrons had current production types. Altogether, 14 different types were represented in this extravagant variety, which in eight years would be replaced by just two supersonic types.

CONVAIR XFY-1
Allison XT40-A-14, 5332 hp +1296 lb. st
DIMENSIONS: Span 27'8", Lg. 32'3", Tail Span 21'8", Wing Area 355 sq. ft.
WEIGHT: Empty 11,139 lb., Combat 13,250 lb., Gross 14,250 lb. Fuel 576 gal.
PERFORMANCE: Speed- Top 474 mph at s.1., 489 mph at 24,000'. Combat Ceiling 37,600', Climb 9980'/1 min., 20',000'/3.4 min., 35,000'/8.9 min. Loiter time 1 hour at 35,000'.

CONVAIR XFY-1 in transition to level flight

Grumman's Jaguar

While it may have seemed that the Navy was buying every fighter type offered during the '50s, there were prototypes too radical for production, but representing unique approaches to fighter development. Grumman stepped out first with the first American fighter with variable-sweep wings, the XF10F-1 Jaguar.

When its wings were extended for takeoff and landing, they had a 50'7" span and 13.5-degree sweep, but in high-speed flight they moved back to 36'8" span and 52.5-degree sweep. This feature was a way to give fast swept-wing aircraft the low-speed stability necessary for carrier operations. The fighter's equipment included APQ-41 radar, four 20-mm guns under a cockpit protected by 346 pounds of armor, and wing points for two 2,000-pound bombs, rocket pods, or 300-gallon drop tanks.

Two XF10F-1 prototypes ordered April 7, 1948, were to have delta wings and a J42 engine, but the J40 engine and variable sweep wing were included by August 18, 1950, when 12 were ordered, and 100 more scheduled for Korean war programs. The first flight was made at Edwards AFB by Corky Meyer on May 19, 1952, with a 6,800-pound thrust J40-WE-6, since the WE-8 specified was not yet available. The high "all flying" T-tail proved unsatisfactory and had to be replaced after 17 flights.

The production contract was terminated on April 1, 1953, because the F3H-1 seemed to offer a less complicated solution for the all-weather mission, and the second prototype was never completed. Grumman, however, had found that variable sweep could work and would use it on their successful F-14 nearly 20 years later; so the 30 million dollars spent on the XF10F-1 project was not entirely without result.

Vertical Takeoff

Alternatives to carrier-based fighters were explored by the vertical takeoff & landing (VTOL) Convair XFY-1 and Lockheed XFV-1, and the water-based Convair XF2Y-1. The only Navy single-seat fighters built by these firms, they were a radical departure from previous concepts, and the Navy invited bids in September 1950.

A VTOL fighter could operate from cargo ship deck to beach, provid-

LOCKHEED XFV-1
Allison XT40-A-14, 5332 +1296 lb. st
DIMENSIONS: Span 27'5", Lg. 37'6", Wing Area 246 sq. ft.
WEIGHT: Empty 11,599 lb., Combat 15,000 lb. Gross 16,221 lb., Fuel 508 gal.
PERFORMANCE: (Est.) Speed- Top 562 mph at s.l., 595 mph at 35,000'. Combat Ceiling 43,600', Climb 10,820'/1 min., 30,000'/5 min. Loiter time 1.17 hour at 35,000'.

ing defense and close support when carriers were unavailable. Powered by an Allison T-40A-14 turning 16-foot diameter, six-bladed contra-props, the delta-wing XFY-l took off vertically from four small wheels at the wing and fin tips, swung into horizontal flight, and hung on its props to back down to a vertical landing. Design armament of four 20-mm guns in wing-tip pods was not actually installed.

Three prototypes ordered March 31, 1951, were test vehicles for a fighter version planned with a more powerful T54 engine and a design speed of 610 mph. Actually, only the first XFY-l flew. J.F. Coleman piloted the first free flight at Brown Field, San Diego, on August 1, 1954, and on November 2, Coleman made the first successful transition from vertical to horizontal flight, returning to the vertical posture to back down to a landing.

The power plant, however, was inadequate to lift a useful payload and backing into the ground was never an attractive prospect. Fearing engine failure on their so-called "Pogo", Convair itself suggested project termination after some 65 flights. Another discouraging factor was the elaborate ground equipment required.

Built at the same time, for the same purpose, and with the same engine, Lockheed's XFV-l had short straight wings with gun pods at the tips, and the intended landing wheels at the tips of a four-fin tail. The XFV-l, however, never made a vertical takeoff or landing, but was tested on an ungainly temporary landing gear by H.R. Salmon, who began taxi trials in December 1953 and flew from a horizontal posture on June 16, 1954.

Every succeeding test was made the same way, the engine never being trusted enough to remove the auxiliary gear and try the tail-down attitude. Performance data accompanying the picture is that expected for the fighter version with a 6,825 hp XT40-A-16, but only the XT40-A-14 was actually available. The Allison XT40 turboprop, like the Westinghouse J40 turbojet was a failure on every aircraft that tried to use it.

As the first of the Navy's new super-carriers entered service, the need to overcome VTOL's multitude problems paused. Lockheed's XFV-1 project was closed on June 16, 1955, and Convair's XFY-1 ended August 1.

Convair Sea Dart

The only water-based jet fighter ever built in America, the XF2Y-l Sea Dart was designed to operate from coastal waters bays, and lakes. It floated on a water-tight belly until enough speed was built up to rise on its retractable twin hydroskis.

Two prototypes based on an October 25, 1950, Navy specification had been ordered January 19, 1951, and a mockup inspected by August 28, 1952, when an initial production order for 12 was given. Anticipated top speed was 724 mph at sea level and 648 mph at 35,000'.

After taxi runs tests begun December 14, 1952, E. D. Shannon made the first XF2Y-l Dart flight from San Diego Bay on April 9, 1953. While that flight used Westinghouse J34-WE-32 engines, they were replaced by the J46-WE-12B with afterburners in 1954.

The second Sea Dart, YF2Y-1, was a Mach .99 aircraft on the level and on August 3, 1954, exceeded Mach 1 in a shallow dive, the only supersonic seaplane ever flown. But in March 1954, the contract had been cut back to five aircraft, and the YF2Y-1 was destroyed in flight on November 4, 1954. While another YF2Y-1 flew on March 4, 1955, the last two were not flown. A fixed single-ski configuration was tested on the original XF2Y-l in 1957.

CONVAIR XF2Y-l Sea Dart
Two Westinghouse J46-WE-12B, 4020 lb. st military, 5725 lb. st/AB
DIMENSIONS: Span 33'8", Lg. 52'7", Ht. 16'2", Wing Area 568 sq. ft.
WEIGHT: Empty 15,900 lb, Gross 21,200 lb. Fuel 615 gal.
PERFORMANCE: Speed- Top 648 mph at 35,000', Stalling 136 mph. Service Ceiling 44,000', Climb 17,100'/1 min.

CONVAIR YF2Y-l
Two Westinghouse J46-WE-12B, 5725 lb. st
DIMENSIONS: Span 35'4", Lg. 51'1", Ht. 16'1", Wing Area 568 sq. ft.
WEIGHT: Empty 16,725 lb, Gross 24,374 lb. Fuel 1000 gal.
PERFORMANCE: Tests incomplete.

Armament on production F2Y-1s was to be 44 2.75-inch rockets in two retractable launchers within the hull behind the pilot, but all Sea Darts were completed as unarmed research aircraft. The program was abandoned because the Navy never approved an operational requirement for a seaplane fighter, as other weapons had a higher budget priority.

The First Supersonic Carrier-based Fighter

The Navy's first supersonic fighter was the Grumman Tiger, which had small, thin swept wings and the first application of area rule design with an indented fuselage to reduce drag.

Begun in January 1953 as Model G-98, and first ordered April 27, the first Tiger was flown July 30, 1954, by Corky Meyer. Three aircraft were accepted in 1954 as F9F-9s with a Wright J65-W-6, and two more accepted before 39 remaining on that contract were redesignated F11F-l in April 1955. A longer nose replaced the short nose of early aircraft and boundary air splitters were added to the intakes.

Mfr

GRUMMAN F9F-9
Wright J65-W-6, 7700 lb. st
DIMENSIONS: Span 31'7", Lg. 44'1", Ht. 13'3", Wing Area 250 sq. ft.
WEIGHT: Empty 13,307 lb., Gross 18,375 lb., Max. 23,459 lb. Fuel 914+300 gal.
PERFORMANCE: Speed- Top 736 mph at s.1., 681 mph at 35,000', Cruising 536 mph, Stalling 153 mph. Service Ceiling 41,900', Climb 11,350'/1 min. Range 1318 miles. (preflight data)

Afterburners tested at Edwards on the second article allowed Mach 1 speeds, but were unsatisfactory until production J65-W-18 engines with afterburners became available in March 1956. Four 20-mm Mk 12 guns with 500 rounds were paired under the intakes and four Sidewinders could be attached under the wings. Two 150-gallon drop tanks or 1,000-pound bombs could be carried on the inner pylons.

The last two planes on that contract were completed with the General Electric YJ79-GE-3, designated F11F-lF Super Tiger, and first flown on May 25, 1956. Despite reaching Mach 2 speeds above 35,000 feet, and setting a World's Altitude Record of 75,550 feet on April 12, 1958, the powerful F11F-1F version was unsuccessful in finding customers. Germany, Switzerland, Canada, and Japan considered that fighter, but it was the Lockheed F-104 that won all those sales in 1958.

USN

GRUMMAN F11F-l (F-11A after 1962)
Wright J65-W-18, 7400 lb. st, 10,500 lb. /AB
DIMENSIONS: Span 31'7", Lg. 46'11", Ht. 13'3", Wing Area 250 sq. ft.
WEIGHT: Empty 14,330 lb., Gross 21,280 lb, 22,160 lb/4 Sidewinders. Max. 27,468 lb. Fuel 1049+300 gal.
PERFORMANCE: Speed- Top 753 mph at s.1., 727 mph at 35,000', Cruising 578 mph, Stalling 118 mph. Service Ceiling 41,900', Climb 18,000'/1 min. Range 1125 miles clean, 900 miles/4 AIM-9.

Mfr

GRUMMAN F11F-lF
General Electric YJ79-GE-3, 9600 lb. st, 15,000 lb. /AB
DIMENSIONS: Span 31'8", Lg. 48', Ht. 13'10", Wing Area 250 sq. ft.
WEIGHT: Empty 16,457 lb., Gross 26,086 lb., Fuel 914+300 gal.
PERFORMANCE: Speed- Top 1325 mph at 35,000'. Service Ceiling 50,300', Climb 8950'/1 min., Combat Range 1136 miles.

Since the J79 engine seemed heavy for the airframe, and had double the fuel consumption of the J65, the Navy retained the Wright engine for 157 more F11F-ls made with a nose lengthened to hold APG-30 radar, a probe that was extended for inflight refueling, and additional internal fuel.

Tigers did not enter squadron service until March 1957 with VA-156, which would be redesignated VF-111 in

1959. Seven squadrons flew Tigers with a good safety record, but when the final F11F-l was delivered January 23, 1959, Grumman had no Navy fighter in production for the first time in its history.

Surpassed in performance by Vought's F8U-l Crusader, Tigers were retired from first-line service in April 1961. The Blue Angels aerobatic team from 1957 to 1969 displayed the Grumman's maneuverability.

Bulinski

GRUMMAN F-11A of "Blue Angels"

The Last Gunfighter, the F-8 Crusader

The first operational carrier-based fighter in the world to exceed 1,000 mph (Mach 1.5) was the Vought F-8 Crusader. This velocity was combined with the low speed limits for flight deck operation by using shoulder-mounted, thin swept-wings with two-position incidence, pivoting on the rear spar so that their angle of attack could be increased seven degrees to get more lift for takeoff or landing.

A Navy requirement for a supersonic single-seat day fighter issued to eight manufacturers on August 19, 1952, resulted in a June 29, 1953, contract for three XF8U-l prototypes designed by the Dallas company team led by John R. Clark. A Pratt & Whitney J57-P-11 of 14,800-pound thrust with a titanium-shrouded afterburner, the power plant of the first-generation supersonic Air Force fighters, gave the Crusader a much easier life than its troublesome F6U and F7U ancestors.

John W. Konrad passed Mach 1 on the first XF8U-l flight at Edwards AFB on March 25, 1955, less than ten years after World War II. A second prototype began tests on June 12, while the third airframe was used for static structure tests.

Production F8U-ls were first flown on September 20, 1955, went to VF-32 and VX-3 for Fleet Indoctrination (FIP) in 1956, and VF-32 became fully operational on March 25, 1957. A 16,000-pound thrust J57-P-12 or P-4, was used and an inflight refueling probe, required on all Navy fighters since September 1955, retracted into the port side. Four 20-mm Mk 12 guns with 500 rounds were mounted behind and below the pilot, together with 16 2.75-in. rockets in a retractable launching pack. Unfortunately, the fighter pitched upward when the pack was lowered, spoiling accuracy, so

Mfr

VOUGHT XF8U-l

the company recommended eliminating the rocket packs in March 1958; they were finally deactivated by June 1960. In the meantime, racks for two Sidewinder missiles were added to fuselage sides.

The 318 F8U-ls built in Dallas had APG-30 gun-ranging radar, which was replaced by an APS-67 search scanner in the F8U-lE flown September 3, 1958, and 130 were accepted by June 1959. Five cameras replaced armament in the F8U-lP first flown December 17, 1956, with 144 accepted by March 1960. Major John Glenn flew one from Los Angeles to New York in 3 hours, 22 minutes on July 16, 1957; the first supersonic transcontinental flight. Low-level missions over Cuba in October 1962 by VFP-62 and VMCJ-2 proved the ballistic missile threat.

A J57-P-16, air scoops for the afterburner, and twin narrow fins under the fuselage for stability, distinguished the F8U-2, first flown as an F8U-l conversion in December 10, 1957. Vought flew the first production F8U-2 on August 20, 1958, and 187 delivered by September 1960 could carry four Sidewinders on the side racks. They entered service in 1959 with VMF-333 and VF-84.

USN

VOUGHT F8U-lP (RF-8A)

VOUGHT F8U-l (F-8A since 1962**)**
Pratt & Whitney J57-P-4, 10,200 lb. st military, 16,000 lb./AB
DIMENSIONS: Span 35'8", Lg. 54'3", Ht. 13'4", Wing Area 375 sq. ft.
WEIGHT: Empty 15,513 lb., Combat 23,659 lb., Gross 26,969 lb., Max. 27,468 lb. Fuel 1273 gal.
PERFORMANCE: Speed- Top 733 mph at s.l., 1013 mph at 35,000', Cruising 570 mph, Stalling 135 mph. Service Ceiling 42,300' (full load), Combat Ceiling 51,500', Climb 20,000'/1 min., Combat Radius 398 miles, Combat Range 1474 miles.

Although the McDonnell Phantom became the Navy's first choice for later procurement, the Crusader remained in production, because the twin-engine Phantom was built for the giant carriers, and the older *Essex*-class carriers still in use required the smaller Voughts.

Under the 1962 designation system, the F8U-l, F8U-lE, and F8U-2 became the F-8A, F-8B, and F-8C Crusaders. The F-8D was first flown February 16, 1960, as the F8U-2N, and introduced an APQ-83 radar and AAS-15 infrared scanner for limited all-weather capability, a Vought-developed autopilot and a J57-P-20. More internal fuel replaced the rocket pack, and the four guns and four Sidewinders were retained on 152 F-8Ds accepted from June 1960 to January 1962. Speed in clean condition increased to Mach 1.9 from the prototype's Mach 1.5.

The last new Crusader for the Navy was the F-8E, first flown at Dallas on June 30, 1961, as the F8U-2NE with new APQ-94 radar. The main addition to the previous model made on 286 F-8Es delivered from October 1961 to September 3, 1964, was a pylon under each wing.

These could handle a 2,000-pound bomb, or six 250-pound bombs, or a Bullpup AGM-12 missile, and, when eight Zuni Mk 32 rocket tubes were attached to the fuselage side stations, up to 5,000 pounds of ground-support weapons were available. One F8U-1NE was converted to an F8U-lT two-place trainer in February 1962.

The French Navy ordered 42 F-8E (FN) Crusaders especially fitted with boundary layer air control, double-

VOUGHT F8U-2 (F-8C)
Pratt & Whitney J57-P-16, 10,700 lb. st military, 16,900 lb./AB
DIMENSIONS: As F8U-l
WEIGHT: Empty 16,483 lb., Combat 24,347 lb., Gross 27,810 lb., 27,938 lb./2 AIM-9. Fuel 1273 gal.
PERFORMANCE: Speed- Top 736 mph at s.l., 1105 mph at 35,000', 1062 mph/2 AIM-9, Cruising 570 mph, Stalling 137 mph. Service Ceiling 41,700', Combat Ceiling 52,000', Climb 21,700'/1 min., Combat Radius 368 miles/2 AIM-9, Combat Range 1490 miles, 1375 miles/2 AIM-9.

VOUGHT F8U-2N (F-8D)
Pratt & Whitney J57-P-20, 10,700 lb. st military, 18,000 lb. AB
DIMENSIONS: as F8U-l
WEIGHT: Empty 17,541 lb., Combat 25,098 lb., Gross 28,765 lb., Max. 29,500 lb. Fuel 1348 gal.
PERFORMANCE: Speed- Top 764 mph at s.l., 1228 mph/guns only,(1194 mph/missiles) at 35,000', Cruising 570 mph, Stalling 162 mph. Service Ceiling 42,900', Combat Ceiling 53,400', Climb 31,950'/1 min. Combat Radius 453 miles/ missiles, Combat Range 1737 miles/guns only.

droop leading edge, and enlarged horizontal tail surfaces to improve landings on the two smaller French carriers. Provided with J57-P-20A engines, and provision for French Matra radar missiles as well as Sidewinders, the first F-8E (FN) flew June 26, 1964, and completion of 42 by January 25, 1965, brought the Crusader total to 1,261.

About 25 Navy and 12 Marine fighter squadrons had received Crusaders when America joined the war in Vietnam. The first to sortie over Vietnam were RF-8A (formerly F8U-lP) Crusader detachments of Light Photographic Squadron VFP-63. Operating continuously from 1964 to 1972, that squadron lost 20 planes and 12 pilots to enemy action. RF-8As were rotated back to Vought for modernization to the RF-8G configuration. They reentered service in October 1965 with an 18,000- pound thrust (with afterburner) J57-P-22, ventral fins, improved navigation and electronics equipment, drop tanks, and four cameras. Top speed was improved from 985 to 1,000 mph, despite a weight increase.

Marine F-8Es operated from Da Nang on close-support missions, but the carrier-based Navy units flew escorts for attack planes. Their first victory was a MiG-17 downed with a Sidewinder from a VF-211 F-8E on June 12, 1966, and 18 more were claimed by VF-211, VF-162, VF-24 (F-8C), VF-51 (F-8H), VF-53, and VF-111 by September 19, 1968. Sidewinders were credited with 15, and guns three, of those kills. The 88 Crusaders lost to enemy action were hit by anti-aircraft missiles and guns, except for three downed by MiG-17s.

VOUGHT F-8E

During the war, Vought remanufactured 448 Crusaders to update their equipment and extend their service life: 73 RF-8Gs were followed by 89 F-8H fighters rebuilt from F-8Ds provided with the J57-P-420 engine, and first flown July 17, 1967. Weapons options included four Sidewinders, or eight 250 or 500-pound bombs.

More extensive work was done on 136 F-8Js in 1968, which were F-8Es with the same P-20As and modified controls used on the French version, as well as adding points for two 300-gallon drop tanks, six 500-pound bombs, or eight Zuni 5-inch rocket packs. Less extensive modernization was made on 87 F-8K and 61 F-8L models, converted from F-8B and C aircraft in 1969 for Reserve stations.

The last Marine F-8 squadron retired its Voughts in December 1975, and first-line Navy fighter squadron service ended March 2, 1976,with the return of the *Oriskany*'s VF-191/194 Crusaders from the last *Essex*-class carrier's

VOUGHT F-8E displays weapons options

VOUGHT F-8H

Pratt & Whitney J57-P-420, 12,400 1b. st military, 19,600 lb./AB
DIMENSIONS: Span 35'8", Lg. 54'3", Ht. 15'9", Wing Area 375 sq. ft.
WEIGHT: Empty 18,824 lb., Combat 25,801 lb. clean, 27,124 lb./4 AIM-9, Gross 29,468 lb. clean, Max. 34,280 lb./8-500 lb. bombs. Fuel 1348 gal.
PERFORMANCE: Speed- Top 768 mph at s.l., 1156 mph at 36,000', Cruising 557 mph, Stalling 166 mph. Service Ceiling 42,000', Combat Ceiling 51,600', Climb 23,300'/1 min. Combat Radius 642 miles clean., 160 miles/8 Mk 81 bombs. Combat Range 1427 miles clean.

final deployment. VFP-63's RF-8Gs remained active at Miramar NAS until 1982. Reserve squadrons flew F-8J fighters until August 1982 and photo Crusaders until March 1987. The Philippines became the second foreign country to get Crusaders with the arrival of 25 reconditioned F-8Hs in 1978.

Lawson

VOUGHT F-8J
Pratt & Whitney J57-P-20A, 12,400 1b. st military, 18,000 lb./AB
DIMENSIONS: Span 35'8", Lg. 54'6", Ht. 15'9", Wing Area 375 sq. ft.
WEIGHT: Empty 19,751 lb., Combat 30,352 lb. (4 AIM-9D), Gross 31,318 lb., Max. 36,587 lb. Fuel 1348+300 gal.
PERFORMANCE: Speed- Top 750 mph at s.l., 1086 mph at 35,000', Cruising 551 mph, Stalling 178 mph. Combat Ceiling 47,800', Climb 21,900'/1 min. Combat Radius 587 miles/4 AIM-9D+2 tanks. Combat Range 1576 miles/4 AIM-9D, Combat Range 838 miles/6 Mk 82 bombs.

New Designations

Promulgation of the current aircraft designation system on September 18, 1962, is a convenient topic to end this chapter on Navy fighter types entering service since 1945. The new system assigned numbers to Air Force and Navy fighters in the same series, and had no manufacturer's symbol.

Most of the first eleven numbers allotted were to Navy fighters already retiring from first-line service; the most notable exception was the F-4 in production for both Air Force and Navy, which will be in chapter 36. New designations of fighter aircraft available in 1962 are given here.

New	Old	New	Old
F-1C	FJ-3	RF-8A	F8U-1D
MF-1C	FJ-3M	TF-8A	F8U-1T
DF-1D	FJ-3D	F-8B	F8U-1E
F-1E	FJ-4	F-8C	F8U-2
AF-1E	FJ-4B	F-8D	F8U-2N
F-2C	F2H-3	F-8E	F8U-2NE
F-2D	F2H-4	F-9F	F9F-6K2
F-3B	F3H-2	QF-9G	F9F-6
MF-3B	F3H-2M	F-9H	F9F-7
F-3C	F3H-2N	F-9J	F9F-8
F-4A	F4H-1F	AF-9J	F9F-8B
F-4B	F4H-1	TF-9J	F9F-8T
RF-4B	F4H-1P	RF-9J	F9F-8P
F-5A	N-156	F-10A	F3D-1
F-6A	F4D-1	F-10B	F3D-2
YF-7A	YF2Y-1	EF-10B	F3D-2Q
F-8A	F8U-1	F-11A	F11F-1

CHAPTER 33

ASW: SEARCH AND ATTACK

GRUMMMAN AF-2W and AF-2S
A "Hunter-Killer" ASW team from VS-25, near San Diego on October 31, 1950.

Since World War II, Navy carrier anti-submarine warfare squadrons have had three aircraft types built for ASW operations: the Grumman AF-2/3 Guardian, the Grumman S-2 Tracker, and the Lockheed S-3 Viking. None carried guns, for they were equipped to find and destroy an enemy usually underwater.

The Guardian began in August 1944 as the Grumman G-70 designed to replace the TBM Avenger, and three prototypes were ordered February 19, 1945. A 2,100-hp R-2800-34W powered the XTB3F-1, with the pilot and radar man sitting side-by-side over an internal weapons bay that accommodated two torpedoes or 4,000 pounds of bombs. The wings had provision for two 20-mm guns, wells for the outward-retracting main wheels, and folded backward in typical Grumman fashion. Instead of a rear gunner, the prototype had a Westinghouse l9XB jet ejecting 1,600-pounds thrust from a tail nozzle, providing an estimated top speed of 356 mph for short bursts.

GRUMMAN XTB3F-1
Pratt & Whitney R-2800-34W, 2100 hp and Westinghouse WE-19-XB-2B, 1600 lb. st
DIMENSIONS: Span 60', Lg. 42'1", Wing Area 549 sq. ft.
WEIGHT: Empty 13,306 lb., Gross 19,065 lb. normal, Max. 21,465 lb. Fuel 370 gal.
PERFORMANCE: Speed- Top 356 mph at s.1., Cruising 160 mph. Service Ceiling 35,500', Climb 3600'/1 min. Range 1280 miles normal, 2880 miles max.

That jet unit was never tested, for just six days after the XTB3F-l's first flight on December 19, 1946, the company received a stop-work order. The Navy saw little need for a torpedo-bomber in the post-war environment. But while hostile surface fleets did not present a substantial threat, submarines certainly did, and the most successful force against them, outside the range of land-based patrol planes, had been the Avengers based on escort carriers.

Adapting the XTB3F to ASW configuration was proposed, using R-2800-46W engines and without the jet's high fuel consumption. A February 20, 1947, Navy order established the remaining two prototypes as ASW aircraft, and a mockup was ready by April 28. The next prototype, the XTB3F-lS with a big belly radome for an APS-20 radar, but no armament, first flew October 1, 1948. On January 12, 1949, the XTB3F-2S flew fitted for offensive weapons in the bomb bay and under the wings.

A production order placed May 3, 1948, was for 30 aircraft designated as AF attack types, divided between search and bombing roles. Powered by a 2,400-hp R-2800-48W, production Guardians came in two versions, AF-2W and AF-2S, with the pilot up front and two radar men in the back. The first AF-2W, flown November 17, 1949, had an APS-20A and added an ECM APR-9 operator, and was followed by the first flight on December 14 of the AF-2S.

They worked in pairs; a four-place AF-2W flew at low altitudes searching the surface for a submarine periscope or snorkel. When a target located, an accompanying AF-2S pinpointed it with APS-31 radar under the starboard wing; if surfaced at night, the target could be illuminated with the ARQ-2A searchlight under the port wing. A submerged target was located with 16 sonobuoys dropped in a pattern to send out a sonar signal that rebounds from a submarine hull and is automatically transmitted back to the operator

The three-place AF-2S could attack with a 1,167-pound Mk 34 or 1,327-pound Mk 41 torpedo from the weapons bay. Four depth charges and up to six rockets carried under the wings were aimed by a periscope bombsight, if the two drop tanks were not needed.

Seven Navy TBM-3E squadrons were designated VS (anti-submarine search) units in April 1950 to fly ASW mis-

USN

GRUMMAN AF-2S
Pratt & Whitney R-2800-48, 2300 hp takeoff and 3500'
DIMENSIONS: Span 60' (24' folded), Lg. 43'5", Ht. 16'7", Wing Area 549 sq. ft.
WEIGHT: Empty 14,658 lb., Combat 18,123 lb., Gross 20,298 lb. normal, Max. 22,565 lb. Fuel 420+300 gal
PERFORMANCE: Speed- Top 265 mph at s.1., 275 mph at 4000', Cruising 166 mph at 1500', Stalling 88 mph. Service Ceiling 22,900', Combat Ceiling 21,600', Climb 2300'/1 min. Combat Range 915 miles normal, 1140 miles max.

sions from the four light and four escort carriers then active. As the largest single-engine aircraft operated from carriers, Guardians entered service with VS-24 at Norfolk in September 1950 and VS-25 at San Diego in October.

During the Korean War, additional 18-plane squadrons were established to serve 12 escort carriers, replacing the TBMs. Grumman delivered 193 AF-2S, 153 AF-2W, and 40 AF-3S Guardians by April 1953, the last model having MAD gear added. The last Guardians were withdrawn from squadron service in August 1955, replaced by the Grumman S-2 Tracker.

S-2 Tracker

The Grumman S-2 (S2F) Tracker was the first aircraft designed from the beginning for the Navy's anti-submarine warfare carriers, whose mission was the destruction of submarines in high priority areas, especially those outside easy reach of shore-based patrol planes. Rather than speed, this mission requires the endurance and detection equipment formerly common only to large patrol bombers. The uneconomical two-plane search and attack partnership of the Grumman AF-2 Guardians was combined into one aircraft in the Grumman G-89 Tracker.

Powered by two Wright R-1820-82 Cyclones, this high-wing monoplane had retractable wheels and long-span flaps to reduce stalling speed for deck landings and for hovering when tracking submarines. Both pilots enjoyed fine visibility from the nose and two electronics operators behind them had APR-9B equipment for detecting enemy radar transmissions and APS-33G or APS-38 radar in a retractable radome for surface search. Underwater detection was by an ASQ-10 MAD in the tail and 16 sonobuoys dropped from the rear of the engine nacelles. A searchlight was under the starboard wing, six rocket racks were installed and a 1,325-pound Mk 41 homing torpedo was accommodated in the weapons bay.

Mfr

GRUMMAN S2F-3 (S-2D)

Two XS2F-1 prototypes and the first 15 production S2F-ls were ordered June 30, 1950, and the XS2F-1 flew December 4, 1952, at Bethpage, with R-1820-76 engines. Successful tests led to a large production order and abandonment of two rival Vought XS2U-l prototypes under construction. Although the first S2F-1 was flown with the R-1820-82 on July 30, 1953, regular monthly deliveries began in September with VS-26 becoming the first squadron to convert to the Tracker in February 1954. By 1959, two 12-plane VS squadrons operated, along with a helicopter squadron, from 10 *Essex*-class carriers (CVS) modified for ASW operations; ships far superior in speed and accommodations to the escort carriers previously used.

Navy acceptances of 755 S2F-ls continued to December 1959, with later aircraft produced for export. Japan purchased 60 S2F-ls minus carrier gear and folding wings in 1957/58, followed by 30 for Italy, with 26 for the Netherlands and 13 for Brazil in 1961. These were new aircraft, but second-hand Navy S2F-1s were also passed on to Argentina (6 in 1962 and 6 S-2Es in 1978), Taiwan (9), Thailand (6), and Uruguay (3). Canada built 42 C2F-ls and 57 C2F-2s for her own Navy, beginning in May 1966.

Sixty 60 S2F-2s with an enlarged weapons bay for a 2,500-pound Mk 90 nuclear depth charge, or two torpedoes, were delivered from July 1954 to November 1955. A second generation of Trackers with more fuel, equipment, and sonobuoy capacity increased from 16 to 32 began with a December 17, 1957, order for the first seven S2F-3s, which were first flown on May 21, 1959. Production aircraft entered service in May 1961, and Grumman delivered 100 by June 1962.

Mfr

GRUMMAN S2F-1 (S-2A) *Wright*

R-1820-82, 1525 hp max, 1275 hp normal

DIMENSIONS: Span 69'8" (27'4" folded), Lg. 42', Ht. 16'4", Wing Area 485 sq. ft.

WEIGHT: Empty 17,357 lb., Combat 22,222 lb., Gross 23,470 lb., Max. 24,408 lb. Fuel 520 gal.

PERFORMANCE: Speed- Top 264 mph at s.l., 272 mph at 3,100', Cruising 150 mph, Stalling 86 mph. Service Ceiling 22,800', Climb 2330'/1 min. Combat Range 968 miles.

When the current designation system was adopted in 1962, the S2F-1 became the S-2A, or the S-2B when the Julie/Jezebel systems were added, the S2F-2 became the S-2C, and the S2F-3 became the S-2D. An ASN-30 computerized tactical navigational system was tested in a modified S2F-3S that became the production S-2E.

The enlarged S-2D had APS-88A radar, Julie active echo ranging, Jezebel passive long-range acoustic search, a "sniffer" for snorkel exhaust fumes, a stronger searchlight and under wing fittings for rockets or torpedoes. A 1,200-pound Mk 101 nuclear depth bomb or two 568-pound Mk 46 torpedoes could be carried internally by the S-2D/E Trackers, while four more torpedoes could be carried on wing racks.

GRUMMAN S2F-2 (S-2C)
Wright R-1820-82, 1525 hp
DIMENSIONS: Span 69'8" (27'4" folded), Lg. 42'3", Ht. 16'4", Wing Area 485 sq. ft.
WEIGHT: Empty 17,640 lb., Combat 23,897 lb., Gross 25,145 lb., max. 25,985 lb. Fuel 520 gal.
PERFORMANCE: Speed- Top 255 mph at s.1., 263 mph at 3100', Cruising 150 mph, Stalling 89 mph. Service Ceiling 21,100', Climb 2040'/1 min., Combat Range 858 miles.

GRUMMAN S-2E (S2F-3S)
Wright R-1870-82A, 1525 hp. takeoff, 1425 hp. military at 2400'
DIMENSIONS: Span 72'7", Lg. 43'6", 16'7", Wing Area 490 sq. ft.
WEIGHT: Empty 18,720 lb., Combat 24,917 lb., Gross 26,664 lb. (Mk 101), Max. 29,734 lb. (Mk 101+4 Mk 46) Fuel 728 gal.
PERFORMANCE: Speed- Top 242 mph at s.l., 251 mph at 4000', Cruising 150 mph at 1500', Stalling 93 mph, Combat Ceiling 18,300', Service Ceiling 20,100', Climb 1830'/1 min., Combat Range 1150 miles/Mk 101, 920 miles/6 Mk 46, Ferry Range 1300 miles. (S-2D similar, but 94 lb. lighter.)

The first S-2Es reached the fleet on August 31, 1962, with 228 completed for the Navy and 14 more for Australia by December 1967, when total production at Lockheed reached 1,169. Later modifications to Navy planes in service produced the S-2F by updating the electronics on 244 S-2Bs, and the S-2G, which were 49 former S-2Es that reappeared in service in December 1972 with new data-processing equipment.

GRUMMAN S-2G (VS-37 in 1975)

The last S-2Gs in service were retired August 30, 1976, after VS-37 received S-3A Vikings. That squadron's last deployment had been on the *Kitty Hawk*, since all the anti-submarine carriers (CVS) had also been retired by 1973. Korea acquired 36 second-hand S-2Es and Peru nine in 1976, while Australia replaced older aircraft with 16 S-2Gs in 1977 and Taiwan acquired 27.

After their retirement from first-line squadrons in 1976, Trackers were modified for a variety of roles, including US-2A target tugs, US-2B utility aircraft, and RS-2C photo aircraft. Very valuable non-combat spin-offs of this type were the C-lA Trader and E-lA Tracer, transport and early warning types. Civilian forest fighters continued flying Trackers for the rest of the century.

S-3 Viking

Lockheed's S-3A Viking was the first carrier-based aircraft to combine jet speed with the specialized characteristics of

LOCKHEED S-3A
Two General Electric TF-34-GE-2, 9275 lb. st
DIMENSIONS: Span 68'8" (29'6" folded), Lg. 53'4", Ht. 22'9", Wing Area 598 sq. ft.
WEIGHT: Empty 26,581 lb., Combat 39,690 lb./4 Mk46, Gross 44,937 lb., Max. 45,516 lb. Fuel 1933+600 gal.
PERFORMANCE: Speed- Top 494 mph at s.l., 515 mph at 20,000', Cruising 409 mph, Stalling 117 mph. Combat Ceiling 38,500', Service Ceiling 39,100', Climb 4550'/1 min. Combat Radius 950 miles/4 Mk46, Combat Range 2886 miles, Ferry Range 3878 miles.

CVS-14, the *Ticonderoga,* was one of 15 antisubmarine carriers operating Grumman S-2 Trackers.

antisubmarine warfare planes. Two new General Electric TF34 turbofans in pods under the 15-degree swept wings had a low-altitude fuel consumption much less than that of conventional jet engines, and allowed a loiter endurance of up to 7.5 hours.

Four crewmen- pilot, copilot, tactical coordinator, and sensor operator- sat in a cabin air-conditioned to protect the delicate electronics, including a Univac 1832 general-purpose digital computer to integrate and store data on the console displays at all crew stations. Sensors included APS-116 high-resolution radar in the nose, a retractable infrared unit, the MAD boom in the tail, wingtip ECM antenna, and an acoustic system with 60 passive and active sonobuoys.

Automatic pilot and carrier landing systems were provided, along with the computerized inertial navigation system and a 1,000-watt transceiver. The weapons bay contains racks for four Mk 46 torpedoes, depth charges, 500-pound bombs, or mines, and a pylon under each wing could carry a 300-gallon drop tank, or weapons, such as three 500-pound bombs on triple ejector racks. Another internal option was two 1,229-pound nuclear depth bombs, or a weapons mixture.

The Viking design was a response to a Navy weapons system requirement dated December 13, 1965, and Lockheed became the contractor on August 1, 1969, teamed with the Vought and Univac corporations. Eight S-3A test aircraft were built at Burbank, with the first flown January 21, 1972, at Palmdale. On April 28, 1972, the Navy ordered the first 13 production S-3As, and 187 Vikings were built by August 1978.

They entered squadron service in February 1974 with VS-41 at NAS North Island, San Diego, where six Pacific Fleet squadrons were stationed by 1978, along with six more at Cecil Field, Florida, for the Atlantic Fleet. Vikings were deployed as ten-plane units with each of the big carriers. In 1992, 16 S-3As were converted to ES-3A types used by Electronic Reconnaissance Squadrons VQ-5 and VQ-6 until 1999.

After VS squadrons changed from antisubmarine to sea control squadrons on September 16, 1993, the force was reduced to ten squadrons, each with eight aircraft. As the ASW mission was downgraded with the Cold War's end, items like the MAD gear were discarded.

While the Viking's external shape had not changed 30 years after its first flight, much improvement has been made with computers, and the ASW mission had less priority. Instead of buying new airframes, the Navy began upgrading surviving S-3As to the S-3B configuration with new engines and electronics. Two AGM-84 Harpoon anti-ship missiles under the wings and APS-137 radar with a new suite of ECM, communication, and navigation systems, were linked to data processing by the AYK-10A digital computer.

USN

LOCKHEED S-3B
Two General Electric TF-34-GE-400, 9275 lb. st
DIMENSIONS: As S-3A
WEIGHT: Empty 26,783 lb. Max. 52,539 lb. Fuel 1933+600 gal.
PERFORMANCE: Speed- Top 506 mph at s.l., Cruising 400 mph. Service Ceiling 40,000'. Range: Patrol 2650 miles, Ferry 3,450 miles.

The prototype conversion arrived for tests at Patuxent River on October 28, 1985, and S-3Bs of VS-30 scored their first Harpoon hit on April 16, 1989. During Desert Storm, S-3B Vikings aboard the carriers played only a minor surveillance role. By July 2000, 112 Navy S-3Bs remained for sea control work.

PART FOUR

AN AWESOME GENERATION

CHAPTER 34

THE COLD WAR, 1963-1991

The Air Force used ex-Navy A-1Es for Vietnam operations.

Kasulka

After the crisis of 1962, the Cold War began a period of Mutual Assured Destruction, as in an exchange of nuclear weapons, both sides would have such losses that neither side could imagine a victory. Instead, a surrogate war in Southeast Asia became the center of conflict.

An undeclared war

Tactical ground support was the most important aspect of Air Force activity in Vietnam. It began on a small scale when the "Farm Gate" detachment began arriving November 4, 1961, their T-28D aircraft carrying Vietnamese markings. As Air Force activity increased, careful "rules of engagement" were developed to avoid provoking the direct Chinese intervention that made Korea so costly.

But after a clash between American and North Vietnamese vessels on August 2, 1964, in the Tonkin Gulf, American involvement escalated into the longest war in our history. In the '60s the struggle in Vietnam diverted funds to the Army and to allied forces. Close ground support missions flown against the Viet Cong were unopposed by fighters, but expanding the air war into the North would become costly.

This F-4E over Laos in January 1969 drops its eight bombs by Loran position, not the most accurate method for a tactical fighter-bomber.

While there were no air force combat units in North Vietnam before the Gulf incident, pilots had been trained in Russia, and 36 MiG-17 fighters and MiG-15UT I trainers had been provided in February 1964 to pilots training in China. Designated the 921st Fighter Regiment, they moved to Noi Bai, near Hanoi, on August 6.

Four MiGs from this unit struck F-105Ds attacking a bridge on April 4, 1965, beginning the USAF's fights over North Vietnam. The VPAF's 923rd Fighter Regiment joined the battle in March 1966 and the 925th came in 1969. MiG-19s also entered combat with the 925th by May 1972.

All VPAF combat sorties were flown by Vietnamese pilots, unlike the Korean War, when most hostile sorties were by Soviet or Chinese nationals. A generous supply of MiGs usually provided more aircraft than the pilot training program could actually fill. In May 1966, Soviet MiG-21s began to replenish the MiG-17 in the 921st FR, which was joined by the 927th in 1972. But while the VPAF's four fighter regiments flew 823 sorties in 1972, losing 52 aircraft in combat, only 47 of their 187 fighters remained operational.

American squadrons superior in numbers, aircraft quality, and especially experience, to the VPAF, found a dangerous enemy with a strong array of anti-aircraft guns and missiles supporting agile fighters using ambush tactics. In 1968, 840,117 combat sorties in support of ground forces were made by the USAF, which had 737 aircraft in Vietnam on June 1 and about 600 in Thailand. Combat operations continued until January 23 1973, in Vietnam, and in Cambodia until August 15.

Air operations then remained the responsibility of the Vietnamese Air Force, which had increased from 362 American-built aircraft in 1968 to 2,075 on January 27, 1973. Although the world's fourth largest air force at the time, it was unable to reverse the situation on the ground, and the battle was over after April 22, 1975; when the VNAF still had 1,492 aircraft, of which the new Communist rulers gained 877, and 132 were evacuated to Thailand.

Navy Air

Navy aircraft inventory declined from 10,586 (5,420 combat) in 1965 to 4,629 (2,146 combat) on September 30, 1991. The average age of Navy aircraft increased from four to ten years from 1957 to 1977, while yearly procure-

Lawson

On the way to Vietnam, November 1970; *Kitty Hawk* with RA-5C, A-6A, A-7E, F-4J, E-1B, and EKA-3B aircraft.

ment dropped from 2,000 to less than 200 aircraft. During the war in Vietnam, Navy aircraft steadily attacked enemy targets from carriers stationed off the coast. Attacks on the enemy mainland, along with operations against hostile submarines, had replaced attacks against surface vessels as the main role of naval aviation.

After the last of eight conventionally powered carriers, the *John F. Kennedy,* was commissioned in September 1968; future super-carriers had nuclear power, as tested on the *Enterprise* commissioned in 1961. On May 3, 1975, the *Nimitz* became the first of six commissioned by July 4, 1992, and three more were laid down by 1998. Their air groups, known since December 20, 1963, as Carrier Air Wings (CVW) carried a mixture of attack, fighter, antisubmarine, early warning and special purpose aircraft.

The last of the *Essex* class attack carriers begun in WW II, the *Oriskany*, was retired on September 30, 1976. Carrier responsibility for nuclear warfare changed, when they were removed from the strategic SIOP program, giving their air groups more flexibility for small wars. With the Cold War winding down, President George H. Bush, on September 27, 1991, announced the removal of all tactical nuclear weapons from Navy aircraft carriers, surface ships, and land-based aircraft.

Submarine hunting was the S–2 Tracker's task from 1954 to 1976.

In the words of Vice Admiral Jerry Miller, "Nuclear weapons are dumb and dangerous for everyone. They create an environment that prevents any user from being a winner. They are weapons of the past, for aircraft carriers at least."* Instead, naval aviation would develop a more rational technology for the new era.

Careful study indicated that destruction of a particular target by an 8,850-pound Mk 53's nine-megaton blast could usually be accomplished by a more accurately aimed 2,120-pound Mk-43's one-megaton yield. The limited-size Mk 57 and 61 would fill nuclear weapons production after 1963 and in 1983 the 2,400-pound B83 entered service.

Smart Bombs

Strategic attack could be made by ballistic or cruise missiles, leaving ground attack squadrons free for a generation of limited warfare. Most tactical targets would be just as disabled by a conventional 2,000-pound Mk 84, when directly hit by that weapon, as by a nuclear weapon of that size.

Accuracy was emphasized and radar guidance was improved. Snakeye tail retarding devices allow closer release points for low-level attacks, and are fitted to Mk 82, 83, and 84 bombs. For soft targets, cluster (CBU) dispensers of bomblets were used.

When VA-75 retired its last Intruder bombers in February 1997, the aircraft's external appearance had not changed in 36 years. Instead, the internal electronics had been completely modernized to improve the crew's ability to find and hit targets. Airframes had become far less changeable than the evolution of computers and radar.

The emphasis on GPU (Guided Precision munitions) and LGB (Laser-aimed bombs began in 1968 with the Paveway I series of electronic guidance elements and fin kits that attach to the nose of standard 500, 1,000, and 2,000-pound bombs. The first LGB combat use was by Navy A-6s in December 1971 and on April 27, 1972, Air Force F-4s used Paveway I bombs to disable the Thanh Hoa bridge that had survived 871 sorties with older weapons.

Paveway II, begun in 1976, provided more accurate guidance for the 2,000-pound GBU-10. In 1980, Paveway III development provided LGB for the GBU-24 and other weapons with midcourse corrections. Laser guided bombs were said to cost ten times more than normal bombs, but are much more accurate. Guidance by GPS was in the near future.

In addition to the LGBs, EO Electro-Optical bombs like the 500-pound AGM-62 Walleye II used by the A-6, and the AGM-84E SLAM had infrared guidance. Use of both air-to-air and air-to-surface missiles added more importance to an aircraft's electronics, radar and miniaturized computers becoming essential for both target search and weapons launching, as well as for navigation at high speeds and altitudes.

LANTIRN, a (Low-Altitude Navigation and Targeting Infrared for Night) system provided night attack capabilities. First tested in July 1984 with a targeting pod on a F-16B, it proved very workable in the Gulf War.

Air-launched Missile Weapons

In 1963, Sidewinder and Sparrow missiles had become so popular that the fastest production fighters, like the F-4A/D Phantoms and Convair F-106A carried no guns at all. But fighter pilots would demand guns be returned and so the F-4E and F-14 had the Vulcan cannons, even though the F-14's Phoenix could hit targets over 100 miles away.

Another missile series was developed for ground attack, the television-guided 465-pound AGM-65A Maverick first tested in Vietnam in 1972 by the 555th TFS. In 1974, an improved AGM-65B guided itself to the target and in 1983 the AGM-65D entered service with an infrared

*J. Miller, op. cit. 234.

Mfr

A television-guided AGM-65 Maverick under the A-7A's left wing and an AGM-45 Shrike under the right wing.

seeker. Marines used the 665-pound AGM-65E. Improved IR seekers in 1989 enabled the Navy's AGM-65F to hit ships ten miles away and the AGM-65G gave Air Force A-10s more power.

The 390-pound anti-radar AGM-45A Shrike would serve until succeeded by the 807-pound AGM-88A HARM. For anti-shipping targets, the Navy's 1,304-pound AGM-84A Harpoon entered service on P-3Cs in 1979. By November 1992, the 2,912-pound AGM-130 missile appeared.

The B-52 goes to War

Instead of nuclear strikes, combat operations with conventional weapons were the norm during the war in Southeast Asia. On June 18, 1965, 27 B-52Fs from the 7th and 320th BWs flew from Guam to attack an enemy base north of Saigon. Each bomber carried 27 750-pound bombs in the bay and 24 more under the wings.

As these operations continued, all B-52Ds in service were modified to carry 42 750-pound or 84 500-pound bombs in the bay, plus 24 of either size under the wings, and these aircraft replaced the B-52F on operations in August 1967. These missions in support of ground operations were unopposed, but the war's most important attack, Linebacker II, would be challenged by stronger means.

Four Sidewinders and four Sparrow IIIs armed the F4H-1 in 1961.

Grumman F-14A launches a Phoenix AIM-54A, but its long range has seldom had tactical application.

Douglas A-4M firing AGM-45 Shrike anti-radiation missile to home in on and destroy enemy radar.

From December 18 to 29, 1972, 700 sorties were flown at night against the Hanoi-Haiphong area, whose principal defense against the high-altitude attacks was surface-to-air missiles. SAMs were blamed for 15 B-52Ds lost, but the few enemy fighters seemed ineffective, and B-52D tail gunners claimed two MiG-21s. Between June 1965 and August 15, 1973, SAC launched 126,615 B-52 sorties against Vietnam, Laos, and Cambodia, losing 29 aircraft-only 17 to hostile action.

While SAC had 639 active B-52s by the end of 1962, attrition and the retirement of the last B-52B in 1966 and the last B-52C in September 1971 reduced the active force. The B-52Es were retired in 1970 and the B-52F retired in 1979.

Development of the B-52's primary strategic mission, however, continued during the war. Overhaul programs were utilized to strengthen the aircraft for low-level, beneath-radar penetrations of hostile territory. An ASQ-151 EVS (Electro-optical Viewing System) allowed the pilots safe low-altitude flight, and ECM sensors, jammers, and expendable chaff and flares were improved.

Another modification, made to 281 late-model aircraft, was the addition of SRAM (Short-range Attack Missile) capability. These 14-foot, 2,247-pound AGM-69A rockets with a 170-kiloton W-59 warhead were first flight-tested from a B-52H on July 29, 1969, and production models reached SAC in March 1972. Eight SRAMs were carried on a rotary launcher in the rear bomb bay, behind the usual gravity bombs, and up to 12 others could be carried on wing pylons.

An A-6E TRAM launches an AGM-84 Harpoon.

SRAM (AGM-69 missiles) added force to the B-52H

The fantastic Blackbird

When the last B-52Hs rolled out of Boeing's factory in October 1962, no one predicted that they would remain in first-line service 40 years later. After all, the previous 40 years since the Martin MB-2 had seen a continuous competition to fly faster, higher, and farther. Already that previous summer saw the first flight of the Lockheed Blackbird, which indeed could fly faster than any other airplane before, or for 40 years, afterwards.

The Lockheed's Blackbird series advanced design and high performance excelled all the century's other aircraft and the SR-71 was the only Mach 3 aircraft in USAF service. Contrasts between Blackbird and Stratofortress history illustrate how Cold War events dominated aviation history.

While the B-52 was publicized as the prime feature of American air power, the Blackbird was kept a strict secret during its early development and its operations remained classified for years. It was not even sponsored by the Air Force, but was instigated by the CIA.

Kelly Johnson's "skunk works", the secretive and unorthodox special design team at the Burbank company's engineering department had produced the U-2 in 1955. High-altitude photographic surveillance of the USSR for the CIA had an enormous impact on the Cold War, including the discovery that the Soviets had forgone mass production of bombers in favor of intercontinental missiles.

Harpoons added anti-shipping weapons to the P-3C, extending the Navy's ASW patrol plane's life cycle.

Boeing B-52F dropping 750-pound bombs on Viet Cong targets in 1965.

A B-52G with an ASQ-151 EVS (Electro-optical Viewing System) to allow safe low-altitude flight, and new ECM devices for low-level, below-radar penetrations of hostile territory.

Johnson studied the CIA's need for Archangel, an invulnerable U-2 replacement and proposed a series of designs labeled A-1 to A-12. The A-12 concept is dated April 21, 1958, in Johnson's diary and was selected on August 29, 1959, with the code name Oxcart. Twelve were ordered for the CIA on January 30, 1960, at a cost then estimated at 96.6 million dollars.

Nearly everything about this aircraft had to be entirely new, for the performance standards included a Mach 3.2 cruise over a 4,120 nautical-mile range up to altitudes over 90,000 feet. Such speeds create skin temperatures so high that 93 percent of the airframe was of expensive titanium alloy. The highest-grade titanium was purchased covertly from the Soviet Union, and composite materials or special steel alloys were used for some parts.

Advanced technology used included two Pratt & Whitney J58 bleed-bypass turbojets designed to run con-

LOCKHEED A-12
Two Pratt & Whitney J58-PW-1, 32,500 lb.
DIMENSIONS: Span 55'7", Lg. 102'3", Ht. 18'4", Wing Area 1795 sq. ft.
WEIGHT: Empty 52,700 lb., Gross 122,500 lb. Fuel 11,130 gal.
PERFORMANCE (Estimated): Speed-Top 2115 mph. Ceiling 87,000', Range 4,150 miles.

tinuously with afterburning, with spiked inlets and ejector nozzles. The long blended body had area rule and fore body lift with chines running back to the 60-degree leading edge sweep of the delta wing. Twin all-movable vertical tails were mounted on the back of each nacelle, and an automatic flight control system provided optimum handling. Flying faster than a rifle bullet, the pilot always wore pressure suits in the air.

Effective use of such performance required development of advanced cameras capable of sharp images from such heights and speeds. A pressure suit was necessary for the single pilot and a periscope enabled him to see below his aircraft. An inertial navigation system (INS) and an automatic flight control system (AFC) and inflight refueling were required.

Lockheed also proposed an interceptor configuration originated in November 1959, and three YF-12A prototypes were ordered for the Air Force in October 1960. Hughes ASG-18 fire control radar and three 815-pound GAR-9 (AIM-47A) semi-active radar homing missiles, originally developed for the XF-108 Rapier, were installed within the fuselage.

A radar officer was added behind the YF-12 pilot, the chines cut back from the nose to clear the radar sweep and infrared seekers added. Ventral fins were added below the nacelles and fuselage for stability.

The remote secret Groom Lake Nevada base redeveloped in 1960-1964, Area 51 was declared a no-fly zone to outsiders. Lou Schalk piloted the first A-12 flight on April 26, 1962, with two J75 engines. A second cockpit for pilot training was provided on the fourth aircraft delivered in November.

A-12 tests with two J58 engines began on January 15, 1963, and special JP-7 fuel were carried in six fuel cells. An accident destroyed the third A-12 on May 24, but an A-12 reached Mach 3.2 at 78,000 feet on November 22. On August 7, 1963, the first YF-12 was flown.

The public first learned of these remarkable Lockheeds through a presidential announcement on February 29, 1964, that an "A-11" experimental aircraft was being tested at Edwards. The false designation and location were intended to conceal the Oxcart program's true nature. Two of the three YF-12s were quickly flown to Edwards to verify that location.

The Air Force wanted a two-place SR-71 reconnaissance version for SAC, so a mockup review was made May 4, 1962, six SR-71As ordered February 18, 1963, and the contract increased to 31 in August. First flown on December 22, 1964, at Palmdale, the SR-71A had chines extending to the tip of the nose and more advanced side-looking radar (SAR) reconnaissance and ECM systems. Computer memory limits blocked progress until the original contractor, Hughes, was dropped in favor of a new navigation system based on star tracking

LOCKHEED SR-71A
Two Pratt & Whitney J58-PW-1, 32,500 lb.
DIMENSIONS: Span 55'7", Lg. 107'5", Ht. 18'6", Wing Area 1795 sq. ft.
WEIGHT: Empty 67,500 lb., Gross 150,000 lb. Fuel 12,219 gal.
PERFORMANCE (Record): Speed-Top 2193 mph. Ceiling 85,069', Range 3,250 miles.

On May 1, 1965, YF-12A prototypes set world records of 2,070 mph straight-course speed, 1,689 mph over a 1,000-kilometer closed course, and 80,257-foot sustained altitude. Seven GAR-9 missiles, without their planned nuclear warheads, were test launched from YF-12s.

Despite its high performance, the YF-12A interceptor program was discontinued January 5, 1967, because there was no bomber threat that could not be met by the existing F-106 force. Unfortunately for the expensive Lockheed, low-level bombing and close fighter combat had become the most desired fighter qualities.

Two more two-place A-12s were added with a pylon on top to hold a 17,000-pound, 40-foot long D-21 reconnaissance drone, but a July 30, 1966 accident caused that plan's end. Instead, D-21 ramjet drones launched by B-52Hs flew over China as late as 1971, but their film packages were lost.

On May 31, 1967, CIA A-12s began the first of 22 Black Shield flights from Okinawa over North Vietnam, photographing airfields, SAM sites, bridges, and sites within China. The *Pueblo* incident in January 1968 prompted a successful A-12 flight over North Korea.

LOCKHEED YF-12A
Two Pratt & Whitney J58-PW-1, 32,500 lb.
DIMENSIONS: Span 55'7", Lg. 105'2", Ht. 18'4", Wing Area 1795 sq. ft
WEIGHT: Empty 60,730 lb., Gross 136,000 lb. Fuel 12,219 gal.
PERFORMANCE (Record): Speed-Top 2070 mph. Ceiling 80,258', Combat Radius 1380 miles/three AIM-47A.

When the first standard SR-71A arrived at Beale AFB for the 9th Strategic Reconnaissance Wing in April 1966, the Air Force began assuming the Blackbird's roles. After the last OXCART mission over North Korea on May 8, 1968, surviving CIA A-12s began retiring to Palmdale for storage. Some original YF-12A records were beaten by a Soviet MiG-25 in 1967, but on July 27, 1976, 9th SRW pilots set new absolute world's records, 2,194 mph over a straight course, 2,092 mph over 1,000 kilometers, and an 85,089-foot altitude in sustained flights.

Blackbird development illustrated the enormous change in aircraft since 1917. Now a multitude of specialists replaced the self-educated designer, computers displaced drawing boards, flight testing measured data points beyond any imagined earlier, and costs were elevated beyond any private corporation's grasp. Government money was required for any prototypes.

SR-71s worked for the USAF until the last training flight on November 7, 1989. Two SR-71As were reactivated in 1995 for limited duties at Edwards and for NASA. But a U-2 squadron, operating with the USAF since June 1957, continued ELINT and other missions outside of the range of hostile SAMS. In fact, the last U-2R was delivered to the USAF on October 3,1989, and 35 U-2s still remained in the Air Force inventory in September 2000.

The century and the Cold War near their end.

As the Cold War gradually wound down, the Air Force shrank in size and its posture changed. Aircraft design had reached a plateau of performance, in which aerodynamics, not power plants, limited top speed. Expensive aircraft could have a long life cycle, if they were carefully upgraded with modernized electronics.

For the Wright brothers, the most important difficulty in flying had been aircraft control. Modern aircraft have multiplied that problem beyond any individual person's ability to calculate and react. Fortunately the 20th century was also the time of enormous progress in mathematics, quantum physics, and electronics. Computer power has made it possible to more accurately position and direct aircraft and their weapons.

The Gulf War

Only a few months after the SR-71 retired, Iraq's invasion of Kuwait on August 2, 1990, gave the Air Force and Navy a new challenge. Operation Desert Shield, deployment of

USN

Commissioned in October 1986, the nuclear-powered *Theodore Roosevelt,* CV-71, and eight sister ships are the world's largest warships and have no fear of running out of fuel. The *Theodore Roosevelt* was among the Navy carriers with Desert Storm in 1991.

RA-5C Vigilantes served the last heavy attack squadrons retired in 1979.

forces to protect Saudi Arabia, began in response to Saudi Arabia's urgent appeal. That build-up led to Desert Storm, the liberation of Kuwait by a United States and United Nations coalition in January-February 1991.

Coalition air strength at the war's beginning totaled 2,614 aircraft, of which 1,990 were American, but Iraqi had strong AAA and SAM forces to protect its 900,000-man army, and the air force had 750 modern combat planes. That air force suffered such a total defeat that American air supremacy at the Cold War's end seemed unquestioned.

During 42 days of 110,000 combat sorties, 59% by the USAF, some 210,000 unguided bombs were dropped. Only 16,000 precision-guided munitions were used, but they demonstrated their increased accuracy.

Six Navy carrier battle groups deployed had 395 combat planes aboard, and 191 Marine combat planes were

A TRAM attack system upgraded this A-6E of VA-34.

The Marines have their unique Harriers, this AV-8B Plus with night-attack capability.

The F-16A, here flown by the 474th TFW at Nellis AFM, became the most widely used American fighter.

The National Air Guard's 119th Fighter-Interceptor squadron used the F-106A until 1988, replacing the last Delta with the F-16A.

present. Tomahawk attacks were made by 288 BGM-109s fired by Navy ships and submarine. Victory in a military sense was complete, but failure to remove Saddam Hussein would extend the problem of Middle Eastern peace into the next century.

When President George H. Bush ordered termination of SAC's alert on September 27, 1991, after 34 years, the Cold War was successfully concluded in the eyes of the United States government. An era of air power rivalry had ended, to be replaced by very different conflicts.

When Desert Storm began, 30-year-old B-52Gs joined the war.

CHAPTER 35

ATTACK PLANES FOR SMALL WARS, 1963-1991

NORTH AMERICAN *T-28D*
Wright R-1820-56S, 1,425 hp
DIMENSIONS: Span 40'7", Lg. 32'10", Ht. 12'8", Wing Area 271 sq. ft. / WEIGHT: Empty 6251 lb., Gross 8118 lb., Max. 8495 lb., Fuel 177 gal. / PERFORMANCE: Speed- Top 298 mph at sea level, 352 mph at 18,000', Cruising 203 mph. Service Ceiling 37,000', Climb 3780'/1 min. Range 1184 miles.

AF

When war began in Vietnam, the Air Force had no ground attack planes in current production, for strategic bombing had been its first priority. The first aircraft sent to Saigon's VNAF had been surplus Navy AD-6s (see Chapter 31), and when the Farm Gate Detachment was sent to train and support the VNAF in November 1961, the Air Force provided aging A-26 light bombers and an armed trainer type, the T-28D.

North American's T-28 Trojan had been built as a two-place Air Force and Navy trainer from 1949 to 1957, when it was replaced by T-37 jets after a propeller-driven trainer was no longer useful. Responding to a French request for a low-cost light ground attack type for their war in Algeria, North American provided the T-28S Nomad, converted from a T-28A by installation of a 1,425-hp R-1820-56S and under wing racks for two 12.7-mm guns, two 500-pound bombs or two rocket pods.

Mfr

NORTH AMERICAN YAT-28E
Lycoming YT-55L-9, 2445 hp
DIMENSIONS: Span 40'7", Lg. 36', Ht. 14'4", Wing Area 271 sq. ft. WEIGHT: Empty 7750 lb., Gross 15,600 lb., Max. 16,300 lb. Fuel 250+220 gal.
PERFORMANCE: Speed- Top 360 mph, Cruising 276 mph, Climb 5130'/1 min. Ferry Range 2760 miles.

The first such conversion had been sent in July 1959 to France as a prototype for 145 surplus T-28As converted to the armed configuration by *Sud Aviation*. Known as the *Fennec* (Desert Fox), they served until the Algerian war was lost, after which 25 were passed to Morocco in 1965 and 40 to Argentina in 1966.

From 1961 to 1969, North American's Columbus factory converted 313 T-28As from the stored surplus to T-28Ds for the Mutual Aid Program. Fairchild modified another 72 T-28Ds from the trainer stockpile. In November 1961, 31 arrived in Saigon for the second VNAF "fighter" squadron, which was trained by the American Farm Gate detachment.

The 1st Air Commando Squadron flew the T-28D against the Viet Cong, using American pilots and Vietnamese crewmen. Its combat role terminated in April 1964, after two American pilots had been killed when their T-28D wings had failed. The Air Commandos were given A-1Es instead, although distribution of T-28Ds to allies continued. Cambodia and Laos each received 60 T-28Ds, and allocations were also made to Thailand, Bolivia, the Congo (Zaire), Ecuador, Ethiopia, Haiti, the Philippines, South Korea, and Taiwan.

An improved version, the YAT-28E with a 2,445-hp Lycoming YT55-L-9 turboprop and taller tailfin, was flown on February 15, 1963. The original aircraft, with two .50-caliber guns and six pylons for stores, was destroyed in a crash. Two more built in 1964 could carry up to 4,000 pounds of stores, but no production was ordered, as the OV-10 was available.

Cessna Dragonfly

The twin-jet Cessna T-37 trainer was chosen as an interim attack type for the Air Force until the more advanced A-7D became available. Cessna first proposed an AT-37D attack version in May 1963, and two T-37Bs became YAT-37Ds, with 2,400-pounds thrust J85-GE-5 engines and weapons installations. First flown October 22, 1963, they were prototypes for the similar A-37A.

The Air Force did not order the attack Cessna into production until August 1966. Thirty-nine new A-37As were built on the T-37B production line, delivery beginning in July 1967. The 604th Special Operations Squadron

AF

CESSNA A-37A
Two General Electric J85-GE-17A, 2400 lb. st
DIMENSIONS: Span 38'5", Lg. 29'4", Ht. 9'6", Wing Area 183.9 sq. ft.
WEIGHT: Empty 5603 lb., Combat 8422 lb., Gross 12,000 lb. Fuel 470+800 gal.
PERFORMANCE: Speed- Top 473 mph at s.l., 479 mph at 15,000', Cruising 317 mph, Stalling 113 mph, Combat Ceiling 41,000', Service Ceiling 42,860'. Climb 9800'/1 min. Combat Radius 336 miles/two 550-lb. bombs & 16 rockets. Ferry Range 1355 miles.

AF

CESSNA YAT-37D and NAA YAT-28E

received 25 and began operations in Vietnam on August 15, 1967.

With two crewmen side-by-side, and two J85-GE-17A jets derated to 2,400-pounds, the A-37A had armor, a 7.62-mm Minigun with 6,000 rounds in the nose, 90-gallon tip tanks, and eight under-wing pylons; the four inner ones could handle 870-pound bombs or 100-gallon drop tanks, the others up to 500 pounds of bombs, bomblet dispensers, or rocket pods, or up to 4,130 pounds of stores. Reliability and weapons delivery were rated as superior during the A-37A's combat tour at Bien Hoa.

The strengthened A-37B Dragonfly was similar but for an inflight refueling probe in the nose and full-rated engines. First ordered January 23, 1967, the A-37B appeared in May 1968. Cessna delivered 577 A-37A/B attack planes by 1977, including 302 for the Mutual Aid Program, some for foreign sales, and 134 served ANG and USAF reserve stations at the end of 1975.

The VNAF got 54 A-37Bs from November 1968 to May 1969 and 140 more in 1970/72, while Cambodia got 24. At the war's end in 1975, 187 remained in service, but

AF

CESSNA A-37B
Two General Electric J85-GE-17A, 2850 lb. st
DIMENSIONS: as A-37A
WEIGHT: Empty 6008 lb., Combat 8422 lb., Gross 14,000 lb. Fuel 457+389 gal.
PERFORMANCE: Speed- Top 478 mph at s.l., 502 mph at 12,000', Cruising 304 mph, Stalling 122 mph, Combat Ceiling 45,100', Service Ceiling 47,400'. Climb 12,120'/1 min. Combat Radius 246 miles /1878-lb. bombs, 132 miles/ 3120 lb. bombs. Ferry Range 1182 miles.

Mfr

NORTH AMERICAN OV-10A (Air Force)
Two Garrett AIResearch T76-G-10/12, 715 hp
DIMENSIONS: Span 40', Lg. 41'7", Ht. 15'1", Wing Area 291 sq. ft.
WEIGHT: Empty 8127 lb., Combat 8659 lb., Gross 10,518 lb. Fuel 252+150 gal.
PERFORMANCE: Speed- Top 284 mph at 5,000', Cruising 207 mph, Stalling 86 mph, Combat Ceiling 26,400', Climb 3240'/1 min. Combat Radius 58 miles/16 rockets, plus 2.5 hours loiter, Ferry Range 1427 miles.

five captured A-37Bs bombed Tan Son Nhat airport on April 28, destroying 24 aircraft, and by May, 95 were captured by the NVAF and 92 VNAF A-37Bs escaped, 16 to Thailand and 27 sent to South Korea.

Other countries receiving Dragonflies after 1974 were Chile (34), Ecuador (12), Guatemala (12), Honduras (15), Iran (12), Uruguay eight, and Peru 36 of the last built. Colombia was given 14 in 1980 for the anti-drug war, and El Salvador received 18 to fight insurgents.

COIN aircraft

Counter-insurgency, or COIN aircraft were intended as low-cost, light planes to strike against guerilla bands. This concept assumed an enemy without sophisticated air defenses, and the sort of aerial police work assigned to the "general purpose" biplanes of the late British Empire. Since the Marines were the American armed force with such experience, beginning with the DH-4s that hit the original Nicaraguan *Sandinistas*, they were given responsibility for the operational requirement, with input from the other services.

A specification for a Light Armed Reconnaissance Aircraft was finalized in September 1963 and proposals invited October 28. The requirements called for a two-place, twin-engine aircraft of minimum size and cost capable of flying from the smallest runways, open fields, roads, or carriers. Four 500-pound bombs and four M60 guns were required for the close support configuration, although armed reconnaissance was the primary role.

Nine companies submitted designs for evaluation by June 1964, but construction of the Convair Model 48 had begun in March as a private venture. Named the Charger, it flew on November 25, with two Pratt & Whitney T74 turboprops, twin booms, a high slab tail-plane, and a short rectangular wing with full-span slotted flaps. Four 7.62-mm M60 guns were mounted on each side of the fuselage, and five external store stations were provided. When holding a 1,200-pound payload and fuel for two hours loiter time over a target 50 nautical miles away, takeoff over 50-foot obstacle could be made in 485 feet, using a deflected slipstream principle. In heavy condition, the Charger could carry cargo, six paratroops, or enough fuel to fly from California to Hawaii.

CONVAIR MODEL 48
Two Pratt & Whitney T74-CP-8, 650 hp
DIMENSIONS: Span 27'6", Lg. 34'10", Ht. 13'7", Wing Area 192 sq. ft.
WEIGHT: Empty 4457 lb., Gross 7100 lb., Max. 10,460 lb. Fuel 208+600 gal.
PERFORMANCE: Speed- Top 319 mph at s.1. Ferry Range 1990 miles.

The Charger proved to be the last airplane from the San Diego factory's 29 years of production since the first PB-2A pursuit. Model 48 was smashed on October 19, 1965, on its 196th flight, but sales chances were already lost before it left the ground.

Shortly before the Charger's first flight test, North American won the design competition with the NA-300, which also was a twin-boomed two-seater. On October 15, 1964, seven prototypes were ordered from the Columbus factory for Marine tests as the YOV-10A; the designation being part of the V series of vertical and short-takeoff aircraft, mostly experimental in nature.

First flown July 16, 1965, by Ed Gillespie, the YOV-10A had two Garrett AiResearch 660-hp T76-G-6/8 turboprops, and sponsons attached on the fuselage carried four 7.62-mm M-60 guns with 500 rpg and hard points for bombs or rockets. The seventh YOV-10A was flown October 7, 1966, with Pratt & Whitney T74 engines for comparison tests.

A production contract was made October 15, 1966, but the original configuration was too light, and additional stores and protection increased weight so much that the wing had to be enlarged and more powerful engines used.

NORTH AMERICAN YOV-10A
Two Garrett T76-G-6, 660 hp at takeoff
DIMENSIONS: Span 30'3", Lg. 40', Ht. 15'1", Wing Area 218 sq. ft.
WEIGHT: Empty 5257 lb., Gross 8000 lb., Max. 10,170 lb. Fuel 210+150 gal.
PERFORMANCE: Speed- Top 305 mph at s.l. Service Ceiling 27,000'. Ferry Range 1380 miles.

A YOV-10A rebuilt to the new standard was flown in March 1967, and the first OV-10A was flown August 6, 1967. A 150-gallon drop tank or 1,200-pound store could be carried on the center station, while four sponson hard points could each carry up to 600 pounds of bombs, rockets, or anti-personnel weapons. Marine aircraft armor weighed 325 pounds.

North American built 157 OV-10As for the USAF and 114 for the Marines by April 1969. The first examples were delivered to each service on the same day, February 10, 1968. Of five Marine OV-10A squadrons, VMO-2 first took the Bronco to Vietnam, flying the first mission from Da Nang on July 6, 1968. Air Force Tactical Air Support OV-10As arrived soon afterwards and were used for forward air control (FAC) missions, locating targets and directing attacks by jet fighter-bombers. There were 96 OV-10As on FAC duty by June 1969.

NORTH AMERICAN OV-10A (Marine VMO-2 at Da Nang)

One Navy light-attack squadron, VAL-4, with 18 OV-10As from the Marines, was commissioned January 3, 1969, to protect river traffic in the Mekong Delta. Pave Nail was an Air Force night observation conversion program for 13 OV-10As that added a laser pod to illuminate targets for accompanying aircraft. Shoulder-launched SA-7 heat-seeking missiles became a serious threat.

Two YOV-10D night observation aircraft were Marine OV-10As modified by addition of an infrared sensor (FLIR) under the nose with a three-barrel 20-mm gun in a ventral turret slaved to the sensor, and under wing pylons for drop tanks. Both fought in Viet Nam from June to August 1971.

Lawson

NORTH AMERICAN YOV-10D (1971)
Two Garrett AIResearch T76-G-420/421, 1040 hp
DIMENSIONS: Span 40', Lg. 44', Ht. 15'1", Wing Area 291 sq. ft.
WEIGHT: Empty 6893 lb., Combat 9908 lb., Max. Gross 14,444 lb. Fuel 252+350 gal.
PERFORMANCE: Speed- Top 288 mph at sea level, Combat Ceiling 30,000', Climb 3020'/1 min. Combat Radius 228 miles/ 3,600-lb. load. Ferry Range 1382 miles.

While ventral turrets were not included on 17 OV-10Ds modified from As for the Marines at the Columbus factory in 1979, new 1,040-hp T76-G-420/421 engines and a laser target designator were fitted. Frequently updated with new electronics, Broncos served in the Gulf War with VMO-1 and VMO-2. They guided air strikes and lost two aircraft to heat-seeking missiles.

USMC

NORTH AMERICAN OV-10A in Gulf War

Air Force OV-10 units were retired in 1991, while the last Marine squadron, VMO-4, retired in June 1994.

Bronco exports began with 18 OV-10B unarmed target tugs built for Germany in 1970, and 32 armed OV-10Cs went to Thailand in 1971. After Venezuela got 16 OV-10Es in 1973, production halted until reinstated by deliveries begun in August 1976 of 16 OV-10Fs for Indonesia. Total OV-10 production was 360 aircraft by 1977. Surplus Broncos were provided to Morocco in 1981 and the Philippines in 1987.

A-4s during the war in Southeast Asia

On August 5, 1964, 64 aircraft, including 15 A-4Es from the *Constellation* and 16 A-4Cs from the *Ticonderoga,* made the Navy's first strike at North Vietnam. Downed by AAA, one unfortunate pilot began the longest POW experience ever endured by an American.

When direct intervention in Vietnam began, the Navy operated 15 attack carriers. Each CAW (Carrier Air Wing) had three attack squadrons; two with A-4s, and A-4s also equipped twelve Marine squadrons.

Continuous carrier air strikes began in February 1965, and in June 1965, Marine A-4 squadrons began rotating to Chu Lai, Vietnam, for land-based close-support missions that continued until June 28, 1973. Every type of non-nuclear weapon available to the A-4 was used during that war.

The need to release Skyhawks for active duty led to a two-place trainer version, retaining most of the armament capabilities. Two prototypes were completed as the TA-4E and the first flew June 30, 1965. Beginning in May 1966, 238 TA-4F two-seaters were produced, followed by 293 TA-4J trainers with J52-P-6 engines.

USN

DOUGLAS A-4F
Pratt & Whitney J52-P-8A, 9300 lb. st
DIMENSIONS: Span 27'6", Lg. 41'4", Ht. 15', Wing Area 260 sq. ft.
WEIGHT: Empty 10,169 lb., Combat 19,356 lb./Mk 28, Gross 19,356 lb., Max. 23,999 lb. Fuel 800+900 gal.
PERFORMANCE: Speed- Top 679 mph at 3500' (clean), 647 mph at 8000'/Mk 28, Cruising 472 mph, Stalling 144 mph. Combat Ceiling 43,900' (clean), 38,600'/Mk 28. Climb 10,200'/1 min. clean; 20,000'/3.6 min./Mk 28. Combat Radius 620 miles/Mk 28/two 300-gal. tanks. Ferry Range 2000 miles.

Both surface-to-air and air-to-air missiles became a serious threat in Vietnam when a Navy VA-23 A-4E was killed by an SA-2 on August 11, 1965. An avionics pod with ECM gear atop the fuselage was soon added to the last new Navy Skyhawk, the A-4F first flown August 31, 1966. With a new engine, ejection seat, and wing landing spoilers, the original A-4F was followed by 146 production examples, beginning in June 1967. Their ECM hump was also retrofitted

DOUGLAS A-4L (retrofit of A-4C)
Wright J65-W-20, 8400 lb. st
DIMENSIONS: as A-4C
WEIGHT: Empty 9861 lb., Combat 16,325 lb./Mk 28, Gross 18,501 lb., Max. 22,500 lb. Fuel 800+900 gal.
PERFORMANCE: Speed- Top 676 mph at s.l.(clean), 648 mph at 2500' (Mk 28), Cruising 495 mph, Stalling 140 mph. Combat Ceiling 41,300'. Climb 10,000'/1 min. clean, 20,000'/3.9 min./Mk 28. Combat Radius 489 miles /Mk 28/two 300-gal. tanks. Ferry Range 1770 miles.

on all A-4Es in service, proving a defense against SAMs, but light AAA still made low-altitude strikes costly.

Skyhawk development continues

The Douglas company had become McDonnell Douglas on April 28, 1967. Production at Palmdale provided Australia with eight new A-4G and two TA-4G trainers for its carrier, the HMAS *Melbourne*. The first flight was on July 19, 1967, with a J52-W-8A engine like those on the A-4F, and ten refurbished A-4Es were added in 1971.

Authority to proceed on 48 single-seat A-4Hs, the first American planes officially sold to Israel, was granted on October 10, 1966. The first was painted with U.S. Navy serial number and markings when it flew on October 27, 1967. It was similar to the A-4F, but for a drag chute and two 30-mm DEFA guns with 150 rpg to replace the 20-mm guns.

Israeli also acquired 60 used A-4E, 17 TA-4F and received a total of 90 A-4H and ten TA-4H aircraft by 1969. Skyhawks became the main IAF attack force during the three-year "War of Attrition" begun in March 1969, targeting hostile radar and weapons sites.

A long Skyhawk life at Navy shore stations was assured by the decision to upgrade 100 A-4Cs to the A-4L configuration. New engines and avionics were installed, and the first flew on August 21, 1969. Weapons options still included a Mk 28 nuclear store, two 564-pound AGM-12B Bullpups, or 12 300-pound bombs.

New Zealand bought ten single-seat A-4Ks and four TA-4K two-seaters for her Navy, the first flown on November 10, 1969, with delivery beginning in the following January. Malaysia and Indonesia acquired second-hand aircraft from Israel.

DOUGLAS A-4H for Israel, October 1967

DOUGLAS A-4K for New Zealand

Although the heavier Vought A-7 had been chosen by the Navy to replace the Skyhawks, the Marines still preferred the smaller type, and procured the A-4M, first flown as a reworked A-4F on April 10, 1970. That model introduced a new engine model, improved canopy, refueling probe, drag chute, and doubled the ammunition load to 200 rpg. Delivery of 134 to five Marine squadrons began in February 1971, and their weapons could include three Bullpups, the usual bomb load, or their choice of nuclear stores.

DOUGLAS A-4M
Pratt & Whitney J52-P-408, 11,187 lb. st
DIMENSIONS: as A-4F
WEIGHT: Empty 10,418 lb., Combat 17,657 lb./Mk 28, Gross 19,833 lb., Max. 24,472 lb. Fuel 800+900 gal.
PERFORMANCE: Speed- Top 687 mph at 5000' (clean), 666 mph at 12,000'/Mk 28, Cruising 483 mph, Stalling 145 mph. Combat Ceiling 46,400' clean, 40,600'/Mk 28. Climb 15,650'/1 min. clean, 20,000'/2.7 min./Mk 28. Combat Radius 524 miles/Mk 28/two 300-gal. tanks. Ferry Range 1860 miles.

DOUGLAS A-4N

Israel also bought 117 designated A-4N, on May 2, 1972, interspersed among A-4M production. Similar to the Marine type, but for 30-mm DEFA guns, their first flight was made June 8. During 1973's Yom Kippur war, 28 refurbished A-4Es and 13 A-4Ms were rushed to the IAF to replace more than 50 Skyhawks lost, mostly to SAM missiles. Altogether the IAF acquired 355 A-4s of different models.

In October 1970, the EA-4F designation was promulgated for two-place TA-4Fs equipped to simulate electronic aggressors. Another TA-4F conversion by the Navy was the OA-4M tactical control model of 1978. While the A-4Fs were retired from fleet squadrons in 1975, the A-4L remained with reserve units, and the renowned Blue Angels team used F-4Fs from 1974 to 1987.

Douglas also made foreign sales by refurbishing retired Navy Skyhawks. The first customer was the *Fuerza Aerea Argentina* (FAA), which bought 25 A-4Bs whose delivery with J65-W-16A engines began in June 1966. These aircraft, plus 25 more in 1969, and 25 A-4Cs in 1976, were redesignated A-4P on May 2, 1972, by the U.S. Navy for book keeping, although the FAA continued using the original names. Sixteen more A-4Bs with W-20 engines became A-4Qs when shipped on the Argentine Navy's light carrier, the *25 de Mayo,* in April 1972.

Reworked Skyhawks sent abroad were 40 A-4S and three TA-4S aircraft with J65-W-20 engines and 30-mm Aden guns for Singapore, refurbished from old A-4Bs in 1974. Kuwait ordered 30 A-4KU and 6 TA-4KU new aircraft on November 7, 1974, and the first flew on July 20, 1976.

The last Skyhawks from the factory were 24 additional A-4Ms, and the last acceptance on February 27, 1979, completed a total of 2,960 Skyhawks, including 555 two-seaters. That nearly 23-year run is one of the great successes of Navy aircraft design. The last Marine Skyhawk squadron, VMA-211, retired its last A-4M in February 1990.

The Skyhawk's last Fight

When the Falklands War began in 1982, 36 A-4B, 16 A-4C, and 10 A-4Q Skyhawks remained available to Argentina. They flew 249 sorties against British ships and positions from May 12 to June 13, sinking the destroyer *Coventry*, two frigates, a landing ship, and lost 22 A-4s in action, mostly to Sea Harriers and SAMs.

GRUMMAN EA-6A

GRUMMAN KA-6D of VA-165 refueling F-4J, 1971.

After older Argentine Skyhawks retired, and the political situation changed, replenishment by 36 upgraded ex-Marine A-4Ms began in October 1997. But the last Skyhawks to fight were 20 A-4KUs that escaped from Kuwait and flew against the Iraqi invaders in January 1991.

The A-6 at war

On July 1, 1965, VA-75 A-6As from the *Independence* began sorties against North Vietnam. As various carriers were rotated into the combat zone, ten Intruder squadrons specializing in night and bad weather strikes hit targets North and South. Deployment to Vietnam of four Marine A-6A squadrons began in December 1967. By 1968, an A-6A medium attack squadron on each carrier had replaced all the prop-driven A-1s.

A-6 development centered on the various electronics systems, but made little change to the basic airframe. Enemy radar was first attacked with AGM-45 Shrikes, but these had a short range, and became lost when the hostile radiation source was turned off. The improved AGM-78 Standard anti-radiation missile was introduced into combat in March 1968 by an A-6B, one of 19 A-6As modified to launch those missiles.

Grumman completed 488 A-6As by December 1970, many of which were modified to later configurations. The second one became an EA-6A ECM type first flown April 26, 1963, and followed by five more EA-6A conversions. Six EA-6As were also converted from production models in 1965, and 15 more new EA-6As delivered in 1969, all going to the Marine's VMAQ-2.

Night attacks on the Ho Chi Minh Trail were possible for 12 A-6As converted to A-6C models in 1970 with a TRIM system, housed in a ventral cupola for infrared and low-light television. Twelve 531-pound Mk-82 Snakeye bombs could be carried to a 575-mile combat radius, or 20 to a 360-mile radius.

Another A-6A system was the Pave Knife pod (AQ-10A) tested by VA-145 from November 1972. Laser-guided Mk 82 and Mk 84 bombs successfully destroyed bridges that had survived ordinary munitions. By the war's end in January 1973, 68 Intruders of all types had been lost in combat, and 15 in operational accidents.

The first KA-6D tanker conversion was flown in May 1966, but 94 were modified by Grumman in 1970/72, providing the Navy with a carrier-based air tanker that could transfer 3,000-gallons of its 3,844-gallon load via a hose reel assembly.

Arc

GRUMMAN EA-6B
Two Pratt & Whitney J52-P-408A, 9300 lb. st
DIMENSIONS: Span 53', Lg. 59'10", Ht. 16'3", Wing Area 529 sq. ft.
WEIGHT: Empty 31,629 lb., Combat 47,656 lb./5 pods, Gross 53,825 lb., Max. 60,059 lb. Fuel 2268+1475 gal.
PERFORMANCE: Speed- Top 583 mph at s.l., 545 mph at 30,000', Cruising 477 mph. Combat Ceiling 37,600', Climb 6,280'/min. Combat Radius 393 miles/4783 lb, 814 miles/ 1927 lb. Ferry Range 2,345 miles.

The Prowlers

The EA-6B Prowler is an ECM version with J52-P-408 jets. Like the EA-6, it has a large fairing atop the tail fin with receivers to pick up enemy radar, but the enlarged front fuselage contained the pilot and three ECM operators for the jamming systems contained in five ALG-99 pods. Electronic equipment inside the EA-6B weighs 8,000 pounds, plus each 950-pound pod. When needed, the pylons carried 300-gallon drop tanks.

The first EA-6B was converted from an A-6A and flown May 25, 1968, followed by six more conversions and then 48 new aircraft beginning service in January 1971. Two Navy squadrons were deployed in 1972 to support strike operations against North Vietnam.

The Navy established 12 electronic attack squadrons with Prowlers to protect carrier, Marine, and Air Force aircraft operations for the rest of the century. As improved electronics were introduced in 1975 and upgraded again in 1984, the production program was increased to 163 for squadrons operating as four-plane units on each carrier.

The first fleet launch of the 780-pound anti-radiation AGM-88A HARM missile was made from an EA-6B on August 5, 1986, by VAQ-131. Over 800 HARMs would be fired during Gulf War ECM missions.

The last EA-6B was delivered on July 29, 1991, but in 2000, 119 Prowlers were still available for ten active carrier-based VAQ units, five land-based squadrons, four Marine VMAQ squadrons, a reserve unit, and a fleet readiness training squadron.

Out-living the Cold War

The first A-6E, converted from an A-6A, and flown February 27, 1970, was identical in appearance to the A, with the J52-P-8A engines used on the last 223 aircraft, but had an entirely new electronics fit, including new APQ-148 radar, ASQ-133 computer, and weapons delivery systems. Later additions included provision for target-finding multi-sensors and laser-guided weapons.

The first of 205 new production A-6Es was accepted on September 17, 1971, and was joined by 241 conversions from earlier aircraft made by March 1980. These conversions were originally expected to cost only 1.6 million dollars each, compared to 9.5 million dollars for each new A-6E.

USN

GRUMMAN A-6E (1979)
Two Pratt & Whitney J52-P-8A, 9300 lb. st
DIMENSIONS: Span 53', Lg. 54'9", Ht. 16'2", Wing Area 529 sq. ft.
WEIGHT: Empty 25,980 lb., Combat 45,525 lb./Mk 43, Gross 54,393 lb., Max. 58,807 lb. Fuel 2344+1477 gal.
PERFORMANCE: Speed- Top 635 mph at s.l. (653 mph clean), Cruising 390 mph, Stalling 142 mph, Combat Ceiling 40,700', Climb 10,150'/min. Combat Radius 450 miles/10,296 lb. bombs/ two 300-gal. tanks, 890 miles/Mk 43/four 300-gal. tanks. Ferry Range 3300 miles.

Entering VA-85 service in December 1971, A-6Es were frequently upgraded with new electronics, and J52-P-408 engines. Improving night bombing accuracy became the main direction of attack technology. Delivery began in December 1978 on new TRAM (Target-Recognition Attack Multi-sensors) A-6Es, including a new ASN-92 inertial navigation system as well as APQ-156 radar, AAS-33 infrared sensor and laser designator in a 20-inch turret under the nose.

Arc

GRUMMAN A-6E TRAM

Enough older models added TRAM suites to become the fleet standard, with combinations up to four AGM-65, AGM-78 and AGM-84 missiles, 28 500–pound or four 2,000–pound bombs. Targets were acquired by radar, image enlarged by infrared and designated by laser beam.

Gann

DOUGLAS AC-47D (Vietnam 1968)
Two Pratt & Whitney R1830-92D, 1200 hp
DIMENSIONS: Span 95'6", Lg. 64'4", Ht. 16'11", Wing Area 987 sq. ft.
WEIGHT: Empty 19,000 lb., Gross Max. 33,000 lb. Fuel 1602 gal.
PERFORMANCE: Speed- Top 230 mph at 8,800', Cruising 160 mph. Service Ceiling 24,000', Range 2,125 miles.

The AGM-84 Harpoon was first used in combat when VA-85 Intruders struck Libyan missile boats on March 24/25, 1986. A conflict at sea with Iran resulted in a frigate being sunk by an A-6E's Harpoon on April 18, 1988. Laser-guided Paveway II bombs (LGB), like the rocket-boosted 1,000-pound AGM-123A Skipper, also became available.

To extend service life, 178 new Boeing composite wings were provided to rebuild Intruders. Five new A-6Fs were built as "Intruder II" in hopes of extending production. First flown on August 26, 1989, they introduced 10,800-pound thrust F404-GE-400D turbofans, APQ-173 radar, and a new fuel system, but the Navy was then committed to the A-12 project, and no more A-6Fs appeared.

Intruders from VA-35 began Gulf War strikes on January 17, 1991, slamming 2,000-pound bombs into the hardened hangars of an Iraqi air base, and launching small ADM decoy gliders to confuse the enemy. Eight Navy A-6E squadrons from carriers were joined in the war by two Marine A-6E squadrons based in Bahrain. EA-6Bs shielded coalition aircraft with radar jamming and HARM missiles, and only four of 115 A-6Es were lost in combat.

The last of 708 Intruders was an A-6E delivered on January 31, 1992. Sixteen A-6E Navy medium attack squadrons and five Marine squadrons were gradually decommissioned. After 36 years of service, VA-75 retired its last Intruder in February 1997. Future carrier attack missions would be assigned to the F/A-18 Hornets.

Gunships

An unusual variation in attack planes was the gunship program improvised for the Vietnam War. The idea was to fit guns into available conventional transport planes that had the endurance for night patrols.

Gunship I was the oldest plane in the USAF, the Douglas C-47 Skytrain with two Pratt & Whitney R-1830-92D Wasps. Two improvised aircraft had been combat tested in Vietnam in December 1964. On July 27, 1965, the Air Force ordered 26 aircraft modified to AC-47D gunships by Air International at Miami, Florida. The first was delivered on August 9, and 53 were completed by December 23, 1967.

Three 7.62-mm GAU-2B/A guns were installed in the port cargo door and the two nearest windows with 21,000 rounds, 45 flares, and up to 1,602 gallons of fuel. Three of the seven crewmen loaded but did not aim the guns; the pilot did that while making a left pylon turn around the target. Slant range, which varied with angle, was about 6,000 feet in a 20-degree bank. The AC-47D would cruise about 140 mph from two to three thousand feet altitude above a threatened friendly outpost, illuminating the enemy with flares and banking left to fire its three 6,000-rounds-per-minute weapons.

Arriving in Vietnam on November 23, 1965, the 4th Air Commando Squadron flew 22,752 combat sorties in its first year's operations. After the 14th Air Commando Squadron was activated in October 1967, AC-47D strength was increased from 22 to 33 aircraft. Of 47 AC-47s sent to Vietnam, 12 were lost to enemy action. When newer AC-130 and AC-119 types arrived, 16 AC-47Ds were transferred to the VNAF in 1969, and eight went to a Royal Laotian squadron.

Gunship II conversions were of the Lockheed C-130 Hercules, powered by four Allison T56-P-9 turboprops. Four 20-mm M-61 Vulcan and four 7.62-mm GAU-2B/A guns were lined up on the port side and the spacious cabin had room for an analog computer fire control, APQ-113

LOCKHEED AC-130H
Four Allison T56-A-15, 4,910 hp at takeoff
DIMENSIONS: Span 132'7", Lg. 97'9", Ht. 38'5", Wing Area 1745 sq. ft.
WEIGHT: Empty 72,890 lb., Gross 160,000 lb. Fuel 6652+2596 gal.
PERFORMANCE: Speed- top 380 mph, Cruising 362 mph. Service Ceiling 25,000'. Range 1500 miles.

computer, infrared sensor, searchlight and image intensification sights.

An AC-130A converted from a C-130A began flight tests on June 12, 1967, at Eglin AFB and arrived in Viet Nam on September 21. Gunship II flew combat missions until November 18, 1968, and then returned to America for repair and evaluation.

Seven more conversions ordered on February 13, 1968, were delivered from August to December, and suffered their first loss to 37-mm AAA on May 24, 1969. A new "Surprise Package" conversion, with improved digital fire control and sensors, laser target designator, and two of the 20-mm guns replaced by 40-mm weapons, began arriving at Ubon, Thailand, in December 1969.

Successful night interdiction missions destroyed thousands of enemy trucks, so Surprise Package modifications were made to five updated AC-130As and ten more C-130As in 1970. Heavier armor and more ammunition were carried by 11 AC-130E Pave Aegis, the first completed in June 1971, with a 105-mm cannon replacing the aft 40-mm gun.

The big Lockheed gunships were effective in Vietnam, but it was evident that they might not survive sophisticated defenses or fighter opposition. In 1973, ten AC-130Es returned home for conversion to AC-130H Spectre models with T56-A-15 engines and added equipment, and were

AF

LOCKHEED AC-130A Close-up of night sights and guns

stationed at Hurlburt Field for TAC's 1st Special Operations Wing.

Gunship III conversions were of the Fairchild Hiller C-119 Flying Boxcars with two Wright R-3350-89 engines. Twenty-six AC-119Gs were delivered from May 21 to October 11, 1968, with four six-barrel 7.62-mm GAU-2 guns pointed out the port sides, 27,000 rounds, flares, and an AVQ-8 illuminator light set and night observation system. They were followed in September by the first of 26

LOCKHEED AC-130E

AC-119K gunships, which added a pair of J85 jets under the wings to boost takeoff power, two 20-mm M61Al guns with 600 rounds, FLIR infrared sensor, and new radar.

The eight-place AC-119G Shadow began combat with the 17th Special Operations Squadrons in January 1969, and the ten-place AC-119K Stinger with the 18th SOSq arrived in Viet Nam on November 3. After many strikes against trucks, boats, and PT-76 light tanks, the AC-119Gs were given to the VNAF in September 1971, and the AC-119Ks were left when the USAF departed in 1973. In April 1975, 37 Fairchild gunships were abandoned to the victorious enemy.

FAIRCHILD HILLER AC-119G

FAIRCHILD HILLER AC-119K 17th SOS, 1969
Two Wright R-3350-89B, 3500 hp, and two General Electric J85-GE-17, 2850 lb. st
DIMENSIONS: Span 109'3", Lg. 86'6", Ht. 26'5", Wing Area 1447 sq. ft.
WEIGHT: Empty 60,277 lb., Combat 70,102 lb., Gross 77,000 lb. Fuel 2488 gal.
PERFORMANCE: Speed- Top 290 mph at 5000', Cruising 170 mph, Stalling 112 mph. Combat Ceiling 22,950', Service Ceiling 26,800', Climb 1772'/1min. Combat Radius 111 miles. Combat Range 692 miles, Ferry Range 1155 miles.

Lockheed Spectre gunships of Special Operations Squadron 16 were upgraded with new digital computer fire controls, FLIR, ECM, and inflight refueling. Fourteen crewmembers handled each of the five AC-130Hs deployed on the Gulf War. One was lost to enemy action, but successful night operations encouraged the conversion of 12 more Hercules to the AC-130U model by 1992.

Based on a C-130H "U-boat" conversion tested at Edwards in January 1991, the AC-130U had one each of the 25-mm, 40-mm, and 105-mm guns and APQ-180 radar to direct a new battle management computer system with ECM flare and chaff dispensers. They would be retained for the rest of the century.

A-7 Corsair II

The Vought A-7 Corsair II was designed to meet a Navy requirement issued in May 1963 for a light single-seat attack plane to replace the A-4. Bomb load and combat radius were to be doubled, without loss of speed. To keep costs as low as possible, improve weapons accuracy, and to expedite operational service, speed was to be limited to subsonic levels.

Vought's design utilizing F-8 experience was declared the design competition winner in February 1964, and a March 19, 1964, contract provided for seven test and the first 35 production aircraft, with severe penalty clauses to guarantee prompt delivery and performance standards. These goals were met when the first A-7A from Dallas began flight tests piloted by John Konrad on September 27, 1965.

VOUGHT A-7A
Pratt & Whitney TF30-P-6, 11,350 lb. st
DIMENSIONS: Span 38'9", Lg. 46'1", Ht. 16', Wing Area 375 sq. ft.
WEIGHT: Empty 15,497 lb., Combat 27,856 lb./3600 lb, Gross 31,936 lb., Max. 34,500 lb. Fuel 1500+900 gal.
PERFORMANCE: Speed- Top 685 mph clean, 559 mph/12 Mk 81 at s.l., 585 mph at 13,000', Cruising 478 mph, Stalling 155 mph. Combat Ceiling 41,500', Climb 5000'/1 min. Combat Radius 655 miles/3600 lb.

Powered by a Pratt & Whitney TF30-P-6, the A-7A had two 20-mm Mk 12 guns with 500 rounds, APQ-116 radar, refueling probe, and electronic bombing and radar systems. A high 35-degree swept wing had six pylons for a wide variety of weapons stores and two Sidewinders could fit on fuselage side rails.

For the nuclear strike mission, a 2,000-pound Mk 28 and three 300-gallon drop tanks were carried, but for the usual close support and interdiction roles, the A-7A could carry six to 24 250-pound Mk 81 bombs, or 12 500-pound Mk 82 plus six Mk 81 bombs. Missile or rocket pods could be substituted as needed, on the pylons.

Vought delivered 199 A-7As and 196 A-7Bs, the latter similar but for a TF30-P-8 and improved flaps. The Corsair II reached VA-174, a training squadron at Cecil Field,

Florida, in October 1966, and on the 40th anniversary of Lindbergh's flight to Paris, two A-7As with two 300-gallon drop tanks flew non-stop from Patuxent NAS to Paris in just seven hours, instead of the 33 hours for that 1927 flight.

Mfr

VOUGHT A-7B
Pratt & Whitney TF30-P-8, 12,200 lb. st
DIMENSIONS: as A-7A
WEIGHT: Empty 16,133 lb., Combat 25,732 lb./1800 lb. bombs, 32,432 lb./7500 lb. bombs, Gross 29,812 lb., Max. 37,027 lb. Fuel 1500+900 gal.
PERFORMANCE: Speed- Top 683 mph clean, 611 mph/6 Mk 81 at s.l., 625 mph at 11,500', Cruising 459 mph, Stalling 147 mph. Combat Ceiling 43,900' (clean), Climb 7290'/1 min. Combat Radius 448 miles/7500-lb. bombs, 799 miles/six Mk 81 bombs, 1393 miles/Mk 28/three 300 gal. tanks. Ferry Range 3190 miles.

Corsair IIs first deployed operationally in November 1967 on the *Ranger* with VA-147. This squadron made the first A-7A attack into North Vietnam on December 4, 1967, and flew 1,400 combat missions in two months, losing one A-7A to an SA-2. First flown February 6, 1968, the A-7B entered combat March 4, 1969, and the last was delivered in May 1969.

There was still no Air Force jet attack type when the A-7A appeared; since World War II funds had been used for strategic offensive and continental defense capabilities. While close support of Army forces was accepted as part of the Air Force mission, it was considered a secondary role for tactical fighters. First control of the air had to be won; only then could the fighter-bombers turn to surface targets.

The concept of limited war in general, and the Southeast Asia war in particular, caused the Army to pressure the Air Force for close support by specialized aircraft, not the multipurpose supersonic fighters favored by the Air Force. The Vought attack plane seemed to be a relatively low cost and quick way to get this capability. On November 5, 1965, the new Secretary of the Air Force, Harold Brown, and USAF Chief of Staff, General John P. McDonnell decided to buy A-7s for Tactical Air Command.

Although the original intention was to save money by retaining most of the original configuration, the Air Force insisted on more power, and in October 1966, contracted with Allison to produce the TF41-A-l, an American version of the Rolls-Royce Spey, for their Corsair version. An M61Al Vulcan with 1,000 20-mm rounds replaced the two Navy guns, plus a computerized navigation/weapons delivery system with APQ-126 radar and a Head-Up Display (HUD) reflecting all steering and attack displays between the pilot's eyes and the windshield.

Two AIM-4E Falcon, AIM-9B Sidewinder, or AGM-65A Maverick missiles could be attached to the fuselage sides, but the basic mission load was eight 800-pound M-117A bombs and two 300-gallon tanks, or a variety of attack stores. A boom receptacle was added on the fuselage top to replace the older nose probe for inflight refueling.

The first A-7D flew at Dallas on April 5, 1968, with a TF-30, since the first production TF-41 was not ready for flight tests until September 26. After that engine production got underway, deliveries to a TAC training unit began in September 1969, and the 354th Tactical Fighter Wing got its first operational A-7Ds in September 1970.

Vought delivered 459 A-7Ds by December 1976 to serve three TAC wings and two ANG squadrons. In October 1972, 354th TFW A-7Ds arrived at Korat, Thailand and began missions into Cambodia, Laos, and North Vietnam. The A-7Ds flew 6,848 sorties with only four losses and the last U.S. air strike in Cambodia was made by an A-7D on August 15, 1973, ending the nation's longest war.

Schoeni

VOUGHT A-7D
Allison TF41-A-1, 14,250 lb. st
DIMENSIONS: Span 38'9", Lg. 46'1", Ht. 16'1", Wing Area 375 sq. ft.
WEIGHT: Empty 19,733 lb., Combat 28,851 lb., Gross 38,008 lb./8 M117, Max. 42,000 lb. Fuel 1425+1200 gal.
PERFORMANCE: Speed- Top 663 mph at 7000', 654 mph at s.l., Cruising 507 mph, Stalling 174 mph. Combat Ceiling 36,700', Service Ceiling 38,800', Climb 10,900'/1 min. Combat Radius 556 miles/6560 lb./two 300-gal. tanks, Combat Range 1330 miles. Ferry Range 3045 miles.

The Navy took advantage of these electronics, power plant, and armament improvements in the A-7E, first flown November 25, 1968. Armed with an M61A-1 gun and rails for two Sidewinders, the A-7E had the advanced electronic provisions, including HUD display and ECM devices used on the A-7D. It could handle a 2,140-pound Mk 43 nuclear store plus drop tanks, but the primary close support mission was delivery of from six to 18 bombs or other stores.

Allison TF41-A-2 engines were specified, but production delays slowed deliveries, so the first 67 aircraft were delivered with TF30-P-8s and designated A-7Cs. Not until March 9, 1970, was an A-7E flown with the TF41-A-2.

The first delivery of the A-7E to a fleet squadron, VA-122, had been made on July 14, 1969, but VA-146 and VA-147 made their first cruise on the *America* with the Allison engine in 1970. Their first combat mission in Vietnam was on May 23, 1970. Of the 54 Corsairs lost in combat during 49 months by 1973, 38 fell to AAA fire, and the rest to SAMs.

VOUGHT A-7E
Allison TF41-A-2, 15,000 lb. st
DIMENSIONS: as A-7D
WEIGHT: Empty 18,546 lb., Combat 28,731 lb./six Mk 81, Gross 32,745 lb., Max. 40,449 lb. Fuel 1476+1200 gal.
PERFORMANCE: Speed- Top 693 mph at s.l. clean, 653 mph at 6000'/ six Mk 81, Cruising 470 mph, Stalling 157 mph. Combat Ceiling 37,910', Climb 8630'/1 min. Combat Radius 295 miles/7500 lb. bombs, 562 miles/six Mk 81, 1054 miles/Mk 43/+3 300-gal tanks. Ferry Range 2860 miles/2676 gal.

Production of 536 A-7Es ended in March 1981, with a total of 931 Corsair IIs for the Navy. Later additions to A-7E electronics added improved ECM with AGM-88A HARM missiles first fired live on October 5, 1981, as well as AGM-65F Mavericks first launched September 20, and FLIR pods for night attacks. In March 1986, A-7Es put a Libyan radar site out of action with AGM-88A missiles.

Navy Corsairs served 27 light attack squadrons with the fleet, usually operating two 14-plane squadrons per carrier. Three replacement training units served ashore, while older models had been retired to six Navy Air Reserve squadrons, beginning in April 1971. The TA-7C designation was applied to a two-seat trainer remanufacture of 60 retired A-7A/B aircraft delivered from 1977 to 1980.

Two A-7Ds modified to export G versions in April 1972 were offered to Switzerland, but the first successful foreign sale was 60 A-7H Corsairs for Greece. Essentially similar to the A-7D, the first A-7H was flown May 6, 1975, the Greeks also buying five TA-7H two-place trainers by 1980. Another two-place version was the YA-7K, converted from an A-7D, which was followed by 30 new A-7Ks for the Air National Guard in 1981.

By October 1986, Vought had completed 1,545 Corsair IIs in total. Post-production rebuilds included 50 A-7As upgraded into A-7Ps for Portugal from 1981 to 1985. An effort to extend sales was to enlarge two A-7Ds to YA-7F configurations with Pratt & Whitney F100-PW-220 afterburning turbofans rated at 23,450-pounds thrust.

VOUGHT A-7H for Greece

While the prototype first flown on November 29, 1989, was said to reach 748 mph, the company, then called LTV, was unable to win funding away from the F-16 program.

Corsair II retirement began when the F/A-18 Hornet was first deployed in 1985. The last two A-7E squadrons were VA-46 and VA-72 on the *Kennedy*. When the Gulf War erupted, they began predawn strikes from the Red Sea on January 17, 1991, and flew 731 sorties with CBUs, AGM-62 Walleye II, and HARM guided missiles, without any combat loss. On May 23, the Corsair's 24-year service ended when both squadrons were decommissioned.

AV-8 Harrier

An entirely new direction in ground attack aircraft was in-

Mfr

HAWKER SIDDELEY AV-8A Harrier
Rolls-Royce Pegasus F402-RR-401, 21,500 lb. st
DIMENSIONS: Span 25'3", Lg. 45'6", Ht. 11'3", Wing Area 201 sq. ft.
WEIGHT: Empty 12,200 lb., Gross 17,050 lb./VTOL, 22,300 lb./STOL, Max. 24,600 lb. Fuel 759+600 gal.
PERFORMANCE: Speed- Top 639 mph at s.l., Cruising 531 mph, Combat Ceiling 40,600'. Combat Radius 447 miles/3 Mk 82 bombs, Ferry Range 1550 miles.

troduced to the Marines in the AV-8A Harrier. The first VSTOL combat type was not an American plane at all, but was begun by Hawker Siddeley (British Aerospace since 1977). Vectored thrust through four rotated nozzles, located two on each side of the fuselage, allowed a single-seat combat type with unique possibilities.

Mfr

VOUGHT YA-7F

When the Harrier was in light condition, thrust from the Rolls-Royce Pegasus could lift the plane vertically upwards (VTOL), or with more weight, a short takeoff (STOL) of 1,000 feet was possible. While a full load would require a lengthier run, only a short landing space was needed after stores were dropped. The tactical opportunities for short-deck or unprepared field operations were apparent to the Marines.

Hawker first flew its VTOL concept in 1960, and a series of Kestrel development aircraft tested the system in the field, including six tested in the U.S. as the XV-6A. Harrier combat versions were already in RAF service when the first Marine order for 12 AV-8s was announced December 23, 1969.

The first AV-8A was delivered at the Kingston-upon-Thames factory January 6, 1971, shipped to the U.S. and began service trials with VMA-513 on April 16. An additional 90 single-seat AV-8A and eight two-seat TAV-8As were ordered and equipped VMA-513, 542, and 231 by 1974. While they demonstrated successful weapons delivery from both land bases and amphibious assault (LPH) ships, they were troubled by a high accident rate over twice that of other jets, 50 aircraft destroyed in 213,000 flying hours.

On June 1, 1975, the AV-8B designation was assigned to the follow-on offensive support Harrier, and McDonnell Douglas was ordered on July 27, 1976, to convert two prototypes from existing AV-8A airframes and the first YAV-8B flew at St. Louis on November 9, 1978. A new larger wing of composite materials and improved engine inlets enabled the AV-8B to double either the payload or radius of action, and a new canopy improved pilot vision.

McDONNELL YAV-8B

Four development AV-8 Harriers followed from 1981 to 1983 with the F402-RR-404. While the new model was made ready, 47 AV-8As reworked with new electronics and lift improvements by the Navy became AV-8Cs from 1979 to 1983.

The *Armada Espanola* ordered a light sea control carrier in June 1977, using a U.S. design and loan to build the *Principe de Asturias* for Spain. Six AV-8As added to the U.S. Marine order and called the AV-8S, or Matador I became a training squadron at Rota in 1976. Twelve Matador IIs (AV-8B) were ordered from McDonnell in March 1983 and delivery began on October 6, 1987, for the new ski-ramp carrier's sea trials. Nine new Harrier II plus models were added in 1990 and the older Matador Is would be sold to Thailand in 1992.

Fighting with Argentina around the Falkland Islands in May 1982 demonstrated the ability of Royal Navy Sea Harriers. Over 2,000 sorties by 28 carrier-based Harriers had resulted in 20 kills claimed, 16 with AIM-9L Sidewinders, without a loss in air-to-air combat, as well as ground attacks that cost two aircraft. This success accelerated confidence in the type.

The United States Marines had also developed evasive maneuvers that can be appreciated by anyone who has watched the Harrier stop in midair, fly backwards, and even sideways, like a helicopter. Two 30-mm Aden guns in pods that could be attached to the fuselage or two Sidewinder missiles under the wings became dangerous to an attacker. Four under-wing pylons could accommodate 1,000-pound bombs, rocket pods, or whatever mission-required stores and takeoff conditions allowed.

The first production AV-8B Harrier II was flown at St. Louis on August 23, 1983, by a British test pilot, and deliveries would begin on an RAF version, the Harrier Mk 5, in 1987. New electronics, with a Head-Up Display, FLIR, and ECM defense was included. A 25-mm five-barrel GAU-12 gun with 300 rounds was fitted along with pylons for six 565-pound Mk 82 Snakeye bombs, or an AGM-65E Maverick missile or drop tank combination. A retractable probe on the port engine intake provided inflight refueling, now required on all American combat planes.

McDONNELL AV-8B
Rolls-Royce F402-RR-406, 21,550 lb. st
DIMENSIONS: Span 30'4", Lg. 46'4", Ht. 11'8", Wing Area 230 sq. ft.
WEIGHT: Empty 12,835 lb., Combat 20,947 lb./4 AIM-9, Gross 24,311 lb.; Combat 23,161 lb./6 Mk 82SE, Gross 26,525 lb., Max. 31,000 lb. Fuel 1187 +1164 gal.
PERFORMANCE: Speed- Top 661 mph clean, 611 mph/four AIM-9 at s.l., 584 mph at 30,000', Cruising 464 mph, Stalling 122 mph. Combat Ceiling 36,550' Climb 13,750'/1min. Combat Radius 173 miles. Speed- Top 635 mph/6 Mk 82SE at s.l., Cruising 465 mph, Stalling 152 mph. Combat Ceiling 36,400'. Climb 13,100'/1min. Combat Radius 221 miles/six Mk 82SE bombs. Ferry Range 2458 miles.

McDONNELL AV-8B before takeoff

The first of eight 20-plane Marine AV-8B attack squadrons was VMA-331, established in January 1985, and began its first Westpac cruise in January 1987 aboard the *Belleau Wood* (LHA-3). Amphibious assault ships of that class could operate up to 20 Harriers and several helicopters.

Weight is especially critical in STOL aircraft. Weighing 21,201 pounds, a clean AV-8B could take off in only 260 feet and top speed was 661 mph, but that was without any weapons at all. When carrying four AIM-9 missiles and its gun, AV-8B takeoff required 510 feet, and top speed was 611 mph. That run was reduced to 275 feet when taking off into a 25-knot wind over an LHA's deck. With six Mk 82SE bombs, 730 or 425 feet are needed.

Production of 256 AV-8B and 20 two-place TAV-8B continued until April 1996. The Gulf War in 1991 involved five Marine squadrons with 60 Harriers flying 3,380 sorties in 42 days. They flew against ground targets from the *USS Nassau* (LHA-4) and a small Saudi Arabian field and lost five planes to enemy ground fire.

In 1993, Marine aircraft modernization programmed a gradual remanufacture to the "Harrier II Plus" standard with APG-65 radar, new ECM, and F402-RR-408 engine. At the century's end, 130 Harriers remained in the inventory.

Italy became the fourth country to try the Harrier II when two TAV-8B trainers were purchased in May 1989 and 16 reworked AV-8B+ models ordered on April 1994. They arrived in time to fly combat missions in Somalia in 1995.

The A-10 Warthog

The A-10 was the first Air Force jet plane in service that was specifically designed for the close air support mission. Low-altitude daylight attack with a heavy load of conventional weapons was its role, and no compromises in favor of high speed or nuclear delivery were made.

Preliminary design study contracts for specialized close air support aircraft had been awarded to General Dynamics, Grumman, Northrop and McDonnell on May 2,1967. The preliminary data received was used to prepare new requirements, and a request for proposals was issued May 7, 1970, for competitive prototype development.

Six companies responded by August 10, and on December 18, the Republic Aviation Division of Fairchild Industries, Farmingdale, New York, and the Northrop Corporation, Hawthorne, California, were selected to build two competing prototypes each. The plan was to "fly-before-buy", as had been done before World War II.

The designations A-9 and A-10 were given the California and New York contenders on March 1, 1971. Both were to be single-place, with two turbofan power plants chosen for fuel economy, not speed, and straight wings to ease into short field landings. A new 30-mm Gatling-type gun was carried, along with ten hard points under the wing for up to 16,000-pounds of mixed ordinance. Low cost was preferred to performance over stated requirements, and high survivability against enemy ground fire was important.

Fairchild Republic's A-10 flew at Edwards AFB May 10, 1972, and Northrop's A-9 on May 30, both ahead of schedule. An intensive competitive flyoff of the four prototypes, involving 635 flying hours, was completed by December 9. In many respects they were similar, but the lighter Northrop had two Lycoming engines under the roots of a high wing and had a single tail. The A-10 had two General Electric turbofans in pods above and behind the low wings and had twin tail fins.

NORTHROP A-9A
Two Lycoming YF102-LD-100, 7500 lb. st
DIMENSIONS: Span 58', Lg. 53'6", Ht. 16'11", Wing Area 580 sq. ft.
WEIGHT: Gross 26,000 lb. (clean), Max. 42,000 lb.
PERFORMANCE: Speed- Top 449 mph at s.l., Cruising 322 mph. Service Ceiling 40,000'. Combat Radius 288 miles/9540 lb. Ferry Range 3622 miles.

Fairchild was announced the winner January 18, 1973, and on March 1, a $159 million cost-plus incentive fee contract for ten preproduction aircraft was made, while General Electric won the engine and gun system contracts. Comparing the prototypes, then designated YA-10A, to the A-7D, led to release of funds for 52 production aircraft July 31, 1974. The first preproduction aircraft flew February 15, 1975, and the first production aircraft, October 21, 1975.

Anti-tank operations were the major A-10 mission, and the seven-barrel 30-mm GAU-8/A cannon and its 1,350 rounds of armor-piercing explosive ammunition, combined with six AGM-65A Maverick missiles, demonstrated a lethal effect on hostile armor. Eight 530-pound bombs were carried on escort missions, and 18 on close air support missions with a 250 nautical mile (288 statute mile) radius and two-hour loiter time. Twenty-eight such bombs could be carried with reduced fuel load, or three 600-gallon ferry tanks, or many other stores options.

Survivability was promised by high maneuverability at low speeds, redundant structural and control elements, foam-protected fuel cells, a titanium armor plate "bathtub" to protect the cockpit, and ECM devices. A two-place all-weather version with radar was converted from a preproduction aircraft and flown May 4, 1979, but was not repeated.

The 354th Tactical Fighter Wing was the first to replace its A-7Ds with A-10s, having one 24-plane squadron fully operational by October 15, 1977, and all 72 planes a year later. Next came the 81st TFW, stationed in Britain, with three more TAC wings and ANG units scheduled.

FAIRCHILD REPUBLIC A-10A
The A-10's gun is this seven-barrel GAU-8/A that fires either 2,100 or 4,200 30-mm rounds per minute, and weighs 1,975 pounds empty and 4,041 pounds with the 1,950 round magazine.

FAIRCHILD REPUBLIC A-10A
Two General Electric TF34-GE-100, 9065 lb. st
DIMENSIONS: Span 57'6", Lg. 53'3", Ht. 14'8", Wing Area 506 sq. ft.
WEIGHT: Empty 19,856 lb., Combat 34,532 lb./8 Mk 82, (38,136 lb./18 Mk 82), Gross 40,269 (45,701) lb., Max. 46,786 lb. Fuel 1638 +1800 gal.
PERFORMANCE: Speed- Top 448 mph at s.l., 460 mph at 10,000'. /8 Mk 82, (433-448 mph/18 Mk 82), Cruising 329 mph, Stalling 120 mph, Combat Ceiling 36,600' (33,400') Climb 6200' (5340')/1 min., Combat Radius 288 (280) miles. Ferry Range 3510 miles.

Thunderbolt II, the name given by the company, was somehow replaced by the pilots by Warthog.

Production of 713 A-10As was completed on March 20, 1985, and none were transferred to other countries. Gulf War deployment of the A-10 included the 10th, 23rd, and 354th TFW, as well as the 706th TFS and 23rd TAS, the latter with OA-10s fitted for FAC work.

A-10s flew 8,100 sorties, firing over 5,000 AGM-65 Maverick missiles, dropping Mk 82 bombs and CBUs, and even two hostile helicopters fell to guns, although no enemy fighters were engaged. Among the score of ground targets claimed were nearly 1,000 tanks, over 3,000 other vehicles, 190 radar sites, and mobile Scud missile launchers.

Of some 144 Warthogs in the Gulf War, only five A-10s were lost in combat and 367 still remained in the active Air Force, ANG and Reserve fleets on September 30, 2000.

A rejected program

A Navy two-seat attack type designated A-12 on October 3, 1988, was designed by a General Dynamics/ McDonnell Douglas team. As a delta-wing design with internal bomb bays and folding wingtips, the A-12 had a 10,800-pound thrust F404-GE-400D turbofan and a potentially stealthy airframe.

Although a program was considered for 858 Navy and Marine aircraft at an estimated cost of 96.2 million each, delays and cost increases discouraged the Pentagon. Defense Secretary Richard Cheney canceled the A-12 on January 12, 1991. While a six-year legal battle over some three billion dollars in development costs occurred, the most important result was that there would be no new carrier-based attack plane for the rest of the century.

Instead, the Navy would rely on the strike fighter concept, completely removed from the slow torpedo seaplanes of the first World War. This book has also shown how the Air Force advanced from 1920's twin-engine GAX ground attack to the A-10's power to strike surface forces, a factor forever changing warfare.

CHAPTER 36

FIGHTERS FOR THE MISSILE ERA

Mfr

Vought F8U-3
Pratt & Whitney J75-P-5A, 16,500 lb. st 29, 000 lb. AB
DIMENSIONS: Span 39'11", Lg. 58'11", Ht. 16'5", Wing Area 450 sq. ft. / WEIGHT: Empty 21,862 lb., Combat 32,318 lb., Gross 37,856 lb. Fuel 2036 gal. / PERFORMANCE: (Estimated) Speed– Top 800 mph at s.l., 1457 mph at 50,000', Cruising 575 mph, Stalling 154 mph. Combat Ceiling 51,500', Climb 35,000'/1.6 min. Loiter time 1.7 hour. Combat Radius 173 miles, Max. Range 2044 miles.

The expanding power of nuclear weapons, land-based bombers, and cruise missiles during the Cold War threatened the Navy's carriers and assault ships. Instead of fighter guns, a more certain defense seemed to be the Sparrow III semi-active radar homing missile, capable of destroying a target 30 miles away with one shot.

That missile's first full guidance flight on February 13, 1953, at Point Mugu, was followed by operational evaluation and deployment with VF-64's F3H Demons in December 1958. When launched from an all-weather, Mach 2 fighter, such Sparrows would provide the long-range fleet air defense essential to the Navy

Chance Vought designers offered the single-seat F8U-3 as such an interceptor. The fuselage was enlarged to accommodate the Pratt & Whitney J75, the chin intake was raked forward, and blown flaps obtained boundary-layer control on the variable-incidence wings. Three Sparrow III missiles were semi-submerged in the fuselage, APQ-50 radar was provided, retractable ventral fins aided stability, and push buttons engaged an automatic flight control system.

Two prototypes were ordered on May 3, 1957, plus 16 F8U-3s on January 16, 1958, and the first prototype flew June 2, 1958, just six days after rival McDonnell's Phantom. A modified J75-P-6 credited with 29,000-pounds thrust powered the first F8U-3, the next was flown September 27 with a 24,500-pound thrust J75-P-5, and a J57-P-8 was scheduled for production aircraft. A proposed auxiliary rocket to be mounted at the tail fin's base was tested on two FJ-4F Fury conversions, but was cancelled before the F8U-3 was flown.

During flight tests a speed of Mach 2.39 (1,600 mph) was obtained, and only the windshield's heat limitation prevented higher speeds. Full performance data is not available, but test pilots reported the F8U-3 a very maneuverable, superior fighter. By December 1958, however, the Navy had chosen the more versatile rival F4H-l for the mission, the Vought contract was canceled, and only the third F8U-3 was flown before termination.

The F-4 Phantom II

McDonnell's Phantom II successfully opened the era of the Mach 2 missile-launching fighter and became the most widely used American supersonic fighter, despite its design as a specialized carrier aircraft.

Two prototypes had, in fact, been ordered in an October 18, 1954, letter contract as twin-engine AH-l attack aircraft, but on May 26, 1955, they were redesignated F4H-l all-weather fighters, and a second crewman, the radar intercept officer (RIO) was added.

USN

McDONNELL F4H-l (F-4A)

The first F4H-l (X prefixes were no longer used on prototypes intended for production) flew May 27, 1958, at St. Louis, piloted by Robert C. Little. Two General Electric J79-GE-3A engines had variable area intakes with flat ramps to shear away the boundary layer from the forward fuselage. The 45-degree swept wing had 12-degree dihedral on the folding outer panel, and 23-degree anhedral on the one-piece stabilator aided stability. Four 400-pound Sparrow III radar missiles recessed under the fuselage had a ten-mile range, while four 200-pound heat-homing Sidewinders (two-mile range), or two more Sparrows, could be added under the outboard wing pylons.

The Navy chose the reliability and weapons potential of the twin-engine, two-seat Phantom II over the single-place F8U-3, so competitive tests resulted in a developmental contract for the St. Louis company by December 17, 1958. Eighteen aircraft delivered by November 1959, with 16,500-pound thrust J79-GE-2 engines and APQ-50 radar with a 24-inch dish in the nose, were followed by 29, accepted from May 1960 to June 1961, whose APQ-72 radar had a 32-inch dish. These aircraft were used for tests and training, joining VF-121 at NAS Miramar in December 1960.

A series of record-breaking flights advertised the Phantom's performance, including a zoom climb to 98,556 feet on December 6, 1959, a sustained altitude of 66,443 feet two years later, and a 1,606 mph (Mach 2.57) world's speed record set by the modified second prototype on November 22, 1961, along with a climb to 49,212 feet in 114 seconds. No armament was fitted for any of these records, of course. On May 10, 1962, a Sparrow III missile fired from an F4H-1 made the first successful head-on attack on a Regulus supersonic cruise missile.

The first operational version, flown on March 27, 1961, became the F-4B on September 18, 1962, while the first 47 F4H-1s became the F-4As, after being known as F4H-1F models for a short time. VF-102 was aboard the shakedown cruise of the *Enterprise*, the first nuclear carrier, from February to April 1962, while in June the first Marine F-4B squadron became VMF (AW)-314. VF-74 became the first full operational F-4B squadron on the *Forrestal* (CV-59) in August, beginning 24 years of carrier deployments.

McDONNELL F-4B
Two General Electric J79-GE-8, 17,000-lb. st AB
DIMENSIONS: Dimensions: Span 38'5", Lg. 58'3", Ht. 16'4", Wing Area 530 sq. ft.
WEIGHT: Empty 27,897 lb., Combat 38,505 lb./4 AIM-7D, Gross 43,907 lb., Max. 55,170 lb. Fuel 1986+740+600 gal.
PERFORMANCE: Speed- Top 845 mph at s.l., 1473 mph at 45,000', Cruising 580 mph, Stalling 95 mph. Combat Ceiling 56,850'. Climb 40,800'/1 min. Combat Radius 472 miles/four AIM-7D, 530 miles/12 500-lb. bombs, 885 miles/Mk 28, Combat Range 1297 miles/1986 gal., 2076 miles max.

Powered by J79-GE-8s, the F-4B had a slightly raised canopy, APQ-72 radar with an infrared detector underneath the nose, and leading and trailing edge flaps for boundary layer control. Four AIM-7D Sparrows and two 370-gallon drop tanks on the inboard pylons was normal, but a 600-gallon tank or a 2,040-pound Mk 28 nuclear bomb could carried on a center-line pylon. Another option allowed from 12 to 24 500-pound Mk 82 bombs or other stores and four AIM-9B Sidewinders could be added when desired. An inflight refueling probe was provided to replenish JP-4 fuel on long flights.

Two 14-plane Navy F-4B squadrons served each of the large carriers, but five *Essex*-class carriers still in service retained Vought F-8 Crusaders. Nine Marine F-4B VMF (AW) all-weather fighter squadrons were redesignated VMFA (Fighter Attack) squadrons in 1964. In 1964, VF-213 tested 12 designated F-4Gs with ASW-21 data systems, but all were converted to standard F-4B configurations in 1966.

By January 27, 1967, 649 F-4Bs were delivered to 22 fleet squadrons. The RF-4B, a photo-reconnaissance version, flew March 12, 1965, and by December 1970, 46 were delivered to three Marine squadrons: VMC-1, -2, and -3. Upgraded electronics kept the RF-4B in service until August 1990.

USAF Phantoms

Air Force intentions to obtain Phantoms were announced January 17, 1962, and 29 F-4Bs were borrowed from the Navy to train instructor pilots. Designated F-110As, the first two arrived at Langley AFB for TAC on January 24. In March, the first production contract was placed for 310 F-4C and 26 RF-4C aircraft, and their first examples were flown on May 27, 1963, and August 20, respectively. McDonnell delivered 583 F-4Cs to 23 TAC squadrons from November 20, 1963, to May 4, 1966.

Essentially, the F-4C was similar to its Navy counterpart except for J79-GE-15 engines, APQ-100 radar, flight controls in the second cockpit, an Air Force boom flight-refueling receptacle, and larger wheels.

McDONNELL F-4C
Two General Electric J79-GE-15, 10,900 lb. st military, 17,000 lb. AB
DIMENSIONS: Span 38'5", Lg. 58'3", Ht. 16'6", Wing Area 530 sq. ft.
WEIGHT: Empty 28,496 lb., Combat 38,328 lb., Gross 51,441 lb., Max. 59,064 lb. Fuel 1972+1340 gal.
PERFORMANCE: Speed- Top 826 mph at s.l., 1433 mph at 40,000', Cruising 587 mph, Stalling 165 mph. Combat Ceiling 55,600', Service Ceiling 56,100'. Climb 40,550'/1 min. Combat Radius 538 miles/Mk-28, 323 miles/11-750 lb. bombs. Ferry Range 1926 miles.

An AJB-7 bombing system directed a Mk 28 nuclear store, six to eleven M117 bombs, or other stores. Four AIM-7D Sparrows were standard, and four AIM-9B Sidewinders or AGM-12B Bullpup missiles could be added on wing pylons.

Two YRF-4Cs with cameras in a longer nose were converted from F-4Bs in 1963 to provide TAC with a supersonic tactical reconnaissance type. The 503 RF-4Cs delivered from June 1964 to January 1974 replaced missiles with cameras, photoflash cartridges, and APQ-99 radar, but retained the nuclear bomb provisions. They entered operational service in September 1964, the 16th Tactical Reconnaissance Squadron becoming the first to be combat ready in August 1965, and served 12 TAC and three ANG squadrons throughout the 1970s.

McDONNELL RF-4C
Two General Electric J79-GE-15, 10,900 lb. st military, 17,000 lb. AB
DIMENSIONS: Span 38'5", Lg. 62'11", Ht. 16'6", Wing Area 530 sq. ft.
WEIGHT: Empty 28,104 lb., Combat 39,788 lb., Gross 52,346 lb., Max. 52,450 lb. Fuel 1889+1340 gal.
PERFORMANCE: Speed- Top 834 mph at s.l., 1460 mph at 40,000', Cruising 587 mph, Stalling 167 mph. Combat Ceiling 55,790', Service Ceiling 56,220'. Climb 38,950'/1 min. Combat Radius 838 miles, 506 miles/Mk 28. Ferry Range 1750 miles.

Flyaway cost was 2.3 million dollars each, but when service life-cycle is considered, the Air Force did well. From October 1965 to April 1973 the RF-4C flew vital reconnaissance missions in Southeast Asia. Many improvements in radar, ECM pods, infrared and optical sensors extended service life. As late as February 1991, six ANG RF-4Cs flew 103 combat sorties into Iraq from Turkey.

The Phantom at War

When Navy F-4Bs began missions over Vietnam, there were no enemy fighters present, so only bombs were expended on early sorties by VF-96 and VMFA-531. But in April 1965 the Americans were challenged by a VPAF fighter regiment's MiG-17s.

Four of those fighters attacked A-1H Skyraiders from the *Midway* on June 17, but Sparrows from two VF-21 F-4Bs shot down two MiGs. By 1968, ten MiGs had been downed in air combat in exchange for four F-4Bs.

War brought F-4Cs of the 45th TFS squadron to Thailand early in 1965, but two MiG-17s downed with Sidewinders on July 10 were their only success that year. Ten F-4C squadrons were in SEA by April 1966, and six victories that month included a MiG-21.

The Phantom's missiles had been designed with bomber interception in mind, and often were evaded with a sharp turn by an alert target. When a gun was desired for close-range work, the 20-mm M61 SUU-16 1,200-round gun pod was introduced in May 1967, but it degraded performance. The F-4Cs downed 42 MiGs; 22 with Sidewinders, 14 with Sparrows, four with gun pods, and two with "maneuvering tactics." Most of the 54 F-4Cs lost in 1965/66 were lost to ground fire.

While the F-4D looked like the F-4C, it was intended for hitting ground targets with a wide variety of attack stores guided by APG-109A radar. The usual four Sparrows could joined by four AIM-4D Falcons, but these were replaced with more reliable Sidewinders. First flown on December 9, 1965, 793 F-4Ds were delivered to the Air Force from March 1966 to February 1968 for 1.7 million dollars each.

F-4Ds replaced the F-4C in SEA squadrons, and were credited, beginning on June 5, 1967, with 44 victories: 26 with Sparrows, six with gun pods, five each for Falcons and Sidewinders, and two with maneuvers. F-4D combat losses by June 1973 were 170, including 127 to AAA, 17 to MiGs, 17 unknown, and 9 to SAMs. Another 24 were lost in accidents.

McDONNELL F-4D
Two General Electric J79-GE-15, 10,900 lb. st military, 17,000 lb. AB
DIMENSIONS: As F4C
WEIGHT: Empty 28,958 lb., Combat 38,781 lb., Gross 51,577 lb., Max. 59,380 lb. Fuel 1889+1340 gal.
PERFORMANCE: Speed- Top 826 at sea level, 1432 mph at 40,000', Cruising 587 mph, Stalling 165 mph. Combat Ceiling 55,400', Service Ceiling 55,850', Climb 40,100'/1 min. Combat Radius 500 miles/MK-28, 527 mph/six M-117. Ferry Range 1844 miles.

The F-4D also introduced new ground attack methods with various rockets and missiles, including the AGM-62A Walleye on August 24, 1967, the GBU-10 laser-guided bomb on May 23, 1968, and widespread enemy SAMs also led to the addition of various ECM devices.

A Gun for the F-4E

After trials of three YF-4Es converted from older aircraft by adding the built-in M61Al gun pilots desired, the Secretary of Defense authorized procurement on July 22, 1966, of the F-4E. First flown on June 30, 1967, the first F-4E had J79-GE-17s, APQ-120 fire control radar and new electronics, with the infrared scanner deleted to make room for the M61A and 639 20-mm rounds. The same

McDONNELL F-4E
Two General Electric J79-GE-17, 11,870 lb. st military, 17,900 lb. AB
DIMENSIONS: Span 38'5", Lg. 63', Ht. 16'6", Wing Area 530 sq. ft.
WEIGHT: Empty 29,535 lb., Combat 38,019 lb./four AIM-7E, Gross 53,848 lb., Max. 61,651 lb. Fuel 1993+1340 gal.
PERFORMANCE: Speed- Top 914 mph at s.l., 1464 mph at 40,000'/4 AIM-7E, (1485 mph clean), Cruising 586 mph, Stalling 158 mph. Combat Ceiling 59,200', Service Ceiling 59,600', Climb 54,200'/1 min. Combat Radius 533 miles/Mk 28, Ferry Range 1885 miles.

weapons and external fuel tank options remained, and the 33rd TFW became the first to fly the type in 1967. Slotted stabilators improved agility.

Production of 1,387 F-4E models, including 959 for the USAF, made them the most numerous Phantom model built, but numerous difficulties delayed their deployment overseas. Sixteen did arrive at Korat, Thailand, to replace F-105Ds of the 469th TFS, in November 1968, and the 4th TFS came to Da Nang in Vietnam, on April 12, 1969. Since the bombing pause suspended attacks on North Vietnam, their work consisted of close support with a wide variety of weapons.

The SAM threat led to the "Wild Weasel" ECM aircraft in 1969. ECM pods were added to 36 F-4Cs, redesignated EF-4C, to detect and attack SAM sites with AGM-45 Shrikes.

Phantoms return to North Viet Nam

The Navy's F-4J was similar in armament to the F-4B, but had APQ-59 radar, AWG-10 fire control, new navigation and bombing systems, refined engines, landing flaps, and slotted stabilators. First flown on May 27, 1966, F-4Js entered service with VF-101 in December 1966, and 522 were delivered by January 7, 1972. A new "Top Gun" program of pilot training at Miramar prepared new tactics.

McDONNELL F-4F

A VF-142 F-4J claimed a MiG-21 on March 28, 1970, but not until January 19, 1972, did a VF-96 F-4J down the next MiG-21. That plane's team of Lt Randy Cunningham and LTJG William Driscoll would use AIM-9 Sidewinders to become the only Navy aces of the war.

From April 1965 to January 1973, Navy F-4 crews claimed 41 MiGs shot down and lost 125 F-4s: 53 to AAA, 13 to SAMs, five to MiGs, and 54 in accidents. Marine losses were 95: 65 to AAA, six to ground attacks, one to a MiG, and 23 in accidents.

An enemy 1972 spring offensive had escalated the war in Viet Nam, and on May 7, President Nixon suspended peace talks and authorized renewal of air strikes throughout North Vietnam. Another four F-4E squadrons joined the seven F-4D and F-4E squadrons in SEA for this campaign. Using new electronic technology and guided bombs the Air Force hit missile sites and transportation targets; one example was the F-4D that cut the tough Paul Doumier Bridge on May 10 with a 3,020-pound M118 smart bomb aimed by an ASQ-153 Pave Knife pod, while other F-4s drove off MiGs and jammed scores of SAMs with a chaff barrier.

On May 23, 1972, the F-4E scored its first victory over a Chinese-built MiG-19 with an AIM-7, but the second kill that day was a MiG-21 hit with the M61 gun. Of 17 MiG-21s and four MiG-19s downed by F-4Es by October 22, 1972, ten fell to Sparrows, six to gunfire, four to Sidewinders, and one to maneuvering. Only 47 of the 187 VPAF MiGs were still operational by autumn 1972, according to the main Russian adviser.

The last American victory over North Vietnam was a MiG-21 destroyed by an F-4D's Sparrow on January 8, 1973. Of 137 enemy aircraft downed by the USAF over Vietnam, Phantoms were credited with 107: 33 MiG-17s, 8 MiG-19s, and 66 MiG-21s. Total Air Force Phantom fighter losses amounted to 442: 307 to AAA, 33 to MiGs, 30 to SAMs, nine to ground attacks, and 63 in accidents. Despite their speed, 83 RF-4Cs were also lost: 65 to AAA, seven to SAMS, four to ground attacks, and seven to accidents.

Vietnamese accounts, as might be expected, contradict some of these figures, especially in asserting that many American losses blamed on AAA should really be credited to MiGs.

Refining the Phantom

After the war ended, the Phantom was the most widely used USAF combat aircraft, with six F-4C, 19 F-4D, and 22 F-4E squadrons. From September 1972 to April 1976, F-4Es added leading edge slats to improve maneuverability while new AIM-7F Sparrows and AIM-9L missiles had more range and higher kill probability. Numerous updates and modifications made during the F-4E's 12-year production life included self-sealing fuel tanks, improved radar, and target-designator systems.

In December 1975, tests began on the first Wild Weasel F-4G model made by fitting 116 F-4Es with an APR-38 warning and attack system. The M61 gun was removed to make room for the ECM gear and controls for AGM-78 or AGM-88 anti-radiation missiles, AGM-75 attack missiles, or cluster bombs. The 35th TFW became the first with F-4Gs in April 1978.

Two F-4G Wild Weasel squadrons flew 2,331 combat sorties in the Gulf War, hitting Iraqi sites with AGM-88 missiles without loss. The last F-4G unit changed to F-16s in October 1994, and the last USAF active duty F-4G was retired in March 26, 1996.

The Navy accepted 1,264 F-4s, extending their service life by equipment updates. On September 13, 1971, the F-4N designation was promulgated for 228 F-4Bs refurbished at North Island NARF in San Diego. First flown on June 4, 1972, the F-4N had new electronics and ALQ-126 ECM.

That facility also modified F-4Js to the F-4S configuration first delivered July 22, 1977, with AWG-10B fire control. Beginning with the 48th of 265 reworked aircraft, leading edge slats were installed. While the F-4S began joining 13 Marine squadrons in June 1978, its improvements also allowed 12 Navy Phantom squadrons to be retained for three *Midway*-class carriers unable to handle the F-14As adopted for all the larger carriers.

McDONNELL F-4J
Two General Electric J79-GE-10, 11,870 lb. st military, 17,859 lb. AB
DIMENSIONS: Span 38'5", Lg. 58'4", Ht. 15'10", Wing Area 530 sq. ft.
WEIGHT: Empty 30,770 lb., Combat 41,399 lb./four AIM-7E, Gross 46,833 lb., Max. 55,896 lb. Fuel 1998+1340 gal.
PERFORMANCE: Speed- Top 875 mph at s.l., 1416 mph at 36,089', Combat Ceiling 54,700', Climb 41,250'/1 min. Combat Radius 596 miles/four AIM-7E/600 gal. tank, Ferry Range 1956 miles.

Navy F-4 carrier operations ended when the *Midway* flew off the last F-4S Phantom of VF-151 on March 25, 1986, and the shore-based VF-202 at NAS Dallas retired its last F-4S on May 14, 1987. The last shore-based Marine squadron, VMFA-112, retired its last Phantom II on January 18, 1992, ending 30 years of service. Retired Phantoms were mostly expended as QF-4 target drones.

McDONNELL YF-4K

Lawson

McDONNELL F-4S

Phantom in Foreign Service

Britain announced an order for the F-4K for the Royal Navy on February 27, 1964, and for the F-4M for the RAF on February 2, 1965. Both were to use British-made Rolls-Royce Spey engines rated at 20,515-pound thrust, with almost half the cost in British-supplied equipment and parts. The first of two YF-4Ks was flown June 27, 1966, with 50 F-4K (Phantom FG.Mk 1) arriving in Britain beginning April 1968.

No 893 Squadron served aboard Britain's last large aircraft carrier, the *Ark Royal*, from 1970 until its final cruise ended December 4, 1978. To fit this carrier's elevators and short deck, the radome could be folded back, and the nose landing gear extension was increased to increase the angle of attack at takeoff. Increased power and enlarged air intakes improved the F-4K's takeoff, acceleration, and combat radius, although top speed decreased from Mach 2.2 to 1.9. Armament was similar to the F-4J.

The RAF's first YF-4M flew February 17, 1967, and the production F-4M on December 26. From July 1968 to August 1969, the RAF received two YF-4M and 116 Ms, which they designated Phantom FGR.Mk 2, as well as 28 of the Ks, and eight squadrons flew Phantoms in 1978. During the Falklands crisis in 1984, 15 surplus F-4Js were added to the RAF inventory. The last FGR.Mk 2 retired from No. 74 Squadron in October 1992.

Iran was the next to order Phantoms on September 30, 1966, and got 32 new F-4Ds, which first reached

SDAM

McDONNELL F-4M

Two Rolls-Royce RB.168-25 Spey 202, 12,250 lb. st military, 20,515 lb. AB
DIMENSIONS: Span 38'5", Lg. 63', Ht. 16'1", Wing Area 530 sq. ft.
WEIGHT: Empty 31,000 lb., Combat 38,019 lb./four AIM-7E, Gross 52,400 lb., Max. 56,000 lb. Fuel 1363 +1340 gal.
PERFORMANCE: Speed- Top 1386 mph at 40,000'/4 AIM-7E, Service Ceiling 60,800', Ferry Range 1750 miles.

Teheran in September 1968, as well as 177 F-4Es and 16 RF-4Es delivered from April 1971 to December 1978. The Shah of Iran was considered to be the strongest obstacle to communist expansion in the Middle East.

The Islamic revolution removed the Shah and turned against Americans, so a February 28, 1979, order stopped production on 47 more Phantoms. Iraq attacked Iran in September 1980 and F-4 pilots began claims for at least 80 kills. After the August 1988 ceasefire, some 95 Phantoms remained, many grounded with parts shortages.

Reacting to Israel's Six-Day War success and the anti-Zionist Soviet position, American governmental opinion swung to military support of Israel. President Lyndon Johnson approved supply of F-4Es on January 7, 1968, and an Israel order for 44 new F-4Es and six new RF-4Es was signed December 27, 1968. These were the first of 428 new F-4Es purchased by foreign air forces.

McDONNELL F-4N

Operation **Peace Echo** began when the first four were flown non-stop by company pilots to Haifa on September 5, 1969. Israeli pilots began attacking Egyptian sites on October 22, and shot down a MiG-21 on November 11. **Peace Echo** deliveries added 36 used-USAF F-4Es from 1970 to 1971, before the ceasefire in the "War of Attrition". In 1972, another **Peace Echo** round brought 24 ex-USAF and 18 new F-4Es for a total of 122 fighters before the Yom Kippur War began on October 6, 1973 with a combined Egyptian-Syrian attack.

Counter-attacking A-4s and F-4s suffered greatly from SAM missiles, and about 37 F-4s were among 109 Israeli aircraft lost in 19 days. As replacements, Operation **Nickel Glass** rushed 48 USAF F-4Es, some Vietnam veterans, to Israel. Tactical lessons learned from that fight shared by both Israelis and Americans resulted in improvements for the Phantom and the last **Peace Echo** resupply provided 24 more ex-USAF 24 new F-4Es, and 12 new RF-4Es by November 1976. By June 1982, 116 Israeli Phantom victories were claimed.

The Republic of Korea is the only Phantom user that got its first aircraft as a gift, 18 F-4Ds paid for by the MAP that began arriving in August 1969. Another 18 arrived in 1972, followed by six more in 1982, and 24 in 1988. Nineteen new F-4Es arrived in 1978 and the last 18 Phantoms built in St. Louis came in 1980.

West Germany's Luftwaffe purchased 88 RF-4E Phantoms, which began arriving there in January 1971, and ordered 175 F-4F fighters in August. First flown May 18, 1973, the F-4F was lighter than the F-4E, with the M61 gun and four Sidewinders, but deleting the Sparrows, and utilizing leading edge slats. They reached Germany from September 1973 to April 1976, and ten standard F-4Es were also purchased for crew training in America. Upgrading F-4F electronics with AIM-120A missiles in 1991 provided Germany with air defense for the rest of the century.

McDONNELL F-4G with Shrikes, Mavericks, and Sparrows.

Japan was unique in building its own Phantoms under license, giving the Japanese Air Self-Defense Force an interceptor version with no bombing provisions. Ordered November 1, 1968, the first of two F-4EJ pattern aircraft flew at St. Louis on January 14, 1971, and both flew to Japan in July. Parts for 11 F-4EJ fighters were shipped for assembly by Mitsubishi, which produced another 127 under license by May 1981. McDonnell also built 14 RF-4EJs for Japan by June 1975.

Beginning in March 1974, 50 new F-4Es and eight RF-4Es were delivered to Greece, and in 1991 28 ex-USAF F-4Es were supplied. Turkey purchased 72 new F-4Es and eight RF-4Es from August 1974 to 1978, and from 1981 to 1991 added 125 ex-USAF aircraft.

Phantoms from ex-USAF stocks went to other countries. Australia leased 24 F-4Es from September 1970 to June 1973 to fill in for deferred F-111Cs. Spain acquired 36 ex-USAF F-4Cs from October 1971 to September 1972. They were retired in April 1979, but 12 RF-4Cs remained in service. Egypt got 35 F-4Es, beginning in September 1979 and found them much more difficult to maintain, compared to MiG-21s.

The Phantom II total reached 5,068 built in St. Louis and 127 in Japan. Used by 12 countries, its multi-purpose armament and performance set a new life cycle expectancy for combat aircraft.

Northrop F-5

The first air force fighter designed primarily for smaller allied nations, the Northrop F-5A was the opposite of the F-4C in weight and cost. From its inception in 1955, the Northrop was designed to have supersonic performance with life cycle costs less than any jet type since the F-80. After the successful parallel development of the T-38 trainer, the Hawthorne company began building the single-seat N156F as a private venture, until a Defense Department letter contract for three prototypes was offered on February 25, 1958.

Although Lewis Neson flew the prototype on July 30, 1959, at Edwards AFB with two General Electric YJ85-GE-ls of 2,100-pounds thrust each, the various official agencies

Mfr

NORTHROP F-5A
Two General Electric J85-GE-13, 2720 lb. st military, 4080 lb. AB
DIMENSIONS: Span 25'10", Lg. 47'2", Ht. 13'2", Wing Area 170 sq. ft.
WEIGHT: Empty 8085 lb., Combat 11,477 lb./two AIM-9B, 14,012lb./two M117, Gross 13,663 lb., Max. 19,728 lb. Fuel 583+546 gal.
PERFORMANCE: Speed- Top 731 mph at s.l., 925 mph at 36,089', 650 mph at 49,000', Cruising 587 mph, Stalling 164 mph. Combat Ceiling 50,600', Climb 28,700'/1 min. Combat Radius 270 miles/two AIM-9B, 420 miles/two 750-lb. bombs. Ferry Range 1318 miles.

Mfr

NORTHROP N156F

involved could not agree on whether the limited performance was balanced by the much lower costs when compared with other potential standard day fighters for the Mutual Aid Program. Freedom Fighter was the name chosen to help sell the F-5 to the MAP market. Not until April 23, 1962, did the Defense Secretary decide to select the Northrop, by which time the F-104G had gotten much of the potential market.

A production contract made on October 22, 1962, was increased August 23, 1963, to 142 F-5A single-seat fighters and 27 F-5B two-seat, unarmed trainers. The third N156F was completed in May 1963 in F-5A configuration, the first production F-5A flew October 1963, and the first F-5B February 24, 1964.

Mfr

NORTHROP F-5F

Powered by two J85-GE-13s with afterburners, the F-5A was armed with two 20-mm M-39 guns with 280 rpg, and two AIM-9B Sidewinders at the wingtips. Two 50-gallon wing tip tanks and three 150-gallon drop tanks could be used on ferry flights, or five external stores stations could accommodate three 1,000-pound and two 750-pound bombs; but only two bombs were carried for a normal ground support mission. Four cameras replaced guns on the RF-5A version appearing in 1968.

The first Northrops completed at Palmdale went to Williams AFB, Arizona, where a USAF training school with 17 F-5As and 15 F-5Bs began in September 1964 to introduce foreign pilots to the new MAP weapon. All F-5 sales were on a government-to-government basis through the MAP and FMS (Foreign Military Sales -direct purchase) programs.

Iran got the first F-5A and F-5B overseas models in January 1965, and in April 1965 deliveries began to South Korea. Norway was the first NATO country in November 1964 to order 78 F-5As, 16 RF-5As, and 14 F-5Bs, and delivery began in June 1965.

USAF pilots flew twelve Freedom Fighters to Vietnam on October 23, 1965, for combat tests. An inflight refueling probe added for the trans-Pacific flights inspired a temporary F-5C redesignation. Belly armor and camouflage were also added. That provisional squadron began the Skoshi Tiger operation from Bien Hoa immediately, dropping four 500-pound bombs and strafing Viet Cong forces on each sortie. No enemy fighters were present during the 2,644 sorties flown in 150 days and ground fire downed one F-5.

In April 1967, 17 F-5C and two F-5Bs were transferred to Vietnamese pilots to replace their A-1 attack prop planes. The VNAF got 102 more F-5As, 10 RF-5As, and six two-seat F-5Bs from the USAF or hurriedly leased from Taiwan, South Korea, and Iran in 1973.

Libya bought eight F-5As and two F-5Bs in 1968, but later transferred them to Pakistan, who passed them next to Greece; illustrating a difficulty the USAF had in controlling the final disposition of the aircraft.

AF

NORTHROP F-5C in Vietnam

USN

NORTHROP F-5E (Marine adversary markings)
Two General Electric J85-GE-21, 3500 lb. st military, 5000 lb. AB
DIMENSIONS: Span 28', Lg. 48'2", Ht. 13'5", Wing Area 186 sq. ft.
WEIGHT: Empty 9588 lb., Combat 13,188 lb./two AIM-9J, Gross 15,745 lb., Max. 20,486 lb. Fuel 671-946 gal.
PERFORMANCE: Speed- Top 753 mph at s.l., 997 mph at 36,089', 720 mph at 50,000', Cruising 548 mph, Stalling 160 mph. Combat Ceiling 53,000', Service Ceiling 53,800'. Climb 28,536'/1 min./two AIM-9J. Combat Radius 351 miles/275 gal. drop tank, 294 miles/four Mk 82. Ferry Range 1350 miles.

Northrop delivered the last of 621 F-5As in March 1972 at a flyaway cost of $756,000 each, compared to $2.4 million for each F-4E Phantom. Production also added 105 RF-5As and 183 F-5B trainers.

Foreign license production began in May 1968 with 36 SF-5A and 34 SF-5B aircraft built in Spain by CASA, 89 CF-5As and 42 CF-5Bs by Canadair for the RCAF, as well as 75 NF-5As and 30 NF-5Bs for the Netherlands by March 1972. In 1972, 16 ex-RCAF CF-5A and four CF-5B fighters were sold to Venezuela.

Recommendations from Vietnam and other experiences led to the F-5E with more powerful J85-GE-21 engines, more internal fuel, leading edge extensions, maneuvering flaps, and an arresting hook. Two 20-mm M-39 guns with 280 rpg and two AIM-9J Sidewinders were on the wingtips. A centerline pylon could hold either a 2,000-pound Mk 84 bomb or a 275-gallon tank, and four wing pylons could hold 750-pound bombs or rocket pods.

Northrop had introduced the new features on a modified F-5B in March 1969, but the Air Force waited until February 26, 1970 to solicit proposals for a new MAP fighter. Northrop's Mach 1.63 design won over competition from a Lockheed F-104 variant, a stripped McDonnell F-4, and a Vought F-8 variant, so the first contract for 325 F-5Es was made December 8, 1970.

While the first F-5E flew August 11, 1972, engine malfunctions delayed operational service to April 1973. The first 26 (called Tiger IIs) went to the USAF for testing and the training squadron for foreign pilots at Williams AFB, while Vietnam was sent 50 to replace F-5As late in 1973.

On April 8, 1975, a defecting F-5A pilot bombed the presidential palace, signaling the war's last days. When the war ended, 22 F-5Es, three F-5As, one RF-5A, and an F-5B were flown out to Thailand, abandoning 27 F-5Es and 60 older models. The VPAF's new 935th Fighter Regiment flew the F-5Es after May 1975.

Tactical Air Command inherited 71 F-5Es from the VNAF schedule and used them to form Fighter Weapons Squadrons specializing in simulation of Soviet combat tactics. These "aggressor" units flew against the larger aircraft of other TAC units to train them to duel dissimilar aircraft like the smaller MiGs. In 1978, TAC had 36 F-5Es at Nellis AFB, 18 at RAF Alconbury, England, and 12 at Clark in the Philippines, as well as a training squadron for MAP pilots. The U.S. Navy also acquired 17 F-5Es and six F-5Fs for a similar unit, VF-43, at the Miramar fighter base in 1977, and another 11 Northrops for Oceana on the Atlantic coast.

The Republic of Korea and Thailand got F-5Es and F-5Fs through MAP, and Taiwan purchased F-5Es and F-5Fs partially manufactured for final assembly in Taichung, while Saudi Arabia bought 70 F-5E fighters delivered from 1972 to 1978 with an inertial navigation system to supplement the usual austere electronics. When Iran purchased 141 F-5Es and 28 F-5Fs, its older models were sold to Greece, Vietnam, and Jordan.

Jordan's second-hand 17 F-5As and nine F-5Fs were joined by 44 F-5Es and two F-5Fs supplied by the MAP. Ethiopia got 13 F-5As and two F-5Bs in 1975, and ordered 14 F-5Es and two F-5Fs, but only eight F-5Es had been delivered when the Ethiopians expelled the American mission in April 1977, ending that program.

Switzerland purchased her first American combat planes with 66 F-5Es and six F-5Fs, the first completed in November 1977, while the Swiss themselves assembled the last 53 by September 1978.

The rest of the 25 recipient countries are listed in Table 12, Taiwan's purchase of 242 F-5E and 30 F-5F Tigers being the largest, and Bahrain's order for 12 F-5E and 4 F-5F Tigers by 1986, the last. Northrop delivered 1,163 F-5E, 238 F-5F, and 12 RF-5Es by 1986.

Table 12 • F-5 International Deliveries to 1986

Location	F-5A	F-5B	RF-5A	F-5E	F-5F	Remarks
AAF/USN:						
Williams	17	15	—	23	9	
Nellis AFB	—	—	—	53	1	
RAF Alconbury	—	—		23	-	
Miramar NAS	—	—	—	11	3	
East Asia:						
Iran	91	23	13	141	28	January 1965
So. Korea	89	36	—	174	40	1965 Co-production
Philippines	19	3	—	—		1966
Taiwan	92	23	—	242	66	Co-production
Thailand	18	5	4	34	6	1966
Vietnam	95	6	9	33	—	October 1965 to 1975
Europe:						
Greece	77	12	16	—	—	1966
Norway	67	14	16	—	—	in June 1965
Turkey	95	13	36	—	—	1966
Switzerland	—	—	—	66	6	1977 Co-production
Others:						
Morocco	24	4	2	16	4	from MAP in 1967
Libya	8	2	-	—	-	1969
Jordan	17	9	-	61	12	F-5As from Iran, 1967
Ethiopia	16	5	-	8	—	1967-1977
Brazil	—	6	-	36	—	1975
Chile	—	-	-	15	3	beginning June 1976
Saudi Arabia	—	16	-	70	24	+8 RF-4E, 1972-1978
Kenya	—	—	—	10	2	1978
Singapore	—	—	—	18	3	1979
Indonesia	—	—	—	12	4	1982
Malaysia	—	—	—	14	-	+2 RF-4E
Yemen (North)	4	—		12	-	1979
Mexico	—	—	—	10	2	ordered 1981
Bahrain	—	—	—	10	4	October 1985

Source: Field Service Inventory Report, 9-30 and 10-9-1986, Northrop Corp., and press reports. Many F-5s transferred from original owners like Iran have been counted twice.

NORTHROP F-20

A single RF-5E demonstrator was flown January 29, 1979 with one gun and cameras, and Saudi Arabia purchased eight, and Malaysia two. Another effort to extend Northrop sales was the F-20 Tigershark, a single-engine refined F-5 first flown on August 30, 1982. While the first prototype had an F404-GE-100, that engine was replaced by a 17,000-pound thrust F404-GE-404. Unfortunately, two of the three prototypes built by May 1984 had crashed, and the F-16C with the same engine won the future contracts.

The Variable-sweep wing F-111

The General Dynamics F-111 was a controversial Air Force fighter-bomber, and only after years of service is it possible to understand the aircraft's place in history. The most conspicuous feature was the variable-sweep wings enabling the big twin-engine two-seater to operate from smaller air bases while achieving Mach 1.2 at sea level and Mach 2.2 at altitude.

From a 16-degree sweep and 63-foot span at takeoff, the wings could be gradually swept back to a 72-degree sweep and 32-foot span. Two crewmen sat side-by-side in a pressurized compartment contained in an escape module that could be ejected at any speed and altitude. An in-flight refueling boom receptacle was behind the cockpit.

While armament provisions included a 20-mm M61Al with 2,000 rounds and two AIM-9B Sidewinders, the F-111A never engaged enemy fighters, but was a tactical bomber. The basic mission was delivery of a nuclear bomb (Mk 43 or 57) in the weapons bay, or four 2,000 or 12 750-pound bombs on four wing pylons. These pylons could also be used for 600-gallon ferry tanks or a variety of bombs or dispensers. Four more outboard pylons for smaller stores were seldom used.

GENERAL DYNAMICS F-111A (First preproduction)

But the F-111's greatest virtue was the accuracy with which bombs could be delivered at night by the AJQ-20 inertial bombing-navigational system and the computerized APQ-113 attack radar. The first USAF aircraft with APQ-110 terrain-following radar was able to fly close to the ground, below the level of radar observation.

Development of the F-111 series was initially based on a July 1960 operational requirement for an all-weather fighter-bomber to replace the F-105 series, utilizing turbofan power plants and a variable-sweep wing. This concept, described as the TFX tactical fighter, was changed when the new Secretary of Defense, Robert S. McNamara, requested in February 1961 that the Air Force try to join with the Navy to produce a common design. Such commonality did work with the F-4s and was an attractive way to control costs.

GENERAL DYNAMICS F-111A of 474th TFW
Two Pratt & Whitney TF30-P-3, 10,750 lb. st military, 18,500 lb. AB
DIMENSIONS: Span 63' (32'swept), Lg. 73'6", Ht.17', Wing Area 525 sq. ft.
WEIGHT: Empty 46,172 lb., Combat 63,051 lb. Gross 82,819 lb./2000 lb., Max. 98,850 lb. Fuel 5043+2400 gal.
PERFORMANCE: Speed- Top 914 mph at s.l., 1453 mph at 53,450', Cruising 1194 mph, Stalling 152 mph. Combat Ceiling 56,650', Climb 25,550'/1 min. Combat Radius 1330 miles/2000-lb. bomb/twoAIM-9B;784miles/12M-117.FerryRange3634 miles.

The Navy had planned a two-place straight-winged fighter with two Pratt & Whitney TF-30 turbofans, designated the Douglas F6D-1 Missileer. Ordered July 21, 1960, it would carry six large Eagle (AAM-N-10) long-range-missiles under the wings. This relatively slow 60,000-pound aircraft would loiter for up to ten hours until its radar spotted targets for the missiles' own radar homing system. That program was cancelled April 25, 1961.

Instead, Secretary McNamara insisted on a common fighter design with the Air Force, proposing on September 1, 1961, a twin-engine, supersonic two-seater with accommodations for either 10,000 lbs. of bombs or six large air-to-air missiles, and weights and dimensions limited by Navy carrier requirements.

The Air Force also insisted on transatlantic ferry capability, with the ability to operate from unprepared fields, as part of its NATO support role. On September 29, new requests for proposals were sent to manufactures, and nine responded by December. The designation F-111, last of the old fighter series, was assigned to the program.

Boeing and General Dynamics each received design data contracts in February 1962, and submitted second, third and fourth proposals that year. Boeing's design used a General Electric engine design (as yet untested) with intakes above the fuselage, and General Dynamics chose Pratt & Whitney TF30 turbofans, with intakes under the wings. The Air Force Selection Board preferred the Boeing design as promising better performance at a lower price, but the Secretary of Defense ordered the TFX contract given to General Dynamics, because of the higher degree of identical structure for the Air Force and Navy versions, and the belief that Boeing's cost estimate was unrealistic.

Senator John L. McClellan directed a widely publicized critical probe of the situation, but F-111 procurement went ahead. Twenty-three developmental aircraft were ordered

Mfr

GENERAL DYNAMICS F-111B
Two Pratt & Whitney TF P-1A, 18,500 lb. st AB
DIMENSIONS: Span 70' (33'11" swept) Lg. 66'9", Ht. 16'8", Wing Area 550 sq. ft.
WEIGHT: Empty 46,000 lb., Combat 63,220 lb./two AIM-54A or 68,365 lb./six AIM-54A, Gross 72,421 lb., Max. 77,566 lb. Fuel 3383+900 gal.
PERFORMANCE: Speed-Top 780 mph at s.l., 1450 mph at 40,000', Cruising 483 mph, Stalling 131 mph. Combat Ceiling 44,900', Climb 21,300'/1 min., Combat Radius 546 miles/six AIM-54A, Ferry Range 3178 miles.

December 21, 1962, from General Dynamics, with Grumman as the subcontractor for the Navy's F-111B version.

The first F-111A flew at Fort Worth on December 21, 1964, the second on February 25, 1965, and on April 12 a letter contract was announced for 431 aircraft. The first 18 preproduction aircraft had no gun provisions and TF30-P-l engines that suffered numerous compressor stalls. A production F-111A first flew on February 12, 1967, but not until September 24 was the TF30-P-3 flown on the 31st production F-111A.

The Navy's F-111B carried two Phoenix (AIM-54A) missiles in the weapons bay and four more under the wings, with the Hughes AWG-9 fire control whose radome nose folded upwards for stowage. A pair of 450-gallon tanks or other weapons stores could be carried on the six under wing pylons, and the wings were lengthened for improved range and loiter performance. A probe could be extended for drogue inflight refueling.

Ordered with the F-111A on December 21, 1962, the first of five Grumman-built preproduction F-111Bs flew May 18, 1965, with TF30-P-l engines, and the last flew on November 16, 1966. Weight had grown from 38,804 pounds empty and 62,788 pounds gross on the 1962 contract to 46,000 pounds empty and 77,566 pounds gross in 1965, degrading performance.

A production contract signed May 10, 1967, included 24 F-111Bs with 12,290-pound thrust TF30-P-12 engines, but this plan was to be frustrated. Range was greatly reduced, and engine stalls were a persistent problem. Desperate measures to reduce weight on succeeding prototypes brought little improvement, and Grumman itself advocated a new fighter design, the strictly Navy future F-14.

The first production F-111B with JF-30-P-12s and new intakes was accepted June 30, 1968, but a stop-work order was issued July 10, 1968, and formal contract termination agreed on December 10. On February 28, 1969, the second and last F-111B was accepted. Over $377 million had failed to produce a carrier fighter, although the swing-wing and the missile system would carry over to the successful F-14.

Readers wishing a detailed analysis of the F-111 commonality concept failure should consult Robert F. Coulam's *Illusions of Choice: The F-111 and the Problem of Weapons Acquisition Reform,* (Princeton NJ: Princeton University Press, 1977).

Air Force F-111As began initial crew training in July 1967 at Nellis AFM, Nevada, where the 474th Tactical Fighter Wing arrived in January 1968. On March 17, 1968, six F-111As of Operation **Combat Lancer** arrived in Thailand to attack targets in North Vietnam. When three aircraft had been lost by April 22, operations were halted after 55 missions and the detachment returned to the U.S.

The last of 158 F-111As was accepted on August 30, 1969, at a cost of $8.2 million dollars per production aircraft. F-111 losses from all causes amounted to 15 by December 1969, and serious doubts about the structure caused the entire force to be grounded until July 31, 1970. All aircraft were returned to the factory for proof testing and modification. Despite criticism, the F-111A had the lowest accident rate, by far, of all supersonic Air Force planes.

Another opportunity to prove itself came with deployment of two squadrons from Nellis AFB to Thailand on October 1, 1972. Flying over 3,000 missions against strong enemy defenses, they operated at night, proved their ability to deliver five times the F-4's bomb load at great accuracy. Of 52 F-111As deployed, seven were lost before the ceasefire in February 1973.

Nellis AFB was also the home of the 347th and 366th TFW, while the F-111A was also flown at Cannon AFGB, New Mexico, by the 27th TFW. Although the F-111 was much heavier and more expensive than planned, it was considered successful as a bomber, so the rest of the F-111 story shall be told among the bombers in the next chapter.

F-14 Tomcat

The first new Navy carrier fighter in squadron service in 14 years, Grumman's two-seat F-14A Tomcat benefited from the F-111B program's development of the variable-sweep wing, Phoenix missile, radar fire control, and Pratt & Whitney TF30 turbofans.

A 20-mm M61 Vulcan with 676 rounds is mounted on the nose's port side for close-in dogfights. The tandem-cockpit canopy design provided better visibility than the F-4, and the F-14A was designed to have the maneuverability necessary for dog fighting. Four Sparrow (AIM-7E/F) missiles for local air superiority missions are carried under the fuselage while two to four heat-seeking Sidewinders for short-distance attacks could be carried under the wings. Two 280-gallon drop tanks and a standard inflight refueling probe could extend the range.

For long-range fleet defense, six 13-foot, 989-pound, AIM-54A Phoenix missiles replaced the smaller weapons. Hostile aircraft can be detected 132 miles away across a 170-mile front (Twice the F-4J's radar range), by the Hughes AWG-9 control system, comprising 1,321 pounds of radar, infrared sensor, computer and displays. Up to 24 targets can be tracked at once, and all six Phoenix missiles could attack separate targets simultaneously.

Lawson

GRUMMAN F-14A (1977 data)
Two Pratt & Whitney TF30-P-412A, 20,900 lb. st/AB
DIMENSIONS: Span 64'2" (38'2" swept), Lg. 61'11", Ht. 16', Wing Area 565 sq. ft.
WEIGHT: Empty 39,037 lb., Combat 51,166 lb. clean, 55,616 lb./four AIM-7E, 62,240 lb./six AIM-54A. Takeoff 57,646 lb. clean, 64.076 lb./four AIM-7E, 70,700 lb./six AIM-54A. Fuel 2382+560 gal.
PERFORMANCE: Speed- Top 914 mph at s.l., 1354 mph at 35,000', Cruising 469 mph, Stalling 132 mph. Combat Ceiling 58,500' clean, 48,400'/six AIM-54A, Climb 47,400'/1 minute clean, 33,500'/six AIM-54A. Combat Radius 850 miles clean, 173 miles/six AIM-54A. Ferry Range 2200 miles.

Successful test hits were scored at supersonic speeds in April 1972 against drone targets as far as 126 miles away, as high as 82,000 feet, and at low altitudes. AIM-54A missiles were claimed to be immune to ECM, with launch and leave capability and proximity fusing. Semi-active homing shifts to active radar homing during the terminal phase.

But although 4,579 $30,000-dollar Navy Phoenix missiles were built from 1972 to 1992, none saw actual Navy combat. Since most Navy missions would require pilots to be close enough for visual target identification, less-expensive missiles could be used. The original concept of defending the fleet at long range from a mass of land-based aircraft had been replaced by the limited war experience of supporting attacks in skies cluttered with more friendly than hostile planes.

Two TF30-P-412A engines gave the Tomcat a rapid acceleration to Mach 2.34 speeds, and the wing sweep varied from 20 degrees at takeoff to 68 degrees in high-speed flight, and back to 75 degrees for shipboard parking. Sweep quickly changed from loiter to high-speed configuration by automatic computer, unlike the slower manual adjustment of the early F-111B.

Compared to the F-4 Phantom, the F-14 had 80 percent more combat radius on internal fuel, 20 percent better rate of climb, 21 percent better acceleration, and 40 percent better turn radius. Titanium was used for 24.4% of the structure, compared to 9% of the F-4, while aluminum was 40%, steel, 18%, and 1% the first boron-epoxy composite material used on a Navy aircraft.

The F-14A was begun as a company proposal (Design 303-60) for a new airframe to replace the failing F-111B. An impressed Navy Fighter Study group issued a request for proposals on June 18, 1968, and by October 1, two-seat, twin-engine fighter proposals were submitted by Grumman, General Dynamics, McDonnell Douglas, North American, and Vought. Grumman got the contract, signed February 3, 1969, for the first six aircraft, later increased to 11 developmental examples.

The first F-14A flew at Calverton, New York, on December 21, 1970, but crashed on its second flight, delaying tests until the second aircraft was ready on May 24, 1971. Eleven test aircraft had been completed by March 1972 and in October the first training squadrons, VF-l and VF-2, were commissioned at NAS Miramar.

VF-124 became the first operational F-14A squadron in January 1973 and the first Navy carrier squadrons were successfully deployed in 1974 on the *Enterprise.* The Navy equipped each of the ten super-carriers with two 24-plane Tomcat squadrons; the remaining fighters were the F-4 Phantoms aboard the *Coral Sea* and *Midway.*

After a very competitive flight demonstration between the F-14 and the F-15 for the Shah of Iran in July 1973, Iran ordered 80 F-14As, lacking only some ECM gear, on January 7, 1974, and an example flew December 5, 1975. The Navy flew the first to Iran on January 24, 1977, and all but one had been delivered before the Shah's overthrow in January 1979 canceled the contract.

Beginning in September 1980, Iranian F-14As flew top cover for F-4 and F-5 fighter-bombers against Iraq's attack. Over 80 Iraqi aircraft were credited to Tomcat Phoenix, Sparrow, and Sidewinder missiles, or guns, by 1988. These successes discouraged Iraqi pilots from fighting Tomcats when United States Navy squadrons arrived in Desert Storm.*

GRUMMAN F-14A for Iran

A 1,750-pound TARPS camera/radar pod were tested in 1979 and 49 F-14As were tailored so each F-14 squadron could provide two for low-altitude tactical reconnaissance when needed. Many accidents caused by the original engines caused their replacement by more reliable TF30-PW-414s of similar power in 1983. Another improvement was a dual chin pod in 1984 for a television camera and infrared system to spot aircraft.

The F-14B designation was assigned in 1970 to the modified seventh Tomcat flown on September 12, 1973, with Pratt & Whitney YF401-PW-400 advanced engines, but that 28,100-pound thrust power plant was unready for production. Instead, the F-14A production program proceeded with annual increments amid severe arguments between the company and the Navy about the 30 million dollar price asked per fighter. New General Electric 27,400-pound thrust F101DFE engines were also installed in that F-14B for tests begun on July 14, 1981, but that program was terminated in September.

Tomcat combat patrols protected fleet concentrations in all the trouble spots of the century's last two decades. On August 19, 1981, F-14As of VF-41 scored their first victories by downing two Libyan Su-22s with AIM-9L Sidewinders. Two Libyan MiG-23s were later hit by VF-32 F-14As on January 4, 1989. An Egyptian airliner carrying terrorists was intercepted and forced to land at a NATO base on October 10, 1985, by a remarkable VF-103 F-14A mission.

In October 1984, VF-301 became the first of four Naval Air Reserve squadrons to receive F-14 Tomcats, but no Marine operational squadrons had F-14s. Carrier air groups began reducing their F-14 complement to one squadron to accommodate F/A-18 strike fighters.

F-14A production was completed March 31, 1987. The first F-14A+ modified with General Electric 28,200-pound thrust F110-GE-400 engines was flown on September 29, 1986, the first production example was accepted November 16, 1987, and assigned to an operational unit, VF-101.

These new engines were fitted to 38 new and 32 reworked F-14A+ aircraft that would receive the old F-14B designation on May 1, 1991. Fuel efficiency was so improved that the F-14B claimed 60% more range and 61% better rate of climb than the F-14A. A Hughes AWG-15 improved fire control and an ALR-67 provided better threat warning.

F-14Bs of VF-74 and VF-103 arrived in the Red Sea on the *Saratoga* in August 1990, the only B models to fight in the Gulf War. Ten Tomcat fighter and 12 Hornet strike fighter squadrons from six carrier battle groups gathered for Desert Storm, with 99 F-14s flying 4,124 escort and TARP sorties. Since Iraqi fighters did not challenge them, only one Mi-8 helicopter fell to their Sidewinders.

GRUMMAN F-14A of VF-32 in Gulf War
Two Pratt & Whitney TF30-P-414A, 20,900 lb. st AB
DIMENSIONS: Span 64'2" (38'2" swept), Lg. 62'8", Ht. 16', Wing Area 565 sq. ft.
WEIGHT: Empty 40,104 lb., Max. 72,000 lb. Fuel 2385+564 gal.
PERFORMANCE: classified. Ferry Range 2000 miles.

While no F-14C model was built, new computers, sensors, APG-71 radar, and AIM-120A or AGM-88A missile fittings were provided for the F-14D. The first of two F-

*Tom Cooper & Farzad Bishop. *Iran-Iraq War in the Air.* (Atglen, PA: Schiffer, 2000), describes Iran's war. Of 58 Iranian F-14As left in 1999, half were still active.

14As modified as F-14D prototypes was tested in 1987, the first production F-14D accepted in November 1990, and 18 more F-14A models were rebuilt to the D configuration with F110-GE-400 engines by 1993. Remanufacture was cheaper than building $38-million new aircraft.

New Tomcat production ended on July 10, 1992, with 712 delivered: 636 as F-14As, one early F-14B prototype, 38 F-14Bs, and 37 F-14Ds. Although all Tomcats could lift four 2,000-pound Mk 84 or 16 500-pound Mk 82 bombs, emphasis on air-to-air tactics delayed the first combat drop of two Mk 84s to a September 5, 1995, sortie in Bosnia.

USN

GRUMMAN F-14B of VF-103
Two Pratt & Whitney TF30-P-400, 13,800 lb. st military, 28,100 lb. /AB
DIMENSIONS: as F-14A
WEIGHT: Empty 41,780 lb., Combat 57,186 lb., Gross 63,666 lb. clean, Max. 72,000 lb./6 AIM-54A/2 drop tanks. Fuel 2382+560 gal.
PERFORMANCE: Speed- Top 1544 mph at 35,000'
Combat Ceiling 54,300'/six AIM-54A, Combat Radius 460 miles/six AIM-54A. Ferry Range 2360 miles.

LANTIRN, a Low-Altitude Navigation and Targeting Infrared for Night system, was introduced to F-14s when VF-103 sailed aboard *Enterprise* in June 1996. This capability was added to 81 Tomcats in fiscal 1998-2000. A Digital Flight Control System (DFCS) introduced to the fleet in June 1998 enhanced flight safety and maneuverability.

At the century's end, the Navy inventory included 52 F-14A, 72 F-14B, and 46 F-14D Tomcats. They were outnumbered by 785 F/A-18 Hornets as strike fighters took a larger Navy role.

F-15 Eagle

The McDonnell Douglas F-15A Eagle was the first Air Force fighter in many years to be designed purely for the air superiority role -destroying enemy fighters in combat. Climb and maneuverability were the first characteristics desired. Without the Navy's strength and weight constraints for catapult launching, arrested and short landings, folding wings, and fuel capacity, a lighter and faster fighter than the F-14 could be achieved.

Air Force concern about Soviet fighter progress was reflected in the request for design proposals sent to seven companies on August 11, 1967. Appearance of the variable-sweep MiG-23 and the very fast MiG-25 threatened the F-4 Phantom's superiority, and indicated that the traditional Soviet point interceptor would be replaced by more versatile types.

Gann

McDONNELL-DOUGLAS F-15A
Two Pratt & Whitney F100-PW-100, 23,480 lb. st/AB
DIMENSIONS: Span 42'10", Lg. 63'9", Ht. 18'5", Wing Area 608 sq. ft.
WEIGHT: Empty 25,780 lb., Combat 36,374 lb./4 AIM-7, Gross 40,327 lb., Max. 52,077 lb. Fuel 1714+1800 gal.
PERFORMANCE: Speed- Top 1028 mph at 10,000', 1650 mph at 45,000', Cruising 578 mph, Stalling 147 mph. Combat Ceiling 63,050', Service Ceiling 63,350', Climb 67,250/ 1 minute. Combat Radius 279 miles/four AIM-7F. Ferry Range 2720 miles.

The Air Force awarded Concept Formulation Study contracts in December 1967 to General Dynamics and McDonnell Douglas*, and on September 30, 1968, began the Contract Definition phase with another Request For Proposals. This document specified one-man operation with 360-degree cockpit visibility and head-up displays, a Mach 2.5 maximum capability with a wing optimized for Mach .9 buffet-free performance and maneuverability at 30,000 feet, high thrust-to-weight ratio, long-range Pulse Doppler radar with look-down capability, low development risk components and systems, and a gross weight in the 40,000-pound class.

Contracts for this phase were awarded in December to Fairchild Hiller (Republic), North American, and McDonnell Douglas, and these companies worked to produce the winning concept until July 1969, when the Air Force began its evaluation of the rival designs, announcing McDonnell the winner on December 23, 1969, and a contract for the first seven developmental aircraft was signed by December 31. This account indicates the lengthy process involved before the St. Louis factory could build the first F-15A and ship it to Edwards AFB for the July 17, 1972, maiden flight by Irving Burrows.

Comparison with the Navy's F-14 Tomcat is natural, the most apparent being that the F-l5A Eagle was a single-place 45-degree sweep fixed-wing fighter without the Phoenix missile system, and therefore a much lighter and

*In April 1967, McDonnell added Douglas to its name when it purchased control of the California firm.

less expensive aircraft. When the Navy asked in 1971 for an F-15N version for carrier landings, the weight estimate was increased 2,300 pounds, degrading design performance and increasing costs to an unacceptable point.

Armament of the F-15A was essentially that of the F-4E Phantom: four Sparrow and four Sidewinder missiles and a 20-mm M61 gun. An APQ-63 radar provided long-range search up to 115 miles and semi-active homing for the 510-pound AIM-7F Sparrows carried below the engine nacelles. The 199-pound AIM-9L heat-seeking Sidewinders were below the wings and the gun with 940 rounds was in the starboard wing root, opposite the inflight refueling receptacle on the port side. Pylons provided for three 600-gallon drop tanks could also accommodate a variety of bombs and stores, although ground attack was not then part of the required mission.

Powered by two Pratt & Whitney F100-PW-100 turbofans, the F-15A's structure included 37.3 percent aluminum, 25.8 percent titanium, and 5.5 percent steel. Twin vertical fins were tipped with ECM antenna, and an air refueling receptacle was in the left wing.

Production go-ahead on a fly-before-buy basis was approved in February 1973 for the first 18 F-15A fighters and two TF-15A trainer development aircraft, and 23 F-15A and seven TF-15B production aircraft. The first two-seater flew July 7, 1973, and all the dual-control trainers were redesignated F-15B. They retained all the combat gear, excepting ECM. Deliveries to TAC's training wing at Luke AFB began in November 1974.

In January 1975, the stripped-down 19th aircraft set world climb records. That F-15A climbed to 12,000 meters (39,372 feet) in 59 seconds; the previous record by an F-4 was 77 seconds. A MiG-25 had set a 30,000 meter (98,430 feet) record in 243.5 seconds; the F-15A did it in 207 seconds, although the Soviet aircraft recaptured the latter record soon after.

The first operational unit delivery was made in January 1976 to the 1st Tactical Fighter Wing at Langley AFB, which formed three 24-plane squadrons during the year. Next came the 36th TFW, which deployed to Germany in April 1977, and the 49th TFW at Holloman, New Mexico. Annual increments to the production program followed regularly until 384 F-15A and 61 F-15B Eagles were built. The safety record was the best of any American fighter.

Israel was the F-15's first foreign customer, buying 23 F-15As and two F-15Bs for $30 million each; the first four being refurbished pre-production F-15As aircraft delivered on December 10, 1976. The F-15's first combat came on June 27, 1979, when Israeli F-15A AIM-9 missiles downed four Syrian MiG-21s. Continued conflicts cost 16 more Syrian aircraft and led to a great air battle over the Bekaa valley in Lebanon in June 1982, when Israeli F-15As were credited with 40 Syrian fighters without loss. Eight F-15As flew 1,280 miles, with air refueling, to bomb a PLO base in Tunis on October 1, 1985.

First flown on February 26, 1979, the F-15C had various refinements, including more fuel and a new ejection

Mfr

McDONNELL DOUGLAS F-15A for Israel

Gann

McDONNELL DOUGLAS F-15C (1979 data)
Two Pratt & Whitney F100-PW-100, 14,670 lb. st military, 23,830 lb. AB
DIMENSIONS: Span 42'10", Lg. 63'9", Ht. 18'7", Wing Area 608 sq. ft.
WEIGHT: Empty 27,762 lb., Combat 40,374 lb./4 AIM-7, Gross 44,899 lb., Max. 56,700 lb. Fuel 2070+1830 gal.
PERFORMANCE: Speed- Top 976 mph at 10,000', 1507 mph at 35,000', Cruising 578 mph, Stalling 154 mph. Combat Ceiling 54,950', Service Ceiling 55,290', Climb 49,410/1 minute. Combat Radius 275 miles/four AIM-7F. Ferry Range 2445 miles.

AF

McDONNELL DOUGLAS F-15C (1992 data)
Two Pratt & Whitney F100-PW-220, 14,370 lb. st military, 23,450 lb. AB
DIMENSIONS: As F-15C
WEIGHT: Empty 28,476 lb., Combat 41,286 lb./4 AIM-7F, Gross 45,713 lb., Max. 57,539 lb. Fuel 2070+1830 gal.
PERFORMANCE: Speed- Top 987 mph at 10,000', 1543 mph at 45,000', Cruising 575 mph, Stalling 155 mph. Combat Ceiling 56,100', Service Ceiling 56,440', Climb 55,960/1 minute. Combat Radius 270 miles/4 AIM-7F, 675 miles/two Mk 841/2680 gal. Ferry Range 2469 miles.
CFT configuration:
WEIGHT: Empty 30,963 lb., Combat 48,704 lb./4 AIM-7, Gross 57,714 lb., Max. 68,000 lb. Fuel 2070+1830+1464 gal.
PERFORMANCE: Speed- Top 831 mph at 10,000', 1294 mph at 35,000', Cruising 572 mph, Stalling 175 mph. Combat Ceiling 52,100', , Service Ceiling 52,490'. Climb 47,100/1 minute. Combat Radius 469 miles/4 AIM-7F, 994 miles/two Mk 84. Ferry Range 2973 miles.

McDONNELL DOUGLAS F-15E (1986)

seat, and the F-15D, a two-place version, first flew on June 19. Twin 732-gallon Conformal Fuel Tanks (CFT) originally developed for Israel could be added next to the engine nacelles and improved F100-PW-220 engines were introduced in 1985.

F-15Cs first joined the18th TFW at Kadena, Okinawa, in September 1979, and they displaced the seven Tactical Fighter Wings' F-15As, which then replaced F-106s in four Fighter Interceptor squadrons and F-4s in five Air National Guard squadrons. Frequent upgrades included advanced central computers, APG-70 radar and AIM-9J Sidewinders. Production paused after the last of 473 F-15Cs and 78 F-15Ds were completed on November 3, 1989. Of these, the USAF got 409 F-15C and 61 F-15D models while Israel added 24 F-15Cs and two F-15Ds.

Japan purchased 131 F-15C and 20 F-15D interceptors without bomb racks, and the first two, designated F-15J, were turned over in July 1980, followed by four F-15DJ two-seaters assembled in St. Louis and eight as knocked-down assemblies to be completed by Mitsubishi along with the remaining fighters. The first Mitsubishi F-15DJ flew on August 26, 1981.

Saudi Arabia was the third country rich enough to buy Eagles, the first of 16 F-15Ds arriving on August 11, 1981. They were joined by 46 F-15Cs, whose first success was to down two Iranian F-4s over the Persian Gulf on June 15, 1984.

While all USAF Eagles could carry four Mk 84 or 16 Mk 82 bombs, the Strike Eagle concept offered a dual-role tactical bomber capable of night attacks with precision-guided weapons. A prototype converted from the second F-15B began tests in August 1981. Production F-15Es had FLIR and LANTIRN pods, strengthened structure, APQ-70 radar, ALQ-135 ECM, and AIM-120A missiles. Internal fuel and gun ammunition was reduced to 2,019 gallons and 450 rounds.

The first of eight development aircraft flew December 11, 1986, and 120 operational F-15Es were ordered. On December 29, 1988, the 4th TFW received one to begin gradual conversion of two strike fighter squadrons.

In response to the invasion of Kuwait, the 1st Tactical Fighter Wing's 71st TFS flew 24 F-15Cs 8,000 miles nonstop from Langley AFM to Dhahran, Saudi Arabia on August 7, 1990, in 15 hours with 11 inflight refueling contacts. That squadron killed a Mirage with an AIM-7M Sparrow on January 17, 1991, the first score of the 120 F-15s in Desert Storm. USAF confidence in the AIM-7M was justified as Sparrows made 28 of the 41 air-to-air kills of Iraqi aircraft, while ten kills were made with AIM-9J Sidewinders.

F-15Cs of the 53rd TFS downed three MiG-23s, two Su-25s two Su-22s, and a Mirage. Eagles from the 58th

TFS, 33rd TFW, downed five MiG-29s, four MiG-23s, three Su-22s, two MiG-25s, and two Mirages by February 7. They were joined by the 525th TFW, which flew from Turkey to down another Mirage. A pilot from the three Saudi F-15C squadrons also downed two Mirages with Sidewinders on January 24.

Two 4th TFW squadrons, the 335th and 336th TFS, brought 48 two-seat F-15Es to Arabia to use their LANTIRN targeting pods for ground attacks, with Mk 82s and GBU-12B Paveway II bombs, losing two planes to AAA.

McDONNELL DOUGLAS F-15E (1991)
Two Pratt & Whitney F100-PW-220, 14,370 lb. st military, 23,450 lb. AB, or F100-PW-229, 29,100 lb. AB
DIMENSIONS: as F-15C
WEIGHT: Empty 32,000 lb., Max. 81,000 lb. Fuel 2019+1446+1830 gal.
PERFORMANCE: Data classified.

F-15 production was revived after the Gulf War to replenish Saudi Arabia with nine F-15Cs and three F-15Ds, with another five F-15Ds for Israel. The last of 221 F-15Es was delivered to the USAF in July 1994, bringing the total to 1,234 Eagles from St. Louis. But the Air Force was reluctant to let the production line close entirely, and ordered 13 more F-15Es, to be delivered on a monthly basis in the new century, as well as a promised South Korean program.

F-16 Fighting Falcon

In several respects, the General Dynamics F-16A represents the opposite of the F-111s previously built at the Fort Worth factory. One man, one engine, and a gun in a compact airframe, the F-16A is a reversal of the greater cost and complexity of American fighters.

The Air Force, on January 6, 1972, issued a Request For Proposals for a lightweight, low-cost, highly maneuverable fighter with Mach 2 speed capability and about 20,000-pounds normal gross weight. Costs per unit should be about three million in then-dollars, because the big disadvantage of the F-14/15 types was that they were too expensive to fill out all the squadrons needed for defense commitments.

Five companies responding by February 18, included Boeing, Lockheed and Vought, but General Dynamics and

GENERAL DYNAMICS YF-16
Pratt & Whitney F100-PW-100, 23,500 lb.
DIMENSIONS: Span 30', Lg. 46'6", Ht. 16'3", Wing Area 280 sq. ft.
WEIGHT: Empty 14,023 lb., Gross 20,665 lb., Max. 31,000 lb. Fuel 1072 gal.
PERFORMANCE: Speed- Top 1320 mph at 36,000'. Combat Radius 600 miles/two AIM-9.

Northrop were awarded contracts on April 13, 1972 for two YF-16 and two YF-17 prototypes. The first YF-16 was flown inside a C-5A transport from Fort Worth to Edwards AFB, where the first planned flight was made February 4, 1974, by Phil Oestricher and the second prototype's tests began May 9. During 330 flights that year in competition with the YF-17, the YF-16 demonstrated a top speed over Mach 2 (1320 mph at 40,000 feet) a climb to 62,000 ft., and a 2 hour, 55 minute flight without refueling. Armament consisted of a 20-mm M61Al in the left side of the fuselage behind the cockpit and an AIM-9 Sidewinder on each wingtip.

On January 13, 1975, the Air Force announced the F-16 was chosen for production that would begin with an April 9 development contract for six single-seat YF-16As and two two-seat YF-16Bs. Both competitors, said Air Force Secretary John L. Lucas, performed well, but the YF-16 had lower drag and excelled in agility, turn rate and endurance. One advantage was having the same F100-PW-100 engine used in the F-15. The simplicity of one pilot and one engine was attractive to Air Force hopes for easier maintenance, and reduced final costs per mission to half those of twin-engine rivals.

The YF-16A first flown December 8, 1976, while the two-place TF-16B trainer first flown August 9, 1977, kept the same weapons capabilities, but had a smaller fuel capacity. A larger nose for APG-65 radar and six pylons under modified wings distinguished them from the original YF-16 prototypes.

While the YF-16A was not as fast as an F-4 or Mig-21, it did claim to have three times the combat radius on internal fuel, better acceleration and turn rates, and instantaneous maneuverability. Wing-body blending and variable wing camber were featured, while the structure included 78.3% aluminum, 10.3% steel, and only 1.6% expensive titanium.

The fly-by-wire control system allowed relaxed stability and maneuver adjustment by computer, an element continually improved during the aircraft's life cycle. A clear canopy provided excellent visibility and a 30-degree inclined seat increased pilot "G" tolerance. An inflight refueling receptacle was standard.

Average flyaway costs were projected in 1975 as less than five million then-dollars, or less than half that of its

GENERAL DYNAMICS F-16A (Block 15)
Pratt & Whitney F100-PW-200, 14,670 lb. st military, 23,830 lb. AB
DIMENSIONS: Span 32'10", Lg. 49'6", Ht. 16'5", Wing Area 300 sq. ft.
WEIGHT: Empty 15,961 lb., Combat 23,768 lb., Gross 29,896 lb./2 AIM-9J/2 tanks, Max. 34,980 lb. Fuel 1073+1040 gal.
PERFORMANCE: Speed- Top 836 mph at s.l., 1346 mph at 36,089', Cruising 577 mph, Stalling 163 mph. Combat Ceiling 54,837', Service Ceiling 47,435'. Climb 52,218'/1 minute. Combat Radius 704 miles/two AIM-9J/2 tanks, 747 miles/two Mk 84 / two AIM-9J/2 tanks. Ferry Range 2385 miles.

GENERAL DYNAMICS F-16A (1980)
Pratt & Whitney F100-PW-100, 23,820 lb.
DIMENSIONS: Span 32'10", Lg. 47'8", Ht. 16'5", Wing Area 300 sq. ft.
WEIGHT: Empty 15,137 lb., Gross 23,357 lb., Max. 35,400 lb. Fuel 1072+1040 gal.
PERFORMANCE: Speed- Top 915 mph at s.l., 1350 mph at 40,000'. Service Ceiling 50,000'. Combat Radius 575 miles/two AIM-9L, 340 miles/two AIM-9L/6 Mk 82. Ferry Range 2415 miles.

twin-engine rivals. These hopes led the Air Force to announce plans in January 1977 to increase its F-16 program to 1,388 aircraft, so TAC could have ten active wings, plus Air Force Reserve squadrons and attrition replacements.

The first F-16A flew on August 7, 1978, and was introduced to TAC service in January 1979 at Hill AFB, Utah, by the 388th TFW, which included a fourth squadron for training foreign pilots. Next, F-16s for the 56th TFW began arriving MacDill AFB on October 22, 1979. Fighting Falcon became the official USAF name on July 21, 1980.

Unsuccessful efforts were made to extend F-16 sales appeal. A cheaper 18,370-pound thrust General Electric J79-GE-17X was flight tested on the second F-16B on October 29, 1980, but no customers responded. No more success was experienced when the first YF-16A flew with a 29,000-pound thrust General Electric F101X on December 19. An advanced F-16XL version with a new wing and more fuel was flown on July 3, 1982, but won no new orders and wound up with NASA in 1989 with three other F-16 technology demonstrators. Fortunately, orders for standard F-16s continued.

GENERAL DYNAMICS F-16B

While production of over 4,000 aircraft in 25 years made little change in their outside appearance, the Block number series tracked frequent upgrades of equipment. Production deliveries began with 94 F-16A Block 1 and 197 Block 5 aircraft for TAC and NATO. Block 10 with 312 aircraft followed, and earlier models were upgraded to that standard in 1982.

Larger horizontal tails and AIM-7 Sparrow missiles distinguished the most numerous F-16A Block 15, with 983 produced, beginning in November 1981, and ending in February 1996 with six for Thailand. To the M61Al behind the cockpit with 512 20-mm rounds, and two AIM-9L Sidewinders on the wingtips, were added AIM-120 missiles directed by an upgraded computer. Westinghouse APG-66 radar fire control weighed only 290 pounds (less than 1/4th that of an F-14's radar), but provided all-weather target detection and tracking, and a threat warning radar antenna was placed on the tail fin. Mach 2.05 was the control speed limit.

External stores for the air-to-ground mission held two 2,000-pound Mk 84 or six 500-pound Mk 82 bombs, two 370-gallon drop tanks, and an ALQ-119 ECM pod. Up to 15,200 pounds of other stores could be lifted for short distances on the seven stations, including a centerline station for a 300-gallon tank or B61 nuclear bomb. Four more Sidewinders or four AGM-65A Mavericks could be carried.

USAF deliveries amounted to 620 F-16As and 122 F-16Bs by 1984. In 1989, 279 Block 15 F-16As were converted to an air defense configuration for the ANG squadrons by adding APG-66A radar, an APX interrogator, and a spotlight.

The F-16C

Block 25, in June 1984, introduced so many improvements like APG-68 radar and new fire control for night attacks and AIM-120 missiles that the F-16C designation was established. All of the 244 B Block 25s went to the USAF with F100-PW-100, but these were upgraded to -220E engines.

Block 30/32 F-16Cs appeared in July 1987 with larger air inlets for an engine bay that could hold either a General Electric FF110-GE-100 (Block 30) or a Pratt & Whitney F100-PW-220 (Block 32). Weapons options included up to eight tons of: six AIM-9M or AIM-120 missiles, four Mk 84 or 12 Mk 82 bombs, four GBU-10B or eight GBU-12B guided bombs, six AGM-65B, AGM-45, or AGM-88A missiles, or 12 chaff/flare dispensers. The 733 Block 30/32 F-16Cs built by 1989 provided pilots with the versatility to handle any type of mission.

GENERAL DYNAMICS F-16C (Block 25)
Pratt & Whitney F100-PW-220, 14,590 lb. st military, 23,770 lb. AB
DIMENSIONS: Span 32'10", Lg. 49'4", Ht. 16'7", Wing Area 300 sq. ft.
WEIGHT: Empty 17,078 lb., Combat 29,803 lb., Gross 32,010 lb./two AIM-9L/two tanks, Max. 35,400 lb. Fuel 1073+740 gal.
PERFORMANCE: Speed- Top 1278 mph at 30,000', Cruising 549 mph, Combat Ceiling 52,450'. Climb 20,300'/1 minute. Combat Radius 722 miles/two AIM-9L. Ferry Range 2159 miles.

The U.S. Navy ordered the first 14 F-16N fighters on January 7, 1984, to serve as adversary fighters. Until those F-16Ns were ready, the Navy borrowed, at no cost, 25 Israeli Kfir fighters, based on the French Mirage 5, but using a J79J-1E engine. Designated F-21A, they arrived in March 1986 to equip VF-43 at Oceana and VMF-401 at Yuma, and the last F-21As were returned to Israel in September 1989.

GENERAL DYNAMICS F-16C with ALQ pod

Similar to Block 30 Cs with the General Electric FF110-GE-100, the first of 22 F-16N fighters and four TF-16N trainers arrived at Miramar in April 1987 with APG-66 radar and no guns, but they suffered structural cracks that led to their 1991 grounding.

Block 40/42 aircraft appeared in 1988 with stronger landing gear to handle a LANTIRN targeting pod's weight and a new digital system for precision night attacks. Some 765 were on order by 1997.

Foreign Service for the F-16

Foreign sales began with a June 7, 1975, announcement of a four-nation European consortium to acquire 348 F-16s for NATO, after rejecting fighter proposals from Dassault, SAAB, and Northrop. Co-production contracts signed in July 1976 called for SABCA in Belgium and Fokker in the Netherlands to divide final assembly. To offset costs, European manufacturers would supply about 40% of the NAT0 aircraft value, and 10% of the USAF aircraft value.

The first Belgian F-16A flew on December 11, 1978, and the last of 96 flew on April 28, 1985, along with 20 F-18Bs and 58 aircraft produced for Denmark. Fokker flew the first Dutch F-16B on May 3, 1979, and also began delivery of 72 aircraft to Norway.

Although Iran ordered 160 F-16s in 1977, that contract's cancellation allowed planes to be allotted to Israel's 75-plane order in August 1978, and the first of 67 Block 5/10 F-16As arrived in July 1980. The first F-16 combat kills were two Syrian Mi-8 helicopters aiding the PLO on April 28, 1981. On June 7, eight F-16As with 16 2,000-pound bombs, escorted by six F-15As, flew 600 miles to destroy the Iraqi Osirak nuclear reactor, eliminating that particular threat for two decades.

ISRAELI F-21A
This *Kfir* still has Marine markings as it remains in the IAF museum.

When Syria moved SAM batteries into the Bekaa valley, an air battle began on June 9, 1982. F-16s shot down 44 of the 85 Syrian aircraft claimed in air-to-air combat, demonstrating the American fighter's superiority.

Pakistan received 28 F-16A and 12 F-16B Block 15 Falcons from January 1983 to March 1986. Two squadrons formed with those fighters patrolled the Afghanistan border during the wartime Soviet occupation, and by November 1988 claimed to have downed about eight intruding Afghan or Soviet aircraft with their AIM-7L missiles. Another Pakistan F-16 order was blocked by the United States in 1990.

The Republic of Korea began with 40 block 32 aircraft from Fort Worth in 1987 and, beginning in 1991, added 120 Block 50 F-16C/Ds with 12 completed at Fort Worth, 36 from kits assembled at Sachon by Samsung, and 72 KF-16s produced under license by Samsung from 1994 to 2000. An order for 20 more Block 50 aircraft from Samsung would be added in July 2002.

Table 13 • F-16s for 18 Foreign Nations

Nation	F-16A	F-16B	F-16C	F-16D	Delivery began*
Europe:					
Belgium	136	24	-	-	Jan 1979
Netherlands	177	36	-	-	June 1979
Norway	60	14	-	-	Jan 1980
Denmark	54	16	-	-	Jan 1980
Turkey	—	-	104	36	July 1987
Greece	—	-	100	30	Nov 1988
Portugal	17	3	-	-	Feb 1989
Others:					
Israel	67	8	81	104	July 1980
Egypt	34	8	136	42	Mar 1982
Venezuela	18	6	—	—	Nov 1985
Bahrain	—	-	18	4	May 1989
Jordan	16	4	—	-	Dec 1997
Asia:					
Korea	—	—	125	55	Oct 1987
Singapore	4	4	22	28	Feb 1988
Thailand	26	10	—	—	May 1988
Indonesia	8	4	—	—	1989
Taiwan	120	30	—	—	1992
Pakistan	28 (13-17 embargoed)	12	—	—	Jan 1983

*Delivery dates refer to arrival in country. Data extracted from various issues of Code One magazine

Desert Storm and after

During Desert Storm, 249 USAF F-16s flew 13,500 sorties, including 40% of coalition bombing sorties. They were employed in close support and interdiction missions, losing five planes in combat to ground fire, since no enemy fighters were encountered. While two squadrons used F-16As, the other eight had F-16Cs with a variety of munitions.

After the war, a 33rd FS F-16D supporting Operation Southern Watch downed an Iraqi MiG-25 on December 27, 1992, in the no-fly zone. This was both the first USAF air-to-air combat victory and the first combat kill by an AIM-120 missile. On January 17, 1993, a MiG-23 became the second victim of an F-16's AIM-120.

F-16 production continued as orders reached 4,285 by the century's end. Block 50/52 versions appeared in 1991 with a new ASQ-213 radar-suppression system using two AGM-88A HARM missiles, and an anti-shipping capability was added by AGM–84 Harpoons. Empty weight had increased from 15,587 pounds for F-16A Block 10 to 19,200 pounds for F-16C Block 50. Factories in Fort Worth, Korea and Turkey produced the new versions.

Mid-Life Update (MLU) kits for the F-16A were provided NATO forces in 1998 to modernize their aircraft with new computers having 12 times more memory, GPS navigation systems, AIM-120 missiles and laser-guided bombs. These upgrades required about 2,500 work hours per aircraft. New F-16s appearing with these features in July 1996 are called Block 20 aircraft. While the Air Force did not request new F-16 buys, Congress "added a few planes per year to maintain a production capability."*

Of 2,233 F-16s ordered for the USAF, 1,412 served 12 Air Force, four Reserve, and 28 ANG Fighter Wings on September 30, 2000. A Common Configuration Implementation Program was planned to update F-16s for the new century, while 30 more Block 50 aircraft were ordered for delivery from 2002-2004.

Some former USAF F-16s had found a new life elsewhere. Israel had received 36 ex-USAF F-16As and 14 F-16Bs in 1994. Jordan signed a peace treaty with Israel in July 1994 and became a non-NATO ally of America. A July 1996 agreement called **Peace Falcon** brought 16 Block 15s out of storage at Davis-Monthan AFB. Upgraded with F100-PW-220E engines and new systems, 12 F-16As and four F-16Bs arrived in Jordan from December 1997 to March 1998.

On July 10, 2000, the United Arab Emirates was authorized 55 single-seat and 25 two-seat Block 60 Desert Falcons with 32,500-pound thrust General Electric F110-GE-132 engines and advanced electronics, ensuring F-16 production into 2006.

The Navy's Hornets

The Navy's desire for a multi-mission fighter of low-cost resulted in ther F/A-18 Hornet, which was the only Navy combat plane in production at the century's end. Although aircraft builders had been asked for proposals in June 1974, it was an Air Force contract that actually produced such a fighter.

Northrop received an Air Force contract on April 13, 1972, for two YF-17 prototypes to compete against the General Dynamic YF-16 for the lightweight fighter contract. Developed from an earlier design study called the P-530 Cobra, Northrop's project differed from the YF-16 in having two engines and twin vertical fins.

Powered by new General Electric YJ101 turbojets, the YF-17 was also armed with an M61 and Sidewinders, and had five stores pylons besides the wingtip missile stations. The first example flew on June 9, 1974, and claimed to be the first U.S. aircraft to fly supersonic in level flight without afterburner, while the second YF-17 flew on August 21.

After learning that the Air Force contract was lost, Northrop focused on the Navy's need for a lightweight fighter to supplement the F-14. Since Northrop's Hawthorne plant lacked experience with carrier-based aircraft, they joined with McDonnell Douglas on October 7, 1974, to jointly prepare a Navy fighter. The St. Louis factory would build the Navy version, and Northrop would work out a land-based variant for NATO. The second YF-17 was turned over to the Navy for thorough testing.

The Navy did not really want to follow the Air Force's lead anyway, and preferred a twin-engine configuration. Adapting the YF-17 to Navy requirements involved increases in fuel load and weapons provisions that added over 10,000 pounds to the weight, and required more wing area. Despite the added weight, speed was to remain about Mach 1.8, and combat radius 460 miles. On May 2, 1975, the Navy announced its selection of that design as the F-14's low-cost counterpart, and a January 22, 1976, letter contract provided for 11 F-18 developmental aircraft, including two two-seat trainers.

An attack version, the A-18, was announced in June 1976 to replace the A-7 Corsairs in the Navy's 24 attack

*Col, Jeffrey Riemer, F-16 SPO director, Code One, July 1998: 16.

USN

McDONNELL DOUGLAS F/A-18A of VFA-131

AF

NORTHROP YF-17
Two General Electric YF101-GE-100, 14,800 lb.
DIMENSIONS: Span 35', Lg. 55'6", Ht. 14'6", Wing Area 350 sq. ft.
WEIGHT: Empty 17,180 lb., Gross 24,580 lb., Max. 34,280 lb. Fuel 946+1200 gal.
PERFORMANCE: Mach 1.95. Service Ceiling 60,000'. Combat Radius 576 miles. Ferry Range 2800 miles.

USN

McDONNELL DOUGLAS F/A-18A (1981)
Two General Electric F404-GE-400, 10,608 lb. st, 16,016 lb. st AB
DIMENSIONS: Span 40'4", Lg. 56', Ht. 15'4", Wing Area 400 sq. ft.
WEIGHT: Empty 23,050 lb., Combat 31,346 lb./clean, 45,915lb./6 Mk 82SE, Gross 35,690 lb. clean, Max. 49,224 lb. Fuel 1597+990 gal.
PERFORMANCE: Speed- Top 795 mph at s.l., 1140 mph at 35,000', Cruising 564 mph, Stalling 123 mph. Combat Ceiling 54,450', Climb 44,300'/1 minute, Combat Radius 647 miles clean, 395 miles/six 512-lb. bombs. Ferry Range 1933 miles.

squadrons. This version had nine weapons stations and electronics chosen for ground targets. An F-18L designation was promulgated for a lighter land-based version offered for export to NATO in November, but no buyers appeared then.

In September 1978, Deputy Chief of Naval Operations (Air) VADM Frederick C. Turner, chose the unusual designation F/A-18 to represent the naval strike fighter. Jack Krings flew the first F/A-18A Hornet on November 18, 1978, at St. Louis, and armament included a 20-mm M61 with 400 rounds in the nose, two AIM-9L Sidewinders on wingtip rails, and a pair of AIM-7F Sparrows under the engine nacelles.

Five other stations could be used for three 330-gallon drop tanks with two more Sparrows or four more Sidewinders. Ground attack weapons could include a choice of four Mk 84 or ten Mk 82 bombs, four AGM-65E or AGM-88 air-to-ground missiles, two B61 nuclear bombs, eight rocket pods, or four laser-guided bombs for precision strikes when a FLIR heat seeker and a laser spot tracker replaced the Sparrows. Up to 13,700 pounds of stores could be lifted, and a retractable refueling probe was provided.

Computer-controlled leading and trailing edge wing flaps are part of the digital fly-by-wire system. Hughes APG-65 multi-mode radar, ASN-130 navigation set and defensive chaff/flare dispensers helped the pilot.

Since the high cost of Grumman's F-14 limited that two-seater program to 18 of the Navy's fighter squadrons on the larger carriers, the first Hornets were expected to equip the remaining six Navy fighter squadrons on the *Midway*-class ships and 12 Marine fighter squadrons would get single-seat F/A-18As to replace their F-4 Phantoms. Production plans for these 18 squadrons, plus six reserve squadrons and an annual attrition of 4.5 percent, were expanded with the decision to replace all 24 light attack squadrons with Hornets.

While a Hornet Fleet Replacement Squadron (FRS) was commissioned as VFA-125 in November 1980, VMFA-314 did not become the first operational F/A-18A Marine squadron until January 1983. Navy Fighter Attack squadrons retained the VFA designation although renamed Strike Fighter squadrons on March 25, 1983. A-7E units converted to F/A-18s as VF-113 and VF-125 first deployed on the *Constellation* on its February to August 1985 WESTPAC cruise.

The St. Louis factory produced 380 single-seat F/A-18A Hornets and 41 two-seat F/A-18B trainers. McDonnell also built 98 CF-18As and 41 CF-18B trainers for Canada from October 1982 to September 1988, and 57 AF/A-18A Hornets with 18 AF/A-18Bs assembled in Australia, beginning in June 1985. Spain began receiving 60 F-18A (C.15) fighters and 12 CE.15 trainers in July 1986.

On September 3, 1987, the first single-seat F/A-18C was flown with a new computer, ECM jammer, and 540 20-mm rounds. That model was first deployed on the carrier *America* by August 1989. A two-seat night attack version, the first F/A-18D, flew on May 6, 1988, and entered Marine squadron service in 1990. The Hornet force increased to 22 Navy and 16 Marine tactical squadrons. Although involved in skirmishes with Libyan forces in 1986, real Hornet fighting began in the Gulf War.

From five Navy carriers, nine squadrons with about 100 Hornets flew 4,439 sorties, mostly anti-radar and battlefield interdiction missions. On the war's first day, two *Saratoga* VFA-81 F-18Cs on a ground attack mission were warned by an E-2 that two MiG-21s were approaching head-on. Without dropping the four 2,000-pound bombs and center drop tank each carried, they destroyed both MiGs with a Sidewinder and two Sparrow missiles. These were the only enemy fighters downed by Navy fighters in the war, while two Hornets were lost to AAA.

USN

McDONNELL DOUGLAS F/A-18C
Two General Electric F404-GE-402, 17,750 lb. st AB
DIMENSIONS: As F-18A
WEIGHT: Empty 23,832 lb., Gross 37,708 lb. Max. 51,900 lb. Fuel 1597+990 gal.
PERFORMANCE: Speed- Top 1360 mph at 35,000', Cruising 530 mph, Combat Radius 393 miles/six Mk 82 bombs.

Hornets in the Gulf War included 84 planes based in Bahrain with six Marine F/A-18A/C squadrons (VMFA-212, 232, -235, -314,-333, and –451) and an F/A-18D squadron, VMFA(AW)-121. They flew 5,239 sorties with HARM and Maverick missiles, Walleye guided bombs, and Rockeye cluster bombs.

Kuwait ordered 32 F/A-18C and eight F/A-18D Hornets in September 1988, becoming in September 1991 the fourth foreign nation with the type. Finland began with seven F/A-18Ds in November 1995, and on May 14, 1996 flew the first of 57 F/A-18Cs to be assembled in Finland by Valmet Aviation. Likewise, Switzerland acquired an F/A-18D flown on January 20, 1996 and ordered 32 Hornets to be assembled in Lucerne. Malaysia and Thailand each ordered eight Hornets.

F404–GE-402 engines with 17,700-pounds thrust and APG-73 radar appeared in 1991 on new Hornets. In 1993, the Sparrows could be replaced with up to eight AIM-120 missiles or four AGM-84A-1C Harpoons for anti-shipping attacks. Marine F-18Ds could be configured for the Advanced Tactical Reconnaissance System (ATARS) tested over Bosnia in May 1999, with 24 pods and 31 conversion kits ordered.

Mfr

McDONNELL DOUGLAS F/A-18E
Two General Electric F414-GE-400, 22,000 lb. st
DIMENSIONS: Span 44'10", Lg. 60'2", Ht. 16', Wing Area 500 sq. ft.
WEIGHT: Empty 30,564 lb., Gross 47,881 lb. Max. 63,500 lb. Fuel 1700+1440 gal.
PERFORMANCE: Combat Radius 600 miles/six Mk 82 bombs. Other data classified.

On July 29, 1991, Defense Secretary Richard Cheney declared that the F/A-18E proposal would be chosen over more F-14s because it was easier to maintain, safer, and less costly. Using more powerful 22,000-pound thrust F414 engines with rectangular intakes, the larger "Super Hornet" version made its first flight November 29, 1995. Two more store pylons are added under the wings, so that six large bombs or missiles can be lifted. A two-seat counterpart, the F-18F, first flew on April 1,1996.

Carrier Air Wings are organized since 1995 to provide each carrier with 36 F/A-18 Hornets in three strike-fighter squadrons, along with a 14-plane F-14 squadron. By June 2000, the inventory included 191 F/A-18 Hornets, along with 31 B, 412 C, and 141 D models, as well as ten of the new F/A-18E and eight F/A-18F Super Hornets.

Total Navy F/A-18A to D production by September 30 was 1,048 aircraft. Cost per plane had risen from 40 million dollars for an F-18C to about 86 million for an F/A-18E, if the 548 planned are built. In fiscal 2000, only 36 were accepted, with an increase to 48 per year planned. The F/A-18E was the only new manufactured combat aircraft scheduled at the new century's beginning.

CHAPTER 37

BOMBERS FROM THE B-70 TO STEALTH

XB-70A Valkyrie taking off

The XB-70

SAC commander General Curtis LeMay recommended on October 14, 1954, that a supersonic replacement for the B-52 be designed, even before Boeing's Stratofortress entered service. On November 8, 1955, both Boeing and North American received letter contracts to design a WS-110A strategic piloted weapons system. The resulting proposals seemed impractical until the appearance of the "compression-lift" theory, which stated that the aircraft shock waves would provide additional lift in supersonic flight. North American's design was favored on December 23, 1957, and a contract for the XB-70 signed January 24, 1958.

The XB-70 Valkyrie was designed to cruise at Mach 3 over 75,000 feet. Such a tremendous advance in performance required both an entirely new aircraft configuration and a radical change in construction. Since the temperatures of up to 600 degrees F encountered on these flights were too much for the usual aluminum alloys, about 69.5 percent of the airframe weight was of welded steel honeycomb sandwich and 9.5 percent was titanium for the forward structure.

Prominent features were the canard foreplane near the long nose, delta wing with tips folding down for stability in supersonic flight, and twin rudders. Six General Electric YJ93-GE-3s with continuous afterburning and two intakes with controlled air induction were mounted under the center section. Boron fuel had been considered, but was replaced by JP-6 in August 1959, and inflight refueling was provided.

Continuous review of future manned-aircraft requirements for the USAF caused many disturbances in the program. While SAC wanted a manned bomber, President Eisenhower and his Defense Department officials said that bomber-penetration chances had been reduced by surface-to-air missile progress, but no defense against our intercontinental and submarine-launched ballistic missiles was in sight.

Expensive bomber programs were becoming unnecessary to deter a nuclear attack. Eisenhower said that "speaking of bombers in the missile age was like talking about bows and arrows in the gunpowder era."*

The conflict among the DoD, Air Force, and Congress swung back and forth. The first cancellation on December 1, 1959, cut back the program to one prototype, so that the next fiscal year's budget could be balanced, but Congress restored funding for a 265 million dollar program in October 1960.

However, on March 28, 1961, the new President, John F. Kennedy, also recommended that the program be limited to research prototypes and considered development as a weapons system unnecessary and economically unjustifiable. Three XB-70 prototypes authorized October 4, 1961, were to have no weapons provisions and only two – not four – crewmen in the pressurized nose with an ASQ-28 Bomb Navigation Subsystem.

Although bays for 25,000 pounds of munitions were provided, guns were no longer part of American bomber designs, as hostile air-to-air missiles were the main threat. But the Valkyrie would not become a bomber, but only an "air vehicle to demonstrate airworthiness in a sustained Mach 3 high altitude environment."

NORTH AMERICAN XB-70A
Six General Electric YJ-93-GE-3, 28,000 lb. st
DIMENSIONS: Span 105', Lg. 185'9", Ht. 30'8", Wing Area 6297 sq. ft.
WEIGHT: Empty 231,215 lb., Combat 341,096 lb., Gross 521,056 lb. Fuel 43,646 gal.
PERFORMANCE: Speed– Top and Cruising 1250 mph at 35,000', 1982 mph at 75,500', Touchdown 184 mph. Combat Ceiling 75,250', Service Ceiling 75,500'. Climb 27,450'/1min. Combat Range 3419 miles. Max. Range 4290 miles.

*Marcelle Knaack, Post-World War II Bombers. op. cit. 568.

An RS-70 (reconnaissance-strike) version was offered to introduce a capability not available in missiles, but the faster SR-71 Lockheed secret development reduced the RS-70's appeal. Defense Secretary Robert McNamara disagreed with General LeMay's advocacy of manned bombers and the third prototype was canceled on February 15, 1964, along with rejection of an Air Force request for 60 RS-70s to be operational in 1969. Nearly four years behind the 1958 schedule, the first XB-70A rolled out of the Palmdale, California, factory with much ceremony on May 11, 1964, and was flown on September 21.

The refined second prototype flown July 17, 1965, was destroyed by a midair collision with an F-104N on June 8, 1966. The first XB-70A made its 83rd and last flight February 4, 1969, to the Air Force Museum at Wright-Patterson AFB, Ohio. Over $1.5 billion had been expended on the B-70 program.

F-111 Aardvarks as bombers

In April 1964 the number of intercontinental missiles on alert surpassed the number of intercontinental bombers on alert, and the destruction of all possible enemy strategic fixed targets seemed assured. No strategic bombers were being produced in the United States. While strategic heavy and medium bomber squadrons decreased from 78 in June 1964 to 40 in June 1968 and 24 in September 1977, Air Force leaders continued to press development of new manned bomber designs.

The next bomber to enter SAC service was the General Dynamics FB-111A, which was developed from the F-111A tactical fighter-bomber. Powered by two Pratt & Whitney TF-30-P-7s, its outstanding feature was variable-sweep wings that could be swept back 72.5 degrees for high-speed attack. Terrain-following radar permitted a low-altitude attack approach that avoided the dangers of a high-altitude approach: early detection by enemy radar and interception by SAMs.

AF

GENERAL DYNAMICS FB-111A
Two Pratt& Whitney TF30-P-7, 20,350 lb. st AB
DIMENSIONS: Span 70', Lg. 75'6", Ht. 17', Wing Area 550 sq. ft.
WEIGHT: Empty 47,481 lb., Combat 70,380 lb., Gross 110,646 lb., Max. 114,277 lb. Fuel 5623+3600 gal.
PERFORMANCE: Speed– Top 838 mph at s. l., 1453 mph at 50,000', Cruising 511 mph, Stalling 183 mph. Combat Ceiling 49,993', Service Ceiling 50,263', Climb 23,418'/1 min. Ferry Range 4786 mph (six 600-gal. tanks/ no refueling.)

Two crewmen sat side by side and depended on speed and electronics for protection rather than any guns. On the basic mission two 2,247-pound nuclear SRAMs (AGM-69As) in the weapons bay and two more under the wings, along with four 600-gallon drop tanks, were carried over a 6,160-mile range, including 3,300 miles added by air refueling. Under wing pylons could hold six drop tanks for ferry flights, 24 750-pound M117A1 bombs, or Mk 43 nuclear bombs.

The FB-111A program was first announced December 10, 1965, as a low-cost interim supersonic replacement for the B-58. A production contract was approved, and an extended wing prototype, converted from the 18th F-111A, flew July 30, 1967. The first production aircraft flew at Fort Worth on July 13, 1968, but on March 19, 1969, a new Defense Secretary, Melvin Laird, cut the program from 263 to 76 aircraft.

SAC formally accepted its first FB-111A on October 8, 1969, and the first FB-111A SRAM launch tests began March 27, 1970. After the last FB-111A was received June 30, 1971, the 380th and 509th Bomb Wing operated them. The cost per production aircraft was listed as 9.8 million dollars.

AF

GENERAL DYNAMICS FB-111A with AGM-69A

In 1989, SAC began to retire their FB-111As, and 34 of these aircraft were transferred to TAC and redesignated F-111Gs with their SRAM provisions replaced by conventional bomb gear. The last SAC FB-111A unit, the 380th BW, was deactivated in July 1991 and the F-111Gs used for training at Cannon AFB.

Australia had contracted October 24, 1963, for 24 F-111Cs to replace their Canberra bombers and the first, which had the longer F-111B wings and FB-111A landing gear, was formally accepted in September 1968. The entire order was then stored pending the results of USAF F-111A testing, and, after becoming a scandal in Australian politics, were not rebuilt and delivered until June to December 1973.

Those were the only F-111s sold abroad, for a 50-plane contract for a Royal Air Force F-111K version announced February 1, 1967, was cancelled in January 1968. The almost completed first two were to be redesignated YF-111A for special tests, but the USAF decided instead to salvage both airframes for useful parts.

Four Australian F-111Cs added cameras to become RF-111C recon types in 1977, and in 1982, four ex-USAF F-111As replaced attrition losses.

AF

GENERAL DYNAMICS F-111E
Two Pratt & Whitney TF30-P-3, 10,750 lb. st military, 18,500 lb. AB
DIMENSIONS: Span 63' (32' swept), Lg. 73'6", Ht.17', Wing Area 525 sq. ft.
WEIGHT: Empty 46,172 lb., Combat 59,620 lb. Gross 82,819 lb./Mk 43, Max. 98,850 lb. Fuel 5043+2400 gal.
PERFORMANCE: Speed- Top 914 mph at s.l., 1453 mph at 53,450', Cruising 1194 mph, Stalling 152 mph. Combat Ceiling 56,650', Climb 25,550'/1 min., Combat Radius 1330 miles/Mk 43/two AIM-9B; 784 miles/12 M-117. Ferry Range 3634 miles.

Other F-111Cs were upgraded with Pave Tack electronics, and 15 used F-111Gs were purchased as replenishments in 1993.

The F-111 becomes more deadly, 1969 to 1986

The USAF ordered F-111Ds on May 10, 1967, with an improved Mark II avionics system and engines, but delayed development led to an interim F-111E model, using the F-111A's engine and radar, but with new air inlets to improve engine operations at high altitudes.

The first of 94 F-111E models replaced the F-111A on the delivery line in August 1969, entering operations with the 27th TFW on September 30. After the grounding and rework period until July 1970, the Fort Worth factory delivered the remaining F-111Es to the 20th TFW in England, which received the first of 79 in September 1970. By May 28, 1971, the last F-111E was accepted.

Bulinski

GENERAL DYNAMICS F-111D
Two Pratt & Whitney TF30-P-9, 12,430 lb. st military, 20,840 lb. AB
DIMENSIONS: Span 63'(32'swept), Lg. 73'6", Ht.17', Wing Area 525 sq. ft.
WEIGHT: Empty 46,631 lb., Combat 61,930 lb. Gross 93,000 lb., Max. 100,000 lb. Fuel 5043+2400 gal.
PERFORMANCE: Similar to F-111F.

The first F-111D was flown May 15, 1970 with a 12,840-pound thrust TF30-P-9, but the remaining 95 had to wait for their advanced APQ-128 terrain-following radar and APQ-30 attack radar. Deliveries delayed to July 1971 were not completed until February 28, 1973. They served the 27th TFW at Cannon AFB, New Mexico, until 1992.

The last new production model, the F-111F, was ordered July 1, 1970, but the new P-100 engines were delayed so that the first 49 entered service with the 347th TFW in September 1971 with TF30-P-9 engines and APQ-144 radar. The 25,100-pound thrust P-100 engines became available in 1972 and 106 F-111Fs were completed by November 1976 at a 10.3 million dollar unit price. Including SAC's FB-111As, 563 F-111 series aircraft were built.

Bulinski

GENERAL DYNAMICS F-111F (347thTFW, 1975)
Two Pratt & Whitney TF30-P-100, 25,100 lb. st AB
DIMENSIONS: Span 63' (32' swept), Lg. 73'6", Ht.17', Wing Area 525 sq. ft.
WEIGHT: Empty 47,450 lb., Combat 62,350 lb., Gross 95,333 lb. Fuel 5035 +2400 gal.
PERFORMANCE: Speed- 914 mph at s.l., Top 1453 mph at 40,000', Cruising 498 mph. Combat Ceiling 57,900', Climb 43,050'/1 minute, Combat Radius 920 miles/2000-lb. bomb, Lo-Lo-Hi mission. Ferry Range 3378 miles.

The proposed FB-111H was a bomber design offered in 1977 as a substitute for the high-cost B-1A program. Using

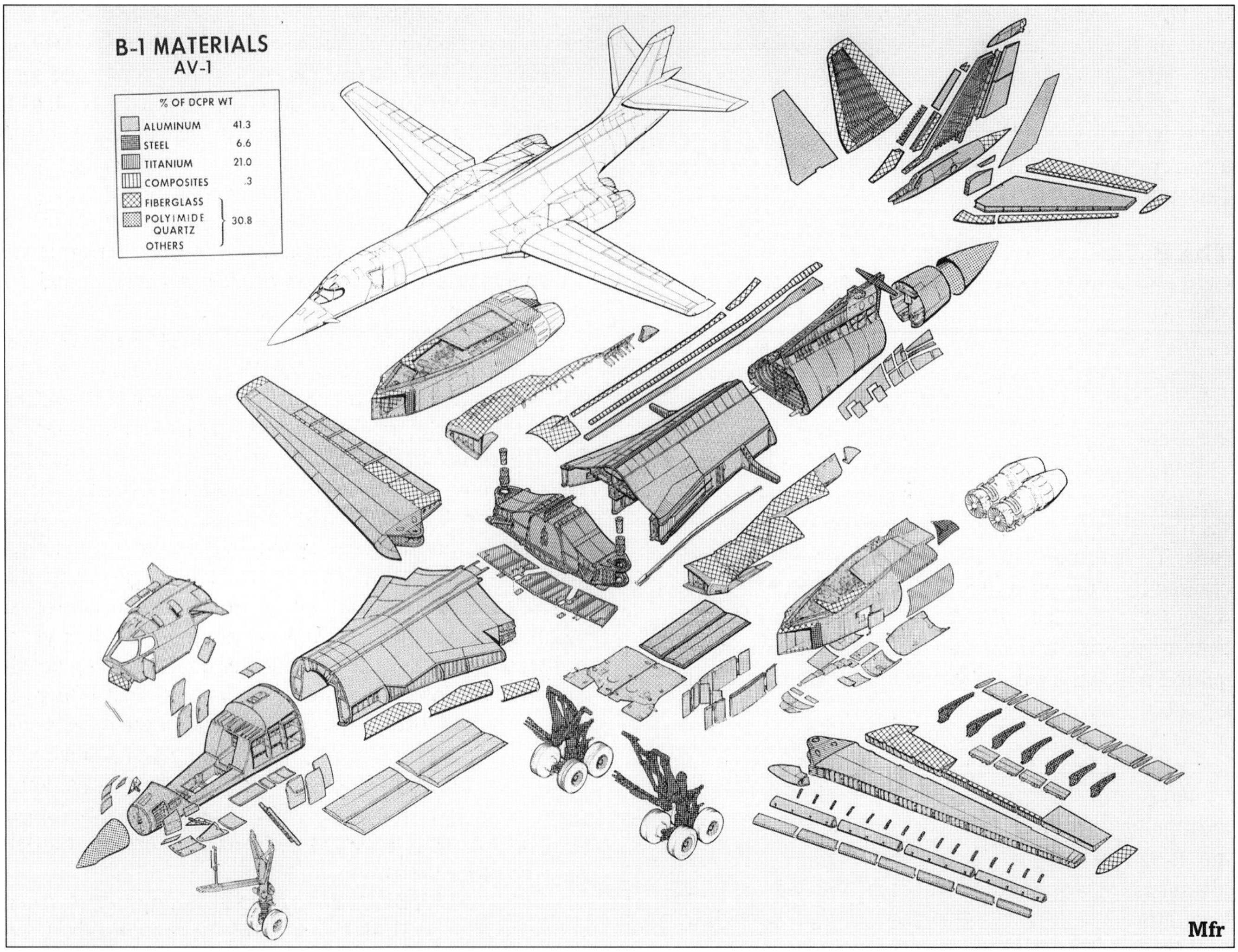

B-1 MATERIALS
AV-1

% OF DCPR WT	
ALUMINUM	41.3
STEEL	6.6
TITANIUM	21.0
COMPOSITES	.3
FIBERGLASS POLYIMIDE QUARTZ OTHERS	30.8

Mfr

ROCKWELL B-1A materials

Mfr

ROCKWELL B-1A
Four General Electric YF-101-GE-100, 16,150 lb., 29,850 lb. st AB
DIMENSIONS: Span 136'8" (78'2" swept), Lg. 150'8", Ht. 33'7". Wing Area 1946 sq. ft.
WEIGHT: Empty 173,000 lb. Combat 229,100 lb. Gross 395,000 lb. Refueled Max. 422,000'. Fuel 30,096 +6614 gal.
PERFORMANCE: Speed- Top 723 mph at 200', 1453 mph at 53,000', Cruising 507 mph. Stalling 182 mph. Combat Ceiling 53,000', Service Ceiling 53,500'. Combat Climb 22,600'/ 1 minute. Combat Range 6,535 miles, Ferry Range 7,188 miles.

the same General Electric F101 engines and radar systems, it was claimed to provide most of the same capabilities as the B-1A, when using air refueling, at less than half the cost. However, the Defense Department was committed to the cruise missile concept for future strategic deterrence.

Two F-111As were converted to EF-111A ECM aircraft by a January 30, 1975, contract with Grumman, who used its EA-6B experience to fit complete tactical radar jamming ALQ-99E gear in a canoe-shaped belly radome and a large fin tip pod for the ECM receivers. After tests of a fully modified prototype began May 17, 1977, the Air Force ordered 40 F-111A aircraft converted to the EF-111A configuration with APQ-160 attack radar.

Delivered from November 1981 to December 1985 and named the Raven, the EF-111A reached operational capability with the 390th Electronic Squadron, 366th TFW, in December 1983. Improved TF-30-P-9 engines and electronics were installed in EF-111As by 1989.

After the F-111F was transferred to the 48th TFW in England in March 1977, the M61A gun was replaced in 1980 by an Pave Tack AVQ-26 pod so that infrared and laser designators could guide weapons like the 2,000-pound GBU-10 or 500-pound GBU-12 bombs. An ALQ-131 ECM pod was also added for protection.

Operation El Dorado Canyon was a reprisal for terrorist attacks that launched 24 F-111F and five EF-111As from England against targets in Libya on April 14, 1986. Inflight refueling allowed 96 Mk 82 and 64 GBU-10 bombs to be carried to Tripoli's airfield, a barracks compound and a terrorist training camp, often aimed by the new Pave Tack pods.

The B-1A

Only one new American bomber, the Rockwell B-1A, appeared during the 1970s. It was intended to replace the B-52 for the SAC mission of penetrating enemy defenses to deliver nuclear or conventional weapons on strategic targets.

After several years of Air Force mission-requirement studies, President Nixon's new Defense Secretary, Melvin Laird, was more sympathetic to a manned bomber program, so in April 1969 the B-1A designation was authorized and on November 3, a Request for Proposals was issued. To rank bids, Air Force Evaluation Boards had increased from three captains and four lieutenants in 1924 to some 600 specialists in 1970, and had returned to a "fly-before-buy" basis which was the pre-1939 system of requiring satisfactory flight-test performance before launching production.

North American Rockwell won the B-1 contract award on June 5, 1970, for five prototypes. Powered by four 29,850-pound thrust General Electric F101 engines with variable intake ramps, the B-1A was two-thirds the size of the B-52, but carried twice the weapons load over a greater range at over twice the high-altitude speed. Low-level attacks, guided by APQ-146 terrain-following radar, could be made at Mach .95 and Mach 2.2 could be reached at high altitudes.

Survival in a surprise missile attack was a prime concern. The B-1A could be dispersed to smaller air bases that could not easily accommodate B-52s and was expected to be able to takeoff from and clear a threatened base within four minutes.

Combining high speed with short takeoff required a swing-wing configuration enabling the wing to fold back, like the F-111, 67.5-degrees during high-speed flight. Four crewmen sat in a self-contained capsule that could be detached for emergency escapes, and a pair of horizontal vanes near the nose was part of a Low-Altitude Ride Control system to reduce the effects of air turbulence.

Each of the three internal weapons bays could accommodate a rotary launcher for eight 2,247-pound AGM-69A missiles, which could be directed by an ASQ-156 system at targets within 100 miles of the aircraft, or up to 50,000 pounds of other stores, such as 12 B-43, 24 Mk 84, 30 M117, or 84 Mk 82 bombs. No guns were carried, but extensive ALQ-161 ECM equipment was provided.

Materials used in the airframe were 41.3% aluminum, 6.6% steel, and 21% titanium, the later percentage limited by cost considerations. Costs also reduced the program on January 18, 1971, to three aircraft and much slippage delayed construction.

Accompanied by an extensive publicity campaign, the first B-1A rolled out of the Palmdale, California, factory on October 26, 1974, before an audience of senior officers, politicians and writers, since the plane's future depended on political actions. Flight tests began on December 23, joined by a second plane on March 26, 1976, and a third on June 14. By November 1977 the prototypes had made 144 flights, had attained Mach 2.1 (1,350 mph) at 50,000 feet, and been up over ten hours on a single flight. From a performance viewpoint, the B-1A seemed entirely successful and far more capable than the B-52.

Air Force leaders such as Chief of Staff General George Brown advocated the B-1 as necessary to the TRIAD concept, in which land-based and submarine-launched missiles are combined with manned bombers to be a deterrent against hostile attack or threats. Manned bombers offer a flexibility of response impossible for missiles, and the B-1 was seen as "the most efficient and effective manned penetrating weapons system ever conceived."

The chief obstacle to a production program was the high cost of the 244 aircraft desired by 1986, quoted at $22.9 billion in 1976 for the total program in "then-year" dollars, or more than $84 million per unit, including development and inflation costs. Questions of cost effectiveness arose, comparing this cost with that of the missiles required to destroy the same targets. The nation, which had just expended some $150 billion on the war in Vietnam – enough to pay for several B-1 programs – no longer seemed willing to accept the inflationary costs of a possibly redundant system.

On June 30, 1977, as President Jimmy Carter faced the beginning of his first fiscal year, he canceled the B-1A production program as unnecessary and too expensive, allowing completion of the flight tests and the fourth prototype. Instead, the emphasis was shifted to cruise missiles (ACLM) that could be carried inside modified B-52s, which could then attack targets without themselves penetrating enemy defense areas.

Cruise missiles

Boeing's ALCM (Air Launched Cruise missile, AGM-86B) was chosen by the Air Force, instead of the Convair AGM-109 Tomahawk preferred by the Navy. Ninety-eight B-52G and 95 B-52H bombers were modified to launch strategic missiles, beginning with the 416th Bomb Wing's B-52Gs.

AF

BOEING B-52G with AGM-86B cruise missiles

Eight AGM-86Bs were carried on a rotary launcher in the internal weapons bay, and pylons mounted under the wings held another twelve. This 21-foot, 3,200-pound missile, speeding a W-80 warhead with a 200-kiloton yield to targets up to 1,500 miles away, made its first operational test with the 416th BW in September 1982.

The last B-52Ds were retired in October 1983, while AGM-84 Harpoon missiles began to add anti-shipping capability to B-52G missions. By July 1985, the active B-52 force was reduced to 264 bombers, but two squadrons, the 69th and 90th, had Harpoons and the 7th BW became the first B-52H unit with AGM-86B cruise missiles. All these Boeings retained their capacity for combinations of conventional or nuclear gravity bombs when conditions allowed them to fly directly over a target

Without new American bomber production, the Seventies saw a shift in the strategic-force balance, as more numerous strategic missiles became the way to deliver nuclear warheads. The most important changes on the U.S. side had been to replace the single-warhead Minuteman II by the Minuteman III, with three independently target able (MIRV) warheads and improved accuracy, upgrade Minuteman silo protection, and provide the bomber force with better electronics and some 1,250 SRAMs to batter their way through enemy defenses. Submarine-launched missiles were also MIRVed. Mass destruction became such a threat that the rival powers negotiated a Strategic Arms Limitation Treaty (SALT).

The SALT II agreement on June 18, 1979, listed the United States strategic inventory as 570 B-52 and 3 B-1A heavy bombers, 1,054 ICBMs, and 656 SLBMs. (Soviet strength was given as 156 Tu-95 and M-4 heavy bombers, 1,398 ICBMs, and 950 SLBMs.)

Reviving the B-1

Meanwhile, the Air Force continued planning to replace the B-52 with B-1s. The fourth B-1A, flown on February 14, 1979, was the only one with an integrated defensive avionic system. Performance of this new electronic countermeasures suite against simulations of hostile detection and missile systems could indicate the future of the manned bomber. Another approach to bomber survivability was the exploration of radar-absorbing materials for aircraft. This caused some excitement in August 1980, when Defense Secretary Harold Brown mentioned a "Stealth" strategic bomber project using such new technology.

Rockwell International also proposed a missile launcher version of the B-1, carrying 16 ACLMs internally and 14 externally. To reduce aircraft costs, this B-1 version would lose its supersonic capability. Fixed wings set at 25-degree sweep would replace the variable-sweep wings, and the aircraft structure could be simplified and lightened. This proposal was rejected.

Another weapon considered for the B-1 and tested on the FB-111A in 1978 was the B77 nuclear bomb, whose yield was adjustable during flight and whose gas generator stabilizor, with lifting and retardant parachute, enables release at altitudes as low as 150 feet. But that was abandoned in favor of the 2,400-pound B83, the last nuclear bomb for SAC.

Ronald Reagan became President and launched an arms expansion that on October 2, 1981, announced the purchase of 100 B-1B bombers. The first production contract was signed on January 20, 1982, and also directed modification of two B-1A prototypes to the new configuration. Additional fuel and bomb load increased the weight. Since supersonic speed was no longer needed and low radar reflection desired, new fixed engine inlets and wing fairings appeared.

Flight tests on the modified second B-1A began March 23, 1983, and the fully modified fourth prototype joined on July 30, 1984. A fatal crash of the older aircraft on August 29, confirmed the wisdom of replacing the escape module with ejection seats for the two pilots, an offensive systems officer (OSO) and a defensive systems officer (DSO).

On October 18, 1984, the first B-1B flew at Palmdale, and the first operational B-1B joined SAC's 96th BW at Dyess AFB, Texas, in July 1985. By 1987, the B-1Bs were also operational in the 28th, 319th, and 384th Bomb Wings. Last of the 100 B-1Bs was delivered, at a total 20.5 billion dollar cost, on May 2, 1988, and Lancer became the official name two years later, but pilots liked "Bone" (for B one).

AF

ROCKWELL B-1B
Four General Electric F-101-GE-102, 30,780 lb. st AB
DIMENSIONS: Span 136'8" (78'2" swept), Lg. 147', Ht. 33'7". Wing Area 1950 sq. ft.
WEIGHT: Empty 192,000 lb., Gross 433,406 lb., Max. 477,000 lb. Fuel 30,085+8925 gal.
PERFORMANCE: Speed- Top 699 mph at 500', 825 mph at 50,000', Cruising 648 mph. Combat Ceiling 60,000', Combat Range 6,800 miles/53,040 lb., 7,455 miles max.

New world records were set in 1987 by carrying a 66,140-pound payload 1,080 nautical miles at 669 mph, and 2,700 nautical miles at 655 mph. Published top speed was Mach .92 at 500 feet and Mach 1.25 at 50,000 feet. The four F101-GE-102 engines had afterburners and normal JP-4 fuel.

Weapons on the three stores bay's 15-foot rotary launchers included up to 24 B61 and B83 nuclear bombs with delayed detonations, 24 AGM-69, eight AGM-86B or four AGM-129A missiles, 24 2,000-pound Mk 84 or 84 500-pound Mk 82 AIR bombs, which could be released altitudes as low as 500 feet. Several combinations of GBU and CBU munitions are also available up to a maximum 75,000-pound load. When proper software is provided to their computers, an ASQ-184 avionics system with APQ-164 radar enables night navigation, terrain following, and weapons delivery.

F-117A refueling from KC-10A

Defense consists of an ALQ-116 system combining threat detection, tail warning, and eight ECM dispensers atop the fuselage, each with either 12 flares or 120 chaff cartridges. An ALE-55 towed decoy system to distract incoming missiles can be deployed. Three 2,975-gallon auxiliary tanks could replace weapons in the bays, but as on all USAF bombers, a receptacle to refuel inflight from KC-10s was provided.

Severe engine problems caused the temporary grounding on December 20, 1990, of all B-1Bs except those needed for alert. This resulted in the absence of the Lancer from **Desert Storm** combat. All were back to flying status by April 1991 and in September they were removed from nuclear alert and all training centered on non-nuclear weapons. Since low-level AAA had become more dangerous than SAMs, most missions would be flown at over 20,000 feet

By 1995, B-1Bs served the 7th Bomb Wing at Dyess, the 34th Bomb Squadron at Ellsworth, and the ANG 116th and 184th BWs at Robins AFB, Georgia, and McConnell AAFB, in Kansas. The first combat sortie would come in 1998, as the last chapter will tell.

Stealth

Doubts about the B-1Bs ability to penetrate well-defended enemy targets led the Air Force to explore the possibility of reducing a night bomber's chances of being detected by radar. Aircraft like the B-1 and the SR-71 had reduced their front cross section enough to make them less reflective to hostile radar, and the advantage of building a nearly invisible night bomber was attractive.

It is not surprising that Kelly Johnson's Skunk Works was selected for this project, beginning with a contract in April 1976 to develop a test vehicle called Have Blue with Very Low Observable (VLO) characteristics. That small-scale, proof-of-concept aircraft began test flights at the secret Groom Lake base on December 1, 1977. A second Have Blue prototype in 1978 refined the VLO concept, which replaced aircraft curves with less-reflective straight facets, and careful engine intake screening.

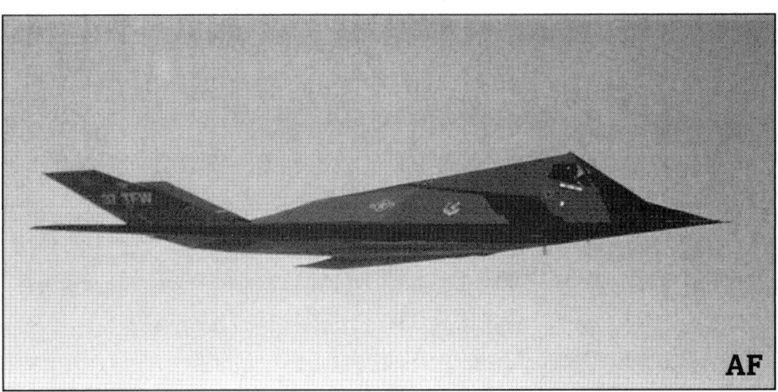

LOCKHEED MARTIN F-117A
Two General Electric F404-GE-F1D2, 10,800 lb. st
DIMENSIONS: Span 65'11", Lg. 43'4", Ht. 12'5". Wing Area 913 sq. ft.
WEIGHT: Empty 29,500 lb., Gross 52,500 lb. Fuel 1,850 gal.
PERFORMANCE: Speed- Top 603 mph at 35,000'. Ceiling 52,000'. Combat Radius 500 miles. Range 1,250 miles
(Data from Miller, F-117. op. cit. 24-25.)

Very strict security protected the program as it advanced to a bomber design. As Oxcart had disguised the A-12, the world's fastest airplane, F-117 was the misleading designation of the secret night bomber. Our first fighters, had been called pursuits, which chased and shot down enemy aircraft, but the F-117 could not catch or shoot anything.

The radical F-117 achieved VLO traits by a faceted delta shape, radar absorbent composite materials, and reduced infrared exhaust emissions. This shape did limit performance, and no radar was allowed, for any emissions must be prevented. Two General Electric F-404 engines like those of the F/A-18, but without afterburners, powered the F-117A, and a unique V-tail was used. No external stations are allowed.

One man flew the Stealth plane, using a built-in computerized inertial navigation and autopilot flight control system. When a target is acquired by infrared detection from a 25,000-foot altitude, a laser target designator releases a 2,000-pound GBU-10 Paveway II or GBU-27 Paveway III bomb.

Piloted by Harold Farley, Jr., the first F-117A flew at Groom Lake on June 18, 1981. Fifty-nine were delivered from January 15, 1982, to July 12, 1990. They achieved operational capability in October 1983 with the 4450th Tactical Group, which became the 37th TFW at the Tonopah Test Range in October 1989.

Armament usually comprised two GBU-27 or GBU-10 bombs in twin bays, and an inflight refueling receptacle allowed movement to any part of the world. Not until November 10, 1988, was the F-117 revealed to the public. Two 37th TFW Nighthawks targeted a Rio Hato military base on December 20, 1989, during the operation against Panama's dictator.

Air Force Bombers in Desert Storm

Desert Storm began on January 17, 1991, when the first ten 415th TFS F-117As based in Saudi Arabia struck Baghdad at 12.22 AM. Since that capital city was so heavily defended, only F-117As and Tomahawk cruise missiles were used against Baghdad itself. During the Gulf War, 42 F-117As flew 1,271 sorties and dropped 2,040 tons of guided bombs, with 79% believed to have hit their targets. Not one F-117A was lost or seriously damaged.

That most modern Air Force bomber was joined by the oldest when seven 2nd BW B-52Gs flew from Barksdale AFB, Louisiana, to launch 35 AGM-86Bs and returned on January 17, after a 35-hour, 14,000-mile flight, the longest combat mission in history. During the Gulf War, 1,624 missions by 86 B-52s were flown with 25,700 tons of iron bombs from Fairford, England; Moron, Spain; and the island of Diego Garcia, as well as SAC bases in the U.S. Twenty-seven 800-pound M117 bombs were inside each B-52G bay, and 18 more could be added on the external beams.

For **Desert Storm**, 22 swing-wing 20th TFW F-111Es were deployed from England to Turkey and 67 48th TFW F-111Fs were based at Taif, Saudi Arabia, on January 17, 1991. The 48th TFW flew 2,417 sorties, dropping 3,650 tons of bombs, including 4,595 LGBs, nearly 80% of those dropped in the war. Pave Tack anti-armor missions used 2,542 GBU-12Bs, while other PGBs, including 2,000-pound GBU-15 infrared glide bombs, hit targets from hardened aircraft shelters to bridges and deep bunkers. No F-111s were lost in combat.

That force also dropped cluster and general purpose bombs, like those used by most of the other USAF aircraft. Twenty-three EF-111A Ravens made over 900 sorties to jam Iraqi radar, with one EF-117A lost.

GENERAL DYNAMICS F-111F PAVE TACK (1990)
Two Pratt & Whitney TF30-P-100, 25,100 lb. st AB
DIMENSIONS: Span 63' (32' swept), Lg. 73'6", Ht.17', Wing Area 525 sq. ft.
WEIGHT: Empty 47,175 lb., Combat 55,620 lb., Gross 83,320 lb., Max. 93,134 lb. Fuel 5035+2405 gal.
PERFORMANCE: Speed- Top 914 mph at s.l., 1453 mph at 60,200', Cruising 508 mph. Combat Ceiling 60,600', Climb 52,370'/1 minute. Combat Radius 1260 miles/1416-lb. bombs, Hi-Lo-Hi mission. Ferry Range 2753 miles.

Down-sizing the Bomber force

After the war, the F-117s were transferred to the 49th TFW at Holloman AFB, acquired new GPS navigation gear, and were named Nighthawks in 1994. On May 3, 1994, the last B-52Gs retired to storage, leaving the B-52H in Air Force squadrons. More combat missions would come in the near future for the B-1B, B-52H and the F-117A, as an advanced GPS/inertial navigation system was added.

The last F-111Fs retired from the 27th FW on July 27, 1996, when the USAF finally accepted Aardvark as the official F-111 name. EF-111A Ravens patrolled during operations in the former Yugoslavia and were finally retired from the USAF in May 1998.

Bomber forces would be gradually reduced until 94 B-52, 84 B-1, and 9 B-2 heavy bombers, 500 Minuteman III and 50 Peacekeeper ICBMs, and 332 Trident SLBMs were listed in 1994.

Northrop B-2A Spirit

The last American bomber of the century is a large four-

NORTHROP GRUMMAN B-2A
Four General Electric F118-GE-100, 19,000 lb. st
DIMENSIONS: Span 172', Lg. 69', Ht. 17'. Wing Area 5,140 sq. ft.
WEIGHT: Empty 153,700 lb., Gross 336,500 lb. Max. 375,000 lb. Fuel 20,770 gal.
PERFORMANCE: Speed- Top 570 mph at s.l., 628 mph at 45,000'. Ceiling 50,000'. Range 6,000 miles/24,000 lb.

engine stealth aircraft whose wingspan happens to be the same 172-feet as that of the Northrop B-35 flying wings flown 46 years before.

Radar Absorbent Materials (RAMs) demonstrated on a Northrop Tacit Blue reconnaissance vehicle were included in the composite materials that were 80% of the structure, along with a blended body and flying wing shape, sharp wing edges, and four buried low-noise F-118 non-afterburning engines with special air intakes and exhaust electors. An elaborate ZSR-63ECM system reacts to outside threats.

Production began at Palmdale with six developmental test aircraft, the first flown on July 17, 1989, the second on October 19, 1990, and the last on February 2, 1993. Fifteen production aircraft followed and deliveries to the 393rd BS, 509th BW, at Whiteman AFB, Missouri, began

AF

GENERAL DYNAMICS EF-111A

on December 17, 1993. Such a small production run increased the most complicated bomber ever built to a cost of nearly a billion dollars each. An elaborate ground support structure is required so that only Whiteman AFB was suitable for launching missions.

Two crewmen are guided by an astro-inertial navigation system and flight computers control the instability that troubled early flying wings. ALQ-181 radar has 21 operation modes from navigation to target detection, and weighs 2,100 pounds.

Up to 40,000 pounds of weapons are carried in two internal bays. The first 10 production aircraft had 16 gravity bombs like the nuclear B83 or conventional Mk 84. Guided AGM-129 cruise missiles linked to a GPS for continual updating were introduced on the next three, while the last two in 1997 had the definitive Block 30 fit, to which all early aircraft were upgraded. While nuclear stores were no longer carried, 80 M 82 bombs or Mk 36 mines were. The GPS-guided 2,000-pound GBU-32 and 4,700-pound GAM-113 developed for the B-2A provided individual target direction for each weapon.

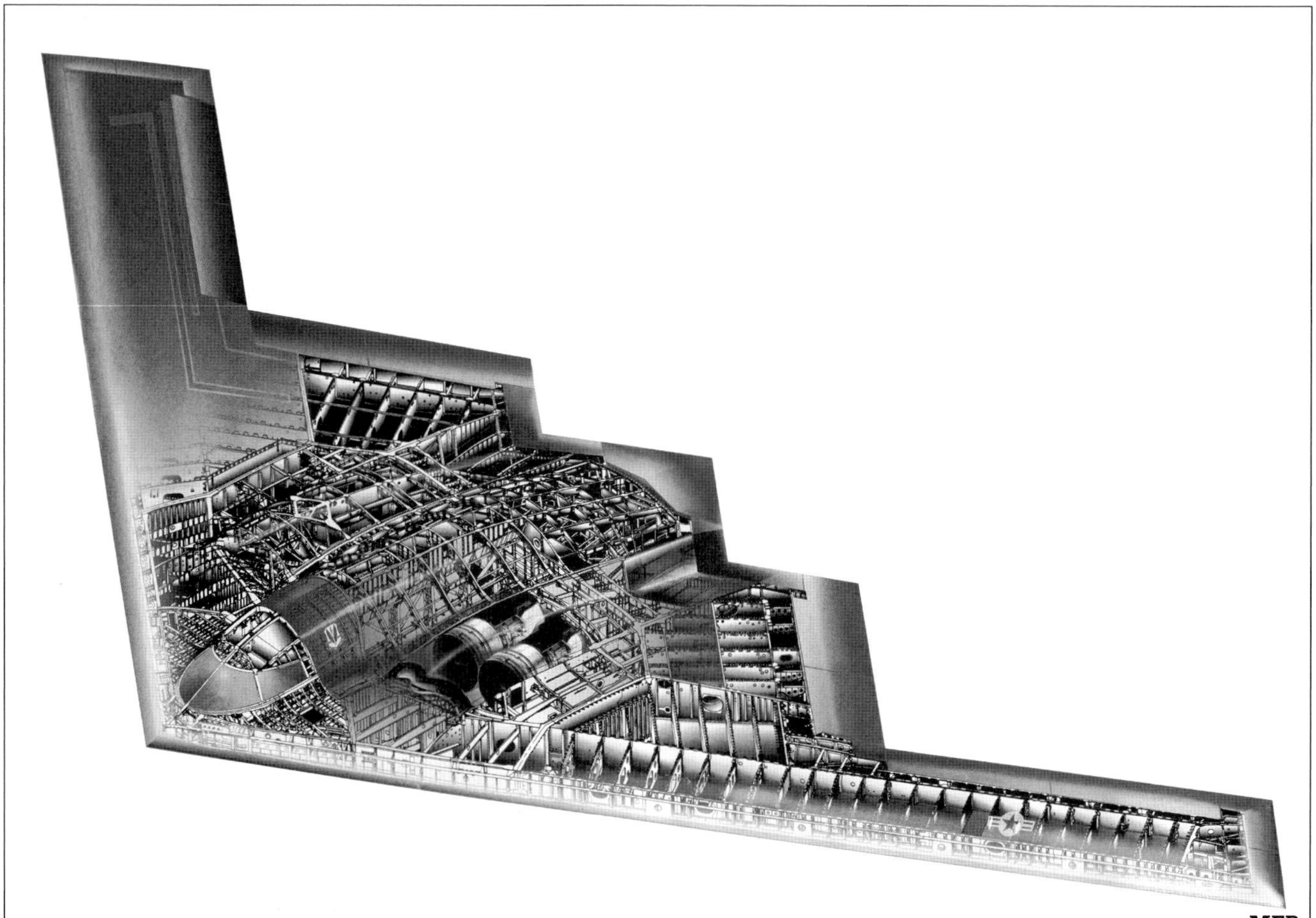

MFR

NORTHROP GRUMMAN B-2A interior

CHAPTER 38

FROM IRAQ TO AFGHANISTAN

Today's F-16 pilot has a very different working environment than those of 1917.

How things have changed for pilots since young Americans flew Spads in 1918! The F-16 pilot in his pressurized air-conditioned cockpit has computer control over flying and navigation, an array of weapons, and has an ejection seat for escaping his plane. Spad pilots had no computer or parachute.

Even more dramatic was the change in the world below him. When Wright's first airplane flew, the United States had only recently become an imperial power after the Spanish-American War. President Theodore Roosevelt had an impressive Navy and small Army, but American forces seemed smaller than those of at least seven other empires that straddled the world.

The century's last decade found the United States the only super power, able to project its strength into any part of the world. At the heart of its power were the airplanes produced by its national wealth and technology. The cost of air power had become too high to allow any other nation to become a credible contender for world power.

The Cold War had vanished by 1992, as the USAF was noticed for humanitarian missions such as flying medical supplies to Mongolia, Lithuania, and other places once considered hostile territory. On March 4, two B-52s landed in Moscow on a friendship mission, and on March 24 the United States signed the Open Skies Treaty, allowing unarmed reconnaissance flights over any of the 25 signatory nations.

Symbolic of the new era was first American military band to parade in Moscow, the AFRES Command Band in May 1992. The "most far-reaching nuclear arms reduction pact in history", START III, was signed by Presidents George H. Bush and Boris Yeltsen on January 3, 1993.

Reorganization of the USAF in June 1992 meant the end of both SAC and TAC as their combat aircraft were combined in the new Air Combat Command (ACC), while cargo and tanker aircraft joined the Air Mobility Command (AMC). The new United States Strategic Command now controlled long-range Air Force and Navy ballistic missiles.

Nuclear weapon capability had been removed from the B-1Bs in 1995, as confirmed by Russian inspectors. So the first combat mission, Operation **Desert Fox,** centered on two Oman-based B-1Bs releasing 63 500-pound Mk 83 bombs each. President Clinton ordered that attack on Iraqi Republican Guards barracks on December 17, 1998, in response to Saddam Hussein's expulsion of United Nations inspectors. Navy fighters supported that mission, as well as a second raid the following night.

An attack on Iraq in 1998 was the first B-1B mission.

Coalition air forces flew 40,000 strike sorties in 30 days as air skirmishes continued over the Iraq no-fly zones and F-16s downed two MiGs and bombed an airfield. Operation **Provide Comfort,** a no-fly zone to protect Kurdish people in Northern Iraq, continued from 1991 into the next century.

The need for precision bombing led to development of the Joint Direct Attack Munition (JDAM) glider bomb family, satellite-guided by their own individual GPS to hit targets up to six miles away. The 2,000-pound GBU-31 is the first of these weapons to be used in combat.

Conflict in the former Yugoslavia led to Operation **Allied Force** with 9,000 NATO sorties being flown in 30 days. Two B-2As flew the first of 45 combat missions all the way from Missouri on March 24, 1999, each launching 16 GBU-31s. Eight B-1Bs and 18 B-52Hs flew from Fairford, England, to drop Mk 82s on Serbian targets. On May 1, B-1Bs dropped 168 bombs on the Novi Sad oil refinery. 86th FW F-16s shot down four Serbian attack planes in Bosnia.

The super-power status of the United States was unequaled in history. No longer were the mass air and sea battles seen in the 20th century possible, for the great air

Serbia became the first B-2 target in 1999.

fleets and most of the factories that built them are gone. The expense of maintaining large, modern, air and naval fleets was beyond the resources of smaller nations not full partners in the global economy. While the threat of war continued, it would come from warlords empowered more by discontent than by their weapons.

Some 40 years after it was built, the B-52H was finding targets in Serbia and in Afghanistan.

As the century ended, the threat to America would come from camps in Afghanistan, where religious fanatics trained to begin a war without airpower. That war would be based on ideology, and technology was only seen as a tool to be turned on its Western promoters. Nearly 60 years after Pearl Harbor, the September 11, 2001, air attack would begin a new century's war on American security and values. Operation **Enduring Freedom** may be a model for the new era.

The ATF program

Development of an Advanced Tactical Fighter (ATF) to replace the F-15 in the next decade has become an extremely lengthy and expensive process. The goal was a multi-mission air superiority fighter to penetrate enemy air space to detect and destroy high-threat targets.

Supersonic cruising speed without afterburners and low radar reflectivity was required and computer directed flight control, navigation and weapons control were essential. The Air Force Flight Dynamics Lab explored design concept contracts with General Dynamics and McDonnell Douglas from 1975 to 1986, and Lockheed separately stressed "super stealth" designs.

After many models had been made of the different concepts, Lockheed and Northrop were named on October 31, 1986, as the winners of 691-million dollar contracts to each build two demonstration prototypes. Since each project required more engineering than one company could do, the YF-22 was produced by a Lockheed, General Dynamics and Boeing team, while the YF-23 would be a joint Northrop and McDonnell Douglas product.

The days of the individual design genius were over, long gone with the drafting table and slide rule. Collective computer analysis, debates, and decisions were continuous, although secure from outside observers. The first YF-22 drawings were formally released to the Fort Worth factory on April 1, 1988. Parts were flown from there and from Seattle to Burbank for assembly.

AF

LOCKHEED MARTIN YF-22

First flown on August 27, 1990, the rival Northrop YF-23 differed in having a flatter fuselage with intakes under the wings for the twin General Electric YF120 engine. The second YF-23 flew on October 26, but the YF-22 would be more successful..

General Electric YF-120-GE-100 vectored-thrust engines powered the first YF-22 flight from Palmdale on September 29, 1990, by Lockheed test pilot Dave Furguson, and the second YF-22 flew October 30 with Pratt & Whitney YF119-PW-100 engines. Supersonic cruise and inflight refueling were soon demonstrated, while AIM-9 and AIM-120 missiles were fired from the weapons bay.

Nine production F-22A Raptors ordered in August 1991, had numerous design modifications. The wing sweep was reduced from 48 to 42 degrees, the main wheels folded sideways, and the cockpit and inlets refined. Seven years after the prototype, the first F-22A flight was on September 7, 1997, at the Lockheed Georgia factory. Weapons arrangements include an M61A gun with 480 rounds, with a bay for six AIM-120C, or two such missiles and two 1,000-pound GBU-32 JDAM guided glider bombs.

SDAM

NORTHROP McDONNELL-DOUGLAS YF-23
Two General Electric F1120-GE-100, 35,000 lb. st AB
DIMENSIONS: Span 43'7", Lg. 67'5", Ht. 14'.
Other data classified.

SDAM

LOCKHEED MARTIN F-22A
Two Pratt & Whitney F119-PW-100, 35,000 lb. st AB
DIMENSIONS: Span 44'6", Lg. 62'1", Ht. 16'7". Wing Area 840 sq. ft.
WEIGHT: Empty 42,974 lb., Gross 65,337 lb. Max. 80,000 lb. Fuel 2820+2400 gal.
PERFORMANCE: Speed- Top 1320 mph, Cruising 1128 mph. Service Ceiling 60,000'. Combat Radius 430 miles. Ferry Range 2073 miles.
Other data classified.

SDAM

LOCKHEED MARTIN X-35A (JSF technology demonstrator)
Pratt & Whitney F119-PW-611
DIMENSIONS: Span 33', Lg. 56'11", Ht. 14'6".
WEIGHT: Gross 34,856 lb.
Other data classified.

How many F-22As will be produced in the 21st century depends on the annual budget. Costs and reliability have become as important as superior performance in selecting the American combat planes of the next decade.

The JSF program

The goal of the Joint Strike Fighter (JSF) program is development of an "affordable, highly common family" of single-engine, single-seat, strike aircraft. Two design teams were selected to build contrasting JSF concepts.

At the century's end, the Concept Demonstration Phase produced an unarmed Lockheed Martin X-35 to explore the possibilities of an aircraft with multi-national appeal, as well as sales to all three American services. Boeing, merged with McDonnell Douglas in 1997, also had a test vehicle built in Palmdale. The X-32 first flew on September 18, 2000.

A Pratt & Whitney JSF119-611 was installed in the X-35, which first flew on October 24, 2000. For the STOVL phase of the tests, which began on June 24, 2001, Lockheed had chosen to use a lift fan, and its advantage over the Boeing system would win the Pentagon's approval. That victory announced on October 26, is expected to have Lockheed begin the 21st century with the largest aircraft contract yet made.

Readers of this book have seen the American combat plane grow in effectiveness from 1917's modest aircraft to today's very expensive machines. Fighter development has been the most fertile, new types appearing at a rapid rate through each period of their history. Successful adaptation to ground attack and reconnaissance missions have strengthened the fighter's role in every air force.

The missile era has sharply curtailed the bomber's role, but seems to have actually enhanced the power of the fighter, whose own missiles now strike air and surface targets from beyond gunfire's range. The fighter's future, like that of the other combat types, will continue to depend on the kind of missions demanded by the direction of international power politics.

LOCKHEED MARTIN X-35B (STOVL demonstrator)

This book ends with the 20th Century, and the new century's events are being recorded by journalism, only the "first draft of history." The Wright Brother's Centennial reminds us that they hoped that aircraft would someday make war impossible. During 2003's new Gulf war, not one Iraqi fighter arose to contest the coalition air force, proving American air power too great to challenge.

The United Nation's Charter in 1945 announced the goal "to save succeeding generations from the scourge of war," and the Security Council's five permanent members have a practical monopoly of air power. A new generation's political and economic growth could make that goal possible.

Table 14 • USAF Active Combat Type Inventory

	September 30, 1991				September 30, 2000			
Type	USAF	ANG	Reserve	Total	USAF	ANG	Reserve	Total
A-7	5	245	—	250	—	—	—	—
A-10	404	124	87	615	213	102	52	367
A-37	6	22	—	28	—	—	—	—
AC-130A	9	—	—	9	—	—	—	—
				(902)				(367)
B-52	191	—	—	191	85	—	9	94
B-1	96	—	—	96	75	—	18	93
B-2	3	—	—	3	21	—	—	21
				(290)				(204)
F-4	190	165	—	353	—	—	—	—
F-15	744	163	—	907	614	126		740
F-16	930	658	150	1738	773	569	60	1402
F-22	1	—		1	3	—	—	3
				(2999)				(1214)
FB-111	39	—		39		—	—	
F-111	289	—		289			—	—
F-117	58	—		58	55			55
				385				55
Total				4577				2771

Source: AIR FORCE magazine has annual USAF Almanac each May issue. Above data selected from 5/92: 34-36, and 5/01: 56-57.

BIBLIOGRAPHY AND READERS' GUIDE

Olive drab replaced natural metal finish in 1941, on this restored P-40E seen at Porterfield, CA, in June 1974.

American combat planes have worn many interesting colors over the years and they are displayed in the specialty books listed in our readers' guide. Air show photos by Ron Bulinski sample the markings enthusiasts can discover.

This section is intended both to describe the data sources for this book and to guide readers seeking more information. A book of this scope does not have room for all the details an enthusiast may be eager to learn about any one of the many planes described here, but this guide can point the way.

B-17G in wartime colors and a P-40M-10 in Royal Canadian Air Force markings at the July 1988 Brown Field show.

A green tail, gray fuselage, and yellow upper wing illustrate pre-war *USS Ranger*'s Wildcat colors at September 1977 Reno show.

Late-1942 Navy blue-gray markings on FM-2 at NAS North Island show in August 1961.

F4U with 1943's sea blue and white scheme at Brown Field, July 1988.

The July 1988 Brown Field show also exhibited P-47D-2 with wartime dark green and gray.

For each chapter, publications are listed that provide details of serial numbers, technical features, markings, and more photographs to delight airplane enthusiasts. History fans seeking the big picture will find a list of official, academic,

Most American warplanes at World War II's end had the natural metal finish of P47D-28 at a 1975 George AFB show.

and popular books for each topic. This history has room only to concentrate on aircraft and omit the human side, but if you want to learn about the people who made and flew these air weapons, they can be found in these books.

Most of the data in this book was gathered by the author from unpublished documentation stored in the National Archives, the Air Force and Navy history offices, and the archives of major aviation museums. In order not to smother the text, footnotes are limited to direct quotations, and primary sources are cited for each chapter, especially those with data that bears on possible disputed points.

Notes on Documentary Sources

Perhaps the most controversial element in a description of military airplanes is the data describing each type's performance. Since the actual data on most military aircraft is kept secret for some time, there is opportunity for unofficial and often inaccurate estimates of each type's capability to be published. Conflicting sets of data have appeared on many of the aircraft described in this book, and therefore it is necessary to specify the sources from which the data here presented was selected.

Every effort has been made to select data based on actual flight tests of a typical example of the type described, or, when test flights are not available, to give the specifications guaranteed by the manufacturer in their contract with the government. Such data, of course, cannot necessarily be true for every article of that type produced because is much variation, by modification or service wear and tear, from the brand-new aircraft tested. Pilots usually regard official figures as being decidedly optimistic.

In this book, much data on aircraft built for United States air services is taken from the once-confidential official characteristics charts prepared by each service for senior officers. These charts were usually issued annually from 1920 to 1942 and included aircraft on hand or on order at the time of issue. Since 1942, charts are issued individually for each aircraft. The Technical Data Branch, Materiel Division, at Wright Field prepared the *"Characteristics and Performance of U.S. Army Airplanes"* charts, and these were examined at the Air Force Museum at the Wright-Patterson Air Force Base, Dayton Ohio. (It should be added that the data selected to accompany this book's photos indicates

Green and tan camouflage on F-84F at Mitchell Field, Milwaukee, July 1967.

Typical 1973 Navy markings on VS-25 S-2E at North Island NAS.

only the outlines of the flight envelope, which encloses a wide range of altitude and load options.)

Serial Technical reports of *Official Airplane Performance Tests* made at McCook & Wright Fields from 1918 to 1938 are the source for most Army plane data of that period. They are listed here as OPT in the chapter references for each aircraft, and were sometimes included in the Air Service Information Circulars printed at Dayton.

The *Index of AF Serial Numbers Assigned to Aircraft 1958 and Prior*, Procurement Division, AAF, April 1961, has Air Force contract data and approval dates. *Model Designations of Army Aircraft and Model Designations of Army Aircraft Engines.* ATSC Wright Field, 1945, indicates differences among models.

Characteristics charts for Naval aircraft were made available by the Office of Technical Information of the Bureau of Aeronautics, U.S. Navy, which also had official flight test reports made at Anacostia Naval Air Station previous to World War Two. These documents are now at the Naval Historical Center in the Washington Navy Yard

The Modern Army Section of the National Archives in Washington, D.C., has been another useful source, with Record Group 18 containing the *Army Air Forces Central Files 1919-45* including valuable memoranda, correspondence, and reports filed under 452.1 Aircraft. The Documentary Collection of the Air Corps Library in the same record group contains under D52.1 many of the old Technical Reports from McCook Field (1918-27) and historical material on early Air Service types.

The hearings before the Morrow Board in 1925, and official reports of the Truman Committee of the Senate,

F-105G Wild Weasel with a Shrike missile at China Lake, May 1978.

South Dakota ANG A-7D at Norton AFB, October 1980.

VX-4 F-4J tested at Point Mugu NATS, November 1973, displayed an unusual black finish.

VF-111 "Sundowners" squadron F-4N at Miramar NAS, October 1975.

Admiral Ernest J. King of the Navy, and General Henry H. Arnold of the Air Force, also provided useful information.

Data on aircraft built for export is drawn from specifications issued by the manufacturers and some were published in annual surveys of the aircraft industry made by *Jane's All the World's Aircraft*, the *Aircraft Yearbook, Aero Digest* and

Point Mugu also flew a Bicentennial celebration F-4J in 1976.

The second F-16XL, the modified 75-0747 with two seats and F101 DFE engine, wears dull blue-gray scheme at Edwards AFB, October 1983.

A YA-10A with lizard dull green at Hill AFB, August 1992.

Bright red color announces QF-4B drone at Point Mugu, October 1975.

Aviation Week magazines. Articles in the American and British aeronautical press provided much data on the production of aircraft for export.

Convair and Ryan company archives are preserved in the San Diego Aerospace Museum (SDAM) library, and Curtiss-Wright aircraft materials are kept in the National Air and Space Museum's (NASM) library annex at Silver Hill. Access was allowed to North American company records, and the historical offices of Boeing and Grumman were especially helpful. Company specialists, like Peter Bowers at Boeing, the late Harry Gann at Douglas, and Art Schoeni at Vought personally contributed information, and several companies supplied information and photographs through helpful public relations offices. We have included a list of the excellent company histories that have been consulted.

The logbooks of company test pilots established the test dates of numerous aircraft models. For example, those of William B. Wheatley, copied in SDAM files, covered Consolidated aircraft from 1932 to 1941. Other test pilot logs cited in these notes are those of Don Armstrong, Lloyd Child, Bob Chilton, Bud Gillies, Harold Harris, Lin Hendrix, Russ Rogers, and Sam Shannon.

On occasion, the author was able to fill in between the lines of official documents with insights gained in conversations with test pilots and engineers like the late Ed Heinemann, known as "Mr. Attack Aviation," and with many veteran aircrew. The author's personal experiences aboard ships, in aircraft factories, and visits to foreign aviation facilities, also helped.

Many individuals, most of them in the American Aviation Historical Society, have contributed information and photographs for this edition, and we have listed them as correspondents. Several of these contributors are personal friends whose help has ranged from modest, but very illuminating items, to the over 500 photos Peter Bowers provided, and the many Navy photos supplied by Robert Lawson.

Books

The following list is limited to those books that were most useful and complete in providing information on the aircraft themselves and their historical background. Omitted are many accounts of operations, theoretical studies, and some secondary sources that have become largely outdated. Works particular to just one chapter are cited with that chapter.

I. General studies

A. Army Air Force and United States Air Force publications

U.S. Army Air Forces. Historical Office. *The Official Pictorial History of the AAF.* New York: Duell, 1947.

Futrell, R. Frank. *Command of Observation Aviation: A Study in Control of Tactical Air Power.* USAF Historical Study #24. Air Historical Office, Washington 1956.

Wright-Patterson AFB, Ohio: USAF Procurement Division, Reports Section, April 1961.

Index of A.F. Serial Numbers Assigned to Aircraft, 1958 and Prior.

Index of Army & Navy Aeronautical Equipment, Vol. 5, Armament.

B. Air Force history

Anderton, David A. *History of the US Air Force.* London: Hamlyn, 1981.

Arnold, Henry H. *Global Mission.* New York: Harper, 1949.

_____. *Winged Warfare.* New York: Harper, 1941.

Boyne, Walter J. *Silver Wings, A History of the USAF.* New York: Simon & Schuster, 1993.

_____. *Beyond the Wild Blue- A History of the USAF 1947-1997.* New York: St. Martin's: 1997.

Copp, Dewitt S. *A Few Great Captains.* Garden City NY: Doubleday, 1980.

Fahey, James C. *U.S. Army Aircraft 1908-1946.* New York: Ships and Aircraft, 1946.

Goldberg. Alfred. ed. *A History of the United States Air Force, 1907-1957.* Princeton, N.J.: Van Nostrand, 1957.

LeMay, Curtis E. and MacKinlay Kantor. *Mission With LeMay: My Story.* Garden City, NY: Doubleday, 1965.

McFarland, Stephen L. *America's Pursuit of Precision Bombing, 1910-1945.* Washington: Smithsonian, 1995.

C. Navy and Marines:

Fry, John. *USS Saratoga CV-3.* Atglen, PA: Schiffer, 1996.

Grossnick, Roy A. *United States Naval Aviation 1910-1995.* Washington DC: Department of the Navy, U.S. Naval Historical Office, 1997. (1970/1980 editions by Lee M. Pearson and Adrian O. Van Wyen.)

Larkins, William T. *U.S. Marine Corps Aircraft 1914-1959.* Concord, CA: Aviation History Pub. 1959.

_____. *U.S. Navy Aircraft 1921-1941.* Concord, CA: Aviation History Pub. 1961.

_____. *Battleship & Cruiser A/c of the USN 1910-1949.* Atglen, PA: Schiffer, 1996.

Pearson, Lee M. *Attack Plane Design History, USN to 1957.* Ms at SDAM.

Polmar, Norman. *Aircraft Carriers.* Garden City, NY: Doubleday, 1969.

Price, Alfred. *Aircraft Versus Submarines.* Annapolis: Naval Institute, 1974.

Turnbull, Archibald D., & C.L. Lord. *History of United States Naval Aviation.* New Haven: Yale Univ., 1949.

Warlick, W.W., & V.F. Grant. *Naval Aviation.* Annapolis MD: Naval Institute, 1929.

D. Aircraft Armament:

Friedman, Norman. *US Naval Weapons.* Annapolis: Naval Institute, 1982.

Gerken, Louis C. *Torpedo Technology.* Chula Vista, CA: ASC, 1989.

Green, C.M. et al. Ordnance Dept. *Planning Munitions for War* Washington DC: Office of Military History, U.S Army. 1955.

Gunston, Bill. *Encyclopedia of Aircraft Armament.* NY: Orion, 1988.

Holley, I.B. Jr. *Development of Aircraft Gun Turrets in the AAF.* USAF Historical Study No. 54. Air Historical Office, Washington: 1947.

Woodman, Harry. *Early Aircraft Armament.* Wash. DC: Smithsonian, 1989

E. Aircraft and their builders

Aircraft Yearbook: Washington, DC: Lincoln Press, annually 1919-1960.

Allen, Richard S. *Revolution in the Sky.* Brattleboro, VT: Stephen Greene Press, 1964.

Anderson, Fred. *Northrop -an Aeronautical History.* Los Angeles: Northrop Corporation, 1976.

Avery, Norm. *North American Aircraft 1934-1998* vol. 1, Santa Ana CA: Narkiewitz /Thompson, 1998.

Boeing Co., *Pedigree of Champions, Boeing Since 1916.* Seattle: 1963.

Bowers, Peter M. *Boeing Aircraft Since 1916.* Annapolis: Naval Inst.1989.

_____. *Curtiss Aircraft 1907-1947.* London: Putnam, 1979.

Breihan, John R., Stan Piet, Roger S. Mason, *Martin Aircraft 1909-1960.* Santa Ana: Narkiewitz/Thompson, 1995.

Brown, K.S., & Robertson, Bruce. *U. S. Army and Air Force Fighters, 1916-1961.* Letchworth: Harleyford, 1961.

Francillon, Rene J. *McDonnell Douglas Aircraft since 1920.* vol.1-2. Annapolis: Naval Institute, 1988-1990.

_____. *Grumman Aircraft since 1929.* Annapolis: Naval Institute, 1989.

_____. *Lockheed Aircraft since 1913.* Annapolis: Naval Institute, 1987

Gunston, Bill. *Night Fighters-A Developmental History.* New York: Scribners, 1976.

Hansen, James. *Engineer in Charge.* NASA, Washington DC: 1987.

Heinemann, Edward. *Combat Plane Designer.* Annapolis: Naval Instit., 1980.

Jones, Lloyd S. *U.S. Bombers.* Fallbrook, CA: Aero, 1980.

_____. *U.S. Fighters.* Fallbrook, CA: Aero, 1975.

_____. *U.S. Naval Fighters.* Fallbrook, CA: Aero, 1977.
Matt, Paul. *Historical Aviation Album.* 18 v., Temple City, CA: 1965-1987.
Mayborn, Mitch. *Grumman Guidebook.* Dallas: Flying Enterprises, 1976.
Moran, Gerald P. *Aeroplanes Vought, 1917-1977.* Temple City, CA: Historical Aviation Album, 1978.
Norton, Donald J. *Larrv-A Biography of Lawrence D. Bell.* Chicago: Nelson-Hall, 1981.
Rubenstein, Murray, & R. M. Goldman. *To Join With the Eagles: Curtiss Wright Aircraft, 1903-1965.* Garden City, NY: Doubleday. 1974.
Schlaifer, Robert. *Development of Aircraft Engines.* Boston: Harvard, 1950.
Schoeni, Arthur. *Vought-Six Decades of Aviation History.* Plano, TX: Aviation Quarterly Pub., 1978.
Sikorsky, Igor. *The Winged S.* New York: Dodd and Mead, 1943.
Stoff, Joshua. *Thunder Factory.* Osceola WI: Motorbooks, 1990.
Stout, William B. *So Away I Went!* New York: Bobbs-Merrill, 1951.
Swanborough, F. G., & Bowers, P. M. *United States Military Aircraft Since 1909.*London: Putnam, 1989.
_____. *United States Navy Aircraft Since 1911.* Annapolis MD: Naval Institute, 1990.
Thetford, Owen. *Aircraft of the Royal Air Force since 1918.* London: Putnam, 1968.
_____ *British Naval Aircraft since 1912.* London: Putnam, 1982.
Thomas, Nigel. Seven albums of materials on Thomas-Morse aircraft, 1915 to 1933. Unpublished ms., SDAM.
Thompson, Kevin. *North American Aircraft 1934-1998* vol.2, Santa Ana CA: Narkiewitz /Thompson, 1999.
Thompson, Jonathan. *Vultee Aircraft 1932-1947.* Santa Ana, CA: Narkiewitz/ Thompson, 1992.
Trimble, William T. *Wings for the Navy, A History of the Naval Aircraft Factory, 1917-1956.* Annapolis: Naval Institute, 1990.
Wagner, William. *Reuben Fleet and the Story of Consolidated Aircraft.* Fallbrook, CA: Aero, 1976.
Wegg, John. *General Dynamics Aircraft.* London: Putnam, 1990.
Welty, Howard O. *History of Convair 1908-1956.* San Diego, CA: Convair Div. 1966.
Who's Who in World Aviation. Wash., DC: American Aviation, 1955.
Yenne, Bill. *Into the Sunset, the Convair Story.* Lyme, CT: Greenwich, 1995.

Monograph series:

Monographs on individual aircraft types have multiplied in the last two decades. My own investigations of original documentation has been limited by life span, so this writer is very grateful that a new generation of authors has appeared to describe in colorful detail the most famous war planes.

These studies began in Britain with the inexpensive *Aircraft in Profile* series edited by Charles W. Cain, and resulted in 262 monographs published in 1974 by Doubleday, Garden City, NY, in 14 volumes. Individual titles are cited as *Profile* in the relevant chapter along with the larger American publications listed below.

Squadron Signal *in action* series, Carrollton, TX. Monographs published since 1973, Individual titles are cited as *Sq/Sg.* in the relevant chapter.

Detail & Scale publications, by Bert Kinsey, also published by Squadron Signal, Carrollton, TX. Individual titles cited as *D&S.*

WarbirdTech, Specialty Press, North Branch, MN. Monographs published since 1973, Individual titles cited as *Warbird.*

Steve Ginter's Naval Fighters series from Simi Valley, CA, is highly recommended, as well as Jay Miller's Aerofax series.

Periodicals

Aero Digest. Washington D.C. Monthly issues from 1935 to 1945 were especially useful.
Aeromilitaria. Shepperton: AIR-BRITAIN. Quarterly.
Air Enthusiast. London. Quarterly since 1976.
Air Force Magazine. Washington D.C. Air Force Association monthly.
Air Power History. (formerly *Aerospace Historian)* Air Force Foundation quarterly since 1954.
Airpower/Wings. Granada Hills, CA. Alternative titles monthly since 1971.
Air & Space. Washington DC. Smithsonian, bi-monthly since 1986.
American Aviation Historical Journal (AAHS). Quarterly since 1956.
Aviation. New York, NY. Monthly 1922-1947. *Aviation Week* since 1947.
Aviation History. Leesburg, VA. Monthly.
Naval Aviation News. Washington DC. Monthly since 1919.
Skyways (Airplanes 1920-1940). Quarterly since 1987. Poughkeepsie, NY.
Wings of Fame . vol. 1-20 London: Aerospace Quarterly 1996-2001.
WW1 Aero. Quarterly since 1976. Poughkeepsie, NY.

II. World War I and the Biplane Era

U.S. government:

Crowell, Benedict. *America's Munitions 1917-1918.* Washington, DC: GPO, 1919.
Maurer, Maurer, ed. *The U.S. Air Service in World War I.* Vols. I-IV. Office of Air Force History. Washington: GPO, 1978/79.
Mixter, George W., & Harold H. Emmons. *United States Army Aircraft Production Facts.* Washington: GPO, 1919.
Van Wyen, Adrian O. *Naval Aviation in World War I.* Washington: GPO, 1969.

Books about 1914-1930 period:

Bruce, J.M. *British Aeroplanes 1914-1918.* New York: Funk, 1957.
Casari, Robert B. *U.S. Army Aviation Serial Numbers & Orders, 1908-1923.* Chillicothe, OH: Military Aircraft, 1995.
_____. *Encyclopedia of U.S. Military Aircraft. Part 1 1908-1917.* (4 vols.); *Part 2, World War I Production Program* (3 vols.) Chillicothe, OH. 1973.
Layman, R.D. *Naval Aviation in the First World War.* Annapolis: Naval Institute, 1996.
Loening, Grover. *Our Wings Grow Faster.* New York: Doubleday, 1935.
_____. *Amphibian; The Story of the Loening Biplane.* Greenwich, CT: New York Graphic Society, 1973.
Davilla, James D. & A.M. Soltan. *French Aircraft of the First World War.* Stratford CT: Flying Machines Press. 1997.
Gorrell, E.S. *The Measure of America's World War Aeronautical Effort.* Burlington, VT: Norwich University, 1940.
Hallion, Richard P. *Rise of the Fighter Aircraft 1914-1918.* Annapolis MD: Nautical & Aviation Pub. 1985.
Holley, I.B. Jr. *Ideas and Weapons.* New Haven: Yale University, 1953.
Hudson, James J. *Hostile Skies: A Combat History of the American Air Service.* Syracuse, NY: Syracuse University, 1968.
Hurley, Alfred F. *Billy Mitchell.* Bloomington: Indiana University, 1974.
Jones, H.A. *The War in the Air.* Oxford: Oxford University Press, 1934. (vol. IV, 16-22,45-55, describes Curtiss flying boat operations)
Lamberton, W. M., & E. F. Cheesman. *Fighter Aircraft of 1914-1918 War.*
_____. *Reconnaissance and Bomber Aircraft of the 1914-1918 War.* Letchworth, UK: Harleyford, 1960.
Morrow, John H. *The Great War in the Air.* Washington: Smithsonian, 1993.
Warlick, William W. and V.F. Grant. *Naval Aviation.* Annapolis: Naval Institute, 1929.
Wildenberg, Thomas. *Destined for Glory: Dive Bombing & the Evolution of Carrier Airpower.* Annapolis: Naval Institute,1998.

Chapter 1 Notes

In addition to the works cited above, see:

U.S. Army Aeronautical Specification No. 1002, August 1, 1916, at SDAM.

Eaton seaplane in *Jane's*, 1917: 235b, and Eaton file at SDAM.

Chapter 2

Official Performance Test (OPT) Reports made by the Army's Engineering Division at Dayton, Ohio, provided most specifications cited in this chapter. The USD-9A report is dated 10-14-18. See OPTs for: BVL-12, 10-24-19; LUSAO-11, 12-22-19; GAX, 10-21-20; LUSAGH-11, 11-20-20; DH-4B, 3-28-21; IL-1, 8-8-21.

Type data not in OPTs is from *Characteristics & Performance of Army Airplanes,* 6-1-20 & 1-1-24.

National Archives Record Group 18 contains the *Army Air Forces Central Files 1919-45,* including reports filed under 452.1 Aircraft and the D52.1 section. DH #95 file in Box 460, had DH-4 OPT 6-10-18, and a "History of DH-4", Maj. Robert Marsh, Memo to Chief, Tech. Sect.; DH #32 file, Box 459, had DH-4M OPT 4-10-24.

Gallaudet #4 file in Box 472, had "Resume of Development of DB-1B", Lt. E.W. Dickman memo, Eng. Div., Dayton, 5-13-24.

R.H. Fleet letter to Engineering Div. on DB-1, 5-14-26, in SDAM.
Harris, Harold R. Biography & flight logs in SDAM.

Monographs:
Boyne, Walter J. *de Havilland DH-4.* Washington: Smithsonian, 1984.
Bruce, J.M., & J. Noel, *BREGUET 14.* Profile #157, Windsor, UK: 1967.
Smart, Lawrence C. *The Hawks That Guided the Guns.* (Privately printed) 1968. Detailed account of 135th Sq. DH-4 operations.

Periodicals:
Jane's All the World's Aircraft 1922: 181-182b, for Junkers JL-12.
Matt, Paul. "Packard-LePere LUSAC-11" *Historical Aviation Album, V.1* Temple, 1965.
_____ "L.W.F. Model G" *Historical Aviation Album, V.2,* Temple City,1965: 52-57.
Mitchell, Glenn D. "The L-W-F Model G-2." *Aviation.* 12-1-18: 554-557.

Chapter 3 Notes

U.S. Army Aeronautical Specification No. 1003, May 1, 1917. At SDAM.
Official Performance Test (OPT) Reports:USB-1, 7-24-18; LUSAC-11, 1-24-19; U.S.XB1A, 2-14-20, 8-11-21; M-8, 2-17-20; Orenco D & MB-3, 2-20-20; FVL-1, 11-23-20; Spad 13, 4-27-21; Curtiss-Orenco, 8-26-21; MB-3A, 3-14-23.
Data not in OPTs from *Characteristics & Performance of Army Airplanes,* 6-1-20,1-1-24.

Periodicals:
AERIAL AGE WEEKLY. 12-30-18, 812-813: The Hispano-Suiza Engine.
_____. 3-17-19, 36-37: Orenco B/C Single Seater.
_____. 3-31-19, 154-155: Curtiss 18-T triplane.
_____. 6-16-19, 676-677: Curtiss 18-B Biplane.
D'Estout, Henri. "Robbins & Schiefer Pursuit." *AAHS* 5-4, 1960: 308-309.
Frandsen, Bert . "Nieuport 28." *W.W.I AERO* #165. 8/99: 33-51.
Hardesty, Bergen. "Nieuport 28." *Model Airplane News.* 3/59: 26-27.
Henry, Wesley B. "Packard-LePere LUSAC-11." *W.W.I AERO* #144. 5/94: 17-34.
Nowarra, H.J. *50 Jahre Deutsche Luftwaffe.* Vol. 1, Berlin 1961. See pp. 170-184 for Fokker fighter introduction.

Chapter 4

Official Performance Test (OPT) Reports: Caproni, 9-22-18; Handley-Page, 11-30-18; Martin NBS-1, 5-6-21; Curtiss NBS-1, 7-4-22; NBS-3, 1-22-25; NBS-4, 11-9-24; LB-1, 7-6-27; XLB-5, 2-23-27; XB-2, 12-1-27, rev. 9-27-28; XLB-2, 1-13-28; XLB-6, 10-30-28; XBL-3A, 12-12-28; LB-7, 5-1-29; B-2, 7-2-29; LB-10, 9-16-29; LB-6, 11-7-29; LB-8, 11-26-29; B-3A, 12-19-30; B-5A, 4-10-31; B-6A, 10-2-31.
Air Service Technical Order #32, March 1923: NBS-1.
Data not in OPTs from *Characteristics & Performance of Army Airplanes,* 6-1-20, 1-1-24, 1-1-27, 1-1-31, & 9-15-34.
National Archives, Record Group 18 contains the *Army Air Forces Central Files 1919-45,* including D52.1 Handley-Page #29. Box 474, and Bomber files.
NBL-2 contract, 6-15-22, in SDAM files.
Details of Caproni bombers in America from Casari, Robert B. *Encyclopedia of U.S. Military Aircraft. Op. cit.* Part 2, 1973. 20-31, 94/5.

Periodicals:
Aircraft Yearbook, 1921: 190-191, LWF Owl.
Aviation 8-9-26: 252-253. "Huff Daland Bomber XLB-1".
2-14-27: 333. "Huff Daland Cyclops".
7-25-27: 200-202. "Curtiss Builds Largest Bomber".
9-12-27: 595-597. "Keystone All-Metal Bomber".
1-16-28: 148-150. "Sikorsky Guardian".
3-26-28: 776, 792. "Keystone Pirate".
Allen, Francis J. "Flying Battleship Barling & NBL-1" *Air Enthusiast #98,* 3/02: 66-73.
Barling, Walter. Interview in *Consolidator,* San Diego, March 1942.
Bowers, Peter M. "Keystone Bombers." *Aero Album,* Summer 1972: 2-22.
Matt, Paul R. "LWF Owl". *Historical Aviation Album* #XI, 1972: 11-21.
McCorrson, Sean & P. Matt."Curtiss B-2." *Historical Aviation Album, v. XVIII.* 1987: 4-20.
Tilford, Earl H. "The Barling Bomber." *Aero Historian,* 6/1979: 91-97.
Underwood, John. "Anglo-American Blockbuster." *Air Classics,* 10/1976.

Chapter 5

Official Performance Test (OPT) Reports: PW-1A, 1-2-22; PW-2, 1-22-22; PW-2A, 11-3-22; PW-2B, 8-24-22; V-40, 3-15-22; PW-6, 10-2-24; PW-7, 3-19-24; PW-8, 4-17-23, 3-18-24, & 8-4-24; XPW-9, 10-8-23; PW-8A, 11-7-24; PW-8B, 7-9-25; PW-9, 6-30-24 & 1-19-26; P-1, 8-17-25; P-1B, 6-28-27; P-2, 8-17-27; XP-8, 1-17-28; XP-6, 5-14-28; PW-9D, 6-16-28; XP-7, 11-30-28; P-3A, 1-2-29; P-1C, 3-27-29; XP-3A, 5-22-29; P-5, 7-8-29; P-12, 3-6-30; Model 100, 3-12-30; P-12B, 4-4-30; XP-15, 6-10-30; XP-17, 6-12-30; XP-13A, 9-24-30; P-12C, 11-25-30; XP-9. 11-26-30; XP-16, 10-31-30; YP-20, 12-4-30; P-6A, 12-19-30; Model 218, 12-18-30; XP-22, 6-30-31; XP-925A, 8-21-31; P-12E, 10-23-31; P-12F, 4-9-31; XP-6E, 1-12-31; YP-16, 4-9-31; P-6E, 5-19-32; XP-6F, 9-20-34.
Other test reports included "Cooling System Flight Tests of VCP-1", 2-18-20; "Static Test of the PA-1", 4-20-22; and "Static Test of the PG-1", 4-20-22. Data not in OPTs is from *Characteristics & Performance of Army Airplanes,* 1-1-24, 1-1-30, and 2-15-32.
Air Service Technical Order #22, February 1922: PW-1, XB-1A; #24 , April 1922: V-40
XP-23 data from Curtiss report, 4-18-32, at SDAM.
Air Corps Central Files in National Archives, under D52.1 Pursuit, has relevant documentation of this period.

Books:
Bowers, Peter. *Boeing Aircraft, op cit,* 78-192.
______. *Curtiss Aircraft,. op cit,* 182-264.
Davis, Larry. *CURTISS ARMY HAWKS in Action,* Carrollton: Sq/Sg. 1992.

Periodicals:
Bowers, Peter. "Early Army Hawks." *SKYWAYS* #5, 1/88: 2-21.
Cavanagh, Robert & K.C. Rust. "Early Air Service Pursuits" *SKYWAYS* Pt. 1, #15, 7/90: 2-24; Pt. 2, #16, 10/90: 2-24.
SKYWAYS #25. "Verville VCP-R." 1/93: 2-15.

Chapter 6

Official Performance Test (OPT) Reports: CO-1, 8-31-22; CK-CO2, 1-1-24, CO-4, 1-2-22, 10-5-23; CO-4A, 11-10-24; CO-5, 10-9-23; AO-1, 11-7-24; XCO-5A, 11-23-24; XCO-6, 12-13-24; XCO-7B, 2-6-25; XCO-8, 12-16-24; XO-1, 12-8-24, 1-16-25; X0-2, 12-18-24, 1-12-25; XCOA-1, 3-16-25; O-1, 4-17-26; O-2, 7-31-26; O-6, 5-18-26; O-7, 10-28-26; O-11, 4-10-28, O-13, 5-9-28; O-17, 5-2-28; O-6B, 5-25-28; XA-4, 2-18-29; XO-15, 4-8-29; XO-14, 5-4-29; O-28, 8-7-29; XO-10, 11-12-29; O-25, 11-23-29; A-3B, 4-23-30; YO-13C, 8-11-30; XO-1G, 10-14-30; OA-2, 10-23-30; O-38, 12-10-30; O-18, 1-14-31; Y1O-33, 1-7-31; O-25A, 1-19-31; O-38B, 5-5-31; O-1G, 5-14-31; Y1O-41, 6-26-31; O-39, 9-4-31; O-25C, 10-23-31.
Data not in OPTs is from *Characteristics & Performance of Army Airplanes,* 1-1-24, 1-1-30, 2-15-32, and 9-15-34.
Proceedings, Officer's Board, Observation planes, Dayton, 11-20-24 ff.
Harris, Harold R. Flight log copies in SDAM.
Curtiss Aeroplane Co., Buffalo, 5/28: *Falcon Handbook, O-1B, A-3 series.*
_____, Report 5533, 3-19-34, Colombia Falcon, at NASM.
Douglas Co., Santa Monica,1926: *O-2 Handbook;* Specifications.
Thomas-Morse Co., Buffalo 1930: *O-19 Instruction Handbook.*
Historical Office, Army Air Forces. *Official Pictorial History of AAF.* Duell Sloan & Pearce, New York, 1947: 180-183.

Periodicals:
Fechet, Maj. Gen James E. "Observation Aviation. "*Aviation* 1/1931: 19-21.
Hagedorn, Dan. "Curtiss types in Latin America, "*Air Enthusiast* #45, 1992: 61-77.
Historical Aviation Album #XI. "Douglas O-2/25." 1972: 22-44.
_____ #XII. "Douglas O-32/38." 1973: 72-98.
Jane's All the World's Aircraft 1933: 280-281c, Export Falcon; O-38P.
_____ 1935: 291-293c, Falcon II.

Chapter 7

USN BuAer Characteristics charts. July 1928: F-5L, HS-2, NC-4, PN-7, PN-9,10,12, PB-1; Jan 1931: PS-3; 3-1-

33: XPH-1, XPN-11; 9-1-33: PD-1, XPY-1; 9-1-35: XP2M-1, XP4N-1,-2, XP2Y-1; 10-1-37: PH-1, PK-1, PM-1,-2, P3M-2; 10-1-40: P2Y-3.
Documents at SDAM:
Glenn L. Martin Co. SD-154, PM-1 spec.; PM-2 actual Group Weight, May 1931; P3M-1 spec.
Hall-Aluminum Aircraft Corp. XPH-1 Description & Photos.
U.S. Navy.,*F-5L Flying Boat Handbook,* 1918.
Wheatley, William. Pilot's Logbooks for 1929-1937.
White, Joel J. *Brief History of Fleet Patrol Squadrons 1919 to 1935.* (Unpublished Navy report.)

Books:
Molson, Ken, & A.J. Shortt. *Curtiss HS Flying Boat.* NAM, Ottawa, 1995.
Pardini, Albert C. *The Legendary Secret Norden Bombsight.* Atglen, PA: Schiffer,1999.
Trimble, William F. *Wings for the Navy.* Annapolis: Naval Institute, 1990.

Periodicals:
Aerial Age Weekly, 4-24-19: 338-340; "Navy HS-1L & 2L Flying Boats."
Aero Digest 3/38: 98, PH-2; 3/1940: 142, PH-3.
Allen, Richard S. "Sikorsky Airplanes." *Skyways* #30, 4/94: 22, XPS-1; #33 1/95: 46, XPS-2; #38 4/1996: 36-38, PS-3.
Andrews, Hal. "PS/RS." *Naval Aviation News,* 4/82, 24-25.
Aviation. "Navy's Giant XP2H-1." 10/34, 317-319.
Bowers, Peter M. "Sea Wings." *Wings* 10/75: 41-49.
Boyne, Walt. "The Flying Hallmarks." *Wings* 5/75: 8-23.
Historical Aviation Album IX, 1971: "Consolidated P2Y boats." 198-214.
Meyers, Roy. "Boeing PB-1." *Skyways #34* . 4/1995, 67-69.
Ostrowski, David W. "Tests of XP2M-1." *Skyways #56,* 10/2000, 2-16.
Over the Front.. "US NAVY F-5-L Flying Boat." Summer 1990: 142-152.
World War I Aeroplanes #165. "Curtiss H-16A." 8/99: 74-80.

Chapter 8

USN BuAer Characteristics charts: 7-1-25, CT-1; 7-1-26, DT-4; 7-1-28, DT-1, -2; 10-1-31, R-6L; 9-1-32, P2D-1, T2D-1, XT3D-1, XTN-1, XT2N-1, XT5M-1; 9-1-36, XT3D-2, TG-1,-2; 10-1-37, BM-1,-2. Army Air Service OPT, Martin MT, 8-31-20.

Books:
Wildenberg, Thomas. *Destined for Glory.* Annapolis: Naval Institute, 1998.

Periodicals:
Aerial Age Weekly, 2-27-22: 586, "Curtiss Navy Torpedo Seaplane."
Andrews, Hal. "CT." *Naval Aviation News,* 1-2-95: 25-25.
_____. "Martin BM-1 & 2" *Naval Aviation News,* 7/96: 44-45.
Blum, Gert P.M. "Early Fokker "torpedoes." *AAHS* 33-4 1988: 266-281.
Elliott, John M. "Martin MBT/MT Story." *AAHS* 32-2, 1987: 144-159.
Matt, Paul. "Martin BM-1/-2."*Historical Aviation Album, v. I,* 1965: 20-24.
_____ "Martin T4M-1."*Historical Aviation Album, v. IV,* 1967:175-180.
Ostrowski, Dave. "Glenn Martin MBT and MT Bombers." *Skyways* #35, 5/95: 27-37.
Pearson, Lee M. "Torpedo Bombers." Naval Aviation Confidential Bulletin, 10/1949
Schreier, Konrad F. "The Davis Gun." *Naval History* Spring 1989: 55-56.

Chapter 9

USN BuAer Characteristics charts: Jan 1925, M-81; Jan 1926, AS-2, EM-2, OL-1, UO-1; July 1, 1926, OL-2/4; Jan 31, XOJ-1, XOK-1, OL-8/9, XO2L-1, O2U-1/4, O3U-1, XO4U-1, XSL-1; Sept 33, O2C-2, OJ-2, XO4U-2; Sept 34, XOJ-3; B/J reports: XOJ-1, #249, 6-23-31, #404, 4-9-34; XOJ-3, #522,4-4-34.
NASA report 117 on S3C-1.

Correspondence:
Tsung Chi Lee, letters to author August 6 & 20, 1991, described 4th Squadron Corsairs, denies any Corsair aerial engagement in the Shanghai Incident. Cf Moran, p. 56, who indicates eight more Corsairs added by 1932.

Books:
Larkins, William T. *Battleship and Cruiser Aircraft of the U.S. Navy* . Atglen, PA: Schiffer, 1996.
Loening, Grover. *Amphibian; The Story of the Loening Biplane.* Greenwich, CT: New York Graphic Society, 1973

Periodicals:
Andrews, Hal."F8C/O2C Helldiver." *Naval Aviation News* .11/92: 18-19.
_____."F9C-1/-2 Sparrowhawk." *Historical Aviation Album, v. VIII.* 1987: 36-57.
Bowers, P.M. "Loening's Flying Shoehorns." *Wings.* 2/74: 48-66.
_____."Vought Corsairs." *Wings.* 2/73: 36-59.
Matt, Paul "Berliner-Joyce OJ" *American A/c Modeler.* 5/68: 27-29, 54-55.
Nye, Willis L. VE-7, UO-1, FU-1 plans, SDAM file.
Ostrowski, Dave. "Anacostia Flight Tests: Stearman XOSS-1." *Skyways* #35, 5/95: 2-14.

Chapter 10

USN Characteristics Charts: July 1925, F4C-1, VE-7SF; July 1926, FB-1/34;
July 1928, XF6C-5 FU-1, TS-1; January 1930, FB-5, F6C-1/2;
January 1931, XFH-1, XF2U-1; July 1931, XF5B-1, Bulldog; October 1931, XFG-1;
1 Sept 1932, F6C-3/4, F3W-1; 1 March 1933, XF9C-1/2; 1 Sept 1933, XF8C-2,-7;
1 Sept 1934, F4B-1,-2, F8C-4; 1 Sept 1935 F3B-1; 1 Oct 1937, F4B-3,-4.
B/J Co. report #259, 5-19-31, on XFJ-1.
Hall, Charles W. *Data & Photos Descriptive of F4C-1.* NY 1924: SDAM.
Hall-Aluminum *Photos & Descriptive of XFH-1.* Buffalo 1929: SDAM
Navy Dept. Report NASA-47, 8-15-29 on XF8C-2, at NASM.

Periodicals:
Aerial Age Weekly, "Curtiss 18-T triplane", 3-31-19: 154/5.
Andrews, Hal. "Curtiss F9C-2",*Historic Av. Album* XVIII, 1987: 36-57.
_____ "Falcon" *Naval Aviation News.* July 1981: 24-25.
_____ "TS-1, Part 1", *Naval Aviation News.* Jan/Feb 1996: 38-39.
Bliss, R.L. & Gene Schmidt. "F2B-1 Fighter". *Skyways* #39. Oct 1996: 2-25.
Bowers, P.M. *Curtiss Navy Hawks in Action,* Sq/Sig #156. Carrollton 1995.
Goodspeed, M.H. "Curtiss F9C" *Wings of Fame #17,* London 1999: 98-105
Matt, Paul R., & Bruce Robertson. *United States & Navy Marine Corps Fighters 1918-1962.* Letchworth, England: Harleyford, 1962.
Ostrowski, Dave. "Anacos. Flight Tests-Boeing F4B-1/2".*Skyways* #48. Oct 1998: 17-43.
_____. "Anacos. Flight Tests-Curtiss F7C-1". *Skyways* #57. Jan 2001: 24-50.
_____ "Anacos. Flight Tests-Curtiss XF9C-1/2".*Skyways* #60.Oct 2001: 2-21.
Owers, Colin A. "75-Day Fighter –Curtiss HA." *Air Enthusiast* #103, 2003.
Smith, Richard K. *Dirigibles Akron & Macon.* Annapolis: Naval Institute, 1965.

III. World War II Period

Data on World War Two aircraft was combined in *Army Airplane Characteristics* (#TSEST-A-2) 1 April 1946, prepared by William Englehardt of the Air Material Command's Design Branch, Characteristics Section. The Airplane Characteristics Charts for 2-15-32, 9-15-34, 1-15-38, 7-1-39, & 8-1-41 are also cited in chapter notes.

The Historical Division of the Air Materiel Command prepared a number of case history monographs of AAF wartime types and some are available at the Air Force Museum and at the AFHRC.

The National Archives in Washington, DC., Modern Army Section, Record Group 18, contains the *Army Air Forces Central Files 1919-45* with correspondence and reports filed under 452.1 Aircraft, while 452.1 *Assignment of Airplanes* has lists for 12-31-34, 12-31-36, 12-15-38, 6-30-40, 1-31-41, 9-30-41, and Aircraft in Overseas possessions, 11-30-41. Navy aircraft reports in the National Archives are located in Record Group 72.

The Department of Air Commerce published a list of *U.S. Military Aircraft Acceptances 1940-1945* (Washington: U. S. Government Printing Office, 1946). Bureau of Aeronautics lists of *Naval Aircraft, Record of Acceptances,* and U. S. Army publications on *Aircraft Model Designations* were used to establish the numbers of aircraft delivered to each service.

U.S. Air Force Historical Division.
(Office of Air Force History)

Carter, Kit C. and Robert Mueller, compilers. *The Army Air Force in World War*

II; A Combat Chronology. Washington: GPO, 1973.
Craven, Wesley F. and James L. Cate, eds. *The Army Air Forces in World War II.* 7 vols. Chicago: University of Chicago Press, 1948-1958.
DuBuque, Jean H. & Robert F. Gleckner. *The Development of the Heavy Bomber, 1918-1944.* USAF Historical Study No. 6: 1951.
Holley, Irving B. *Buying Aircraft: Material Procurement for the Army Air Forces (U.S. Army in World War II series).* Washington: GPO, 1964.
Maurer Maurer, ed. *Air Force Combat Units of World War II.* New York: Watts, 1963.
Maurer Maurer, ed. *Combat Squadrons of the Air Force, World War II.* Washington DC: GPO, 1969.

Air Forces at war

Arakaki, Leatrice R. and John R. Kuborn. *7 December 1941: The Air Force Story.* Washington: GPO, 1991.
Boyne, Walter J. *Clash of Wings-WWII in the Air.* New York: Touchstone 1994.
Cloe, John H. *The Aleutian Warriors, History of 11th Air Force & FAW 4.* Missoula, MT: Pictorial, 1995.
Dorr, Robert F. *7th Bombardment Group/Wing.* Paducah: Turner 1996.
Freeman, Roger A. *The Mighty Eighth: Units, Men, and Machines.* Garden City, NY: Doubleday, 1970.
_____ *Mighty Eighth War Diary.* New York: Jane's, 1981.
_____. *Mighty Eighth War Manual.* New York: Jane's, 1984.
Hagedorn, Daniel P. *ALAE SUPRA CANALEM The Sixth Air Force & Antilles Air Command.* Paducah, KY: Turner 1995.
Rust, Kenn C. *The 9th Air Force in World War II.* Fallbrook, CA: Aero, 1967.
_____. World War II series, Temple City, CA: Historical Aviation,
Fifth Air Force Story. 1975.
Seventh Air Force Story. 1979
Tenth Air Force Story. 1980
Twelfth Air Force Story, 1975.
Thirteenth Air Force Story. 1981.
Fourteenth Air Force Story. 1977.
Fifteenth Air Force Story, 1976.
Twentieth Air Force Story. 1979.
Smith, Blake W. *Warplanes to Alaska.* Blaine WA: Hancock 1997.
Van Wagner, R.D. *Any Place, Any Time, Any Where, 1st Air Commandos.* Atglen, PA: Schiffer, 1998.

The U.S. Navy in WW II

Buchanan, Albert. *The Navy's Air War.* New York; Harper, 1946.
Lundstrom, John B. *The First Team: Pacific Naval Air Combat from Pearl Harbor to Midway.* Annapolis: Naval Institute 1984.
_____. *The First Team: Guadalcanal Campaign.* Annapolis: Naval Institute, 1994.
Morison, Samuel Eliot. *History of the United States Naval Operations in World War II,* 11 Vols. Boston: Little, Brown. 1947-1960.
Office of Naval Operations, *U.S. Naval Aviation in the Pacific.* Washington, DC: GPO 1947.
Sherrod, Robert. *History of Marine Corps Aviation in World War II.* Washington, DC: Combat Forces Press, 1952.

Wartime Industry:

Dean, Francis H. *America's Hundred-Thousand Production Fighters.* Atglen, PA: Schiffer, 1997.
Kelsey, Benjamin S. *The Dragon's Teeth? Creation of American Air Power for World War II.* Washington, DC: Smithsonian, 1982.
Lindbergh, Charles A. *The Wartime Journals of Charles A. Lindbergh.* New York: Harcourt, 1970.
Whitney, Daniel. *Vee's For Victory! Story of Allison V-1710 Engine.* Atglen, PA: Schiffer, 1998.

American aircraft in World War II Era Foreign Service:

British Air Commission aircraft purchases for 1938-41 are filed at the Air University, Office of Air Force History library under 512.861D. This data is more reliable than totals based on serial number block assignments.

The author is also grateful for information learned on his visits to the Imperial War Museum and the RAF Museum in London, as well as to the museum at Duxford and the splendid national air museums at Beijing, Beersheba, Istanbul, Linkoping, Moscow, and Paris.

Chennault, Claire L. *Way of a Fighter.* New York: Putnam, 1949.
Cuny, Jean & Raymond Danel. *L'aviation de chasse franchais, 1918-1940.* Paris: Larivere, 1976
_____. *L'aviation franchais de Bombardment,* Paris: Larivere, 1980
Ford, Daniel. *Flying Tigers* . Washington, DC: Smithsonian, 1991.
Hagedorn, Daniel P. *Central American & Caribbean Air Forces.* Tonbridge, UK: Air-Britain, 1993.
Haight, John M. *American Aid to France.* New York: Atheneum, 1970.
Halley, James J. *RAF Aircraft AA100 to AZ999.* Tunbridge Wells, Air-Britain: 2001.
Hayes, Otis Jr. *The Alaska-Siberian Connection.* Texas A&M Univ., 1996.
Howson, Gerald. *Aircraft of the Spanish Civil War 1936-39.* Washington, DC: Smithsonian, 1990.
Johnson, Brian, & Terry Heffernan. *A MOST SECRET PLACE Boscombe Down 1939-45.* London: Jane's, 1982.
Lukas, Richard C. *Eagles East, The AAF and the Soviet Union. 1941-46.* Tallahasse: Florida State Univ., 1970.
Meekcoms, K.J. *British Air Commission and Lend-Lease.* Tunbridge Wells, Air-Britain: 2001.
Moulin, Jean et al. *Le Bearn et le Commandant Teste* . Boug-en-Bresse: Marines, 1997.
Nordeen, Lon. *Fighters Over Israel.* New York: Orion, 1990.
Petrov, G.F., et al. *Americanski v Russii.* Moscow: Rusavia, 1999.
Pickler, Gordon K. *U.S. Aid to the Chinese Air Force.* Florida State Univ. PhD dissertation, 1971. At SDAM.
Robertson, Bruce. *British Military Aircraft Serials,* 1912-1969. London: Ian Allen, 1969.
Rosholt, Malcolm. *Flight in the China Airspace,1910-50.* Rosholt. WI: 1984.
Turk Hava Kuvvetleri. *Ucak Albumu Vol. II. 1923-1950.* Ankara: 1984.
Widfeldt, Bo, & Ake Hall. *SVENSKA VIGAR 1 Svenska militaria flygplan 1911-1999.* Nassjo, Sweden, 1999.
Xu, Guangqui. *War Wings; U.S. & Chinese Military Aviation, 1929-1949.* Westport: Greenwood, 2001.
Young, Edward M. "American Aircraft in Siam" *AAHS* 1983: 216-227.

Chapter 11

This chapter makes wide use of sources cited above, as well as statistics given in the *Aircraft Yearbook for 1946*: Washington, DC: 454-194.
For GHQ 1938 war games, see:
Caldwell, Cy. "Knighthood in Flower *"Aero Digest* 6/38: 45/46, 99. Compare this humorous attack with Fletcher Pratt's favorable, "Our Air Force Tests its Strength", *Model Airplane News* 8/38: 4-5, 48-50.

Chapter 12

Official Performance Test (OPT) Reports made by the Army's Engineering Division at Dayton, Ohio, provided these specifications cited in this chapter.
XO-27, 10-22-30; Y1O-27, 9-10-32; XO-31, 5-30-31; XO-35, 12-16-31; YO-40, 5-3-32; YO-40A, 8-30-33; Y1O-40B, 8-31-33; Y1O-43, 4-7-33; O-43A, 9-10-34; O-46A, 5-7-36; XO-47, 11-16-36.
Characteristics & Performance of Army Airplanes, charts dated 2-15-32: XO-27, YO-31; 9-15-34: Y1O-35; 7-1-39: Y1O-31A/C; 8-1-41: O-47A/B, O-49, YO-50, YO-51, O-53; 3-15-46, O-52.
Army Air Corps: Officer's Board, Observation types, September 15, 1933.
Case, H.W. "Final Report on YO-51..." ACTR #4656, June 12, 1941.
Fechet, Majgen James E. "Observation Aviation." *Aviation,* Jan 1933:19-21.
Francillon, Rene *The Air Guard.* Austin, TX, Aerofax 1983.
Holley, I.B. *Evolution of the Liaison-type Airplane,* 1917-1944. USAFHS Study #44, April 1946.
Kohn, Leo J. "Vigilant" *ARMCHAIR AVIATOR* Dec 1972: 41-45.
Krauskopf, Robert. "National Guard Av." *AAHS* 5-1, 1960:14-19.
Matt, Paul. "North American O-47." *Historical A/c Album* XIII, 1974: 182-206.
Morley, Richard A. "Curtiss O-52 Owl." *AAHS* 40-1, 1995: 36-44.
Ryan Company YO-51 files, SDAM.
Westburg, Peter W. "Douglas Observation Planes." *Air Classics,* Pt. 1, Nov. 1976, 18-24, 68-77; Pt. 2, Dec 1976, 18-25, 64-67; Pt. 3, Jan 1977, 18-25, 68-74; Pt. 4, Mar 1977, 20-31, 83-91.

Chapter 13

Official Performance Test (OPT) Reports made by the Army's Engineering

Division at Wright Field Dayton, Ohio, provided these specifications cited in this chapter.
XA-8, #3535, October 14, 1931; YA-8, #3664, July 1, 1932; Y1A-8A, #3766, February 17, 1933; A-11, #4054, January 18, 1935; A-12, #3958, April 10, 1934; XA-13, #3886, September 9, 1933; XA-14, October 20, 1936; A-17, #4219, May 7, 1936; A-17A, #4292, February 8, 1937; Y1A-18, #4370, January 25, 1938.
Characteristics & Performance of Army Airplanes, February 15, 1932, has XA-7. July 1, 1939 and August 1, 1941, charts have pre-war data & estimates. See also the company histories cited below.
Army Aircraft Characteristics, Wright Field, 4-1-1946: pp. 6-8A, is the major source of A-20 through A-41 data, along with material added in the following sources.
Douglas A/c Co.
T.R. Smith, Report SM10908 "History of Light Bomber Airplanes" 12-4-44, and Airplane Delivery Record, 1940-41; B. Hite, Airplane Record, 7-11-41, Rev. 6-218-43; Harry Gann, Douglas A/c Production, 9-23-83.
Handbook... A-20A Wright Field, March 15, 1941.
Pilot's Flight Operating Instructions, A-20G, J, P-70, AAF Nov. 1944.
DB-7 data from Musee De L'Air undated document.
Pilot's Notes, HAVOC II, British Air Ministry, April 1942.
Deed Levy letter to RW, 12 Feb. 1986, gives A-21 dates.
G.L. Martin to SecWar, 5-27-39: NA, *AAF Central Files,* 1939, 452.1 Attack Bombers.

While the original Martin 167F specification dated February 3, 1939, has the data shown in previous publications, data here is from the December 1, 1939, revision based on the actual weight and tests of production aircraft. Top speed is given as 298 mph, instead of 304 mph. Comparable data for the Maryland II was unavailable.

Curtiss Co. spec for A-25, 4-3-41; also A-25A from SB2C-1A, 1 Apr 44
Contract for Vultee V-72 made with UK 7-3-40, SDAM.
McKenzie, Maj. Melvin A. Report on XA-32. Eglin Field 29 Sept 1943.
Documents prepared by Historical Section, Air Material Command, Wright Field and filed at Air Force Historical Research Center, Air University, Maxwell AFB, Alabama:
Summary of A-24 Project, AAF MD, Feb. 1945: 202.1-14.
Summary of A-25 Project, AAF MD, June 1945: 202.2-15.
Summary of A-26 Project, AAF MD, February 1946: 202.1-23.
Summary of XA-41 Project, AAF MD, Sept 1945: 202.1-22 in AFHRC.
Moss, Capt. Roy E. Final Report on the...XA-38. AMC, 4 Dec 1947.
Case History of Hughes D-2, D-5, F-11 Project, AMC Wright Field, August 1946, 202.1-32 in AFHRC.

Books:

Barton, Charles. *Howard Hughes and his Flying Boat.* Fallbrook 1982: 103, 130, 259.
Cortesi, Lawrence. *Grim Reapers, History of the 3rd Bomb Group.* Temple City, 1985.
Haight, *op cit* 242-245, and Charles Christienne, *History of French Military Aviation,* 1986: 316 through 413 for details of French use of DB-7 and M-167.
Jane's All the World's Aircraft, 1936: 302c, for Northrop 2E.
Peek, Chet. *The Spartan Story,* 1994: 120-122.
Smith, Peter C. *VENGEANCE.* Washington DC. Smithsonian Press 1987.
Widfeldt, Bo, & Ake Hall. *B-5 -stort-bombekopen.* Nassjo, Sweden. 2000.

Periodicals:

Aero Digest March 1937: 106, for Shrike Model 60, and March 1940: 238 for 8A-3,-4; and 196, 210 for Pratt & Whitney data.
Aeromilitaria 2/84: 31-36, lists Marylands in RAF & SAAF service. Dr. John R. Breihan kindly supplied copies of RAF veteran's letters with Maryland experience.
Aeromilitaria 2/79: 36-40, lists Baltimores in RAF and SAAF service.
Aviation , February 1938: 54, for 8A-1, -2.
Casius, Gerard J. "Royal Netherlands Navy DB-7s." *AAHS.* Summer 1979: 158/9.
Hagedorn, Dan. "Lend-Lease to Latin America". *AAHS Journal*_34-2,1989: 108-123.
Hagedorn, Dan. "Postscript with a Vengence". *AAHS* 43-1 1989: 222-224.
Jeffries, Walter & Ken Rust, "Curtiss Shrike." *AAHS Journal*_10-2,1965: 129-139.
Medvyed, Alexandr & Viktor Marskovski. "Night Radar fighters of VVS." *Aviatiya & Vrema,* Kiev 1995 #2: 14-20; describes use of A-20G-1. Erik Pilawski kindly translated text for SDAM files.
Pelletier, Alain J. "Northrop's Connection." *Air Enthusiast #77,* 1998: 2-13.
Thompson, Warren B. "B-26 Invader in Korea." *Wings of Fame* v.13, London: Aerospace 1998:112-125.
Tulsa Airman.. "Spartan Zeus." July 1937: 6-7.
Young, Edward M. "Demise of NA-68/69." *AAHS Journal* 25-3, 1980: 194-198.

Chapter 14

Materiel Division, Wright Field, Dayton: Official Performance Test (OPT) Reports:
Ford XB-906, 6-27-31; Douglas XB-7, 12-19-31; XB-901, 8-21-31; YB-9 1-13-31; Y1B-9, 2-10-32; YB-9A, 10-31-32; Martin XB-907A, 3-30-33; YB-10, 7-16-34; YB-12, 11-15-34; DB-1, 12-20-35; B-18, 7-24-37; XB-15, 8-8-38.
Characteristics & Performance of Army Airplanes,: 2-15-32, 9-15-34, 7-1-39, 4-1-46.
Bunker, Col. Howard G. *Final Report of Douglas XB-19.* July 18,1942.
Martin B-10B spec. 4-26-35, Handbook of YB-10, 12, 12A, 11-15-34.
Air Corps Central Files, (National Archives) 452c Bombers.
Boeing Y1B-17 Test manual, 4-15-37
Douglas B-23 manual
Hagedorn, Dan. "Flying Fort's Big Brother", *SKYWAYS* Oct. 1997, 32-56.
Westburg, Peter W. "B-7: Gull-winged Bomber" *Air Classics,* June 1975: 18-25, 66-73.

Chapter 15

Army Airplane Characteristics (AAC), 1 April 1946, is the source for most specifications here, supplemented by the more detailed Tactical Planning Characteristics & Performance Chart dated 29 June 1945, and the following:

AMC historical reports at AFHRC (Air Force Historical Center) Maxwell AFB, file 202.
Final report on the XB-38, MDR 5163, 8 November 1944.
Summary of the XB-40 Project, 21 August 1945.
Summary of the XB-41 Project, 24 August 1945
Snodgrass, R.J. Case History_XA-42, XB-42A, XB-42A: March 1948.
History of the B-24 Airplane A 33-page study by AAF-ATSC Wright Field, at SDAM.
B-26 Marauder Historical Society: *A Bibliography & Guide to Sources,* Esther M. Oyster & John O. Moench, 1992.
Boeing A/c Co., Seattle, Report D-3163: B-17C, 3-18-41.
Consolidated A/c Corp., San Diego, reports at SDAM: Model 32 report, 6-30-39; Weight & Balance: XB-24, 2-19-40.
Flight Tests XB-24, January 2 to August 9,1940. B-24 Series Airplanes-Army Contracts 25 May 1944, 35p.
Detail Weight Statement: B-24A, 6-5-41.
Model Specifications: LB-30 rev. 12 Apr 41; B-24C rev. 10 Sept. 41; B-24D: rev. 1 Feb 42, 3 Dec 42 & 22 Mar 43; B-24K 24 May 43; B-24L 20 Aug. 43; B-24M 1 Aug 44 & 1 July 45.
Block Descriptions, B-24D & B-24J. 1942/44.
Flight Manual, B-24D, December 1942.
Service Manual, Armament B-24D, April 1943.
G.L. Martin Co. Pilot's Flight Instructions: B-26, B-26A, and B-26B, March 1942. B-26B1 and -26C, 25 December 1943.
North American Av. *A Brief History of the B-25.* 31 pp. n.d.
Pilot's Notes for Fortress GR. II, IIA & III, Air Ministry, May 1944.
Pilot's Notes for Liberator III,V,VI,VIII, Air Ministry, October 1944.

Books and Monographs:

Avery, Norman. *B-25 Mitchell.* St. Paul: Phalanx Pub. 1992.
Birdsall, Steve. *Log of the Liberators.* Garden City, NY: Doubleday, 1973.
_____. *Pride of Seattle The first 300 B-17Fs.* Carrollton, TX: Sq/Sig, 1998.
Blue, Allen G. *The B-24 Liberator.* New

York: Scribners, 1974.
Bowers, Peter M. *Fortress in the Sky.* Granada Hills, CA: Sentry, 1976.
_____ *50th Anniversary Boeing B-17.* Seattle: Museum of Flight, 1985.
Breihan, John R. at al. *Martin Aircraft 1909-1960.* Narkiewicz/Thompson, Santa Ana, CA: 1995, 101-119.
Dorr, Robert L. *B-24 Liberator Units of the Pacific War.* Oxford,UK: Osprey 1999.
Freeman, Roger A. *B-17 Fortress at War.* NY: Scribners, 1977.
_____. *B-26 Marauder at War.* Garden City: Doubleday, 1978.
_____. *B-24 Liberator at War.* London: Ian Allan, 1983.
_____. *Mighty Eighth War Manual.* NY: Jane's, 1984.
Glines, Carroll V. *Doolittle's Tokyo Raiders.* Princeton, NJ: Van Nostrand, 1964.
General Dynamics Corp. *Liberator.* San Diego, CA: 1989.
Havener, J.K. *Martin B-26 Marauder.* Blue Ridge Summit, PA: TAB, 1988.
Hess, William N. *B-17 Flying Fortress.* Osceola, WI: Motorbooks, 1994.
Hickey, Lawrence J. *Warpath Across the Pacific-345th BG.* Boulder: IRPC, 1986.
Holley, I.B. *Development of Aircraft Gun Turrets in AAF, 1917-1944.* USAFHO 1947.
Johnsen, Frederick A. *B-24 Liberator.* Osceola, WI: Motorbooks, 1993.
_____ *Consolidated B-24..* WarbirdTech #1. N. Branch, MN: 1996.
_____*Boeing B-17 Fortress.* WarbirdTech #7. N. Branch, MN: 1996.
_____ *North American B-25.* WarbirdTech #12. N. Branch, MN: 1996.
_____ *Martin B-26 Marauder.* WarbirdTech #29. N. Branch, MN: 2000.
Lloyd, Alwyn T. *Liberator, America's bomber.* Missoula, MO: Pictorial, 1993.
Kidder, Warren B. *Willow Run.* Lansing, MI, KFT, 1995.
McDowell, Ernest R. *Flying Fortress.* Carrollton, TX: Sq/Sg, 1987.
Mitchell, John H. *On Wings We Conquer, the 19th & 7th Bomb Groups in the Southwest Pacific.* Springfield, MO: G.E.M Pub. 1990.
Moench, John O. *Marauder Men.* Longwood, FL, Malia Ent. 1989
Pace, Steve. *B-25 Mitchell,.* Osceola: Motorbooks., 1994.
Scutts, Jerry. *B-25 Mitchell at war.* London: Ian Allen, 1983
_____. *Marine Mitchells.* St. Paul: Phalanx Pub., 1993.
Tannehill, Victor C. *Martin Marauder B-26.* Arvada, CO: Boomerang, 1997.
Thompson, Scott A. *B-17 in Blue.* Elk Grove, CA: Aero Vintage, 1993.
Unger, Ulrich. *Pe-8, Der Sowjet Fernbomber.* Berlin: Brandenburgish, 1993.

Periodicals:

Arnold, H.H. "The Air Corps in National Defense," *Aero Digest* Aug. 1939: 28-31.
AEROMILITARIA #2:78 "MITCHELLS in RAF Service." 41-48.
AEROMILITARIA #4:79 "Royal Air Force Fortresses." 87-90.
AEROMILITARIA #2:83 "RAF Marauders." 31-37.
Bowyer, Mike." Fortress Is of Bomber Command." *Aviation News,* 1 Aug 1991: 218-224.
Gallacher, Ian."B-17C, an Uneasy Evaluation." *Wingspan* Feb. 1993: 16-17.
Hansen, C.L. "Design Analysis of B-25." *Aviation* March 1945: 119-141.
Akilianov,Alexander. "Mitchell in the USSR." *Mir Aviatii* . (World Aviation) 1.94: 33-36.
Ratkin, Vladimir. "B-25" *Mir Aviatii* . (World Aviation) Moscow, 2.94: 32-37.
Wood, Carlos C. "Design of the XB-42." *Aviation.* February 1947: 37-42.

Chapter 16

Official Performance Test (OPT) Reports: Y1P-26,#3684 5-10-32; P-26A, #3949 3-2-34; P-31, #3749 12-12-32; YP-29, #4121 6-28-35; V-141, #4222 6-23-36; PB-2A, #4238 6-25-36; P-35, #4358 11-18-37; Y1P-36, #4338 8-27-38.
Army Aircraft Characteristics, ATSC Wright Field. H.H. 1 April, 1946. AAF a/c data from this source, unless otherwise cited. Characteristics charts dated 9-15-1934: has P-30; 7-1-1939: YP-29; 8-1-1941: P-36B, P-36F.
Documents in the Air Force Historical Research Center (AFHRC) at Air University, Maxwell AFB were consulted, as well as the *Army Air Corps Central Files* (see 452.1P Boxes 976ff) in the National Archives.

Memos and letters of special importance:

H.H. Arnold to J.J. Honan, 4-15-37. Questions Seversky claims.
B.S. Kelsey to ChiefEng. 11-15-37. Delay on P-35s.
F.M. Kennedy to ChAC. 11-5-37. Contract penalty.
NA 452.1G Box 993, A. Seversky to Chief Air Corps, 6-7-38; and other letters. Burdette Wright to LtCol Spatz, April 1, 1939, on H75Q.
452.1 Pursuit, Box 976 has 4-17-36 chart of mfr. guarantees.
M/Gen. Foulois to Assit.SecWar, 1-11-35. "No use for 2-seat pursuit" see Langley Field Conference of Pursuit Group COs Feb 21-25, 1938; and Armament Laboratory files.
National Air & Space Museum (NASM) has AAF Aircraft Record Cards on microfilm, and Curtiss-Wright Corp. Engineering Reports of Buffalo Division (hereafter CW) are stored in NASM's Garber Facility.
CW 5887, 5907, 5910, 5911, 5916/18, 5962, 5973 6162 on early Hawk 75 development. Actual weights are given, performances are as estimated.
CW 7886, H75R; CW 7897/98, 7996 on H75A-4;
CW 7908, 7991, H75A-7; CW 8225, 8241, H75A-8.
H. Lloyd Child's pilot log giving Curtiss test flight dates was shared by Mauno Salo.
P-24 documents at SDAM (San Diego Aerospace Museum) include: R.J. Woods to H.G. Welty, May 4, 1956; MD ACES Report on XP-900, 10-20-31; & XP-900 brochure.
The Hoover Institute at Stanford University has the Chennault file, including CW-21 contract data and W.D. Pawley letters.
Letters to author by Raymond Cheung, 6/92, described P-26 service in China, and Malcolm Rosholt, 2-18-84, told of H75Q there.

Books:

Allen, Richard S. *Revolution in the Sky.* NY: Orion, 1988.
Beauchamps, Gerry, & Jean Cuny. *Curtiss Hawk 75.* Colorado Springs: V-P Pub., 1995.
Bodie,Warren M. *Republic P-47 THUNDERBOLT.* Hayesville, NC: Widewing, 1993.
Gwynn-Jones, Terry. "Forgotten Air War." (Thailand) *Aviation History* 9/00: 50-56.
Jane's 1938: 260, H75H; 295, Sev 2PA-A, 2PA-L; 306 V-143.
_____ 1939: 239, H75Q.
_____ 1941: 155, H-75A-4.
Shamburger, Page and Joe Christy. *The Curtiss Hawks.* Kalamazoo: Wolverine, 1972.
Widfeldt, Bo, & Ake Hall. *B-5 stortbombekopen.* Nassjo, Sweden. 2000: 46-50, 135.

Periodicals:

Aero Digest 3/35: 38, on Model 281; 4/36: 116, Sev -3M; 3/39: 135/6, EP-1, 2PA-200; 3/41:144, NA-50; 158, Vanguard 48; 178, 2-AP;
Aeroplane Monthly Dec 1984: 655-659, Has RAF test of 2PA-202.
Beauchamps, Gerry. "Futuristic Hawks, the X/YP-37." *AAHS* 22-1 1977: 12-25.
Berlin, Don R. "Development of the Curtiss P-36A." *Aero Digest..* Dec. 1937: 54-58.
Bowers, Peter M. *Boeing P-26 Variants.* Arlington TX: Aerofax, 1984.
Casius, Gerard, "St. Louis Lightweight." *Air Enthusiast #16,* 1981: 33-44.
Eberspacher, Warren. "Consolidated PB-2." *Skyways* #57, Jan 2001: 2-23.
Fausel, Robert, & Richard A. Morley. "China Odyssey". *AAHS* 43-1 1989: 200-221.
Hazen, R. M. "The Allison Aircraft Engine." *SAE Journal.* V.49,#5, Nov. 1941: 498-500.
Hyer, Charles R. "Curtiss P-36 in Service," *AAHS* 33-4 1988: 242-257.
Jyoko, Noburo. "Japanese Severskys." *AAHS* 30-3 1985: 214-217.
Morareau, Lucien. "Forgotten Aircraft of the Antilles." *Small Air Forces Observer* #97, 4/2001:5-11.

Chapter 17

Delivery dates are from individual Aircraft Record cards on microfilm at the US-AFHC, Maxwell AFB. Fighter characteristics are from TSEST-A2, 1 April 1946, unless selected from the primary materials cited below.

Air Corps:

Type Specification, C-616, Interceptor Pursuit, January 25, 1939.
Type Specification, C-619, Pursuit, June 24, 1939.
Curtiss-Wright company reports at NASM Silver Hill facility provided the spe-

cifications for the H81A-2 and H87A-2 (4-10-41) and H86A spec. 5-1-40.
Actual Weight & Balance Reports on P-40, P-40B,C, D,E, F, K, L, & M.

SDAM files on P-40 include:
B. S. Wright to H.H. Arnold, May 16,1940, bomb racks for P-40.
Sam Spaulding to M.L. Kearny, July 29, 1941; Tomahawks in RAF.
Logan, W.G. *Final report...of the XP-46*: AAF MD #4832, October 17, 1942.

Lockheed:
Foreign Release Agreements: Lockheed P-38, 17 April 1940; at USAFHC.
Hibbard, Hall L. "Design Analysis, Lockheed P-38." Reprint from *Aviation*.

Bell:
XP-39 data selected from the AMC Inspection Report, March 27, 1939; Bell A/c Corp. Handbook for the XP-39, n.d.; and Characteristics chart dated July 1, 1939. The common assertion that the XP-39 reached 390 mph is not supported by official documentation.
Bell reports 4Y003-C, 6-1-40 on YP-39; 12Y005, 2-14-40, & 4Y003-G, 11-1-40 on P-39C; 14-943-903, 6-12-42 on P-39D-2; Spec C-619-33, 10-9-44 on N-5.
Model 14 weights, 14-942-001, 7-25-41; performance 943-009, 8-18-41.
Weight & Balance reports, 12-18-42: P-39D-1, D-2, K-1, L-1, M-1, and N-1.
Larry Bell to MD engineering chief, 8-30-39, on NACA study.
Larry Bell to George Lewis, NACA, 1-17-40; cited in Hansen, 200.
Larry Bell to MajGen. Echols, Chief MD, 5-24-41, on P-400 speed.
Historical Division, Air Materiel Command, Wright Field, Dayton:
Hall, C.L. ACTR #5022, 1 Sept. 1943: Final report...XP-39E.
Hall, C.L. *Final report...of the XP-51B*: ACTR #5134, July 29, 1944:
Logan, W.G. *Final report...of the XP-51*: #4801, July 15, 1942.
Kesley, Capt. B.S. to MD engineering chief, 10-25-40 on 37-mm gun.

North American:
See notes in Wagner, Ray. *Mustang Designer, Schmued and the P-51*, cited below.
Republic: Detail specifications and block numbers for P-47D series. SDAM.
Pilot's handbooks for P-43, P-43A, P-66. SDAM.

Books:
Bodie, Warren M. *Lockheed P-38 Lightning*. Hayesville, NC: Widewing, 1991.
_____. *Republic P-47 THUNDERBOLT*. Hayesville, NC: Widewing, 1993.
Boylan, Bernard. *Development of the Long-range Escort fighter. USAF Historical Study #136,* Maxwell AFB: Air Univ. 1955.
Christy, Joe, & Jeff Ethell. *P-40 Hawks at War*. NY: Scribners, 1980.
Dienst, John, and Dan Hagedorn. *North American Mustang in Latin America*. Arlington, TX: Aerofax, 1985.
Ethell, Jeffrey. *Mustang: A Documentary History*. New York: Jane's 1981.
Freeman, Roger A. *Mustang at War*. Garden City, NY: Doubleday, 1974.
_____. *Thunderbolt, Documentary P-47 History*. NY: Scribners, 1979.
Gruenhagen, Robert W. *Mustang: The Story of the P-51*. New York: Genesis, 1969.
Hellstrom, Leif. *J26 Mustang*, 2nd ed. Stockholm, Sweden 1997.
Hess, William N. *Fighting Mustang: The P-51 Chronicle*. Garden City: Doubleday, 1970.
Matthews, Birch *Cobra!, Bell A/c, 1934-1946*. Atglen, PA: Schiffer, 1996.
Molesworth, Carl. P-40 *Warhawk Aces of MTO*. Oxford: Osprey 2002.
Morgan, E.B. & E. Shacklady, *SPITFIRE - the History*. Stamford, UK 1987.
Shamburger, Page, & Joe Christy, *Curtiss Hawks*. Kalamazoo, MI: Wolverine, 1972.
Wagner, Ray. *Mustang Designer, Schmued and the P-51,* New York: Orion, 1990.

Monographs:
Davis, Larry. *P-51 Mustang*. Sq/Sg, 1995.
Johnsen, Frederick A. *Lockheed P-38 Lightning,* Warbird, 1996.
_____. *Bell P-39/P-63,* Warbird #17, 1998.
Kinsey, Bert. *P-51 Mustang in detail & scale. Parts 1 & 2*. Carrollton TX: Sq/Signal, 1997.
McDowell, Ernest R. *Thunderbolt, The P-47 in European Theater*. Carrollton: Sq/Sg,1998.
_____ *Thunderbolt, The P-47 in the Pacific Theater*. Carrollton: Sq/Sg, 1999.
Stafford, Gene B. *Thunderbolt in Action #18*. Sq/Sg, 1975.

Periodicals:
Aero Digest 3/40: 158. "Vultee Vanguard"
Air Enthusiast 8/71: 134-139, "The Calamitous Cobra".
Carter, Dustin, "Vultee's P-38" *AAHS 33-1,* 1988: 18-22.
Bell, Larry, *Aviation 7*/41: 74-75,90, "Fighter Philosophy".
_____ *Air Trails* 7/41: 12-13,46-48, "We Built the Giant Killer".
Dorr, Robert F. "Bell P-39/63" *Wings of Fame #10*. 1998: 116-148.
Eberspacher, Warren. "Vultee P-66 Vanguard", *SKYWAYS #59,* 7/01: 2-18.
Foss, R.L. & Roy Blair. "From Propellers to Jets in Fighter Design". *LOCKHEED HORIZONS:* 3-23.
Gordon, Yefim. "P-39 in the USSR". *Wings of Fame #10*. 1998: 149-151.
Martin, R. "The Vitiated Vanguard". *AAHS 29-2*. 1984: 102-115.
Miller, E. E. "Design Analysis of Bell Airacobra". *Aviation* 5/43: 126-155,
Roman, V. *Aerokobry vstupayut y boy*. Kiev 1993. English translation by Dr. David C. Montgomery in *AAHS Journal* 43-4, 1998: 282-293.
Woods, R. J. "Why a Rear Engine Installation." *Aviation*. 3/41: 36-37, 142.

Chapter 18
War Department, Office of Chief of Air Corps:
MajGen Arnold to GHQ AF, Nov. 14, 1939, Requests new pursuit emphasis.
GHQ AF to MajGen Arnold, Jan. 11, 1940, Reply to above.
Air Corps, Materiel Div.: Air Corps Specification XC-622.Nov. 27, 1939.
Request for Data R40-C, February 20, 1942
Report on R40-C, May 15, 1940 (Declassified 7-18-89)
Historical Division, Air Materiel Command, Wright Field:
History of XP-52 Project. June 19, 1942. (Declassified 8-5-92)
Review of XP-53 Project. June 6, 1942.
Case History of XP-54. November 1944.
Case History of XP-56. January 1946.
Final Report of Development,...XP-55. Maj. C.R. Polk, 22 October 1945.
Final Report of Development,...XP-56. Capt. O.B. Thornton, 30 July 1948.
Summary of Case History of the XP-58.
Summary of Case History of the P-59 series. Nov. 14, 1945.
Final Report on XP-59A, XP-59. Capt. D.T. Tuttle, 28 June 1945.
Case History of the P-60 series.
Final Report on the XP-61D. A.K. Dillon, 27 April 1948.
Final Report on the XP-67. Major J.F. Aldridge, Jr., 31 Jan 1946.
Young, James O. "Riding England's Coattails", AFFTC History Office, 24 Oct 1995.

Books:
Carpenter, Davis M. *Flame Powered Bell XP-59A*. Jet Pioneers, 1992.
Pape, Garry R. & John M. Campbell. *Northrop Flying Wings*. Atglen, 1995: 54-69.
Pape, Garry R. & Ronald C. Harrison. *Queen of the Midnight Skies*. Atglen: Schiffer 1992.

Periodicals:
Balzer, Gerald. Six-part article in *AAHS Journal,* Vol. 40-4, 41-1/4, 42-1. is the most detailed account of the R40-C program aircraft.
Alain Pelletier, "French Kings", *Air Enthusiast #72,* Nov/Dec 1997: 57-63.
_____."Not So Ideal -the XP-67", *Air Enthusiast #96,* Nov/Dec 2001: 2-8.

Chapter 19
U.S. Navy, BuAer, Characteristics charts. 9-1-35: XP3D-1, XP3Y-1; 9-1-36: XPBY-1, XP3D-2; 10-1-37: XPTBH-2, XPBS-1; 10-1-39: XPB2Y-1; 10-1-40: XPBM-1, PBM-1, PBO-1, PBY-1/2/3, XPBY-5A; 8-1-41: PBY-4/5, PB2Y-2; 9-1-42: PBM-3C; 5-1-43: XPBB-1; 9-1-43: PBY-5A; 5-1-44: PBN-1; 8-1-44: PBY-5/5A, PB2Y-3; 10-1-44: PBM-5S; 11-1-44: PBY-6A, PB4Y-1; 12-1-44: PV-1; 11-1-45: PV-2; 2-1-45: PB2Y-5; 5-1-45: PBM-3D; 8-1-45: PBY-5; 3-1-46: PB4Y-2; 9-1-47, PBM-5.
BuAer Type Specifications: VPM Design 137, (4-engine) 14 Feb 35, VPB airplane P3D-1, 21 May 1935, P3D-2, 27 July 1936; VPB (Consolidated) 28 July 1936, 18 March 37, PBB-1 21 Aug 41.
Naval Aviation Confidential Bulletin April 1946: BuAer,Washington, DC
U.S. Senate, 75th Congress: Report No.

859 on Consolidated XP3Y-1 contract and factory wages.
Consolidated A/c Detail Specifications: PBY-2 final, 1 Feb 38; PBY-3 14 Sep 38, PBY-4 19 Apr 38, and all models to 5 Nov 41.
Model 31 reports, Flight Test Record, Patrol bomber 3-12-40. P4Y-1 proposal, 12-12-42.
Laddon to BuAir on Model 31, Sept 9, 1941.
Model 30 and 34 reports.
General Arrangement drawings: XPBS, PBY, PB2Y, XPB3Y-1 & P4Y-1.
Actual Weight & Balance reports: All PBY and PB2Y models from 11 Feb 38 to 6 Aug 42, and XPB2Y-1 12-7 -37
PB4Y-2 Familiarization Training Manual 6-1-44.
Letters from SDAM files:
G. McVickers to Frank Fink, Nov. 26, 1942. "empty weight grew from 15,534 pounds on the first PBY-5 to 17,751 pounds."
Cameron T. Robertson to R.L. Cormier, Aug. 3, 1942, on XPB2M-1R.
I.M. Laddon, various notes at SDAM
Logbooks of test pilots Douglas Kelly, Richard A. McMakin, Phil Prophett, and Russell R. Rogers were used to establish 1937/42 Convair flight test dates.

Books:
Carlisle, Robert L. *Cats Over the Atlantic VPB-73.* Santa Barbara: Fithian, 1995.
Creed, Roscoe. *PBY The Catalina Flying Boat.* Annapolis: Naval Institute, 1985.
Crocker, Mel. *Black Cats and Dumbos.* Blue Ridge Summit, PA: Tab, 1987.
Ginter, Steve. *Martin Mars Flying Boats.* Simi Valley, CA: Ginter, 1995.
Hendrie, Andrew. *Flying Cats.* Annapolis: Naval Institute, 1988.
_____. *Seek & Strike- The Lockheed Hudson.* London: Kimber, 1983.
Knott, Richard C. *Black Cat Raiders of WW II.* Annapolis: Nautical, 1981.
Mariner Association. *Mariner/Marlin Flying Boats.* Paducah KY: Turner, 1993.
Messimer, Dwight R. *In the Hands of Fate Story of Patrol Wing Ten.* Annapolis: Naval Institute, 1985.
Pember, Harry E. *Sikorsky VS-44 Flying Boat.* Stratford: Flying Machines, 1998.
Price, Alfred. *Aircraft versus Submarine.* Annapolis: Naval Institute, 1973.
Scarborough, W.E. *PBY Catalina in Action..* Carrollton TX: Sq/Sig, 1983.
Scrivner, C.L. & Scarborough, W.E. *PV-1 Ventura in Action.* Carrollton: Sq/Sig, 1981.
Smith, Bob. *PBM Mariner in Action..* Carrollton TX: Sq/Sig, 1987.
Stanaway, John C. *Vega Ventura* . Atglen, PA: Schiffer, 1996.
Vincent, David. *Catalina Chronicle, History of RAAF ops.* Adelaid: LPH, 1981.

Periodicals:
Aeromilitaria, "Consolidated Catalina in RAF Service." March 1977.
"Lockheed Ventura in RAF Service." April 1982: 82, 87-98.
Boyne, Walter. "Hall's XPTBH-2." *Wings.* June 1975: 8-25.
Northrop Co. *Norcrafter.* Hawthorne, March-April 1941: 15-17.
Ostrowski, David. "XPTBH-2 tests" *Skyways #40* Oct. 1966: 45-52.
Ragnarsson, Ragnar J. "Northrop seaplane" *Wings.* February 1941: 24-38, 50.
Russian booklet:
V.R. Kotjebnikov, *Petaioya Lodka Konsolidated Katalina. Morskoj Oruzie 6* Flying boat Consolidated Catalina. Maritime Weapons. Biblioteka Gangut, 1995
Video: Robert Burgener. *Project Zebra.* Rockville, MD: 1998.

Chapter 20
U.S. Navy, BuAer, Characteristics charts. 9-1-32: XSE-1, XSG-1; 9-1-33: SU-1/2/3, O3U-3, XO4U-2, XS2C-1, XSE-2, XSS-1; 9-1-34: XO3C-1, XO2D-1, XSOE-1, XO5U-1; 9-1-35: XSF-2, XSBU-1; 9-1-36: SU-4, O3U-6, XS2C-1; 10-1-39: XOSN-1, XOSS-1, SOC-1, SOC-3, SON-1, XOS2U-1, OS2U-1, XSO2U-1, XSO3C-1, SBU-1. 8-1-41: OS2U-2; 11-20-42, SOC-3A; 11-1-43: SO3C-1,-2,-2C,-3; 1-1-44: XSC-1; 1-1-46: SC-1; 1 Mar 46: SC-2; 1 Jan 47: XOSE-1.

USN Reports on XSG-1: NASA 136, April 14, 1933; SF-1: NASA 169.
USN Type Specification class VSO 5 Dec 1934, 27 Feb 1936.
USN Contract Correspondence: National Archives: RG 72, Box 699/700 for XSOE-1 contract 38637, including 4-16-36 weight report; also J. Underwood to RW, 7-26-77.
USN contract NO-LL-96676 for SOR-1, 6-30-42, at SDAM.
Chance Vought Company Reports: Vought Aircraft 1917-1971; First Flights of Vought planes; CV report dated 3-14-33, V-65F; report #3454, V-93S.
The *BEE HIVE* 3/34: 5, V-93.
Curtiss blueprints: VSO P-1009, 012/13, 8-9-37, at SDAM.
Karaberis,Lt. C.A. Memo on SO3C: describes type's failure. 1 April 1943. At SDAM.
B. A.Gillies logbook has XS2L-1, XSF-2 dates.
Deed Levy to RW, 12 Feb 86, on XOSS tests.

Books:
Adcock, Al. *OS2U Kingfisher in Action.* Carrolton: Squad/Sig, 1991.
Jane's 1934: 340c, V-92; 1935: 341c; V-80F.
Larkins, William T. *Battleship and Cruiser Aircraft of the USN.* Atglen: Schiffer, 1996.
_____ *Curtiss SOC.* Profile #194, England: 1967.
Moran, Gerard. *AEROPLANES VOUGHT.* op cit.
Scutts, Jerry, *Fantail Fighters..* St. Paul: Phalanx, 1995
Periodicals:
Aeroplane Monthly. "Vought V-66E."12/97: 28-33.
Aero Digest 7/33: V-80P; 3/39: V-99M.
Airpower. "Voughts." 11/79: 37-55.
Andrews, Harold. "S2C-1."*Skyways #28,* 10/93: 14-15.
_____*Naval Aviation News.* 9/93: 18-19, XSG-1; 11/93: 18-19, 2; XS2L-1, XSS-2.
Ostrowski, David. "Anacostia flight tests of XOSS-1."*Skyways #35,* 7/95: 2-14.
_____.XSE-2."*Skyways #45,* 1/98: 51-55.

Chapter 21
U.S. Navy, BuAer, Characteristics charts: 1 Sept 32, XBY-1; 1 Sept 33, XB2Y-1; 1 Sept 35: XSBU-1, XSBC-2; 3 Jan 36: XTBD-1; 1 March 36: XBT-1, XSB2U-1, XTBG-1; 1 Sept 36, XBF-1, XB2G-1; 1 Oct 37: BG-1, XBA-1, XSB3U-1; 1 Oct 39, , SBU-1, SB2U-1,-2, XBT-2; 1 Oct 40: BT-1, SBC-3, SBC-4, XSB2A-1; 1 Aug 41: TBD-1; 1 April 42: SB2A-1; 6 Aug 42: SBD-3; 8 Aug 42, TBF-1; 11 Nov 42: SBN-1; 30 Nov 42: SBD-1, -2; 1 Mar 43: SB2A-2, SB2A-4; 1 July 43: TBF-1C; 1 Sept 43 SB2C-1; 1 June 44: SBD-5; 1 Aug 44: TBM-3, XBTC-2; 1 Sept 44: TBY-2; 1 Nov 44: SB2C-3,-4; 1 July 45, XBTK-1; 1 Oct 45: SBD-6; 1 Dec 45, XBTM-1; 1 Feb 46: TBM-3E; 1 Oct 46, SB2C-5.
AAF Characteristics Chart, 1942, (AFHRC 168.11-18) for A-34.

Documents:
Pearson, Lee. US Navy ms. in SDAM "Attack Plane History to 1957". The most useful single source for this chapter.
US Navy Dept. Type Specification for VB dive bomber (BuAer Design No.110) Washington 30 October, 1931. 42-page copy at SDAM.
US Navy Reports: XBY-1 NASA 134; XBG-1, BG-1, NASA 146, 169.
US Navy BuOrd #1207, Aircraft Torpedoes, 27 June 1944.
US Navy Confidential Bulletin, Jan 1946: 32-36,April 46, 26-28..
Heinemann, E. H. papers, collection at SDAM:
Douglas A/c Co. B. Hite. Airplane Record, Rev. 6-28-43.
Specification DS 120 & dr. 519137, XTB2D-1.
Glenn E. Smith & E.H. Heinemann. "Sugar Baker Dog." ms.1987.

Monographs:
Adcock, Al. *TBD DEVASTATOR in action.* Carrollton: Sq/Sig, 1989.
Andrews, Hal. *Curtiss SB2C-1.* Profile #124, Leatherhead, UK: 1966.
Doll, Thomas E. *Douglas TBD DEVASTATOR.* Aero #23, Fallbrook: 1973.
_____ *SBC Helldiver in action.* Carrollton, Sq/Sig, 1995.
_____ *SB2U Vindicator in action.* Carrollton: Sq/Sig, 1992.
_____ *Grumman TBF/TBM Avenger.* Fallbrook: Aero, 1984.
Ginter, Steve et al, *XBTU-1 & TBY-2 Sea Wolf.* Simi Valley, CA: Ginter, 1997.
Kinzey, Bert, *SB2C Helldiver in detail & scale.* Carrollton: Sq/Sig, 1997.
_____ *TBF/TBM Avenger in detail & scale.* Carrollton: Sq/Sig, 1997.
Kowalkski, Bob. *Douglas XSB2D-1 & BTD-1.* Simi Valley, CA: Ginter, 1995.
_____ *Douglas XTB2D-1 Skypirate.* Simi Valley, CA: Ginter, 1996.
_____ *Martin AM-1 Mauler.* Simi Valley,

CA: Ginter, 1994.
_____ *Kaiser Fleetwings XBTK-1.* Simi Valley, CA: Ginter, 1999.
Scrivner, Charles. *TBF/TBM Avenger in action.* Carrollton: Sq/Sig, 1987.
Smith, Peter C. *Curtiss SB2C Helldiver.* Wiltshire: Crowood, 1968.
Tillman, Barret. *SBD Dauntless Units in WW 2.* Oxford, UK: Osprey, 1993.

Periodicals:
Andrews, Hal. "Vought SBU-1"*Historical Aviation Album #3.* Temple City 1966:122-127.
Brown, E. "Valediction for Vought" *Air International*. 12/78: 275-281.
_____. "Ill-favoured Helldiver" *Air International*. 9/79: 281-288.
Fleetwings News. "Our Dive Bomber" Bristol, PA: 10-22-46: 1-2.
Goodspeed, M.H. "Grumman TBF/TBM Avenger" *Wings of Fame #13.*AIRtime, 1998: 32-91.
Kernahan, G. "Trials of Helldiver." *AAHS Journal*. 36-4, 1991: 242-257.
Martin, B. et al. "Brewster Blaster." *AAHS Journal.* 32-1,1987: 58-73.
Mass, Jim. "Fall from Grace -Brewster". *AAHS Journal.* 30-2, 1985: 118-135.
Miska, Kurt. "XTB2F-1", *Air Combat 1939-45,* V.4, #6, 1972: 117-174.
Ostrowski, David, "Anacostia flight tests of XSB2U-1." *Skyways* #13, 1/90: 42-55.
_____ XBS2U-3. *Skyways* #37, 1/96: 10-17.
_____ XSBA-1. *Skyways* #41, 1/97: 2-17.
Peletier, Alain J. "A Tracker before its time? XTB2F-1". *Air Enthusiast #98,* 3/02: 48-53,

Chapter 22
U.S. Navy, BuAer, Characteristics charts.1 Jan 32: XFF-1;
1 Sep 33: XF2J-1, XF12C-1, XF6B-1, XF11C-1,-2,-3, XF2F-1;
1 Sep 34: XFD-1, XF3U-1, XF3J-1;
1 Mar 35: XF7B-1, XF13C-1/2/3; 1 Sep 35: FF-1, BF2C-1;
1 Mar 36: XF3F-1; 1 Oct 37: F2F-1; 1 Oct 40: F3F-1/2/3.
U.S. Navy, BuAer, Detail Specification: SD-202-1, 30 Jan 34, F2F-1;
SD-112-7, 22 April 35, XF13C-3; SD-112-9, 25 August 36, XF3F-2.
Curtiss Report 6138, 3-24-36, Hawk III; at NASM.

Publications:
Bowers, Peter. *Curtiss Navy Hawks in action.* Carrollton: Sq/Sg 1995.
Dann, Richard. *Grumman Biplane Fighters in action.* Carrollton: Sq/Sg, 1996.
Howson, Gerald. *Aircraft of the Spanish Civil War.* 1990:161-163 on G-23.
Jane's 1935: 292c for Hawk II; 1937, 289c for Hawk IV.

Periodicals:
Andrews, Harold. "B/J Navy Fighters". *Skyways* #34. Apr 1995: 28-32.
_____ "Northrop Fighters" *Skyways* #48. Oct 1998: 2-10.
Matt, Paul. "Grumman FF-1." *Aero Album.* Winter 1970: 32-37.
_____"Berliner-Joyce XF3J-1."*Historical Aviation Album #XV,* 1977: 311-318.

Chapter 23
U.S. Navy, BuAer, Characteristics charts.
1 Oct 1937: XF4F-2 (& Jan. 1938 test report)
1 Oct 1940: XF4F-3, XF4U-1; 26 Dec 40, XF5F-1
1 Aug 1941: F2A-2,-3; F4F-3, -3A;
1 April 1942: F4F-4. (Cf 14 Aug 1942 for heavier weights)
17 Dec 1942: XF4U-3; 26 Dec 1942, XFL-1;
1 May 1943: F4U-2; 1 July 1943, FM-1;
1 March 1944: F4U-1; 1 Sept 1944, FM-2; 1 Oct 1944, F4U-1D;
1 Nov 44, F6F-3; 1 Dec 1944, F2G-1.
1 Oct 1945, F6F-3N; 1 Nov 1945, F6F-5, F5F-5N;
1 March 1946, F4U-4; 1 July 1947.

U.S. Navy, BuAer, Detail Specification: SD-112-12, 18 Nov 37, F2A-1.

Grumman Historical Office provided much data to SDAM and the authors of the works cited below. Grumman Report 1420A, April 6, 1941, on F4F-3, -3A, was especially helpful. Weights on F4F models increased as production changes were made; data cited here represents F4F-3 and -4 as they entered combat in early 1942. Navy and BAC schedules show 81, not 91, G-36As to Britain. G-36B & 339E data from Johnson & Hefferman, 83-87. See Lundstrom, *op. cit.* 441-447 for F4F-4 critique.

Books:
Abrams, Richard. *F4U Corsair at War.* New York: Scribners, 1977.
Guyton, Boone T. *Whistling Death..* NY: Orion, 1990.
Tillman, Barrett. *Wildcat in WWII.* Annapolis: Nautical Pub. 1983.
_____ *Hellcat, the F6F in WWII.* Annapolis: Naval Institute, 1979.

Monographs:
Ginter, Steve. *Ryan FR-1 Fireball & XF2R-1.* Simi Valley, CA: Ginter 1995.
Greene, Frank L. *History of Grumman Wildcat F4F.* 42-page reprint by Grumman Co. of article abridged in *AAHS Journal,* 3-4, 1961: 223-245.
Keskinen, Kalevi, *Brewster B-239.* Helsinki, Finland 1970.
Kinzey, Bert. *F4F Wildcat in detail,* D & S. Vol. 65, Carrollton: Sq/Sig, 2000
_____ *F4U Corsair in detail.* D & S. Vol. 55/56, Carrollton: Sq/Sig, 1998.
_____ *F6F Hellcat in detail.* D & S. Vol. 49, Carrollton: Sq/Sig, 1998.
Linn, Don. *F4F Wildcat in action,* Carrollton TX: Sq/Sig, 1988.
Lucabaugh, Dave, & Bob Martin. *Grumman XF5F-1,* Simi Valley, CA: Ginter 1995.
Mass, Jim. *F2A Buffalo in action.* Carrollton TX: Sq/Sig, 1987.
Sullivan, Jim. *F4U Corsair in action.* Carrollton TX: Sq/Sig, 1994.
Tillman, Barrett. *Vought F4U Corsair.* North Branch, MN: Specialty Press, 2001.

Periodicals:
Mass, Jim. "Fall from Grace-Brewster Co." *AAHS* 30-2, 1985: 118-135.
Martin, Bob. "The Bell XFL-1".
_____ 38-3, 1993: 204-215.
Ostrowski, David, "Anacostia flight tests:XF2A-1,F2A-1."*Skyways* #55, 7/00: 2-11,31-9.
_____, "Anacostia flight tests: XF5F-1." *Skyways* #62, 4/02: 2-22.
Scarborough, W.E. Fighting Two- the Flying Chiefs" Pt. 1, *The Hook* Sum 91: 16-35.
Stenman, Kari. "Brewster in Finnish ser." *Air Enthusiast* #48, 1992: 40-51.
Wixey, Ken. "Corpulent Feline." *Air Enthusiast* #68, 1997: Pt. 1,16-25, #70, 1997: Pt. 2, 51-56

Chapter 24
Official Documents
United States Strategic Bombing Survey, Summary, (Pacific War) Washington. 1 July 1946: 16-20 for B-29 effect on the war and Japanese casualties.
Craven, Wesley F. and James L. Cate, Eds. *The Army Air Forces in World War II.* Vol V.3-178, 507-758; Vol VI: 208-211.
USAF Historical Studies: No. 6, *Development of the Heavy Bomber,* 1918-1944, Air University, 1951, (reprinted at Kansas State Univ.)
Army AC Type Specification, Heavy Bomber XC-218A, April 8, 1940.
_____ Tactical Planning Characteristics, B-29, 28 June 1945.

So many modifications were made during a long service life that variations in weight and performances makes selection of "typical" B-29 characteristics difficult. Data accompanying this text is for early wartime models.

B-29 Airplane Commander's Manual, 1944.
Pilot's Operating Manual, B-29, 24 April 1951
AFHRC Case History File 202 on B-33.
Consolidated Vultee A/c Corp.:
Pilot's Instructions for XB-32. 10-23-43, with Weight Chart, 12-18-42.
Specification for XB-32, ZD-33-001-D, Revised 6-1-44.
Model Specification for B-32, FZD-33-015A, 2-6-45. (Weights based on a/c. #55)
Company files on Model 33 (B-32) including operations, at SDAM, with memos, like H. A. Sutton to R. C. Sebold, 10-27-42.
Logbooks of test pilots and engineers: Bill Chana, Beryl Erickson, Richard A. McMachin, Russell Rogers.

Books:
Gurney, Gene. *Journey of the Giants.* New York: Coward, 1961.
Hansen, Chuck. *U.S. Nuclear Weapons.* New York: Orion, 1988.
Morrison, Wilbur H. *Point of No Return-The Story of the 20th Air Force.* New York: Times, 1979.
Rhodes, Richard. *Dark Sun.* New York: Touchstone, 1999: (pp.307-348 for B-29 nuclear role.)
Rust, Ken. *Twentieth Air Force story.* Temple City: Historical Aviation, 1979.
Thomas, Gordon, & Max M. Witts. *Enola Gay.* New York: Stein & Day, 1977.

Monographs:
Bowers, Peter M. *Boeing B-29.* North Branch,MN: Warbird Specialty, 1999.

Campbell, Richard H. *Brief History of the Enola Gay.* Albuquerque, National Atomic Museum, 1998.

Davis, Larry. *B-29 Superfortress in action.* Carrollton TX: Sq/Sig, 1997.

Harding, Stephen & James Long. *Dominator B-32.* Missoula: Pictorial,1983.

Lloyd, Alwyn T. *B-29 Superfortress in Detail & Scale,* Pt. 1,1983, Pt. 2, 1987.

Periodicals:

Hazen, R. M. "Development of the Allison 3420." *Aero Digest.*. 10-1-45: 75-79, 106.

Thompson, Warren. "B-29 Superfortress in Korea." *Wings of Fame* v.16. 1999: 12-27.

Part IV.
Chapter 25

Standard Aircraft Characteristics Charts, B-26B, 11 July 1952; A-26A, April 67, F4U-5; 1 June 1953;

Official histories:

Berger, Carl, et al. *The United States Air Force in Southeast Asia, An Illustrated Account.* Washington: Office of Air Force History, 1977.

Bohn, John T. *Development of SAC, 1946-1971.* Offutt AFB, 1972.

Field, James A. *History of United States Naval Operations Korea.* Washington: GPO, 1962.

Futrell, Robert F. *The United States Air Force in Korea, 1950-1953.* New York: Duell, Sloan & Pearce, 1961.

Shaw, Frederick J., & A. Timothy Warnock. *Cold War and Beyond Chronology of the USAF 1947-1997.* Washington: GPO, 1997.

Warnock, A. Timothy. *The USAF in Korea, A Chronology 1950-1953.* Washington: GPO, 2000.

Books:

Boyne, Walter J. *Beyond the Wild Blue- A History of the USAF 1947-1997.* New York: St. Martin's: 1997.

Brown, Anthony C. *Dropshot: The American Plan for World War III.* New York: Dial Press/Wade. 1978.

Crosnier, Alorin, & Jean-Michel Guhl. *L'Armee de L'Air en Indochine.* Vol. 1. Paris: SUP AIR 1981: 40-52.

Ellis, John *Brute Force: Allied Strategy & Tactics in the Second World War.* New York: Viking, 1990.

Hagedorn, Dan & Leif Hellstrom. *Foreign Invaders, Douglas in foreign service.* Leicester: Midland 1994.

Hansen, Chuck *U.S. Nuclear Weapons: The Secret History.* Arlington: Aerofax, 1988.

Miller, Jay. *Lockheed U-2.* Austin, Aerofax, 1983.

_____. *Lockheed Martin's Skunk Works.* Leicester: Aerofax, 1997.

Miller, Jerry. *Nuclear Weapons & Aircraft Carriers.* Washington: Smithsonian 2001.

Polmar, Norman. *US Naval Weapons.* Annapolis: Naval Institute, 1982.

_____. *SPYPLANE The U-2 History Unclassified.* Osceola, WI: MBI, 2001.

Procock, Chris. *Dragon Lady The History of the U-2.* Osecola, WI: MBI, 1989.

Rhodes, Richard, *DARK SUN: The Making of the Hydrogen Bomb.* New York: Simon & Schuster, 1996.

Thompson, Warren. *B-26 Invader Units over Korea.* Botley, UK: Osprey 2000.

Zhang, Xiaoming. *Red Wings over the Yalu.* College Stat.: Texas A&M Univ. Press, 2002.

Monographs:

Gordon, Yefim. *Mikoyan-Gurevich MiG-15.* Hinckley: Aerofax, 2001.

_____ . *Myasishev M-4 and 3M.* Hinckley: Midland, 2003.

_____ & V. Rigamant. *Tupolev Tu-95/142 Bear.* Leicester: Aerofax, 1997.

Periodicals:

Hua, Hsichun Mike. "Black Cat Squadron". *Air Power History* 49-1, 2002: 4-19. Details of Chinese U-2 flights.

Chapter 26

Air Force Documents:

Army Airplane Characteristics (AAC),1 April 1946, is the source for XB-44 and estimated XB-35 & XB-36 specifications.

Standard Aircraft Characteristics: XB-35, 15 June 47; B-29A, B-50A, 11 July 1952;

B-50D, 25 Jan 57; B-36A, 13 April 50; B-36B, 20 Oct 50; RB-36D, RB-36E, 8 Sept 50;

B-36D 12 August 52; B-36F, 26 Mar 54; B-36H, 15 January 54; B-36J III, 3 Oct 54.

Air Materiel Command Historical Office, Wright-Patterson AFB:

Report on Preliminary Design Studies, Long Range Bombardment Airplane, 10-3-41.

Case History of the XB-36, YB-36 and B-36. 28 May 1948.

Morrow, Ardath M. Case History of the YB-35, YB-49. February 1950.

Office of AF History, USAF:

Bohn, John T. *Development of SAC, 1945-1971.* Offutt AFB, MT. 1972.

Knaack, Marcelle S. *Encyclopedia of USAF Aircraft and Missile Systems. Vol. 2, Post-World War II Bombers 1945-1973.* Washington: GPO, 1988.

Steadfast & Courageous: FEAF Bomber Command & the Air War in Korea. GPO, 2000.

Convair documents in SDAM:

I.M. Laddon to MajGen. O.F. Echols, 8-1-43

Performance Summary, 8-1-44 & 7-10-46.

Acceptance and Delivery chart, Model B-36, 9-13-48.0p.

B-36 flight chronology, H.C. Tafe to Major J.D. Brady, 1 July 1949

B-36 Model Improvements, 13 February 1957.

History of the B-36. 2-12-59.

Northrop Aircraft Co. Drawing 5060665, XB-35.

Books:

Arsenbev, E. *Istrebitelb MiG-15.* Moscow, Armada #10, 1999

Barlow, Jeffrey G. *Revolt of the Admirals.* Washington, Naval Historical Center, 1994.

Brown, Anthony C. *Dropshot: The American Plan for World War III.* New York. Dial Press/Wade. 1978.

Duffy, Paul, & Andrei Kandalov. *Tupolev, The Man and His Aircraft,.* Shrewsberry, England: Airlife, 1996. Kandalov, former first deputy director of the Tupolev Design Bureau, also told the Tu-4 story while visiting this author's home in 1995.

Hansen, Chuck. *US Nuclear Weapons.* New York, Orion 1988.

Jacobsen, Meyers K., ed. *Convair B-36, A Comprehensive History.* Atglen, Schiffer 1997.

Lashmar, Paul. *Spy Flights of the Cold War.* Annapolis: Naval Institute, 1996.

Pape, Garry R. & John M. Campbell. *Northrop Flying Wings.* Atglen, Schiffer 1995.

Polmar, Norman & Timothy Laur, *Strategic Air Command.* Baltimore, N & A. 1990.

Smith, Richard K. *75 Years of Inflight Refueling.* Washington, GPO. 1998.

Periodicals:

Hardesty, Von. "Made in the USSR." *Air & Space* 2/2001: 68-79. Washington DC.

Northrop, John K. "Northrop XB-35 Flying Wing". *Aviation* August 1946: 55-61.

Thompson, Warren. "B-29 in Korea" *Wings of Fame #16,* Airtime 1999: 12-27.

Chapter 27

Air Force Documents:

Army Airplane Characteristics (AAC),1 April 1946, is the source for original specifications of 1945-46 types.

Standard Aircraft Characteristics: F-80B May 49; F-80C, Jul 50; F-82E, F-82F, F-82G, 22 Sep 50; F-84B/C/D, 5/50; F-84E, 24 Oct 49, 24 March 52; YF-84F, 7/50;

F-84F-25, 2 Sep 55; F-84G Dec 53; XF-84H, 10 May 54; XF-85, 6 Jul 49;

F-86A/E, 27 April 54; F-86D, 1 Oct 56, 16 Nov 60; F-86F, 17 Feb 54, 1 Oct 56;

F-86H, 16 Nov 60; F-86K, 15 Jul 55; F-86L, 16 Nov 60; XF-88, Nov 49;

XF-89, May 49; F-89A, 29 May 1950; F-89C, 11 July 52; XF-90, Jan 50;

XF-91, 10 Nov 50; XF-91, May 51; XF-92A , 27 Jan 50; YF-93A, 9 May 50;

F-94A, 7 Nov 49; F-94C, 1 Oct 56.

AMC Historical Office reports at AFHRC (Air Force Historical Center) Maxwell AFB, file 202.

Final report on the XP-79, #5509. P.B. Smith, 11 July 1946.

Final report on the XP-80, #5235. Lt. B. Hello, 28 June 1945.

Final report on the XP-83, #5536. Maj. W.G. Logan, 6 January 1947.

Final report on the XP-82, #5673. Werner R. Rankin, 19 February 1948.

Case History of the F-82E, F, and G. Martin J. Miller, Jr. January 1951.

Case History of the F-84 Airplane. Dorothy L. Miller, April 1950.

Case History of the XF-87 Airplane. Helen W. Shulz, January 1950.

Case History of the XF-92. Ardath M. Morrow, June 49.

Boyd, Robert J. *SAC Fighter Planes.* Offutt AFB: OH, HQ SAC, 1988.

Chilstrom, Maj. K.O. *Performance Test on XP-86.* MCRFT-2126, 15 Jan 1948.

Knaack, Marcelle S. *Encyclopedia of USAF Aircraft and Missile Systems.*

Vol. 1, Post-World War II Fighters 1945-1973. Washington, GPO. 1978.

Other Sources:

Bradley, Robert E. The XP-92 Story, 2001: ms at SDAM with NACA RM L53J23.
Chana, Bill. World's First Delta Wing Airplane- Convair XF-92A. SAE/AIAA 2000.
Consolidated Vultee Corp. "Convair Designs AAF's Newest Jet" San Diego, 1-25-46. Model 105 (P-81) test files in SDAM, including XP-81 brochure & Spec. 613-B. dated September 1944.
Hendrix, Lin. Republic test pilot. Interview with author about XP-84H, etc. 11-18-77.
North American Aviation. Report NA54-389, *F-86 projects*, 1 May 1955.
Report No. NA-8564, *XP-86 Estimates.* 15 May 1945.
Canary, Jack. *Brief History, Chronological Summary of F-86.* 24 March 53.
Greene, L.P. *F-86 Preliminary Design.* 25 February 1959.
NA-140 Model Summary. May 28, 1952.
Patch, A.C. & J.E. Thompson. *Changes & Improvements of the F-86D.* n/d.
Brown, Anthony C. *Dropshot: The American Plan for World War III. op. cit.*

Monographs:

Balzer, Gerald & Mike Darlo. *Northrop F-89 Scorpion.* Arlington: Aerofax, 1993.
Davis, Larry, & Dave Menard. *F-89 Scorpion in Action.* Carrollton TX: Sq/Sig, 1990.
Davis, Larry. *F-86 SABRE in action.* Carrollton TX: Sq/Sig, 1992.
Francillon, Rene, & Kevin Keaveney. *Lockheed F-94 Starfire.* Arlington: Aerofax, 1986.
Johnson, C.L. *Development of the Lockheed P-80.* Burbank: Lockheed, 1946.
Keaveney, Kevin. *Republic F-84 (Swept-wing Variants).* Arlington: Aerofax, 1987.
McLaren, David R. *Double Menace P/F-82 Twin Mustang,* Colorado Springs: ViP, 1994.
_____. *Lockheed P-80/F-80 Shooting Star.* Atglen, Schiffer, 1996.
_____. *Republic F-84 Thunderjet.* Atglen, Schiffer, 1998.
_____. *Lockheed F-94 Starfire.* Atglen, Schiffer, 1993.
Pace, Steve, *McDonnell XF-88 Voodoo.* Simi Valley: Ginter, 1999.
_____ , *Republic XF-91 Thunderceptor.* Simi Valley: Ginter, 2000.
Pape, Garry R. & John M. Campbell. *Northrop Flying Wings.* op cit: 93-107.
Wagner, Ray. *North American Sabre.* New York: Hanover House, 1963.
_____. *North American F-86D/K/L, Pt. 1.* Simi Valley: Ginter, 1999.
Wooldridge, E.T. *P-80 Shooting Star:* Washington: Smithsonian, 1979.

Periodicals:

Bodie, Warren M. "Penetration Fighter." Pt. 1 *Airpower* 3/81: 20-36, 49-51, (Story of F-90) Pt. 2 *Wings* 4/81: 8-22.
Foss, R.L. & Roy Blair. "From Propellers to Jets in Fighter Design." *LOCKHEED HORIZONS 1987:* :3-23.
Hallion, Richard P. "P-80: Story of a Star" *Air Enthusiast. #11,* London, 11/79: 54-70.
Powers, Richard D. "Monstro and the Goblins". *AAHS* 18-1, 1973: 146-159.
Rochdort, Gary L. "Republic XF-91". *AAHS* 34-1, 1989: 16-31.
Sunday, Terry L. "Convair's Flying Compromise XP-81". *Wings* 10/87: 36-47.

Chapter 28

Air Force Documents
Army Airplane Characteristics (AAC), 1 April 1946, is the source for estimated XB-43 to XB-48 specifications. Actual weights and performance from Edwards AFB Historical office.
Standard Aircraft Characteristics: B-45A, 11 July 52; B-45C, 11 July 52; XB-47 Nov 49; B-47B, 20 Nov 56; B-47E, 10 July 56; B-47E-IV, 16 Nov 59; RB-47H, 15 Sep 60;
YB-49, 20 Dec 49; XB-52, Oct 50; B-52B/C/E, 1 Oct 58; B-52F, 12 Oct 58;
B-52G, Oct 61; B-52H, June 63; RB-57A, 1 Mar 57; B-57B, 22 Apr 59;
RB-57, May 68; B-57G, Apr 71; B-58A, May 64; YB-60, 11 July 52;
B/EB/RB-66B, Feb 65; RB-66C, 15 Nov 60; XB-68, 12 Sept 56.

Books:

Boyne, Walter J. *Boeing B-52.* London: Janes, 1981.
Knaack, Marcelle S. *Encyclopedia of USAF Aircraft and Missile Systems. Vol. 2, Post-World War II Bombers 1945-1973.* Washington, GPO. 1988.
Mikesh, Robert C. *B-57 Canberra at War.* New York: Scribners, 1980.
Pape, Garry R. & John M. Campbell. *Northrop Flying Wings.* op cit 148-193, 253-4.
Tegler, Jan. *B-47 STRATOJET.* New York: McGraw: 2000.

Monographs:

Bowers, Peter M. *Boeing B-52A/H.* Profile #245. Windsor, Berks, 1972.
Drendel, Lou. *B-47 Stratojet in Action..* Carrollton TX: Sq/Sig, 1976.
_____ *B-52 Stratofortress in Action..* Carrollton TX: Sq/Sig, 1975.
Libis, Scott. *Martin XB-51.* Simi Valley: Ginter 1998.
Mesko, Jim. *B-57 CANBERRA in Action..* Carrollton TX: Sq/Sig, 1986.
Miller, Jay. *Convair B-58 Hustler.* Leicester: Aerofax, 1997.

Periodicals:

Aero Digest 11/50: 22-25, 62-65. "Boeing B-47 Stratojet".
Aviation Week 12/5/55: 23. "Quarles Defends Air Force Policy".
Boyne, Walter J. "Convair's Needle-Nosed Orphan." *Airpower* 9/1976: 4-19, 80.
Dorr, Robert F. Boeing B-52 & the DOOMSDAY Detonations." *Aviation News* 15 July 94: 162-172.
Hall, C. Cargill. "Strategic Reconnaissance in Cold War." *Prologue* 1996, 28-2: 107-125.
_____ . "Truth About Overflights." *Quarterly Journal of Military History.* Spring 1997, 9-3: 24-39.
Yenne, Bill. "Convair B-58". *International AIR POWER v.2,* 2001:116-149.

Chapter 29

Standard Aircraft Characteristics: YF-100A, 22 May 53; F-100A, 20 Jan 63;
F-100C, F-100D, Sept 63; F-101A/C, Nov 62; RF-*101A*, 11 Sept 60; F-101B, Nov 74;
YF-102, 2 Nov 53; F-102A, Aug 62; XF-103, 5 Jan 54; F-104A, May 59;
F-104G, Sept 64; YF-105A, 23 Nov 55; F-105B, Mar 64; F-105D, Jul 65;
F-106A, Oct 62; F-107A, 12 Mar 54; F-108A, 12 June 59.
North American Aviation. Report on the F-100, n.d.
Republic Aviation Corp. *F-105D-25 Weapons System.* Farmingdale *1963 F-105F Two-Place Thunderchief.* Farmingdale 1963

Books:

Anderton, David. *Republic F-105 Thunderchief.* Osceola, Motorbooks, Osprey 1983.
Davis, Larry. *Wild Weasel, SAM Suppression.* Carrollton: Squadron Signal, 1993.
Drendel, John T. *And Kill MIGS, Air to Air Combat in the Vietnam War.* Carrollton, Squadron Signal: 1997.
_____. *Aircraft of the Vietnam War.* New York, NY. Arco, 1971.
_____. *TAC- A Pictorial History 1970-1977.* Warren, Mich.: Squad/Signal 1978.
Francillon, Rene J. *McDonnell Douglas Aircraft since 1920. Vol. 2.* Annapolis: Naval Institute, 1990.
Knaack, Marcelle S. *Encyclopedia of USAF Aircraft and Missile Systems. Vol. 1, Post-World War II Fighters 1945-1973.* Washington, GPO. 1978.
Mutza, Wayne. *Convair F-102 Delta Dagger.* Atglen, Schiffer, 1999.
Reed, Arthur. *F-104 Starfire.* New York: Scribners, 1981
Thompson, Kevin, *North American Aircraft 1934-1998* vol. 2. Santa Ana CA: Narkiewitz /Thompson, 1999.

Monographs:

Davis, Larry, & David Menard. *Republic F-105 THUNDERCHIEF.* North Branch, MN: Specialty Tech #18, 1998.
Holder, William G. *Convair F-106.* Fallbrook, CA: Aero, 1977.
Keaveney, Kevin. *McDonnell F-101B/F.* Arlington: Aerofax, 1984.

Periodicals:

Dean, Jack. "F-105, All-Out Warrior". *Wings* 4/91: 10-38, 48-55.
Dorr, Robert F. "Convair F-102 Delta" *WINGS OF FAME, #17.* AIRtime, 1999: 30-67.
_____ . "Convair F-106 Delta" *WINGS OF FAME, #12.* AIRtime, 1998: 36-97.
Mizrahi, Joe. "F-100 Super Sabre". *Wings* 6/91: 12-41, 54-55.
Spick, Mike. "Starfighter -the Early Years" *Air Enthusiast #46.* 1992: 26-45.

Chapter 30

Navy Dept., BuAer. Naval Aircraft Record of Acceptance, 1947-1954.
Standard Aircraft Characteristics: XP2V-1, 1 Jan 47; P2V-5, 1 Mar 55; P2V-5F Jan 59; P2V-6, 1 Feb 54; P2V-7, 15 Apr 57; XP4M-1, 1 Aug 47; XP4M-1, 1 Sep 47;

XP5M-1, 1 June 1947; XP5Y-1, 1 Oct 47; P5M-2, 1 Mar 55; P5M-2S, 15 Oct 62;
YP6M-1, 15 Apr 57; P-3A, 12 June 1962; P-3B, P-3C Jan 70; P-3C UD II. May 84.
CVAC Report ZC-117-006, Summary of XP5Y-1 Power Plant Testing. 24 Feb 53.
CVAC P6Y-1 Specification, 29 May 1957. SDAM files.

Books:
Barth, Bruce B. *The Martin P5M "Marlin"*. Castro Valley: Pacific Aero, 1994.
Breihan, John R., Stan Piet, Roger S. Mason, *Martin Aircraft 1909-1960.* Santa Ana: Narkiewitz/Thompson, 1995.
Francillon, Rene J. *Lockheed Aircraft since 1913.* Annapolis: Naval Institute,1987.
Mutza, Wayne. *Lockheed P2V Neptune.* Atglen, Schiffer, 1996.
Reade, David. *Age of Orion -Lockheed P-3.* Atglen, Schiffer, 1998.

Monographs:
Ginter, Steve. *Martin P4M-1/-1Q Mercator.* Simi Valley, CA, 1996.
_____. *Convair XP5Y-1 & R3Y-1/-2.* Simi Valley, CA, 1996.

Periodicals:
Aero Digest. "Lockheed P2V Neptune" April, 1953: 29-48.
Allen, Francis J. "Poseidon's Giant (Story of P6M)" *AAHS* 34-2, 1989: 144-153.
Dorr, Robert F. "Ferreting Mercators" *Air International,* 10/93: 215-222.
Hansen, Chuck. "Nuclear Neptunes" *AAHS* 24-4, 1979: 262-268.
Nicolaou, Stephane. "Master of the Seas-P6M-1". *Airpower* 12/86: 12-27, 50-55.
Poling, George E. "On the Trail of the Tradewind". *Airpower* 5/78: 10-18,22-42.
Stone, Irving. "How Martin Tailored P5M to ASW Job". *Aviation Week, 1*-17-55: 28-34.
Wassall, John B. "How the P2V Meets Patrol Objectives". *Aviation Week,* 7-2549: 20-28.

Chapter 31

Navy Dept., BuAer. Naval Aircraft Record of Acceptance, 1947-1954.
Pearson, Lee M. "Development of the Attack Concept" US Navy ms. in SDAM.
Standard Aircraft Characteristics: XBT2D-1, 1 May 45; 1 Oct 46, AD-1; AD-2, 1 Aug 49; AD-4, 1 June 54; , AD-4B, 30 Sep 57; AD-5/5N/5Q/5W, 1 Feb 56: , AD-6, 18 Nov 55;
A2D-1, 11 Dec 53; A-1H/J, Jan 66; A-1E, Oct 68; AJ-1, 30 June 57; A3D-1, 15 Apr 57;
A3D-2, 15 Apr 61; A4D-1, 30 June 57 & 5 Sep 58; A-4B, 30 Aug 63; A-4C, Jan 70;
A-4E, 3 Dec 62; A3J-1, 15 Apr 61; RA-5C, 15 Aug 63; A-6A, Aug 65.

Books:
Heineman, Edward H. *Ed Heineman, Combat Plane Designer.* Annapolis: Naval Institute, 1987. Also various papers at SDAM.
Kilduff, Peter. *Douglas A-4 Skyhawk.* London: Osprey, 1983.
Miller, Jerry. *Nuclear Weapons and Aircraft Carriers.* Washington: Smithsonian, 2001.
Smith, Peter C. *Douglas AD Skraider.* Ramsbury: Crowood, 1999.

Monographs:
Cunningham, Bruce. *DOUGLAS A3D SKYWARRIOR.* Simi Valley, CA: Ginter, 1998.
Drendel, Lou. *A-4 Skyhawk in Action.* Warren, Sq/Sig, 1973.
_____ , *A-6 Intruder in Action.* Warren, Sq/Sig, 1975.
Francillon, Rene J. *DOUGLAS A3D SKYWARRIOR.* ARLINGTON, TX: AEROFAX, 1987.
Jenkins, Dennis R. *Grumman A-6 Intruder.* North Branch,MN: Specialty Tech 33, 1999.
Ginter, Steve. *North American AJ-1 Savage.* Simi Valley, CA: Ginter, 1992.
Grove, Michael & Jay Miller. *North American A3J/A-5 Vigilante.* Arlington: Aerofax,1989.
Sullivan, Jim. *AD Skyraider in Action.* Carrollton, TX: Sq/Sig, 1983.

Periodicals:
Gann, Harry. "Besides, It's Fun to Fly- A-4 Skyhawk". *HOOK* 1990: 18-4, 16-29.
Markgraf, Gerry. "Skyshark, Son of SpAD". *AAHS* 22-3, 1977: 200-215.
Ramage, RADM James D. "Taking A-Bombs to Sea" *Naval History* 1/95: 29-34.
Scarborough, CAPT W.E. "North American AJ Savage". *HOOK,* 1989: 17-3, Pt. 1, 28-43; 17-4, Pt. 2, 16-37.

Chapter 32

Standard Aircraft Characteristics: XFD-1, 1 Sep 45; FH-1, 1 Mar 46;
XF6U-1, XFJ-1, 1 Jan 47; F6U-1, FJ-1, 1 May 49; F2H-1, 1 Apr 48; F2H-2, 1 Nov 49; F2H-2B, 1 Oct 55; F2H-3, 1 May 51;XF9F-2, 1 April 47; F9F-2, 1 Feb 52;
F9F-4, 1 Nov 52; F9F-5, 1 Jun 52; F3D-1, 1 Jul 52; F3D-2, 16 Apr 54; F7U-1, 1 Jun 49; F7U-3, 15 May 55; F4D-1, 1 Dec 59; F5D-1, 1 Feb 57; F9F-6, 1 Jul 53; F9F-7, 1 Feb 56; F9F-8, 15 Apr 57; F9F-8B, 15 Oct 56; F3H-1N, 1 Dec 54; F3H-2M, 15 Aug 55;
F3H-2, 30 Apr 63; FJ-2, 1 Oct 55; FJ-3, 30 Apr 58; FJ-4, 30 Aug 58, FJ-4B, 30 Jan 59; F10F-1, 1 May 51; XFY-1, Jul 54; XFV-1, 1 Oct 52; F2Y-1, 10 Dec 52, XF2Y-1, 1 Jan 55; F9F-9 15 Feb 52; F8U-1, 15 Apr 57; F8U-2, 30 Jan 59; F-8D, 1 Feb 63; F-8J, Jan 70.

Company reports:
BuAer report; "Narrative history of F10F fighter", Barton E. Day, 9 July 57.
Convair corp. XF2Y contract file, Flight Handbook,YF2Y-1,14 March 55 in SDAM.
LTV Corp. "F-8 Crusader". Dallas PR-68-77.

Monographs:
Ginter, Steve. *McDonnell Banshee F2H-1/4.* Simi Valley, CA: Ginter, 1980.
_____. *Douglas F3D Skyknight.* Simi Valley, CA: Ginter, 1980.
_____. *North American FJ-1 Fury.* Simi Valley, CA: Ginter 1983.
_____. *Chance Vought F7U Cutlass.* Simi Valley, CA: Ginter 1982.
_____. *McDonnell F2H DEMON.* Simi Valley, CA: Ginter 1985.
_____. *North American FJ-4/4B Fury.* Simi Valley, CA: Ginter 1994.
_____. *Douglas F5D-1 Skylancer.* Simi Valley, CA: Ginter 1996.
_____. *Lockheed XVL-1 VTOL.* Simi Valley, CA: Ginter 1996.
Ginter, Steve & Nick Williams. *Douglas F4D Skyray.* Simi Valley, CA: Ginter 1986.
Koehnen, Richard. *Chance Vought F6U Pirate.* Simi Valley, CA: Ginter 1983
Long, B.J. *Convair XF2Y-1 & YF2Y-1 SeaDart.* Simi Valley, CA: Ginter 1992.
Meyer, Corwin. *Grumman XF10F-1 Jaguar.* Simi Valley, CA: Ginter 1993.
_____. *Grumman F11F Tiger.* Simi Valley, CA: Ginter 1997.
_____. *Grumman XF11F-1 Tiger.* Simi Valley, CA: Ginter 1998
_____. *Grumman P9F-1 Panther, Pt. One. Simi Valley,* CA: Ginter 2002
Pace, Steve. *Vought's F-8 Crusader Pt. 1.* Simi Valley, CA: Ginter, 1988.
Sullivan, Jim. *F9F Panther/Cougar.* Carrollton, TX: Sq/Sig, 1982.

Periodicals:
Andrews, Harold."Grumman F11F-1 Tiger". *Historical Av. Album Vol. 2,* 1965: 86-91.
Aviation Week. "BuAer Admits, Defends Error on Demon". 10-31-55: 10-13.

Chapter 33

Standard Aircraft Characteristics: AF-2S, 15 Feb 52; S2F-1/-2, 15 June 56; S-2E, Jan 66; S-3A, Jan 73.

Books:
Francillon, Rene J. *Grumman Aircraft since 1929.* 1989. 274-285, 350-375. *op. cit.*
_____. *Lockheed Aircraft since 1913.* 1987 *op. cit.*

Monographs:
Grumman Aircraft Corp. *Grumman S-2E Tracker.* Bethpage: n.d.
Kowalski, Robert J. *Grumman AF Guardian.* Simi Valley, CA: Ginter, 1991.
Lockheed-California Co. *Lockheed S-3A.* Burbank: October 1971.
Sullivan, Jim. *S2F Tracker in Action.* Carrollton, TX: Sq/Sig, 1990.

Chapter 34

Standard Aircraft Characteristics: B-26B/C, July 1952; F4U-5; 1 June 1953;
Office of Air Force History: *Aces and Aerial Victories* . Washington, DC:, GPO, 1976
Berger, Carl. Ed.*USAF in Southeast Asia, 1965-1977.* Washington, DC: GPO, 1976
Strategic Air Command Missile Chronology 1939-1973. Offut AFB, NE; Hdq. SAC 1975.
USAF Southeast Asia Monograph Series:
Vol I, *Tale of Two Bridges, and Battle for the Skies Over North Vietnam*

Vol. 3, *The Vietnameses Air Force 1951-1975.* Washington, DC: GPO, 1975.
Shaw, Frederick J., & Timothy Warnock. *Cold War and Beyond Chronology of the USAF 1947-1997.* Washington 1997.

Books:
Boyne, Walter J. *Beyond the Wild Blue- A History of the USAF 1947-1997.* NY. *op. cit.*
Byrnes, Donn A. & Ken D. Hurley. *Blackbird Rising.* Los Lunas, NM: Saga Mesa, 1999.
Cohen, Col. Eliezer. *Israel's Best Defense-the Story of the Air Force.* NY: Orion, 1993.
Crickmore, Paul F. *Lockheed SR-71 Secret Missions Exposed.* London: Osprey, 1993.
Friedman, Norman. *Desert Victory –war for Kuwait.* Annapolis: Naval Institute, 1991.
Hallion, Richard. *Storm over Iraq.* Annapolis: Naval Institute, 1992.
Miller, Jay. *Lockheed Martin's Skunk Works.* Leicester, Aerofax, 1997, *op. cit.*
Miller, Jerry. *Nuclear Weapons and Aircraft Carriers.* Washington: Smithsonian, 2001.
Morse, Stan, Ed. *Gulf War Debrief.* Westport, CT: Airtime, 1993.
Polmar, Norman. *Ships and Aircraft of U.S. Fleet.* 14th Ed., Annapolis: Naval Instit., 1987.
_____. *Ships and Aircraft of U.S. Fleet.* 17th Ed., Annapolis: Naval Instit., 2001.

Monographs:
Jenkins, Dennis R. *Lockheed SR-71/YF-12 Blackbirds.* North Branch, MN: Specialty Tech 33, 1997.
Maydew, Randy. *Recovering the Lost H-Bomb at Palomares, Spain.* Albuquerque, National Atomic Museum Foundation: 1995.
Miller, Jay. *Lockheed SR-71(A-12/YF-12/D21).* Arlington, TX: Aerofax, 1985.
Remak, Jeanette, & Joseph Ventolo, Jr. *A-12 Blackbird Declassified.* St. Paul, MN: MBI, 2001.
Toperczer, Istvan. *MiG-17 & MiG 19 Units of Vietnam War.* Oxford, UK: Osprey, 2001.
______. *Mig-21 Units of the Vietnam War.* Oxford, UK: Osprey, 2001.

Periodicals:
Air Force Magazine "Black Shield". Jan 95: 66-71.

Chapter 35

Standard Aircraft Characteristics: A-37A. Dec 67; A-37B, Jun 69; OV-10A, Jan 68;
A-4F, Jan 68, Jun 71; A-4L, Jan 70; A-4M, March 70, June 71; A-6C Mar 72;
A-6E, Nov 71; EA-6B, Dec 71; A-7A, May 65; A-7B, Jan 1970; A-7D, Jan 73;
A-7E, Apr 72; A-10, Nov 74; AV-8B, Oct 86.

Books:
Smith, Peter C. *Lockheed C-130 Hercules.* Shrewsbury, Airlife: 2001.
Thompson, Kevin. *North American Aircraft 1934-1998* vol. 2, *op. cit.*

Monographs:
Adcock, Al. *A-7 Corsair II in action.* Carrollton, TX: Sq/Sig, 1991.
Bell, Dana. *A-10 Warthog.* Blue Ridge Summit, PA: Tab D & S, 1986.
Ginter, Steve et al. *Convair Model 48 Charger.* Simi Valley, CA: Ginter, 1997.
Jenkins, Dennis R. *Boeing/BAe Harrier.* North Branch, MN: Specialty Tech 21, 1998.
Jenkins, Dennis R. *Grumman A-6 Intruder.* North Branch, MN: Specialty Tech 33, 1999.
Kinsey, Bert, & Ray Leader. *A-6 Intruder.* Blue Ridge Summit, PA: Tab D & S, 1988.
Linn, Don. *AV-8 Harrier in detail.* Blue Ridge Summit, PA: Tab D & S, 1988.
Love, Terry. *A-37 Dragonfly in action.* Carrollton, TX: Sq/Sig, 1991.
Mesko, Jim. *OV-10 Bronco in action.* Carrollton, TX: Sq/Sig, 1999.
Neubeck, Ken. *A-10 Warthog Mini in action #4.* Carrollton, TX: Sq/Sg,, 1995.
Wogstad, James & P. Friddell. *Grumman EA-6B Prowler.* San Antonio: Aerophile 1985.

Periodicals:
North American "OV-10A Bronco". *Service News.* Columbus Div. 7/70: 53-96.
Huertas, S.M. & D. D."A-4 Skyhawk in Falklands" *WINGS OF FAME, #12.* 1998: 4-29.
Morgan, LT Mark L. "A-7 Corsair in Fleet Service" Pt. One, *The Hook.* Sum 91: 36-57. Pt. Two, *The Hook.* Fall 91: 28-41.
Willing, Martin J. "A Moment in Time - Sud Fennec". *Air Enthusiast #99,* 5/02: 53-59.

Chapter 36

Standard Aircraft Characteristics: F8U-3, 2 June 58; F-4B, 31 May 65;
F-4C/D/RF-4C, Dec 67; F-4E, Feb 71; F-4J, Aug 73; F-5A, Nov 72; F-5E, Nov 74;
F-111A, Jan 73; F-111B, Aug 65;
F-14A, Apr 77; F-14B, 1 July 91; F-15A, Nov 74, F-15C, Feb 92;
F-16A, Mar 84; F-16C, Mar 91; F/A-18A, Oct 84;
Office of Air Force History: *Aces and Aerial Victories.* Washington, DC:, GPO, 1976.
U.S. Congress Senate Committee on Government Operations *TFX Contract Investigation:* Report to 91st Congress, 2nd Session. Washington: GPO, 1970.
Company publications: Many brochures and booklets have been issued describing aircraft in this chapter. Hughes Aircraft Co, AWG-9/ Phoenix System, Feb 1974, is an example. Another is "The Superb F-5", a 56-page study from Northrop dated July 1986.
Continuing periodicals about these aircraft include the especially high quality of *Code One.* Lockheed Martin, Fort Worth.

Books:
Cooper, Tom, & Farzad Bishop. *Iran-Iraq War in the Air.* Atglen, PA: Schiffer, 2000.
Donald, David, Ed. *McDonnell F-4 Phantom –Spirit in the Skies.* Norwalk: AIRtime, 2002.
Drendel, John T. *And Kill MIGS, Air to Air Combat in Vietnam.* Carrollton: Sq/Sg, 1997.
Francillon, Rene J. *McDonnell Douglas Aircraft since 1920.* vol. 2. op. cit.
_____. *Grumman Aircraft since 1929.* 1989. op. cit.
_____. *Lockheed Aircraft since 1913.* 1987 op. cit.
Gillchrist, RADM Paul T. *TOMCAT! Grumman F-14 Story.* Atglen, PA: Schiffer, 1994.
Gunston, Bill. F-111. New York: Scribners, 1978.
Logan, Don. *General Dynamics F-111 Aardvark.* Atglen, PA: Schiffer, 1998.
Scutts, Jerry. *Northrop F-5/F-20.* London: Ian Allen, 1986

Monographs:
Drendel, Lou. *F-16 Fighting Falcon in action.* Carrollton, TX: Sq/Sg, 1982.
Holder, Bill & Mike Wallace. *McDonnell DouglasF/A-18 Hornet.* Atglen, PA: Schiffer, 1997.
Jenkins, Dennis R. *McDonnell Douglas F-15A/B/C/D/E.* Arlington, TX: Aerofax, 1990.
Kinsey, Bert. *F-111 Aardvark.* Blue Ridge Summit, PA: TAB, 1989
McGovern Tim. *McDonnell F-4E Phantom II.* Leicester: Aerofax, 1987.
Miller, Jay. *General Dynamics F-16 Fighting Falcon.* Austin TX: Aerofax, 1982
Stevenson, James P. *Grumman F-14.* Fallbrook, CA: 1975.
Tambani, Anthony J. *F-5 Tigers over Vietnam.* Wellesly, MA: Branden, 2001.
Wallace, Mike & Bill Holder. *Lockheed-Martin F-22 Raptor.* Atglen, PA: Schiffer, 1998.

Periodicals:
Francillon, Rene J. "From Strength to Strength -the F-16", Air International, 1/01:21-70.
Hehs, Eric. "F-16 Evolution". *Code One.* Lockheed Martin, Fort Worth. 7/97; 22-35.

Chapter 37

Standard Aircraft Characteristics: XB-70, Nov 65/Jan 72; FB-111A, Nov 74.
F-111F, Jun 73/Mar 90; B-1A, Dec 86; B-52H, Mar 90. Data on classified aircraft selected from published sources listed below.
Northrop Grumman Corp. *B-2 1996 -The Revolution is here.*
Rockwell International, Los Angeles, 1974: *B-1 Media press kit.*

Books:
Campbell, John M. & Gary Pape. *North American XB-70.* Atglen, PA: Schiffer, 1996.
Holder, Bill. *Northrop Grumman B-2 Spirit.* Atglen, PA: Schiffer, 1998.
Logan, Don. *Rockwell B-1B.* Atglen, PA: Schiffer, 1995.
_____. *General Dynamics F-111 Aardvark.* Atglen, PA: Schiffer, 1998.

Remak, Jeanette, & Joseph Ventolo,Jr. *XB-70 Valkyrie.* Osceola, WI: MBI, 1998.

Monographs:

Drendel, Lou. *Bone B-1 in action.* Carrollton, TX: Sq/Sg, 2002.
Goodall, Jim. *F-117 Stealth in action.* Carrollton, TX: Sq/Sg, 1991.
Greer, Don. *B-2 Spirit in action.* Carrollton, TX: Sq/Sg, 2002.
Miller, Jay. *Lockheed Martin's Skunk Works.* Leicester: Aerofax, 1997, *op. cit.*
_____. *Lockheed Martin F-117 Nighthawk.* Leicester: Aerofax, 1999.
_____. *Northrop B-2 Spirit.* Leicester: Aerofax, 1995.

Periodicals:

Air Force Magazine Almanac. USAF Fleet tables. May 1985: 50-54.
Congressional Digest. "The Strategic Arms Limitation Treaty". Washington DC: Aug-Sept. 1979. p. 201.
Lockheed Horizons "We own the Night". May 92.

Chapter 38

Since Standard Aircraft Characteristics usually remain classified for 12 years, this last chapter is the author's analysis of the last decade's published reports.

Periodicals:

Air Force Magazine Almanac. USAF Fleet tables. May 2001: 56-57.
Dorr, Robert F. "B-2 Stealthy Global Bomber". *Air Forces Monthly* May 02: 42-47.

Photo Credit List: The following code indicates the providers of prints used in this book. Note that print collections do not always indicate the original origin of each image, for in most cases the photographers are unknown or out of business. For example, Curtiss images were usually obtained from collectors like Pete Bowers, or from those stored at the National Air and Space Museum's annex. The San Diego Aerospace Museum has the Convair and Ryan corporate photo files, as well as images made by the Navy's talented J.M.F. Hasse. Other photos collected over the years by the author are credited to the original source, when possible.

AF: United States Air Force photograph
AMC: Prints made by Peter Bowers from the old Air Materiel Command files at Wright Field. (Original negatives were destroyed)
Arc: National Archives, Washington, D.C.
Besecker: Roger F. Besecker, Allentown, PA.
Bodie: Warren M. Bodie, Hayesville, GA.
Boyne: Walter J. Boyne, Ashburn, Virginia
Bulinski: Ron Bulinski, El Cajon, CA
Gann: Harry Gann, Buena Park, Calif.
GP: Gennady Petrov, St. Petersburg, Russia
GSW: Gordon Sear Williams, Seattle, WA.
IWM: Imperial War Museum, London
Lawson: Robert L. Lawson, Utah
Levy: Howard Levy, Brooklyn, NY.
MdA: Musee de L'Air, Paris
Mitchell: John Mitchell, Los Angeles
Mfr: Manufacturer of aircraft supplied print
NACA: National Advisory Committee on Aeronautics (now NASA)
NASM: National Air and Space Museum, Washington D.C.
PMB: Peter M. Bowers collection, Seattle, WA.
SDAM: San Diego Aerospace Museum
USN: United States Navy official photograph
WES: William E. Scarborough,
WL: William T. Larkins, Concord, CA.
WT: Warren Thompson, Germantown, TN

INDEX

Italics indicate illustrated matter.

A

B

C

D

E

F

G

H

I

J

K

L

M

N

O

P

Q

R

S

T

U

V

W

X

Y

Z